OCÉANO ATLÁNTICO
Estrecho de la Florida
LAS BAHAMAS
La Habana
Matanzas
Cienfuegos
CUBA
Camagüey
Guantánamo
Santiago de Cuba
REPÚBLICA DOMINICANA
HAITÍ
Port-au-Prince
Santo Domingo
Mayagüez
San Juan
Ponce
PUERTO RICO
Islas Vírgenes
Kingston
JAMAICA
Antigua
Guadalupe
Dominica
Martinica
Santa Lucía
Barbados
San Vicente
Granada
Antillas Menores
Mar Caribe
NICARAGUA
Managua
L. de Nicaragua
COSTA RICA
San José
Canal de Panamá
Colón
Panamá
PANAMÁ
Golfo de Panamá
Curaçao
Aruba
Bonaire
Isla Margarita
Trinidad y Tobago
Caracas
Río Orinoco
VENEZUELA
GUYANA
COLOMBIA
Bogotá
Río Magdalena
BRASIL
ECUADOR
PERÚ

A GUIDE TO MOSAICOS ICONS

Readiness Check
This icon, located at the beginning of the first *Funciones y formas* section, reminds students to take the Readiness Check in MySpanishLab to test their understanding of the English grammar related to the Spanish grammar concepts in the chapter. A Study Plan with English Grammar Tutorials is generated for those topics students might need to review.

eText Activities
This icon indicates that a version of the activity is available in MySpanishLab. eText activities are automatically graded and provide detailed feedback on incorrect answers.

Video
This icon indicates that a video segment is available for the *¡Cineastas en acción!* video that accompanies the *Mosaicos* program. The video is available on DVD and in MySpanishLab.

Text Audio Program
This icon indicates that recorded material to accompany *Mosaicos* is available online. In addition, audio for all in-class listening activities and *En directo* dialogues is available on CD.

Pair Activity
This icon indicates that the activity is designed to be done by students working in pairs.

Group Activity
This icon indicates that the activity is designed to be done by students working in small groups or as a whole class.

Interactive Globe
This icon indicates that additional cultural resources in the form of videos, web links, interactive maps, and more, relating to a particular country, are organized on an interactive globe online.

Art Tour
This icon accompanies the works of art highlighted in each chapter opener. It links to a virtual art tour and interactive activity in MySpanishLab about the work of art.

MediaShare
This icon, presented with all *Situación* activities, refers to the video-posting feature available online.

Mosaicos:

Spanish as a World Language

It's time to talk! …and have a cultured conversation. Providing the truly communicative, deeply culture-focused approach professors believe in along with the guidance and tools students need to be successful using a program with highly communicative goals—with ***Mosaicos***, there is no need to compromise. Recognizing the primacy of the relationship between culture and language, the new Sixth Edition of ***Mosaicos*** places culture up front and center, and everywhere in-between!

- Over 1,000 language instructors have partnered with Pearson to create solutions that address the needs of today's students and instructors.
- 100 Faculty Advisors have reviewed, tested, and collaborated with colleagues across North America to make Pearson's **MyLanguageLabs™** the most effective online learning and assessment college language learning system available today.

Challenge:

8 out of 10 language instructors told us that better tools are needed to help students develop oral proficiency so that they will be confident in speaking Spanish.

Solution:

- Almost 1,000,000 students have used Pearson's **MyLanguageLabs** to help them succeed in learning Spanish, French, Italian, German, Russian, Chinese, Portuguese, and Latin.
- **MyLanguageLabs** helps to **improve student results** by offering a robust set of tools that allow students to hear native speakers, and practice their speaking. We include pronunciation guides, Blackboard™ Voice, videos, and audio recordings and are the only online learning and assessment system that includes Versant™ Test of Spanish and MediaShare.

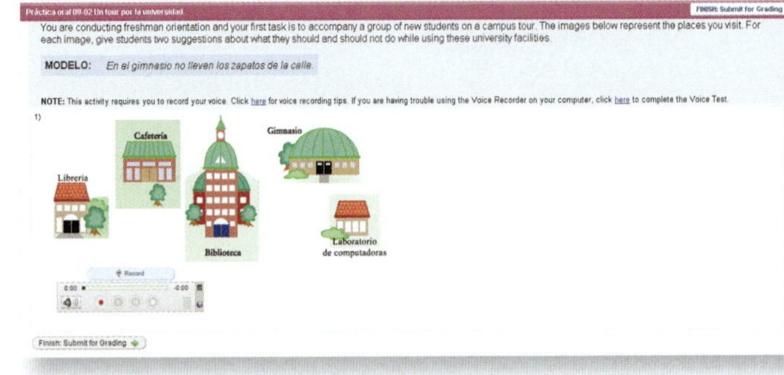

Students love the recording aspect of MyLanguageLabs, which allows them to listen to their own pronunciations, compare, and adjust to match the native speakers. Students' communicative skills have improved significantly with MyLanguageLabs.

—Charles Hernando Molano Álvarez

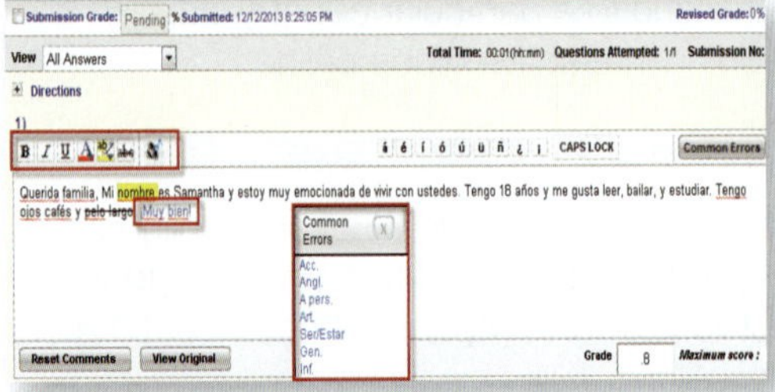

MyLanguageLabs automates teaching chores that are non-meaningful. Let MyLanguageLabs grade homework and quizzes. This gives you time to spend on meaningful pedagogical activities like engaging and interacting with your students.

—Anne Prucha, University of Central Florida

Challenge:

8 out of 10 language instructors voiced that they are teaching more students than ever before, and consequently feel that they no longer have time to provide students with careful guidance to foster speaking and writing skills.

Solution:

- **MyLanguageLabs** allows instructors to easily create the course syllabus, and assign and grade homework, providing you with the time to work with individual students, helping them **achieve higher proficiency levels** in speaking and writing, in particular.

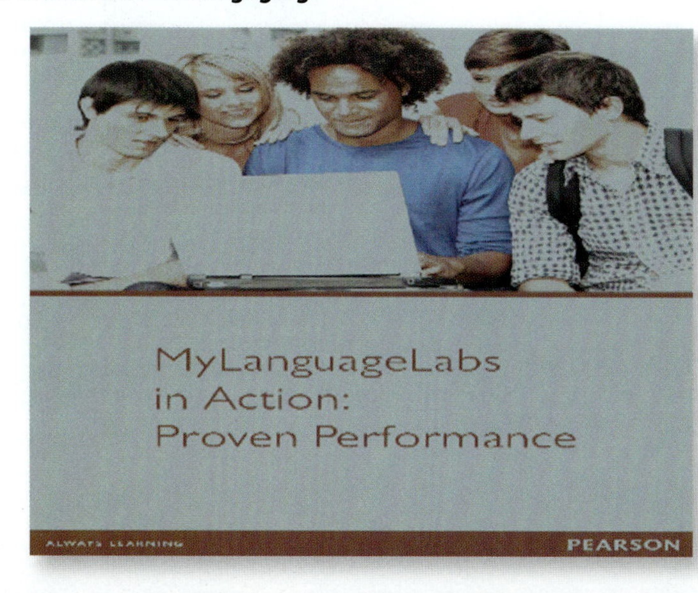

MyLanguageLabs
in Action:
Proven Performance
ALWAYS LEARNING
PEARSON

LEARN SMARTER

Boost performance with powerful, personalized learning!

Powered by **amplifier** and accessible in MySpanishLab, new Dynamic Study Modules combine leading brain science with big-data adaptivity to engage students, drive proficiency, and improve outcomes like never before.

As the language learning and teaching community moves to digital learning tools, Pearson is supercharging its Spanish content and optimizing its learning offerings with personalized Dynamic Study Modules, powered by **amplifier** and MySpanishLab. And, we're already seeing significant gains. Developed exclusively for *Mosaicos*, each study module offers a differentiated digital solution that consistently improves learning results and increases levels of user confidence and engagement with the course materials.

Language instructors observe that they are able to maximize their effectiveness, both in and out of the classroom, because with they are freed from the onerous task of basic knowledge transfer and empowered to:

- reclaim up to 65% more class time for peer to peer communication in the target language;
- tailor presentation and focused practice to address only the most prevalent student knowledge gaps;
- enable livelier, more engaged classrooms.

How does *amplifire* improve learning?

Dynamic Study Modules consist of a comprehensive online learning process that starts with modules of 25 vocabulary and grammar questions that drive deep, contextual knowledge acquisition and understanding.

Based on a Test–Learn–Retest adaptive module, as students respond to each question the tool assesses both knowledge and confidence to identify what students do and don't know. Asking students to indicate their level of confidence engages a different part of the brain than just asking them to answer the question.

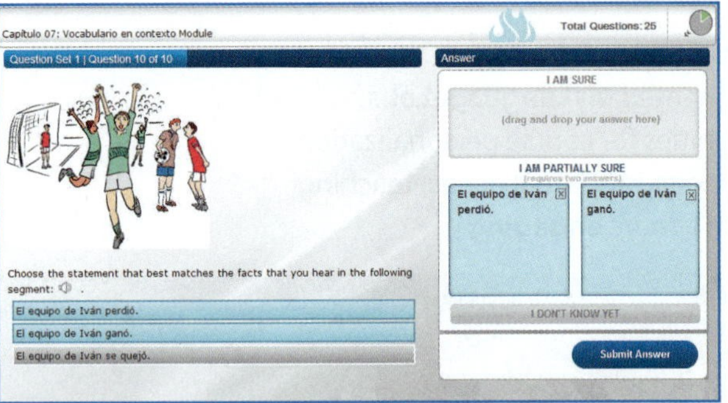

amplifire **results, embedded explanations, and review opportunities are extremely comprehensive and ideal for fast learning and long-lasting retention.**

After completing the first question set, students are given embedded and detailed explanations for their correct answers, as well as why other answer choices were incorrect. This approach, taken directly from research in cognitive psychology, promotes more accurate knowledge recall. Embedding the learning into the application also saves students valuable study time because they have the learning content at their fingertips!

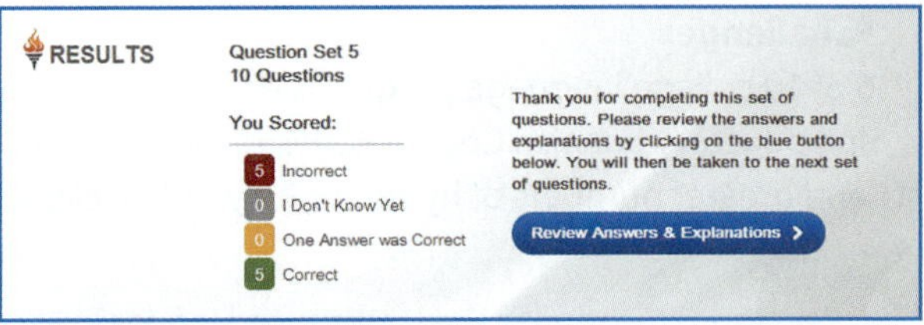

Dynamic Study Modules cycle students through learning content until they demonstrate mastery of the information by answering all questions confidently and correctly two times in a row.

Once students have reviewed the first set answers and explanations, modules ***amplifire*** presents them with a new set of questions. The ***amplifire*** methodology cycles students through an adaptive, repetitive process of test-learn-retest, until they achieve mastery of the material.

RESULTS!

Based on GAMING and LEARNER ENGAGEMENT techniques, AMPLIFIRE DYNAMIC STUDY MODULES take basic knowledge transfer out of the classroom and improve performance.

Improved student performance and long-term retention of the material ensures students are not only better prepared for their exams, but also for their future classes and careers.

Sixth Edition

mosaicos

SPANISH AS A WORLD LANGUAGE

Annotated Instructor's Edition

MATILDE OLIVELLA DE CASTELLS (LATE)
Emerita, California State University, Los Angeles

ELIZABETH E. GUZMÁN
University of Iowa

PALOMA LAPUERTA
Central Connecticut State University

JUDITH E. LISKIN-GASPARRO
University of Iowa

PEARSON

Boston Columbus Indianapolis New York San Francisco Upper Saddle River
Amsterdam Cape Town Dubai London Madrid Milan Munich Paris Montréal Toronto
Delhi Mexico City São Paulo Sydney Hong Kong Seoul Singapore Taipei Tokyo

Senior Acquisitions Editor: Tiziana Aime
Senior Digital Product Manager: Samantha Alducin
Development Editor: Scott Gravina, Celia Meana
MyLanguageLabs Development Editor: Bill Bliss
Director of Program Management: Lisa Iarkowski
Team Lead Program Management: Amber Mackey
Program Manager: Nancy Stevenson
Team Lead Project Managers: Melissa Feimer
Media Coordinator: Regina Rivera
Project Manager: Lynne Breitfeller
Project Manager: Jenna Gray, PreMediaGlobal
Front Cover Design: Black Sun
Cover Image: Maxim Tupikov / Shutterstock
Senior Art Director: Kathryn Foot
Operations Manager: Mary Fischer
Operations Specialist: Roy Roickering
Editorial and Marketing Assistant: Millie Chapman
Editor in Chief: Bob Hemmer
Director of Market Development: Kristine Suárez
World Languages Consultants: Yesha Brill, Mellissa Yokell, Denise Miller

This book was set in 10/13 Serifa Std.

Credits and acknowledgments borrowed from other sources and reproduced, with permission, in this textbook appear on appropriate page within text (or on pages CR-1 to CR-3).

Library of Congress Cataloging-in-Publication Data

Mosaicos : Spanish as a world language / Matilde Olivella de Castells (Late), Emerita, California State University, Los Angeles, Elizabeth E. Guzmán, University of Iowa, Paloma Lapuerta, Central Connecticut State University, Judith E. Liskin-Gasparro, University of Iowa. — sixth Edition.
pages cm
Text is in English and Spanish.
Includes index.
ISBN-13: 978-0-205-25540-5 (alk. paper)
ISBN-10: 0-205-25540-X (alk. paper)
1. Spanish language—Textbooks for foreign speakers—English. I. Castells, Matilde Olivella de. II. Guzmán, Elizabeth E. III. Lapuerta, Paloma. IV. Liskin-Gasparro, Judith E.
PC4129.E5M69 2013
468.2'421—dc23

2013042619

10 9 8 7 6 5 4 3 2 1

Annotated Instructor's Edition ISBN - 10: 0-205-25543-4
Annotated Instructor's Edition ISBN - 13: 978-0-205-25543-6

BRIEF CONTENTS

CAPÍTULO PRELIMINAR Bienvenidos 2

CAPÍTULO 1 ¿Qué estudias? 30

CAPÍTULO 2 ¿Quiénes son tus amigos? 64

CAPÍTULO 3 ¿Qué hacen para divertirse? 100

CAPÍTULO 4 ¿Cómo es tu familia? 136

CAPÍTULO 5 ¿Dónde vives? 170

CAPÍTULO 6 ¿Qué te gusta comprar? 204

CAPÍTULO 7 ¿Cuál es tu deporte favorito? 240

CAPÍTULO 8 ¿Cuáles son tus tradiciones? 276

CAPÍTULO 9 ¿Dónde trabajas? 310

CAPÍTULO 10 ¿Cuál es tu comida preferida? 346

CAPÍTULO 11 ¿Cómo te sientes? 380

CAPÍTULO 12 ¿Te gusta viajar? 414

CAPÍTULO 13 ¿Qué es arte para ti? 448

CAPÍTULO 14 ¿Cómo vivimos los cambios sociales? 478

CAPÍTULO 15 ¿Qué nos trae el futuro? 510

APPENDIX 1 Stress and Written Accents in Spanish A-1

APPENDIX 2 Verb Charts A-3

APPENDIX 3 Spanish-English Glossary A-11

APPENDIX 4 English-Spanish Glossary A-25

Text & Photo Credits A-39

Communicative Functions and Learning Strategies Index A-43

Index A-45

SCOPE & SEQUENCE

Capítulo preliminar
The Preliminary chapter is designed to maximize the comfort level of students and to enhance motivation. It focuses on vocabulary and common expressions to establish a communicative environment and encourage student-to-student talk. Students use the singular forms of ***ser*** and ***estar*** to construct simple sentences.

Capítulo 1
The present tense of regular verbs and the use of articles with nouns facilitate vocabulary building and get students talking about their activities. Interrogative words allow for simple oral exchanges.

Capítulo 2
Students can now describe themselves and others using ***ser*** and ***estar,*** possessive adjectives, and expressions with ***gustar***.

Capítulo	Learning Outcomes	Culture
Preliminar Bienvenidos 2	• Introduce yourself, greet others, and say good-bye • Identify people and classroom objects and tell where they are in the classroom • Listen to and respond to classroom expressions and requests • Spell names and addresses and share phone numbers • Express dates, and tell time, and comment on the weather • Share information about the Spanish language and where it is spoken	**Enfoque cultural:** *El mundo hispano* 3
1 ¿Qué estudias? 30	• Talk about studies, campus, and academic life • Describe daily routines and activities • Specify gender and number • Express location and states of being • Ask and answer questions • Talk about Spain in terms of products, practices, and perspectives • Share information about student life in Hispanic countries and compare cultural similarities	**Enfoque cultural:** *España* 31 **Mosaico cultural:** *La vida universitaria en el mundo hispano* 41
2 ¿Quiénes son tus amigos? 64	• Describe people, places, and things • Express origin and possession • Talk about where and when events take place • Describe what someone or something is like • Express emotions and conditions • Identify what belongs to you and others • Discuss the people, things, and activities you and others like and dislike • Present information about Hispanic influences in the United States	**Enfoque cultural:** *Estados Unidos* 65 **Mosaico cultural:** *Los estereotipos y la cultura hispana* 75

	Vocabulario en contexto	Funciones y formas	Mosaicos
	Las presentaciones 5 *Los saludos y las despedidas* 7 *¿Qué hay en el salón de clase?* 10 *Los meses del año y los días de la semana* 12 *El tiempo* 14 *Expresiones útiles en la clase* 15 *El alfabeto* 18	Identifying and describing people: **Singular forms of *ser* 19** **Cognates 20** Locating people and things: ***Estar* + location 21** Using numbers: **Numbers 0 to 99 23** Expressing time in Spanish: **Telling time 26**	
	Los estudiantes y los cursos 33 *La universidad* 35 *Las actividades de los estudiantes* 38	Talking about academic life and daily occurrences: **Present tense of regular *-ar* verbs 42** Talking about academic life and daily occurrences: **Present tense of regular *-er* and *-ir* verbs 46** Specifying gender and number: **Articles and nouns 50** Expressing location and states of being: **Present tense of *estar* 53** Asking and answering questions: **Interrogative words 55**	**Escucha** • Listen for the gist 59 **Habla** • Ask questions to gather information 60 **Lee** • Identify the format of a text 61 **Escribe** • Brainstorm key ideas before writing 62
	Mis amigos y yo 67 *Las descripciones* 69 *El origen* 72	Describing people, places, and things: **Adjectives 76** Identifying and describing; expressing origin, possession, location of events, and time: **Present tense of *ser* 80** Expressing qualities, emotions, and conditions: ***Ser* and *estar* with adjectives 83** Expressing ownership: **Possessive adjectives 87** Expressing likes and dislikes: ***Gustar* 90**	**Escucha** • Listen for specific information 94 **Habla** • Describe a person 95 **Lee** • Scan a text for specific information 96 **Escribe** • Use adjectives to enrich your descriptions 98

Capítulo 3
Students learn to use the common irregular verbs ***hacer, poner, salir, traer,*** and ***oír*** and expand their communicative horizons with ***ir*** + ***a*** + infinitive to express future plans and activities. The differences between ***saber*** and ***conocer*** introduce important insights about differences in word meanings between English and Spanish.

Capítulo 4
Students learn to use ***tener que*** + infinitive to express intentions and obligations. Along with ***ir*** + ***a*** + infinitive in *Capítulo 3* and ***hace*** with expressions of time in this chapter, students build their ability to use compound structures for more complex meaning. Reflexive verbs with pronouns are introduced in the context of daily routines and will appear in past contexts in *Capítulo 7*.

Capítulo 5
The verb ***tener*** is recycled with additional expressions with ***tener,*** and ***estar*** is recycled with the introduction of the present progressive. These structures, along with direct object and demonstrative pronouns, expand students' ability to talk about their feelings and activities, as well as those of others. With pronouns, students can express themselves beyond the sentence level more smoothly.

Capítulo	Learning Outcomes	Culture
3 ¿Qué hacen para divertirse? 100	• Describe free-time activities and food • Plan your daily activities and express intentions • Identify prices and dates • State what and whom you know • Talk about places to visit in Peru • Share information about free-time activities in Hispanic countries and identify cultural similarities	**Enfoque cultural:** *Perú 101* **Mosaico cultural:** *Los hispanos y la vida social 110*
4 ¿Cómo es tu familia? 136	• Talk about family members and their daily routines • Express opinions, plans, preferences, and feelings • Express obligation • Express how long something has been going on • Talk about Colombia in terms of its products, practices, and perspectives • Share information about families and family life in Hispanic countries and compare cultural similarities	**Enfoque cultural:** *Colombia 137* **Mosaico cultural:** *Las familias de la televisión 146*
5 ¿Dónde vives? 170	• Talk about housing, the home, and household activities • Express ongoing actions • Describe physical and emotional states • Avoid repetition in speaking and writing • Point out and identify people and things • Compare cultural and geographic information of Nicaragua, El Salvador, and Honduras	**Enfoque cultural:** *Nicaragua, El Salvador y Honduras 171* **Mosaico cultural:** *Las viviendas en centros urbanos 181*

	Vocabulario en contexto	Funciones y formas	Mosaicos
	Las diversiones 103 *Los planes* 105 *La comida* 107	Talking about daily activities: **Present tense of *hacer*, *poner*, *salir*, *traer*, and *oír* 111** Expressing movement and plans: **Present tense of *ir* and *ir a* + infinitive 115** Talking about quantity: **Numbers 100 to 2,000,000 119** Stating what you know: ***Saber* and *conocer* 123** Expressing intention, means, movement, and duration: **Some uses of *por* and *para* 127**	**Escucha** • Use background knowledge 131 **Habla** • Inform yourself before you do a survey 132 **Lee** • Look for and use key words 133 **Escribe** • Identify your audience 134
	Los miembros de la familia 139 *¿Qué hacen los parientes?* 143 *Las rutinas familiares* 144	Expressing opinions, plans, preferences, and feelings: **Present tense of stem-changing verbs: *e* → *ie*, *o* → *ue*, and *e* → *i* 147** Talking about daily routine: **Reflexive verbs and pronouns 153** Expressing obligation: ***Tener que* + infinitive 157** Expressing how long something has been going on: ***Hace* with expressions of time 160**	**Escucha** • Listen for a purpose 163 **Habla** • Organize information to make comparisons 164 **Lee** • Use title and illustrations to anticipate content 165 **Escribe** • Use language appropriate for your reader 167
	¿Dónde vives? 173 *La casa, los muebles y los electrodomésticos* 177 *Las tareas domésticas* 179	Expressing ongoing actions: **Present progressive 182** Describing physical and emotional states: **Expressions with *tener* 185** Avoiding repetition in speaking and writing: **Direct object nouns and pronouns 188** Pointing out and identifying people and things: **Demonstrative adjectives and pronouns 193**	**Escucha** • Create mental images 197 **Habla** • Plan what you want to say 198 **Lee** • Inform yourself about a topic before you start to read 199 **Escribe** • Select the appropriate content and tone for a formal description 202

Capítulo 6
Those who use *Mosaicos* over 3 semesters may start a new semester with this chapter. Talking about the past is the focus of this and upcoming chapters. The introduction of the preterit of familiar verbs allows them to start spiraling up into a higher level of performance by recycling vocabulary and expanding their communicative repertoire. Indirect object pronouns are presented to be used with ***gustar*** and similar verbs so they can be immediately used for self-expression.

Capítulo 7
Reflexive verbs and stem-changing verbs, which were introduced in earlier chapters, are now recycled in past contexts. Some irregular preterits are also introduced to expand students' ability to talk about past actions.

Capítulo 8
The imperfect is presented here to allow students to differentiate between narration and description in the past. The preterit and the imperfect will be combined after ample practice with each one. Comparisons (introduced briefly in *Capítulo 2*) are formally presented to expand the possibility of contrasting present and past experiences.

Capítulo	Learning Outcomes	Culture
6 ¿Qué te gusta comprar? 204	• Talk about shopping and clothes • Talk about events in the past • Indicate to whom or for whom an action takes place • Express likes and dislikes • Describe people, objects, and events • Share information about shopping practices in Hispanic countries and compare cultural similarities	**Enfoque cultural:** *Venezuela* 205 **Mosaico cultural:** *Las tiendas de barrio* 215
7 ¿Cuál es tu deporte favorito? 240	• Talk about sports • Emphasize and clarify information • Talk about past events • Talk about practices and perspectives on sports in Argentina and Uruguay • Share information about sporting events in Hispanic countries and compare cultural similarities	**Enfoque cultural:** *Argentina y Uruguay* 241 **Mosaico cultural:** *Los hinchas y el superclásico* 250
8 ¿Cuáles son tus tradiciones? 276	• Discuss situations and celebrations • Describe conditions and express ongoing actions in the past • Tell stories about past events • Compare people and things • Talk about Mexico in terms of practices and perspectives • Share information about celebrations in Hispanic countries and compare cultural similarities	**Enfoque cultural:** *México* 277 **Mosaico cultural:** *Los carnavales y las tradiciones* 285

	Vocabulario en contexto	Funciones y formas	Mosaicos
	Las compras *207* *La ropa* *210* *¿Qué debo llevar?* *213*	Talking about the past: **Preterit tense of regular verbs 216** Talking about the past *ir* and *Ser*: **Preterit of *ir* and *ser* 219** Indicating to whom or for whom an action takes place: **Indirect object nouns and pronouns 222** Expressing likes and dislikes: ***Gustar* and similar verbs 226** Describing people, objects, and events: **More about *ser* and *estar* *230***	**Escucha** • Take notes to recall information 235 **Habla** • Negotiate a price 236 **Lee** • Use context to figure out the meaning of unfamiliar words 237 **Escribe** • Recount events in sequence 238
	Los deportes *243* *El tiempo y las estaciones* *246* *¿Qué pasó ayer?* *248*	Talking about the past: **Preterit of reflexive verbs 251** Talking about the past: **Preterit of *-er* and *-ir* verbs whose stem ends in a vowel 256** Talking about the past: **Preterit of stem-changing *-ir* verbs 259** Emphasizing or clarifying information: **Pronouns after prepositions 263** Talking about the past: **Some irregular preterits 266**	**Escucha** • Differentiate fact from opinion 270 **Habla** • Focus on key information 271 **Lee** • Predict and guess content 272 **Escribe** • Use supporting details 274
	Las fiestas y las tradiciones *279* *Otras celebraciones* *281* *Las invitaciones* *283*	Expressing ongoing actions and describing in the past: **The imperfect 286** Narrating in the past: **The preterit and the imperfect 290** Comparing people and things: **Comparisons of inequality 293** Comparing people and things: **Comparisons of equality 297** Comparing people and things: **The superlative 300**	**Escucha** • Draw conclusions based on what you know 304 **Habla** • Conduct an interview 305 **Lee** • Make inferences 306 **Escribe** • Select and sequence details 308

Capítulo 9
Direct and indirect pronouns are recycled from *Capítulos 5* and *6* to be used together to provide practice with more complex structures. Formal commands are also presented in this chapter so that students may learn to give advice and make suggestions.

Capítulo 10
Impersonal constructions with ***se*** allow students to talk about events beyond their direct experience. To expose the students to all of the major time frames, the present perfect (to talk about the recent past) and the future tenses are also presented in this chapter.

Capítulo 11
Those who use *Mosaicos* over 3 semesters may start a new semester with this chapter. The subjunctive mood is introduced in this chapter and its major functions are introduced in upcoming chapters. The chapter presents the verb forms and its use with expressions of hope, emotion, and influence.

Capítulo	Learning Outcomes	Culture
9 ¿Dónde trabajas? 310	• Talk about careers and employment • Avoid repetition • Describe past events in more detail • Give instructions and suggestions • Compare demographic and economic changes in Guatemala and in the United States	**Enfoque cultural:** *Guatemala 311* **Mosaico cultural:** *¿Trabajas o estudias? 321*
10 ¿Cuál es tu comida preferida? 346	• Talk about ingredients, recipes, and meals • State impersonal information • Talk about the recent past • Give instructions in informal settings • Talk about the future • Present information, concepts, and ideas about food and public health in Ecuador and other Latin American countries	**Enfoque cultural:** *Ecuador 347* **Mosaico cultural:** *Comida callejera 356*
11 ¿Cómo te sientes? 380	• Discuss health and medical treatments • Express expectations and hopes • Describe emotions, opinions, and wishes • Express goals, purposes, and means • Share information about public health and medical practices in Cuba and the Dominican Republic, and compare cultural similarities	**Enfoque cultural:** *Cuba y República Dominicana 381* **Mosaico cultural:** *Los remedios caseros 390*

	Vocabulario en contexto	Funciones y formas	Mosaicos
	El trabajo 313 *Los oficios y las profesiones* 315 *Buscando trabajo* 318	Avoiding repetition: **Review of direct and indirect object pronouns 322** Avoiding repetition: **Use of direct and indirect object pronouns together 326** Talking about the past: **More on the imperfect and the preterit 330** Giving instructions or suggestions: **Formal commands 334**	**Escucha** • Use contextual guessing 339 **Habla** • Gather information strategically to express a decision 340 **Lee** • Organize textual information into categories 342 **Escribe** • Focus on purpose, content, and audience 344
	Los productos y las recetas 349 *En el supermercado* 351 *La mesa* 354	Stating impersonal information: ***Se* + verb constructions 357** Talking about the recent past: **Present perfect and participles used as adjectives 360** Giving instructions in informal settings: **Informal commands 364** Talking about the future: **The future tense 368**	**Escucha** • Make notes of relevant details 374 **Habla** • Give and defend reasons for a decision 375 **Lee** • Learn new words by analyzing their connections with known words 376 **Escribe** • Summarize information 378
	Médicos, farmacias y hospitales 383 *Las partes del cuerpo* 386 *La salud* 388	Expressing expectations and hopes: **Introduction to the present subjunctive 391** Expressing requests: **The subjunctive with expressions of influence 395** Expressing emotions, opinions, and attitudes: **The subjunctive with expressions of emotion 398** Expressing goals, purposes, and means: **Uses of *por* and *para* 401**	**Escucha** • Listen for the main idea 407 **Habla** • Select appropriate phrases to offer opinions 408 **Lee** • Focus on relevant information 409 **Escribe** • Persuade through suggestions and advice 411

Capítulo 12
Students use the subjunctive in affirmative and negative expressions, expressions of doubt, and with adjective clauses to expand their ability to talk about situations that may not or do not exist. The longer forms of possessive pronouns are also presented in this chapter.

Capítulo 13
Students continue to learn how to talk about uncertain and nonexistent situations with the introduction of the conditional. The preterit and the imperfect are also recycled to reinforce the use of the past tense.

Capítulo 14
To allow students to express hypothesis and conjecture, some adverbial conjunctions that require the subjunctive are introduced. The use of the past tense is further reinforced through the presentation of the past perfect.

Capítulo 15
Additional ways of making hypothesis are introduced after the presentation of the imperfect subjunctive. The presentation of ***se*** for unplanned occurrences recycles the use of the indirect object pronouns, concluding the logical sequence and a solid foundation that have prepared students for further practice and learning.

Capítulo	Learning Outcomes	Culture
12 ¿Te gusta viajar? 414	• Talk about travel arrangements and preferences • Express possession and clarify what belongs to you and to others • Express affirmation and negation • Express doubt and uncertainty • Talk about travel experiences • Share information about the social and economic impact of the Panama Canal	**Enfoque cultural:** *Costa Rica y Panamá* 415 **Mosaico cultural:** *El mochilero* 425
13 ¿Qué es arte para ti? 448	• Talk about art and culture • Express doubt and uncertainty • Hypothesize about the future • Describe states and conditions • Talk about Bolivia and Paraguay in terms of products, practices, and perspectives • Share information about art and culture in Hispanic countries and identify cultural similarities	**Enfoque cultural:** *Bolivia y Paraguay* 449 **Mosaico cultural:** *El grafiti y la identidad urbana* 460
14 ¿Cómo vivimos los cambios sociales? 478	• Discuss demographics and social conditions • Indicate conditions, goals, and purposes • Express conjecture • Talk about the past from a past perspective • Share information about social change, gender roles, and migration in Hispanic countries and identify cultural similarities	**Enfoque cultural:** *Chile* 479 **Mosaico cultural:** *La migración interna en el mundo hispano* 487
15 ¿Qué nos trae el futuro? 510	• Talk about advances in science and technology • Express wishes and recommendations in the past • Hypothesize and share information about the present and the future • Express unexpected occurrences • Talk about Puerto Rico in terms of its advances in science and technology	**Enfoque cultural:** *Puerto Rico* 511 **Mosaico cultural:** *La investigación tecnológica en Latinoamérica* 520

	Vocabulario en contexto	Funciones y formas	Mosaicos
	Los medios de transporte 417 *El alojamiento y las reservaciones 421* *Viajando en coche 423*	Expressing affirmation and negation: **Affirmative and negative expressions 426** Talking about things that may not exist: **Subjunctive in adjective clauses 430** Expressing possession: **Possessive pronouns 434** Expressing doubt and uncertainty: **Subjunctive with expressions of doubt 437**	**Escucha** • Use background knowledge to support comprehension 442 **Habla** • Make your presentations comprehensible and interesting 443 **Lee** • Focus on logical relationships 444 **Escribe** • Use facts to offer good advice 446
	La literatura y el cine 451 *La pintura y el arte 454* *La música y la cultura popular 457*	Talking about the past: **Review of the preterit and imperfect 461** Hypothesizing: **The conditional 464** Expressing reciprocity: **Reciprocal verbs and pronouns 468**	**Escucha** • Identify the speaker's intentions 472 **Habla** • Make your presentations comprehensible and interesting 473 **Lee** • Focus on multiple meanings when reading poetry 474 **Escribe** • Write to spark interest 476
	Cambios en la sociedad 481 *El papel de la mujer 484* *Temas de hoy: los jóvenes y la emigración 485*	Expressing conjecture: **Adverbial conjunctions that require the subjunctive 488** Expressing conjecture or certainty: **Adverbial conjunctions that take the subjunctive or indicative 491** Talking about the past from a past perspective: **The past perfect 496** Expressing actions: **The infinitive as subject or object 499**	**Escucha** • Identify the speaker's point of view 503 **Habla** • Organize ideas to present solutions to problems 504 **Lee** • Identify the tone of a text 505 **Escribe** • Use language to express emotions 507
	La ciencia y la tecnología en el mundo de hoy 513 *La conservación del medio ambiente 515* *Otros retos del futuro 517*	Expressing wishes and recommendations in the past: **The imperfect subjunctive 521** Hypothesizing about the present and the future: ***If*-clauses 525** Expressing the unexpected: ***Se* for unplanned occurrences 529**	**Escucha** • Identify the speaker's intention through the main idea and specific information 533 **Habla** • Use drama and humor in telling a personal anecdote 534 **Lee** • Identify the narrator's perspective 536 **Escribe** • Use imagination and humor in writing a narrative 538

NEW to *Mosaicos,* Sixth Edition

Students and instructors will benefit from a wealth of new content and features in this edition. Detailed, contextualized descriptions are provided in the features walk-through that follows.

- **amplifire Dynamic Study Modules,** available in MySpanishLab, are designed to improve learning and long-term retention of vocabulary and grammar via a learning tool developed from the latest research in neuroscience and cognitive psychology on how we learn best. Students master critical course concepts online with **amplifire,** resulting in a livelier classroom experience centered on meaningful communication.
- ***¡Cineastas en acción!,*** a new video program created especially for ***Mosaicos,* sixth edition,** brings together five young filmmakers from different Spanish-speaking countries to attend a summer program at the Los Angeles Film Institute. As part of the program, each will produce documentaries on Hispanic culture in the United States or abroad while competing for a prestigious scholarship for best documentary. Who will win? Students using the ***Mosaicos*** program will decide!

  And, of course, our five young filmmakers will not only learn about making documentaries, but will also learn about each other, and create new bonds as they experience the diversity of Hispanic cultures in Los Angeles.
- Each chapter begins with a robust and interesting two-page cultural section—***Enfoque cultural***—which introduces students to the country of focus and starts the cultural integration that continues throughout the chapter.
- Midway through the chapter, ***Mosaico cultural*** provides a journalistic, thematic cultural presentation. The focus is not on a specific country, but rather on the chapter's theme and how it is reflected in different Spanish-speaking countries, including Hispanic communities in the United States.
- Relevant and interesting cultural information is presented as the introduction to many activities through brief ***Cultura*** sections. Rather than just a boxed aside, the cultural information presented through text and photographs forms the precursor to the activity, making clear and direct connections between language and culture. Accompanying *Comparaciones, Conexiones,* or *Comunidades* questions encourage meaningful communication and cross-cultural reflection.
- Teacher notes provide **additional cultural information** relevant to specific activities that the instructor may wish to highlight to further enrich the cultural aspect of the activities.
- **Learning Outcomes** are provided at the beginning of the chapter giving students a clear idea of the expected performance goals.
- Care has been taken to ensure that the **ACTFL Performance Descriptors**—Presentational, Interpretive, and Interpersonal—are put to consistent use throughout the chapter. A boxed Teacher's Note at the beginning of each chapter details precisely which activities fulfill the requirements for each mode. Additionally, the ***Mosaicos*** skills section is organized around the modes.
- **Advance organizers** accompany the ***Situación*** role plays, providing guidance for students to increase their success in communicating. Each grammar module now culminates with one rather than two *Situaciones* activities with careful attention given to the activity's "situation" being realistic and encouraging meaningful communication among students. Additional ***Situación*** activities are available in MySpanishLab and via the *Situaciones* mobile app including rubrics for activities intended to be completed in real time with Pearson's network of native speakers from around the world.
- The **visual aspect** of the vocabulary presentation has been enhanced providing even more contextualization for the new vocabulary.
- Guided **Vocabulary Tutorials** are provided within **MySpanishLab.** Students work through a series of word recognition activities, most of which culminate with a pronunciation activity in which students compare their pronunciation to that of a native speaker.
- **Pronunciation presentation and practice** is provided for each chapter within MySpanishLab with accompanying text and audio followed by activities.
- Each vocabulary section now begins with an input-based comprehension check. The first vocabulary presentation is followed by an audio-based activity, ***Escucha y confirma***. ***Para confirmar*** follows the second two vocabulary presentations, providing students with the first step towards achieving comprehension.
- A new form-focused activity, ***¿Comprendes?***, follows the presentation of each grammatical structure. This quick, form-focused activity provides students with the opportunity to test themselves in order to ensure they have understood the form of the structure before moving on. ***¿Comprendes?*** activities are also available to be completed online in MySpanishLab.
- ***En directo*** boxes, which provide colloquial expressions for specific activities making speech more native-like, now include **audio** so that students can listen to the expressions used in realistic conversational contexts.
- The ***Mosaicos*** skills section has been edited to make it more manageable for students. Some of the readings for the *Lee* section have been updated, ensuring consistently high-interest readings at the appropriate level. Additionally, the texts featured in the *Lee* section of chapters 13–15 are now pieces of **authentic literature** including stories and a poem.
- ***Comprueba lo que sabes,*** found in MySpanishLab is interactive and encourages students to self-check their mastery of chapter content. Additional practice and games that reinforce chapter vocabulary and grammar is available online.
- **Annotated Scope and Sequence** The authors share their thinking through annotations in the Scope and Sequence of the Annotated Instructor's Edition, explaining the rationale of the grammar scope and sequence.

WHY *MOSAICOS*? WHY THEN... AND WHY NOW?

It has been twenty years since ***Mosaicos*** first appeared in 1994, ushering in a new and evolved vision of how the elements that comprise basic language instruction could be combined in a highly communicative, culturally based language program. Its vision was complete and synthetic, both in the integrity of each element as well as the gathering of these elements into an integrated, connected whole. This vision of wholeness was transformed to become a sound and compelling approach, reflecting the nature of language and how it is learned. The ***Mosaicos*** title was carefully chosen to reflect the principles upon which it was founded and the manner in which it was structured.

The most basic elements of this approach were the following:

- A **guided communicative approach** based on solid methodological principles combined with years of empirical classroom experience, creating an informed and sensible pedagogy that works not only in theory, but also in practice.
- Learning **language in context** with a **focus on meaning.**
- The **integration of culture** as an essential part of language and of the experience of learning it.
- A **synthetic and focused approach** to listening, speaking, reading, and writing.
- The interweaving throughout the program of these elements.

The innovative and evolved approach taken in ***Mosaicos*** set a new standard for language programs and changed basic language publishing. Most important, ***Mosaicos*** has continued to evolve in response to current standards of language teaching, the recommendations of our many reviewers and their experiences in the classroom, as well as the new technologies that transform the potential for achieving more and better communication in the classroom. The new sixth edition of ***Mosaicos*** is more solid and more integrated than ever before, creating for students a multifaceted experience of the intricate mosaic of the Spanish language and its cultures.

Over the past twenty years, many new and reimagined Beginning Spanish programs have appeared, but ***Mosaicos*, sixth edition** continues to offer a unique approach for this reason:

Mosaicos *offers instructors the truly communicative, deeply culture-focused approach they seek while providing the guidance and tools students need to be successful using a program with highly communicative goals. With* Mosaicos*, there is no need to compromise.*

This inclusiveness of ***Mosaicos*, sixth edition** extends to the broad range of students often found in many Spanish-language classrooms. Accommodating the needs and abilities of all students, from struggling learners to gifted ones, without compromising either group, is a perpetual dilemma for instructors. ***Mosaicos*, sixth edition** provides a highly communicative program with an articulated focus on culture, built in such a way that all students receive the guided learning support they need to succeed and become accomplished learners as they benefit from the rich program and opportunities for communication. Even the struggling student's individual possibilities for learning and communication are not shortchanged; the ***Mosaicos*, sixth edition** program offers the opportunity for achieving more than these students may have thought possible, allowing them to fulfill their true potential.

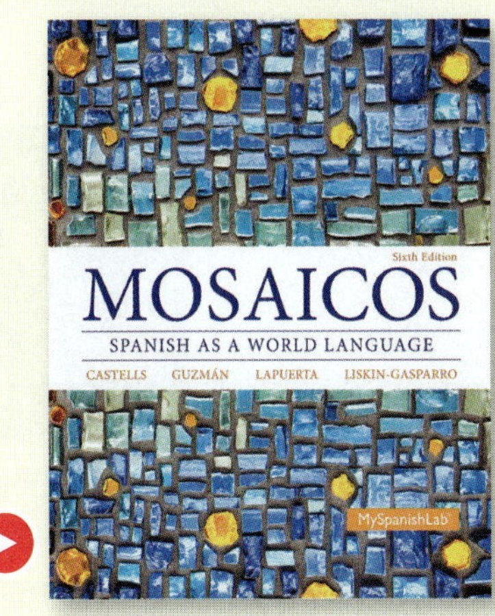

HOW DOES MOSAICOS *DO THIS?*

Integrated Culture | Context | Communication and Guidance | Four-Skills Synthesis

These words have appeared in many programs, but we believe the sixth edition of ***Mosaicos*** meticulously elaborates those simple words into a beautifully conceived, tightly woven, highly articulated program.

CULTURE

Up front and center, and everywhere in between!

All language is enveloped by and imbued with culture—it is the very substance of language. Culture is found both at the forefront and embedded throughout every chapter in ***Mosaicos*, sixth edition.** From its first edition, the authors of ***Mosaicos*** emphasized the link between culture and language and, in response to the broad and emphatic desire from our many users and reviewers, the new sixth edition has taken this coverage to new levels. Let's look at the many ways in which culture is integrated throughout the new ***Mosaicos*, sixth edition** program by looking at examples from Chapter 4.

NEW! *Enfoque cultural:* Each chapter begins with a robust and interesting two-page cultural section that

ENFOQUE *cultural* COLOMBIA

Enfoque cultural
To learn more about Colombia, go to MySpanishLab to view the *Vistas culturales* videos.

¿QUÉ TE PARECE?

- Medellín recibe el premio a "la ciudad más innovadora del 2012" en reconocimiento de su planificación urbana.
- El 95% (por ciento) de las esmeraldas del mundo vienen de Colombia.
- Colombia es el país más biodiverso por metro cuadrado (*square meter*) del planeta.
- Colombia produce el 12% (por ciento) del café del mundo.

Fernando Botero, uno de los pintores contemporáneos más famosos de Colombia, pinta a unos padres con sus hijos en este cuadro titulado *En familia.*

¿Cómo es tu familia? **137**

introduces students to the country of focus, giving students a real sense of the vibrancy and uniqueness of the Hispanic cultures. The cultural presentation has been significantly increased at the beginning of the chapter for two reasons. First, many students lack cultural knowledge of the countries in focus, including their geographic location, and thus benefit from this orientation before delving into the chapter. Second, leaving the main cultural presentation for the end of the chapter (as many programs do) makes culture look like an afterthought that is separate from the language itself.

Maps provide geographic location and shared borders with surrounding countries, along with visuals of some cultural and geographic features.

A **work of art** from the country in focus is provided, along with cultural information about the work, and it is enhanced online with a fully **Interactive Art Tour** in MySpanishLab. These tours, developed by experts in language and culture, feature Spanish narrations, offer an in-depth look at the work of art, and enable students to zoom in on details they couldn't otherwise see. At the same time, the tours provide further cultural information.

The **Interactive Globe**, located in the ***Enfoque cultural*** sections and found in MySpanishLab, allows students to further explore the country of focus and the cultural theme of each chapter through ***Vistas culturales*** videos and popular newspapers and magazines.

NEW! *¿Qué te parece?* Far from a dry list of statistics, these interesting and memorable cultural facts, serve to pique students' interest and begin to give shape to the individual countries.

NEW! A full page is devoted to a country-focused, cultural photomontage with captioned readings, giving students a sense of the richness and the accomplishments of the country's culture and facilitates a discussion around culture. Language is carefully controlled, which ensures that students can comfortably comprehend the content. Vocabulary and grammar from previous chapters are recycled, but no new structures are introduced. Any new, non-active vocabulary is either a cognate or is glossed. The photographs also provide context with visual clues.

ENFOQUE cultural

El carnaval de Barranquilla se celebra cada año cuatro días antes de la Cuaresma (*Lent*). Atrae a personas de todas partes que desean disfrutar de las tradiciones, la música y el baile colombianos.

El escritor colombiano y ganador del Premio Nobel de Literatura, Gabriel García Márquez, cuenta con grandes éxitos literarios, entre ellos, su obra maestra, *Cien años de soledad* (*One Hundred Years of Solitude*).

Dieciocho millones de bombillos multicolores iluminan el paseo del río Medellín. Este espectáculo de luces dura (*lasts*) desde el 1 de diciembre hasta el 7 de enero.

Bogotá, la capital de Colombia, está situada en el centro del país, a 2.600 metros sobre el nivel del mar. Es una ciudad moderna, y a la vez tradicional.

¿CUÁNTO SABES?

Completa estas oraciones (*sentences*) con la información correcta.

1. Ecuador, __Perú__ y Brasil están al sur de Colombia.
2. Las casas pintadas de diferentes colores son típicas en la ciudad de __Cartagena de Indias__.
3. __Fernando Botero__ es un pintor colombiano.
4. El 95% de las __esmeraldas__ del mundo y el 12% del __café__ vienen de Colombia.
5. En Barranquilla se celebra __el carnaval__ con música y baile en las calles.

138 Capítulo 4

NEW! ***¿Cuánto sabes?*** Brief questions on the two chapter-opening cultural pages serve as a classroom warm-up and help ensure that students are accountable and that they read for meaning.

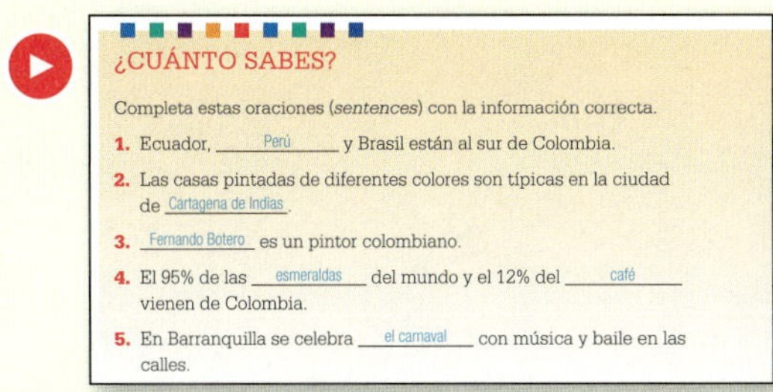

¿CUÁNTO SABES?

Completa estas oraciones (*sentences*) con la información correcta.

1. Ecuador, __Perú__ y Brasil están al sur de Colombia.
2. Las casas pintadas de diferentes colores son típicas en la ciudad de __Cartagena de Indias__.
3. __Fernando Botero__ es un pintor colombiano.
4. El 95% de las __esmeraldas__ del mundo y el 12% del __café__ vienen de Colombia.
5. En Barranquilla se celebra __el carnaval__ con música y baile en las calles.

MOSAICO cultural — Las familias de la televisión

Al igual que en Estados Unidos y en muchos países del mundo, la familia ocupa un lugar importante en los programas televisivos. La telenovela *Los Reyes* es una de las más famosas de la televisión colombiana. Esta serie es sobre una familia de clase media que tiene que trabajar mucho para tener una vida tranquila. Los diálogos de esta telenovela son realistas y las situaciones también.

Los Reyes es una crítica social, habla de los conflictos de clase y de los problemas de la sociedad colombiana. Sin embargo, usa a la familia como núcleo de esa discusión. La serie muestra que Colombia es un país moderno y complejo.

Naturalmente, estos conflictos no son exclusivos de Colombia. En México, Argentina y España, este tipo de programa es también muy popular. En España, por ejemplo, la serie *Los Serrano* cuenta la historia de Diego Serrano, un viudo (*widower*) con tres hijos. La historia se complica cuando Diego se casa con Lucía, madre divorciada con dos hijas. Las dos familias tienen que adaptarse para convivir juntas. Al final, como es el caso en muchas familias, la convivencia requiere paciencia y comprensión entre todos los miembros.

La familia ve otro episodio divertido de la serie *Los Reyes*.

El elenco (*cast*) de la serie *Los Serrano*

Compara

1. ¿Qué familias famosas hay en la televisión de tu país? ¿Cuál es tu favorita?
2. Escoge a una familia de una serie televisiva que te gusta. Describe a esta familia.
3. Compara la familia de la serie televisiva con tu propia familia. ¿Qué tienen en común? ¿Qué diferencias hay entre ellas?

146 Capítulo 4

NEW! Chapter theme, learning outcomes, and culture all come together in ***Mosaico cultural***. Midway through the chapter (between the vocabulary and grammar sections), ***Mosaico cultural*** provides a journalistic, thematic, cultural presentation. The focus here is not on a specific country but rather on different cultural aspects of the Hispanic world, including Latinos in the United States, which are relevant to the chapter theme. The communicative *Compara* questions that follow the readings provide the opportunity for cross-cultural reflection.

NEW! ***Cultura*** Relevant and interesting cultural information is presented when appropriate as the introduction to an activity. The cultural input through text and photographs forms the first step to doing the activity, making the clear and direct connection between language and culture. Accompanying *Comparaciones, Conexiones,* or *Comunidades* questions encourage meaningful communication and cross-cultural reflection.

Cultura

La familia real española

Spain is the only Spanish-speaking country that is a parliamentary system with a constitutional monarchy. The Spanish Royal Family consists of King Juan Carlos, Queen Sofía, and their children Prince Felipe, Infanta Elena and Infanta Cristina. The monarchy is part of the Bourbon Dynasty and has been in Spain since the year 1700.

Conexiones. ¿Sabes qué otros países tienen una monarquía hoy? Busca información en Internet sobre una de ellas y describe a los miembros de su familia para presentar en clase.

4-5

¿Quién es y cómo es?

PREPARACIÓN. Escojan (*Choose*) un miembro de una familia famosa (los Obama, los Jackson, los Kennedy, los Kardashian, etc.) y preparen su árbol familiar.

INTERCAMBIOS. Túrnense (*Take turns*) para describir el árbol familiar de esta persona.

MODELO EL PRÍNCIPE FELIPE

E1: *Es el hijo de los Reyes de España. Su esposa es Leticia. Tienen dos hijas.*

E2: *Sus hijas se llaman Leonor y Sofía. Elena y Cristina son las hermanas mayores del Príncipe Felipe.*

4-6

El arte de preguntar. **PREPARACIÓN.** Túrnense para preparar las preguntas a estas respuestas.

MODELO Mi madre se llama Dolores.

¿Cómo se llama tu madre?

1. Tengo dos hermanos.
2. Vivo con mi madre y mi padrastro.
3. Tengo dos abuelas y un abuelo.
4. Mis abuelos no viven con nosotros.
5. Tengo muchos primos.
6. Tengo una media hermana, pero no vive con nosotros.

INTERCAMBIOS. Ahora háganse (*ask each other*) preguntas para obtener información sobre la familia de su compañero/a. Después, compartan (*share*) esta información con la clase.

Cultura

Los apellidos

In Hispanic culture, people offically use two surnames, the first is their father's and the second is their mother's. For example, in Pablo's family, his father's name is Jaime Méndez and his mother's name is Elena Sánchez. Pablo's official name, then, is Pablo Méndez Sánchez.

Comparaciones. ¿Cuántos nombres y apellidos tienes? En la cultura hispana, ¿cuál sería (*would be*) tu nombre oficial?

4-7

Mi familia. Busca fotos de tus familiares en tu celular o en Facebook. Luego, muéstrale las fotos a tu compañero/a y describe a tus familiares.

1. nombre y apellido
2. relación familiar
3. personalidad
4. actividades que haces con la persona

142 Capítulo 4

4-27 

Un viaje (*trip*) a Colombia. **PREPARACIÓN.** Tu familia va a viajar a Colombia. Selecciona la mejor recomendación para cada persona. Después añade (*add*) algo que quieres hacer tú y explica por qué.

1. ___b___ Mi hermana quiere visitar un lugar religioso muy original.
2. ___c___ A mis padres les gustaría ver joyas (*jewels*) precolombinas.
3. ___a___ Mi prima quiere escuchar música colombiana.
4. ___d___ Mis abuelos prefieren las actividades al aire libre.

a. Tiene que asistir a un concierto de Los Príncipes del Vallenato.
b. Tiene que ir a la Catedral de Sal.
c. Tienen que ir al Museo del Oro.
d. Tienen que conocer el Parque Ecológico El Portal.

INTERCAMBIOS. Busca información en Internet y prepara una breve descripción de uno de los lugares, grupos o eventos siguientes. Incluye la ubicación (*location*) y las actividades asociadas con el lugar, el grupo o los eventos. Luego, comparte la información con la clase.

1. Los Príncipes del Vallenato
2. la Catedral de Sal
3. el Museo del Oro
4. el Parque Arqueológico de San Agustín

Culture Integrated within Activities: Chapter-relevant culture is often integrated within the activities. In this example, the activities for learning to "express obligation with *tener que* + infinitive" are related to the culture of Colombia.

VIDEO

cineasta 1. com. Persona que se dedica al cine, especialmente como director.

¡Cineastas en acción!: *Where people and cultures come together!*

The Cast

All aspiring documentary filmmakers

Esteban [Costa Rica]

Artistic, free-spirited surfer

Yolanda [Mexico]

Vegan. Green. Hipster.

Esteban's good looks catch her eye, but Federico tries to touch her heart.

Vanesa [Spain]

Madrileña. Trasnochadora. Full of fun and high spirits. Who cannot love fashionista Vanesa?

Federico [Argentina]

Meat lover. A little macho and full of himself. Can he win over vegan Yolanda who finds him just plain annoying?

Héctor [Peru]

The nice guy and everyone's friend.

THE LOCATION

The Los Angeles Film Institute

Our protagonists' rendezvous point: Blanca's house, their home for the summer

The city of Los Angeles and a myriad of sites throughout the Hispanic world

THE SET-UP

Our five aspiring young filmmakers attend the Los Angeles Film Institute's summer program on documentary filmmaking. Each explores, learns, and then documents the wealth of Hispanic culture in the United States and abroad as part of their course work. Each has also brought previously shot footage from Spanish-speaking countries around the world. Lots of cultural exchange goes on among these new friends as they share aspects of their native cultures and personal experiences through video.

However, our friendly *amigos* are in competition with each other for a prestigious scholarship—spending the next academic year at the Institute—awarded to the student who produces the best work over the course of the summer. Who decides who deserves to win the coveted *beca*? Students using the ***Mosaicos*, sixth edition** program will decide!

Technology also opens up further cultural exchange. The filmmakers are able to virtually share their various projects using tablets and smartphones. In addition, when Vanesa's cousin contacts her on Skype from Guatemala, they hop onto her Facebook page to view her photo album of Guatemala while she narrates her experiences working there. *¡El mundo se convierte en un pañuelo!*

Put five eclectic young filmmakers together and of course some drama will ensue—friendships, rivalries, and maybe even some romance. Watch the dramas unfold!

THE PEDAGOGY

The central theme of each video segment expands on the overarching theme of each ***Mosaicos*, sixth edition** chapter. In the chapter *¿Qué hacen para divertirse?*, we'll visit a Peruvian restaurant in Los Angeles where the chef shares her recipe for *pescado encebollado*. We learn through Federico's eyes what his neighborhood and house in Buenos Aires look like in the chapter *¿Dónde vives?*. In *¿Qué te gusta comprar?*, we'll view a Latino fashion show in Los Angeles and in *¿Cuáles son tus tradiciones?*, we get a close-up look at the exuberance of the La Mercé festival in Barcelona. Tapas culture in Spain, gay marriage in Argentina, surfing in Perú—just a few of the many worlds our friends explore and share!

- Dialogues reinforce each chapter's vocabulary and grammar.
- In-text activities in the ***En acción*** section of the chapter provide pre-, during, and post-viewing activities (continuing the process approach of the ***Mosaicos*** four-skills section).
- Instructors can—at their discretion and reflecting their own methodology—choose whether Spanish captions are available to students. A variety of different types of auto-graded interactive activities are provided within MySpanishLab that assess listening comprehension and cultural knowledge.
- Additional culturally-based video activities are found in MySpanishLab.

CONTEXT

Vocabulary and grammar where they belong—in communicative and cultural context!

In addition to presenting language in the context of culture, one of the hallmarks of ***Mosaicos*** has always been the presentation of vocabulary and grammar in context through a communicatively rich format.

Vocabulario en contexto

New vocabulary is presented in contexts that reflect the chapter theme. Vocabulary is chunked into three modules per chapter so students can learn and practice a manageable amount. Language samples, photos, line drawings, and realia are used to present new material, rather than word lists and translations. Vocabulary is then consistently **recycled in new contexts,** within and across the chapters, blending it with new words and structures.

Boldface type is used within the language samples to highlight key words and phrases that students will need to learn to use actively. Audio icons remind students that recorded versions of the language samples are available online or on CD. A convenient list of these words and phrases with their translation is provided at the end of the chapter with accompanying audio.

NEW! Learning Outcomes clearly listed at the beginning of the chapter give students a clear idea of their goals for this section.

Strategically placed *Lengua* boxes provide students with succinct information right at the point of need to support self-expression.

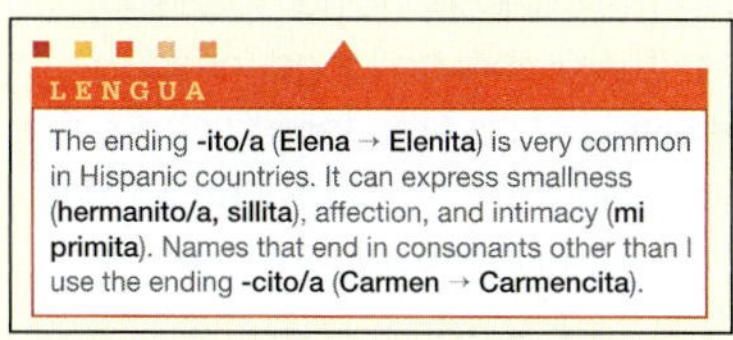

LENGUA

The ending **-ito/a** (**Elena** → **Elenita**) is very common in Hispanic countries. It can express smallness (**hermanito/a, sillita**), affection, and intimacy (**mi primita**). Names that end in consonants other than l use the ending **-cito/a** (**Carmen** → **Carmencita**).

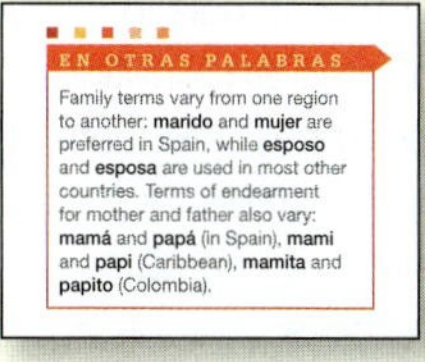

EN OTRAS PALABRAS

Family terms vary from one region to another: **marido** and **mujer** are preferred in Spain, while **esposo** and **esposa** are used in most other countries. Terms of endearment for mother and father also vary: **mamá** and **papá** (in Spain), **mami** and **papi** (Caribbean), **mamita** and **papito** (Colombia).

En otras palabras boxes give examples of regional variations of the language.

Vocabulario en contexto

Talking about family members, what they do, and their daily routines

Los miembros de la familia

NEW! Online Vocabulary Tutorials. Guided online vocabulary tutorials offer students opportunities to work through a series of word recognition activities that help them tie words to images. Most tutorials culminate with a pronunciation activity where students compare their pronunciation to that of a native speaker.

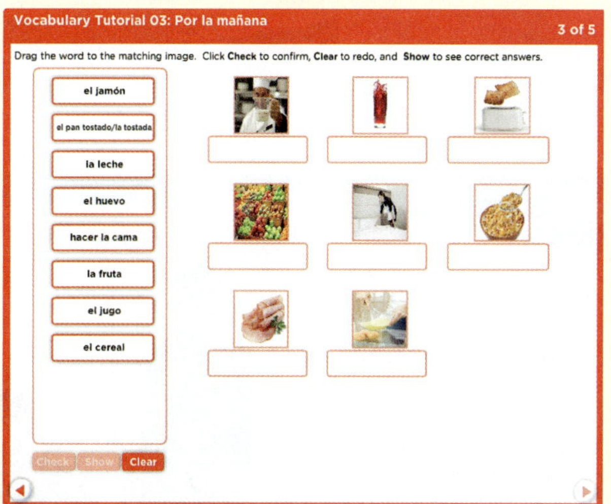

NEW! Pronunciation Presentation and Practice. Within MySpanishLab, a pronunciation topic is presented with accompanying text and audio, followed by three sets of activity types: *Identificación, Las palabras que faltan, Repetición*. In the Annotated Instructor's Edition, notes indicate the specific pronunciation topic covered in that chapter.

Funciones y formas

In ***Mosaicos*, sixth edition,** grammar is presented as a means to effective communication, **moving from meaning to form** and providing an understanding that is both functional and structural. Students are first presented with new structures in meaningful contexts through visuals and brief language samples. The new structures are highlighted in boldface type.

NEW! Audio is provided in MySpanishLab for all of the language samples.

A short, comprehension-based *Piénsalo* activity follows each language sample. These activities form part of the presentation of grammar in context. Students use comprehension and reasoning skills to figure out the answers, by focusing on the connection between meaning (*función*) and the new grammatical structure (*forma*).

Charts and bulleted explanations—clear, concise, and easy to understand—are designed to be studied at home or used for reference in class.

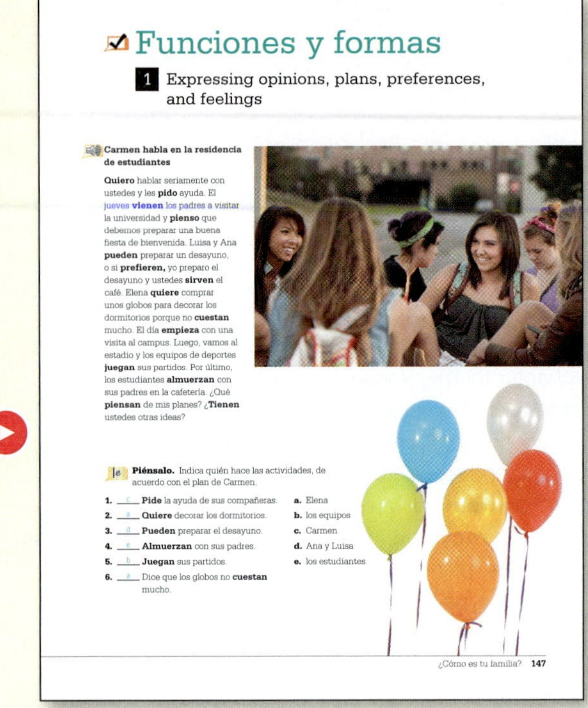

Funciones y formas

1 Expressing opinions, plans, preferences, and feelings

Carmen habla en la residencia de estudiantes

Quiero hablar seriamente con ustedes y les **pido** ayuda. El jueves **vienen** los padres a visitar la universidad y **pienso** que debemos preparar una buena fiesta de bienvenida. Luisa y Ana **pueden** preparar un desayuno, o si **prefieren,** yo preparo el desayuno y ustedes **sirven** el café. Elena **quiere** comprar unos globos para decorar los dormitorios porque no **cuestan** mucho. El día **empieza** con una visita al campus. Luego, vamos al estadio y los equipos de deportes **juegan** sus partidos. Por último, los estudiantes **almuerzan** con sus padres en la cafetería. ¿Qué **piensan** de mis planes? ¿**Tienen** ustedes otras ideas?

Piénsalo. Indica quién hace las actividades, de acuerdo con el plan de Carmen.

1. __c__ **Pide** la ayuda de sus compañeras.
2. __a__ **Quiere** decorar los dormitorios.
3. __d__ **Pueden** preparar el desayuno.
4. __e__ **Almuerzan** con sus padres.
5. __b__ **Juegan** sus partidos.
6. __a__ Dice que los globos no **cuestan** mucho.

a. Elena
b. los equipos
c. Carmen
d. Ana y Luisa
e. los estudiantes

¿Cómo es tu familia? 147

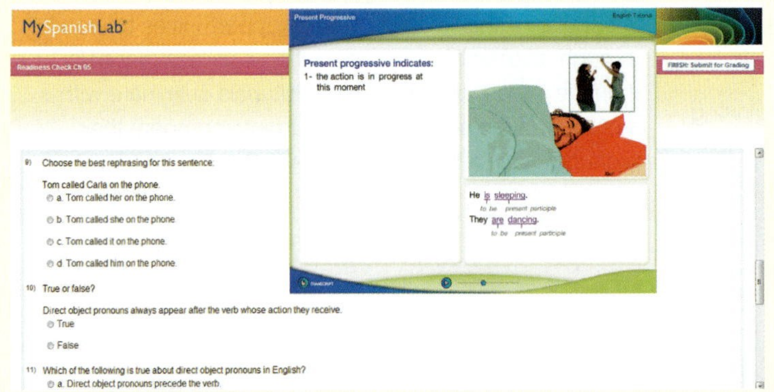

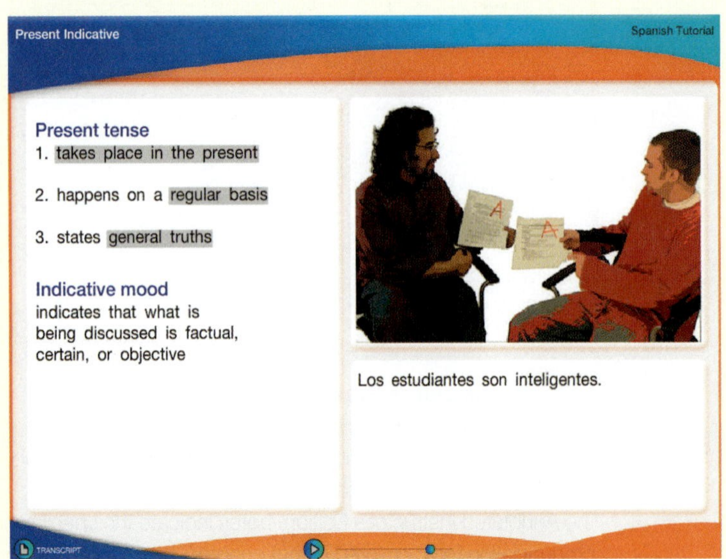

Online English Grammar Readiness Checks and Tutorials: Online English Grammar Readiness Checks assess students' understanding of the English Grammar topics needed to successfully understand the Spanish ones in the chapter and provide personalized remediation via animated English Grammar Tutorials in MySpanishLab. Understanding English grammar terminology greatly facilitates learning of the corresponding Spanish concepts. Instructors no longer need to spend valuable class time talking about the language of language . . . they can instead use the language in meaningful ways.

Online Spanish Grammar Tutorials: Online interactive grammar tutorials in MySpanishLab offer narrated explanations and illustrated examples to help students further comprehend the concepts they are learning. The tutorial ends with an auto-scored comprehension check.

These multiple and complementary means of grammar presentation provide students with different portals for understanding, while serving different learning styles and ensuring that students grasp the concepts.

COMMUNICATION AND GUIDANCE

Providing students the guidance they need to express themselves with confidence!

Just as language and culture are inseparable in ***Mosaicos,* sixth edition,** communication and the guidance provided to foster communication are inseparable as well. Since both the vocabulary and grammar sections contribute unique aspects to the guidance provided, we will look at each one.

With ***Mosaicos,* sixth edition,** almost all of the activities provided in the textbook are communicative in nature. Discrete point practice is primarily provided online through MySpanishLab or in the printed Student Activities Manual. Classroom time is devoted to communicative practice.

The progression within each activity set moves the student along gradually from comprehension to open-ended expression. This carefully stepped progression ensures students are guided through the process and not rushed to produce before they are ready.

COMMUNICATING AND PRACTICING WITH VOCABULARY

NEW! *Escucha y confirma:* A listening activity follows the first of the three vocabulary presentations per chapter. This input-based comprehension check gives students listening practice while allowing them to assess their understanding of the vocabulary and determine if they are ready to move on to additional vocabulary practice in meaningful contexts.

4-1

Escucha y confirma. Listen to the following questions about Pablo's family and select the correct response based on his family tree.

A	B
1. su abuelo	su padre
2. su prima	su hermana
3. su hijo	su nieto
4. Elena	María
5. Jorge	Jaime

NEW! *Para confirmar:* The first activity of the second two vocabulary presentations is always an input-based comprehension check allowing students to ensure their grasp of the vocabulary before moving on to additional vocabulary practice in meaningful contexts.

NEW! Brief ***Cultura*** presentations introduce selected vocabulary activities to raise awareness of the cultural contexts in which language is used. Accompanying *Comparaciones, Conexiones,* or *Comunidades* questions encourage meaningful communication and cross-cultural reflection.

The activity sequence fosters the use of new and previously learned vocabulary in natural, thematically relevant contexts. Activities foster personalization as students are encouraged to talk about what is known to them, themselves, and the people they know and gradually increase in expectation of output as students become comfortable using the new vocabulary. The vast majority of the activities are done in pairs or groups so that students spend their classroom time in conversation.

COMMUNICATING AND PRACTICING WITH GRAMMAR

NEW! *¿Comprendes?* A new form-focused activity follows the grammar presentation. Students can do the activity in class with the instructor or as graded online homework before coming to class as all *¿Comprendes?* activities are auto-graded and include immediate feedback when completed within MySpanishLab. In these quick, form-focused activities students check that they are able to produce the new grammatical forms before moving to the contextualized and communicative activities.

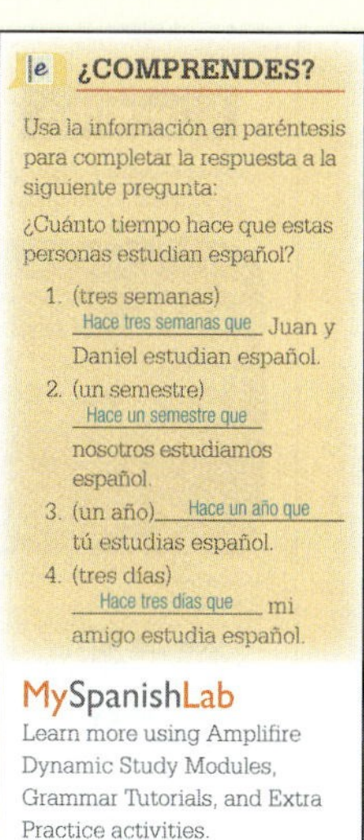
¿COMPRENDES?

Usa la información en paréntesis para completar la respuesta a la siguiente pregunta:

¿Cuánto tiempo hace que estas personas estudian español?

1. (tres semanas) Hace tres semanas que Juan y Daniel estudian español.
2. (un semestre) Hace un semestre que nosotros estudiamos español.
3. (un año) Hace un año que tú estudias español.
4. (tres días) Hace tres días que mi amigo estudia español.

MySpanishLab
Learn more using Amplifire Dynamic Study Modules, Grammar Tutorials, and Extra Practice activities.

The continuing activity sequence moves students gradually from meaningful, form-focused activities towards production of open-ended, personalized communication. The activities focus attention on the communicative purpose of the linguistic structures while invoking culturally relevant contexts. All activities require students to process meaning as well as form so that they develop skill in using their linguistic knowledge to gather information, answer questions, and resolve problems. For example, even the form-focused activities require students to process meaning, not just fill in the blank with the correct response, making the connection between meaning and form. For good reason, the grammar section is called *Funciones y formas*—a hallmark of the *Mosaicos* approach.

Instructor annotations offer suggestions on how to personalize and expand the activities, guide students through multi-stage activities, and encourage students to engage in metalinguistic processing.

NEW! Brief ***Cultura*** presentations introduce selected grammar activities to raise awareness of the cultural contexts in which language is used. Accompanying *Comparaciones, Conexiones,* or *Comunidades* questions encourage meaningful communication and cross-cultural reflection.

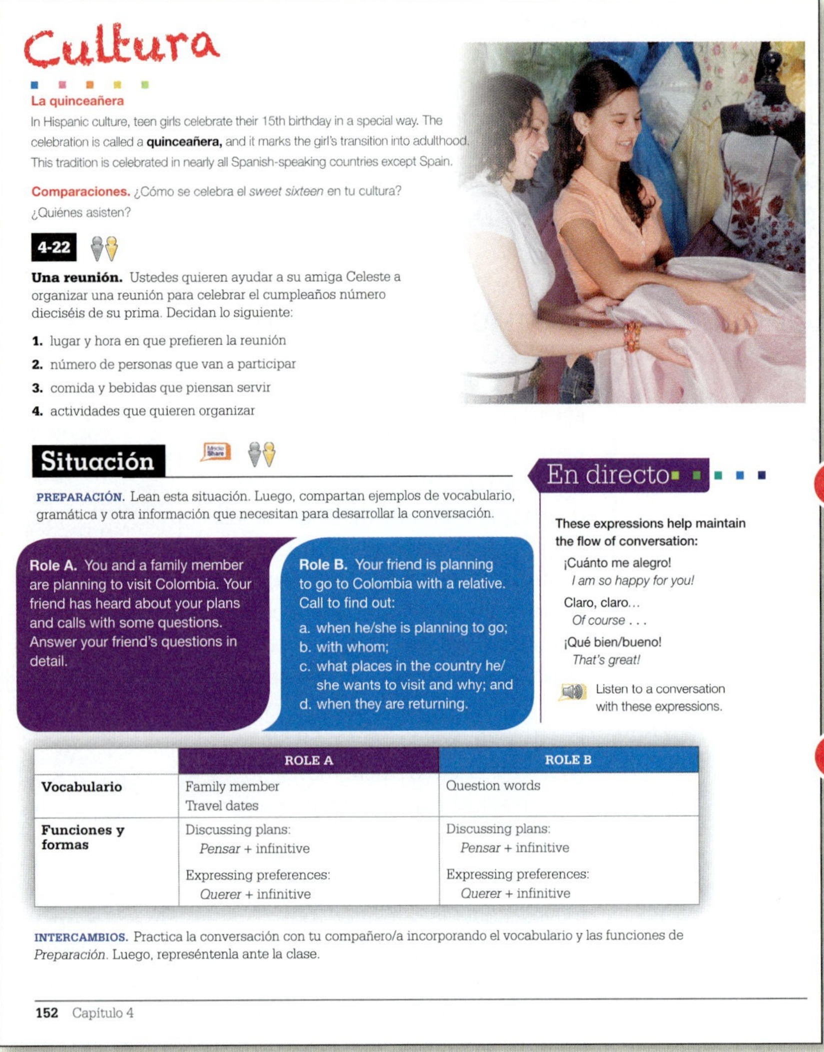

Cultura

La quinceañera

In Hispanic culture, teen girls celebrate their 15th birthday in a special way. The celebration is called a **quinceañera,** and it marks the girl's transition into adulthood. This tradition is celebrated in nearly all Spanish-speaking countries except Spain.

Comparaciones. ¿Cómo se celebra el *sweet sixteen* en tu cultura? ¿Quiénes asisten?

4-22

Una reunión. Ustedes quieren ayudar a su amiga Celeste a organizar una reunión para celebrar el cumpleaños número dieciséis de su prima. Decidan lo siguiente:

1. lugar y hora en que prefieren la reunión
2. número de personas que van a participar
3. comida y bebidas que piensan servir
4. actividades que quieren organizar

Situación

PREPARACIÓN. Lean esta situación. Luego, compartan ejemplos de vocabulario, gramática y otra información que necesitan para desarrollar la conversación.

Role A. You and a family member are planning to visit Colombia. Your friend has heard about your plans and calls with some questions. Answer your friend's questions in detail.

Role B. Your friend is planning to go to Colombia with a relative. Call to find out:

a. when he/she is planning to go;
b. with whom;
c. what places in the country he/she wants to visit and why; and
d. when they are returning.

En directo

These expressions help maintain the flow of conversation:

¡Cuánto me alegro!
I am so happy for you!

Claro, claro...
Of course . . .

¡Qué bien/bueno!
That's great!

Listen to a conversation with these expressions.

	ROLE A	ROLE B
Vocabulario	Family member Travel dates	Question words
Funciones y formas	Discussing plans: *Pensar* + infinitive Expressing preferences: *Querer* + infinitive	Discussing plans: *Pensar* + infinitive Expressing preferences: *Querer* + infinitive

INTERCAMBIOS. Practica la conversación con tu compañero/a incorporando el vocabulario y las funciones de *Preparación.* Luego, represéntenla ante la clase.

152 Capítulo 4

NEW! The *En directo* boxes, which provide colloquial expressions for the activity, now include **audio** so that students can listen to the expressions used in meaningful conversational context.

NEW! *Situación* Advance Organizers. The encompassing goal of these activities has always been embraced by our users. To provide students with guidance to increase their success in communicating through open-ended role plays, the authors have provided advance organizers for the *Situación* activities. Each student prepares by listing specifics for the indicated topics of vocabulary, grammar, and culture (where appropriate) that will facilitate their conversation with their classmate.

NEW! *Situaciones* app. Additional *Situación* role-play activities are available in MySpanishLab and via a mobile app that can be easily accessed on tablets and smartphones.

Situación. Another of the hallmarks of ***Mosaicos*** has always been the culminating role-play activities for each grammar section. Students have the opportunity to converse in realistic contexts by putting together everything they have learned. These open-ended communicative activities prompt students to integrate relevant grammatical structures, vocabulary, and culture with contexts drawn from the chapter theme. Students also have the opportunity to complete activities and communicate "live" with native speakers around the world.

NEW! Each grammar module now culminates with one rather than two *Situación* activities with careful attention to creating realistic situations for the students to enact.

FOUR-SKILLS SYNTHESIS

Bringing it ALL together!

Mosaicos* section:** Not only are listening, speaking, reading, and writing practiced throughout the chapters of ***Mosaicos*, sixth edition** but the final culminating section of each chapter—*Mosaicos*—is devoted to the development and practice of each of these communication skills in a highly focused manner. True to the synthetic nature of this section, the chapter's thematic content and vocabulary are brought together with its linguistic structures and cultural focus. Hence the name, *Mosaicos,* whereby students have the opportunity to bring it ***all together into a coherent whole.

To enhance the development of these skills, **guidance** is provided for each section. First, specific **strategies** are presented for each of the four skills. The strategies build on each other within and across the chapters. Activities are designed so that students systematically practice implementing the strategies presented. Second, a **process approach**, with pre-, during, and post-activities, is applied for all four skills through the *Preparación* and *Un paso más* steps. The cumulative effect of the fifteen *Mosaicos* sections throughout the text will greatly increase students' abilities to effectively listen, speak, read, and write.

Mosaicos

ESCUCHA

4-34 Presentational

Preparación. Antes de escuchar el mensaje de Pedro para Julio sobre una fiesta sorpresa (*surprise*), prepara tus ideas sobre la siguiente información. Después, presenta tus notas a la clase.

1. el posible propósito (*purpose*) de este mensaje
2. la información específica que puede ser importante

ESTRATEGIA

Listen for a purpose

Listening with a purpose in mind will help you focus your attention on the most relevant information. As you focus your attention, you screen what you hear and select only the information you need.

4-35 Interpretive

Escucha. First read the information you will need to attend the party Pedro is organizing. Then, as you listen, complete the sentences with the rest of the information. Don't worry if you do not understand every word.

1. La fiesta es para... Josefina
2. La fiesta va a ser en la casa de... Pedro
3. El día de la fiesta es... el domingo
4. Julio debe llevar (*take*)... música típica de Colombia
5. Julio tiene que llegar a la casa a las... ocho y media
6. La dirección es... calle 12, número 127

Comprueba

I was able to . . .

____ recognize the names of people.

____ identify specific information about an event.

4-36 Interpersonal

Un paso más. Vas a organizar una fiesta sorpresa para tu profesor/a de español y deseas invitar a tu compañero/a. Llama a tu compañero/a por teléfono y explícale lo siguiente:

1. cuándo y dónde va a ser la fiesta
2. qué van a comer y beber
3. qué música van a escuchar
4. otros planes

¿Cómo es tu familia? 163

NEW! *Comprueba* boxes provide a self-check guide for students to help them determine if they have covered the main points accurately and sufficiently.

NEW! Each set of activities is now organized around the three ACTFL Performance Descriptors of the three Modes of Communication: Presentational, Interpretive, and Interpersonal. This organization maximizes learning as three parts of a single goal: communication. By consistently using all three interrelated modes, students' opportunity to use the language in relation to the theme is multiplied. Instructor annotations indicate the mode for each activity.

NEW! Based on pre-revision survey feedback from our users, some readings for the Lee section have been updated, ensuring consistently **high-interest readings at the appropriate level.** Additionally, the last three chapters, 13–15, now introduce students to **authentic literature,** enriching the program while giving those students who go on to the intermediate level an introduction to reading and interpreting literature.

If students need more practice with any of the four skills, **additional practice** is provided for each skill within the Student Activities Manual, available in print or in Pearson's award-winning online learning and assessment MySpanishLab platform.

CHAPTER SELF-ASSESSMENT

A check to ensure that all the pieces are firmly in place!

Within the MySpanishLab online learning and assessment system, at the end of each chapter, students can check their mastery of chapter content through further practice in a variety of activities, resources, and games that reinforce chapter vocabulary, grammar, and culture in different ways. Examples of available resources are:

- **NEW! amplifire Online Dynamic Study Modules** are designed to improve learning and long-term retention of vocabulary and grammar. With **amplifire** study modules, students not only master critical concepts, but they **study faster, learn better, and remember longer.** Based on the latest research in neuroscience and cognitive psychology on how we learn best, learners cycle through a process of test/learn/retest until they achieve mastery of the content. The result is a personalized, adaptive approach—tailored to individual students' needs.

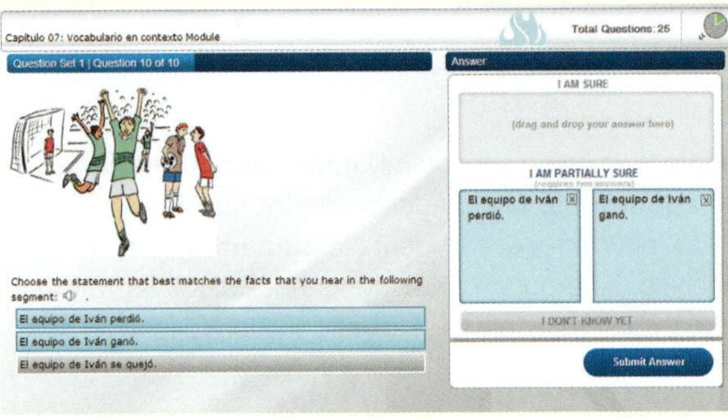

amplifire is the only assessment available that is able to quickly and effectively pinpoint knowledge gaps and areas of misinformation—where learners were confident but incorrect about their answer choices. Instructors can use the results to determine what information the learners retained and where misinformation and gaps still exist, and adjust their curricula accordingly.

- **Vocabulary Flashcards** with audio recordings by a native speaker help students review words and quiz themselves on the active vocabulary. Flashcards can be accessed via mobile devices for practice on the go.
- **NEW! Games** are a painless, enjoyable, and effective way to practice new skills. Games vary from *Concentration* (flip cards to match words to visuals), to *Soccer* (provide the appropriate word in a context), to a *Quiz Show* game in which students choose the appropriate response in a multiple-choice format. Questions are contextualized and move beyond simple form-based exercises to more meaningful, engaging activities.
- **Oral Practice:** Provides two oral activities. Students record their response to the activity and submit it for instructor grading.
- **NEW!** The **Practice Test with Study Plan** is an auto-scored, full-length test that reviews chapter vocabulary and grammar. Students are given a study plan based on their performance. The study plan refers them to explanations in the eText, extra practice activities, and tutorials to help them review concepts where they need additional practice.

And, finally, *Why* **Mosaicos**? Because ***Mosaicos*** has the ribbon…ensuring you never lose your place…

Informed by National Standards

The National Standards for Foreign Language Learning: Preparing for the 21st Century, whose five goal areas (Communication, Cultures, Connections, Comparisons, and Communities) have served as an organizing principle for language instruction for more than a decade, inform the pedagogy of the sixth edition of ***Mosaicos.*** Marginal notes throughout the Annotated Instructor's Edition draw attention to the way specific activities and other elements of the program help students develop proficiency in the five goal areas. A number of strategies have been implemented to achieve success.

Communication. Students are prompted to engage in meaningful conversations throughout the text, providing and obtaining information, expressing their opinions and preferences, and sharing their experiences. Readings and listening activities invite them to interpret language on a variety of topics, while *presentaciones* and writing assignments call on them to present information and ideas in both written and oral modes. The **ACTFL Performance Descriptors of the three Modes of Communication**—Presentational, Interpretive, and Interpersonal—are used consistently throughout the chapters and are the organizing principle for the *Mosaicos* skills' section. By consistently using all three modes, students' opportunity to use the language in relation to the theme is multiplied.

Cultures. Many features of the ***Mosaicos*** program give students an understanding of the relationship between culture and language: The ***Enfoque cultural*** opening spread; the maps, the art, and the accompanying Art Tour; the ***Mosaico cultural*** section; the cultural vignettes in the ***¡Cineastas en acción!*** video; the *Cultura* sections; and the culture integrated within the activities.

Connections. Ample opportunities are provided for students to makes connections with other disciplines through realia, readings, the ***Enfoque cultural*** section, the ***Mosaico cultural*** section, the *Conexiones* questions which accompany the *Cultura* sections, the diverse cultural vignettes of the ***¡Cineastas en acción!*** video, and the conversation activities throughout the text. Students gain information and insight into the distinctive viewpoints of Spanish speakers and their culture.

Comparisons. *Lengua* and *En otras palabras* boxes, the *Compara* questions in each ***Mosaico cultural*** section, and the *Comparaciones* questions in the *Cultura* sections—all provide students with points of comparison between English and Spanish (and among the varieties of Spanish spoken in different parts of the world). Readings and activities frequently juxtapose U.S. and Hispanic cultural products, practices, and perspectives.

Communities. Students are encouraged to extend their learning through guided research on the Internet and/or other sources, and many of the topics explored in ***Mosaicos*** can stimulate exploration, personal enjoyment, and enrichment beyond the confines of formal language instruction. *Comunidades* questions which accompany many of the *Cultura* sections encourage reaching out to the community and cross-cultural reflection.

The Complete *Mosaicos* Program

Mosaicos is a complete teaching and learning program that includes a variety of resources for students and instructors, including an innovative offering of online resources.

FOR THE STUDENT

Student Text (ISBN 10: 0-205-25540-X)

The ***Mosaicos*, sixth edition** Student Text is available in a complete, hardbound version, consisting of a preliminary chapter followed by Chapters 1 through 15. The program is also available as three paperback volumes rather than the single hardcover version. Volume 1 of the paperback series contains the preliminary chapter plus Chapters 1 to 5; Volume 2, Chapters 5 to 10; and Volume 3, Chapters 10 to 15. All three volumes include the complete front and back matter.

Student Activities Manual (ISBN 10: 0-205-24796-2)

The Student Activities Manual (SAM), thoroughly revised for this edition, includes workbook activities together with audio- and video-based activities, all designed to provide extensive practice of the vocabulary, grammar, culture, and skills introduced in each chapter. The organization of these materials parallels that of the student text and include a *Repaso* section at the end that provides additional activities designed to help students review the material of the chapter as well as to prepare for tests.

The online Student Activities Manual found in MySpanishLab now features premium content which includes a variety of interactive activities not available in print.

Answer Key to Accompany Student Activities Manual (ISBN 10: 0-205-25544-2)

An Answer Key to the Student Activities Manual is available separately, giving instructors the option of allowing students to check their homework. The Answer Key now includes answers to all SAM activities.

Audio CDs to Accompany Student Text (ISBN 10: 0-205-25542-6)

A set of audio CDs contains recordings of the *Vocabulario en contexto* and *Funciones y formas* language samples, the ***Mosaico cultural*** reading passages, and the audio material for the *Escucha y confirma* listening activities included in the student text. These recordings are also available online.

Audio CDs to Accompany Student Activities Manual (ISBN 10: 0-205-25541-8)

A second set of audio CDs contains audio material for the listening activities in the Student Activities Manual. These recordings are also available online.

Video on DVD (ISBN 10: 0-205-25545-0)

¡Cineastas en acción! is a newly shot video filmed to accompany the sixth edition of ***Mosaicos.*** Vocabulary and grammar structures of each chapter are used in realistic situations while gaining a deeper understanding of Hispanic cultures.

Pre-viewing, viewing, and post-viewing activities are found in the ***¡Cineastas en acción!*** sections of the textbook and the Student Activities Manual. The video is available for student purchase on DVD, and it is also available within MySpanishLab.

MySpanishLab with Pearson eText, Access Card, for *Mosaicos*: Spanish as a World Language (multi-semester access) (ISBN 10: 0-205-99724-4)

MySpanishLab, part of our MyLanguageLabs suite of products, is an online homework, tutorial, and assessment product designed to improve results by helping students quickly master concepts, and by providing educators with a robust set of tools for easily gauging and addressing the performance of individuals and classrooms. **MyLanguageLabs** has helped almost one million students successfully learn a language by providing them everything they need: full eText, online activities, instant feedback, **amplifire** dynamic study modules, and an engaging collection of language-specific learning tools, all in one online program. For more information, including case studies that illustrate how MyLanguageLabs improves results, visit www.mylanguagelabs.com.

FOR THE INSTRUCTOR

Annotated Instructor's Edition (ISBN 10: 0-205-25543-4)

The Annotated Instructor's Edition contains an abundance of marginal annotations designed especially for novice instructors, instructors who are new to the ***Mosaicos*** program, or instructors who have limited time for class preparation. The format allows ample space for annotations alongside full-size pages of the student text. Marginal annotations suggest warm-up and expansion exercises and activities and provide teaching tips, additional cultural information, and audioscripts for the in-text listening activities. Answers to discrete-point activities are printed in blue type for the instructor's convenience.

Instructor's Resource Manual (available online)

The Instructor's Resource Manual (IRM) contains complete lesson plans for all chapters, integrated syllabi for regular and hybrid courses, as well as helpful suggestions for new and experienced instructors alike. It also provides videoscripts for all episodes of the ***¡Cineastas en acción!*** video, audioscripts for listening activities in the Student Activities Manual, and a complete guide to all ***Mosaicos*** supplements. The Instructor's Resource Manual is available to instructors online at the ***Mosaicos*** Instructor Resource Center and in MySpanishLab.

Supplementary Activities (available online)

Available in MySpanishLab, the Supplementary Activities ancillary consists of a range of engaging activities that complement the vocabulary and grammar themes of each chapter. It offers instructors additional materials that can serve to energize and enrich their students' classroom experience.

Testing Program (available online)

The Testing Program has been thoroughly revised and expanded for this edition. The testing content correlates with the vocabulary, grammar, culture, and skills material presented in the student text. For each chapter of the text, a bank of testing activities is provided in modular form; instructors can select and combine modules to create customized tests tailored to the needs of their classes. Two complete, ready-to-use tests are also provided for each chapter. The testing modules are available to instructors online in MySpanishLab for those who wish to create computerized tests (MyTest) or in the ***Mosaicos*** Instructor Resource Center as downloadable Word documents.

Testing Audio CD (ISBN 10: 0-205-25549-3)

A special set of audio CDs, available to instructors only, contains recordings corresponding to the listening comprehension portions of the Testing Program.

PowerPoint™ Presentations (ISBN 10: 0-205-99712-0)

A PowerPoint™ Presentation is available for each chapter of the text. These dynamic, visually engaging presentations allow instructors to enliven class sessions and reinforce key concepts. The presentations are available to instructors online in MySpanishLab or in the ***Mosaicos*** Instructor Resource Center.

Situaciones adicionales (available online)

The downloadable *Situaciones adicionales* provide instructors with additional opportunities for reinforcing and assessing students' speaking skills. The activities are also available via the *Situaciones* mobile app.

Instructor Resource Center

Several of the instructor supplements listed above—the Instructor's Resource Manual, the Testing Program, the PowerPoint™ Presentations,—are available for download at the access-protected ***Mosaicos*** Instructor Resource Center (www.pearsonhighered.com/mosaicos). An access code will be provided at no charge to instructors once their faculty status has been verified.

ONLINE RESOURCES

MySpanishLab with Pearson eText—Access Card—for *Mosaicos*: Spanish as a World Language

MySpanishLab, part of our MyLanguageLabs suite of products, is an online homework, tutorial, and assessment product designed to improve results by helping students quickly master concepts, and by providing educators with a robust set of tools for easily gauging and addressing the performance of individuals and classrooms. **MyLanguageLabs** has helped almost one million students successfully learn a language by providing them everything they need: full eText, online activities, instant feedback, **amplifire** dynamic study modules, and an engaging collection of language-specific learning tools, all in one online program. For more information, including case studies that illustrate how MyLanguageLabs improves results, visit www.mylanguagelabs.com.

COMPANION WEBSITE

The open-access Companion Website (www.pearsonhighered.com/mosaicos) includes audio to accompany listening activities and sample language from the textbook and audio to accompany the listening activities in the Student Activities Manual.

Acknowledgments

Mosaicos is the result of a collaborative effort among the authors, our publisher, and our colleagues. In particular, the cultural content of the sixth edition has been enhanced by the work of the contributors who created content and activities for the program: María Lourdes Casas, Óscar Martín, Frances Matos-Shultz, Sergio Salazar, Kristine Suárez, Lilián Uribe, and U. Theresa Zmurkewycz. We also extend our thanks to Alicia Muñoz Sánchez and Raúl J. Vázquez-López, who wrote ancillary materials. We are also indebted to the members of the Spanish teaching community for their time, candor, and insightful suggestions as they reviewed drafts of the sixth edition of ***Mosaicos.*** Their critiques and recommendations helped us to sharpen our pedagogical focus and improve the overall quality of the program. We gratefully acknowledge the contributions of the following reviewers:

Sissy Alloway, Morehead State University

Debra Ames, Valparaiso University

Ashlee S. Balena, University of North Carolina at Wilmington

Fleming L. Bell, Valdosta State University

Talia Bugel, Indiana University-Purdue University, Fort Wayne

Stephen Buttes, Indiana University-Purdue University, Fort Wayne

Sara Casler, Sierra College

Jens Clegg, Indiana University-Purdue University Fort Wayne

Hilda Coronado, Glendale Community College

Lisa DeWaard, Clemson University

Neva Duffy, Chicago State University

Ari Gutman, Auburn University

Crista Johnson, University of Delaware

Keith Johnson, California State University, Fresno

Maribel Manzari, Washington & Jefferson College

Bryan Miley, Glendale Community College

John Andrew Morrow, Ivy Tech Community College

Margarita Orro, Miami Dade College, North Campus

Claudia Ospina, Wake Forest University

Leon Palombo, Miami Dade College, North Campus

Yelgy Parada, Los Angeles City College

Kristina Primorac, University of Michigan

Terri Rice, University of South Alabama

Lee J. Rincón, Moraine Valley Community College

Pamela Rink, Tulsa Community College

Angelo J. Rodriguez, Kutztown University of Pennsylvania

Felipe E. Rojas, Chicago State University

Anita Saalfeld, University of Nebraska at Omaha

Michael Sawyer, University of Central Missouri

Rachel Showstack, Wichita State University

Gayle Vierma, University of Southern California

Maida Watson, Florida International University

Amanda Wilcox, Auburn University

Kelley L. Young, University of Missouri-Kansas City

Hilma-Nelly Zamora-Breckenridge, Valparaiso University

U. Theresa Zmurkewycz, Saint Joseph's University

Mosaicos Advisory Board

Silvia Arroyo, Mississippi State University

Donna Binkowski, Southern Methodist University

Joelle Bonamy, Columbus State University

Robert Cameron, College of Charleston

Susana Castillo-Rodríguez, University of New Hampshire

Juliet Falce-Robinson, University of California, Los Angeles

Ronna Feit, Nassau Community College, SUNY

Chris Foley, Liberty University

Leah Fonder-Solano, University of Southern Mississippi

Muriel Gallego, Ohio University

Kathryn Grovergrys, Madison Area Technical College

Marie Guiribitey, Florida International University

Todd Hernández, Marquette University

Yun Sil Jeon, Coastal Carolina University

Lauri Kahn, Suffolk County Community College

Rob Martinsen, Brigham Young University

Teresa McCann, Prairie State College

Eugenia Muñoz, Viriginia Commonwealth University

Michelle Orecchio, University of Michigan

Susana García Prudencio,
Pennsylvania State University

Bethany Sanio,
University of Nebraska, Lincoln

Virginia Shen,
Chicago State University

Julie Sykes,
University of Oregon

Kelley L. Young,
University of Missouri - Kansas City

Gabriela C. Zapata,
University of Southern California

Nancy Zimmerman,
Kutztown University

We are also grateful for the guidance of Celia Meana and Scott Gravina, the Developmental Editors, for all of their work, suggestions, attention to detail, and dedication to the text. Their support and efficiency helped us achieve the final product. We are very grateful to the many other members of the Pearson World Languages team who provided guidance, support, and fine attention to detail at all stages of the production process: Samantha Alducin, Senior Digital Product Manager, and Regina Rivera, Media Editor, for helping us produce the new MySpanishLab program, the new video, audio programs, and Companion Website. Thanks to Jonathan Ortiz and Millie Chapman, Editorial Assistants, for their hard work and efficiency in managing the reviews and attending to many editorial details.

We are very grateful to our World Languages Consultants, Denise Miller, Yesha Brill, and Mellissa Yokell, for their creativity and efforts in coordinating marketing campaigns and promotion for this edition. Thanks, too, to our program and project management team, Nancy Stevenson and Lynne Breitfeller, who guided *Mosaicos, sixth edition,* through the many stages of production; to our partners at PreMediaGlobal, especially Jenna Gray, for her careful and professional production services and to the PreMediaGlobal design team for the gorgeous interior. A special thank you to Kathryn Foot, Senior Art Director and designer Michael Black of Black Sun for their creative work on the cover. Finally, we would like to express our sincere thanks to Steve Debow, Senior Vice President for World Languages, Bob Hemmer, Editor in Chief, Tiziana Aime, Senior Acquisitions Editor, and Kristine Suárez, Director of Market Development, for their guidance and support through every aspect of this new edition.

About the Authors

Elizabeth with her husband in Petra, Jordan

ELIZABETH E. GUZMÁN

I did my graduate studies in Spanish Applied Linguistics at the University of Pittsburgh.

One of my proudest teaching moments was… when my former students have shown me what a difference I can make in my students through my love of teaching.

My favorite vacation spots in the Hispanic world are… the lake regions of my native Chile and Peru.

I can't live without… my laptop and Pandora radio.

My favorite feature in Mosaicos is… that it opens the doors to the fascinating Spanish-speaking world, its people, and its diverse cultures.

My favorite activities are… traveling, gardening, and listening to music.

The people closest to my heart are… my family, my friends, and the people who value freedom and justice as much as I do.

What makes me happy is… knowing that my work transcends me.

The people I admire are… those from whom I can learn something.

My favorite classroom is… one in which students and I become part of one community working toward common goals.

PALOMA LAPUERTA

My Ph.D. is from… Université de Genève, Switzerland, but I did my "licenciatura" in Universidad de Salamanca, Spain.

My research area is… Spanish Language and Peninsular Literature.

One of my proudest teaching moments was… when I noticed that everybody was having a good time... and learning!

My favorite vacation spot in the Hispanic world is… I have two: Castellón, Spain, which is by the sea, and Pereira, Colombia, which is near the Andes.

I can't live without my… Moleskine®.

My favorite feature in Mosaicos is… that it takes you to places beyond the textbook.

The movie I have seen most often is... *Volver*, by Pedro Almodóvar.

My favorite activity is... to travel.

The site that I found most beautiful was... Machu Picchu.

The landscape I found most impressive was... Namibia.

Paloma in Istanbul, Turkey

Judy with student Jia and her first apple pie

JUDITH E. LISKIN-GASPARRO

My Ph.D. is from… the University of Texas–Austin

My research area is… classroom-based second language acquisition.

One of my proudest teaching moments was… when my doctoral student won the ACTFL-MLJ Birkmaier Award for Doctoral Dissertation Research. There have been four proudest moments, because four of my SLA students have won this award since 2007.

My favorite vacation spot in the Hispanic world is… For its mystery and sheer beauty, Machu Picchu. For the lifestyle and amazing *tortillas de patatas*, San Sebastián.

I can't live without my… laptop.

My favorite feature in Mosaicos is… its clickability (my made-up word). It invites students and instructors to challenge linear patterns of learning.

My public talent is... baking cookies—all kinds, and for all occasions. I also give pie workshops.

My secret talent is... making up cool games to play with toddlers.

I am thrilled when... people think I am a native speaker of Spanish.

mosaicos

SPANISH AS A WORLD LANGUAGE

Goals
Capítulo preliminar is designed to make students' first exposure to the Spanish classroom a successful and enjoyable experience. Establish a comfortable atmosphere by using supportive techniques to lower students' anxiety level. Give frequent praise and encouragement. Help students access meanings of unknown words by using gestures or visuals, particularly in the early stages of learning.

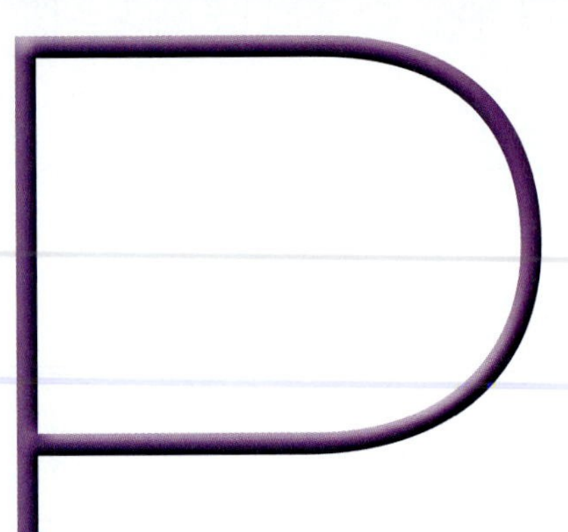

Preliminar Bienvenidos

ENFOQUE CULTURAL
El mundo hispano

VOCABULARIO EN CONTEXTO
Las presentaciones
Los saludos y las despedidas
¿Qué hay en el salón de clase?
Los meses del año y los días de la semana
El tiempo
Expresiones útiles en la clase
El alfabeto

FUNCIONES Y FORMAS
Singular forms of *ser*
Estar + location
Numbers 0 to 99
Telling time

EN ESTE CAPÍTULO...
Comprueba lo que sabes
Vocabulario

LEARNING OUTCOMES

By the end of the chapter, you will be able to:

- introduce yourself, greet others, and say good-bye
- identify people and classroom objects and tell where they are in the classroom
- listen to and respond to classroom expressions and requests
- spell names and addresses and share phone numbers
- express dates, tell time, and comment on the weather
- share information about the Spanish language and where it is spoken

Integrated Performance Assessment: Three Modes of Communication

Presentational: See activities P-1, P-9, P-17, and P-21.

Interpretive: See activities P-1, P-2, P-5, P-6, P-10, P-11, P-15, P-16, P-21, P-22, P-25, P-26, and P-29.

Interpersonal: See activities P-2, P-3, P-4, P-7, P-8, P-10, P-12, P-13, P-14, P-18, P-19, P-20, P-23, P-24, P-27, P-28, and P-30.

ENFOQUE cultural EL MUNDO HISPANO

Personas que hablan español (en millones) ▶

Enfoque cultural

To learn more about the Spanish-speaking world, go to MySpanishLab to view the *Vistas culturales* videos.

¿QUÉ TE PARECE?

- Spanish is a highly phonetic language, which means that in most cases if you can spell a word, you can pronounce it.
- Minor differences exist between the Spanish in Latin America and the Spanish in Spain but not enough to get in the way of communication.
- Historically, Latin and Arabic have had the biggest influence on the Spanish language. Today, Spanish has adopted hundreds of words relating to technology and pop culture from English.
- Since 1904, there have been eleven Nobel Prizes for Literature in Spanish.
- It is projected that by 2050, the United States will become the largest Spanish-speaking country in the world.

▲ Bienvenidos al mundo hispano.

Suggestions for photos
Point to the page or project the image and ask if students understand the word *bienvenidos.* Introduce the words *hablan* and *lengua.* Then point to photos and ask questions such as the following (you may write questions and answers on the board): *¿Qué lengua hablan estas personas? Hablan español.* Personalize by asking: *¿Qué lengua hablas tú? ¿Hablas inglés? ¿Estudias español? ¿Qué lengua hablamos en clase? ¿Hablamos inglés o español en clase?* Help students come up with answers that use cognates (*porque es una lengua importante, para comunicarse con muchas personas,* etc.).

Suggestion for map
Project the map and call attention to the number of Spanish speakers in different countries: *Muchas personas en el mundo hablan español. ¿Cuántas personas hablan español en Estados Unidos?, ¿En México?,* etc. Explain that in Spanish the comma is used in place of the decimal point and vice-versa so that 3,5 is equal to 3.5 in English.

Suggestions for *Enfoque cultural*
Project the map from the previous page and point out these locations to show the vastness of the Spanish-speaking world or have students locate them on the map.

Note for *¿Cuánto sabes?*
The first activity in each chapter is called *¿Cuánto sabes?* Encourage students to look at the map and photos that precede *¿Cuánto sabes?* before they do the activity. It is also a good idea to do a warm-up to activate students' prior knowledge about the featured country or countries. The instructor's notes on this page suggest questions you may ask for this purpose.

Suggestions for *¿Cuánto sabes?*
Ask students questions about the Spanish language using cognates and allow them to answer in English. *¿Qué otras lenguas son similares al español? ¿El francés o el ruso?, ¿el italiano o el chino?, ¿el portugués o el árabe?, ¿el catalán o el alemán?* Introduce the word *mundo.* Point to the map and call attention to the number of Spanish speakers in different countries: *Muchas personas en el mundo hablan español. ¿Cuántas personas hablan español en Estados Unidos?, ¿en México?*, etc.

El mundo hispano es muy grande y diverso:

desde el río Grande al norte de México,

hasta Tierra del Fuego al sur de Argentina;

desde la ciudad de Barcelona en el Mediterráneo, al este de España,

hasta las islas Galápagos en el Pacífico, al oeste de Ecuador.

Vamos a explorar este mundo y aprender (*learn*) más.

¿CUÁNTO SABES?

Use the information in the map, the photos and captions to determine whether each statement is true (**Cierto**) or false (**Falso**).

1. ___Cierto___ Más de (*More than*) 350 millones de personas hablan español en el mundo.
2. ___Cierto___ El español se habla en 23 países (*countries*).
3. ___Falso___ El río Grande separa México de España.
4. ___Falso___ Las islas Galápagos están en el mar Mediterráneo.
5. ___Cierto___ En Estados Unidos hablan español más personas que (*more than*) en Argentina.

Vocabulario en contexto

Making introductions and talking about the classroom

MySpanishLab **PRONUNCIATION TOPIC:** Vowels
Learn more using Amplifire Dynamic Study Modules, Pronunciation, and Vocabulary Tutorials.

Las presentaciones

ANTONIO: **Me llamo** Antonio Mendoza. **Y tú, ¿cómo te llamas?**

BENITO: Me llamo Benito Sánchez.

ANTONIO: **Mucho gusto.**

BENITO: **Igualmente.**

LAURA: María, **mi amigo** José.

MARÍA: Mucho gusto.

JOSÉ: **Encantado.**

PROFESOR: **¿Cómo se llama usted?**

ISABEL: Me llamo Isabel Contreras.

PROFESOR: Mucho gusto.

- Spanish has more than one word meaning *you*. Use **tú** when talking to someone on a first-name basis (a child, close friend, or relative).
- Use **usted** when talking to someone you address in a respectful or formal manner; for example, **doctor/doctora; profesor/profesora; señor/señora.** Also use **usted** to address people you do not know well.
- People of college age or younger normally use **tú** when speaking to each other.
- **Mucho gusto** is used by both men and women when they are meeting someone for the first time. A man may also say **encantado,** and a woman, **encantada.**
- You may respond to **mucho gusto** with either **encantado/a** or **igualmente.**

PRÁCTICA

P-1 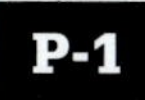  **Presentaciones. PREPARACIÓN.** With a partner complete the following conversation with the appropriate expressions from the list.

Encantado	Igualmente	mi amigo Pedro	Mucho gusto

ALICIA: Me llamo Alicia. Y tú, ¿cómo te llamas?

ISABEL: Isabel Pérez. ___Mucho gusto___.

ALICIA: ___Igualmente___.

ALICIA: Isabel, ___mi amigo Pedro___.

ISABEL: Mucho gusto.

PEDRO: ___Encantado___.

 **INTERCAMBIOS.** Move around the classroom, introducing yourself to several classmates and introducing classmates to each other.

Suggestions for *Las presentaciones*
Model *Me llamo* by pointing to yourself and saying your name. Then write *Me llamo* on the board and repeat the sentence. Now ask students for their names. Accept answers if they say only their names, but encourage them to use *Me llamo…*, pointing to the board to guide them. Introduce yourself to a student, asking his/her name; answer with *Mucho gusto*. Write *Mucho gusto* on the board, and encourage the same response from the student. You can shake the student's hand to make the introduction more realistic. Repeat with another student. Again, encourage the student to say *Mucho gusto* after his or her name; this time respond with *Igualmente*. Repeat it again before asking students to introduce themselves to a classmate. They may refer to the dialogue if needed. You may wish to spend a few minutes having students introduce themselves to several students sitting near them.

Suggestion
Project images of people of various ages to quickly compare the uses of *tú* and *usted*. Tell students to use *tú* when addressing each other. Then model the second dialogue by acting it out with a female and a male to show the change in *encantado/a*. Write both forms on the board.

Alternate
Model the third dialogue. Write *amigo/a* on the board. Do the dialogue again with a female student, using *amiga*. Then, in groups of three, one student introduces the other two, using their real names.

Expansion
You may introduce the phrase *Tu nombre, por favor*. For further practice, have a student ask you your name or the names of two classmates.

Suggestion
When the need arises, use the *Expresiones útiles en la clase*, page 15. Try to speak Spanish as much as possible from the first day of class.

Suggestion for P-2, *Preparación*
When doing the pre-listening activity explain that in some Spanish-speaking countries children are brought up to address their parents as *usted.*

Note for P-2, *Escucha*
The listening activity audioscripts appear in the margins for instructors. You may wish to use the following procedure: 1) Play the conversations; students mark their answers; 2) have students check their answers with a partner; and 3) play the conversations again, repeating difficult parts.

Audioscript for P-2
Conversación 1
—Buenos días, señora Gómez.
—Buenos días. ¿Cómo está usted, señor Jiménez?
—Bastante bien, gracias. ¿Y usted?
—Bien, gracias.
Conversación 2
—¡Hola, Felipe! ¿Qué tal? ¿Cómo estás?
—Regular, ¿y tú?
—Bien, gracias.
Conversación 3
—Buenas tardes, señora Mena. ¿Cómo está usted?
—Bastante bien, gracias. Y usted, ¿cómo está, señora?
—Regular, regular.
—Lo siento.
Conversación 4
—Me llamo Carlos Martínez. Y tú, ¿cómo te llamas?
—Me llamo Cristina Camacho.
—Mucho gusto.
—Igualmente.

P-2 

Escucha y confirma. PREPARACIÓN. Before you listen to four brief conversations in which people greet each other, complete the following chart with the pronoun you think you would use in each case. Compare your answers with those of a classmate and explain why you chose **tú** or **usted.**

WHEN TALKING TO YOUR . . .	TÚ	USTED
1. brother or sister	✓	
2. doctor		✓
3. coach		✓
4. parent	✓	

ESCUCHA. As you listen to the four conversations, mark (✓) the appropriate column to indicate whether the greetings are formal (with **usted**) or informal (with **tú**).

	FORMAL	INFORMAL
1.	✓	
2.		✓
3.	✓	
4.		✓

LENGUA

When you talk to people, you address them with various degrees of formality, depending on how well you know the person and the context of the conversation. For example, when you talk to a professor, you probably use more formal language than when you talk to classmates or friends. In Spanish, one way to mark this difference is by using **tú** (informal) and **usted** (formal).

Los saludos y las despedidas

SEÑOR GÓMEZ: **Buenos días, señorita** Rivas.

SEÑORITA RIVAS: Buenos días. **¿Cómo está usted, señor** Gómez?

SEÑOR GÓMEZ: **Bien, gracias,** ¿y usted?

SEÑORITA RIVAS: **Muy** bien, gracias.

MARTA: ¡**Hola,** Inés! **¿Qué tal? ¿Cómo estás?**

INÉS: **Regular,** ¿y tú?

MARTA: **Bastante** bien, gracias. Bueno, **hasta mañana.**

INÉS: **Chao.**

SEÑORA MOYA: **Buenas tardes,** Clara. ¿Cómo estás?

CLARA: Bien, gracias. Y usted, ¿cómo está, **señora?**

SEÑORA MOYA: **Mal,** Clara, mal.

CLARA: ¡Qué lástima!

Los saludos

- Use **buenos días** until lunchtime.
- Use **buenas tardes** from noon until nightfall. After nightfall, use **buenas noches** (*good evening, good night*).
- **¿Qué tal?** is less formal than **buenos días, buenas tardes,** etc.
- Use **está** with **usted** and **estás** with **tú.**

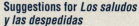

Suggestions for *Los saludos y las despedidas*
Write different times of the day on the board and model possible greeting(s) for each. Students respond *sí* or *no.*

Suggestions
Introduce *buenos días, buenas tardes,* and *buenas noches* with visuals or by drawing the sun and the moon or writing times on the board. You may mention that in Spain people normally use *buenos días* until 2:00 P.M., their customary lunchtime. In other countries it is used until noon. Model and practice each greeting before moving to the next.

Suggestions
Present the first dialogue, modeling the parts of both characters; students follow along in their books. Personalize the dialogue by addressing some students by name. Then pair students up, assign roles, and have them practice the dialogue. Have them change roles for further practice.

Suggestion
Model the *despedidas,* using hand gestures while speaking. Point out that some Spanish speakers use a different hand gesture when saying good-bye: palm facing out, fingers moving up and down. With a student, model the use of *adiós* meaning "hello" when two people pass each other, but do not stop to talk.

Suggestion
Model correct pronunciation of the *d* in *adiós:* Students should place the tip of tongue against the back of the upper front teeth. (English d is pronounced with the tip of the tongue on the ridge behind the upper teeth.) Explain that the word has only two syllables: *a-diós.*

Suggestion
Have students move around the room, greeting one another, asking how the other is, and saying good-bye.

Suggestion
Model *por favor.* Give a student a pencil and say *El lápiz, por favor,* indicating that you would like it back. When the student returns the pencil, say *Gracias.* Coach students to reply with *De nada.* Repeat with other classroom objects. Then ask them to continue in small groups or pairs. Write useful words on the board.

Suggestion
Model the difference between *con permiso* and *perdón* by walking in front of a student and saying *con permiso,* and by lightly stepping on a student's toe or bumping into him/her and saying *perdón.*

Note
Whenever possible, students should work in pairs, taking turns to answer. This provides additional opportunities to communicate in Spanish. Then the whole class reviews the activity.

Las despedidas

Use the following expressions to say good-bye:

adiós	*good-bye*
chao	*good-bye*
hasta luego	*see you later*
hasta mañana	*see you tomorrow*
hasta pronto	*see you soon*

- **Adiós** is generally used when you do not expect to see the other person for a while. It is also used as a greeting when people pass each other but have no time to stop and talk.
- **Chao** (also spelled **chau**) is an informal way of saying good-bye and when passing on the street, similar to **adiós**. It is popular in South America.

Expresiones de cortesía

Here are other expressions of courtesy:

por favor	*please*
gracias	*thanks, thank you*
de nada	*you're welcome*
lo siento	*I'm sorry (to hear that)*
con permiso	*pardon me, excuse me*
perdón	*pardon me, excuse me*

- **Con permiso** and **perdón** may be used before the fact, as when asking a person to allow you to go by or when trying to get someone's attention. Only **perdón** is used after the fact, as when you have stepped on someone's foot or have interrupted a conversation.

PRÁCTICA

P-3   

Para confirmar. Alternate greetings (**buenos días, buenas tardes, buenas noches**) with your classmate according to the time given.

1. 9:00 A.M. Buenos días.
2. 11:00 P.M. Buenas noches.
3. 4:00 P.M. Buenas tardes.
4. 8:00 A.M. Buenos días.
5. 1:00 P.M. Buenas tardes o buenos días.
6. 10:00 P.M. Buenas noches.

P-4 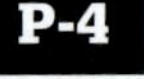 

Despedidas. With a classmate, create short two-line exchanges for the following situations.

You run into a good friend on campus.
E1: *Adiós.*
E2: *Chao.*

Answers may vary. Possible answers:

1. You'll see your friend tomorrow. Hasta mañana.
2. You arrange to meet your classmate at the library in ten minutes. Hasta pronto.
3. Your roommate is leaving for a semester abroad. Adiós.

P-5

¿Perdón o con permiso? Would you use **perdón** or **con permiso** in these situations? Decide with a classmate which is more appropriate. Then create a similar situation to act out for the class.

1. 

Perdón.

2. 

Perdón. / Con permiso.

3. 

Perdón.

4. 

Perdón.

5. 

Con permiso.

P-6

Despedidas y expresiones de cortesía. With a classmate, decide which expression is best for each situation. Then create another situation and act it out.

Adiós.	Gracias.
Por favor.	De nada.
Hasta luego.	¡Qué lástima!
Lo siento.	

1. Someone thanks you. De nada.
2. You say good-bye to a friend you will see later this evening. Hasta luego.
3. You ask if you can borrow a classmate's notes. Por favor.
4. You hear that your friend is sick. Lo siento, ¡qué lástima!
5. You receive a present from your cousin. Gracias.
6. ... adiós, hasta luego

Cultura

When saying *hello* or *good-bye* and when being introduced, Spanish-speaking men and women almost always shake hands, embrace, or kiss each other on the cheek. Girls and women most often kiss each other on the cheek, as do men and women who are close friends or acquaintances. In Spain they kiss on both cheeks. Men who are close friends normally embrace and pat each other on the back while in Argentina, it is common for them to kiss each other on the cheek.

Comunidades. What are common greetings in your culture? Do you greet your family and your friends in the same way?

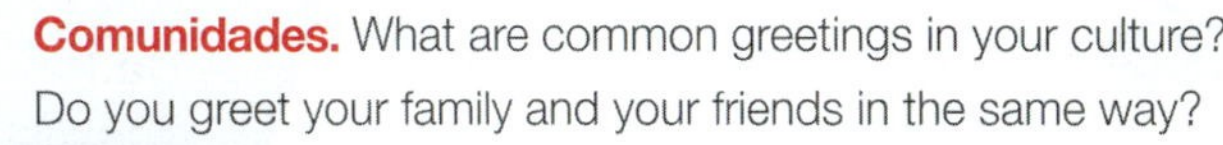

P-7

Encuentros (*Encounters*). Create short conversations with the following people, whom you meet on the street. Then switch roles.

1. tu (*your*) amigo Miguel
2. tu profesor/a
3. tu amiga Isabel
4. tu doctor/a

Note for P-6
An ellipsis (...) next to an item number in an activity signals an opportunity for students to provide their own cue or response.

Note for Cultura
The questions included in the *Cultura* boxes direct students to reflect on and discuss cultural practices by comparing them with practices in other cultures. Starting in *Capítulo 4*, the questions accompanying the *Cultura* boxes are in Spanish while the information remains in English. Cultural information and questions go to all Spanish in *Capítulo 8*.

Standard 2.1
Students demonstrate an understanding of the relationship between the practices and perspectives of the culture studied.

This culture note gives students information about some everyday cultural practices, including both appropriate phrases and appropriate actions. Instructors may wish to have students talk about the cultural perspectives (social distance, courtesy, etc.) enacted in these common cultural practices.

Warm-up for P-7
Model the exchange with a student before beginning the activity.

Suggestion

Strive to present new vocabulary in context, introducing 3–4 items at a time and checking for understanding before continuing. The vocabulary in this chapter will be recycled in the next few chapters.

Use the images as a springboard for presenting people and items typically found in the classroom. To check for recognition, mention objects in the classroom and have students identify them.

Note

You may wish to point out that both *computador* and *computadora* are used (also *ordenador* in Spain). The gender of nouns is presented in *Capítulo 1;* for now, use *un* and *una* without detailed explanation.

Write the sentence *¿Qué hay en el salón de clase?*, highlighting the verb *hay* and using it in different contexts: *Hay un/a profesor/a en la clase; hay una pizarra; hay estudiantes…*

Suggestion for P-8

Introduce the forms *tengo/no tengo* of the verb *tener* to facilitate conversation.

Follow-up for P-8

Have students identify additional objects or furniture in the classroom.

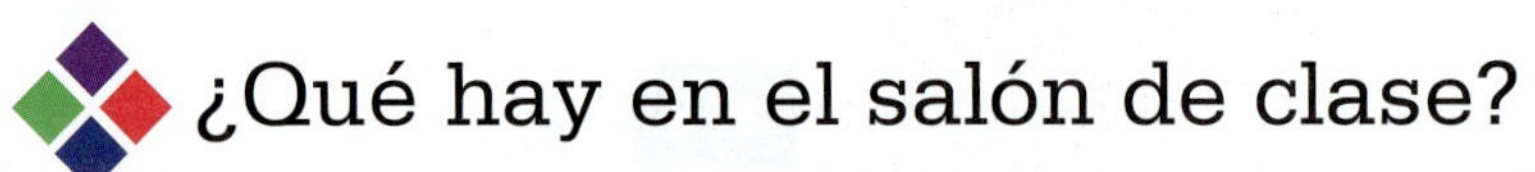

¿Qué hay en el salón de clase?

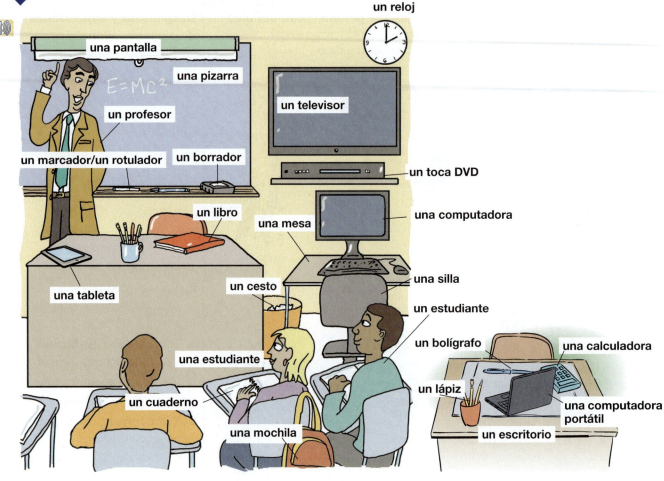

un reloj
una pantalla
una pizarra
un profesor
un televisor
un marcador/un rotulador
un borrador
un toca DVD
un libro
una mesa
una computadora
una tableta
un cesto
una silla
un estudiante
una estudiante
un bolígrafo
una calculadora
un lápiz
un cuaderno
una computadora portátil
una mochila
un escritorio

PRÁCTICA

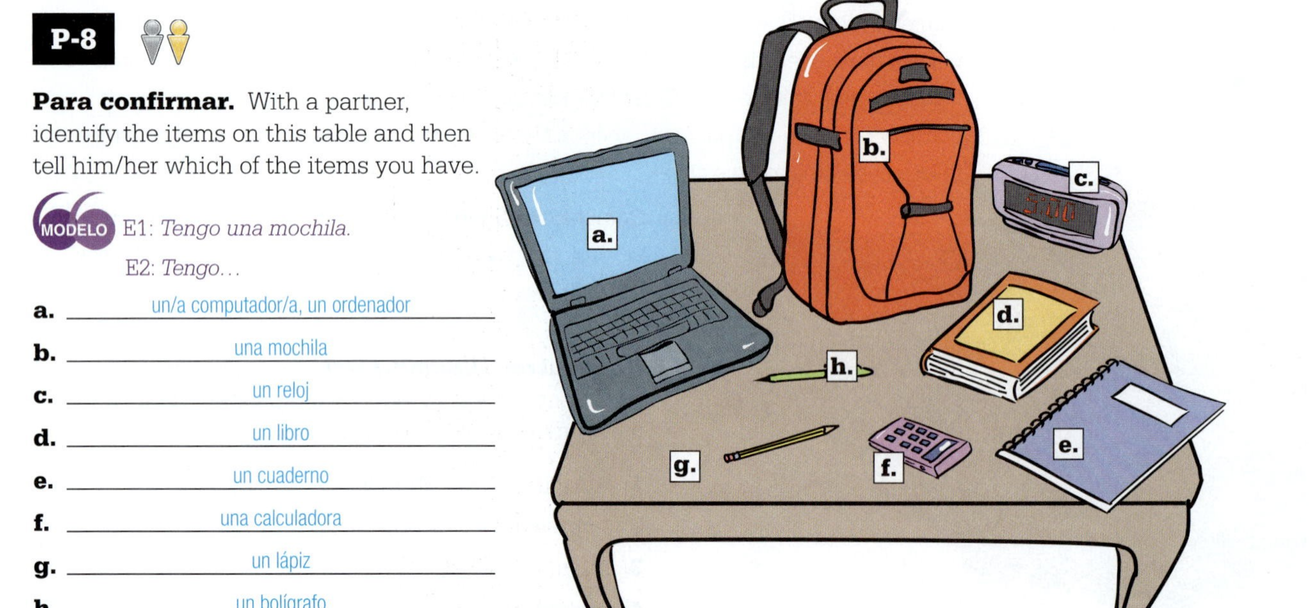

P-8

Para confirmar. With a partner, identify the items on this table and then tell him/her which of the items you have.

MODELO E1: *Tengo una mochila.*
E2: *Tengo…*

a. un/a computador/a, un ordenador
b. una mochila
c. un reloj
d. un libro
e. un cuaderno
f. una calculadora
g. un lápiz
h. un bolígrafo

P-9

Para la clase de español. Write down a list of the things you need for this class. You and your partner should then compare your lists.

Suggestion for P-9
Provide additional vocabulary if needed (e.g., *un diccionario*).

P-10

¿Qué hay en el salón de clase? Use the clues below to complete the crossword puzzle in Spanish. Working with a partner, compare your responses, then look around the room and take turns telling each other what objects you see.

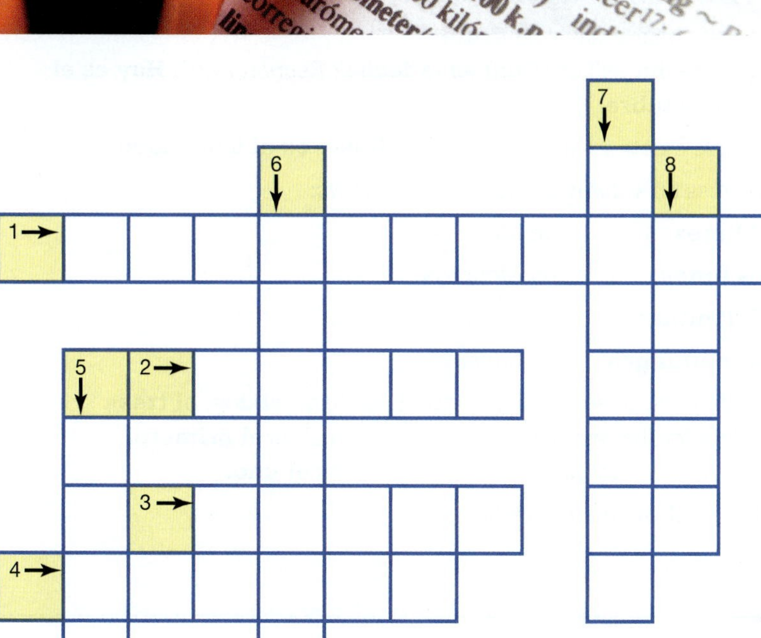

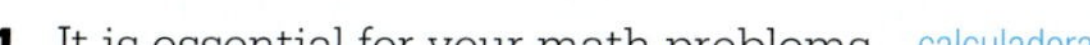

1. It is essential for your math problems. calculadora
2. Without it, you cannot write. lápiz
3. Waste material goes here. cesto
4. You need them to study. libros
5. You sit on it. silla
6. You write your notes on it. cuaderno
7. You pack and carry your books in it every morning. mochila
8. It tells the time. reloj

Suggestion
Use a Spanish-language calendar or project one from the Internet and model days of the week. Point out that Monday is normally the first day of the week. You may preview ordinal numbers (presented in *Capítulo 5*) by saying *El lunes es el primer* [hold up index finger] *día de la semana. El martes es el segundo día*, etc. Introduce *último: el último día es el domingo.*

Suggestion
Introduce *Hoy es…* and *Mañana es…* by modeling appropriate days. You may also wish to introduce *Ayer fue…*

Note
You may want to point out that the spelling *setiembre* is also correct.

Follow-up
Use a hypothetical class schedule and ask questions: *¿Qué días hay clase de español? ¿Cuándo es la clase de economía? ¿Y la de filosofía?* This will help students practice more cognates and serve as a preview for the vocabulary presented in *Capítulo 1*.
You may also use cognates that refer to students' interests: *¿Qué día es el ballet? ¿Cuándo es el concierto?*

Note for *Lengua*
Mention that the U.S. military also uses this format for writing dates.

Suggestion for P-11
Show students a Spanish-language calendar (paper or from the web).

Note for *Lengua*
The numbers from 1 to 31 are presented here so students can say the date. When reviewing sixteen to nineteen, emphasize the *i* sound linking *diez* and rest of number.
At this point, students are not expected to know these numbers perfectly. Numbers to 100 are introduced later in this chapter.

Los meses del año y los días de la semana

Los meses del año

enero	*January*
febrero	*February*
marzo	*March*
abril	*April*
mayo	*May*
junio	*June*
julio	*July*
agosto	*August*
septiembre	*September*
octubre	*October*
noviembre	*November*
diciembre	*December*

Los días de la semana

lunes	*Monday*
martes	*Tuesday*
miércoles	*Wednesday*
jueves	*Thursday*
viernes	*Friday*
sábado	*Saturday*
domingo	*Sunday*

Days of the week and months of the year are not generally capitalized in Spanish, but sometimes they are capitalized in advertisements and invitations.

ENERO
CALENDARIO
lunes martes miércoles jueves viernes sábado domingo
1 AÑO NUEVO 2 3 4 5
6 LOS SANTOS REYES 7 8 9 10 11 12
13 14 15 16 17 18 19
20 21 22 23 24 25 26
27 28 29 30 31

- Monday (**lunes**) is normally considered the first day of the week.
- To ask what day it is, use **¿Qué día es hoy?** Answer with **Hoy es…**
- To ask about today's date, use **¿Qué fecha es?** or **¿Cuál es la fecha?** Respond with **Hoy es el 14 de octubre.**
- To give a date for an event, say **La fiesta es el 5 de mayo.**
- Express *on* + *a day of the week* as follows:

el lunes	*on Monday*
los lunes	*on Mondays*
el domingo	*on Sunday*
los domingos	*on Sundays*

- Cardinal numbers are used with dates (e.g., **el dos, el tres**), except for the first day of the month, which is **el primero.** In Spain the first day is also referred to as **el uno.**
- Hoy es **el primero** de julio.

PRÁCTICA

El calendario hispano
In Spanish-speaking countries, the first day of the week on a calendar is Monday. Sunday appears at the end of the week and it is generally marked by red numbers. Many calendars bear the saint's name for each day.

Comparaciones. What dates are typically highlighted on your calendar?

P-11 

Para confirmar. Using the calendar, take turns asking: **¿Qué día de la semana es…?** Then tell your partner your favorite day of the week.

1. el 2
2. el 5
3. el 22
4. el 18
5. el 10
6. el 13
7. el 28
8. el…

LENGUA

Here are the numbers you need when giving a date:

1 uno	17 diecisiete
2 dos	18 dieciocho
3 tres	19 diecinueve
4 cuatro	20 veinte
5 cinco	21 veintiuno
6 seis	22 veintidós
7 siete	23 veintitrés
8 ocho	24 veinticuatro
9 nueve	25 veinticinco
10 diez	26 veintiséis
11 once	27 veintisiete
12 doce	28 veintiocho
13 trece	29 veintinueve
14 catorce	30 treinta
15 quince	31 treinta y uno
16 dieciséis	

P-12 

Preguntas. Take turns asking and answering these questions.

1. ¿Qué día es hoy?
2. Hoy es… ¿Qué día es mañana?
3. Hoy es el… de… ¿Qué fecha es mañana?
4. ¿Hay clase de español los domingos? ¿Y los sábados?
5. ¿Qué días hay clase de español?

LENGUA

When dates are written using only numerals, the day normally precedes the month: *11/8* = **el 11 de agosto.**

 **P-13** 

Fechas importantes. Take turns asking your partner the dates on which these events take place.

 MODELO la reunión de estudiantes (10/9)

E1: *¿Cuándo es la reunión de estudiantes?*

E2: *(Es) el 10 de septiembre.*

1. el concierto de Juanes (12/11) (Es) el 12 de noviembre.
2. el aniversario de Carlos y María (14/4) (Es) el 14 de abril.
3. el banquete (1/3) (Es) el primero / el 1 de marzo.
4. la graduación (22/5) (Es) el 22 de mayo.
5. la fiesta de bienvenida (24/8) (Es) el 24 de agosto.

P-14 

El cumpleaños (*birthday*). Find out when your classmates' birthdays are. Write their names and birthdays in the appropriate spaces in the table.

 MODELO E1: *¿Cuándo es tu cumpleaños?*

E2: *(Es) el 3 de mayo.*

LENGUA

You may have noticed that the word **tú** (meaning *you*) has a written accent mark, and that the word **tu** (meaning *your*) does not. In this book, boxes similar to this one will help you focus on when to use accent marks. You will find all the rules for accentuation in Appendix 1.

CUMPLEAÑOS			
enero	febrero	marzo	abril
mayo	junio	julio	agosto
septiembre	octubre	noviembre	diciembre

Warm-up for P-12
Ask *¿Hoy es…?* using the wrong day; students will answer *no.* Then say *¡Ah! Hoy es…* using another wrong day. Students answer *no.* Then ask *¿Qué día es hoy?*

Note for P-13
Both *el primero de marzo* and *el uno de marzo* are used.

Suggestion for P-13
Provide additional vocabulary or suggestions for other events in Spanish if needed (e.g., *el último día de clase, el Día de la Independencia, el cumpleaños de…,* etc.)

Suggestion
Explain that *tiempo* is used to talk about weather. Write the word on the board, then point to the window or to the drawing on this page. Say *hace buen tiempo* or *hace mal tiempo*. Ask *¿Qué tiempo hace hoy?* You may need to remind students what the word *hoy* means. Ask this question every day when you arrive in class and after greetings. Students will learn now how to answer simple weather questions as a preview to the weather expressions that they will learn in *Capítulo 7*.

El tiempo

Hoy hace sol. Hace buen tiempo.

- Use **¿Qué tiempo hace?** to inquire about the weather. To answer, you may use the following expressions that start with **hace:**

Hace buen tiempo.	*The weather is good.*
Hace mal tiempo.	*The weather is bad.*

Hoy llueve. Hace mal tiempo.

- To express that it is sunny or that it is raining use the following:

Hace sol.	*It is sunny.*
Llueve./Está lloviendo.	*It is raining.*

PRÁCTICA

Cultura

El tiempo y los hemisferios

Seasons in the northern and southern hemispheres are inverted. That is, when it is winter in the United States, it is summer in Argentina. This applies to the school year as well. In Argentina for example, the academic year starts in March and ends in December, right before Christmas. The Christmas holidays are often spent on the beach or outdoors.

Conexiones. Why do you think the academic year is arranged in that way in the southern hemisphere? Would it be a good idea to change this arrangement?

P-15 

¿Qué tiempo hace hoy? Take turns with your partner asking about the weather in these cities. Then ask about the weather in your city.

MODELO Miami:

E1: *¿Qué tiempo hace en Miami?*

E2: *En Miami hace buen tiempo. Hace sol.*

1. Madrid: 
2. Quito:
3. Lima: 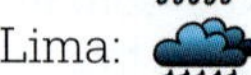
4. Ciudad de México: 
5. Bogotá: 
6. Nueva York: 
7. (your city:)

Expresiones útiles en la clase

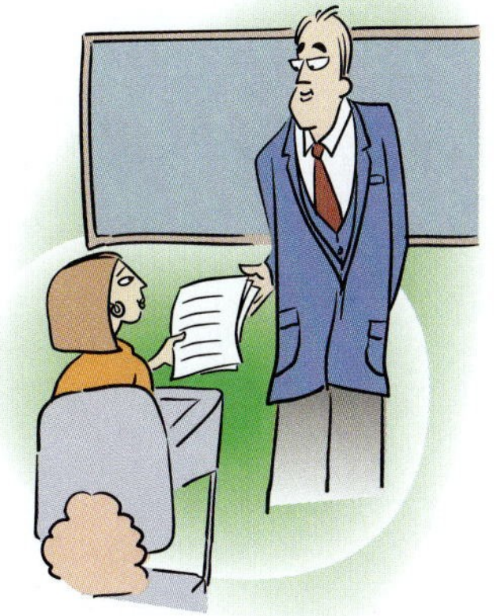

 ▲ La tarea, por favor.

▲ Ve a la pizarra.

▲ Contesta.

▲ Repite.

▲ Levanta la mano.

▲ Escribe.

▲ Lee.

■ When asking two or more people to do something, the verb forms are **ve → vayan, contesta → contesten, repite → repitan.**

Suggestions
Introduce the meaning of the expressions in the section through gestures: *escuchen* (cup hand behind ear); *contesten* (make motion of talking); *abran el libro* (open a book); *vayan a la pizarra* (go to the board). Point to students, ask them to follow your instructions, and write the expressions on the board.

Note
If you use the *usted* form with students, introduce the following expressions with *usted:*

¿Comprende? ¿Tiene preguntas? Conteste, por favor. Vaya a la pizarra.

■ Although you may not use all of these expressions, it is useful to recognize them and to know how to respond. Other expressions that you may hear or say in the classroom include the following:

Expressions in plural

¿Comprenden?	*Do you understand?*
¿Tienen preguntas?	*Do you have any questions?*
Contesten, por favor.	*Please answer.*
Vayan a la pizarra.	*Go to the board.*
Túrnense.	*Take turns.*
Hablen (sobre...)	*Talk (about ...)*

Expressions with *tú*

¿Comprendes?	*Do you understand?*
¿Tienes preguntas?	*Do you have any questions?*
Contesta, por favor.	*Please answer.*
Ve a la pizarra.	*Go to the board.*
Dile a tu compañero/a...	*Tell your partner ...*

Other useful expressions

Más despacio, por favor.	*More slowly, please.*
Más alto, por favor.	*Louder, please.*
¿En qué página?	*On what page?*
¿Cómo se dice... en español?	*How do you say ... in Spanish?*
Otra vez.	*Again.*
Presente.	*Here.*
No comprendo.	*I don't understand.*
No sé.	*I don't know.*

PRÁCTICA

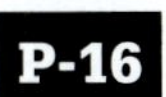

Las expresiones útiles. Match the following expressions with their pictures and compare your answers with those of a classmate. Then take turns telling your partner three things he/she needs to do and your partner will act them out.

1. __e__ Ve a la pizarra.
2. __a__ Abre el libro.
3. __c__ Pregúntale a tu compañero.
4. __d__ Repite.
5. __b__ Siéntate.
6. __f__ Lee.

a.

b.

c.

d.

e.

f.

Note
Although *ch* and *ll* used to be considered independent letters of the Spanish alphabet because they represent distinct sounds, the present-day Spanish alphabet consists of 27 letters.

Note
You may want to introduce other names for the letters *v* and *w*. In 2010 the RAE affirmed *uve* and *uve doble*, respectively, as the official names for these letters, although it recognizes other usages. Since *b* and *v* are pronounced alike (*be*), many Spanish speakers say *be larga* or *be de burro* for *b* and *ve corta* or *ve de vaca* for *v* when spelling. Other commonly used names for *w* are *doble v*, *v doble*, and *doble uv*.

Note
Point out the importance of good pronunciation and remind students of the pronunciation guide in MySpanishLab.

Note for P-17
Point out that because Spanish words are spelled much like they sound, Spanish speakers often do not spell out the whole word, but instead give only the letter(s) that may cause confusion, such as *b* and *v*. Model the activity by using some Spanish last names.

Suggestion for P-18
Have students move around the classroom for this activity. You may wish to bring students' attention to the use of *usted* in the question, due to the formal context of the interaction.

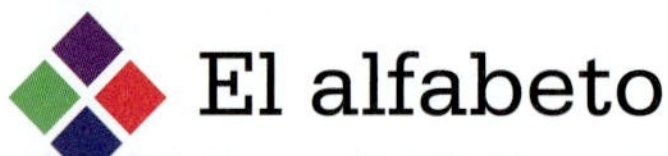

El alfabeto

a a	**j** jota	**r** erre
b be	**k** ka	**s** ese
c ce	**l** ele	**t** te
d de	**m** eme	**u** u
e e	**n** ene	**v** uve
f efe	**ñ** eñe	**w** uve doble
g ge	**o** o	**x** equis
h hache	**p** pe	**y** ye, i griega
i i	**q** cu	**z** zeta

- The Spanish alphabet includes **ñ,** a letter that does not exist in English. Its sound is similar to the pronunciation of *ni* and *ny* in the English words *onion* and *canyon.*
- The letters **ch** and **ll** were considered independent letters in the Spanish alphabet until 1994.
- The letters **k** and **w** appear mainly in words of foreign origin.

PRÁCTICA

EN OTRAS PALABRAS

Like English speakers, Spanish speakers have different accents that reflect their region or country of origin. For example, the letter **c** before vowels **e** and **i** and the letter **z** are pronounced like **s** except in certain regions of Spain, where they are similar to the English *th.*

P-17  

Para confirmar. Take turns spelling the name of the street where you live in Spanish. Then check if your partner wrote it correctly.

P-18  

Los nombres. You are at the admissions office of a university in a Spanish-speaking country. Spell your first or last name for the clerk. Take turns.

E1: *¿Cómo se llama usted?*
E2: *Me llamo Jill Robinson.*
E1: *¿Cómo se escribe Robinson?*
E2: *erre-o-be-i-ene-ese-o-ene*

Funciones y formas

1 Identifying and describing people

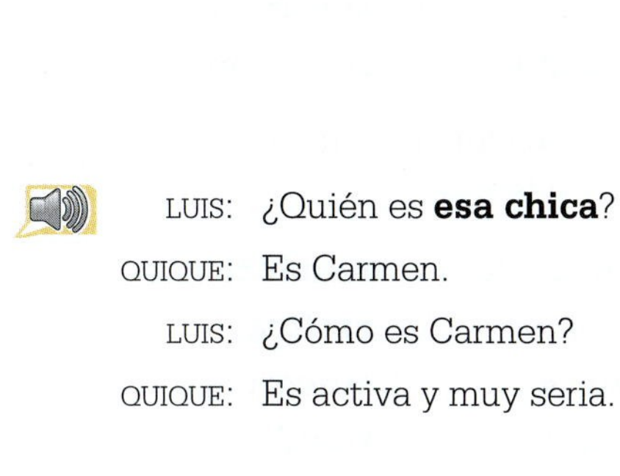

CARLOS: **¿Quién es ese chico?**
SANDRA: **Es** Julio.
CARLOS: ¿**Cómo es** Julio?
SANDRA: **Es** romántico y sentimental.

LUIS: ¿Quién es **esa chica**?
QUIQUE: Es Carmen.
LUIS: ¿Cómo es Carmen?
QUIQUE: Es activa y muy seria.

Piénsalo. Indicate (✓) the true statements.

1. _____ El chico se llama Carmen.
2. __✓__ Julio es romántico.
3. __✓__ Carmen es muy seria.
4. _____ Carmen no es activa.

Singular forms of *ser*

The verb **ser** is used to identify and describe.

Esa chica **es** Carmen.	*That girl is Carmen.*
Es activa y muy seria.	*She is active and very serious.*
Rodolfo **es** su amigo.	*Rodolfo is her friend.*
Es atractivo.	*He is attractive.*

Here are the forms of **ser** you will use in this chapter.

SER (*to be*)			
yo	**soy**	*I*	*am*
tú	**eres**	*you*	*are*
Ud.	**es**	*you*	*are*
él, ella	**es**	*he, she*	*is*

To make a sentence negative, place **no** before the appropriate form of **ser.** When responding negatively to a question, say **no** twice.

Ella es inteligente. → Ella **no** es inteligente.
¿Es rebelde? → **No, no** es rebelde.

Note for *Piénsalo*
All grammar presentations are accompanied by an introductory activity, *Piénsalo.* Here students are asked to read a short dialogue or text and do a comprehension-based activity before reading the grammar explanation. The activity, which can be done in class or online, will get students to think about the grammar point before they read the explanation.

Suggestions
Use pictures of your students and of well-known people to practice *¿Quién es?* Use the pictures again to ask: *¿Cómo es X, serio/a o cómico/a? ¿X es activo/a o no es activo/a? ¿Es sentimental o práctico/a? ¿Es optimista o pesimista?* When presenting cognates with *-o* and *-a* endings, write words on the board, point to a male student using the appropriate adjective, and then point to a female student. Contrast with *¿Cómo está?* (e.g., *¿Cómo es Carmen? Es inteligente y seria. ¿Cómo está Carmen? Está muy bien.*) Model and personalize the short dialogues by pointing to individual students and having classmates respond. (Use only positive traits.)

Note
The verb *ser* is introduced for the first time here although students need only the forms *yo, tú, usted, él,* and *ella* for communication at this stage. The formal presentation of *ser* is in *Capítulo 2.*

Suggestion
Introduce *soy* by pointing to yourself as you describe yourself, sometimes using *yo* and omitting it where appropriate: *Yo soy activo/a y serio/a. No soy impulsivo/a. Soy optimista. No soy pesimista.*

Introduce *eres* and *es* by substituting names of students in exchanges like those at the beginning of *Identifying and describing people.*

Note for *¿Comprendes?*
A *¿Comprendes?* activity appears after each grammar presentation. Students can complete them in class or online to see if they have understood the grammar structure and are ready to move on to the communicative practice. Additional activities are available for practice in MySpanishLab.

Suggestion
Explain how students can make good use of Spanish cognates. Ask if they can come up with words they already know in Spanish that have English cognates. Focus attention on adjectives by introducing *elegante, importante,* and *inteligente.* To introduce new cognates, use well-known people and visuals (e.g., a secretary *es responsable, es muy eficiente;* a poet or a writer *es idealista y sentimental, es creativo/a;* a musician or singer *es rebelde y romántico/a;* a priest *es religioso y tranquilo*). Well-known fictional characters may also be used (e.g., *Sherlock Holmes es inteligente, es paciente y es muy eficiente*). Ask yes/no questions to check understanding.

Note
You may wish to add that the equivalent in Spanish for "lecture" is *conferencia,* and for "exit" is *salida.*

Warm-up for P-19
Give a photo of a well-known person to each pair of students, and have them describe his/her personality.

Suggestion for P-19
Ask students to come up with other words they know in Spanish that have English cognates. Focus attention on adjectives by providing examples such as: a secretary *es responsable, es muy eficiente;* a poet *es idealista y sentimental, es creativo/a;* a musician *es rebelde y romántico/a.* Ask yes/no questions to check understanding.

Follow-up for P-20
After doing this activity, have students get together in groups of four to exchange information.

Cognates

Cognates (*Cognados*) are words from two languages that have the same origin and are similar in form and meaning. Since English and Spanish have many cognates, you will discover that you already recognize many Spanish words. Here are some cognates that you may use to describe people.

The following cognates use the same form to describe a man or a woman.

arrogante	**importante**	**optimista**	**popular**
eficiente	**independiente**	**paciente**	**responsable**
elegante	**inteligente**	**perfeccionista**	**sentimental**
idealista	**interesante**	**pesimista**	**tradicional**

The following cognates have two forms. The **-o** form is used to describe a male, and the **-a** form to describe a female.

activo/a	**creativo/a**	**introvertido/a**	**romántico/a**
ambicioso/a	**dinámico/a**	**moderno/a**	**serio/a**
atlético/a	**extrovertido/a**	**nervioso/a**	**sincero/a**
atractivo/a	**generoso/a**	**pasivo/a**	**tímido/a**
cómico/a	**impulsivo/a**	**religioso/a**	**tranquilo/a**

Some words appear to be cognates but do not have the same meaning in both languages. These are called false cognates. **Lectura** (*Reading*) and **éxito** (*success*) are examples. You will find other examples in future chapters.

¿COMPRENDES?

Describe the following people using the appropriate form of **ser**.

1. Yo __soy__ inteligente.
2. Usted __es__ interesante.
3. Él __es__ cómico.
4. Isabel __es__ atlética.
5. Tú __eres__ paciente.
6. Carlos __es__ sincero.

MySpanishLab
Learn more using Amplifire Dynamic Study Modules, Grammar Tutorials, and Extra Practice activities.

PRÁCTICA

P-19  

Yo soy... Ask your partner about his/her personality. Use the cognates provided or others that you know.

MODELO E1: *¿Eres pesimista?*
E2: *No, no soy pesimista.*
E1: *¿Cómo eres?*
E2: *Soy activo, optimista y creativo.*

generoso/a	optimista
independiente	responsable
inteligente	tímido/a
nervioso/a	

P-20

Descripciones. Ask each other about your classmates. Describe them by using cognates.

MODELO E1: *¿Cómo es...?*
E2: *Es...*

2 Locating people and things

 **¿Dónde está** la profesora?

¿Está **sobre** la mesa? No.

¿Está **debajo de** la mesa? No.

¿Está **entre** Juan y María? No.

¿Está **al lado de** María? No.

¿Está **enfrente de** María? Sí, la profesora está **enfrente de** María.

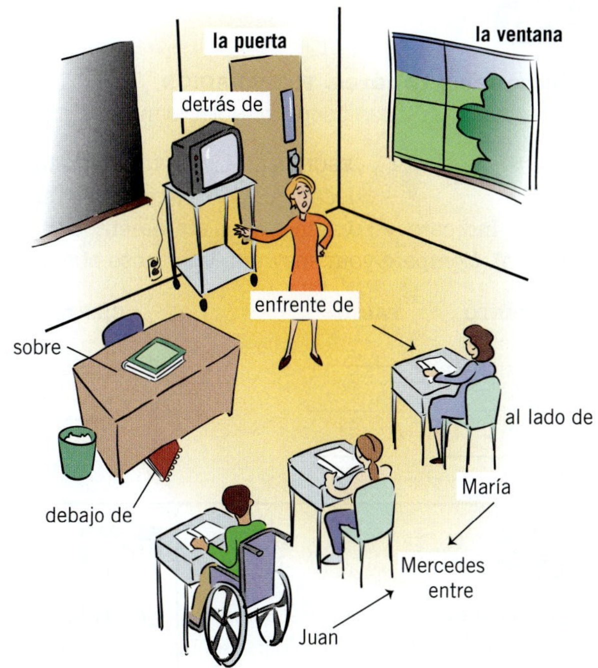

e **Piénsalo.** For each pair, select the sentence that is true according to the drawing.

1. ____ El cuaderno está al lado de la mesa.

__✓__ El cuaderno está debajo de la mesa.

2. __✓__ La puerta está detrás de la profesora.

____ La puerta está delante de la profesora.

3. ____ Mercedes está enfrente de María.

__✓__ Mercedes está al lado de María.

Estar + location

To express location the verb **estar** is used:

El libro **está** sobre la mesa.	*The book is on the desk.*
María **está** en la clase.	*Maria is in the classroom.*

To ask about the location of a person or an object, use **dónde + está.**

¿**Dónde está** la profesora?	*Where is the professor?*
Está en la clase.	*She is in class.*
¿**Dónde está** el libro?	*Where is the book?*
Está sobre la mesa.	*It is on the table.*

Here are some expressions that describe location:

al lado de	*next to*
debajo de	*under*
detrás de	*behind*
enfrente de	*in front of, facing*
entre	*between*
sobre	*on, on top of*

e **¿COMPRENDES?**

Complete the following sentence with the appropriate option based on the position of people in the drawing.

1. __b__ La profesora está…
2. __a__ Juan está…
3. __d__ El libro está…
4. __c__ Mercedes está…

a. al lado de Mercedes.
b. enfrente de María.
c. entre Juan y María.
d. sobre el escritorio.

MySpanishLab

Learn more using Amplifire Dynamic Study Modules, Grammar Tutorials, and Extra Practice activities.

Note

Spanish has two words for "in front of." *Marta está delante de Pedro* means that Marta is in front of (ahead of) Pedro when they are facing in the same direction. *Marta está enfrente de Pedro* means that they are facing each other. Also use *enfrente* to express "in front of" with objects or buildings. *Los turistas están enfrente de la catedral.* (The tourists are in front of the cathedral.)

Suggestions

Present the contrasting pair *enfrente de/detrás de* by standing in front of a student. Say *¿Dónde está el/la profesor/a? Está enfrente de...* Then move behind a student and ask the same question. *Está detrás de...* Reinforce understanding by asking three students to form a line in front of the class. Make statements about their positions. The remaining students respond with *sí* or *no*, according to whether your statements are correct.

Ask either/or questions about students and objects: *¿Está Manuel enfrente de Carolina o detrás de ella?*

Ask questions using *¿Dónde está...?* You may want to review *quién;* introduce other expressions such as *encima de, dentro de, a la derecha (de), a la izquierda (de).* Or preview *están* by asking questions regarding the location of students: *¿Dónde están David y Elena?*

PRÁCTICA

P-21 

Personas y lugares. **PREPARACIÓN.** Take turns telling your partner the location of three people or objects in the classroom scene.

   **ESCUCHA.** Listen to the statements about the location of people and objects in the classroom scene. Indicate (✓) whether each statement is true (**Cierto**) or false (**Falso**). Compare your answers with those of a classmate.

	CIERTO	FALSO
1.		✓
2.	✓	
3.	✓	
4.	✓	
5.		✓
6.	✓	

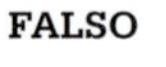

P-22 

En la clase. Look at the student name tags in Professor Gallegos's class below. Ask your partner where Juan, Pedro, Cristina, Mercedes, and Roberto are sitting and he/she will ask you about María, Susana, Carlos, and Profesor Gallegos.

 E1: *¿Dónde está Roberto?*
E2: *Está al lado de Mercedes.*

P-23 

¿Dónde está? Take turns asking where several items in your classroom are. Answer by giving their position in relation to a person or another object.

 E1: *¿Dónde está el libro?*
E2: *Está sobre el escritorio.*

P-24 

¿Quién es? Based on what your partner says regarding the location of another student, guess who the student is.

 E1: *Está al lado de Juan. ¿Quién es?*
E2: *Es María.*

Standard 1.2 Students understand and interpret written and spoken language on a variety of topics. In P-21 the pre-listening activity and the drawing aid comprehension of the spoken word at this early learning stage. Students can understand more than they can say, so instructors should focus on comprehension, rather than limit input to only the words and structures that students can produce orally.

Audioscript for P-21, *Escucha*

1. *El televisor está detrás del profesor.*
2. *La pantalla está sobre la pizarra.*
3. *Marcos está al lado de Elisa.*
4. *La pizarra está al lado del televisor.*
5. *La tableta está debajo del escritorio.*
6. *El cesto está entre el escritorio y la mesa de la computadora.*

Suggestion for P-22

Start by saying where some of the students are seated (e.g., *Pedro está al lado de Carlos*). Students answer *sí* or *no*. Point out that several statements are possible for each name. Then students do the activity.

Alternative for P-22

You may create an information gap activity by preparing two partially filled seating charts (in which version A includes the information missing in version B and vice versa). Pairs of students ask each other questions to fill in their respective charts, e.g., *¿Quién está delante de Cristina?*

Warm-up for P-24

Model the activity with students before they pair up. You may wish to introduce the expressions *cerca (de)* and *lejos (de)* and use them in this guessing game: *Está lejos de Susana. Está lejos de Arturo. Está muy cerca de Amelia. ¿Quién es?* Students take turns providing information and guessing.

3 Using numbers

 Los números 0 a 99

0	**cero**	11	**once**	22	**veintidós**
1	**uno**	12	**doce**	23	**veintitrés**
2	**dos**	13	**trece**	30	**treinta**
3	**tres**	14	**catorce**	31	**treinta y uno**
4	**cuatro**	15	**quince**	40	**cuarenta**
5	**cinco**	16	**dieciséis**	50	**cincuenta**
6	**seis**	17	**diecisiete**	60	**sesenta**
7	**siete**	18	**dieciocho**	70	**setenta**
8	**ocho**	19	**diecinueve**	80	**ochenta**
9	**nueve**	20	**veinte**	90	**noventa**
10	**diez**	21	**veintiuno**		

 **Piénsalo.** Match the word to the correct number.

1. __e__ dieciocho　　**a.** 60
2. __c__ veintiuno　　**b.** 9
3. __d__ treinta y uno　　**c.** 21
4. __a__ sesenta　　**d.** 31
5. __b__ nueve　　**e.** 18

Note
Students worked with the numbers 1–31 in giving dates earlier in this chapter. Those numbers are repeated here for reinforcement.
Project text image of the calendar and review numbers 0 to 31 by pointing to different dates and asking: *¿Qué fecha es?* Give addresses using numbers from one to ten while pointing to the correct or incorrect number on the board. Students answer *sí* or *no.* Do the same with other numbers.
Point out the written accents (*dieciséis,* etc.). Rules of accentuation are presented in Appendix 1.

Numbers 0 to 99

Numbers from sixteen through twenty-nine are usually written as one word. Note the spelling changes and the written accent on some forms.

18: **dieciocho**　　22: **veintidós**

Beginning with thirty-one, numbers are written as three words.

31: **treinta y uno**　　45: **cuarenta y cinco**

The number *one* has three forms in Spanish: **uno, un,** and **una.** Use **uno** when counting: **uno, dos, tres...** Use **un** or **una** before nouns.

un borrador
una mochila
veintiún libros
veintiuna mochilas

Use **hay** for both *there is* and *there are.*

Hay un libro sobre la mesa.　　*There is one book on the table.*
Hay dos libros sobre la mesa.　　*There are two books on the table.*

¿COMPRENDES?

Write the numerals for the following words.

1. diez __10__
2. treinta __30__
3. noventa y cuatro __94__
4. sesenta y seis __66__
5. veinticinco __25__

MySpanishLab
Learn more using Amplifire Dynamic Study Modules, Grammar Tutorials, and Extra Practice activities.

PRÁCTICA

Suggestion for P-25
Have students hold up one, two, three, or four fingers to represent each number's position. Or have them write each number down on the board, as you read them again.

Suggestion for P-26
Point out that *una* is used before feminine nouns by modeling examples. Write numbers on the board, making sure to include *uno* (*un bolígrafo, una silla, veintiún relojes*).

Suggestion for P-28
Introduce the word *calle*. Explain that when a street name does not specify that it is an *avenida*, *paseo*, etc., it is understood that it is a *calle*; e.g., *Rosa vive en Serrano* (*en la calle Serrano*).

Suggestion for P-28
Clarify the meaning of *dirección* by giving addresses of places with which students are familiar. You may want to explain the use of both paternal and maternal surnames in most Spanish-speaking countries (Argentina is an exception). Say *La dirección de... es...* Write the numbers as you say them.

P-25 

¿Qué número es? Your instructor will read a number from each group. Circle the number you hear. Then compare your responses with those of your partner and tell him/her your favorite number.

a.	8	4	3	5
b.	12	9	16	6
c.	37	59	41	26
d.	54	38	76	95
e.	83	62	72	49
f.	47	14	91	56

P-27 

Problemas. Take turns solving the following arithmetic problems. Use **y** (+), **menos** (–), and **son** (=). Then create a new arithmetic problem and ask your partner to solve it.

 MODELO 12 – 5 =
Doce menos cinco son siete.

a. 11 + 4 = 15
b. 8 + 2 = 10
c. 13 + 3 = 16
d. 20 – 6 = 14
e. 39 + 50 = 89
f. 80 – 1 = 79
g. 50 – 25 = 25
h. 26 + 40 = 66
i. ... ...

P-26 

Para la oficina. You and your partner have to check a shipment of equipment and supplies delivered to the Spanish department. Take turns asking your partner how many of each there are. Then ask each other about the items without a number and respond with your own amount.

 MODELO 4 relojes E1: *¿Cuántos relojes hay?*
E2: *Hay 4 relojes.*

- 10 teléfonos
- 12 escritorios
- 20 cestos
- 95 bolígrafos
- 70 rotuladores
- 34 libros
- ... diccionarios
- ... cuadernos

Cultura

In Spanish-speaking countries, the name of the street precedes the house or building number. Sometimes a comma is placed before the number.

Calle (*Street*) Bolívar, 132 Avenida (*Avenue*) de Gracia, 18

Telephone numbers are generally not stated as individual numbers, but in groups of two, depending on how the numbers are written or on the number of digits, which varies from country to country.

12–24–67: **doce, veinticuatro, sesenta y siete**
2–43–89–07: **dos, cuarenta y tres, ochenta y nueve, cero siete**

Comunidades. How do you say or write a street address in your language? How do you say a phone number?

P-28 

Los números de teléfono y las direcciones (*addresses*). Take turns asking each other the phone numbers and addresses of the people listed in the following directory. Then ask your partner for his/her address and phone number (real or imaginary).

Cárdenas Alfaro, Joaquín	General Páez 40	423–4837
Cárdenas Villanueva, Sara	Avenida Bolívar 7	956–1709
Castelar Torres, Adelaida	Paseo del Prado 85	218–3642
Castellanos Rey, Carlos	Colón 62	654–6416
Castelli Rivero, Victoria	Chamberí 3	615–7359
Castillo Montoya, Rafael	Santa Cruz 73	956–3382

 MODELO Castellanos Rey, Carlos

E1: *¿Cuál es la dirección de Carlos Castellanos Rey?*
E2: *Calle Colón, número 62.*

E1: *¿Cuál es su número de teléfono?*
E2: *(Es el) 6–54–64–16.*

4 Expressing time in Spanish

¿Qué hora es?

Es la una.

Son las once.

Son las siete y diez.

Son las ocho y media.

Son las dos menos diez.
Es la una y cincuenta.

Piénsalo. Match the following times.

1. __d__ Las dos y cinco. **a.** 1:30

2. __c__ Las tres. **b.** 3:50

3. __a__ La una y media. **c.** 3:00

4. __b__ Las cuatro menos diez. **d.** 2:05

Suggestions
Model *¿Qué hora es?* by using a clock with movable hands or pointing to a clock or watch. Answer *Es la una, Son las…* Then give true or erroneous times using a clock with movable hands; students respond *sí* or *no*. Follow with either/or questions (e.g., *¿Son las tres o las cuatro?*) while indicating times. Finally, introduce and practice *y cuarto / y quince* and *y media / y treinta.*

Suggestions
Point out that there are alternate expressions for the time after the half hour: *son las tres menos diez; son las dos y cincuenta.*

Present *en punto* and *más o menos* using gestures. Follow with an introduction of *de la mañana/tarde/noche* and indicate A.M. or P.M. on the board.

Explain that it is also common to say *siete de la tarde* if there is still daylight.

You may introduce the expressions *el mediodía* for noon and *la medianoche* for midnight.

Telling time

Use **¿Qué hora es?** to inquire about the time. To tell time, use **Es la...** and **Son las...** with the other hours.

Es la una.	*It is one o'clock.*
Son las tres.	*It is three o'clock.*

To express the quarter hour, use **y cuarto** or **y quince.** To express the half hour, use **y media** or **y treinta.**

Es la una **y media.**	*It is one-thirty.*
Es la una **y treinta.**	
Son las dos **y cuarto.**	*It is two-fifteen.*
Son las dos **y quince.**	

To express time after the half hour, subtract minutes from the next hour, using **menos** for analog clocks. It is becoming more common, especially with digital clocks, to use **y** + **minutos**.

Son las cuatro **menos** diez.	*It is ten to four.*
Son las tres **y cincuenta.**	*It is three fifty.*

Add **en punto** for the exact time and **más o menos** for approximate time.

Es la una **en punto.**	*It is one o'clock on the dot/sharp.*
Son las cinco menos cuarto, **más o menos.**	*It is about a quarter to five.*

For A.M. and P.M., use the following:

de la mañana	(from midnight to noon)
de la tarde	(from noon to nightfall)
de la noche	(from nightfall to midnight)

e ¿COMPRENDES?

Give the time in numerals.

1. Son las tres y cinco 3:05.
2. Son las seis y cuarenta y cinco 6:45.
3. Es la una y cuarto 1:15.
4. Son las once en punto 11:00.
5. Son las cinco menos veinte 4:40.

MySpanishLab

Learn more using Amplifire Dynamic Study Modules, Grammar Tutorials, and Extra Practice activities.

PRÁCTICA

P-29 

¿Qué hora es en...? Take turns telling your partner what time it is in the following cities. Then draw another time clock and ask your partner to give you the time.

México, P.M.

San Juan, A.M.

Buenos Aires, P.M.

Madrid, P.M.

Cultura

In Spanish-speaking countries, events such as concerts, shows, classes, and professional meetings generally begin on time. Medical appointments are also kept at the scheduled hour. However, informal social functions, such as parties and private gatherings, do not usually begin at the announced time. In fact, guests are expected to arrive at least 30 minutes after the appointed time. When in doubt, you may ask **¿En punto?** to find out whether you should be punctual.

Comparaciones. What is the convention in your culture regarding the time you should get to someone's house for a social gathering? Is it polite to arrive right on time, or should you arrive later? In what other situations are you expected to be punctual?

P-30 

El horario de María. Take turns asking and answering questions about María's schedule. Then write down your own Monday schedule, omitting the time each class meets. Exchange schedules with your partner, and find out what time each of his/her classes starts.

MODELO E1: *¿A qué hora es la clase de español?*
E2: *Es a las nueve.*

LUNES	
9:00	la clase de español
10:00	la clase de matemáticas
11:00	la clase de psicología
12:00	el laboratorio
1:00	el almuerzo
2:30	la clase de física
5:00	la clase de tenis

LENGUA

To ask the time at which an event takes place or something happens, use **¿A qué hora es...?** To answer, use **Es a la(s)...** or simply **A la(s)...**

¿A qué hora es la clase de español? *At what time is Spanish class?*
(Es) a las nueve y media. *It is at 9:30.*

Warm-up for P-30
Introduce *¿A qué hora es...?* and *(Es) a la(s)...* by writing on the board (in appropriate order):
la clase de español (time)
el almuerzo 12:30 P.M.
la clase de física 1:00 P.M.
Clarify *almuerzo* by using appropriate gestures for eating and by writing *cafetería* on the board. Then model questions and answers for the schedule.
Students will have additional opportunities to practice telling time in *Capítulo 1*.

Note for *Vocabulario*
End-of-chapter vocabulary lists are designed for students to know which words are considered active for each chapter.

En este capítulo...

Comprueba lo que sabes

Go to ***MySpanishLab*** to review what you have learned in this chapter. Practice with the following:

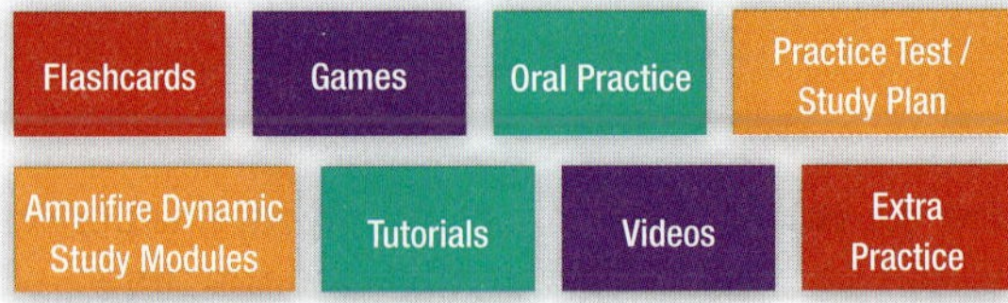

Vocabulario

LAS PRESENTACIONES
Introductions

¿Cómo se llama usted? *What's your name?* (formal)

¿Cómo te llamas? *What's your name?* (familiar)

Encantado/a. *Pleased/nice to meet you.*

Igualmente. *Likewise.*

Me llamo... *My name is ...*

Mucho gusto. *Pleased/nice to meet you.*

LOS SALUDOS
Greetings

bastante *rather*

bien *well*

buenas tardes/buenas noches *good afternoon/good evening, good night*

buenos días *good morning*

¿Cómo está? *How are you?* (formal)

¿Cómo estás? *How are you?* (informal)

hola *hi, hello*

mal *bad*

muy *very*

regular *fair*

¿Qué tal? *What's up? What's new?* (informal)

LAS DESPEDIDAS
Leavetaking

adiós *good-bye*

chao/chau *good-bye*

hasta luego *see you later*

hasta mañana *see you tomorrow*

hasta pronto *see you soon*

EXPRESIONES DE CORTESÍA
Courtesy expressions

con permiso *pardon me, excuse me*

de nada *you're welcome*

gracias *thanks*

lo siento *I'm sorry (to hear that)*

perdón *pardon me, excuse me*

por favor *please*

EN EL SALÓN DE CLASE
In the classroom

el bolígrafo *ballpoint pen*

el borrador *eraser*

la calculadora *calculator*

el cesto *wastebasket*

la computadora *computer*

la computadora portátil *laptop*

el cuaderno *notebook*

el toca DVD *DVD player*

el escritorio *desk*

el lápiz *pencil*

el libro *book*

el marcador/el rotulador *marker*

la mesa *table*

la mochila *backpack*

la pantalla *screen*

la pizarra *chalkboard*

la puerta *door*

el reloj *clock*

la silla *chair*

la tableta *tablet*

el televisor *television set*

la ventana *window*

LAS PERSONAS
People

el amigo/la amiga *friend*

el chico/la chica *boy/girl*

el doctor/la doctora *doctor*

él *he*

ella *she*

el/la estudiante *student*

el profesor/la profesora *professor, teacher*

el señor (Sr.) *Mr.*

la señora (Sra.) *Ms., Mrs.*

la señorita (Srta.) *Ms, Miss*

tú *you* (familiar)

usted *you* (formal)

yo *I*

LEARN Assess yourself at the end of the chapter

At the end of each chapter MySpanishLab features ample opportunity for you to assess if you have achieved the learning outcomes presented at the beginning of each chapter. Go to MySpanishLab to access these practice resources:

- An **Audio-enhanced Vocabulary Flashcard** tool that can be exported to your mobile phone.
- **Games:** *Concentración* (Concentration), *Un partido de fútbol* (soccer-inspired hangman), and *Un concurso* (Quiz Show), which test your knowledge of the chapter's vocabulary and structures.
- **Oral Practice:** Record your answers to the **Oral Practice** comprehensive speaking activities to practice the vocabulary and grammar from the chapter.
- A comprehensive **Practice Test** that generates a personalized Study Plan with support materials.
- **Amplifire Dynamic Study Modules** that will help you better retain the information you learn.

See page 20 for cognates.
See page 23 for numbers.
See page 26 for telling time.

LA POSICIÓN
Position

al lado (de) *next to*
debajo (de) *under*
detrás (de) *behind*
enfrente (de) *in front of*
entre *between, among*
sobre *on, above*

EL TIEMPO

Hace buen/mal tiempo. *The weather is good/bad.*
Hace sol. *It's sunny.*
Llueve./Está lloviendo. *It's raining.*
¿Qué tiempo hace? *What's the weather like?*

VERBOS
Verbs

eres *you are* (familiar)
es *you are* (formal), *he/she is*
está *he/she is, you are* (formal)
estás *you are* (familiar)
hay *there is, there are*
soy *I am*

PALABRAS Y EXPRESIONES ÚTILES
Useful words and expressions

a *at, to*
el año *year*
¿Cómo es? *What is he/she/it like?*
el día *day*
¿Dónde está...? *Where is ... ?*
el/la *the*
en *in*
ese/a *that* (adjective)
el/la *the*
hoy *today*
la mañana *morning*
mañana *tomorrow*
más o menos *more or less*
el mes *month*
mi(s) *my*
¿Quién es...? *Who is ... ?*
la semana *week*
sí *yes*
tu(s) *your* (familiar)
un/una *a, an*
y *and*

LOS MESES DEL AÑO
Months of the year

enero *January*
febrero *February*
marzo *March*
abril *April*
mayo *May*
junio *June*
julio *July*
agosto *August*
septiembre *September*
octubre *October*
noviembre *November*
diciembre *December*

LOS DÍAS DE LA SEMANA
Days of the week

lunes *Monday*
martes *Tuesday*
miércoles *Wednesday*
jueves *Thursday*
viernes *Friday*
sábado *Saturday*
domingo *Sunday*

EXPRESIONES ÚTILES EN LA CLASE

¿Cómo se dice... en español? *How do you say ... in Spanish?*
¿Comprenden?/¿Comprendes? *Do you understand?*
Contesten, por favor./Contesta, por favor. *Please answer.*
¿En qué página? *On what page?*
Dile a tu compañero/a... *Tell your partner...*
Escribe. *Write.*
Hablen (sobre...) *Talk (about ...)*
Lee. *Read.*
Levanta la mano. *Raise your hand.*
Más alto, por favor. *Louder, please.*
Más despacio/lento, por favor. *More slowly, please.*
No comprendo. *I don't understand.*
No sé. *I don't know.*
Otra vez. *Again.*
Presente. *Here (present).*
Repite./Repitan. *Repeat.*
Túrnense. *Take turns.*
La tarea, por favor. *Homework please.*
¿Tienen preguntas?/¿Tienes preguntas? *Do you have any questions?*
Vayan a la pizarra./Ve a la pizarra. *Go to the board.*

Introduction to chapter
Introduce the chapter theme about student life and ask questions to recycle content from the previous chapter. Help students access meaning by making frequent use of gestures or visuals.

Related questions: *¿Cómo se llama tu universidad? ¿Cómo es? ¿Es moderna o tradicional? ¿Es grande o pequeña? ¿Hay muchos o pocos estudiantes en la universidad? ¿Hay muchos estudiantes en las clases? Normalmente, ¿hay más de 20?, ¿más de 30? ¿Cómo son las clases? ¿Son interesantes o aburridas?*

Standard 3.1
Students reinforce and further their knowledge of other disciplines through the foreign language. The map and photos at the beginning of each chapter reinforce students' general cultural knowledge; remind them of facts about history, art, and geography that they may have learned in the past; and help them to integrate disparate pieces of information into a culturally coherent frame.

Integrated Performance Assessment: Three Modes of Communication
Presentational: See activities 1–15, 1–17, 1–19, 1–37, 1–39, 1–42, 1–45, and 1–47.
Interpretive: See activities 1–1, 1–2, 1–9, 1–12, 1–16, 1–17, 1–18, 1–20, 1–21, 1–22, 1–23, 1–27, 1–29, 1–32, 1–38, 1–40, 1–44, and 1–48.
Interpersonal: See activities 1–3, 1–4, 1–5, 1–7, 1–8, 1–9, 1–10, 1–11, 1–12, 1–13, 1–14, 1–15, 1–16, 1–17, 1–19, 1–20, 1–21, 1–22, 1–23, 1–24, 1–25, 1–26, 1–27, 1–28, 1–29, 1–30, 1–31, 1–32, 1–33, 1–39, 1–41, 1–43, and 1–46 and all *Situación* activities.

1 ¿Qué estudias?

ENFOQUE CULTURAL
España

VOCABULARIO EN CONTEXTO
Los estudiantes y los cursos
La universidad
Las actividades de los estudiantes

MOSAICO CULTURAL
La vida universitaria en el mundo hispano

FUNCIONES Y FORMAS
Present tense of regular *-ar* verbs
Present tense of regular *-er* and *-ir* verbs
Articles and nouns
Present tense of *estar*
Interrogative words

EN ACCIÓN
Saludos

MOSAICOS
ESCUCHA Listen for the gist
HABLA Ask questions to gather information
LEE Identify the format of a text
ESCRIBE Brainstorm key ideas before writing

EN ESTE CAPÍTULO...
Comprueba lo que sabes
Vocabulario

LEARNING OUTCOMES

You will be able to:

- talk about studies, campus, and academic life
- describe daily routines and activities
- specify gender and number
- express location and states of being
- ask and answer questions
- talk about Spain in terms of products, practices, and perspectives
- share information about student life in Hispanic countries and compare cultural similarities

ENFOQUE cultural ESPAÑA

Enfoque cultural

To learn more about Spain, go to MySpanishLab to view the *Vistas culturales* videos.

Un fresco del siglo XVI en la Universidad de Salamanca

¿QUÉ TE PARECE?

- Muchos turistas visitan España; es el cuarto (4°) país más visitado del mundo.
- El fútbol es muy popular en España; España es el campeón de la Copa Mundial (2010) y Real Madrid ha ganado la Copa de Europa nueve (9) veces.
- En España se hablan castellano (español), catalán, gallego y euskera (vasco).
- España produce mucho vino; es el tercer (3er) productor de vino en el mundo.
- España forma parte de la Unión Europea.

Note
The 16th-century fresco, originally created for the dome of the library at the University of Salamanca, features the Chariot of Mercury and Virgo.

Suggestion for art
Project the image of the painting and ask if students understand the words *fresco* and *universidad*, which are cognates. (You may have to explain what a *fresco* is.) Use easily understandable sentences and help students make connections: *Este fresco está en la Universidad de Salamanca, en España. El fresco es muy grande.* Using gestures, preview some words that students will learn in the chapter to describe and locate the painting: *Los estudiantes estudian en la universidad; ustedes son estudiantes; ustedes estudian en una universidad. ¿Cómo se llama su universidad?* Point to the map. *¿Dónde está España? ¿Dónde está Salamanca?* Write on the board 1218, the year the *Universidad de Salamanca* was founded. *¿Es una universidad antigua o nueva?* Explain *antiguo/a* and *nuevo/a: la universidad es antigua; el fresco es antiguo; está en un edificio antiguo de la universidad.* Ask students about your college or university: *¿Es antigua o nueva? ¿Cuál es la universidad más antigua de Estados Unidos?*

Note for *Córdoba*
La *Mezquita de Córdoba*, a World Heritage Site, is known today as the Cathedral of Our Lady of the Assumption. It stands as a symbol of the many religious changes that the city of Cordoba has undergone.

Note for *Segovia*
The aqueduct, believed to have been built in the first century A.D., is one of the best preserved Roman aqueducts in all of Europe. It was used to bring water to the city from the Frío River, over 14 kms. away, up until the twentieth century.

Note for *Parque Güell*
Built between 1900 and 1914, *Parque Güell* forms part of the World Heritage Site *Works of Antoni Gaudí*. Originally conceived as an upscale housing development, it has since been transformed into an open municipal park and garden.

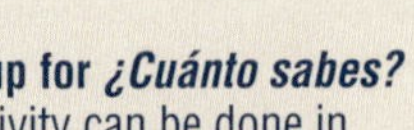

Warm-up for *¿Cuánto sabes?*
This activity can be done in pairs or as a class warm-up. Project the image of the map to introduce the activity in class. Point out the photos on the map and introduce vocabulary as you ask questions. Use gestures to make yourself understood: *¿Qué es este edificio? Es un museo de arte moderno. ¿Conocen la paella? La paella es muy buena*, etc.

La influencia musulmana es evidente en la Mezquita–catedral de Córdoba.

El acueducto de Segovia es un monumento romano del siglo I. Tiene 760 metros de largo.

Antoni Gaudí, el arquitecto modernista, diseña el Parc Güell, uno de los parques más grandes de Europa. El parque está en Barcelona. Gaudí recicla productos de cerámica para la decoración del parque.

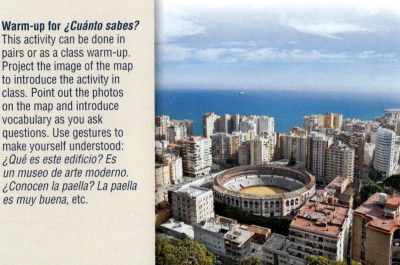

Málaga es una ciudad moderna y antigua. La Plaza de Toros es parte de la tradición española. El Museo Picasso de Málaga se funda en el año 2003.

¿CUÁNTO SABES?

Match the following items based on the information from the map, text, and photos.

1. __d__ la capital de España
2. __e__ el arquitecto del Parc Güell
3. __a__ construcción romana
4. __c__ producto importante
5. __f__ ejemplo de la influencia musulmana
6. __b__ un artista importante de Málaga

a. acueducto de Segovia
b. Picasso
c. vino
d. Madrid
e. Antoni Gaudí
f. Mezquita–catedral de Córdoba

Vocabulario en contexto

Talking about students, their studies, and their activities

Los estudiantes y los cursos

MySpanishLab

Pronunciation topic:
Consonants p, t, c, q, s, and z

Learn more using Amplifire Dynamic Study Modules, Pronunciation, and Vocabulary Tutorials.

Me llamo Rosa Pereda. **Estudio sociología** en la **Facultad de Humanidades** de la **Universidad** de Salamanca. Mis clases son muy temprano. **Llego** a la universidad a las ocho y media. Este semestre mis cursos son **economía, ciencias políticas, psicología, antropología** y **estadística.** Mi clase **favorita** es economía. La clase de estadística es **difícil, pero** el profesor es muy **bueno.** La clase de psicología es **fácil** y muy **interesante.** Por las tardes **trabajo** en una **oficina.**

Este chico es mi amigo. Se llama David Thomas. Es **norteamericano** y estudia español en mi universidad. **También** estudia **literatura, historia** y **geografía.** David es un chico muy responsable y **estudioso.** Generalmente llega a la universidad a las diez. **Practica** español **todos los días** con sus **compañeros** de clase, sus profesores y sus amigos de la universidad. Por la tarde, **escribe** sus **tareas** en la computadora, estudia en el **laboratorio** con uno de sus compañeros y **escucha** música o **mira** programas en español en la televisión.

Note
Vocabulario en contexto provides a richly contextualized cultural framework for learning and practicing vocabulary. New material is presented in thematic groups, accompanied by photographs, illustrations, and authentic documents. The Annotated Instructor's Edition provides an array of teaching techniques for this and other sections. Active vocabulary appears in boldface. The vocabulary list at the end of the chapter contains that vocabulary, as well as other key words that are used in the chapter.

Suggestion
Introduce this section by describing Rosa Pereda. Use gestures, cognates, and visuals to facilitate comprehension: *Rosa Pereda es estudiante. Es inteligente, activa y muy popular entre los estudiantes. Estudia sociología en la Universidad de Salamanca.* Recycle some additional cognates from *Capítulo preliminar.* Use connectors such as *pero, entonces,* and *ahora,* as needed. Finally, ask yes/no and either/or questions to check comprehension: *¿Llega Rosa a la universidad a las once? ¿Estudia economía? ¿Estudia psicología o matemáticas?* Follow a similar procedure to introduce David.

PRÁCTICA

Audioscript for 1-1
1. *Rosa estudia economía en la universidad.*
2. *La clase de psicología es fácil para Rosa.*
3. *Rosa trabaja por las tardes.*
4. *David es norteamericano.*
5. *David estudia antropología.*
6. *Por las tardes, David estudia en la biblioteca.*

1-1  

Escucha y confirma. Listen to the statements about Rosa and David, then answer **sí** or **no** based on what you have read.

1. **a.** sí **b.** no
2. **a.** sí **b.** no
3. **a.** sí **b.** no
4. **a.** sí **b.** no
5. **a.** sí **b.** no
6. **a.** sí **b.** no

1-2 

¿Qué sabes de los estudiantes? Decide if the following information refers to Rosa (**R**) or David (**D**).

1. __R__ Llega temprano a la universidad.
2. __D__ Practica español en el laboratorio.
3. __D__ Estudia geografía.
4. __D__ Escucha música por la tarde.
5. __R__ Su clase favorita es economía.
6. __D__ Escribe tareas en la computadora.

1-3 

Preguntas. Take turns asking and answering the following questions.

1. ¿Quién es Rosa Pereda? una estudiante
2. ¿Qué estudia Rosa? sociología
3. ¿Cuál es su clase favorita? economía
4. ¿Cómo se llama el amigo de Rosa? David
5. ¿Dónde estudian los estudiantes? en la Universidad de Salamanca
6. ¿Quién practica español en el laboratorio? David

Suggestion for 1-4
Question words will be formally presented later in this chapter. Tell students to follow the model, since every question begins with *¿Cuál es...*

1-4 

¿Qué sabes de tu compañero/a? Use **¿Cuál es...?** to ask each other the following information.

E1: *¿Cuál es...?*
E2: *Es...*

1. tu nombre completo
2. el nombre de tu universidad
3. tu clase más (*most*) difícil
4. tu clase más fácil
5. el nombre de tu profesor favorito/profesora favorita

Suggestion for 1-5
Ask additional questions using cognates: *¿Tu compañero/a habla portugués? ¿Estudia álgebra/física?*

1-5 

Más información. To learn more about your partner, take turns asking him/her the following questions.

1. ¿De dónde eres?
2. ¿A qué hora llegas a la universidad?
3. ¿Dónde está la universidad?
4. ¿Cómo es la universidad?
5. ¿Cómo es tu profesor favorito/profesora favorita?

La universidad

Carlos y Carmen hablan de sus clases.

CARLOS: Hola, Carmen. ¿Cómo estás?

CARMEN: Hola, Carlos. **¿Cómo te va?**

CARLOS: Bueno… bastante bien, pero tengo problemas con mi clase de **informática.**

CARMEN: ¿Quién es tu profesor?

CARLOS: Se llama Pedro Hernández. Es inteligente y dedicado, pero la clase es **aburrida** y **saco malas notas.**

CARMEN: ¡Vaya! Lo siento. ¿Estudias suficiente?

CARLOS: Estudio mucho.

CARMEN: **¡Qué lástima!** Mis cinco clases son **excelentes.** Y tú, **¿cuántas clases tienes?**

CARLOS: **Tengo solo** cuatro.

CARMEN: ¡Uy! Son las once. Tengo un **examen** de economía **ahora.** Hasta luego.

CARLOS: Hasta pronto. **¡Buena suerte!**

Mapa de la universidad

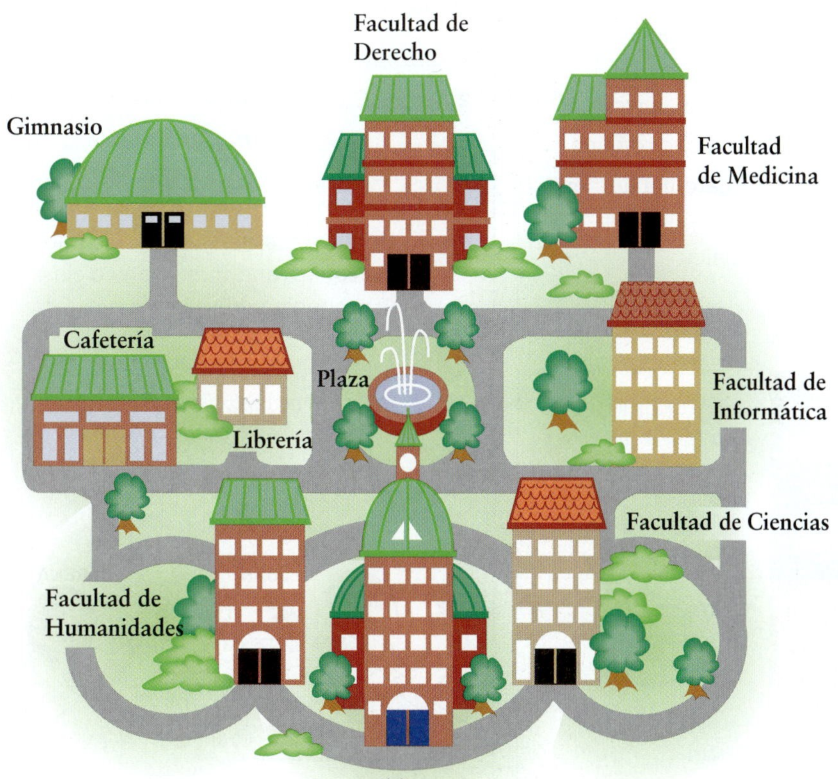

Dialogue
Talk about the dialogue to familiarize students with the content: *Carmen está muy bien. Carlos no está bien. Está preocupado. Estudia mucho para su clase de informática, pero saca malas notas.* Check for comprehension. You may wish to have students practice the dialogue in pairs, personalizing as much as possible.

Suggestion
Explain that *¿Cómo te va?* is a common informal greeting equivalent to *¿Cómo estás?* and *¿Qué tal?*, and that *¡Vaya!* has no specific meaning in this context. It is a filler that denotes Carmen's empathy for her friend's predicament.

Suggestion
You may want to project the campus map and explain that *facultad* is the equivalent of "school" (e.g., School of Art and Architecture) or "department" in U.S. colleges and universities. Point to various buildings, and recycle expressions from *Capítulo preliminar: La Facultad de Humanidades está al lado de la cafetería. La plaza está detrás de la biblioteca.* Remind students: *La librería es donde compramos los libros. La biblioteca es donde estudiamos y consultamos libros.*

Suggestion for *La universidad*
Project image of the campus map and ask students if the following statements are true (*Cierto*) or false (*Falso*). Ask students to correct false statements to make them true.

1. *La plaza está en el centro del campus.* (C)
2. *La Facultad de Humanidades está enfrente de la biblioteca.* (F)
3. *La cafetería está detrás del gimnasio.* (F)
4. *La librería está al lado de la cafetería.* (C)
5. *La Facultad de Medicina está al lado del gimnasio.* (F)
6. *La Facultad de Derecho está entre el gimnasio y la Facultad de Medicina.* (C)

Suggestion for *La universidad*
Bring in copies of your school's campus map, and have students label buildings in Spanish. Have students work with a partner and ask each other questions to locate places.

Expansion for 1-6
Introduce additional courses (*informática, química*). Use the verb *estudiar* to preview introduction of names of courses. You can talk about yourself by saying *Yo no estudio economía. No estudio español. Soy profesor/a de español. Enseño español. Ustedes estudian español.* Ask yes/no questions and either/or questions: *¿Estudias informática?, ¿español? ¿Estudias mucho o poco?*

PRÁCTICA

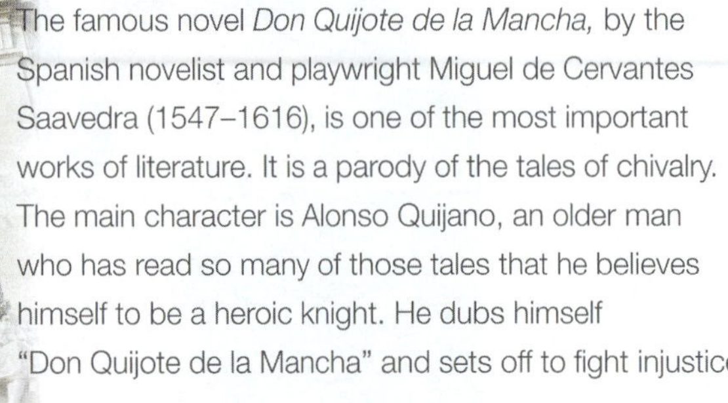

Cultura

The famous novel *Don Quijote de la Mancha,* by the Spanish novelist and playwright Miguel de Cervantes Saavedra (1547–1616), is one of the most important works of literature. It is a parody of the tales of chivalry. The main character is Alonso Quijano, an older man who has read so many of those tales that he believes himself to be a heroic knight. He dubs himself "Don Quijote de la Mancha" and sets off to fight injustice.

Conexiones. Name a famous literary character in your culture. In your opinion, who is the most famous writer in your language?

1-6 

Para confirmar. Match the words with the appropriate class.

1. c *Don Quijote* (Cervantes)
2. e números
3. a mapa digital
4. b animales
5. f Freud
6. d Napoleón

a. geografía
b. biología
c. literatura
d. historia
e. matemáticas
f. psicología

1-7 

¿Qué clases toman? Write the subjects next to the school where they are offered.

Historia medieval	Química I
Administración electrónica	Creación de páginas web
Fisiología II	Derecho romano
Biología	Anatomía humana
Filosofía clásica	Laboratorio de física
Literatura latinoamericana	Criminología

FACULTAD DE CIENCIAS	Biología, Química I, Laboratorio de física
FACULTAD DE HUMANIDADES	Literatura latinoamericana, Filosofía clásica, Historia medieval
FACULTAD DE DERECHO	Derecho romano, Criminología
FACULTAD DE MEDICINA	Fisiología II, Anatomía humana
FACULTAD DE INFORMÁTICA	Creación de páginas web, Administración electrónica

1-8 

¿En qué facultad estudian? **PREPARACIÓN.** Match the names of the university students pictured with the school where they study.

1. b Juan
2. a Carmen
3. d Lorena
4. c Álvaro

a. Facultad de Medicina
b. Facultad de Informática
c. Facultad de Humanidades
d. Facultad de Ciencias

INTERCAMBIOS. Exchange information with a classmate and indicate two classes that each student is probably taking.

E1: *¿Dónde estudia Carmen?*
E2: *Carmen estudia en la Facultad de... Probablemente tiene clases de... y de...*

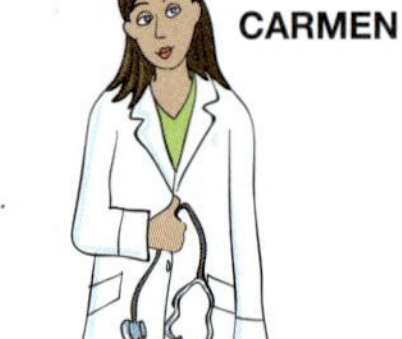

1-9

Mis clases. **PREPARACIÓN.** Make a list of your classes. Indicate the days and time each class meets and whether it is easy or difficult, interesting or boring. A list of some common courses follows.

Algunas materias o asignaturas:

Artes plásticas	Contabilidad	Historia del arte
Astronomía	Economía	Informática
Bioquímica	Estadística	Negocios
Cálculo	Filosofía	Seminario de...
Comunicaciones	Física	Sociología

CLASE	DÍAS	HORA	¿CÓMO ES?

INTERCAMBIOS. Tell your partner about your classes. Take turns completing the following ideas.

1. Mis clases comienzan (*start*) a la(s)...
2. Mi clase favorita es...
3. El profesor/La profesora se llama...
4. La clase es muy...
5. Practico español en...
6. En mi clase de español hay...

EN OTRAS PALABRAS

Words related to computers and computing are often borrowed from English (e.g., **software, e-mail**), and they vary from country to country. As you have already learned, one word for *computer* is **la computadora,** used mainly in Latin America, along with **el computador.** Computer is **el ordenador** in Spain. *Computer science* is **la informática** in Spain and **la computación** in some countries in Latin America.

Suggestion for 1-9
Provide the names of additional courses, using as many cognates as possible. Be prepared to assist students with vocabulary while they write down the subjects they are taking. You may explain the meaning of *contabilidad* and *negocios.*

Suggestion for 1-9, *Intercambios*
This activity may be done in groups of three or four. Students listen to each other's answers and compare the information. They may present their information to the class.

1-10

Las clases de mis compañeros/as. **PREPARACIÓN.** Use the following questions to interview your partner. Then switch roles.

1. ¿Qué estudias este semestre?
2. ¿Cuántas clases tienes?
3. ¿Cuál es tu clase favorita?
4. ¿Qué día y a qué hora es tu clase favorita?
5. ¿Cómo es tu clase de español? ¿Es fácil o difícil? ¿Es interesante o aburrida?
6. ¿Sacas buenas notas?
7. ¿Tienes muchos exámenes?

INTERCAMBIOS. Introduce your partner to another classmate and state one piece of interesting information about him/her. Your classmate will ask your partner about his/her classes.

E1: *Él es Pedro. Estudia ciencias políticas y tiene cuatro clases este semestre.*

E2: *Mucho gusto. ¿...?*

Warm up for 1-10
Before this activity you may want to have students practice the first-person singular of *-ar* verbs and *tengo, tienes,* and *tiene,* which appear in the photo presentations and dialogue at the beginning of this section. Make comparisons with Carmen and Carlos: *Carmen tiene 5 clases. ¿Cuántas clases tienes? Carlos saca malas notas, ¿y tú?*

Suggestion for 1-10
Have students share the information they get with other classmates. You may wish to preview third-person plural forms: *Los estudiantes de esta clase estudian mucho. Trabajan en las computadoras del laboratorio. Ustedes estudian español.*

Note
Point out that some Spanish speakers say *tomar notas* in place of *tomar apuntes.*

Las actividades de los estudiantes

En la biblioteca

Unos **alumnos** estudian en la biblioteca. **Toman apuntes** y trabajan en sus tareas. A veces **buscan** palabras en el **diccionario.** Frecuentemente **conversan** sobre sus clases.

Los fines de semana

Los estudiantes **toman algo** en un **café.**

Miran televisión en **casa.**

Bailan en una **discoteca** con amigos.

Ignacio **camina** en la **playa.**

Luciana **monta** en bicicleta.

Suggestion
Introduce the new vocabulary in this conversation by describing the photograph: *Estos hombres están en una librería. Hay un estudiante y un dependiente en la foto. El estudiante se llama Alberto García Girón. Necesita comprar un diccionario de español para su clase de literatura española. El diccionario cuesta 48 euros. Alberto busca los 48 euros en su cartera (billetera) y compra el diccionario.* Show students a wallet to demonstrate the meaning of *cartera.*

Follow-up
Ask short yes/no and either/or questions to check comprehension and to recycle vocabulary. Students can then work in pairs to personalize this dialogue, substituting what they need to buy at the bookstore.

En la librería

ESTUDIANTE: **Necesito comprar** un diccionario para mi clase de literatura española.
DEPENDIENTE: **¿Grande** o **pequeño?**
ESTUDIANTE: Grande, y completamente en español.
DEPENDIENTE: **Este** diccionario es muy **bueno.**
ESTUDIANTE: **¿Cuánto cuesta?**
DEPENDIENTE: Cuarenta y ocho **euros.**

PRÁCTICA

1-11   

Para confirmar. Complete the following sentences with the correct option to indicate what students do. Then ask your partner about his/her activities.

 E1: *Los estudiantes buscan palabras en el diccionario. ¿Y tú?*

E2: *Yo, en Internet.*

1. Los estudiantes ___b___ en la biblioteca.
   - **a.** toman café
   - **b.** estudian
   - **c.** hablan
2. Miran televisión en ___c___.
   - **a.** la biblioteca
   - **b.** la playa
   - **c.** casa
3. Montan en bicicleta ___a___.
   - **a.** los fines de semana
   - **b.** en el café
   - **c.** en una discoteca
4. Practican deportes como el básquetbol en ___b___.
   - **a.** el laboratorio
   - **b.** el gimnasio
   - **c.** la Facultad de Artes

1-12 

Otra conversación. PREPARACIÓN. Read the conversation between a student and a clerk. Then complete the sentences.

ESTUDIANTE: Necesito comprar un diccionario para mi clase de literatura española.

DEPENDIENTE: Aquí hay un diccionario muy bueno.

ESTUDIANTE: ¿Cuánto cuesta?

DEPENDIENTE: Cuarenta y ocho euros.

1. El estudiante necesita… ___un diccionario___.
2. Es un diccionario… ___muy bueno___.
3. Es para su clase de… ___literatura española___.
4. El diccionario cuesta… ___cuarenta y ocho euros___.

 **INTERCAMBIOS.** With a partner, change the conversation to role play a similar situation.

1-13 

¿Cuánto cuesta? During your semester in Spain, you go to the university bookstore. Take turns with a partner asking how much the pictured items cost and responding as the salesclerk.

 ESTUDIANTE: *¿Cuánto cuesta el diccionario?*

DEPENDIENTE/A: *Cuesta cuarenta y siete euros.*

Suggestion for 1-12
Ask short yes/no and either/or questions to check comprehension and to recycle classroom vocabulary before students begin the activity. Students can then work in pairs to personalize this dialogue, substituting what they need to buy at the bookstore.

Cultura

Since 2002, the euro has been the official monetary unit of the Eurozone, which includes France, Germany, Greece, Ireland, Italy, and Spain, among others. The euro currency sign is € and the banking code is EUR.

Comunidades. What are the advantages and disadvantages of several countries sharing the same currency?

Note for *Cultura*
As of 2012 the countries using the euro as their official monetary unit include Austria, Belgium, Cyprus, Estonia, Finland, France, Germany, Greece, Ireland, Italy, Kosovo, Luxembourg, Malta, Monaco, Montenegro, Netherlands, Portugal, San Marino, Slovakia, Slovenia, Spain, and Vatican City. Andorra and Latvia start using the euro in 2014, and Lithuania plans to adopt it in 2015.

Suggestion for 1-14
Make sure that students understand *dónde* and *cuándo.* You may ask: *¿Cuándo es la clase de español, el lunes o el martes? ¿Dónde es?*

Note for 1-15
Students have already practiced conjugating *-ar* verbs in previous activities. You may wish to go over them before starting activity 1-15 or ask students to review verb endings in *Funciones y formas.*

Suggestion for 1-15
Monitor the interviews and help with vocabulary as needed.

Note for 1-16, *Escucha*
Listening activities provide many learning opportunities when done in the classroom and they can be used to enhance communication. You may, for example, play the audio once and ask students to communicate in pairs about what they have understood. Then play it again and change the pairs successively until the main ideas have been completely understood by most.

Note for 1-16, *Escucha*
In the listening activities in *Mosaicos,* all directions are in English. This enables students to listen to content without being distracted by difficulty in understanding the directions.

Suggestion for 1-16
Mention that students will hear the word *fútbol* and that in Spanish this word usually refers to soccer.

Audioscript for 1-16
1. *Por las mañanas camino a la oficina. Trabajo en el departamento de informática de una compañía muy importante. Llego a la oficina a las nueve menos diez, y a las nueve ya estoy frente al ordenador. Mi trabajo es muy interesante.*
2. *Estudio biología, química e italiano. Mis clases son por la mañana y por la tarde. La clase de biología es difícil, pero no es aburrida. Hay muchos alumnos en mis clases de biología y de química, pero hay menos alumnos en las prácticas de laboratorio.*

1-14

Entrevista (*Interview*). Ask where and when your classmate does each of the following activities. Then share your findings with the class.

MODELO practicar básquetbol

E1: *¿Dónde practicas básquetbol?, ¿y cuándo?*

E2: *Practico básquetbol en el gimnasio por la tarde.*

ACTIVIDAD	DÓNDE	CUÁNDO
1. estudiar para un examen difícil		
2. mirar televisión		
3. tomar café		
4. conversar con tus amigos		
5. escuchar música		
6. comprar unos libros para tus clases		

1-15

Las actividades de tus compañeros.

PREPARACIÓN. Go around the classroom and interview three people. Take notes to report back to the class.

1. ¿Qué haces (*do you do*) los fines de semana?
2. ¿Dónde miras tu programa de televisión favorito?
3. ¿Qué compras en la librería?
4. ¿Dónde estudias normalmente?
5. ¿Trabajas los fines de semana? ¿Dónde trabajas?

INTERCAMBIOS. Now share with the class two pieces of information you got from your classmates.

MODELO *María estudia normalmente en casa. No trabaja los fines de semana.*

1-16

¿Qué hacen? (*What do they do?*)

PREPARACIÓN. You will hear three people talking about their activities during the week and on weekends. Before you listen, list your own activities in the chart. Ask your partner if he/she does the same things. What do you have in common?

MIS ACTIVIDADES DIARIAS (*DAILY*)	MIS ACTIVIDADES DEL FIN DE SEMANA

ESCUCHA. Now pay attention to the general idea of what is said in the conversation. Then write the number of the speaker (1, 2, 3) next to each topic.

__2__ los estudios
__3__ el tiempo libre (*free time*)
__1__ el trabajo

MOSAICO cultural La vida universitaria en el mundo hispano

 ¿Cómo es tu universidad? ¿Tiene un campus grande? ¿Hay residencias para los estudiantes? Hay muchas diferencias entre la vida de los estudiantes universitarios en los países hispanos y en Estados Unidos. Normalmente, las universidades de España y Latinoamérica no tienen un campus sino que (*but rather*) tienen diferentes edificios o facultades en la ciudad.

▲ Universidad de Viña del Mar, Chile

▲ Universidad de Oviedo, España

Las residencias de estudiantes no son comunes en el mundo hispano. Muchas veces, los jóvenes viven en la casa de sus padres o alquilan (*rent*) una habitación en casa de una familia cerca de la universidad. Otros jóvenes buscan apartamentos con otros estudiantes.

Otra diferencia importante son las actividades extracurriculares como los deportes y las organizaciones estudiantiles. La universidad hispana no tiene fraternidades. En general, la vida deportiva no es tan importante como en las universidades de Estados Unidos. Los estudiantes practican los deportes en su tiempo libre.

Por supuesto (*of course*), existen diferencias entre las universidades según el país. Por ejemplo, en las universidades latinoamericanas, las relaciones con los profesores son más formales que en Estados Unidos. Sin embargo (*Nevertheless*), en España las relaciones son mucho más informales. Los estudiantes usan el "tú" cuando hablan con los profesores y usan el nombre de los profesores, ¡no el apellido!

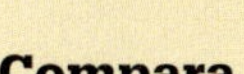

Compara

1. ¿Qué aspectos son similares entre tu universidad y las universidades del mundo hispano?
2. ¿Qué aspectos son diferentes?
3. ¿Qué actividades extracurriculares hay para los estudiantes en tu universidad?

▼ Universidad de Guanajuato, México

3. Los sábados por la mañana, practico fútbol con mis amigos. Por la tarde, miro televisión y hablo con mi amiga Alicia. Por la noche, Alicia y unos amigos toman algo en un café y yo bailo en una discoteca.

Funciones y formas

1 Talking about academic life and daily occurrences

REPORTERO: Hola, buenos días, soy Pablo Brito del canal 6. ¿Su nombre, por favor?

SARA: Yo soy Sara González y ella es Marta Figueroa.

REPORTERO: ¿Tienen ustedes una vida muy activa?

MARTA: Sí, nosotras somos (*are*) atletas. **Practicamos** muchos deportes (*sports*). Sara **participa** en maratones y **practica** tenis. Yo **practico** fútbol y baloncesto.

SARA: Y los fines de semana **montamos** en bicicleta.

REPORTERO: ¡Qué interesante! Muchas gracias.

Piénsalo. Indicate which statements are true (**Cierto**) or false (**Falso**), based on the reporter's interview with Sara and Marta.

1. Falso Pablo es un reportero de radio.
2. Cierto Marta y Sara **practican** muchos deportes.
3. Falso Marta **participa** en maratones.
4. Cierto Marta **practica** fútbol.
5. Falso Sara **practica** baloncesto.
6. Cierto Sara y Marta **montan** en bicicleta.

Present tense of regular *-ar* verbs

To talk about actions, feelings, and states of being, you need to use verbs. In both English and Spanish, the infinitive is the base form of the verb that appears in vocabulary lists and dictionaries. In English, infinitives are preceded by *to: to speak.* Infinitives in Spanish belong to one of three groups, depending on whether they end in **-ar, -er,** or **-ir.** Verbs ending in **-ar** are presented here, and verbs ending in **-er** and **-ir** are presented in the next section.

HABLAR (*to speak*)			
yo	habl**o**	nosotros/as	habl**amos**
tú	habl**as**	vosotros/as	habl**áis**
él, ella, Ud.	habl**a**	ellos, ellas, Uds.	habl**an**

- Use the present tense to express what you and others generally or habitually do or do not do. You may also use the present tense to express an ongoing action. Context will tell you which meaning is intended.

Ana **trabaja** en la oficina.	*Ana works in the office.* *Ana is working in the office.*
Luis **practica** el piano todos los días.	*Luis practices the piano every day.*

Note
In *Funciones y formas,* structures are presented in context to stress their functions in communication. Each structure is presented first as meaningful input through a visual and a short dialogue or text, and is accompanied by *Piénsalo,* a comprehension-based activity designed to highlight function/form connections. Brief grammar explanations come next and are followed by practice within a focused, contextualized framework. Additional practice is given online through MySpanishLab and in the Student Activities Manual (SAM). To use class time efficiently, have students look at the input-oriented visual and introductory dialogue or text, do the comprehension-based activity, and then read the grammar explanations as homework. This way they will come to class ready for the communicative/task-oriented activities, and instructor presentations of grammar points in class can be brief.

Suggestion
Review subject pronouns (*Capítulo preliminar*) by pointing to a student or students and having classmates provide the appropriate pronouns.

Note
Vosotros/as forms are presented in charts throughout *Mosaicos;* however, activities do not require students to produce *vosotros/as* forms since the majority of Spanish speakers do not use them. Instructors who wish to use *vosotros/as* in class can easily incorporate them into the activities.

Suggestion
To familiarize students with the verb forms, say: *Yo hablo español.* Point to a student or to a picture of a well-known Hispanic person and say: *Él/Ella habla español.* Point to the student or picture and to yourself and say: *Nosotros hablamos español en clase.*

- Here are some expressions you may find useful when talking about the frequency of actions.

siempre	*always*	**muchas veces**	*often*
todos los días/meses	*every day/ month*	**a veces**	*sometimes*
todas las semanas	*every week*	**nunca**	*never*

- Here are some common **-ar** verbs and expressions.

bailar	*to dance*	**mirar**	*to look (at)*
buscar	*to look for*	**montar (en bicicleta)**	*to ride (a bicycle)*
caminar	*to walk*	**necesitar**	*to need*
comprar	*to buy*	**participar**	*to participate*
conversar	*to talk*	**practicar**	*to practice*
escuchar	*to listen (to)*	**sacar buenas/ malas notas**	*to get good/ bad grades*
estudiar	*to study*	**tomar apuntes/ notas**	*to take notes*
llegar	*to arrive*	**trabajar**	*to work*

e ¿COMPRENDES?

These activities appear after each grammar presentation. Complete them in class or online to see if you have understood the gramatical structure and have learned the forms.

Insert the person or persons to whom the statements below most likely apply: **yo, tú, usted, ella, nosotros, los estudiantes.**

1. _Los estudiantes_ compran libros para las clases que toman.
2. _Nosotros_ necesitamos computadoras para estudiar en línea.
3. _Usted_, señorita, necesita comprar bolígrafos para tomar apuntes.
4. Y _tú_, ¿qué necesitas para el proyecto de química?
5. _Yo_ compro memoria USB en la librería de la universidad.
6. _Ella/Usted_ necesita hablar de sus problemas de horario con la administración.

MySpanishLab
Learn more using Amplifire Dynamic Study Modules, Grammar Tutorials, and Extra Practice activities.

PRÁCTICA

1-17

Preferencias. PREPARACIÓN. Rank these activities from 1 to 9, according to your preferences (1 = most interesting, 9 = least interesting).

_____ bailar en una discoteca
_____ mirar televisión en casa
_____ estudiar otras culturas
_____ comprar DVD y CD
_____ caminar en la playa
_____ montar en bicicleta cuando hace sol
_____ escuchar música rock
_____ conversar con los amigos por mensajes de texto
_____ bajar (*download*) música de Internet

INTERCAMBIOS. Now compare your answers with those of a classmate. Follow the model.

E1: *Para mí, bailar en una discoteca es la actividad número 1. ¿Y para ti?*

E2: *Para mí, caminar en la playa es número 1.*

1-18

Mi rutina. PREPARACIÓN. Indicate (✓) the activities that are part of your routine at school.

1. _____ Llego a la universidad a las nueve de la mañana.
2. _____ Llamo a mis amigos por teléfono.
3. _____ Nunca tomo notas en las clases.
4. _____ Hablo con mis compañeros en Facebook.
5. _____ Estudio en la biblioteca por la mañana.
6. _____ Trabajo en mis tareas todas las noches.
7. _____ Miro dramas policiacos en la televisión.
8. _____ A veces practico un deporte con mis amigos/as.

INTERCAMBIOS. Now compare your answers with those of a classmate. Report your findings to the class.

Daniel y yo somos parecidos (similar). *Miramos dramas policiacos en la televisión.*

Ben y yo somos diferentes. Yo estudio por la mañana; él estudia por la tarde.

Ocasionalmente hablamos inglés. No hablamos italiano. Write *hablamos* on the board, circling the *-amos* ending. Point to another student and to yourself, and give another example: *Nosotros miramos televisión.* Write *miramos* on the board, again circling *-amos.* Point to one student and say: *Él/Ella habla inglés.* Point to another student and repeat the same sentence. Then point to both students and say: *Ellos/Ellas hablan inglés, pero no hablan portugués.* Write *hablan* on the board, circling the *-an.*

Note
The use of the present tense to express future actions is presented in *Capítulo 3.*

Suggestion
Model the use of *nunca* before the verb: *Juan nunca llega a las ocho.*

Suggestion
As a summary activity after presenting the verb conjugation in context, brainstorm with students the verbs they have seen so far. Write them on the board, organizing them by conjugation group (*-ar* verbs vs. other). Ask them to choose three verbs and write sentences to share with the class.

Suggestions for 1-17
Additional items: *estudiar por la noche, tomar notas en mis clases, hablar con mis amigos en el café, llegar en taxi/caminar a la universidad, escuchar la radio.*

The inclusion of *para mí* and *para ti* in the model in the *Intercambios* gives students the opportunity to use more authentic language. Students do not learn them as active vocabulary at this stage; they follow the model.

Suggestion for 1-18
Students can work in small groups to determine the group's most and least interesting activity. The whole class can then tally the responses.

Warm-up for 1-19
Model the activity by asking one student: *¿Practicas español con tus amigos?* If he/she responds *Sí*, say: *Yo escribo el nombre de… en el libro.* If he/she says *No*, ask another student. Then say: *Ahora ustedes pregunten a sus compañeros. Levántense, por favor.* Signal for them to get up and move around to interview their classmates.

Follow-up for 1-19
After students complete the activity, have them report their results to the class. To practice plural verb forms, students can work in groups and pull together their findings: *David y Amanda llegan a la universidad a las 9:30.*

Note for *En directo*
Before doing activity 1-19, first have students read the expressions in *En directo*. Then have them listen to the dialogue and encourage them to use the expressions in their own conversation.

Audioscript for *En directo*
JILL: *¡Oye! ¡Profesora Enríquez!*
JAKE: *Jill, tienes que ser más formal con la profesora. Dile, "Oiga, por favor" o "Perdón, tengo una pregunta".*
JILL: *Está bien… ¡Profesora Enríquez! Tengo una pregunta para usted.*
PROFESORA ENRÍQUEZ: *Con mucho gusto.*

Suggestion for 1-20, *Intercambios*
Encourage students to focus on using appropriate verb forms in the *Intercambios*. Explain the logic of the *ustedes* form in the follow-up question in the model; i.e., E1 is asking about E2 and his/her friends.

1-19 

A preguntar. **PREPARACIÓN.** Find four different classmates, each of whom does one of the following activities. Write each name on the appropriate line. The *En directo* expressions will help you.

mirar televisión por la tarde

E1: *¡Oye! ¿Miras televisión por la tarde?*

E2: *No, no miro televisión por la tarde. Miro televisión por la noche.*

INTERCAMBIOS. Now report to the class your findings about your classmates' activities.

PERSONA	ACTIVIDAD
________	estudiar español todos los días
________	llegar a clase a las 9:30 de la mañana
________	escuchar música en español
________	trabajar en una oficina por la tarde

En directo

To get someone's attention:

¡Oye! *Hey! (to someone your age or younger)*

Oiga, por favor. *Excuse me. (to someone older than you or someone you do not know)*

To interrupt to ask a question:

Perdón, tengo una pregunta. *Sorry, I have a question.*

To agree to answer:

Con mucho gusto. *It would be a pleasure.*

Listen to a conversation with these expressions.

1-20

Mis actividades. **PREPARACIÓN.** Indicate (✓) how often you do the following activities:

ACTIVIDADES	A VECES	MUCHAS VECES	SIEMPRE	NUNCA
estudiar con amigos				
usar Internet para hacer investigación				
montar en bicicleta los fines de semana				
mirar videos en YouTube				
bailar los sábados				
tomar café				

INTERCAMBIOS. Now tell each other how often you do these activities, and then ask your partner where he/she does them.

E1: *Yo estudio con mis amigos a veces. ¿Y tú?*

E2: *Yo siempre estudio con mis amigos.*

E1: *¿Dónde estudian ustedes?*

E2: *Estudiamos en la biblioteca.*

A popular social activity in Spain is **ir de tapas** (to go out for *tapas*). **Tapas** are small portions of different dishes that are served in most bars with wine or beer. They range from a piece of bread with an anchovy to elaborate appetizers. People usually walk from bar to bar tasting different tapas.

Comparaciones. Do you know of other cultures in which small portions are shared among friends or family in restaurants or bars?

1-21 

Un día típico en la vida de Luisa. Take turns describing what Luisa does on a typical day. Then select two of the times to tell your partner what you do at those times.

Luisa llega a la oficina a las nueve menos diez.

1.

2.

3.

4.

Situación

PREPARACIÓN. Read the following situation with your partner. Then brainstorm the vocabulary, structures, and other information you will need for both roles in the conversation.

Role A. Besides studying, your new friend works. Ask:

a. where he/she works;
b. the days of the week and the hours he/she works; and
c. if the job (**trabajo**) is interesting/boring/difficult/easy.

Then answer your friend's questions about your job.

Role B. Answer your friend's questions about your job. Then ask similar questions about his/her job (**trabajo**).

	ROLE A	ROLE B
Vocabulario	Routine work activities Places Days of the week and time Adjectives to describe one's work Question words	Routine work activities Places Days of the week and time Adjectives to describe one's work Question words
Funciones y formas	Asking and answering questions Giving an opinion Present tense of *ser* Present tense	Asking and answering questions Giving an opinion Present tense of *ser* Present tense

INTERCAMBIOS. Using the information in *Preparación,* act out the conversation with your partner.

Suggestion for 1-21
Have students observe the whole series of pictures to figure out the context of the scene. Encourage them to describe the setting and action in each picture. Emphasize the importance of guessing when they lack vocabulary (e.g., the words in illustrations). Point out that part of the routine of many Spaniards is meeting with friends at a *bar de tapas* after work or school, before going home for dinner (*cena*). Explain that a) many offices close from 1:30 to 4:30 P.M., especially outside the major cities; b) employees usually work until 8:00 P.M.; and c) dinner is late by U.S. standards, about 9:30 P.M.

Note for 1-21
This activity provides additional practice telling time, which was presented in *Capítulo preliminar.*

Expansion for 1-21
Based on a typical day in Luisa's life, have students describe her personality.

This is a good opportunity to recycle cognates presented in *Capítulo preliminar* (*eficiente, independiente, inteligente, activa, moderna*), as well as others presented in this chapter (*estudiosa, interesante*).

Note
Students are given an interactive task in *Situación.* The task is presented in English to ensure that students understand what is requested and that they produce the necessary vocabulary and structures on their own. The *Situación* sections provide students with ample opportunities for practice within realistic contexts and will always appear at the end of each *Funciones y formas* section.

Suggestions for *Situación*
This activity can be organized in a variety of ways. In addition to grouping students in pairs, you may want to divide the class into Group A to play Role A and Group B to play Role B.

You may want to assign partners and have pairs create mini-skits using the video-posting feature, *MediaShare,* online. You may want to have students present their role plays to the class.

2 Talking about academic life and daily occurrences

REPORTERO: Hola, buenas tardes. Estoy entrevistando a jóvenes estudiantes. ¿Qué hacen ustedes durante el día?

PEDRO: Antonio estudia ciencias en la universidad. **Asiste** a sus clases y luego **corre** al laboratorio, donde trabaja todos los días. Habla con el profesor y **aprende** (*learns*) mucho. Los estudiantes de ciencias **leen** mucho, **escriben** trabajos de investigación y sacan buenas notas. Yo soy un estudiante de arquitectura, y mis compañeros y yo **leemos** y **escribimos** mucho también. Yo casi (*almost*) **vivo** (*live*) en la biblioteca cuando estudio para los exámenes.

Piénsalo. Indicate which statements are true (**Cierto**) or false (**Falso**), based on the reporter's interview with Pedro.

1. Falso Antonio estudia arquitectura.
2. Cierto Antonio trabaja en el laboratorio y **aprende** mucho.
3. Cierto Los estudiantes **leen** y **escriben** mucho.
4. Falso Antonio no **asiste** (*attends*) a sus clases porque trabaja mucho.
5. Cierto Los estudiantes de ciencias sacan buenas notas.
6. Cierto Pedro estudia arquitectura.
7. Cierto Pedro casi **vive** en el laboratorio.

Suggestions
Review *-ar* verbs and person markers (*-s*, *-mos*, *-n*).
Point out the similarities and differences between *-er* and *-ir* verbs. Contextualize your language as you review the verbs: *Antonio asiste a sus clases todos los días. Y tú, ¿asistes a tus clases todos los días? Antonio aprende mucho con el profesor. Y tú, ¿aprendes mucho en tus clases? Antonio y Pedro escriben muchos trabajos de investigación. Y ustedes, ¿escriben mucho también?*
Point out the similarities and differences between *-er* and *-ir* verbs. *¿Lees mucho? ¿Qué libros lees? Y tus amigos, ¿leen mucho también? ¿Lees el periódico por la mañana? ¿Lees el periódico en Internet o en papel? ¿Dónde vives? ¿Vives en una casa o en un apartamento?*

Present tense of regular *-er* and *-ir* verbs

- You have learned in this chapter that the present tense is used to express activities and ongoing actions. You have also learned the present tense forms for verbs whose infinitives end in **-ar.** Now you will learn those forms for verbs whose infinitives end in **-er** and **-ir.**

APRENDER (*to learn*)			
yo	aprend**o**	nosotros/as	aprend**emos**
tú	aprend**es**	vosotros/as	aprend**éis**
él, ella, Ud.	aprend**e**	ellos, ellas, Uds.	aprend**en**

- Note that **-er** and **-ir** verbs have the same endings, except for the **nosotros/as** and **vosotros/as** forms.

VIVIR (*to live*)			
yo	viv**o**	nosotros/as	viv**imos**
tú	viv**es**	vosotros/as	viv**ís**
él, ella, Ud.	viv**e**	ellos, ellas, Uds.	viv**en**

- Other common **-er** and **-ir** verbs are:

comer	*to eat*	**responder**	*to respond*
comprender	*to understand*	**asistir**	*to attend*
correr	*to run*	**escribir**	*to write*
leer	*to read*		

- The verb **ver** has an irregular **yo** form:

VER (*to see*)			
yo	ve**o**	nosotros/as	ve**mos**
tú	ve**s**	vosotros/as	ve**is**
él, ella, Ud.	ve	ellos, ellas, Uds.	ve**n**

Veo películas los fines de semana. *I see movies on weekends.*

- Use **deber** + *infinitive* to express that you should/must/ought to do something.

Los atletas **deben beber** mucha agua. *Athletes should drink a lot of water.*

¿COMPRENDES?

Provide the forms of **comer** and **escribir** to complete the following ideas.

1. Los estudiantes __comen__ con sus amigos en un restaurante en el campus todos los días.
2. Yo __como__ en casa porque cuesta dinero comer en los restaurantes.
3. Y tú, ¿ __comes__ tu almuerzo (*lunch*) en casa o en la cafetería de la universidad?
4. La profesora __escribe__ los exámenes en su computadora portátil.
5. Mis amigos y yo __escribimos__ la tarea de español en la computadora.

MySpanishLab

Learn more using Amplifire Dynamic Study Modules, Grammar Tutorials, and Extra Practice activities.

PRÁCTICA

1-22

Mi profesor/a modelo. PREPARACIÓN. Indicate (✓) which of the following activities are part of the routine of an ideal instructor inside and outside the classroom.

	SÍ	NO
1. Lee el periódico (*newspaper*) en clase.	_____	_____
2. Escucha los problemas de los estudiantes.	_____	_____
3. Bebe café y come en la clase.	_____	_____
4. Escribe buenos ejemplos en la pizarra.	_____	_____
5. Nunca prepara sus clases.	_____	_____
6. Siempre asiste a clase.	_____	_____
7. Responde a las preguntas de los estudiantes.	_____	_____
8. Habla con los estudiantes en su oficina.	_____	_____

INTERCAMBIOS. Compare your answers with those of a classmate. Together write two more activities typical of an ideal instructor.

Note for *solo*
A rule published by the RAE (2010) eliminated the accent mark on *solo* when used as an adverb: ***Solo*** tengo una hermana.

Suggestion for 1-23
Pasarlo bien is introduced as a lexical item. Before the activity, expand on the meaning by giving examples: *Hay muchas maneras de pasarlo bien. Yo, por ejemplo, para pasarlo bien, escucho música, corro en el parque cuando hace buen tiempo, preparo comida mexicana en casa,* etc. *¿Y tú, lees o bailas para pasarlo bien? ¿Cuáles son tus actividades los fines de semana para pasarlo bien?*

Audioscript for *En directo*
RUBY: *Cristián y yo tomamos una clase para aprender a hacer tapas.*
ZULI: *¡Qué interesante! Yo tengo clase de cocina francesa.*
RUBY: *¡Qué divertido!*
ZULI: *Al contrario, ¡qué aburrido! No me gusta la comida francesa.*
RUBY: *¡Qué increíble! Y, ¿por qué tomas la clase?*

Note for 1-24
In this activity students use *¿Qué (no) haces?* as a fixed phrase. Using the phrase gives students broader opportunities for communication, but they do not use *hacer* in their responses. Be prepared to help with vocabulary if necessary.

Expansion for 1-24
Additional places: *la librería, el laboratorio, el trabajo, el gimnasio, el parque.* You can also ask questions with *dónde;* students answer by giving the appropriate place: *¿Dónde comes los sábados? ¿Dónde escribes?*

 **Standard 1.1 and Standard 1.3**
Students engage in conversations, provide and exchange information, and exchange opinions (1.1). Students present information, concepts, and ideas to an audience of listeners or readers (1.3). In activity 1-24, students converse with each other (1.1) and then make a brief presentation to the class (1.3) on what they have learned in the interaction. Students build their linguistic knowledge and communication skills when

1-23

Para pasarlo bien (*To have a good time*).
PREPARACIÓN. Indicate (✓) which of the following activities you do to have a good time.

1. _____ Leo libros en español todas las semanas.
2. _____ Escribo mensajes de texto.
3. _____ Practico deportes con los amigos.
4. _____ Asisto a clase a las ocho de la mañana.
5. _____ Corro en el gimnasio y en el parque.
6. _____ Veo películas y programas de televisión en casa.
7. _____ Charlo con mis amigos y con mi familia por Skype.
8. _____ Bebo solo Coca-Cola en las fiestas.

 **INTERCAMBIOS.** Compare your answers with those of a classmate. Then exchange information with another pair about the activities you all do to have a good time. Use the expressions in *En directo.*

E1: *Nosotros bailamos en discotecas para pasarlo bien. ¿Y ustedes?*
E2: *Bebemos café y conversamos con los amigos.*

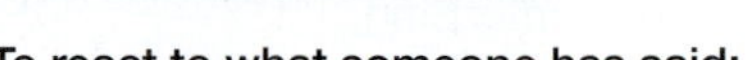

To react to what someone has said:
¡Qué interesante! *That's so interesting!*
¡Qué increíble! *That's unbelievable!*
¡Qué casualidad! *What a coincidence!*
¡Qué divertido! *How funny!*
¡Qué aburrido! *How boring!*

 Listen to a conversation with these expressions.

1-24

Lugares y actividades. Ask what your classmate does in the following places. He/She will respond with one of the activities listed. Then ask what your classmate does not do in those places.

en la clase
E1: *¿Qué haces en la clase?*
E2: *Veo películas en español.*
E1: *¿Qué no haces en la clase?*
E2: *No leo mensajes de texto.*

LUGARES	ACTIVIDADES
en la playa	beber cerveza
en un café	caminar
en una discoteca	bailar salsa
en una fiesta	mirar televisión
en el cine	leer el periódico (*newspaper*)
en la casa	ver películas de horror
en un restaurante	escribir mensajes de texto
en la biblioteca	comer un sándwich y tomar un café

1-25 

A preguntar. PREPARACIÓN. Find four different classmates, each of whom does one of the following activities. Write each name on the appropriate line.

ver videos en la computadora
E1: *¿Ves videos en la computadora?*
E2: *Sí, veo videos en la computadora.*

PERSONA	ACTIVIDAD
_________	asistir a conciertos de música rock
_________	beber café todos los días
_________	vivir en casa con tu familia
_________	escribir mensajes de texto por la noche

INTERCAMBIOS. Now report to the class your findings about your classmates' activities.

1-26 

¿Qué deben hacer? Take turns giving advice to the people in the following situations. Then create your own situation and your partner will give you advice.

 Maricela desea sacar buenas notas.
Debe estudiar todos los días.

1. Carlos desea aprender sobre cine español.
2. Luisa y Jorge beben muchos refrescos.
3. Los estudiantes desean comer tapas.
4. Óscar desea aprender a bailar.
5. Carolina desea preparar tacos y enchiladas.
6. ...

Situación  

PREPARACIÓN. Read the following situation with your partner. Then brainstorm the vocabulary, structures, and other information you will need for both roles in the conversation.

Role A. You see a classmate at a coffee shop with a laptop and books spread out on the table. Ask if he/she:

a. drinks coffee in the coffee shop every day;
b. how often **(con qué frecuencia)** he/she studies there; and
c. whether he/she reads the newspapers **(los periódicos)** there.

Role B. You are sitting at a table with your laptop and books at your favorite coffee shop. A classmate walks over, greets you, and starts a conversation. Answer your classmate's questions about what you usually do there.

	ROLE A	ROLE B
Vocabulario	Greetings After class activities Question words	Greetings After class activities
Funciones y formas	Asking questions Present tense Addressing someone your age	Answering questions Present tense Addressing someone your age

INTERCAMBIOS. Using the information in *Preparación,* act out the conversation with your partner.

they convey information, feelings, or opinions that are not already known to the listener, because these authentic communicative situations push learners to synthesize their linguistic knowledge in new ways to get their point across.

Follow-up for 1-25, *Intercambios*
After students complete the activity, have them report their results to the class. Make students accountable for attending to the reports of their classmates by asking questions; e.g., *¿Qué hacen Susan y David? ¿Qué beben?*

Suggestion for *Situación*
You may want to assign partners and have pairs create mini-skits using the video-posting feature, *MediaShare,* online.

Suggestions
Write *el/un* on the board or on a visual next to the word *libro,* circling or underlining the *o.* Write *la/una* and the word *tarea,* circling the *a.* Give other examples of vocabulary presented in the chapter. Write *el mapa* and say *excepción;* do the same thing with *el día* and *la mano.* Continue with *la actividad, la lección,* and *la televisión,* underlining the endings *-dad, -ción,* and *-sión,* pointing out that words with these endings use the articles *la/una.*

As a mnemonic device, write the following words in a vertical column on the board: *el cereal, el libro, el salón, el postre, el borrador, el tenis.* Circle the final letters of each word to spell "loners"; point out that words ending in these letters are usually masculine. Common exceptions to this rule are *la noche* and *la clase.*

3 Specifying gender and number

MANUEL: Hola, Rocío. Tengo **un** plan. ¿Estudiamos español en **la** universidad esta tarde? Necesitamos **un** diccionario para **la** tarea.

ROCÍO: ¡Buena idea! ¿En **la** biblioteca? **El** profesor de español es bueno, pero es **una** clase difícil. ¿Invitamos a Marcos?

MANUEL: Fenomenal. Usamos **la** pizarra y **el** escritorio **del** salón 12 de **la** biblioteca.

Piénsalo. Match the words with the correct article. Use the conversation and the endings of the nouns as clues.

1. __d__ clase
2. __c__ diccionario de español
3. __b__ pizarra
4. __a__ escritorio
5. __b__ universidad

a. el
b. la
c. un
d. una

Articles and nouns

Gender

- Nouns are words that name a person, place, or thing. In English all nouns use the same definite article, *the*, and all singular nouns use the indefinite articles *a* and *an*. Spanish nouns, whether they refer to people or to things, have either masculine or feminine gender. Masculine singular nouns use **el** or **un** and feminine singular nouns use **la** or **una.**
- The terms *masculine* and *feminine* are used in a grammatical sense and have nothing to do with biological gender.

	Masculine	Feminine	
Singular Definite Articles	**el**	**la**	*the*
Singular Indefinite Articles	**un**	**una**	*a/an*

- Generally, nouns that end in **-o** are masculine and require **el** or **un,** and those that end in **-a** are feminine and require **la** or **una.**

el/un libr**o** **el/un** cuadern**o** **el/un** diccionari**o**
la/una mes**a** **la/una** sill**a** **la/una** ventan**a**

- Nouns that end in **-dad, -ción, -sión** are feminine and require **la** or **una.**

la/una universi**dad** **la/una** lec**ción** **la/una** televi**sión**

- Nouns that end in **-ma** are generally masculine.

el/un progra**ma** | **el/un** proble**ma**
el/un dra**ma** | **el/un** poe**ma**

- In general, nouns that refer to males are masculine, and nouns that refer to females are feminine. Masculine nouns ending in **-o** change the **-o** to **-a** for the feminine; those ending in a consonant add **-a** for the feminine.

el/un amig**o** | **la/una** amig**a**
el/un profeso**r** | **la/una** profesor**a**

- Nouns ending in **-ante** and **-ente** may be feminine or masculine. Gender is signaled by the article (**el/la estudiante**).
- Use definite articles with titles when you are talking about someone. Do not use definite articles when addressing someone directly.

La señorita Andrade es **la** secretaria en el Departamento de Lenguas Europeas. **El** profesor Campos es **el** director del departamento. | *Ms. Andrade is the secretary in the Department of European Languages. Professor Campos is the chair of the department.*

Todos los días, **el** profesor Campos dice "Buenos días, señorita Andrade". | *Every day, Professor Campos says "Good morning, Ms. Andrade."*

Ella contesta: "Buenos días, profesor Campos". | *She responds, "Good morning, Professor Campos."*

Number

	Masculine	Feminine	
Plural Definite Articles	**los**	**las**	*the*
Plural Indefinite Articles	**unos**	**unas**	*some*

- Add **-s** to form the plural of nouns that end in a vowel. Add **-es** to nouns ending in a consonant.

la sill**a** → las silla**s** | el cuadern**o** → los cuaderno**s**
la activida**d** → las activida**des** | el seño**r** → los seño**res**

- Nouns that end in **-z** change the **z** to **c** before **-es.**

el lápi**z** → los lápi**ces**

- To refer to a mixed group, use masculine plural forms.

los chic**os** | *the boys and girls*

¿COMPRENDES?

Provide the correct definite article and indefinite article as indicated for the following nouns.

Definite articles: **el, la, los, las**

1. __la__ compañera
2. __el__ escritorio
3. __las__ clases
4. __los__ profesores
5. __la__ mochila

Indefinite articles: **un, una, unos, unas**

6. __una__ mesa
7. __un__ señor
8. __unas__ universidades
9. __unos__ relojes
10. __un__ mapa

MySpanishLab
Learn more using Amplifire Dynamic Study Modules, Grammar Tutorials, and Extra Practice activities.

Suggestion for 1-27
Students may do this activity individually and then check answers with a partner, noting discrepancies that they cannot resolve on their own. That way class time is reserved for items that students find most difficult.

Suggestion for 1-28
Remind students of the verb *deber,* which they used in activity 1-26, and can use in this activity as well.

Note for 1-28
The expression *tener que* + infinitive is presented here for recognition only and to provide a context for each situation. Students are not expected to use it. A complete presentation of *tener* and *tener que* + infinitive appears in *Capítulos 3* and *4.* Since students have seen and used *tiene(s)* they should have no difficulty in recognizing *tienen.*

Suggestion for *Situación*
You may wish to have students review the phrases in the *En directo* boxes in this chapter to increase the amount of language they produce and to make their exchanges sound more natural.

Suggestion
Remind students that they have already used two verbs that translate as "to be" in English. Write *ser* and *estar* on the board. Ask students basic questions they practiced in the previous chapter (*¿Cómo estás? ¿Dónde está…? ¿Cómo es…?*) while pointing to the appropriate verb.

Suggestion
Use photos or illustrations of people in various places to practice forms of *estar,* some of which students have already seen: *Ellos están en un café, y estas chicas están en una oficina* (write *están* on the board). *Pero ustedes están en la clase de español. Yo estoy aquí también. Nosotros* (use gesture) *estamos en la clase de español.*

Cross-reference
The uses of *ser* and *estar* are contrasted in *Capítulo 2.* You have already been using some forms of *estar.* All the present tense forms are presented here.

PRÁCTICA

1-27  

Conversaciones incompletas. PREPARACIÓN. Complete the conversations. Then, compare answers with a classmate.

1. Supply the definite articles (**el, la, los, las**).

En la universidad

E1: ¿Dónde está María?

E2: Está en ___la___ clase de ___la___ profesora Sánchez.

E1: ¡Qué lástima! Necesito hablar con ella. Es urgente. ¿A qué hora llega?

E2: Llega a ___las___ dos, más o menos.

2. Supply the indefinite articles (**un, una, unos, unas**).

En la librería

E1: Necesito comprar ___unos___ lápices.

E2: Y yo necesito ___un___ cuaderno. ¿Qué más compro?

E1: Para el curso de español, ___unos___ profesores usan ___un___ diccionario electrónico.

INTERCAMBIOS. With a partner, select one of the conversations to create and act out a similar situation.

1-28 

¿Qué necesitan? Take turns saying what these classmates need. Then tell your partner what you should do and he/she will tell you what you need.

MODELO E1: *Alicia debe buscar unas palabras.*
E2: *Necesita un diccionario.*

1. Mónica debe tomar apuntes en la clase de historia.
2. Carlos y Ana deben hacer la tarea de matemáticas.
3. Alfredo debe estudiar para el examen de geografía.
4. Isabel debe escribir una composición para su clase de inglés.
5. Blanca y Lucía deben buscar las capitales de Sudamérica.
6. David debe marcar las partes importantes del libro de texto.
7. Yo debo…

Situación

PREPARACIÓN. Read the following situation with your partner. Then brainstorm the vocabulary, structures, and other information you will need for both roles in the conversation.

Role A. You have missed the first day of class. Ask a classmate:
a. what time the class meets;
b. who the professor is; and
c. what you need for the class.

Role B. Tell your classmate:
a. the time the class meets;
b. the name of the professor and what he/she is like; and
c. at least three items that your classmate needs for the class.

	ROLE A	ROLE B
Vocabulario	Time Question words	Time Class materials Words to describe a person
Funciones y formas	Asking questions Thanking someone Getting the attention of an acquaintance	Answering questions Telling the time Describing someone Definite and indefinite articles Reacting to what someone says

INTERCAMBIOS. Using the information in *Preparación,* act out the conversation with your partner.

4 Expressing location and states of being

ELISA: ¿Humberto? Te habla Elisa.

HUMBERTO: ¡Elisa! ¡Qué sorpresa! ¿Dónde **estás?**

ELISA: **Estoy** en el aeropuerto de Barajas, en Madrid. ¿Y tú?

HUMBERTO: Mi padre y yo **estamos** de vacaciones en Nueva York. En este momento, mi padre **está** en la tienda Best Buy. ¿Y cómo **están** todos en tu familia?

ELISA: Todos **estamos** muy bien. ¡Qué bueno escucharte! Lo siento, Humberto, pero el vuelo (*flight*) sale (*leaves*) pronto. Hablamos más mañana. Adiós.

Piénsalo. Indicate whether each statement is true (**Cierto**) or false (**Falso**), based on the conversation.

1. Falso Humberto **está** en el aeropuerto.
2. Falso Elisa **está** de vacaciones en Nueva York.
3. Cierto Humberto **está** en una ciudad grande con una persona de su familia.
4. Falso La tienda Best Buy de esta conversación **está** en Madrid.
5. Cierto Elisa y Humberto **están** contentos de hablar por teléfono.

Present tense of *estar*

- You have already been using some forms of **estar.** Here are all the present tense forms of this verb.

ESTAR (*to be*)			
yo	**estoy**	nosotros/as	**estamos**
tú	**estás**	vosotros/as	**estáis**
Ud., él, ella	**está**	Uds., ellos, ellas	**están**

- Use **estar** to express the location of persons or objects.

¿Dónde **está** Humberto? — *Where is Humberto?*

Está en Nueva York. — *He is in New York.*

- Use **estar** to talk about states of health or being.

¿Cómo **está** la familia de Elisa? — *How is Elisa's family?*

Está muy bien. — *They are very well.*

¿COMPRENDES?

Complete the sentences with the correct forms of **estar.**

1. El profesor está en la oficina.
2. Nosotros estamos bien.
3. Yo estoy en el gimnasio.
4. ¿Cómo están ustedes?
5. Mis amigos están en la biblioteca.
6. Mi compañero está bien también.

MySpanishLab

Learn more using Amplifire Dynamic Study Modules, Grammar Tutorials, and Extra Practice activities.

Note for 1-29
Activity 1-29 engages students in active learning. Rather than memorize a set of rules, they articulate to themselves and to their partners how a rule applies to a particular statement. This metalinguistic approach—thinking and talking about the language—pushes students to take their understanding of a grammatical concept to a deeper level. Metalinguistic talk, termed "languaging" by researchers (e.g., Swain, 2006) in second language acquisition, has been shown to contribute to language learning.

Suggestions for 1-31
Encourage students to guess how to say the location in drawing 4 (*el hospital, la clínica*), telling them only that it is a cognate. Once a student guesses one of the words, model pronunciation and spelling of both. Do the same thing for *básquetbol* in drawing 3. You may also mention *baloncesto.*

Introduce the phrases *¿Qué hace?* and *¿Qué hacen?*, which students will need in their interactions. Remind them that they have already used the phrase *¿Qué haces?* earlier in the chapter.

Suggestion for *Situación*
Students should switch roles, so they can each play both people. To save time in class, you may assign *Situación* for homework and have pairs post their presentations using the videoposting feature, *MediaShare,* online.

PRÁCTICA

1-29 

En la cafetería. Complete the conversation between Roberto and Carlos, using the correct forms of **estar.** Then indicate in parentheses if **estar** signals location (**L**) or a state of being (**S**). Compare answers with a classmate and create a similar conversation.

ROBERTO: Hola, Carlos. ¿Qué tal? ¿Cómo __estás (S)__?

CARLOS: __Estoy (S)__ muy bien. ¿Y tú?

ROBERTO: Muy bien, muy bien. ¿Y cómo __está (S)__ tu hermana (*sister*) Ana?

CARLOS: Bien, gracias. Ella y mamá __están (L)__ en España ahora.

ROBERTO: ¡Qué suerte! Y nosotros __estamos (L)__ en la universidad, ¡y en la semana de exámenes!

1-30 

Horas y lugares favoritos. **PREPARACIÓN.** Choose two different times of day and ask your partner where he/she usually is at that time.

E1: *¿Dónde estás generalmente a las 10:00 de la mañana?*
E2: *Estoy en...*
E1: *¿Y dónde estás a la 1:00 de la tarde?*

INTERCAMBIOS. Compare your responses with those of your partner. Identify the similarities and/or differences in your schedules.

1-31 

Conversación. Ask a classmate where any of the people in these drawings are and what they are doing. Then draw where you would like to be and your partner will say where you are and what you do there.

María Luisa
E1: *¿Dónde está María Luisa?*
E2: *Está en la biblioteca.*
E1: *¿Qué hace?*
E2: *Estudia.*

María Luisa

Berta Lorena

Marcelo Eduardo

Carlos El Dr. Núñez

Yo

Situación

PREPARACIÓN. Read the following situation with your partner. Then brainstorm the vocabulary, structures, and other information you will need for both roles in the conversation.

Role A. You are a new student at the university, and you do not know where some of these buildings are located. Introduce yourself to a classmate and ask where the following buildings are:

a. la biblioteca
b. la cafetería
c. la Facultad de Ciencias
d. la Facultad de Humanidades

Role B. You meet a new student on campus. Answer his/her questions about the location of certain buildings.

	ROLE A	ROLE B
Vocabulario	Places on campus Question words	Places on campus Words to express location
Funciones y formas	Introducing oneself Using *estar* to talk about location	Reacting to what you hear Answering questions Giving information about location

INTERCAMBIOS. Using the information in *Preparación,* act out the conversation with your partner.

5 Asking and answering questions

Andrea Pérez conversa con su consejera (*advisor*) en la Universidad de Salamanca. La consejera debe rellenar (*fill out*) algunos formularios con información sobre Andrea. Aquí están algunas de las preguntas de la consejera, y en la columna de la derecha, las respuestas de Andrea.

Consejera	Andrea
¿**Cómo** se llama tu residencia estudiantil?	Se llama Residencia Oviedo.
¿**Dónde** está?	Está en la calle San Narciso.
¿**Cuándo** son tus clases?	Por la mañana y por la tarde.
¿**Cuánto** cuesta tu pase de autobús al mes?	Aproximadamente 35 euros.
¿**Quién** es tu compañera de cuarto?	Cristina Zapatero.
¿**Por qué** deseas (*want to*) estudiar psicología?	Para ayudar (*help*) a otras personas.

e **Piénsalo.** Match Andrea's responses with other questions her advisor asked her.

1. __c__ Es el profesor Agustín Reyes Torres.
2. __d__ Se llama Cristina Zapatero.
3. __a__ En la Residencia Oviedo.
4. __e__ 400 euros al mes.
5. __b__ Por la tarde.

a. ¿**Dónde** vives?
b. ¿**Cuándo** es tu clase de psicología?
c. ¿**Quién** es tu profesor favorito?
d. ¿**Cómo** se llama tu compañera de cuarto?
e. ¿**Cuánto** cuesta vivir en la residencia?

Interrogative words

- Interrogative words are used to ask questions or to obtain specific information. You have already been using many of these words.

¿cómo?	*how/what?*	**¿cuál(es)?**	*which?*
¿qué?	*what?*	**¿quién(es)?**	*who?*
¿cuándo?	*when?*	**¿cuánto/a?**	*how much?*
¿por qué?	*why?*	**¿cuántos/as?**	*how many?*
¿dónde?	*where?*	**¿para qué?**	*why?/what for?*

- If a subject is used in a question, it normally follows the verb.

¿Dónde trabaja **Elsa?** — *Where does Elsa work?*

Suggestion
Encourage students to guess the meanings of the question words in the exchanges between Andrea and her advisor, based on the context as well as on their own experience filling out similar forms.

Suggestions
Ask questions such as the following: *¿Dónde está la pizarra? ¿Y quién(es) está(n) al lado de la pizarra? ¿Cuántos alumnos hay en esta fila? ¿Quiénes son? ¿Cómo es…?* Point out the difference in stress and meaning between *¿por qué?* and *porque.*

To practice asking for definitions, provide students with words such as *lugar* and *objeto: ¿Qué es una librería? Es un lugar donde compramos libros. ¿Qué es un lápiz? Es un objeto que usamos para escribir.* In small groups, have students practice giving simple definitions (e.g., *oficina, tiza*).

Ask questions using *cuál(es): ¿Cuál es la mochila de Alberto? ¿Y cuáles son los libros de Ana y Pedro?*

Point out that intonation rises at the end of yes/no questions. Lift your hand as you raise intonation asking yes/no questions with subjects before and after the verb.

To practice interrogative tags ask several questions of the same student: *Tú eres David, ¿verdad? Y tú eres norteamericano, ¿no?*

Practice *¿cómo?* to request repetition or clarification.

Some speakers accept *cuál + noun*, as in *¿Cuál mochila es tuya?*, whereas others do not. *Mosaicos* uses *cuál(es) + ser* (or phrase, as in *¿Cuál de las mochilas es tuya?*).

- Use **por qué** to ask *why* and **porque** to answer *because*.

¿**Por qué** está Pepe en la biblioteca?	*Why is Pepe at the library?*
Porque necesita estudiar.	*Because he needs to study.*

- Use **qué + ser** when you want to ask for a definition or an explanation.

¿**Qué es** la sardana?	*What is the sardana?*
Es un baile típico de Cataluña.	*It is a typical dance of Catalonia.*

- Use **cuál(es) + ser** when you want to ask which one(s).

¿**Cuál es** tu mochila?	*Which (one) is your backpack?*
¿**Cuáles son** tus papeles?	*Which (ones) are your papers?*

- Questions that may be answered with **sí** or **no** do not use a question word.

¿Trabajan ustedes los sábados?	*Do you work on Saturdays?*
No, no trabajamos.	*No, we do not.*

- Another way to ask a question is to place an interrogative tag after a statement.

Tú hablas inglés, **¿verdad?**	*You speak English, don't you?*
David es norteamericano, **¿no?**	*David is American, isn't he?*

LENGUA

All question words have a written accent over the stressed syllable:

cómo, dónde

When these words are used in a non-interrogative context, they do not have a written accent.

¿Dónde está la biblioteca?
Where is the library?

Esta es la biblioteca donde estudio todos los días.
This is the library where I study every day.

LENGUA

To request repetition or clarification of a statement, use **¿Cómo?** or **¿Perdón?** The use of **¿Qué?,** the equivalent of English *What?,* is generally considered rude by native speakers.

¿COMPRENDES?

Complete the following questions with the appropriate interrogative word.

1. ¿ __Cómo__ te llamas?
2. ¿ __Cuál__ es tu clase favorita?
3. ¿ __Cuándo__ es la clase, por la mañana o por la tarde?
4. ¿ __Cuántas__ personas viven en la residencia?
5. ¿ __Qué__ estudias en esta (*this*) universidad?

MySpanishLab
Learn more using Amplifire Dynamic Study Modules, Grammar Tutorials, and Extra Practice activities.

PRÁCTICA

Follow-up for 1-32
Have students create more questions using the interrogative words in the directions.

1-32 

Preguntas. First look at the cues after each question and then complete each question with **quién, cuándo, cuántos/as, cuál,** or **por qué** as logical. Use your questions to interview two people as you walk around the room.

1. ¿ __Cuántas/Qué__ clases tomas? Tomo...
2. ¿ __Cuándo__ son tus clases? Por la...
3. ¿ __Cuál__ es tu clase favorita? La clase de...
4. ¿ __Quién__ es tu profesor/a favorito/a? El profesor/La profesora...
5. ¿ __Por qué__ estudias español? Porque...
6. ¿ __Cuántos__ estudiantes hay en tu clase de español? Hay...

1-33 

Entrevista. Take turns asking each other questions to find out the following information. Use appropriate phrases to express disbelief, interest, etc.

 razón para estudiar español

¿Por qué estudias español?

1. número de clases que toma este semestre
2. tu clase favorita y razón (por qué)
3. número de alumnos en la clase favorita
4. nombre del profesor favorito/de la profesora favorita
5. lugar donde estudia generalmente y cuántas horas estudia por (*per*) día
6. lugar donde trabaja

Suggestion for 1-33
Students can interview each other in pairs, and then report to other students in groups of four. Encourage them to be creative and ask additional questions.

Situación

PREPARACIÓN. Read the following situation with your partner. Then prepare examples of the vocabulary, structures, and other information you will need for your role in the conversation.

Role A. It is the beginning of the term, and you need to add a history class. One of your friends is in a class that looks promising. Ask:

a. who the professor is;
b. where the class is;
c. if there is a lot of homework;
d. when the class meets; and
e. how many exams the class has.

Role B. Your friend wants some information about your history class. Reply as specifically as possible to all of his/her questions. Then offer some additional information about the class.

	ROLE A	ROLE B
Vocabulario	Expressions related to school and people at school Question words	Expressions related to school and people at school
Funciones y formas	Asking questions with appropriate interrogative words Thanking someone for information provided	Answering questions with appropriate information Reacting to what you hear

INTERCAMBIOS. Using the information in *Preparación,* act out the conversation with your partner.

Suggestion for *Situación*
You may wish to have students review the phrases in the *En directo* boxes in this chapter to increase the amount of language they produce and to make their exchanges sound more natural.

Note for *En acción*
This original storyline video will introduce students to five young filmmakers from different Spanish-speaking countries. While attending a summer program at the Los Angeles Film Institute, these aspiring artists will learn a great deal not only about documenting Hispanic cultures, but about themselves as well.

Suggestions for *En acción*
Throughout the video, the filmmakers compete for a prestigious scholarship to be awarded to the student who produces the best documentary during the summer course. Write the word *beca* on the board. In groups, have students create a semantic map by associating as many related words as they can. You might want to start them out with a few associations, such as *educación, dinero, estudiar, universidad*, etc. Then, have groups collaborate in creating a master map on the board by sharing their ideas.

Depending on available class time, you may wish to have students watch the video and complete some, or all of the related activities outside of class.

EN ACCIÓN

Saludos

1-34 Antes de ver

Los buenos estudiantes. In this video segment, you will be introduced to five college students. Mark (✓) the activities that you associate with a responsible college student.

1. _✓_ Asiste a clase todos los días.
2. ____ Llega tarde a sus clases.
3. _✓_ Habla con sus profesores.
4. ____ Usa su teléfono en clase.
5. _✓_ Levanta la mano y participa.
6. _✓_ Saca buenas notas.
7. ____ Escucha música en clase.
8. _✓_ Estudia para los exámenes.

1-35 Mientras ves 

Un curso de verano. As you watch the video, indicate whether the following statements refer to Esteban (**E**), Yolanda (**Y**), Federico (**F**), or Vanesa (**V**).

1. _E_ Es de Costa Rica.
2. _F_ Es de Buenos Aires.
3. _Y_ Es de México.
4. _V_ Es de España.
5. _E_ Estudia arte.
6. _V_ Baila y escucha música.
7. _E_ Hace *surf*.

1-36 Después de ver 

¿De qué hablan? **PREPARACIÓN.** Mark (✓) the topics that the students discuss in this video segment.

1. _✓_ la competición por la beca (*scholarship*)
2. _✓_ los países (*countries*) de origen
3. _✓_ el profesor de cine
4. _✓_ los estudios
5. ____ las familias
6. _✓_ las universidades

INTERCAMBIOS. Take turns describing the two university campuses shown in the video, la UNAM and la Universidad VERITAS. In what ways are they similar or different from your campus?

Mosaicos

ESCUCHA

1-37 Presentational

Preparación. You will hear two college students talking about their classes. Before you listen, think about the topics they may talk about and make a list of the things you may expect to hear, based on your experience as a student. Present your ideas to the class.

ESTRATEGIA

Listen for the gist

You can get the gist of what others are saying by relying on what you do understand, your knowledge of the topic, and your expectations of what happens in different types of conversations. You will find these techniques helpful when listening to Spanish.

1-38   Interpretive

Escucha. Listen to the conversation between Ana and Mario and indicate whether each statement is true (**Cierto**) or false (**Falso**).

1. Cierto Mario y Ana estudian en la misma (*same*) universidad este semestre.
2. Cierto Mario toma clases de ciencias y humanidades.
3. Cierto Ana lee en la biblioteca para sus clases.
4. Falso Mario realmente visita otros países en una de sus clases.
5. Cierto Ana toma clases por la tarde.

Comprueba

I was able to …

____ **recognize the names of academic subjects.**

____ **recognize places at the university.**

____ **identify actions that refer to students' routines.**

1-39  Interpersonal / Presentational

Un paso más. Ask your classmate what he/she usually does on the following days and times. Then switch roles. Talk to the class about the activities that you and your classmate do during the week. Explain if you do activities at similar or different times.

LUNES	MARTES	MIÉRCOLES	JUEVES	VIERNES
8:00 DE LA MAÑANA	3:00 DE LA TARDE	5:00 DE LA TARDE	9:00 DE LA TARDE	1:00 DE LA TARDE

E1: *¿Qué clases tienes los lunes a las 8:00?*

E2: *Los lunes a las 8:00 estudio en la biblioteca.*

Note for *Mosaicos*
The design of the activities in this section follows some of the principles that inform the Integrated Performance Assessment model (IPA): a) students "do something with the language" (complete a task); b) tasks assess knowledge and skills within realistic contexts; and c) tasks reflect a sequence that integrates the three modes of communication: interpretive, interpersonal, and presentational. When completing these tasks, students monitor their progress through a simplified standards box that will focus on some aspects of a given task.

Audioscript for *Escucha*
ANA: *Hola Mario, ¿qué tal? ¿Cómo estás?*
MARIO: *Muy bien, ¿y tú?*
ANA: *Bien, gracias. ¿Estudias aquí este año?*
MARIO: *Sí, solo este semestre.*
ANA: *¿Y qué clases tomas?*
MARIO: *Matemáticas, inglés, historia y geografía. ¿Y tú?*
ANA: *Yo tomo cinco clases: física, química, matemáticas, biología…*
MARIO: *¿Todas de ciencias? ¿No tomas clases de humanidades?*
ANA: *¡Oh, sí! También estudio literatura. Es una clase muy interesante, pero necesitamos leer mucho. Pasamos horas y horas en la biblioteca.*
MARIO: *¿Y quién es tu profesor?*
ANA: *Es una profesora que se llama Catalina Gómez. Es excelente. Pero mi clase favorita es la de biología. Trabajamos mucho en el laboratorio. ¿Y cuál es tu clase favorita, Mario?*
MARIO: *Pues, la clase de geografía.*
ANA: *¿Geografía?*
MARIO: *Sí, es excelente. Es una clase con computadoras. Visitamos un país diferente en cada clase: España, México, Colombia, Chile, Perú… Es una clase muy popular entre los estudiantes.*
ANA: *¡Qué interesante! ¡Uy! Son las tres menos diez. Mi clase de física es a las tres. Hablamos otro día.*

Suggestion for 1-39, *Preparación*
Give students a couple of minutes to write down their questions. Then, put them in pairs to take turns asking and answering.

Note for *Preparación*
This activity helps students focus on both the rhetorical aspects of their text (i.e., gathering and organizing ideas), as well as on form, accurate use of vocabulary, language structures (tense, agreement), and mechanics of writing in Spanish.

Suggestions for *Habla*
As a warm up activity, give students some relevant information. *Este es un anuncio de una librería de Málaga. Málaga está al sur de España, en la región de Andalucía.* (Point to *Málaga* on a map of Spain.) *En la Universidad de Málaga, hay un programa muy importante para estudiantes extranjeros: alemanes, ingleses, franceses,* estadounidenses, etc. *Muchos estudiantes de este programa compran los materiales para sus clases en la Librería Cervantes.* Point out differences between addresses written in Spanish and in English: placement of the number after the street name (introduced in *Capítulo preliminar*), and placement of the zip code (*código o zona postal*). Clarify words in the ad, as necessary. Have students perform the conversation at least twice so they can switch roles.

Note for *En directo*
Before doing activity 1-41, first have students read the expressions in *En directo.* Then have them listen to the dialogue and encourage them to use the expressions in their own conversation.

Audioscript for *En directo*
SEÑOR SANZ: *¿Diga?*
LUCIANO: *Buenos días. ¿Es la librería Luna? Necesito comprar un diccionario para…*
SEÑOR SANZ: *Lo siento. Aquí no es.*
LUCIANO: *Ay, perdón.*

HABLA

1-40 Interpretive

Answers for *Preparación* Some questions may vary.
1. ¿Cuál es la dirección de la librería?/¿Dónde está la librería?
2. ¿Tiene libros de historia de España en español?
3. ¿Tiene diccionarios en español?
4. ¿Cuánto cuesta el diccionario bilingüe?

Preparación. Write the questions answered by the clerk at your campus bookstore.

1. ____________ La dirección de la librería es Calle Mayor, número 50.
2. ____________ Sí, tengo libros de historia de España en español.
3. ____________ Sí, tengo diccionarios en español.
4. ____________ El diccionario bilingüe cuesta 40 euros.

ESTRATEGIA

Ask questions to gather information

Asking questions is a good way to start a conversation, but also to get the information you need. To ask questions, you need to remember question words and common phrases, like **¿Cómo es/son…? ¿Cuánto cuesta…? ¿Dónde…? ¿Qué…?** and **¿Quién…?**

1-41  Interpersonal

Habla. Read the ad and make a list of five items you need for your classes that you may be able to buy in this bookstore. Then take turns playing the following roles with your partner.

Role A. Call the bookstore and ask if they have those items, and how much they cost.

Role B. You are the bookstore clerk. Answer your client's questions. Ask for details.

En directo

To answer the phone in Spain:
¿Diga?/¿Sí?

To greet someone formally:
Buenos días./Buenas tardes.

To ask if he/she has what you need:
Necesito/Busco un/una…/ ¿Tiene(n)…?

 Listen to a conversation with these expressions.

LIBRERÍA CERVANTES

Papelería • Fotocopias • Accesorios de informática

Libros de texto • Revistas

Casa especializada en cartuchos y toners

Plaza Constitución, 3
29005 Málaga
Teléfono 221 19 99

Comprueba
In my conversation …

- ____ **I used question words appropriately.**
- ____ **I gave relevant information when answering.**
- ____ **I incorporated chapter vocabulary.**
- ____ **I used verbs accurately.**

1-42 Presentational

Un paso más. Write an e-mail to your best friend explaining the things that you need to buy for your classes, where to find them, and how much they cost.

 Interpersonal

Preparación. Discuss with a classmate which courses from the list students in the following majors (**carreras**) should take.

MEDICINA	BELLAS ARTES	FARMACIA	PSICOLOGÍA	FILOLOGÍA
Fisiología, Anatomía	Diseño gráfico, Muralistas mexicanos	Drogas tóxicas, Medicinas alternativas	Conflictos sociales	Estructura del español, Historia de la lengua

Anatomía
Conflictos sociales
Diseño gráfico
Drogas tóxicas
Estructura del español
Fisiología
Historia de la lengua
Medicinas alternativas
Muralistas mexicanos

ESTRATEGIA

Identify the format of a text

You have lots of reading experience in your first language with different types of texts. Before you start to read a text in Spanish, look at the illustrations, headings, and layout to help you make educated guesses about the content of the text.

 Interpretive

Lee. Choose the word or phrase that best completes each statement, based on the information of the text below.

1. Esta es una...
   a. página de un libro.
   (b.) página web.
2. El logo indica que esta institución es...
   a. muy nueva.   **(b.)** muy antigua.
3. Este texto presenta una lista de...
   (a.) carreras.   **b.** clases.
4. La información de este texto es...
   a. muy específica.
   (b.) muy general.
5. Esta institución tiene...
   a. una facultad.
   (b.) más de una facultad.

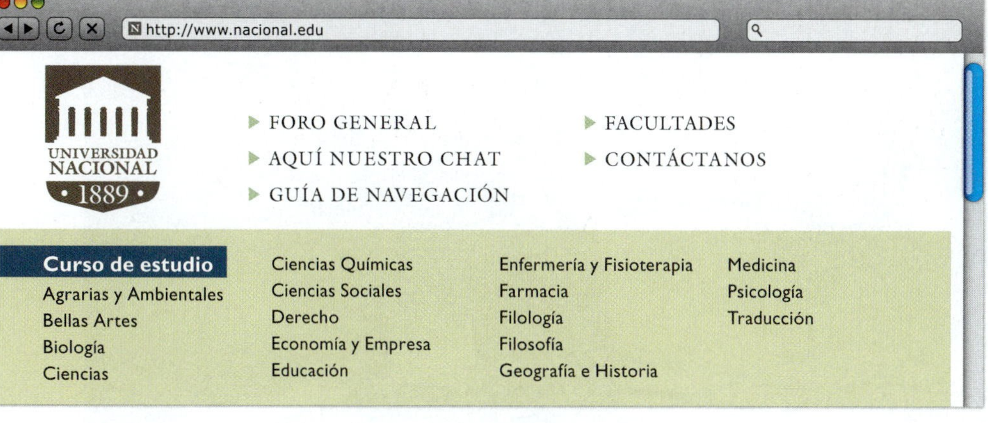

Comprueba
I was able to ...

____ **make informed guesses.**
____ **recognize important words.**
____ **recognize contexts.**

1-45  Presentational

Un paso más. Use the Internet to access the Universidad de Salamanca website and explore the **Servicio Central de Idiomas** page. Explain to your classmates: a) what languages you can study in Salamanca; b) what the address of this office is; and c) why you would or wouldn't like to study at this university in Spain. Your classmates should ask you questions.

Suggestion for 1-43
Show students how to rely on the words they understand to complete the table. If they do not understand *Filología*, they can figure out by elimination which courses are associated with this major; or, if they do not know *diseño*, for example, the cognate *gráfico* will help them place the course correctly.

Suggestions for *Estrategia*
Suggest students set a time limit (5–10 minutes) to relax and let their minds explore the ideas they associate with the topic. Remind students to keep their reader in mind and the questions the reader may have as they read the text.

Suggestions for 1-44
Since this is a reading activity, students should read their responses directly from the text; do not expect them to respond in their own words, unless they volunteer to do so. Direct students to read every text at least twice. Repeated readings with a focus on meaning can help them understand without word-for-word translation.

Note for 1-45, *Un paso más*
These activities may ask students to use the strategies they have practiced by focusing on a part of the text or by reading a different text of the same type (i.e., learning-to-read activities); or they may ask students to do something with the information they have learned from the text (i.e., reading-to-learn activities). The *Un paso más* activity in this chapter belongs to the learning-to-read category. Encourage students to guess the meanings of language names that are near cognates, such as *inglés, francés, italiano*. For language names they cannot guess (*alemán, neerlandés*), or that may be unfamiliar to them (*gallego, euskera*), they should use their dictionaries.

Suggestions for 1-46
You may wish to have students do *Preparación* in pairs. You may also want to model the brainstorming process. Keep input (teacher-talk) as natural and spontaneous as possible so students become comfortable with discussing the writing process. Accept any complete or partial response. Keep in mind that this is probably the students' first formal experience writing in Spanish. Elicit information from them rather than give it yourself. If you decide to have students do the task in pairs, have them approach it as if they were one writer, using the first-person singular.

Suggestion for 1-48, *Un paso más*
Have students check the following after they've written their e-mail:
1. They have provided the information their Spanish friend may need or any other they deem necessary.
2. They have checked any errors in language use, spelling, punctuation, accentuation, and so on.
3. They have used the *nosotros* form when talking about activities they share.

ESCRIBE

1-46 Interpersonal

Preparación. For your Spanish class, you have to respond to an e-mail from a university student in Spain. Read the e-mail and write four questions to ask the student about his college life in Spain.

Hola, me llamo Pedro. Estudio historia en la universidad. Tengo cuatro clases. Por las tardes practico deportes en el gimnasio.

¡Hasta pronto!
Pedro

ESTRATEGIA

Brainstorm key ideas before writing

Brainstorming helps you come up with good ideas for your writing. To brainstorm, write down a topic or a concept that you want to write about. Then list words and phrases that come to mind. Once you see your ideas laid out on paper, you can start to organize them for your writing.

1-47 Presentational

Escribe. Now write the Spanish student an e-mail about life at your college or university. Do the following:

- Introduce yourself.
- Describe your school and your classes.
- Describe your daily routine at school, what you do after classes and on weekends, etc.
- Ask some questions about college life in Spain.

Comprueba
I was able to …

_____ **present main ideas clearly with adequate details.**
_____ **use a wide range of vocabulary words.**
_____ **use correct gender and number agreement with nouns and adjectives.**
_____ **conjugate verbs correctly and make them agree with their subjects.**
_____ **use accurate spelling, capitalization, and punctuation.**

1-48  Interpretive

Un paso más. Exchange your e-mail with a classmate. Then respond with a brief note and ask two additional related questions.

En este capítulo…

Comprueba lo que sabes

Go to ***MySpanishLab*** to review what you have learned in this chapter. Practice with the following:

Vocabulario

LAS MATERIAS O ASIGNATURAS
Subjects

la antropología *anthropology*
la arquitectura *architecture*
las ciencias políticas *political science*
la economía *economics*
el español *Spanish*
la estadística *statistics*
la geografía *geography*
la historia *history*
la informática/la computación *computer science*
la literatura *literature*
la psicología *psychology*
la sociología *sociology*

LOS LUGARES
Places

la biblioteca *library*
el café *cafe, coffee shop*
la cafetería *cafeteria*
la casa *house, home*
la discoteca *dance club*
el gimnasio *gymnasium*
el laboratorio *laboratory*
la librería *bookstore*
la oficina *office*
la playa *beach*
la plaza *plaza, square*
la universidad *university*

LAS FACULTADES
Schools, Departments

de Ciencias *of Sciences*
de Derecho *of Law*
de Humanidades *of Humanities*
de Informática *of Computer Science*
de Medicina *of Medicine*

LAS PERSONAS
People

el alumno/la alumna *student*
el compañero/la compañera *partner, classmate*
el dependiente/la dependienta *salesperson*
ellos/ellas *they*
nosotros/nosotras *we*
ustedes *you* (plural)
vosotros/as *you* (plural)

PALABRAS Y EXPRESIONES ÚTILES
Useful words and expressions

ahora *now*
algo *something*
¡Buena suerte! *Good luck!*
¿Cómo te va? *How is it going?*
con *with*
¿Cuántas clases tienes? *How many classes do you have?*
¿Cuánto cuesta? *How much is it?*
el diccionario *dictionary*
este/a *this*
el examen *test*
el euro *euro*
el fin de semana *weekend*
el mapa *map*
para *for, to*
pero *but*
porque *because*
¡Qué lástima! *What a pity!*
solo *only*
también *also*
la tarea *homework*
tengo/tienes *I have/you have*
¿verdad? *right?*

LAS DESCRIPCIONES
Descriptions

aburrido/a *boring*
antiguo/a *old*
bueno/a *good*
difícil *difficult*
estudioso/a *studious*
excelente *excellent*
fácil *easy*
favorito/a *favorite*
grande *big*
interesante *interesting*
malo/a *bad*
norteamericano/a *North American*
pequeño/a *small*

PALABRAS INTERROGATIVAS
Interrogative words

¿cómo? *how?/what?*
¿cuándo? *when?*
¿cuál(es)? *which?*
¿cuánto/a? *how much?*
¿cuántos/as? *how many?*
¿dónde? *where?*
¿para qué? *why?/what for?*
¿por qué? *why?*
¿qué? *what?*
¿quién(es)? *who?*

EXPRESIONES DE FRECUENCIA
Expressions of frequency

a veces *sometimes*
muchas veces *many times*
nunca *never*
siempre *always*
todas las semanas *every week*
todos los días/meses *every day/month*

VERBOS
Verbs

aprender *to learn*
asistir *to attend*
bailar *to dance*
beber *to drink*
buscar *to look for*
caminar *to walk*
comer *to eat*
comprar *to buy*
comprender *to understand*
conversar *to talk, to converse*
correr *to run*
deber *should*
escribir *to write*
escuchar *to listen (to)*
estar *to be*
estudiar *to study*
hablar *to speak*
leer *to read*
llegar *to arrive*
mirar *to look (at)*
montar (en bicicleta) *to ride (a bicycle)*
necesitar *to need*
participar *to participate*
practicar *to practice*
responder *to respond*
sacar buenas/malas notas *to get good/bad grades*
tomar *to take, to drink*
tomar apuntes/notas *to take notes*
trabajar *to work*
ver *to see*
vivir *to live*

Note for *Vocabulario*
End of chapter vocabulary lists are designed for students to know which words are considered active for each chapter.

Introduction to chapter
Introduce the chapter theme about how we identify and talk about ourselves and others.

Ask questions to recycle content from the previous chapter. Help students access meaning by making frequent use of gestures or visuals. *¿Cómo eres? ¿Eres independiente? ¿Eres optimista? ¿Eres paciente o impulsivo? ¿Estudias mucho? ¿Eres muy estudioso o solo un poco? ¿Cómo son tus amigos? ¿Son generosos? ¿Son atléticos? ¿Son inteligentes? ¿Sacan buenas notas? ¿Hablan español tus amigos? ¿Viven todos en Estados Unidos? ¿Dónde están tus amigos ahora?*

Integrated Performance Assessment: Three Modes of Communication

Presentational: See activities 2-7, 2-8, 2-12, 2-23, 2-27, 2-30, 2-34, 2-39, 2-42, and 2-45.

Interpretive: See activities 2-5, 2-6, 2-9, 2-10, 2-13, 2-14, 2-16, 2-17, 2-21, 2-22, 2-23, 2-29, 2-35, 2-37, 2-41, and 2-43.

Interpersonal: See activities 2-3, 2-4, 2-5, 2-6, 2-7, 2-8, 2-12, 2-13, 2-14, 2-15, 2-16, 2-17, 2-18, 2-19, 2-20, 2-21, 2-22, 2-23, 2-24, 2-25, 2-26, 2-27, 2-29, 2-30, 2-36, 2-38, 2-40, 2-46 and all *Situación* activities.

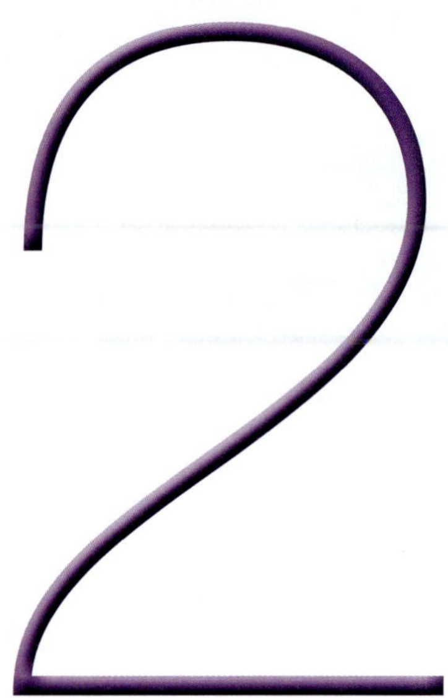

¿Quiénes son tus amigos?

ENFOQUE CULTURAL
Estados Unidos

VOCABULARIO EN CONTEXTO
Mis amigos y yo
Las descripciones
El origen

MOSAICO CULTURAL
Los estereotipos y la cultura hispana

FUNCIONES Y FORMAS
Adjectives
Present tense of *ser*
Ser and *estar* with adjectives
Possessive adjectives
Gustar

EN ACCIÓN
Entre amigos en Los Ángeles

MOSAICOS
ESCUCHA Listen for specific information
HABLA Describe a person
LEE Scan a text for specific information
ESCRIBE Use adjectives to enrich your descriptions

EN ESTE CAPÍTULO...
Comprueba lo que sabes
Vocabulario

LEARNING OUTCOMES

You will be able to:

- describe people, places, and things
- express origin and possession
- talk about where and when events take place
- describe what someone or something is like
- express emotions and conditions
- identify what belongs to you and others
- discuss the people, things, and activities you and others like and dislike
- present information about Hispanic influences in the United States

ENFOQUE *cultural* ESTADOS UNIDOS

CANADÁ
OCÉANO PACÍFICO
OCÉANO ATLÁNTICO
ESTADOS UNIDOS
MÉXICO
Golfo de México
San Francisco
Los Angeles
Phoenix
Tucson
Santa Fe
Houston
San Antonio
Chicago
Philadelphia
New York
Miami

Los actores hispanos Rico Rodriguez y Sofía Vergara

Un rapero latino, Daddy Yankee

Una margarita con guacamole y *chips*

Calle Ocho, in Miami

El Álamo, San Antonio, Texas

Enfoque cultural

To learn more about Hispanics in the United States, go to MySpanishLab to view the *Vistas culturales* videos.

¿QUÉ TE PARECE?

- El español es la segunda lengua del mundo y la más estudiada en las universidades de Estados Unidos.
- Muchos estudiantes estudian español para su futuro trabajo, para conversar con otras personas y para los viajes y vacaciones.
- En 1988 el presidente Reagan declaró el período entre el 15 de septiembre y el 15 de octubre el Mes de la Hispanidad, días dedicados a celebrar la herencia y cultura hispanas en Estados Unidos.
- Los hispanos en Estados Unidos son el grupo minoritario más grande del país. El 63% de la población hispana es de México.

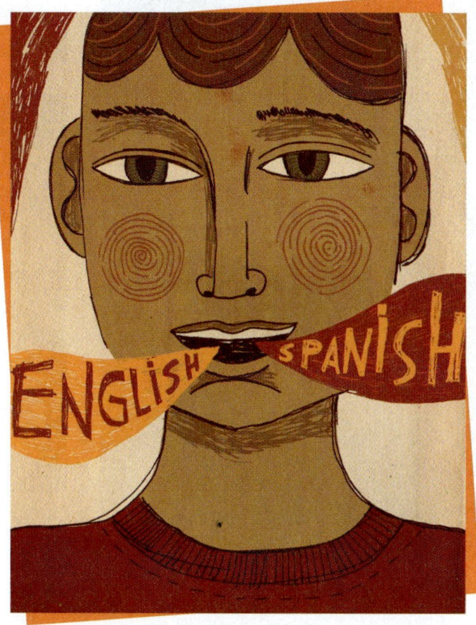

Este cuadro anónimo representa el mundo bilingüe en el que vive mucha gente en Estados Unidos.

Note for map
Place names for cities are in English since the United States is a majority English-speaking country. Point out that Hispanic cultural influence dates back to the 15th century and is evident in place names, historical monuments, foods, music, dance, literature, and architecture. Both English and Spanish have borrowed words from the other language.

Suggestion
Preview nationalities and recycle numbers by showing the following figures for the Hispanic population in the United States, according to origin: *mexicano: 63%; puertorriqueño: 9,2%; centroamericano: 7,9%; sudamericano: 5,5%; cubano: 3,5%; dominicano: 2,8%; español: 1,3%; otros hispanos: 6,8%*. Hispanics as a group make up 16.3% of the total U.S. population. (Source: U.S. Census, 2010)

Suggestion for map
Project the online image of the map, found in the Instructor's Resources folder, and point to the photos. Work on cognates as you make statements and ask questions. *En Estados Unidos hay muchos hispanos. ¿Qué hispanos famosos hay? ¿Quién es Sofía Vergara? ¿Ves su programa,* Modern Family, *en la televisión? El Álamo es un fuerte mexicano. ¿Dónde está El Álamo? ¿Conocen músicos hispanos? ¿Es buen músico Daddy Yankee? ¿Qué otros músicos hispanos hay en Estados Unidos?*

Suggestion for art
Have students look at the painting and explain what it makes them think of. Introduce the word *bilingüe* and ask them related questions: *¿Cuántas lenguas habla una persona bilingüe? ¿Eres bilingüe? ¿Hay bilingües en la clase? ¿Qué palabra usamos para nombrar a una persona que habla tres o más lenguas? ¿Conocen personas bilingües o trilingües?* Use this opportunity to advocate for the advantages of learning languages. *¿Por qué es bueno hablar varias lenguas?*

Note for *El barrio Pilsen*
The Pilsen neighborhood was first populated by Czech and Polish immigrants. The Hispanic presence began to establish itself in the 1950s, and by the 1970s it had grown to become the majority population in this vibrant area of Chicago.

Note for *San Agustín*
There is a fountain in St. Augustine that represents Ponce de León's search for the Fountain of Youth.

Note for *Narciso Rodríguez*
Designs by Narciso Rodríguez can be found in Neiman Marcus, Barneys and Kohl's. His perfume is sold in Sephora and Nordstrom.

Note for musicians
Hispanic musicians born in the United States often use Spanglish in the lyrics of their songs. This artistic practice follows in the footsteps of Chicana writers such as Sandra Cisneros who adopted Spanglish as their creative language.

ENFOQUE cultural

El barrio Pilsen de Chicago cuenta con numerosos murales inspirados en el movimiento muralista mexicano. Los murales coloridos de Francisco Mendoza representan escenas de la vida diaria de esta comunidad hispana.

Narciso Rodríguez es un diseñador cubanoamericano. Aquí está con la actriz Jessica Alba. Isabel Toledo es otra famosa diseñadora cubanoamericana. Michelle Obama es cliente de los dos.

Don Pedro Menéndez de Avilés es el fundador de San Agustín (St. Augustine), en el norte de Florida. Es la ciudad más antigua de Estados Unidos.

Pitbull (Armando Pérez) es cubanoamericano. En esta fotografía recibe el premio Lo Nuestro, presentado por Univisión, la cadena de televisón en español con más audiencia en todo el mundo.

¿CUÁNTO SABES?

Using the map, photos, and accompanying text, provide the following information.

1. Un cantante hispano famoso
   - **a.** Armando Pérez
   - **b.** don Pedro Menéndez de Avilés
   - **c.** Narciso Rodríguez
2. Se celebra las dos últimas semanas de septiembre y las dos primeras de octubre.
   - **a.** el Mes de la Hispanidad
   - **b.** los premios Lo Nuestro
   - **c.** fiesta en la Calle Ocho
3. Una ciudad de los tiempos coloniales
   - **a.** Pilsen
   - **b.** Miami
   - **c.** St. Augustine
4. Patrocinador de los premios Lo Nuestro
   - **a.** Francisco Mendoza
   - **b.** Univisión
   - **c.** el mundo bilingüe
5. El 63%
   - **a.** el porcentaje de estudiantes que estudian español
   - **b.** el porcentaje de personas bilingües en Estados Unidos
   - **c.** el porcentaje de hispanos de Estados Unidos de origen mexicano

Vocabulario en contexto

Describing yourself and others

MySpanishLab **Pronunciation Topic:** Linking (*enlace*)
Learn more using Amplifire Dynamic Study Modules, Pronunciation, and Vocabulary Tutorials.

Mis amigos y yo

¿Quiénes somos?

Me llamo Mario Quintana. Soy de Puerto Rico y **tengo** veintidós **años. Me gusta** escuchar música y mirar televisión. Estudio en una universidad de Nueva York y **deseo** ser profesor de historia. Los chicos en estas fotografías son mis amigos. Ellos también son **hispanos** y estudian en la universidad. **Todos** somos **bilingües.**

Esta chica es Amanda Martone. Es **alta, delgada** y **morena.** Tiene los **ojos** de color café y el **pelo negro** y muy **largo.** Amanda es una chica muy **agradable.** Estudia **mucho** y desea ser economista. Su familia es dominicana, pero vive en Estados Unidos.

Esta chica se llama Ana Villegas. No es alta ni baja. Es **de estatura mediana** y usa **lentes de contacto.** Es **pelirroja** y tiene los ojos **oscuros.** Ana es **callada, trabajadora** y muy inteligente. Sus padres son cubanos.

Esta chica es Marta Chávez Conde. Es española y tiene veintiún años. Es **rubia,** tiene los ojos **azules** y es muy **divertida.** Este año está en Estados Unidos con su familia.

Este chico se llama Ernesto Fernández. Ernesto es moreno y tiene los ojos **castaños** y el pelo **corto.** Es **bajo, fuerte,** muy **conversador** y **simpático. Le gusta usar** la computadora para conversar con sus amigos de aquí y de México.

Suggestions
Introduce the people in the photos, focusing on specific information in the descriptions that accompany each one. Point to Mario and describe his origin, age, and preferences. Then describe yourself, ask questions, and personalize: *Yo no soy de Puerto Rico, soy… No tengo ventidós años. ¿Cuántos años tengo?* You may introduce additional vocabulary when personalizing: *Mario es alto y moreno* (use gestures). Point to a student and say: *… es moreno también, pero…* (point to another) *… no es moreno. Es rubio.* To present *desear,* add: *Mario no desea ser piloto* (write *piloto* on the board and cross it out). *No desea ser dentista/policía* (do the same for *dentista* and *policía*). Then ask simple questions about students' goals: *¿Deseas tú ser piloto? ¿Profesor/a?* Point to Puerto Rico on a map: *Mario es de Puerto Rico. Y tú, ¿eres de Argentina? ¿Eres de Puerto Rico? No, eres de Estados Unidos* (or appropriate country). Give additional information about Mario to review material from *Capítulo 1: Mario es bilingüe. Habla español y también habla inglés. Él camina a la universidad todos los días. Está en la universidad desde las nueve de la mañana hasta las tres de la tarde. Los fines de semana practica fútbol con sus amigos.* Check comprehension. Do the same with the other photos. You may point out the *diéresis* in the word *bilingüe.*

Suggestion
Use posters or digital photos online to demonstrate age and *tener… años.* Ask *¿Cuántos años tiene?* using the pictures to elicit responses. Then ask students their age. You may also wish to preview the use of *gustar* with some examples: *Me gusta esta clase. ¿Te gusta el chico en esta foto?,* etc.

Suggestion
Use the ID card to explain the use of two last names in Spanish.

Audioscript for 2-1
1. *Mi amigo Pedro es muy conversador y muy divertido.*
2. *Elena es una chica rubia, tiene los ojos castaños y es muy alta.*
3. *Juan y Roberto son muy trabajadores y estudian mucho.*
4. *Patricia es hispana y es bilingüe.*
5. *Rosa María es muy agradable.*

Follow-up for 2-3
Have students name the person described by the following questions: *¿Quién tiene veintiún años? (Marta), ¿… es alta? (Amanda), ¿… es muy conversador? (Ernesto)*, etc.

Note for 2-3, *Intercambios*
You may do this activity in small groups (four students) or with the whole class. If students talk in English, guide them back to Spanish, providing vocabulary as needed.

Note for 2-4
The *gustar* construction is presented in *Funciones y formas* in this chapter and in *Capítulo 6*. Here students should use phrases with *gustar* as set expressions. Refer to page 245 for a preview.

Warm-up for 2-4
Say what you like/do not like to do: *(No) Me gusta caminar. Por las noches me gusta mirar televisión.* Ask students: *¿Te gusta estudiar español? ¿Te gusta estudiar en la biblioteca/caminar/mirar televisión por las noches/bailar en las discotecas?* Have students take turns asking and answering.

Suggestion for 2-4
Ask students to describe the type of people their classmates are according to their answers.

PRÁCTICA

2-1  

Escucha y confirma. Listen to the following people describe their friends. Then, decide whether the statements are true (**Cierto**) or false (**Falso**).

1. Falso Pedro es callado y estudia mucho.
2. Cierto Elena es rubia y alta.
3. Cierto Juan y Roberto son muy trabajadores.
4. Cierto Patricia es hispana y bilingüe.
5. Falso Rosa María es muy divertida.

2-2 

Asociaciones. Match the descriptions on the left with the person they describe.

1. b Tiene el pelo largo.
2. a Tiene veintidós años.
3. e Es de España.
4. c Es bajo y fuerte.
5. d Usa lentes de contacto.
6. c Habla mucho.
7. b Tiene los ojos de color café.
8. b Tiene el pelo negro y es muy agradable.
9. e Tiene los ojos azules y el pelo rubio. Es muy divertida.
10. a Desea ser profesor de historia.

a. Mario Quintana
b. Amanda Martone
c. Ernesto Fernández
d. Ana Villegas
e. Marta Chávez Conde

2-3 

¿Quién es? **PREPARACIÓN.** With a partner, write a list of eight expressions to describe people, including physical appearance (height, hair, eye color, etc.) and personality traits (shy, fun, etc.).

INTERCAMBIOS. Without mentioning his/her name, describe a classmate. The rest of the group will try to guess who this person is.

E1: *Es delgado y de estatura mediana. Tiene el pelo negro. Es fuerte y callado.*
E2: *¿Es…?*

LENGUA

Depending on the region or country, people use **moreno/a** or **negro/a** to refer to African ancestry and skin color or to hair color. The word **trigueño/a** (from **trigo,** wheat) is used to describe light brown skin color. **Corto/a** generally refers to length (**pelo corto**), while **bajo/a** refers to height (**Ella es baja**).

2-4  

¿Qué me gusta? Tell your classmate if you like each of the following activities. Then compare your responses.

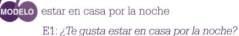

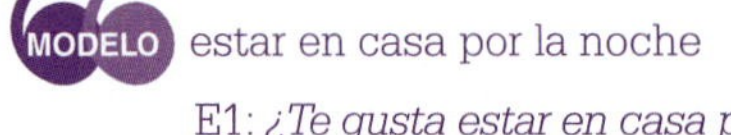

estar en casa por la noche
E1: *¿Te gusta estar en casa por la noche?*
E2: *Sí, me gusta.*

- bailar los sábados por la noche
- comer en restaurantes italianos
- escribir mensajes de texto
- estudiar español
- practicar tenis/fútbol/béisbol
- tener animales en casa
- tomar café por la noche
- trabajar los fines de semana

2-5 

Mi ídolo. Select a well-known person or celebrity and describe him/her to your partner. Your partner will ask questions until he/she guesses the name.

Las descripciones

 **¿Cómo son estas personas?**

triste **alegre**

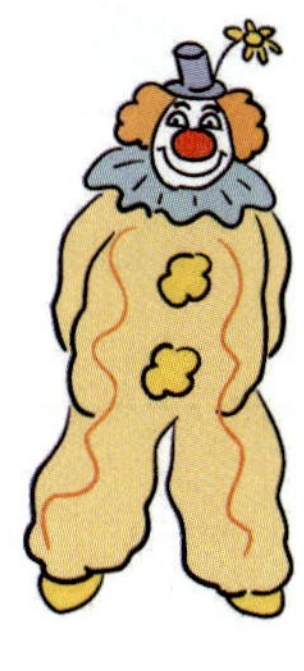

simpático

antipático

trabajador **perezoso**

pobre **rica**

fuerte **débil**

lista **tonto**

joven **vieja/mayor**

casado **soltero**

LENGUA

The word **la pierna** (*leg*) is used with humans. A human foot is **el pie**. For animals and furniture, **la pata** is used to express both leg and foot.

 **¿Cómo son estos animales?**

Este perro es **gordo** y **feo**, pero muy cariñoso.

Esta gata es **bonita** pero está demasiado **delgada**.

Este perro es gordo y feo, pero muy cariñoso. Esta gata es bonita pero está demasiado delgada.

Warm-up
Describe yourself and/or students using adjectives and expressions introduced in this and the previous section, or describe people in photos that you and/or students bring in. For words such as *alto/bajo, rubio/moreno,* and *tengo* or *tiene el pelo negro/castaño/corto/largo,* point to students who fit those descriptions. To check comprehension of new vocabulary, describe students correctly or incorrectly, and ask the class to indicate the accuracy of your description with *sí* or *no*. To recycle *¿quién?* ask questions using adjectives: *¿Quién es alto y moreno? ¿Quién tiene el pelo castaño?* Students can answer using names of classmates. Recycle numbers: *¿Cuántos son altos?, ¿morenos?,* etc.

Suggestion
Describe famous people using adjectives from this chapter. Ask students to do the same.

Alternate
Ask students to describe themselves using the adjectives in this section.

Expansion
Tape the name and photo of a famous person to the back of each student. Students move around the room asking yes/no questions about their new identity to help them discover who they are. You may demonstrate by having them choose a name for you and answering your yes/no questions.

Alternate
Have students complete the following sentences with an adjective: *Me gusta trabajar. Soy…; Berta tiene quince años. Es muy…; Manuela y Marcos siempre están en el laboratorio. Son muy…*

Note
Explain that some Spanish speakers consider *viejo/a* impolite when describing people and prefer to use *mayor.*

Suggestion
Use the drawings to introduce some body parts. Then point to your body or use photos to show: *la cabeza, las piernas,*

las manos, los pies. Other parts of the body appear in *Capítulo 11.*

Suggestion
Have students work in groups to describe themselves by giving physical characteristics or other traits.

Suggestion
Show pictures of flowers and describe them to introduce colors. Also use brochures/ads for cars. Ask students about their preferences. Encourage them to describe the cars, giving colors and features. You may also introduce words such as *suéter, blusa, camisa,* and ask: *¿De qué color es el suéter de...? ¿Y la blusa de...?*

 **¿De qué color son estas cosas?**

Este auto es **rojo** y es muy bueno.

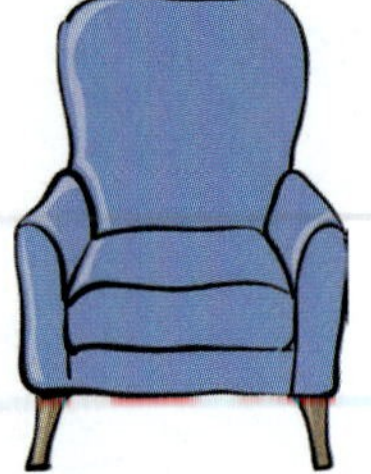

Esta **flor** es **amarilla** y **blanca.** Es muy bonita.

La silla **azul** es alta.

La silla **verde** es baja.

 **Otros colores**

marrón | gris | rosado | morado | anaranjado | negro

EN OTRAS PALABRAS

Depending on the country and what is described, Spanish has various words to express the color brown: **café, marrón, carmelita, castaño/a,** and **pardo/a.** The words **naranja** and **rosa** are also used instead of **anaranjado/a** and **rosado/a.**

PRÁCTICA

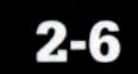 **2-6** 

Para confirmar. Complete the following statements about these famous people. Then describe yourself to your partner in two affirmative and two negative statements.

 Shakira no es mayor, es *joven.*

1. __c__ Penélope Cruz no es gorda, es...
2. __a__ Sofía Vergara no es perezosa, es...
3. __f__ Jennifer López no es antipática, es...
4. __b__ Madonna no es tonta, es...
5. __d__ Bill Gates no es pobre, es...
6. __e__ Enrique Iglesias no es feo, es...
7. _____ Yo soy..., no soy...

a. trabajadora
b. lista
c. delgada
d. rico
e. guapo
f. simpática

EN OTRAS PALABRAS

Depending on the region, Spanish speakers may use **bonita, linda,** or **guapa** to refer to a female. **Bien parecido, buen mozo,** and **guapo** usually refer to a male.

2-7  

¿De qué color son estas banderas (*flags*)?

PREPARACIÓN. Read each description and then write the name of the country under its flag. Check your answers with a partner.

a. Colombia

b. España

c. México

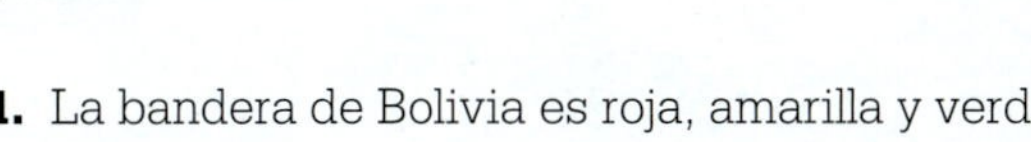

d. Estados Unidos

e. Bolivia

1. La bandera de Bolivia es roja, amarilla y verde.
2. La bandera de Estados Unidos es roja, blanca y azul.
3. La bandera de España es roja y amarilla.
4. La bandera de México es verde, blanca y roja.
5. La bandera de Colombia es amarilla, azul y roja.

INTERCAMBIOS. Invent a flag of different colors and describe it to your partner. He/She will recreate it based on your description. Limit your colors to the pens, pencils, markers, etc. that you and your partner have available. He/She will recreate it based on your description. Write the name of the colors on the flag if necessary.

Suggestions for 2-7, *Intercambios*
For a group activity, mix and distribute the flags randomly for students to describe them. Then, display all flags and have students decide which is the best and why. For classrooms with smartboards, have student pairs create a flag and then direct a classmate to recreate it on the board. You can also substitute *Mi mochila ideal,* for flags.

2-8 

Vamos a describir. Take turns describing the people in these photos. Then describe your best friend to your partner.

Eva

Alicia y Raquel

Alejandro

José Luis

Suggestion for 2-8
You may wish to introduce the words *mujer/hombre.* Brainstorm with students to get them started by asking questions based on the photos: *¿Cómo es esta mujer? ¿Es joven o mayor? ¿Este hombre es simpático o antipático?* Encourage students to recycle vocabulary by imagining personality traits for the people in the four photos.

2-9

¿Quién soy? Write a brief description of yourself including at least three physical traits, two personality traits, and two activities you like to do. Do not include your name on the paper.

Follow-up for 2-9
Collect the papers with students' descriptions. Ask each student to pick a description, read it, and try to guess who wrote it.

Suggestions
Refer students to the maps on the inside covers of their books or project the globe from the Interactive Globe folder online. Spin the globe using the cursor and zoom in/out to point out where Spanish is spoken. Recycle names of Spanish-speaking countries by pointing to them on the map. Name the capital or a well-known city and have students name the country.

Note
Point out that the most commonly used words for U.S. citizens are *norteamericano/a* and *americano/a,* although Canada and Mexico are also part of North America. *Estadounidense* is also used.

El origen

¿De dónde son...?

▲ Shakira y Gerard Piqué

Shakira es de Colombia, es **colombiana.** Su **esposo** Gerard Piqué no es colombiano, es **español.** Es futbolista en el equipo de Barcelona.

▲ Marc Anthony y Pitbull en los Latin Grammys

Marc Anthony y Pitbull (o Armando Pérez) son de Estados Unidos, pero la familia de Marc Anthony es **puertorriqueña** y la familia de Pitbull es **cubana.** Marc Anthony y Pitbull son bilingües; cantan en inglés y en español.

LENGUA

These are other examples of nationalities:

alemán/alemana (*German*), **canadiense, francés/francesa, japonés/japonesa, marroquí, nigeriano/a, polaco/a, portugués/portuguesa.**

PRÁCTICA

Para confirmar. **PREPARACIÓN.** Indicate the origin of the following people. Check your answers with a partner.

 Mónica Puig es una famosoa tenista de Puerto Rico.
Es *puertorriqueña*.

1. Hanley Ramírez es un jugador de béisbol de República Dominicana. Es ___dominicano___.
2. Sofía Vergara es una modelo y actriz de Colombia, protagonista de la serie *Modern Family*. Es ___colombiana___.
3. Rigoberta Menchú es una activista de Guatemala, Premio Nobel de la Paz, 1992. Es ___guatemalteca___.
4. El Dr. José Manuel Pérez, de Puerto Rico, investiga el uso de la nanotecnología para detectar el cólera. Es ___puertorriqueño___.
5. Isabel Allende es escritora, originaria de Chile, autora de *La casa de los espíritus*. Es ___chilena___.
6. Jorge Ramos es un presentador de noticias (*news*) de México. Es ___mexicano___.
7. Gabriel García Márquez es un escritor de Colombia, autor de *Cien años de soledad*, Premio Nobel, 1982. Es ___colombiano___.
8. Enrique Iglesias es un cantante de España. Es ___español___.

INTERCAMBIOS. Tell your partner why one of the people in *Preparación* is interesting to you.

 *Para mí, Enrique Iglesias es interesante. Es un cantante bilingüe.*

2-11

Adivinanzas (*Guesses*). Think of a well-known person. A classmate will try to guess the person by asking you questions.

 E1: *¿De dónde es?*

E2: *Es de Estados Unidos.*

E1: *¿Cómo es?*

E2: *Es moreno y muy cómico.*

E1: *¿Qué es? / ¿En qué trabaja?*

E2: *Es actor.*

E1: *¿Es Jack Black?*

E2: *¡Sí!*

En directo

To explain why a person might interest you:

Me gustan sus libros. *I like his/her books.*

Escribe novelas fascinantes. *He/She writes fascinating novels.*

Trabaja por los pobres. *He/She works for/helps the poor.*

Es muy guapo/bonita/elegante. *He is handsome./She is pretty/elegant.*

Baila muy bien. *He/She dances very well.*

 Listen to a conversation with these expressions.

Cultura

Puerto Rico

Puerto Rico was a Spanish colony for almost four centuries until it was ceded to the United States following the Spanish–American War in 1898. Puerto Rico is a commonwealth (**estado libre asociado**) of the United States, and its people have been U.S. citizens since 1917. However, Puerto Rico remains geographically and culturally part of Latin America and almost all of its residents speak Spanish as their primary language. English is also widely spoken. Being bilingual opens doors to better economic opportunities in Puerto Rico and on the mainland.

Comunidades. What other Hispanic groups have an important presence in the United States? Where is that presence evident—in business, music, art, food?

Suggestion for 2-10, *Preparación*
Practice nationalities, contrasting nationality with country: *Es chileno/a, es de Chile.* To practice what students have learned in the chapter you may ask questions such as: *¿Quién es Oprah Winfrey? ¿Cómo es? ¿De dónde es?* Let students know that they will learn more about some of these people in later chapters.

Note for *En directo*
Before doing activity 2-10, *Intercambios*, first have students read the expressions in *En directo*. Then have them listen to the dialogue and encourage them to use the expressions in their own conversation.

Audioscript for *En directo*
ANA: *Dime, Celia, ¿por qué te gusta Isabel Allende?*
CELIA: *Bueno, me gustan sus libros.*
ANA: *Es cierto. Escribe novelas fascinantes.*
CELIA: *Exactamente. Y, también es muy elegante.*

Note for 2-12
This activity guides students to use a maximum of the vocabulary and resources learned in this and the two previous chapters. Students can practice questions and develop interpersonal skills in *Preparación*. The information they gather will allow them to write a description in *Intercambios*, which they will then share. Encourage them to use as many details as possible in this description.

Alternate for 2-12
Have students interview a Hispanic person on campus or in the community. Alternatively, have them read online (in English or Spanish) about a prominent Hispanic figure in the United States and then answer the questions in the activity. Finally, have them report findings to the class. You may wish to provide a list of names to choose from. Have students write their questions individually before interviewing. To check for accuracy, have them read their questions aloud.

Warm-up for 2-13
As a pre-listening activity, divide the class in pairs or small groups and have them draw four columns: Hispanic names, nationalities, physical descriptions, areas of study. Ask them to write—in three minutes—as many words as possible that they can associate with each column. Or, you may provide words and have students sort them to the appropriate columns.

Audioscript for 2-13
¡Hola! Me llamo Miguel Jiménez. Soy argentino, de Buenos Aires, y tengo veintiséis años. Estudio medicina en la Universidad de Virginia. Estoy en el tercer año de la carrera. Soy alto, delgado y muy trabajador.

PRÁCTICA

2-12

Entrevista. **PREPARACIÓN.** Prepare at least five questions to interview a classmate and get the following information.

1. his/her name
2. his/her age
3. what he/she is like (his/her personality)
4. the things he/she likes to do
5. where he/she is from

 **INTERCAMBIOS.** Interview your classmate. Then share your findings with the class. Finally, write a short description of your classmate.

2-13

¡Hola! **PREPARACIÓN.** You will hear a student introduce and describe himself to his new classmates. Before you listen, mark (✓) in the *Antes de escuchar* column the information you think you will hear. Then tell your partner what other information you would give about yourself.

	ANTES DE ESCUCHAR	DESPUÉS DE ESCUCHAR
1. name		✓
2. age		✓
3. parents' names		
4. physical description		✓
5. nationality		✓
6. place where he intends to work		

 **ESCUCHA.** As you listen, pay attention to the general idea of what is said. Then, in the *Después de escuchar* column, indicate what information the speaker provided.

MOSAICO cultural

Los estereotipos y la cultura hispana

▲ ¿Comes hamburguesas todos los días?

¿Es verdad que los estadounidenses comen hamburguesas todos los días, que todos tienen armas y que no les gusta el ejercicio? Por otra parte, ¿es cierto que muchos españoles son toreros (*bullfighters*), que los mexicanos comen solo (*only*) tacos y enchiladas o que todos los argentinos solo bailan tango? La respuesta a las dos preguntas es, ¡de ninguna manera (*absolutely not*)!

Una sola característica no define una cultura completamente. Este tipo de comentarios causa conflictos en la comunicación entre culturas, especialmente en casos donde las personas viven en la misma (*same*) comunidad. Para comprender la diversidad cultural es necesario evitar (*avoid*) ideas clichés porque no representan la totalidad de una comunidad o cultura.

▲ ¿Eres torero?

El diálogo honesto entre las personas de diferentes culturas es una manera de terminar con los estereotipos. Recuerda (*Remember*) que existen muchos españoles que no asisten a las corridas de toros (*bullfights*), muchos argentinos que no bailan tango y muchos estadounidenses que no comen hamburguesas todos los días.

▲ ¿Bailas el tango?

Compara

1. ¿Cuáles son algunos adjetivos que en tu opinión describen a una persona típica de Estados Unidos? Prepara una lista en español.
2. De tu lista, ¿qué adjetivos sirven también para describir a un hispano típico?
3. ¿Son siempre negativos los estereotipos? Explica con ejemplos.

Note
Adjectives and adjective agreement have been previewed in the *Vocabulario en contexto* section of this chapter. Guide students to notice that adjective endings usually indicate gender and number and that masculine plural adjectives are used for mixed-gender groups.

Suggestions
Use visuals to practice noun–adjective agreement or personalize by describing students: *José es un chico alto y simpático.* Write *chico alto* on the board, underlining the *o*. Do the same with a feminine noun and adjective. Write the plural. Ask yes/no and either/or questions regarding students. Ask about courses with adjectives ending in *-e*, such as *interesante: ¿Es interesante la historia? Y el español, ¿es interesante? Y las ciencias, ¿son interesantes?* Have students work in pairs to find out courses or subject areas that their partners find *interesante(s)* or *aburrido/a(s)* and share opinions with the class. Practice adjectives that end in a consonant and adjectives of nationality: *Javier Bardem es español. Penélope Cruz es española. Ella es una actriz excelente. Javier Bardem y Penélope Cruz son muy famosos.* Students in groups may discuss their favorite programs, sports figures, actors, or singers in groups and compare findings.

Standard 4.1
Students demonstrate an understanding of the nature of language through comparisons of the language studied and their own.
Students encounter many opportunities to reflect on the different ways that languages accomplish the same function. The characteristics of adjectives in Spanish—different forms for masculine/feminine, singular/plural; placement before/after the noun—can serve as the starting point for reflection on the fact that languages express meanings in different ways.

Funciones y formas

1 Describing people, places, and things

Ana, Patricia y Teresa estudian mucho. Son inteligent**es** y trabajador**as.** Son de España.

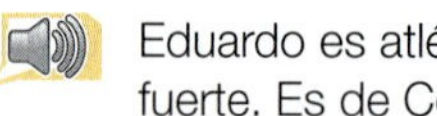
Eduardo es atlétic**o** y fuerte. Es de Colombia. Adriana es muy elegant**e.** Es perüan**a.**

Carlos, Luis y Carmen son sociabl**es** y activ**os.** Conversan y bailan mucho en las discotecas.

Piénsalo. Complete the descriptions of the people in the drawings by supplying their names.

1. Adriana es pelirroj**a** y joven.
2. Luis es rubi**o** y alt**o.**
3. Ana, Patricia y Teresa son estudios**as** y responsabl**es.**
4. Carlos, Luis, y Carmen son simpátic**os** y popular**es.**
5. Eduardo es colombian**o.**
6. Ana, Patricia, y Teresa son español**as.**

Adjectives

Adjectives are words that describe people, places, and things. Like articles (**el, la, los, las**) and nouns (**chica, chicas; libro, libros**), they generally have more than one form. In Spanish an adjective must agree in gender (masculine or feminine) and number (singular or plural) with the noun or pronoun it describes. Adjectives that describe characteristics usually follow the noun.

Most masculine adjectives end in **-o,** and most feminine adjectives end in **-a.** To form the plural, these adjectives add **-s.**

	MASCULINE	FEMININE
singular	el chic**o** alt**o**	la chic**a** alt**a**
plural	los chic**os** alt**os**	las chic**as** alt**as**

Adjectives that end in **-e** and some adjectives that end in a consonant have the same form for both masculine and feminine. To form the plural, adjectives that end in **-e** add **-s;** those that end in a consonant add **-es.**

	MASCULINE	FEMININE
singular	un libr**o** interesant**e**	una revist**a** interesant**e**
	un cuadern**o** azul	una mochil**a** azul
plural	unos libr**os** interesant**es**	unas revist**as** interesant**es**
	unos cuadern**os** azul**es**	unas mochil**as** azul**es**

Other adjectives that end in a consonant add **-a** to form the feminine and **-es** or **-as** to form the plurals.

	MASCULINE	FEMININE
singular	el alumn**o** españo**l**	la alumn**a** españo**la**
	el alumn**o** hablado**r**	la alumn**a** hablado**ra**
plural	los alumn**os** españo**les**	las alumn**as** españo**las**
	los alumn**os** hablado**res**	las alumn**as** hablado**ras**

Adjectives that end in **-ista** are both masculine and feminine. To form the plurals, add **-s.**

Pedro es muy optim**ista,** pero Alicia es pesim**ista.** — *Pedro is very optimistic, but Alicia is pessimistic.*

Ellos no son material**istas.** — *They are not materialistic.*

¿COMPRENDES?

Complete each sentence with the correct form of the adjective.

1. Los habitantes de Puerto Rico son puertorriqueños. (puertorriqueño)
2. Ariana vive en Madrid. Es española. (español)
3. Los alumnos estudian mucho. Son muy trabajadores. (trabajador)
4. El color favorito de Javier es el negro. Su mochila también es negra. (negro)
5. Mis clases de economía no son interesantes; son muy aburridas. (aburrido)
6. Me gusta mucho mi profesora de historia. Es muy inteligente. (inteligente)

MySpanishLab
Learn more using Amplifire Dynamic Study Modules, Grammar Tutorials, and Extra Practice activities.

Note
Point out that *bueno/a, malo/a, grande* may precede or follow the noun. Explain that *bueno* and *malo* are shortened before a masculine singular noun: *un buen gimnasio, un mal profesor.* Also mention that *grande* is shortened to *gran* before a masculine or feminine singular noun: *una gran casa.*

PRÁCTICA

Cultura

Hispanos

In Spanish-speaking countries, the adjective **hispano/a** emphasizes the common background among peoples, cultures, and countries where Spanish is spoken. In the United States, the word has come to mean somebody with roots in Spain or the Spanish-speaking countries of Latin America. In the Southwest, it refers to people who trace their ancestry to Spaniards who settled there when that area was part of Mexico. **Hispano** is not the same as **español,** which refers either to the Spanish language or to the nationality of people from Spain.

Conexiones. Can you name a famous Hispanic person? A famous Spaniard?

2-14  

¿Cómo son estas personas? Choose the correct option to describe the following people. Check your answers with a partner and then share your own opinion about a classmate.

1. Muchos estudiantes de mi universidad son…
- **a.** latinoamericano.
- **b.** hispanos.
- **c.** norteamericanas.
- **d.** mexicana.

2. Mi profesora favorita es muy…
- **a.** jóvenes.
- **b.** activo.
- **c.** inteligente.
- **d.** delgado.

3. Mi amigo Nicolás es…
- **a.** español.
- **b.** dominicana.
- **c.** peruanos.
- **d.** mexicana.

4. Las dos chicas más inteligentes de la clase son…
- **a.** activos y sociables.
- **b.** trabajadoras y estudiosas.
- **c.** altos y morenos.
- **d.** interesante y optimista.

5. Para mí, el/la estudiante más… es…

Note for 2-14
Guide students to focus on the endings of the adjectives and their corresponding nouns to select the correct responses.

Expansion for 2-15

Remind students to pay attention to whether they are describing males or females, or one or more persons.

Encourage them to provide additional positions and adjectives. Model or brainstorm adjectives they can use for variety. They may also use the negative with the opposite quality: *La asistente no es antipática. Por el contrario, es muy simpática.*

Also encourage students to ask questions, such as: *¿Es joven/Son jóvenes? ¿Habla(n) español bien? ¿Cómo se llama(n)?*

Expansion for 2-16

Ask students to describe other well-known people, such as actors or people prominent in public affairs. Introduce *¿Estás/Están de acuerdo?* to ask students if they agree with the descriptions given.

Have students practice plural forms by using one adjective to describe two people: *Selena Gómez y Julia Roberts son bonitas y simpáticas.*

Suggestion for 2-16, *Intercambios*

Since asking questions is a difficult skill for beginners, you may wish to have students write down some questions before they do *Intercambios*. Remind them to listen attentively to what their classmates say in order to ask appropriate follow-up questions. Be prepared to provide additional vocabulary as needed.

Cultura

Bilingüismo

While Spanish is the common language spoken in Spain and most of Latin America, other languages are also spoken. In Spain, people in different regions speak Galician, Basque or Catalan. In Latin America, large communities speak indigenous languages in Mexico, Guatemala, Peru, and Bolivia. Paraguay is officially a bilingual country, and most of the people speak both Spanish and Guarani.

Conexiones. Do you know somebody who is bilingual? What are the advantages of being bilingual?

Señal de tráfico de estacionamiento en euskera (vasco) y castellano.

2-15 

Cualidades necesarias. Your school has hired some recent graduates who were language majors. Mark (✓) the qualities these new employees have and describe them to your partner. Your partner will mention additional qualities.

MODELO dos empleados bilingües en inglés y español

E1: *Los empleados bilingües hablan bien inglés y español. Son activos y extrovertidos.*

E2: *Sí. Son simpáticos, no son antipáticos. Hablan con los estudiantes y los padres de los estudiantes.*

1. dos especialistas en computadoras para el laboratorio de lenguas

_____ activos _____ pasivos _____ extrovertidos
_____ bilingües _____ agradables _____ trabajadores
_____ competentes _____ callados _____ listos

2. una recepcionista para la Oficina de Admisiones

_____ imparcial _____ simpática _____ interesante
_____ perezosa _____ habladora _____ perfeccionista

2-16 

Personas importantes. **PREPARACIÓN.** Take turns reading the descriptions of the people in the photos. Then add one or two more sentences with additional details about them.

Jimmy Smits es un actor famoso de cine (*movies*) y televisión.

Tish Hinojosa es una cantante mexicoamericana. Canta y escribe canciones también.

Miguel Cabrera es un jugador de béisbol muy bueno. Es venezolano.

Julia Álvarez es una novelista y poeta dominicana. También es profesora.

INTERCAMBIOS. Now take turns describing someone important in your life. Your classmates will ask questions to get more information about that person.

Situación

Llamadas de teléfono

Although there are differences among countries, as a general rule people in Spanish-speaking countries do not usually call each other before 9:00 A.M. but they may often call after 9:00 P.M. In the case of Spain or Argentina, it may be acceptable to call people as late as 10:30 or 11:00 P.M.

Comparaciones. What's a reasonable time to call a friend in the United States in the morning or at night? What do these telephone practices tell us about hours and schedules in daily life?

En directo

To address someone you don't know on the phone:

Hola, buenos días/buenas tardes.

To respond:

Buenos días /Buenas tardes...

To greet someone you know on the phone:

Hola, ¿qué tal?

Soy María.../Habla María...

To respond:

Ah, ¡hola!

¿Qué tal, María?/¿Cómo estás?

 Listen to a conversation with these expressions.

PREPARACIÓN. Read the following situation with your partner. Then brainstorm the vocabulary, structures, and other information you will need for both roles in the conversation.

Role A. Your friend calls to tell you that he/she is dating someone new. Ask:

a. where your friend's new boyfriend/girlfriend (**novio/a**) is from;
b. what he/she is like;
c. what he/she studies; and
d. if he/she has a car, what it is like.

Role B. You call your friend to talk about your new boyfriend/girlfriend. Your friend asks a lot of questions. Answer in as much detail as possible.

	ROLE A	ROLE B
Vocabulario	Adjectives to describe people and things Adjectives of nationality Colors School subjects Question words	Adjectives to describe people and things Adjectives of nationality Colors School subjects
Funciones y formas	Asking questions Noun–adjective agreement Present tense *Ser (de)* Using *tú* to talk to a friend	Giving information Noun–adjective agreement Present tense *Ser (de)* Using *tú* to talk to a friend

INTERCAMBIOS. Using the information in *Preparación,* act out the conversation with your partner.

Suggestion for *Situación*
You may want to assign partners and have pairs create mini-skits using the video-posting feature, *MediaShare,* online.

Note for *En directo*
Before doing the *Situación,* first have students read the expressions in *En directo.* Then have them listen to the dialogue and encourage them to use the expressions in their own conversation.

Audioscript for *En directo*
FERNANDO: *Hola, buenos días, llamo por el anuncio del apartamento en la Avenida Campos.*
SR. RIVERA: *¡Ah, sí, hola! Buenos días. Yo soy el señor Rivera. ¿Te interesa mi apartamento?*
FERNANDO: *Sí, mi amigo y yo necesitamos un apartamento.*
SR. RIVERA: *Muy bien. ¿Desean verlo esta tarde a las 3?*
FERNANDO: *¡Sí! A las 3.*
[*un minuto más tarde...*]
FERNANDO: [phone rings] *Hola Jorge, soy Fernando.*
JORGE: Hola, ¿qué tal?...
FERNANDO: *Bien. Mira, hay un apartamento muy interesante. Necesitamos verlo hoy a las 3.*
JORGE: *¡Perfecto!*

Note
You may wish to explain to students that the term **neoyorquino** refers to a Puerto Rican who lives in New York, usually New York City.

Warm-up
Review forms already familiar by asking students to identify classmates: *¿Quién es ese/a estudiante?* To review time, write various times of day on the board and ask: *¿Qué hora es?* Ask students when they arrive at school, this class, home, and so on. Remind them that they have already used *ser* to identify persons and things (*es profesora, es un libro*), to tell time, and to describe (*Manuel es alto; La clase es interesante*).

Suggestion
Ask questions to practice the use of *ser* to express possession: *¿De quién es esa mochila? ¿Y de quién es ese bolígrafo?*

Suggestion
Point out that events that take *ser* include such things as a class, a gathering of friends in a café, and a meal. Make sure students understand the difference between location of an event and location of a person or object: *¿Dónde es la clase de español? ¿Dónde está el profesor de español?/ La reunión es en la biblioteca. La biblioteca está en la avenida Independencia.*

2 Identifying and describing; expressing origin, possession, location of events, and time

Marc Anthony **es** un artista neoyorquino muy talentoso y versátil. **Es** cantante y actor. Sus padres **son** de Puerto Rico. También **es** compositor. Canta y escribe canciones de salsa, pop y pop latino, y **es** un actor de cine y teatro muy bueno. Sus (*His*) conciertos **son** en Estados Unidos y en **muchos** países latinoamericanos.

Piénsalo. Read the statements about Marc Anthony. Select the meaning expressed by **es** or **son** in each sentence from the list.

1. __c__ Marc Anthony **es** de ascendencia puertorriqueña.
2. __e__ El próximo (*next*) concierto de Marc Anthony **es** en California.
3. __b__ Las películas de Marc Anthony **son** muy populares.
4. __d__ Este álbum de Marc Anthony **es** de Daniel. Es su álbum favorito.
5. __a__ Marc Anthony **es** un cantante de salsa muy famoso.

a. identificación
b. descripción
c. nacionalidad/origen
d. posesión
e. eventos (localización, hora)

Present tense of *ser*

- You have practiced some forms of **ser** and have used them for identification (**Esta señora es la profesora de historia**) and to tell time (**Son las cuatro**). Here are other uses of this verb.

Ser (*to be*)			
yo	**soy**	nosotros/as	**somos**
tú	**eres**	vosotros/as	**sois**
Ud., él, ella	**es**	Uds., ellos/as	**son**

- As you have seen, **ser** is used with adjectives to describe an intrinsic feature of a person, place, or thing.

¿Cómo **es** ella?	*What is she like?*
Es atlética y extrovertida.	*She is athletic and outgoing.*
¿Cómo **es** el apartamento?	*What is the apartment like?*
El apartamento **es** pequeño pero **es** muy cómodo.	*The apartment is small, but it is very comfortable.*

- **Ser** is used to express nationality.

Gonzalo **es** chileno.	*Gonzalo is Chilean.*
Adriana **es** venezolana.	*Adriana is Venezuelan.*

LENGUA

Adjectives of nationality that end in a consonant form the feminine by adding **-a.**

español → español*a*

Note that the feminine and plural forms do not have a written accent.

portugués → portugues*a*
portugueses → portugues*as*
alemán → aleman*a*
alemanes → aleman*as*

Adjectives of nationality are not capitalized.

- **Ser + de** is used to express origin.

¿De dónde **son** Gonzalo y Adriana?	*Where are Gonzalo and Adriana from?*
Gonzalo **es** de Chile.	*Gonzalo is from Chile.*
Adriana **es** de Venezuela.	*Adriana is from Venezuela.*

- **Ser + de** is used to express possession. The equivalent of the English word *whose?* is **¿de quién?**

¿**De quién es** el apartamento?	*Whose apartment is it?*
El apartamento **es de** Marta.	*The apartment is Marta's.*

LENGUA

De + el contracts to **del**, but **de + la** and **de + los/las** do not contract.

El diccionario **es del** profesor, no **es de la** estudiante.	*The dictionary is the professor's, not the student's.*

- **Ser + de** is also used to express the material of which something is made.

El reloj **es de** oro.	*The watch is (made of) gold.*
Las sillas **son de** madera.	*The chairs are made of wood/ wooden.*

- **Ser** is also used to express where an event takes place or the time of an event.

El concierto **es** en el estadio.	*The concert is (takes place) in the stadium.*
La clase **es** a las nueve.	*The class is (takes place) at nine.*

¿COMPRENDES?

Complete the sentences with the correct form of the verb **ser.**

1. Muchos jugadores de béisbol __son__ de República Dominicana.
2. Nosotros __somos__ de la Ciudad de Guatemala. ¿De dónde __eres__ tú?
3. Mi amiga __es__ extrovertida y habladora.
4. Las esculturas (*sculptures*) del artista __son__ de madera.
5. El concierto de música clásica __es__ mañana a las 8:00.
6. Estos libros __son__ de Jorge.

MySpanishLab

Learn more using Amplifire Dynamic Study Modules, Grammar Tutorials, and Extra Practice activities.

PRÁCTICA

2-17

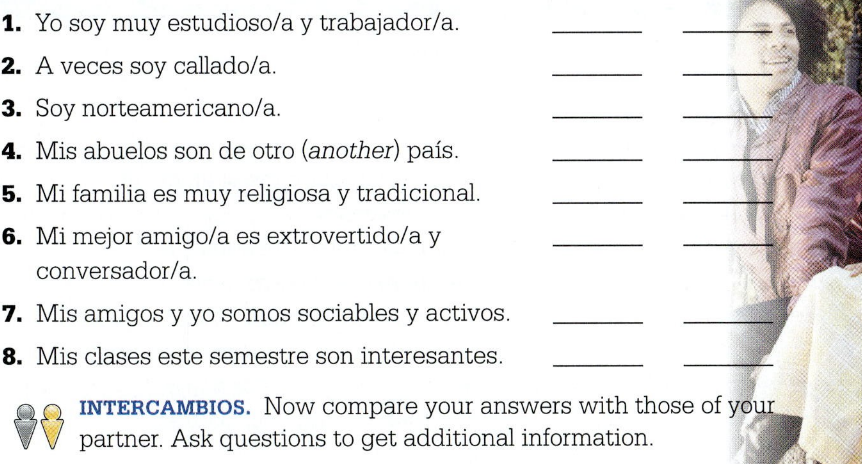

¿Cómo somos? PREPARACIÓN. Look at the following statements and indicate if the descriptions are true for you.

	Sí	No
1. Yo soy muy estudioso/a y trabajador/a.	______	______
2. A veces soy callado/a.	______	______
3. Soy norteamericano/a.	______	______
4. Mis abuelos son de otro (*another*) país.	______	______
5. Mi familia es muy religiosa y tradicional.	______	______
6. Mi mejor amigo/a es extrovertido/a y conversador/a.	______	______
7. Mis amigos y yo somos sociables y activos.	______	______
8. Mis clases este semestre son interesantes.	______	______

INTERCAMBIOS. Now compare your answers with those of your partner. Ask questions to get additional information.

Suggestion for 2-17, *Intercambios*
Before students begin, brainstorm possible questions: *¿Quién es/Cómo se llama tu mejor amigo/a? ¿Es extrovertido/a y hablador/a? ¿Cómo es?* Point out that *No* responses to yes/no questions should lead to additional questions.

Follow-up for 2-17
Have students in pairs or groups write as many questions as they can about one of the topics in the *Preparación*. Then each partner asks 1–2 questions.

Follow-up for 2-18
Students change partners. Each new partner should tell the other the information he/she gathered. To facilitate the reporting of information, you may wish to model the following: *X dice que el laboratorio de computadoras es grande. Tiene muchas computadoras.*

Expansion for 2-18
You may ask students to give additional information, using *estar* for location (*Capítulo 1*): *El laboratorio de computadoras está en la biblioteca.*

Warm-up for 2-19
Ask students questions about classroom objects with *¿De quién es/son...?* and *¿De qué es?* Before students begin the activity, encourage variety by brainstorming questions they may ask their partners.

Note for 2-20
This activity offers a good opportunity to recycle the expressions for location presented in the *Capítulo preliminar* and *Capítulo 1.* You may wish to review them before doing the activity.

Follow-up for 2-20
Students may also ask for the time of the various events, which will give them the opportunity to practice again *¿A qué hora...?*

Suggestion for *Situación*
Review greetings and introductions presented in the *Capítulo preliminar* so students can use them to make the conversation sound more natural.

2-18 

¿Cómo es? Ask what the following people, places, and objects are like.

 MODELO tu profesor/a de inglés

E1: *¿Cómo es tu profesor de inglés?*

E2: *Es alto, moreno y muy simpático.*

1. tus amigos
2. tu cuarto (*bedroom*)
3. tu compañero/a de cuarto (*roommate*)
4. el auto de tu mejor amigo/a
5. los salones de clase de la universidad

2-19 

¿Qué es esto? Take turns describing an object and its location in the classroom. Your partner will ask you questions and guess what it is.

 MODELO E1: *Es grande, es de plástico, está al lado de la ventana...*

E2: *¿De qué color es?*

E1: *Es roja.*

E2: *¿Es la mochila de Juan?*

LENGUA

Madera (*wood*), **plástico, tela** (*fabric*), **metal, oro** (*gold*), and **vidrio** (*glass*) are some words used to describe the material things are made of.

2-20 

Eventos y lugares. You are working at the university's information desk, and a visitor (your classmate) stops by. Answer his/her questions. Then switch roles.

 MODELO la exposición de fotografía

E1: *Perdón, ¿dónde es la exposición de fotografía?*

E2: *Es en la biblioteca.*

E1: *¿Dónde está la biblioteca?*

E2: *Está enfrente de la Facultad de Ciencias.*

1. el concierto de música
2. la conferencia sobre el arte mexicano
3. la fiesta para los estudiantes internacionales
4. la reunión de los exalumnos
5. la ceremonia de graduación

Situación

PREPARACIÓN. Read the following situation with your partner. Then brainstorm the vocabulary, structures, and other information you will need for both roles in the conversation.

Role A. A friend has invited you to a party at his/her house on Saturday. Ask:
a. where the house is located;
b. what it looks like (so you can find it easily); and
c. the time of the party.

Role B. You have invited a friend to a party at your house on Saturday. Answer your friend's questions. Then explain that the house belongs to your parents (**padres**), and tell your friend why your parents are not at home that weekend.

	ROLE A	ROLE B
Vocabulario	Question words Greetings Adjectives to describe the house	Time expressions Greetings
Funciones y formas	*Ser* for events *Estar* to express location Asking questions Accepting an invitation appropriately	Expressing the time of an event *Ser* for events *Estar* to express location *Ser* to express possession Giving information Extending an invitation appropriately

INTERCAMBIOS. Using the information in *Preparación,* act out the conversation with your partner.

3 Expressing qualities, emotions, and conditions

Todos los estudiantes **están** aburridos porque la profesora **es** aburrida.

Piénsalo. Read the statements below and classify them as to whether they describe either **a)** a personality trait/ physical characteristic or **b)** a feeling or perception that may change.

1. __a__ La película (*movie*) **es** aburrida. No tiene mucha acción.
2. __b__ Sofía **está** delgada en esa foto.
3. __b__ Los estudiantes **están nerviosos.** Tienen un examen difícil hoy.
4. __a__ Normalmente, las modelos **son** altas y muy delgadas.
5. __b__ Hoy los niños **están** contentos. Van (*They are going*) al parque.
6. __a__ Roberto **es** estudioso y trabajador. Estudia mucho todos los días.

Warm-up
Use questions with *ser* to ask for descriptions of people and objects in photos and in the classroom: *¿De qué color es la mochila de Nancy? ¿Cómo es este señor? ¿Es alto o bajo? ¿Es joven o mayor?* Make statements using *estar* and adjectives (*cansado/a, contento/a, furioso/a, triste*) to convey emotional or physical states. Use gestures or visuals to explain meaning as needed.

Suggestion
To help students develop their metalinguistic awareness, you may wish to ask why *contento/a, cansado/a,* and *enojado/a* are always used with *estar.*

Ser and *estar* with adjectives

Ser and **estar** are often used with the same adjectives. However, the choice of verb determines the meaning of the sentence.

- **Ser** + *adjective* states the norm—what someone or something is like.

Jorge **es** delgado.	*Jorge is thin.* (He is a thin man.)
Sara **es** muy nerviosa.	*Sara is very nervous.* (She is a nervous person.)
El libro **es nuevo.**	*The book is new.* (It is a new book.)

- **Estar** + *adjective* expresses a change from the norm, a condition, or how the speaker feels about or perceives the person or object.

Jorge **está** delgado.	*Jorge is/looks thin.* (He lost weight recently, or he looks thin in a picture or because of the clothes he is wearing.)
Sara **está** muy nerviosa.	*Sara is very nervous.* (She is feeling nervous.)
El libro **está** nuevo.	*The book is/looks new.* (It is used, but it seems like a brand new book.)

- The adjectives **contento/a, cansado/a, enojado/a** are always used with **estar.**

Ella **está contenta** ahora.	*She is happy now.*
Los niños **están cansados.**	*The children are tired.*
Carlos **está enojado.**	*Carlos is angry.*

- Some adjectives have one meaning with **ser** and another with **estar.**

Ese señor **es** malo.	*That man is bad/evil.*
Ese señor **está** malo.	*That man is ill.*
La chica **es** lista.	*The girl is clever/smart.*
La chica **está** lista.	*The girl is ready.*
La manzana **es** verde.	*The apple is green.*
La manzana **está** verde.	*The apple is not ripe.*
La profesora **es** aburrida.	*The professor is boring.*
La profesora **está** aburrida.	*The professor is bored.*

¿COMPRENDES?

Complete the sentences with the correct form of **ser** or **estar.**

1. Nosotros ___estamos___ aburridos en la clase de física.
2. El profesor de la clase ___es___ malo.
3. Las manzanas Granny Smith ___son___ verdes. Es su color natural.
4. Isabela y Martín ___son___ muy listos. Sacan buenas notas en todas sus materias.
5. Julia, ¿ ___estás___ cansada?
6. Mis amigos ___están___ enojados porque no hablo mucho con ellos.

MySpanishLab
Learn more using Amplifire Dynamic Study Modules, Grammar Tutorials, and Extra Practice activities.

PRÁCTICA

2-21  

Suggestions for 2-21
You may wish to remind students to focus on adjective agreement. Have partners exchange roles. Encourage them to use as many adjectives as possible.

¿Qué pasa aquí? Look at the drawing and then complete the description in each paragraph with the appropriate form of **ser** or **estar.** Check your answers with a partner. Take turns explaining why you chose **ser** or **estar** in each case.

1. Esteban (1) ___es___ un joven listo y estudioso. Este semestre saca buenas notas, excepto en la clase de economía. (2) ___Es___ una clase muy difícil. Esteban (3) ___está___ nervioso porque mañana hay un examen sobre la Unión Europea, pero él no (4) ___está___ listo. Debe estudiar toda la noche.

2. ¡Pobres niños! (*Poor children!*) La fruta (5) ___es___ buena y saludable (*healthful*), pero estas manzanas (6) ___están___ verdes, no (7) ___están___ buenas. Ahora los niños no (8) ___están___ contentos. Una niña (9) ___está___ mala porque le duele el estómago (*her stomach hurts*).

¿Cómo está ahora? You and your partner know the people mentioned in the table. One of you will describe a person, using an adjective from the list. The other explains how the person has changed and why. Then switch roles.

Arturo, fuerte/por su enfermedad (*illness*)

E1: *Arturo es fuerte.*

E2: *Pero por su enfermedad, ahora está muy débil.*

PERSONAS	CARACTERÍSTICAS	RAZONES
1. Ramón	alegre	por sus problemas
2. Laura y Gustavo	callado/a	por la dieta
3. Cristina	conversador/a	por el ejercicio
4. Andrés	débil	por el exceso de estudio
5. Ana y Sofía	extrovertido/a	por la falta (*lack*) de motivación
6. Teresa	feliz	por su depresión
	fuerte	por sus buenas notas
	introvertido/a	
	optimista	
	perezoso/a	
	pesimista	
	trabajador/a	
	triste	

2-23

Termómetro emocional. **PREPARACIÓN.** Indicate (✓) how you feel in each situation.

LUGARES	ABURRIDO/A	CONTENTO/A	TRANQUILO/A	TRISTE	RELAJADO/A	NERVIOSO/A
en la cafetería con mis compañeros						
en los exámenes finales						
en la oficina de un/a profesor/a						
en un concierto con mis amigos						
en una fiesta formal						
en mi casa por la noche						

Follow-up for 2-22
Brainstorm with the class the conditions that might have prompted the changes in the persons listed by asking questions such as *¿Por qué está delgado ahora Arturo?* (e.g., *dieta*). Focus on the concept that a change of state/condition prompts the switch from *ser* to *estar*.

INTERCAMBIOS. Talk with your partner about how you each feel in the situations given in *Preparación*. Then write a brief paragraph in which you compare your feelings and reactions.

MODELO *Yo estoy nervioso/a en un concierto, pero mi compañero/a está tranquilo/a.*

Suggestion for *Situación*
Before students begin *Situación*, brainstorm with them the questions they will need to ask. You may want to bring in some extra photos from magazines or the Internet for students to use in class.

Situación

PREPARACIÓN. Read the following situation with your partner. Then brainstorm the vocabulary, structures, and other information you will need for both roles in the conversation.

Role A. Show your classmate a photo (from your phone or the Internet). Identify the people and give some information about them. Then respond to your friend's questions and react to his/her comments about them.

Role B. After your classmate tells you about the people in the photo, ask and comment about:

a. how they seem to be feeling, based on their facial expressions or what they are doing; and
b. where they appear to be.

	ROLE A	ROLE B
Vocabulario	Adjectives to describe people Professions	Question words Adjectives to describe people
Funciones y formas	Giving information *Ser* with adjectives to describe people *Estar* with adjectives to express perceptions about people *Estar* to express location	Asking questions *Estar* with adjectives to express perceptions about people *Estar* to express location

INTERCAMBIOS. Using the information in *Preparación,* act out the conversation with your partner.

4 Expressing ownership

Mis amigos y yo

Mi nombre es Pablo Ramos. Soy estudiante en la universidad. Soy simpático, listo y sincero; por eso tengo muchos amigos. Estos son **mis** amigos. **Mi** mejor amigo se llama Luis. Tiene pelo corto y es muy guapo. En esta foto está entre Carmen y Teresa. **Nuestras** amigas de la universidad son activas y muy trabajadoras. Al lado de Teresa está **su** amigo Juan, con la camiseta rosa. Juan estudia en otra universidad. Por último está **nuestra** amiga Ángela. Es la hermana (*sister*) de Luis. Es muy divertida. Y **tus** amigos, ¿cómo son?

Suggestions
Students were introduced to *mi(s), tu(s), su(s)* as lexical items in *Capítulo preliminar*. You may wish to go over these forms by pointing to objects: *mi libro, mi escritorio, mis lápices, mis bolígrafos*. Use *tu(s)* and *su(s)* by pointing to objects and asking questions to check comprehension. You may also wish to explain to students that *vuestro(s)* and *vuestra(s)* are used only in Spain, whereas *su(s)* is used in Latin American varieties of Spanish.

Piénsalo. Complete the following statements about Pablo and his friends.

1. Pablo Ramos es estudiante. En la foto están ____ .
   a. Carmen y Ramón **b.** sus amigos **c.** sus hermanas
2. Ángela es ____ de Luis.
   a. la hermana **b.** la amiga **c.** la profesora
3. ____ amiga Teresa es muy trabajadora.
   a. Tu **b.** Su **c.** Mi
4. Pablo tiene una foto de Carmen y Luis porque son ____ amigos.
   a. mis **b.** sus **c.** nuestros

Possessive adjectives

Possessive adjectives modify nouns to express possession. They always precede the noun they modify.

mi amigo **tu** familia

POSSESSIVE ADJECTIVES	
mi(s)	*my*
tu(s)	*your* (familiar)
su(s)	*your* (formal), *his, her, its, their*
nuestro(s), nuestra(s)	*our*
vuestro(s), vuestra(s)	*your* (familiar plural)

- Possessive adjectives change number to agree with what is possessed, not with the possessor.

mi clase **mis clases**

- The **nosotros/as** and **vosotros/as** forms must agree also in gender.

nuestro profesor	**nuestros amigos**
nuestra profesora	**nuestras amigas**

- **Su** and **sus** have multiple meanings. To ensure clarity, you may use **de +** *the name of the possessor* or *the appropriate pronoun* instead of **su/sus.** For example, the multiple meanings of **su compañera** can be expressed as follows:

	de ella (la compañera de Elena)
	de él (la compañera de Jorge)
la compañera **+**	**de usted**
	de ustedes
	de ellos (la compañera de Elena y Jorge)
	de ellas (la compañera de Elena y Olga)

¿COMPRENDES?

Complete the sentences with the appropriate possessive adjective.

1. __Mis__ amigos y yo somos estudiantes.
2. Carla y __su__ mejor amiga son muy activas.
3. Oye, Marcos, ¿cuándo es __tu__ clase de sociología?
4. Marcos y __sus__ amigos estudian sociología y español.
5. Elena, ¿son difíciles __tus__ clases este semestre?
6. Nosotros estudiamos en la biblioteca con __nuestros__ amigos todos los días.

MySpanishLab

Learn more using Amplifire Dynamic Study Modules, Grammar Tutorials, and Extra Practice activities.

PRÁCTICA

¿De quién es? Explain to your partner to whom each sentence refers. Follow the model.

Su libro es muy difícil. (Laura)

El libro de Laura es muy difícil.

1. Sus bicicletas son nuevas. (ellos) — Las bicicletas de ellos...
2. Su clase de química es en el laboratorio. (Eva y Rosa) — La clase de química de Eva y Rosa...
3. Su coche es viejo pero es muy bueno. (Mario) — El coche de Mario...
4. Su mochila está en el escritorio. (ella) — La mochila de ella...
5. Sus amigas toman café juntas (*together*) todos los días. (ellas) — Las amigas de ellas...

2-25

Mi mundo (*world*). **PREPARACIÓN.** Write down two things you own (**pertenencias**) and two people you value. You may use the words in the box or choose others.

Pertenencias:	**Personas:**
un carro	un/a amigo/a
una computadora portátil	un/a profesor/a ideal
un iPad	un actor/una actriz

INTERCAMBIOS. Take turns describing your selections. Then share with the class the similarities and differences between you and your classmate.

Pertenencias

E1: *Yo tengo un auto. Es rápido y moderno. Y tu auto, ¿cómo es?*

E2: *Mi auto es rojo y muy viejo.*

Personas

E1: *Mi madre es importante en mi vida (life). Es muy alegre. Y tu mamá, ¿cómo es?*

E2: *Mi madre es tranquila y muy inteligente.*

2-26 

¿Cómo es/son...? Which of these statements apply to you and which apply to your friends? Mark (✓) your answers in the spaces under **Yo.** Then interview a classmate.

	Yo	Mi compañero/a
1. El carro de mi mejor amiga es blanco.	_____	_____
2. Mi compañero/a de cuarto es colombiano/a.	_____	_____
3. Mis amigos hablan español.	_____	_____
4. Nuestro deporte favorito es el tenis.	_____	_____
5. Nuestra ciudad es muy grande.	_____	_____
6. Mis amigos son aburridos.	_____	_____

EN OTRAS PALABRAS

The word for *car* in Spanish varies. The most widely accepted word is **el auto,** commonly used in the southern half of South America. **El coche** is used in Spain, Cuba, and Chile, and in most other places, **el carro** is frequently used.

2-27

Nuestra universidad.

PREPARACIÓN. With a partner, list some words that generally describe the following aspects of your university: **los profesores, las clases, los estudiantes, el campus, los equipos** (*teams*) **de fútbol, baloncesto, béisbol,** etc.

INTERCAMBIOS. Now write one or two sentences about each topic in *Preparación*. Present your sentences to the class. The class will decide which sentences a) describe the school most accurately and b) present an appealing view of the school for prospective students.

Situación  

PREPARACIÓN. Read the following situation with your partner. Then brainstorm the vocabulary, structures, and other information you will need for both roles in the conversation.

Role A. Call your best friend from high school and tell him/her about your new friends on campus. Describe each of them, including their ages, appearance, personalities, the things you do together, and your favorite places.

Role B. Your best friend from high school calls you to tell you about his/her new friends in college. Ask questions about them and about their favorite activities and places.

	ROLE A	ROLE B
Vocabulario	Age Adjectives to describe people Activities	Age Adjectives to describe people Activities Question words
Funciones y formas	Giving information about people, activities, and places	Asking questions

 **INTERCAMBIOS.** Using the information in *Preparación,* act out the conversation with your partner.

Suggestions for 2-26
After interviewing each other, students should compare answers, and then write one similarity and one difference between them. Students can share their findings with the class.

Standard 1.1
Students engage in conversation and provide and obtain information.
Activity 2-26 provides for three levels of conversation: between students in a pair, among students in a group, and whole-class discussion. Conversations are valuable for beginners, who learn to ask questions for clarification or to indicate comprehension problems, thus strengthening the speaking and listening skills of all conversation partners.

Suggestion for 2-27, *Intercambios*
You may wish to have each pair of students present two of their sentences, one for each competition listed. The presentations can be oral, or you may wish to have students write them on the board. This second option may lead to more discussion, since the sentences will be available for reference and comparison.

Note
In *Vocabulario en contexto,* students used *me gusta, te gusta,* and *le gusta* as lexical terms. Here they will find a brief explanation of the forms that they will need for communication at this stage. A detailed grammar explanation is not necessary at this point.

Suggestion
Explain that Mexico City is located in *el Distrito Federal* (*D.F.*) of Mexico.

Suggestion
Be sure to point out that the singular *gusta* is always used with infinitives, even when there is more than one infinitive in the sentence.

Explain that the expression *me cae bien* is often used to refer to people because in some contexts *gustar* may have a sexual connotation.

5 Expressing likes and dislikes

Marisa, una estudiante mexicana, chatea con Carla por Internet. Carla es mexicoamericana y vive en El Paso, Texas.

Piénsalo. Indicate whether each statement refers to Marisa (**M**) or Carla (**C**).

1. C **Me gustan** las posibilidades académicas que ofrece Estados Unidos.
2. M **Me gusta** vivir en la capital de México.
3. C **Me gusta** ser bilingüe.
4. M **Me gustan** las actividades al aire libre (*open air*).
5. M **Me gusta** el arte.

Marisa: Hola. ¿Quién eres? ¿Cómo te llamas?

Carla: Carla Chandía. Mucho gusto, Marisa.

Marisa: Y tú, ¿de dónde eres? ¿Dónde vives?

Carla: Mi familia y yo somos de Guanajuato, pero vivimos en El Paso, Texas.

Marisa: ¿**Te gusta** vivir en Estados Unidos?

Carla: **Me gusta** este país y en particular El Paso. Hay muchas actividades interesantes para los jóvenes. **A mí me gusta** hablar español e inglés con mis amigos. **Me gustan** las oportunidades para estudiar y trabajar. Y tú, ¿dónde vives?

Marisa: Vivo en la Ciudad de México y **me gusta** mucho vivir aquí. El D.F. es una ciudad enorme y muy bonita. **Me gusta** caminar por el parque Chapultepec y jugar con mi perro, Lassie.

Carla: ¿Qué **te gusta hacer** en tu tiempo libre?

Marisa: **Me gustan** muchas cosas, como escuchar música, ir a los museos, mirar tele y más…

Gustar

- To express what you like to do, use **me gusta** + *infinitive.* To express what you don't like to do, use **no me gusta** + *infinitive.*

Me gusta hablar español.	*I like to speak Spanish.*
No me gusta mirar televisión.	*I don't like to watch television.*
Me gusta practicar deportes y salir con mis amigos.	*I like to play sports and go out with my friends.*

- To express that you like something or someone, use **me gusta** + *singular noun* or **me gustan** + *plural noun.*

Me gusta la música clásica.	*I like classical music.*
Me gustan las personas alegres.	*I like happy people.*

- To ask a classmate what he/she likes, use **¿Te gusta(n)...?** To ask your instructor, use **¿Le gusta(n)...?**

¿Te gusta/Le gusta tomar café?	*Do you like to drink coffee?*
¿Te gustan/Le gustan los chocolates?	*Do you like chocolates?*

- To state what another person likes, use **a** + *name of person* + **le gusta(n)...** When you are talking about the preferences of more than one person, use **a** + *names* + **les gusta(n)...**

A Diego le gustan las fiestas.	*Diego likes parties.*
A Carlos le gusta el fútbol.	*Carlos likes soccer.*
A Diego y a Carlos les gusta ir de vacaciones con sus padres.	*Diego and Carlos like to go on vacation with their parents.*

¿COMPRENDES?

Complete the mini-conversations about people's likes and dislikes with the appropriate phrase: **me gusta(n), te gusta(n),** or **le gusta(n).**

1. LAURA: ¿__Te gusta__ el básquetbol, Gonzalo?
   GONZALO: Sí, __me gustan__ todos los deportes.
2. JULIÁN: A Carmen __le gusta__ bailar salsa y merengue.
   ALEJANDRA: A mí no __me gusta__ bailar.
3. FRANCISCO: ¿__Te gusta__ mirar televisión, Horacio?
   HORACIO: Un poco. __Me gustan__ las comedias y las telenovelas.

MySpanishLab
Learn more using Amplifire Dynamic Study Modules, Grammar Tutorials, and Extra Practice activities.

PRÁCTICA

2-28 **Mis preferencias.** **PREPARACIÓN.** Indicate (✓) your preferences in the following chart.

ACTIVIDAD	ME GUSTA MUCHO	ME GUSTA UN POCO	NO ME GUSTA
escribir correos electrónicos en español			
comer en restaurantes de comida mexicana			
bailar salsa			
escuchar música rock en español			
aprender sobre la cultura de otros países			
visitar lugares históricos			

INTERCAMBIOS. Compare your answers with those of a classmate. Share with the class one similarity and one difference in your preferences.

Suggestion for 2-28
Tell students about the kind of music you like. Ask about their preferences. Play some traditional music from the Spanish-speaking world (*pasodoble* from Spain, *ranchera* from Mexico, *cumbia* from Colombia, *tango* from Argentina, *son* and *chachachá* from Cuba, hip-hop from Puerto Rico/ Dominican Republic, Andean music, etc.). Ask students if they have listened to local radio programming in Spanish in areas with large Hispanic populations, and if so, what kind of music those stations play.

2-29 

¿Te gusta...? **PREPARACIÓN.** Ask a classmate if he/she likes the following. Be sure to ask follow-up questions as appropriate.

1. el gimnasio de la universidad
2. la informática
3. los autos híbridos
4. los gatos
5. los conciertos de música clásica
6. la clase de español

INTERCAMBIOS. Write a brief note to another classmate in which you share two pieces of information about yourself and two pieces of information you discovered about your partner.

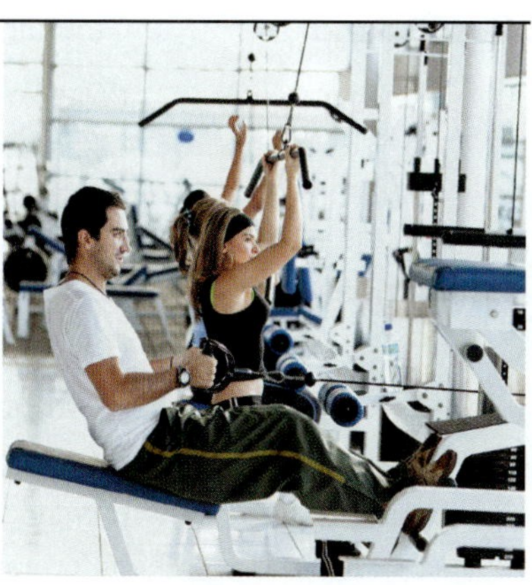

2-30

¿Qué te gusta hacer? **PREPARACIÓN.** Write down some questions that you would ask a classmate to find out the following.

1. what he/she likes to do in his/her free time
2. in what restaurants he/she likes to eat with his/her friends

INTERCAMBIOS. Interview two classmates and ask each of them the questions you prepared in *Preparación.* Compare their responses and share your conclusions with the class.

Situación

PREPARACIÓN. Read the following situation with your partner. Then brainstorm the vocabulary, structures, and other information you will need for both roles in the conversation.

Role A. You are at a park where you hear someone giving commands to a dog in Spanish. Break the ice and introduce yourself. Ask:

a. the person's name;
b. the dog's name and age; and
c. if the dog is friendly (**manso**).

Compliment the dog (smart, strong, very pretty, etc.). Tell the person that you like dogs very much and that you also like cats. Answer the questions this person asks.

Role B. You are in the park with your dog and someone approaches. Answer this person's questions and:

a. ask if he/she has a dog, and if so, what it looks like;
b. say that you don't like cats and say why you don't like them; and
c. ask where this person is from and where he/she is studying Spanish.

	ROLE A	ROLE B
Vocabulario	Greetings and introductions Adjectives to describe pets Likes and dislikes Question words	Greetings and introductions Adjectives to describe pets Likes and dislikes Question words
Funciones y formas	Asking questions Giving information Describing animals *(No) Gustar* to express likes and dislikes	Giving information Asking questions Describing animals *(No) Gustar* to express likes and dislikes

INTERCAMBIOS. Using the information in *Preparación,* act out the conversation with your partner.

EN ACCIÓN

Entre amigos en Los Ángeles

Suggestions for *En acción*
Remind students that they may not understand everything that is said in the video the first time they watch it. They should try to listen for the main ideas and understand key differences between the characters.

If your students watch the video outside of class, remind them that they may need to replay specific parts and go back and watch the entire segment several times to increase their comprehension. If necessary, you may also want to activate the captions so students can read the dialogue (in Spanish) as they watch.

2-31 Antes de ver

La cultura hispana. Mark (✓) the items typically associated with Hispanic culture in the United States.

1. ✓ el guacamole
2. ____ la lasaña
3. ✓ la salsa
4. ____ el 4 de julio
5. ✓ el festival de la Calle Ocho
6. ____ el lacrosse
7. ✓ los tostones
8. ✓ el español

2-32 Mientras ves

Dos ciudades. As you watch, first mark (✓) the qualities that describe Los Angeles according to the characters in the video.

1. ✓ Es una ciudad muy grande.
2. ✓ Tiene mercados con productos latinos.
3. ____ Es una ciudad colonial.
4. ✓ La mitad (*half*) de la población es hispana.
5. ✓ Hay muchos puertorriqueños.
6. ____ Tiene edificios muy antiguos.

Then, make a list of the activities that Blanca likes to do when she returns to San Juan, Puerto Rico.

____

____

____

2-33 Después de ver

¿Quién es? **PREPARACIÓN.** After watching the video, indicate whether the following statements refer to Esteban (**E**), Yolanda (**Y**), Federico (**F**), or Blanca (**B**).

1. Y Es estudiosa.
2. F Es muy hablador.
3. F Es listo y simpático.
4. Y Es vegana.
5. B Es puertorriqueña.
6. E Está triste.

INTERCAMBIOS. Take turns describing your best friend to your partner. Include two personality traits, two physical characteristics, and at least one activity that he/she likes to do.

Mosaicos

Integrated Performance Assessment (IPA)
The activities in each *Mosaicos* section correspond to the three modes of communication as indicated by the tag next to each activity.

Suggestion for audio
Listening activities in class provide many learning opportunities. Instructors can guide students' attention to certain passages, and vary how the listening activity is presented. For example, you may choose to have students listen to the audio more than once to listen for different types of information or to help them develop their overall listening skills.

Audioscript for *Escucha*
ESTUDIANTE: *¡Hola, mamá! ¿Cómo estás?*
MAMÁ: *Bien, muy bien. Y tú, ¿cómo estás, hija?*
ESTUDIANTE: *Aquí muy contenta con mis nuevas compañeras de la universidad. Son muy agradables, pero muy diferentes.*
MAMÁ: *¿Sí? ¿Por qué?*
ESTUDIANTE: *Bueno, Rita es mexicana y estudia economía. Es muy seria y trabajadora. Ella es baja, delgada y tiene el pelo rubio. Es callada y muy tranquila. No le gusta salir mucho. Marcela es de Honduras. Es alta, morena, tiene el pelo largo y los ojos negros. Ella es muy activa y le gustan la música moderna, el rock y la salsa. Le gusta bailar y salir con sus amigos todos los fines de semana.*
MAMÁ: *¿Y qué estudia Marcela?*
ESTUDIANTE: *Estudia arte moderno.*
MAMÁ: *Bueno, veo que son diferentes, pero las dos son agradables, ¿no?*
ESTUDIANTE: *Sí, y las dos me caen muy bien.*
MAMÁ: *Bueno, me alegro, hija.*

ESCUCHA

ESTRATEGIA

Listen for specific information

When you ask someone questions, he/she may provide not only the answers you need, but also additional information. To listen effectively, focus on the information you requested. This will help you remember it afterwards.

2-34 Presentational

Preparación. You will listen to a student tell her mother about how different her two roommates are. Before listening to their conversation, write the name(s) of your two best friends and a sentence that describes each one.

2-35   Interpretive

Escucha. Listen to the conversation between a student and her mother. Mark (✓) the appropriate column(s) to indicate whether the following statements describe Rita or Marcela.

	RITA	MARCELA
1. Estudia economía.	✓	
2. Le gusta bailar.		✓
3. Es alta, morena y tiene los ojos negros.		✓
4. Es muy seria, baja y delgada.	✓	
5. Estudia arte moderno.		✓

Comprueba
I was able to …

____ recognize the names of people.

____ associate specific information to each person.

____ hear and remember descriptive words.

____ recognize words that refer to actions.

2-36  Interpersonal / Presentational

Un paso más. Ask a classmate what his/her friends are like, what they like to do, and what they study. Then complete the following sentences with the information you gathered and report to the class.

1. Los mejores amigos de mi compañero/a son…
2. A ellos les gusta…
3. Sus amigos y yo somos semejantes/diferentes porque…

HABLA

2-37 Interpretive

Preparación. Find photos and research information online about one of the following public figures.

1. Shakira
2. Eva Longoria
3. Selena Gómez
4. Marco Rubio
5. William Levy
6. Sonia Sotomayor

En directo

To introduce information about physical characteristics:

En cuanto a lo físico.../ Físicamente, es...

To introduce information about personality:

Es una persona.../Tiene un carácter...

Listen to a conversation with these expressions.

2-38  Interpersonal

Habla. Share information with your partner about the person you researched. Then switch roles. Describe the physical characteristics and personality traits of this person. Be prepared to respond to your partner's questions and comments.

2-39 Presentational

Un paso más. Write a paragraph describing the person your classmate has described to you.

ESTRATEGIA

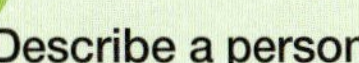

Describe a person

Descriptions are most effective when they are well organized. For example, you may want to include demographic information (e.g., age, nationality/origin), physical characteristics, personality traits, and accomplishments. A well-organized description presents information by category, beginning with an introductory statement to orient your listener.

Comprueba

In my conversation ...

- ____ my description was well organized.
- ____ I used a variety of descriptive words.
- ____ I made nouns and adjectives agree in gender and number.
- ____ I asked questions that were clear and easy to answer.
- ____ I gave clear information in response to questions.

Suggestion for 2-37
Provide students with websites in Spanish. Give them a guide to help them focus when they read the information about a person: *¿De dónde es? ¿Cuántos años tiene? ¿Cómo es? ¿Qué le gusta hacer?*

Suggestion for 2-37
To avoid having many students choose the same person, you can project images from the Internet in class and have students in pairs/small groups make their choices.

Suggestion for 2-38
Students should find a partner who has chosen a different person. Brainstorm with students how the listener can ask questions to elicit clarification and details.

Note for *En directo*
Before doing activity 2-38, first have students read the expressions in *En directo*. Then have them listen to the dialogue and encourage them to use the expressions in their own conversation.

Audioscript for *En directo*
ÁNGELES: *Julia, ¿conoces a mi amiga Marisa?*
JULIA: *No estoy segura. ¿Cómo es?*
ÁNGELES: *Físicamente, no es muy alta, pero es muy guapa.*
JULIA: *¡Ah, sí! Es una persona muy divertida.*
ÁNGELES: *Sí, es muy simpática y ahora va a estudiar aquí en nuestra universidad.*
JULIA: *¡Qué bien!*

Suggestion for 2-39
For the presentational part of this activity, students should write about the person that a classmate has described to them. Encourage students to organize the information that they have gathered from their classmate's description, as well as from their own questions. To make this activity more challenging, you may ask students to draw comparisons between their classmate's chosen famous Hispanic and their own.

LEE

2-40 Interpersonal

Preparación. Read the title of the text and examine its format. What type of text is it: a series of e-mail messages, personal ads, or ads for items for sale? Then with a classmate mark (✓) the qualities that you appreciate most in a partner/friend and say why.

a. _______ sociable
b. _______ simpático/a
c. _______ divertido/a
d. _______ perfeccionista
e. _______ mayor
f. _______ flexible
g. _______ trabajador/a
h. _______ ocupado/a

2-41 Interpretive

Lee. Read the ads on the next page and scan them for the information needed in the form below. In some cases, it may not be possible to provide all of the information requested.

	PERSONA 1	PERSONA 2	PERSONA 3	PERSONA 4
nombre				
edad				
nacionalidad				
estado civil				
personalidad (uno o dos adjetivos)				
le gusta…				

ESTRATEGIA

Scan a text for specific information

When you read in Spanish, you can search for particular pieces of information you think will be in the text. Often the comprehension questions after the text will help you decide what information to search for as you read. This approach to reading, called *scanning*, works best if you a) focus on the information you are seeking, and b) read the text through quickly at least twice, looking for specific information each time.

Comprueba

I was able to …

____ **identify the type of text.**

____ **find the information I was looking for in each text.**

____ **recognize important words.**

Suggestion for 2-41
Before the activity, make sure students have figured out that the text is a series of personal ads. Explain that they will now scan the ads for specific information about each person and that they should not worry about words they do not understand. You may wish to explain the meaning of the following words before students read the ads: *fronteras, compromiso,* and *viajo* as follows: *Mi familia y yo viajamos por carro entre…* [your state] *y…* [a neighboring state] *para visitar a mis abuelos. Siempre cruzamos la frontera entre… y…* [the two states] *durante el día. No nos gusta viajar por la noche.*

Follow-up for 2-41
To check comprehension, students can compare their forms with a partner and report discrepancies. You may wish to teach phrases such as *En su anuncio, Susana dice que…* Make the activity as communicative as possible by having students answer *No sé* or *No se dice* when the information is not provided.

Amigos sin fronteras

Soltera, sin hijos y sin compromiso. Me llamo Susana y tengo 24 años. Soy guatemalteca. Busco amigos extranjeros, solteros, separados o divorciados, jóvenes o mayores. Soy amable, cariñosa y muy trabajadora. Por mi trabajo, viajo mucho, pero me gusta la compañía de otras personas. Soy bilingüe. Hablo español e inglés. Escriban a sincompromiso@yahoo.net.

Soy Ricardo Brown. 21 años, sincero, dedicado. Me gustan las fiestas. Soy soltero. Deseo conocer a una chica de unos 23 años, preferiblemente venezolana como yo. Prefiero una mujer activa e independiente. Me gusta practicar deportes y explorar lugares nuevos. Escríbanme a amigosincero@hotmail.org.

Me llamo Pablo Sosa, tengo 31 años, y soy chileno. Soy agradable y muy trabajador. Me gusta hacer mi trabajo a la perfección, pero soy tolerante. Los autos convertibles son mi pasión. Deseo mantener correspondencia por correo electrónico con jóvenes del extranjero para intercambiar información sobre los convertibles europeos o americanos. Mi dirección electrónica es locoporlosautos@yahoo.com.

Soy Xiomara Stravinsky, decoradora y fotógrafa argentina. Me gusta el arte, especialmente el impresionismo. Tengo 27 años y soy divorciada. Soy dinámica, agradable y generosa, pero tengo pocos amigos porque tengo dos trabajos y paso muchas horas con mis clientes. Necesito un cambio en mi vida. ¿Deseas ser mi amigo/a? Por favor, escríbeme a xiomarastravinsky@hotmail.com.

2-42  Presentational

Un paso más. Find the best match for Susana, Ricardo, Pablo, and Xiomara from the following responses received. Then write your own personal ad including a description of your personality and the things you like to do. Share your ad with the class.

1. Tengo 22 años y me gustan todos los deportes. Mis padres viven en Caracas pero yo vivo en Miami.
2. Enseño arte en la escuela secundaria. Tengo tiempo para mis amigos los fines de semana.
3. Soy de Nicaragua. Soy muy sociable y deseo perfeccionar mi inglés.
4. Trabajo para *Autos de hoy*, una revista de Internet.

LENGUA

The letter **y** changes to **e** when it precedes a word beginning with the *i* sound (which may include words that start with *hi*): **inglés y español,** but **español e inglés; inteligente y agradable,** but **agradable e inteligente.**

Suggestion for 2-43
Accept any logical, well-supported answer. To review and expand vocabulary, you may ask students to provide synonyms (or related words) and/or antonyms of the descriptive adjectives in the ads.

Suggestion for 2-44
Students who prefer not to talk about themselves can assume a different identity for this activity.

Suggestions for 2-45
Have students proofread to correct spelling and grammatical errors.

You may wish to provide students with a list of kinds of movies such as *películas de: acción, terror, ciencia ficción, suspenso, aventura, comedia, amor*, etc.

ESCRIBE

2-43 Interpretive

Preparación. Read the following personal ad and indicate the adjectives used to describe the author's physical appearance or personality traits.

> Soy un fanático del cine y necesito amigos para conversar sobre películas los fines de semana. Tengo 24 años y estudio cinematografía. Me fascinan las películas de acción y también las románticas. Soy fuerte, activo, atlético y aventurero. Me gusta practicar deportes, especialmente el tenis y el esquí. Siempre estoy muy ocupado, pero tengo unas horas todas las semanas para conversar sobre películas. Interesados, favor de enviar correo electrónico a **fanaticodelcine@yahoo.com.**

ESTRATEGIA

Use adjectives to enrich your descriptions

You may enrich a description by using a variety of descriptive adjectives. When describing objects you may use adjectives to describe shapes or colors. When describing people you may refer to their looks or the way they are. Make sure the adjectives agree in gender and number with the objects and people they describe.

2-44 Presentational

Antes de escribir. Before starting your e-mail in response to the ad from fanaticodelcine, prepare a list of:

1. adjectives that describe you physically
2. adjectives that describe your personality
3. activities that you like to do
4. the kinds of movies you like

2-45 Presentational

Escribe. Write an e-mail to fanaticodelcine in response to the ad.

Comprueba

I was able to …

___ introduce myself.

___ explain the purpose of my e-mail.

___ give details about myself.

___ share my taste in movies.

2-46  Interpersonal

Un paso más. Exchange e-mails with your partner and write a possible response from fanaticodelcine. Include the following and follow up with other information.

1. a greeting
2. the description of a film you would like to discuss
3. whether you like the film or not, and why

En este capítulo...

Comprueba lo que sabes

Go to ***MySpanishLab*** to review what you have learned in this chapter. Practice with the following:

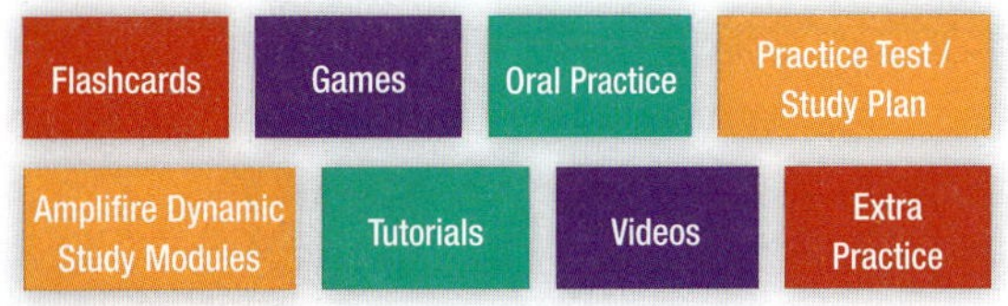

Vocabulario

LAS DESCRIPCIONES *Descriptions*

agradable *nice*
alegre *happy, glad*
alto/a *tall*
antipático/a *unpleasant*
bajo/a *short (in stature)*
bilingüe *bilingual*
bonito/a *pretty*
callado/a *quiet*
cansado/a *tired*
casado/a *married*
contento/a *happy, glad*
conversador/a *talkative*
corto/a *short (in length)*
de estatura mediana *average, medium height*
débil *weak*
delgado/a *thin*
divertido/a *funny, amusing*
enojado/a *angry*
feo/a *ugly*
fuerte *strong*
gordo/a *fat*
guapo/a *good-looking, handsome*
hispano/a *Hispanic*
joven *young*
largo/a *long*
listo/a *smart; ready*
mayor *old*
moreno/a *brunette*
nervioso/a *nervous*
nuevo/a *new*
oscuro/a *dark*
pelirrojo/a *redhead*
perezoso/a *lazy*
pobre *poor*
rico/a *rich. wealthy*
rubio/a *blond*
simpático/a *nice, charming*
soltero/a *single*
tonto/a *silly, foolish*
trabajador/a *hardworking*
triste *sad*
viejo/a *old*

LOS COLORES *Colors*

amarillo/a *yellow*
anaranjado/a *orange*
azul *blue*
blanco/a *white*
castaño/a *brown*
gris *gray*
marrón *brown*
morado/a *purple*
negro/a *black*
rojo/a *red*
rosado/a, rosa *pink*
verde *green*

LAS NACIONALIDADES *Nationalities*

alemán/alemana *German*
argentino/a *Argentinian*
boliviano/a *Bolivian*
canadiense *Canadian*
chileno/a *Chilean*
chino/a *Chinese*
colombiano/a *Colombian*
costarricense *Costa Rican*
cubano/a *Cuban*
dominicano/a *Dominican*
ecuatoriano/a *Ecuadorian*
español/a *Spanish*
estadounidense *U.S. citizen*
francés/francesa *French*
guatemalteco/a *Guatemalan*
hondureño/a *Honduran*
japonés/japonesa *Japanese*
marroquí *Moroccan*
mexicano/a *Mexican*
nicaragüense *Nicaraguan*
nigeriano/a *Nigerian*
panameño/a *Panamanian*
paraguayo/a *Paraguayan*
peruano/a *Peruvian*
polaco/a *Polish*
portugués/portuguesa *Portuguese*
puertorriqueño/a *Puerto Rican*
salvadoreño/a *Salvadoran*
uruguayo/a *Uruguayan*
venezolano/a *Venezuelan*

VERBOS *Verbs*

desear *to wish, to want*
ser *to be*
usar *to use*

PALABRAS Y EXPRESIONES ÚTILES *Useful words and expressions*

el auto, el coche, el carro *car*
de *of, from*
¿de quién? *whose?*
del *of the (contraction of* de+ el)
el esposo/la esposa *husband/wife*
la flor *flower*
le gusta(n) *you (formal) like*
los lentes de contacto *contact lenses*
me gusta(n) *I like*
mucho (adv.) *much, a lot*
mucho/a (adj.) *many*
el ojo *eye*
el pelo *hair*
te gusta(n) *you (familiar) like*
Tengo... años. *I am ... years old.*
tiene *he/she has; you (formal) have*
todos/as *everybody*

See page 87 for possessive adjectives.

Introduction to chapter
Introduce the chapter theme about what people do in their free time and ask questions to recycle content from the previous chapter. Facilitate comprehension by using gestures or visuals. *¿Qué te gusta hacer en tu tiempo libre? ¿Usas tu tiempo libre para estudiar? ¿Te gusta estar con tus amigos? ¿Comes en restaurantes con tus amigos o preparas comida en casa? ¿Ves la televisión o escuchas música? ¿Qué programas te gusta ver? ¿Qué música te gusta escuchar?*

Integrated Performance Assessment: Three Modes of Communication

Presentational: See activities 3-5, 3-6, 3-7, 3-17, 3-19, 3-25, 3-26, 3-37, 3-40, 3-46, 3-47, and 3-50.

Interpretive: See activities 3-3, 3-4, 3-7, 3-8, 3-10, 3-12, 3-15, 3-16, 3-18, 3-20, 3-21, 3-22, 3-24, 3-27, 3-31, 3-32, 3-33, 3-37, 3-38, 3-39, 3-41, 3-43, 3-46, and 3-49.

Interpersonal: See activities 3-1, 3-2, 3-3, 3-4, 3-5, 3-6, 3-7, 3-8, 3-9, 3-10, 3-11, 3-12, 3-13, 3-14, 3-15, 3-16, 3-17, 3-18, 3-19, 3-20, 3-21, 3-22, 3-23, 3-24, 3-25, 3-26, 3-27, 3-28, 3-29, 3-30, 3-31, 3-32, 3-33, 3-34, 3-35, 3-36, 3-39, 3-42, 3-44, 3-48, 3-51, and all *Situación* activities.

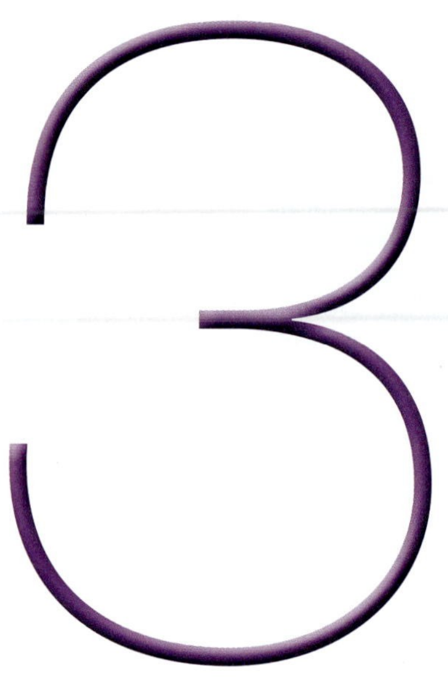

3 ¿Qué hacen para divertirse?

ENFOQUE CULTURAL
Perú

VOCABULARIO EN CONTEXTO
Las diversiones
Los planes
La comida

MOSAICO CULTURAL
Los hispanos y la vida social

FUNCIONES Y FORMAS
Present tense of *hacer, poner, salir, traer,* and *oír*
Present tense of *ir* and *ir a + infinitive*
Numbers 100 to 2,000,000
Saber and *conocer*
Some uses of *por* and *para*

EN ACCIÓN
¡A comer!

MOSAICOS
ESCUCHA Use background knowledge
HABLA Inform yourself before you do a survey
LEE Look for and use key words
ESCRIBE Identify your audience

EN ESTE CAPÍTULO...
Comprueba lo que sabes
Vocabulario

LEARNING OUTCOMES

You will be able to:

- describe free-time activities and food
- plan your daily activities and express intentions
- identify prices and dates
- state what and whom you know
- talk about places to visit in Peru
- share information about free-time activities in Hispanic countries and identify cultural similarities

ENFOQUE cultural

PERÚ

Enfoque cultural

To learn more about Peru, go to MySpanishLab to view the *Vistas culturales* videos.

En este detalle de un cuadro anónimo del siglo XVIII, vemos a unos invitados a la boda entre la princesa inca Ñusta Beatriz y un noble español, D. Martín de Loyola.

¿QUÉ TE PARECE?

- La papa es original de Perú. Existen más de 3.000 variedades de este tubérculo.
- Desde la época de los incas hasta ahora, Perú es el principal productor de oro en el mundo.
- El periódico *El Peruano,* fundado por Simón Bolívar en 1825, es el más antiguo de Latinoamérica.
- Inca Kola es el refresco más popular en Perú por su sabor y vibrante color amarillo producido por infusiones de diferentes hierbas naturales.
- El surf es uno de los deportes más populares en Perú. La playa de Punta Hermosa, en el sur, atrae a surfistas de todas partes.

Note
Both *Perú* and *el Perú* are widely accepted. In *Mosaicos, Perú* is used. Both Cuzco and Cusco are accepted spellings for the Peruvian city that was the capital of the Inca Empire.

Suggestion for map
Brainstorm with students the information they may already know about Peru. You may want to project the map from the Interactive Globes. Zoom in and out as desired or spin the globe using the cursor to ask questions. *¿Qué países están al norte de Perú? ¿Cuáles están al sur?, ¿y al oeste?* Also ask: *¿Cómo se llama el océano que está al lado de Perú? ¿Qué países no tienen costa? ¿Cómo se llaman las montañas que hay en Perú, Bolivia y otros países latinoamericanos?* Explain *cordillera* by drawing a chain of mountains or by pointing to them on the map.

Note for art
Writings and paintings like this one document marriages between members of Incan and European nobility. Introduce the word **boda** by pointing to the couple and the word **casarse**. Ask questions to elicit vocabulary: *¿Cómo es el hombre del cuadro? ¿Cómo es la mujer? ¿Qué hacen las personas en una boda normalmente? ¿Comen mucho o poco? ¿Beben? ¿Bailan?*

Standard 2.1
Students demonstrate an understanding of the relationship between the practices and perspectives of the culture studied. This painting depicts a wedding between people from different cultures. Have students reflect on how practices of both cultures are combined (or not) when members of one culture are the conquerors and members of the other culture have been conquered.

Note for *Machu Picchu*
The "lost city" was discovered nearly intact in 1911 by Hiram Bingham of Yale University. The site includes hundreds of agricultural terraces, many stone houses, and several ceremonial temples, also constructed of stone. Machu Picchu is truly a marvel. Machu Picchu was declared a Peruvian Historical Sanctuary in 1981 and a UNESCO World Heritage Site in 1983. It was also voted one of the New Seven Wonders of the World in a worldwide Internet poll in 2007.

Note for *el lago Titicaca*
Lake Titicaca is a sacred place for the Inca civilization, as the Incan mythology says that the first Inca king, Manco Capac, was born here. According to Incan mythology, this is the place where the world originated when the god Viracocha came out of the lake and created the sun, the stars, and the first people.

Note for *Trujillo*
The Mansiche Arena in Trujillo is the stage for the National Marinera Contest, where different categories and choreographic styles are judged. The traditional accompaniment for the dance is provided by the Peruvian *cajón,* a kind of box drum played by slapping the front face with the hands, and guitars clarinets, drums and bugles. During the festival, the city also hosts processions involving floats, and the whole town takes on a festive air. The people of Trujillo gather at the main square to dance and celebrate.

Note for *Mario Vargas Llosa*
Mario Vargas Llosa's writings include a variety of literary genres, literary criticism, and journalism. His novels include comedies, murder mysteries, historical novels, and political thrillers. Several, such as *La tía Julia y el escribidor* (*Aunt Julia and the Scriptwriter*) have been adapted as feature films.

ENFOQUE cultural

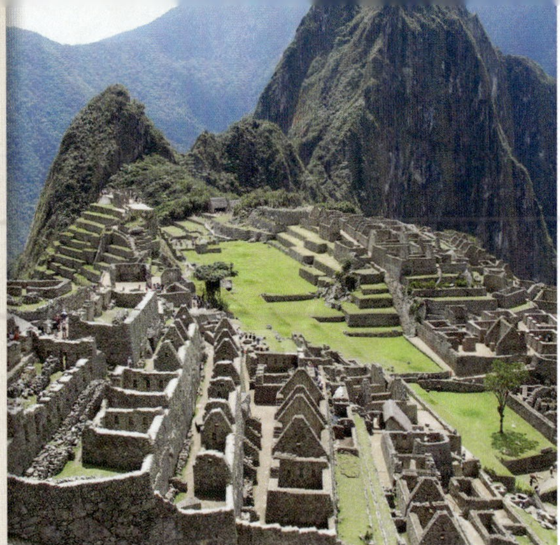

Machu Picchu es una de las ruinas arqueológicas más importantes del mundo. Fue construida en el siglo XV como fortaleza y santuario religioso para los emperadores incas. El mundo recibe las primeras noticias de este lugar en 1911 por medio del explorador Hiram Bingham.

La marinera es uno de los bailes más hermosos y populares que existen en Perú. Todos los años se realiza un festival de marinera en la ciudad de Trujillo (en la costa norte del país), donde compiten parejas para ganar el título de rey y reina de la marinera del año.

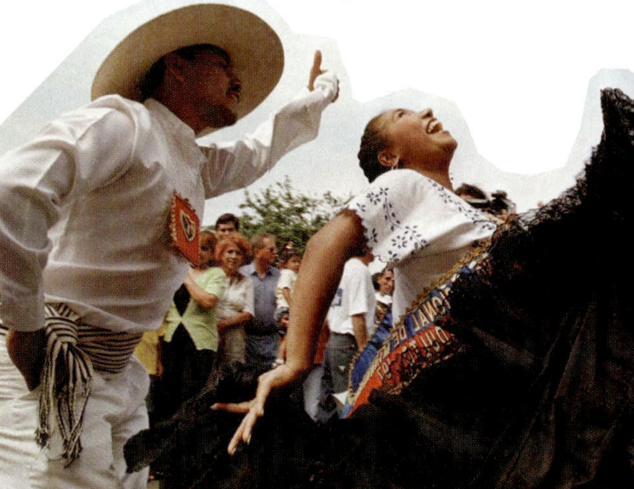

El lago Titicaca se encuentra entre los territorios de Perú y Bolivia a una altura de 12.500 pies sobre el nivel del mar. Allí se encuentran 36 islas flotantes (artificiales) construidas de totora (*reeds*), que abunda en el lago. En las islas flotantes de Uro, Taquile y Amantaní viven comunidades indígenas que mantienen sus costumbres ancestrales.

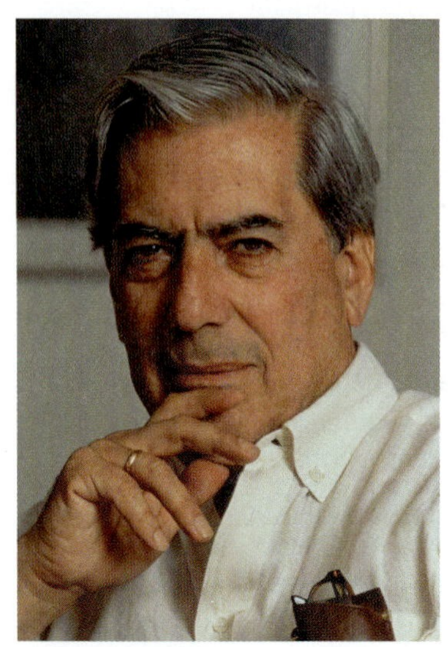

El escritor, novelista, periodista y político peruano Mario Vargas Llosa recibe el Premio Nobel de Literatura en el año 2010. Publica su primera obra, *Los jefes,* a los veintitrés años. Llega a la fama mundial con la novela *La ciudad y los perros.* Sus obras reflejan su percepción de la sociedad peruana y sus experiencias personales.

¿CUÁNTO SABES?

Using the map, photos, and accompanying text, complete the sentences with the correct word.

1. __Machu Picchu__ es una antigua e importante ciudad inca en Perú.
2. El lago Titicaca está localizado entre __Perú__ y __Bolivia__.
3. __La llama__ es un animal que vive en los andes peruanos.
4. Inca Kola es un __refresco__ de color __amarillo__.
5. Mario Vargas Llosa recibe __el Premio Nobel de Literatura__ en el 2010 por ser un prestigioso escritor.
6. En Perú existen más de 3.000 variedades de __papas__.

Vocabulario en contexto

Talking about free-time activities, plans, and food

Las diversiones

MySpanishLab **PRONUNCIATION TOPIC:** Consonant *h* and sequence *ch*

Learn more using Amplifire Dynamic Study Modules, Pronunciation, and Vocabulary Tutorials.

En todos los **países** hispanos hay **fiestas** y **reuniones.** Los **jóvenes** bailan, escuchan **música** o conversan. A veces **tocan la guitarra** y **cantan canciones** populares.

Muchas personas van a la playa en su **tiempo libre** y también **durante** las **vacaciones.** Aquí en la playa Mancora en Perú, estas personas **toman el sol** y **descansan mientras otras** personas **nadan en el mar,** corren o caminan por la playa.

Un **hombre** y una **mujer** leen el **periódico** en un café de su **ciudad.** Y tú, ¿lees el periódico? ¿Qué periódicos o **revistas** lees? ¿Lees el periódico en papel o en línea?

Muchos **jóvenes** van al **cine,** especialmente los fines de semana. También es común **alquilar** DVD o bajar películas de Internet.

PRÁCTICA

Escucha y confirma. Indicate the places where people do the activities you hear.

	(house)	(beach)	(cinema)
1.	✓		
2.		✓	
3.			✓
4.	✓		
5.	✓		
6.			✓

3-2 

Asociaciones. Match the places to the activities you most likely do there. Compare your answers with those of a classmate and say what other activities you do in those places.

1. __c__ la playa
2. __e__ la discoteca
3. __a__ el cine
4. __b__ la biblioteca
5. __a, b, d, e__ la casa

a. ver una película
b. leer el periódico
c. caminar por la arena
d. mirar televisión
e. bailar y conversar

Suggestion for *Vocabulario en contexto*
Introduce each photo to demonstrate new vocabulary. Then ask yes/no, either/or, and information questions to personalize the material: *¿Bailas salsa? ¿Bailas bien? ¿Qué música te gusta? ¿Tocas la guitarra o el piano? ¿Cantas canciones populares? ¿Quién es tu artista favorito/a?*
Talk about yourself and ask questions: *Yo leo el periódico por la mañana. Me gusta leer* (name of newspaper). *Y tú, ¿lees el periódico por la mañana, por la tarde o por la noche? ¿Qué periódico te gusta más? Yo también leo revistas. Mis revistas favoritas son… ¿Qué revista te gusta más?*
Ask about specific pastimes. *¿Vas al cine los fines de semana? ¿Vas por la tarde o por la noche? A mí me gusta ver películas románticas. También me gustan las películas de misterio, pero no me gusta ver películas de ciencia ficción. Y a ti, ¿te gusta ver películas de acción? ¿Cuáles son tus películas favoritas?*

Note for 3-1
To maximize the communicative experience, encourage students to compare answers with a classmate and to discuss (in the target language) differences in their responses.

Audioscript for 3-1
1. *Los jóvenes alquilan películas los fines de semana.*
2. *Marisa y Paola toman el sol durante las vacaciones.*
3. *En su tiempo libre, Mario y sus amigos van al cine.*
4. *Cuando sus padres están de vacaciones, Gabi invita a sus amigos a fiestas.*
5. *Después de clase, los estudiantes necesitan descansar.*
6. *Hay películas muy buenas en las ciudades grandes.*

Suggestion for 3-2
To make this activity challenging, you may want to write key vocabulary on the board and have students do the second part of the activity with their books closed.

Suggestion for 3-3
The expression *¿Qué hacen los estudiantes?* was introduced in *Capítulo 1.* Remind students what *hacer* means by writing on the board: *¿Qué haces los fines de semana?* Ask questions to review the verb and recycle vocabulary: *¿Qué haces en la universidad? ¿Qué hace Elisa en el gimnasio? ¿Qué hacemos en la clase de español?*

Expansión for 3-3
7. *en una reunión;* 8. *en el cine;* 9. *en un restaurante elegante;* 10. *en el auto;* 11. *en el centro de la ciudad;* 12. *en el gimnasio*

Suggestion for 3-4
This is a good opportunity to recycle vocabulary from previous chapters and to use new vocabulary. Before the *Intercambios,* brainstorm with students the vocabulary related to free-time activities that they have learned (*mirar televisión, practicar básquetbol/baloncesto, montar en bicicleta*). You may introduce new words, such as *piano, trompeta, violín.*

3-3 

Nuestro tiempo libre. What do you do in the following places? Take turns asking one another, and take notes on the responses. Then prepare a report to share with the class about the most popular activities in your group.

en las vacaciones

E1: *¿Qué haces en tus vacaciones?*

E2: *En mis vacaciones generalmente voy a la playa. ¿Y tú?*

	COMPAÑERO/A 1	COMPAÑERO/A 2	COMPAÑERO/A 3	YO
1. en la universidad después de clase				
2. en la biblioteca pública de tu ciudad				
3. en casa el fin de semana				
4. en un parque de tu ciudad				
5. en la playa durante las vacaciones				
6. en la discoteca con tus amigos				

3-4 

¿Qué hacen Pedro y Carmen?

PREPARACIÓN. Look at the drawings and take turns explaining what Pedro and Carmen do on weekends.

INTERCAMBIOS. Each of you will write a message to an e-pal in Peru explaining what you and your friends do on weekends.

Hola, Rafael:

¿Cómo estás? Nosotros estamos muy bien. Los fines de semana mis amigos y yo…

¡Hasta pronto!

Carmen

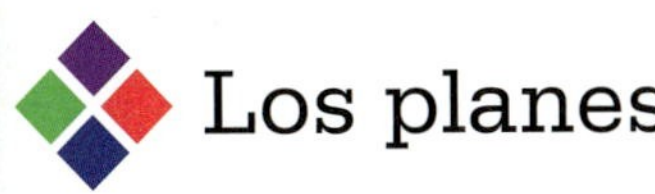

Los planes

Una conversación por teléfono entre Manuel y Liliana

LILIANA: ¿Aló?

MANUEL: Hola, mi amor, ¡**felicidades** por tu **cumpleaños!**

LILIANA: Ay, gracias, Manuel.

MANUEL: **¿Qué te parece** si **vamos** al cine esta tarde y **después** a un restaurante para **cenar?**

LILIANA: Me parece **fabuloso.** ¿Qué película vamos a ver?

MANUEL: Hay una nueva de Augusto Tamayo.

LILIANA: Muy bien. Me gustan mucho sus películas. ¿Dónde **ponen** la película?

MANUEL: **Cerca de** El Jardín Limeño, tu restaurante favorito.

LILIANA: **Estupendo,** ¿entonces **luego** vamos a cenar allí?

MANUEL: **¡Claro!** ¿Nos vemos en tu casa a las cinco?

EN OTRAS PALABRAS

Telephone greetings vary from country to country. **¿Diga?** and **¿Dígame?** are used to answer the phone in Spain; **¡Bueno!** in Mexico; **¿Aló?** in Argentina, Peru, and Chile; **¡Oigo!** and **¿Qué hay?** in Cuba. Terms of endearment such as **mi amor, corazón, mi vida, querido/a,** and **mi cielo** also reflect regional preferences.

PRÁCTICA

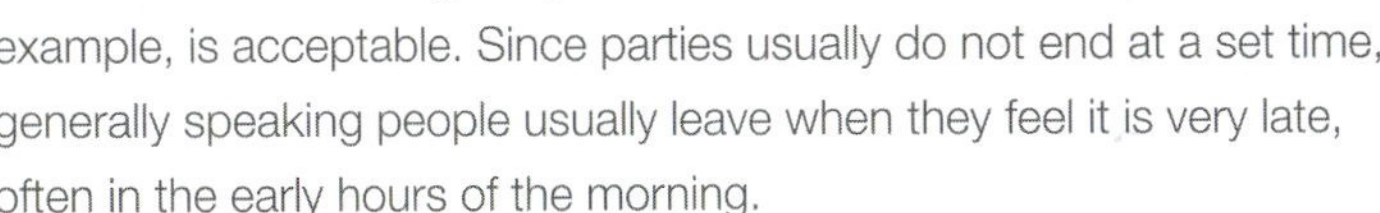

Cultura

La puntualidad

Many people in Spain and Latin America have a flexible concept of time when it comes to informal settings. Arriving on time for parties and social gatherings is not expected, and it can even be considered rude. Being thirty minutes late, for example, is acceptable. Since parties usually do not end at a set time, generally speaking people usually leave when they feel it is very late, often in the early hours of the morning.

Comparaciones. What is considered late for a party in your country? What is the host's reaction if you leave a party early?

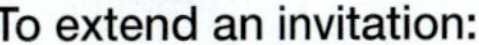

En directo

To extend an invitation:

Te llamo/escribo para invitarte a + *infinitive...*

I am calling/writing to invite you to...

To accept an invitation:

¡Estupendo! ¿Dónde quedamos? *Great! Where will we meet?*

Sí, gracias/¡Ah, qué bien!/¡Qué buena idea!

Yes, thanks/How great!/What a great idea!

¡Fabuloso! *Fabulous!*

To decline an invitation:

Lo siento, pero no tengo tiempo/tengo mucha tarea... *I'm sorry, but I don't have time/I have too much homework...*

Ese día no puedo, tengo un examen. *I can't on that day, I have an exam.*

Listen to a conversation with these expressions.

3-5 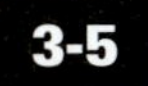 

Para confirmar. PREPARACIÓN. Using the preceding conversation as a model, call a classmate and invite him/her to join you in a weekend activity. He/She should accept or decline the invitation.

INTERCAMBIOS. Repeat the activity with two other classmates. Then explain to the class your weekend plans and who is joining you.

MODELO *El sábado por la tarde, Juan, Verónica y yo vamos al gimnasio para ver un partido de voleibol.*

3-6 

Un plan para el sábado. Write a text message to a classmate inviting him/her to go to the movies on Saturday. Respond to your classmate's message.

Note
Vamos a + infinitive appears in the dialogue as a lexical item. *Van a + infinitive* appears in the suggested comprehension check that follows. Students will be able to preview other forms of this construction elsewhere in *Vocabulario en contexto.*

Note
Augusto Tamayo San Román is a Peruvian screenwriter, director, and producer. His best known films include *El bien esquivo* (2001), *La sombra al frente* (2005), and *La vigilia* (2010).

Suggestion for dialogue
Model pronunciation and intonation in the dialogue with a student. Then ask two students to read it aloud and have the class practice it in pairs. Mention that *fabuloso, estupendo,* and *perfecto* express enthusiastic agreement and should be said with emphasis.

After students read the dialogue you may do this *cierto o falso* comprehension check.

1. *Liliana llama por teléfono a Manuel por el cumpleaños de él.* (F) 2. *Manuel y Liliana van a ver una película en el cine.* (C) 3. *Liliana piensa que las películas de Augusto Tamayo son malas.* (F) 4. *Liliana y Manuel viven juntos.* (F) 5. *Liliana acepta la invitación de Manuel.* (C)

Suggestion
You may want to point out that some Spanish speakers use *dar la película / pasar la película* rather than *poner la película.*

Suggestion for 3-5
Before the activity you may review the expressions in *En directo* and listen to the conversation in the eText. Provide other ways to accept or reject an invitation. For example, *Aceptar: ¡Cómo no! ¡Estupendo! Me gustaría mucho. No aceptar: No puedo. Debo estudiar.* You may also brainstorm with students about their plans for the weekend: *¿Qué planes tienen este fin de semana? ¿Van al cine? ¿Van a un concierto?, ¿a un partido de béisbol? ¿Van a escuchar música en su casa?*

Audioscript for *En directo*

INÉS: *Hola, Roberto. Te llamo para ver si quieres ir al cine el jueves.*
ROBERTO: *Ese día no puedo, tengo un examen el viernes y tengo que estudiar mucho.*
INÉS: *Está bien. ¿Por qué no vamos el viernes?*
ROBERTO: *Sí, el viernes sí puedo. ¿Cenamos primero y luego vamos al cine?*
INÉS: *¡Qué buena idea! ¿Dónde quedamos?*
ROBERTO: *En la biblioteca a las siete. ¿De acuerdo?*
INÉS: *¡Sí, estupendo!*

Suggestion for 3-7

This *Agenda cultural* is from a Peruvian newspaper. Ask students to read the *Cultura* box before they do the activity. Go over some key points in the *Agenda cultural* to facilitate comprehension. Write down the abbreviations and ask if students can guess what they mean: *Dir.* (*director*); *cll (calle)*; *av.* (*avenida*). Ask them to guess the meaning of *Ingreso libre* (free, no charge) and *Entrada general* (General admission). Point out cognates (*Homicidio, contrato, Conferencia*, etc.) and *S/.*, which stands for *Nuevo Sol*, the Peruvian monetary unit. If you wish, assign students to look up the exchange rate for this currency. Explain the expression *a cargo de*, which refers to the director or the actors of a theatrical production.

▲ Alejandro González Iñárritu, Guillermo del Toro y Alfonso Cuarón

Cultura

El cine

Traditionally, Mexico, Spain, and Argentina have had important film industries, but films are made in other Spanish-speaking countries as well. Outstanding Spanish-language film directors like Pedro Almodóvar and Icíar Bollaín in Spain, Alfonso Cuarón, Guillermo del Toro, and Alejandro González Iñárritu in Mexico, Sergio Cabrera in Colombia, and Juan Carlos Tabío in Cuba, among others, are internationally known.

Conexiones. What other famous directors (American or foreign-born) can you name? What do you like best about their style?

3-7 

¿Adónde vamos? Identify three activities on this page from a newspaper in Lima that you and your classmate find interesting. Then fill in the chart, including time for each activity. Be prepared to share this information with the class.

¿Adónde vamos?	¿Qué vamos a hacer?	¿Cuándo?

AGENDA CULTURAL

La guía de Lima

Cine

Cine arte: Películas de culto, presenta:

1:00 PM. “Dementia” (56'–1955) Dir.: John Parker (Estados Unidos).

4:30 PM. “Homicidio por contrato” (81'–1958) Dir.: Irving Lerner (Estados Unidos).

7:30 PM. Festival de Cine al Este de Lima, presenta: “Milos Forman, lo que no te mata” (100'–2010) Dir.: Miloslav Smidmajer (República Checa).

Ingreso libre.

Libros

Casa de la Literatura Peruana (cll. Jr. Ancash 207–Lima)

11:00 AM. Títeres: “La Achique”. Ingreso libre.

7:00 PM. Conversando con mi autor favorito, presenta: Fernando Ampuero. Ingreso libre (previa inscripción: Tlf.: 426–2573, anexo 104 / actividadesliterariascaslit@gmail.com).

Música

Auditorio del Colegio Santa Úrsula (av. Santo Toribio 150–San Isidro)

Música: Temporada de Abono 2013, presenta: “Recital de viola y violín” a cargo de Domenico Nordio y Francesca Dego (Italia); a las 7:30 PM. Entrada general: S/.140

Auditorio del Británico de San Borja (av. Javier Prado Este 2726–San Borja)

Música: “Industrial pop” a cargo de Bocanegra; a las 7:30 PM.

Ingreso libre.

Exposiciones

“NEVADOS” pintura de Alejandro Jaime, en Sala de Arte del Centro Cultural El Olivar (cll. La República 455, El Olivar–San Isidro) de lunes a sábado de 10 AM a 8 PM. Hasta el 28 de mayo.

Teatro

Teatro Nadal (cll. Mártir José Olaya 139, int. 112–Miraflores)

Unipersonal: “Conferencia magistral” de Antón Chéjov (Rusia), a cargo de Carlos Gassols; a las 8:00 PM. Entrada general: S/.45

Teatro de Lucía (cll. Bellavista 512–Miraflores)

Teatro: “De repente el verano pasado” de Tennessee Williams (Estados Unidos), a cargo de Lucía Irurita y Mirna Bracamonter, Dir.: Alberto Isola; a las 8:00 PM. Entrada general: S/.30–Estudiantes: S/.25

Conferencias

Nueva Acrópolis Breña (av. Bolivia 568–Breña)

Charla: “La física cuántica: el lado esotérico de la naturaleza”; a las 8:30 PM. Ingreso libre (previa inscripción: www.acropolisperu.org).

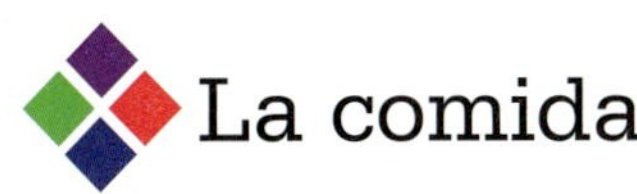

La comida

En el restaurante. Ahora Liliana y Manuel están en el restaurante El Jardín Limeño para **celebrar** el cumpleaños de Liliana. Hablan con el **camarero.**

CAMARERO: Buenas noches. ¿Qué desean los señores?

MANUEL: Liliana, ¿qué vas a comer?

LILIANA: Para mí, primero una **ensalada** y después **pollo** con **verduras.**

MANUEL: Yo, para empezar, ceviche de **pescado.** Y luego un **bistec** con **papas.**

CAMARERO: ¿Y para beber?

LILIANA: Para mí, **vino** tinto. Y también **agua** con gas, por favor.

CAMARERO: ¿Algo más?

MANUEL: Nada más, gracias.

ESPECIALIDADES DE LA CASA

ENTRADAS

Ensalada de la casa	S/.10
Ceviche de pescado	S/.15
Papa a la huancaína	S/.10
Causa a la limeña	S/.12

PLATOS PRINCIPALES

Chupe de camarones	S/.22
Ají de gallina	S/.18
Lomo saltado	S/.17
Bistec con papas	S/.17
Pollo con verduras	S/.16

POSTRES

Suspiro de limeña	S/.8
Alfajor	S/.8
Mazamorra morada	S/.6

BEBIDAS

Chicha morada	S/.4
Jugo de maracuyá	S/.4
Inca Kola	S/.3

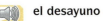

Más comidas y bebidas

el desayuno

el almuerzo

la comida/la cena

Notes for *la comida*
This chapter presents foods common to students' experience. The theme of food is revisited in *Capítulo 10.* Introduce the words *pescado, carne, pimientos, papas, plátanos.* Explain that *vegetales* and *verduras* are used for vegetables.
Explain that *entradas* in a menu is a false cognate, meaning appetizers, not entrées. Explain the sections of the menu: *entradas, platos principales, postres.* Write on the board *comidas* and *bebidas* and the related verbs (*comer, beber*). Introduce food vocabulary as you talk about some of the dishes (*queso, huevos, atún, aguacate, pollo, nuez, arroz, leche*) and some methods of cooking (*frito, cocido, estofado*).

Suggestion for *Más comidas y bebidas*
Use online images of the meals to review food vocabulary and ask questions such as: *¿Tomas café o té en el desayuno? ¿Comes cereal? ¿Qué comes a la hora del almuerzo? ¿Qué comida no te gusta? ¿Cuál es tu bebida/comida favorita? ¿Qué comida es rica en vitaminas?* Introduce *caliente* and *frío/a: La sopa está caliente. La cerveza está fría. Y el café, ¿está frío o está caliente?* Explain that in several countries of Latin America the word *comida* is also used to mean the late afternoon/ evening meal.

Suggestion for 3-8
Ask if students know which item in each group has the fewest calories.

Follow-up for 3-9
Ask additional questions: *¿A qué hora es el desayuno? ¿El almuerzo? ¿La cena? ¿Cuándo tomamos vino? ¿Leche? ¿Jugo de naranja? ¿Cerveza?...*

PRÁCTICA

3-8 

Para confirmar. **PREPARACIÓN.** Decide which item in each group contains the most calories.

1. la sopa de tomate, la hamburguesa, la sopa de pollo — la hamburguesa
2. el pollo frito, el pescado, la ensalada — el pollo frito
3. las verduras, las frutas, las papas fritas — las papas fritas
4. la cerveza, la leche desnatada (*skim*), el café — la cerveza
5. el helado de chocolate, el cereal, el arroz — el helado de chocolate

 **INTERCAMBIOS.** Compare with your partner to see if you agree which foods have the most calories. Then, ask each other about your preferences.

E1: *Frecuentemente como ensaladas y bebo cerveza. ¿Y tú?*
E2: *Yo frecuentemente como hamburguesas con papas fritas y bebo refrescos.*

3-9 

Las comidas. **PREPARACIÓN.** Discuss with your classmate what you usually have for breakfast, lunch, and dinner.

 *En el desayuno, como tostadas y bebo café. ¿Y tú?*

INTERCAMBIOS. Write a paragraph explaining what you and your classmate eat frequently for breakfast, lunch, and dinner.

 *Para desayunar yo frecuentemente como cereal y bebo café con leche. Mi compañero…*

Cultura

La comida rápida

Fast food is popular among young Hispanics, and American-style hamburger places may be found in Hispanic countries. They often adapt to local tastes, and it is not unusual to have hamburgers served with rice and black beans instead of fries. Beer and wine may be sold in addition to soft drinks.

Comunidades. Do you know of any fast food places in your community that are not American style? What types of food do they serve?

Bembos en Lima

MENÚ

SOPAS

Sopa de pollo	S/. 9
Sopa de tomate	S/. 7
Sopa de vegetales	S/. 7
Sopa de pescado	S/. 12

ENSALADAS

Ensalada de lechuga y tomate	S/. 8
Ensalada de pollo	S/. 14
Ensalada de atún	S/. 12

PLATOS PRINCIPALES

Bistec con papas y vegetales	S/. 20
Hamburguesa con papas fritas	S/. 16
Pescado con papas fritas	S/. 18
Arroz con vegetales	S/. 15

Suggestion for 3-10
Recycle *deber* + *infinitive* by asking questions: *¿Qué debes hacer después de la clase? ¿Qué deben hacer por la mañana?*, etc. Ask if anyone in class is a vegetarian (*vegetariano/a*). Discuss vegetarian diets.

Alternate for 3-10
Have pairs discuss the following situations: 1. *Tu amigo Pedro está a dieta porque está un poco gordo. ¿Qué debe comer en el desayuno, en el almuerzo y en la cena?* 2. *Tu padre tiene un nivel de colesterol muy alto. ¿Qué comidas no debe comer? (huevos, leche, bistec, queso, helado)*

3-10 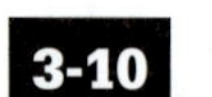 

¿Qué debe comer? Take turns asking each other which items from the menu are the best options for the following people.

1. Tu amiga Luisa desea subir de peso (*gain weight*).
2. Tu mamá es alérgica a los mariscos (*seafood*).
3. Tu amigo José necesita bajar de peso (*lose weight*).
4. El profesor Méndez está enfermo (*sick*) del estómago hoy.

3-11 

¿Qué te gusta más? Using the words below, discuss with your partner what you each prefer to drink **por la mañana, para el almuerzo, por la noche.** Then explain your partner's preferences to the class.

 E1: *¿Qué te gusta beber por la mañana, té o café?*

E2: *Me gusta más beber café.*

- agua mineral con gas
- un refresco
- agua mineral sin gas
- un té (helado)
- un batido (*shake*) de yogur y fruta
- un vaso (*glass*) de leche
- una copa de vino
- una cerveza
- un chocolate caliente
- jugo de naranja

3-12 

En el café. **PREPARACIÓN.** It is 9:00 on Saturday morning, and you and a friend are in a café in Lima. Look at the menu and decide what you want to order.

INTERCAMBIOS. Ask your friend what he/she would like to order, then explain your order to a waiter.

 E1: *El desayuno es muy bueno aquí. ¿Qué deseas comer?*

E2: _________ *¿Y tú?*

E1: *Yo* _________ *¿Y qué vas a tomar?*

E1: *Camarero, mi amigo/a… y yo…*

DESAYUNOS

café	S/.3
té	S/.3
café con leche	S/.5
jugo de naranja	S/.5
chocolate	S/.6
tostadas	S/.5
pan con mantequilla	S/.5
pan dulce	S/.6
cereal	S/.8
huevos fritos	S/.10

En directo

Expressions to order food:

Para mí, unas tostadas, café…
For me, some toast, coffee...

Me gustaría/Quisiera comer/tomar… *I would like to eat/drink …*

Yo quiero/deseo…
I want...

 Listen to a conversation with these expressions.

3-13 

Nuestro menú. You and your roommate want to have guests over for dinner tonight. Decide whom each of you is going to invite and what you are going to serve. Finally, compare your menu with that of another pair of classmates.

- Vamos a invitar a
  ____
  ____
  ____
- Vamos a servir
  ____
  ____
  ____

3-14 

Un viaje (*trip*). You and your partner are in Peru and are planning a day trip to Machu Picchu. Arrange to take some food and beverages with you.

1. Make a list of the food and beverages that you need to take.
2. Talk in detail about at least five activities that you are going to do.

3-15 

¿Qué hacen estos estudiantes?

PREPARACIÓN. Rafael and Miguel talk about their activities and weekend plans. Before you listen, write down three activities you normally do during the week, and three that you plan to do this weekend. Then, ask your partner if he/she is going to do the same things.

 **ESCUCHA.** Listen to Rafael and Miguel's conversation. Indicate (✓) the activities they say they will do during the weekend.

1. _____ estudiar para los exámenes
2. __✓__ comer en un restaurante
3. __✓__ descansar y tomar el sol
4. _____ trabajar en la librería
5. _____ celebrar el cumpleaños de Rafael

Suggestions for 3-12
Bring menus to class. Have pairs of students play the roles of diner and server in a restaurant.

Note for *En directo*
Before doing activity 3-12, *Intercambios*, first have students read the expressions in *En directo*. Then have them listen to the dialogue and encourage them to use the expressions in their own conversation.

Audioscript for *En directo*
CAMARERO: *Buenas noches. ¿Qué desean los señores?*
LUISA: *Para mí, unas tostadas y un café con leche.*
ESTEBAN: *Yo quiero una ensalada de pollo. También quisiera tomar agua bien fría.*
CAMARERO: *Muy bien. Regreso pronto con sus bebidas.*

Suggestion for 3-14
Review *ir + a + infinitive* to help students talk about their plans.

Audioscript for 3-15
RAFAEL: *Hola, Miguel, ¿cómo estás?*
MIGUEL: *Muy bien, Rafael. ¿Y tú?*
RAFAEL: *Bien, pero cansado. Tomo muchas clases este semestre y estudio mucho porque mi clase de economía es muy difícil. Además trabajo en una librería los martes y jueves por la tarde. Esta semana tenemos exámenes y voy a la biblioteca todos los días.*
MIGUEL: *¿Y qué vas a hacer este fin de semana?*
RAFAEL: *No sé. Me gustaría descansar.*
MIGUEL: *Perfecto. Mira, Rafael, mi familia tiene una casa en la playa. El viernes vamos un grupo de amigos, después del último examen. Vamos a descansar, nadar y tomar el sol. Por la noche vamos a comer en un restaurante. La comida es excelente, especialmente el pescado, y los camareros son muy amables. ¿Por qué no vienes con nosotros? Te va a gustar.*
RAFAEL: *¡Ah! ¡Qué bien! Me gusta mucho descansar en la playa. ¡Y también me gusta la buena comida!*
MIGUEL: *¡Estupendo! Nos vemos el viernes, entonces.*
RAFAEL: *Sí, y gracias, ¿eh?*

MOSAICO cultural Los hispanos y la vida social

Los hispanos utilizan su tiempo libre para hacer actividades en grupo. Los españoles van de tapas, los argentinos y uruguayos organizan grandes asados y los colombianos van a fiestas donde bailan toda la noche. Pero no participan solo en actividades típicas de sus países. La globalización y la influencia de la cultura norteamericana en el mundo hispano han cambiado (*have changed*) la vida social de muchos.

▲ **Salir de tapas en Madrid**

▲ **Asador de carne en Argentina**

Hoy en día, los centros comerciales son un lugar muy importante para las personas jóvenes. Es común ver a grupos de amigos pasear, ir al cine, tomar un café o ir a un restaurante en estos centros después de la escuela o del trabajo. La música también tiene una gran influencia estadounidense. Muchas veces los jóvenes cantan las canciones que suenan en la radio, y bailan al ritmo de la música electrónica en las discotecas.

Sin duda, Internet tiene un impacto muy fuerte en cómo los jóvenes utilizan su tiempo libre. Los jóvenes de 12 a 18 años pasan a veces de tres a cuatro horas al día en Internet. Las redes sociales (*social networks*) son una pasión entre los latinoamericanos. En Argentina, por ejemplo, hay 40 millones de personas; 20 millones utilizan Facebook. Y tú, ¿pasas muchas horas en Facebook? ¿Paseas con tus amigos en los centros comerciales?

▼ **Real Plaza en Lima**

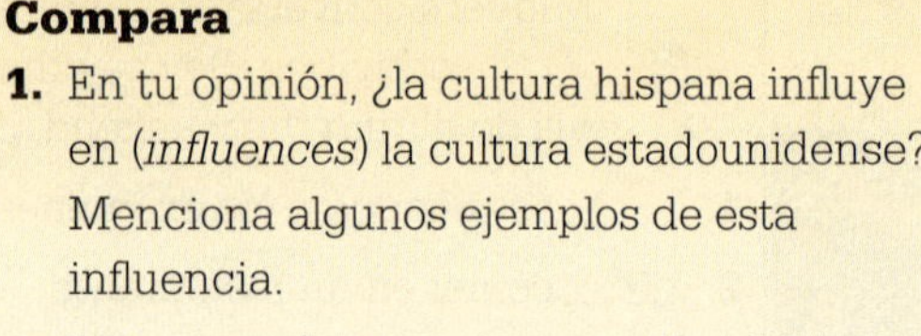

Compara

1. En tu opinión, ¿la cultura hispana influye en (*influences*) la cultura estadounidense? Menciona algunos ejemplos de esta influencia.
2. Menciona dos semejanzas y dos diferencias de cómo pasan el tiempo los jóvenes en Estados Unidos y en el mundo hispano.

Funciones y formas

1 Talking about daily activities

Unos nuevos amigos conversan sobre sus actividades

CAROLINA: Bueno, para conocernos mejor, ¿por qué no jugamos a Decir la verdad? José Manuel, la primera pregunta es para ti. ¿Qué **haces** cuando estás aburrido?

JOSÉ MANUEL: **Pongo** la tele para ver películas. Y tú, Tomás, ¿adónde **sales** cuando tienes tiempo? ¿Y con quién?

TOMÁS: Bueno, **salgo a** comer con mi novia Pilar. Pero cuando tengo exámenes, debo **salir para** la biblioteca. Carolina, cuando **oyes** música salsa, ¿qué **haces?**

CAROLINA: Eso es muy fácil. Siempre bailo cuando **oigo** música salsa. Mi pregunta es para ustedes dos. ¿Qué **hacen** ustedes en casa que no les gusta **hacer?**

TOMÁS: No me gusta, pero **hago la cama** porque me gusta el orden.

JOSÉ MANUEL: Mis hermanitos me **traen** su ropa y lavo su ropa sucia (*dirty*) todo el fin de semana. ¿Y tú, Carolina?

CAROLINA: ¿Yo? Pues, **pongo la mesa** todos los días, pero no me gusta. ¡Qué lata!

Piénsalo. Match each idea with its most logical ending.

1. c, e **Pongo** la tele...
2. d **Pongo la mesa...**
3. b, c **Oigo** música...
4. f Debo **salir para** la biblioteca...
5. a, d **Hago** la cama...
6. d Lavo la ropa que **traen** mis hermanos...

a. porque me gusta el orden.
b. cuando **salgo** con mis amigos.
c. para pasarlo bien (*have a good time*).
d. para ayudar (*help*) en casa.
e. porque me gusta ver películas.
f. porque necesito buscar unos libros.

Present tense of *hacer, poner, salir, traer,* and *oír*

- In the present tense, the verbs **hacer, poner, salir, traer,** and **oír** have irregular **yo** forms, but are regular in all other forms.

HACER (*to make, to do*)			
yo	**hago**	nosotros/as	**hacemos**
tú	**haces**	vosotros/as	**hacéis**
Ud., él, ella	**hace**	Uds., ellos/as	**hacen**

- **Hacer** means *to do* or *to make.* It is used frequently in questions to ask in a general sense what someone does, is doing, or likes to do.

¿Qué **haces** para sacar buenas notas? *What do you do to get good grades?*

Hago la tarea para mis clases todos los días. *I do the homework for my classes every day.*

Suggestion
Explain that the game "Decir la verdad" is played by young people who want to get to know each other by exploring areas of interest. Each player asks one question on any subject, to which the interviewee must respond truthfully. Explain *¡Qué lata!* and review *¡Qué asco! Hay ideas, cosas o actividades que no nos gustan porque son desagradables, feas. Por ejemplo, a mí no me gusta lavar los platos. Están sucios con comida. Cuando tengo que lavar platos, yo siempre digo: ¡Qué asco estos platos! Otras actividades son aburridas: por ejemplo, no me gusta estudiar los fines de semana. ¡Qué lata estudiar los fines de semana!* Check comprehension by asking students to provide the expression that fits each situation. *Ahora ustedes van a usar ¡Qué lata! o ¡Qué asco! 1. Tienes un examen el día de tu cumpleaños. 2. Tienes que escribir una composición en tu clase de inglés. 3. Tu sopa tiene un insecto. 4. El/La profesor/a de español anuncia un examen sorpresa.*

Suggestion for *Funciones y formas*
Use visuals and comprehensible input to review the verb forms. Project the image and talk about the activities of the people in the illustration, as well as your own activities. For example, *Mi esposo pone la mesa. Yo no pongo la mesa; yo cocino. Mi hijo pone las películas para nosotros. Y en tu casa, ¿quién pone las películas?*

- **Poner** means *to put.* When used with some electrical appliances, **poner** means *to turn on;* **poner la mesa** means *to set the table.*

PONER (*to put*)			
yo	**pongo**	nosotros/as	**ponemos**
tú	**pones**	vosotros/as	**ponéis**
Ud., él, ella	**pone**	Uds., ellos/as	**ponen**

Por la mañana **pongo** mis libros en mi mochila. — *In the morning I put my books in my backpack.*

Mi abuelo **pone** la televisión después de la cena. — *My grandfather turns on the TV after dinner.*

Yo **pongo la mesa** a la hora de la cena. — *I set the table at dinner time.*

- **Salir** can be used with several different prepositions. To express that you are leaving a place, use **salir de;** to express your destination, use **salir para;** to express with whom you go out or the person you date, use **salir con;** to express intention, use **salir a.**

SALIR (*to leave*)			
yo	**salgo**	nosotros/as	**salimos**
tú	**sales**	vosotros/as	**salís**
Ud., él, ella	**sale**	Uds., ellos/as	**salen**

Yo **salgo de** mi cuarto a las 7:15 de la mañana. — *I leave my room at 7:15 in the morning.*

Salgo para la cafetería. — *I am leaving for the cafeteria.*

Mi mejor amiga **sale con** Mauricio. — *My best friend is dating Mauricio.*

Ellos **salen a** bailar los sábados. — *They go out dancing on Saturdays.*

TRAER (*to bring*)			
yo	**traigo**	nosotros/as	**traemos**
tú	**traes**	vosotros/as	**traéis**
Ud., él, ella	**trae**	Uds., ellos/as	**traen**

Yo siempre **traigo** un postre a estas fiestas. — *I always bring a dessert to these parties.*

- **Oír** means *to hear* in the sense of *to perceive sounds.* Note the spelling and the accent marks in the infinitive, **nosotros/as,** and **vosotros/as** forms.

OÍR (*to hear*)			
yo	**oigo**	nosotros/as	**oímos**
tú	**oyes**	vosotros/as	**oís**
Ud., él, ella	**oye**	Uds., ellos/as	**oyen**

Yo **oigo** música. — *I hear music.*

—¿**Oyes** la alarma? — *—Do you hear the alarm?*

—No, no **oigo** nada. — *—No, I don't hear anything.*

¿COMPRENDES?

Complete the sentences to say what these people do on the weekend.

1. Los sábados, Marcos y Victoria __salen__ (salir) a la discoteca. __Oyen__ (Oír) buena música y bailan mucho.
2. Yo no __salgo__ (salir) mucho los sábados. __Traigo__ (Traer) mis libros a casa y __hago__ (hacer) tareas todo el fin de semana.
3. A veces (*Sometimes*) nosotros __hacemos__ (hacer) fiestas en mi apartamento. Mis amigos __traen__ (traer) comida y nosotros __oímos__ (oír) música o __ponemos__ (poner) una película.

MySpanishLab

Learn more using Amplifire Dynamic Study Modules, Grammar Tutorials, and Extra Practice activities.

PRÁCTICA

3-16

La perfección andante (*Perfection in motion*). **PREPARACIÓN.** Decide if you are organized, considerate, studious, and punctual. Check (✓) the statements that refer to things you do or don't do regularly.

1. _____ Yo **hago** mi cama temprano por la mañana.
2. _____ Cuando **oigo** que un amigo está triste, lo invito a salir.
3. _____ Siempre **pongo** música rock cuando estudio.
4. _____ Generalmente, **traigo** mi iPad a clase para tomar apuntes.
5. _____ En general, no **traigo** mi iPod porque necesito escuchar al profesor.
6. _____ Por las mañanas, **hago** ejercicio y luego **salgo** para la universidad.

INTERCAMBIOS. Take turns talking about the activities you both do that show off your best qualities.

MODELO E1: *Yo soy organizado/a. Siempre hago mi cama por la mañana. ¿Y tú?*

E2: *Pues, yo también…*

3-17

¿Usas bien tu tiempo libre? **PREPARACIÓN.** Check (✓) the version of each pair of activities that fits you.

1. _____ Pongo la mesa para cenar.
   _____ Como en cualquier lugar de la casa.
2. _____ Hago el desayuno.
   _____ Salgo a desayunar fuera de casa.
3. _____ Hago la cama todos los días.
   _____ Hago la cama una vez por semana.
4. _____ Traigo el periódico a casa.
   _____ Leo el periódico en Internet.
5. _____ Pongo la televisión para ver películas.
   _____ Salgo al cine para ver películas.

INTERCAMBIOS. Share your answers with a classmate and describe what else you do in that situation.

MODELO *Pongo la mesa para cenar y traigo las bebidas también.*

3-18

Para pasarlo bien. **PREPARACIÓN.** Indicate (✓) the activities that, in your opinion, your classmates probably do to have fun. Compare your answers with those of your partner.

1. ____ Alquilan películas los fines de semana.
2. ____ Oyen música y bailan mientras estudian para los exámenes.
3. ____ Frecuentemente hacen fiestas con sus amigos.
4. ____ Asisten a conciertos y exposiciones de arte.
5. ____ Hacen ejercicio en el gimnasio o en el parque.
6. ____ Escuchan programas en la Radio Pública Nacional (*NPR*).
7. ____ Salen a comer en grupo.
8. ____ Hablan por Skype constantemente.

INTERCAMBIOS. Using the activities you marked in *Preparación*, ask your instructor if he/she does these activities to have fun.

MODELO E1: *Para pasarlo bien, nosotros asistimos a conciertos de música rock. ¿Usted asiste a conciertos de música rock para pasarlo bien?*

INSTRUCTOR: *No, no asisto a conciertos de música rock. Para pasarlo bien escucho conciertos de música jazz en la radio pública.*

E1: *¡Qué interesante!*

Suggestion for 3-16, *Intercambios*
Have students work with different partners as often as possible.

Suggestion for 3-16, *Intercambios*
You may want to point out the spelling of *traigo*, as well as the accent mark and the use of *y* in some forms of the verb *oír*.

Alternate for 3-18
Students may ask partners if and when they do some of the activities listed. Then they switch partners and tell each other the information they gathered.

Suggestion for 3-18
Para pasarlo bien appeared earlier in the chapter. You may wish to reinforce its meaning: *Hay muchas maneras de pasarlo bien. Yo, por ejemplo, para pasarlo bien, escucho música, voy al cine con amigos, tengo/hago fiestas en mi casa y otras actividades similares. ¿Y tú, lees o bailas para pasarlo bien? ¿Qué haces para pasarlo bien los fines de semana/durante las vacaciones? ¿Qué hacen ustedes para pasarlo bien en casa?*

Suggestion for 3-18, *Intercambios*
Encourage students to be creative in their questions about your activities, and use humor to exaggerate similarities and/or differences between students' leisure activities and your own.

Note for *En directo*
Before doing activity 3-19, first have students read the expressions in *En directo.* Then have them listen to the dialogue and encourage them to use the expressions in their own conversation.

Audioscript for *En directo*
VERÓNICA: *Hay una exposición de las primeras obras de Picasso.*
CHELA: *¡Qué interesante! A mí me encanta Picasso.*
VERÓNICA: *Después ponen una película sobre la vida de Picasso. ¿Vamos esta tarde?*
CHELA: *Lo siento. Tengo mucho trabajo.*
VERÓNICA: *¡Qué lata!*

Suggestion for *Situación*
Encourage students to make their conversations sound natural and realistic. To help them compensate for possible lack of vocabulary, review greetings and communication strategies, such as asking for repetition, asking questions, and using synonyms/opposite (*Repite, por favor; No comprendo; Más despacio, por favor; ¿Qué significa?*).

Suggestion for *Situación*
You may want to assign partners and have pairs create mini-skits using the video-posting feature, *MediaShare,* online.

Suggestion for *Situación*
Additional situations are available in the Instructor's Resource folder online.

3-19 

Mi rutina. **PREPARACIÓN.** Talk about the activities you routinely do. Then ask your classmate about his/her activities.

tener clases (por la mañana/por la tarde)

E1: *Yo tengo clases por la mañana. ¿Y tú?*

E2: *Yo tengo clases por la mañana y por la tarde.*

1. salir de casa (temprano/tarde) por la mañana
2. poner (el iPod/la computadora) para escuchar música por la mañana
3. hacer la tarea (en casa/en la biblioteca)
4. salir a (comer/ver películas) con amigos por la noche
5. traer muchos (libros/amigos) a casa después de las clases

INTERCAMBIOS. Write a brief paragraph comparing your routine with that of your classmate. In your opinion, who has a more interesting routine, and why? Provide a few reasons.

En directo

To react to what someone has said:

¡Qué interesante! *How interesting!*

¡Qué divertido! *How fun!*

¡Qué aburrido! *How boring!*

¡Qué lata! *What a nuisance!*

 Listen to a conversation with these expressions.

Situación

PREPARACIÓN. Read the following situation with your partner. Then brainstorm the vocabulary, structures, and other information you will need for both roles in the conversation.

Role A. You have made a new friend, and you are asking him/her about the things he/she likes to do in his/her free time. Ask him/her:

a. if he/she goes out a lot and where;
b. if he/she does any sports;
c. if he/she goes to parties and what does he/she bring; and
d. if he/she likes to listen to music and what music he/she listens to.

Role B. You are new in town, and you have just met someone who is interested in knowing more about you. Answer the questions in as much detail as possible and ask some questions of your own.

	ROLE A	ROLE B
Vocabulario	Free-time activities Question words Movies, music, or other forms of entertainment	Free-time activities Question words Movies, music, or other forms of entertainment
Funciones y formas	Verbs *hacer, poner, traer, oír* Asking and answering questions Reacting to what one hears	Verbs *hacer, poner, traer, oír* Asking and answering questions Reacting to what one hears

INTERCAMBIOS. Using the information in *Preparación,* act out the conversation with your partner.

2 Expressing movement and plans

Elena, la chica en el centro de la foto, habla de sus amigos

Mis amigos y yo somos diferentes, pero estamos muy unidos. Para mi cumpleaños, nosotros **vamos a** un restaurante todos los años. Los sábados, yo **voy a** la casa de mi amiga Estela, y luego ella **va** conmigo **al** gimnasio para hacer ejercicio. A veces Rafael, Humberto y Rodrigo también **van al** gimnasio con nosotras. Mi amiga Teresa, no sale mucho porque prefiere estudiar. Yo siempre bromeo (*joke*) con ella: "Tere, ¿**vas a** la biblioteca a pasarlo bien?" Fernando es muy tranquilo y le fascina el arte. Con frecuencia él y Estela **van a** la librería a comprar libros.

Piénsalo. Read the following statements about Elena and her friends. Then indicate (✓) if the statement is **Probable** or **Improbable,** based on the information Elena provides.

	Probable	Improbable
1. Elena y sus amigos **van a** restaurantes juntos para celebrar su cumpleaños.	✓	
2. Fernando **va a** los conciertos de música rock.		✓
3. Estela afirma: "Frecuentemente, yo **voy a** la librería a comprar libros".		✓
4. Teresa comenta: "Fernando y yo **vamos al** museo de arte esta tarde".	✓	
5. Elena no **va a** las fiestas de cumpleaños de sus amigos.		✓

Present tense of *ir* and *ir a + infinitive*

- After the verb **ir,** use **a** to introduce a noun that refers to a place. When **a** is followed by the article **el,** the two words contract to form **al.**

IR (*to go*)			
yo	**voy**	nosotros/as	**vamos**
tú	**vas**	vosotros/as	**vais**
Ud., él, ella	**va**	Uds., ellos/as	**van**

Voy **a la** fiesta de María. — *I am going to Maria's party.*

Vamos **al** gimnasio. — *We are going to the gym.*

- Use **¿adónde?** when asking *where* (*to*)? with the verb **ir.**

¿**Adónde** vas ahora? — *Where are you going now?*

- To express a future action or condition, use the present tense of **ir a +** the infinitive form of the verb.

Mis amigos **van a nadar** después. — *My friends are going to swim later.*

¿**Vas a ir** a la fiesta? — *Are you going to go to the party?*

- The expression **vamos a +** *infinitive* can mean *let's.*

Vamos a cenar en mi casa. — *Let's have dinner at my house.*

Vamos a bailar después. — *Let's go dancing afterward.*

LENGUA

The following expressions denote future time:

después, más tarde, esta noche, mañana, pasado mañana, la próxima semana, el próximo mes/año.

Suggestion for *Funciones y formas*
You may project a calendar to practice *ir a + infinitive* to refer to future events. Say what you or another person will do tomorrow, on Saturday, and so on. Personalize by asking students about themselves. When asking questions, point out that in normal speech, *va a hacer* ("*vaacer*") sounds like one word. Explain that this linking of sounds is similar to what happens in English ("Whaddayagonnado?").

Suggestion for *ir a + infinitive*
Emphasize to students here and throughout the chapter that *ir + a + infinitive* is the most common way to express futurity in Spanish.

¿COMPRENDES?

Complete the conversation with the correct form of the verb **ir.**

LUIS: Hola, Lorena, ¿adónde (1) ___vas___?

LORENA: Hola, Luis. (2) ___Voy___ a la biblioteca porque debo estudiar para el examen de mañana.

LUIS: Ah, pues yo también (3) ___voy___ para allá. ¿Por qué no (4) ___vamos___ juntos (*together*)?

LORENA: Sí, claro. Pero ¿qué tal si primero (5) ___vamos___ a tomar un café a la cafetería?

MySpanishLab

Learn more using Amplifire Dynamic Study Modules, Grammar Tutorials, and Extra Practice activities.

PRÁCTICA

Note for 3-20
Las líneas de Nazca are a series of figures, including complex hummingbirds, spiders, monkeys, fish, sharks, llamas, and lizards, that were etched into the earth in the Nazca Desert in southern Peru by members of the Nazca culture between 200 B.C. and 700 A.D. The lines can be recognized as coherent figures only from the air, and the question of how and why they were created remains a mystery.

3-20 

¿Adónde van? **PREPARACIÓN.** Josh and Steve are North American students visiting Peru for their summer vacation. Match the descriptions with the places they plan to see.

a. Machu Picchu

b. las líneas de Nazca

c. la Universidad de San Marcos

d. una peña

1. ___c___ Steve estudia historia. Por eso, busca una institución prestigiosa. Está en Lima. Va a…
2. ___b___ Los dos amigos van a visitar uno de los lugares más misteriosos del planeta. Allí hay enormes figuras geométricas trazadas (*drawn*) en la tierra que son visibles solamente desde el aire. Ellos van a…
3. ___d___ Josh conoce (*meets*) a Susana en Perú. Ella lo invita a un evento folclórico donde las personas oyen poesía, música tradicional y comen y bailan también. Josh y Susana van a…
4. ___a___ Steve y Josh van a un lugar histórico imposible de ignorar. Es considerado el símbolo del imperio inca. Está cerca de Cuzco. Steve y Josh van a…

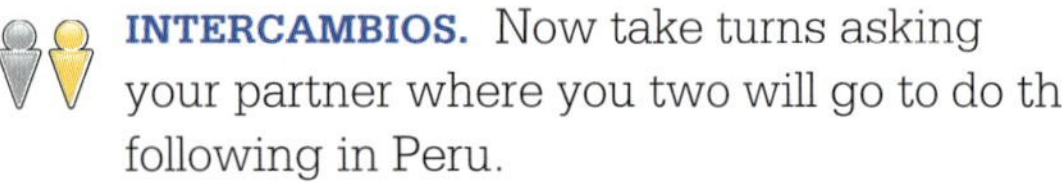

INTERCAMBIOS. Now take turns asking your partner where you two will go to do the following in Peru.

1. ¿Adónde vamos para hacer amigos, conversar y bailar ritmos peruanos? una peña
2. ¿Adónde vamos para tomar fotos de los alumnos y el edificio de una universidad muy antigua? la Universidad de San Marcos
3. ¿Adónde vamos para escalar unas montañas altas de mucha importancia histórica? Machu Picchu

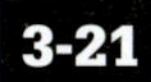

3-21

Los horarios. **PREPARACIÓN.** Your classmate's friends Bob, Juan, Alicia, and Sofía are busy today. Ask your classmate when each friend is leaving the place listed and where he/she is going afterward.

MODELO E1: *¿A qué hora sale del trabajo tu amigo Bob?*

E2: *(Sale) a las seis de la tarde.*

E1: *¿Adónde va después?*

E2: *Va al cine.*

NOMBRE	HORA	LUGAR	DESTINO
Juan	8:00 de la mañana	gimnasio	clase
Alicia	9:30 de la mañana	laboratorio de computadoras	biblioteca
Sofía	8:30 de la mañana	oficina	cafetería
Tú	...	...	...

INTERCAMBIOS. Exchange information with your partner about what each of you does at the times listed in *Preparación*.

MODELO E1: *¿Qué haces a las 8:00 de la mañana?*

E2: *Salgo de mi casa para la universidad.*

E1: *¿Adónde vas después?*

E2: *Voy al gimnasio. ¿Qué haces tú a las 8:00 de la mañana?*

3-22

¡Qué desorden! (*What a mess!*) **PREPARACIÓN.** Cristina had a party at her house, and now her friends are helping her clean up. Match each situation with its probable solution. Compare answers with a partner.

1. __b__ Hay muchos platos sucios.
2. __c__ Cristina ve mucha comida en la mesa.
3. __a__ La casa está desordenada.
4. __d__ Cristina y sus amigos necesitan energía para limpiar la casa.
5. __e__ Los amigos de Cristina están cansados después de la fiesta.

a. Dos chicos van a ordenar todo.

b. Algunos amigos van a recoger (*pick up*) los platos.

c. Una amiga va a poner la comida en el refrigerador.

d. Una amiga va a preparar café.

e. Van a descansar.

INTERCAMBIOS. Brainstorm how Cristina's parents are going to react when they find out about her party. Some reactions may include: *cancelar su tarjeta de crédito/su teléfono celular, prohibir fiestas/amigos, estar enojados...*

MODELO E1: *Sus padres no van a estar contentos.*

E2: *Sí, y van a conversar muy seriamente con Cristina.*

3-23

Mi agenda para la semana. Invite six classmates individually to do the following activities with you. They are going to accept or refuse your invitation.

MODELO estudiar en la biblioteca el lunes por la noche

E1: *¿Vamos a estudiar en la biblioteca el lunes por la noche?*

E2: *Lo siento, Miguel, el lunes por la noche voy a ir al cine con David. Pero ¿por qué no estudiamos el martes por la mañana?*

E1: *Buena idea. Vamos a estudiar el martes temprano por la mañana.*

1. ir a un concierto el viernes por la noche
2. mirar una buena película en casa el lunes a mediodía
3. tomar algo en un café el sábado por la mañana
4. estudiar para un examen difícil el miércoles por la tarde
5. bailar en la discoteca el jueves por la noche
6. hacer ejercicio el domingo a mediodía

Expansion for 3-21
You may wish to have groups of students create schedules and repeat the activity using the real-life information they learn from their partners.

Suggestion for 3-22, *Intercambios*
You may wish to ask students to support their responses. Model as follows: *Los padres van a conversar seriamente con Cristina sobre las fiestas secretas. Creen que no es correcto hacer fiestas secretas*, etc.

Suggestion for 3-23
Before students do the activity, model with a few of them how to extend, accept, and refuse invitations. Refer students to the *En directo* box on p. 105.

Expansion for 3-23
Have students prepare their schedules for the upcoming week and then take turns asking questions to find out what their classmates are going to do. Model as follows: *¿Qué vas a hacer la próxima semana? ¿Adónde vas a ir?*

Warm-up for 3-24
Use posters of people engaged in a variety of activities to solicit spontaneous descriptions of what each person is going to do. Then ask students to compare their activities with those shown in the drawings.

3-24 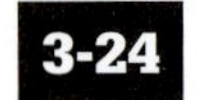 

Los planes de Maribel. **PREPARACIÓN.** Take turns telling each other what Maribel is going to do at the times indicated.

INTERCAMBIOS. Chat with your classmate about what you are going to do at those times on Friday.

Situación  

Suggestion for *Situación*
You may want to assign partners and have pairs create mini-skits using the video-posting feature, *MediaShare*, online.

PREPARACIÓN. Read the following situation with your partner. Then brainstorm the vocabulary, structures, and other information you will need for both roles in the conversation.

Role A. You call to invite a friend to a café tonight where a mutual friend is going to sing. After your friend responds, ask about his/her plans for later in the evening:

a. where he/she is going;
b. with whom; and
c. what time, etc.

Role B. A friend calls to invite you to a café tonight where a mutual friend is going to sing. Inquire about the event to find out:

a. what time and where it will be; and
b. if other friends are going to go.

Accept the invitation and mention your plans for later in the evening.

	ROLE A	ROLE B
Vocabulario	Free-time activities	Free-time activities
Funciones y formas	Making plans Verb *ir* *ir* + *a* + *infinitive* Extending an invitation Asking the time Reacting to what one hears	Verb *ir* *ir* + *a* + *infinitive* Accepting an invitation Telling time Asking questions

INTERCAMBIOS. Using the information in *Preparación*, act out the conversation with your partner.

3 Talking about quantity

Adriana va a comprar un billete de lotería. Si gana (*If she wins*) dos millones de dólares, va a comprar un boleto de avión por **mil setecientos dólares** para visitar a su familia en Perú. Además va a comprar un carro deportivo por **cuarenta y dos mil cuatrocientos dólares** y muchas cosas más. Y para sus padres, **mil dólares.** Adriana puede imaginar a su padre contando (*counting*) el dinero... **quinientos, seiscientos, setecientos, ochocientos, novecientos...** y a su madre pensando en (*thinking about*) la fiesta que va a preparar.

Piénsalo. Select the numbers that correspond to the cost of the other items Adriana is hoping to buy.

1. __b__ una casa por setecientos cincuenta mil dólares
2. __d__ una computadora portátil por dos mil ciento diez dólares
3. __a__ un teléfono celular por quinientos dólares
4. __c__ tres televisores plasma por cinco mil cuatrocientos dólares

a. 500
b. 750.000
c. 5.400
d. 2.110

Numbers 100 to 2,000,000

- You have already learned the numbers up to 99. In this section you will learn the numbers to talk about larger quantities.

100	**cien/ciento**	1.000	**mil**
200	**doscientos/as**	1.100	**mil cien**
300	**trescientos/as**	2.000	**dos mil**
400	**cuatrocientos/as**	10.000	**diez mil**
500	**quinientos/as**	100.000	**cien mil**
600	**seiscientos/as**	150.000	**ciento cincuenta mil**
700	**setecientos/as**	500.000	**quinientos mil**
800	**ochocientos/as**	1.000.000	**un millón (de)**
900	**novecientos/as**	2.000.000	**dos millones (de)**

- Use **cien** to say 100 when used alone or when followed by a noun. Use **ciento** for numbers from 101 to 199.

100	**cien**
100 chicos	**cien** chicos
120 profesoras	**ciento** veinte profesoras
177 libros	**ciento** setenta y siete libros

- Multiples of 100 agree in gender with the noun they modify.

200 periódicos	**doscientos** periódicos
1.400 revistas	**mil cuatrocientas** revistas

Suggestion for *Funciones y formas*
Use the following activity to check comprehension of numbers. Project the numbers and then say one number aloud from each row. Students identify the number by holding up 1, 2, 3, or 4 fingers to show if the number they hear is the first, second, third, or fourth in the group. As a follow-up, say numbers again in random order and ask students to write each one.

1	2	3	4
114	360	850	524
213	330	490	919
818	625	723	513
667	777	984	534
1.310	1.420	3.640	6.860
10.467	50.312	100.000	2.000.000
7.1492	1776	1890	2001

Suggestion
When reviewing the numbers, point out the exceptions: *quinientos, setecientos, novecientos*. Also point out that *y* is not used after *cien, ciento, mil*, or *millón*, only between tens and units (*ciento cuarenta y cinco*).

- Use **mil** for *one thousand.* Multiples of 1,000 are also **mil.**

1.000	**mil** alumnos, **mil** alumnas
12.000	**doce mil** residentes

- Use **un millón** to say *one million.* Use **un millón de** when a noun follows.

1.000.000	**un millón**
1.000.000 de personas	**un millón de personas**
12.000.000 de dólares	**doce millones de dólares**

- In many Spanish-speaking countries, a period is used to separate thousands, and a comma is used to separate decimals.

$1.000	$19,50

- Numbers higher than one thousand, such as dates or street addresses, are not stated in pairs as they often are in English.

1942 (*nineteen forty-two*)	**mil novecientos cuarenta y dos**

e **¿COMPRENDES?**

Complete each sentence with the appropriate number.

1. Aproximadamente __d__ de personas hablan español.
2. El dólar tiene __a__ centavos.
3. El profesor Hiram Bingham de Yale llega a Machu Picchu por primera vez (*for the first time*) en el año __b__ .
4. La Constitución de Estados Unidos tiene más de __e__ años.
5. El próximo milenio va a empezar en el año __c__ .

a. cien
b. mil novecientos once
c. tres mil uno
d. trescientos cincuenta millones
e. doscientos veinte

MySpanishLab
Learn more using Amplifire Dynamic Study Modules, Grammar Tutorials, and Extra Practice activities.

Expansion for 3-25
Pass out a card to each student with a number ranging from 100 to 2,000,000. After the students have written out their numbers on separate pieces of paper, collect their original cards and place them in a bag. Have a student select a card and read the number aloud. The student whose number was called must show written proof of the number. Check that it is correct. If it's not written correctly, then have a different student call a new number and continue until the number called has been written out correctly by the student. Time permitting, have the student write the number out on the board just as it appears on his/her paper, and ask the class if it's written correctly.

PRÁCTICA

Cantidades. Alternate asking each other the following questions. Then report the most surprising amounts to the class.

1. ¿Cuántos mensajes de texto envías (*send*) y recibes al día?
2. ¿Cuánto dinero vas a ganar después de la universidad?
3. ¿Qué cantidad máxima vas a gastar por un coche usado?
4. ¿Qué cantidad máxima vas a pagar para tu boda?
5. ¿Cuánto vas a gastar por tu carrera universitaria?
6. ¿Cuántos estudiantes van a graduarse de tu universidad este año?
7. ¿Cuánto dinero vas a gastar en diversiones este semestre?
8. ¿Cuántas personas viven en la residencia estudiantil más grande de tu universidad?

3-26 

Unas vacaciones. PREPARACIÓN. Your classmate has chosen one of the destinations in the ad below for an upcoming vacation. To find out where he/she is going, ask the following questions and react to what you hear. Then switch roles.

1. ¿Adónde vas?
2. ¿Qué lugares vas a ver?
3. ¿Cuántos días vas a estar allí?
4. ¿Cuánto cuesta la excursión?
5. ¿Cuánto dinero vas a necesitar?

INTERCAMBIOS. Based on your classmate's answers, write an e-mail to your instructor informing him/her of your classmate's plans.

En directo

To call attention to an unusual fact:

¡Fíjate qué noticia! *How about that!*

¡Imagínate! *Imagine that!*

To react to good news:

¡Qué suerte! *How lucky!*

¡Qué maravilla! *How wonderful!*

¡Qué bien! *How nice!*

To convince someone:

¡Venga/Anda, anímate! *Come on, cheer up!*

Lo vamos a pasar muy bien. *We are going to have a good time.*

 Listen to a conversation with these expressions.

AGENCIA MUNDIAL

A SU SERVICIO SIEMPRE *20 años de experiencia, responsabilidad y profesionalidad.*

TODOS LOS PRECIOS INCLUYEN PASAJES AÉREOS Y SERVICIOS TERRESTRES POR PERSONA

PERÚ Y BOLIVIA

LIMA, AREQUIPA, CUZCO, MACHU PICCHU, PUNO, LA PAZ, 15 días. La Ruta del Inca. Hoteles de 3 y 4 estrellas. Desayuno incluido. **$2.760**

PERÚ

LIMA, CUZCO, MACHU PICCHU, NAZCA, 12 días. Visite fortalezas incas. Vea las misteriosas líneas de Nazca desde el aire. Hoteles de primera. Desayuno y cena incluidos. **$3.150**

LIMA, NAZCA, AREQUIPA, LAGO TITICACA, 10 días. Admire la arquitectura colonial de Lima y Arequipa. Vea las líneas de Nazca desde el aire. Navegue en el lago más alto del mundo. Hoteles de primera. **$2.620**

ARGENTINA

BUENOS AIRES, BARILOCHE, MENDOZA, 12 días. Disfrute de una gran metrópoli. Esquíe en uno de los lugares más bellos del mundo. Hoteles de 4 y 5 estrellas. Desayuno y cena. **$3.590**

CHILE Y ARGENTINA

SANTIAGO, PUERTO MONTT, BARILOCHE, BUENOS AIRES, 12 días. Excursión a Viña del Mar y Valparaíso. Cruce de los Andes en minibús y barco. Hoteles de 3 y 4 estrellas. **$4.075**

CARIBE

JAMAICA, 7 días. Happy Inn, todo incluido. Exclusivo para parejas. **$2.480**

PUERTO RICO

SAN JUAN, 5 días. Hotel de 5 estrellas. Excursión a Ponce. Visita con guía al Viejo San Juan. Desayuno incluido. **$1.995**

MÉXICO

MÉXICO, TAXCO, ACAPULCO, 7 días. Hoteles de 3 y 4 estrellas. Excursión a Teotihuacán. Desayuno bufet incluido. **$1.800**

CANCÚN, 5 días. Hotel de 4 estrellas. Excursión a Cozumel. Visita a ruinas mayas. Las mejores playas. **$1.510**

Solicite los programas detallados con variantes de hoteles e itinerarios a su agente de viajes.

Tel. 312-785-4455 Fax: 312-785-4456

Suggestion for 3-26
Before doing activity 3-26, first have students read the expressions in *En directo*. Then have them listen to the dialogue and encourage them to use the expressions in their own conversation.

Audioscript for *En directo*
FRANCISCO: *¡La Academia de Idiomas aceptó mi propuesta! ¡Voy a estudiar en Perú el semestre que viene!*
CELESTE: *¡Fíjate qué noticia! ¡Qué bien!*
FRANCISCO: *¡Imagínate! ¿Por qué no presentas una propuesta tú también y así vamos juntos?*
CELESTE: *Pues, no sé…*
FRANCISCO: *¡Anda, anímate! Lo vamos a pasar muy bien.*
CELESTE: *Está bien.*

Note for *Situación*
Now that students have been doing the *Situación* activities for several chapters, you may wish to give them guidance on how to maximize the communicative potential of this activity. Pairs of students should work together to read the instructions for both roles, brainstorm how they will approach the task, and fill out the advance organizer table with the words, phrases, and structures they will need. They should then practice the role-plays without writing anything else down, since the goal is for them to speak, not read from a script. As an oral assessment, ask several pairs to perform for the class. (Other pairs may perform for a different role-play in the chapter.) If time permits, you may ask them to switch roles and perform the role-plays again for additional communicative practice. Direct students to pay attention to their use of register (*usted* or *tú*), vocabulary, and negotiation strategies (to clarify meaning, to agree, disagree, refuse politely, etc.) in their role-plays.

Situación

PREPARACIÓN. Read the following situation with your partner. Then brainstorm the vocabulary, structures, and other information you will need for both roles in the conversation.

Role A. You have been working hard, and you would like to splurge on a weekend trip to do some special (but expensive) activities, like rent a car, go to a professional sports event or rock concert, eat in good restaurants, and shop (**ir de compras**). Call and invite your friend to go. Explain your plan and be prepared to answer questions about the cost of this weekend adventure.

Role B. Your friend calls to invite you on a weekend trip. It sounds like a lot of fun, but also very expensive.

Accept or refuse your friend's invitation and ask questions to get an idea of the cost. Decide whether you can afford it, and either accept or decline the invitation. Thank your friend for the invitation.

	ROLE A	ROLE B
Vocabulario	Food Free-time activities Numbers	Food Free-time activities Numbers
Funciones y formas	Answering questions Extending an invitation Reacting to what one hears	Accepting and refusing invitations Asking questions Reacting to what one hears

INTERCAMBIOS. Using the information in *Preparación*, act out the conversation with your partner.

4 Stating what you know

ALFREDO: Me gustan mucho los músicos y ella **sabe** cantar muy bien.

ELENA: Sí, es una cantante fabulosa.

MARIO: Luisa, **conoces** a Liliana, ¿no?

LUISA: Sí, las dos estamos en la clase de arte de la profesora Ruiz.

Piénsalo. Indicate (✓) in the appropriate box whether each sentence refers to knowing a fact, knowing how to do something, knowing a person, or being familiar with a place, an event, or a thing.

	knowing a fact	knowing how to do something	knowing a person	being familiar with a place, event, etc.
1. ¿**Conoces** la música afroperuana?				✓
2. Me gusta mucho la música, pero no **sé** bailar.		✓		
3. ¿**Sabes** los nombres de esos grupos musicales?	✓			
4. ¿**Conoces** a Alfredo Roncal? Toca la guitarra.			✓	
5. ¿**Sabes** si hay un club de música hispana en la ciudad?	✓			

Saber and *conocer*

- Both **saber** and **conocer** mean *to know,* but they are not used interchangeably.

	SABER	CONOCER
yo	**sé**	**conozco**
tú	**sabes**	**conoces**
Ud., él, ella	**sabe**	**conoce**
nosotros/as	**sabemos**	**conocemos**
vosotros/as	**sabéis**	**conocéis**
Uds., ellos/as	**saben**	**conocen**

- Use **saber** to express knowledge of facts or pieces of information.

  Él **sabe** dónde está el club. *He knows where the club is.*

- Use **saber** + *infinitive* to express knowing how to do something.

  Yo **sé** tocar la guitarra. *I know how to play the guitar.*

- Use **conocer** to express familiarity with someone or something. **Conocer** also means *to meet* someone for the first time. Remember to use the personal **a** when referring to people.

  Conozco a los músicos. *I know the musicians.*

  Conozco bien ese club. *I am very familiar with that club.*

  Ella va a **conocer a** Luis. *She is going to meet (be introduced to) Luis.*

LENGUA

Sé, the **yo** form of the verb **saber,** has a written accent to distinguish it from the pronoun **se.**

Yo **sé** que su hermano **se** llama José.

¿COMPRENDES?

Complete each sentence with the correct form of **saber** or **conocer.**

1. Yo no __sé__ tocar la guitarra, ¿y tú?
2. Yo no __conozco__ personalmente al presidente de Estados Unidos.
3. Andrés, ¿__conoces__ París?
4. Emilio y Gustavo __saben__ mucho sobre la historia.
5. Nosotros __conocemos__ a muchas personas en esta ciudad.
6. La profesora __sabe__ hablar español muy bien.

MySpanishLab

Learn more using Amplifire Dynamic Study Modules, Grammar Tutorials, and Extra Practice activities.

Suggestion for *Funciones y formas*

Use visuals of well-known people to practice *saber* and *conocer*. For example, use a picture of Sofía Vergara: *Yo sé quién es esta persona. Es Sofía Vergara. Sé que es una actriz famosa y que es de Colombia. Sé que vive en Hollywood. Sé quién es, pero no la conozco.*

Point out that *saber* can be followed by *que*, but *conocer* cannot.

Remind students that both verbs are irregular in the *yo* form and that *conozco* adds a *z* because *c* is pronounced *k* before *o*.

PRÁCTICA

3-27  

Un encuentro entre dos estudiantes. Raúl just arrived on campus, and he asks Sergio some questions. Select the correct words to complete their conversation. Then practice the conversation with a partner to compare your answers and take turns telling each other what you know about your own university. Who knows more?

RAÚL:	Soy un nuevo estudiante y no (1) __a__ dónde está la biblioteca.	**a.** sé	**b.** conozco
SERGIO:	Es muy fácil. Tú (2) __a__ dónde está la cafetería, ¿no? Pues, está al lado.	**a.** sabes	**b.** conoces
RAÚL:	Gracias. ¿Y (3) __a__ si hay un club de español?	**a.** sabes	**b.** conoces
SERGIO:	Sí, claro, y (4) __a__ que esta noche tiene una reunión.	**a.** sé	**b.** conozco
RAÚL:	Magnífico. Solo (5) __b__ a dos o tres personas en la universidad.	**a.** sé	**b.** conozco
SERGIO:	Pues allí vas a (6) __b__ a muchos estudiantes.	**a.** saber	**b.** conocer

Note for 3-28
Students should have no difficulty in understanding cognates (e.g., *representante, gobernador*). Other words may need some explanation, for example, *decano* (dean).

3-28 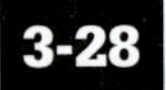 

¿Sabes quién es...? Ask your classmate if he/she knows who is being referred to and say what you know about the person. Take turns asking questions.

MODELO la actriz principal de *Los juegos del hambre*

E1: *¿Sabes quién es la actriz principal de* Los juegos del hambre?

E2: *Sí, sé quién es; es Jennifer Lawrence.*

E1: *¿Conoces a Jennifer Lawrence en persona?*

E2: *No, no conozco a Jennifer Lawrence pero sé que es muy guapa.*

1. el/la representante de la Cámara de Representantes (*Congress*) de tu distrito
2. el/la decano/a de la Facultad de Humanidades/ Ciencias
3. tu profesor/a de español
4. el escritor más famoso de Perú
5. el gobernador de tu estado
6. el vicepresidente de Estados Unidos

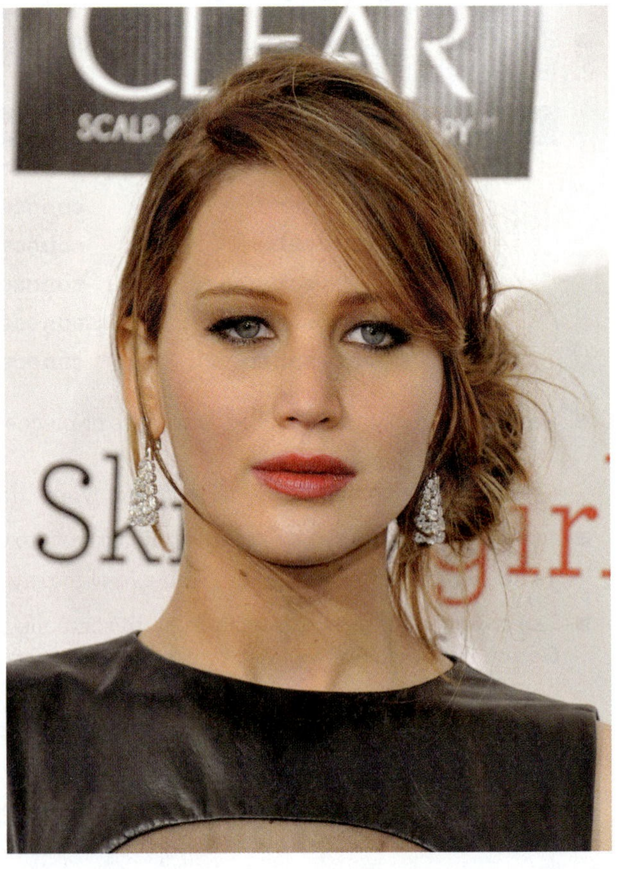

3-29 

Adivina, adivinador. In small groups, take turns reading the descriptions and guessing who is being described. Then, create your own description and ask another group to guess.

MODELO E1: *Es una chica muy pobre que va a un baile. Allí conoce a un príncipe, pero a las 12:00 de la noche ella debe volver a su casa.*

E2: *Sé quién es. Es Cenicienta* (Cinderella).

1. Es un gorila gigante con sentimientos (*feelings*) humanos. En una película aparece en el edificio Empire State de Nueva York. King Kong
2. Es una cantante muy famosa. Tiene el pelo largo y rubio. Canta, baila, escribe canciones y también participa en organizaciones benéficas. Es de Colombia. Shakira
3. Es una película de ciencia ficción. Los personajes son altos y azules y viven en los árboles. Es impresionante ver la película en tres dimensiones. Avatar
4. Es...

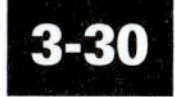 

¿Qué sabes hacer? Ask your classmate if he/she knows how to do the following things. If your classmate says yes, ask more questions to get additional information.

MODELO preparar platos peruanos

E1: *¿Sabes preparar platos peruanos?*

E2: *No, no sé preparar platos peruanos. ¿Y tú?*

1. tocar un instrumento musical
2. cantar karaoke
3. bailar salsa y merengue
4. hablar otras lenguas
5. cantar en español
6. ...

3-31 

Bingo. To win this game, you have to fill in three boxes (horizontal, vertical, or diagonal) with the names of classmates who answer the questions correctly.

¿Quién sabe dónde está la ciudad de Cuzco? ______	¿Quién sabe cuál es la capital de Perú? ______	¿Quién sabe qué es Machu Picchu? ______
¿Quién sabe quién es el presidente de Bolivia? ______	¿Quién sabe cuál es la unidad monetaria de Perú? ______	¿Quién sabe el nombre de un lago importante que está entre Perú y Bolivia? ______
¿Quién conoce unos platos típicos de la cocina (*cuisine*) peruana? ______	¿Quién conoce algún país hispanoamericano? ______	¿Quién sabe cómo se llama la cadena de montañas de Perú? ______

Note for 3-29
Gigante is not glossed since it is a near cognate. Context will help students guess meaning.

Expansion for 3-29
Use gestures as needed to clarify the following:

- *Es un animal de los dibujos animados. Es gris, corre muy rápido y tiene orejas muy largas* (Bugs Bunny).
- *Es una chica muy bonita y buena que vive en el bosque con siete enanitos. Tiene una madrastra muy mala* (*Blancanieves*).

Suggestion for 3-29
Use visuals and personalized questions to elicit the use of *saber + infinitive: ¿Sabe bailar esta persona? Y tú, ¿sabes bailar? ¿Sabes bailar muy bien?* Ask some students to name one thing they can do.

Suggestion for 3-31
Students may consult the *Enfoque cultural* reading or read about these countries on the Internet prior to doing this activity so they will be able to answer the questions. Options for doing this activity: 1. Students close their books, and the instructor asks the questions, calling on the first student to raise his/her hand. 2. In groups of 4 or 5, students spend 5 minutes preparing answers to the questions. Then they close their books and the game proceeds as above, but groups take turns giving the first response to the question.

Answers for 3-31
Top row: *en Perú; Lima; las ruinas de los incas*
Middle row: *Evo Morales; Nuevo Sol; el lago Titicaca*
Bottom row: Possible answers: *ceviche de pescado, yuca frita, adobo de chancho, chupe de camarones;* Answers may vary; *los Andes*

Suggestion for 3-32
Completing this activity in class allows students to discuss their answers while you observe. Encourage students to explain to their partner why they selected *saber* or *conocer*.

Note for 3-32
This activity engages students in active learning. Rather than memorize a set of rules, they articulate to themselves and to their partners how a rule applies to a particular statement. This metalinguistic approach—thinking and talking about the language—pushes students to take their understanding of a grammatical concept to a deeper level. Metalinguistic talk, termed "languaging" by researchers (e.g., Swain, 2006) in second language acquisition, has been shown to contribute to language learning.

3-32 

***Saber* y *conocer*.** Complete the conversation with the correct forms of **saber** and **conocer.** Then practice the conversation with your partner to review your answers. Be sure to explain why you selected **saber** or **conocer** in each case.

PACO: ¿(1) __Conoces__ a esa chica?
AUGUSTO: Sí, yo (2) __conozco__ a todas las chicas aquí.
PACO: Entonces, ¿(3) __sabes__ dónde vive?
AUGUSTO: No, no (4) __sé__ dónde vive.
PACO: ¿(5) __Sabes__ cómo se llama?
AUGUSTO: Lo siento, pero no (6) __sé__.
PACO: Pero ¿cómo dices que (7) __conoces__ a la chica? Tú no (8) __sabes__ dónde vive y además (*in addition*), no (9) __sabes__ su nombre.

Situación

PREPARACIÓN. Read the following situation with your partner. Then prepare examples of the vocabulary, structures, and other information you will need to present your role in the conversation.

Role A. You are looking for a new roommate for your apartment. Your partner knows a student from Peru who is looking for a place to live. Ask your partner:

a. the Peruvian student's name;
b. where in Peru he/she is from; and
c. if your partner knows the Peruvian student well.

Also find out if the Peruvian student knows how to cook Peruvian dishes and how to play soccer (**fútbol**).

Role A. Your partner is looking for a new roommate for his/her apartment. Mention that you know a student from Peru who is looking for a place to live. Answer your partner's questions about that person.

	ROLE A	ROLE B
Vocabulario	Food Free-time activities Question words Peruvian food	Food Free-time activities Peruvian food
Funciones y formas	Asking questions Reacting to what one hears Talking about what or who you know (*saber* vs. *conocer*)	Answering questions Reacting to what one hears Talking about what or who you know (*saber* vs. *conocer*)

INTERCAMBIOS. Using the information in *Preparación*, act out the conversation with your partner.

5 Expressing intention, means, movement, and duration

CARLOS: Papá, necesito tu auto **por** una semana. ¿Está bien?

PADRE: ¿**Por** una semana? ¿**Por** qué?

CARLOS: **Porque** mis amigos y yo vamos a ir la playa **para** las vacaciones de primavera.

PADRE: ¡Ni lo pienses!

Piénsalo. Indicate whether each statement is true (**Cierto**) or false (**Falso**) according to the conversation. If the statement is false, supply the correct information.

1. Cierto Carlos necesita el auto de su padre **por** una semana.
2. Cierto El padre pregunta **por qué** Carlos desea el auto.
3. Cierto Carlos desea ir a la playa **para** las vacaciones de primavera.
4. Falso Los amigos de Carlos necesitan el auto **para** trabajar.
5. Falso El padre está alegre **porque** Carlos le pide su auto.

Some uses of *por* and *para*

- **Por** and **para** have different meanings in Spanish, though sometimes they are both translated into English as *for.* The uses presented here include some you have already seen, as well as some new ones.
- **Para** expresses *for* when you mean *intended for* or *to be used for.* It can refer to a person, an event, or a purpose.

Necesito un diccionario **para** la clase.	*I need a dictionary for the class.*
Este diccionario es **para** David.	*This dictionary is for David.*

- **Para +** *infinitive* means *in order to.*

Uso el autobús **para** ir a la universidad.	*I use the bus (in order) to go to the university.*
El restaurante hace publicidad **para** atraer clientes.	*The restaurant does advertising (in order) to attract customers.*

Note
Since the uses of *por* and *para* are not easy for students to master, these prepositions are presented more than once in *Mosaicos.* This first presentation gives only those uses necessary for communication about the theme of the chapter. *Capítulo 11* has a complete presentation of *por* and *para,* including uses that students are familiar with.

Suggestion for *Funciones y formas*
Use visuals to contrast the use of *por* and *para* to express movement: *Josefina está en su casa ahora. Ella va para la playa* (show visual of a beach) *después. Ella camina con su amiga por la playa* (show online image of young women walking on the beach).

Suggestion for 3-33
Have students explain their answers to a partner as a way to develop a metalinguistic awareness of language and meaning.

¿COMPRENDES?

Complete the conversation with **por** or **para.**

—Hola Ana, ¿(1) _para_ dónde vas?

—Hola Juan, voy a montar en bicicleta (2) _por_ el parque.

—Tu bicicleta es muy bonita, ¿(3) _por_ cuánto la vendes? Es que debo comprar una bicicleta (4) _para_ ir a mi trabajo.

—Si quieres, puedes usar esta bicicleta (5) _por_ tres días.

MySpanishLab
Learn more using Amplifire Dynamic Study Modules, Grammar Tutorials, and Extra Practice activities.

- **Por** appears in expressions such as **por favor, por teléfono,** and **por la mañana/tarde/noche.** Other expressions with **por** that you will find useful include the following:

por ciento	*percent*	**por fin**	*finally, at last*
por ejemplo	*for example*	**por lo menos**	*at least*
por eso	*that is why*	**por supuesto**	*of course*

- **Por** and **para** can also be used to express movement in space and time.

Para indicates movement toward a destination.

Caminan **para** la playa.	*They walk toward the beach.*
Vamos **para** el túnel.	*We are going toward the tunnel.*

- **Por** indicates movement through or by a place.

Caminan **por** la playa.	*They walk along the beach.*
Vamos **por** el túnel.	*We are going through the tunnel.*

- You may also use **por** to indicate length of time or duration of an action. Many Spanish speakers omit **por** in this case, or they use **durante.**

Necesito el auto **por** tres días.	*I need the car for three days*

PRÁCTICA

3-33  

¿Por o para? With a partner, choose the use of **por** and **para** in the following text with its appropriate meaning from the list. Then ask your partner what he/she does on Friday nights and what he/she does to celebrate a birthday.

Mis amigos y yo siempre estamos ocupados los fines de semana. Los viernes **por**[1] la noche, siempre vamos a un cine cerca de nuestro barrio. Cuando vamos **para**[2] el cine, caminamos **por**[3] el parque. Después del cine, a veces hacemos fiestas en casa. Si es una fiesta de cumpleaños, compro un regalo especial **para**[4] mi amigo. **Para**[5] celebrar, también invito a todos nuestros amigos.

1. por _c_	**a.** intended for (person)
2. para _d_	**b.** in order to
3. por _e_	**c.** length of time
4. para _a_	**d.** movement toward a destination
5. Para _b_	**e.** movement through or by a place

3-34 

¿Para dónde van? Take turns guessing where these people are going. Then find out where your classmate is going after class, and why.

Jorge tiene su guitarra.
Va para la fiesta.

1. Es la una de la tarde y Pedro desea comer.
2. Sebastián lleva una mochila con sus libros de química.
3. Lola y Pepe van a consultar unos libros porque tienen un examen.
4. Gregorio va a comprar un libro para su clase de español.
5. Ana María va a ver una película de su actor favorito.
6. Amanda y Clara están muy elegantes y contentas.

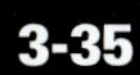 

Caminante. Your classmate likes to walk. Ask him/her the following questions. Then switch roles.

1. ¿Te gusta caminar con amigos o solo/a? ¿Por qué?
2. ¿Por dónde caminas cuando quieres estar solo/a?
3. ¿Te gusta caminar por la playa o por un parque?
4. ¿Caminas por la mañana o por la tarde?
5. Cuando sales a caminar, ¿por cuánto tiempo caminas?

¿Para quiénes son los regalos (*gifts*)? You are very generous and have bought the following gifts. Your partner asks for whom they are.

la revista

E1: *¿Para quién es la revista?*

E2: *Es para mi hermana.*

1. tres libros de español
2. dos billetes de avión
3. el teléfono celular
4. el iPad
5. la computadora portátil
6. el buen vino chileno

Suggestions for 3-36
You may wish to provide words for some family members, so students can use them for gift recipients: *hermano/a, primo/a, tío/a,* etc. This will serve as a warm-up for the presentation of kinship terms in *Capítulo 4.* Have students alternate roles or change roles halfway through. Ask them to elaborate on their responses by identifying the recipient as well as the purpose of the gift.

Situación

PREPARACIÓN. Read the following situation with your partner. Then prepare examples of the vocabulary, structures, and other information you will need to present your role in the conversation.

Role A. You run into a friend who is carrying a big gift box. You ask what it is and whom it is for.

Role B. You are walking out of a store carrying a big gift box. You run into a friend who asks you about the gift. Answer and explain to whom you are giving the gift and for what occasion.

	ROLE A	ROLE B
Vocabulario	Gifts and gift-giving occasions	Question words
Funciones y formas	*Por* and *para* Asking questions	*Por* and *para* Answering questions

INTERCAMBIOS. Using the information in *Preparación,* act out the conversation with your partner.

Suggestion for *Situación*
You may want to assign partners and have pairs create mini-skits using the video-posting feature, *MediaShare,* online.

EN ACCIÓN

¡A comer!

Suggestion for 3-37
You may want to have students learn more about the food items by researching them online. Students could be asked to show photos and share information about foods that may be unfamiliar to them.

If you do this activity in class, tell students to use their previous knowledge to help narrow down the possibilities and make an educated guess.

3-37 Antes de ver

Comida típica. Match the foods in the left column with the countries most commonly associated with them on the right.

1. __d__ paella	a. Estados Unidos
2. __e__ dulce de leche	b. Perú
3. __b__ papas a la huancaína	c. Venezuela
4. __a__ hamburguesas con papas fritas	d. España
5. __c__ arepas	e. Argentina
6. __f__ tacos	f. México

3-38 Mientras ves

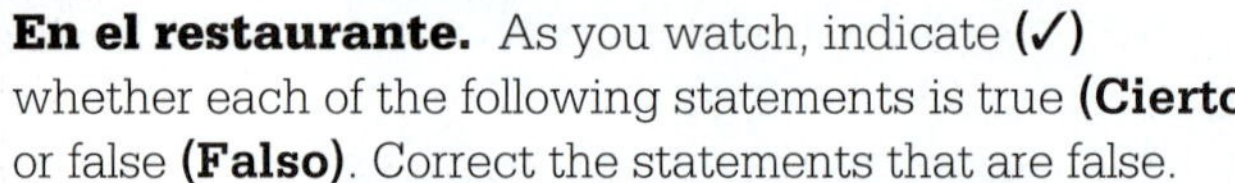

En el restaurante. As you watch, indicate (✓) whether each of the following statements is true **(Cierto)** or false **(Falso)**. Correct the statements that are false.

	CIERTO	FALSO
1. Héctor, Vanesa y Yolanda van a un restaurante para almorzar.	✓	
2. Yolanda está contenta porque hay muchos platos vegetarianos en el menú.		✓
Hay muchos platos con productos de animales.		
3. Una comida típica de Perú es arroz chaufa con vegetales.	✓	
4. Vanesa va a comer ceviche.	✓	
5. Héctor va a beber chicha morada.		✓
Héctor va a beber Inca Kola.		
6. La cocinera del restaurante es de Lima.	✓	

3-39 Después de ver

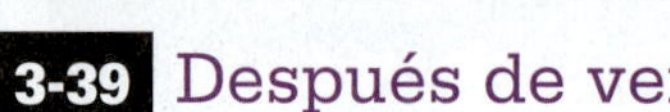

¡Qué rico! **PREPARACIÓN.** After watching the video, indicate whether the following items are associated with Peruvian food (**P**) or with Mexican food (**M**).

1. __P__ el ceviche
2. __M__ las frutas y verduras frescas
3. __P__ las papas
4. __M__ las pastas
5. __P__ el tallarín saltado con vegetales
6. __M__ los tacos

INTERCAMBIOS. You and several classmates have decided to eat at the same restaurant featured in the video. Take turns asking your classmates what they are going to order and why they have made that choice.

Mosaicos

ESCUCHA

3-40 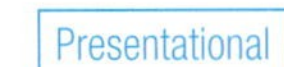 Presentational

Preparación. Before you listen to an ad for the travel agency *ViajaMás*, use what you already know about Latin America to write down the name of one large city in Peru, Argentina, and Venezuela, and the likely cost of a plane ticket to each city. Compare answers with the class.

ESTRATEGIA

Use background knowledge

When you listen to a conversation, you can use your experience and your knowledge of the situation to enhance your comprehension.

Audioscript for 3-41
Agencia ViajaMás anuncia sus precios especiales de ida y vuelta para las siguientes ciudades desde Miami: Lima, vuelo número 881, solo sábados y domingos, precio especial: $730. Buenos Aires, vuelo número 479, todos los días, precio: $980. Caracas, vuelo número 963, todos los días, precio especial: $250. Bogotá, vuelo 1247, lunes, martes y sábados, precio: $455. ¡Gracias por llamar a la Agencia ViajaMás y buen viaje!

3-41   Interpretive

Escucha. Now listen to the ad and complete the chart with the information you hear.

Ciudad	Vuelo #	Días	Precio del boleto $
Lima	881	sábados y domingos	730
Buenos Aires	479	todos los días	980
Caracas	963	todos los días	250
Bogotá	1247	lunes, martes y sábados	455

Comprueba

I was able to ...

_____ **recognize names of places.**

_____ **identify numbers.**

_____ **recognize days of the week.**

3-42  Interpersonal

Un paso más. Read the following role-plays and take turns practicing each part with a partner. Then write an e-mail to your best friend explaining your travel plans. Include destination, date, time, and cost of your flight.

Role A. You are interested in one of the trips that you heard in the ad. Call the airline customer service center to ask for further details: a) at what time the flight leaves, and b) at what time it arrives at its destination.

Role B. You are the airline agent. Provide the information requested by your client and add further details: a) approximate duration of the flight, and b) if the flights are direct or not.

Suggestion for 3-42
Make sure that the students use the information they heard in the recording and that they attempt to create with language by adding some information of their own.

Suggestions for 3-43
Students will interpret an authentic text before they prepare the questions that they will use in a survey. Make comments and ask students questions based on the text to make sure they understand the information and to model for their own questions: *Yo como mucha fruta. Me gustan las naranjas, las manzanas, las fresas. Como fruta todos los días. ¿Y tú comes manzanas regularmente? ¿Cuántas veces a la semana?*

Suggestion for 3-44
Have each student survey at least 5 classmates, and encourage them to ask and answer the questions according to the model. Students should also ask their interviewees about favorite foods that are not included in the grid: *¿Qué más comes en el desayuno/el almuerzo/ la cena?*

Note for *En directo*
Before doing activity 3-44, first have students read the expressions in *En directo*. Then have them listen to the dialogue and encourage them to use the expressions in their own conversation.

Audioscript for *En directo*
NADIA: *¿Qué traes para comer hoy?*
PILI: *Ensalada, como todos los días.*
NADIA: *¿No comes carne?*
PILI: *Muy poca. Solo una vez al mes. ¿Y tú?*
NADIA: *Sé que no es bueno, pero como carne dos veces a la semana.*
PILI: *Es mucho, ¿no?*

Suggestions for 3-45
Students will now present the information gathered in the previous section of the activity. Encourage them to organize the information well before they present it to the class. They should draw conclusions by comparing the findings from their survey with the recommendations from the text they read.

HABLA

ESTRATEGIA

Inform yourself before you do a survey

When preparing to do a survey, it is helpful to gather as much information as you can about the topic to ask questions.

3-43 Interpretive

Preparación. Read the following recommendations provided by an organization that wants to promote healthy habits in the schools, and prepare five related questions to ask students in your university about their own eating habits.

Tabla 1 Frecuencia de consumo recomendada

Frutas, verduras, ensaladas, lácteos y pan	**Todos los días.**
Legumbres	**2 a 4 veces por semana.** (2 como primer plato y 2 de acompañamiento)
Arroz, pasta, papas	**2 a 4 veces por semana.** Alternar su consumo.
Pescados y carnes	**3 a 4 veces por semana.** Alternar su consumo.
Huevos	**4 unidades a la semana.** (alternando con carnes y pescados)
Dulces, refrescos, comida rápida	**Ocasionalmente.** Sin abusar.

SOURCE: Eroski Consumer, Fundación Eroski

3-44  Interpersonal

Habla. Use your questions to find out what your classmates normally eat and drink and how many times a week.

MODELO E1: *¿Cuántas veces por semana bebes refrescos?*
E2: *Bebo refrescos todos los días.*

En directo

To express frequency

todos los días *every day*

dos veces por semana *twice a week*

una vez al mes *once a month*

cada día *each day*

 Listen to a conversation with these expressions.

Comprueba

In my conversation . . .

_____ my questions were easily understood.

_____ I mentioned lots of foods in my responses.

_____ I used expressions of frequency.

3-45  Presentational

Un paso más. Compare the recommendations with the answers you gathered and present the findings to the class. Include in your report answers to the following questions.

1. ¿Tienen los estudiantes una dieta equilibrada? ¿Por qué?
2. ¿Qué productos comen en exceso? ¿Qué productos consumen poco?

LEE

  Interpretive

Preparación. The three ads below come from a newspaper in Lima, Peru. Look them over quickly without reading them. Then mark which ad goes with each of the following descriptions. What word(s) in each ad helped you select your responses?

1. __C__ un restaurante de comida china
2. __A__ actividades para niños
3. __B__ un restaurante de comida tradicional peruana

ESTRATEGIA

Look for and use key words

Even though you may not know all the words when you read a text in Spanish, identifying and focusing on key words can help you understand the main ideas. Look the text over before starting to read to get a sense of what type of text it is and what it may be about.

3-47  Presentational

Lee. Read the ads below to get a sense of what each is about. Then offer a solution for each of the situations that follow. Explain your reasoning to the class.

NIÑOS

CORPORACIÓN CULTURAL DE LIMA. Santa María y Gálvez. 2209451. A las 12 y 16 horas. Bagdhadas. S/. 12.

TEATRO INFANTIL A DOMICILIO. 2390176. El patito feo. Adaptación del cuento de Andersen. Compañía Arcoíris.

CENTRO LIMA. Av. Grau y Velásquez. A las 12, show especial de Navidad.

FANTASÍA DISNEY. Desde las 15. Niños, S/. 8; adultos, S/. 14. Parque de entretenimientos.

EL MUNDO FANTÁSTICO DE MAFALDA. Desde las 10. Entrada general a todos los juegos. Niños, S/. 12. Calle Domingo Sarmiento 358.

PLANETARIO DEL MORRO SOLAR. A las 12, 17 y 19. Gratis para niños; adultos, S/. 15. Circunvalación, Nuevo Perú. Tel. 5620841.

PARQUE DE LAS LEYENDAS (ZOO). De 9 a 19 hrs. Niños y 3ra edad, S/. 5; S/. 10, otro público. Cerro Tongoy, 3701725.

A.

Costa Verde
Sabrosa comida tradicional peruana
Menú especial los fines de semana
Aperitivo
Entrada
Segundo
Postre
Café y plus café (crema de café, crema de menta, anisado)
Valor: S/. 75
Carnes, pescados y mariscos preparados por los mejores cocineros del país
Avenida Arequipa 357
Reservas: 428 9654
Fax: 428 9655

B.

La más exquisita, variada y exótica carta de comida cantonesa-peruana: finas carnes, pescados y todo tipo de mariscos.

SÁBADOS Y DOMINGOS:

Almuerzos y cenas familiares

...los esperamos

AIRE ACONDICIONADO
MÚSICA AMBIENTAL
CAMAREROS PROFESIONALES
AV. REPÚBLICA DE PANAMÁ 8720
RESERVAS 3817543, 3816532, 3814241

C.

1. Los señores Molina tienen cuatro hijos de entre tres y ocho años. A los niños les fascinan los animales. ¿Adónde van a ir probablemente? ¿Por qué?
2. Carlos está triste porque se fracturó una pierna y no puede (*he can't*) salir de la casa. Su mamá tiene una sorpresa para él. ¿Qué es?
3. Cuatro médicos franceses visitan el Hospital Central. El Dr. Moreira, director del hospital, desea invitar a sus colegas a cenar en un restaurante cómodo con comida tradicional peruana. ¿A qué restaurante va a invitarlos? ¿Por qué?

Comprueba

I was able to ...

____ recognize important words.

____ identify the main ideas.

____ recognize contexts.

Suggestion for 3-46
To assess students' understanding, ask additional questions regarding the ads: 1. *¿Qué palabras indican que las actividades son para los niños? ¿Qué significa "3ra edad"? ¿Qué significa "otro público"?;* 2. *¿Qué expresión indica que este restaurante prepara comida nacional? ¿Cuánto cuesta el menú especial de los fines de semana?;* 3. *¿Cuál de los dos restaurantes sirve comida que a ustedes les gusta más, Costa Verde o El Chifa Lungfung?*

Suggestion for 3-47
You may wish to have each pair of students present a solution to the class, including key words that helped them make their decision. Pairs who have a different solution to the one presented should be encouraged to present their alternative.

Suggestion for 3-51
Depending on your teaching approach or your students' writing proficiency, you may wish to give this activity a more cultural orientation. To that end, you may ask students to do some research on the Internet. Students may take a virtual tour of a specific place such as a museum, historical landmark, or vacation spot. They should describe the place and indicate its importance.

Suggestions for 3-51
If you want students to revise their first drafts in class, have them exchange e-mails with a peer editor, one whom you appoint or whom they choose. Give students enough time to read their classmate's message so they can discuss it later. If time is limited, you may assign students to read their partners' text as homework, followed by a class discussion. Remind peer editors to concentrate on content only. They may check that their classmate's message contains the date, a salutation, and a closing.

Suggestion for 3-51
After students have written their e-mails, have them check the following:

1. Did they include the date?
2. Are their salutation and closing appropriate?
3. Did they include a brief introduction and enough information in the body of the message?
4. Did they check for spelling and grammatical errors?

Note for *En directo*
Before doing activity 3-51, first have students read the expressions in *En directo*. Then have them listen to the message and encourage them to use the expressions in their own e-mail.

Audioscript for *En directo*
Hola, Rebeca, ¿cómo van tus vacaciones? ¿Qué haces? ¿Adónde vas? Quiero saberlo todo, ¡así que llámame en cuanto puedas!
Hasta pronto, Alex

3-48  Interpersonal

Un paso más. With a classmate, answer the following questions about the three ads from Peru on page 133.

1. ¿Cuál de las siguientes actividades desean hacer ustedes en Lima: ir a un parque de atracciones (*amusement park*), comer comida tradicional peruana, ver teatro o comer comida china? ¿Por qué?
2. ¿Cuál de los dos restaurantes sirve comida que a ustedes les gusta más, Costa Verde o Chifa Lungfung? ¿Por qué?

ESCRIBE

3-49 Interpretive

Preparación. Choose a vacation spot that you know well (or find information online) and that you like a lot. Then make a list of words (adjectives) that describe the place, write some enjoyable activities (verbs) that people do there.

ESTRATEGIA

Identify your audience

When you write an e-mail to a friend it is essential to include the parts of the e-mail (To, From, Subject, the salutation or greeting, the body, and the closing farewell). Address your friend with the **tú** form.

 **3-50** Presentational

Escribe. Now write an e-mail to your friend, telling about your vacation. Use the information you prepared in *Preparación* and other information that may be of interest to your friend.

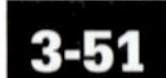 **3-51**  Interpersonal

Un paso más. After completing your e-mail, exchange it with a classmate, read his/hers and take notes to answer the following questions: a) where your classmate is spending his/her vacation; and b) what he/she does during the vacation. Inform the class.

En directo

Salutations for casual correspondence:

Querido/a...: *Dear...*

Hola...: *Hi...*

Closings for casual correspondence:

Tu amigo/a, *Your friend,*

Hasta pronto, *See you soon,*

 Listen to a recorded message with these expressions.

Comprueba

I was able to ...

- _____ **present main ideas clearly, with some details.**
- _____ **use a wide range of learned vocabulary.**
- _____ **conjugate verbs appropriately and make the right agreements.**
- _____ **use accurate spelling, capitalization, and punctuation.**

En este capítulo…

Comprueba lo que sabes

Go to ***MySpanishLab*** to review what you have learned in this chapter. Practice with the following:

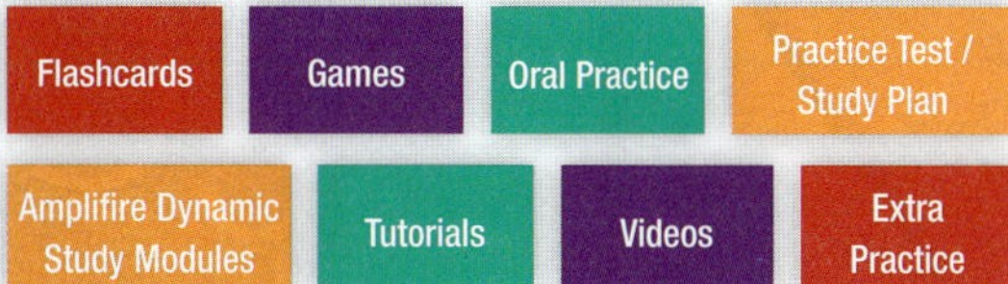

Vocabulario

LAS DIVERSIONES Y LAS CELEBRACIONES
Entertainment and celebrations

la canción *song*
el cumpleaños *birthday*
la fiesta *party*
la guitarra *guitar*
la música *music*
la película *film*
la reunión *meeting, gathering*
el tiempo libre *free time*
las vacaciones *vacation*

LAS PERSONAS
People

el/la camarero/a *server, waiter/waitress (restaurant)*
el hombre *man*
el/la joven *young man/woman*
la mujer *woman*

LA COMUNICACIÓN
Communication

el periódico *newspaper*
la revista *magazine*
el teléfono *telephone*

LOS LUGARES
Places

el cine *movies*
la ciudad *city*
el mar *sea*
el país *country, nation*

LAS DESCRIPCIONES
Descriptions

caliente *hot*
fabuloso/a *fabulous, great*
frío/a *cold*
frito/a *fried*

VERBOS
Verbs

alquilar *to rent*
bajar *to download*
cantar *to sing*
celebrar *to celebrate*
cenar *to have dinner*
descansar *to rest*
hacer *to do*
hacer la cama *to make the bed*
ir *to go*
nadar *to swim*
oír *to hear*
poner *to put*
poner la mesa *to set the table*
poner una película *to show a movie*
salir *to leave*
tocar (un instrumento) *to play (an instrument)*
tomar el sol *to sunbathe*
traer *to bring*

EN UN CAFÉ O RESTAURANTE
In a coffee shop or restaurant

la aceituna *olive*
el agua *water*
el almuerzo *lunch*
el arroz *rice*
la bebida *drink*
el bistec *steak*
el café *coffee*
la cena *dinner, supper*
el cereal *cereal*
la cerveza *beer*
el ceviche *dish of marinated raw fish*
la comida *food; meal; dinner, supper*
el desayuno *breakfast*
la ensalada *salad*
los espaguetis/los tallarines *spaghetti*
los frijoles *beans*
la fruta *fruit*
la hamburguesa *hamburger*
el helado *ice cream*
el huevo *egg*
el jamón *ham*
el jugo *juice*
la leche *milk*
la lechuga *lettuce*
la naranja *orange*
el pan tostado/la tostada *toast*
la papa *potato*
las papas fritas *French fries*
el pescado *fish*
el pollo *chicken*
el queso *cheese*
el refresco *soda, soft drink*
el sándwich *sandwich*
la sopa *soup*
el té *tea*
el tomate *tomato*
el vegetal/la verdura *vegetable*
el vino *wine*

EXPRESIONES CON POR
Expressions with por/para

por ciento *percent*
por ejemplo *for example*
por eso *for this reason*
por fin *at last*
por lo menos *at least*
por supuesto *of course*

PALABRAS Y EXPRESIONES ÚTILES
Useful words and expressions

¿adónde? *where (to)?*
al (contraction of **a** + **el**) *to the*
¡claro! *of course!*
cerca de *close to, near*
después, luego *after, later*
durante *during*
¡estupendo! *fabulous!*
felicidades *congratulations*
mientras *while*
otro/a *other, another*
¿qué te parece? *what do you think?*
si *if*

See *Lengua* box on page 115 for expressions that denote future time.

See page 119 for numbers from 100 to 2,000,000.

Introduction to chapter
Introduce the chapter theme about family and family activities. Ask questions to recycle content from the previous chapter. Help students access meaning by making frequent use of gestures or visuals. Related questions: *¿Cómo es tu familia? ¿Es grande o pequeña? ¿Cuántas personas hay en tu familia? ¿Dónde viven? ¿Viven en otros países? ¿Hablas mucho con ellos? ¿Vas a ver a tu familia este fin de semana? ¿Sabes dónde está Colombia? ¿Está en Norteamérica, en Centroamérica, en Sudamérica o en Europa? ¿Cómo se llama la gente de Colombia? ¿Conoces a alguien de este país?*

Integrated Performance Assessment: Three Modes of Communication

Presentational: See activities 4-5, 4-7, 4-19, 4-21, 4-27, 4-28, 4-29, 4-34, 4-39, 4-40, and 4-44.

Interpretive: See activities 4-1, 4-2, 4-3, 4-4, 4-3, 4-8, 4-10, 4-12, 4-13, 4-15, 4-16, 4-17, 4-22, 4-23, 4-26, 4-27, 4-28, 4-29, 4-32, 4-35, 4-37, 4-41, and 4-43.

Interpersonal: See activities 4-3, 4-5, 4-6, 4-9, 4-11, 4-12, 4-13, 4-14, 4-16, 4-18, 4-19, 4-20, 4-21, 4-22, 4-24, 4-25, 4-26, 4-28, 4-36, 4-42, 4-45, and all *Situación* activities.

4 ¿Cómo es tu familia?

ENFOQUE CULTURAL
Colombia

VOCABULARIO EN CONTEXTO
Los miembros de la familia
¿Qué hacen los parientes?
Las rutinas familiares

MOSAICO CULTURAL
Las familias de la televisión

FUNCIONES Y FORMAS
Present tense of stem-changing verbs: *e* → *ie, o* → *ue,* and *e* → *i*
Reflexive verbs and pronouns
Tener que + infinitive
Hace with expressions of time

EN ACCIÓN
Una fiesta en familia

MOSAICOS
ESCUCHA Listen for a purpose
HABLA Organize information to make comparisons
LEE Use the title and illustrations to anticipate content
ESCRIBE Use language appropriate for your reader

EN ESTE CAPÍTULO...
Comprueba lo que sabes
Vocabulario

LEARNING OUTCOMES

You will be able to:

- talk about family members and their daily routines
- express opinions, plans, preferences, and feelings
- express obligation
- express how long something has been going on
- talk about Colombia in terms of its products, practices, and perspectives
- share information about families and family life in Hispanic countries and compare cultural similarities

ENFOQUE cultural COLOMBIA

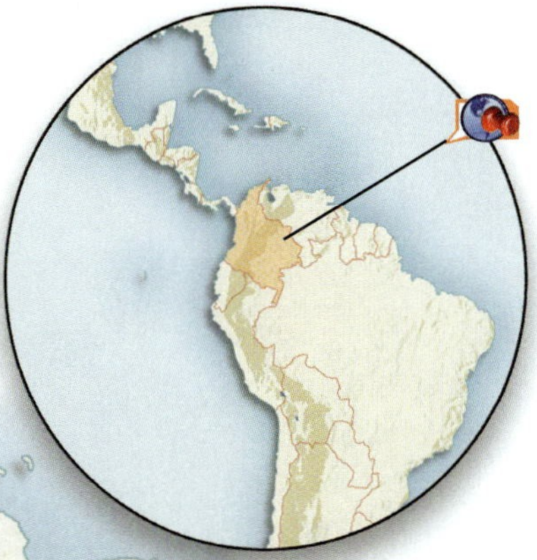

Las casas pintadas de Cartagena de Indias

Mar Caribe

Barranquilla

Cartagena de Indias

PANAMÁ

VENEZUELA

Medellín

Bucaramanga

CORDILLERA DE LOS ANDES

Río Magdalena

Pereira

Bogotá

Pieza antigua del Museo del Oro de Bogotá

El Parque Nacional del Café, Departamento El Quindío

Cali

COLOMBIA

Popayán

OCÉANO PACÍFICO

ECUADOR

BRASIL

Arepas de queso

PERÚ

Cordillera de Los Andes

Enfoque cultural

To learn more about Colombia, go to MySpanishLab to view the *Vistas culturales* videos.

¿QUÉ TE PARECE?

- Medellín recibe el premio a "la ciudad más innovadora del 2012" en reconocimiento de su planificación urbana.
- El 95% (por ciento) de las esmeraldas del mundo vienen de Colombia.
- Colombia es el país más biodiverso por metro cuadrado (*square meter*) del planeta.
- Colombia produce el 12% (por ciento) del café del mundo.

Fernando Botero, uno de los pintores contemporáneos más famosos de Colombia, pinta a unos padres con sus hijos en este cuadro titulado *En familia.*

Suggestion for art
Present *familia, padre, madre, hijo/a, hijos* and project the text image of the painting. Ask questions about the family in the painting: *¿Cómo es el padre? ¿Cómo es la madre? ¿Y el hijo mayor?* Show other paintings by Botero that you may find online. Write his name on the board and explain that he features mostly rotund people in his paintings. Compare this painting with *La familia presidencial* and others in which he depicts families. Use cognates to talk about the themes of some of his other paintings: *la injusticia social, la violencia, la tortura, el abuso de poder,* etc.

Note for *Barranquilla*
Barranquilla hosts other significant cultural events as well. Among the most important is *Barranquijazz,* a music festival held in September that highlights top jazz musicians. The *Carnaval de las Artes* is another noteworthy event that draws artists and thinkers of both national and international renown. Yet another event rooted in Barranquilla is the *Festival Internacional de Cuenteros,* which celebrates the whimsy and talent of storytellers.

Note for *Bogotá*
Bogotá is the largest city in Colombia and has the largest population of any city in the country. It is also the primary industrial and economic center of Colombia, thanks in great part to its central location.

Note for *Gabriel García Márquez*
García Márquez is by far the most celebrated Colombian writer. Author of novels, short stories and screenplays, he began his career as a law student and journalist. His works have been embraced not only by his fellow Colombians, but also by people throughout Latin America and the world.

Note for *Alumbrado navideño*
Encourage students to search for videos online of this spectacular event that takes place each year. You may want to project some of the television coverage available online.

Note
Beginning in *Capítulo 4,* direction lines for activities are in Spanish. Some of these will be glossed.

ENFOQUE cultural

El carnaval de Barranquilla se celebra cada año cuatro días antes de la Cuaresma (*Lent*). Atrae a personas de todas partes que desean disfrutar de las tradiciones, la música y el baile colombianos.

El escritor colombiano y ganador del Premio Nobel de Literatura, Gabriel García Márquez, cuenta con grandes éxitos literarios, entre ellos, su obra maestra, *Cien años de soledad* (*One Hundred Years of Solitude*).

Dieciocho millones de bombillos multicolores iluminan el paseo del río Medellín. Este espectáculo de luces dura (*lasts*) desde el 1 de diciembre hasta el 7 de enero.

Bogotá, la capital de Colombia, está situada en el centro del país, a 2.600 metros sobre el nivel del mar. Es una ciudad moderna, y a la vez tradicional.

¿CUÁNTO SABES?

Completa estas oraciones (*sentences*) con la información correcta.

1. Ecuador, __Perú__ y Brasil están al sur de Colombia.
2. Las casas pintadas de diferentes colores son típicas en la ciudad de __Cartagena de Indias__.
3. __Fernando Botero__ es un pintor colombiano.
4. El 95% de las __esmeraldas__ del mundo y el 12% del __café__ vienen de Colombia.
5. En Barranquilla se celebra __el carnaval__ con música y baile en las calles.

Vocabulario en contexto

Talking about family members, what they do, and their daily routines

Los miembros de la familia

MySpanishLab **TOPIC FOR PRONUNCIATION:** Rules for Written Accents

Learn more using Amplifire Dynamic Study Modules, Pronunciation, and Vocabulary Tutorials.

En Colombia, como en otros países hispanos, las familias generalmente son extensas, y muchas veces varias generaciones conviven en una misma casa. Los **abuelos** juegan un papel muy importante y tienen mucho contacto con los **nietos.**

Aunque tradicionalmente las **madres** hacen el trabajo doméstico, muchos **padres** piensan que la colaboración es necesaria y se ocupan de sus **hijos,** cocinan o lavan los platos.

En los pueblos pequeños de Colombia no es extraño ver a familias enteras usar una motocicleta como vehículo de transporte familiar. En esta **foto** vemos a los **esposos** con sus **niños.**

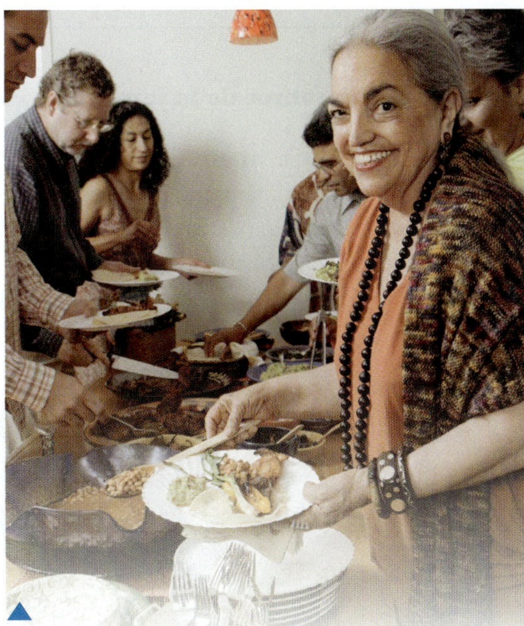

Las reuniones familiares forman parte central en la vida de las familias hispanas. En ocasiones importantes, como los cumpleaños, los **bautizos** o los **matrimonios,** hay comida y, con frecuencia, baile.

Suggestion for *Vocabulario en contexto*
This section works as an advance organizer for the chapter. Students will find vocabulary and grammatical forms to which they will be introduced more formally later. It is important to make them get a general sense of the chapter theme and of some cultural aspects of the featured region.

Suggestion
Talk about the families in the photo, pointing out the grandparents, children, and grandchildren. Personalize by talking about your family and/or asking about theirs. Remind students about gender variations: *hijo/hija, abuelo/abuela,* etc. Ask: *¿Tienes una familia extensa o pequeña? ¿Cuántos miembros de tu familia viven en la misma casa?*

Suggestion
The family photos are an opportunity to use *izquierda, derecha, delante* and *detrás* to locate the people in the image. You may also recycle *entre, al lado de, junto a,* etc.

Suggestion
You may wish to provide students with some sample family types, such as: *la familia monoparental, familias de padres divorciados, familias de padres separados,* etc. Ask: *¿Conoces diferentes tipos de familias? ¿Puedes dar ejemplos? ¿Cuántos niños hay en la familia de la tercera foto? ¿Y en tu familia?*

Suggestion
You may introduce the words *ahijados* and *padrinos.* Explain that in some Hispanic countries these relationships are often related to religious celebrations, such as baptism or weddings. You may also explain the meaning of compadrazgo (the relationship between the parents of the child and the godparents). Ask: *¿Qué reuniones importantes celebran ustedes en familia? ¿Se reúnen frecuentemente?*

Suggestions
Use images to present family relationships. You may want to write them on the board. Pause to ask yes/no questions to check comprehension: *Don José y doña Olga son los padres de Elena. También son los abuelos de Pablo.*

Personalize by asking questions such as: *¿Quién tiene cuatro abuelos? ¿Tres?* For now, just strive for recognition; later students will describe their family in detail.

Note
Explain that *don* and *doña* are titles roughly equivalent to Mr. and Mrs./Ms. They are followed by a person's first name (*don José, doña Olga*). They are often used to address someone older in a familiar yet respectful manner.

Point out that *novio/a* means "fiancé/e," as well as "groom/bride," and in many places, "boy/girlfriend." Introduce the terms of endearment *abuelito/a; mamá, papá; mami, papi;* etc.

Suggestions
To help students build confidence in discussing families: 1) ask questions to identify different members in Pablo's family; 2) using the board, describe your own family tree and ask: *¿Es mi nieto o mi abuelo? ¿Es mi hermana o mi madre?;* 3) ask questions about magazine pictures of people of different ages; 4) have students bring pictures of their families and explain them to the class.

Note for 4-1
Since listening activities are often done outside of class, their directions are in English to ensure that students understand what they have to do.

Audioscript for 4-1
1. *¿Es don José el abuelo de Pablo o es su padre?*
2. *¿Es Sofía la hermana de Pablo o es su prima?*
3. *¿Es Jorge el hijo de doña Olga o es su nieto?*
4. *¿Cómo se llama la tía de Pablo, Elena o María?*
5. *¿Quién es el hijo de don José, Jorge o Jaime?*

Pablo habla de su familia

Me llamo Pablo Méndez Sánchez y vivo con mis padres, mi **hermana** y mis **abuelos** en un apartamento en Bogotá, la capital de Colombia.

Mi **madre** tiene un **hermano,** mi **tío** Jorge. Su **esposa** es mi **tía** María. Tienen tres hijos y viven también en Bogotá. Mi **primo** Jorgito es **el menor.** Mis **primas** Elenita y Ana son **gemelas.** Mis primos son muy simpáticos y **pasamos** mucho tiempo **juntos.**

Mis tíos tienen solo dos **sobrinos** en Bogotá, mi hermana Inés y yo. Su otra **sobrina,** Sofía, vive en Cartagena, al norte del país. Sofía es **la mayor** de todos los primos.

La **nieta** favorita de mis abuelos es mi hermanita Inés. Tiene solo tres años y es la menor de todos sus **nietos.**

EN OTRAS PALABRAS

Family terms vary from one region to another: **marido** and **mujer** are preferred in Spain, while **esposo** and **esposa** are used in most other countries. Terms of endearment for mother and father also vary: **mamá** and **papá** (in Spain), **mami** and **papi** (Caribbean), **mamita** and **papito** (Colombia).

Otros miembros de la familia de Pablo

La única hermana de mi **mamá** es mi tía Gloria. Gloria y Sergio están **divorciados** y tienen una hija, mi prima Sofía. Ahora la tía Gloria está casada con Osvaldo, el **padrastro** de Sofía. Sergio está casado con Paula y tienen un hijo, Roberto. Paula es la **madrastra** de Sofía, y Roberto es su **medio hermano.**

PRÁCTICA

4-1

Escucha y confirma. Listen to the following questions about Pablo's family and select the correct response based on his family tree.

	A	B
1.	su abuelo	su padre
2.	su prima	su hermana
3.	su hijo	su nieto
4.	Elena	María
5.	Jorge	Jaime

Asociación. Asocia cada expresión con el miembro de la familia que describe. Después, nombra a estos miembros de tu familia.

1. __c__ la esposa de mi padre
2. __a__ el hermano de mi prima
3. __d__ los padres de mi padre
4. __b__ el hijo de mi hijo
5. __e__ el hermano de mi madre

a. mi primo
b. mi nieto
c. mi madre
d. mis abuelos
e. mi tío

La familia de Pablo. PREPARACIÓN. Con tu compañero/a, completa las oraciones de acuerdo con (*according to*) la información que tienes sobre la familia de Pablo.

1. La hermana de Pablo se llama __Inés__.
2. Don José y doña Olga son los __abuelos__ de Pablo.
3. Pablo es el __hijo__ de Jaime.
4. Jaime es el __padre__ de Pablo, y Elena es su __madre__.
5. Inés y Ana son __primas__. Elenita y Ana son __hermanas gemelas__.
6. Elena es la __tía__ de Jorgito, Elenita y Ana.
7. Gloria es la __hermana__ de Jorge y Elena.

LENGUA

The ending **-ito/a** (**Elena** → **Elenita**) is very common in Hispanic countries. It can express smallness (**hermanito/a, sillita**), affection, and intimacy (**mi primita**). Names that end in consonants other than l use the ending **-cito/a** (**Carmen** → **Carmencita**).

INTERCAMBIOS. Túrnense (*Take turns*) para hacerse preguntas sobre la familia de Pablo.

MODELO E1: *¿Quién es Osvaldo?*
E2: *Es el esposo de Gloria y el...*

4-4 

¿Cierto o falso? Marca (✓) la columna adecuada de acuerdo con la información sobre la familia de Gloria.

	CIERTO	FALSO
1. La tía Gloria está casada con Sergio.		✓
2. Osvaldo es el papá de Roberto.		✓
3. Paula es la madrastra de Roberto.		✓
4. Gloria es la madre de Sofía.	✓	
5. Sofía tiene un medio hermano.	✓	

Suggestion for 4-1
To check comprehension, with the class as a whole, have students indicate their selections by using a thumbs up for A, thumbs down for B. If your classroom is equipped with a SMART Board, you may use a clicker.

Note for *Lengua*
Another way to form diminutives is by adding *-cillo/a* to nouns ending in *-o, -a,* and *-l.* You may want to point out that there is a good deal of variation from region to region regarding which diminutive to use.

Note for 4-4
Mention that *hermanastro/a* is used in some countries in place of *medio hermano/ media hermana,* despite the differences between the terms. *Medios hermanos/ medias hermanas* have one parent in common; *hermanastros/as* do not.

Follow-up for 4-4
Have students describe members of their own families. Be prepared for blended and/or non-traditional families.

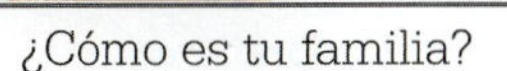

Note for *Cultura*
Beginning with this chapter, reflection questions are given in Spanish.

Note for *Cultura*
Identify the members of the Spanish Royal family in the image: *A la izquierda de la imagen está el Príncipe Felipe, seguido por su padre, el Rey Juan Carlos y su madre, la Reina Sofía. A la derecha de la imagen esta la hija mayor de los reyes, la Infanta Elena. Las Infantas Sofía y Leonor están delante de sus abuelos. Son las hijas del Príncipe Felipe y su esposa, Leticia, la cual no aparece en la foto.*

Note for 4-6
In the *Preparación*, students can practice formulating questions in preparation for the *Intercambios*.

Follow-up for 4-6
Remind students that you will ask them to describe the families of their classmates afterward, so they should take notes.

La familia real española

Spain is the only Spanish-speaking country that is a parliamentary system with a constitutional monarchy. The Spanish Royal Family consists of King Juan Carlos, Queen Sofía, and their children Prince Felipe, Infanta Elena and Infanta Cristina. The monarchy is part of the Bourbon Dynasty and has been in Spain since the year 1700.

Conexiones. ¿Sabes qué otros países tienen una monarquía hoy? Busca información en Internet sobre una de ellas y describe a los miembros de su familia para presentar en clase.

¿Quién es y cómo es?
PREPARACIÓN. Escojan (*Choose*) un miembro de una familia famosa (los Obama, los Jackson, los Kennedy, los Kardashian, etc.) y preparen su árbol familiar.

INTERCAMBIOS. Túrnense (*Take turns*) para describir el árbol familiar de esta persona.

EL PRÍNCIPE FELIPE

E1: *Es el hijo de los Reyes de España. Su esposa es Leticia. Tienen dos hijas.*

E2: *Sus hijas se llaman Leonor y Sofía. Elena y Cristina son las hermanas mayores del Príncipe Felipe.*

4-6

El arte de preguntar. **PREPARACIÓN.** Túrnense para preparar las preguntas a estas respuestas.

Mi madre se llama Dolores.
¿Cómo se llama tu madre?

1. Tengo dos hermanos.
2. Vivo con mi madre y mi padrastro.
3. Tengo dos abuelas y un abuelo.
4. Mis abuelos no viven con nosotros.
5. Tengo muchos primos.
6. Tengo una media hermana, pero no vive con nosotros.

INTERCAMBIOS. Ahora háganse (*ask each other*) preguntas para obtener información sobre la familia de su compañero/a. Después, compartan (*share*) esta información con la clase.

Los apellidos

In Hispanic culture, people offically use two surnames, the first is their father's and the second is their mother's. For example, in Pablo's family, his father's name is Jaime Méndez and his mother's name is Elena Sánchez. Pablo's official name, then, is Pablo Méndez Sánchez.

Comparaciones. ¿Cuántos nombres y apellidos tienes? En la cultura hispana, ¿cuál sería (*would be*) tu nombre oficial?

Mi familia. Busca fotos de tus familiares en tu celular o en Facebook. Luego, muéstrale las fotos a tu compañero/a y describe a tus familiares.

1. nombre y apellido
2. relación familiar
3. personalidad
4. actividades que haces con la persona

¿Qué hacen los parientes?

Mis abuelos viven en una casa al lado del parque. Normalmente, ellos **pasean** por las mañanas y **almuerzan** muy temprano. Después, **duermen la siesta** y por la tarde **visitan** a sus **parientes.**

Jorgito es mi primo favorito. Es **un poco** menor que yo. Nosotros corremos y jugamos mucho **juntos.** También nos gusta ver el fútbol en la televisión y montar en bicicleta los domingos.

Hace dos años que mi prima Ana tiene **novio,** y **frecuentemente dice** que **quiere casarse** muy pronto. Elenita, su hermana gemela, **piensa** que Ana no debe casarse porque es muy joven.

LENGUA

In Spanish, the direct object of a verb is normally introduced without a preposition. However, the preposition **a** is required when the direct object is a person or a specific animal: **los abuelos visitan a los parientes; la hija pasea al perro.**

Mi tío Jorge es un hombre muy **ocupado.** Sale de casa muy **temprano** y **vuelve tarde** todos los días. Mi tía María, su esposa, dice que él **prefiere** el trabajo a su familia. Pienso que en todas las familias hay problemas. En mi familia también, pero eso es normal.

PRÁCTICA

4-8

Para confirmar. Contesta (*Answer*) de acuerdo con la información adicional sobre la familia de Pablo.

	CIERTO	FALSO
1. Normalmente los abuelos están muy ocupados.		✓
2. Jorgito y Pablo montan en bicicleta frecuentemente.	✓	
3. Elenita piensa que su hermana es muy joven para casarse.	✓	
4. El tío Jorge cree que Elenita tiene problemas.		✓
5. El tío Jorge trabaja mucho.	✓	
6. El tío Jorge llega temprano a su casa.		✓

4-9 

¿Y qué hace tu familia? Pídele (*Ask for*) la siguiente información a tu compañero/a sobre su familia.

1. número de personas en la casa, edad (*age*) y relación de parentesco (*kinship*)
2. ocupación y descripción (física y de personalidad) de dos miembros de la familia
3. actividades de estas personas en su tiempo libre
4. nombre del pariente favorito, relación familiar y razón (*reason*) de su preferencia

Suggestion
You may want to point out that *pariente* is a false cognate. Use visuals to practice *pasear* and *almorzar.* Personalize: *Me gusta pasear por el parque por las tardes. ¿Y a ti, te gusta pasear? ¿Paseas por las calles o por el parque? ¿Duermes la siesta alguna vez? Yo duermo la siesta en las vacaciones. ¿Visitas a tus parientes frecuentemente?* Recycle *correr* and *jugar.* Personalize: Follow a similar procedure for the other illustrations. You may also use additional visual aids.

Suggestion for 4-9
Tell students that if they don't feel comfortable talking about their families they can talk about an imaginary family. To ensure students will ask questions accurately, give them a minute or two to write down the questions first. Ask for volunteers to read their questions out loud. Have students work in small groups to list the advantages/disadvantages (*ventajas/desventajas*) of a large family. Have them compare lists.

Follow-up for 4-9
Have students report to the class what a classmate has said about his/her family, reinforcing *él/ella* verb forms: *Mi compañera dice que vive con su familia. Tiene tres hermanos. Su tía vive con ellos.*

Suggestion
The vocabulary of daily routines associated with reflexive verbs is presented here for recognition in the context of family life. Students do not conjugate reflexive verbs at this point. To preview this vocabulary, model the activity by talking about your daily routine with the help of gestures: *Me despierto a las 6:30, me levanto, me ducho, me visto, me lavo los dientes,* etc. Use *temprano* and *tarde: No me acuesto tarde porque me levanto temprano.* Also ask yes/no questions or questions that do not require students to produce structures they have not studied, such as: *¿A qué hora te levantas? ¿Te levantas temprano? ¿Te duchas por las mañanas o por las noches?*

Suggestion
The drawings present an opportunity to preview some vocabulary related to housing that students will learn in *Capítulo 5.* Introduce *cocina* and *cuarto de baño*, then ask: *¿Dónde desayuna la familia? ¿Dónde se lavan?*, etc.

Introduce the expression *Poco después* by comparing it to *luego* and *más tarde.*

Introduce the expression *no sale hasta…* You may also show with gestures what *ropa* means.

Suggestions for 4-11
Students will learn the conjugation of reflexives in *Funciones y formas.* Students may respond to questions with information words only, rather than with complete sentences, e.g., *¿A qué hora se levanta tu madre?* Answer: *A las siete.*

Las rutinas familiares

En casa de Pablo hay mucha actividad por la mañana.

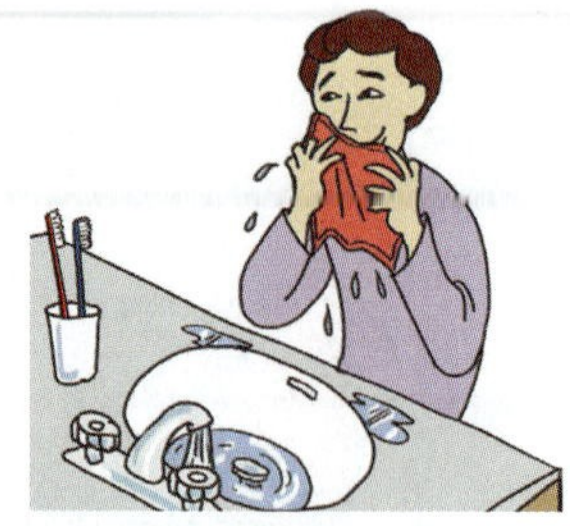

Los niños **se despiertan** a las siete. **Se levantan, se lavan** y luego **desayunan** en la cocina con sus padres. Después salen para la escuela.

Poco después, la madre **se ducha, se seca, se viste** y **se maquilla.**

Más tarde, el padre **se afeita, se baña** y **se pone la ropa,** y sale de casa a las ocho menos cuarto.

PRÁCTICA

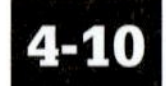

Para confirmar. Pon (*Put*) en orden cronológico las siguientes oraciones según (*according to*) las escenas.

__4__ La madre se maquilla.
__1__ Los niños se despiertan a las siete.
__5__ El padre se baña y luego se pone la ropa.
__3__ La madre se ducha.
__6__ El padre sale de casa a las nueve.
__2__ Los niños desayunan y después salen para la escuela.

Las rutinas diarias. Túrnense y contesten las siguientes preguntas sobre la rutina diaria de la familia de Pablo.

1. ¿Con quién desayunan los niños? con sus padres
2. ¿Quién se maquilla por las mañanas? la madre
3. ¿A qué hora se despiertan los niños? a las siete
4. ¿Quién sale de casa a las nueve? el padre
5. ¿Quién se afeita por las mañanas? el padre
6. ¿Qué hace la madre después de ducharse? Se seca, se viste y se maquilla

4-12 

Mañanas ocupadas (*busy*). Marca (✓) las acciones diarias de los miembros de tu familia. Después, compara la rutina de tu familia con la de tu compañero/a.

	SE DESPIERTA TEMPRANO	SE DUCHA POR LA MAÑANA	SE PONE ROPA ELEGANTE	DESAYUNA CON LA FAMILIA
Mi padre (padrastro)				
Mi madre (madrastra)				
Mi hermano/a				
Mi abuelo/a				
Mi tío/a				

Suggestions for 4-12
Although students do not have to produce conjugated verbs in this activity, you may wish to preview the infinitives and the first, second, and third persons of the conjugation to help them understand the questions.

4-13 

¿Y tú? Completa el siguiente párrafo con las expresiones de la lista para describir tu rutina. Compara tus respuestas con las de tu compañero/a para ver qué tienen en común.

me ducho
salgo para la universidad
me despierto
me levanto
desayuno

Primero __me despierto__, luego __me levanto__.
Poco después __me ducho__, más tarde __desayuno__.
Por último __salgo para la universidad__.

LENGUA

Use the following expressions to organize time sequentially: **primero, luego, poco después, más tarde,** and **por último.**

4-14 

¿A qué hora? Túrnense para hacerse las siguientes preguntas sobre la rutina diaria.

1. ¿Te duchas por la mañana o por la noche?
2. ¿Quién se levanta temprano en tu familia?
3. ¿Te vistes antes o después de desayunar?
4. ¿Te pones ropa elegante o informal para ir a clase?
5. ¿A qué hora te acuestas durante la semana?
6. ¿A qué hora te acuestas los fines de semana?
7. ¿A qué hora te levantas los fines de semana?
8. ¿A qué hora tienes la clase de español?

4-15  

La rutina de Gloria. Listen as Gloria describes her family's routine and mark (✓) the actions that she mentions.

1. __✓__ Nos levantamos temprano durante la semana.
2. ____ Los fines de semana desayunamos juntos.
3. ____ Primero se levanta Osvaldo.
4. __✓__ Mientras Osvaldo se ducha, Sofía se despierta, se levanta y sale para la escuela.

Warm-up for 4-15
As a pre-listening activity, have students work in groups of four to describe their family routines. Then, each student writes a description of his/her family routine.

Audioscript for 4-15
En mi familia nos levantamos temprano durante la semana, pero dormimos mucho los fines de semana. Primero me ducho yo y me maquillo. Después se levanta Osvaldo, mi esposo, y mientras él se ducha, mi hija Sofía se despierta, se levanta y sale para la escuela.

MOSAICO cultural

Las familias de la televisión

Al igual que en Estados Unidos y en muchos países del mundo, la familia ocupa un lugar importante en los programas televisivos. La telenovela *Los Reyes* es una de las más famosas de la televisión colombiana. Esta serie es sobre una familia de clase media que tiene que trabajar mucho para tener una vida tranquila. Los diálogos de esta telenovela son realistas y las situaciones también.

Los Reyes es una crítica social, habla de los conflictos de clase y de los problemas de la sociedad colombiana. Sin embargo, usa a la familia como núcleo de esa discusión. La serie muestra que Colombia es un país moderno y complejo.

Naturalmente, estos conflictos no son exclusivos de Colombia.

▲ **La familia ve otro episodio divertido de la serie *Los Reyes*.**

En México, Argentina y España, este tipo de programa es también muy popular. En España, por ejemplo, la serie *Los Serrano* cuenta la historia de Diego Serrano, un viudo (*widower*) con tres hijos. La historia se complica cuando Diego se casa con Lucía, madre divorciada con dos hijas. Las dos familias tienen que adaptarse para convivir juntas. Al final, como es el caso en muchas familias, la convivencia requiere paciencia y comprensión entre todos los miembros.

▼ **El elenco (*cast*) de la serie *Los Serrano***

Compara

1. ¿Qué familias famosas hay en la televisión de tu país? ¿Cuál es tu favorita?
2. Escoge a una familia de una serie televisiva que te gusta. Describe a esta familia.
3. Compara la familia de la serie televisiva con tu propia familia. ¿Qué tienen en común? Qué diferencias hay entre ellas?

Funciones y formas

1 Expressing opinions, plans, preferences, and feelings

Suggestions
To introduce stem-changing verbs, highlight the stem with a different color or use capital letters when writing the stem on the board. Point out that the stem change is in the stressed stem vowel, not in the preceding vowel (e.g., *preferir, almorzar*).

Use visuals and comprehensible input to present some of the verbs: *Este chico almuerza con sus amigos en una cafetería. Ellos almuerzan a la una. Yo no almuerzo a la una, almuerzo a las doce y media. Tú también almuerzas a las doce y media, ¿verdad? Ah, entonces nosotros (no) almorzamos a la misma hora. ¿Quién (más) almuerza más temprano/tarde?*

Carmen habla en la residencia de estudiantes

Quiero hablar seriamente con ustedes y les **pido** ayuda. El jueves **vienen** los padres a visitar la universidad y **pienso** que debemos preparar una buena fiesta de bienvenida. Luisa y Ana **pueden** preparar un desayuno, o si **prefieren,** yo preparo el desayuno y ustedes **sirven** el café. Elena **quiere** comprar unos globos para decorar los dormitorios porque no **cuestan** mucho. El día **empieza** con una visita al campus. Luego, vamos al estadio y los equipos de deportes **juegan** sus partidos. Por último, los estudiantes **almuerzan** con sus padres en la cafetería. ¿Qué **piensan** de mis planes? ¿**Tienen** ustedes otras ideas?

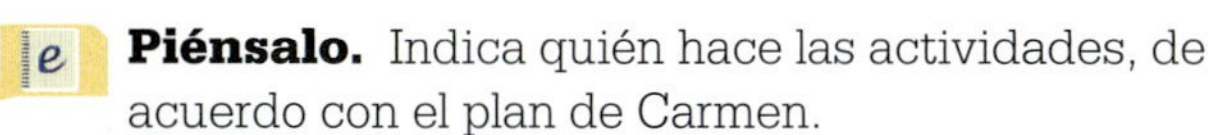

Piénsalo. Indica quién hace las actividades, de acuerdo con el plan de Carmen.

1. __c__ **Pide** la ayuda de sus compañeras.
2. __a__ **Quiere** decorar los dormitorios.
3. __d__ **Pueden** preparar el desayuno.
4. __e__ **Almuerzan** con sus padres.
5. __b__ **Juegan** sus partidos.
6. __a__ Dice que los globos no **cuestan** mucho.

a. Elena
b. los equipos
c. Carmen
d. Ana y Luisa
e. los estudiantes

Present tense of stem-changing verbs: *e → ie, o → ue,* and *e → i*

- Some common verbs in Spanish undergo a vowel change in all forms of the present tense except **nosotros/as** and **vosotros/as.**

PENSAR (e → ie) (*to think*)			
yo	p**ie**nso	nosotros/as	pensamos
tú	p**ie**nsas	vosotros/as	pensáis
Ud., él, ella	p**ie**nsa	Uds., ellos/as	p**ie**nsan

VOLVER (o → ue) (*to return*)			
yo	v**ue**lvo	nosotros/as	volvemos
tú	v**ue**lves	vosotros/as	volvéis
Ud., él, ella	v**ue**lve	Uds., ellos/as	v**ue**lven

PEDIR (e → i) (*to ask for*)			
yo	p**i**do	nosotros/as	pedimos
tú	p**i**des	vosotros/as	pedís
Ud., él, ella	p**i**de	Uds., ellos/as	p**i**den

- Other common verbs that have vowel changes in the stem are the following:

e → ie	**o → ue**	**e → i**
cerrar *to close*	**almorzar** *to have lunch*	**repetir** *to repeat*
empezar *to begin*	**costar** *to cost*	**servir** *to serve*
entender *to understand*	**dormir** *to sleep*	
preferir *to prefer*	**encontrar** *to find*	
querer *to want; to love*	**poder** *to be able to, can*	

- Use **pensar** + *infinitive* to express what you or someone else is planning to do.

Pienso estudiar esta noche. — *I plan to study tonight.*

Pensamos comer a las ocho. — *We are planning to eat at 8:00.*

- Note the irregular **yo** form in the following **e → ie** and **e → i** stem-changing verbs.

tener (*to have*)	**tengo**, t**ie**nes, t**ie**ne, tenemos, tenéis, t**ie**nen
venir (*to come*)	**vengo**, v**ie**nes, v**ie**ne, venimos, venís, v**ie**nen
decir (*to say, to tell*)	**digo**, d**i**ces, d**i**ce, decimos, decís, d**i**cen
seguir (*to follow*)	**sigo**, s**i**gues, s**i**gue, seguimos, seguís, s**i**guen

- In the verb **jugar** (*to play a game or sport*) **u** changes to **ue.**

Mario j**ue**ga muy bien al tenis. — *Mario plays tennis very well.*

Nosotros jugamos todas las semanas. — *We play every week.*

¿COMPRENDES?

Completa las oraciones con la forma correcta del verbo.

preferir (e → ie)

1. Yo _prefiero_ café.
2. Mis padres _prefieren_ té.

dormir (o → ue)

3. Mi perro _duerme_ mucho.
4. ¿_Duermes_ tú mucho?

servir (e → i)

5. Nosotros _servimos_ refrescos.
6. Usted no _sirve_ cerveza.

MySpanishLab

Learn more using Amplifire Dynamic Study Modules, Grammar Tutorials, and Extra Practice activities.

PRÁCTICA

4-16

Los planes. **PREPARACIÓN.** Marca (✓) tus preferencias y planes.

1. ¿Prefieres tener una familia grande o pequeña?
   _____ grande
   _____ pequeña
2. ¿Quieres tomar cursos en el verano o prefieres trabajar?
   _____ Tomar cursos en el verano.
   _____ Prefiero trabajar.
3. ¿Sigues las tradiciones de tu familia o quieres ser más independiente?
   _____ Sigo las tradiciones de mi familia.
   _____ Quiero ser más independiente.
4. Cuando tienes amigos en casa, ¿sirves vino, cerveza o refrescos?
   _____ vino y cerveza
   _____ agua y refrescos
5. Cuando terminas las vacaciones, ¿vuelves a casa deprimido/a o contento/a?
   _____ deprimido/a
   _____ contento/a

INTERCAMBIOS. Ahora pregúntale a tu compañero/a sobre sus planes y preferencias. Debes pedir más información.

E1: *¿Prefieres tener una familia grande o pequeña?*

E2: *Prefiero tener una familia pequeña.*

E1: *¿Cuántos hijos quieres tener?* o *¿Por qué prefieres una familia pequeña?*

E2: . . .

Cultura

Las bodas hispanas

Weddings are very important celebrations for Hispanic families. Many relatives and friends attend the ceremony, which can be a religious event or a civil union. When a Hispanic woman marries, she does not take her husband's surname but rather continues to use that of her parents.

Comparaciones. En tu cultura, ¿qué apellido usan las mujeres cuando se casan? ¿Qué sistema prefieres y por qué?

4-17

Planes para la boda. Beatriz y Miguel se casan en un mes. Completa la descripción de los planes para la boda con un verbo de la lista y en la forma correcta.

empezar	poder	querer	servir
entender	preferir	seguir	volver

Beatriz y Miguel (1) quieren/prefieren tener una boda pequeña, pero elegante. La ceremonia (2) empieza a las 7:00. Los sobrinos y primos jóvenes de los novios no asisten a la ceremonia. Ellos no (3) entienden la ceremonia y (4) pueden/prefieren jugar con una niñera en otra parte de la iglesia. Después de la ceremonia, todos van a un restaurante, donde los invitados (5) pueden bailar y cenar. Los camareros (6) sirven una cena italiana porque los padres de Miguel son de Italia. Después de la cena, la familia (7) vuelve a la casa de los padres de la novia. Los invitados (8) siguen en la fiesta, pero Beatriz y Miguel salen para su luna de miel (*honeymoon*) a Colombia.

Follow-up for 4-16
Each group chooses the best reply for each item and shares them with the class. You may wish to stage a competition for replies that are the most sensible, the most creative, etc.

Follow-up for 4-16
As a follow-up, you may wish to have students report the information they obtained from their classmates. This will provide them with the opportunity to use the third-person singular. You may also want to have them identify some areas in which they have similar or different preferences or plans.

4-18 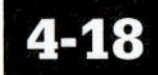 

¿Qué piensan hacer? Túrnense para decir qué piensa hacer cada (*each*) miembro de la familia en las situaciones siguientes.

 Mi hermano quiere estar delgado.

E1: *Tu hermano probablemente piensa correr mucho.*

E2: *Probablemente piensa empezar una dieta.*

E3: *Y probablemente piensa ir al gimnasio todos los días.*

1. Mi hermana tiene un teléfono celular que no funciona (*works*).
2. Mi mamá trabaja mucho y quiere descansar.
3. Mi tía está enferma, por eso se siente muy débil y cansada.
4. Mis abuelos están de vacaciones en Colombia.
5. Mis primos quieren ir a Cartagena para visitar a los abuelos.
6. Mi tío lee y escucha las noticias sobre Colombia porque quiere aprender más sobre el país.

LENGUA

- **Pensar en** is the Spanish equivalent of *to think about someone or something.*

  ¿**Piensas en** tu familia cuando estás fuera de casa?
  Do you think about your family when you are away from home?

  Sí, **pienso** mucho **en** ellos.
  Yes, I think about them a lot.

- **Pensar de** is used to ask for an opinion. **Pensar que** is normally used in the answer.

  ¿Qué **piensas de** los planes de ayuda familiar?
  What do you think of the plans to help families?

  Pienso que son excelentes.
  I think they are excellent.

Suggestion for 4-19
Encourage students to give their partners as much information as possible so they can identify the similarities and differences between the gatherings in their respective families.

Follow-up for 4-19
Intercambios
You may wish to have the pairs share their similarity/difference with the class, and then find out which activities, roles, or customs are the most prevalent among your students.

4-19  

¿Qué pasa en las reuniones familiares?

PREPARACIÓN. Descríbele las reuniones de tu familia a tu compañero/a. Deben tomar nota de las semejanzas y las diferencias.

 preparar la comida

E1: *En las reuniones de mi familia, mi abuela prepara mucha comida.*

E2: *En las reuniones de mi familia, tenemos mucha comida también. Pero mi madre y mi tía preparan la comida.*

1. servir la comida
2. jugar con los niños
3. venir de muy lejos
4. dormir en el sofá
5. preferir hablar de deportes (*sports*)
6. volver a casa para el Día de Acción de Gracias

INTERCAMBIOS. Hablen de una semejanza y una diferencia entre las reuniones de sus familias. Compartan la información con la clase.

Cultura

Las comidas

Meal times vary according to the region but, generally, lunch is the largest and most important meal of the day. In the Hispanic world, people have lunch between 1 and 3 P.M. while dinner is a light meal enjoyed between 7 and 10 in the evening.

Comparaciones. ¿Cuál es la comida más importante en tu cultura? ¿Cómo es?

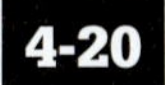 

Entrevista. Túrnense para entrevistarse (*interview each other*). Hablen sobre los siguientes temas (*topics*) y después compartan la información con otro compañero/otra compañera.

1. la hora del almuerzo, qué prefiere comer y dónde
2. los deportes que prefiere practicar o mirar en la televisión
3. a qué hora empieza a hacer la tarea generalmente
4. si duerme una siesta durante el día
5. si vuelve a la casa de sus padres para las vacaciones
6. qué piensa hacer después de graduarse de la universidad

Suggestion for 4-20
Provide time for students to prepare the questions they are going to ask. Make sure they pay attention to the conjugation of verbs when asking the questions.

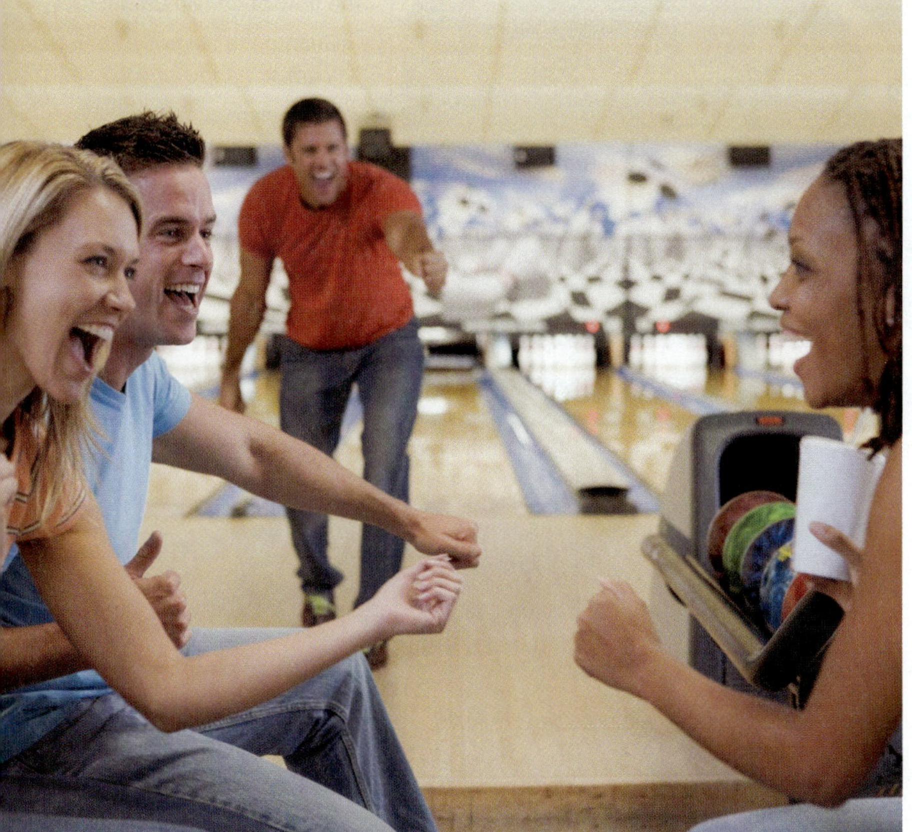

4-21 

¿Cuándo y con quién?

PREPARACIÓN. Habla con tu compañero/a para obtener la siguiente información.

1. qué actividades prefiere hacer con miembros de su familia y cuándo
2. qué actividades hace con sus amigos los fines de semana
3. qué actividades hace con sus amigos durante la semana

INTERCAMBIOS. Preparen una lista de las actividades que tienen en común y otra lista de las que son diferentes. Comparen sus listas con las de otra pareja (*pair*).

Durante la semana, almorzamos en la cafetería de la universidad. ¿Y ustedes?

Follow-up for 4-21
Preparación
Encourage students to try to get as much information as possible from their partners.

La quinceañera

In Hispanic culture, teen girls celebrate their 15th birthday in a special way. The celebration is called a **quinceañera,** and it marks the girl's transition into adulthood. This tradition is celebrated in nearly all Spanish-speaking countries except Spain.

Comparaciones. ¿Cómo se celebra el *sweet sixteen* en tu cultura? ¿Quiénes asisten?

4-22 

Una reunión. Ustedes quieren ayudar a su amiga Celeste a organizar una reunión para celebrar el cumpleaños número dieciséis de su prima. Decidan lo siguiente:

1. lugar y hora en que prefieren la reunión
2. número de personas que van a participar
3. comida y bebidas que piensan servir
4. actividades que quieren organizar

Situación

PREPARACIÓN. Lean esta situación. Luego, compartan ejemplos de vocabulario, gramática y otra información que necesitan para desarrollar la conversación.

Role A. You and a family member are planning to visit Colombia. Your friend has heard about your plans and calls with some questions. Answer your friend's questions in detail.

Role B. Your friend is planning to go to Colombia with a relative. Call to find out:

a. when he/she is planning to go;
b. with whom;
c. what places in the country he/she wants to visit and why; and
d. when they are returning.

	ROLE A	ROLE B
Vocabulario	Family member Travel dates	Question words
Funciones y formas	Discussing plans: *Pensar* + infinitive Expressing preferences: *Querer* + infinitive	Discussing plans: *Pensar* + infinitive Expressing preferences: *Querer* + infinitive

INTERCAMBIOS. Practica la conversación con tu compañero/a incorporando el vocabulario y las funciones de *Preparación*. Luego, represéntenla ante la clase.

These expressions help maintain the flow of conversation:

¡Cuánto me alegro!
I am so happy for you!

Claro, claro…
Of course . . .

¡Qué bien/bueno!
That's great!

 Listen to a conversation with these expressions.

Suggestions for *En directo*
Before doing the *Situación,* first have students read the expressions in *En directo.* Then have them listen to the dialogue and encourage them to use the expressions in their own conversation.

Audioscript for *En directo*
DAVID: *¿Qué tal, Paula? ¿Cómo estás?*
PAULA: *Muy bien. Empiezo a trabajar en la librería esta semana, así que estoy muy contenta.*
DAVID: *¡Cuánto me alegro!*
PAULA: *Voy a trabajar muchas horas, porque necesito dinero para comprar un carro.*
DAVID: *Claro, claro… Bueno, tengo que irme porque hoy es la graduación de mi hermano.*
PAULA: *¡Qué bien!*

Suggestion for *Situación*
In order to provide a cultural context for the *Situación* you may ask the students to prepare for the activity by researching at least two places of interest to tourists who visit Colombia and at least three activities that people usually do in each place.

Suggestion for *Situación*
Have students use the chart provided to jot down words and expressions that they have learned.

2 Talking about daily routine

Me llamo Óscar Torres. Mi esposa Rosa y yo tenemos una vida muy ocupada. **Nos levantamos** a las seis todos los días.

Yo **me ducho** mientras Rosa **se viste** rápidamente.

Después, Rosa **despierta** a Carlitos y a Roberto, nuestros hijos. Roberto se viste, y Rosa **viste** a Carlitos.

Desayunamos y luego todos **nos lavamos** los dientes y a las siete salimos de la casa.

Piénsalo. Para cada acción, indica si la persona se hace la acción a sí misma (*himself/herself/themselves*) o a otra persona.

ACCIÓN	A SÍ MISMO/A	A OTRA PERSONA
1. Óscar **se ducha** por la mañana.	A sí mismo	
2. Rosa **despierta** a Carlitos.		A otra persona
3. La madre **viste** al niño porque es muy pequeño.		A otra persona
4. Roberto **se viste** rápidamente.	A sí mismo	
5. Nosotros **nos lavamos** los dientes después de desayunar.	A sí mismos	
6. Rosa probablemente **se baña** por la noche, porque no tiene tiempo por la mañana.	A sí misma	

Suggestions
You may mention that *cepillarse los dientes* is also used.
Write different times on the board and say what you do on a typical morning, using gestures to help students' comprehension: *Por la mañana, a las siete y cuarto más o menos, yo busco el periódico y preparo el café. A las siete y media me baño, me lavo el pelo y me visto. A las ocho desayuno cereal y bebo otra taza de café. A las nueve salgo para la universidad.* Ask questions to check comprehension. Then ask at what time students do each activity: *¿Qué haces a las ocho? ¿A qué hora desayunas? ¿Te bañas por la mañana o por la noche? ¿A qué hora?*

Suggestions
Remind students that they have been using the reflexive *¿Cómo te llamas? Me llamo… ¿Cómo se llama usted?* since the beginning of the course, as well as many other reflexive forms in *Vocabulario en contexto.*

Suggestion
Explain the concept of reflexive/non-reflexive actions. Point out that some verbs can be used reflexively or non-reflexively: *La mamá peina a su hija. La mamá se peina. Roberto baña a su perro. Roberto se baña.* If possible, use visuals. You may create a story about a sports figure, for example, using a series of visuals.

Suggestion
You may tell students that *acostarse* literally means to put oneself to bed and that *dormirse* means to fall asleep.

Reflexive verbs and pronouns

- Reflexive verbs express what people do to or for themselves.

LAVARSE (*to wash oneself*)			
yo	**me lavo**	nosotros/as	**nos lavamos**
tú	**te lavas**	vosotros/as	**os laváis**
Ud., él, ella	**se lava**	Uds., ellos/as	**se lavan**

Reflexive:

Mi hermana **se** lava las manos. — *My sister washes her hands.*

Non-Reflexive:

Mi hermana **lava** el auto. — *My sister washes the car.*

- A reflexive pronoun refers back to the subject of the sentence. English sometimes uses the pronouns ending in *-self/-selves* to express reflexive meaning. In many cases, Spanish uses reflexives where English does not.

Yo **me levanto, me ducho, me seco** y **me visto** rápidamente. — *I get up, take a shower, dry myself, and get dressed quickly.*

- Place reflexive pronouns after the word **no** in negative constructions.

Rosa **no se levanta** temprano los fines de semana. — *Rosa does not get up early on weekends.*

- The pronoun **se** attached to the end of an infinitive indicates the verb is reflexive.

vestir — *to dress (someone else)*
vestirse — *to get dressed (oneself)*

- With a conjugated verb followed by an infinitive, place the reflexive pronoun before the conjugated verb or attach it to the infinitive.

Yo **me** voy a levantar a las siete. — *I am going to get up at seven.*
Yo voy a levantar**me** a las siete.

- When referring to parts of the body and articles of clothing, use definite articles rather than possessives with reflexive verbs.

Me lavo **los** dientes. — *I brush my teeth.*
Roberto se pone **la** chaqueta. — *Roberto puts on his jacket.*

- Some verbs change meaning when used reflexively.

dormir	*to sleep*	**dormirse**	*to fall asleep*
levantar	*to raise, to lift*	**levantarse**	*to get up*
llamar	*to call*	**llamarse**	*to be called*
poner	*to put, to place*	**ponerse**	*to put on*
quitar	*to take away*	**quitarse**	*to take off*

- Here is a list of common reflexive verbs. Note the stem changes that occur in many of them.

acostarse (ue)	*to go to bed, to lie down*	**lavarse**	*to wash (oneself)*
afeitarse	*to shave (oneself)*	**maquillarse**	*to put on makeup*
bañarse	*to take a bath*	**peinarse**	*to comb (one's hair)*
casarse	*to get married*	**secarse**	*to dry (oneself)*
conectarse a	*to connect to*	**sentarse (ie)**	*to sit down*
despertarse (ie)	*to wake up*	**sentirse (ie)**	*to feel*
ducharse	*to take a shower*	**vestirse (i)**	*to get dressed*

¿COMPRENDES?

Completa las oraciones con el pronombre reflexivo o el verbo indicado.

me, te, se, nos

1. Yo __me__ baño por la mañana.
2. Los estudiantes __se__ bañan por la noche.
3. Usted __se__ baña después de desayunar.

despertarse

4. Mis abuelos se __despiertan__ temprano.
5. Mi hermana y yo nos __despertamos__ tarde.
6. Y tú, ¿cuándo te __despiertas__?

MySpanishLab
Learn more using Amplifire Dynamic Study Modules, Grammar Tutorials, and Extra Practice activities.

PRÁCTICA

¿Qué hacemos todos los días? Pon estas actividades en el orden más lógico (1 = primero; 6 = finalmente). Luego, comparte tus respuestas con tu compañero/a. ¿Hace tu compañero/a las actividades en el mismo orden? Comenten las diferencias.

_______ Me duermo.
_______ Me levanto.
_______ Salgo para mis clases.
_______ Me acuesto.
_______ Me ducho y me lavo la cara (*face*).
_______ Desayuno.

¿Tenemos las mismas rutinas? Hablen sobre sus actividades diarias.

despertarse

E1: *Yo me despierto a las siete. ¿Y tú?*

E2: *Generalmente, me despierto a las ocho.*

1. levantarse
2. ducharse
3. vestirse
4. desayunar
5. acostarse
6. dormirse

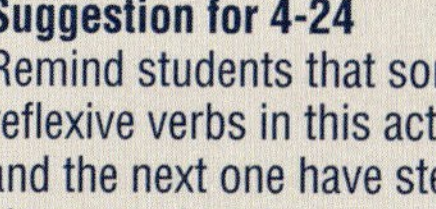

Suggestion for 4-24
Remind students that some reflexive verbs in this activity and the next one have stem changes: *dormirse, acostarse, despertarse, vestirse.*

Follow-up for 4-24
You may wish to ask the pairs of students if their routines for any of these activities are the same, so that they respond using *nosotros/as* forms.

Suggestion for 4-25
As an alternative, make this a group activity by having students share their paragraphs with the class. Then have students ask each other questions to find out who wakes up the earliest/ gets up immediately after awakening/gets dressed before eating breakfast, etc.

4-25 

Los horarios. Usen la información de la actividad 4-24. Completen la tabla y escriban un párrafo sobre sus horarios. ¿Qué tienen en común? ¿Qué diferencias hay entre sus horarios?

	YO	MI COMPAÑERO/A
despertarse		
levantarse		
ducharse		
vestirse		

Situación  

PREPARACIÓN. Lean esta situación. Luego, compartan ejemplos de vocabulario, gramática y otra información que necesitan para desarrollar la conversación.

Role A. You are going to a summer language school (**programa de verano**) in **Bogotá**. Ask the director:

a. where the students live;
b. what time they go to bed and get up; and
c. where and when they eat their meals.

Role B. You are the director of a summer language school (**programa de verano**) in **Bogotá.** Answer the questions of a prospective student, giving as much information as possible.

Suggestion for *Situación*
To provide cultural context have students research the times of meals and other daily routines of Colombia before working on their dialogue.

	ROLE A	ROLE B
Vocabulario	Daily routines Question words	Daily routines
Funciones y formas	Talking about routines: Reflexive verbs Stem-changing verbs	Talking about routines: Reflexive verbs Stem-changing verbs

INTERCAMBIOS. Practica la conversación con tu compañero/a incorporando el vocabulario, las funciones y demás información. Luego, represéntenla ante la clase.

3 Expressing obligation

La Sra. Rojas está de mal humor hoy. Se siente muy frustrada con el estilo de vida de su familia. Acaba de poner esta nota en la puerta del refrigerador.

Planes para nuestra familia

De hoy en adelante, todos **tenemos que ser** más organizados. Verónica **tiene que ver** menos televisión. Luis **tiene que practicar** el piano todos los días. Papá **tiene que hacer** más ejercicio. Agustín y Toño **tienen que terminar** su tarea antes de jugar videojuegos. Finalmente, todos **tenemos que ayudar** con las tareas domésticas.

Mamá

Piénsalo. Asocia las situaciones con las obligaciones según la nota de la Sra. Rojas.

1. __f__ La madre piensa que la familia debe cambiar su estilo de vida.
2. __d__ Verónica mira mucha televisión.
3. __c__ El padre tiene una vida sedentaria.
4. __e__ Luis no es muy perseverante con la música.
5. __b__ Agustín y Toño probablemente prefieren practicar deportes y no estudian.
6. __a__ No todos colaboran para mantener la casa limpia (*clean*).

a. Todos **tienen que ayudar** con las tareas domésticas.
b. **Tienen que dedicar** suficiente tiempo a sus estudios.
c. **Tiene que hacer** más actividades físicas.
d. **Tiene que leer** más o **ser** más activa.
e. **Tiene que practicar** regularmente.
f. La familia **tiene que** organizar sus actividades.

Tener que + infinitive

- Use **tener que** to express what someone *has to, needs to,* or *must* do.

Eliana, **tienes que estudiar más.**	*Eliana, you have to study more.*
Tengo que visitar a mis abuelos este fin de semana.	*I have to visit my grandparents this weekend.*

¿COMPRENDES?

Completa las oraciones con la palabra o expresión correcta.

1. Tengo que __d__ a mis abuelos.
2. Mi madre __e__ que trabajar.
3. Nosotros tenemos __c__ ir de compras.
4. Mis amigos __a__ que estudiar.
5. Y tú, ¿qué tienes __b__ hoy?

a. tienen
b. que hacer
c. que
d. visitar
e. tiene

MySpanishLab

Learn more using Amplifire Dynamic Study Modules, Grammar Tutorials and Extra Practice activities.

Suggestion for 4-26
To preview some new vocabulary, talk about your own (real or imaginary) personal obligations. *Soy una persona con muchas obligaciones y necesidades. Por las mañanas, tengo que preparar el desayuno para mis hijos. También tengo que poner la correspondencia en el buzón antes de salir al trabajo. En la oficina tengo que escribir mucho, ayudar a los alumnos, responder a correos electrónicos, asistir a reuniones, etc. Cuando llego a casa, estoy cansado/a; por eso, necesito descansar. A veces, tengo que acostarme temprano porque tengo que levantarme a las 5:30 de la mañana.* Have students take notes on the similarities and differences between their responsibilities and those of their partners. As a follow-up, you may have them use this information as the basis of a writing activity or report the information to the class.

Standard 3.2
Students acquire information and recognize distinctive viewpoints that are only available through the foreign language and its cultures. In activity 4-27, students learn about places and events that are popular in Colombia but not widely known outside that country. You may wish to have students make a list of places in the U.S. that they would recommend to visitors, and give their reasons. What do they want visitors to know about the U.S.?

Follow up for 4-27 *Intercambios*
Have students prepare a PowerPoint presentation with photos of one of the events, groups, or places mentioned in the *Preparación.* Each member of the group should be responsible for 1–2 slides and related information and express a reaction to/opinion about the information he or she has presented. After the groups have presented, ask: *¿Qué lugar les gusta más? ¿Por qué? ¿Piensas visitar… algún día?*

PRÁCTICA

4-26 

Mis obligaciones. PREPARACIÓN. Marca (✓) las tareas que tienes que hacer regularmente. Con tu compañero/a, comparen sus obligaciones.

_________ pasear al perro
_________ hacer ejercicio
_________ comprar comida
_________ hacer la tarea para mis clases
_________ llamar por teléfono a mi familia
_________ poner los platos sucios en el lavaplatos (*dishwasher*)
_________ leer y contestar el correo electrónico
_________ ir a la universidad
_________ trabajar por las tardes
_________ conectarme a Skype para hablar con mis padres

INTERCAMBIOS. Ahora dile a tu compañero/a cuándo tienes que hacer estas tareas. Luego, comparen sus obligaciones. ¿Quién de ustedes tiene más obligaciones?

MODELO E1: *Tengo que pasear al perro todos los días. ¿Y tú?*
E2: *Yo no tengo que pasear al perro, pero tengo que preparar la comida los domingos...*

Cultura

El Parque Ecológico El Portal

El Portal is an ecological park near Bucaramanga, Colombia. It is a popular destination for ecotourism. There, tourists can partake in a number of different activities such as mountain biking and hang gliding.

Comunidades. ¿Hay lugares en tu región o país dedicados al ecoturismo? ¿Qué puedes hacer allí?

4-27  

Un viaje (*trip*) a Colombia. PREPARACIÓN. Tu familia va a viajar a Colombia. Selecciona la mejor recomendación para cada persona. Después añade (*add*) algo que quieres hacer tú y explica por qué.

1. __b__ Mi hermana quiere visitar un lugar religioso muy original.
2. __c__ A mis padres les gustaría ver joyas (*jewels*) precolombinas.
3. __a__ Mi prima quiere escuchar música colombiana.
4. __d__ Mis abuelos prefieren las actividades al aire libre.

a. Tiene que asistir a un concierto de Los Príncipes del Vallenato.
b. Tiene que ir a la Catedral de Sal.
c. Tienen que ir al Museo del Oro.
d. Tienen que conocer el Parque Ecológico El Portal.

INTERCAMBIOS. Busca información en Internet y prepara una breve descripción de uno de los lugares, grupos o eventos siguientes. Incluye la ubicación (*location*) y las actividades asociadas con el lugar, el grupo o los eventos. Luego, comparte la información con la clase.

1. Los Príncipes del Vallenato
2. la Catedral de Sal
3. el Museo del Oro
4. el Parque Arqueológico de San Agustín

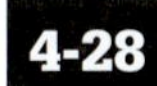 

4-28

Sugerencias. **PREPARACIÓN.** ¿Qué tienen que hacer (o no) las personas en estas circunstancias?

 Luis no tiene dinero (*money*).

E1: *Tiene que buscar trabajo en Internet.*

E2: *No tiene que perder el tiempo en Facebook.*

1. Mi amigo Juan tiene un examen muy difícil el lunes.
2. Francisco nunca tiene energía. Siempre está cansado.
3. Manuel y Victoria no tienen una buena relación de pareja (*couple*).
4. Mi hermana Marta ve televisión todos los días y saca malas notas en sus clases.
5. Luis y Emilia quieren aprender español.
6. Isabel y Lucía desean visitar un país hispano, pero no hablan español.

INTERCAMBIOS. Escribe tres problemas personales. Explícale tus problemas a tu compañero/a y dile qué tienes que hacer.

 *Vivo en un apartamento muy feo. Tengo que buscar un apartamento bonito…*

Suggestion for 4-28
To model, do one of the scenes partially with the class and then assign the scenes to individual groups to present in class.

Situación

PREPARACIÓN. Lean esta situación. Luego, compartan ejemplos de vocabulario, gramática y otra información que necesitan para desarrollar la conversación.

Role A. Your parents are angry at you because you a) stay out late; b) do not study enough; c) prefer to spend all your time with your friends; and d) play with your phone at mealtimes. You ask a friend for advice.

Role B. A friend calls you to discuss family problems. Listen and ask appropriate questions, then offer some advice.

	ROLE A	ROLE B
Vocabulario	Family Leisure activities	Family Leisure activities
Funciones y formas	Talking about routines: Stem-changing verbs Present tense of verbs	Asking questions: Stem-changing verbs Giving advice: *Tener* + *que* + infinitive

INTERCAMBIOS. Practica la conversación con tu compañero/a incorporando el vocabulario y las funciones de *Preparación*. Luego, represéntenla ante la clase.

Note
You may want to point out that some Spanish speakers add the word *desde* when the sentence begins with the present tense: *Trabajan (desde) hace dos horas.*

Suggestion
Explain that other interrogative time expressions may also be used: e.g., *¿Cuántos años...? ¿Cuántos días...? ¿Cuántas horas...?*

4 Expressing how long something has been going on

PATRICIA: Señora, **¿cuánto tiempo hace que** practico esta sonata? ¡Estoy muy cansada!

SRA. ESCOBEDO: **Hace dos horas que** trabajas en ella. Pero una vez más, por favor, Patricia. El recital es en dos días.

(*El día del recital*)

SRA. ESCOBEDO: Les presento a Patricia Suárez. Estudia el violín conmigo **hace cinco años.** Ahora va a tocar la Sonata n.° 4 de Mozart.

Suggestion for *Piénsalo*
After students have studied the sentence patterns and have done the activities, you may wish to go back to *Piénsalo* and have them form the questions that can be answered by the sentences.

Note for *Hace* with expressions of time
In order to simplify the use of *hace* with expressions of time, *desde hace* is not presented in this chapter. You may choose to introduce the use of *desde hace* with time expressions by giving students the following structure: *present tense + desde hace + length of time.*
Estudiamos español desde hace tres semanas.

¿COMPRENDES?

Usa la información en paréntesis para completar la respuesta a la siguiente pregunta:

¿Cuánto tiempo hace que estas personas estudian español?

1. (tres semanas) Hace tres semanas que Juan y Daniel estudian español.
2. (un semestre) Hace un semestre que nosotros estudiamos español.
3. (un año) Hace un año que tú estudias español.
4. (tres días) Hace tres días que mi amigo estudia español.

MySpanishLab
Learn more using Amplifire Dynamic Study Modules, Grammar Tutorials, and Extra Practice activities.

Piénsalo. Indica si las siguientes afirmaciones son ciertas (**C**) o falsas (**F**).

1. C **Hace cinco años que** Patricia estudia con la Sra. Escobedo.
2. F **Hace tres años que** Patricia aprende la Sonata n.° 4 de Mozart.
3. F Patricia conoce a su profesora de violín **hace dos años.**
4. C **Hace dos horas que** Patricia practica la sonata de Mozart.
5. F **Hace cinco años que** la Sra. Escobedo toca el violín.
6. F La Sra. Escobedo enseña clases de violín **hace un año.**

Hace with expressions of time

- To say that an action/state began in the past and continues into the present, use **hace** + *length of time* + **que** + *present tense.*

  Hace dos horas que juegan. — *They have been playing for two hours.*

- If you begin the sentence with the present tense of the verb, do not use **que.**

  Juegan **hace dos horas.** — *They've been playing for two hours.*

- To find out how long an action/state has been taking place, use **cuánto tiempo** + **hace que** + *present tense.*

  ¿Cuánto tiempo hace que juegan? — *How long have they been playing?*

PRÁCTICA

4-29 

Este soy yo. **PREPARACIÓN.** Lee esta descripción de Jaime y completa las oraciones. Compara tus respuestas con las de tu compañero/a.

Me llamo Jaime Caicedo y soy de Cartagena, Colombia. Quiero aprender inglés para poder trabajar en una compañía internacional. Estudio inglés **hace dos años,** pero tengo que estudiar más para hablar correctamente. Siempre miro programas de televisión en inglés. Mi favorito es *NCIS*. **Hace cinco años que** miro este programa y me gusta mucho. Tengo un auto **hace un año,** y salgo en él con mis amigos y también con mi novia. **Hace seis meses que** somos novios. Somos muy felices.

1. Jaime Caicedo es de... Cartagena
2. Hace dos años que Jaime... mira televisión en inglés.
3. Hace seis meses que Jaime... tiene novia.

INTERCAMBIOS. Escribe tu propia descripción, siguiendo el modelo en *Preparación*. Luego, comparte tu descripción con tu compañero/a.

4-30 

¿Cuánto tiempo hace que...? Túrnense para hacerse las siguientes preguntas. Después, compartan la información con otra pareja.

1. ¿Dónde vive tu familia? ¿Cuánto tiempo hace que vive allí?
2. ¿Dónde trabajas? ¿Cuánto tiempo hace que trabajas allí?
3. ¿Cuánto tiempo hace que estudias en esta universidad? ¿Y por qué estudias español?
4. ¿Practicas algún deporte? ¿Cuánto tiempo hace que juegas al...? ¿Juegas bien?

Suggestion for 4-30
Tell students that those who do not have a job may respond to question 2 with information about a friend or family member: *Yo no trabajo, pero mi amiga Susana trabaja en...*

Situación

PREPARACIÓN. Lean esta situación. Luego, compartan ejemplos de vocabulario, gramática y otra información que necesitan para desarrollar la conversación.

Role A. A friend is visiting you from out of town. Give him/her a tour and then suggest going to the local Colombian restaurant for dinner. Give details about the places you visit and answer your friend's questions.

Role B. You are visiting a friend and he/she gives you a tour. Ask your friend questions: a) how long he/she has lived here; and b) how long the stores, restaurants, and other places you see on the tour have been there.

	ROLE A	ROLE B
Vocabulario	Places in town Length of time	Question words Length of time
Funciones y formas	Expressing length of time of an event or condition: Hace + *time* + que + *present tense verb* Making a suggestion	Asking questions about length of time of an event or condition: ¿Cuánto tiempo + hace que + *present tense verb?* ¿Cuántos años + hace que + *present tense verb?*

INTERCAMBIOS. Practica la conversación con tu compañero/a incorporando el vocabulario y las funciones de *Preparación*. Luego, represéntenla ante la clase.

Suggestion for *Situacion*
To provide cultural context ask students to research Colombian restaurants in their area, and their menus.

EN ACCIÓN

Una fiesta en familia

Note for 4-31
If students are completing this activity in class, you may want to ask them to work in pairs and compare their answers. Have some pairs report on their answers and invite the class to ask follow-up questions. *¿Qué haces típicamente para celebrar tu cumpleaños? ¿Con quién almuerzas los domingos?* etc.

4-31 Antes de ver

¿A solas (*alone*) o en familia? Marca las actividades que haces típicamente a solas (**S**) o en familia (**F**).

1. _____ Celebro mi cumpleaños.
2. _____ Me cepillo los dientes.
3. _____ Almuerzo los domingos.
4. _____ Escucho música en mi teléfono.
5. _____ Me visto.
6. _____ Salgo para mis clases.
7. _____ Duermo la siesta en el sofá.
8. _____ Visito a mis parientes.
9. _____ Converso sobre temas políticos.
10. _____ Me ducho.

4-32 Mientras ves  

A celebrar. Marca (✓) la columna adecuada de acuerdo con la información en el segmento de video. Corrige las afirmaciones falsas.

	CIERTO	FALSO
1. Blanca prepara un típico desayuno colombiano.	_____	✓
2. Los estudiantes quieren conocer a la familia de Blanca.	✓	_____
3. Yolanda habla de la celebración de la independencia colombiana en Nueva York.	✓	_____
4. Esteban muestra un video de sus amigos.	_____	✓
5. El hijo de Blanca llega a la fiesta con su esposa.	✓	_____
6. Yolanda quiere comer la carne que prepara Federico.	_____	✓

4-33 Después de ver 

Lejos de casa. PREPARACIÓN. Marca (✓) los temas que aparecen en este episodio, implícita o explícitamente.

1. ✓ La importancia de la familia.
2. _____ Las oportunidades de trabajo en el extranjero.
3. ✓ Las tradiciones culturales.
4. ✓ La separación física entre los padres y los hijos.
5. ✓ La tecnología como medio de comunicación.

INTERCAMBIOS. Comparen sus respuestas de *Preparación* y háganse las siguientes preguntas relacionadas.

1. ¿Qué fiestas celebras siempre en familia? Describe una fiesta típica con tu familia.
2. ¿Qué fiestas prefieres celebrar con tus amigos/as? ¿Son distintas a las fiestas que celebras con tu familia? Explica.
3. Describan cómo celebra la gente la independencia colombiana en Nueva York. ¿De qué manera es similar a la celebración del cuatro de julio? ¿Hay alguna diferencia? Expliquen.

Mosaicos

ESCUCHA

4-34 Presentational

Preparación. Antes de escuchar el mensaje de Pedro para Julio sobre una fiesta sorpresa (*surprise*), prepara tus ideas sobre la siguiente información. Después, presenta tus notas a la clase.

1. el posible propósito (*purpose*) de este mensaje
2. la información específica que puede ser importante

ESTRATEGIA

Listen for a purpose

Listening with a purpose in mind will help you focus your attention on the most relevant information. As you focus your attention, you screen what you hear and select only the information you need.

Suggestion
Before students listen, model the pronunciation of CD (*cedé*).

4-35  Interpretive

Escucha. First read the information you will need to attend the party Pedro is organizing. Then, as you listen, complete the sentences with the rest of the information. Don't worry if you do not understand every word.

1. La fiesta es para... Josefina
2. La fiesta va a ser en la casa de... Pedro
3. El día de la fiesta es... el domingo
4. Julio debe llevar (*take*)... música típica de Colombia
5. Julio tiene que llegar a la casa a las... ocho y media
6. La dirección es... calle 12, número 127

Comprueba

I was able to . . .

____ **recognize the names of people.**

____ **identify specific information about an event.**

Audioscript for 4-35
¡Hola, Julio! Habla Pedro. Te llamo porque mi prima Josefina llega hoy de Colombia y mi hermano y yo queremos darle una fiesta sorpresa. Mi hermana y mi madre van a preparar la comida, así que te va a gustar. Yo solo me ocupo de las bebidas. La fiesta va a ser el domingo, en mi casa. Debes llegar temprano, a las ocho y media, más o menos, porque Josefina va a venir a las nueve y, como es una sorpresa, todos tenemos que estar aquí antes que ella. Dice mi hermano que tienes unos CD de vallenatos y otra música típica de Colombia. ¿Puedes traer algunos? Bueno, recuerda, la hora: ocho y media, en mi casa: calle 12, número 127. Te esperamos el domingo. Chao.

Note for 4-35
As mentioned in ***Vocabulario en contexto***, directions for listening activities are given in English to ensure that students understand what they have to do.

4-36  Interpersonal

Un paso más. Vas a organizar una fiesta sorpresa para tu profesor/a de español y deseas invitar a tu compañero/a. Llama a tu compañero/a por teléfono y explícale lo siguiente:

1. cuándo y dónde va a ser la fiesta
2. qué van a comer y beber
3. qué música van a escuchar
4. otros planes

Note for *Estrategia*
The focus here is on organizing information for a purpose. You may wish to introduce as lexical items *más… que, menos… que,* if you think the phrases will help students converse more naturally. (Comparisons are presented in *Capítulo 8.*)

Preparation for 4-37
Make sure students notice that the sample response in the model includes three pieces of information: name (*David*), relationship (*primo*), and activity (*come*). They should follow the model. Encourage them to include more than one family member in each response.

Warm-up for 4-37
Ask questions about students' families: *¿Cuántos hermanos tienes? ¿Dónde viven?* Ask other students to recall information given by their classmates.

Note for *En directo*
Before doing activity 4-38, first have students read the expressions in *En directo*. Then have them listen to the dialogue and encourage them to use the expressions in their own conversation.

Audioscript for *En directo*
ROBERTO: *Oye, Jaime. Tengo un problema con mi hermano y necesito tu opinión.*
JAIME: *Por supuesto. Dime, ¿qué pasa?*
ROBERTO: *Pues, mi hermano quiere usar mi carro. Por un lado, no me importa porque ahora estoy en la universidad. Por otro lado, mi hermano no es cuidadoso.*
JAIME: *Entiendo lo que dices. En cambio, pienso que en esta ocasión tu hermano va a tener mucho cuidado y comprende que es un gran favor.*
ROBERTO: *Tienes razón, Jaime.*

HABLA

4-37 Interpretive

Preparación. Completa las siguientes afirmaciones con los nombres de tus parientes, la relación de parentesco (*kinship*) y sus actividades.

Mi primo David come en restaurantes los fines de semana.

1. … mucho y con frecuencia está(n) cansado/a(s).
2. … en casa los fines de semana. Descansan, leen, escuchan música, etc.
3. … ejercicio físico tres o cuatro veces por semana.
4. … con amigos o con la familia en casa el día de su cumpleaños.
5. … por Skype o Facebook. Se conecta(n) con su familia y amigos cada día.

ESTRATEGIA

Organize information to make comparisons

In *Capítulo 3,* you practiced organizing information for a presentation. Now you will focus on organizing information for a conversation about a specific topic—your family. Follow these steps in organizing your information.

- List the names of family members you are going to talk about.
- Indicate the family relationships.
- Decide on possible categories for your comparisons (**aburridos, divertidos; extrovertidos, tímidos; trabajadores, perezosos**).

4-38  Interpersonal

Habla. En grupos pequeños, háganse las siguientes preguntas y comparen la información.

1. ¿Quiénes son tus parientes más artísticos? Expliquen (*Explain*).
2. ¿Quiénes son las personas más activas en tu familia? Expliquen.
3. ¿Qué miembros de la familia pasan mucho tiempo en casa? Expliquen.

En directo 

To make comparisons and contrasts:

Por un lado… *On the one hand . . .*

Por otro lado… *On the other hand . . .*

En cambio… *On the other hand . . .*

En contraste… *In contrast . . .*

 Listen to a conversation with these expressions.

Comprueba

In my conversation . . .

____ **I used question words appropriately.**

____ **I described and compared family members.**

____ **I gave relevant information when answering.**

____ **I used adjectives accurately.**

4-39  Presentational

Un paso más. En los mismos grupos, comparen sus respuestas y completen un pequeño informe (*report*) con la información anterior. Luego, presenten su informe a la clase.

LEE

4-40 Presentational

Preparación. Lee el título y los subtítulos del artículo en la página siguiente y observa las fotos. Luego, usa la información del título, los subtítulos y las fotos para contestar las siguientes preguntas. Presenta tus respuestas a la clase. Answers may vary.

1. ¿Cuál es el tema del artículo?
   - **a.** la comunicación entre amigos
   - **(b.)** la comunicación entre los miembros de una familia
   - **c.** la comunicación con los colegas en el trabajo
2. En tu opinión, ¿cuáles de las siguientes ideas va a incluir el artículo? (Hay más de una respuesta correcta).
   - **a.** Hoy en día la comunicación entre padres e hijos es mejor que (*better than*) en el pasado.
   - **(b.)** Los jóvenes no hablan con sus padres sobre sus problemas porque los padres siempre están ocupados.
   - **(c.)** La vida moderna afecta la comunicación entre padres e hijos.
   - **(d.)** La tecnología tiende a reducir la comunicación sobre temas importantes.
3. Marca (✓) las actividades de la siguiente lista que asocias con una buena relación entre padres e hijos.
   - **a.** __✓__ conversar
   - **b.** __✓__ pasar tiempo juntos
   - **c.** __✓__ hablar por teléfono
   - **d.** _____ pelear (*to argue*)
   - **e.** __✓__ escribir correos electrónicos a un miembro de la familia que vive lejos (*far*)
   - **f.** __✓__ comprar regalos con frecuencia
   - **g.** __✓__ expresar cariño (*affection*) verbalmente
   - **h.** _____ no hablar de sus problemas con los padres

ESTRATEGIA

Use title and illustrations to anticipate content

Before you start to read, gather as much information about the text as possible. The title, section headings, and illustrations can help you anticipate content, so pay special attention to them. Write down what you think the text is about, and refer to your notes as you are reading, correcting them as necessary. This will help you focus your attention as you read.

Suggestion for 4-40
Have students present their responses to the class or exchange them with a classmate. Question 3 lends itself to discussion, since the concept of communication may be interpreted differently in different families. To help students compare responses to question 3, you may write on the board: *Es necesario...; No es necesario...* and give an example: *Es necesario estar en contacto con la familia. No es necesario hablar por teléfono todos los días.*

4-41 Interpretive

Lee. Lee el artículo e indica...

1. una palabra asociada con los problemas de comunicación familiares. tecnología
2. por qué la tecnología probablemente afecta las relaciones de la familia. el uso excesivo
3. dos productos que son ejemplos de cómo la tecnología puede causar problemas en la familia. Internet/el correo electrónico, el teléfono celular
4. dos palabras que indican la calidad de la comunicación cuando usamos el correo electrónico o los mensajes de texto. breve, superficial
5. dos formas de usar la tecnología positivamente en la comunicación con la familia. para pasar tiempo con sus familiares y para expresar el amor y el cariño que siente por ellos

Comprueba

I was able to . . .

_____ **use headings and photos to identify the main idea.**

_____ **focus on one piece of information at a time.**

_____ **write effective notes.**

Suggestion for 4-41
Remember that students may comprehend more than they can verbalize or write. Therefore, it is advisable not to force them to respond to questions in their own words or paraphrase at this stage. Let them quote their answers directly from the text if they prefer.

LA IMPORTANCIA DE LA COMUNICACIÓN FAMILIAR

LA FAMILIA EN CRISIS

Los expertos afirman que la familia de hoy está en crisis porque no hay buena comunicación entre sus miembros. También dicen que la comunicación es vital en todas las relaciones, especialmente en las relaciones familiares.

La comunicación crea relaciones familiares fuertes y cariñosas.

AUSENCIA DE LOS PADRES

¿Por qué hay problemas de comunicación en las familias? Hay varias razones. Una razón es que la madre y el padre trabajan largas horas fuera de casa y los hijos están solos mucho tiempo, sin la compañía y la supervisión de sus mayores. La ausencia de los padres puede crear cierta independencia en los hijos y una distancia emocional que causa dificultades en la comunicación entre padres e hijos.

LA TECNOLOGÍA

Un segundo factor es la tecnología. Nuestro mundo está controlado por la tecnología. Evidentemente la tecnología facilita muchas cosas, pero su uso excesivo puede complicar la vida. Muchos jóvenes tienen acceso ilimitado a Internet, sobre todo a los sitios web de comunicación social y entretenimiento, como Facebook y YouTube. Idealmente, el bajo costo de la conexión debería afectar positivamente la comunicación en la familia, pero la realidad indica que la comunicación moderna (por ejemplo, mensajes de texto, entradas de Twitter) tiende a ser más breve y más superficial. Los hijos prefieren no discutir sus problemas por correo electrónico o mensajes de texto. Prefieren hablar directamente con sus padres, si es que sus padres tienen el tiempo.

Lo mismo ocurre con el teléfono celular. Es cierto que los jóvenes usan celulares para llamar a sus padres, pero muy pocos usan el celular para conversar largamente con sus padres sobre temas personales importantes.

CONCLUSIÓN

En conclusión, el tiempo limitado que los padres pueden dar a sus hijos y la tendencia a usar la tecnología para comunicaciones muy breves pueden afectar negativamente las relaciones familiares. Por eso es importante crear oportunidades para una comunicación real y profunda dentro de la familia. Si usas la tecnología de manera positiva para pasar tiempo con tus familiares y para expresar el amor y el cariño que sientes por ellos, tu familia va a ser más fuerte y unida.

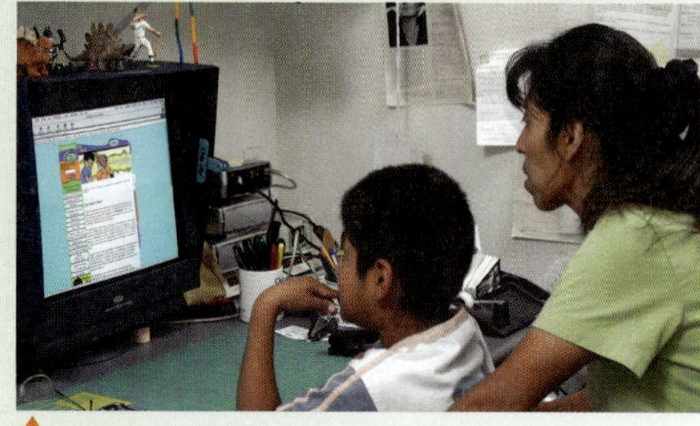

La tecnología puede facilitar la comunicación familiar.

Follow-up for 4-42
Students may share their ideas with another pair. Or you may wish to have a class discussion that focuses on making connections between the content of the article and the reality of students' lives: the process of establishing and maintaining communication with family when they are no longer living at home.

4-42  Interpersonal

Un paso más. Habla con tu compañero/a sobre el impacto de la tecnología en la comunicación familiar entre los estudiantes universitarios y sus padres. Fíjate (*Focus*) en los dos temas principales del artículo:

- la separación física entre los padres y los hijos
- el uso de la tecnología como medio de comunicación

ESCRIBE

4-43 Interpretive

Preparación. Tu madre está preocupada porque estudias este semestre en la Universidad Javeriana en Bogotá. Lee el correo electrónico que te escribe. Después identifica las preguntas de tu madre que quieres contestar y prepara algunas ideas.

Querido hijo:

¿Qué tal estás? Hace dos semanas que no sabemos nada de ti. ¡No escribes correos electrónicos, no te conectas a Skype o a Facebook! ¿Qué ocurre? ¿Estás desconectado de Internet?

Bueno, sé que es el fin del semestre y debes tener mucho trabajo. ¿Tienes mucho estrés? ¿Duermes bastante? ¿Comes bien en la universidad? ¿Tienes problemas en tus clases?

Tu padre y yo pensamos mucho en ti. ¿Tienes tiempo para pasear por la ciudad y conocer muchos sitios nuevos? Debes visitar el Museo del Oro y el de Botero. Creo que la Candelaria es muy bonita también. Por favor, escribe o llama pronto.

Un beso de papá y mamá,

Tu madre

ESTRATEGIA

Use language appropriate for your reader

Even though you are just starting to learn Spanish, you know enough words and phrases to write e-mails that are polite or casual, depending on who will read your message. Use the expressions in *En directo* when writing to people in your family. When you write an e-mail to your instructor, use salutations like **Estimado profesor Gallegos** and closings like **Atentamente** or **Un cordial saludo.**

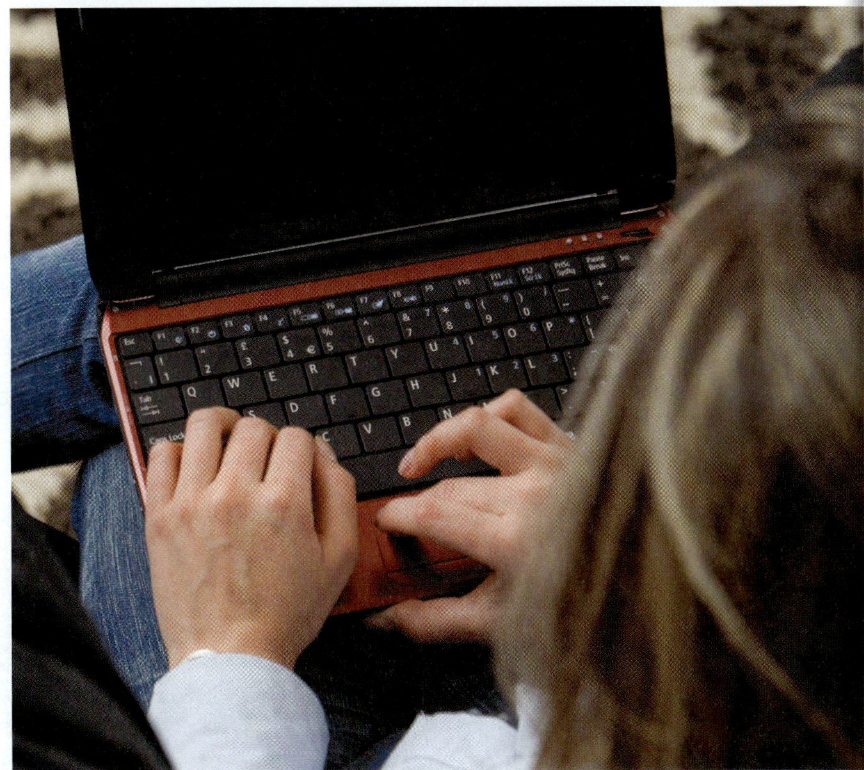

Suggestion for 4-43
In recognition of blended and/or non-traditional families, tell students that they can address their letters to their father, a grandparent, or a favorite aunt/uncle.

Note for *En directo*
Before doing activity 4-44, first have students read the expressions in *En directo*. Then have them listen to the dialogue and encourage them to use the expressions in their own message.

Audioscript for *En directo*

Querido papá:

Mamá me dice que estás muy ocupado. Trabajas muchas horas y te acuestas muy tarde. Por favor, descansa más. Pasa más tiempo con mamá y duerme al menos ocho horas cada noche. Te lo pido porque te quiero.

Abrazos y besos,
Brenda

4-44 Presentational

Escribe. Ahora responde a la carta de tu madre.

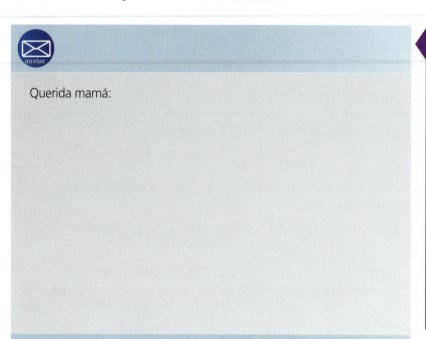

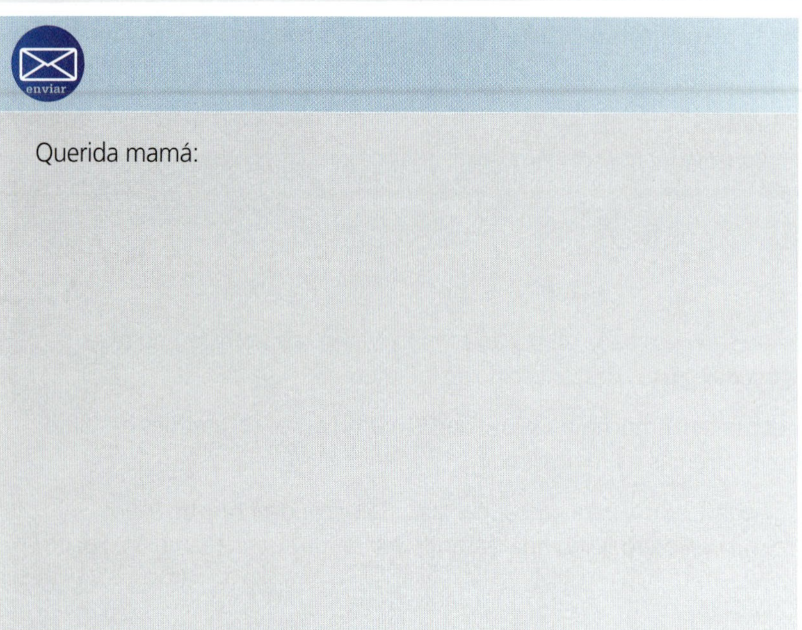

En directo

To write a salutation:

Querido papá/abuelo: *Dear . . . ,*

Querida mamá/abuelita: *Dear . . . ,*

To close correspondence:

Con cariño, *Affectionately,*

Con mucho cariño, *With much love,*

Abrazos y besos, *Hugs and kisses,*

Te recuerdo con cariño, *I remember you (familiar) with affection,*

 Listen to an e-mail with these expressions.

Comprueba

I was able to . . .

_____ present main ideas clearly with adequate details.

_____ use a wide range of vocabulary words.

_____ use correct gender and number agreement with nouns and adjectives.

_____ conjugate verbs correctly and make them agree with their subjects.

_____ use accurate spelling, capitalization, and punctuation.

_____ close the message properly.

4-45 Interpersonal

Un paso más. Lee la respuesta de tu compañero/a a su madre. Escríbanse (*Write to each other*) un correo electrónico en el que hacen una lista de las semejanzas y diferencias entre sus cartas.

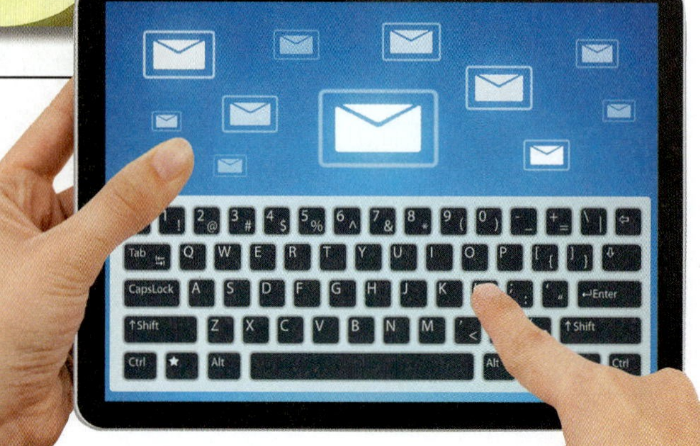

En este capítulo...

Comprueba lo que sabes

Go to ***MySpanishLab*** to review what you have learned in this chapter. Practice with the following:

Vocabulario

LA FAMILIA
The family

la abuela *grandmother*
el abuelo *grandfather*
la esposa *wife*
el esposo *husband*
la hermana *sister*
el hermano *brother*
la hija *daughter*
el hijo *son*
la madrastra *stepmother*
la madre *mother*
la mamá *mom*
la media hermana *half-sister*
el medio hermano *half-brother*
la nieta *granddaughter*
el nieto *grandson*
el niño/la niña *child*
la novia *fiancée; girlfriend*
el novio *fiancé; boyfriend*
el padrastro *stepfather*
el padre *father*
los padres *parents*
el papá *dad*
el pariente *relative*
el primo/la prima *cousin*
la sobrina *niece*
el sobrino *nephew*
la tía *aunt*
el tío *uncle*

LAS DESCRIPCIONES
Descriptions

casado/a *married*
divorciado/a *divorced*
gemelo/a *twin*
ocupado/a *busy*

VERBOS
Verbs

acostar(se) (ue) *to put to bed; to go to bed*
afeitar(se) *to shave; to shave (oneself)*
almorzar (ue) *to have lunch*
ayudar *to help*
bañar(se) *to bathe; to take a bath*
casar(se) *to get married*
cerrar (ie) *to close*
conectar(se) *to connect to*
costar (ue) *to cost*
decir (g, i) *to say, to tell*
dedicar *to dedicate*
desayunar *to have breakfast*
despertar(se) (ie) *to wake (someone up); to wake up*
dormir (ue) la siesta *to take a nap*
dormir(se) (ue) *to sleep; to fall asleep*
duchar(se) *to give a shower to; to take a shower*
empezar (ie) *to begin, to start*
encontrar (ue) *to find*
entender (ie) *to understand*
llamar(se) *to call; to be called*
hacer *to do*
jugar (ue) *to play (a game, sport)*
lavar(se) *to wash (oneself)*
levantar(se) *to raise; to get up*
maquillar(se) *to put makeup on (someone); to put makeup on (oneself)*
pasar *to spend (time)*
pasear *to take a walk, to stroll*
pedir (i) *to ask for; to order*
peinar(se) *to comb (someone's hair); to comb (one's hair)*
pensar (ie) *to think*
pensar (ie) + *infinitive* *to plan to + verb*
poder (ue) *to be able to, can*
poner(se) (g) la ropa *to put one's clothes on*
preferir (ie) *to prefer*
querer (ie) *to want*
quitar(se) *to take away; to take off*
repetir (i) *to repeat*
secar(se) *to dry (oneself)*
seguir (i) *to follow, to go on*
sentarse (ie) *to sit down*
sentir(se) (ie) *to feel*
servir (i) *to serve*
tener (g, ie) *to have*
terminar *to finish*
venir (g, ie) *to come*
vestir(se) (i) *to dress; to get dressed*
visitar *to visit*
volver (ue) *to return*

PALABRAS Y EXPRESIONES ÚTILES
Useful words and expressions

el bautizo *baptism, christening*
la foto(grafía) *photo(graph)*
frecuentemente *frequently, often*
juntos/as *together*
el/la mayor *the oldest*
el matrimonio *marriage*
el/la menor *the youngest*
tarde *late*
temprano *early*
un poco *a little*

See *Lengua* box on page 145 for time expressions.
See *Lengua* box on page 150 for other expressions with **pensar.**
See page 160 for time expressions with **hacer.**

Introduction to chapter
Introduce the chapter theme. Help students access meaning by making frequent use of gestures or visuals.
Ask related questions: *¿Dónde vives? ¿Vives en una casa o en un apartamento?, ¿o alquilas un cuarto en una casa? ¿Vives con tu familia o con otros estudiantes? ¿Te gusta el lugar donde vives ahora? Después de graduarte, ¿dónde quieres vivir? ¿En la ciudad o en el campo?*

Integrated Performance Assessment: Three Modes of Communication

Presentational: See activities 5-6, 5-13, 5-34, 5-37, 5-40, and 5-44.

Interpretive: See activities 5-1, 5-2, 5-3, 5-4, 5-5, 5-9, 5-10, 5-11, 5-14, 5-16, 5-17, 5-18, 5-19, 5-20, 5-21, 5-23, 5-24, 5-25, 5-27, 5-28, 5-29, 5-31, 5-32, 5-33, 5-35, 5-38, 5-41, and 5-43.

Interpersonal: See activities 5-3, 5-4, 5-5, 5-6, 5-7, 5-8, 5-9, 5-10, 5-11, 5-12, 5-13, 5-14, 5-15, 5-16, 5-17, 5-18, 5-19, 5-20, 5-21, 5-22, 5-23, 5-24, 5-25, 5-26, 5-27, 5-28, 5-29, 5-30, 5-33, 5-36, 5-38, 5-39, 5-42, 5-45, and all *Situación* activities.

5 ¿Dónde vives?

ENFOQUE CULTURAL
Nicaragua, El Salvador y Honduras

VOCABULARIO EN CONTEXTO
¿Dónde vives?
La casa, los muebles y los electrodomésticos
Las tareas domésticas

MOSAICO CULTURAL
Las viviendas en centros urbanos

FUNCIONES Y FORMAS
Present progressive
Expressions with *tener*
Direct object nouns and pronouns
Demonstrative adjectives and pronouns

EN ACCIÓN
En casa

MOSAICOS
ESCUCHA Create mental images
HABLA Plan what you want to say
LEE Inform yourself about a topic before you start to read
ESCRIBE Select the appropriate content and tone for a formal description

EN ESTE CAPÍTULO...
Comprueba lo que sabes
Vocabulario

LEARNING OUTCOMES

You will be able to:

- talk about housing, the home, and household activities
- express ongoing actions
- describe physical and emotional states
- avoid repetition in speaking and writing
- point out and identify people and things
- compare cultural and geographic information of Nicaragua, El Salvador, and Honduras

ENFOQUE cultural

Enfoque cultural

To learn more about Nicaragua, El Salvador, and Honduras, go to MySpanishLab to view the *Vistas culturales* videos.

Cuadro de Fernando Llort, pintor de El Salvador

NICARAGUA, EL SALVADOR Y HONDURAS

¿QUÉ TE PARECE?

- El 90% de la población de Honduras es mestiza, el 7% indígena, el 2% negra y el 1% blanca. Los mayas son el principal grupo indígena.
- El Salvador declaró la guerra contra Honduras, en 1969, después de un partido de fútbol. Se conoce como la Guerra de las Cien Horas.
- El café es un producto de exportación importante en esta región.
- El lago Nicaragua es el único lago del mundo donde hay tiburones (*sharks*).

Suggestion for map
Brainstorm with students what they already know about Nicaragua, El Salvador, and Honduras. Project the image of the map and ask them to locate the countries: *¿Qué países están al norte de El Salvador? ¿Cuál está al sur de Nicaragua?* Explain that *mango verde con limón y sal* is a refreshing snack found in these countries. Ask questions to help students make connections: *¿Tienen algún amigo de Honduras/Nicaragua/El Salvador? ¿Conocen a alguna persona famosa de estos países?* Recycle adjectives that refer to nationalities: *hondureño, nicaragüense, salvadoreño. Rubén Darío es un escritor nicaragüense muy importante.*

Note for art
Fernando Llort is a well-known painter from El Salvador. His childlike and colorful style has often been compared with that of the Spanish painters Pablo Picasso and Joan Miró.

Suggestions
Recycle previously learned vocabulary by asking questions about the painting: *¿Cuántas personas hay en este cuadro? ¿Qué hacen? ¿Qué colores hay en el cuadro? ¿Hay animales? ¿Cómo son? ¿Cuántas casas hay? ¿Cómo son? ¿Piensan que esto es un pueblo o una ciudad? ¿Por qué? ¿Les gusta el cuadro? ¿Por qué?* Encourage students to take the virtual art tour online to learn more about this painting.

Note about *Suchitoto and Santa Ana*
Many Salvadorans visit Suchitoto for its cultural events and for Suchitlán, a large lake known for fishing, boating, and bird watching. Santa Ana is known for its coffee production and its proximity to the Santa Ana and Izalco volcanoes.

Note about *turismo*
The recent growth in tourism—now bigger than the coffee industry—has helped the Nicaraguan economy to prosper. Tourists from the United States, Europe, and Central and South America are drawn to the ecotourism activities, the beaches on both the Caribbean and Pacific coasts, and the colonial cities.

Note about *Copán*
Although Copan may have been founded as early as 2000 B.C., it reached its peak in 300–900 A.D. The city was abandoned in the 10th century. The Spanish explorer Diego García de Palacio reached the ruins in 1570, but the site was not excavated until the 19th century. It has been designated a UNESCO World Heritage site.

ENFOQUE cultural

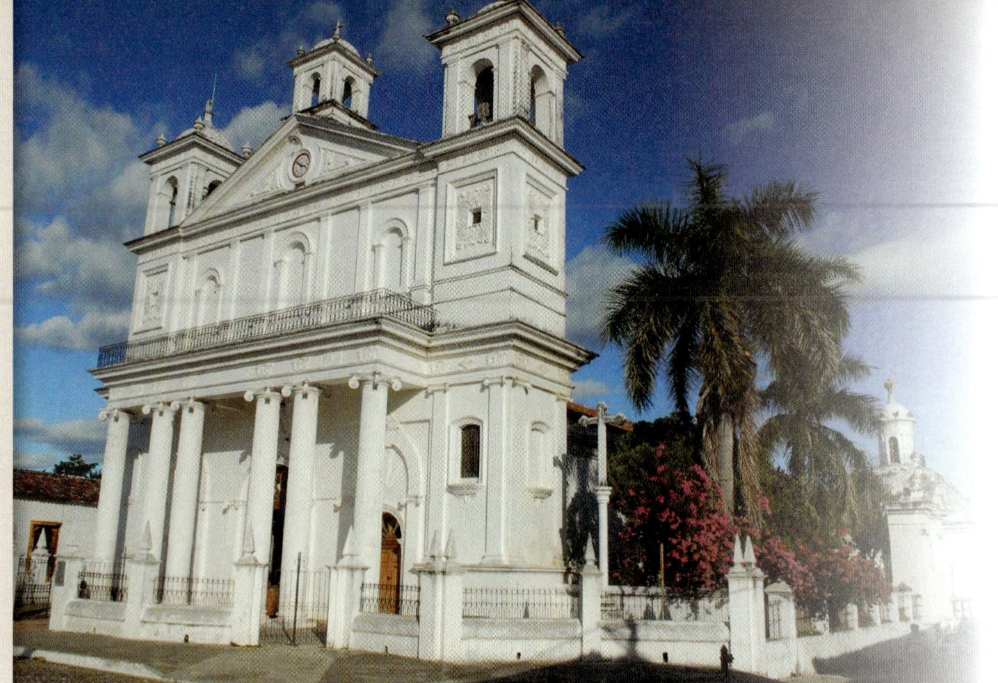

Suchitoto y Santa Ana son dos ciudades coloniales de El Salvador. Aquí se encuentran casas coloniales, museos, galerías de arte e iglesias.

El turismo es la segunda industria más importante de Nicaragua. El número de turistas que visitan Nicaragua aumenta cada año un 15% desde el 2007 y se espera llegar a 2,6 millones de turistas para el año 2020.

En el valle de Copán, en Honduras, se encuentran las ruinas más importantes de la civilización maya. Este antiguo centro de actividad y cultura es ahora el Parque Arqueológico Copán e incluye vestigios de plazas, templos y un estadio para el juego de pelota. Aquí vemos uno de los marcadores (*scoreboards*).

¿CUÁNTO SABES?

Completa estas oraciones con la información correcta.

1. El Salvador tiene frontera con ___Guatemala___, ___Honduras___ y ___Nicaragua___.
2. Hay tiburones en ___el lago Nicaragua en Nicaragua___.
3. Los mayas son el grupo indígena principal de ___Honduras___.
4. El pintor Fernando Llort es de ___El Salvador___.
5. La mayor parte de la población de Honduras es ___mestiza___.
6. El ___café___ de Honduras se exporta a muchos países.

Vocabulario en contexto

Talking about housing, the home, and household activities

¿Dónde vives?

MySpanishLab **Pronunciation Topic:** Consonants *b*, *v*, and *d*.
Learn more using Amplifire Dynamic Study Modules, Pronunciation, and Vocabulary Tutorials.

En las ciudades de Nicaragua, El Salvador y Honduras hay **viviendas** de diferentes **estilos.** La ciudad de Granada, en Nicaragua, tiene **calles** y plazas como esta, con casas coloniales de colores alegres. En Tegucigalpa, la capital de Honduras, hay **edificios** de **apartamentos.** Algunas personas prefieren vivir **cerca** del **centro. Creen** que los **barrios** de las **afueras** están muy **lejos** del **trabajo** y de los centros de diversión.

Una calle en el centro de Granada, Nicaragua

EN OTRAS PALABRAS

Some words for the parts of a house vary from one region to another in the Spanish-speaking world. Here are some examples:

habitación → dormitorio, cuarto, alcoba, recámara
sala → salón, living
planta → piso
piscina → pileta, alberca

¿En qué piso viven?

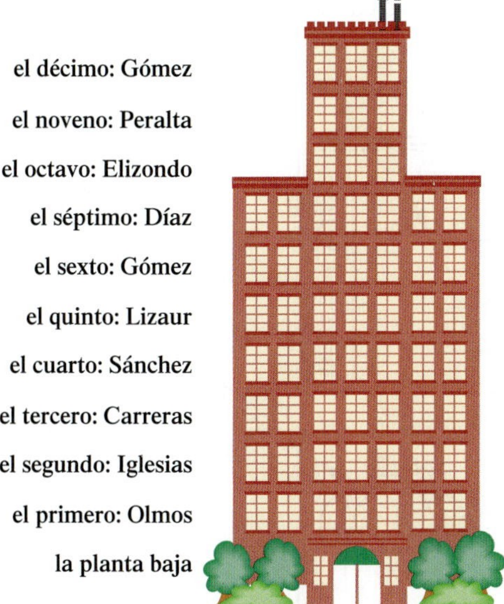

Cultura

La planta baja

In most Hispanic countries the term **planta baja** is used for the American first floor/lobby. **El primer piso** or **primera planta** is usually what in the United States is the second floor, and so on.

Comparaciones. Si presionas el botón "1" en un ascensor (*elevator*) en un país hispano, ¿a qué piso llegas? ¿Y en Estados Unidos?

LENGUA

Ordinal numbers are adjectives and agree in gender and number with the noun they modify (e.g., **la segunda casa, el cuarto edificio**). **Primero** and **tercero** drop the final **-o** when used before a masculine singular noun.

el **primer** apartamento el **tercer** piso

Suggestion for *¿Dónde vives?*
You may want to project the image of Granada in class and ask questions to review the vocabulary.
Ask questions so that students describe the street and the buildings in the photo. *¿Qué hay en esta foto? ¿Les gusta esta calle? ¿Cómo son los edificios?* Point to the street arcades, which are typical of Granada in Nicaragua.
Explain: *Estos corredores son típicos de Granada, son para pasear. Las casas en esta ciudad son antiguas. En la capital, Managua, hay edificios modernos y rascacielos* (write word on board).
Then personalize by asking: *Y tú, ¿vives en el centro o en las afueras de la ciudad? ¿Vives en un apartamento o en una casa? ¿Tu casa tiene arcos/puertas/ventanas grandes?*

Suggestion
The reference to colonial style is a good opportunity to introduce Culture, Comparisons, and Connections of the National Standards. Ask students what they understand by the term colonial style: *¿Hay casas de estilo colonial en tu vecindario o en tu ciudad? ¿Cómo son esas casas? ¿Dónde hay estilo colonial español en Estados Unidos? ¿Es similar o diferente el estilo colonial de California y el de Nueva Inglaterra? ¿Por qué?*

Suggestion for *¿En qué piso viven?*
You may want to project the image of this building to review ordinal numbers. Ask questions about the drawing to check comprehension: *¿Es este un edificio moderno o antiguo? ¿Tiene piscina/pileta/alberca? ¿En qué planta/piso está la piscina probablemente: en la planta baja o en el décimo piso? ¿Hay terrazas en este edificio? ¿Dónde están? En este edificio hay una oficina de administración. ¿En qué piso está probablemente?*

Suggestion for ad
Explain the word *anuncio* by showing the ad. Ask questions to check comprehension: *¿Qué hacemos en el comedor? ¿Y en la cocina?*

Note
The monetary unit of Honduras is *el lempira,* named in honor of Lempira (1497–1537), a Lenca chieftain who fought against the Spanish. House prices are often given in dollars as well as in *lempiras* (Lps). As of July, 2013 1 $US = 20.4 Lps, approximately. You may ask students to find the current rate of exchange.

El apartamento del anuncio

MARTA DÍAZ: Hola, buenos días. Me llamo Marta Díaz. Me gustaría visitar el apartamento del anuncio.

DIEGO LÓPEZ: Sí, claro. Mucho gusto, señorita Díaz. Yo soy Diego López. Pase, pase. Como usted puede ver, el apartamento es muy alegre.

MARTA DÍAZ: ¡Ah, sí! Tiene muchas ventanas y luz natural.

DIEGO LÓPEZ: Esta es la **sala.** Es muy grande. Junto a la sala hay un **comedor** pequeño y al lado está la **cocina.**

MARTA DÍAZ: ¡La cocina es lindísima!

DIEGO LÓPEZ: Sí, todos los **electrodomésticos** son nuevos. A la izquierda del **pasillo** hay dos **habitaciones** y un **baño.**

MARTA DÍAZ: Esta habitación tiene muy buena **vista** a la **piscina** y al **jardín.** Además, los **muebles** son de buena calidad. Me gusta mucho el apartamento. ¿Cuánto es el **alquiler?**

DIEGO LÓPEZ: 12.000 lempiras al mes.

MARTA DÍAZ: Pues, señor López, me encantan el apartamento y esta **zona** céntrica. Y el precio es muy bueno. Voy a decidir esta noche y lo llamo mañana.

DIEGO LÓPEZ: Perfecto, señorita Díaz. Hasta mañana.

ALQUILERES

Categoría:	Alquiler apartamentos
Ciudad:	Tegucigalpa
Ubicación:	Palmira
Descripción:	PALMIRA ALQUILER DE APARTAMENTO MUY AMPLIO, CÉNTRICO Y ACCESIBLE, 2 HABITACIONES, SALA-COMEDOR, COCINA, 1 BAÑO, ÁREA DE LAVANDERÍA, ESTACIONAMIENTO, PISCINA.
Precio:	$ 12.000

EN OTRAS PALABRAS

The Spanish word for *apartment* varies according to the country. **El apartamento** is used in Central America, Colombia, and Venezuela, and **el departamento** is common in Mexico, Argentina, Peru, and Chile. The word used in Spain is **el piso.**

EN OTRAS PALABRAS

The expressions **Pase(n)** and **Adelante** invite people to enter a room or a house in many Spanish-speaking countries. In others, like Colombia, the expression **Siga(n)** is preferred.

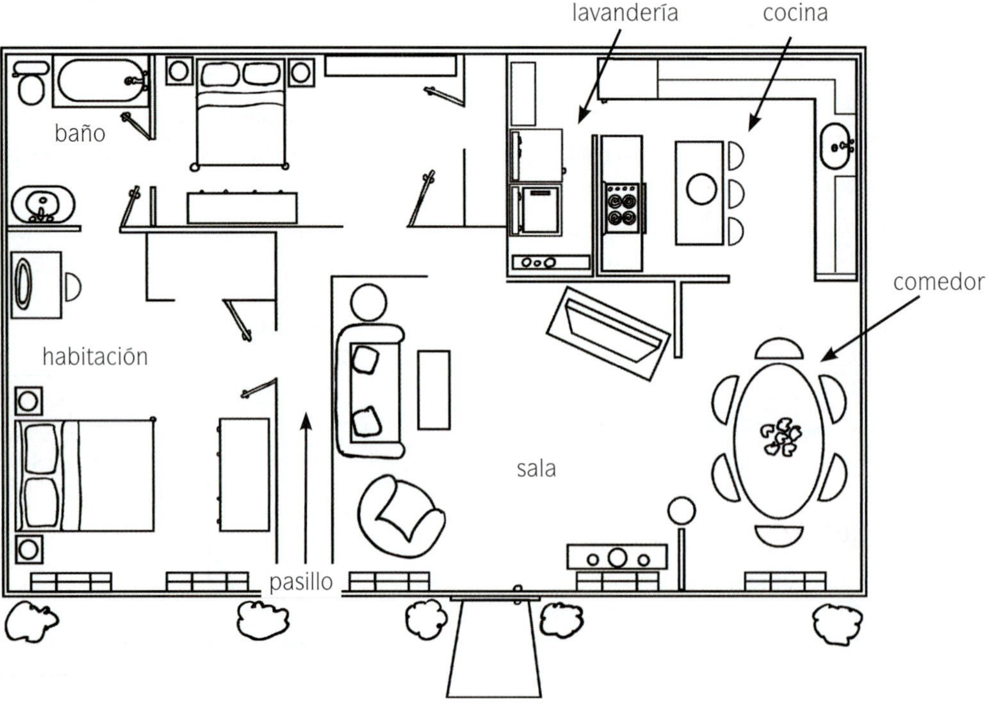

PRÁCTICA

5-1   

Escucha y confirma. Look at the floor plan of the house on page 174 and decide if each of the sentences you hear is cierto (**C**) or falso (**F**).

1. F
2. C
3. F
4. C
5. F
6. F

5-2

Asociación. Indica si las siguientes afirmaciones son ciertas (**C**) o falsas (**F**), según la conversación entre Diego y Marta.

1. F Marta Díaz quiere comprar el apartamento.
2. F La sala es pequeña.
3. F El apartamento tiene dos baños.
4. C Los electrodomésticos son nuevos.
5. C Los muebles son de buena calidad.
6. F A Marta no le gusta la zona céntrica.

5-3 

¿En qué piso viven? Túrnense y pregúntense dónde viven las diferentes personas. Tu compañero/a debe contestar de acuerdo con el dibujo (*drawing*) en la página 174.

 MODELO E1: *¿Dónde viven los Girondo?* E2: *Viven en el cuarto piso, en el apartamento 4-A.*

Cultura

Hoteles de lujo

In many Hispanic countries, the tourism industry is one of the most important drivers of the economy. As a result, most beach and ski resorts tend to be similar everywhere, and, with some exceptions, do not reflect local architecture or building styles. A booming tourism industry also sparks controversy. Although it brings jobs to local communities, most of the economic benefits are enjoyed by the multinational companies that own the resorts, not by the communities themselves.

Comparaciones. En Estados Unidos, ¿hay zonas de playa donde hay turismo masivo? ¿Dónde están? En general, ¿son zonas ricas o pobres?

5-4  

Un hotel de lujo. Tu amigo/a (tu compañero/a) es un/a arquitecto/a que va a construir un hotel de lujo en la Bahía de Jiquilisco, cerca de San Salvador, y te pide consejo (*advice*) sobre cómo distribuir los siguientes espacios del hotel.

 MODELO el restaurante

E1: *¿En qué piso vamos a poner el restaurante?*

E2: *Debe estar en la planta baja.*

1. la discoteca
2. la recepción
3. el gimnasio
4. la oficina de seguridad
5. las habitaciones
6. la piscina
7. la cafetería con vistas a la playa
8. el salón de computadoras

Audioscript for 5-1
1. *En el apartamento hay tres habitaciones.*
2. *El comedor está al lado de la sala.*
3. *El baño está al lado de la cocina.*
4. *En el apartamento hay una lavandería.*
5. *El pasillo está entre la habitación y el baño.*
6. *Hay cuatro sillas en el comedor.*

Suggestion for 5-3
Before doing this activity, ask questions to personalize: *¿Quién vive en un edificio de apartamentos? ¿En qué piso vives? ¿Te gusta vivir en un edificio de apartamentos muy alto? ¿Por qué?*

Suggestion for 5-4
Before doing this activity you may brainstorm with students a list of rooms or spaces that you may find in a big hotel: *salas de conferencias, terraza, baños, cocina, lavandería, tiendas, bar, gimnasio (sala de ejercicio).* These may be added to the ones listed in the activity.

Suggestion for 5-5
You may want to have students compare their housing with the drawing by asking them about these features: *tipo de vivienda, número de baños, número de habitaciones, ubicación,* etc.

5-5 

La casa de alquiler. **PREPARACIÓN.** Ustedes van a mudarse (*move*) a un apartamento porque la casa donde viven es muy grande y la quieren alquilar. Escriban un anuncio para alquilar su casa. Incluyan la siguiente información:

Exterior de la casa

- número de habitaciones y de baños
- distribución (*layout*) de los cuartos
- color de la sala
- otras características (garaje, jardín, sótano [*basement*], ático, etc.)
- ubicación (*location*) de la casa en relación al centro de la ciudad, a la universidad, etc.
- precio

Interior de la casa

INTERCAMBIOS. Presenten su anuncio a la clase y contesten las preguntas de sus compañeros sobre la casa que quieren alquilar.

Cultura

Terremoto en Managua

Managua, the capital of Nicaragua, like many cities, has been shaped by its history, economy and natural disasters. As a result of the devastating earthquake in 1972, most of the city has been rebuilt in the outskirts, which are geographically safer areas. The traditional downtown area, although rebuilt, focuses on government and tourism, but lacks residential and commercial activity.

Conexiones. ¿En qué regiones de tu país ocurren desastres naturales? ¿De qué tipos: huracanes, terremotos (*earthquakes*), tornados? ¿Qué hacen las personas para proteger (*protect*) su vivienda de los desastres naturales?

▲ Casa en el centro de Managua

Suggestion for 5-6
You may wish to have students prepare their advantages and disadvantages as lists of simple sentences to facilitate the exchange of views; e.g., *Las casas son grandes. Hay más espacio; preferimos los apartamentos porque no tenemos que cortar el césped.*

5-6 

Ventajas y desventajas. Hablen de las ventajas y desventajas de los temas relacionados con las viviendas. Escriban las más importantes y luego compartan sus opiniones con la clase.

	VENTAJAS	DESVENTAJAS
1. vivir en un apartamento		
2. vivir en una casa		
3. tener una piscina		
4. compartir una casa con 3 o 4 compañeros/as		

La casa, los muebles y los electrodomésticos

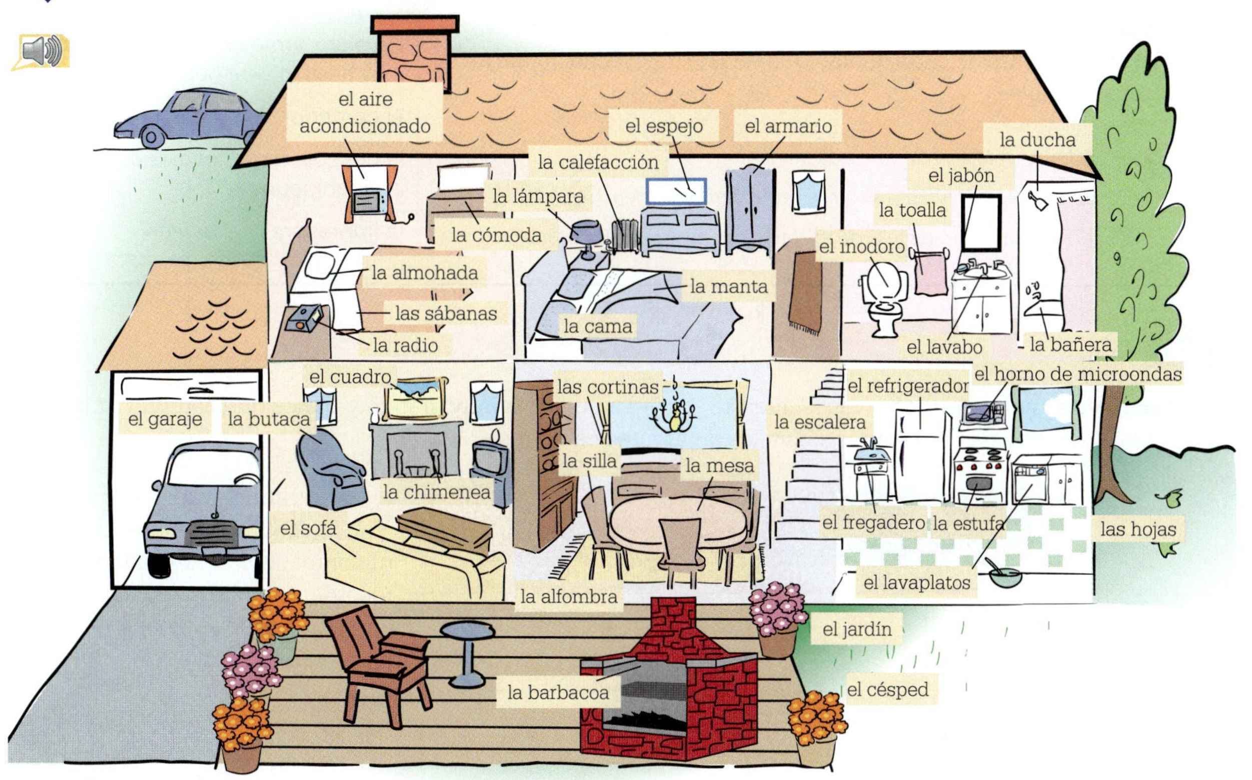

PRÁCTICA

5-7 

Para confirmar. **PREPARACIÓN.** Escribe las siguientes palabras en la columna apropiada.

la alfombra	las cortinas	el/la radio
el armario	el cuadro	el refrigerador
la butaca	el horno	las sábanas
la cómoda	el lavaplatos	la silla

APARATOS ELÉCTRICOS	MUEBLES	ACCESORIOS
el refrigerador	el armario	el cuadro
el/la radio	la cómoda	las cortinas
el horno	la silla	la alfombra
el lavaplatos	la butaca	las sábanas

EN OTRAS PALABRAS

Words for household items often vary from one region to another, for example:

manta → cobija, frazada
armario → clóset
bañera → bañadera, tina
refrigerador → nevera, heladera
estufa → cocina

 **INTERCAMBIOS.** Contesten las siguientes preguntas relacionadas con *Preparación.*

1. Según ustedes, ¿qué aparato eléctrico cuesta más dinero?
2. ¿Qué muebles necesitan todos los días los estudiantes?
3. ¿Qué accesorios tienen ustedes en su cuarto?
4. ¿En qué parte de la casa generalmente están estos accesorios?

Suggestion for *La casa, los muebles y los electrodomésticos*
Tell students to imagine that the classroom is a house. Walk around and "identify" the different "rooms." First, whisper to individual students what activities they will act out in pantomime in each part of the house. Later, you may ask the rest of the class questions: *Mark y Susan están en la cocina. ¿Qué hacen? (Preparan la comida). Esta es la sala y aquí están María y Carlota. ¿Qué hacen en la sala? (Miran televisión).* Encourage students to include items from each room in their responses. You may also review colors using the illustration, and/or by having students give the colors of rooms in their houses or apartments.

Suggestion
You may introduce some additional vocabulary, such as *pared, congelador, ventilador.*

Note
When referring to a microwave oven, people usually shorten it to *el microondas,* instead of saying *el horno de microondas.*

Note for 5-7
Point out that some Spanish speakers prefer to say *el radio.* In Spain, *la radio* is more common.

Standard 4.1
Students demonstrate understanding of the nature of language through the language studied and their own. The information in the *En otras palabras* box shows students that different words are used for the same entity in different parts of the Spanish-speaking world. Instructors may wish to have students brainstorm words they know for apartment in English (flat, rooms) as well as other items (e.g., soda = soft drink, pop; long sandwich with meat, lettuce, etc. = sub, hero, hoagie, grinder, po' boy).

Follow-up for 5-8
You may wish to have students report the most interesting feature of their partners' house/apartment. This type of follow-up makes students accountable for focusing on the pair work.

Follow-up for 5-9
To give students additional practice talking about housing, you may wish to ask them about what they bought when they moved into their dorm room or apartment, and things (besides basic furniture items) they found most useful.

Suggestion for 5-10
The expressions *más que* and *menos que* will be useful to students in this activity. Introduce them here as a preview to the section on comparisons of inequality in *Capítulo 8*. Most of the adjectives and expressions in the box are a review. Students have the opportunity to recycle them in the context of the house and furnishings in this activity. Encourage students to use the cardinal and ordinal numbers.

5-8 

El curioso. Intercambien preguntas para describir los cuartos de la casa/del apartamento de cada uno/a. Traten (*Try*) de obtener la mayor información posible.

E1: *¿Cómo es la sala de tu casa?*

E2: *Es pequeña. Hay una alfombra verde y un sofá blanco grande.*

E1: *¿También hay una mesa de cristal? ¿Y cómo es tu dormitorio?*

LENGUA

Here are some electronics that you may have in your house:

el cargador	*charger*
la consola de videojuegos	*games console*
la impresora	*printer*

5-9

Preparativos. **PREPARACIÓN.** Vas a mudarte (*move*) a una casa muy grande y tienes que comprar muchas cosas. Organiza tu lista de compras según las siguientes categorías.

	MUEBLES	ACCESORIOS	ELECTRODOMÉSTICOS/ APARATOS ELECTRÓNICOS
para el dormitorio			
para la sala			
para el comedor			
para la cocina			

INTERCAMBIOS. Comparte tu lista de compras con tu compañero/a. Él/Ella te va a recordar (*remind you about*) otras cosas que probablemente vas a necesitar.

E1: *Voy a comprar una cama nueva para el dormitorio.*

E2: *¿No vas a comprar sábanas y mantas? ¿Y no necesitas un sofá?*

5-10 

Por catálogo. Miren los objetos del catálogo y elijan (*choose*) un producto de cada categoría. Describan sus preferencias y expliquen dónde van a poner estos accesorios.

barato/a	cómodo/a	grande
bonito/a	de buena calidad	lindo/a
caro/a	de color…	pequeño/a

E1: *Me gusta la toalla gris porque no es cara y es muy linda. Es para el cuarto de baño.*

E2: *Yo prefiero la toalla azul porque es más grande.* Voy a poner la toalla en mi baño.

Las tareas domésticas

Gustavo **lava** los **platos** todos los días.

Beatriz a veces **seca** los platos.

Beatriz **cocina** frecuentemente. Ella usa mucho los electrodomésticos.

Gustavo **limpia** el baño y **pasa** la **aspiradora** una vez por semana.

Gustavo **saca** la **basura** todas las noches.

Gustavo **barre** la **terraza** por las tardes.

Beatriz **tiende** la ropa después de lavarla.

Después la **dobla** cuando está **seca.**

LENGUA

The following expressions denote frequency:

- a veces *sometimes*
- frecuentemente *frequently*
- los domingos (lunes, martes, …) *on Sundays (Mondays, Tuesdays, …)*
- todos los días *every day*
- una vez por semana *once a week*
- todas las mañanas (tardes, noches) *every morning (afternoon, night)*

Beatriz **plancha** la ropa los sábados.

PRÁCTICA

5-11 

Para confirmar. Pon estas actividades en el orden que las haces por la mañana. Después, compara tus respuestas con las de tu compañero/a. Usa las siguientes expresiones para indicar el orden: **primero, luego, más tarde, después, finalmente.** ¿Hacen las mismas cosas y en el mismo orden?

MODELO E1: *Primero preparo el café. ¿Y tú?*

E2: *Primero hago la cama.*

______ lavar los platos	______ desayunar
______ preparar el café	______ secar los platos
______ salir para la universidad	______ hacer la cama

Suggestion for *Las tareas domésticas*
You may want to project the images in class and ask the following questions as a warm-up: *¿Quién limpia tu casa? ¿Qué días limpias la casa? ¿Barres la terraza? ¿Y pasas la aspiradora también? ¿Quién cocina en tu familia? ¿Lavas los platos? ¿Quién lava la ropa?, ¿… dobla la ropa? ¿… plancha la ropa? ¿… saca la basura?* Point out that the verb **colgar** is also used: *Beatriz cuelga (tiende) la ropa.*

Suggestion for 5-11
Make sure that students use the given expressions to organize their answers and to recycle vocabulary when communicating with each other.

Warm-up for 5-12
Have students name rooms of a house or places associated with the following activities: *preparar la comida, pasar tiempo con los amigos, almorzar, cultivar vegetales, leer el periódico, ver televisión, escuchar música, relajarse, jugar con el perro.*

Suggestion for 5-13
This activity provides a good opportunity to recycle *ir + a + infinitive.* Students work together on their lists and then role-play their conversation on the distribution of chores. You may ask questions to elicit some ideas: *¿Quién va a preparar la comida? ¿Quién va a pasar la aspiradora?*, etc.

Audioscript for 5-14
AGENTE: *Señor Mena, creo que esta casa es una buena compra. Además, está cerca de su trabajo.*
SRA. MENA: *Sí, pero no me gusta la zona donde está. Nosotros preferimos comprar algo más pequeño, pero en una buena zona, especialmente por los niños.*
AGENTE: *Es que una casa con tres habitaciones, dos baños, sala, comedor y garaje para dos autos en un barrio bueno cuesta bastante... ¿Y un apartamento? Hay unos apartamentos nuevos, muy buenos, en la calle Sol.*
SR. MENA: *Mire, preferimos una casa. Los niños necesitan estar al aire libre para jugar. Por eso queremos una casa con un jardín pequeño.*
AGENTE: *Pues hay una casa en la Colonia La Mascota que no es muy grande, 200 metros cuadrados, pero que tiene dos habitaciones grandes, una tercera habitación más pequeña y dos baños.*
SR. MENA: *La Mascota es un barrio muy bueno. ¿La casa tiene jardín?*
AGENTE: *Sí, uno pequeño.*
SRA. MENA: *¿Y cuánto piden?*
AGENTE: *Déjeme ver... 1.200.000 colones, un buen precio para esa zona.*
SR. MENA: *Pues, creo que debemos verla.*

5-12 

Actividades en la casa. Pregúntale a tu compañero/a dónde hace estas actividades normalmente cuando está en casa.

 E1: *¿Dónde lavas la ropa?*
E2: *Lavo la ropa en la lavandería. ¿Y tú?*

1. dormir la siesta
2. escuchar música
3. ver la televisión
4. pasar la aspiradora
5. estudiar para un examen
6. hablar por teléfono con amigos/as

¡A compartir las tareas! **PREPARACIÓN.** Ustedes van a compartir una casa el próximo año académico. Preparen una lista de todas las tareas domésticas que van a hacer.

INTERCAMBIOS. Discutan qué tareas va a hacer cada uno/a de ustedes según sus gustos. Finalmente, hagan un calendario de tareas y compártanlo con el resto de la clase.

 *A mí me gusta tener la cocina limpia. Por eso, yo voy a lavar los platos todas las noches.*

5-14

El agente de bienes raíces. **PREPARACIÓN.** The Mena family and their two children live in San Salvador. They have decided to move to a larger place and they are talking to a real estate agent. Before listening, write down with your partner the kind of housing and the characteristics of the neighborhood they may be looking for.

  **ESCUCHA.** As you listen, circle the letter next to the correct information and compare your answers with those of your classmate.

1. Los señores Mena quieren comprar...
   - **(a.)** una casa.
   - **b.** un apartamento.
2. El señor y la señora Mena prefieren vivir...
   - **(a.)** en una buena zona.
   - **b.** lejos de un parque.
3. El agente de bienes raíces...
   - **a.** no sabe cómo ayudarlos.
   - **(b.)** tiene una casa buena para ellos.
4. El agente dice que la casa del barrio La Mascota...
   - **a.** cuesta mucho.
   - **(b.)** tiene un buen precio.
5. El señor Mena dice que...
   - **(a.)** los niños necesitan estar al aire libre para jugar.
   - **b.** los niños no necesitan jugar al aire libre.

Cultura

Tareas domésticas

Nowadays it is more common in many Spanish-speaking countries to see male family members doing the household chores traditionally assigned to women, such as shopping for groceries, cooking, cleaning the house, and taking care of the children.

Comparaciones. ¿Hay tareas domésticas solo para hombres o solo para mujeres en tu familia y en otras familias que conoces? Explica con ejemplos.

MOSAICO cultural Las viviendas en centros urbanos

Las ciudades del mundo hispano son complejas, multiculturales y un poco caóticas. Debido a la falta de espacio en las áreas metropolitanas, muchas personas viven en apartamentos. Algunas prefieren vivir cerca del centro para disfrutar de la vida cultural de la ciudad: teatros, centros comerciales, centros educativos, etc. En ciudades como Bogotá, Lima, Quito y Buenos Aires, existe una tendencia a construir altos edificios de apartamentos para solucionar el problema de espacio.

▲ **Edificios de apartamentos en Bogotá**

Con el crecimiento (*growth*) de las ciudades, también crece el costo de vida. ¿Sabías que, según un estudio del 2012, comprar vivienda en zonas exclusivas de Bogotá es más caro que comprar un apartamento en Manhattan? Por esta razón, algunas personas deciden vivir en un tipo de vivienda colectiva. En esta vivienda urbana vive una familia o un grupo de amigos, que comparten un baño y la cocina con otros. Estos lugares se llaman *conventillos* en Argentina, *casas de vecindad* en España o *inquilinatos* en Uruguay, Bolivia y Colombia.

En Uruguay y Argentina, por ejemplo, en estos tipos de vivienda residen inmigrantes y trabajadores de pocos recursos. Sin embargo, los conventillos son importantes centros de cultura popular porque reúnen a personas de diferentes nacionalidades, regiones y clases sociales. En los conventillos del barrio de la Boca de Buenos Aires, por ejemplo, se origina el tango.

Compara

1. ¿Cómo son las ciudades en tu región o estado? ¿Hay problemas de espacio?
2. Generalmente, ¿dónde viven las personas en tu ciudad, en casas o en apartamentos? ¿Hay altos edificios de apartamentos como en Bogotá?
3. ¿Existen viviendas colectivas o algo similar en tu ciudad? ¿Dónde están? ¿Quiénes viven allí?
4. Busca fotos de las viviendas típicas de tu ciudad y describe cómo son.

▲ **Conventillo en el barrio de la Boca en Buenos Aires**

Funciones y formas

1 Expressing ongoing actions

ÓSCAR: ¿Aló?

CATALINA: Hola, Óscar. Te habla Catalina. ¿Qué **estás haciendo?**

ÓSCAR: Hola, Catalina. ¡**Estoy trabajando** mucho!

CATALINA: ¿Por qué?

ÓSCAR: Mis padres **están pasando** sus vacaciones en la playa y vuelven mañana. ¡La casa es un desastre total!

CATALINA: ¿Así que **estás limpiando?**

ÓSCAR: ¡Claro! **Estoy barriendo** el piso, **ordenando** la sala, **recogiendo** la ropa… de mi cuarto. Y tú, ¿qué **estás haciendo?**

CATALINA: ¿Yo?… Nada. **Estoy leyendo** el periódico y **tomando** un café.

Piénsalo. Indica a quién o a quiénes se refieren las siguientes afirmaciones. ¿A Catalina (**C**), a Óscar (**O**) o a ambos (**C y O**)?

1. __O__ **Está trabajando** mucho.
2. __C__ **Está descansando.**
3. __O__ **Está limpiando** la casa de sus padres.
4. __O__ No está contento porque **está trabajando** mucho en casa.
5. __C__ **Está bebiendo** algo.
6. __C y O__ **Están haciendo** actividades diferentes.

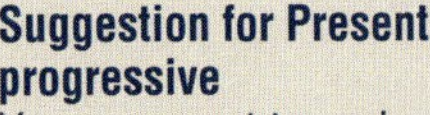

Suggestion for Present progressive
You may want to project the images for *Piénsalo* to review the present progressive. *En este dibujo, el chico está trabajando mucho y la chica está tomando un café. Él está arreglando su casa y ella está leyendo el periódico.* Give additional examples in context referring to your class. For example: *Ahora yo estoy hablando y ustedes están escuchando.* Point out that the present participle is invariable, always ending in *-o*. Use the present progressive to ask yes/no and either/or questions based on the visuals.
You may personalize presentation of the present progressive: *Yo estoy hablando español. Y tú, ¿estás escuchando o estás hablando?* (Ask a student to erase the board.) Then say: *Pedro está trabajando en la pizarra. ¿Está escribiendo o está borrando la pizarra?* (Ask a student to write his/her name on a piece of paper.) Then say: *María está escribiendo en su cuaderno. ¿María está escribiendo la tarea o está escribiendo su nombre?* Then ask: *Yo estoy hablando. Y ustedes, ¿están escuchando? ¿Están contestando preguntas? ¿Están tomando notas?*

Present progressive

- Use the present progressive to emphasize that an action or event is in progress at the moment of speaking, rather than a habitual action.

  Óscar **está limpiando** la casa. — *Oscar is cleaning the house.* (at this moment)

  Óscar **limpia** la casa. — *Oscar cleans the house.* (habitually)

- Form the present progressive with the present tense of **estar** + *present participle.* To form the present participle, add **-ando** to the stem of **-ar** verbs and **-iendo** to the stem of **-er** and **-ir** verbs.

	Estar	Present Participle
yo	**estoy**	
tú	**estás**	habl**ando**
Ud., él, ella	**está**	com**iendo**
nosotros/as	**estamos**	escrib**iendo**
vosotros/as	**estáis**	
Uds., ellos/as	**están**	

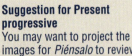

- When the verb stem of an **-er** or an **-ir** verb ends in a vowel, add **-yendo.**

  leer → leyendo

  oír → oyendo

- Stem-changing **-ir** verbs (**o → ue, e → ie, e → i**) change **o → u** and **e → i** in the present participle.

dormir (ue)	(**o → u**)	d**u**rmiendo
sentir (ie)	(**e → i**)	s**i**ntiendo
pedir (i)	(**e → i**)	p**i**diendo

- Spanish does not use the present progressive to express future time, as English does; Spanish uses the present tense instead.

  Salgo mañana. — *I am leaving tomorrow.*

  ¿**Te levantas** temprano mañana? — *Are you getting up early tomorrow?*

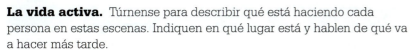

> **e ¿COMPRENDES?**
>
> Indica qué están haciendo los estudiantes en este momento. Usa la forma correcta de los verbos en el presente progresivo.
>
> 1. Alicia y sus compañeros __están trabajando__ mucho para su clase de astronomía. (trabajar)
> 2. Ellos __están leyendo__ información sobre los planetas. (leer)
> 3. En este momento Alicia __está haciendo__ investigación en Internet. (hacer)
> 4. Pero Cristina no __está estudiando__ en este momento. (estudiar)
> 5. Cristina __está hablando__ con Alicia. (hablar)
> 6. Alicia piensa: Cristina __está perdiendo__ tiempo. ¡Tenemos que terminar este trabajo! (perder)
>
> **MySpanishLab**
>
> Learn more using Amplifire Dynamic Study Modules, Grammar Tutorials, and Extra Practice activities.

PRÁCTICA

5-15

Un día ocupado. Hoy es un día de mucha actividad para la familia Villa. Asocia las actividades de la izquierda con las explicaciones de la columna de la derecha, para averiguar (*find out*) por qué las están haciendo.

1. __d__ La Sra. Villa está preparando una cena deliciosa y un pastel (*cake*) especial.
2. __e__ Su hijo Marcelo está barriendo la terraza.
3. __b__ Su hija Ana está lavando los platos en el fregadero.
4. __c__ Alicia está decorando la mesa.
5. __a__ Pedro está hablando por teléfono.

a. Está llamando a su mejor amigo para invitarlo a la fiesta.
b. El lavaplatos no está funcionando.
c. Es una ocasión especial.
d. Es el cumpleaños de su esposo.
e. Está muy sucia (*dirty*) y unos amigos vienen a celebrar el cumpleaños.

5-16

La vida activa. Túrnense para describir qué está haciendo cada persona en estas escenas. Indiquen en qué lugar está y hablen de qué va a hacer más tarde.

MODELO E1: *Rodrigo y Soledad están cantando en una fiesta. Están en la terraza.*

E2: *Después van a bailar y conversar con sus amigos.*

Rodrigo Soledad

Pepe

Arturo

Carlos

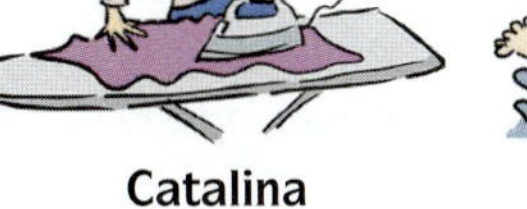

Catalina

Gonzalo

Suggestion for 5-16
Distribute small pieces of paper with different activities to students in small groups. Activities must be associated with an event (watching a football game, cleaning the house on the weekend, preparing a surprise party for someone, etc.) The group as a whole must perform the actions simultaneously. Members of the other groups must describe the action of each person in the group and guess what the event is.

Expansion for 5-16
Have students guess what various classmates are doing at specific moments during the day. Provide the following model:
Son las 8:00 de la noche del viernes. ¿Qué está haciendo [classmate's name]*?* The student whose name was mentioned can agree or disagree with their classmates. You may wish to introduce: *Estoy de acuerdo* or *No estoy de acuerdo.*
Other options: *las 12 de la noche del lunes, la mañana del 25 de diciembre, el día del cumpleaños de papá, la noche antes de un examen,* etc.

Standard 3.1
Students reinforce and further their knowledge of other disciplines through the foreign language. In activity 5-17, students use the information in the photos and their knowledge of Hispanic cultures to figure out which cultural activity each photo depicts. Instructors will provide additional cultural information. The information they gain through this activity, as well as the skill of focusing on cultural information in visual material, may be useful to them in their courses in art, history, and other disciplines.

Suggestion for 5-17
You may divide the class into groups of 3 or 4 and assign one photo to each group. To make the activity more communicative, students should interact with classmates in other groups.

Follow-up for 5-17
You may wish to have students repeat this activity with photos of places and celebrations they bring from home, or with culturally relevant photos that you bring to class or that are in the chapter.

Suggestion for *Situación*
Review with students phone etiquette in Spanish. For example, when people answer the phone, they may say: *aló, diga, hola, sí.* The person at the other end of the line can reply: *Habla…* You may wish to remind students that with family members people tend to be less formal. Students may address their mother or father as *tú.*

Suggestion for *Situación*
You may want to assign partners and have pairs create mini-skits using the video-posting feature, *MediaShare,* online.

5-17

Lugares y actividades. Mira las siguientes fotografías de celebraciones y descríbele a tu compañero/a dos o tres actividades que las personas están haciendo en una de las fotos. Tu compañero/a va a hacer lo mismo (*the same*) con otra fotografía.

Situación

PREPARACIÓN. Lean esta situación. Luego, compartan ejemplos de vocabulario, gramática y otra información que necesitan para desarrollar la conversación.

Role A. There is a big family gathering at your aunt's house today, but you are away at school. Call and greet the family member who answers the phone. Explain that you cannot attend, and express your regret for not being there. Ask how everyone is and what each family member is doing at the moment.

Role B. You are at a big family gathering today. A family member calls to say he/she cannot attend. Answer the phone. Greet the caller and answer his/her questions. Finally, tell the caller that everyone says hello (**todos te mandan saludos**) and say good-bye.

	ROLE A	ROLE B
Vocabulario	Words for family relationships Question words	Words for family relationships Activities that family members do at family gatherings
Funciones y formas	Present progressive Expressing regret Asking questions Observing phone etiquette	Present progressive Expressing regret Giving information Observing phone etiquette

INTERCAMBIOS. Practica la conversación con tu compañero/a incorporando el vocabulario y las funciones de *Preparación.* Luego, represéntenla ante la clase.

2 Describing physical and emotional states

Hoy es un día de verano y los Robledo se están mudando. **Tienen prisa** porque ya son las tres de la tarde. El señor Robledo y su hija Isabel **tienen calor** porque hace cuatro horas que trabajan bajo (*under*) el sol. Ella **tiene mucha sed** y está bebiendo agua. El bebé, Nicolás, llora porque **tiene hambre.** La señora Robledo le da de comer mientras la abuelita Rosa duerme la siesta. Después de empacar su ropa y todas sus fotografías, libros y plantas, Rosa **tiene mucho sueño.** ¡Qué día para los Robledo!

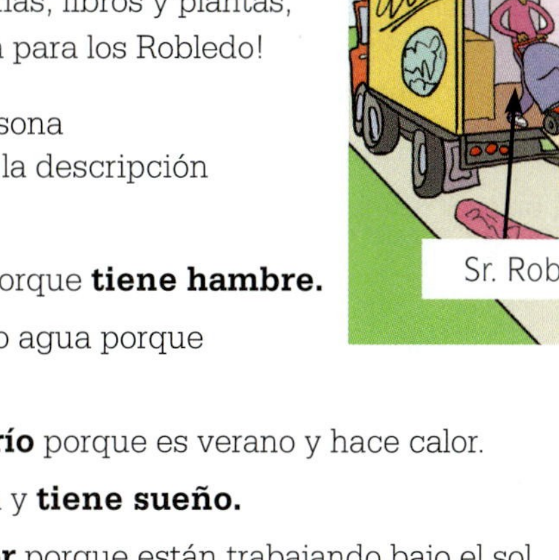

Piénsalo. Identifica a la persona (o personas) del dibujo según la descripción de su estado físico.

1. ___Nicolás___ Va a comer porque **tiene hambre.**
2. ___Isabel___ Está tomando agua porque **tiene sed.**
3. ___los Robledo___ No **tienen frío** porque es verano y hace calor.
4. ___Rosa___ Está cansada y **tiene sueño.**
5. ___el señor Robledo e Isabel___ **Tienen calor** porque están trabajando bajo el sol.
6. ___los Robledo___ **Tienen prisa** porque quieren salir pronto.

Expressions with *tener*

- Spanish uses **tener** + *noun* for many conditions and states where English uses *to be* + *adjective*. You have already seen the expression **tener... años: Eduardo tiene veinte años.** Here are some other useful expressions.

Tener + *noun*			
tener	**hambre**	*to be*	*hungry*
	sed		*thirsty*
	sueño		*sleepy*
	miedo		*afraid*
	calor		*hot*
	cuidado		*careful*
	frío		*cold*
	suerte		*lucky*
	prisa		*in a hurry/rush*
	razón		*right, correct*

- With these expressions, use **mucho/a** to indicate *very.*

Tengo **mucho** calor (frío, miedo, sueño, cuidado).	*I am very hot (cold, afraid, sleepy, careful).*
Tienen **mucha** hambre (sed, suerte).	*They are very hungry (thirsty, lucky).*

¿COMPRENDES?

Completa las oraciones con **tener** y una expresión lógica para describir cómo está Olivia.

1. Son las 12:00 de la noche. Olivia ___tiene sueño___.
2. Hace 95 °F y no puede dormir. ___Tiene calor___.
3. Oye ruidos (*noises*) en la casa. ___Tiene miedo___.
4. Pero los ruidos desaparecen y no vuelven. Olivia piensa que ___tiene suerte___.

MySpanishLab
Learn more using Amplifire Dynamic Study Modules, Grammar Tutorials, and Extra Practice activities.

Suggestion for Expressions with *tener*
Personalize these expressions as follows: *¿Tienes calor en este momento?, ¿Tienes sed? ¿Qué tomas cuando tienes sed? ¿A qué hora tienes sueño generalmente?* Ask students about their classmates' answers.

Suggestion
You may wish to explain that *mucha prisa* is the Spanish equivalent of being in a rush/great hurry. Provide an example: *Son las ocho menos cinco y Emilio está corriendo por el pasillo para llegar a su clase de español. Hay un examen a las ocho y no quiere llegar tarde. Emilio tiene mucha prisa.*
Review *ser* and *estar* with *frío* and *caliente* versus *tener frío/calor.* Visuals will be helpful.

PRÁCTICA

5-18 

Asociaciones. Lee las situaciones y luego asocia cada una de ellas con una expresión lógica de la derecha.

1. Mi hermano siempre tiene __f__ y, por eso, está comiendo ahora.
2. Mi hermana duerme a todas horas porque siempre tiene __d__.
3. En este momento mis primos están visitando la Antártida; probablemente tienen __e__.
4. Mis abuelos están bebiendo agua en la cocina porque tienen __a__.
5. Mi mamá tiene __c__; siempre gana (*wins*) cuando juega a la lotería.
6. ¡Uf! Todavía estoy planchando mi blusa y mis amigos van a llegar en cinco minutos. Yo tengo __b__.

a. sed
b. prisa
c. suerte
d. sueño
e. mucho frío
f. hambre

Suggestion for 5-19
Encourage students to talk about the illustrations before using the *tener* expressions. Provide additional vocabulary as needed.

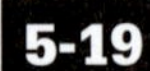

5-19 

¿Qué están haciendo, dónde están y cómo se sienten?

PREPARACIÓN. Túrnense y describan qué están haciendo las personas en los dibujos. Indiquen dónde están y cómo se sienten.

 *El padre y su hijo están durmiendo en el sofá. Tienen sueño.*

1.

2.

3.

4.

INTERCAMBIOS. Respondan a las siguientes preguntas sobre las escenas de *Preparación*.

1. ¿Cuál de los dibujos describe mejor cómo se sienten ustedes en este momento?
2. ¿Qué dibujo refleja (*reflects*) el clima de su región en diciembre?
3. ¿A qué hora se sienten ustedes como las personas del dibujo del modelo?

Estados físicos y estados de ánimo (*moods*). PREPARACIÓN. Termina las siguientes ideas y luego compara tus respuestas con las de tu compañero/a. Usa expresiones con **tener.**

1. Generalmente, cuando mis hermanos y yo hacemos una barbacoa, nosotros . . .
2. Cuando mi madre pasa mucho tiempo limpiando nuestra casa, ella . . .
3. En las mañanas de invierno, yo siempre . . .
4. Cuando yo leo un libro aburrido, siempre . . .
5. Cuando llego a casa y mi compañero/a está preparando mi plato favorito, yo siempre . . .

INTERCAMBIOS. Usando tus apuntes de *Preparación,* escribe una semejanza y una diferencia entre tu compañero/a y tú.

Suggestion for 5-20, *Intercambios*
You may wish to have pairs present their most striking difference to the class to serve as the starting point for additional interaction using expressions with *tener.*

Situación

PREPARACIÓN. Lean esta situación. Luego, compartan ejemplos de vocabulario, gramática y otra información que necesitan para desarrollar la conversación.

Role A. You are staying at a hotel. You call the front desk and say the following:

a. you are very tired, but you cannot sleep because the people in the next room are making a lot of noise (**ruido**);
b. you are cold and need more blankets (**mantas**); and
c. you want to know what time the dining room opens because you are always hungry in the morning.

Role B. You work at the front desk in a hotel. A guest calls you with two complaints and a question. Be as understanding and helpful as possible in responding to the guest.

	ROLE A	ROLE B
Vocabulario	Words that describe physical states	Words and expressions to express reassurance
Funciones y formas	Lodging a complaint Observing phone etiquette	Reacting appropriately to a complaint Using a professional speech style Observing phone etiquette

INTERCAMBIOS. Practica la conversación con tu compañero/a incorporando el vocabulario y las funciones de *Preparación.* Luego, represéntenla ante la clase.

Suggestion for *Situación*
You may want to assign partners and have pairs create mini-skits using the video-posting feature, *MediaShare,* online.

Suggestion for *Situación*
You may wish to review with students ways to address someone formally over the phone and how to place a complaint in Spanish. For example: *Llamo para informarle que no hay calefacción/las personas en el cuarto están haciendo mucho ruido,* etc.
You may also review how to identify oneself over the phone as follows: *Me llamo.../Mi nombre es.../ Llamo del cuarto número...*

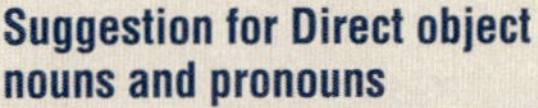

Suggestion for Direct object nouns and pronouns
You may want to project the images in class and have students identify the direct object nouns in the photos by asking questions using *¿Qué?*; e.g., *El padre lava los platos. ¿Qué lava el padre? (Lava) los platos. Los niños secan los platos. ¿Qué secan los niños? (Secan) los platos. Ellas preparan la comida. ¿Qué preparan? (Preparan) la comida.* Ask questions using *¿Quién?* and *¿A quién?* with the photo of the grandmother and child, e.g., *La abuela cuida a la niña. ¿Quién cuida a la niña? ¿A quién cuida la abuela? (Cuida) a la niña.* For additional practice with *¿A quién?*, have one student look at another and ask questions, e.g., *Juan, mira a María. ¿A quién mira Juan? (Mira) a María.*

Suggestion
To practice direct object pronouns, distribute some of your classroom items among the students and then ask questions: *¿Tienes mi lápiz? Sí, lo tengo./No, no lo tengo. Y tú, ¿tienes mi libro?* Ask students if they use certain household items, e.g., *¿Usas la aspiradora en tu casa? Sí, la uso./No, no la uso. ¿Y el horno de microondas?* Help them if necessary. You may also ask if they eat certain items, e.g., *¿Comes cereal en el desayuno? Sí, lo como. ¿Y frutas? Si tienes frío, ¿bebes chocolate caliente?* Introduce *me* afterwards by asking *¿Me ves? ¿Me escuchas?*, and then guide students to ask each other the same questions to practice both *me* and *te*. During the rest of the course be sure to integrate direct object pronouns into regular speech.

3 Avoiding repetition in speaking and writing

¿Qué hacen estas personas?

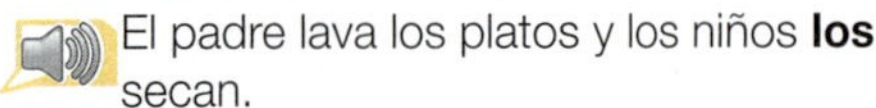

El padre lava los platos y los niños **los** secan.

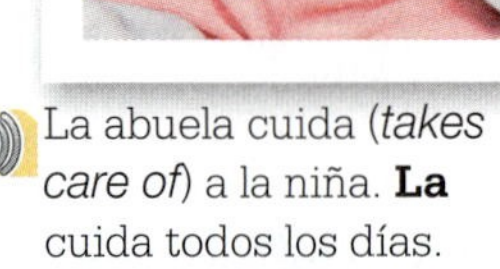

La abuela cuida (*takes care of*) a la niña. **La** cuida todos los días.

Los cocineros (*cooks*) preparan la comida en la cocina del restaurante y después **la** sirven.

Piénsalo. Asocia la descripción con la foto correcta, **A, B** o **C.**

1. __b__ La niña está contenta porque su abuela **la** cuida.
2. __a__ El padre trabaja y los niños **lo** ayudan.
3. __c__ Los cocineros tienen una cocina enorme. **La** usan todos los días.
4. __c__ Ellos están preparando mucha comida. Después, los clientes van a comer**la.**
5. __b__ La abuela está cuidando a la niña. La abuela **la** quiere mucho.
6. __a__ El padre está en la cocina con sus hijos. **Los** mira con cariño y habla con ellos mientras trabajan.

Direct object nouns and pronouns

- Direct objects answer the question *what?* or *whom?* in relation to the verb.

¿Qué dobla Pedro?	*What does Pedro fold?*
(Pedro dobla) **las toallas.**	(*Pedro folds*) *the towels.*

- Direct objects may be nouns or pronouns. When direct object nouns refer to a specific person, a group of persons, or a pet, the word **a** precedes the direct object. This **a** is called the **a personal** and has no equivalent in English. The **a personal** followed by **el** contracts to **al.**

Amanda seca **los platos.**	*Amanda dries the dishes.*
Amanda seca **al perro.**	*Amanda dries off the dog.*

¿Ves la piscina?	*Do you see the swimming pool?*
¿Ves **al** niño en la piscina?	*Do you see the child in the swimming pool?*

- The **a personal** is not used with the verb **tener.**

María tiene un hijo.	*María has a child.*

- Since the question word **quién(es)** refers to people, use the **a personal** when **quién(es)** is used as a direct object.

¿**A quién** vas a ayudar?	*Whom are you going to help?*
Voy a ayudar **a** Pedro.	*I am going to help Pedro.*

- Direct object pronouns replace direct object nouns and are used to avoid repeating the noun while speaking or writing. These pronouns refer to people, animals, or things already mentioned.

Direct Object Pronouns			
me	*me*	**nos**	*us*
te	*you* (familiar, singular)	**os**	*you* (familiar plural, Spain)
lo	*you* (formal, singular), *him, it* (masculine)	**los**	*you* (formal and familiar, plural), *them* (masculine)
la	*you* (formal, singular), *her, it* (feminine)	**las**	*you* (formal and familiar plural), *them* (feminine)

- Place the direct object pronoun before the conjugated verb form.

¿Barre la cocina Mirta?	*Does Mirta sweep the kitchen?*
No, no **la** barre.	*No, she does not sweep it.*
¿Cuidas a tu hermanito?	*Do you take care of your little brother?*
Sí, **lo** cuido.	*Yes, I take care of him.*

- With compound verb forms (a conjugated verb and an infinitive or present participle), a direct object pronoun may be placed before the conjugated verb, or may be attached to the accompanying infinitive or present participle.

¿Vas a ver a Rafael?	*Are you going to see Rafael?*
Sí, **lo** voy a ver mañana. Sí, voy a ver**lo** mañana.	*Yes, I am going to see him tomorrow.*
¿Están limpiando la casa?	*Are they cleaning the house?*
Sí, **la** están limpiando. Sí, están limpiándo**la.**	*Yes, they are cleaning it.*

LENGUA

You have seen that words that stress the next-to-the-last syllable do not have a written accent if they end in a vowel: **lavando.** If we attach a direct object pronoun, we are adding a syllable, so the stress now falls on the third syllable from the end and a written accent is needed: **lavándolo.**

¿COMPRENDES?

Completa las oraciones con el pronombre correcto según la información.

MARIO: Rosario, ¿cuándo vamos a visitar el apartamento?

ROSARIO: (1) __Lo__ vamos a visitar el jueves. ¿Leíste el anuncio del periódico?

MARIO: Sí, (2) __lo__ leí. El apartamento parece grande pero no sé si tiene lavandería.

ROSARIO: (3) __La__ debe tener porque dice el anuncio que los apartamentos que alquilan tienen área de servicio.

MARIO: Sí, debemos (4) visitar__los__ todos para estar seguros.

MySpanishLab

Learn more using Amplifire Dynamic Study Modules, Grammar Tutorials, and Extra Practice activities.

Suggestion for 5-21
You may point out that although all options are grammatically correct, only one of them contains the direct object pronoun appropriate to the context.

Suggestion for 5-23, *Intercambios*
Encourage students to expand on their descriptions to each other. You may wish to have them share them with the class or with another pair.

PRÁCTICA

5-21 

La división del trabajo. Tus compañeros Martín, Pedro y Julio comparten un apartamento y tú quieres saber cómo dividen las tareas domésticas entre ellos. Indica la respuesta más apropiada a cada pregunta que le haces a Julio.

1. ¿Quién limpia la nevera?
   - **a.** Yo lo limpio.
   - **b.** Pedro la limpia.
   - **c.** Nosotros las limpiamos.
2. ¿Quién hace las camas?
   - **a.** Pedro la hace.
   - **b.** Yo los hago.
   - **c.** Martín las hace.
3. ¿Quién tiende la ropa?
   - **a.** Los tres lo tendemos.
   - **b.** Pedro los tiende.
   - **c.** Martín la tiende.
4. ¿Quién saca la basura?
   - **a.** Martín lo saca.
   - **b.** Pedro las saca.
   - **c.** Yo la saco.
5. ¿Quién pasa la aspiradora?
   - **a.** Martín y yo las pasamos.
   - **b.** Pedro la pasa.
   - **c.** Ellos lo pasan.

5-22 

En casa. Adivina (*Guess*) a qué o a quién se refiere tu compañero/a en el contexto de la casa y la familia.

 **Los** lava después de comer
E1: *Los lava después de comer.*
E2: *Los platos.*
E1: *¡Sí, tienes razón!*

Possible answers:

1. La madre **la** plancha cuando está seca. 1. la ropa
2. Los hijos **lo** ordenan todos los sábados. 2. el cuarto, el baño, el comedor
3. Los niños **las** hacen después de levantarse. 3. las camas
4. El padre **los** llama porque necesita ayuda. 4. a sus hijos, a los niños
5. Cada uno **las** limpia en su cuarto para tener más luz natural. 5. las ventanas
6. El esposo **la** pasa por la alfombra de la sala. 6. la aspiradora
7. El hermano mayor **los** ayuda con su tarea. 7. a sus hermanos

5-23 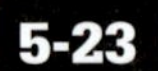 

¿Qué es lógico? **PREPARACIÓN.** Mira el dibujo y asocia las situaciones con las acciones más lógicas.

SITUACIÓN

1. __b__ Las camas están sin hacer.
2. __d__ La ropa está seca.
3. __a__ Los dormitorios están desordenados.
4. __f__ El aire acondicionado no funciona.
5. __c__ Las ventanas están sucias.
6. __e__ No pueden poner el auto en el garaje porque hay muchos muebles viejos y cajas con libros.

ACCIÓN

a. Los hijos los van a ordenar.
b. La madre las hace después de leer el periódico.
c. El padre las va a limpiar.
d. La hija va a plancharla.
e. Los hijos lo van a organizar y limpiar.
f. El hijo mayor lo va a reparar (*fix*).

 **INTERCAMBIOS.** Dile a tu compañero/a cuáles de las afirmaciones de *Preparación* describen mejor tu apartamento o tu casa en este momento.

5-24  

Mis responsabilidades en casa. PREPARACIÓN. Averigua (*Find out*) si tu compañero/a es responsable de las siguientes tareas domésticas en su casa. Añade una más.

 doblar la ropa

E1: *¿Doblas la ropa?*

E2: *Sí, normalmente la doblo. ¿Y tú?*

1. sacar la basura
2. ordenar el garaje
3. limpiar la bañera
4. lavar las sábanas
5. cortar el césped (*grass*)
6. …

 INTERCAMBIOS. Comparen sus respuestas. Después, díganle a otra pareja cuáles son las tareas domésticas que ustedes dos hacen y averigüen si ellos las hacen también.

 E1: *Nosotros no lavamos los platos en casa porque tenemos lavaplatos. ¿Y ustedes los lavan?*

E2: *Sí, los lavamos y los secamos también.*

5-25  

El apartamento de mi compañero/a. Vas a cuidar el apartamento de tu compañero/a por una semana y quieres saber cuáles van a ser tus obligaciones y qué cosas tu amigo/a te permite hacer allí.

 **Para saber tus obligaciones:**

E1: *¿Debo sacar la basura?*

E2: *Sí, la debes sacar todos los días.*

Para saber qué es permitido (*allowed*):

E1: *¿Puedo lavar mi ropa en tu lavadora?*

E2: *Sí, puedes lavarla.*

1. regar las plantas
2. alquilar películas con tu cuenta de Netflix
3. pasear al perro
4. usar los electrodomésticos
5. limpiar el apartamento
6. hacer una fiesta
7. hacer la tarea en tu computadora

5-26 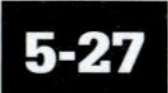

Los preparativos para la visita. La familia Granados está muy ocupada porque espera la visita de unos parientes. Túrnense para preguntar y contestar sobre lo que está haciendo cada miembro de la familia.

 E1: *¿Quién está preparando la comida?*

E2: *La madre está preparándola.*

5-27 

Una mano amiga. PREPARACIÓN. Tu compañero/a te va a hacer preguntas sobre tus relaciones con otras personas. Contesta, escogiendo a una de las personas de la lista.

mi madre	mi novio/a	mi padre
mi mejor amigo/a	mis abuelos	¿…?

 ayudar económicamente

E1: *¿Quién te ayuda económicamente?*

E2: *Mis padres me ayudan económicamente.*

1. querer mucho
2. escuchar en todo momento
3. llamar por teléfono con frecuencia
4. ayudar con los problemas
5. aconsejar (*advise*) cuando estás indeciso/a
6. entender siempre

Suggestion for 5-24
Encourage student 1 to use *también* when answering a question affirmatively if his/her partner has given the same answer previously (e.g., E1: *¿Sacas la basura?* E2: *Sí, la saco. ¿Y tú?* E1: *Sí, yo la saco también.*). You may wish to preview *tampoco* for negative answers (e.g., E2: *No, no la saco. ¿Y tú?* E1: *No, yo no la saco tampoco.*).

Follow-up for 5-24, *Intercambios*
Have students compare their answers and then tell another pair what chores both of them do or do not do in their homes. Also as follow-up, ask students how often they do these tasks—*todos los días, cada tres días*, etc.—and which tasks are their favorites.

Note for 5-25
Many Spanish speakers say *sacar al perro* instead of *pasear al perro.*

Suggestion for 5-25
You may wish to use visuals for this activity, supplementing the actions with additional ones depicted in photos or drawings.

Suggestion for 5-26
You may wish to have students take turns asking the questions. To expand the activity, you may have pairs of students come up with additional questions (to ask other pairs) whose answers cannot be found in the drawing; e.g., *¿Qué plato está preparando la señora Granados? ¿Qué parientes vienen de visita?*, etc.

Suggestions for 5-27
Have students do *Preparación* in pairs, taking note of similarities and differences. As a follow-up, pairs can get together in small groups and share their answers to both parts of the activity.

Note for *En directo*
Before doing the *Situación*, first have students read the expressions in *En directo*. Then have them listen to the dialogue and encourage them to use the expressions in their own conversation.

Audioscript for *En directo*
MARISA: *Pablo, vamos a hacer algo constructivo hoy. Yo voy a limpiar mi cuarto. Y tú, ¿por qué no lavas los platos?*
PABLO: *Oye, ¡no me des órdenes!*
MARISA: *No te quejes. Solo hay dos platos en el fregadero.*
PABLO: *Bueno, entonces, ¿por qué no los lavas tú?*

Suggestion for *Situación*
Before students begin *Situación*, you may wish to remind them to use direct object pronouns to avoid repetition. You may write the pronouns on the board for students to use during the activity.

INTERCAMBIOS. Dile a tu compañero/a qué haces por las siguientes personas. Indica en qué circunstancias lo haces.

tu amigo/a

E1: *Lo/La ayudo cuando está cansado/a.*

E2: *Y yo lo/la escucho cuando tiene problemas en el trabajo.*

1. tu papá
2. tu mamá
3. tu novio/a
4. tus vecinos (*neighbors*)
5. tu compañero/a de cuarto
6. tu mejor amigo/a

Situación

PREPARACIÓN. Lean esta situación. Luego, compartan ejemplos de vocabulario, gramática y otra información que necesitan para desarrollar la conversación.

Role A. You and your brother/sister have to do some chores at home. Since you are older, you tell your sibling three or four things that he/she has to do. Be prepared to respond to complaints and questions.

Role B. You and your older brother/sister have to do some chores at home. Because you are younger, you get some orders from your sibling about what you have to do. You do not feel like working, and you especially do not like being bossed around, so respond to everything you hear with a complaint or a question.

	ROLE A	ROLE B
Vocabulario	Words for house chores Household items	Words for house chores Household items
Funciones y formas	Enlisting the help of another person Telling someone what to do *Deber* + verb infinitive Responding to complaints Direct object pronouns	Reacting to orders from a family member Complaining to a family member Direct object pronouns

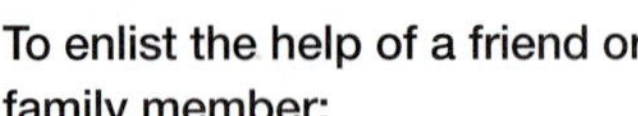

To enlist the help of a friend or family member:

Vamos a + *infinitive*... *Let's...*

Yo voy a... *I'm going to...*

Y tú, ¿por qué no...? *And how about if you...?*

To complain to a friend or family member:

Oye, no me des más órdenes. *Look, don't order me around.*

Basta de órdenes. *Stop ordering me around.*

Yo sé qué debo hacer. *I know what I have to do.*

To respond to a complaint from a friend or family member:

Es importante hacerlo. *It has to be done.*

No te quejes demasiado. *Don't complain so much.*

No seas perezoso. *Don't be so lazy.*

Listen to a conversation with these expressions.

INTERCAMBIOS. Practica la conversación con tu compañero/a incorporando el vocabulario y las funciones de *Preparación*. Luego, represéntenla ante la clase.

4 Pointing out and identifying people and things

AGENTE: **Esta** casa blanca es muy moderna y el precio es muy bueno.

CLIENTE: Pero **esa** tiene jardín, ¿verdad?

AGENTE: Es verdad. **Esta** casa y **aquella** no tienen jardín. Por eso, **esa** casa con jardín es más cara.

Piénsalo. El agente les está presentando diferentes tipos de viviendas a sus clientes. Indica si cada descripción se refiere a la imagen de la vivienda que está cerca (**C**), un poco lejos (**P**) o lejos (**L**) del agente.

1. __C__ **Esta** casa de dos pisos está en una ciudad. Tiene muchas ventanas en cada piso, pero no tiene jardín.
2. __L__ **Aquella** casa donde están la madre y su hija es de material sólido y de un color alegre.
3. __P__ **Esa** casa es de construcción sólida y tiene dos pisos y un garaje. Está en una zona muy verde.

Demonstrative adjectives and pronouns

- Demonstrative adjectives agree in gender and number with the noun they modify. English has two sets of demonstratives (*this, these* and *that, those*), but Spanish has three sets.

Demonstrative Adjectives

Demonstrative Adjectives

this	**este** cuadro **esta** butaca	*these*	**estos** cuadros **estas** butacas
that	**ese** horno **esa** casa	*those*	**esos** hornos **esas** casas
that (over there)	**aquel** camión **aquella** casa	*those (over there)*	**aquellos** camiones **aquellas** casas

- Use **este, esta, estos,** and **estas** when referring to people or things that are close to you in space or time.

Este escritorio es nuevo.	*This desk is new.*
Traen el sofá **esta** tarde.	*They will bring the sofa this afternoon.*

- Use **ese, esa, esos,** and **esas** when referring to events, people, or things that are not relatively close to you. Sometimes they are close to the person you are addressing.

Esa lámpara es muy bonita.	*That lamp is very pretty.*
Ese amigo de Lola vende su auto, ¿verdad?	*That friend of Lola's is selling his car, isn't he?*

- Use **aquel, aquella, aquellos,** and **aquellas** when referring to people or things that are more distant, or to events that are distant in time.

Aquel edificio es muy alto.	*That building (over there) is very tall.*
En **aquella** ocasión los niños jugaron en el parque.	*On that (long ago) occasion, the children played in the park.*

Suggestion
To introduce demonstratives, point to objects in class, relating demonstrative adjectives to their location and stressing the demonstrative adjectives as you speak: *Este libro es mi libro de español. Ese cuaderno es su cuaderno de ejercicios, ¿no? Aquellas mochilas son de los estudiantes.* Walk around the room to show how demonstratives change in relation to the speaker and the person spoken to.

Suggestion
As you walk around the classroom pointing to different objects, you may introduce the words *aquí, acá, allí,* and *allá* along with the corresponding demonstrative adjective.

Note
According to the *Real Academia de la Lengua Española* (2010), the use of accent marks with demonstrative pronouns is no longer recommended. They are not used in Mosaicos.

Demonstrative Pronouns

- Demonstratives can be used as pronouns to mean *this one/these* or *that one/those,* thus avoiding repetition when speaking or writing.

Demonstrative Pronouns

this	**este** **esta**	*these*	**estos** **estas**
that one	**ese** **esa**	*those*	**esos** **esas**
that one (over there)	**aquel** **aquella**	*those (over there)*	**aquellos** **aquellas**

- To refer to a general idea or concept, or to ask for the identification of an object, use **esto, eso,** or **aquello.** These forms are invariable.

Trabajan mucho y **eso** es muy bueno.	*They work a lot, and that is very good.*
¿Qué es **esto**? Es un espejo.	*What is this? It is a mirror.*
Aquello es un edificio de la universidad.	*That (over there) is a university building.*

PRÁCTICA

5-28 

Cerca, relativamente cerca o lejos. Decide cuál de las opciones debes usar según el lugar donde están los siguientes objetos. Compara tus respuestas con las de tu compañero/a y explica la razón de tu preferencia.

Cerca de ustedes

1. _____ mesa es de Honduras.
   a. Esta **b.** Esa **c.** Aquella

2. _____ cuadros también son de Honduras.
   a. Estos **b.** Esos **c.** Aquellos

Relativamente cerca de ustedes

3. _____ sofá es muy grande.
   a. Este **b.** Ese **c.** Aquel

4. _____ alfombra tiene unos colores muy alegres.
   a. Esta **b.** Esa **c.** Aquella

Lejos de ustedes

5. _____ espejo es nuevo.
   a. Este **b.** Ese **c.** Aquel

6. _____ lámparas son antiguas.
   a. Estas **b.** Esas **c.** Aquellas

5-29

En una mueblería en Managua. Tu compañero/a y tú deciden vivir juntos/as en Nicaragua y van a una mueblería para comprar muebles y accesorios. Usen las siguientes expresiones para hablar sobre lo que ven. Sigan el modelo.

bonito/a
feo/a
(no) me gusta(n)
cómodo/a
caro/a
me encanta(n)

MODELO
E1: *¿Te gusta el sofá?*
E2: *¿Cuál? ¿Aquel sofá verde?*
E1: *No, ese sofá azul.*
E2: *Sí, me encanta.*

¿COMPRENDES?

Escribe la forma correcta de los adjetivos demostrativos en cada caso.

este, esta, estos, estas

1. esta butaca
2. este cuarto
3. estas ventanas
4. estos sofás

ese, esa, esos, esas

5. esas sábanas
6. esos cuadros
7. ese jardín
8. esa piscina

aquel, aquella, aquellos, aquellas

9. aquel sofá
10. aquella cortina
11. aquellas mesas
12. aquellos teléfonos

MySpanishLab
Learn more using Amplifire Dynamic Study Modules, Grammar Tutorials, and Extra Practice activities.

Note for 5-28
This activity heightens students' metalinguistic awareness by having them think and talk about the language and not just memorize rules. Metalinguistic talk has been shown to contribute to language learning.

Preparation for 5-28
Have students bring 1 or 2 photos of famous people to class for this activity. Organize students into groups of 3 or 4 and have members of each group tape their photos to desks, walls, board, etc., around the room to facilitate their use of the 3 demonstrative adjectives. Then ask students to describe the famous person using demonstrative adjectives for the rest of the group to guess:
Aquel actor vive en... Tiene...

Suggestion for 5-28
You may wish to prompt students to consider the distance between themselves and the object to which they are referring.

Note for 5-29
You may explain that the *córdoba* (currency of Nicaragua) takes its name from the Spanish conquistador Francisco Hernández de Córdoba. The symbol for the *córdoba* is a C followed by a dollar sign, as shown in the illustration. Prices in Nicaragua and Honduras (*lempira*) are often given in both the national currency and in U.S. dollars. El Salvador now uses the U.S. dollar as its national currency.

5-30 

Descripciones. Piensa en tres objetos o muebles y el lugar de la casa donde están. Tu compañero/a va a hacerte preguntas para adivinar qué mueble u objeto es.

E1: *Este mueble está generalmente en el comedor.*

E2: *¿Es grande?*

E1: *Puede ser grande o pequeño.*

E2: *¿Lo usamos para comer?*

E1: *Sí.*

E2: *Es la mesa.*

Situación

PREPARACIÓN. Lean esta situación. Luego, compartan ejemplos de vocabulario, gramática y otra información que necesitan para desarrollar la conversación.

Role A. You want to sublet an apartment for one semester. You answer an ad from a student who is helping two friends sublet their apartments while they are studying abroad. The student has already shown you pictures of one apartment (**ese apartamento**) and is now showing you pictures of the second one (**este apartamento**). Discuss with the person:

a. the rent (**el alquiler**);
b. the number of bedrooms; and
c. the facilities of both apartments, such as the laundry room (**lavandería**), garage, and pool. Say which of the two apartments you want to see and explain why.

Role B. You have agreed to help two friends sublet their apartments for one semester while they are studying abroad. You have already shown a potential subletter pictures of one apartment (**ese apartamento**) and now are showing pictures of a second one (**este apartamento**). Answer his/her questions by saying that:

a. the rent of the first apartment is $900 per month and the second one is $1,100;
b. both apartments have two bedrooms; and
c. the first apartment comes with a one-car garage, while the other one has a two-car garage. Also tell him/her the advantages of each of the two apartments.

	ROLE A	ROLE B
Vocabulario	Rooms of a house/apartment Facilities of a house/apartment Numbers (prices)	Rooms of a house/apartment Facilities of a house/apartment Numbers (prices)
Funciones y formas	Describing a house or apartment Verbs that describe: *ser, tener,* etc. Talking about price of an apartment Expressing a wish to do something Asking and answering questions Observing phone etiquette	Describing a property for rental Verbs that describe: *ser, tener,* etc. Talking about price of an apartment Asking and answering questions Observing phone etiquette

INTERCAMBIOS. Practica la conversación con tu compañero/a incorporando el vocabulario y las funciones de *Preparación.* Luego, represéntenla ante la clase.

Suggestion for *Situación*
Students should use *ese apartamento* to refer to the first apartment (the one they saw before) and *este apartamento* or *este* to refer to the pictures of the apartment they are looking at now.

EN ACCIÓN

En casa

Expansion for 5-31
Add more appliances or rooms in a house to this list. Have students work in groups to describe or define the words. The groups then compare notes to create better definitions.
Alternatively, each group has a different set of words to define. They read their definitions aloud and members of other groups guess what appliances or rooms are being described.

Note for *César Pelli*
César Pelli is an internationally recognized Argentine American architect who has designed several of the world's most renowned buildings, such as the Petronas Towers in Kuala Lumpur, the *Torre de Cristal* in Madrid, and the World Financial Center in Manhattan.

5-31 Antes de ver

¿Qué es? Asocia las palabras de la primera columna con las definiciones a la derecha.

1. __b__ el microondas
2. __c__ el barrio
3. __e__ la aspiradora
4. __a__ el baño
5. __d__ la cocina

a. Es el cuarto donde te lavas la cara o te duchas.
b. Lo usas para calentar la comida.
c. Es una parte de la ciudad donde vive la gente.
d. Es el cuarto donde preparas la comida.
e. Sirve para limpiar las alfombras.

5-32 Mientras ves  

La casa de Federico. Indica si las siguientes afirmaciones sobre la casa de Federico y su barrio son ciertas (**C**) o falsas (**F**). Corrige las afirmaciones falsas.

1. __C__ La casa de Federico está cerca del puerto en un barrio de Buenos Aires.
2. __F__ El barrio de Federico es principalmente una zona residencial. Hay mucha industria, rascacielos y tiendas también.
3. __F__ El Puente de la Mujer es una obra del arquitecto argentino César Pelli. El Puente de la Mujer es obra del arquitecto español Santiago Calatrava.
4. __F__ Federico y su familia comen siempre en el comedor. Federico y su familia comen en el salón, en el comedor y también en la cocina.
5. __C__ Federico usa el microondas con frecuencia porque siempre tiene hambre.

5-33 Después de ver 

¿Qué están haciendo? **PREPARACIÓN.** Federico describe el barrio y la casa donde vive. Asocia los lugares con las actividades que Federico y su familia probablemente están haciendo allí.

1. __d__ En los restaurantes al aire libre...
2. __a__ Frente al Puente de la Mujer...
3. __b__ En el salón...
4. __e__ En la cocina...
5. __c__ En los dormitorios...

a. están caminando.
b. están mirando la tele.
c. están durmiendo la siesta.
d. están disfrutando de la vista y comiendo.
e. están lavando los platos.

INTERCAMBIOS. Hagan una lista de por lo menos (*at least*) dos cuartos de una casa o apartamento y dos lugares de la ciudad donde viven ustedes. Describan las actividades que hacen los niños, los adultos y las personas mayores en estos lugares.

Mosaicos

ESCUCHA

 Presentational

Preparación. Vas a escuchar la descripción de una casa. Antes de escuchar, piensa en las casas que conoces y prepara una lista de cuatro cuartos y de tres objetos (muebles, aparatos eléctricos/electrónicos o accesorios) que esperas encontrar en cada uno de los cuartos. Compártela con la clase.

ESTRATEGIA

Create mental images

You have already learned that visual cues can increase your listening comprehension. For example, seeing the pictures or objects that a speaker refers to can help you understand what is being said. You can also create mental pictures by using your imagination or by making associations with familiar things or experiences. As you listen, practice creating mental images to help you develop your listening skills in Spanish.

5-35  Interpretive

ESCUCHA. Listen to the different statements about the location of pieces of furniture and objects. Indicate whether each statement is true (**Cierto**) or false (**Falso**) according to the drawing.

1. Falso
2. Cierto
3. Falso
4. Falso
5. Cierto
6. Cierto
7. Falso
8. Cierto

Comprueba

I was able to ...

____ create mental images based on my experience with houses.

____ associate items in the drawing with what I heard.

____ understand key words.

Audioscript for 5-35

1. *La casa de los Pérez Esquivel tiene dos dormitorios y un baño.*
2. *En la sala hay un televisor y un sofá grande.*
3. *En el comedor hay una alfombra.*
4. *Un dormitorio tiene una cama grande y dos mesas de noche.*
5. *En los baños de esta casa hay bañera.*
6. *Hay cuadros en la sala y en el comedor.*
7. *La ventana del comedor no tiene cortinas.*
8. *La cocina está entre un dormitorio y el comedor.*

5-36  Interpersonal

Un paso más. Descríbele tu vivienda (número de cuartos, colores, muebles, etc.) a tu compañero/a. Él/Ella va a tomar notas para describirle tu vivienda a otra persona de la clase. Comprueba si la información es correcta. Luego, intercambien roles.

Suggestion for 5-36

Model this activity with one of your better students. Providing students with a model of how to report is useful. You may present the following expressions for the reporting phase:

Acabo de conversar con... y dice que su casa/apartamento tiene.../es...

For the *Comprueba* portion of 5-36, you may introduce the following expressions: *Tú dices que tu apartamento tiene.../es...*

Suggestions for 5-38
Have students read the ads and talk about the apartments with their partner as though they were talking on the phone. You may wish to review the formulaic expressions used in phone conversations.
Review ways to describe different options, for example: *Hay un apartamento que cuesta… Tiene dos habitaciones. También hay otro apartamento que tiene muebles finos.* Point out the meaning of *despensa* (pantry) in the first ad. Direct students to look up the exchange rate between the U.S. dollar and the Salvadoran *colón* (SVC) on the Internet. Explain to them that although the *colón* is still accepted, it is not widely used since the U.S. dollar has been the national currency since 2001. Students should have 2 conversations, and each member of the pair must ask and answer questions about 2 ads. Remind them that the goal is to decide which apartment they want to follow up on.

Suggestion for 5-39
This is a follow-up activity to *Habla,* so students should work in the same pairs. You may want to have the class vote on the most appealing apartment(s) and give their reasons.

Note for *En directo*
Before doing activity 5-39, first have students read the expressions in *En directo.* Then have them listen to the dialogue and encourage them to use the expressions in their own conversation.

Audioscript for *En directo*
SR. RUIZ: *Agencia Salvador. Buenos días.*
PABLO: *Buenos días. ¿Con quién hablo?*
SR. RUIZ: *Se ha comunicado con la Agencia Salvador. Soy el señor Ruiz.*
PABLO: *¿Está la señora Barrios, por favor? Deseo hablar con ella sobre el anuncio.*
SR. RUIZ: *Sí. Ahora mismo lo comunico con su oficina.*

HABLA

5-37 Presentational

Preparación. Necesitas alquilar un apartamento. Escribe algunas características esenciales y algunas secundarias del apartamento que necesitas. Compártelas con la clase.

ESTRATEGIA

Plan what you want to say

Speaking consists of more than knowing the words and structures you need. You also have to know what you want to say. Planning what you want to say—both the information you want to ask for or convey and the language you will need to express yourself—before you start to speak will make your speech more accurate and also more coherent.

5-38  Interpersonal, Interpretive

Habla. Tu mejor amigo/a y tú estudian en San Salvador este año y quieren alquilar un apartamento. Lean los anuncios y decidan qué apartamento prefieren y por qué. Hablen sobre las ventajas y desventajas de uno u otro.

ALQUILERES

1. Se alquila condominio residencial privado, 3er nivel, 2 dormitorios, 1 baño, cuarto y baño, empleada, cocina con despensa, sala y comedor separados, garaje 2 carros, área recreación niños. SVC 4.500 vigilancia incluida. 22 24 46 30.
2. Alquilo apartamento cerca de centro comercial. Transporte público a la puerta. Ideal para profesionales. 1 dormitorio, 1 baño con jacuzzi, con muebles y electrodomésticos, terraza, sistema de seguridad, garaje doble. SVC 7.500. Tfno. 22 65 16 92.
3. Alquilo apartamento, cerca zona universitaria. 3 dormitorios. 1ra planta. Ideal para estudiantes. (SVC 1.800) Llamar al 22 35 37 83.
4. Alquilo preciosa habitación en casa particular. Semi amueblada. Amplia, enorme clóset, cable gratis. Alimentación opcional. Información al teléfono 22 63 28 07.

Comprueba

In my conversation …

____ I was able to convey my preferences.

____ I asked appropriate questions.

____ I gave relevant responses.

____ I was able to come to an agreement with my partner.

5-39  Interpersonal

Un paso más. Ya que (*Since*) saben qué apartamento les gusta más, tienen que dar el próximo paso (*next step*). Conversen para decidir lo siguiente:

1. ¿Por qué es este apartamento el favorito de ustedes?
2. ¿Qué preguntas quieren hacerle al dueño del apartamento para obtener más información?

En directo

To find out who is answering your call:

¿Con quién hablo? *Who is this?*

To request to talk with someone specific:

¿Está… [nombre de la persona], por favor?

Is … [person's name] there, please?

Deseo hablar con… [nombre de la persona].

I would like to speak with … [person's name].

 Listen to a conversation with these expressions.

LEE

5-40    Presentational

Preparación. ¿Qué sabes sobre el tema? Indica si las afirmaciones son ciertas (**C**) o falsas (**F**). Luego, escribe tu opinión sobre este tema en un párrafo y preséntalo a la clase.

1. __C__ Hoy en día muchos jóvenes viven con sus padres después de graduarse de la universidad.
2. __F__ Los jóvenes de hoy desean independizarse (*become independent*) de sus padres más que hace 10 o 15 años.
3. __F__ Vivir en la casa de los padres es un fenómeno estadounidense solamente.
4. __C__ El desempleo (*unemployment*) entre los jóvenes es una razón importante para vivir con los padres después de graduarse.
5. __C__ Más hombres que mujeres viven con sus padres después de graduarse.

ESTRATEGIA

Inform yourself about a topic before you start to read

To get acquainted with a topic, you should think about what you already know, read something about it on the web (in English or in Spanish), talk with people who know about the topic; a combination of these three approaches is the best preparation. The goal is to build your knowledge about the topic before you start to read. Then, when you read the text, try to apply that knowledge to support your comprehension.

Suggestion for 5-40
You may wish to have students correct the false statements so that they articulate what they know about the topic.

5-41 Interpretive

Lee. El siguiente artículo describe un nuevo fenómeno social. Léelo y sigue las instrucciones.

1. En el primer párrafo, el autor del artículo presenta el nuevo fenómeno social. Explícalo con tus propias palabras.
2. El segundo párrafo presenta tres causas del fenómeno. ¿Cuáles son?
3. El tercer párrafo menciona los sobrenombres (*nicknames*) que se les dan a los adultos que viven con sus padres en varios países. ¿Cuáles son?
4. En el último párrafo se presenta la perspectiva de los padres. ¿Cuál es?

Comprueba

I was able to …

- ____ anticipate content related to the topic.
- ____ use the statistics to confirm my comprehension of the main ideas.
- ____ identify the two main reasons that adults live with their parents.
- ____ find other countries where the phenomenon is common.

Answers for 5-41
1. Answers may vary.
2. *Es mucho más barato no tener que pagar un alquiler o comprar comida, los jóvenes disfrutan de la comodidad de la casa familiar, los padres hoy son más tolerantes.*
3. basement dwellers, *solteros parásitos, bamboccioni (bebés grandes)*
4. *Muchos padres están contentos de tener la compañía de los hijos. A veces los padres prefieren irse de la casa para independizarse de sus hijos.*

Un nuevo fenómeno social

No abandonar el nido (nest) *familiar*

Cada vez hay más adultos entre los 20 y los 34 años que viven en la casa de sus padres. En el pasado, esto era (*used to be*) bastante normal en los países hispanos pero no en Estados Unidos donde, tradicionalmente, los jóvenes se independizaban más pronto. Según un estudio de la Oficina del Censo de Estados Unidos, en 2011 un 59% de los chicos de entre 18 y 24 años y un 50% de las chicas vivían (*lived*) todavía en el domicilio familiar en comparación con el 53% y el 46%, respectivamente, en 2005.

Las causas principales de este fenómeno son variadas. Para algunos jóvenes es mucho más barato no tener que pagar un alquiler o comprar comida, sobre todo si no tienen un trabajo estable. Pero la razón para otros jóvenes es que disfrutan (*enjoy*) de la comodidad (*comfort*) de la casa familiar. Además, los padres hoy son más tolerantes que en el pasado, por eso los hijos no sienten la necesidad de irse.

Esta tendencia social no solo se limita a Estados Unidos, donde estos jóvenes se llaman *basement dwellers* porque muchos tienen su habitación en el sótano de la casa, sino que se encuentra en todo el mundo. En América Latina los jóvenes generalmente vivían con los padres antes de casarse (*get married*), pero ahora hay muchos que después de casarse y de tener hijos continúan viviendo en la misma casa. En Japón a los hijos adultos que prefieren vivir en casa con sus padres les llaman solteros (*unmarried*) parásitos, y en Italia, *bamboccioni* (bebés grandes).

Curiosamente, en Estados Unidos esta tendencia afecta más a los hombres que a las mujeres. El porcentaje de hombres de entre 25 y 34 años que viven con sus padres creció (*grew*) de un 14% en 2005 a un 19% en 2011 y de un 8% a un 10% para las mujeres en el mismo periodo.

¿Qué opinan los padres de esta situación? Muchos padres están contentos de tener la compañía de los hijos. Pero a veces la situación cambia y son los padres quienes tienen que irse de la casa para independizarse de sus hijos.

Suggestion for 5-42
To increase student engagement with the activity, you may wish to have the groups share their results with the class.

5-42 Interpersonal

Un paso más. Hablen sobre los temas siguientes y escriban sus respuestas en la tabla.

1. ¿Qué significa para ustedes independizarse de sus padres?
2. ¿Cuáles son las ventajas y desventajas de vivir con los padres después de graduarse? ¿Bajo qué circunstancias es necesario vivir con ellos?

Ser independientes de los padres significa…	_____ no vivir con ellos _____ pagar todos nuestros gastos (teléfono, carro, apartamento, etc.) _____ hablar con ellos solamente 1 o 2 veces por semana _____ hablar con los amigos cuando necesitamos consejos (*advice*), no con ellos _____ (otro) ________________________________
Ventajas de vivir con los padres	**1.** **2.** **3.**
Desventajas de vivir con los padres	**1.** **2.** **3.**

Cultura

Desempleo juvenil

In Hispanic countries, unemployment among young people (ages 18–35) is high. Spain has been one of the countries hardest hit in recent years, even among university graduates. In addition to the social and economic strains caused by unemployment, there are other social consequences, like young people having to live with their parents and being forced to postpone marriage and starting a family.

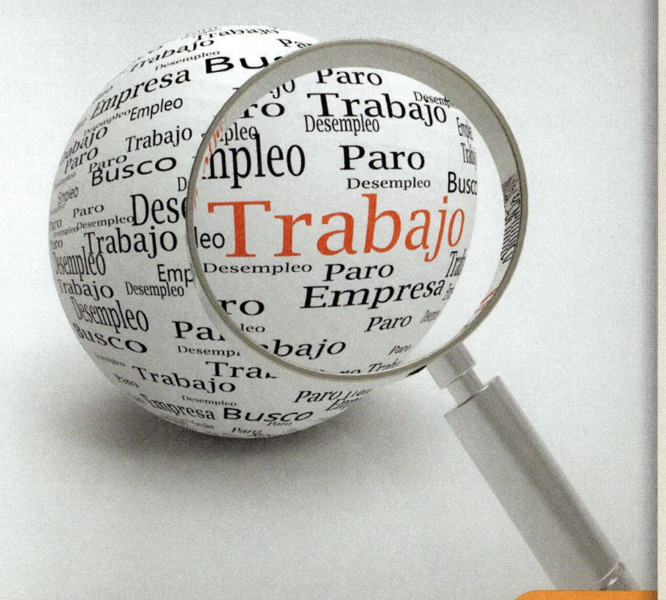

Comparaciones. ¿Es el desempleo juvenil un gran problema en tu país o región? ¿Hay muchos universitarios desempleados que tienen que vivir con sus padres después de graduarse de la universidad?

ESCRIBE

5-43 Interpretive

Preparación. Lee los requisitos sobre el concurso (*contest*) "La casa ideal para las familias multigeneracionales" que aparece en el periódico *La Prensa* de Tegucigalpa, Honduras.

El diario *La Prensa* invita al público a participar en el concurso "La casa ideal para las familias multigeneracionales".

Bases del concurso:

Los participantes deben enviar la siguiente información por correo electrónico al Comité de Selección de "La casa ideal para las familias multigeneracionales":

1. información personal: nombre completo, dirección, teléfono y correo electrónico
2. un panfleto descriptivo de la casa para varias personas adultas y niños con la siguiente información: tamaño de la casa, número y nombre de las habitaciones, distribución del espacio, aparatos electrónicos y un dibujo o foto digital de la casa

Fecha límite: el 30 de marzo

Premio: una computadora portátil de último modelo y alta resolución, con programas de alta capacidad y funcionalidad

ESTRATEGIA

Select the appropriate content and tone for a formal description

To write a description using a formal tone, you will need to anticipate what your audience may know about the topic, including relevant details; adapt the language of your text to the level of your readership. If you wish to address your reader(s) directly, use **usted/ustedes.**

Suggestion for 5-44
Remind students that they are writing this pamphlet for a jury of experts. Depending on your students' skill, you may wish to have them do this writing task in pairs. If possible, students with artistic skills should be paired with those who may not be so artistic.

Suggestion for 5-45
Before doing *Un paso más*, have students check their texts in relation to the following items that you may write on the board:

1. *la claridad de ideas*
2. *la cantidad de información*
3. *el tono apropiado para un comité de periodistas*
4. *la precisión gramatical*

5-44 Presentational

Escribe. Decides participar en el concurso con un proyecto excepcional. Prepara un panfleto incluyendo toda la información que pide el concurso. Considera la cantidad de información necesaria y el tono apropiado para tus lectores, los miembros del Comité de Selección. ¡Buena suerte!

Comprueba

I was able to ...

____ **include relevant details about the topic.**

____ **provide the appropriate amount of information.**

____ **use the appropriate form to address the audience.**

5-45 Interpersonal

Un paso más. Habla con tu compañero/a sobre tu panfleto. Descríbanse sus proyectos y averigüen lo siguiente:

1. tamaño de la casa
2. estilo de la decoración
3. características originales

En este capítulo...

Comprueba lo que sabes

Go to ***MySpanishLab*** to review what you have learned in this chapter. Practice with the following:

Flashcards | Games | Oral Practice | Practice Test / Study Plan | Amplifire Dynamic Study Modules | Tutorials | Videos | Extra Practice

Vocabulario

LA ARQUITECTURA *Architecture*

el alquiler *rent*
el apartamento *apartment*
el edificio *building*
el estilo *style*
la vivienda *housing*

EN EL BAÑO *In the bathroom*

la bañera *bathtub*
la ducha *shower*
las cortinas *curtains*
el inodoro *toilet*
el jabón *soap*
el lavabo *bathroom sink*
la toalla *towel*

EN LA COCINA *In the kitchen*

la estufa *stove*
el fregadero *kitchen sink*
el plato *dish, plate*

PALABRAS ÚTILES *Useful words*

la desventaja *disadvantage*
el trabajo *work*
la ventaja *advantage*
la vista *view*

EN UNA CASA *In a home*

el aire acondicionado *air conditioning*
el armario *closet, armoire*
el baño *bathroom*
la basura *garbage, trash*
la calefacción *heating*
la chimenea *fireplace*
la cocina *kitchen*
el comedor *dining room*
el cuarto *room; bedroom*
la escalera *stairs*
el garaje *garage*
la habitación *bedroom*
la lavandería *laundry room*
el pasillo *corridor, hall*
la piscina *swimming pool*
el piso *floor; apartment*
la planta baja *first floor, ground floor*
la sala *living room*
la terraza *deck, balcony*

EN EL JARDÍN *In the garden*

la barbacoa *barbecue pit; barbecue (event)*
el césped *lawn*
la hoja *leaf*

LOS LUGARES *Places*

las afueras *outskirts*
el barrio *neighborhood*
la calle *street*
el centro *downtown, center*
cerca (de) *near, close (to)*
lejos (de) *far (from)*
la zona *area*

LOS NÚMEROS ORDINALES *Ordinal numbers*

primero / primer *first*
segundo *second*
tercero / tercer *third*
cuarto *fourth*
quinto *fifth*
sexto *sixth*
séptimo *seventh*
octavo *eighth*
noveno *ninth*
décimo *tenth*

LOS MUEBLES Y ACCESORIOS *Furniture and accessories*

la alfombra *carpet, rug*
la butaca *armchair*
la cama *bed*
la cómoda *dresser*
la cortina *curtain*
el cuadro *picture, painting*
el espejo *mirror*
la lámpara *lamp*
la mesa *table*
la silla *chair*
el sofá *sofa*

LOS ELECTRODOMÉSTICOS *Appliances*

la aspiradora *vacuum cleaner*
el lavaplatos *dishwasher*
el (horno de) microondas *microwave (oven)*
el/la radio *radio*
el refrigerador *refrigerator*

LAS DESCRIPCIONES *Descriptions*

limpio/a *clean*
ordenado/a *tidy*
seco/a *dry*
sucio/a *dirty*

PARA LA CAMA *For the bed*

la almohada *pillow*
la manta *blanket*
la sábana *sheet*

EXPRESIONES CON *TENER* *Expressions with **tener***

tener... calor *to be hot*
cuidado *careful*
frío *cold*
hambre *hungry*
miedo *afraid*
prisa *in a hurry*
razón *right*
sed *thirsty*
sueño *sleepy*
suerte *lucky*

VERBOS *Verbs*

barrer *to sweep*
cocinar *to cook*
creer *to believe*
doblar *to fold*
lavar *to wash*
limpiar *to clean*
ordenar *to tidy up*
pasar la aspiradora *to vacuum*
planchar *to iron*
recoger (j) *to pick up*
sacar *to take out*
secar *to dry*
tender (ie) *to hang (clothes)*

See *Lengua* box on page 178 for more electronic items.
See page 189 for direct object pronouns.
See pages 193–194 for demonstrative adjectives and pronouns.

Introduction to chapter
Introduce the chapter theme about shopping and ask questions to recycle content from the previous chapter. Help students access meaning by using gestures or pointing to the items. Related questions: *¿Qué te gusta comprar? ¿Ropa? ¿DVD? ¿Zapatos? ¿Aparatos electrónicos? ¿Prefieres comprar en tiendas o por Internet? ¿Por qué?*

Integrated Performance Assessment: Three Modes of Communication

Presentational: See activities 6-10, 6-15, 6-17, 6-31, 6-36, 6-39, and 6-41.

Interpretive: See activities 6-1, 6-2, 6-4, 6-5, 6-6, 6-7, 6-8, 6-9, 6-10, 6-11, 6-12, 6-13, 6-14, 6-16, 6-18, 6-19, 6-21, 6-22, 6-23, 6-24, 6-25, 6-26, 6-28, 6-29, 6-30, 6-32, 6-34, 6-38, and 6-40.

Interpersonal: See activities 6-2, 6-3, 6-4, 6-6, 6-7, 6-8, 6-9, 6-10, 6-11, 6-12, 6-13, 6-14, 6-15, 6-16, 6-17, 6-19, 6-20, 6-21, 6-22, 6-23, 6-24, 6-26, 6-27, 6-30, 6-33, 6-35, 6-37, 6-42 and all *Situación* activities.

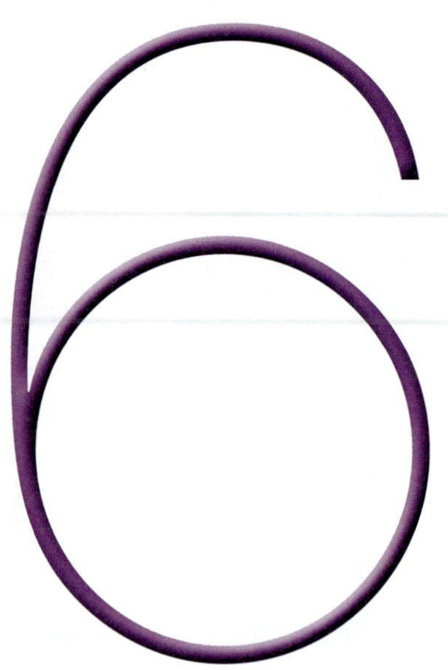

6 ¿Qué te gusta comprar?

ENFOQUE CULTURAL
Venezuela

VOCABULARIO EN CONTEXTO
Las compras
La ropa
¿Qué debo llevar?

MOSAICO CULTURAL
Las tiendas de barrio

FUNCIONES Y FORMAS
Preterit tense of regular verbs
Preterit of *ir* and *ser*
Indirect object nouns and pronouns
Gustar and similar verbs
More about *ser* and *estar*

EN ACCIÓN
De moda

MOSAICOS
ESCUCHA Take notes to recall information
HABLA Negotiate a price
LEE Use context to figure out meaning of unfamiliar words
ESCRIBE Recount events in sequence

EN ESTE CAPÍTULO...
Comprueba lo que sabes
Vocabulario

LEARNING OUTCOMES

You will be able to:

- talk about shopping and clothes
- talk about events in the past
- indicate to whom or for whom an action takes place
- express likes and dislikes
- describe people, objects, and events
- share information about shopping practices in Hispanic countries and compare cultural similarities

ENFOQUE cultural VENEZUELA

Enfoque cultural

To learn more about Venezuela, go to MySpanishLab to view the *Vistas culturales* videos.

Simón Bolívar (1783–1830), nacido en Caracas, Venezuela, es un héroe de la independencia latinoamericana.

¿QUÉ TE PARECE?

- En el área de los Andes venezolanos hay una gran concentración de personas de herencia italiana. Un plato típico es espaguetis con caraotas negras (frijoles).
- *Venezuela* significa pequeña Venecia. El italiano Américo Vespucio le dio el nombre al país. Los palafitos (*houses on stilts*) en el lago Maracaibo le recordaron a Venecia, Italia.
- El Salto Ángel es la catarata más alta del mundo. Tiene este nombre porque el aviador estadounidense Jimmie Angel fue la primera persona en volar (*fly*) sobre ella.

Standard 2.2 Students demonstrate an understanding of the relationship between the products and perspectives of the culture studied. Venezuela's status as an oil-rich nation has changed its political position in the western hemisphere in recent years. You may wish to have students look up such facts as which countries import oil from Venezuela, changes in the gross national product of Venezuela, and the retail price of gasoline in Venezuela as indicators of the impact of a product (oil) on a country and its culture.

Suggestion for map
Brainstorm with students the information they may already know about Venezuela. Project the map and ask questions. Ask about its geographic characteristics according to the map: *¿Qué países limitan con Venezuela? (Colombia, Brasil, Guyana) ¿Cuál es el río más grande de Venezuela? (el Orinoco) ¿Qué mar hay al norte de Venezuela? (el mar Caribe)* Recycle weather expressions: *¿Cómo es el clima, frío o tropical? ¿Qué tiempo hace en el Caribe?* Personalize: *¿Conocen a alguna persona famosa de Venezuela?*

Suggestion
Mention the geographic diversity of Venezuela: tropical islands (*isla de Margarita* and *Los Roques*); mountains (*Cordillera de Mérida*); one of the longest rivers in South America (*el Orinoco*); the biodiversity of the *sabana* area south of the Orinoco where *Salto Ángel* is located. Talk about the photos. Explain that *hayacas* (also known as *hallacas*) are similar to Mexican *tamales,* but are wrapped in banana leaves instead of corn husks: *Se hacen de carne, vegetales y masa de maíz. Generalmente se preparan para la Navidad.*

Suggestion
This painting of Simón Bolívar by an unknown artist shows the Venezuelan hero in military uniform. Explain that Bolívar was the principal architect of South American independence movements.

Ask students to describe the subject of the painting by asking questions. Recycle vocabulary for colors and physical features: *¿Cómo es Simón Bolívar? ¿De qué color son sus ojos? Bolívar lleva un uniforme porque es militar. ¿De qué color es su uniforme?* Model *llevar* and vocabulary from this chapter by pointing out students who are wearing jewelry: *Isabel lleva unos pendientes*, etc.

Note for *Los tepuis*
Tepui means *casa de los dioses.* This photo shows *Monte Roraima* in the Canaima National Park.

Suggestion for *Los tepuis*
The Disney animated movie *Up!* was inspired by the *tepui* mountains in Venezuela. Ask students: *¿Conocen la película* Up!*?*, etc.

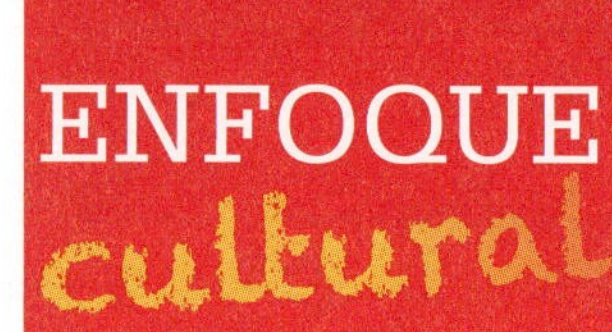

ENFOQUE cultural

◀ El turpial es el ave nacional de Venezuela. Es un pajarito pequeño que mide entre 15 y 20 centímetros. Tiene un canto muy melodioso y, por eso, de una persona que canta muy bien que se dice que "canta como un turpial".

Los tepuis (*mesas*) venezolanos son formaciones geológicas impresionantes. En Venezuela se encuentran los más altos de toda América y son las formaciones más antiguas del planeta Tierra. Se cree que tienen billones de años. Sir Arthur Conan Doyle se inspiró en estos tepuis para escribir su novela, *El mundo perdido*. ▶

Las arepas son la base de la cocina y la dieta diaria de los venezolanos. Se preparan con una masa de maíz similar a las pupusas centroamericanas. Tienen nombres muy variados según sus ingredientes. La Reina pepiada se rellena con pollo, cebolla, aguacate (*avocado*) y mayonesa. La arepa Tumbarranchos es para el desayuno. Se prepara con queso, repollo (*cabbage*), mostaza y mortadela. ▶

▲ El producto más valioso de Venezuela no es el petróleo, sino el cacao. Se considera uno de los más exquisitos y raros del mundo. Los conocedores del chocolate y las chocolaterías más exclusivas de Europa importan el cacao de Venezuela para sus productos.

¿CUÁNTO SABES?

Completa estas oraciones con la información correcta.

1. El turpial es un ___ave / pájaro___ que se distingue por sus colores brillantes.
2. Los ___tepuis___ son un tipo de montaña plana, pero muy alta.
3. La ___arepa___ Tumbarranchos no lleva aguacate .
4. La persona que le dio a Venezuela su nombre fue ___Américo Vespucio___.
5. La influencia ___italiana___ es muy evidente en la comida de la región andina.
6. El Salto Ángel es la ___catarata___ más alta del mundo.
7. La exportación más exclusiva de Venezuela es el ___cacao___.

Vocabulario en contexto

Talking about shopping and clothes

MySpanishLab **PRONUNCIATION TOPIC:** Diphthongs.
Learn more using Amplifire Dynamic Study Modules, Pronunciation, and Vocabulary Tutorials.

Las compras

▲ Muchas personas **van de compras** a los **mercados** al aire libre. En esta calle en Sabana Grande, Venezuela, hay tiendas y mercados. En los mercados tradicionales venden **telas,** objetos de **artesanía, joyas, bolsos,** etc., pero a veces también hay discos, aparatos electrónicos y otras **cosas** para la casa.

▲ En los mercados tradicionales los turistas a veces compran **regalos** para su familia y sus amigos. A esta señora le gustan las joyas artesanales. Compra un **collar** de **plata** para su mejor amiga, una **pulsera** para su hermana, unos **aretes** para su hija y un **anillo** de **oro** para sí misma (*herself*).

▲ En este **centro comercial venden** de todo. Hay tiendas de **ropa** y de **zapatos.** También hay **tiendas** de muebles y accesorios para la casa, hay librerías, tiendas de **juguetes** para los niños e incluso hay un **supermercado.**

De compras

José Manuel va a un **almacén** a comprar un regalo para su novia. Necesita la ayuda de la dependienta.

DEPENDIENTA: **¿En qué puedo servirle?**

JOSÉ MANUEL: **Quisiera** comprar un regalo para mi novia. Un bolso o una **billetera,** por ejemplo.

DEPENDIENTA: Hay unos bolsos de **cuero** preciosos y no son muy **caros. Enseguida** le **muestro** los que tenemos.

[*La dependienta trae unos bolsos*].

JOSÉ MANUEL: No sé. **Me gustaría** comprar este bolso, pero no puedo **gastar** mucho. ¿Cuánto cuesta?

DEPENDIENTA: Solo **vale** 500 bolívares. Es bastante **barato.**

JOSÉ MANUEL: Sí, no es mucho **dinero.** Es un buen **precio.**

DEPENDIENTA: Y **están** muy **de moda.** Las chicas jóvenes los **llevan** mucho.

JOSÉ MANUEL: Bueno, lo voy a comprar.

DEPENDIENTA: Muy bien, señor. ¿Va a **pagar** con **tarjeta de crédito** o **en efectivo?**

JOSÉ MANUEL: En efectivo.

LENGUA

To soften requests, Spanish uses the forms **me gustaría** (instead of **me gusta**) and **quisiera** (instead of **quiero**). English does this with the phrase *would like*. ***Me gustaría/Quisiera* ir a ese almacén.** *I would like to go to that department store.*

Suggestion for *Las compras*
Project the images in class and ask the following to review new vocabulary: *Esta foto es de un centro comercial. En todas las capitales del mundo hispano hay grandes almacenes, como, por ejemplo, Macro en Venezuela y El Corte Inglés en España. En estos almacenes hay tiendas de todo: de ropa, zapatos, libros, juguetes y mucho más.*

Suggestion
Explain that the currency of Venezuela is the *bolívar.* Call students' attention to the name. In 2007 the *bolívar* was revalued by the government at a ratio of 1 to 1,000 and was renamed the *bolívar fuerte* (BsF) in 2008. The equivalent is approximately $1.00 = BsF 6.28, but the rate varies widely. You may wish to ask students to find the current equivalent to BsF 500 in dollars.

Suggestion for *Lengua*
Introduce and compare *quisiera* and *me gustaría.* Use the *De compras* dialogue from the online Learning Module as a model for students to create new interactions. Have students select a different item, substituting *me gustaría* for *quisiera,* and paying with a credit card instead of cash.

PRÁCTICA

Audioscript for 6-1
1. *José Manuel quiere comprar un regalo para su novia.*
2. *La dependienta le muestra unas billeteras.*
3. *Los bolsos son de cuero.*
4. *Los bolsos son muy caros.*
5. *Los bolsos están de moda.*
6. *José Manuel va a pagar con tarjeta de crédito.*

Suggestion for 6-2
Students should have no problem guessing the meaning of *juguetería, joyería,* and *zapatería.* Call their attention to the word endings. Ask what would be sold in *una carnicería, una pescadería, una papelería,* etc.

6-1  

Escucha y confirma. Indicate whether the statement you hear is true (**Cierto**) or false (**Falso**) according to the conversation between José Manuel and the salesperson.

	Cierto	Falso
1.	✓	
2.		✓
3.	✓	
4.		✓
5.	✓	
6.		✓

6-2  

¿Adónde van? Las siguientes personas necesitan comprar algunas cosas. Indica a qué tienda deben ir.

1. __f__ María necesita unos libros para su clase de literatura.
2. __d__ Juan quisiera cocinar comida venezolana para sus amigos.
3. __b__ Rosa piensa comprar unos regalos para sus sobrinos.
4. __a__ Felipe necesita una cómoda para su cuarto.
5. __c__ Olga necesita unos zapatos nuevos para una entrevista de trabajo.
6. __e__ Catalina va a comprar un collar elegante para ir a una fiesta.

a. mueblería **d.** supermercado
b. juguetería **e.** joyería
c. zapatería **f.** librería

Comprar por Internet

The use of the Internet varies widely between countries and generations. Online shopping is less frequent, in some Hispanic countries, even among younger people. This is certainly the case for electronics or clothing purchases. Shopping at stores for clothes, appliances, or electronics is preferred, since most people like the personal interaction and the expertise of sales associates at those stores.

Conexiones. ¿Qué ventajas y desventajas hay en comprar a través de Internet? ¿Qué productos o servicios es mejor comprar en una tienda personalmente? ¿Por qué?

Suggestion for 6-3
Students saw the expression *Necesito comprar* in *Capítulo 1.* You may reintroduce here *tener que + infinitive* to express obligation, which they learned in *Capítulo 4.* This is also an opportunity to recycle *ir + a + infinitive/pensar + infinitive* that appeared in *Capítulos 3* and *4.*

6-3  

¿Qué tienen que hacer? Ustedes tienen que hacer muchas cosas esta semana antes de su viaje a Venezuela. Hablen de qué necesitan hacer o comprar y por qué. Luego indiquen a qué tiendas van a ir.

MODELO comprar zapatos para nuestro viaje
E1: *Necesitamos comprar unos zapatos cómodos porque vamos a caminar mucho.*
E2: *Podemos comprarlos en una zapatería.*

1. necesitar maletas (*suitcases*) grandes
2. comprar una guía turística
3. planear y pagar el viaje
4. comprar un regalo para nuestra amiga venezolana
5. leer blogs sobre Venezuela
6. necesitar ropa de verano

Cultura

Mercados tradicionales

People in many cultures engage in some form of haggling (**regatear**), a business-like transaction between a customer and a vendor that has rules (usually unspoken) about when, where, and how it is done. In Spanish-speaking countries, haggling is not expected or acceptable in a pharmacy, a supermarket, a restaurant, or a governmental office, for example. However, people often haggle at outdoor markets.

Comparaciones.

¿Se regatea en tu país? ¿En qué situaciones? ¿Alguna vez regateaste? ¿Dónde? ¿Cuánto te pidieron por el producto? ¿Cuánto pagaste finalmente?

6-4

En el mercado tradicional. PREPARACIÓN. Mira los productos que hay en este mercado tradicional. Escoge por lo menos tres recuerdos (*souvenirs*) que quieres comprar y llena la siguiente tabla.

PRODUCTO QUE QUIERES COMPRAR	PRECIO QUE QUISIERAS PAGAR POR EL PRODUCTO
collar de plata	*550 bolívares*
__________	__________
__________	__________

INTERCAMBIOS. Ahora, túrnense para comprar unos recuerdos. Pregunten el precio de los productos. Regateen (*Haggle*) para obtener un precio más barato.

MODELO

E1: *Quisiera comprar este collar. ¿Cuánto cuesta?*

E2: *Cuesta 650 bolívares.*

E1: *¡Uy, es muy caro! Lo compro por 550.*

E2: *Pero, es muy bonito.*

E1: *Sí, es muy bonito, pero no tengo suficiente dinero.*

E2: *Bueno, está bien. Se lo vendo por 575.*

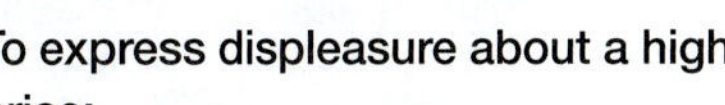

En directo

To express displeasure about a high price:

¡Qué caro/a! *How expensive!*

To show pleasure at a bargain:

¡Qué barato/a! *How cheap!*

¡Qué ganga! *What a bargain!*

Listen to a conversation with these expressions.

Note for 6-4
Argentina, Paraguay, and Uruguay are known for their leather goods. In Bolivia, Peru, Ecuador, and Guatemala, one can find beautiful Indian weavings. Chile and Argentina produce excellent wines. Some countries are famous for the high quality of their gems and silver work: Colombia (emeralds) and Peru and Mexico (silver). Isla de Margarita in Venezuela is known for its miniature handicrafts.

Suggestion for 6-4
Discuss shopping at markets. Introduce the word *regatear* (haggling) or have students read the *Cultura* box, answer the *Comparaciones* questions, and give examples (house, car, flea markets, garage sales, eBay). Model haggling with a student by pretending you want to buy something and bargaining for a lower price. To avoid spending too much time on this activity, you may time it and indicate when students should change roles.

Note for *En directo*
Before doing activity 6-4, *Intercambios*, first have students read the expressions in *En directo*. Then have them listen to the dialogue and encourage them to use the expressions in their own conversation.

Audioscript for *En directo*
IVÁN: *Me encanta esta camisa, pero cuesta 85 dólares.*
LUPE: *¡Qué cara! Mira esta. Solo cuesta 30 dólares.*
IVÁN: *¡Qué ganga! Y me gusta mucho también.*

Suggestions for *La ropa*
You may use fashion magazines when introducing clothing. Identify and describe each piece. Ask questions to check comprehension. Describe the clothes you're wearing and then comment on students' clothes: *¿De qué color es el vestido de…? Es bonita la blusa de…, ¿no?* Use expressions such as *de lunares, de cuadros, de rayas,* and *de color entero/de un solo color.*

Describe a student's clothing without mentioning his or her name. Other students guess who the person is.

You may introduce additional vocabulary such as: *ropa interior, de manga corta/larga, bolsillo, de tacón alto, elegante.*

Suggestion for *La ropa*
Review vocabulary by commenting on clothing students are wearing: *Pedro lleva una camisa de cuadros. Es muy bonita. Y Juan, ¿lleva una camisa de cuadros? No, es de rayas. Le queda muy bien. No le queda ancha.* Introduce the word *vestido.*

La ropa

La ropa formal **La ropa informal** **La ropa interior y de estar en casa**

Telas y diseños

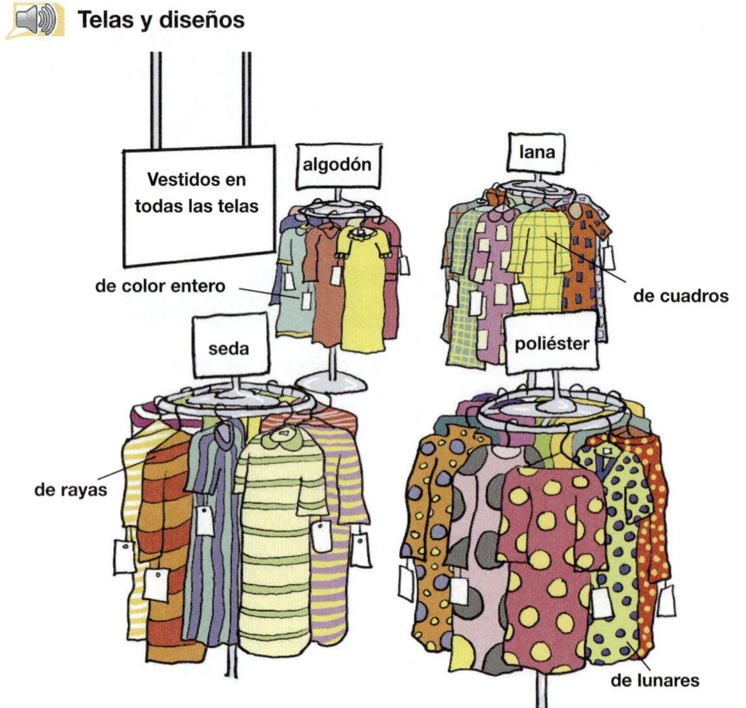

EN OTRAS PALABRAS

Some words referring to clothing differ from one region to another. For example, in Spain **el/la piyama** is **el pijama,** and **medias** means *stockings,* but in parts of Latin America it also means *socks.* Depending on the country, the words **aros, aretes, pendientes, pantallas,** or **zarcillos** are used for *earrings.* In Argentina and Uruguay **pollera** is used instead of **falda,** and in Colombia **vestido** may mean *suit* or *dress*.

Las rebajas

MARTA: Las **rebajas** son **magníficas.** Mira esa falda de rayas. Está **rebajada** de 840 bolívares a 775. ¿Por qué no vemos si tienen tu **talla?**

ANA: Sí, y **me pruebo** la falda para ver si **me queda** bien. Uso la talla 38 y a veces es difícil **encontrarla.** Esta falda es de algodón y es **preciosa.**

MARTA: O te pruebas la falda en casa y si te queda mal, la **cambias.**

[***Entran en*** *la tienda*].

ANA: Buenos días, señorita, **quisiera** probarme la falda que está en el **escaparate** en la talla 38.

DEPENDIENTA: Lo siento, pero las únicas tallas que **nos quedan** son más grandes, la 42 y la 44.

ANA: ¡Qué lástima! Gracias.

▲ Le queda **estrecha.**

▲ Le queda **ancha.**

LENGUA

The word **talla** is normally used when talking about clothing size; **número** refers to shoe size. **Tamaño** means size in all other contexts: **¿Cuál es tu número de zapatos?**

The word **calzado** means footwear in general: **Chik's es el calzado oficial de Miss Venezuela.**

The verb **calzar** is also used to ask about someone's shoe size. **¿Qué número calzas? ¿Cuánto calzas?**

PRÁCTICA

6-5

Para confirmar. Asocia las afirmaciones para describir la experiencia de Ana en las rebajas.

1. __c__ Ana necesita una falda en la talla 38.
2. __e__ La falda no es de color entero.
3. __f__ Ana prefiere las telas naturales.
4. __a__ Ana entra en la tienda, pero no se prueba la falda.
5. __b__ La falda no es muy cara.
6. __d__ Marta dice que Ana puede probarse la falda antes de comprarla.

a. La dependienta dice que no tienen su talla.
b. Está rebajada.
c. Sabe que la talla 42 le va a quedar ancha.
d. No se prueba la falda porque prefiere comprar un vestido.
e. Es de rayas.
f. Le gusta la falda porque es de algodón.

6-6

¿Qué llevas? **PREPARACIÓN.** Indica qué prendas de vestir (*articles of clothing*) usas en cada situación.

1. Para ir a correr o al gimnasio me pongo ________.
2. Para dormir llevo ________.
3. Para ir a una fiesta me pongo ________.
4. Después de ducharme y antes de vestirme llevo ________.

INTERCAMBIOS. Ahora, túrnense para preguntarse qué prendas de vestir usan en cada situación.

MODELO para venir a clase

E1: *¿Qué usas para venir a clase?*

E2: *Uso unos vaqueros.*

1. para salir los sábados con tus amigos
2. para ir a una fiesta de cumpleaños
3. para una entrevista de trabajo
4. para ir a la playa en verano

Suggestion for *Las rebajas*
Explain *rebajas: A veces hay rebajas* (write word on the board) *muy buenas. ¿Saben ustedes qué es una rebaja? Pues, si un reloj normalmente cuesta 50 dólares, en una rebaja pueden comprarlo por 40 dólares o menos.* Ask questions to check comprehension.

Use visuals and comprehensible input to review vocabulary. *¿Te pruebas la ropa en las tiendas? ¿Vas a las tiendas cuando hay rebajas? ¿Cuál es tu tienda favorita?* You may explain that the approximate equivalent of a women's size 38 is an 8. Sizes 40, 42, and 44 are similar to women's sizes 10, 12, and 14, respectively.

Industria textil

Spanish-speaking countries used to have robust local or regional clothing industries. With globalization, however, clothing has become an international product, usually manufactured in distant countries and distributed via multinational business networks. As in the United States, people in Latin America and Spain usually buy clothes made in other countries or continents, although in open markets or specialized clothing stores people can still buy locally manufactured clothing. It is important to note that Zara, a Spanish textile group, is currently the biggest clothing company in the world.

Conexiones. ¿En qué tiendas compras ropa generalmente? ¿Dónde está manufacturada la ropa que llevas hoy? ¿Dónde se puede encontrar ropa artesanal en tu ciudad? ¿Crees que es necesario pagar más por ropa de marca (*brand name*)?

Suggestion for 6-7
Before this activity, talk about the different parts of the body by pointing to yourself or to the people in the drawings. Call attention to the *Lengua* box. Then ask questions to relate clothing to parts of the body: *¿Qué lleva Marisa en la mano? ¿Cuántos aretes lleva Miguel en la oreja?*

6-7 

¿Qué ropa llevan? PREPARACIÓN. Cuenten (*Count*) cuántas personas de la clase llevan los siguientes accesorios y prendas de vestir. Después, comparen sus resultados.

1. aretes en las orejas ________
2. camisetas con el logotipo de la universidad ________
3. zapatillas de deporte ________
4. vaqueros rotos (*with holes*) ________
5. corbatas ________
6. collares de oro ________

LENGUA

Here is some useful vocabulary for the body (**el cuerpo**): **la cabeza** (head), **las orejas** (ears), **la nariz** (nose), **los brazos** (arms), **las manos** (hands), **las piernas** (legs), **los pies** (feet), **el cuello** (neck). You will learn more words related to parts of the body in *Capítulo 11.*

INTERCAMBIOS. Túrnense para describir la ropa que llevan algunas personas de la clase para adivinar (*guess*) quiénes son.

Suggestion for 6-8
To help students' speech sound more natural, you may wish to review ways to express agreement/disagreement as they work together to solve the problems presented in the chart.
Encourage students to be creative and expand on their answers in this activity: *En el almacén El Encanto hay unos collares muy bonitos. ¿Por qué no miramos los collares allá?* Have them think of other gifts and come to a conclusion: *¿Le vamos a regalar una camisa? ¿Le interesan las zapatillas? ¿Qué le vamos a dar?* They can do this exercise in groups of 3 or 4.

6-8 

El cumpleaños de Nuria. Ustedes van a una tienda para comprarle un regalo a una buena amiga, pero cada artículo que ven presenta un problema. Piensen en la solución.

ARTÍCULO	PROBLEMA	SOLUCIÓN
collar	Es muy caro.	*Debemos buscar uno más barato.*
impermeable	Le queda ancho.	
vaqueros	Son de poliéster.	
sudadera	Es pequeña.	
blusa	Las rayas son muy anchas.	
bolso	No es de cuero.	

¿Qué debo llevar?

 En el **invierno** hace frío. ¿Qué ropa llevamos?

 Cuando hace calor en el **verano,** ¿qué nos ponemos para ir a la playa?

Y cuando llueve en la **primavera** y en el **otoño,** usamos impermeable y paraguas.

PRÁCTICA

 **6-9** 

Para confirmar. PREPARACIÓN. Asocia las prendas de vestir con las afirmaciones más lógicas.

1. __b__ los guantes
2. __d__ el traje de baño
3. __f__ las botas
4. __e__ el suéter
5. __c__ los pantalones cortos
6. __a__ el sombrero

a. Sirve para protegernos del sol.
b. Los llevamos en las manos cuando hace frío.
c. Son más cómodos cuando hace buen tiempo.
d. Nos lo ponemos para ir a la playa.
e. Es de lana, para llevar cuando hace frío.
f. Las llevamos en los pies en invierno.

 INTERCAMBIOS. Túrnense y pregunten qué ropa o accesorios usan ustedes en las siguientes situaciones. Añadan (*Add*) otras opciones en sus respuestas.

MODELO cuando llueve

E1: *¿Qué usas/llevas cuando llueve?*

E2: *Uso un paraguas. ¿Y tú?*

E1: *Uso un impermeable.*

1. cuando montas en bicicleta
2. para caminar por el parque en invierno
3. para ir a la playa con tus amigos
4. en los pies cuando hace calor
5. cuando hace mucho sol en verano
6. en otoño cuando hace viento (*wind*)

Suggestion for *¿Qué debo llevar?*
Use visuals to illustrate weather expressions and clothes. Tell students what you wear in winter: *En el invierno, yo llevo un suéter y pantalones largos. Cuando hace mucho frío, me pongo un abrigo y unos guantes. A veces llevo una bufanda.* Ask yes/no and either/or questions to check understanding. Personalize by asking what students wear and do in winter and in summer.

Note
More weather-related terms are introduced in *Capítulo 7*.

Suggestion for 6-9
Recycle vocabulary of body parts that was presented before. You may ask: *¿Dónde se pone el sombrero?* Or *Llevamos un sombrero en… ¿Qué llevamos en los pies, las botas o los guantes? En los pies nos ponemos…*

Suggestions for 6-10
Point out *isla de Margarita* on a map and explain that it is an island in the Caribbean, north of Venezuela, and that Canaima is in western Venezuela. You may also mention that the highest waterfall in the world, Salto Ángel, is there.

Students can expand their lists by describing the items. Have students plan a trip in another season, focusing on the different clothing they will need. Point out that there are only two seasons in Venezuela, dry (December to April) and rainy (May to November).

Note for 6-11
A *guayabera* is a loose short- or long-sleeved man's shirt that is not tucked in. It is worn in place of a shirt or jacket and tie in areas where the weather is very hot.

Warm-up for 6-12
As a prelistening activity, have students in groups of 4 describe the clothes they wear for parties, classes, family reunions, weddings, and graduations.

Audioscript for 6-12, *Escucha*
BERTA: *Alfredo, dime una cosa, ¿vas a la fiesta en la embajada esta noche?*
ALFREDO: *Sí. Tú también vas, ¿verdad?*
BERTA: *Sí, y no sé qué me voy a poner. Supongo que es formal.*
ALFREDO: *Sí, es formal. Yo voy a ir con un traje azul y mi hermana va a llevar un traje de la diseñadora Carolina Herrera, sencillo pero elegante.*
BERTA: *¡Qué bien! Yo no sé todavía qué me voy a poner. ¿Y a qué hora van a ir?*
ALFREDO: *A las nueve más o menos.*
BERTA: *Bueno, nos vemos entonces.*

6-10 

Vacaciones en Venezuela. Tu amigo/a y tú van a pasar unas vacaciones en Venezuela. Escojan el plan que más les interesa y preparen una lista de la ropa y accesorios que van a necesitar. Presenten su plan a la clase.

Plan A. Quince días en isla de Margarita. Por el día: ir a la playa; por la noche: ir a las discotecas.

Plan B. Tomar un curso de verano en la Universidad Central de Venezuela en Caracas. Por la mañana: clases de español; por la tarde: lugares de interés turístico.

Plan C. Explorar la fauna y flora de la región de Canaima. Por el día: caminar mucho; por la noche: estar en un campamento.

Vamos a ir a isla de Margarita. Yo necesito un traje de baño y mi compañera necesita unos pantalones cortos.

6-11 

Ropa para todos. Cada uno/a debe comprar ropa para hacer unos regalos a tres personas diferentes de la lista siguiente. Explícale a tu compañero/a qué vas a comprar, dónde y para quién son estos regalos.

1. tu sobrina de seis años
2. tu mamá para el Día de la Madre
3. un/a amigo/a que necesita ropa informal
4. tu padre para su cumpleaños
5. tu novio/a para el Día de los Enamorados

6-12 

Ropa para cada ocasión. PREPARACIÓN. Tell your classmate what you wear on the following occasions: **una fiesta elegante** and **una fiesta informal**.

  ESCUCHA. Listen to the conversation and indicate (✓) the clothes and the event mentioned.

ROPA	EVENTO
✓ ropa elegante	____ entrevista de trabajo
____ falda y chaqueta	____ reunión de jóvenes
____ traje pantalón y blusa	____ excursión de fin de semana
____ pantalones cortos y camiseta	✓ fiesta formal

MOSAICO cultural

Las tiendas de barrio

Los centros comerciales son lugares importantes en las ciudades hispanas. Como en Estados Unidos, los centros comerciales son también centros de ocio y entretenimiento donde se va a comprar, a comer o a ver películas. Los centros comerciales están en zonas urbanas donde vive mucha gente y, por eso, también hay grandes supermercados. En algunas ciudades, los supermercados son cadenas (*chains*) nacionales, como Éxito en Colombia y Coto en Argentina. Pero también hay otros de origen europeo, como Carrefour, o estadounidense, como Walmart.

Lo importante es que los hispanos compran comida, ropa, instrumentos para el trabajo y productos para sus casas y mascotas en estos supermercados y centros comerciales.

Sin embargo (*However*), los grandes supermercados compiten con los lugares más tradicionales. En América Latina, existen centros de comercio llamados tiendas de barrio (o quioscos en México, Argentina y Uruguay). Las tiendas de barrio tienen una variedad de productos, pero son mucho más pequeñas que los supermercados. Ocasionalmente, las personas prefieren estas tiendas porque son mucho más personales y es posible regatear.

Las tiendas de barrio tienen una gran importancia cultural en los países hispanos. En estos lugares se establecen relaciones de amistad (*friendship*) y solidaridad entre las personas y la comunidad. Las tiendas de barrio también ofrecen otros servicios: recepción y transmisión de mensajes y publicación de información importante.

Hipermercado Éxito en Bogotá, Colombia

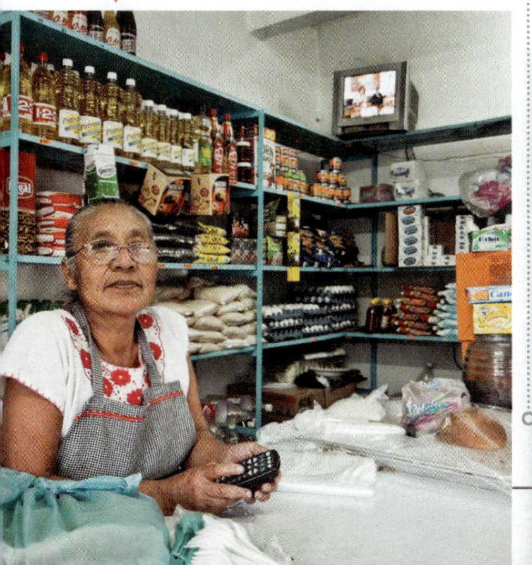
Una tienda de barrio en Venezuela

Compara

1. ¿Qué ofrecen los centros comerciales en tu comunidad?
2. ¿Hay tiendas de barrio o alguna tienda similar donde vives?
3. ¿Cómo se llaman y qué compras allí?
4. ¿Qué importancia tienen las tiendas de barrio en la comunidad?

Note for *Funciones y formas*
This chapter presents the preterit tense of regular verbs and of *ser* and *ir*. The preterit of irregular and reflexive verbs is presented in *Capítulo 7*.

Suggestion for *Funciones y formas*
Describe what you generally do each morning and mention how today differed from your routine: *Normalmente desayuno en casa, pero hoy desayuné en la cafetería. Generalmente tomo té, pero hoy tomé un café y conversé con unos estudiantes* (write preterit forms on the board). *Después caminé a mi oficina y hablé por teléfono.* Ask questions to check understanding and then ask personal questions using the verb forms on the board: *¿Tomaste café en el desayuno? Y tú, ¿tomaste café o té? ¿Desayunaste en casa o en un café?* If necessary, write the verb forms on the board. Repeat information provided by students using the *él/ella* verb form: *Pedro tomó té, pero Arturo tomó café.*

Funciones y formas

1 Talking about the past

Querido diario:

Hoy Álvaro y yo **gastamos** mucho dinero en ropa para vernos bien en la fiesta de boda de mi cuñada Gabriela esta tarde. Yo **compré** un hermoso vestido de fiesta y un chal de encaje (*lace shawl*). Álvaro **compró** un traje, una camisa y una corbata.

A las 7:00 de la tarde, **empezó** la ceremonia religiosa. La fiesta con la familia y los amigos **comenzó** a las 9:00 y **terminó** a las 4:00 de la mañana. Todos **comimos, bailamos** y **cantamos** mucho. Vamos a recordar este día especial por mucho tiempo. Gabriela y Gonzalo son una pareja perfecta.

Ahora voy a dormir. Estoy muy cansada.
Camila

Piénsalo. ¿Qué pasó el día de la boda? Ordena cronológicamente la siguiente información (1 = primer evento, etc.), según el diario de Camila.

1. __2__ La fiesta con la familia y los amigos **comenzó** a las 9:00.
2. __1__ Camila **compró** un hermoso vestido de fiesta.
3. __4__ La fiesta **terminó** a las 4:00 de la mañana.
4. __3__ Todos **comieron, bailaron** y **cantaron** mucho.

Preterit tense of regular verbs

- Spanish has two simple tenses to express the past: the preterit (**el pretérito)** and the imperfect (**el imperfecto**). Use the preterit to talk about past events, actions, and conditions that are viewed as completed or ended.

	HABLAR	COMER	VIVIR
yo	habl**é**	com**í**	viv**í**
tú	habl**aste**	com**iste**	viv**iste**
Ud., él, ella	habl**ó**	com**ió**	viv**ió**
nosotros/as	habl**amos**	com**imos**	viv**imos**
vosotros/as	habl**asteis**	com**isteis**	viv**isteis**
Uds., ellos/as	habl**aron**	com**ieron**	viv**ieron**

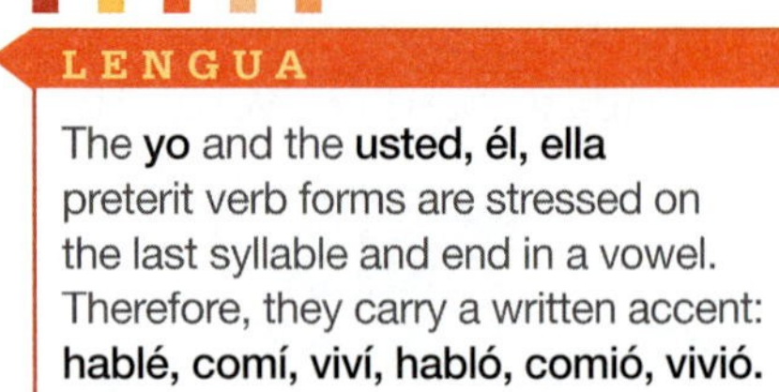
LENGUA

The **yo** and the **usted, él, ella** preterit verb forms are stressed on the last syllable and end in a vowel. Therefore, they carry a written accent: **hablé, comí, viví, habló, comió, vivió.**

- Note that the **nosotros/as** forms of the preterit of **-ar** and **-ir** verbs are the same in the present and the preterit tenses. Context will help you determine if **nosotros/as** verb forms are present or past.

Llegamos a la tienda a las tres.	*We arrive at the store at three. We arrived at the store at three.*
Salí de la universidad a las dos, y **llegamos** a casa a las tres.	*I left the university at two, and we arrived home at three.*

- Stem-changing verbs ending in **-ar** and **-er** do not have a stem change in the preterit.

  pensar: pensé, pensaste, pensó, pensamos, pensasteis, pensaron

  volver: volví, volviste, volvió, volvimos, volvisteis, volvieron

- Verbs ending in **-car** and **-gar** have a spelling change in the **yo** form of the preterit that reflects how the word is pronounced. Verbs ending in **-zar** have a spelling change in the **yo** form because Spanish rarely uses a **z** before **e** or **i.**

  sacar:
  sa**qué,** sacaste, sacó...

  llegar:
  lle**gué,** llegaste, llegó...

  empezar:
  empe**cé,** empezaste, empezó...

- There are some expressions you can use with the preterit to denote when an event took place.

anoche	*last night*
anteayer	*day before yesterday*
ante(a)noche	*the night before last*
ayer	*yesterday*
el año/mes pasado	*last year/month*
la semana pasada	*last week*
una semana atrás	*a week ago*
hace un día/mes/año (que)	*it has been a day/month/year since*

e ¿COMPRENDES?

Completa las oraciones con la forma correcta del verbo.

1. El año pasado Pablo y Elisa __comieron__ (comer) muchas veces en el restaurante venezolano de la ciudad.
2. La semana pasada Elena y yo __estudiamos__ (estudiar) juntas para el examen de geografía.
3. Ayer yo __compré__ (comprar) unos calcetines y una falda en los Almacenes Arias.
4. Anoche Luis __escribió__ (escribir) muchos correos electrónicos.
5. Hace un año Carlota __comenzó__ (comenzar) a estudiar español.
6. La semana pasada tú __llegaste__ (llegar) tarde a clase todos los días.

MySpanishLab

Learn more using Amplifire Dynamic Study Modules, Grammar Tutorials, and Extra Practice activities.

PRÁCTICA

6-13

Ayer yo... PREPARACIÓN. En el cuadro, marca (✓) tus actividades de ayer y añade una actividad en cada columna.

POR LA MAÑANA	POR LA TARDE	POR LA NOCHE
_____ Desayuné.	_____ Almorcé en la cafetería.	_____ Preparé la cena.
_____ Llegué a tiempo a mis clases.	_____ Saqué libros de la biblioteca.	_____ Miré televisión.
_____ Estudié varias horas.	_____ Lavé la ropa.	_____ Planché mi ropa.
_____ Llamé por teléfono a un/a amigo/a.	_____ Compré comida para toda la semana.	_____ Salí con mis amigos.
...	...	...

INTERCAMBIOS. Ahora escríbele un correo electrónico a tu compañero/a explicándole lo que hiciste (*you did*) ayer. Intercambien sus mensajes en la clase para comparar lo que hicieron.

Suggestion for 6-13, *Intercambios*
Practice the third person by asking students to report back on what their classmate did. This activity provides a preview of the strategy, recounting events in sequence, students will be using in *Escribe.*

Follow-up for 6-14
Assign students in pairs or small groups to write as many sentences as they can about the activities of Carmen and Rafael in one subset of the drawings. Encourage them to use as many different verbs in the preterit as possible. Then create a detailed story of the couple's day by combining the work of all. Copies of the story (with verbs removed) can be used as an activity for a future class.

6-14 

El sábado pasado. **PREPARACIÓN.** Miren las siguientes escenas. Túrnense para explicar cómo pasaron el sábado Carmen y Rafael.

▲ El sábado por la mañana

▲ El sábado por la tarde

▲ El sábado por la noche

INTERCAMBIOS. Escriban un párrafo para describir las actividades de Carmen y Rafael. Después, compártanlo oralmente con la clase.

6-15 

¿Cómo pasaron el fin de semana? **PREPARACIÓN.** Conversen sobre el fin de semana de ustedes para conocer detalles sobre:

- las actividades que hizo (*did*) cada uno/a
- dónde las hizo
- con quién
- qué día, a qué hora
- un detalle más

INTERCAMBIOS. Determinen quién de ustedes pasó el mejor fin de semana. Describan las actividades de esta persona a la clase.

Situación

PREPARACIÓN. Lean la situación. Luego, compartan ejemplos de vocabulario, gramática y otra información que necesitan para desarrollar la conversación.

Role A. Your classmate and a friend went on a shopping spree last weekend. Ask:

a. what store(s) they shopped in;
b. what each of them bought;
c. what time they returned home; and
d. what your classmate's plans are for wearing or using the items.

Role B. Answer your classmate's questions about your shopping spree with a friend over the weekend. Then find out if your classmate went shopping over the weekend, played a sport, or watched a lot of TV.

	ROLE A	ROLE B
Vocabulario	Shopping: clothes, shoes, or other	Shopping: clothes, shoes, or other
Funciones y formas	Past tense Recounting events in the past Asking questions	Past tense Recounting events in the past Asking questions Talking about future plans

INTERCAMBIOS. Practica la conversación con tu compañero/a incorporando el vocabulario y las funciones de *Preparación*. Luego, represéntenla ante la clase.

2 Talking about the past: *ir* and *ser*

CLIENTA: Compré este vestido aquí el sábado pasado. Pero ahora me queda estrecho.

SUPERVISORA: ¿Quién **fue** el vendedor que le vendió el vestido, señorita?

CLIENTA: No sé su nombre, pero **fue** su compañero, un señor alto y delgado.

SUPERVISORA: ¿Qué pasó? ¿Lavó el vestido en casa?

CLIENTA: Claro que no. Hay que limpiar este vestido en seco (*dry clean*). **Fui** a una lavandería (*dry cleaner*).

SUPERVISORA: Los irresponsables **fueron** los empleados de la lavandería. No limpiaron en seco su vestido. Lo lavaron.

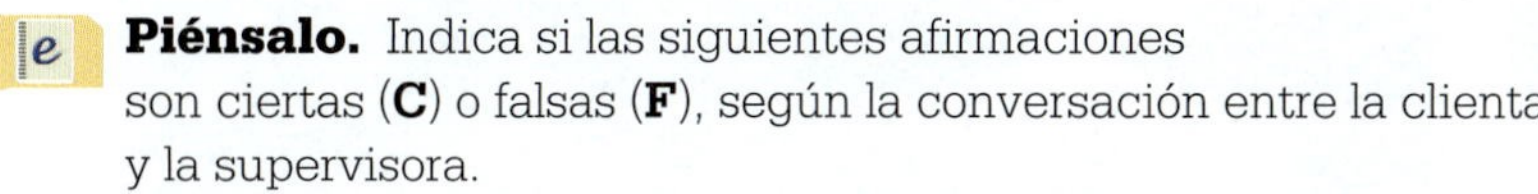

Piénsalo. Indica si las siguientes afirmaciones son ciertas (**C**) o falsas (**F**), según la conversación entre la clienta y la supervisora.

1. __C__ El vendedor **fue** el compañero de la supervisora.
2. __C__ La clienta **fue** a una tienda especializada para limpiar el vestido.
3. __C__ Lavar el vestido **fue** un error de los empleados de la lavandería.
4. __C__ La supervisora **fue** amable con la clienta porque trató de comprender el problema.
5. __F__ Los vendedores de la tienda de ropa **fueron** las personas responsables del problema con el vestido.

Preterit of *ir* and *ser*

- The verbs **ir** and **ser** have identical forms in the preterit. They are used often in speaking and writing, and the context will help you to determine the meaning.

IR *and* SER			
yo	**fui**	nosotros/as	**fuimos**
tú	**fuiste**	vosotros/as	**fuisteis**
Ud., él, ella	**fue**	Uds., ellos/as	**fueron**

- You will also be able to differentiate between **ir** and **ser** in the preterit because **ir** is often followed by the preposition **a.**

Ernesto **fue** a la tienda. — *Ernesto went to the store.*

Fue vendedor en esa tienda por dos años. — *He was a salesclerk at that store for two years.*

¿COMPRENDES?

Completa la conversación con la forma correcta del verbo **ser** o **ir** en el pretérito.

ANA: Hola, mamá. ¿Adónde (1) __fuiste__ esta mañana?

MAMÁ: (2) __Fui__ a ver a la tía Luisa, que se rompió una pierna.

ANA: Ay, no, ¿cómo (3) __fue__ ?

MAMÁ: Se resbaló (*slipped*) en el hielo al salir de su casa.

ANA: ¡Qué mal! Y, ¿cuándo (4) __fue__?

MAMÁ: Ayer por la tarde.

ANA: ¿(5) __Fuiste__ a verla con papá?

MAMÁ: No. (6) __Fui__ sola.

MySpanishLab
Learn more using Amplifire Dynamic Study Modules, Grammar Tutorials, and Extra Practice activities.

Suggestion for Talking about the past
Ask: *¿Adónde fueron las siguientes personas?* 1. *Ayer fue el cumpleaños de Javier. Su novia le compró un traje de muy buena calidad. (una boutique)* 2. *Javier invitó a Paula a escoger su anillo de boda. (una joyería)* 3. *Marcela, la hermana de Javier, fue a comprar las últimas* (the latest) *fragancias de Óscar de la Renta y Paloma Picasso. (una perfumería)* 4. *Paula compró sus zapatos blancos. (una zapatería)*

Suggestion for 6-16
In the class before the one in which you do this activity, you may ask students to research the places mentioned so that they can contribute more in class. They should be ready to answer the following questions: *¿En qué región de Venezuela está este lugar? ¿Cuándo se fundó? ¿Qué hacen los turistas que visitan este lugar?*

Note for 6-16
You may want to mention that *cataratas* (*Cataratas de Niágara*) in question #2 is another word for *salto* (*Salto Ángel*).

Follow-up for 6-16
Ask students to 1. explain why they think each person chose that particular place, and 2. tell about 3 or 4 activities that each person probably did there.

PRÁCTICA

6-16 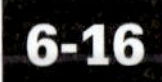  

¿Quién fue a este lugar? Las siguientes personas fueron a Venezuela para conocer algunos lugares famosos. Primero, lean cada situación y luego, relacionen las fotos con cada una de ellas.

A. Salto Ángel

B. Isla de Margarita

C. Maracaibo

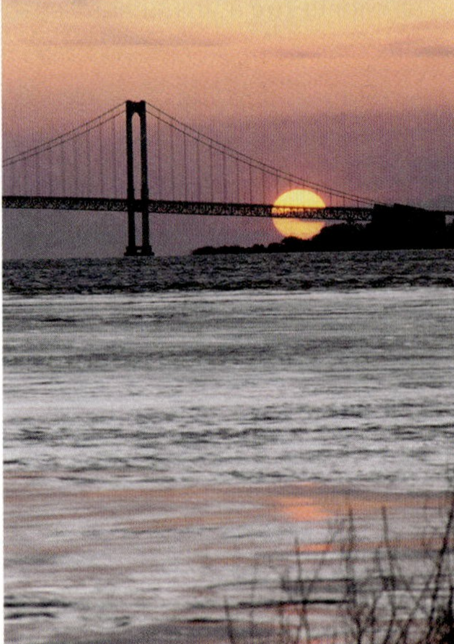

D. El puente Angostura sobre el río Orinoco

1. __D__ Andrés visitó un lugar con agua para navegar. Le fascinan los deportes acuáticos, pero no le gusta el mar. ¿Adónde fue Andrés?
2. __A__ Alguien te habló sobre este lugar espectacular y único en el mundo. Es semejante a las cataratas de Niágara y tú decidiste ir para verlo. ¿Adónde fuiste?
3. __B__ Los estudiantes del primer año de español de tu universidad fueron de viaje a una playa exótica. Allí conocieron a otros turistas de muchas partes del mundo. ¿Adónde fueron los estudiantes?
4. __C__ Los ingenieros Roberto y Angélica decidieron ir a este lugar para investigar las últimas tecnologías en el procesamiento del petróleo. ¿Adónde fueron Roberto y Angélica?

6-17

¿Quiénes fueron? Escojan a uno de estos personajes famosos y hagan una breve presentación en clase. Respondan a las siguientes preguntas.

Atahualpa	Roberto Clemente	Pablo Casals
Frida Kahlo	Simón Bolívar	Nicolás Guillén
Ernesto Guevara	Mario Molina	

1. ¿Quién fue esta persona?
2. ¿Dónde nació, vivió y murió (*died*)?
3. ¿Por qué fue famoso/a? Indiquen como mínimo dos o tres hechos (*facts*) sobre su vida.

Suggestion for 6-17
Three students per group is optimal to maximize student-to-student communication. You can assign this activity ahead of time or bring information to class about these people. Explain in advance the format and guidelines for the presentations.

Situación

PREPARACIÓN. Lean esta situación. Luego, compartan ejemplos de vocabulario, gramática y otra información que necesitan para desarrollar la conversación.

Role A. A classmate tells you that he/she went to a concert last weekend. Ask:

a. where the concert was;
b. what time it started;
c. with whom he/she went;
d. what time the concert ended; and
e. where he/she went afterwards.

React to the information you hear and answer your classmate's questions about your weekend activities.

Role B. Your classmate wants to know about the concert you went to last weekend. Answer your classmate's questions. Then ask your classmate about his/her weekend activities: if he/she went to a party or concert over the weekend, if he/she went out with friends, and so on. Ask for details about where, when, and with whom he/she went.

	ROLE A	ROLE B
Vocabulario	Time, days of the week, leisure activities	Time, days of the week, leisure activities
Funciones y formas	Recounting past events Past tense of *ir* and *ser* Asking questions Reacting to what you hear	Recounting past events Past tense of *ir* and *ser* Reacting to what you hear

INTERCAMBIOS. Practica la conversación con tu compañero/a incorporando el vocabulario y las funciones de *Preparación*. Luego, represéntenla ante la clase.

3 Indicating to whom or for whom an action takes place

LUCY: Oye, Panchito, ¿qué **te** compran tus padres para tu cumpleaños: ropa, chocolates o qué?

PANCHITO: No **me** dan ni ropa ni chocolates. Siempre **me** compran libros superinteresantes. Y tus padres, ¿qué **te** compran a ti, Lucy?

LUCY: Mi mamá siempre **nos** compra ropa a mi hermano y a mí. A mí **me** gusta mucho la ropa nueva.

PANCHITO: ¿Y qué **les** das tú a tus padres para su cumpleaños?

LUCY: ¡A mi mamá **le** doy muchos besitos y a mi papá **le** doy muchos problemas porque no hago mi tarea!

Piénsalo. Primero, identifica quién hace la acción: **Lucy, Lucy y su hermano, la mamá de Lucy, el papá de Lucy, Panchito** o **los padres de Panchito.** Luego, en la segunda línea, indica **quién recibe** la acción.

1. Los padres de Panchito **le** compran libros a Panchito.
2. La mamá de Lucy **les** compra ropa a Lucy y a su hermano.
3. Lucy **le** da muchos besos a su mamá.
4. Lucy **le** causa problemas a su papá porque no hace la tarea.

Suggestions
Act out this and similar situations in class: *Yo le doy el bolígrafo a Mercedes. Mercedes le da el bolígrafo a Juan. ¿Qué le da Mercedes a Juan? ¿A quién le da el bolígrafo Mercedes?* (Point to Juan.) *Mercedes le da un lápiz a Lisa. ¿Qué le da Mercedes a Lisa? ¿A quién le da un lápiz Mercedes?* Write on the board one or two sentences you have used. Circle *le* and the indirect object noun. Draw an arrow to connect *le* to the indirect object noun.

Start a chain activity by saying: *Le doy mi lápiz a X. X, ¿qué le das a Y?* The next student continues the chain: *Yo le doy ___ a Y. Y, ¿qué le das a Z?*, etc.

Indirect object nouns and pronouns

- Indirect object nouns and pronouns tell *to whom* or *for whom* an action is done; in other words, who is affected by an action.

Indirect Object Pronouns			
me	*to/for me*	**nos**	*to/for us*
te	*to/for you* (familiar)	**os**	*to/for you* (familiar)
le	*to/for you* (formal), *him, her, it*	**les**	*to/for you* (formal), *them*

- Indirect object pronouns have the same form as direct object pronouns except in the third person: **le** and **les.**

Mi madre **me** compró ropa la semana pasada.	*My mother bought me clothes last week. [My mother bought clothes for me last week.]*
Yo **te** presto mis zapatos para la fiesta.	*I will lend you my shoes for the party. [I will lend my shoes to you for the party.]*
¿El dependiente? Ella **lo** ve todas las mañanas. (*direct object*)	*The salesperson? She sees him every morning.*
¿El dependiente? Ella **le** da los recibos por la mañana. (*indirect object*)	*The salesperson? She gives him the receipts in the morning.*

- Place the indirect object pronoun before a conjugated verb form. It may be attached to a present participle, in which case an accent mark is added, or to an infinitive.

Les voy a vender mi carro. Voy a vender**les** mi carro.	*I am going to sell them my car.*
Juan **nos** está preparando la cena. Juan está preparándo**nos** la cena.	*Juan is preparing dinner for us.*

- Use indirect object pronouns even when the indirect object noun is stated explicitly.

Yo **le** presté mi libro a **Victoria.** — *I lent my book to Victoria.*

- To eliminate ambiguity, **le** and **les** are often used with the preposition **a** + *pronoun*.

Le hablo **a usted.** — *I am talking to you.* (not to *him/her*)

Siempre **les** cuento mis secretos **a ellos.** — *I always tell my secrets to them.* (not to *you*/**ustedes**)

- For emphasis, use **a mí, a ti, a nosotros/as,** and **a vosotros/as** with indirect object pronouns.

Pedro **te** habla a **ti.** — *Pedro is talking to you.* (not to someone else)

- **Dar** is almost always used with indirect object pronouns.

DAR (*to give*)			
yo	**doy**	nosotros/as	**damos**
tú	**das**	vosotros/as	**dais**
Ud., él, ella	**da**	Uds., ellos/as	**dan**

LENGUA

Dar uses the same endings as **-er** and **-ir** verbs in the preterit: **di, diste, dio, dimos, disteis, dieron**

Jorge le **dio** a Elena una copia de sus apuntes.
Jorge gave Elena a copy of his notes.

Mis padres me **dieron** dinero para la matrícula.
My parents gave me money for tuition.

- Notice the difference in meaning between **dar** (*to give*) and **regalar** (*to give as a gift*).

Ella le **da** el cinturón a Pedro. — *She gives Pedro the belt* (hands it to him).

Ella le **regala** el cinturón a Pedro. — *She gives Pedro the belt* (a gift).

- Other verbs of transmission (of things, ideas, words) that are generally used with indirect object pronouns include:

decir	*to say, to tell*
describir	*to describe*
escribir	*to write*
explicar	*to explain*
mostrar (ue)	*to show*
prestar	*to lend*
regalar	*to give* (a present)
vender	*to sell*

¿COMPRENDES?

Completa las oraciones con el pronombre correcto según la información entre paréntesis.

1. Yo _le_ doy un regalo. (a mi madre)
2. Yo _les_ doy un juguete. (a los niños)
3. Los niños _me_ dan un beso. (a mí)
4. El profesor _les_ da una buena nota. (a ustedes)
5. Mi tía Carla _nos_ da unos libros. (a mi hermano y a mí)
6. Felisa _te_ da las gracias. (a ti)

MySpanishLab

Learn more using Amplifire Dynamic Study Modules, Grammar Tutorials, and Extra Practice activities.

Suggestion
Mention that the pronoun is used when the indirect object noun is stated, but the reverse is not true. The indirect object pronoun can stand alone.

Note
Double object pronouns are introduced in *Capítulo 9.*

PRÁCTICA

6-18 

Las compras. Asocia la acción con la persona que la recibe.

1. __d__ Para su cumpleaños, le regalé una corbata
2. __a__ Julia fue a Venezuela y les compró unos aretes muy bonitos
3. __e__ Después de probarnos los pantalones de rayas le preguntamos el precio
4. __f__ Los zapatos nuevos me quedan muy bien
5. __b__ Cuando fuimos a Italia te envié una postal
6. __c__ Nos compraron unas bufandas muy lindas en Berlín

a. a todas sus amigas.
b. a ti.
c. a nosotros.
d. a mi padre.
e. al dependiente.
f. a mí.

Follow-up for 6-19
Have students change partners and share the recommendations they received. You may model the exchange with a student: *Mi compañero/a me recomienda sandalias de Teva porque son muy cómodas. ¿Qué te recomienda tu compañero/a?*

6-19 

Para estar a la última moda. Cada uno/a de ustedes desea o necesita lo que se indica en la lista siguiente. Explíquense (*Explain to each other*) la situación y después pidan y den una recomendación.

E1: *Quiero llevar zapatos muy cómodos. ¿Qué me recomiendas?*

E2: *Te recomiendo unas sandalias de la marca Teva.*

1. Quiero llevar pantalones de moda (*in style*).
2. Deseo protegerme del sol.
3. Quiero ropa buena y barata.
4. Quiero verme (*look*) más delgado/a.
5. Me gustaría llevar ropa elegante y fina a la entrevista de trabajo.

Cultura

Tiendas locales en pueblos o ciudades pequeñas

Throughout most of Latin America and Spain, big department stores are more commonly found in large, metropolitan areas. People who live in small towns may make a trip to the city if they want to visit big chain stores, but more often they shop at local, smaller stores or markets to buy gifts. Many people who live in less-populated areas enjoy the benefit of shopping at a store where they have a longstanding, personal relationship with the owner and employees.

Comparaciones. ¿Te gusta hacer tus compras en tiendas pequeñas? ¿Qué productos prefieres comprar en estas tiendas? ¿Qué productos prefieres comprar en los grandes almacenes?

Suggestion for 6-20
As preparation, have students think of gifts for an elderly person, an athlete, a baby, a boyfriend/girlfriend.

Suggestion for 6-20
You may write down some gift ideas and have students decide in groups to whom in the class they will give them as awards and why: 1. *una invitación para un desfile de moda* (fashion show); 2. *una suscripción a una revista;* 3. *800 bolívares para gastar en el Centro Sambil en Caracas;* 4. *el libro más vendido* (bestseller) *del mes.*

6-20 

Afortunados. Ustedes ganaron la lotería ayer y quieren compartir su fortuna con su familia y sus compañeros de clase.

1. Hagan una lista de dos o tres personas a quienes desean regalarles algo.
2. Indiquen el regalo que piensan hacerle a cada uno/a y expliquen por qué.

E1: *A nuestros padres les vamos a regalar un crucero por el Caribe.*

E2: *A Sara vamos a comprarle una mochila.*

6-21 

Entrevista. **PREPARACIÓN.** Basándose en la siguiente lista, pregúntense sobre sus hábitos de compras y los regalos que ustedes hacen y reciben de otras personas. Tomen notas.

1. ir de compras: ¿Qué? ¿Con qué frecuencia? ¿Tienda(s) favorita(s)?
2. comprar regalos caros: ¿A quién(es)? ¿Cuándo?
3. comprarte regalos: ¿Quién(es)?

INTERCAMBIOS. Escribe una comparación entre tus hábitos de compras y los de tu compañero/a. Usa las siguientes preguntas como guía (*as a guide*).

1. ¿Tienen ustedes hábitos de compras semejantes o diferentes?
2. ¿Compran en las mismas tiendas? ¿Compran regalos semejantes o diferentes?
3. ¿A quién(es) le(s) dan regalos? ¿Quiénes les dan regalos a ustedes? ¿Qué tipos de regalos reciben?

Suggestion for 6-21
You may encourage students to talk about changes in their gift-giving practices and tastes. *¿Dónde les gusta comprar regalos, en los grandes almacenes o por Internet? ¿Prefieren recibir regalos o tarjetas regalo* (gift cards), *para escoger su propio regalo?*

Situación  

PREPARACIÓN. Lean esta situación. Luego, compartan ejemplos de vocabulario, gramática y otra información que necesitan para desarrollar la conversación.

Role A. You are a customer at a department store. Tell the salesperson:

a. you are looking for a present for a friend (specify male or female);
b. you are not sure what you should buy for him/her; and
c. the amount that you can spend.

Role B. You are a salesperson. A customer asks you for advice about a gift for a friend. Inquire about the friend's age, taste, size, favorite color, and other pertinent information. Make suggestions and offer information about the quality of the products, prices, sales, and so forth.

	ROLE A	ROLE B
Vocabulario	Clothes, shopping, prices	Age, likes and dislikes, sizes, colors, shopping, prices
Funciones y formas	Expressing what you need Indirect object pronouns Addressing a salesperson	Indirect object pronouns Addressing a customer

INTERCAMBIOS. Practica la conversación con tu compañero/a incorporando el vocabulario y las funciones de *Preparación*. Luego, represéntenla ante la clase.

Suggestion for *Situación*
You may want to assign partners and have pairs create mini-skits using the video-posting feature, *MediaShare*, online.

Suggestions for Expressing likes and dislikes
You may want to recycle food vocabulary to practice with *gustar.* Using visuals, identify a few of your favorite foods. Poll students, eliciting responses as to what they like and dislike (and why).

Point out that the definite article is used with *gustar,* and that the subject usually follows the verb: *Me gustan los colores brillantes. Nos gusta la música.*

To reinforce the *gustar* construction, practice *interesar, encantar, fascinar,* and *parecer,* whose structure is parallel to English: Your opinion interests me. *Me interesa tu opinión.*

Note for Expressing likes and dislikes
Many Spanish speakers use *caer bien/caer mal* exclusively to talk about liking/disliking people in a general sense, reserving the use of *gustar* for talking about physical attraction.

4 Expressing likes and dislikes

DEPENDIENTE: ¿**Le gustan** estas camisas?

JORGE: No, no **me gustan,** pero **me gusta** esta chaqueta.

DEPENDIENTE: Es una buena chaqueta para el otoño. ¿**Le interesan** los deportes, señor? Tenemos unas zapatillas de deporte muy baratas.

JORGE: **Me encanta** practicar deportes, pero no **me gusta** mirar los partidos en televisión. **Me fascinan** el tenis, el béisbol y el fútbol.

Piénsalo. Indica si cada afirmación es cierta (**C**) o falsa (**F**), según la conversación. Si no hay información suficiente, contesta no sé (**NS**).

1. __F__ A Jorge **le gusta** una de las camisas que le muestra el dependiente.
2. __C__ A Jorge **le interesa** comprar una chaqueta.
3. __NS__ A Jorge **le queda** poco dinero, porque compró la chaqueta cara.
4. __C__ A Jorge **le encantan** varios deportes.
5. __F__ A Jorge **le gusta** mirar los partidos de fútbol en la televisión.
6. __NS__ A los amigos de Jorge **les interesa** jugar al fútbol con él.

Gustar and similar verbs

- In previous chapters you have used the verb **gustar** to express likes and dislikes. As you have seen, **gustar** is not used the same way as the English verb *to like.* **Gustar** is similar to the expression *to be pleasing* (*to someone*).

Me gusta esta chaqueta.	*I like this jacket.* (lit, *This jacket is pleasing to me.*)

- The subject of **gustar** is the person or thing that is liked. The indirect object pronoun shows to whom the person or thing is pleasing.

me	gusta el traje.	*I*	*like(s) the suit.*
te		*you* (familiar)	
le		*you* (formal), *he/she*	
nos		*we*	
os		*you* (familiar)	
les		*they, you* (formal and familiar)	

- The most frequently used forms of **gustar** in the present tense are **gusta** and **gustan** and for the preterit **gustó** and **gustaron.** If one thing is liked, use **gusta/gustó.** If two or more things are liked, use **gustan/gustaron.**

Me **gusta** ese **collar.**	*I like that necklace.*
No me **gustaron** los anillos.	*I did not like the rings.*

- To express what people like or do not like to do, use **gusta** followed by one or more infinitives.

Nos **gusta caminar** por la mañana.	*We like to walk in the morning.*
¿No te **gusta correr** y **nadar?**	*Don't you like to run and swim?*

- Some other Spanish verbs that follow the pattern of **gustar** are:

encantar	*to like a lot, to love*
fascinar	*to like a lot, to love*
interesar	*to interest; to matter*
parecer (zc)	*to seem*
quedar	*to fit; to have something left*
Leí la novela y me **encantó.**	*I read the novel and I loved it.*
Nos **fascina** la moda europea.	*We love European fashion.*
No te **interesan** las humanidades.	*You are not interested in the humanities.*
El curso me **parece** muy difícil.	*The course seems very difficult to me.*
No me **queda** mucho dinero.	*I don't have much money left.*
No le **quedan** bien los pantalones.	*His/Her pants don't fit well.*

- To express that you like or dislike a person, use **caer bien** or **caer mal,** which follow the pattern of **gustar.**

Les cae bien Miriam.	*They like Miriam.*
Esa dependienta **me cae mal.**	*I do not like that salesclerk.*

- To emphasize or clarify to whom something is pleasing, use **a + mí, a + ti, a + él/ella, a usted(es),** etc., or **a** + *noun.*

A mí me gustaron los zapatos, pero **a Pedro** no le gustaron.	*I liked the shoes, but Pedro did not like them.*

¿COMPRENDES?

Completa las oraciones con la forma correcta del verbo.

1. A Carmen le _interesan_ (interesar) mucho las ciencias.
2. Esta película nos _parece_ (parecer) muy interesante.
3. Diego es muy simpático. A mí me _cae_ (caer) muy bien.
4. El regalo que les di a mis padres les _encantó_ (encantar).
5. A Inés no le _gustan_ (gustar) los pimientos.

MySpanishLab

Learn more using Amplifire Dynamic Study Modules, Grammar Tutorials, and Extra Practice activities.

PRÁCTICA

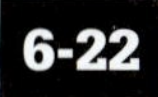

Preferencias en la ropa. **PREPARACIÓN.** Indiquen si les encanta, les gusta o no les gusta la siguiente ropa. Luego, comparen sus preferencias.

INTERCAMBIOS. Expliquen si coinciden en sus gustos.

E1: *A nosotros nos gusta la ropa deportiva.*

E2: *Y a mí me encantan los vaqueros.*

- la ropa deportiva
- los suéteres de lana
- los vaqueros
- las chaquetas de cuero
- las gorras
- los pantalones cortos
- las sudaderas
- los anillos
- las camisetas de rayas

Follow-up for 6-23
Play a game to see who can follow money transactions and answer quickly. 1. *Tienes $26. Compras un video por $21. ¿Cuánto dinero te queda?* 2. *Sales de casa con $75. Gastas $10 en el almuerzo, compras un suéter que cuesta $35 y pagas $20 por unas gafas de sol. ¿Cuánto dinero te queda?* 3. *Tengo $200 y quiero salir esta noche. Gasto $40 en el restaurante, las entradas al teatro cuestan $60 y le pago $15 al taxista. ¿Cuánto dinero me queda?* 4. *Tienes $150 en total, $50 en la cartera y $100 en la chaqueta. Alguien te roba la chaqueta. ¿Cuánto dinero te queda?*

Expansion for 6-24
You may extend this activity by providing additional photos of famous people or by having students bring photos to class.
You may wish to introduce *no pega* and *no combina* as alternates for *no va.*

Note for *En directo*
Before doing activity 6-24, first have students read the expressions in *En directo.* Then have them listen to the dialogue and encourage them to use the expressions in their own conversation.

Audioscript for *En directo*
PEDRO: *Mamá, ¿qué te parece si llevo esta camiseta para la boda de Marisa?*
SRA. MÉNDEZ: *Pedro, sabes que no es apropiado llevar ropa informal para una boda.*
PEDRO: *Pero el único traje que tengo me queda muy estrecho.*
SRA. MÉNDEZ: *No te preocupes, hijo. Ahora mismo vamos a comprarte uno nuevo.*

6-23 

¿Cuánto dinero les queda? Lean estas situaciones. Túrnense para preguntar y calcular cuánto dinero les queda a estas personas.

 Adriana tiene 500 bolívares. Paga 250 bolívares por un vestido y 200 por unos aretes.

E1: *¿Cuánto dinero le queda?*

E2: *Le quedan 50 bolívares.*

1. Ernesto tiene 750 bolívares. Le da 150 a su hermano. 600 bolívares
2. Érica tiene 550 bolívares. Va al cine con una amiga y luego cenan en un restaurante. El cine cuesta 55 y la cena 120. 375 bolívares
3. Gilberto tiene 700 bolívares. Compra un suéter por 300. 400 bolívares
4. Marco y Luisa tienen 300 bolívares. Van a la playa y almuerzan en un restaurante por 140 bolívares por persona. 20 bolívares

Cultura

¿Ropa formal o ropa informal?

People in Spanish-speaking countries usually dress more formally than in the United States for school or work, or even when they go out shopping. This is the case for many middle and high school students because they wear uniforms. At the workplace, men are expected to dress formally in jackets and ties. Most people would never wear flip-flops, sneakers, shorts, or jeans to work or school.

Comparaciones. ¿En qué contextos te vistes formalmente? ¿Informalmente? Explica las costumbres de los estudiantes de tu universidad.

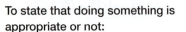

6-24  

¿Qué les parece? Las siguientes personas trabajan en una oficina de relaciones públicas. Den su opinión sobre su ropa y sus accesorios.

 E1: *No me gusta la falda de Violeta porque no es apropiado llevar una falda corta a la oficina.*

E2: *Pues a mí me encanta.*

En directo

To state that doing something is appropriate or not:

(No) Es apropiado + *infinitivo*...

Es inapropiado + *infinitivo*...

To explain why some clothes are inappropriate:

... no es apropiado/a porque la ocasión es formal/informal.

En un/a... (*evento*) no es elegante/apropiado llevar...

(*Ropa*)... no va bien con... (*accesorio*).

 Listen to a conversation with these expressions.

Situación

PREPARACIÓN. Lean esta situación. Luego, compartan ejemplos de vocabulario, gramática y otra información que necesitan para desarrollar la conversación.

Role A. You are shopping at a community crafts fair where haggling is the norm. You select an item that you plan to give as a gift. In your interaction with the vendor:

a. say how much you like what the vendor is selling;
b. ask the price of the item you are interested in;
c. react to what you hear and offer a lower price;
d. comment on the item, saying whom you plan to give it to; and
e. come to an agreement on the price.

Role B. You are selling your handicrafts and jewelry at a community crafts fair. A customer is interested in one of your items. In your interaction with the customer:

a. respond to his/her compliments;
b. give the price of the item;
c. explain why you cannot accept the customer's offer of a lower price;
d. respond to his/her comments on the item; and
e. come to an agreement on the price.

	ROLE A	ROLE B
Vocabulario	Numbers (prices)	Numbers (prices)
Funciones y formas	Haggling over the price of an item Direct and indirect object pronouns Complimenting an artisan on his/her work	Haggling over the price of an item Direct and indirect object pronouns Refusing an offer

INTERCAMBIOS. Practica la conversación con tu compañero/a incorporando el vocabulario y las funciones de *Preparación*. Luego, represéntenla ante la clase.

Suggestion for *Situación*
You may want to assign partners and have pairs create mini-skits using the video-posting feature, *MediaShare,* online.

Suggestion for Describing people, objects, and events Ask students which verb they use to talk about events, nationality, possession, and characteristics (*ser*) or location, perceptions, and appearance (*estar*).

Suggestion for More about *ser* and *estar* You may want to project images in class to help students understand the function of *ser* in sentences like *Es muy alta para su edad* and compare it to the use of *estar* in *La niña está muy grande.* Explain that the child is tall in comparison to others of her age (which is a characteristic of the child), whereas in the second sentence, *estar* is used because the comparison is not with others, but with the child herself at a different moment in time. Point out the contrast between *El café está caliente* and *La nieve en las montañas es fría.* In the first sentence the temperature of coffee varies according to circumstances (and therefore *estar* is used), but a cold temperature is an intrinsic characteristic of snow (and therefore *ser* is used).

5 Describing people, objects, and events

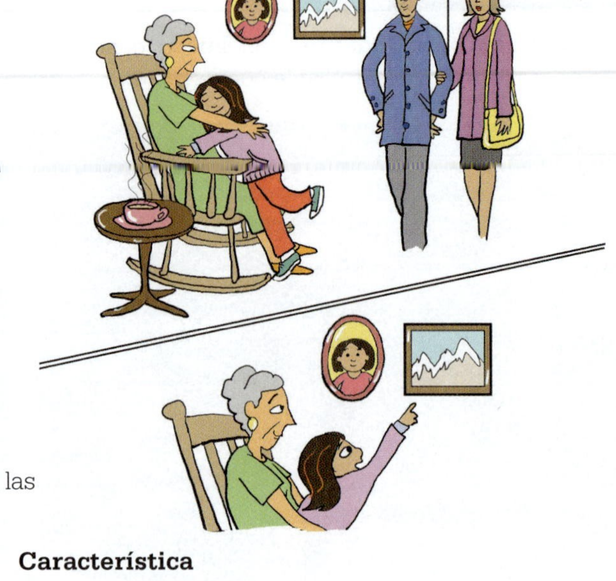

ABUELA: Cuidado, Susana, el café **está** muy caliente. [*A la madre*] ¡La niña **está** muy grande!

MADRE: Claro, tiene cinco años. **Es** muy alta para su edad.

SUSANA: Abuelita, ¿qué **es** ese cuadro?

ABUELA: **Son** montañas de la Cordillera de los Andes en Chile.

Piénsalo. Indica la función de **ser** o **estar** en las siguientes afirmaciones.

	Condición	Característica
1. El café **está** caliente.	✓	
2. ¡La niña **está** muy grande!	✓	
3. Es muy alta para su edad.		✓
4. Son montañas de los Andes.		✓
5. El aire en las montañas **es** muy frío por las noches.		✓

More about *ser* and *estar*

- In *Capítulo 2,* you learned to use **ser** to identify and describe, and to express nationality, ownership, and origin. You also learned to use **ser** to talk about dates and time and to tell where an event takes place.

Víctor **es** de Venezuela.	*Victor is from Venezuela.* (nationality)
Es un diseñador de ropa para hombres.	*He is a designer of men's clothing.* (profession)
Es alto y delgado y **es** muy fuerte.	*He is tall and thin, and he is very strong.* (distinguishing characteristics)
Estas figuras pintadas **son** de Víctor, tiene una colección grande.	*These painted figures belong to Victor; he has a big collection.* (possession)
El próximo desfile de moda con su ropa **es** mañana a las ocho.	*The next fashion show of his clothing is tomorrow at eight o'clock.*
Va a ser en el Teatro El Rey.	*It is going to take place in the El Rey Theater.* (time/location of event)

- **Ser** is also used to talk about what something is made of.

El reloj **es** de oro.	*The watch is (made of) gold.*

- You also learned in *Capítulo 2* that **estar** is used to indicate location, to talk about health and similar conditions, and to describe changes in feelings or perceptions. It is also used to express ongoing actions, presented in *Capítulo 4*.

El Teatro El Rey **está** en el centro.	*The El Rey Theater is downtown.* (location)
Víctor fue al doctor la semana pasada, pero ahora **está** bien.	*Victor went to the doctor last week, but now he is fine.* (health)
Víctor **está** nervioso antes de los desfiles, pero siempre **está** contento después.	*Victor is nervous before fashion shows, but he is always happy (feels good) afterward.* (feelings, condition)
Los modelos se **están** vistiendo ahora.	*The models are getting dressed now.* (ongoing action)

- When describing people or objects, use **ser** to convey an intrinsic characteristic. Use **estar** to convey a feeling or perception. The difference in meaning is sometimes so pronounced that the adjectives have different English translations.

Adjective	With *Ser*	With *Estar*
aburrido/a	*boring*	*bored*
bueno/a	*good* (character)	*well* (health); *physically attractive*
grave	*serious* (situation)	*seriously ill*
listo/a	*clever*	*ready*
malo/a	*bad* (character)	*ill*
muerto/a	*dead* (atmosphere)	*deceased*
rico/a	*rich, wealthy*	*delicious* (food)
verde	*green*	*unripe*
vivo/a	*lively* (personality)	*alive*

Javier **es** malo, les roba dinero a sus compañeros y dice mentiras.	*Javier is bad; he steals money from his classmates and tells lies.*
Roberto Tovares **es** rico. Tiene una casa en California y un apartamento en París.	*Roberto Tovares is wealthy. He has a house in California and an apartment in Paris.*
¡Esta sopa **está** riquísima! ¿Usaste una receta diferente?	*This soup is delicious! Did you use a different recipe?*

e ¿COMPRENDES?

Completa las oraciones con la forma correcta de **ser** o **estar.**

1. Pedro no vino a clase hoy, __está__ malo.
2. Me encanta este postre, __está__ muy rico.
3. No comas esa naranja porque __está__ verde.
4. Manuel __es__ listo y saca buenas notas.
5. La situación __es__ grave porque llueve mucho.
6. Desafortunadamente, Carolina tuvo un accidente y __está__ grave en el hospital.

MySpanishLab

Learn more using Amplifire Dynamic Study Modules, Grammar Tutorials, and Extra Practice activities.

PRÁCTICA

Follow-up for 6-25
Have students work in pairs to compare their answers and figure out the function of each use of *ser* and *estar*.

6-25 

La mañana horrible de Javier. Lee el cuento sobre la mañana de Javier y complétalo con la forma apropiada de **ser** o **estar.**

Javier se despierta temprano. (1) ___Son___ las seis de la mañana. La casa (2) ___está___ muy fría, y el agua en la ducha (3) ___está___ fría también. ¡Javier no (4) ___está___ nada contento! Su reunión con la profesora de historia (5) ___es___ a las 10:00 y él no (6) ___está___ listo. Necesita leer un artículo antes de la reunión, pero no sabe dónde (7) ___está___. Tiene hambre, pero no hay pan, los plátanos (8) ___están___ verdes y (9) ___es___ demasiado tarde para hacer café. La situación (10) ___es___ grave, piensa Javier. Finalmente (11) ___son___ las diez en punto y Javier entra en la oficina de la profesora Guzmán. Por su expresión, Javier sabe que ella (12) ___está___ tensa. Le dice a Javier que su borrador (*draft*) no (13) ___es___ bueno y que tiene que trabajar mucho más. Cuando sale de la reunión, Javier (14) ___está___ muy preocupado.

Suggestion for 6-26
To ensure that photos are not described more than once, you may show other photos of your own and assign a photo secretly to each group. Each student in the group must contribute to the description and must take notes.

6-26 

De compras. Las personas en las fotos siguientes fueron de compras. Escojan una de las fotos y escriban una breve descripción usando la siguiente información. Después, la clase va a adivinar qué foto describen.

1. nombre de las personas y la relación entre ellas (usen su imaginación)
2. probable lugar de origen de las personas
3. lugar donde las personas están en esta foto y por qué están allí
4. su estado de ánimo (*mood*)
5. artículos que compraron y dos o tres actividades que hicieron en este lugar

6-27 

¿Quiénes son y cómo están? Describan qué hacen estas personas, cómo son probablemente y cómo están en estas situaciones.

1.

2.

3.

Situación  

PREPARACIÓN. Lean esta situación. Luego, compartan ejemplos de vocabulario, gramática y otra información que necesitan para desarrollar la conversación.

Role A. Your classmate asks about the photo of your family (or friends) on your cell phone. Explain:

a. who the people are;
b. where they are;
c. what they are like; and
d. how they are feeling in the photo.

Role B. Ask your classmate to see the cell phone photo he/she is looking at. Ask as many questions as you can about the people in the photo, their activities, and the setting.

	ROLE A	ROLE B
Vocabulario	Descriptions of people, places, and events	Descriptions of people, places, and events
Funciones y formas	Describing people, places, and events *Ser* and *estar* Asking questions	Describing people, places, and events *Ser* and *estar* Asking questions

INTERCAMBIOS. Practica la conversación con tu compañero/a incorporando el vocabulario y las funciones de *Preparación.* Luego, represéntenla ante la clase.

Preparation for *Situación*
Have students bring a photo of family or friends to class to use for this *Situación.* They can also use a photo from their cell phones. Have them change partners and act out the situation a second time so that everyone can take both roles.

EN ACCIÓN

De moda

Suggestion for 6-28
You may want to review common vocabulary for articles of clothing before completing this activity. You could also have students come up with other situations or places (such as the university cafeteria, a wedding, etc.) and describe what would be appropriate clothing to wear.

6-28 Antes de ver 

¿Es apropiado? En este episodio, Esteban va a un restaurante con una chica de su clase. Indica la ropa y accesorios que son apropiados (**A**) y no apropiados (**NA**) para esta ocasión. Explica por qué no son apropiados.

1. __A__ una camisa
2. __NA__ una bata — No se usa en lugares públicos.
3. __NA__ unas zapatillas — Son muy informales.
4. __NA__ un traje de baño — No es apropiado para un restaurante.
5. __A__ un saco/una chaqueta
6. __NA__ unos guantes — No es elegante usar guantes en un restaurante.
7. __A__ unos zapatos
8. __A__ una corbata
9. __A__ un cinturón
10. __A__ unos calcetines

Suggestion for 6-29
You may want to have students review the verbs in these sentences before they begin this activity. Then, have students identify the subject of each verb and indicate whether it is singular or plural.

6-29 Mientras ves  

¿Y qué pasó después? Los chicos están muy ocupados hoy. Indica el orden en que ocurrieron las siguientes actividades en este segmento (**A–F**).

1. __D__ Esteban se probó la ropa que compró en el centro comercial.
2. __E__ Blanca y Yolanda hablaron sobre la ropa de Esteban.
3. __B__ La modelo habló sobre el festival de moda en Los Ángeles.
4. __F__ Llegó Amber.
5. __C__ Yolanda y Esteban fueron al centro comercial.
6. __A__ Vanesa y Yolanda le mostraron a Esteban un video sobre un festival de moda.

6-30 Después de ver 

PREPARACIÓN. Indica si las siguientes afirmaciones son ciertas (**C**) o falsas (**F**), según el contenido del segmento de video.

1. __C__ A Yolanda le interesa salir con Esteban.
2. __F__ Esteban viste siempre a la moda.
3. __C__ La casa Pineda Covalín es de la Ciudad de México.
4. __F__ Muchos vestidos de la casa Pineda Covalín están inspirados en diseños árabes.
5. __C__ Según la modelo, Suzy Diab, el *Latino Fashion Week* es una buena manera de conectarse con su cultura.
6. __F__ Blanca piensa que Yolanda tiene un buen plan.

INTERCAMBIOS. Hablen de una mala experiencia que tuvieron (real o imaginaria) cuando fueron de compras a una tienda o centro comercial. ¿Qué compraron? ¿Para qué ocasión? ¿Dónde? ¿Cuál fue el problema? ¿Qué hicieron para solucionarlo?

Mosaicos

ESCUCHA

ESTRATEGIA

Take notes to recall information

When you want to remember something that you are listening to, like a class lecture, you benefit from taking notes. Taking notes can also be helpful when you want to remember a homework assignment or other instructions.

6-31 Presentational

Preparación. En esta conversación, Andrea habla con sus padres sobre la ropa que necesita durante el año académico. Antes de escuchar, prepara una lista de la ropa y accesorios que tuviste que comprar antes de empezar las clases este año. Comparte esta lista con la clase.

6-32  Interpretive

Escucha. Listen to the conversation between Andrea and her parents. As you listen, take notes on what she needs. Write at least three items for each category that Andrea mentions.

1. Para ir a clases Andrea necesita… botas, guantes, una chaqueta, una bufanda y un abrigo
2. Para practicar deportes Andrea tiene que comprar… pantalones cortos, camisetas, una sudadera, medias
3. Para salir con sus amigos Andrea quiere… pantalones vaqueros, blusas, zapatos y muchas cosas más

Comprueba

I was able to …

___ **recognize clothing vocabulary.**

___ **identify the correct categories.**

___ **take notes to remember the information.**

6-33  Interpersonal

Un paso más. Túrnense para responder oralmente a las siguientes preguntas y tomen notas de sus respuestas. Después, compartan la información con otra pareja.

1. ¿Qué accesorios, muebles para tu cuarto y/o aparatos electrónicos compraste antes de comenzar tus clases en la universidad este semestre?
2. ¿Qué libros o artículos compraste para estudiar? ¿Dónde los compraste?
3. ¿Fuiste a las rebajas? ¿Qué compraste? ¿Cuánto gastaste?

Integrated Performance Assessment (IPA) The activities in each *Mosaicos* section correspond to the three modes of communication as indicated by the tag next to each activity.

Audioscript for *Escucha*

ANDREA: *Mamá, ustedes saben que necesito muchas cosas. Por ejemplo, para ir a mis clases ahora en invierno, necesito unas botas, guantes y una chaqueta. También necesito una bufanda y un abrigo.*
MAMÁ: *Pero, Andrea, si el año pasado te compramos ropa de invierno. Todavía la puedes usar.*
ANDREA: *No, mamá. Quiero estar a la última moda, y mi ropa ya está vieja. Quiero ir a una boutique elegante y comprarme toda mi ropa allí.*
PAPÁ: *Me parece muy bien, Andrea. Puedes comprar todo lo que quieras, pero dime, ¿de dónde vas a sacar dinero para pagar por esa ropa? Tú no trabajas.*
ANDREA: *¡Papá, por favor! Tú me puedes prestar dinero o me puedes dar tu tarjeta de crédito. Además necesito ropa para practicar deportes. Quiero comprar pantalones cortos, camisetas, una sudadera, medias y…*
MAMÁ: *Andrea, ¿estás loca? Nosotros no tenemos tanto dinero. No podemos pagar todo eso ni prestarte dinero ni mucho menos darte la tarjeta de crédito.*
ANDREA: *Mamá, escucha, para salir con mis amigos necesito pantalones vaqueros, blusas, zapatos y muchas cosas más.*
PAPÁ: *Todo me parece muy bien, Andrea. Trabaja, ahorra y gasta tu dinero, pero yo no te voy a dar ni un solo bolívar.*
ANDREA: *Pero, papá, comprende, por favor.*
PAPÁ: *Ni una palabra más.*

HABLA

6-34 Interpretive

Preparación. Quieres comprar unos regalos o algunas cosas para tu cuarto/apartamento en un mercado al aire libre. Completa la tabla siguiente.

¿QUÉ QUIERES COMPRAR?	¿PARA QUIÉN(ES)?	DESCRIPCIÓN Y PRECIO DEL PRODUCTO

6-35 Interpersonal

Habla. Estás en un mercado al aire libre. Pregúntale al vendedor/a la vendedora (tu compañero/a) el precio de los productos que deseas comprar. Regatea (*Haggle*) para obtener el mejor precio posible. Luego, cambien de papel.

Comprueba

In my conversation …

_____ I discussed the price.

_____ I showed my desire to buy the item if we could agree on a price.

_____ I gave clear information in response to questions.

_____ I negotiated the price successfully.

6-36 Presentational

Un paso más. Comparte con la clase tu experiencia de regateo en el mercado al aire libre. Incluye la siguiente información:

1. qué productos compraste y para quién los compraste
2. qué precio te dio el/la vendedor/a por cada producto
3. cuánto dinero ofreciste por cada producto
4. cuánto pagaste finalmente

ESTRATEGIA

Negotiate a price

In Hispanic cultures, negotiating the price of an item in an outdoor market or other location in which the price is not fixed follows both linguistic and cultural rules. You should haggle over the price only if you intend to buy the item. Your initial offer, while lower than the selling price given by the vendor, should be reasonable, because an excessively low price may be insulting. In your negotiation, which may last several turns, you may include a brief comment about the desirability of the item and a reaction to the price suggested by the vendor.

En directo

To haggle:

CLIENTE/A

Me gusta este/a _____, pero no tengo tanto dinero. *I like this _____, but I don't have enough money.*

Solo puedo pagar… *I can only pay...*

¡Es muy caro/a! *It is very expensive!*

¿Qué le parece(n)… bolívares/dólares (etc.)? *How about... bolivars/dollars?*

Le doy… bolívares/dólares. *I will give you... bolivars/dollars.*

VENDEDOR/A

¡Imposible! *Impossible!*

El material es importado/de primera calidad. *The material is imported/top quality.*

Lo siento, pero no puedo darle… por ese precio. *I'm sorry, but I cannot give you... for that price.*

Listen to a conversation with these expressions.

Note for *En directo*
Before doing activity 6-35, first have students read the expressions in *En directo*. Then have them listen to the dialogue and encourage them to use the expressions in their own conversation.

Audioscript for *En directo*
VENDEDOR: *Buenas tardes, ¿en qué puedo servirle?*
CLIENTA: *Me gusta este bolso de cuero, pero no tengo tanto dinero. Solo puedo pagar la mitad.*
VENDEDOR: *¡Imposible! El material es de primera calidad. Lo siento, pero no puedo darle el bolso por ese precio.*
CLIENTA: *Está bien. Le pago la cantidad completa si usted incluye este cinturón. ¿Qué le parece?*
VENDEDOR: *De acuerdo.*

Suggestion for 6-35
Remind students about where haggling over a price is appropriate (see *Cultura* box on p. 209). Before starting the activity, you may wish to review haggling and phrases used when negotiating price.

Suggestion for 6-36
Have students change partners so they can hear about each other's experiences.

LEE

6-37   Interpersonal

Preparación. Habla con tu compañero/a sobre lo siguiente:

1. ¿Te gusta comprar en Internet o prefieres ir a las tiendas? ¿Por qué?
2. ¿Qué ropa compras por Internet? ¿Qué ropa no compras por Internet? ¿Por qué?
3. ¿Cuáles son las ventajas principales de comprar por Internet? ¿Las desventajas?
4. Si compras por Internet, ¿cuáles son tus sitios o tiendas favoritas? ¿Por qué te gustan?

ESTRATEGIA

Use context to figure out the meaning of unfamiliar words

When you come across unfamiliar words and phrases while reading, use the context and your understanding of the text so far to figure out the meaning. Reread the last line or two, focusing on overall meaning. In many cases, this strategy will help you understand the unknown word without using a dictionary.

Suggestion for 6-37
Ask students to scan the text and use their background knowledge to answer the following questions: *¿Qué tipo de texto es? ¿Qué información les ayudó a identificarlo? Según su experiencia, ¿qué esperan encontrar en el texto: la opinión del escritor o información objetiva?*

Hombres, ropa e Internet

MIÉRCOLES, 10 DE MARZO DE 2013 / 2 comentarios

El año pasado descubrí un nuevo hobby: la compra de ropa por Internet. Si ir al centro comercial les molesta a ustedes tanto como a mí, van a comprender que veo muchas ventajas en la compra online. Como a todos, me encanta la ropa bonita y estilosa, pero ir de tienda en tienda buscando rebajas me parece ridículo. No me gusta estresarme buscando tallas y modelos. Ni buscar en cada prenda la etiqueta con el precio. Yo solo uso ropa de algodón y es muy difícil encontrarla si no miras con cuidado la información sobre la tela, que aparece en etiquetas pequeñas y difíciles de leer.

No. Nunca más. Mi vida cambió cuando decidí explorar la compra online. Comencé tímidamente comprando varios pares de calcetines. Las compras online deben funcionar, me dije. Sé el número que calzo, y quiero calcetines negros y de algodón. Bueno, pues hice una búsqueda rápida y encontré varias páginas que me garantizan la mejor calidad de algodón —hilo de Escocia, para los entendidos— en mi talla y con envío inmediato a domicilio. ¿Qué más puedo pedir?, me dije.

Entonces decidí comprar los calzoncillos, que me gustan variados: de rayas, de cuadros, ¡o incluso de flores! No hay problema: 5 pares de calzoncillos de bellos colores y diseños fue mi siguiente compra. Tengo que confesar que luego compré 20 camisas, varios pantalones, un traje de chaqueta y un impermeable. Una vez tuve que devolver una prenda porque pedí una talla demasiado pequeña, pero créanme, las ventajas son muchas más que las desventajas. Si quieren evitar las colas y la frustración de no encontrar el material o los colores que les gustan, les recomiendo comprar por Internet. Es el consejo que les da un amigo…

6-38   Interpretive

Lee. Lee el texto y luego, indica si las siguientes afirmaciones son correctas (**C**) o incorrectas (**I**). Si son incorrectas, corrige la información.

1. __I__ Al autor del texto le gusta comprar ropa en las tiendas. (No le gusta ir a los centros comerciales).
2. __C__ El autor se pone tenso cuando tiene que buscar una prenda de su talla.
3. __I__ Al autor le gusta la ropa de lana. (Solo usa ropa de algodón).
4. __I__ La primera compra que hizo el autor por Internet fueron unas camisas de rayas. (Compró calcetines).
5. __I__ El autor decidió no comprar zapatos por Internet. (No dice nada acerca de los zapatos)
6. __C__ Al autor le gusta comprar por Internet porque es rápido.

Comprueba
I was able to …

____ **use context to decipher meaning of unknown expressions.**

____ **identify specific information correctly.**

6-39  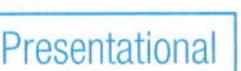 Presentational

Un paso más. Busca un sitio web en el mundo hispano que venda productos que te interesan. Toma nota de la siguiente información de la lista. Después, presenta la página web a la clase. Tus compañeros/as van a hacerte preguntas sobre los productos, los precios y cómo se compra.

1. el nombre y la dirección del sitio y el país donde se encuentra
2. los productos principales, sus precios y cómo se comparan estos precios con los de Estados Unidos
3. instrucciones para realizar las compras

Suggestions for 6-38
You may wish to discuss responses with the whole class. Encourage students to support their answers.

Suggestion for 6-39
Model giving instructions, using the simple present indicative: *Primero, vas a…, pulsas* (click)*…, buscas…, indicas la talla/el color/el estilo, etc. Finalmente, pagas con una tarjeta de crédito.*

ESCRIBE

6-40   Interpretive

Preparación. Lee el siguiente correo electrónico de Laura a su amiga Cristina, contándole su última experiencia comprando ropa. Después, pon en orden cronológico la secuencia de eventos.

> Querida Cristina:
>
> ¿Recuerdas el vestido que compré el jueves pasado cuando fuimos con mi hermana al centro comercial? Cuando me lo probé, ella pensó "le queda ancho", pero no me dijo (*said*) nada. Luego me escribió un correo electrónico y me explicó que tampoco le gustó el color ni el estilo. Esto me enojó mucho, pero después volví a probarme el vestido y pensé que mi hermana tenía razón (*was right*). Y devolví el vestido.

__5__ Laura devolvió el vestido.

__2__ Laura se probó el vestido.

__1__ Laura fue de compras con Cristina y su hermana.

__3__ Su hermana le explicó a Laura por qué no le gustó el vestido.

__4__ A su hermana no le gustó el estilo del vestido.

ESTRATEGIA

Recount events in sequence

When we tell a story either orally or in writing, we almost always organize the events in chronological order. Using appropriate connectors to indicate the order of the events will make your writing clearer.

En directo

To indicate the succession of events or temporal transitions, you may use the following connectors: **primero, luego, más tarde, antes de eso, después (de eso), finalmente.**

 Listen to a conversation with these expressions.

Audioscript for *En directo*

MARÍA: *Tomás, no puedes imaginarte cómo me fue hoy en el centro comercial.*

TOMÁS: *Uf, cómo te encanta ir de compras. Dime, ¿qué pasó esta vez?*

MARÍA: *Bueno, fui a mi tienda favorita para comprar una blusa y unos jeans. Primero, vi una blusa preciosa, pero no tenían mi talla. Luego, encontré unos jeans baratos y bonitos, pero cuando me los probé, me quedaban anchos. Después, vi otra blusa espectacular, pero era muy cara. Finalmente, encontré unos zapatos divinos de rebaja y los compré. ¡Qué suerte!*

TOMÁS: *Ay María, ¡tú y tus aventuras en el centro comercial me fascinan!*

Note

Writing an e-mail is usually considered a presentational activity because it does not involve an immediate interaction between two or more speakers.

Suggestion for 6-41

Ask students to re-read their e-mail and provide them with a checklist:

1. *¿Incluiste toda la información necesaria?*
2. *¿Organizaste los eventos cronológicamente para contar paso a paso lo que ocurrió? ¿Usaste expresiones que indican transición temporal?*
3. *¿Revisaste la gramática, el vocabulario, la concordancia* (agreement), *el tiempo (presente, pasado)?*
4. *¿Usaste la puntuación y ortografía correctas?*

6-41 Presentational

Escribe. Cuéntale a tu mejor amigo/a en un correo electrónico tu última experiencia comprando un producto.

INCLUYE:

1. el nombre de la tienda donde compraste el producto
2. el producto que compraste y una descripción del producto
3. un recuento de lo que ocurrió en orden cronológico; ¿Cuándo hiciste (*did you make*) la compra?: ¿Qué ocurrió después?: ¿Cuánto costó y cómo pagaste?
4. la razón de tu satisfacción o insatisfacción con el producto

Comprueba

I was able to ...

____ describe the parts of the event in order.

____ use connectors to indicate the order.

____ open and close the message properly.

6-42   Interpersonal

Un paso más. Comparte con tu compañero/a la experiencia de una mala compra. Utilicen las siguientes preguntas como guía y añadan otras. Túrnense para hacerse preguntas y responder.

1. ¿Qué compraste? ¿Cuándo? ¿Dónde?
2. ¿Qué pasó primero? ¿Qué pasó después?
3. ¿Cómo resolviste la situación finalmente?

En este capítulo…

Comprueba lo que sabes

Go to ***MySpanishLab*** to review what you have learned in this chapter. Practice with the following:

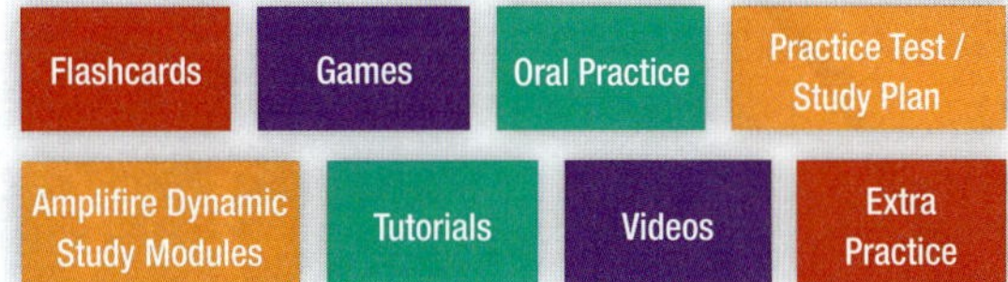

Vocabulario

LOS ACCESORIOS
Accessories

el anillo *ring*
el arete *earring*
la billetera *wallet*
la bolsa/el bolso *purse*
la bufanda *scarf*
el cinturón *belt*
el collar *necklace*
las gafas de sol *sunglasses*
la gorra *cap*
el guante *glove*
la joya *piece of jewelry*
el pañuelo *handkerchief*
el paraguas *umbrella*
la pulsera *bracelet*
el sombrero *hat*

LA ROPA
Clothes

el abrigo *coat*
la bata *robe*
la blusa *blouse*
las botas *boots*
los calcetines *socks*
el calzado *footwear*
los calzoncillos *boxer shorts*
la camisa *shirt*
la camisa de manga corta *short sleeve shirt*
la camiseta *T-shirt*
el camisón *nightgown*
la chaqueta *jacket*
la corbata *tie*
la falda *skirt*
el impermeable *raincoat*
las medias *stockings, socks*
los pantalones *pants*
los pantalones cortos *shorts*
las pantimedias *pantyhose*
el/la piyama *pajamas*
la ropa interior *underwear*
el saco *blazer, jacket*
las sandalias *sandals*
el sostén *bra*
la sudadera *sweatshirt; jogging suit*
el suéter *sweater*
el traje *suit*
el traje de baño *bathing suit*
el traje *suit*
los vaqueros/los jeans *jeans*
el vestido *dress*
las zapatillas *slippers*
las zapatillas de deporte *tennis shoes*
los zapatos *shoes*
los zapatos de tacón *high-heeled shoes*

DISEÑOS
Designs

de color entero *solid*
de cuadros *plaid*
de lunares *dots*
de rayas *stripes*

PALABRAS Y EXPRESIONES ÚTILES
Useful words and expressions

la artesanía *handicrafts*
la cosa *thing*
el cuero *leather*
el dinero *money*
en efectivo *in cash*
¿En qué puedo servirle(s)? *How may I help you?*
enseguida *immediately*
estar de moda *to be fashionable*
ir de compras *to go shopping*
el juguete *toy*
Me gustaría… *I would like…*
el número *size (shoes)*
el oro *gold*
la plata *silver*
Quisiera… *I would like…*
la talla *size (clothes)*
el tamaño *size*

VERBOS
Verbs

caer bien/mal *to be liked*
calzar *to wear (shoes)*
cambiar *to change, to exchange*
dar *to give, to hand*
encantar *to delight, to love*
encontrar (ue) *to find*
entrar (en) *to go in, to enter*
fascinar *to fascinate, to be pleasing to*
gastar *to spend*
gustar *to be pleasing to, to like*
interesar *to interest*
llevar *to wear, to take*
mostrar (ue) *to show*
pagar *to pay (for)*
parecer (zc) *to seem*
prestar *to lend*
probarse (ue) *to try on*
quedar *to fit; to be left over*
regalar *to give* (a present)
regatear *to haggle*
valer *to be worth*
vender *to sell*

LAS COMPRAS
Shopping

el almacén *department store; warehouse*
el centro comercial *shopping center*
el escaparate *store window*
el mercado *market*
el precio *price*
la rebaja *sale*
el regalo *present*
el supermercado *supermarket*
la tarjeta de crédito *credit card*
la tienda *store*

TELAS
Fabrics

el algodón *cotton*
la lana *wool*
el poliéster *polyester*
la seda *silk*

EXPRESIONES DE TIEMPO
Time expressions

anoche *last night*
anteayer *the day before yesterday*
ante(a)noche *the night before last*
el año/mes pasado *last year/month*
ayer *yesterday*
hace un día/mes/año (que) *it has been a day/month/year since*
una semana atrás *a week ago*
la semana pasada *last week*

LAS ESTACIONES DEL AÑO
Seasons of the year

el invierno *winter*
el otoño *fall*
la primavera *spring*
el verano *summer*

LAS DESCRIPCIONES
Descriptions

ancho/a *wide*
barato/a *inexpensive, cheap*
caro/a *expensive*
estrecho/a *narrow, tight*
magnífico/a *great*
precioso/a *beautiful*
rebajado/a *marked down*

Introduction to chapter Introduce the chapter theme about sports and other physical activities. Ask questions to recycle content from the previous chapter. Related questions: *¿Te gusta más el béisbol o el básquetbol? ¿Prefieres jugar deportes o verlos en la televisión? ¿Qué otras actividades físicas haces? ¿Corres? ¿Montas en bicicleta? ¿Corriste ayer? ¿Montaste en bicicleta ayer? ¿Cuándo fue la última vez? ¿Caminas mucho por el campus? ¿Eres atlético/a? ¿Crees que debes ser más activo/a? ¿Por qué?*

Integrated Performance Assessment: Three Modes of Communication

Presentational: See activities 7-4, 7-10, 7-15, 7-36, 7-40, 7-44, and 7-47.

Interpretive: See activities 7-1, 7-2, 7-3, 7-5, 7-6, 7-7, 7-9, 7-10, 7-11, 7-12, 7-14, 7-15, 7-16, 7-19, 7-20, 7-21, 7-23, 7-24, 7-25, 7-26, 7-28, 7-30, 7-37, 7-39, 7-43, and 7-46.

Interpersonal: See activities 7-2, 7-3, 7-4, 7-5, 7-6, 7-7, 7-8, 7-9, 7-10, 7-12, 7-13, 7-14, 7-15, 7-16, 7-17, 7-18, 7-19, 7-20, 7-22, 7-23, 7-24, 7-25, 7-26, 7-28, 7-29, 7-30, 7-31, 7-32, 7-35, 7-38, 7-42, 7-45, and all *Situación* activities.

7 ¿Cuál es tu deporte favorito?

ENFOQUE CULTURAL
Argentina y Uruguay

VOCABULARIO EN CONTEXTO
Los deportes
El tiempo y las estaciones
¿Qué pasó ayer?

MOSAICO CULTURAL
Los hinchas y el superclásico

FUNCIONES Y FORMAS
Preterit of reflexive verbs
Preterit of *-er* and *-ir* verbs whose stem ends in a vowel
Preterit of stem-changing *-ir* verbs
Pronouns after prepositions
Some irregular preterits

EN ACCIÓN
Vamos a hacer surf

MOSAICOS
ESCUCHA Differentiate fact from opinion
HABLA Focus on key information
LEE Predict and guess content
ESCRIBE Use supporting details

EN ESTE CAPÍTULO...
Comprueba lo que sabes
Vocabulario

LEARNING OUTCOMES

You will be able to:

- talk about sports
- emphasize and clarify information
- talk about past events
- talk about practices and perspectives on sports in Argentina and Uruguay
- share information about sporting events in Hispanic countries and compare cultural similarities

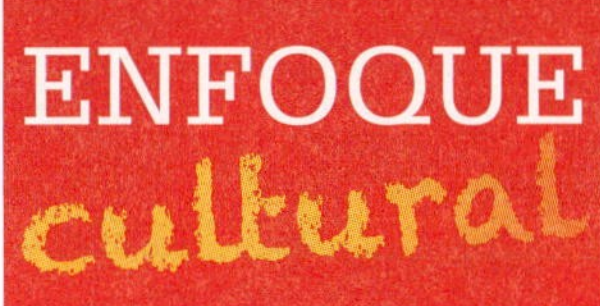

ARGENTINA Y URUGUAY

Enfoque cultural

To learn more about Argentina and Uruguay, go to MySpanishLab to view the *Vistas culturales* videos.

Hamlet & Ophelia de Juan Carlos Liberti, pintor argentino (1930)

¿QUÉ TE PARECE?

- La influencia italiana en Argentina se nota en palabras como *chau*, el acento y la entonación, la comida, los nombres y apellidos.
- Los porteños son los habitantes de Buenos Aires.
- La Celeste, el equipo nacional de fútbol de Uruguay, ganó la Copa América en 2011. Ha ganado la Copa América 15 veces.
- Muchos argentinos van en buquebús (*ferry*) de Buenos Aires a Montevideo solo para ver un partido de fútbol. El viaje dura menos de tres horas.
- Punta del Este, Uruguay, es un centro turístico muy popular entre los cantantes, actores y diseñadores, como Shakira y Ralph Lauren. Es el Miami de Uruguay.
- Muchos argentinos y uruguayos usan *vos* en vez de *tú.* Por ejemplo, dicen: *Vos decís* y no *Tú dices*.

Suggestion for map
Brainstorm with students the information they may already know about Argentina and Uruguay. Project the map (available in the Instructor Resources folder online), and point to the photos. Make comments as you ask what students know: *¿Cuál es la capital de Uruguay? ¿Y la de Argentina? ¿Qué países hay al norte de Argentina? ¿Y al oeste?* Introduce weather expressions: *Cuando en el hemisferio norte es verano, ¿qué estación tienen en el hemisferio sur? ¿Qué tiempo hace ahora probablemente en Argentina y Uruguay?* Personalize questions: *¿Conocen a alguna persona famosa de estos países? ¿Saben cuál es la comida típica de Argentina y Uruguay?* Introduce some vocabulary of the chapter while pointing to Bariloche on the map. *¿Qué deportes practican los argentinos? En Argentina hay buenas pistas de esquí. ¿A ustedes les gusta esquiar?*

Note for art
Juan Carlos Liberti was born in Buenos Aires, Argentina. A self-taught painter in the surrealist tradition, Liberti has exhibited in museums in Argentina, Spain, Puerto Rico, and the continental United States.

Suggestion for art
Ask students to interpret the meaning of the painting: *¿Es una obra realista o surrealista? ¿Qué elementos son más realistas? (el vestido de Ophelia y el traje de Hamlet, la barandilla* [railing]*) ¿Y qué elementos son más irreales? (el pelo, no tienen caras) ¿Les gusta el cuadro? ¿No les gusta? ¿Por qué?*

ENFOQUE cultural

Note about *las Cataratas de Iguazú*
Iguazú Falls are on the border between Argentina and Brasil. The falls are over 80 meters high and over 2500 meters in diameter. The first inhabitants were the Caingangues and later the Tupi-Guaranies. Álvar Nuñez Cabeza de Vaca was the first Spaniard to see the falls. The falls and the Iguazú National Park in which it is located have been designated a UNESCO World Heritage Centre.

Note about *Palacio Barolo*
The Palacio Barolo was the tallest building in South America when it was built.

Note about *las Madres y Abuelas de la Plaza de Mayo*
The Madres de la Plaza de Mayo have protested in the Plaza de Mayo, in front of the Casa Rosada, the Argentine Presidential palace every Thursday since 1977. They protest against the Dirty War and attempt to get information about their disappeared children, spouses, and other relatives, including grandchildren born in captivity.

Note about *Casapueblo*
Casapueblo is a favorite spot for viewing sunsets. Both tourists and locals visit the museum to sit on a balcony and watch the sunsets.

La Garganta del Diablo es una de las cascadas de las Cataratas de Iguazú en Argentina. Las cataratas están en la frontera entre Argentina y Brasil y forman parte del Parque Nacional Iguazú. En el parque se encuentra una variedad de animales exóticos, como tapires, jaguares, caimanes, osos hormigueros, ocelotes y monos aulladores.

Los Palacios Salvo y Barolo fueron diseñados por el arquitecto italiano Mario Palantí, que emigró a Buenos Aires. Se dice que son edificios hermanos.

La Plaza de Mayo en Buenos Aires es un lugar con mucha historia por sus manifestaciones tanto políticas como populares. El pañuelo blanco es el símbolo de las Madres y Abuelas de la Plaza de Mayo. Enfrente queda la Casa Rosada, el palacio presidencial de Argentina.

Palacio Barolo, Buenos Aires, Argentina

Palacio Salvo, Montevideo, Uruguay

En Punta Ballena, Uruguay, cerca de Punta del Este, se encuentra Casapueblo, la casa y museo del pintor, escultor, arquitecto y muralista Carlos Páez Vilaró. Esta escultura habitable dispone de hotel, café literario y tienda para los turistas que la visitan.

¿CUÁNTO SABES?

Completa las oraciones con la información correcta.

1. Las playas de Punta del Este en Uruguay son famosas.
2. El fútbol es uno de los deportes más populares en ambos países
3. Los porteños viven en Buenos Aires.
4. Carlos Páez Vilaró es un distinguido arquitecto uruguayo.
5. El parque nacional que se encuentra en la frontera de Argentina y Brasil es el Parque Nacional Iguazú.
6. Una de las cascadas más impresionantes de Iguazú se llama la Garganta del Diablo.

Vocabulario en contexto

Talking about sports, the weather, and the past

Los deportes

MySpanishLab Pronunciation Topic: Consonants *g* and *j*

Learn more using Amplifire Dynamic Study Modules, Pronunciation, and Vocabulary Tutorials.

El **fútbol** es el **deporte** número uno en muchos países hispanos.

En España, Argentina, Uruguay, Colombia, México y otros países hispanos hay excelentes **equipos** de fútbol. Los mejores **jugadores** de los equipos locales forman la selección nacional. Esta selección representa al país en los **partidos** de los **campeonatos** internacionales y participa, **cada** cuatro años en la Copa Mundial.

En la zona del Caribe, el **béisbol** es el deporte más popular, y jugadores como Félix Hernández y Miguel Cabrera son conocidos mundialmente.

En Argentina, Chile y España, el **esquí** es un deporte muy popular. Aquí vemos a unos jóvenes que van a **esquiar** en las **pistas** de Bariloche, Argentina, uno de los centros de esquí más importantes de América del Sur.

El **ciclismo,** el **tenis** y el **golf** son otros deportes que cuentan con figuras renombradas en Hispanoamérica y España. Los españoles Miguel Indurain, Roberto Heras y Alberto Contador fueron **campeones** del Tour de France. En esta **carrera,** que **dura** más de 20 días, los **ciclistas recorren** a veces unos 200 kilómetros, el equivalente de 120 millas, en un solo día. Por otro lado, España ha dado también jugadores de golf muy buenos, como Severiano Ballesteros, José María Olazábal y Sergio García.

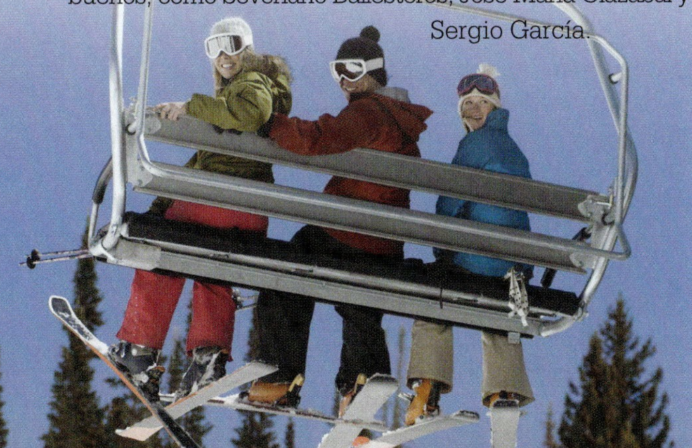

En cuanto al tenis, Juan Martín del Potro, argentino, y Nicolás Massú, chileno, son actualmente dos de los **tenistas** más conocidos del Cono Sur. La argentina Gabriela Sabatini, quien se retiró en 1995, es considerada la mejor tenista sudamericana de todos los tiempos. La figura más importante del tenis hispano en la actualidad es el español Rafael Nadal.

EN OTRAS PALABRAS

While the majority of Spanish speakers use **jugar al + deporte** some omit **al (jugar tenis, jugar golf,** etc.).

Some speakers say **básquetbol,** with the stress on the first syllable, rather than **baloncesto. Vóleibol** has several variants, including **volibol,** with the stress on the last syllable.

Suggestions for *Los deportes*
Talk about the photos to provide comprehensible input. Ask questions to emphasize the differences between *el fútbol americano* and *el fútbol* (soccer): *¿Cómo es el uniforme? ¿Cuántos jugadores hay en el equipo? ¿Cómo es el balón?* (Use gestures to explain *alargado, redondo.*) *¿Qué parte del cuerpo usan los jugadores para jugar al fútbol?*
Show news reports, photos, and video clips of Latin American and Spanish teams. Explain that the word *selección* as used in the presentation means team.
Talk about the photo of the ski slopes: *El esquí es un deporte popular en España. Hay centros de esquí importantes en los Pirineos, las montañas del norte. En Argentina el esquí también se practica mucho.* Check comprehension: *¿Dónde se puede esquiar en España? ¿Y dónde se puede esquiar en América del Sur?* Then personalize and review the seasons. *¿Esquías en el invierno? ¿Dónde esquías? Y a ti, ¿te gusta nadar? ¿Qué prefieres hacer: esquiar o nadar?*
En Estados Unidos hay muchos beisbolistas profesionales de República Dominicana, de Puerto Rico y de Cuba. ¿Conoces a algún beisbolista famoso? ¿Juegas al béisbol? ¿Y al baloncesto?

Note
Contador's career, like that of other famous cyclists, has been marked by allegations of doping. In 2010 he was stripped of his title as winner of the *Tour de France* and banned from competing for two years.

Deportes y equipos deportivos

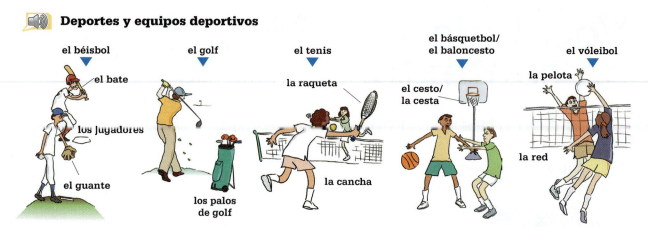

el béisbol: el bate, los jugadores, el guante

el golf: los palos de golf

el tenis: la raqueta, la cancha

el básquetbol/el baloncesto: el cesto/la cesta

el vóleibol: la pelota, la red

PRÁCTICA

Héroes del deporte

Soccer (**fútbol**) stars in Spanish-speaking countries have an astonishing popularity and importance in everyday life. Soccer stars have unrivalled popularity as celebrities in their countries and beyond and, unlike many prominent sports figures in the United States, serve as social role models as well. Some soccer stars, such as Lionel Messi and Iker Casillas, have capitalized on their social status to start nonprofit organizations to address social poblems.

Conexiones. Piensa en un deportista que es un ídolo para tu generación. Explica por qué es importante.

▲ Lionel Messi con sus *fans* en Colombia

Escucha y confirma. Identify the sport most closely associated with the information you hear. Write the number of the sentence next to the sport.

2 el fútbol	5 el béisbol
4 el esquí	6 el tenis
___ el vóleibol	___ el básquetbol
1 el ciclismo	3 el golf

Deportes: ¿Quién es? **PREPARACIÓN.** Asocia los deportes con los jugadores hispanos. Compara tus respuestas con las de tu compañero/a.

1. d ciclismo	**a.** Sergio García
2. c tenis	**b.** Félix Hernández
3. b béisbol	**c.** Rafael Nadal
4. a golf	**d.** Miguel Indurain

INTERCAMBIOS. Ahora hablen de dos de sus deportistas favoritos/as. Expliquen quiénes son y a qué deporte juegan, dónde juegan, qué campeonatos ganaron y por qué son sus deportistas favoritos/as.

Audioscript for 7-1

1. *En algunas carreras, los ciclistas recorren unos 200 kilómetros en un día.*
2. *La Copa Mundial es un campeonato que se celebra cada cuatro años.*
3. *El español Severiano Ballesteros fue tres veces campeón del Open Británico.*
4. *Las pistas de Bariloche son populares en toda América del Sur.*
5. *Hay excelentes jugadores del Caribe que juegan en los equipos de Estados Unidos.*
6. *Entre las figuras más conocidas se destaca la argentina Gabriela Sabatini.*

Suggestions for 7-2

Involve the entire class in an additional information-sharing activity. Ask: *¿Quién es un famoso ciclista norteamericano? ¿Sabes quién es Pau Gasol?* (a famous Spanish basketball player)

7-3

¿Qué necesitamos para jugar? **PREPARACIÓN.** Escribe el equipo que se necesita para practicar cada deporte.

DEPORTE	EQUIPO
el béisbol	
el golf	
el vóleibol	
el baloncesto	
el tenis	

INTERCAMBIOS. Entrevista a tu compañero/a para conversar sobre deportes.

1. ¿Qué deporte(s) practicas? ¿Por qué?
2. ¿Qué equipo necesitas para practicarlo(s)?
3. ¿Dónde compras el equipo y la ropa que necesitas?

EN OTRAS PALABRAS

Different words are used in Spanish for *ball,* depending on the context. The ball in basketball and volleyball is usually called **un balón.** Both **la pelota** and **el balón** are used for the soccer ball. **La pelota** is used in golf and tennis. **La bola** is used in bowling.

7-4

¿Qué deporte es? Túrnense para identificar los siguientes deportes. Después, pregúntale a tu compañero/a cuál es su deporte favorito y por qué.

1. Hay nueve jugadores en cada equipo y usan un bate y una pelota. el béisbol
2. Es un juego para dos o cuatro jugadores; necesitan raquetas y una pelota. el tenis
3. En este deporte los jugadores no deben usar las manos. el fútbol
4. Para practicar este deporte necesitamos una bicicleta. el ciclismo
5. En cada equipo hay cinco jugadores que lanzan (*throw*) el balón a un cesto. el baloncesto
6. Para este deporte necesitamos una red y una pelota. Mucha gente lo juega en la playa. el vóleibol

7-5

Tu deporte favorito. Háganse preguntas para averiguar lo siguiente.

MODELO E1: *¿Qué deporte te gusta practicar?*
E2: *Me gusta practicar el tenis, ¿y a ti?*

1. el deporte que te gusta practicar
2. el lugar donde lo practicas, con quién y cuándo
3. el deporte que te gusta ver
4. el lugar y las personas con quienes lo ves
5. los nombres de tus equipos favoritos
6. la marca (*brand*) de ropa deportiva que más te gusta

7-6

Concurso. Van a participar en un concurso sobre deportes. En grupos de tres o cuatro, escojan a uno/a de los/las deportistas de las fotos.

1. Identifiquen al/a la atleta y su deporte.
2. Digan algún campeonato/torneo (*tournament*) que este/a atleta ganó.
3. Digan el equipo que necesita para practicar su deporte.
4. Cuenten algún dato personal o profesional de esta persona.

INTERCAMBIOS. Compartan con la clase la información sobre este/a atleta. El grupo con la información más completa gana el concurso.

Note for 7-3
Remind students that *equipo* means both "team" and "equipment." *El equipo es el grupo de jugadores: por ejemplo, el equipo de los Medias Rojas de Boston. Pero equipo también quiere decir lo que necesitan los jugadores para jugar. ¿Qué equipo necesitan los jugadores de béisbol? (bates, pelotas y guantes)*

Suggestion for 7-4
You may wish to have students work in pairs on identifying the sports and talking about their favorites. Alternatively, you can have them do the first part individually and then talk with a partner about the sports they like the most.

Expansion for 7-4
Have students jot down notes to describe two different sports and then exchange them with other classmates to see if they can guess the sport.

Follow-up for 7-5
Find out how many students attend sports events and how many watch them on TV: *¿Van ustedes a los partidos de... o prefieren verlos por televisión? ¿A qué partidos van?*

Suggestion for 7-6
In this activity students will make connections with what they know. Many will be able to contribute a considerable amount of information about Victor Cruz, LeBron James, and Lindsey Vonn. To encourage competition, subtract points from teams whose members speak English. Alternatively, divide the class into groups and have them take turns answering the questions about the 3 athletes. If one group does not know an answer, the other group may respond. Record each group's points on the board.

Notes for 7-6
Victor Cruz was born in Paterson, New Jersey. He made his National Football League (NFL) debut in 2010 for the New York Giants, where he currently plays wide receiver. He won the 2011 Super Bowl with the Giants.

LeBron James plays basketball for the Miami Heat. He is nicknamed "The King" for his outstanding performance on the court; currently, he has 4 NBA Most Valuable Player titles, 2 NBA Championships, 1 NBA Rookie of the Year award, and 1 NBA scoring champion title. Lindsey Vonn is considered to be the most successful female alpine ski racer in American history. Vonn made her way to the World Cup at the early age of 16 in 2000. Since then she has gone on to set the U.S record for 59 World Cup wins.

Suggestion for *El tiempo y las estaciones*
Use visuals to illustrate and review weather expressions. Ask when certain weather patterns are likely to occur and present: *templado, cálido,* etc. Personalize: *¿Prefieres, el frío o el calor? ¿Te gusta la lluvia? ¿Y la nieve? ¿Qué deportes practicas cuando nieva?*

Suggestions
Recycle months by asking when the following occur; for each item ask what the weather is like both in your area and in the Southern Hemisphere: 1. *Termina el año escolar.* 2. *Empieza la temporada* (season) *de béisbol.* 3. *Celebras tu cumpleaños.* 4. *Sales de vacaciones.* 5. *Se juega el campeonato de fútbol americano Super Bowl.* 6. *Se celebra el día de San Patricio.* 7. *Se celebra el cumpleaños de Martin Luther King, Jr.* 8. *Es el cumpleaños de tu mejor amigo/a.* 9. *Este mes tiene el día más corto del año.*

Note
Some Spanish speakers use *hay* instead of *hace: Hay mucho sol.*

Suggestions for 7-7, *Intercambios*
You may wish to recycle the present progressive and expressions with *tener.* Have students work in pairs and suggest other situations: 1. *Hace mucho calor y no tienes aire acondicionado en la casa;* 2. *Tienes que hacer la tarea pero hace muy buen tiempo;* etc.

El tiempo y las estaciones

Verano

En verano generalmente hace buen tiempo y hace calor. Es la **estación** perfecta para practicar vóleibol en la playa, o **natación** al aire libre. Algunos prefieren **hacer surf** en el mar o **parapente** en las montañas.

Invierno

En invierno hace frío y a veces **nieva.** Pero la **nieve** es necesaria para esquiar. Cuando se **congelan** los **lagos,** se puede **patinar** sobre **el hielo.**

Otoño

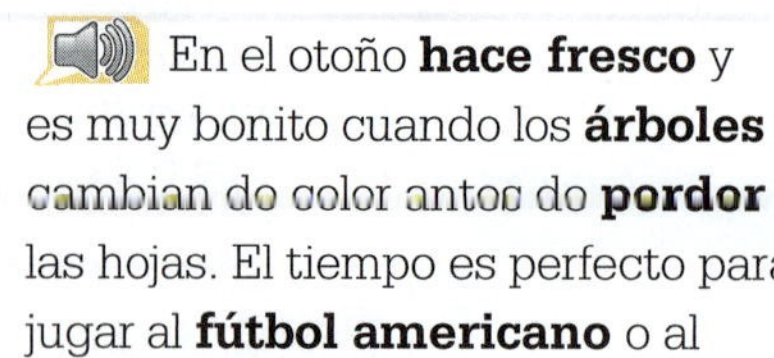

En el otoño **hace fresco** y es muy bonito cuando los **árboles** cambian de color antes de **perder** las hojas. El tiempo es perfecto para jugar al **fútbol americano** o al **hockey sobre hierba,** pero no es fácil jugar al golf cuando **hace viento.**

Primavera

En la primavera **llueve** bastante y es difícil practicar **atletismo** u otros deportes. Pero la **lluvia** es muy buena para las plantas y las flores. Como **hace mal tiempo,** muchas personas **juegan a los bolos** o **levantan pesas** en el gimnasio.

LENGUA

Replace **o** with **u** when the word that follows starts with **o.**

Pedro u Osvaldo   *Pedro or Osvaldo*

Likewise **y** is replaced with **e** when the word that follows begins with **i.**

Juan e Isabel   *Juan and Isabel*

EN OTRAS PALABRAS

In some Spanish-speaking countries, the expressions **jugar (al) boliche** or **ir de bowling** are preferred to **jugar a los bolos.**

PRÁCTICA

 **7-7** 

Para confirmar. **PREPARACIÓN.** Asocia cada descripción con la condición meterológica más lógica.

1. __e__ Las calles están blancas.
2. __c__ Las personas llevan impermeable y paraguas.
3. __d__ La casa es un horno y vamos a ir a la playa.
4. __b__ Los árboles se mueven (*move*) mucho.
5. __a__ Vamos a celebrar mi cumpleaños en el parque porque el clima está perfecto.
6. __f__ El cielo (*sky*) está cubierto (*overcast*) y parece que va a llover.

a. Hace muy buen tiempo.
b. Hace mucho viento.
c. Está lloviendo.
d. Hace mucho calor.
e. Está nevando.
f. Está nublado.

 **INTERCAMBIOS.** Habla con tu compañero/a de lo que haces en estas situaciones.

1. Quieres hacer un plan con tus amigos. Hace sol y mucho calor.
2. Tienes que jugar un partido de fútbol pero anoche llovió mucho y la cancha está mojada (*wet*).
3. Está nevando y hace frío pero quieres hacer deporte.

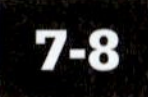 **7-8** 

¿Qué tiempo hace? Tu amigo/a te llama por teléfono desde otra ciudad. Pregúntale qué tiempo hace allí y averigua cuáles son sus planes. Tu amigo/a debe hacerte preguntas también.

 MODELO

E1: *¡Qué sorpresa! ¿Dónde estás?*
E2: *Estoy en…*
E1: *¿Qué tiempo hace allí?*
E2: *Hace…*

En directo

To thank a friend for calling:

Mil gracias por llamar. ¡Fue un gusto escucharte! *Thanks so much for calling. It was great to hear your voice!*

Gracias por llamar. ¡Qué placer escucharte! *Thanks for calling. How nice to hear from you!*

 Listen to a conversation with these expressions.

7-9 

El tiempo y las actividades. PREPARACIÓN. Túrnense para explicar qué hacen o qué les gusta hacer a estas personas en las siguientes condiciones.

1. Cuando llueve yo…
2. Cuando hace mucho calor me gusta…
3. A veces cuando nieva…
4. Mis amigos y yo… cuando hace mal tiempo.
5. En invierno…
6. Los estudiantes… cuando hace buen tiempo.
7. Cuando está nublado…
8. Hoy hace viento pero…

INTERCAMBIOS. Preparen una breve conversación que incluya al menos (*at least*) una pregunta, tres expresiones de tiempo y un deporte.

 MODELO

E1: *Hola, Carmen. ¿Vamos a la playa esta tarde? Hace mucho calor.*
E2: *Sí, pero en la televisión dicen que esta tarde va a llover.*
E1: *Está nublado pero pienso que no va a llover.*
E2: *Bueno, pues vamos. Es mejor jugar al vóleibol cuando está nublado.*

Cultura

The Celsius system is used in Hispanic countries. To convert degrees Fahrenheit to degrees Celsius, subtract 32, multiply by 5, and divide by 9.

86 °F − 32 = 54
54 × 5 = 270
270 ÷ 9 = 30 °C

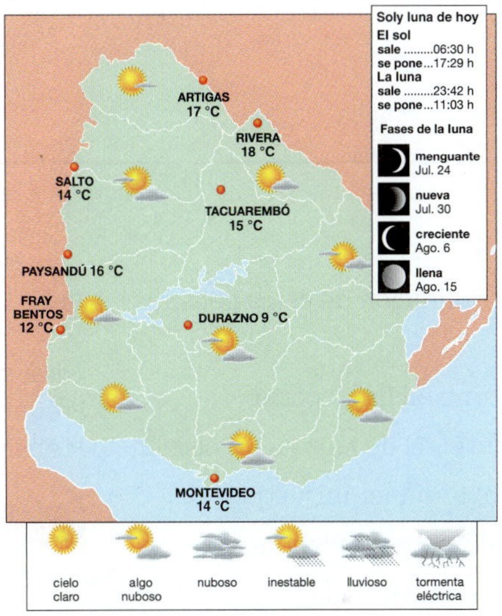

Comparaciones. ¿Qué temperatura hace ahora en tu ciudad? ¿Cambia mucho el clima con las estaciones? ¿Cuál es tu estación del año favorita? ¿Por qué? ¿Practicas distintos deportes según la época del año? ¿Cuáles?

7-10

Las temperaturas.

PREPARACIÓN. Escojan una ciudad del mapa de Uruguay y túrnense para completar la conversación.

 MODELO

E1: *¿Qué temperatura hace en…?*
E2: *… grados. Su equivalente en Fahrenheit es…*
E1: *¿Y qué tiempo hace donde estás tú?*
E2: *… ¿Y qué temperatura hace en…?*

INTERCAMBIOS. Preparen un pronóstico del tiempo (*weather forecast*) de la región donde viven. Indiquen la temperatura de tres ciudades, el tiempo que hace hoy y el tiempo que va a hacer mañana. Después, compártanlo con la clase.

Suggestions for 7-8
Review Spanish telephone etiquette. To make the conversation more realistic, pairs use their cell phones. You may wish to assign students to look up the current weather in a Hispanic city and then do the dialogue in class again using that information.
You may wish to present: *tornado, ciclón, humedad, huracán, granizo, nevada, llovizna, sequía, neblina, escampar, lloviznar, truenos, relámpagos.*

Note for *En directo*
Before doing activity 7-8, first have students read the expressions in En *directo*. Then have them listen to the dialogue and encourage them to use the expressions in their own conversation.

Audioscript for *En directo*
JULIÁN: *¿Coach Pérez? Soy yo, Julián Gil.*
COACH PÉREZ: *¡Ah, sí, Julián! Mi portero estrella. ¿Cómo estás?*
JULIÁN: *Muy bien. Tengo buenas noticias. ¡Me aceptaron en la universidad y voy a formar parte de su equipo de fútbol!*
COACH PÉREZ: *¡Felicidades! ¡Cuánto me alegro! Mil gracias por llamar. ¡Qué gusto escucharte!*
JULIÁN: *Al contrario, gracias a usted por toda su ayuda.*

Suggestion for 7-9, *Intercambios*
Ask students to work orally on this dialogue and then present it to the class.

Suggestion for 7-10
Have students tell how they describe the weather at the following Celsius temperatures: *0 °C (hace mucho frío); 0–10 °C (hace frío); 20 °C (hace fresco); 30 °C (hace calor); 40 °C (hace mucho calor).*
You may wish to introduce vocabulary related to moon phases: *menguante, nueva, creciente, llena* by showing the box on the right of map. *Hoy hay luna llena. La luna está menguante.* Encourage students to prepare for the *Intercambios* by discussing

weather in their area: *¿Cuál es la temperatura máxima aquí en el verano? ¿Y la temperatura mínima en el invierno?* Then give students time to prepare their weather reports and present them to the class as if they were on television.

Note
This section reintroduces reflexive verbs and adds others that may be conjugated with a pronoun. These verbs appear here in the preterit in boldface as lexical items; the purpose is to offer students a contextualized preview of the forms, which are presented in *Funciones y formas.*

Suggestion for *¿Qué pasó ayer?*
Project the images in class to review vocabulary in context. Talk about the illustrations and ask: *¿Se despertó temprano Iván? ¿A qué hora se levantó? ¿Desayunó mucho o poco?,* etc.

Note
Point out that Spanish often borrows English sports words, giving them a Spanish pronunciation and spelling: *penalti, gol, cacher, nocaut, jonrón.* A penalty in sports is *un penal* in some parts of Latin America.

¿Qué pasó ayer?

Un partido importante

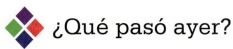

Ayer fue el partido decisivo del campeonato de fútbol.

▲ Iván **se despertó** temprano.

▲ **Se levantó.**

▲ **Se vistió.**

▲ **Se sentó** a comer un buen desayuno. Después, **se fue** para el **campo** de fútbol.

▲ Durante el partido, el árbitro **pitó** un **penalti.**

▲ Un jugador del equipo **contrario se enfadó** y **discutió** con el **árbitro,** pero el equipo de Iván **metió un gol** y **ganó.**

▲ Después del partido, Iván **se quitó** el uniforme, **se bañó** y **se puso la ropa.**

▲ Luego fue a una fiesta para celebrar el triunfo.

▲ **Volvió** a casa muy tarde, **se acostó** y **se durmió** enseguida.

PRÁCTICA

7-11 

Para confirmar. **PREPARACIÓN.** Busca la definición de estas palabras relacionadas con los deportes.

1. __c__ ganar
2. __f__ equipo
3. __e__ gol
4. __d__ partido
5. __b__ árbitro
6. __a__ campeón

a. el jugador número uno en un deporte
b. la persona que hace el rol de juez en un partido
c. tener más puntos al terminar un juego
d. el juego entre dos equipos o individuos
e. el punto en un partido de fútbol
f. un grupo de jugadores

INTERCAMBIOS. Hazle preguntas a tu compañero/a para ver si sabe las respuestas. Pregúntale sobre las palabras en *Preparación*.

MODELO E1: *¿Cómo se llama un equipo que gana?*
E2: ...

Hispanic sports fans generally do not boo opposing teams or particular players. Instead they whistle to show their displeasure. This behavior may occur at a soccer game, boxing match, or other popular sports events.

Comparaciones. En tu comunidad, ¿cómo demuestran descontento los hinchas (*fans*) con los jugadores o con un partido? ¿Alguna vez viste una escena un poco violenta durante o después de un partido? ¿Qué ocurrió? ¿Qué hiciste tú?

7-12 

El partido de Iván. Trabajen juntos para contestar las preguntas sobre las actividades de Iván (en la página 248) el día del partido.

1. ¿Qué hizo (*did*) Iván primero? Se despertó.
2. ¿Qué hizo después de levantarse? Se vistió.
3. ¿Qué desayunó Iván? un buen desayuno
4. ¿Por qué se enfadó un jugador del equipo contrario? porque el árbitro pitó un penalti
5. ¿Quién ganó el partido? el equipo de Iván
6. ¿Adónde fue Iván después del partido? Fue a una fiesta.

7-13 

¿Las actividades de ayer? **PREPARACIÓN.** Háganse preguntas para obtener la siguiente información sobre sus actividades de ayer.

 E1: *¿A qué hora te despertaste ayer?*
E2: *Me desperté a las once.*

1. hora de despertarse y de levantarse
2. desayuno que tomó
3. número de horas de estudio
4. deporte(s) que practicó y por cuánto tiempo
5. hora de acostarse

INTERCAMBIOS. Comparen sus actividades.

1. ¿Quién de ustedes se levantó más temprano?
2. ¿Quién tomó un desayuno más nutritivo?
3. ¿Quién estudió más?
4. ¿Quién practicó deportes por más tiempo?
5. ¿Quién se acostó más tarde?

7-14 

El tiempo y los deportes. **PREPARACIÓN.** Write down the information you might hear in a weather forecast in your area in each season. Remember to include temperatures. Then ask your partner what weather conditions he/she listed and if you agree.

primavera ___________ otoño ___________

verano ___________ invierno ___________

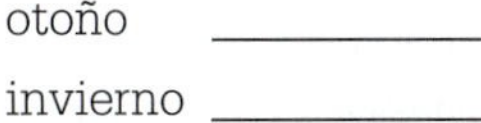

 E1: *¿Qué tiempo tienes para...? ¿Qué temperatura hace?*
E2: *Tengo...*

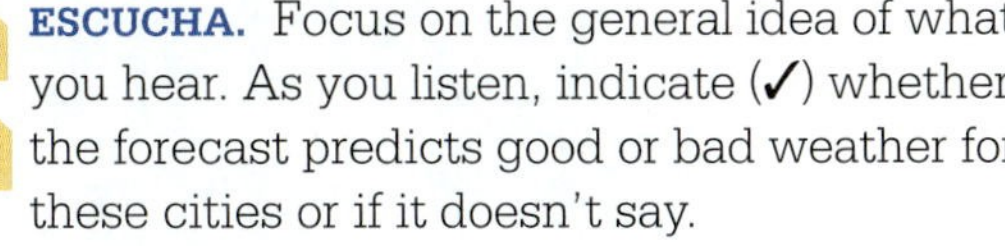

ESCUCHA. Focus on the general idea of what you hear. As you listen, indicate (✓) whether the forecast predicts good or bad weather for these cities or if it doesn't say.

	BUEN TIEMPO	MAL TIEMPO	NO SE DICE
Montevideo		✓	
Buenos Aires		✓	
México			✓
Caracas	✓		

Suggestion for 7-12
Brainstorm things students did yesterday and write some sentences on the board. You may use the third person of reflexive and non-reflexive verbs: *Pablo se despertó a las 6. Leonardo comió en un restaurante argentino. Paula fue a clase de matemáticas.* Then model the first person by talking about your day: *Ayer por la mañana me levanté temprano, trabajé en mi oficina, después comí con mi amigo. Por la tarde fui al gimnasio*, etc.

Suggestion for 7-12
Explain that formulating questions is an important skill. In this activity students formulate questions in the past tense, using regular verbs only. They will learn the past tense of some irregular verbs in *Funciones y formas.*

Suggestion for 7-14, *Escucha*
Listening activities provide many learning opportunities when done in the classroom and they can be used to enhance communication. You may, for example, play the audio once and ask students to communicate in pairs about what they have understood.

Audioscript for 7-14
Anunciador:
Están escuchando Radio Hispanoamérica. Ahora les informamos sobre los próximos acontecimientos deportivos y sobre el pronóstico del tiempo. En Montevideo, se va a celebrar esta tarde el último partido de fútbol de la Copa Mundial. La selección nacional de Argentina juega hoy contra la selección de México. El tiempo en esta ocasión no va a ayudar al equipo mexicano. No llueve, pero el día está muy nublado y hace frío. La temperatura es de 14 grados centígrados. Por otra parte, en Buenos Aires está lloviendo y la temperatura es de 10 grados centígrados. Los jugadores del equipo argentino salieron temprano para Montevideo y afortunadamente, no les afectó la lluvia.

En Caracas se celebra otro campeonato importante: el campeonato hispanoamericano de hockey sobre hierba. Aunque hoy hace sol, la temperatura es de 20 grados centígrados, es decir, no hace demasiado calor. Eso es bueno porque no hay nada peor que un partido de hockey con lluvia y frío.

MOSAICO cultural Los hinchas y el superclásico

El fútbol es más que un simple deporto para los hispanos, es una pasión. El sueño común entre muchos niños es jugar fútbol profesionalmente.

Los fines de semana los clubes de fútbol juegan en grandes estadios y miles de *fans* los apoyan (*support*). Existen intensas rivalidades entre los seguidores de los clubes más populares y ganadores. Estos encuentros se llaman los superclásicos. En México, por ejemplo, los equipos rivales son el Club América y el Deportivo Guadalajara, más conocido como el Chivas. En España son el Real Madrid y el FC Barcelona. En Colombia, los equipos del superclásico son el Santa Fe y el Millonarios de Bogotá. Sin embargo la experiencia deportiva más intensa ocurre entre Boca Juniors y River Plate de Argentina. La rivalidad entre estos equipos es enorme. Los hinchas de River se burlan de (*make fun of*) los jugadores de Boca y los llaman "chanchos" (*pigs*). En respuesta, los hinchas de Boca llaman "gallinas" (*chickens*) a los jugadores de River.

Cuando Boca y River juegan, la ciudad de Buenos Aires se viste con los colores de los equipos y canta con entusiasmo. Ser hincha de River o de Boca es una tradición familiar. Es normal ver a los niños con camisetas azules cantando: "Boca es entusiasmo y valor, Boca Juniors… a triunfar…". También es común ver a niños y niñas con camisetas rojas y blancas cantando: "Boca: River es tu papá… Olé, olé, River, River…" Por estas razones, el "superclásico" es más que futbolístico: es también una tradición social. Porque el fútbol es más que un deporte. El fútbol es una parte importante de la identidad de los hispanos.

▲ Los hinchas de River Plate (de rojo y blanco) se burlan de sus rivales con el chancho (de azul y amarillo).

▲ Los *fans* de River Plate proclaman su devoción con pancartas y los colores de su equipo.

Este *fan* de Boca Junior expresa el sentimiento de muchos otros como él. ▶

Compara

1. ¿En tu país hay algún evento deportivo comparable al superclásico? ¿Cuál? ¿Cuándo ocurre? ¿Qué equipos se enfrentan normalmente?
2. ¿Qué rivalidades son famosas en los deportes profesionales o universitarios de tu país?
3. ¿Eres hincha de algún equipo deportivo? ¿Cómo expresas tu apoyo (*support*)? ¿Cómo es tu relación con los hinchas de los equipos rivales?

Notes for Mosaico cultural
Remind students that every country has two teams that share a similar rivalry. Almost every soccer fan, regardless of what team they support, will feel an affinity for one team or another. The Argentinian *superclásico* is followed by many across Latin America and Spain. *Boca Juniors* is the fourth most famous soccer team in the world (behind *Barcelona, Real Madrid,* and *Manchester United*).

Soccer as a social phenomenon affects the daily lives of Hispanic people, even if they directly engage with it or not. Streets close and traffic is rerouted whenever there is an important soccer match. There are professional soccer matches four or five days a week, and there are TV channels entirely devoted to covering the soccer arena. ESPN and Fox Sports, which air twice a day every day to keep up with soccer happenings, are viewed widely by Hispanics.

You may want to remind students about important Hispanic soccer figures and their relevance in the construction of a Hispanic identity. Lionel Messi and

Funciones y formas

1 Talking about the past

REPORTERO: ¡Felicitaciones por el triunfo! ¡Jugaron como campeones!

RODOLFO: Gracias. El triunfo es de todo el equipo. Fue un partido difícil, pero **nos preparamos** bien.

REPORTERO: ¿Y cómo empezó este día de victoria para ti, Rodolfo?

RODOLFO: Bueno, anoche **me acosté** temprano. Hoy, **me levanté** a las 5:30, **me duché** muy rápido para el entrenamiento, **me vestí** y **me fui** a la cancha.

REPORTERO: ¿Y cómo **se prepararon** ustedes para enfrentar al equipo rival?

RODOLFO: Eh… Primero, es fundamental **sentirse** ganador y también es importante tener un buen entrenador como el nuestro.

Piénsalo. Indica si las siguientes afirmaciones son probables (**P**) o improbables (**I**) según la conversación entre Rodolfo y el reportero.

1. __I__ Todos los jugadores del equipo **se acostaron** tarde la noche antes del partido.
2. __P__ Rodolfo **se levantó** temprano el día del partido.
3. __P__ Rodolfo **se duchó** rápidamente para llegar a tiempo a la cancha.
4. __I__ El equipo no **se preparó** bien para el partido y ganó.
5. __I__ Según Rodolfo, lo más importante para ganar es **sentirse** nervioso.

Preterit of reflexive verbs

- In *Capítulo 4* you learned about reflexive verbs. Now you will use these verbs in the preterit. The rules that apply to reflexive verbs are the same in the past tense as in the present.

  As you have seen, reflexive verbs express what people do *to* or *for themselves.*

LEVANTARSE	
yo	**me levanté**
tú	**te levantaste**
Ud., él, ella	**se levantó**
nosotros/as	**nos levantamos**
vosotros/as	**os levantasteis**
Uds., ellos/as	**se levantaron**

Los jugadores **se levantaron** a las cinco.	*The players got up at five o'clock.*
Yo **me preparé** rápidamente.	*I got ready quickly.*

Diego Armando Maradona, both Argentinian, are by far the most important soccer players in the history of Hispanic soccer. Explain to students that their importance is equivalent to that of Michael Jordan in basketball or Babe Ruth in baseball. Students should access some of the many YouTube videos on this topic for additional information.

Note
Reflexive verbs were presented and practiced in *Capítulo 4* and appeared in *Vocabulario en contexto* of this chapter. You may wish to review the present and model the past tense as follows: *Siempre me levanto temprano, pero hoy no me levanté muy temprano porque no sonó el reloj despertador. Me desperté 30 minutos tarde. Y tú, ¿a qué hora te despertaste esta mañana? Y, ¿a qué hora te levantas normalmente? ¿Te levantaste temprano o tarde hoy?*

Standard 4.1 Students demonstrate an understanding of the nature of language through comparisons of the language studied and their own. Draw students' attention to this difference between English and Spanish: When the meaning is clear from the context, Spanish uses the definite article to refer to parts of the body and to clothing (e.g., *Me lavo **el** pelo, Alicia se quitó **la** sudadera*) in contrast to English, which uses possessive adjectives (e.g., **my** hair, **her** sweatshirt).

- With a conjugated verb followed by an infinitive, place the reflexive pronoun before the conjugated verb or attach it to the infinitive.

Yo **me** empecé a preparar a las cinco.
Yo empecé a preparar**me** a las cinco.
} *I started to get ready at five.*

- Remember that when referring to parts of the body and clothing, the definite articles are used with reflexive verbs.

Me lavé **el** pelo.	*I washed my hair.*
Alicia se quitó **la** sudadera.	*Alicia took off her sweatshirt.*

- Some verbs that use reflexive pronouns do not necessarily convey the idea of doing something to or for oneself. These verbs normally convey mental or physical states.

María **se enfermó** gravemente la semana pasada.	*María got seriously sick last week.*
Nos preocupamos mucho cuando fue al hospital.	*We got very worried when she went to the hospital.*

- Reflexive verbs that convey mental or physical states do not take an object. The following verbs are in that category.

arrepentirse	*to regret*
atreverse	*to dare*
divertirse	*to have fun*
disculparse	*to apologize*
enfadarse	*to get upset, angry*
quejarse	*to complain*
sentirse	*to feel*

La entrenadora **se disculpó** por no asistir a la práctica del viernes pasado.	*The coach apologized for not attending last Friday's practice.*
El público **se quejó** del pobre desempeño de los jugadores.	*The public complained about the poor performance of the players.*

e ¿COMPRENDES?

Completa las oraciones con el pretérito de los verbos.

1. Ayer Marta __se enfermó__ (enfermarse).
2. Pero hoy __se levantó__ (levantarse) para ir a clase.
3. Los estudiantes no __se prepararon__ (prepararse) para el examen.
4. Yo __me disculpé__ (disculparse) con el profesor porque no fui a clase.
5. Nosotros __nos quejamos__ (quejarse) porque el examen fue muy difícil.
6. ¿Por qué __te sentaste__ (sentarse) tú en la última fila (*row*)?

MySpanishLab

Learn more using Amplifire Dynamic Study Modules, Grammar Tutorials, and Extra Practice activities.

PRÁCTICA

7-15 

¿Cómo te fue (*did it go*) ayer? Pon estas actividades en el orden más lógico y compara tus respuestas con las de tu compañero/a. ¿Tienen el mismo orden? Presenten sus diferencias a otro grupo.

__6__ Me preparé para un examen.	__1__ Me desperté temprano.
__9__ Me dormí.	__4__ Me senté a desayunar.
__2__ Me levanté.	__3__ Me bañé.
__5__ Me fui a la universidad.	__7__ Al final del día, me sentí cansado/a.
__8__ Me acosté.	

7-16 

¿Cómo reaccionaron los jugadores? **PREPARACIÓN.** Jorge, Enrique y Raúl tuvieron un partido de fútbol el sábado. Completen las afirmaciones de Jorge sobre sus actividades.

MODELO Jorge: Yo me acosté muy temprano la noche anterior, pero Enrique... *se acostó a la hora de siempre.*

1. Yo me desperté tarde para estar bien descansado, pero Enrique...
2. Yo me preparé por dos horas en el gimnasio, pero Enrique y Raúl...
3. Yo me quejé cuando el árbitro pitó un penalti, pero Raúl...
4. Cuando el árbitro cometió un error en la cancha, yo me enojé mucho, pero Enrique...
5. Después del partido yo me reuní con los aficionados, pero Enrique y Raúl...
6. Cuando los tres llegamos a casa...

INTERCAMBIOS. La última vez (*the last time*) que ustedes tuvieron un partido importante, ¿hicieron actividades semejantes o diferentes a las de Jorge y sus amigos? Comparen sus actividades y reacciones.

MODELO E1: *Yo me desperté muy temprano el día del partido. ¿Y ustedes?*

E2: *Yo me desperté temprano también.*

E3: *Yo me desperté tarde y me levanté tarde.*

Suggestion for 7-16
If your students need to refresh their knowledge of reflexive constructions before doing this activity, you may wish to reframe the sentences in the present.

Note
As mentioned in *Vocabulario en contexto,* the forms *hizo* and *hicieron* appear in the direction lines of activities, but students do not have to produce the preterit of *hacer* until it is presented later in this chapter.

Suggestions for 7-17
Have students tell the class what they did. You may direct discussion to see who did the most for their health. You may also ask students to offer recommendations to their classmates.

Expansion for 7-18
You may wish to increase the amount of student talk by inviting them to use their imagination to interpret the situations in original and amusing ways.

Suggestion for 7-19
Personalize by asking athletes in the class what they normally do to prepare for a game and what they did for their last important match or game.

Cultura

Una actividad física

In Spanish-speaking countries, the most common physical activity is walking—as light exercise after work or after a meal, as a family activity, or simply to be outside in one's neighborhood. It is often a social activity where friends and neighbors meet and greet each other. As in the United States, professional people with busy work schedules join gyms or sports clubs, especially in metropolitan areas.

Comparaciones. ¿Consideras que andar es una actividad física? ¿Dónde pasea la gente de tu comunidad?

7-17 

Mis actividades. Para cuidar tu salud decidiste cambiar tu rutina y empezar cada día con un poco de ejercicio antes de ir a clase. Habla con tu compañero/a y cuéntale qué hiciste esta mañana. Usa por lo menos cuatro de los siguientes verbos.

despertarse	caminar
ducharse	correr
levantarse	jugar
prepararse	nadar

7-18 

¿Qué les ocurrió? Lean las siguientes situaciones y digan lo que probablemente hicieron (*did*) estas personas después. Usen los verbos de la lista. Luego, comparen sus opiniones con las de sus compañeros.

afeitarse	lavarse	perfumarse
bañarse	maquillarse	probarse
despertarse	mirarse	quitarse
enfadarse	peinarse	secarse

MODELO Bernardo se despertó cuando sonó el despertador.

E1: *Luego se levantó lentamente. En tu opinión, ¿qué pasó después?*

E2: *Probablemente se afeitó.*

1. Teresa se miró en el espejo.
2. Juan y Tomás entraron en el vestuario (*locker room*) del gimnasio después del partido.
3. Marisa y Erica salieron de una tienda deportiva.
4. Ramón salió de la ducha.
5. Marta no está contenta. Habló con la capitana del equipo de unos temas personales y luego la capitana les contó todo a otras jugadoras.
6. Pablo llegó tarde al estadio.

7-19 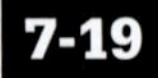 

El campeonato. El mes pasado ustedes representaron a su universidad en un campeonato de tenis en Montevideo. Digan lo que hicieron (*what you did*)...

1. para prepararse físicamente.
2. para prepararse mentalmente.
3. para cumplir (*to fulfill*) con las responsabilidades académicas.

7-20 

Loreta se levantó con el pie izquierdo (*got up on the wrong side of the bed*). Observen las siguientes escenas. Túrnense y cuenten lo que ocurrió. Usen su imaginación y los verbos de la lista u otros, si es necesario.

acostarse	ducharse	explicar	practicar
despertarse	enfadarse	golpear (*to knock*)	sentarse
disculparse	enojarse	levantarse	sonar

Situación  

PREPARACIÓN. Lean la situación. Luego, compartan ejemplos de vocabulario, gramática y otra información que necesitan para desarrollar la conversación.

Role A. You are the star player for your university's soccer team. You spend a lot of your free time promoting sports and physical activity for children in your community. A reporter for a local TV station interviews you for a special feature on student athletes. Answer the reporter's questions as fully as possible. Remember that you are considered a role model for young athletes.

Role B. You are a television reporter. Today you are interviewing the star soccer player for the university team who is also a role model for young athletes in the community. After introducing yourself and greeting the athlete, find out:

a. what school he/she went to;
b. when he/she started to play;
c. what his/her daily routine is to keep in shape (**estar en forma**); and
d. what sports he/she practiced yesterday.

	ROLE A	ROLE B
Vocabulario	Activities to keep oneself fit Sports routines	Question words Sports-related vocabulary Sports routines
Funciones y formas	Answering questions Present tense Reflexive verbs Addressing someone formally	Introducing oneself Asking questions Present tense Past time (Preterit) Addressing someone formally

INTERCAMBIOS. Practica la conversación con tu compañero/a incorporando el vocabulario y las funciones de *Preparación*. Luego, represéntenla ante la clase.

Suggestions for 7-20
You may wish to present some of the verbs listed after the directions for this activity: *enojarse, disculparse, golpear, recriminar.* Ask students to name the characters and tell what each scene shows. You may ask them to use their imagination to explain the what, why, how of each event. Guide them through the scenes by asking questions: Scene #1: *¿A qué hora salió el sol? ¿Sonó el reloj despertador?* Scene #2: *La entrenadora, ¿se levantó antes que Loreta? ¿Cómo llegó la entrenadora al cuarto de...? ¿Quién abrió la puerta?* Scene #3: *¿Por qué se levantó tarde...? ¿Qué excusa le dio... a la entrenadora? ¿Por qué se acostó tarde...?* Scene #4: *¿A qué hora llegó la tenista a la cancha?*

Suggestion for *Situación*
You may want to assign partners and have pairs create mini-skits using the video-posting feature, *MediaShare,* online.

2 Talking about the past

VÍCTOR: Federico, ¿miraste el partido entre la selección de Argentina y la de Colombia?

FEDERICO: No, Víctor. Pero **oí** las noticias por la radio, y mi hermano **leyó** la crónica del partido en el periódico. La selección colombiana ganó dos a uno. Los argentinos no jugaron bien. Y tú, ¿viste el partido?

VÍCTOR: Desafortunadamente no, pero **leí** en Internet que los jugadores argentinos no **oyeron** las instrucciones de su entrenador y cometieron muchos errores. Por eso, el árbitro les marcó un penalti.

FEDERICO: Tienes razón, yo **oí** que la estrategia de defensa que **construyeron** no fue buena. Ellos **creyeron** que ganarles a los colombianos es fácil, pero son muy buenos.

Piénsalo. **¿QUIÉN LO HIZO?** (*Who did it?*): Federico (**F**), Víctor (**V**), el hermano de Federico (**HF**) o los jugadores argentinos (**JA**).

1. __F__ **Oyó** las noticias del partido por la radio.
2. __HF__ **Leyó** la crónica en el periódico.
3. __V__ **Leyó** en Internet comentarios sobre el partido.
4. __JA__ No **oyeron** las instrucciones.
5. __JA__ **Creyeron** que ganar es fácil.
6. __JA__ **Construyeron** (*They built*) una mala estrategia de defensa.

Suggestion
You may wish to introduce additional verbs: *caer, concluir, contribuir, destruir, incluir.* All but *caer* are cognates that students will readily understand.

LENGUA

Note that **-er** and **-ir** verbs whose stems end in a vowel (**creer, leer, oír**) have an accent mark on the **i** in the infinitive and in the preterit endings that begin with **i.**

No la **oímos** llegar anoche.
We didn't hear her arrive last night.

Preterit of *-er* and *-ir* verbs whose stem ends in a vowel

- You have already learned the preterit forms of regular **-er** and **-ir** verbs. For verbs whose stem ends in a vowel, the preterit ending for the **usted/él/ella** form is **-yó** and for the **ustedes/ellos/ellas** form, the ending is **-yeron.**

LEER			
yo	leí	nosotros/as	leímos
tú	leíste	vosotros/as	leísteis
Ud., él, ella	le**y**ó	Uds., ellos/as	le**y**eron

OÍR			
yo	oí	nosotros/as	oímos
tú	oíste	vosotros/as	oísteis
Ud., él, ella	o**y**ó	Uds., ellos/as	o**y**eron

Los jugadores **oyeron** los comentarios negativos de los reporteros deportivos. — *The players heard the negative comments of the sports commentators.*

Cuando el entrenador **oyó** el pitazo final, abrazó a los jugadores. — *When the coach heard the final whistle, he hugged the players.*

Los miembros del equipo **construyeron** una casa con la organización Hábitat para la Humanidad. — *The members of the team built a house with Habitat for Humanity.*

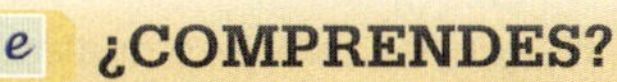

¿COMPRENDES?

Completa las oraciones con el pretérito de los verbos.

1. Pablo y Miguel ____oyeron____ (oír) la noticia en la radio.
2. Ellos no la ____creyeron____ (creer).
3. Carmen ____leyó____ (leer) la información en Internet.
4. Nosotros no ____creímos____ (creer) lo que Carmen nos contó.
5. Los arquitectos ____construyeron____ (construir) un edificio muy feo.
6. ¿Asististe al partido ayer o ____leíste____ (leer) el libro de historia?

MySpanishLab

Learn more using Amplifire Dynamic Study Modules, Grammar Tutorials, and Extra Practice activities.

PRÁCTICA

7-21

¿Cómo se enteraron (*found out*) de los resultados? El fin de semana pasado se jugó la Copa Davis. Indica cómo se enteraron estas personas de los resultados. Usa los verbos **creer, leer** y **oír.**

1. Paula y su novio pasaron el fin de semana en las montañas y ____oyeron____ los resultados en la radio durante su viaje de regreso a la ciudad.

2. Mercedes trabajó en la biblioteca todo el fin de semana. Cuando su hermano le contó los resultados, ella no le ____creyó____.

3. Ricardo participó en un partido de fútbol entre su universidad y una universidad rival. Él ____leyó____ los resultados de la Copa Davis en el periódico.

4. Los Belmar salieron a hacer ejercicio a la hora del partido. Prefieren el aire libre a mirar televisión y ____leyeron____ los resultados en el periódico al día siguiente.

Additional practice for Preterit of *-er* and *-ir* verbs

In groups, have students find out how many students did the following:

1. *Leyeron el periódico ayer.*
2. *Oyeron las noticias esta mañana.*
3. *Fueron a un partido de tenis o béisbol recientemente.*
4. *Practicaron un deporte esta semana.*
5. *Se levantaron antes de las ocho esta mañana.*
6. *Contribuyeron con por lo menos una hora a una actividad de voluntariado* (volunteer) *esta semana.*

Then have each group report their findings to the rest of the class.

7-22 

Las noticias. Dile a tu compañero/a cuándo y cómo te enteraste de las siguientes noticias. ¿Lo leíste, lo oíste o lo miraste?

 el equipo ganador del Super Bowl

E1: *Lo miré en la televisión. ¿Y tú?*

E2: *Yo lo leí en Internet.*

1. el equipo ganador de la última serie mundial de béisbol
2. los resultados de las últimas elecciones presidenciales
3. la muerte de Amy Winehouse
4. tu admisión a esta universidad

7-23

La semana pasada. **PREPARACIÓN.** Mira la lista de actividades e indica (✓) en cuáles participaste la semana pasada. Añade detalles sobre cada actividad.

_____ concluir un proyecto importante para la clase de...

_____ ir a la biblioteca para...

_____ leer el blog de...

_____ mirar una película con...

_____ oír música de...

_____ contribuir a la organización sin fines de lucro (*non-profit*)...

 **INTERCAMBIOS.** En grupos de tres o cuatro, comparen sus respuestas para ver quién hizo más actividades la semana pasada.

Situación

PREPARACIÓN. Lean la situación. Luego, compartan ejemplos de vocabulario, gramática y otra información que necesitan para desarrollar la conversación.

Role A. Call a friend to invite him/her to go to a sports event with you. Mention:

a. what the event is;
b. that you read about it in the newspaper; and
c. that you want to see the city's new stadium (**estadio**).

Role B. Your friend calls to invite you to a sports event. Respond to the invitation with questions and comments. Then decide if you want to go and either accept or decline the invitation.

	ROLE A	ROLE B
Vocabulario	Sports events	Question words
Funciones y formas	Inviting someone to do something	Accepting or declining an invitation Reacting to what you hear Asking questions

INTERCAMBIOS. Practica la conversación con tu compañero/a incorporando el vocabulario y las funciones de *Preparación.* Luego, represéntenla ante la clase.

3 Talking about the past

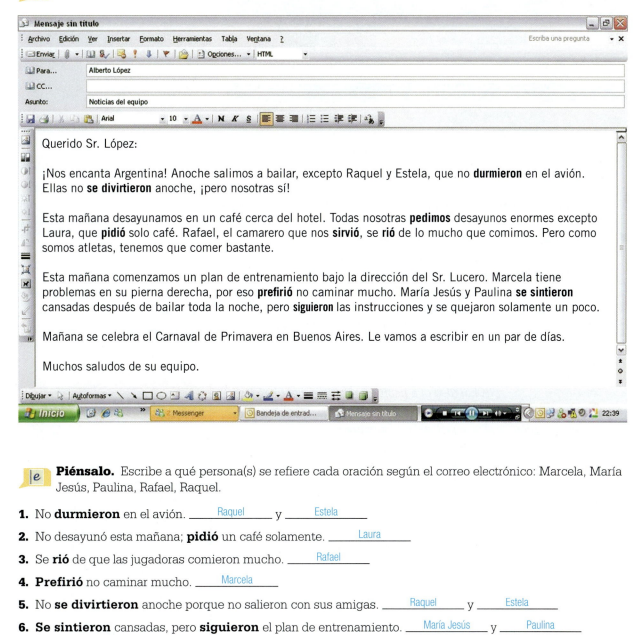

Mensaje sin título

Archivo Edición Ver Insertar Formato Herramientas Tabla Ventana ?

Para... Alberto López

CC...

Asunto: Noticias del equipo

Querido Sr. López:

¡Nos encanta Argentina! Anoche salimos a bailar, excepto Raquel y Estela, que no **durmieron** en el avión. Ellas no **se divirtieron** anoche, ¡pero nosotras sí!

Esta mañana desayunamos en un café cerca del hotel. Todas nosotras **pedimos** desayunos enormes excepto Laura, que **pidió** solo café. Rafael, el camarero que nos **sirvió**, se **rió** de lo mucho que comimos. Pero como somos atletas, tenemos que comer bastante.

Esta mañana comenzamos un plan de entrenamiento bajo la dirección del Sr. Lucero. Marcela tiene problemas en su pierna derecha, por eso **prefirió** no caminar mucho. María Jesús y Paulina **se sintieron** cansadas después de bailar toda la noche, pero **siguieron** las instrucciones y se quejaron solamente un poco.

Mañana se celebra el Carnaval de Primavera en Buenos Aires. Le vamos a escribir en un par de días.

Muchos saludos de su equipo.

Piénsalo. Escribe a qué persona(s) se refiere cada oración según el correo electrónico: Marcela, María Jesús, Paulina, Rafael, Raquel.

1. No **durmieron** en el avión. Raquel y Estela
2. No desayunó esta mañana; **pidió** un café solamente. Laura
3. Se **rió** de que las jugadoras comieron mucho. Rafael
4. **Prefirió** no caminar mucho. Marcela
5. No **se divirtieron** anoche porque no salieron con sus amigas. Raquel y Estela
6. **Se sintieron** cansadas, pero **siguieron** el plan de entrenamiento. María Jesús y Paulina

Suggestion for *Piénsalo*
To draw students' attention to the stem change in the third-person forms of the preterit, you may wish to have students write the infinitive for each verb and circle the vowel change: *dormir → durmieron (o → u).* Noticing the vowel change serves as a warm-up for the grammar presentation that follows.

Note
According to the *Real Academia,* monosyllabic words do not usually carry a written accent, unless their meaning or function needs to be differentiated, e.g., *el* (article) vs. *él* (pronoun). Depending on regional pronunciation, some words can be monosyllabic or bisyllabic, and in this case, a written accent is helpful to clarify pronunciation norms. As an example, the preterit of *reír, rió,* is pronounced as one syllable in large areas of Latin America, including Mexico and Central America. In other regions, like Spain, Argentina, Ecuador, Colombia, and Venezuela, the bisyllabic pronunciation is more common. To avoid confusion about how it should be pronounced, *Mosaicos* treats it as a bisyllabic word and thus writes it with an accent. Other examples are the preterit forms of *criar, freír,* and *guiar.*

Suggestion for Preterit of stem-changing *-ir* verbs
Do a quick review of the verbs before starting the *Práctica* activities. Ask questions such as: *¿Cómo dormiste anoche, Alex? ¿Cómo durmió Alex?*, etc.

Preterit of stem-changing *-ir* verbs

- In the preterit, stem-changing **-ir** verbs change **e** → **i** and **o** → **u** in the **usted, él, ella,** and **ustedes, ellos/as** forms. The endings are the same as those of regular **-ir** verbs.

PREFERIR (e → i)			
yo	preferí	nosotros/as	preferimos
tú	preferiste	vosotros/as	preferisteis
Ud., él, ella	pref**i**rió	Uds., ellos/as	pref**i**rieron

DORMIR (o → u)			
yo	dormí	nosotros/as	dormimos
tú	dormiste	vosotros/as	dormisteis
Ud., él, ella	d**u**rmió	Uds., ellos/as	d**u**rmieron

Marta **prefirió** salir temprano. — *Marta preferred to leave early.*

Las jugadoras **durmieron** tranquilamente. — *The players slept peacefully.*

- The following are other stem-changing **-ir** verbs:

despedirse *to say good-bye* — Los hinchas se desp**i**dieron de su equipo. *The fans said good-bye to their team.*

divertirse *to have fun/ enjoy* — Todos se div**i**rtieron con la presentación de las barras paralelas. *Everyone enjoyed the performance on the parallel bars.*

morir *to die* — Un hincha m**u**rió de un ataque al corazón cuando su equipo perdió. *A fan died of a heart attack when his team lost.*

pedir *to ask for/order* — El entrenador p**i**dió agua para los jugadores. *The coach asked for water for the players.*

reír *to laugh* — El árbitro se r**i**ó cuando un perro cruzó la cancha. *The referee laughed when a dog crossed the field.*

repetir *to repeat* — El reportero rep**i**tió el nombre del jugador que marcó el gol. *The reporter repeated the name of the player who scored the goal.*

seguir *to follow* — Los jugadores s**i**guieron las instrucciones de su entrenador. *The players followed the instructions of their coach.*

sentirse *to feel* — Todos se s**i**ntieron felices con el triunfo. *Everyone felt happy about the victory.*

servir *to serve* — Los hinchas le s**i**rvieron perros calientes gratis al público. *The fans served free hot dogs to the public.*

vestirse *to get dressed* — Los jugadores se v**i**stieron para ir a celebrar. *The players got dressed to go out and celebrate.*

¿COMPRENDES?

Completa las oraciones con el pretérito de los verbos.

1. Durante la recepción, los jugadores prefirieron (preferir) beber cerveza.
2. El entrenador siguió (seguir) la tradición de servirles champaña.
3. Un jugador pidió (pedir) agua.
4. Los otros jugadores se rieron (reírse) de él.
5. Cuando recibieron sus medallas, los jugadores se sintieron (sentirse) orgullosos.
6. Todos se divirtieron (divertirse) mucho.

MySpanishLab
Learn more using Amplifire Dynamic Study Modules, Grammar Tutorials, and Extra Practice activities.

PRÁCTICA

7-24

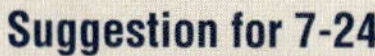

Suggestion for 7-24
You may wish to return to this activity after the uses of the preterit and imperfect are presented in *Capítulo 8* and *Capítulo 9* because it provides examples of the preterit to describe activities in a period in the past (The athlete's career in sports is now over).

Carrera de un campeón. **PREPARACIÓN.** Un famoso deportista recibió muchas medallas durante su carrera. ¿Cómo lo logró (*accomplished*)? Marca (✓) la alternativa más apropiada.

1. **a.** _____ Durmió poco antes de cada partido.
   b. _____ Siempre durmió por lo menos ocho horas.
2. **a.** _____ Prefirió evitar el alcohol.
   b. _____ Prefirió beber alcohol moderadamente.
3. **a.** _____ Se preparó solo.
   b. _____ Prefirió prepararse con un entrenador.
4. **a.** _____ Siguió las recomendaciones de su entrenador.
   b. _____ Les pidió consejos a sus amigos.
5. **a.** _____ Cuando no ganó un partido, se sintió deprimido.
   b. _____ Se sintió triste cuando no ganó un partido, pero pidió ayuda para mejorar.

INTERCAMBIOS. Usen la imaginación para hablar de la carrera del deportista.

se divirtió...

E1: *Yo creo que no se divirtió mucho durante su carrera. Y tú, ¿que crees?*

E2: *Yo creo que se divirtió porque le gusta mucho competir.*

1. durmió...
2. siguió una dieta especial de...
3. pidió...
4. se sintió...

7-25 

Momentos cruciales. **PREPARACIÓN.** Indica lo que hicieron las siguientes jugadoras del equipo femenino de básquetbol unos minutos antes del partido.

1. Marta ___se vistió___ (vestirse) con la camiseta número 3.
2. Ana y Luisa Fernanda ___siguieron___ (seguir) con atención los pasos del calentamiento (*warm-up*).
3. Carmen ___prefirió___ (preferir) no comer antes del partido.
4. Las jugadoras del equipo contrario ___se rieron___ (reírse) cuando su entrenadora les contó un chiste (*joke*).
5. La entrenadora les ___repitió___ (repetir) las instrucciones a todas las jugadoras.
6. El equipo ___se sintió___ (sentirse) animado (*encouraged*) con los aplausos del público.

INTERCAMBIOS. Piensa en un momento crucial en tu vida relacionado con los deportes y compártelo con tu compañero/a. Cuéntale cinco acciones o emociones relacionadas con el evento. Usa las siguientes preguntas como guía:

¿Qué pasó? ¿Cómo te sentiste? ¿Con qué número te vestiste? ¿Cuántos puntos marcaste? ¿Qué tipo de entrenamiento seguiste?...

Mi momento crucial fue cuando ganamos la final de básquetbol. Me sentí...

7-26  

Celebrando la victoria. Uno de los equipos de su universidad ganó un campeonato importante y ustedes hicieron una fiesta en su honor. Explíquenle a otra pareja los siguientes detalles de la fiesta. Usen los verbos de la lista.

despedirse	pedir	repetir	servir
divertirse	reír	sentirse	vestirse

1. hora y lugar de la fiesta
2. número de personas que asistieron y cómo se vistieron para la fiesta
3. tipo de cooperación que ustedes pidieron para los gastos de la fiesta
4. cómo se divirtieron en la fiesta
5. comida y bebida que sirvieron en la fiesta y tipo de música que escucharon
6. reconocimiento (*recognition*) que les dieron a los jugadores
7. sentimientos de los jugadores durante la fiesta
8. a qué hora se despidieron y se fueron de la fiesta los invitados

Situación

PREPARACIÓN. Lean la situación. Luego, compartan ejemplos de vocabulario, gramática y otra información que necesitan para desarrollar la conversación.

Role A. You had to work late last night and missed an important basketball game at your school. Call a friend who went to the game. After greeting your friend:

a. explain why you did not go;
b. ask questions about the game;
c. answer your friend's questions; and
d. accept your friend's invitation to go to another game next Saturday.

Role B. A friend calls to find out about last night's basketball game. Answer your friend's questions and then:

a. say that there is another game on Saturday;
b. find out if your friend is free that evening; and
c. if free, invite him/her to go with you.

	ROLE A	ROLE B
Vocabulario	Question words	Formulaic expressions related to making an invitation
Funciones y formas	Explaining the reason for something Past tense (preterit) Asking and answering questions Accepting an invitation Observing phone etiquette in Spanish	Asking and answering questions Past tense (preterit) Inviting someone to do something together: Present tense Reacting to what you hear

INTERCAMBIOS. Practica la conversación con tu compañero/a incorporando el vocabulario y las funciones de *Preparación*. Luego, represéntenla ante la clase.

4 Emphasizing or clarifying information

ROBERTO: Estas flores son **para ti,** Cristina.

CRISTINA: **¿Para mí?** Gracias, Roberto.

***

ROBERTO: Oye, Cristina. El partido es mañana. ¿Quieres ir **conmigo?**

CRISTINA: No puedo ir **contigo,** Roberto. Mis primos están aquí, y voy al partido **con ellos.**

Piénsalo. Indica quién dice cada oración, Roberto (**R**) o Cristina (**C**).

1. __R__ ¿Quieres ir **conmigo?**
2. __R__ Estas flores son **para ti.**
3. __C__ No puedo ir **contigo.**
4. __C__ **¿Para mí?**
5. __C__ Voy al partido **con ellos.**

Suggestion for *Piénsalo*
You may wish to have students connect the preposition (*para*) with the pronoun (*mí/ti* or *-migo/-tigo*) to prepare for the grammar explanation.

Pronouns after prepositions

- In *Capítulo 6* you used **a + mí, a + ti,** and so on, to clarify or emphasize the indirect object pronoun: **Le di el suéter a él.** These same pronouns are used after other prepositions, such as **de, para,** and **sin.**

a	+	mí
de		ti
para		usted, él, ella
por		nosotros/as
sin		vosotros/as
sobre		ustedes, ellos/as

Siempre habla **de ti.**	*He is always talking about you.*
Las raquetas son **para mí.**	*The racquets are for me.*
No quieren ir **sin nosotros.**	*They do not want to go without us.*

- In a few cases, Spanish does not use **mí** and **ti** after prepositions. After **con,** use **conmigo** and **contigo.** After **entre,** use **tú** y **yo.**

¿Vas al partido **conmigo?**	*Are you going to the game with me?*
Sí, voy **contigo.**	*Yes, I am going with you.*
Entre tú y **yo,** ella tiene unos problemas serios.	*Between you and me, she has some serious problems.*

Suggestion
You may want to mention that the prepositional pronoun *mí* has an accent mark to distinguish it from the possessive adjective *mi.*

¿COMPRENDES?

Completa las oraciones con los pronombres apropiados.

1. A __mí__ me gusta el café.
2. Susana no bebe café. A __ella__ le gustan solamente los refrescos.
3. Tenemos vecinos muy divertidos. Conversamos mucho con __ellos__.
4. Jorge, no puedo ir al partido __contigo__. Lo siento mucho.
5. Entre __tú__ y __yo__, esas chicas son terriblemente chismosas (*gossipy*).
6. Si no estás con ellas, hablan mal de __ti__.

MySpanishLab
Learn more using Amplifire Dynamic Study Modules, Grammar Tutorials, and Extra Practice activities.

PRÁCTICA

7-27 

Un amigo preguntón. Un amigo de Rosario le hace muchas preguntas. Asocia sus preguntas con un comentario lógico de Rosario.

1. __c__ ¿Con quién vas a ir al partido de tenis, Rosario?
2. __f__ ¿Por qué no vemos las finales del campeonato con Sofía?
3. __a__ Rosario, ¿para quién es esta raqueta de tenis?
4. __b__ ¿Pueden ir mis amigos a la cancha con nosotros?
5. __d__ Después del partido de ayer encontramos una sudadera. ¿Es de Carlos?
6. __e__ ¿De quién van a recibir el trofeo los ganadores?

a. La compré para ti.
b. Imposible. No podemos ir con ellos. Tengo solo dos billetes.
c. Contigo, ¡por supuesto!
d. Sí, es de él.
e. De nosotros. De ti y de mí. ¡Qué emocionante!
f. Prefiero verlas sin ella. Habla mucho y no puedo concentrarme.

Cultura

La plaza

Plazas play a prominent role in everyday life throughout Latin America and Spain. Most cities and towns have a main square downtown, but it is also common to find smaller plazas in every neighborhood where families go to walk and socialize. In addition to cafés and shops, plazas also host open-air markets, concerts, and fairs. Many plazas are also used as the starting or ending points for bike races or other athletic competitions.

Comparaciones. ¿En qué lugares de tu ciudad prefiere reunirse la gente? ¿Existe algún lugar histórico en tu ciudad? ¿Qué actividades se pueden hacer allí?

▲ La Plaza Mayor en Salamanca, España

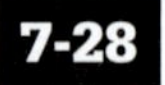 

¿Con quién va? **PREPARACIÓN.** Completa la siguiente conversación usando pronombres.

JULIA: Salgo ahora para la plaza a tomar algo y mirar escaparates. ¿Vienes conmigo?

CELIA: No, no puedo ir (1) __contigo__. Tengo que trabajar hasta muy tarde.

JULIA: ¡Cuánto lo siento! Entonces, ¿vas a salir después con Roberto?

CELIA: Sí, voy a ir con (2) __él__ más tarde.

JULIA: ¡Ah, claro! No puede salir sin (3) __ti__. Tú eres su mejor amiga.

CELIA: Sí, somos muy buenos amigos. Entonces, ¿con quién vas a salir?

JULIA: Pues, mi hermana está aquí, y voy a ir con (4) __ella__.

 **INTERCAMBIOS.** Cambien la conversación entre Julia y Celia para hablar de sus propios planes.

7-29 

Haciendo planes. Escoge una de las dos actividades e invita a tu compañero/a a hacerla.

MODELO ir al cine/teatro

E1: *¿Cuándo puedes ir al cine conmigo?*

E2: *Puedo ir contigo el sábado.*

1. estudiar español/historia/biología
2. ir al parque/al partido de béisbol/al concierto
3. jugar al golf/al tenis/al vóleibol
4. preparar una fiesta de cumpleaños/una cena para un amigo

Situación

PREPARACIÓN. Lean la situación. Luego, compartan ejemplos de vocabulario, gramática y otra información que necesitan para desarrollar la conversación.

Role A. One of your friends is a basketball player. He gave you two tickets for today's game, but you have no transportation. Call a friend who has a car. After greeting him/her:

a. explain how you got the tickets for the game;
b. invite your friend to go with you; and
c. explain that you have no transportation.

Role B. A friend calls you to invite you to today's basketball game. After exchanging greetings:

a. thank your friend for the invitation;
b. respond that you would be delighted to go with him/her;
c. say that you can pick him/her up in your car; and
d. agree on a time and place.

	ROLE A	ROLE B
Vocabulario	Sports-related expressions	Sports-related expressions
Funciones y formas	Explaining the reason for something Preterit Present tense Inviting someone to do something with you Making arrangements to meet with someone	Thanking someone Accepting an invitation Making arrangements to meet with someone

INTERCAMBIOS. Practica la conversación con tu compañero/a incorporando el vocabulario y las funciones de *Preparación*. Luego, represéntenla ante la clase.

5 Talking about the past

ABUELA: ¡Bienvenidos! Pasen, por favor. ¿No **vino** Carmencita? ¿Está enferma?

MADRE: Está trabajando. **Estuvo** en la biblioteca hasta muy tarde anoche, pero no **pudo** terminar su proyecto. Nos **dijo** que es largo y difícil.

***

CARMENCITA: ¿Mis padres? **Tuvieron** que ir a la casa de mi abuela, pero yo no **quise** ir a otra cena aburrida. Les **dije** una pequeña mentira sobre un proyecto…

Piénsalo. Marca (✓) si las afirmaciones probablemente expresan la **verdad,** una **mentira** (*lie*) o **no se sabe,** según la conversación.

	VERDAD	MENTIRA	NO SE SABE
1. Carmencita **tuvo** que terminar un proyecto.		✓	
2. Los padres de Carmencita **tuvieron** que ir a la casa de la abuela.	✓		
3. Carmencita no **quiso** ir a la casa de su abuela.	✓		
4. Carmencita **estuvo** en la biblioteca por muchas horas.			✓
5. Carmencita **hizo** un proyecto para una clase.			✓
6. Carmencita les **dijo** la verdad a sus padres.		✓	

Some irregular preterits

- Some verbs have irregular forms in the preterit because they use different stems than in the present tense. The preterit endings are added to those stems. Note that the **yo, usted, él,** and **ella** preterit endings of these verbs are unstressed and therefore do not have written accents.
- The verbs **hacer, querer,** and **venir** have an **i** in the preterit stem.

INFINITIVE	NEW STEM	PRETERIT FORMS
hacer	**hic-**	hice, hiciste, hizo, hicimos, hicisteis, hicieron
querer	**quis-**	quise, quisiste, quiso, quisimos, quisisteis, quisieron
venir	**vin-**	vine, viniste, vino, vinimos, vinisteis, vinieron

The verbs **estar, tener, poder, poner,** and **saber** have a **u** in the preterit stem.

INFINITIVE	NEW STEM	PRETERIT FORMS
estar	**estuv-**	estuve, estuviste, estuvo, estuvimos, estuvisteis, estuvieron
tener	**tuv-**	tuve, tuviste, tuvo, tuvimos, tuvisteis, tuvieron
poder	**pud-**	pude, pudiste, pudo, pudimos, pudisteis, pudieron
poner	**pus-**	puse, pusiste, puso, pusimos, pusisteis, pusieron
saber	**sup-**	supe, supiste, supo, supimos, supisteis, supieron

LENGUA

- The verb **querer** in the preterit followed by an infinitive normally means *to try* (*but fail*) *to do something.*

  Quise hacerlo ayer. *I tried to do it yesterday.*
- **Poder** used in the preterit usually means *to manage to do something.*

  Pude hacerlo esta mañana. *I managed to do it this morning.*
- **Saber** in the preterit normally means *to learn* in the sense of *to find out.*

  Supe que llegó anoche. *I learned (found out) that he arrived last night.*

Suggestion
Provide additional input by relating a recent experience (real or imaginary) and using visuals to introduce the preterit of these verbs and others. Example: *El año pasado estuve en Miami. Estuve en un hotel en la playa y pude hablar español en los restaurantes y en las calles, porque en Miami viven muchos hispanos. Jugué a la lotería pero no tuve suerte. No gané nada, y además gasté mucho dinero en las tiendas y los clubes. Pero me divertí mucho.* Personalize: *¿Dónde estuviste el verano pasado? ¿Te gustó el lugar? ¿Qué hiciste allí?*

Follow-up for Some irregular preterits
After students have practiced producing irregular preterit forms in the activities in this section, you may wish to go back to the *Piénsalo* activity to have students correct the lies that Carmencita told and create an alternative account of her activities.

- The verbs **decir, traer,** and all verbs ending in **-ducir** (e.g., **traducir** *to translate*) have a **j** in the stem and use the ending **-eron** instead of **-ieron. Decir** also has an **i** in the stem.

INFINITIVE	NEW STEM	PRETERIT FORMS
decir	**dij-**	di**j**e, di**j**iste, di**j**o, di**j**imos, di**j**isteis, di**j**eron
traer	**traj-**	tra**j**e, tra**j**iste, tra**j**o, tra**j**imos, tra**j**isteis, tra**j**eron
traducir	**traduj-**	tradu**j**e, tradu**j**iste, tradu**j**o, tradu**j**imos, tradu**j**isteis, tradu**j**eron

e ¿COMPRENDES?

Completa las oraciones con el pretérito de los verbos.

1. Ayer Luis __tuvo__ (tener) un accidente de automóvil.
2. Por eso, sus amigas Laura y Elena no __pudieron__ (poder) usar su auto.
3. Ellas __tuvieron__ (tener) que tomar el autobús.
4. Las amigas __pidieron__ (pedir) una ambulancia para Luis.
5. Laura __hizo__ (hacer) los trámites para su admisión en el hospital.
6. Las amigas __se despidieron__ (despedirse) después de dejarlo en el hospital.

MySpanishLab
Learn more using Amplifire Dynamic Study Modules, Grammar Tutorials, and Extra Practice activities.

PRÁCTICA

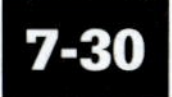

¿Qué hicieron? **PREPARACIÓN.** Marca (✓) las tareas que probablemente hicieron los miembros de un equipo de hockey antes del partido, y las que probablemente no hicieron.

	SÍ	NO
1. poder lavar las sudaderas	______	______
2. ver videos de partidos anteriores	______	______
3. ponerse los uniformes nuevos	______	______
4. hacer ejercicios de calentamiento (*warm-up*)	______	______
5. traer los nuevos cascos (*helmets*) a la cancha	______	______
6. tener tiempo para estudiar las nuevas estrategias del partido	______	______

INTERCAMBIOS. Después, háganse las preguntas para compartir sus respuestas.

E1: *¿Compraron zapatos nuevos para jugar?*
E2: *Sí, probablemente los compraron.*

Follow-up for 7-30
Have students ask each other what they really did yesterday.

7-31 

Unos días de descanso. Tu compañero/a estuvo unos días en Argentina (o Uruguay). Hazle preguntas para saber más de su viaje.

1. lugares adonde fue
2. tiempo que estuvo allí
3. cosas interesantes que hizo
4. los lugares que le gustaron más
5. si pudo hablar español y con quién(es)

Suggestion for 7-31
Students can consult the *Enfoque cultural* section in this chapter for information on these countries, or they can make up details of their trip.

Suggestions for 7-32
You may use visual aids to teach students to construct a cohesive oral narration. Present and model the following expressions: *pero, por eso/por esa razón, primero, después,* etc. Encourage students to use a variety of verbs by brainstorming verbs they will need and writing the infinitives on the board.

Suggestion
You may wish to assign one drawing to each pair so they can develop a detailed story about it.

Note for En *directo*
Before doing activity 7-32, first have students read the expressions in *En directo.* Then have them listen to the dialogue and encourage them to use the expressions in their own conversation.

Audioscript for *En directo*
BELKIS: *Ay, Sara. Ayer conocí al amor de mi vida.*
SARA: *¡No me digas! ¿Qué pasó?*
BELKIS: *Estaba en un café en el centro cuando lo vi. Me miró y enseguida ¡vino a saludarme!*
SARA: *¿Y qué más pasó?*
BELKIS: *Me sentí tan nerviosa.*
SARA: *¡Cuenta, cuenta!*
BELKIS: *Por fin se me pasaron los nervios y le toqué la cabeza y el pelo y las orejas. ¡Qué perrito tan cariñoso!*
SARA: *¡¿Cómo?!*

Suggestions for *Lengua*
Hace meaning *ago.* To clarify the concept, ask *¿Qué hora es?* Students reply *Es/Son la(s)...* Then ask *¿Cuándo empezó esta clase?* Then say *La clase empezó hace... minutos.* Write the formula *pretérito + hace +* (*minutos, horas,* etc.) on the board and give other examples. Then repeat the process with the second formulation: *hace +* (*minutos, horas, etc.*) *+ que + pretérito.*
You may write on the board several years and actions: *1990–llegar a San Antonio; 1992–empezar a estudiar; 1996–casarse; 2000–tener el primer hijo.* Then create a story and ask questions: *¿Cuándo llegó a San Antonio? Ah, hace... años que llegó a*

7-32 

¿Qué ocurrió? Miren los dibujos. Túrnense y expliquen con detalles todo lo que le ocurrió a Javier el día de su cumpleaños. Después, cuéntale a tu compañero/a lo que hiciste tú el día de tu cumpleaños.

LENGUA

Hace, meaning *ago*

- To indicate the time that has passed since an action was completed, use **hace** + *length of time* + **que** + *preterit verb.*

  Hace dos meses **que** fui a la Copa Mundial. *I went to the World Cup two months* ago.

  Hace una hora **que** empezó el partido. *The game started an hour* ago.

- When **hace** + *length of time* ends the sentence, omit **que.**

  Fui a la Copa Mundial **hace** dos meses.

  El partido empezó **hace** una hora.

En directo

To express interest and to ask for details:

¡No me digas! ¿Qué pasó? *You don't say! What happened?*

¿Y qué más pasó? *And what else happened?*

¡Cuenta, cuenta! *Tell me more!*

 Listen to a conversation with these expressions.

Situación  

PREPARACIÓN. Lean la situación. Luego, compartan ejemplos de vocabulario, gramática y otra información que necesitan para desarrollar la conversación.

Role A. Congratulations! You entered a contest (**concurso**) and won an all-expenses-paid trip to attend the World Cup. Tell your classmate that you won the contest and that you went to the World Cup. Answer all of his/her questions in detail.

Role B. Your classmate won a contest and tells you about it. Ask
a. how he/she found out about the contest;
b. how long he/she was away;
c. how many games he/she attended;
d. with whom he/she went; and
e. details about the last game.

	ROLE A	ROLE B
Vocabulario	Expressions related to a contest and traveling Sports	Expressions related to a contest and traveling Sports
Funciones y formas	Telling someone some good news Answering questions	Reacting to what you hear Asking follow-up questions

INTERCAMBIOS. Practica la conversación con tu compañero/a incorporando el vocabulario y las funciones de *Preparación.* Luego, represéntenla ante la clase.

EN ACCIÓN

Vamos a hacer surf

San Antonio. ¿Y cuántos años hace que empezó a estudiar? ¿Cuántos años hace que se casó? ¿Cuántos años hace que tuvo su primer hijo? Personalize and encourage students to tell their partners about their experiences.

Expansion for 7-33
You may wish to expand this activity by giving students a list of sports. Have them work in groups to create a list of words that they associate with each sport.

7-33 Antes de ver 

El surf. En este segmento, Esteban va a enseñarles a hacer surf a sus amigos. Marca (✓) las palabras que asocias con este deporte.

1. ✓	el traje de baño	**5.** ____	la pista
2. ✓	el buen tiempo	**6.** ✓	el equilibrio
3. ✓	las olas (*waves*)	**7.** ✓	la playa
4. ____	la pelota	**8.** ____	los palos

7-34 Mientras ves 

¿Qué pasó? Indica (✓) si las siguientes oraciones son ciertas o falsas. Corrige las falsas.

	CIERTO	FALSO
1. Federico llega tarde porque está trabajando en su proyecto. *No se despertó a tiempo.*		✓
2. Hace buen día para hacer surf.	✓	
3. Héctor practica el tenis y el béisbol.	✓	
4. A Esteban le gusta hacer surf.	✓	
5. En Lima hay una playa que se llama Waikiki Beach.	✓	
6. En Perú hace buen tiempo durante los meses de junio, julio y agosto. *Hace fresco y generalmente está nublado.*		✓
7. El deporte de *sandboard* empezó en Brasil.	✓	

7-35 Después de ver 

¡Al agua! PREPARACIÓN. En este segmento de video, los chicos fueron a la playa a hacer surf. Numera las actividades según el orden en que ocurrieron en el video.

a. __3__ Héctor mostró un video sobre las playas de Lima.

b. __5__ Los chicos se rieron mucho de Esteban.

c. __2__ Los chicos hablaron de sus deportes preferidos.

d. __4__ Esteban corrió hacia el agua con la tabla de surf.

e. __1__ Héctor y Esteban esperaron a los otros por mucho tiempo.

 **INTERCAMBIOS.** Hablen sobre la primera vez que practicaron un deporte nuevo. ¿Qué deporte fue? ¿Cuándo fue y con quién(es) lo hicieron? ¿Necesitaron comprar un equipo o ropa especial? ¿Qué dificultades tuvieron? ¿Continúan practicándolo hoy?

Mosaicos

Suggestions for audio
Listening activities provide many learning opportunities when done in the classroom and can be used to enhance communication. Instructors are also encouraged to guide students' attention to certain passages, and to vary the ways in which the listening activity is presented.

Audioscript for *Escucha*
REPORTERO: *Nicolás, bienvenido al Programa de Deportes. Sabemos que acabas de regresar de Bariloche, donde te entrenaste por algún tiempo.*
NICOLÁS: *Sí, efectivamente. Estuve dos meses esquiando, junio y julio. Me encantó el lugar. Me gustó mucho Cerro Catedral; es un lugar maravilloso, con 65 kilómetros de pistas para esquiar. La ciudad de Bariloche es fantástica y la gente es muy amable.*
REPORTERO: *¿Fue tu primera visita a Bariloche?*
NICOLÁS: *No. En mi infancia fui con mis padres varias veces.*
REPORTERO: *¿Y las pistas? ¿Estuvieron bien?*
NICOLÁS: *Sí, estuvieron maravillosas, porque la primera semana de junio nevó mucho, unos 30 centímetros de nieve, y pude esquiar muy bien. Al final llovió dos días y no pude esquiar mucho. Por eso regresé a Buenos Aires. Pero me entrené y me siento muy bien.*
REPORTERO: *¡Qué bien! Y, dime, ¿a qué distancia está Cerro Catedral de Bariloche?*
NICOLÁS: *Está muy cerca, a solo 20 kilómetros.*
REPORTERO: *¿Y cuándo regresas a Bariloche?*
NICOLÁS: *El próximo año. Voy a ir con unos amigos que quieren prepararse allí también.*
REPORTERO: *Muy bien y buena suerte en la próxima competencia.*
NICOLÁS: *Muchas gracias.*

ESCUCHA

ESTRATEGIA

Differentiate fact from opinion

When you listen to or watch the news or a talk show, you need to distinguish facts from opinions. Facts are provable pieces of information based on statistics, data, and other verifiable evidence. Opinions are personal points of view that combine attitudes and beliefs with factual information.

7-36 Presentational

Preparación. Vas a escuchar una conversación entre un reportero y Nicolás, un esquiador argentino que habla sobre su viaje a Bariloche, Argentina. Antes de escuchar la conversación, escribe sobre el tiempo que probablemente hizo durante su estadía en Bariloche. Después, escribe una opinión sobre la gente del lugar que Nicolás probablemente va a conocer. Finalmente, escribe dos afirmaciones que reflejan la opinión de Nicolás sobre el lugar que va a visitar.

1. el tiempo que probablemente hizo
2. una opinión sobre la gente que conoció
3. una opinión sobre el lugar que visitó

7-37  Interpretive

Escucha. Listen to the interview and write in Spanish three pieces of factual information and three opinions Nicolás offered about the place and/or the people.

Información concreta: Cerro Catedral tiene 65 kilómetros de pistas para esquiar; nevó unos 30 centímetros de nieve; llovió dos días; Cerro Catedral está a 20 kilómetros de Bariloche.
Opinión personal: Me gustó mucho Cerro Catedral; Cerro Catedral es un lugar maravilloso; la ciudad es fantástica; la gente es muy amable.

Comprueba
I was able to ...

____ **listen for specific information.**

____ **take good notes while listening.**

____ **distinguish facts from opinions.**

7-38  Interpersonal

Un paso más. Hazle preguntas a tu compañero/a para averiguar la siguiente información.

1. un deporte que practica y su opinión sobre ese deporte
2. el nombre de su deportista favorito/a y su opinión sobré él/ella
3. algún dato interesante sobre este deporte
4. una experiencia personal positiva que tuvo relacionada con este deporte

HABLA

  Interpretive

Preparación. Investiguen en Internet la siguiente información sobre un deporte que se practica en Argentina o Uruguay.

1. el nombre del deporte
2. dos o tres datos históricos sobre el deporte: cuándo empezó a practicarse; dónde empezó; algo interesante sobre los comienzos (*origin*) del deporte
3. una persona argentina o uruguaya famosa en la historia de este deporte: nombre, fecha y lugar de nacimiento; datos sobre su carrera deportiva

ESTRATEGIA

Focus on key information

In *Capítulo 6* you practiced taking notes to understand and remember something you heard. Here you will take the next step: turning your notes into a brief report to present to the class. Follow these steps: 1) Decide what aspects of the topic you want to report on; 2) then listen for and take notes on those aspects; and 3) organize your notes for your presentation.

7-40  Presentational

Habla. Hagan una breve presentación sobre el deporte y el/la deportista que investigaron.

Comprueba

In our preparation and presentation . . .

____ **I spoke in Spanish as much as my partners.**

____ **I took good notes and contributed useful information.**

____ **My part of the presentation was clear and easy to understand.**

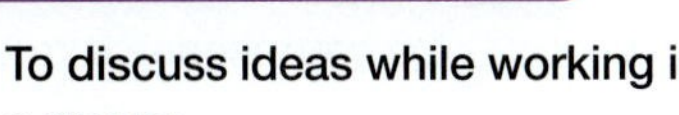

En directo

To discuss ideas while working in a group:

¿Qué te/le/les parece esto?
What do you think about this?
¿Qué te/le/les parece si decimos/organizamos…?
How about if we say/organize . . . ?
¿Por qué no lees/hablas/miras…?
Why don't you read/say/look at . . . ?

To propose a new idea:
¡Oigan, tengo una idea!
Listen, I have an idea.

Listen to a conversation with these expressions.

7-41  Interpersonal

Un paso más. De las presentaciones en clase, elijan un deporte y un/a deportista y preparen preguntas para hacer a otros compañeros. Incluyan la información indicada en las fichas (*note cards*) siguientes.

Deporte	Deportista
Nombre:	Nombre y nacionalidad:
Dónde y cuándo empezó a practicarse:	Fecha de nacimiento:
Dónde se practica ahora:	Campeonatos que ganó:
Su popularidad:	Su reputación nacional e internacional:

En directo

To maintain the interest of listeners:

Hay hechos/datos interesantes sobre…
La información que tenemos sobre… es increíble.
¡Imagínense! Ganó el primer puesto en…
Este/a deportista juega al… como nadie.

 Listen to a conversation with these expressions.

Suggestions for 7-40
Guide students to share equitably among group members the preparation and presentation tasks. Remind students that the goal is a clear, comprehensible presentation in their own words, since classmates will take notes and prepare a brief report on what they have heard.
To encourage classmates to participate as active listeners, have them write at least two follow-up questions or comments for the presenters, and encourage them to ask for clarification when necessary.

Audioscript for *En directo*
LUIS: *Pienso que debemos hacer algo para animar a nuestro equipo. ¿Qué les parece esto? Hacemos un afiche para cada jugador.*
HÉCTOR: *Me parece bien, pero ¿qué les parece si organizamos un baile para obtener fondos? Necesitan nuevos uniformes.*
OLIVIA: *¡Me encanta esa idea! ¿Por qué no hablas con John? Él es muy buen* disc jockey.
ANDREA: *¡Oigan, tengo una idea! Vamos a hacer las dos cosas. Yo ayudo a Luis con los afiches y Olivia y Héctor organizan el baile.*

Suggestion for 7-41
To enable students to give their brief reports (no more than 1 minute long), you may wish to have several simultaneous presentations to different small groups, or you may ask 2 or 3 students to give reports at the beginning or end of several future class sessions.

Audioscript for *En directo*
PROFESORA LYNCH: *Chicos, hay datos interesantes sobre la alimentación y el éxito en los deportes. La información que tenemos sobre la importancia de la buena nutrición es increíble.*
CHRIS: *La profesora tiene razón. Mi prima se convirtió en campeona cuando decidió comer cosas más saludables y eliminar la comida basura. Ahora practica karate como nadie. ¡Imagínense! Ganó el primer puesto en su clase después de entrenarse por solo dos meses.*

Suggestion for 7-42
As a warm-up, review and reinforce some key words in the activity by asking: *¿Con qué palabras asocian ustedes los siguientes deportes, con agua, nieve o arena?* (Write words on the board.) 1. *el esquí;* 2. *la natación;* 3. *el vóleibol en la playa;* 4. *el surf.* You may also have students brainstorm popular sports in the U.S. For each sport, ask students where it is practiced, what equipment or clothing is needed, and what weather conditions favor its practice.

Standard 1.2 Students understand and interpret written and spoken language on a variety of topics. In this section students read a text about the passion for sports in Uruguay, which is followed by comprehension and production activities. Both types of activities help students build their analytical skills and their overall comprehension of written Spanish.

LEE

7-42 Interpersonal

Preparación. Mira el texto "Los deportes: Una pasión uruguaya". Lee el título y examina las fotos. Busca nombres de lugares y deportes conocidos. Luego, responde a las preguntas.

1. Después de examinar el texto, selecciona el posible tema.
   - **a.** los lugares en Uruguay donde se practican los deportes
   - **b.** los atletas más famosos de Uruguay
   - **c.** el amor de los uruguayos por los deportes
2. Marca (✓) las ideas que probablemente vas a encontrar en el texto.
   - **a.** _✓_ los deportes más populares de Uruguay
   - **b.** ____ el origen de los deportes de Uruguay
   - **c.** _✓_ los lugares donde se practican algunos deportes en Uruguay
   - **d.** ____ los campeonatos que ganaron los equipos de fútbol uruguayo
   - **e.** ____ los deportes favoritos de los uruguayos en comparación con los de otros países latinoamericanos

ESTRATEGIA

Predict and guess content

You may enhance your comprehension of a text by predicting and guessing its content before you start to read. Begin by brainstorming the information you are likely to find in the text and identifying the text format.

Intercambios. Háganse preguntas y compartan la información que recogieron.

1. ¿Te gustan los deportes individuales o prefieres los de equipo? ¿Por qué?
2. ¿Sabes esquiar? ¿Esquías en la nieve o en el agua? ¿Esquías bien o regular?
3. ¿Qué tipos de surf conoces? ¿Alguna vez oíste hablar (*Have you heard about*) del surf en la arena? ¿Qué sabes de ese deporte?

7-43 Interpretive

Lee. Lee el artículo y haz lo siguiente:

1. Indica dos razones que explican la popularidad del fútbol en Uruguay.
2. Nombra tres deportes de equipo, dos individuales y uno que no requiere una pelota.
3. Explica por qué Punta del Este es un lugar ideal para practicar el surf acuático.

Comprueba
I was able to ...

____ use my knowledge of sports to anticipate the content of the reading.

____ distinguish between facts and opinions.

____ understand most of the information in the text.

LOS DEPORTES, UNA PASIÓN URUGUAYA

Uruguay es un país pequeño donde los deportes son fundamentales en la vida de las personas.

Entre las grandes pasiones nacionales está el fútbol. Desde su infancia, muchos uruguayos acompañan fielmente[1] a sus equipos. En varias ocasiones, la selección nacional uruguaya ganó títulos y campeonatos importantes.

Pero los uruguayos también tienen otras pasiones. El básquetbol, el ciclismo, el fútbol de salón, el rugby, el boxeo y la pelota de mano son otros deportes muy populares.

Las hermosas playas del Uruguay también favorecen los deportes acuáticos, como el surf, que es muy popular. En 1993 Uruguay participó en el Primer Campeonato Panamericano del Surf en Isla de Margarita, Venezuela. Hoy en día los surfistas uruguayos participan en competencias nacionales e internacionales, hasta[2] en los Juegos Olímpicos.

Uno de los lugares favoritos para practicar el surf es Punta del Este. Ubicada al sureste del Uruguay, a 140 kilómetros de Montevideo, Punta del Este es una hermosa península de enormes playas, con arenas finas y gruesas, rocas y un entorno de bosques y médanos[3].

Precisamente en estos médanos nació una variante del surf: el surf en la arena o *sandsurf*. Los brasileños inventaron este deporte en los años ochenta para divertirse en las playas cuando no había olas grandes. El deporte creció rápidamente en Uruguay, ya que tiene muchas playas bonitas con médanos enormes. Por ejemplo, los médanos de Valizas son los más grandes de Sudamérica, algunos con 30 metros de altura y una longitud de bajada[4] de aproximadamente 125 metros. Sin embargo, el tema del surf en la arena es polémico[5]. Las autoridades uruguayas están controlando e incluso prohibiendo la práctica de este deporte por el posible deterioro ecológico que causa. La prohibición del surf en la arena no va a detener el espíritu activo de los uruguayos, quienes van a buscar o inventar otras opciones para entretenerse.

La costa de Valizas

[1] *faithfully* [2] *even* [3] *sand dunes* [4] *slope* [5] *controversial*

7-44 Presentational

Un paso más. Seleccionen algún deporte. Preparen una ficha sobre ese deporte sin mencionar el nombre, y luego intercambien su ficha con la de otro grupo. Traten de adivinar el deporte de sus compañeros.

1. lugar donde se practica
2. deporte individual o en grupo (número de personas en el equipo)
3. en qué clima o estación se practica
4. un jugador famoso/una jugadora famosa del deporte
5. otra información relevante

Note for En *directo*
Before doing activity 7-45, first have students read the expressions in En *directo*. Then have them listen to the dialogue and encourage them to use the expressions in their interviews.

Audioscript for *En directo*
DOCTOR VALLE: *Los expertos afirman que es más importante comer bien que hacer ejercicio. Sin embargo, la investigación que terminé indica que ambos son igual de importantes.*
DELIA: *A mí me parece que depende de la persona. A algunas personas les hace falta más ejercicio mientras que a otros les conviene más tener una dieta equilibrada.*

ESCRIBE

7-45  Interpersonal

Preparación. Entrevista a tres compañeros sobre los siguientes temas.

1. las ventajas o desventajas de hacer ejercicio físico durante la infancia (*childhood*)
2. las ventajas o desventajas de unos deportes sobre otros
3. los deportes y actividades físicas que practicaron de niños
4. los deportes que practican ahora

En directo

To express facts:

Los expertos afirman/dicen/ aseguran que…

La investigación indica que…

Los estudios muestran que…

To express an opinión:

A mí me parece que…

 Listen to a conversation with these expressions.

ESTRATEGIA

Use supporting details

Supporting details are facts and examples that follow the topic sentence and make up the body of a paragraph. They should support the main idea of the paragraph and be placed in a logical order. You should then write a closing sentence that summarizes your main point.

7-46 Interpretive

Escribe. Escribe un informe sobre el papel del ejercicio en la salud de los niños. Usa la información de 7-45 para escribir tu informe. Incluye lo siguiente:

1. los beneficios del ejercicio físico para los niños
2. los tipos de actividad física que son divertidos y beneficiosos para los niños
3. las estrategias para aumentar la actividad física

Comprueba

I was able to …

____ present my main idea clearly, using relevant vocabulary.

____ use facts and examples to develop my main ideas.

____ provide the supporting details in a logical order.

Suggestion for 7-47
Before presenting their information to the class, have students check the following:
1. *la organización y la cantidad de información;*
2. *el vocabulario y las estructuras;*
3. *las expresiones para presentar hechos u opiniones;*
4. *la ortografía y los acentos.*

7-47  Presentational

Un paso más. Presenta tu informe a la clase. Tus compañeros van a hacerte preguntas.

En este capítulo...

Comprueba lo que sabes

Go to ***MySpanishLab*** to review what you have learned in this chapter. Practice with the following:

Vocabulario

LOS DEPORTES
Sports

el atletismo *track and field*
el baloncesto/el básquetbol *basketball*
el béisbol *baseball*
el ciclismo *cycling*
el esquí *skiing, ski*
el fútbol (americano) *soccer (football)*
el golf *golf*
el hockey sobre hierba *field hockey*
la natación *swimming*
el tenis *tennis*
el vóleibol *volleyball*

LAS PERSONAS
People

el árbitro *umpire, referee*
el campeón/la campeona *champion*
el/la ciclista *cyclist*
el/la entrenador/a *coach*
el equipo *team; equipment*
el/la hincha *fan*
el/la jugador/a *player*
el/la tenista *tennis player*

LA NATURALEZA
Nature

el árbol *tree*
el lago *lake*

PALABRAS Y EXPRESIONES ÚTILES
Useful Words and Expressions

cada *each*
conmigo *with me*
contigo *with you* (familiar)
contrario/a *opposing*
el penalti *penalty* (in sports)

EL TIEMPO
Weather

está despejado *it's clear*
está nublado *it's cloudy*
hace fresco *it's cool*
hace viento *it's windy*
el hielo *ice*
la lluvia *rain*
la nieve *snow*

LOS LUGARES
Places

el campo *field*
la cancha *court, golf course*
la piscina/la pileta *pool*
la pista *slope; court; track*

EL EQUIPO DEPORTIVO
Sports equipment

el bate *bat*
el balón/la pelota *ball*
el cesto/la cesta *basket, hoop*
los palos *golf clubs*
la raqueta *racquet*
la red *net*

VERBOS
Verbs

congelar(se) *to freeze*
construir *to build, to develop*
discutir *to argue*
durar *to last*
enfadarse *to get angry*
esquiar *to ski*
ganar *to win*
hacer parapente *to go paragliding*
hacer surf *to surf*
ir(se) *to go away, to leave*
jugar (ue) a los bolos *to bowl*
levantar pesas *to lift weights*
llover (ue) *to rain*
meter un gol *to score a goal*
nevar (ie) *to snow*
oír *to hear*
patinar *to skate*
perder (ie) *to lose*
pitar *to whistle*
preparar(se) *to train*
recorrer *to travel, to cover (distance)*
traducir (zc) *to translate*

LOS EVENTOS
Events

el campeonato *championship*
la carrera *race*
el juego/el partido *game*

LAS ESTACIONES
Seasons

el invierno *winter*
el otoño *fall*
la primavera *spring*
el verano *summer*

See page 252 for other reflexive verbs.

See page 260 for other stem-changing **-ir** verbs.

Introduction to chapter
Introduce holidays and celebrations, the chapter theme, and ask questions to recycle content from the previous chapter. Related questions: *¿Cuándo es tu cumpleaños? ¿Cómo lo celebras? ¿Te enfadas si tus amigos no te felicitan? ¿Cómo lo celebraste el año pasado? ¿Qué te regalaron tus amigos o familiares? ¿Qué otras festividades celebras?*

Integrated Performance Assessment: Three Modes of Communication

Presentational: See activities 8-8, 8-34, 8-37, 8-42, and 8-44.

Interpretive: See activities 8-1, 8-2, 8-3, 8-4, 8-5, 8-8, 8-9, 8-10, 8-11, 8-13, 8-14, 8-15, 8-19, 8-21, 8-22, 8-24, 8-27, 8-29, 8-31, 8-32, 8-33, 8-35, 8-39, 8-41, and 8-45.

Interpersonal: See activities 8-2, 8-3, 8-4, 8-5, 8-6, 8-7, 8-8, 8-9, 8-10, 8-11, 8-12, 8-13, 8-14, 8-15, 8-16, 8-17, 8-18, 8-19, 8-20, 8-21, 8-23, 8-24, 8-25, 8-26, 8-27, 8-28, 8-29, 8-33, 8-36, 8-38, 8-40, 8-43, and all *Situación* activities.

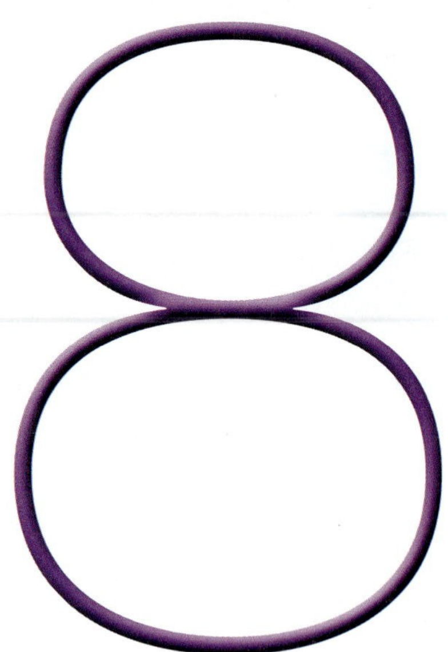

8 ¿Cuáles son tus tradiciones?

ENFOQUE CULTURAL
México

VOCABULARIO EN CONTEXTO
Las fiestas y las tradiciones
Otras celebraciones
Las invitaciones

MOSAICO CULTURAL
Los carnavales y las tradiciones

FUNCIONES Y FORMAS
The imperfect
The preterit and the imperfect
Comparisons of inequality
Comparisons of equality
The superlative

EN ACCIÓN
Hay que celebrar

MOSAICOS
ESCUCHA Draw conclusions based on what you know
HABLA Conduct an interview
LEE Make inferences
ESCRIBE Select and sequence details

EN ESTE CAPÍTULO...
Comprueba lo que sabes
Vocabulario

LEARNING OUTCOMES

You will be able to:

- discuss situations and celebrations
- describe conditions and express ongoing actions in the past
- tell stories about past events
- compare people and things
- talk about Mexico in terms of practices and perspectives
- share information about celebrations in Hispanic countries and compare cultural similarities

ENFOQUE cultural

MÉXICO

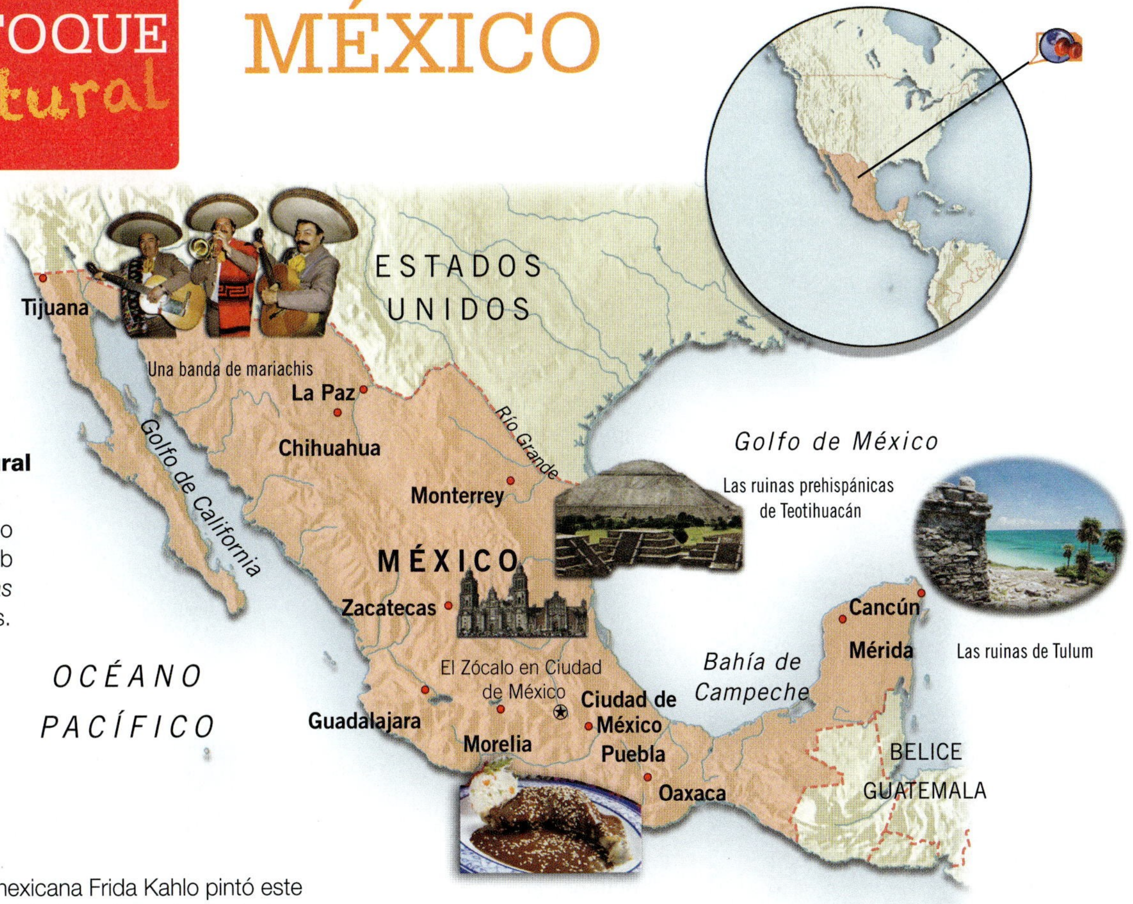

Enfoque cultural

To learn more about Mexico, go to MySpanishLab to view the *Vistas culturales* videos.

La pintora mexicana Frida Kahlo pintó este cuadro en 1932. Su título es *Autorretrato entre México y Estados Unidos.*

¿QUÉ TE PARECE?

- El Día de la Independencia de México es el 16 de septiembre, no el 5 de mayo como muchos piensan.
- El nombre completo del país es Estados Unidos Mexicanos. Hay 31 estados más la capital, México D.F. (Distrito Federal).
- Millones de mariposas monarcas migran cada año a México desde Estados Unidos y Canadá.
- Antes del año 1953, las mujeres mexicanas no podían votar en las elecciones nacionales.
- México D.F. se hunde (*sinks*) entre 0,2 y 1,3 pies al año debido a que el 70% del agua para la ciudad viene de fuentes (*sources*) subterráneas.

Suggestion for map
Brainstorm with students the information they may already know about Mexico. Project the map and ask: *¿Qué países tienen frontera con México? ¿Qué ciudades estadounidenses están cerca de la frontera mexicana? ¿Cuál es la capital de México? ¿Qué otras ciudades mexicanas conocen? ¿Qué comida tradicional mexicana les gusta? ¿Qué tradiciones de México conocen?* Point out the pre-Columbian pyramid of Teotihuacán on the map, which is called *la Pirámide del Sol,* and relate it to Frida Kahlo's painting.

Note for art
Frida Kahlo painted *Autorretrato entre México y Estados Unidos* in 1932 during her stay in the U.S. Dressed in pink, she is at the center of a self-portrait that contrasts traditional culture and modernity: Mexico is represented in warm colors, whereas the U.S. abounds in buildings, industries, and electric gadgets are depicted in grays and blues. The inscription on this pedestal says "*Carmen* (Frida's baptismal name) *Rivera pintó su retrato en el año 1932.*"

Suggestion for art
Project text image of the painting and ask questions to elicit vocabulary: *¿Cómo es Frida Kahlo? ¿Qué lleva? ¿De qué color es su vestido?* Recycle colors by asking students to describe the flags. Ask about the ruins and pre-Columbian figures on the Mexican side: *¿Qué edificio es este probablemente? ¿Qué representa esta figura?* (The feminine figure represents fertility.) Point out the skull on the ground and ask what they know about *El Día de los Muertos.* Explain that *sol* and *luna* are symbols from the Aztec religion. (The blood from the sun's mouth is a reminder of Aztec sacrifices.) Ask students to describe what they see on the U.S. side (*fábrica, humo, contaminación, aparatos eléctricos*).

Note for *Tulum*
The majority of the Mayan cities were built in the western part of the Yucatán Peninsula; Cobá and Tulum are in the east.

Note for *Cabo San Lucas*
Cabo San Lucas and Puerto Vallarta, on the Pacific Coast, have overtaken Acapulco and Cancún, on the Caribbean, in popularity.

Note for *Bosque de Chapultepec*
Located in Mexico City, Chapultepec Park is the largest urban forest in all of Latin America. It is a very important natural reserve for the city with an extensive history dating back to at least the 15th century. Thanks to its many attractions, such as a zoo, amusement parks, and museums, the park welcomes an estimated 15 million visitors annually.

Note for *San Miguel de Allende*
San Miguel de Allende is located in the state of Guanajuato in central Mexico. A century ago, the town was fading away into irrelevance. Foreign artists, captivated by its history and stunning architecture, initiated the resurgence of this now thriving city. These artists are credited with establishing vital art and cultural institutions, such as the Allende Institute and the School of Fine Arts, which today continue to contribute to the city's appeal.

◀ Tulum es la única ciudad maya construida en la costa de la península del Yucatán. Al igual que en otras ciudades mayas y aztecas, en Tulum también hay pirámides.

Cabo San Lucas es una de las muchas playas que atraen a los turistas a México. Es especialmente popular entre actores y actrices de Estados Unidos y otros países. ▶

▲ La ciudad de San Miguel de Allende es reconocida por la UNESCO como Patrimonio de la Humanidad por sus contribuciones tanto culturales como arquitectónicas.

El Museo Nacional de Antropología, situado dentro del Bosque de Chapultepec en México D.F., exhibe la mayor colección de piezas arqueológicas de la cultura precolombina. Aquí hay una réplica del templo maya de Hochob dentro de los jardines del museo. ▶

¿CUÁNTO SABES?

Completa las oraciones con la información correcta.

1. Las ruinas de la ciudad de Tulum se encuentran en ___la península del Yucatán___.
2. El 16 de septiembre se celebra ___la independencia de México___.
3. La capital mexicana está en ___el ditrito Federal (D.F.)___.
4. Una playa que atrae a muchos turistas es ___Cabo San Lucas___.
5. Tulum se diferencia de otras ciudades mayas porque ___está en la costa___.
6. Cada año llegan a México millones de ___mariposas monarcas___.

Vocabulario en contexto

Discussing traditions and celebrations

MySpanishLab **Pronunciation Topic:** Consonants *r* and *rr*.

Learn more using Amplifire Dynamic Study Modules, Pronunciation, and Vocabulary Tutorials.

Las fiestas y las tradiciones

▲ **La romería de El Rocío, España**

En Almonte, un pequeño pueblo de la provincia de Huelva, España, se celebra todos los años la romería de El Rocío. Los **peregrinos** se visten con trajes tradicionales de muchos colores y van hasta la ermita (*sanctuary*) de la Virgen del Rocío a **caballo,** andando y en carretas **adornadas.** En estas fiestas religiosas populares la **gente** expresa su devoción pero también es una ocasión para **pasarlo bien.**

▲ **El Día de los Muertos, México**

El Día de los **Muertos,** también conocido como el Día de los **Difuntos,** se conmemora el 2 de noviembre. Mucha gente va al **cementerio** ese día o el día anterior para **recordar** y llevarles flores a sus familiares o amigos difuntos. En México, los **preparativos** para el Día de los Muertos **comienzan** con mucha anterioridad. Algunas familias acompañan a sus muertos en el cementerio la noche del 1 al 2 de noviembre.

▲ **La Diablada, Bolivia**

Las fiestas y los bailes que se celebran en diversas partes del mundo ayudan a **mantener** las **costumbres** de los **antepasados.** La Diablada es uno de los **festivales** folclóricos con más colorido en Hispanoamérica. Se celebra durante el **carnaval** de Oruro en Bolivia y también en el norte de Chile y en otros países, entre ellos, Perú.

▲ **Carnaval**

La música, el baile y la **alegría** reinan en los carnavales. Hay **desfiles** de **carrozas** y **comparsas** que bailan en las calles, muchas personas **se disfrazan** y todo el mundo se divierte. El **último** día de Carnaval es el martes antes del **comienzo** de la Cuaresma (*Lent*).

▲ **Semana Santa, Guatemala**

Esta es una de las **procesiones** de Semana Santa en Antigua, Guatemala. Esta ciudad fue la antigua capital de Guatemala y es famosa por su arquitectura colonial y las **maravillosas** alfombras que se hacen con flores, **semillas** y aserrín (*sawdust*) para el paso de las procesiones.

▲ **El Día de San Fermín, España**

El Día de San Fermín, el 7 de julio, se inicia la **celebración** de los sanfermines en Pamplona, España. Esta celebración, que dura del 7 al 14 de julio, es famosa mundialmente por los encierros. Los jóvenes corren por las calles seguidos de los **toros.**

Warm-up
Have students provide as much information as possible about holidays that are celebrated in both the U.S. and the Hispanic world.

Suggestion for *Las fiestas y las tradiciones*
Use the images to ask questions as a warm-up. Provide additional information.

- Locate on a map the province of Huelva (southwestern Spain), where *El Rocío* takes place. Explain that many worshippers arrive in wagons, on horseback, or on foot; that is, *hacen el camino* from various regions in Spain to attend the festival.
- Point out that Christianity's Holy Week (*Semana Santa*) is the week from Palm Sunday to Easter Sunday. The photograph shows *una hermandad,* a religious brotherhood in Guatemala, whose members wear traditional clothing and carry religious icons mounted on heavy wooden floats as an act of religious devotion, walking on beautiful carpets of flowers, seeds, and tinted sawdust.

Suggestion
Point out similarities and differences of special days in both cultures: April Fool's Day/*el Día de los Inocentes, 28 de diciembre;* Friday the 13th/*martes 13.*

Audioscript for 8-1

1. *La fiesta termina el martes antes del comienzo de la Cuaresma.*
2. *También se conoce como el Día de los Difuntos.*
3. *Muchos de los peregrinos van hasta la ermita a caballo.*
4. *Los toros corren por las calles.*
5. *Las familias decoran el cementerio con flores.*
6. *Hay comparsas, carrozas y desfiles.*

Standard 4.2 Students demonstrate understanding of the concept of culture through comparisons of the cultures studied and their own.

The photos of festivals in this section, especially of *Carnaval*, and students' mental images of Mardi Gras in New Orleans provide the opportunity to compare how this event is celebrated in Latin America and the U.S. Students who observe Lent will be able to explain to their classmates the timing of *Carnaval*/Mardi Gras and the contrast between the secular and the religious character of these observances.

Alternate for 8-3

This may be done as a research activity. You may assign students different festivals, have them bring the images to class and do the following: 1. Locate the festival on a map. 2. Talk about the purpose of the festival and when it is celebrated. 3. Describe what people do there. 4. Give their opinion about the activities associated with the festival. Other festivals that you may assign include: *la Guelaguetza* (Oaxaca, Mexico); *las Fallas* (Valencia, Spain); *el Carnaval de Barranquilla* (Colombia); *la Fiesta de la Fruta y de las Flores* (Ambato, Ecuador); *el Festival de la Vendimia* (Perú, Chile, Argentina); *el Festival de la Pollera* (Panamá); *el Festival de la Frutilla* (Chile).

PRÁCTICA

8-1  

Escucha y confirma. Indicate (✓) whether the descriptions you hear relate to **el Día de los Muertos, Carnaval,** or neither of the two.

CARNAVAL	EL DÍA DE LOS MUERTOS	NINGUNO DE LOS DOS
1. ✓		
2.	✓	
3.		✓
4.		✓
5.	✓	
6. ✓		

Cultura

Fiestas

El Día de Acción de Gracias (*Thanksgiving*) no se celebra en los países hispanos y tampoco es tradicional el Día de las Brujas (*Halloween*), aunque empieza a celebrarse en algunas ciudades de Hispanoamérica y de España. Por otro lado, debido a la importancia e influencia de la religión católica en los países hispanos, algunas fiestas católicas se consideran también fiestas oficiales y son días feriados. Pero lo más importante es la gran diversidad de fiestas locales. Muchas personas trabajan todo el año para garantizar el éxito de estas celebraciones.

Comparaciones. ¿Hay fiestas religiosas en tu comunidad? ¿Son fiestas oficiales? ¿Cómo se celebran? ¿Hay feriados religiosos y seculares? ¿Cuáles son?

8-2   **Definiciones.** Asocia el nombre de la festividad con su descripción. Después, compara tus respuestas con las de tu compañero/a y dile a cuáles de ellas te gustaría (*would like*) asistir y por qué.

1. __e__ San Fermín
2. __a__ La Diablada
3. __f__ El Rocío
4. __b__ Carnaval
5. __c__ El Día de los Muertos
6. __d__ Semana Santa

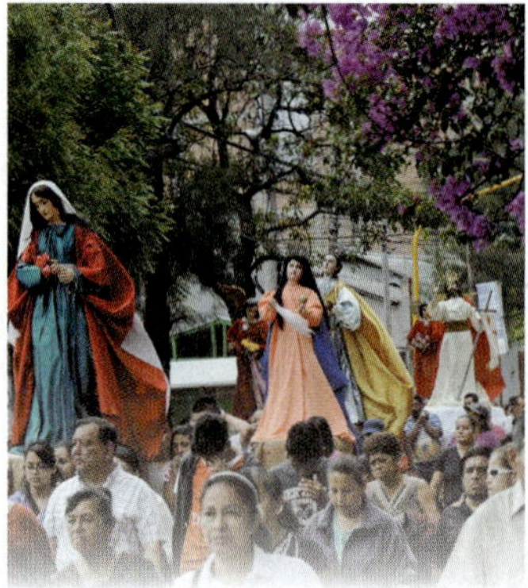

▲ Procesión de Semana Santa en Tegucigalpa, Honduras

a. Se celebra durante el carnaval de Oruro en Bolivia. Muchas personas bailan en las calles disfrazadas de demonios.
b. Muchas personas se disfrazan y bailan en comparsas por las calles.
c. Todos van al cementerio a hacer ofrendas a los seres queridos que están muertos.
d. Hay procesiones por las calles y en Antigua, Guatemala, se hacen unas alfombras de aserrín, flores y semillas.
e. Los jóvenes corren por las calles delante de los toros.
f. Es una fiesta en el sur de España. La gente va en carretas hasta una ermita.

8-3 

Imágenes. Escojan una de las fotos de las fiestas y descríbanla detalladamente contestando las siguientes preguntas.

1. ¿Qué están haciendo las personas?
2. ¿Qué ropa llevan estas personas? ¿Qué colores hay?
3. ¿Qué objetos hay? ¿Para qué sirven?
4. ¿Piensan que esta festividad es religiosa? ¿Por qué?
5. Según ustedes, ¿es la festividad divertida? ¿Por qué?

8-4 

Contextos. PREPARACIÓN. Hablen sobre las ideas, sentimientos o costumbres que se relacionan con las siguientes palabras.

el carnaval

música, baile, alegría, mucha gente por la calle, carrozas…

1. los cementerios
2. los toros
3. los disfraces
4. el baile

INTERCAMBIOS. Escriban por lo menos 6 oraciones usando las palabras que anotaron en *Preparación*.

El carnaval es una fiesta muy alegre. La gente se disfraza y baila por las calles.

Otras celebraciones 

la Nochebuena

la Navidad

la Nochevieja

el Año Nuevo

el Día de la Independencia de México

la Pascua

el Día de la Madre

el Día del Padre

el Día de Acción de Gracias

el Día de las Brujas

el Día de los Enamorados/del Amor y la Amistad

Cultura

La Navidad

En muchos países hispanos, los niños reciben regalos de Papá Noel o del Niño Dios el día de Navidad. Sin embargo, la Nochebuena se considera el día más importante. Muchos católicos van a la iglesia a la medianoche para asistir a la Misa del Gallo (*midnight mass*). El 6 de enero, día de la Epifanía, se celebra la llegada de los Reyes Magos con sus regalos para el Niño Jesús. La noche del 5 de enero, muchos niños se acuestan esperando la visita de los tres reyes que llegan montados en sus camellos con regalos para ellos.

▲ Los Reyes Magos en México

Comparaciones. En tu cultura, ¿existen celebraciones en las que se hacen regalos? ¿Hay alguna tradición especial para los niños? ¿Hay celebraciones infantiles que no son religiosas? ¿En qué se inspira esta celebración?

PRÁCTICA

8-5   

Para confirmar. PREPARACIÓN. Asocia las fechas con los días festivos. Compara tus respuestas con las de tu compañero/a.

1. __h__ el 25 de diciembre
2. __g__ el 2 de noviembre
3. __f__ el 6 de enero
4. __a__ el 4 de julio
5. __c__ el 24 de diciembre
6. __d__ el 31 de diciembre
7. __e__ el 14 de febrero
8. __b__ el 31 de octubre

a. el Día de la Independencia de Estados Unidos
b. el Día de las Brujas
c. la Nochebuena
d. la Nochevieja/el Fin de Año
e. el Día de los Enamorados/del Amor y la Amistad
f. el Día de los Reyes Magos
g. el Día de los Muertos
h. la Navidad

 **INTERCAMBIOS.** Comenten entre ustedes las respuestas a las siguientes preguntas.

1. ¿Cuál(es) de las fiestas de *Preparación* celebra cada uno/a de ustedes?
2. ¿Cuál es la fiesta favorita de la mayoría de las personas del grupo, y por qué?
3. ¿En cuál de estas fiestas reciben regalos? ¿Qué tipo de regalos?
4. ¿En cuál de estas fiestas hay una comida especial?

Note
Pascuas can refer to both Christmas and Easter: *la Pascua Florida* refers to Easter, *las Pascuas Navideñas* refers to Christmas.

In many countries, on New Year's Eve people eat 12 grapes at the stroke of midnight to ensure good fortune in the New Year.

September 16 is Mexico's Independence Day. Remind students that the date of Independence Day varies from country to country, and have them research the date in several Latin American countries.

Suggestion
Talk about one Hispanic holiday in detail. Mention that *El Día de los Muertos* in Mexico is on November 1 and 2, All Saints' Day and All Souls' Day, respectively. Families go to cemeteries to decorate the graves of departed loved ones with flowers. Stores sell candy skulls and fanciful skeletons; bakeries make *pan de muerto.* Souls of the departed are believed to return to visit their families on this occasion. Many families place altars, called *ofrendas,* in their homes, on which they place candles and the favorite food and drink of their loved ones.

Suggestion for 8-5
As a preview, compare holiday traditions using comparatives/superlatives: *¿Qué costumbre es la más/menos importante para tu familia? ¿Por qué tiene más/menos importancia ese día?* For *Intercambios,* ask students to talk among themselves in groups of 3 or 4 and then share the information with the class.

Suggestions for 8-6
Talk about parades with which students are familiar and ask questions. Encourage students to look for additional information. Some people mistakenly connect this date to Mexico's independence from Spain, which took place in 1810 and is celebrated on September 16. *Cinco de Mayo* is a festival about patriotism and unity, and it is celebrated mostly by Mexicans and Mexican Americans in the U.S. You may wish to model the activity with a proficient student.

Alternate for 8-7
Preview the imperfect by asking students yes/no questions regarding holiday celebrations as children: *De niño/a, ¿celebrabas el Día de las Brujas? ¿Comías mucho el Día de Acción de Gracias? ¿Te gustaba recibir regalos el día de Navidad? ¿Recibías juguetes? ¿Dinero? ¿Ropa?*

Follow-up for 8-7
¿Qué día festivo te gusta más? ¿Por qué? ¿A quién no le gustan los días festivos? ¿Por qué?

Suggestion for 8-8
Assign students to do brief, structured presentations about celebrations they are familiar with, such as Kwanzaa, Hanukkah, Christmas, Ramadan, and Eid.

Alternate for 8-8
Recycle the preterit by asking students to describe their last birthday, what they did last New Year's Eve, and so on: *¿Qué hiciste el día de tu cumpleaños el año pasado? ¿Celebró la Navidad tu familia? ¿Fuiste a una fiesta para la Nochevieja?*

Suggestion for 8-8
You may have students choose a celebration or festivity in advance so they come to class prepared to talk about it.

8-6 

Festivales o desfiles. Piensa en algunos festivales o desfiles importantes y completa el cuadro siguiente. Tu compañero/a va a hacerte preguntas sobre ellos.

FESTIVAL O DESFILE	FECHA	LUGAR	DESCRIPCIÓN	OPINIÓN

E1: *¿En qué fiesta o desfile importante estás pensando?*
E2: *En el Cinco de Mayo.*
E1: *¿Dónde lo celebran?*
E2: *En México y en algunas ciudades de Estados Unidos, como Austin, Texas.*
E1: *¿Cómo es...?*
E2: ...
E1: *¿Qué opinas de...?*
E2: ...

8-7 

Unos días festivos. Hablen sobre cómo celebran ustedes estas fechas.

 tu cumpleaños
E1: *¿Cómo celebras tu cumpleaños?*
E2: *Lo celebro con mis amigos. Salimos a cenar o los invito a mi apartamento para ver una película. A veces voy a casa para celebrarlo con mi familia.*

1. la Nochevieja/el Fin de Año
2. el Día de las Brujas
3. el Día de Acción de Gracias
4. el Día de la Independencia
5. el Año Nuevo
6. el Día de la Madre

LENGUA

The words **fiesta, festividad,** and **festival** are often used interchangeably. **Fiesta** may mean a holiday or a party or celebration. **Festividad** normally refers to a public festivity or a holiday. **Festival** often involves a series of events or celebrations of a public nature. Another term for holiday is **día festivo. Día feriado** is a legal holiday.

Cultura

Tradiciones curiosas

Existen diferentes tradiciones relacionadas con el último día del año. En España a las doce en punto de la noche del 31 de diciembre suenan doce campanadas (*bell chimes*) y se comen doce uvas. En México hay personas que salen a la calle con maletas vacías para hacer muchos viajes durante el nuevo año. En Argentina se encienden tres velas: verde para la esperanza, roja para espantar malas energías y amarilla para la abundancia.

Comparaciones. ¿Qué tradiciones existen en tu país en la última noche del año? ¿Existe alguna tradición especial en tu familia?

Una celebración importante.

PREPARACIÓN. Escojan una celebración importante del mundo hispano (Carnaval, Semana Santa, Año Nuevo, las Posadas, la Diablada, Día de la Independencia, etc.) y, si necesitan, busquen información en Internet sobre los siguientes aspectos:

1. el lugar donde se celebra
2. la época del año
3. las actividades
4. los vestidos o disfraces
5. la comida u otro aspecto relevante de la festividad

INTERCAMBIOS. Preparen una presentación de 1 o 2 minutos sobre la celebración que escogieron y preséntenla a la clase.

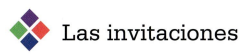

Las invitaciones

 **¿Quieres salir conmigo?**

LUISA: Hola, Arturo, ¿qué tal?

ARTURO: Bien, Luisa, ¿y tú?

LUISA: **Estupendamente.** ¿Qué planes tienes para Nochevieja? Debemos hacer algo juntos.

ARTURO: Me gustaría mucho, pero no puedo porque esa noche tenemos la cena familiar.

LUISA: ¡Qué lástima! ¿Y qué tal si hacemos algo después de cenar?

ARTURO: Sí, **¿cómo no?** Si quieres, podemos ir de discoteca por la noche. Las discotecas tienen música **en vivo**, con buenos grupos musicales, y la gente está muy **animada.**

LUISA: ¡Qué buena idea! Creo que hay **fuegos artificiales** en la plaza a las doce. Podemos **dar una vuelta** por allí.

ARTURO: Bueno, **entonces** nos vemos en mi casa el 31 a eso de las once y media.

LUISA: Fenomenal, Arturo. Me hace mucha ilusión comenzar el Año Nuevo contigo.

PRÁCTICA

8-9

Para confirmar. Con tu compañero/a, lee la conversación entre Luisa y Arturo. Después, invita a tu compañero/a a hacer algo juntos. Luego, tu compañero/a va a invitarte a ti.

LUISA: Hola, Arturo, ¿cómo estás?

ARTURO: Bien, Luisa, ¿y tú?

LUISA: Estupendamente. Mira, me gustaría invitarte a cenar el sábado para hablar de tu viaje a México.

ARTURO: Mañana no puedo porque tengo un partido de fútbol.

LUISA: ¡Qué lástima! ¿Y el domingo?

ARTURO: El domingo está bien. Si quieres, podemos vernos antes para dar un paseo.

LUISA: ¡Qué buena idea! Nos vemos en el centro a las seis.

ARTURO: Hasta el domingo.

En directo

To accept an invitation:

Gracias. Me encanta la idea.

Con mucho gusto.

Encantado/a.

Será un placer. *It will be a pleasure.*

To decline an invitation:

Me gustaría ir, pero…

¡Qué lástima/pena! Ese día tengo que…

No puedo, tengo un compromiso. *I can't. I have a prior engagement.*

 Listen to a conversation with these expressions.

Suggestion
If students have already researched different festivals as suggested as an alternative to 8-3, they can either do more research on those celebrations or choose others to research for 8-8.

Standard 5.2
Students show evidence of becoming lifelong learners by using the language for personal enjoyment and enrichment. This chapter, with its focus on Mexico, helps students make connections between their academic experience with Spanish and the many aspects of Mexican and Mexican American culture in their daily lives. There are Mexican restaurants throughout the U.S.; supermarket shelves dedicated to Mexican food items and activities and products related to *Cinco de Mayo* are increasingly available.

Note for En directo
Before doing activity 8-9, first have students read the expressions in *En directo.* Then have them listen to the dialogue and encourage them to use the expressions in their own conversation.

Audioscript for *En directo*
MANNY: *Lily, ¿te gustaría ir conmigo a la fiesta de Érica?*
LILY: *Con mucho gusto, Manny. Será un placer.*
MANNY: *Oye, pensaba ir al cine después de la fiesta. ¿Quieres acompañarme?*
LILY: *Pues, me gustaría ir, pero tengo que ayudar a Érica a ordenar su apartamento después de la fiesta.*

Warm-up for 8-9
Before students invite each other to attend events, brainstorm with the class as a whole some possible activities that people do with others. You may wish to provide one example: *ir al cine.* Then model the activity with a proficient student. Encourage students to use the expressions presented in *En directo.*

Warm-up for 8-12
As a prelistening activity, have students in groups of 4 share in Spanish what their favorite holidays are and narrate what they usually do on those days.

Suggestion for 8-12
Remind students to pay attention to the general idea of what is said and then identify the holiday described in each conversation.

Audioscript for 8-12
Conversación 1.
MUJER: *¿Por qué hay tantos niños en la calle? Y están disfrazados.*
HOMBRE: *Hoy es una fiesta muy importante para los niños de Estados Unidos.*
MUJER: *¿Y qué hacen en la calle?*
HOMBRE: *Les piden caramelos a los vecinos.*

Conversación 2.
MUJER: *Ahora salgo para la iglesia y después voy al cementerio para llevarle flores a mi padre.*
HOMBRE: *¿Cuándo murió tu padre?*
MUJER: *En el año 2001.*
HOMBRE: *¿Y haces esto todos los años?*
MUJER: *Sí, todos los años, por supuesto.*

Conversación 3.
MUJER: *¿Qué le vas a regalar a tu novia mañana?*
HOMBRE: *Todavía no sé. Quizás un perfume, un collar.*
MUJER: *¿Y van a salir por la noche?*
HOMBRE: *Bueno, es un día muy especial para los novios. La voy a invitar a su restaurante favorito.*

Conversación 4.
MUJER: *¿Qué te trajeron anoche?*
NIÑO: *Me trajeron una bicicleta. Yo les pedí muchas cosas, pero solo me trajeron la bicicleta.*
MUJER: *Es que hay muchos niños en el mundo y ellos tienen que llevarles regalos a todos.*
Explain to students that *el Carnaval de Barranquilla* is the second largest in the world after Rio de Janeiro's. Remind them that, as with most carnivals, Barranquilla's takes place one week before Lent.

8-10 

Fiestas en Querétaro. Lean el programa de fiestas de fin de año y contesten las preguntas. Luego, preparen una lista con las diferencias que encuentran entre estas festividades y las de su país en esta época del año.

1. ¿ En qué país se celebran estos eventos?
2. ¿Cuáles de estos eventos son gratis?
3. ¿Qué festividad se celebra con fuegos artificiales?
4. ¿Cuál de las festividades se celebra más de un día?
5. ¿Para qué evento se necesita tener un boleto?

1. México
2. el Encendido del Árbol de Navidad, el Desfile del Carro de la Posada y la Fiesta de Fin de Año y Pirotecnia
3. la Fiesta de Fin de Año
4. el Desfile del Carro de la Posada
5. el Concierto Navideño

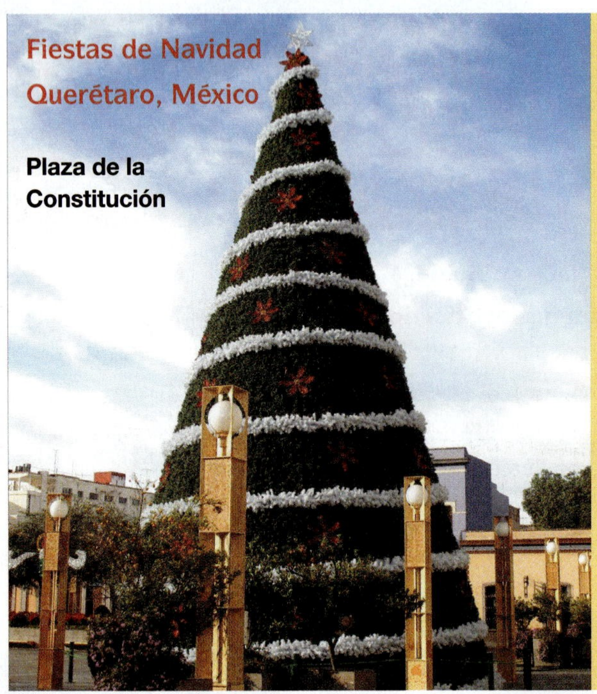

Encendido del Árbol de Navidad
FECHA: 5 de diciembre
LUGAR: Jardín Zenea
DIRECCIÓN: Parque Central
HORA: 14:00 h

Desfile del Carro de la Posada
FECHA: 20-23 de diciembre
LUGAR: Calles del Centro Histórico
DIRECCIÓN: Centro Histórico
HORA: 18:00 h

Concierto Navideño
FECHA: 18 de diciembre
LUGAR: Teatro Municipal
DIRECCIÓN: Avenida República 2051
HORA: 20:00 h
VENTA DE BOLETOS: Caja N.° 10

Fiesta de Fin de Año y Pirotecnia
FECHA: 31 de diciembre
LUGAR: Jardín Zenea
DIRECCIÓN: Parque Central
HORA: 21:00 h

8-11 

Una fiesta especial. **PREPARACIÓN.** Piensa en una celebración o fiesta en la que participaste recientemente y descríbele la fiesta a tu compañero/a. Usa las siguientes preguntas como guía.

1. ¿A qué fiesta asististe?
2. ¿Dónde se celebró? ¿Cuántos invitados asistieron?
3. ¿Cuándo fue la fiesta? ¿A qué hora empezó? ¿Cuánto tiempo duró?
4. Describe la comida que sirvieron.
5. ¿Cómo se divirtió la gente? ¿Qué música tocaron?

INTERCAMBIOS. Ahora compara tu fiesta con la de tu compañero/a y busquen algunas diferencias entre las dos fiestas.

8-12  

La fiesta. **PREPARACIÓN.** Before you listen to four short conversations about different holidays, tell your partner one or two things you know about each holiday listed below.

  **ESCUCHA.** Identify each holiday below according to the corresponding conversation you hear and write the appropriate number next to it. Check answers with a classmate.

__3__ el Día del Amor y la Amistad/Día de los Enamorados
__2__ el Día de los Muertos
__4__ el Día de los Reyes Magos
__1__ el Día de las Brujas

MOSAICO cultural Los carnavales y las tradiciones

¿Sabías que el carnaval más grande del mundo hispano es el de Barranquilla en Colombia? ¿Sabías que dura una semana entera? Es cierto. Aproximadamente dos millones de personas de todo el mundo se reúnen para presenciar los desfiles, comparsas, disfraces, bailes y alegría que llenan las calles cada día. "¡Güepajé!" grita la gente en lo que es hoy una celebración con sus orígenes en diferentes tradiciones.

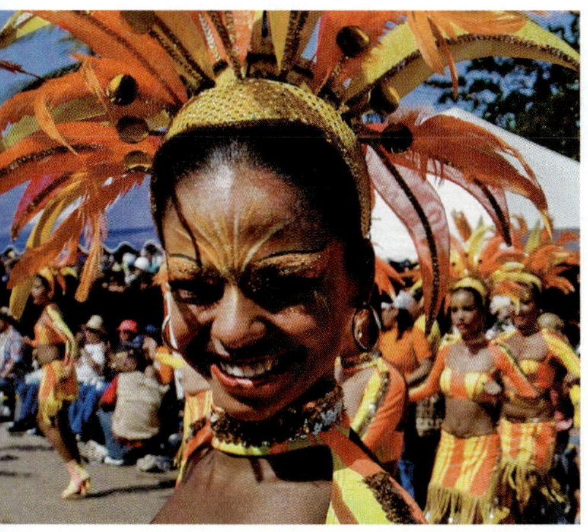

Los carnavales latinoamericanos comenzaron como un medio para unir las celebraciones tradicionales (usualmente paganas) con las celebraciones religiosas que llegaron de Europa. En el Carnaval de Barranquilla se celebra la diversidad cultural del Caribe con sus tradiciones indígenas, africanas y europeas. Cada país tiene sus propios carnavales y celebra la diversidad de maneras diferentes.

Otra tradición que se mantiene y se pasa de generación en generación es la de los papalotes o cometas (*kites*). En los meses de agosto y septiembre, cuando hace más viento, es común ver a familias en los parques y en las playas jugando con cometas. También hay grandes festivales, como el Festival Internacional de Cometas Ciudad de Valencia, en España. Allí se reúnen equipos y aficionados de todo el mundo para exhibir sus cometas en la playa y competir en modalidad acrobática. ¡Quién se pierde (*misses out on*) cualquiera de estas festividades y tradiciones!

You may wish to tell students that *papalote* comes from the náhuatl *papálotl* which means butterfly. This may be a good moment to point out how the Hispanic world is characterized by diversity in linguistic expressions and cultural traditions. You may also wish to tell students that they should not assume from the cultural readings about festivals in *Mosaicos* that people in the Hispanic world live in a constant state of celebration. These cultural events are colorful and are interesting to learn about, but they are just one of many aspects of the cultures of the Hispanic world.

Compara

1. ¿Qué tipo de carnavales o fiestas tradicionales existen en tu país o región? ¿Qué tienen en común con las del mundo hispano? Explica.
2. Cuando eras niño/a, ¿participabas en tradiciones familiares como elevar cometas? ¿Qué tradiciones son importantes en tu cultura?
3. ¿Qué celebración se transmite de generación en generación en tu familia? ¿Cómo es esta celebración?

Suggestion for *Funciones y formas*
Project the illustrations and ask students: *¿Cómo era la vida cuando la abuela era joven? Según la abuela, la música era mejor porque tenía más melodía y era más suave y romántica. Ella cree que hoy no hay música, que hay solo ruido.* Ask questions to check understanding.

Suggestions
Give examples of some uses of the imperfect: what you used to do while in college, descriptions of places or people, including their ages. You may wish to write some verb forms on the board and use visuals. Ask yes/no and either/or questions with the imperfect.

Suggestions
Bring photos to class or assign students to bring in photos and ask: *¿Qué hacía/hacías/hacían cuando tomaron esta foto?* to preview imperfect/preterit contrast. Allow students to guess what was happening in the photos before you tell them.

Note
Compare time expressions such as *mientras, a veces, siempre, generalmente,* and *frecuentemente* to those related to the preterit: *ayer, una vez, la semana pasada, de repente.*

Note
Point out that the *yo, él, ella, usted* forms of the imperfect are identical.

Funciones y formas

1 Expressing ongoing actions and describing in the past

ABUELA: **Antes** la música **era** suave y romántica. **Tenía** más melodía y las orquestas **eran** magníficas. **Hoy en día** no **hay** música, solo ruido, y a la gente **no le interesa** bailar.

NANCY: **Antes** las familias **cenaban** juntas. **Conversaban** mientras **comían,** y los hijos **se aburrían** (*got bored*) mucho. ¡**Era** una tortura! **Ahora es** mucho mejor. Cuando **tengo** hambre, **preparo** algo para comer. Además, los padres no **controlan** tanto la vida de sus hijos.

Piénsalo. Indica a qué función se refiere cada afirmación.

CONDICIÓN O ACTIVIDAD	DESCRIPCIÓN DE UN ESTADO EN EL PASADO	ACCIÓN HABITUAL EN EL PASADO	ACCIÓN EN EL PRESENTE
1. La música del pasado **tenía** más melodía.	✓		
2. Antes las familias **cenaban** juntas.		✓	
3. Los hijos **se aburrían** mucho.	✓		
4. Cuando tengo hambre, **preparo** algo para comer.			✓
5. Los padres no **controlan** tanto la vida de sus hijos.			✓

The imperfect

- You have already learned to use the preterit to talk about actions in the past. In these scenes, the grandmother and granddaughter use a different past tense, the **imperfect,** because they are focusing on how things used to be and what usually took place 50 or 60 years ago. If they were talking about a specific completed action, like something they did yesterday, they would use the preterit.

  Generally, the imperfect is used to:

- express habitual or repeated actions in the past (without focus on the completion of a specific action).

  Nosotros **íbamos** a casa para cenar todos los días a las seis. — *We used to go home to eat dinner every day at six o'clock.*

- express an action or state that was in progress in the past (not whether the action or state was completed).

  Todos los invitados **hablaban** y **bailaban.** — *All the guests were talking and dancing.*

  Estaban muy contentos. — *They were very happy.*

- describe characteristics and conditions in the past.

El desfile **era** muy largo y **había** muchos espectadores.	*The parade was very long and there were many spectators.*

- tell time in the past.

Era la una de la tarde; no **eran** las dos.	*It was one in the afternoon; it was not two.*

- express a person's age in the past.

Ella **tenía** quince años entonces.	*She was fifteen years old then.*

- Note that the endings for **-er** and **-ir** verbs are the same and have a written accent over the **í** of the ending.

IMPERFECT			
	Hablar	**Comer**	**Vivir**
yo	habl**aba**	com**ía**	viv**ía**
tú	habl**abas**	com**ías**	viv**ías**
Ud., él, ella	habl**aba**	com**ía**	viv**ía**
nosotros/as	habl**ába**mos	com**ía**mos	viv**ía**mos
vosotros/as	habl**aba**is	com**ía**is	viv**ía**is
Uds., ellos/as	habl**aba**n	com**ía**n	viv**ía**n

- Some expressions of time and frequency that often accompany the imperfect to express ongoing or repeated actions or states in the past are:

mientras	*while*
a veces	*sometimes, at times*
siempre	*always*
generalmente	*generally*
frecuentemente	*frequently*

- The Spanish imperfect has several English equivalents.

Mis amigos **bailaban** mucho.
- *My friends danced a lot.*
- *My friends were dancing a lot.*
- *My friends used to dance a lot.*
- *My friends would dance a lot.*
- (implying a repeated action)

- There are no stem changes in the imperfect.

Ella no d**ue**rme bien ahora, pero antes d**o**rmía muy bien.	*She does not sleep well now, but she used to sleep very well before.*

- Only three verbs are irregular in the imperfect.

ir	iba, ibas, iba, íbamos, ibais, iban
ser	era, eras, era, éramos, erais, eran
ver	veía, veías, veía, veíamos, veíais, veían

- The imperfect form of **hay** is **había** (*there was, there were, there used to be*). It is invariable.

Había una invitación en el correo.	*There was an invitation in the mail.*
Había muchas personas en la fiesta.	*There were many people at the party.*

e ¿COMPRENDES?

Completa las oraciones con el imperfecto.

1. Marcos siempre ___bailaba___ (bailar) en las fiestas.
2. Nosotros siempre ___comíamos___ (comer) mucho cuando ___íbamos___ (ir) a la casa de nuestros abuelos.
3. A los hermanos les ___gustaba___ (gustar) cantar cuando ___estaban___ (estar) en la primaria.
4. Cuando tú ___eras___ (ser) niño, ¿___hacías___ (hacer) tus disfraces del Día de las Brujas, o los ___comprabas___ (comprar)?

MySpanishLab
Learn more using Amplifire Dynamic Study Modules, Grammar Tutorials, and Extra Practice activities.

Suggestion
Present the preterit form *hubo* and explain to students that it is most often used in recounting sudden events, e.g., *hubo un accidente, hubo un tornado.*

PRÁCTICA

8-13 

Cuando yo tenía cinco años. Marca (✓) las actividades que hacías cuando tenías cinco años y añade una más. Compara tus respuestas con las de tu compañero/a. ¿Cuántas actividades tienen en común?

1. _____ Jugaba en el parque con mi perro.
2. _____ Invitaba a mis amigos a dormir en mi casa.
3. _____ Salía con mis padres los fines de semana.
4. _____ Iba a la playa en el verano.
5. _____ Veía televisión hasta muy tarde.
6. _____ Celebraba el Año Nuevo con mis amigos.
7. _____ Participaba en las fiestas de mi escuela.
8. . . .

Suggestion for 8-14
Students should add to the chart an additional activity that they used to do very often and one they did infrequently.

Follow-up for 8-14
Find out which activities the whole class enjoyed most and least.

8-14 

En mi escuela secundaria. **PREPARACIÓN.** Marca (✓) la frecuencia con que tus amigos/as y tú hacían estas actividades. Añade otra actividad y compara tus respuestas con las de tu compañero/a.

ACTIVIDADES	SIEMPRE	FRECUENTEMENTE	A VECES	NUNCA
jugar juegos en línea				
organizar reuniones para animar al equipo de la escuela (*pep rallies*)				
ir a los partidos de fútbol y otros deportes				
asistir a conciertos y obras de teatro				
participar en un equipo, en la banda, etc.				
otra actividad				

 MODELO decorar los salones de clase

E1: *Frecuentemente decorábamos los salones de clase.*

E2: *Pues, nosotros los decorábamos solo a veces.*

INTERCAMBIOS. Hablen de los siguientes temas.

1. Tradicionalmente, ¿cómo celebraban y animaban al equipo de su escuela?
2. ¿Cuáles eran las actividades favoritas de cada uno/a ustedes?

Follow-up for 8-15
Have students share their descriptions with the class.

8-15 

Se fue la luz. (*There was a blackout.*) El sábado pasado los señores Herrera organizaron una fiesta en su casa. Durante la fiesta hubo un apagón en su barrio. Según el dibujo, describan lo que hacían las personas cuando se fue la luz. ¿Te pasó algo similar alguna vez? Cuéntaselo a tu compañero/a.

Follow-up for 8-16
Ask students to describe their childhood memories of grandparents, parents, or other relatives. Starting with a phrase like *Cuando era niño/a, mi abuelo/a vivía/era...*, etc., anchors the descriptions in the past (imperfect), rather than in the present.

Variation for 8-16
As an alternative, give students names of famous people and ask for descriptions, using verbs such as *era, vivía, se dedicaba a, pintaba,* and *escribía* (Frida Kahlo, William Shakespeare, Simón Bolívar, George Washington).

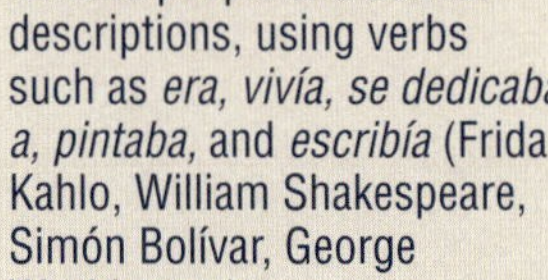

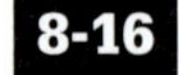 8-16 

Mi casa. Descríbele a tu compañero/a la casa o apartamento donde vivías cuando eras niño/a. Después, tu compañero/a debe hacer lo mismo.

Las fiestas infantiles. Comenten cómo eran las fiestas de cumpleaños cuando ustedes eran pequeños/as. Hablen de los siguientes aspectos y añadan uno más.

1. lugar de la celebración
2. horas (comienzo y final)
3. dos o tres actividades que hacían
4. personas que participaban
5. comida y bebida que servían
6. ropa que llevaban
7. ...

8-18

Antes y ahora. Explícale a tu compañero/a cómo era tu vida antes de la universidad y cómo es ahora con respecto a los siguientes temas. Háganse preguntas para obtener más detalles.

1. tus relaciones con tus padres
2. tus relaciones sociales
3. tus estudios
4. tu tiempo libre
5. tus amigos
6. tus vacaciones

E1: *Antes yo vivía con mis padres, pero ahora no los veo mucho porque estudio en una universidad en otro estado. ¿Y tú?*

E2: ...

En directo

To talk about how things used to be:

Entonces... *Then. . .*

Por aquel entonces... *Back then. . .*

En aquellos tiempos… *In those days. . .*

En esos años… *During those years. . .*

Listen to a conversation with these expressions.

Situación

PREPARACIÓN. Lean la situación. Luego, compartan ejemplos de vocabulario, gramática y otra información que necesitan para desarrollar la conversación.

Role A. You are an exchange student from Mexico and want to find out about your American host brother's/sister's weekend and summer activities when he/she was in high school. Ask:

a. what activities there were for high school students in the community,
b. what he/she generally did with friends on the weekends; and
c. what he/she usually did in the summer.

Role B. You are the American host brother/sister of an exchange student from Mexico (your classmate). Answer his/her questions about your weekend and summer activities when you were in high school. Provide lots of detail to give your guest a good idea of your activities and of life in your community.

	ROLE A	ROLE B
Vocabulario	Free-time and summer activities Question words Expressions to react to what one hears	Free-time and summer activities Expressions to react to what one hears
Funciones y formas	Asking questions Imperfect	Answering questions in detail

INTERCAMBIOS. Practica la conversación con tu compañero/a incorporando el vocabulario, las funciones y demás información. Luego, represéntenla ante la clase.

Suggestion for 8-17
Ask students what holiday or other event was celebrated most in their families. Have them talk about that holiday with their partner.

Note for *En directo*
Before doing activity 8-18, first have students read the expressions in *En directo.* Then have them listen to the dialogue and encourage them to use the expressions in their own conversation.

Audioscript for *En directo*
STEPHEN: *Abuelo, cuando eras niño, ¿cuál era tu celebración favorita?*
ABUELO: Mi'jo, *por aquel entonces se celebraban muchas fiestas y me divertía en todas. Sin embargo, mi favorita era el desfile que hacíamos todos los años en honor a la Virgen de Guadalupe. Toda la gente del pueblo participaba. Preparábamos carrozas; había desfiles, comida rica y orquestas que tocaban música festiva. En aquellos tiempos yo era muy buen bailarín y formaba parte de las comparsas. Eran unos tiempos maravillosos.*

Suggestion for *Situación*
Encourage students to use the imperfect preceded by the expressions listed in *En directo* to describe what used to happen in the past.

Suggestion for *Situación*
Review with students ways to react to what they hear and ask for more information: *Qué interesante; Quiero saber más sobre… ¿Me puedes explicar más?*

Suggestion
Retell the story of *Cenicienta* from the *Piénsalo* activity and explain how the events move the story forward in time, and that the background information gives interesting and important details to flesh out the story, but does not advance the action. Ask students to identify the preterit and imperfect forms they recall from the story and help them see that the preterit recounts the events and the imperfect gives information about context and characters.

Suggestion
Create a brief narration to exemplify the use of both preterit and imperfect or use the following: *Juan y su hermano Carlos fueron a Sonora, México, para pasar el verano con la familia de su padre. Sus tíos tenían una casita en la playa. El lugar era muy bonito. Las playas eran tranquilas y no había muchos turistas. Todos los días se levantaban a las ocho más o menos, desayunaban y se iban a pescar y a conversar con sus primos. Por la tarde, nadaban o hacían buceo y se reunían con sus amigos mexicanos. Pasaron las últimas dos semanas en la ciudad de Hermosillo. En Hermosillo salían por las noches y bailaban mucho en los clubes. Su último día fue muy triste para todos. Almorzaron con sus tíos y sus primos y después todos los llevaron al aeropuerto. Fue un verano maravilloso para estos chicos.*

2 Narrating in the past

Había una vez una chica que **vivía** con su padre, porque su madre **estaba** muerta. La chica **se llamaba** Cenicienta. **Era** muy bella y muy buena, y todos los vecinos la **querían** mucho. Pero un día, su vida **cambió.** Su padre **se casó** con una mujer muy mala que **tenía** dos hijas. La mujer y sus hijas **vinieron** a vivir a la casa de Cenicienta. Las hijas **eran** muy crueles y **odiaban** (*hated*) a Cenicienta, su hermanastra...

Piénsalo. Lee las afirmaciones e indica su función en la historia de Cenicienta: **contar los eventos** o **dar información de fondo** (*background information*).

	CONTAR LOS EVENTOS	DAR INFORMACIÓN DE FONDO
1. La chica **se llamaba** Cenicienta.		✓
2. Era muy bella y muy buena.		✓
3. Todos los vecinos la **querían** mucho.		✓
4. Pero un día, su vida **cambió.**	✓	
5. Su padre **se casó** con una mujer muy mala.	✓	
6. La mujer y sus hijas **vinieron** a vivir a la casa de Cenicienta.	✓	

The preterit and the imperfect

- The preterit and the imperfect are not interchangeable. They fulfill different functions when telling a story or talking about an event in the past.
- Use the preterit:

1. to express a sequence of actions completed in the past (note that there is a forward movement of narrative time).

Oyeron un ruido, **se levantaron** y **bajaron** las escaleras.	*They heard a noise, got up, and went downstairs.*

2. to talk about the beginning or end of an event, action, or condition.

Pepito **leyó** a los cinco años.	*Pepito read* (began to read) *at age five.*
El niño **se enfermó** el sábado.	*The child got sick* (became sick) *on Saturday.*
Pepito **leyó** el cuento.	*Pepito read* (finished) *the story.*
El niño **estuvo** enfermo ayer.	*The child was sick yesterday* (and is no longer sick).

3. to talk about an event, action, or condition that occurred over a specified period of time.

Vivieron en México por diez años.	*They lived in Mexico for ten years.*

- Use the imperfect:

1. to talk about customary or habitual actions, events, or conditions in the past.

Todos los días **llovía** y por eso **leíamos** mucho.	*It used to rain every day, and that's why we read a lot.*

2. to express an ongoing part of an event, action, or condition.

En ese momento **llovía** mucho y los niños **estaban** muy tristes.	*At that moment it was raining a lot, and the children were very sad.*

- In a story, the imperfect provides the background information, whereas the preterit tells what happened. Frequently an action or situation (expressed with the imperfect) is going on when something else (expressed with the preterit) suddenly happens.

Era Navidad. Todos **dormíamos** cuando los niños **oyeron** un ruido en el techo.	*It was Christmas. We were all sleeping when the children heard a noise on the roof.*

PRÁCTICA

8-19 **¡Qué día más malo!** Ayer iba a ser un día especial para Pedro, pero sus planes terminaron mal. Marca (✓) las tres cosas más graves que le ocurrieron a Pedro, según tu opinión. Compara tus respuestas con las de tu compañero/a.

1. _____ Mientras se bañaba por la mañana, se cayó.

2. _____ Mientras desayunaba tranquilamente, el teléfono sonó y no pudo terminar de comer.

3. _____ Iba a la tienda para comprarle un anillo a su novia cuando alguien le robó el dinero.

4. _____ Mientras llamaba por teléfono a un restaurante para reservar una mesa, el restaurante se incendió.

5. _____ Iba a proponerle matrimonio a su novia cuando su exnovia lo llamó por teléfono.

6. _____ Mientras preparaba una cena deliciosa para celebrar el cumpleaños de su novia, el perro se comió el pastel.

e ¿COMPRENDES?

Completa las oraciones con la forma correcta del verbo en el pretérito o el imperfecto según el contexto.

1. Cuando yo ___tenía___ (tener) diez años, mis padres nos ___llevaron___ (llevar) a México.
2. Todos los días nosotros ___nadábamos___ (nadar) y ___jugábamos___ (jugar) al voleibol en la playa.
3. Un día mi hermano ___aprendió___ (aprender) a volar en parapente.
4. Mis padres no me ___permitieron___ (permitir) tomar lecciones porque yo ___era___ (ser) desmasiado joven.

MySpanishLab

Learn more using Amplifire Dynamic Study Modules, Grammar Tutorials, and Extra Practice activities.

8-20 

La última vez. Túrnense para preguntarse cuándo fue la última vez que cada uno/a de ustedes hizo estas actividades y cómo se sentía mientras las hacía.

MODELO ver un partido de béisbol

E1: *¿Cuándo fue la última vez que viste un partido de béisbol?*

E2: *Vi un partido de béisbol la semana pasada.*

E1: *¿Y cómo te sentías mientras veías el partido?*

E2: *Estaba aburrido/a, porque no me gusta mucho el béisbol.*

1. participar en un campeonato

2. ganar un premio

3. estar en un desfile

4. disfrazarse

5. bailar en un carnaval o en una fiesta

6. ...

8-21 

¿Qué les pasó? Miren las fotos y expliquen qué hacían estas personas y qué les pasó. Describan con detalle la situación.

MODELO Meriel: caminar por el mercado, ver pulseras, discutir precio, empezar a llover

E1: *Meriel caminaba por el mercado cuando vio unas pulseras.*

E2: *Y discutía el precio cuando empezó a llover.*

1. María: caminar, ladrón (*thief*) robar el bolso, hablar por teléfono, parar

2. Luisito: jugar con su hermana, caerse, hacerse daño (*hurt himself*), llorar (*to cry*), ayudar

3. Ángela: ir de viaje, caminar por el aeropuerto, abrirse la maleta, salirse la ropa

Suggestion for 8-19
You may wish to have students share their responses with another pair. Alternatively, you may have the whole class compare their responses and defend their choices.

Suggestion for 8-20
Recycle *sentirse* in the context of a situation or story. Example: Say how you reacted to hearing bad/good news: *Cuando escuché la noticia del accidente me sentí muy mal. Fue un accidente terrible y no pude dormir esa noche.* Then say how you were feeling later. *Por la mañana todavía me sentía mal y llamé a mi mejor amiga.*

Note
You may want to point out that *ver* uses the same preterit endings as other *-er* verbs but the *yo* and *usted/él/ella* forms do not have an accent mark.

Suggestion for 8-21
Before doing this activity you may ask pairs to take turns writing descriptions and actions for each photo. Then have them work together on a detailed narration.

Suggestion for 8-22
After students have done the activity, you may wish to have them compare their answers with those of another pair and decide the function of the preterit or the imperfect in each case.

Warm-up for 8-23
Model this activity by describing an event and an unexpected occurrence, using visuals or gestures to facilitate comprehension: *El sábado pasado fui a una boda. La novia llevaba un velo muy largo. Después de la ceremonia fuimos a un hotel para el banquete. Todos estábamos muy contentos y bailábamos mientras la orquesta tocaba. Una pareja se movía mucho mientras bailaba y tropezó con la mesa donde estaban el pastel de boda y los platos de postre. ¡Total que el pastel se cayó al piso! La madre de la novia corrió hacia donde estaba el pastel y también se cayó. Los novios fueron adonde estaba la señora, pero esta se levantó y dijo que estaba bien. La orquesta empezó a tocar y la fiesta continuó, pero sin pastel. Fue una boda inolvidable.*

Follow-up for 8-23
After each student in the pair finishes narrating, the other should ask questions to obtain more information about the event.

8-22  

Una leyenda. Completa esta narración usando el pretérito o el imperfecto. Compara tus respuestas con las de tu compañero/a e intercambien las razones por las que es preferible usar el pretérito o el imperfecto.

Según una leyenda mexicana, (1) __había__ (haber) antiguamente una mujer indígena que (2) __caminaba__ (caminar) por las calles. Siempre (3) __se vestía__ (vestirse) de blanco. (4) __Tenía__ (tener) el pelo negro y largo. (5) __Estaba__ (estar) muy triste y (6) __lloraba__ (llorar) mucho, por eso muchas personas la (7) __llamaban__ (llamar) la Llorona. La leyenda cuenta que ella (8) __se enamoró__ (enamorarse) de un caballero español. De su romance (9) __nacieron__ (nacer[1]) tres hijos. Luego el caballero (10) __abandonó__ (abandonar) a su familia y (11) __se casó__ (casarse) con otra mujer. Entonces ella (12) __estaba__ (estar) tan desesperada que (13) __mató__ (matar[2]) a sus hijos. Luego (14) __se arrepintió__ (arrepentirse) y (15) __vivió__ (vivir) el resto de su vida con mucho sufrimiento. Todavía hoy en día se oye al fantasma[3] de la mujer llorando por sus hijos.

[1]*to be born* [2]*to kill* [3]*ghost*

8-23 

Un evento inolvidable.
Cuéntale a tu compañero/a algo inesperado que te ocurrió el año pasado. Indica qué pasó, dónde y cuándo. Describe la escena con detalles.

Situación  

PREPARACIÓN. Lean la situación. Luego, compartan ejemplos de vocabulario, gramática y otra información que necesitan para desarrollar la conversación.

Role A. You have just come back from a vacation. Tell your classmate about a particular place you visited. Explain what it was like and what you did there.

Role B. Your classmate has just returned from a vacation. Ask about a particular place he/she visited while there. Find out

a. what the place looked like;
b. what he/she did there; and
c. what special event he/she can tell you about.

	ROLE A	ROLE B
Vocabulario	Words associated with vacations Words to describe a place	Question words
Funciones y formas	Describing a vacation spot Adjectives Narrating and describing in the past Preterit and imperfect	Asking questions about a past event Preterit and imperfect Reacting to what one hears

INTERCAMBIOS. Practica la conversación con tu compañero/a incorporando el vocabulario, las funciones y demás información. Luego, represéntenla ante la clase.

3 Comparing people and things

Para planificar el Carnaval de la Primavera debemos mirar las estadísticas de los años recientes. ¿Vamos a celebrar el carnaval **más de** dos días? En el año 2012, la asistencia fue **mayor que** la del 2013. En el 2012, había **más** mujeres **que** hombres, pero en el 2013 participaron **menos** mujeres **que** en el año anterior. En el 2013, el presupuesto era **más** pequeño **que** en el 2012. Para tener un **mejor** carnaval **que** en años anteriores, vamos a necesitar **más** dinero **que** en los años pasados.

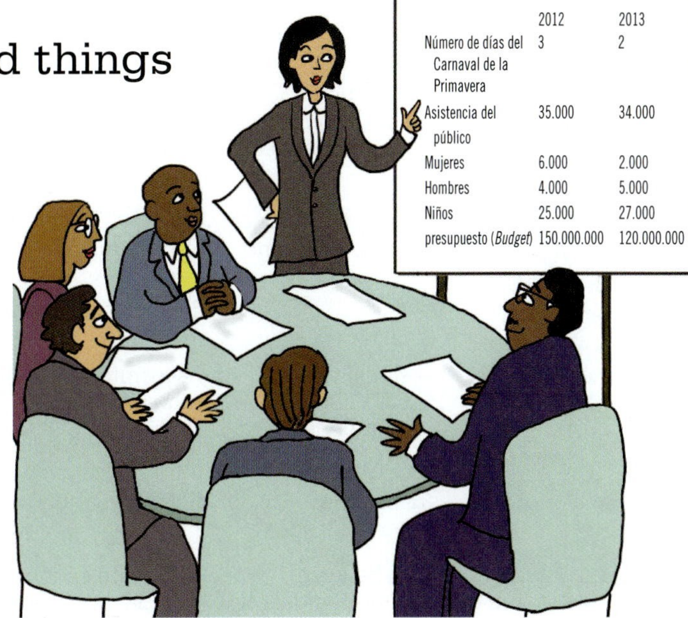

	2012	2013
Número de días del Carnaval de la Primavera	3	2
Asistencia del público	35.000	34.000
Mujeres	6.000	2.000
Hombres	4.000	5.000
Niños	25.000	27.000
presupuesto (*Budget*)	150.000.000	120.000.000

Note
The structure of comparisons in Spanish is similar to that of English. Students will find this grammar point easier than many others in *Mosaicos*. You may wish to focus on the irregular comparatives (see next page), as well as on high-frequency comparisons, such as *A + verb + mejor que B* and *Me gusta más + infinitive + que + infinitive.*

Piénsalo. Indica si las siguientes afirmaciones son ciertas (**C**), falsas (**F**) o posibles (**P**), según las estadísticas. Si la respuesta es falsa, corrige la información.

1. __C__ En el año 2012 participaron **menos** hombres **que** en el 2013.
2. __F__ En el año 2012 participaron **menos** niños **que** adultos en el carnaval. children: 25,000; adults: 10,000
3. __C__ Los organizadores gastaron **más** dinero en el año 2012 **que** en el 2013.
4. __P__ En el futuro el carnaval va a durar **más de** dos días.
5. __P__ Los carnavales del futuro van a ser **mejores que** los del pasado.

Comparisons of inequality

- Use **más... que** or **menos... que** to express comparisons of inequality with nouns, adjectives, and adverbs.

COMPARISONS OF INEQUALITY					
Cuando Alina era joven tenía	**más** / **menos**	amigos que Pepe.	*When Alina was young she had*	*more* / *fewer*	*friends than Pepe.*
Ella era	**más** / **menos**	activa que él.	*She was*	*more* / *less*	*active than he.*
Salía	**más** / **menos**	frecuentemente que él.	*She went out*	*more* / *less*	*frequently than he.*

- Use **de** instead of **que** before numbers.

En el año 2013, había **más de** diez carrozas en el desfile.	*In 2013, there were* more than *ten floats in the parade.*
En el siguiente año había **menos de** diez carrozas.	*The following year there were* fewer than *ten floats.*

- The following adjectives have both regular and irregular comparative forms. Use **mayor** to refer to a person's age. **Más viejo/a** is used to refer to the age of nouns other than people; e.g., a city, a building, a tree.

- Some adjectives have both regular and irregular comparative forms but with different uses:

más bueno/a *better* más malo/a *worse*	refer to a person's moral qualities	Jorge es más bueno que su hermano Esteban. *Jorge is a better person than his brother Esteban.*
mejor *better* peor *worse*	refer to skills and abilities	Esta orquesta es mejor que aquella. *This orchestra is better than that one.*
más viejo *older*	generally used with nouns other than people	La ermita es más vieja que la iglesia. *The sanctuary is older than the church.*
mayor *older*	refers to a person's age	Soy mayor que tú. *I am older than you.*
Exception: más joven o menor *younger*	can be used interchangeably	Mi madre es más joven que mi tía. Mi madre es menor que mi tía. *My mother is younger than my aunt.*

- **Bien** and **mal** are adverbs. They have the same irregular comparative forms as the adjectives **bueno** and **malo.**

bien → mejor	Yo canto **mejor** que Héctor.	*I sing better than Héctor.*
mal → peor	Héctor canta **peor** que yo.	*Héctor sings worse than I.*

¿COMPRENDES?

Completa las oraciones con la forma correcta del comparativo.

1. Mi hermano canta bien, pero Justin Bieber canta ___mejor___.
2. Lucía tiene 15 años y su hermana tiene 20. Lucía es ___menor___ que su hermana.
3. Yo estudio mucho. Paso ___más___ horas en la biblioteca ___que___ mis amigos.
4. El auto es muy caro. Cuesta ___más___ ___de___ cuarenta mil dólares.
5. El primer edificio se construyó en 1800. Es ___más___ ___viejo___ que los otros edificios de la universidad.

MySpanishLab

Learn more using Amplifire Dynamic Study Modules, Grammar Tutorials, and Extra Practice activities.

Cultura

Veracruz y Mérida

Veracruz y Mérida son dos ciudades mexicanas importantes. Veracruz, que está a 400 kilómetros (250 millas) al sureste de la Ciudad de México, fue fundada por el conquistador Hernán Cortés en 1519. Por su puerto, que es el más importante del país, Veracruz es conocida como *la puerta al mundo.*

▲ Desfile en Mérida

Mérida es la ciudad principal del estado de Yucatán, en el sureste del país. Está a más de 1.550 kilómetros (965 millas) de la capital. En el 2000 Mérida fue nombrada *la Capital Americana de la Cultura* a causa de su alta calidad de vida y su extraordinario desarrollo en las artes.

Comparaciones. ¿Cuáles son las ciudades más turísticas de tu país? ¿Por qué? ¿Dónde están los puertos más importantes? ¿Hay ciudades que han recibido (*have received*) nombres o títulos especiales en tu país? ¿Cuáles?

▲ Desfile en Veracruz

PRÁCTICA

8-24

Comparación de dos desfiles.

PREPARACIÓN. Lee la siguiente información sobre dos desfiles mexicanos. Completa las afirmaciones con **más que, menos que, más de** o **menos de,** según la información en la tabla. Compara tus respuestas con las de tu compañero/a.

	VERACRUZ	MÉRIDA
habitantes	568.313	970.377
promedio (*average*) de público que participa	15.000 personas	13.000 personas
número de bandas	9	7
número de policías	220	185

1. Mérida tiene __más__ habitantes __que__ Veracruz.
2. __Más__ personas asisten al desfile de Veracruz __que__ al desfile de Mérida.
3. Los dos desfiles tienen __más__ __de__ cinco bandas.
4. Mérida gasta __menos__ dinero en seguridad (*security*) __que__ Veracruz.
5. __Más__ __de__ medio millón de personas viven en Veracruz.
6. Probablemente el público de Mérida es __menos__ entusiasta __que__ el de Veracruz.

INTERCAMBIOS. La banda de tu universidad piensa participar en uno de estos desfiles, pero no puede gastar mucho dinero. Con tu compañero/a, decidan a qué desfile debe asistir y expliquen por qué.

COSTO POR PERSONA	DESFILE DE VERACRUZ	DESFILE DE MÉRIDA
transporte	5.824,50 pesos	6.552,60 pesos
hotel por día	880,50 pesos	915,25 pesos
comidas por día	450,00 pesos	348,00 pesos

Suggestions for 8-24
Point to the location of Veracruz and Mérida on a map. Students read that Mérida was chosen as *la Capital Americana de la Cultura* in 2000 by the *Organización Capital Americana de la Cultura.* Recycle weather expressions by asking students to guess what the weather is like in these cities. Ask them to compare the weather in Veracruz and Mérida with that of their own city: *En invierno, ¿hace más o menos frío en Mérida que en tu ciudad? ¿Dónde hay menos humedad, en tu ciudad o en Veracruz?*

Suggestion for 8-24, *Intercambios*
You may wish to check (or ask students to check) the exchange rate between the American dollar and the Mexican *peso* so students have a better understanding of the cost per person.

Cultura

La Calavera Catrina

La Calavera Catrina es un relieve en zinc realizado en 1910 por José Guadalupe Posada. Las calaveras representaban de manera humorística figuras contemporáneas en forma de esqueletos y a menudo iban acompañadas de un poema. Hoy en día la imagen se incorpora a las representaciones artísticas del Día de los Muertos en México.

Comparaciones. ¿Se usan las calaveras y los esqueletos humorísticamente en tu cultura? Explica tu respuesta.

8-25 

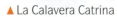

La Calavera (*skull*) Catrina. Los mexicanos celebran el Día de los Muertos con la imagen de la Calavera Catrina y en Estados Unidos se celebra el Día de las Brujas con la figura de una bruja. Comparen las dos imágenes usando el vocabulario de la lista y los criterios indicados.

adornado/a	bonito/a	fuerte
alegre	colorido/a	horroroso/a
alto/a	elegante	joven
bajo/a	feo/a	mayor

 MODELO *La bruja es más horrorosa que la Calavera Catrina.*

1. la apariencia física
2. los colores
3. el estilo
4. lo que más te gusta de una de ellas

▲ La Calavera Catrina

▲ La bruja

Suggestion for 8-25
Remind students to use the appropriate form of the adjectives in doing this activity. After students do the activity, you may want to have each pair compare its reactions with that of another pair.

Suggestion for 8-26, *Preparación*
You may wish to present some background information about Eva Longoria and Christina Aguilera. Ask the following questions: *¿Qué hace…? ¿Cómo se hizo famosa…?* (Eva Longoria, by playing the role of Gabrielle Solís in *Desperate Housewives;* Christina Aguilera by recording the song "Reflection" for the animated film *Mulan*). Ask the students to provide any additional information they may know about these artists or other famous Hispanic artists. You may also ask students to use their digital devices and provide you, in Spanish, with the information they find.

Suggestion for 8-26, *Intercambios*
Before this activity, you may want to brainstorm with the class some ways to present a proposal or new idea to someone in authority. Remind them of the proper register (use of *usted*). To open the conversation the following expressions may be useful: *En representación de… vengo a presentar… En nombre de… le presento…/quisiera discutir con usted…*

Suggestion for *Situación*
You may want to assign partners and have pairs create mini-skits using the video-posting feature, *MediaShare*, online.

8-26 

Personas famosas.

PREPARACIÓN. Comparen a Eva Longoria con Christina Aguilera según los siguientes criterios.

1. su aspecto físico
2. su edad
3. el tipo de trabajo que hacen
4. el dinero o popularidad que tienen

INTERCAMBIOS. Escoge a una de estas famosas y compárate con ella. Tu compañero/a te va a decir si está de acuerdo o no.

Situación

PREPARACIÓN. Lean la situación. Luego, compartan ejemplos de vocabulario, gramática y otra información que necesitan para desarrollar la conversación.

Role A. You are a student government representative presenting a proposal to the dean to change the graduation ceremony. Compare the ceremony at your school with one at a rival institution. Say that the other ceremony is better because it is smaller, better organized, less expensive, and usually has better music and speeches (**discursos**).

Role B. You are the dean. A student government representative is proposing changes in the graduation ceremony. Listen to the presentation and ask questions to compare the advantages of both types of ceremonies.
Then either accept or reject the proposal, and justify your decision.

	ROLE A	ROLE B
Vocabulario	Expressions associated with size, organization, cost, and other amenities of a graduation ceremony	Expressions associated with size, organization, cost, and other amenities of a graduation ceremony
Funciones y formas	Presenting a group proposal to someone in authority Comparing to pinpoint better qualities Convincing/persuading Addressing someone in authority properly	Asking questions Drawing conclusions to make a decision

INTERCAMBIOS. Practica la conversación con tu compañero/a incorporando el vocabulario, las funciones y demás información. Luego, represéntenla ante la clase.

4 Comparing people and things

 PRESIDENTA DEL COMITÉ ORGANIZADOR:

Este año tuvimos un Carnaval de Primavera **tan** espectacular **como** el del 2013, que hasta este año era nuestro carnaval más grande. En los tres días del carnaval asistió **tanto** público **como** en el año 2013, un total de 25.400 personas. Además, los grupos musicales tocaron música **tan** buena **como** la música del carnaval del 2013. También el número de bailarines se mantuvo igual. Hubo **tantos** bailarines **como** en el 2013. Estoy muy agradecida, porque ustedes colaboraron **tanto como** en otros años. Vamos a planificar el carnaval del próximo año **tan bien como** el de este año.

Piénsalo. Indica si las siguientes afirmaciones representan correctamente la información que dio la presidenta del comité. Usa **(C)** para las afirmaciones correctas o **(I)** para las incorrectas.

1. __C__ En 2013 asistieron 25.400 personas al carnaval y este año asistió el mismo número de personas.
2. __I__ Este año los grupos musicales tocaron música que al público le gustó **menos que** en otros años.
3. __C__ Este año el comité organizador hizo un trabajo **tan bueno como** el trabajo de otros años.
4. __C__ La planificación del carnaval fue buena este año y la del próximo año va a ser buena también.

Comparisons of equality

- In the previous section you learned to express comparisons of inequality. In this section you will learn how to indicate that two people, things, or activities are equal in some way.

COMPARISONS OF EQUALITY	
tan... como	*as ... as*
tanto/a... como	*as much ... as*
tantos/as... como	*as many ... as*
tanto como	*as much as*

- Use **tan... como** to express comparisons of equality with adjectives and adverbs.

La boda fue **tan** elegante **como** la fiesta. — *The wedding was as elegant as the party.*

El padre bailó **tan** bien **como** su hija. — *The father danced as well as his daughter.*

- Use **tanto/a... como** and **tantos/as... como** to express comparisons of equality with nouns.

Había **tanta** alegría **como** en el Carnaval. — *There was as much joy as at Mardi Gras.*

Había **tantos** invitados **como** en mi fiesta de graduación. — *There were as many guests as at my graduation party.*

- Use **tanto como** to express comparisons of equality with verbs.

Los invitados bailaron **tanto como** nosotros. — *The guests danced as much as we did.*

¿COMPRENDES?

Completa las oraciones con las expresiones que indican igualdad.

1. El año pasado, el Día de la Independencia fue __tan__ emocionante __como__ el año anterior.
2. En mi casa tuvimos __tanta__ comida __como__ en la última celebración.
3. La ciudad organizó __tantos__ desfiles __como__ en años anteriores.
4. La gente comió y bebió __tanto__ __como__ el año pasado.

MySpanishLab
Learn more using Amplifire Dynamic Study Modules, Grammar Tutorials, and Extra Practice activities.

Suggestion for Comparisons of equality
You may project the online image to review comparisons of inequality. Ask students to compare people at the meeting; e.g., *La presidenta del comité organizador trabaja más que los otros miembros del comité.*

Suggestion
You may give students additional examples: *En la fiesta había tanto ruido como en el Carnaval* and *Había tantas flores como en mi fiesta de cumpleaños.*

Suggestion
You may wish to tell students that the coat of arms that appears on Mexican coins and bills is the national symbol that also appears on the flag. The coat of arms was inspired by the Aztec legend about the founding of Tenochtitlán. According to the legend, the war god Huitzilopochtli had commanded the Aztec people to build their capital at the spot where they found an eagle perched on a prickly pear cactus (*nopal*) growing on a rock submerged in a lake. The eagle would have a snake trapped in its mouth that it had just caught. After 200 years of wandering, they found the promised sign on a small island in the swampy Lake Texcoco. Here they founded their new capital, Tenochtitlán, which was later known as Mexico City.

Follow-up for 8-27
Ask questions to summarize: *¿Pedro tiene tantas clases como Vilma? ¿Tiene Pedro tanto dinero como ella? ¿Vilma tiene tantos hermanos como él?* Then personalize by asking:

1. *¿Cuántos hermanos tiene cada uno/a de ustedes?*
2. *¿Reciben ustedes dinero de sus padres para sus gastos personales o trabajan para ganar* (earn) *dinero?*
3. *¿Coleccionan ustedes DVD o CD? ¿Son las películas tan importantes para ustedes como la música? ¿Qué otras cosas coleccionan?*

PRÁCTICA

Cultura

El peso mexicano

La moneda mexicana es el peso. Tanto en los billetes como en las monedas de metal está el escudo nacional, que tiene un águila parada sobre un nopal (un tipo de cacto), devorando a una serpiente.

Comparaciones. ¿Sabes cuál es la tasa de cambio (*exchange rate*) entre el peso mexicano y el dólar estadounidense? ¿Qué imágenes hay en los billetes de tu país? ¿Y en las monedas? ¿Qué importancia histórica y simbólica tienen esas imágenes?

8-27  

Unos estudiantes afortunados. **PREPARACIÓN.** Lean algunos datos personales sobre cuatro estudiantes e indiquen si las afirmaciones a continuación son ciertas (**C**) o falsas (**F**). Si son falsas, corrijan la información.

	PEDRO	VILMA	MARTA	RICARDO
hermanos	2	3	3	2
clases	5	5	4	6
dinero para gastos personales cada mes	5.000 pesos	8.500 pesos	5.000 pesos	8.500 pesos
películas en DVD	20	18	18	21
viajes a otros países	3	8	3	8

1. __F__ Pedro tiene **tantos** hermanos **como** Vilma. Pedro tiene menos hermanos que Vilma.
2. __F__ Vilma tomó **tantas** clases este semestre **como** Ricardo. Vilma tomó menos clases que Ricardo.
3. __C__ La familia de Marta es **tan** grande **como** la familia de Vilma.
4. __C__ Cada mes, Ricardo recibe **tanto** dinero de sus padres **como** Vilma.
5. __F__ Pedro viaja **tanto como** Ricardo. Pedro viaja menos que Ricardo.
6. __F__ Vilma ve al mes **tantas** películas **como** Ricardo. Vilma ve al mes menos películas que Ricardo.

INTERCAMBIOS. Escoge a uno de los estudiantes de *Preparación* y dile a tu compañero/a las cosas que tienes en común con él/ella.

8-28

Opiniones. **PREPARACIÓN.** Selecciona a dos personas famosas, dos festividades en tu cultura y dos programas cómicos de la televisión.

 **INTERCAMBIOS.** Ahora, expresen su opinión sobre ellos y compárenlos.

E1: *Tom Cruise es tan buen actor como Johnny Depp.*

E2: *No, desde mi punto de vista Johnny Depp es mejor actor que Tom Cruise.*

Situación

PREPARACIÓN. Lean esta situación. Luego, compartan ejemplos de vocabulario, gramática y otra información que necesitan para desarrollar la conversación.

Role A. You are reminiscing about Independence Day celebrations when you were a child. Tell your classmate that you think that:

a. in the past people were more patriotic (**patrióticos**);
b. the celebrations were less expensive; and
c. the celebrations were more family oriented (**se celebraban en familia**) than today.

Role B. Your classmate argues that today's Independence Day celebrations are less family oriented than in the past. You disagree. State that:

a. today people are just as patriotic as they were in the past;
b. people used to spend less money because they made less money; and
c. today families celebrate Independence Day together as much as in the past.

	ROLE A	ROLE B
Vocabulario	Independence Day activities Phrases to express agreement and disagreement	Independence Day activities Phrases to express agreement and disagreement
Funciones y formas	Making comparisons of equality and inequality Expressing agreement and disagreement	Making comparisons of equality and inequality Expressing agreement and disagreement

INTERCAMBIOS. Practica la conversación con tu compañero/a incorporando el vocabulario, las funciones y demás información. Luego, represéntenla ante la clase.

Additional practice with Comparisons
Have a group discussion on the impact of the media and changes students may have observed. Ask:

1. *¿Creen ustedes que hoy hay tanto sexo y violencia en las películas como en el pasado?*
2. *¿Piensan ustedes que hoy hay más violencia social porque la gente ve más televisión?*

Suggestion for *Situación*
Additional situations are available in the Instructor's Resource folder.

Suggestion
Draw 3 people on the board of different heights, weights, and ages or use visuals to present the superlative: *Ella es la más alta de las tres. Él es el más alto del grupo.*

Suggestion
Show visuals of people, places, or things. Describe them and confirm your description by using a superlative: *Creo que es muy feo. Sí, es feísimo.* Then have students describe the visuals.

Suggestion
You may wish to point out the spelling changes in such adjectives as *rico* → *riquísimo* and *largo* → *larguísimo.*

5 Comparing people and things

PERLA: Lupita, ¿tienes algún plan especial para el Día de los Muertos?

LUPITA: Claro que sí. En mi comunidad, vamos al cementerio para visitar a familiares y amigos muertos. Les llevamos **la mejor** música mexicana y su comida preferida. Es **el** día **más importante del** año para recordarlos. Creemos que ellos vuelven a su tumba el 1 y 2 de noviembre para disfrutar de **la mejor** compañía, la de su familia y amigos.

PERLA: ¡Qué interesante! Para mi familia **el** acto **más** importante es recordarlos con **las** flores **más** hermosas **de** la estación.

Piénsalo. Completa las siguientes oraciones con el nombre de la persona que expresa la información.

1. ___Lupita___ lleva al cementerio **la mejor** música mexicana.
2. Según ___Lupita___, el Día de los Muertos es **el** día **más importante del** año para recordar a los familiares y amigos muertos.
3. ___Lupita___ dice que **la** compañía **más** agradable para los muertos es la de sus familiares y amigos.
4. ___Lupita___ dice que su familia lleva la comida que les gustaba **más** a sus familiares muertos.
5. ___Perla___ dice que para su familia, **la** manera **más** apropiada **de** recordar a los muertos es llevarles flores.

The superlative

- Use superlatives to express *most* and *least* as degrees of comparison among three or more entities. To form the superlative, use *definite article* + *noun* + **más/menos** + *adjective.* To express *in* or *at* with the superlative, use **de.**

Es **el** disfraz **menos** creativo (**de** la fiesta).	*It is the least creative costume (at the party).*
México es **el** país con **más** fiestas **de** América del Norte.	*Mexico is the country with the most holidays in North America.*

- Do not use **más** or **menos** with **mejor, peor, mayor,** or **menor.**

¿Esos desfiles? Son **los mejores** desfiles **del** país.	*Those parades? They are the best parades in the country.*
Ivonne es **la mejor** bailarina **del** grupo.	*Ivonne is the best dancer of the group.*

- You may delete the noun when it is clear to whom or to what you refer.

Son **los mejores del** país.	*They are the best (ones) in the country.*

- To express the idea of *extremely*, add the ending **-ísimo (-a, -os, -as)** to the adjective. If the adjective ends in a consonant, add **-ísimo** directly to the singular form of the adjective. If it ends in a vowel, drop the vowel before adding **-ísimo.**

fácil	Este baile es **facilísimo.**	*This dance is extremely easy.*
grande	La carroza es **grandísima.**	*The float is extremely big.*
bueno	Las orquestas son **buenísimas.**	*The orchestras are extremely good.*

LENGUA

A Spanish word can have only one written accent. Therefore, an adjective with a written accent loses the accent when **-ísimo/a** is added.

fácil > facilísimo/a rápido > rapidísimo/a

¿COMPRENDES?

Completa las oraciones para expresar el superlativo.

1. En mi opinión, los deportes acuáticos son _los_ _más_ divertidos. Me encanta nadar, bucear y pescar.
2. Miguel es fenomenal. Es _el_ _mejor_ jugador del equipo.
3. Laura tiene 30 años, Marisol tiene 28 y Susana tiene solo 18. Laura es _la_ _mayor_ de las tres.
4. Mi abuela hace _las_ enchiladas _más_ deliciosas del mundo.

MySpanishLab

Learn more using Amplifire Dynamic Study Modules, Grammar Tutorials, and Extra Practice activities.

PRÁCTICA

Estadísticas demográficas. **PREPARACIÓN.** Lee la información de la tabla siguiente e indica a qué país de la columna B se refiere cada oración de la columna A. Compara tus respuestas con las de tu compañero/a.

	MÉXICO	GUATEMALA	ESTADOS UNIDOS
Población (aprox.) del país	115.000.000 habitantes	14.400.000 habitantes	313.900.000 habitantes
Población de la capital	México D. F.: 8.836.045	Ciudad de Guatemala: 1.110.100	Washington D. C.: 601.723
Número de lenguas indígenas	62	23	aprox. 150
Religión predominante	76.5% son católicos (aprox. 88.000.000)	49% son católicos (aprox. 7.058.000)	51.3% son protestantes (aprox. 161.004.000)
Número de estados o departamentos	32 estados	22 departamentos	50 estados

COLUMNA A

1. _c_ Este país tiene **el mayor número** de habitantes.
2. _a_ La población de la capital de este país es **la más** numerosa.
3. _c_ Es el país donde existe **el mayor** número de lenguas indígenas.
4. _b_ Este es el país con **menos** lenguas indígenas.
5. _c_ Este país tiene **el menor** porcentaje de personas que profesan el catolicismo.
6. _c_ Este país tiene **el mayor** número de gobiernos estatales o departamentales.

COLUMNA B

a. México
b. Guatemala
c. Estados Unidos

Note for 8-29
Students will have to extrapolate from the information in the table. If 51.3% of U.S. residents are Protestants and students know that there are people of several different religions, then they will figure out that the percentage of Catholics is below 49%.

Additional practice with Superlatives
Have students share their answers to the following questions: *¿Cuál es…*
1. *la clase más difícil en tu facultad?*
2. *la fiesta universitaria más popular entre los alumnos?*
3. *el/la profesor/a de español más interesante?*
4. *la lengua más estudiada por los alumnos?*
5. *el horario menos deseado por los estudiantes?*
6. *la facultad con más mujeres/hombres?*

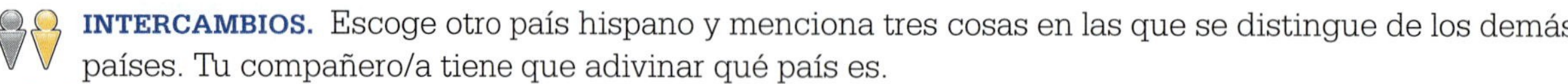

INTERCAMBIOS. Escoge otro país hispano y menciona tres cosas en las que se distingue de los demás países. Tu compañero/a tiene que adivinar qué país es.

MODELO E1: *Es el país de América del Sur que tiene* ***el mayor*** *número de habitantes.*

E2: *Es Colombia. Tiene más de 47 millones de habitantes.*

8-30 

¿En qué pueblo o ciudad? Respondan a las siguientes preguntas y luego comparen sus respuestas con las de otra pareja. ¿Están de acuerdo o tienen opiniones diferentes?

¿En qué pueblo o ciudad de tu país...

1. sirven la mejor comida étnica?
2. se come la comida más picante (*spicy*)?
3. se vende el café cubano más fuerte?
4. celebran las mejores fiestas de Año Nuevo?
5. hay el mayor número de desfiles hermosos?
6. tocan la mejor música folclórica?

Suggestion for *Situación*
You may want to assign partners and have pairs create mini-skits using the video-posting feature, *MediaShare*, online.

Situación

PREPARACIÓN. Lean esta situación. Luego, compartan ejemplos de vocabulario, gramática y otra información cultural que necesitan para desarrollar la conversación.

Role A. You took your traditional trip for spring break and had a great time. Tell your classmate the five most interesting places you saw or activities you did. Provide details about at least one place or activity.

Role B. Ask several questions about your classmate's spring break trip to learn about his/her interesting and enjoyable activities. Then say where you went during spring break, and share the favorite parts of your trip.

	ROLE A	ROLE B
Vocabulario	Words related to places Expressions associated with trips Descriptive words	Question words
Funciones y formas	Narrating an event Describing in detail: Preterit and imperfect Adjectives Expressing the utmost feature of a place or an experience	Reacting to what you hear Asking follow-up questions Narrating an event Describing an experience Expressing the utmost feature of a place or an experience

INTERCAMBIOS. Practica la conversación con tu compañero/a incorporando el vocabulario, las funciones y demás información. Luego, represéntenla ante la clase.

EN ACCIÓN

Hay que celebrar

8-31 Antes de ver 

Las tradiciones. Marca (✓) las tradiciones que asocias con la cultura hispana. Luego, compara tus respuestas con las de tu compañero/a.

1. ✓ el Día de los Muertos
2. ✓ el Cinco de Mayo
3. ✓ la corrida de toros
4. ____ el Día de las Brujas
5. ____ el Día de Acción de Gracias
6. ✓ el fútbol
7. ✓ el festival de la Calle Ocho
8. ____ el Cuatro de Julio

Expansion for 8-31
Have students work in groups to discuss how they celebrate any of the traditions mentioned in this activity. They should elaborate on special food, people (family, friends, etc.), rituals, or events that they may associate with each one. To practice with the preterit and the imperfect, have students share what they did last year to celebrate Halloween, Cinco de Mayo, or any particular holiday.

8-32 Mientras ves  

Unas celebraciones importantes. Indica si las siguientes afirmaciones se refieren a la fiesta de La Mercé (**LM**) o al Día de los Muertos (**DM**), según el contenido de este segmento.

1. LM Es una fiesta en honor a la Virgen.
2. DM Se celebra el primero y el dos de noviembre.
3. DM Las familias hacen procesiones hasta el cementerio.
4. LM Hay espectáculos con música, bailes y desfiles con dragones.
5. LM Algunas personas forman castillos o torres humanas.
6. DM Las calaveras de azúcar son típicas de esta celebración.

8-33 Después de ver  

Días festivos. PREPARACIÓN. Marca (✓) las afirmaciones que contienen ideas que aparecen en el video. Después, compara tus respuestas con las de tu compañero/a.

1. ✓ Muchas celebraciones de América Latina muestran el sincretismo de la cultura española y de las culturas precolombinas.
2. ✓ Algunas fiestas hispanas se celebran también en Estados Unidos.
3. ✓ El Día de los Muertos es una celebración en homenaje (*homage*) a las personas que murieron.
4. ____ Las fiestas del mundo hispano son diferentes según la clase social.

 **INTERCAMBIOS.** Háganse las siguientes preguntas relacionadas con las celebraciones.

1. Piensen en una celebración del mundo hispano. ¿Cómo se celebra? ¿Qué características tiene?
2. ¿Qué diferencias hay entre las celebraciones personales o familiares (cumpleaños, Día del Santo, bautismo, Bar Mitzvah, boda, etc.) y las celebraciones cívicas (carnaval, fiestas de independencia, Día de las Brujas, etc.)?

Mosaicos

Warm-up for 8-35
As a pre-listening activity, have students work in groups of 4 and narrate what they did last year to celebrate their favorite holiday.

Audioscript for 8-35
DANIEL: *Estoy encantado de poder pasar las Navidades contigo y tu familia aquí en México.*
SANDRA: *Y te tenemos muchas sorpresas. Esta noche empiezan las Posadas.*
DANIEL: *¿Y qué es eso?*
SANDRA: *Aquí en México empezamos a celebrar la Navidad nueve días antes y nos reunimos un grupo de familiares y personas cercanas y pedimos posada.*
DANIEL: *¿Piden posada?*
SANDRA: *Sí, un lugar para pasar la noche, igual que hicieron José y María cuando llegaron a Belén. Vamos a casa de un pariente o alguien conocido, cantamos canciones típicas de Navidad y pedimos posada. Los parientes o amigos responden que no podemos entrar. Nosotros seguimos pidiendo posada hasta que nos dejan entrar. Entonces empieza la fiesta, y al final se rompe una piñata con regalos y dulces.*
DANIEL: *Parece ser divertido.*
SANDRA: *Sí, es muy divertido. Hacemos esto todas las noches durante nueve días. Y ustedes, ¿qué hacen en Navidad?*
DANIEL: *En casa nos reunimos la noche de Nochebuena. Viene toda la familia e intercambiamos regalos.*
SANDRA: *Bueno, esta Navidad va a ser muy diferente para ti, pero te va a gustar mucho.*

Suggestion for 8-35
You may wish to have students listen to the conversation twice, the first time to get the gist of the conversation and the second time to take notes on what contextual cues in the conversation helped them to infer information that was not stated overtly. You may wish to provide an example.

ESCUCHA

ESTRATEGIA

Draw conclusions based on what you know

Understanding what someone says involves using the context and the information the speaker provides to draw conclusions that go beyond literal comprehension. This process is called inferencing, or making inferences. For example, if you are driving with a friend and get lost, you may say, "There is a gas station up there on the right." Your friend will probably infer that you want to stop to ask for directions.

8-34 Presentational

Preparación. Es el 22 de diciembre y dos amigos conversan sobre las celebraciones del fin de año. Antes de escuchar su conversación, describe en un párrafo cómo celebras tú el fin de año.

8-35   Interpretive

Escucha. First, read the statements below, and then listen as two friends talk about a Mexican holiday. After listening, mark (✓) the statements that provide information you can infer from what you heard.

1. _____ Daniel es mexicano.
2. _____ Sandra es una persona muy tímida.
3. __✓__ Sandra no es estadounidense.
4. _____ Daniel está triste porque no va a celebrar la Navidad con su familia.
5. _____ Pedir posada es una costumbre en la que participa solamente la familia.
6. __✓__ Daniel no conoce algunas costumbres mexicanas.

Comprueba
I was able to …

___ make inferences based upon what I heard.

___ use contextual and factual information to draw conclusions.

8-36  Interpersonal

Un paso más. Comparte tus respuestas a estas preguntas con tu compañero/a.

1. ¿Qué fiesta o tradición religiosa te gustaría celebrar en un país hispano? ¿Por qué?
2. ¿Celebras esa fiesta en tu ciudad o país? ¿Cómo se celebra?
3. ¿Qué fiesta o tradición celebras con tus amigos?

HABLA

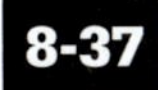

8-37 Presentational

ESTRATEGIA

Conduct an interview

To conduct an interview, you need to ask two types of questions: a) questions to open up a topic; and b) follow-up questions to get additional information. Questions that can be answered with **Sí** or **No** are not likely to elicit much information, unless you follow up with **¿Por qué?** Listen carefully to what your interviewee says so that you can ask relevant follow-up questions.

Preparación. Escriban una pregunta de seguimiento (*follow-up*) para cada una de las afirmaciones. Luego, compártanlas con la clase.

1. Cuando yo tenía doce años practicaba muchos deportes.
2. En mi familia celebrábamos fiestas.
3. Algunas costumbres familiares me gustaban y otras no.

8-38  Interpersonal

Habla. Entrevista a tu compañero/a sobre su infancia y adolescencia. Hazle preguntas para iniciar temas y obtener más información. Toma notas de sus respuestas.

Comprueba

In my conversation ...

_____ **I asked both topic opening questions and follow-up questions.**

_____ **I took effective notes.**

8-39  Interpretive

Un paso más. Escriban un breve informe comparativo sobre los siguientes aspectos de la infancia y adolescencia de cada uno/a de ustedes. Otros compañeros van a leer su informe y tratar de averiguar quiénes son ustedes. Mantengan su identidad en secreto.

1. Durante la infancia/adolescencia...
2. Con respecto a los deportes/las fiestas...
3. La persona A y la persona B tuvieron una niñez/adolescencia semejante/diferente porque...

ALMAS GEMELAS

Somos dos almas gemelas. Tanto mi compañero/a como yo nacimos en...

MUNDOS APARTES

Somos dos mundos apartes. Mi compañero/a nació en... Yo nací en...

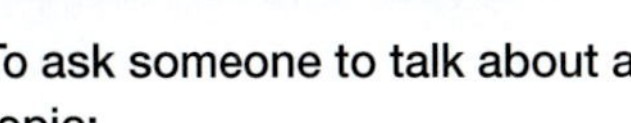

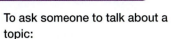

To ask someone to talk about a topic:

¿Me podrías hablar sobre...?
Can you talk to me more about ...?

¿Qué me puede decir usted sobre/de...?
What can you tell me about ...?

Me gustaría saber...
I would like to know ...

To ask someone to expand on a topic:

¿Podrías hablar más sobre...?

¿Qué más me puedes decir sobre...?

To show empathy when responding:

¡Oh! ¡Qué lástima! ¡Cuánto lo siento!
How sad! I'm so sorry.

To share someone's happiness:

¡Qué fabuloso/bueno!
How fabulous/great!

¡Cuánto me alegro!
I'm so happy to hear that!

To express interest in what someone said:

¡Qué interesante!
How interesting!

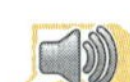 Listen to a conversation with these expressions.

Suggestion for 8-37
You may want to give students some examples of open-ended questions that encourage the other person to talk, such as *¿Podrías hablar de los deportes que practicabas de niño/a?* This type of question elicits long and more detailed responses than direct, close-ended questions like *¿Qué deportes practicabas cuando eras niño/a?*

Suggestion for 8-37
Have students work in small groups helping each other prepare open-ended initial and follow-up questions for their interviews.

Note for *En directo*
Before doing activity 8-38, first have students read the expressions in *En directo*. Then have them listen to the dialogue and encourage them to use the expressions in their own conversation.

Audioscript for *En directo*
ERNESTO: *Profesora, me gustaría saber en qué países de América Latina se celebra la Navidad. ¿Me podría hablar sobre ello?*
PROFESORA: *En verdad, la Navidad se celebra por toda América Latina pero las tradiciones varían. Es decir, la gente celebra este día de diferentes formas; tienen diferentes costumbres.*
ERNESTO: *¡Qué interesante! ¿Qué más me puede decir sobre estas tradiciones?*

Suggestions for 8-39
To keep identities of the interviewees hidden, pairs can type their reports, referring to each other as *Persona A* and *Persona B*. You may wish to use your course management system to post the reports and have students try to figure out the identity of the pairs as homework and then compare notes in class.

You may wish to have students read aloud the anonymous reports (randomly handed out), and the class together guesses the identities of the pairs.

LEE

8-40   Interpersonal

Preparación. Las creencias sobre la muerte varían de una cultura a otra. Indica si las siguientes creencias y prácticas se asocian con la cultura egipcia (**E**), con alguna cultura indígena americana (**I**) o con ambas (**A**). Intercambien la información y compárenla con su propia cultura.

1. __A__ Creían que había vida después de la muerte.
2. __A__ Construían pirámides para honrar a los muertos.
3. __I__ Vestían a los muertos con ropa funeraria especial.
4. __A__ Ponían una máscara sobre la cara del muerto.
5. __A__ Enterraban (*They buried*) al muerto en las pirámides, en tumbas o sepulcros, de acuerdo al estatus social de la persona muerta.
6. __A__ La familia de la persona muerta depositaba joyas y objetos de valor en la tumba o pirámide.
7. __I__ Rociaban (*They sprayed*) el cadáver con un polvo de color rojo para simbolizar el renacimiento (*rebirth*).

ESTRATEGIA

Make inferences

Understanding a text, like listening to a speaker, involves both comprehending the words literally and using information provided to make inferences. To make inferences when you read, use your knowledge, understanding of context, and active thinking skills, as well as your ability to understand the printed words on the page.

Suggestion for 8-41
To check that students understand the content of the reading, you might suggest they use the information from it as a basis for comparison with other cultures they may know about, such as Native American culture.

8-41 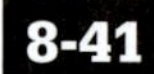  Interpretive

Lee. Determina si las siguientes afirmaciones representan información explícita (**E**) o si son inferencias (**I**) basadas en el contenido del texto. Si es una inferencia, indica la oración o las oraciones en el texto en que se basa(n).

1. __E__ Los expertos no saben de dónde vinieron los mayas.
2. __I__ Los mayas crearon una gran civilización.
3. __I__ Las comunidades mayas tenían autoridades que los gobernaban.
4. __I__ Como los egipcios, los mayas construyeron edificios magníficos para honrar la memoria de personas de alto estatus en su comunidad.
5. __E__ Los mayas, como otros grupos indígenas, pensaban que la vida continuaba después de la muerte.
6. __E__ Para los mayas, el tipo de muerte determinaba el destino de una persona.
7. __I__ No todos los mayas iban al mismo destino después de la muerte.
8. __E__ La comida, el agua y los amuletos ayudaban al espíritu del muerto a llegar a su destino final.

Comprueba

I was able to …

___ **use literal as well as implied information to make inferences.**

___ **differentiate between explicit facts and information provided indirectly.**

CREENCIAS Y COSTUMBRES MAYAS SOBRE LA MUERTE

El origen de los mayas es incierto. Sin embargo, se sabe que esta civilización ocupó y se desarrolló[1] en los actuales territorios de Guatemala, México, Belice, Honduras y El Salvador. Durante su período de mayor esplendor, los mayas construyeron ciudades y pirámides, donde enterraban[2] a sus gobernantes[3] y los veneraban[4] después de muertos.

Los mayas compartían con otras culturas mesoamericanas algunas creencias y costumbres. Entre otras cosas, creían en la vida después de la muerte y en la interacción entre el mundo humano y el mundo espiritual. Creían que el destino de una persona después de la muerte dependía de la forma en que moría y no de su conducta mientras vivía. Las tumbas y la ropa de los muertos confirman que los mayas creían que el espíritu se prolongaba más allá de la muerte. La mayoría de los muertos iba a Xibalbá, un lugar en el mundo de abajo.

Para llegar a Xibalbá había que superar numerosos peligros[5]. El espíritu debía comer bien y cuidarse. Por eso, los mayas dejaban en la tumba ropa funeraria. También ponían comida, agua y amuletos protectores, de acuerdo con el estatus social del muerto.

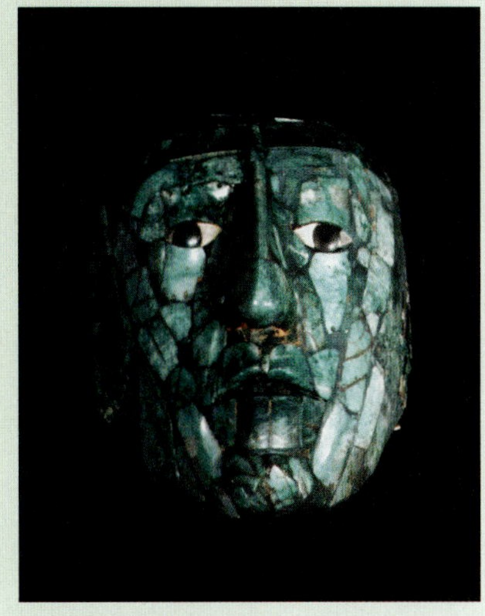

Los mayas rociaban[6] el cadáver con un polvo rojo que simbolizaba el renacimiento. También lo adornaban con joyas, collares, pulseras y anillos de jade, hueso[7] o concha[8] y un cinturón ceremonial. En muchas tumbas ponían una máscara sobre la cara del muerto para ocultar su identidad. En la boca le ponían una cuenta[9] de jade, símbolo de lo precioso y lo perenne, para preservar su espíritu inmortal.

Algunas de estas creencias y costumbres todavía se conservan, con ciertas variaciones, en algunas comunidades de Guatemala, México y El Salvador.

[1]*developed* [2]*buried* [3]*rulers* [4]*worshipped* [5]*dangers* [6]*sprinkled* [7]*bone* [8]*shell* [9]*bead*

8-42 Presentational

Un paso más. Escribe un párrafo e indica qué objetos probablemente ponían los mayas en la tumba o pirámide de un gobernante con las siguientes características:

- Era físicamente activo.
- Le gustaba mucho el arte.
- Estudiaba astronomía.
- Le fascinaba la guerra.
- Tenía ocho hijas, todas muy bellas.

ESCRIBE

8-43  Interpersonal

Preparación. Vas a narrar una historia personal, real o imaginaria. Habla con tu compañero/a para determinar lo siguiente:

1. ¿Cuál es el objetivo de tu narración?
2. ¿Cuántos protagonistas hay? ¿Qué características físicas y de personalidad tienen?
3. ¿Cómo vas a organizar los hechos? ¿En orden cronológico?
4. ¿Qué información vas a presentar en la introducción? ¿Cuál va a ser el conflicto?
5. Escribe una lista de verbos que te ayuden a describir el ambiente (*setting*) y otros que narren la acción. Intercambien sus listas y háganse sugerencias.

ESTRATEGIA

Select and sequence details

A successful narrative is characterized by a logical, clear, and believable sequence of events, and a good description of setting and characters. Structure your narration as follows:

- Introduce the characters, describe the setting, and begin the action.
- Present the unfolding of the action. Describe the characters and the tensions caused by their actions or by the events around them.
- Either resolve the actions/tensions, or leave the ending unresolved so your reader can imagine what happens.

Note for *En directo*
Before doing activity 8-44, first have students read the expressions in *En directo.* Then have them listen to the dialogue and encourage them to use the expressions in their own writing.

Audioscript for *En directo*
MARIO: *¡Felicidades, Pati! El carnaval internacional fue increíble.*
PATI: *Gracias, Mario. La verdad es que nos divertimos mucho.*
MARIO: *Dime, ¿cómo fueron los preparativos?*
PATI: *Bueno, primero todos los participantes nos reunimos y hablamos del plan. Después, quedamos todos los martes a la una de la tarde para practicar. Luego, el día antes del carnaval, decoramos las carrozas. Por fin, llegó el día del carnaval y ¡todo nos fue perfectamente bien!*

8-44  Presentational

Escribe. Usa la información de la actividad 8-43 y escribe tu narración.

Comprueba
I was able to ...

___ **successfully develop a story, including the characters and the events.**

___ **recount the order of events chronologically.**

En directo

To indicate chronological order:

Primero...

Después.../Después de (un tiempo)...

Luego...

Más tarde...

Finalmente.../Por fin...

 Listen to a conversation with these expressions.

8-45 Interpretive

Un paso más. Intercambia tu narración con un/a compañero/a. Mientras leen, escriban tres preguntas de seguimiento para hacerle a su compañero/a sobre los personajes, el conflicto o la resolución.

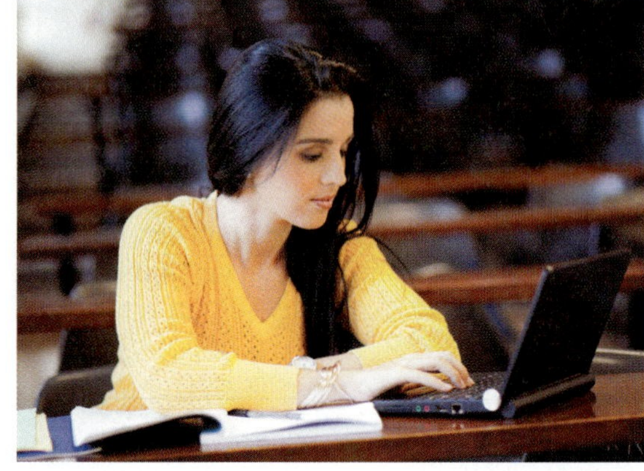

En este capítulo...

Comprueba lo que sabes

Go to ***MySpanishLab*** to review what you have learned in this chapter. Practice with the following:

Vocabulario

LAS FIESTAS Y LAS CELEBRACIONES
Holidays and celebrations

la alegría *joy*
el aserrín *sawdust*
el carnaval *carnival*
la carreta *cart, wagon*
la carroza *float (in a parade)*
la celebración *celebration*
la comparsa *group dressed in similar costumes*
la corrida (de toros) *bullfight*
la costumbre *custom*
el desfile *parade*
el día feriado *legal holiday*
el día festivo *holiday*
el festival *festival*
la festividad, la fiesta *festivity; holiday; celebration*
los fuegos artificiales *fireworks*
la invitación *invitation*
el preparativo *preparation*
la procesión *procession*
la semilla *seed*
el toro *bull*
la tradición *tradition*

VERBOS
Verbs

acompañar *to accompany*
comenzar (ie) *to begin*
dar una vuelta *to take a walk*
disfrazarse (c) *to wear a costume*
encerrar (ie) *to lock up, shut in*
enterrar *to bury*
invitar *to invite*
mantener (g, ie) *to maintain*
matar *to kill*
pasarlo bien *to have a good time*
quedar *to arrange to meet*
recordar (ue) *to remember*
reunirse *to get together*

LAS PERSONAS
People

el antepasado *ancestor*
la gente *people*
el/la peregrino/a *pilgrim*

LOS LUGARES
Places

el cementerio *cemetery*
la iglesia *church*
el teatro *theater*

OTRAS CELEBRACIONES
Other celebrations

el Año Nuevo *New Year's Day*
el Día de Acción de Gracias *Thanksgiving Day*
el Día de las Brujas *Halloween*
el Día de los Enamorados/del Amor y la Amistad *Valentine's Day*
el Día de la Independencia de México *Mexican Independence Day*
el Día de la Madre *Mother's Day*
el Día del Padre *Father's Day*
la Navidad *Christmas*
la Nochebuena *Christmas Eve*
la Nochevieja *New Year's Eve*
la Pascua *Easter*

EL TIEMPO
Time

antes *before*
el comienzo *beginning*
entonces *then*
hoy en día *nowadays*
mientras *while*

LAS DESCRIPCIONES
Descriptions

adornado/a *decorated*
animado/a *lively*
difunto/a, muerto/a *dead*
horroroso/a *horrific*
malévolo/a *malevolent*
maravilloso/a *marvelous*
suave *soft*
último/a *last*

PALABRAS Y EXPRESIONES ÚTILES
Useful words and expressions

cómo no *of course*
estupendamente *marvellously*
en vivo *live*

See pages 293, 297, and 300 for expressions used to make comparisons.

EXPRESIONES DE TIEMPO
Time expressions

a veces *sometimes, at times*
frecuentemente *frequently*
generalmente *generally*
mientras *while*
nunca *never*
siempre *always*

¿Dónde trabajas?

Introduction to chapter
Introduce the chapter theme about what people do for a living and ask questions to recycle content from the previous chapter. Related questions: *¿Cuáles son algunos días feriados en que normalmente no trabaja la gente? Sin embargo, hay gente que por su profesión siempre está trabajando. ¿Pueden nombrar algunas de estas profesiones? ¿Qué otras profesiones saben decir en español? ¿Te gustaría llevar traje de chaqueta todos los días para ir a trabajar? ¿Cómo te gustaría vestir para ir a trabajar? ¿Trabajaste el verano pasado? ¿Qué trabajo tenías? ¿Qué hacías en tu trabajo?*

Integrated Performance Assessment: Three Modes of Communication

Presentational: See activities 9-19, 9-32, 9-37, 9-40, and 9-42.

Interpretive: See activities 9-1, 9-2, 9-3, 9-4, 9-5, 9-8, 9-9, 9-10, 9-11, 9-13, 9-14, 9-15, 9-17, 9-20, 9-21, 9-22, 9-25, 9-26, 9-27, 9-28, 9-29, 9-30, 9-31, 9-33, 9-35, 9-39, and 9-41.

Interpersonal: See activities 9-2, 9-3, 9-4, 9-5, 9-6, 9-7, 9-8, 9-10, 9-11, 9-12, 9-13, 9-14, 9-15, 9-16, 9-17, 9-18, 9-19, 9-20, 9-21, 9-22, 9-23, 9-24, 9-25, 9-28, 9-31, 9-34, 9-36, 9-38, 9-43 and all *Situación* activities.

ENFOQUE CULTURAL
Guatemala

VOCABULARIO EN CONTEXTO
El trabajo
Los oficios y las profesiones
Buscando trabajo

MOSAICO CULTURAL
¿Trabajas o estudias?

FUNCIONES Y FORMAS
Review of direct and indirect object pronouns
Use of direct and indirect object pronouns together
More on the imperfect and the preterit
Formal commands

EN ACCIÓN
Buscando trabajo

MOSAICOS
ESCUCHA Use contextual guessing
HABLA Gather information strategically to express a decision
LEE Organize textual information into categories
ESCRIBE Focus on purpose, content, and audience

EN ESTE CAPÍTULO...
Comprueba lo que sabes
Vocabulario

LEARNING OUTCOMES

You will be able to:

- talk about careers and employment
- avoid repetition
- describe past events in more detail
- give instructions and suggestions
- compare demographic and economic changes in Guatemala and in the United States

ENFOQUE cultural GUATEMALA

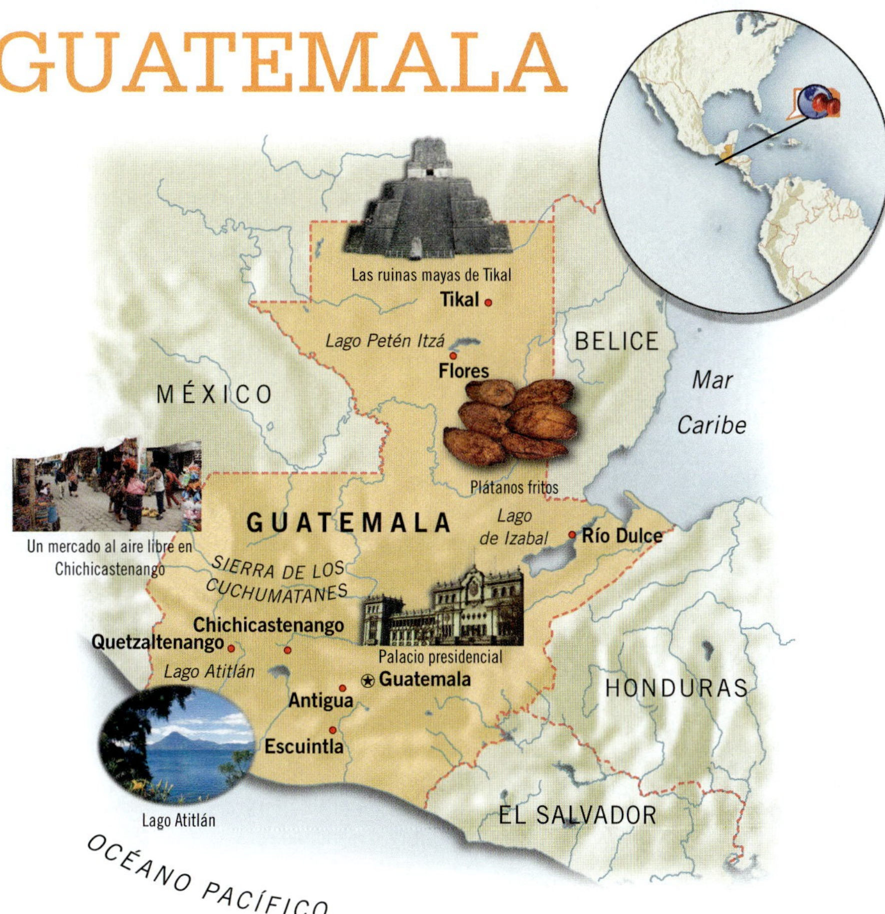

Enfoque cultural

To learn more about Guatemala, go to MySpanishLab to view the *Vistas culturales* videos.

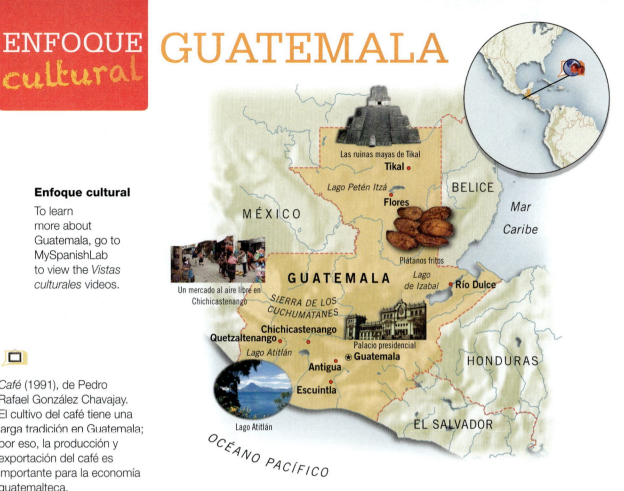

Café (1991), de Pedro Rafael González Chavajay. El cultivo del café tiene una larga tradición en Guatemala; por eso, la producción y exportación del café es importante para la economía guatemalteca.

¿QUÉ TE PARECE?

- El nombre Guatemala viene del náhuatl y significa lugar de muchos árboles.
- En la bandera de Guatemala la franja (*stripe*) blanca con el escudo (*coat of arms*) entre las dos azules representa al país entre el océano Pacífico y el mar Caribe.
- Guatemala cuenta con 33 volcanes. Algunos de ellos, como el volcán Pacaya, siguen en actividad eruptiva.
- La guerra civil de Guatemala duró 36 años; terminó en 1996.
- La mitad de la población de Guatemala tiene menos de veinte años.
- El fiambre es una ensalada típica que puede tener hasta 50 ingredientes. Se come el 1 de noviembre para celebrar el Día de Todos los Santos.

Suggestion for map

Brainstorm with students information about Guatemala. Ask: *¿Cómo se llaman los ciudadanos de Guatemala?* Project the map, draw students' attention to Antigua, and have them guess the meaning. (Antigua was formerly the capital of Guatemala.) Ask which major civilization existed in Guatemala before the Spaniards arrived. Call their attention to the names of some cities and ask them to guess what languages are probably spoken in Guatemala.

Use photos to explain that indigenous and mestizo people are the majority and that many Guatemalans do not speak Spanish as their first language. Mention Rigoberta Menchú, Nobel Peace Prize winner, and Miguel Ángel Asturias, winner of the Nobel Prize in Literature. Mention two major natural disasters that have affected the country: Hurricane Mitch in 1998; and an earthquake in 1976 that killed 23,000 people. Explain that these disasters and political instability have forced many Guatemalans to leave the country in search of better living conditions.

Note for art

This painting and the ones on p. 313 are by the Guatemalan painter Pedro Rafael González Chavajay. He comes from a family of painters of Mayan descent. They have created a school of primitive art with paintings that meticulously show the life and traditions of the Mayan people.

Note for *Cobán*
Cobán celebrates its annual festival during the last week of July with parades, expositions, and rodeos, as well as the crowning of the *Rabín Ajau*. Mayan girls from around the country are first selected as princesses in their local communities, then compete for the national title.

Note for *Tikal*
Tikal is a UNESCO World Heritage Site. It is believed that the city was abandoned in 900 A.D. during a drought. Antigua and *Parque arqueológico y ruinas de Quiriguá* are other UNESCO sites in Guatemala.

El Mirador was first seen in 1926, but it wasn't until 1978 that excavations began. Distinguished American archaeologists and historians have worked on its excavations. Hiking through jungles is one of the only ways to reach the site.

Note for *Miguel Ángel Asturias*
Through his work, Miguel Ángel Asturias (1899–1974) helped bring about international awareness of the indigenous peoples of Guatemala and is widely recognized as one of the greatest Latin American writers of the 20th century.

ENFOQUE cultural

En la ciudad de Cobán, en el centro de Guatemala, se celebra anualmente la Fiesta Nacional Indígena de Guatemala (un festival folclórico). Incluye un certamen (*contest*) de belleza para mujeres indígenas de Guatemala. Participan aproximadamente 100 señoritas que expresan sus ideales en su idioma materno y en español. La ganadora es coronada con el título de *Rabín Ajau,* que significa Hija del Rey en Q'eqchi', un idioma maya.

El quetzal, el ave nacional de Guatemala, tiene un papel mitológico en su historia. El nombre del dios supremo, Quetzalcóatl, está formado por dos palabras de origen náhuatl: *quetzal,* que se refiere a la pluma larga y verde del ave, y *coatl,* que quiere decir serpiente. Para los mayas, las plumas del quetzal eran sagradas. El quetzal aparece en el escudo nacional y es también el nombre de la moneda oficial.

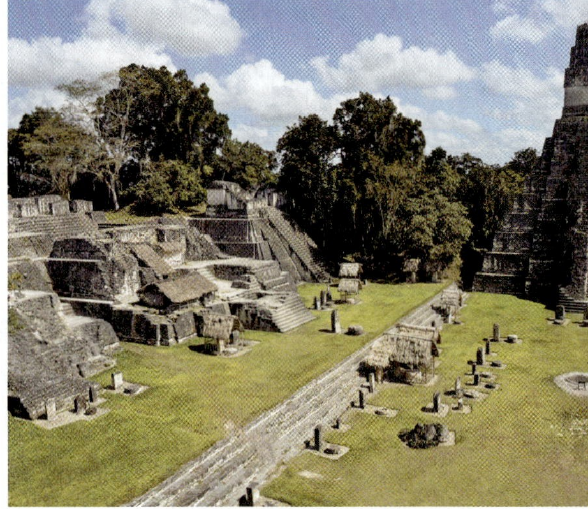

Tikal es la ciudad maya más conocida en Guatemala. Fue construida en 200 d.C. Hay miles de estructuras pero la mayoría de ellas no han sido excavadas. Otras, como el Mirador, están en medio de la selva y no es fácil llegar a verlas.

Miguel Ángel Asturias Rosales, quien ganó el Premio Nobel de Literatura en 1967, vivió en el exilio durante gran parte de su vida por criticar en sus obras la represión y las dictaduras (como en *El señor presidente*). En *Hombres de maíz* defendió las tradiciones y cultura mayas. En el centro de la Ciudad de Guatemala esta estatua conmemora la vida del gran escritor guatemalteco.

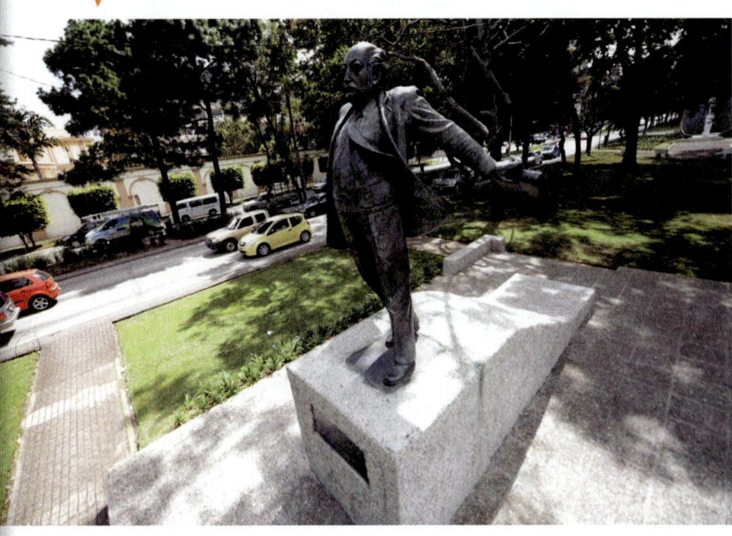

¿CUÁNTO SABES?

Contesta las siguientes preguntas según la información que tienes sobre Guatemala.

1. ¿Cuál es la capital de Guatemala? la Ciudad de Guatemala
2. ¿Cómo se llama el océano que está al oeste del país? el océano Pacífico
3. ¿Qué comida es típica para el Día de Todos los Santos? el fiambre
4. ¿Quién es un escritor famoso? Miguel Ángel Asturias Rosales
5. ¿De qué lengua vienen las palabras "quetzal" y "Guatemala"? náhuatl
6. ¿Qué civilización construyó la ciudad de Tikal? la civilización maya

Vocabulario en contexto

Talking about careers and employment

El trabajo

Pronunciation topic: Consonants l, m, n, and ñ

Learn more using Amplifire Dynamic Study Modules, Pronunciation, and Vocabulary Tutorials.

▲ El sector más grande en la economía guatemalteca es la **agricultura.** Esta representa dos tercios (*thirds*) de las **exportaciones** y la mitad de la **fuerza laboral** del país. Los productos **agrícolas** principales son el café, la caña de azúcar y los plátanos. Antes, los **agricultores** plantaban y **cosechaban** sus cultivos (*crops*) en **terrenos** pequeños. Ahora el café y otros productos agrícolas se **cultivan** en **fincas** grandes.

▲ Fincas de café

▲ Antes, los productos del **campo** y los productos artesanales, como las telas, se vendían solo en los mercados locales como en el de Chichicastenango. Sin embargo, ahora se exportan a otros países. En concreto, la **industria textil** es una importante **fuente de ingresos** para muchas familias.

▲ Un mercado en Chichicastenango

▲ El terreno fértil es el **recurso natural** más importante de Guatemala. En sus tierras también se encuentran minerales como el **hierro,** el **petróleo** y el níquel, que muchas veces **se explotan** a través de compañías extranjeras. Antes, los **carpinteros** hacían muebles solamente para el consumo local. Gracias a los abundantes **bosques** de Guatemala, hoy en día se exportan la **madera** y sus productos derivados.

▲ Una mina de níquel en El Estor, Guatemala

Suggestion
Have students describe the images and the actions depicted in them. Focus on the contrast between the past (paintings) and the present (photos).

Standard 2.2
Students demonstrate an understanding of the relationship between the products and perspectives of the culture studied.

The paintings by Pedro Rafael González Chavajay and the photos of Guatemalan industry today depict aspects of the work life of the people of Guatemala. Have students say as much about the paintings and the photos as they can. What do the work, facial expressions, and objects depicted in the paintings say about Mayan culture? What aspects of the Guatemalan economy of the 21st century are depicted in the photos?

Audioscript for 9-1

1. *La agricultura es una importante fuente de ingresos en Guatemala.*
2. *Productos como el café, el azúcar y los plátanos se cultivan en fincas grandes.*
3. *Los productos artesanales se vendían solo en los mercados locales.*
4. *Algunas compañías extranjeras explotan minerales como el hierro o el níquel.*
5. *Los carpinteros hacían muebles para el consumo local.*
6. *Los bosques de Guatemala son abundantes.*

PRÁCTICA

9-1  

Escucha y confirma. Listen to the following statements and decide if they refer to the past (**antes**), or to the present (**ahora**).

1. antes (ahora)
2. antes (ahora)
3. (antes) ahora
4. antes (ahora)
5. (antes) ahora
6. antes (ahora)

9-2  

Los trabajos y los trabajadores. Indica si las siguientes afirmaciones son ciertas (**C**) o falsas (**F**). Corrige las falsas y compara tus respuestas con las de tu compañero/a.

1. __C__ Los agricultores hacen los trabajos del campo.
2. __C__ Los artesanos elaboran telas.
3. __F__ Los carpinteros trabajan con los metales. Trabajan con la madera.
4. __C__ Guatemala exporta muebles y otros productos hechos de madera.
5. __F__ El oro y la plata son los minerales más abundantes de Guatemala. hierro, níquel
6. __F__ Los agricultores plantan y cosechan productos para el consumo local solamente. Los productos agrícolas se exportan también.

LENGUA

The suffix **-ero/-era** is often used in Spanish to designate trades and professions, e.g., **camarero/a** (*server*), **plomero/a** (*plumber*), **peluquero/a** (*hairdresser*). Another common suffix is **-ista,** e.g., **electricista** (*electrician*); **contratista** (*contractor*).

9-3  

Productos y lugares. Asocia las descripciones con las definiciones. Luego, compara tus respuestas con las de tu compañero/a.

1. __d__ los productos que se venden a otros países
2. __a__ las telas y otros productos artesanales que se exportan a los mercados internacionales
3. __f__ el conjunto de personas que trabajan
4. __b__ el lugar en el campo donde se encuentran los cultivos
5. __c__ los depósitos minerales y el terreno fértil
6. __e__ el material básico que usan los carpinteros

a. la industria textil
b. la finca
c. los recursos naturales
d. las exportaciones
e. la madera
f. la fuerza laboral

Suggestions for 9-4

You may wish to model the type of description you are looking for by projecting the painting from the chapter opener and leading the class in a description of it. You may want to have partners change roles and describe a second painting, or have them take turns describing different aspects of the same painting.

9-4 

Descripciones. Escoge uno de los cuadros en la página 313 para describírselo a tu compañero/a. Describe las escenas con el mayor detalle posible e incluye las siguientes ideas:

1. lugar donde están las personas
2. rasgos físicos
3. edad aproximada
4. ropa que llevan
5. qué están haciendo
6. qué están pensando
7. cómo se sienten

Los oficios y las profesiones

Dra. Alicia Gonica de Pérez
CARDIÓLOGA

Consultorio
La Concepción 81
Calle 18, 402, Ciudad de Guatemala
Teléfono: (502) 23622001
Fax: (502) 23670721

▲Una **médica** le inyecta antibióticos a una paciente en su **consultorio.**

▲Una **ejecutiva** llama por teléfono a un **cliente.**

▲Una **locutora espera** la **señal** para comenzar un programa de noticias en una estación de radio.

▲Un **técnico** revisa los controles de una **compañía** petrolera.

▲Unos **bomberos apagan** un **incendio** en la Ciudad de Guatemala.

◀Un **peluquero** le corta el pelo a una clienta.

Otras ocupaciones

la juez (el juez)

el abogado (la abogada)

la bibliotecaria (el bibliotecario)

el policía (la policía)

el ama de casa (el amo de casa)

el actor (la actriz)

el chofer (la chofer)

la cajera (el cajero)

la científica (el científico)

el psicólogo (la psicóloga)

el plomero (la plomera)

la arquitecta (el arquitecto)

la enfermera (el enfermero)

la mujer de negocios (el hombre de negocios)

el ingeniero (la ingeniera)

la periodista (el periodista)

la electricista (el electricista)

el intérprete (la intérprete)

el contador (la contadora)

el obrero (la obrera)

Suggestion for *Vocabulario en contexto*
You may want to project the images in class and ask questions to provide comprehensible input. You may expand by having students describe the workers' job/task and the kind of preparation or education required. Personalize when possible: *¿Quién es la persona de la primera foto? ¿Dónde trabaja? Y ustedes, ¿trabajan? ¿Dónde trabajas? ¿Quién trabaja mucho en tu familia? ¿Conoces a alguien desempleado?*

Follow-up for *Vocabulario en contexto*
Working in pairs, have students ask each other about their jobs, what they do at work, what they like or do not like about their jobs. (If students do not work, they may talk about the job of someone in their family or an imaginary job.)

Suggestion for *Vocabulario en contexto*
Mention that in most industrialized countries employees get four to seven weeks of paid vacation: *En la mayoría de los países industrializados los empleados tienen de cuatro a siete semanas de vacaciones pagadas.* Ask: *¿Piensan que en dos semanas de vacaciones hay tiempo para viajar, estar con la familia, descansar? ¿Cómo pueden pasar más tiempo con sus hijos y relajarse los padres que tienen vacaciones cortas?*

Suggestion for *Otras ocupaciones*
Use visual aids or project images from the online Learning Module to review the various professions. Ask questions to elicit information about them. *¿Qué trabajo hace un abogado? ¿Dónde trabaja un bibliotecario?*, etc. Point out that the opposite gender is given in parentheses. Let students know that both forms *la juez* and *la jueza* are accepted in Spanish.

PRÁCTICA

9-5  

Para confirmar. Lean las siguientes descripciones y digan qué profesión u oficio deben tener las personas con estas características.

abogado/a	artista	mecánico/a	plomero/a
actor/actriz	ingeniero/a	médico/a	psicólogo/a

1. psicólogo A Pablo le gusta observar y analizar el comportamiento (*behavior*) de las personas.
2. mecánicos Los hermanos Pedraza siempre resuelven los problemas del auto de su padre. Lo examinan y lo reparan a la perfección.
3. abogadas Eva y Ana tienen facilidad para resolver los problemas de otras personas y la habilidad de exponer oralmente ante una corte.
4. ingeniero A Jaime le fascina desarmar (*disassemble*) aparatos electrónicos para estudiar cómo funcionan.
5. actriz/artista Daniela es una chica muy sensible y una gran observadora. Le fascina expresar sus sentimientos y experiencias de manera artística.
6. médica Adela siempre lee libros sobre anatomía. Ella sabe el nombre de cada parte del cuerpo humano.

EN OTRAS PALABRAS

In Spain the words for **contador, chofer,** and **plomero** are **contable, chófer,** and **fontanero.**

Warm-up for 9-6
Recycle previously taught occupations and comparative expressions by having students compare occupations: *¿Un peluquero gana tanto dinero como un médico? ¿Es mejor ser ingeniero o actor? ¿Por qué? ¿Un profesor trabaja más o menos que un médico?*

Suggestion for 9-6
Add additional occupations that are cognates: *el/la astronauta, el/la mecánico/a, el/la dentista, el/la piloto, el/la recepcionista, el/la secretario/a, el/la veterinario/a.*

Inform students that *el amo de casa* has come into usage in Spanish, as has *house husband* in English.

Cultura

La mujer y el trabajo

Un cambio social importante en los países hispanos en las últimas décadas es la entrada masiva de las mujeres al mercado laboral. Sin embargo, aún existen desigualdades. Por ejemplo, los salarios de las mujeres son en muchos casos más bajos que los de los hombres. Algunos países, como Perú y Chile, tienen un Ministerio de la Mujer para proteger los derechos de las mujeres.

Conexiones. En tu opinión, ¿por qué existen diferentes oportunidades en el mercado laboral para hombres y mujeres? ¿Qué medidas se toman para acabar con esta desigualdad?

9-6  

Las profesiones y la personalidad. PREPARACIÓN. Digan cómo deben ser estos/as profesionales. Seleccionen las palabras de la lista para describirlos/las.

un bombero / una bombera

E1: *Debe ser valiente, serio y responsable.*

E2: *Sí, y no debe ser perezoso.*

autoritario/a	detallista	perezoso/a
calculador/a	estudioso/a	responsable
cuidadoso/a	guapo/a	romántico/a
dedicado/a	inteligente	serio/a
delgado/a	irónico/a	simpático/a
descuidado/a	paciente	valiente

1. un médico/una médica
2. un actor/una actriz
3. un hombre/una mujer de negocios
4. un peluquero/una peluquera
5. un locutor/una locutora
6. un amo/ama de casa
7. un ejecutivo/una ejecutiva
8. un mecánico/una mecánica
9. un cocinero/una cocinera
10. un abogado/una abogada

INTERCAMBIOS. Intercambien ideas sobre lo siguiente.

1. ¿Conoces a algún/alguna... (*nombre de la profesión*)? ¿Cómo se llama? ¿Dónde trabaja?
2. ¿Qué características personales o especiales, en tu opinión, lo/la ayudan en su profesión?

9-7 

Asociaciones. Asocien una o más profesiones con los siguientes lugares de trabajo. Túrnense y digan lo que hacen estas personas.

LUGAR	PROFESIÓN	¿QUÉ HACE?
1. el hospital	*enfermero/a, médico/a*	*Atiende a los pacientes.*
2. el restaurante	chef, camarero/a	
3. la clase	profesor/a	
4. la estación de radio	locutor/a, ingeniero/a	
5. la tienda de ropa	dependiente/a, vendedor/a	
6. el consultorio médico	médico/a	
7. la peluquería	peluquero/a	

Note for 9-7
Answers may vary but likely answers are included in column 2. Column 3 answers will depend on the students' answers to column 2.

9-8 

¿Cuál es la profesión? Escribe la ocupación o profesión y una ventaja y una desventaja para cada una. Después, túrnense para compartir sus ideas.

 Trabaja en una biblioteca.

E1: *Es un bibliotecario.*

E2: *Una ventaja de ser bibliotecario es tener acceso a muchos libros y una desventaja es trabajar muchas horas frente a la computadora.*

E1: *Para mí una ventaja es trabajar en un lugar tranquilo y una desventaja es la falta de ejercicio físico.*

	PROFESIÓN	VENTAJAS	DESVENTAJAS
1. Escribe artículos para el periódico.	periodista		
2. Presenta programas de televisión.	locutor/a		
3. Traduce simultáneamente.	intérprete		
4. Mantiene el orden público.	policía		
5. Apaga incendios.	bombero/a		
6. Defiende o acusa a personas delante de un/a juez/a.	abogado/a		

Suggestions for 9-8
In groups of 3, have students brainstorm at least 3 advantages and 3 disadvantages of specific jobs. Model the activity: *¿Cuáles son las ventajas y desventajas de los siguientes trabajos: médico, enfermero, profesor, piloto?* Introduce the words *estrés* and *peligro* to talk about disadvantages. Have them switch roles so that all can practice identifying and describing. Alternatively, you may want to do only the identification part of the activity.

Suggestion for 9-8
Model the activity with one of your better students. Provide plenty of examples of the infinitive as the subject of a sentence as follows:

Trabajar al aire libre, ¿es una ventaja o una desventaja para un constructor? Tienes razón. Trabajar... es una... porque...

Preparar comida, ¿es una ventaja o una desventaja para alguien que tiene adicción a la comida? ¿Qué es mejor para ustedes, trabajar en una oficina o trabajar al aire libre?, etc.

Buscando trabajo

La entrevista de trabajo

SRA. ARCE: Buenos días, Sr. Solano. Soy Marcela Arce, presidenta de la compañía.

SR. SOLANO: Mucho gusto, señora.

SRA. ARCE: Siéntese, por favor. Usted **solicitó** el **puesto** de **gerente de ventas** en línea, ¿verdad?

SR. SOLANO: Sí, señora. Hice una búsqueda en Internet y vi que había una **vacante.** Así que **llené** una **solicitud.**

SRA. ARCE: Sí, aquí la tengo, y también su **currículum. Por cierto,** es excelente.

SR. SOLANO: Muchas gracias.

SRA. ARCE: **Actualmente** usted trabaja en la empresa Badosa. ¿Por qué quiere **dejar** su puesto?

SR. SOLANO: Bueno, **en realidad** estoy muy contento allí, pero a mí me gustaría trabajar en una compañía internacional para poder hablar otras lenguas. Como usted ve en mi currículum, hablo español, inglés y francés.

SRA. ARCE: En su solicitud, usted indica que desea un **sueldo** de 35.000 quetzales al mes. **Sin embargo,** para el puesto que tenemos, el sueldo que **se ofrece** es de 30.000 quetzales.

SR. SOLANO: Sí, lo sé, pero la diferencia no es tan importante. **Lo importante** es que aquí puedo tener la oportunidad de comunicarme con los clientes en su **propia** lengua. Creo que esto puede mejorar las ventas de Computel notablemente.

SRA. ARCE: Pues, si le parece bien el sueldo, ¿por qué no pasamos a la oficina del director general para seguir hablando?

SR. SOLANO: ¡Cómo no!

LENGUA

In Spanish, **actualmente** means *now, at present.*

> **Actualmente** yo trabajo en Antigua.
>
> *At the present time/Now I work in Antigua.*

Therefore, **actualmente** is a false cognate of *actually.* The equivalents of *actually* in Spanish are **realmente** or **en realidad.**

> **Realmente/En realidad** yo solo trabajé en la Ciudad de Guatemala un mes.
>
> *Actually I worked in Guatemala City for only a month.*

PRÁCTICA

Cultura

El quetzal

El quetzal es la moneda nacional de Guatemala y su símbolo es GQT. La tasa de cambio es aproximadamente, 8 quetzales por dólar. Queztal es una palabra de origen náhuatl y se refiere al pájaro de vivos colores que es símbolo de Guatemala.

Comparaciones. ¿Sabes cuál es el origen de la palabra dólar?

Suggestion for 9-9
Encourage students to make the following changes: the job being offered, languages spoken, and salary (using currencies of other countries). If possible, check the current exchange rate of the quetzal, the currency of Guatemala. This salary translates to approximately $4,000 U.S. per month.

9-9 

Para confirmar. Busquen los siguientes datos en la conversación anterior.

1. nombre de la presidenta de la compañía Marcela Arce
2. puesto que solicita el Sr. Solano gerente de ventas
3. nombre de la compañía donde desea trabajar Computel
4. lenguas que habla 3: español, inglés, francés
5. sueldo que desea el Sr. Solano treinta y cinco mil quetzales (35.000)
6. sueldo que se ofrece en el nuevo puesto treinta mil quetzales (30.000)
7. motivo para cambiar de puesto trabajar en una compañía internacional y usar otras lenguas

9-10  

¿En qué orden? Cuando alguien busca un trabajo, normalmente, ¿en qué orden ocurren las siguientes actividades? Ordénalas de 1 a 8. Después, compara tus respuestas con las de tu compañero/a y dile si haces las mismas cosas y en el mismo orden.

__1__ Leo los anuncios del periódico *El Diario de Centro América*.

__4__ Me llaman de la Compañía Rosell para una entrevista.

__7__ Les contesto que no, que se cerró el almacén.

__3__ Con un clic del ratón, envío mis materiales a la Compañía Rosell.

__5__ Voy a la compañía para la entrevista.

__6__ Me preguntan si me despidieron (*fired*) del trabajo anterior.

__2__ Lleno la solicitud en línea para la Compañía Rosell y subo (*upload*) mi currículum.

__8__ Me ofrecen el puesto de vendedor/a.

9-11 

El arte de entrevistarse. PREPARACIÓN. Escoge el anuncio que te parece más interesante y solicita ese puesto. Tu compañero/a, en el papel de jefe/a de personal, debe entrevistarte y tomar notas para obtener la siguiente información. Luego, cambien de papel.

1. nombre de la persona que solicita el puesto
2. estudios
3. lenguas que habla
4. lugar donde trabaja y responsabilidades
5. experiencia anterior
6. razones para querer trabajar en esta compañía

INTERCAMBIOS. Ahora informa al presidente/a la presidenta de la empresa (otro/a compañero/a) sobre las calificaciones del candidato/de la candidata que acabas de entrevistar.

INSTITUTO DE CIRUGÍA PLÁSTICA: CLÍNICA CÁRDENAS

Necesita enfermera

Prótesis:
implantes faciales (Botox, silicona)
liposucción papada
abdomen
muslos

Informes:
Clínica Centro, Zona 10
Tel: (502) 2534147

Llamar a secretaria: Marta

EMPRESA MINERA

Requiere
3 Ingenieros de sistemas

REQUISITOS:
1. Mayor de 25 años
2. Experiencia en minas de cobre
3. Flexibilidad horaria (incluidos fines de semana)

OFRECEMOS:
1. Ingreso superior a 40.000 quetzales
2. Capacitación profesional
3. Bonos de participación

Interesados enviar currículum a: Minas de Guatemala S.A.

Oficina de Personal
Diagonal 19, 29-78, Zona 11
Ciudad de Guatemala, Guatemala
Teléfono: (502) 2762147
Fax: (502) 2763482

Hotel VILLA ANTIGUA

Necesita

RECEPCIONISTA
- Experiencia
- Bilingüe español-inglés

CAMARERA
- Mín. 2 años de experiencia
- Disponible trabajar por las mañanas y tardes

Dirigirse al Hotel VILLA ANTIGUA
Jefe de Personal
9a. Calle Poniente, Carretera a Ciudad Vieja
Antigua, Guatemala
Teléfono: +(502) 78323956 o +(502) 78323955

EMPRESA EXPORTADORA DE ARTESANÍAS
Requiere

CONTADOR

Requisitos:
- Experiencia mínima de 5 años
- Graduado del Colegio de Contadores Públicos
- Para cita llamar al Sr. López al (502) 2764532

Note for 9-10
Founded in 1880, *El Diario de Centro América* is one of the main newspapers in Guatemala.

Follow-up for 9-10
Have students go through this process in small groups, step by step, as though they were seeking jobs, either imaginary or taken from classified ads.

Warm-up for 9-11
Model the activity with one of your stronger students, projecting the image of a job ad as the starting point. Encourage students to answer giving as much information as possible.

Expansion for 9-11, *Preparación*
7. *fecha en que puede empezar a trabajar;* 8. *sueldo que desea ganar;* 9. *habilidades especiales.*

Suggestion for 9-11, *Intercambios*
Remind students that they will be reporting on an interview that already took place, so they will need to use the preterit or imperfect. You may model this phase for them as follows: *Yo entrevisté a X. X estudió contabilidad en la Universidad de… y se graduó en el año…*, etc.

Follow-up for 9-12
Ask pairs to share some of their recommendations with the class. The class as a whole may choose the best ones.

Warm-up for 9-13
As a pre-listening activity, have students talk in small groups about their future professions and the schedules they expect to have in their jobs.

Audioscript for 9-13
Me llamo Julieta Odriozola y trabajo para el periódico La República. *Mi trabajo es muy interesante porque escribo artículos sobre los eventos notables de la comunidad. Por ejemplo, les hago entrevistas a personalidades políticas, personas del mundo de los negocios o artistas, y esto me da la oportunidad de conocer a mucha gente fascinante. Después, estas entrevistas se publican en el periódico. Uno de los problemas de mi trabajo es que no tengo horario fijo, pues dependo de los horarios de los eventos o de las personas que voy a entrevistar. A veces trabajo los fines de semana o por la noche. Por ejemplo, la semana pasada, entrevisté a una mujer de negocios muy importante. Esta señora tenía varias reuniones de negocios el día que la entrevisté; por eso la tuve que entrevistar en su auto cuando íbamos de una reunión a otra. Las entrevistas a los artistas son completamente diferentes. Para la mayoría de ellos, el tiempo no es una obsesión, y es muy agradable hablar con ellos.*

9-12

¿Comportamiento apropiado? Preparen una lista de cinco acciones que se deben hacer antes de una entrevista y cinco que no se deben hacer durante una entrevista. Después, comparen su lista con la de otros/as compañeros/as.

LO QUE SE DEBE HACER ANTES DE UNA ENTREVISTA	LO QUE NO SE DEBE HACER DURANTE UNA ENTREVISTA

Cultura

Documentos a presentar

En muchos países hispanos, en una solicitud de trabajo además de un CV es común incluir una foto reciente de la persona que solicita el trabajo. Hasta hace poco tiempo, también era necesario agregar en el CV datos como la nacionalidad o el estado civil.

Comparaciones. ¿Cuáles son las ventajas y desventajas de incluir una foto en el CV? ¿Por qué en tu país no se exige foto?

9-13  

Mi profesión. **PREPARACIÓN.** You will listen to Julieta Odriozola talk about her profession. Before listening, each of you will write down the names of four professions that have traditionally been associated with women and four professions traditionally associated with men. Share your answers.

ESCUCHA. Pay attention to the general idea of what is said. As you listen mark (✓) the appropriate ending to each statement. Check answers with a classmate.

1. Julieta Odriozola es…
_____ artista.
_____ política.
__✓__ periodista.

2. Julieta tiene un horario…
_____ de 9 a 5.
__✓__ variable.
_____ de lunes a sábado.

3. Julieta hace casi todo su trabajo en…
_____ su auto.
_____ su casa.
__✓__ diferentes lugares.

4. Julieta trabaja con…
_____ artistas jóvenes.
__✓__ personas importantes.
_____ empleados de la comunidad.

MOSAICO cultural

¿Trabajas o estudias?

Carlos, un estudiante de publicidad, empezó a hacer malabarismos (*juggling*) en los parques y en las calles de la Ciudad de Guatemala a los 18 años. Algunos de sus amigos cantaban en las estaciones de tren y así pagaron sus estudios. El caso de Carlos y sus amigos es bastante común para los hispanos jóvenes. En general es complicado encontrar un trabajo mientras se estudia, especialmente cuando los jóvenes no tienen experiencia. En los centros metropolitanos el nivel de competencia para tener acceso a un puesto vacante es alto.

En Perú y Ecuador, por ejemplo, es posible ver a estudiantes universitarios vendiendo artesanía, collares y pulseras para ganar dinero. Un caso similar es el de Matías, un joven de Buenos Aires, que tuvo este tipo de empleo informal por cinco años, antes de graduarse de dentista. Matías bailaba tango con su novia en las estaciones del metro de Buenos Aires. Dice Matías: "fue una experiencia bonita, hacíamos el espectáculo y la gente nos daba algo de dinero; todos se divertían mucho". Este tipo de trabajo se llama en el Cono Sur "trabajo a la gorra" porque al final del espectáculo, los jóvenes pasan una gorra (o un sombrero) para recolectar el dinero de los espectadores.

Es cierto que muchos estudiantes trabajan en restaurantes o supermercados, pero cada vez más estos otros tipos de trabajos informales son comunes entre los adolescentes. Los trabajos de medio tiempo los ayudan a pagar sus estudios y a tener dinero para pasar tiempo con amigos y familia.

▲ Los estudiantes hacen malabarismos y cantan para ganar dinero.

▲ Este joven toca la guitarra en una estación de tren.

◀ Tango en la calle

Compara

1. ¿Qué tipo de trabajos son frecuentes entre los estudiantes universitarios en tu país?
2. ¿Existe el trabajo informal entre los jóvenes en tu país? ¿Qué actividades son comunes?
3. ¿Conoces algún tipo de "trabajo a la gorra" en tu comunidad? Explica.
4. ¿Qué piensas de estos jóvenes y del trabajo informal? Explica.

Note for *Mosaico cultural*
Underemployment is a serious problem in the fast-growing societies of the Hispanic world. People who cannot find professional work often turn to the informal economy, making ends meet through commissions, tips, and occasional jobs. In some countries this process of eking out a living through a variety of seasonal and low-paying jobs is known as *rebusque*.

Students may choose to start up informal businesses at their universities. Some buy packaged food and sell it on campus; others sell CDs and DVDs. This practice is controversial, because although these small-scale entrepreneurs need to earn money to support themselves in college, their activities take valuable time away from their academic pursuits.

You may wish to remind students that participation in the informal economy is most common among young people who are trying to live on their own for the first time.

Suggestion for *Funciones y formas*
This section reviews direct and indirect objects and pronouns, presented in *Capítulos 5* and *6,* in anticipation of the introduction of the double object pronoun structure in the next section. Help students focus their attention on the pronouns and their referents.

Funciones y formas

1 Avoiding repetition

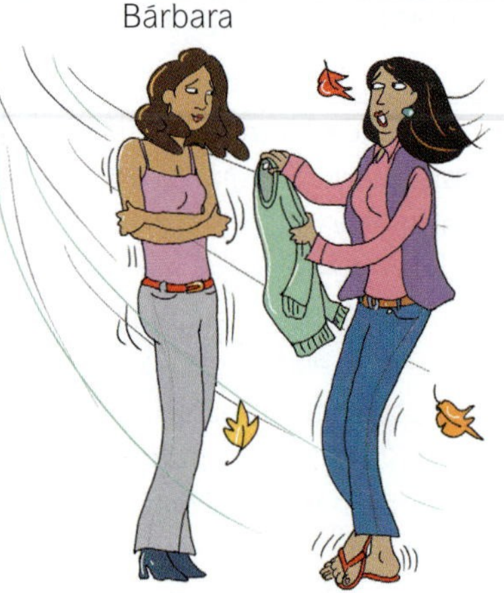

BÁRBARA: Carlota, ¿por qué llevas chanclas (*flip-flops*)?

CARLOTA: **Le** di mis zapatos al zapatero porque se rompieron.

BÁRBARA: ¿Y no tienes frío?

CARLOTA: Sí, pero no tengo otra opción. El zapatero va a arreglar**los** en una hora. Y tú, Bárbara, ¿por qué no trajiste chaqueta? Hace frío.

BÁRBARA: **La** dejé en casa.

CARLOTA: Bueno, yo **te** presto mi suéter.

Piénsalo. Para cada oración, escribe las palabras en negrita (*boldface*) en la columna apropiada. En algunas oraciones hay más de un objeto directo u objeto indirecto.

	OBJETO DIRECTO	OBJETO INDIRECTO
1. **Le** di mis **zapatos** al **zapatero.**	zapatos	le, zapatero
2. El zapatero va a arreglar los **zapatos** de Carlota.	zapatos	none
3. El zapatero va a arreglar**los.**	los	none
4. ¿Por qué no trajiste **chaqueta?**	chaqueta	none
5. **La** dejé en casa.	la	none
6. **Te** presto mi **suéter.**	suéter	te

Review of direct and indirect object pronouns

- In *Capítulo 5* you learned that direct objects answer the question *what?* or *whom?* in relation to the verb. They can refer to people, animals, or objects. When a direct object noun refers to a specific person, a group of people, or a pet, the personal **a** precedes the direct object. To avoid repetition in speaking or writing, direct object pronouns can replace direct object nouns if the noun has already been mentioned.

¿Ves **al chef?**	*Do you see the **chef?***
Sí, **lo** veo. Está al lado de la cocina.	*Yes, I see **him.** He is next to the kitchen.*
La Dra. Martín recibe **a sus pacientes** en la clínica.	*Dr. Martín sees **her patients** in the clinic.*
Los recibe todos los días.	*She sees **them** every day.*

- In *Capítulo 6* you learned that indirect object nouns and pronouns tell *to whom* or *for whom* an action is done. They most often occur in the context of transferring information or objects, such as giving someone a gift, telling someone a story, or asking someone for something.

La maestra siempre **les** dice la verdad a los niños.	*The teacher always tells the children the truth.*
El camarero no **nos** trajo la sopa.	*The waiter did not bring us the soup.*

- Direct and indirect object pronouns are placed before conjugated verbs. When a conjugated verb is followed by an infinitive or present participle, the pronouns can either precede the conjugated verb or be attached to the infinitive or present participle.

¿Las fotos de la casa? La arquitecta está organizándo**las.** La arquitecta **las** está organizando.	*The photos of the house?* *The architect is compiling them.*
Su asistente va a mandar**nos** todos los documentos. Su asistente **nos** va a mandar todos los documentos.	*Her assistant is going to send us all the documents.*

- Direct and indirect object pronouns have the same form, except in the third person. Note that **le/les** refer to either males or females.

DIRECT OBJECT PRONOUNS		INDIRECT OBJECT PRONOUNS	
me	nos	me	nos
te	os	te	os
lo	los	le	les
la	las		

¿COMPRENDES?

Completa las oraciones con el pronombre correcto.

1. No tengo mi cartera. __La__ dejé en casa.
2. Juan __le__ dio a Marisol una bolsa guatemalteca.
3. Pero Juan no __nos__ trajo regalos a nosotros.
4. Me encantan tus fotos en Facebook. Estoy mirándo__las__ ahora.
5. ¿Los intérpretes? __Los__ voy a llamar ahora.

MySpanishLab

Learn more using Amplifire Dynamic Study Modules, Grammar Tutorials, and Extra Practice activities.

PRÁCTICA

9-14

Los preparativos para la evaluación. **PREPARACIÓN.** Trabajas en la oficina de una arquitecta y mañana empieza la evaluación anual. Indica si la arquitecta (**A**) o el asistente administrativo (**AA**) está haciendo estos trabajos.

1. ___A___ Está terminando el último informe.
2. ___A___ Está firmando el contrato.
3. ___AA___ Está sacando las fotocopias.
4. ___AA___ Está organizando el horario.

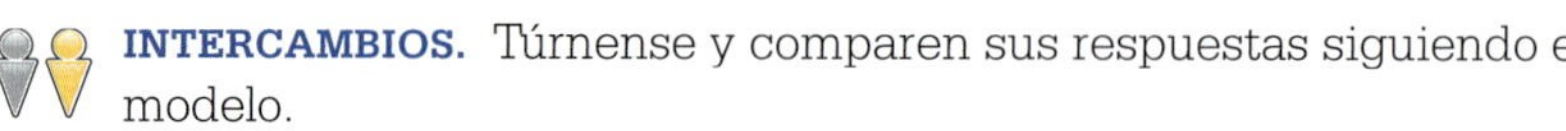

INTERCAMBIOS. Túrnense y comparen sus respuestas siguiendo el modelo.

MODELO E1: *¿Quién está examinando el contrato?*

E2: *La arquitecta está examinándolo.*

Suggestion for 9-14, *Intercambios*
Remind students about the need for a written accent on the present participle when a pronoun is attached.

Note for 9-15
Students should focus their attention on the indirect objects—form and placement. In the next section they will use pronouns as both direct and indirect objects.

9-15

Comunicaciones y transacciones. Miren los dibujos y expliquen dónde ocurren las escenas y qué pasa en cada una.

MODELO enviar/flores

E1: *Pancho está en la floristería.*

E2: *Sí. Le va a enviar flores a su esposa porque es el Día de los Enamorados.*

1. mandar/mensaje de texto

Juan le manda a María un mensaje de texto.

2. dar/documentos

La jefa le da a su asistente los documentos.

3. vender/telas tradicionales

La artesana les vende a los turistas unas telas tradicionales.

9-16 

El jefe ideal. **PREPARACIÓN.** Hablen sobre lo que hace (o no hace) un/a jefe/a ideal por sus empleados.

MODELO darles las gracias por la calidad de su trabajo

Les da las gracias por la calidad de su trabajo.

1. sugerir estrategias de trabajo eficientes
2. mandar correos electrónicos durante el fin de semana
3. ofrecer ayuda para resolver conflictos
4. subir el salario
5. dar un mes de vacaciones
6. hacer trabajar horas extras sin recompensa

INTERCAMBIOS. Ahora túrnense para hacerse preguntas sobre lo que ustedes van a hacer por sus empleados cuando sean jefes de una empresa.

MODELO E1: *¿Vas a darles las gracias a tus empleados?*

E2: *Sí, les voy a escribir una carta de reconocimiento todos los años.*

Situación

Suggestion for *Situación*
Encourage students to use object pronouns whenever possible.

PREPARACIÓN. Lean la situación. Luego, compartan ejemplos de vocabulario, gramática y otra información que necesitan para desarrollar la conversación.

Role A. You have come back from a trip to Guatemala and have brought with you the following items that you bought at an outdoor market: blouses, tapestries, and jewelry. With your classmate, decide who in your class will be the recipients of your gifts.

Role B. One of your classmates has come back from a trip to Guatemala, and he/she has a few gifts to distribute among your classmates. Help him/her decide for whom each gift is most appropriate.

	ROLE A	ROLE B
Vocabulario	Handicrafts	Handicrafts Question words
Funciones y formas	Asking and answering questions Direct and indirect object pronouns	Asking and answering questions Direct and indirect object pronouns Giving suggestions

INTERCAMBIOS. Practica la conversación con tu compañero/a incorporando el vocabulario, las funciones y demás información. Luego, represéntenla ante la clase.

Warm-up
In this chapter students have reviewed direct and indirect objects as single objects in a sentence in preparation for double object pronouns. Although they can recognize these pronouns and some may produce them correctly in controlled situations, learners at this stage rarely use them when speaking freely. Assure students that there will be ample opportunities to practice object pronouns throughout the course.

Note
Explain that the phrase *a + noun* or *a + pronoun* may be used to clarify the meaning of *se: Se lo da a ella. Se lo da a Ana.*

2 Avoiding repetition

CONSEJERA: ¿Ya **le** mandó su currículum al director?
CLIENTE: Sí, **se lo** mandé la semana pasada.
CONSEJERA: ¿Recibió alguna confirmación?
CLIENTE: Sí, ellos **me la** mandaron rápidamente. **La** recibí hoy.

Piénsalo. Lee las oraciones e indica los objetos directos y los indirectos, tanto los pronombres como los sustantivos (*nouns*).

	OBJETO INDIRECTO	OBJETO DIRECTO
MODELO La secretaria **me** dio una cita para el lunes.	*me*	*cita*
1. ¿Ya **le** mandó su currículum al director?	le, director	currículum
2. **Se lo** mandé la semana pasada.	se	lo
3. Ellos **me la** mandaron rápidamente.	me	la
4. **La** recibí hoy.	none	la

Use of direct and indirect object pronouns together

- You have already learned how to use indirect object pronouns or direct object pronouns in sentences. In this section you will learn how to use both types of pronouns in the same sentence.

INDIRECT OBJECT PRONOUNS		DIRECT OBJECT PRONOUNS	
me	nos	me	nos
te	os	te	os
le (se)	les (se)	lo	los
		la	las

- When direct and indirect object pronouns are used in the same sentence, the indirect object pronoun goes before the direct object pronoun. Place double object pronouns before conjugated verbs.

Ella **me** dio **la solicitud.** (i.o. = me, d.o. = la solicitud) — *She gave me the application.*

Ella **me la** dio. (i.o. = me, d.o. = la) — *She gave it to me.*

- In compound verb constructions, you may place double object pronouns before the conjugated verb or attach them to the accompanying infinitive or present participle.

Él quiere dar**me** **el contrato.** i.o. d.o.	*He wants to give me the contract.*
Él quiere dár**melo.** i.o. d.o. Él **me** **lo** quiere dar. i.o. d.o.	*He wants to give it to me*
Ella **te** está haciendo **la oferta de trabajo.** i.o. d.o.	*She is making you the job offer.*
Ella **te** **la** está haciendo. i.o. d.o. Ella está haciéndo**tela.** i.o. d.o.	*She is making it to you.*

- The indirect object pronouns **le** and **les** change to **se** before **lo, los, la,** or **las.**

Le dio **el puesto** a Verónica. i.o. d.o.	*He gave the job to Veronica.*
Se **lo** dio. i.o. d.o.	*He gave it to her.*
Les va a mostrar **el anuncio.** i.o. d.o.	*She is going to show them/you* (ustedes) *the ad.*
Se **lo** va a mostrar. i.o. d.o.	*She is going to show it to them/you* (ustedes).

- When a direct object pronoun and a reflexive pronoun are used together, the reflexive pronoun precedes the direct object pronoun.

Siempre **me** envío **correos electrónicos** i.o. d.o. para recordar lo que debo hacer.	*I always send myself e-mails to remember what I have to do.*
Siempre **me** **los** envío. i.o. d.o.	*I always send them to myself.*

LENGUA

You have learned that when the stress falls on the third syllable from the end of a word, a written accent is required. Therefore, you need to add one on the verb when double object pronouns are attached to an infinitive.

¿Va a darme la solicitud?
→ ¿Va a dármela?

When double object pronouns are attached to a present participle, the stress falls on the fourth syllable from the end, and a written accent is also required:

Se la está dando.
→ Está dándosela.
4 3 2 1

¿COMPRENDES?

Completa las oraciones con los pronombres de objeto directo e indirecto.

1. (los informes) La secretaria __se__ __los__ dio a Javier.
2. (las bebidas) El camarero __nos__ __las__ trajo a nosotros.
3. (el collar de plata) Yo __se__ __lo__ regalé a mi hermana.
4. (sus problemas) Laura __se__ __los__ contó al psicólogo.
5. (el puesto) El jefe __me__ __lo__ dio a mí, no a él.
6. (la información) ¿Cuándo __se__ __la__ vas a dar a ellos?

MySpanishLab
Learn more using Amplifire Dynamic Study Modules, Grammar Tutorials, and Extra Practice activities.

Suggestion for 9-17, *Intercambios*
If students have chosen the same response as their partners in *Preparación*, encourage them to come up with different justifications.

PRÁCTICA

9-17

¿Qué haces? **PREPARACIÓN.** La imparcialidad, la amabilidad y la confidencialidad son fundamentales en el trabajo. Lee las siguientes situaciones y selecciona lo que harías (*would do*) en cada una.

1. Un cliente te pide el teléfono de la oficina del presidente de la compañía.
   a. ____ Se lo doy. **b.** ____ No se lo doy.
2. Alguien quiere leer un documento confidencial.
   a. ____ Se lo muestro. **b.** ____ No se lo muestro.
3. La nueva jefa de personal viene a una reunión de su departamento. Alguien tiene que presentarla a los empleados.
   a. ____ Se la presento. **b.** ____ No se la presento.
4. Una empleada nueva te dice que quiere dos semanas de vacaciones después de trabajar solo tres meses.
   a. ____ Se las doy. **b.** ____ Decido no dárselas.

INTERCAMBIOS. ¿Estás de acuerdo con tu compañero/a? Intercambien sus respuestas y expliquen por qué.

Un cliente te pide información personal sobre las finanzas de otro cliente. Los dos clientes son hermanos.

E1: *No se la doy porque no le gustaría al segundo cliente.*

E2: *Yo se la doy porque los dos clientes son hermanos.*

Suggestion for 9-18
Remind students that the owner of a company and a new employee would address each other as *usted.* Analyze the model interaction with them so they are aware of the use of *le* rather than *te* in E1's turn.

9-18

¿Qué hizo el supervisor? Eres el/la dueño/a de una compañía. Habla con tu nuevo/a empleado/a (tu compañero/a) para saber si el supervisor le explicó cómo funciona su departamento.

darle el manual de la compañía

E1: *¿Le dio el manual de la compañía?*

E2: *Sí, me lo dio.*

1. explicarle la campaña de publicidad
2. mostrarle los anuncios
3. traerle las revistas
4. pedirle un documento que faltaba
5. dejarle las fotos
6. describirle los modelos que se necesitan

9-19 

¡El cliente siempre tiene razón! **PREPARACIÓN.** Cada uno de ustedes comió recientemente en un restaurante. Comparen su experiencia.

1. ¿Cuándo te sirvieron el agua?
2. ¿Te trajeron pan?
3. ¿Te dijo el camarero cuáles eran los platos especiales del día?
4. ¿Te describió los platos?
5. ¿Te ofreció postres y café?
6. ¿Aceptaron tu tarjeta de crédito?

INTERCAMBIOS. Presenten a la clase un breve resumen del servicio en sus respectivos restaurantes.

Suggestions for 9-19, *Preparación*
Have students start the activity by explaining to their partners to which recent restaurant experience (where, when, with whom) they will be referring in *Preparación.* Students can alternate asking and answering the questions.

Suggestion for 9-19, *Intercambios*
You may use students' summaries as the basis for conducting a discussion on the service at restaurants that students frequent.

Situación

PREPARACIÓN. Lean la situación. Luego, compartan ejemplos de vocabulario, gramática y otra información que necesitan para desarrollar la conversación.

Role A. It is the end of the day, and you just finished a report for your new supervisor, who has been in meetings all day. You have to leave, so you ask your co-worker to turn it in (**entregar**) for you. You call your friend from the car to ask:

a. if he/she gave the report (**el informe**) directly to the supervisor;
b. what time he/she turned it in; and
c. what the supervisor said to him/her.

Role B. A co-worker asks you to turn in his/her report to your supervisor because he/she has to leave. Your friend is nervous about turning in the report by the end of the day. When your friend calls you, answer all of his/her questions.

	ROLE A	ROLE B
Vocabulario	Greetings Question words Expressions of thanks	Expressions of reassurance
Funciones y formas	Asking questions Direct and indirect object pronouns Opening and closing a phone conversation Expressing gratitude for a favor	Answering questions Direct and indirect object pronouns Opening and closing a phone conversation Acknowledging gratitude

INTERCAMBIOS. Practica la conversación con tu compañero/a incorporando el vocabulario y las funciones de *Preparación*. Luego, represéntenla ante la clase.

Suggestions for More on the imperfect and the preterit
You may want to project the dialogue and explain to students that the statements with the verbs in bold refer to background activities for the narrative event (*el asalto*).
Students can invent other background information to describe the scene in the bank (i.e., what was going on) when the robbery started. Point out to students that the imperfect is used to establish the context for an event or series of events that will be narrated.

You may wish to use the interview of one of the witnesses to the bank robbery in *Piénsalo* to show students additional uses of *iba a* + infinitive and the preterit of *poder, querer,* and *saber.*

Contrast the use of preterit and imperfect by giving examples: *El año pasado ustedes no estaban en mi clase de español. Yo no los conocía. Yo los conocí en... cuando vinieron a mi clase. Yo no sabía entonces si eran buenos estudiantes, pero después de tener una o dos clases con ustedes supe que eran buenos.*

3 Talking about the past

PERIODISTA: Sr. Mario Parada, usted estaba en el Bancafé cuando entraron los ladrones (*robbers*), ¿verdad? ¿Qué **estaba haciendo?**

SR. PARADA: Yo **estaba hablando** con la cajera. **Iba a** hacer un depósito, pero claro, no **pude** realizar la transacción.

PERIODISTA: ¿Qué hicieron los empleados cuando **supieron** que había ladrones en el banco?

SR. PARADA: Todo pasó muy rápido. En el momento del robo, los cajeros **estaban atendiendo** a los clientes. Los oficiales de seguridad vieron a los ladrones y **quisieron** detenerlos (*stop them*) pero no **pudieron.**

Piénsalo. Indica (✓) si cada afirmación representa una **actividad en progreso** o un **evento terminado** en el pasado.

	ACTIVIDAD EN PROGRESO	EVENTO TERMINADO
1. Yo **estaba hablando** con la cajera.	✓	
2. No **pude** hacer la transacción.		✓
3. Los empleados lo **supieron.**		✓
4. Los cajeros **estaban respondiendo** a las preguntas de los clientes.	✓	
5. Los oficiales **quisieron** detenerlos.		✓
6. No **pudieron** hacerlo.		✓

More on the imperfect and the preterit

- You have used the imperfect to express an action or event that was in progress in the past. You may also use the imperfect progressive to emphasize the ongoing nature of the activity in the past. Form the imperfect progressive with the imperfect of **estar** and the present participle (**-ndo**).

  Mario **estaba hablando** con la cajera cuando entraron los ladrones. — *Mario was talking to the teller when the robbers came in.*

  Los gerentes del banco **estaban trabajando** en el segundo piso cuando oyeron los gritos. — *The managers of the bank were working on the second floor when they heard the shouts.*

- To express intentions in the past, use the imperfect of **ir** + **a** + *infinitive.*

  Iba a salir, pero era muy tarde. — *I was going to go out, but it was very late.*

- In *Capítulo 7* you practiced the preterit of **saber** with the meaning of finding out about something. You also practiced the preterit of **querer** with the meaning of wanting or trying to do something, but failing to accomplish it. In the negative, the preterit of **querer** conveys the meaning of refusing to do something.

  Supe que Jorge consiguió trabajo. — *I found out that Jorge got a job.*

  Quise entrevistarme con el gerente, pero fue imposible. — *I wanted (and tried) to get an interview with the manager, but it was impossible.*

  No quise ir. — *I refused to go.*

- Other verbs that convey a different meaning in English when the preterit is used are **conocer** and **poder.**

IMPERFECT		PRETERIT	
Yo **conocía** a Ana.	*I knew Ana.*	**Conocí** a Ana.	*I met Ana.*
Podía hacerlo.	*I could (was able to) do it.*	**Pude** hacerlo.	*I accomplished (managed to do) it.*
No podía hacerlo.	*I couldn't (wasn't able to) do it.*	**No pude** hacerlo.	*I couldn't do it. (I tried and failed.)*
Quería ir con ellos.	*I wanted to go with them.*	**Quise** ir con ellos.	*I tried to go with them (but didn't go).*
		No **quise** ir con ellos.	*I refused to go with them.*

¿COMPRENDES?

Completa las oraciones con la forma correcta del verbo en el pretérito o el imperfecto.

1. El proyecto fue difícil, pero nosotros ___pudimos___ (poder) hacerlo.
2. Pablo no ___quiso___ (querer) compartir los comentarios del jefe y no dijo nada.
3. Ellas ___estaban conversando/conversaban___ (conversar) cuando entró el gerente.
4. Alfredo y Sandra ___se conocieron___ (conocerse) en una recepción.
5. Después Alfredo ___supo___ (saber) que Sandra ya conocía a su hermano.

MySpanishLab
Learn more using Amplifire Dynamic Study Modules, Grammar Tutorials, and Extra Practice activities.

PRÁCTICA

9-20 

Las memorias de Arturo. Completa el párrafo de Arturo, un profesor de antropología, con la forma apropiada de los verbos. Luego, compara tus respuestas con las de tu compañero/a.

En el año 2007, yo (1) ___conocí___ (conocí/conocía) a mi novia Elizabeth en mi primer viaje a Guatemala. En ese momento, yo solo (2) ___conocía___ (conocí/conocía) Antigua y un par de lugares de interés para los turistas. Después de nuestro encuentro, yo inmediatamente (3) ___supe___ (supe/sabía) que mis visitas a Guatemala (4) ___iban___ (fueron/iban) a ser más frecuentes. Ese año nosotros no (5) ___pudimos___ (pudimos/podíamos) viajar juntos por el país, pero el año siguiente lo hicimos. Su familia, ella y yo (6) ___pudimos___ (pudimos/podíamos) explorar juntos la reserva ecológica Calahuar. Caminamos todo el día por el bosque. Después de caminar tantas horas, yo no (7) ___podía___ (pude/podía) dar un paso más, pero al día siguiente (8) ___pudimos___ (pudimos/podíamos) continuar el viaje a San Pedro La Laguna en Atlitán.

Suggestion for 9-20
Students may work individually first and then in pairs, or you may prefer to have them work in pairs from the beginning. Asking students to verbalize to their partners the reasons for their choices will increase their analytical skills.

9-21 

Una oficina muy ocupada. Ustedes visitaron la oficina que aparece en la siguiente escena. Túrnense para preguntar qué estaban haciendo las personas cuando cada uno/a de ustedes llegó.

E1: *¿Qué estaba haciendo Alicia cuando llegaste a la oficina?*

E2: *Estaba conversando con un cliente.*

Suggestion for 9-21
Encourage students to provide as many explanations as possible. Then have pairs share their answers with the class.

Expansion for 9-22
5. *Un hombre miraba por un microscopio en un laboratorio donde había computadoras y diferentes productos químicos.* (científico); 6. *Una señora estaba enfrente de un micrófono en un estudio. Tenía unos papeles sobre un escritorio y observaba con mucha atención una señal para empezar a hablar.* (locutora); 7. *Una mujer vestida de uniforme corría detrás de un hombre que escapaba de una tienda.* (la policía)

9-22

¡A usar la imaginación! Estas descripciones indican lo que estaban haciendo varias personas ayer. Identifiquen cuál era el oficio o profesión de ellos y qué iban a hacer después.

 Esta persona llevaba un traje espacial, guantes, botas muy grandes y un plástico transparente frente a los ojos para poder ver.

E1: *Era un astronauta.*

E2: *Iba a caminar en la Luna.*

1. Un hombre joven tenía un secador en la mano y hablaba con una clienta mientras le arreglaba el pelo. peluquero
2. Unos señores iban en un camión rojo con una sirena. El camión iba muy rápido y los autos le daban paso (*yielded*). bomberos
3. Una joven que llevaba un vestido similar a los que se llevaban en la época de Cleopatra hablaba frente a una cámara. Tenía pelo negro y estaba muy maquillada. actriz
4. Un señor estudiaba los planos de un edificio y decía que ciertas cosas no estaban bien. arquitecto; *Answers for the second part may vary.*

9-23

Un día extraño. Trabajen juntos para completar las oraciones, explicando por qué ayer fue un día diferente a los otros días.

 Siempre desayuno, pero ayer…

E1: *Siempre desayuno bien, pero ayer no pude desayunar.*

E2: *¿Por qué?*

E1: *Me desperté a las 8:45 y tuve que pasar por el cajero automático antes de clase.*

1. Mis padres siempre me mandan mensajes de texto, pero ayer…
2. Siempre termino mi tarea antes de las diez de la noche, pero ayer…
3. Generalmente duermo muy bien, pero anoche…
4. Con frecuencia practico deportes por la tarde, pero ayer…
5. Generalmente acepto las invitaciones de mis amigos, pero ayer…
6. Casi siempre hago la tarea de matématicas sin ningún problema, pero ayer…

9-24  

¡Malas sorpresas! Lean las siguientes situaciones e inventen historias breves: los planes probables de las personas, qué intentaron (quisieron) hacer y qué pudieron (o no pudieron) hacer.

 Martín está enfadado porque su bicicleta se descompuso (*broke*).

E1: *Martín no pudo ir al parque con sus amigos.*

E2: *Él quiso arreglar su bicicleta, pero...*

1. Lorena está molesta porque la fotocopiadora de la oficina no funciona.
2. Fuiste a tu restaurante favorito, pero el restaurante estaba cerrado.
3. El jefe de producción llamó a una reunión urgente ayer. Anoche comenzó a nevar y muchos empleados no llegaron a su trabajo.
4. Al carro de Marta y Francisco se le acabó (*ran out of*) la gasolina cerca de la playa. Tuvieron que dejarlo en la carretera.
5. Esteban tenía una entrevista con el jefe de personal a las nueve pero no llegó a tiempo.

Situación

PREPARACIÓN. Lean la situación. Luego, compartan ejemplos de vocabulario, gramática y otra información que necesitan para desarrollar la conversación.

Role A. You work as a server at a restaurant near your campus. While you were working last night, there was a power outage (**un apagón**). In the darkness of the crowded restaurant, servers dropped trays (**bandejas**), some customers stole purses, cell phones, and other items from nearby tables, and other people started to fight (**pelearse**). A reporter for the school newspaper interviews you about the incident.

Role B. You are a reporter for your school newspaper, and you are investigating an incident that took place at a restaurant near campus. Ask the server (your classmate) for details:

a. what people were doing when the power went out (**cortarse la luz**);
b. what happened next; and
c. what people tried to do and were able (or not able) to do.

	ROLE A	ROLE B
Vocabulario	Words and expressions related to restaurants	Question words Words and expressions related to restaurants
Funciones y formas	Telling a story in the past Preterit and imperfect Answering questions	Asking questions Preterit and imperfect

INTERCAMBIOS. Practica la conversación con tu compañero/a incorporando el vocabulario y las funciones de *Preparación*. Luego, represéntenla ante la clase.

Suggestions for Giving instructions or suggestions
Remind students that they are already familiar with commands: some were introduced in the preliminary chapter and have been used in activity directions, beginning in *Capítulo 4*. Review some of these: *contesten, escriban, indiquen, compartan, busquen, escojan, completen, lean.*

Suggestion for Giving instructions or suggestions
Point out the difference in syllable stress between *hable* and *hablé.*

4 Giving instructions or suggestions

RICARDO: Buenos días, señorita. Me llamo Ricardo Roldán Díaz. ¿Podría darme una solicitud para el puesto de asistente de contador?

SECRETARIA: Claro que sí, Sr. Roldán. Por favor, **llene** la solicitud y **mándenosla** pronto.

RICARDO: ¿Puedo mandársela por correo electrónico?

SECRETARIA: Sí, **envíela** por correo electrónico, o **súbala** a nuestra página web.

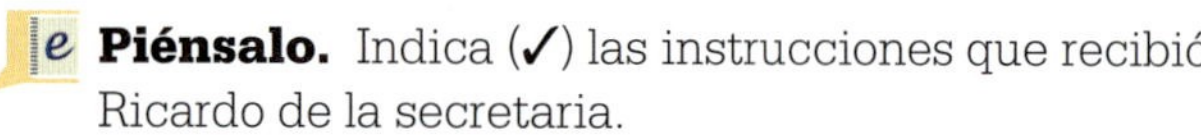

Piénsalo. Indica (✓) las instrucciones que recibió Ricardo de la secretaria.

1. __✓__ Llene la solicitud.
2. _____ Envíe una foto.
3. _____ Mándeme flores.
4. __✓__ Suba la solicitud a nuestra página web.
5. __✓__ Mande pronto la solicitud.
6. _____ No deje ningún espacio en blanco.

Suggestion for Formal commands
Remind students that they saw some of these orthographic changes while practicing the preterit in *Capítulo 6.*

Formal commands

- Commands (**los mandatos**) are the verb forms used to tell others to do something. Use formal commands with people you address as **usted** or **ustedes.** To form these commands, drop the final **-o** of the **yo** form of the present tense and add **-e(n)** for **-ar** verbs and **-a(n)** for **-er** and **-ir** verbs.

			USTED	USTEDES	
firmar	→	firmø	firme	firmen	*sign*
leer	→	leø	lea	lean	*read*
abrir	→	abrø	abra	abran	*open*

Firme aquí, por favor.	*Sign here, please.*
Lean los informes antes de la reunión.	*Read the reports before the meeting.*
Abra la sesión a las 14:00 horas en punto.	*Open the session at 2:00* P.M. *sharp.*

- The stem of the command form is the same as the stem of the **yo** form of the present tense, even for stem-changing and most irregular verbs.

			USTED	USTEDES	
pensar	→	pienso	piense	piensen	*think*
dormir	→	duermo	duerma	duerman	*sleep*
repetir	→	repito	repita	repitan	*repeat*
poner	→	pongo	ponga	pongan	*put*

- The use of **usted** and **ustedes** with command forms is optional. When used, they normally follow the command.

Pase/Pase **usted.**	*Come in.*

- To make a formal command negative, place **no** before the affirmative command.

No salga ahora.	*Do not leave now.*

- Object pronouns and reflexive pronouns are attached to the end of affirmative commands. (Note the written accent over the stressed vowel.) Object pronouns and reflexive pronouns precede negative commands and are not attached.

Cómpre**la.**	*Buy it.*
No **la** compre.	*Do not buy it.*
Háblen**le.**	*Talk to him/her.*
No **le** hablen.	*Do not talk to him/her.*
Siénte**se.**	*Sit down.*
No **se** siente.	*Do not sit down.*

- The verbs **dar, ir, ser,** and **saber** have irregular command forms.

dar:	**dé, den**
ir:	**vaya, vayan**
ser:	**sea, sean**
saber:	**sepa, sepan**

- Verbs ending in **-car, -gar, -zar, -ger,** and **-guir** have spelling changes in command forms.

sacar	saco	→	sa**qu**e, sa**qu**en
jugar	juego	→	jue**gu**e, jue**gu**en
almorzar	almuerzo	→	almuer**c**e, almuer**c**en
recoger	recojo	→	reco**j**a, reco**j**an
seguir	sigo	→	si**g**a, si**g**an

e ¿COMPRENDES?

Completa las oraciones con la forma correcta del mandato formal.

1. ___Lea___ (Leer) el informe, por favor, Sr. Flores.
2. Luego, ___de___ me (dar) un resumen de los puntos principales.
3. No ___incluya___ (incluir) información innecesaria.
4. Manuel y Clara, no ___salgan___ (salir) antes de las cinco.
5. ___Sigan___ (Seguir) Uds. mis instrucciones, por favor.
6. Clara, al terminar el proyecto, ___mánde___ melo (mandar) por *e-mail*.

MySpanishLab

Learn more using Amplifire Dynamic Study Modules, Grammar Tutorials, and Extra Practice activities.

PRÁCTICA

9-25 

Instrucciones a un/a estudiante. No fuiste a clase durante la semana dedicada a Guatemala y quieres ponerte al día. Túrnense para hacer cada uno un rol: el estudiante que pregunta y el profesor que responde. Añadan una pregunta más.

E1: *¿Estudio el capítulo 9?*

E2: *Sí, estúdielo.*

1. ¿Contesto las preguntas sobre los lugares turísticos en Guatemala?
2. ¿Miro los DVD de bailes folclóricos de Guatemala?
3. ¿Busco más información en línea sobre la cultura de Guatemala?
4. ¿Hago la tarea sobre las culturas indígenas de Guatemala?
5. ¿Leo el artículo sobre Rigoberta Menchú?
6. ¿...?

Cultura

En Guatemala, los jóvenes se dirigen normalmente a sus padres, a sus profesores y a otras personas mayores con la forma **usted.** El uso de **tú** y de **usted** varía mucho en el mundo hispano. En general la forma **tú** es más común para comunicarse con los padres, pero **usted** se usa frecuentemente para la comunicación con los profesores.

Comparaciones. No todas las lenguas tienen el equivalente de las formas **tú** y **usted.** ¿Cómo se dirige la gente a otras personas en tu cultura para demostrar respeto?

Suggestion for 9-26
Model the use of pronouns with negative commands. You may wish to direct students to respond negatively to some of the situations.

En el hospital. Un/a enfermero/a entra en la habitación y le hace las siguientes preguntas al/a la paciente. Túrnense para hacer los papeles de enfermero/a y paciente, y añadan una pregunta más.

E1: *¿Le abro las cortinas?*

E2: *Sí, ábramelas, por favor. Quisiera leer.*

1. ¿Le pongo la televisión?
2. ¿Le preparo un café?
3. ¿Le doy otra almohada?
4. ¿Me llevo estas flores?
5. ¿Le traigo el teléfono?
6. ¿...?

Mandatos del entrenador de un equipo. Preparen una lista de sugerencias que el/la entrenador/a puede darles a los miembros de su equipo para lograr los objetivos siguientes. Comparen su lista con la de otra pareja.

para mantenerse en buen estado físico

E1: *Practiquen todos los días.*

E2: *No se acuesten tarde.*

1. para tener mejor rendimiento (*performance*)
2. para prepararse mentalmente para un partido difícil
3. para evitar problemas con el árbitro
4. para dormir bien cuando tienen mucho estrés
5. para ser buenos alumnos y también buenos deportistas

9-28

¿Qué deben hacer estas personas? Busquen una solución a los siguientes problemas y díganle a cada persona qué debe hacer.

MODELO El Sr. Álvarez dice: "No estoy contento en mi trabajo".

E1: *Sr. Álvarez, busque otro trabajo inmediatamente.*

E2: *Hable con su jefe y explíquele la situación.*

1. La Sra. Jiménez dice: "Necesito más vendedores en mi compañía".
2. El Sr. Jiménez se queja: "Tengo que terminar un informe económico pero mi computadora no funciona".
3. Unos hombres de negocios van a ir a la Ciudad de Guatemala, pero no saben hablar español.
4. La Sra. Peña tuvo un accidente serio con su auto; el chofer que provocó el accidente no quiere darle la información que ella necesita para informar a su seguro.
5. La Sra. Hurtado entra en su apartamento y ve que hay agua en el piso de la cocina.
6. La Sra. Fernández quiere ir al Festival Folclórico Nacional de Cobán, pero el Sr. Fernández no se siente bien.

Suggestions for 9-28
Describe personal situations and elicit student advice: *¿Qué debo hacer? No tengo dinero. (Trabaje. Pídales dinero a sus padres). Tengo hambre. (Prepare algo. Coma). Estoy triste. (Salga con nosotros. Practique deportes).*
Give students 5–10 minutes to write a *Querida Antonia* (Dear Abby) letter. Then collect the letters and redistribute them, so other students can take the role of Antonia, giving advice using commands.

Situación

Suggestion for *Situación*
Additional role plays are available in the Instructor's Resource folder.

PREPARACIÓN. Lean esta situación. Luego, compartan ejemplos de vocabulario, gramática y otra información que necesitan para desarrollar la conversación.

Role A. Tell your neighbor that you are leaving for three days for job interviews. Ask if your neighbor can do a few things for you. After he/she agrees, tell him/her to:

a. feed (**dar de comer a**) the cat and play with her every day;
b. water the plants;
c. pick up the mail (**correspondencia**); and
d. anything else you may need.

Thank him/her for helping you out.

Role B. Your neighbor tells you that he/she is going to be away. Agree to help him/her out. After you find out what you will have to do:

a. ask whom you should call if there is an emergency (**emergencia**); and
b. get the telephone number of the vet (**veterinario/a**).

	ROLE A	ROLE B
Vocabulario	Household chores	Household chores Question words
Funciones y formas	Formal commands Answering questions Expressing gratitude Using formal commands politely	Asking questions Answering questions

INTERCAMBIOS. Practica la conversación con tu compañero/a incorporando el vocabulario y las funciones de *Preparación*. Luego, represéntenla ante la clase.

EN ACCIÓN

Buscando trabajo

Expansion for 9-29
You might want to have students work in groups to share their future professional aspirations. Tell students to discuss what they would like to do with their career, and to explain why they have chosen this particular path.

9-29 Antes de ver 

Las profesiones. Asocia las definiciones de la columna de la izquierda con las profesiones, oficios u ocupaciones de la columna de la derecha.

1. __e__ Trabaja con madera y con frecuencia hace muebles.
2. __g__ Sirve comida en un restaurante.
3. __a__ Se dedica a cortar el pelo y a peinar a sus clientes.
4. __b__ Defiende a un acusado en la corte.
5. __f__ Ayuda a otras personas u organizaciones sin cobrar sueldo.
6. __d__ Dirige películas.
7. __h__ Estudia las sociedades y culturas del mundo.
8. __c__ Asiste a las personas que tienen problemas de salud.
9. __i__ Cobra y devuelve dinero a los clientes.
10. __j__ Construye casas y edificios.

a. peluquero/a
b. abogado/a
c. enfermero/a
d. director/a de cine
e. carpintero/a
f. voluntario/a
g. camarero/a
h. antropólogo/a
i. cajero/a
j. arquitecto/a

9-30 Mientras ves  

En Guatemala. En este segmento, Vanesa y Héctor miran la página de Facebook de Pilar, la prima de Vanesa. Indica si las siguientes oraciones son ciertas (**C**) o falsas (**F**) según la información que da Pilar. Corrige las oraciones falsas.

1. __F__ Pilar recibe un salario muy alto por el trabajo que hace en Guatemala. Pilar hace trabajo voluntario.
2. __C__ Las estufas ecológicas son menos peligrosas que las estufas de leña.
3. __C__ El lago Atitlán es el lago más profundo de Centroamérica.
4. __C__ El café y el maíz son importantes recursos de Guatemala.
5. __F__ Las ruinas de Tikal son ejemplo de la arquitectura española en Guatemala. Las ruinas de Tikal son un ejemplo de la cultura maya.
6. __C__ Chichicastenango es un famoso mercado de productos naturales y artesanía.

9-31 Después de ver 

¿Qué dijeron? **PREPARACIÓN.** Marca (✓) lo que dijeron los personajes en este segmento de video.

1. ____ Vanesa dijo que estaba buscando un trabajo relacionado con la moda.
2. __✓__ Héctor dijo que él ayudaba a su madre con las cuentas en su peluquería.
3. __✓__ Héctor le contó a Vanesa que cuando era más joven se cortó el pelo.
4. ____ Pilar dijo que estaba haciendo trabajo de voluntaria en Honduras.
5. __✓__ Héctor y Vanesa dijeron que iban a pensar seriamente en trabajar de voluntarios también.

INTERCAMBIOS. Cuéntense alguna anécdota relacionada con un trabajo que tuvieron en el pasado. Usen las siguientes preguntas como guía.

1. ¿Qué trabajo era?
2. ¿Era un trabajo de voluntario(a) o remunerado (*paid*)?
3. ¿Ocurrió algo interesante en ese trabajo? ¿Qué pasó?
4. ¿Qué hiciste?

Mosaicos

ESCUCHA

  Presentational

Preparación. En la siguiente conversación, dos amigas hablan sobre las ventajas y desventajas de su trabajo. Antes de escuchar, escribe el nombre de una profesión relacionada con los negocios y otra con la salud. Luego, escribe una ventaja y una desventaja para cada una de las profesiones. Comparte tus notas con la clase.

PROFESIÓN	VENTAJA	DESVENTAJA

ESTRATEGIA

Use contextual guessing

When you have a conversation in a second language, it is common not to understand everything the other person says. You can figure out the overall message by using contextual cues; that is, by paying attention to the topic or to the words that precede or follow what you did not understand.

9-33  Interpretive

Escucha. Read the words in the left column and then listen to the conversation between Estela and Susana. State the probable meaning of each word in English based on the contextual cues you heard in the conversation. Finally, write down the cue words that helped you understand.

ESCUCHÉ…	POSIBLE SIGNIFICADO	ADIVINÉ EL SIGNIFICADO PORQUE…
1. neuróloga	neurologist	*neuralgias, nervios* (cognados); *dolores de cabeza*
2. primordial	prime, fundamental	*se conecta con lo que es de primera importancia*
3. guardias	to be on duty	*una vez a la semana, quedarse en el hospital 24 horas*

Comprueba

I was able to …

____ comprehend the overall meaning by focusing on what I understood.

____ use context to figure out the meaning of unknown words.

9-34  Interpersonal

Un paso más. Comparte con tu compañero/a las respuestas a las siguientes preguntas.

1. ¿Cuáles son las ventajas y desventajas de la profesión que más te gusta?
2. En general, ¿qué profesión u ocupación te parece menos estresante?
3. ¿Qué profesión u ocupación da más satisfacciones personales? ¿Por qué?

Note for 9-32
This brief presentational activity will help students focus on the conversation they are going to hear. By reflecting on the advantages and disadvantages of certain professions and then sharing their ideas they will familiarize themselves with the context of the interpretive activity that follows. In *Un paso más* students will practice their interpersonal skills by talking informally about the same topic at a personal level.

Audioscript for 9-33
ESTELA: *Susana, te digo que me encanta ser mujer de negocios. El sueldo es excelente y los beneficios son estupendos. Imagínate, tengo un seguro médico maravilloso y cuatro semanas de vacaciones al año. Lo que no me gusta mucho es que tengo que viajar por lo menos treinta semanas al año y que no tengo tiempo para estar mucho con mi familia.*
SUSANA: *Me alegro de que te guste tu trabajo, Estela. A mí también me encanta el mío, pero es diferente, por supuesto.*
ESTELA: *Sí, como neuróloga ayudas a muchas personas. Eso debe ser maravilloso. Es horrible tener neuralgias o dolores de cabeza. ¡Tener un buen médico especialista si uno está mal de los nervios es primordial!*
SUSANA: *Sí, me encanta ayudar a la gente. El único problema que tengo es que el horario es muy variable. Si alguien se enferma de noche, me tengo que levantar para ir a verlo al hospital si es necesario. También tengo guardias una vez a la semana, cuando me tengo que quedar 24 horas en el hospital.*
ESTELA: *Comprendo. No hay nada perfecto.*
SUSANA: *Pero, no me quejo. Me gusta mi trabajo y gano un buen sueldo.*

Note for 9-35
In *Preparación* students will interpret the information in some job ads to find some requirements that they may meet to apply for the jobs and to prepare for the interpersonal activity that follows. In *Un paso más* students will present a report to the class informing about the results of the job interviews.

Audioscript for *En directo*
MATEO: *Buenas tardes, Sra. Durán. Soy Mateo Williams.*
SRA. DURÁN: *Buenas tardes, Sr. Williams. Adelante, por favor. Siéntese aquí.*
MATEO: *Gracias. Aquí le entrego una copia de mi currículum.*
SRA. DURÁN: *Muchas gracias. Por favor, póngase cómodo.*
MATEO: *Gracias.* [brief pause, allowing Sra. Durán to quickly scan his resume] *Como puede ver, tengo mucha experiencia en ventas y mi especialidad son los aparatos electrónicos.*
SRA. DURÁN: *Sí, ya veo. También sé que usted tiene muy buena reputación como vendedor, que trata muy bien a sus clientes. Para nuestra empresa, el trato de nuestros clientes es lo más importante.*
MATEO: *¡Cómo no! Hacen falta buenos productos como los que produce su compañía. Sin embargo, es igual de importante hacer que se sientan bien los clientes.*
SRA. DURÁN: *De acuerdo. Bueno, Sr. Williams, ahora tengo que entrevistar a otro candidato. Fue un placer conocerlo.*
MATEO: *Igualmente. Muchísimas gracias.*

Suggestions for 9-36
To do the interpersonal activity you will need to organize students into groups of 3: *1 jefe/a de personal* and *2 personas que buscan trabajo.* In the preceding activity, students selected 1 job ad from the 3 ads presented; the 2 job seekers in this activity should be applying for the same job.

HABLA

9-35  Interpretive

Preparación. Lee los siguientes anuncios con ofertas de trabajo. Escoge un anuncio y prepara una lista con los requisitos que cumples (*that you meet*).

JEFE DE SERVICIO
necesita importante empresa
MANUFACTURERA DE PLÁSTICOS

Nos urge un buen diseñador gráfico
Requisitos: Conoce al 100% PhotoShop y Freehand. Maneja ambiente Mac y PC. De preferencia estudiante de diseño en la U, con ideas frescas. Dispuesto a trabajar bajo presión.
Ofrecemos: Salario a convenir. Capacitación constante. Desarrollo dentro de la organización. Horario flexible. Seguro de vida y médico.
Interesados, enviar currículum y fotografía reciente, especificando pretensiones de sueldo, a Casilla 2568, Correo Guatemala, zona 1, Guatemala

INSTITUTO PRIVADO

necesita
DIRECTOR/A
Lugar de residencia, Región de los Lagos

Empresa de Hotelería necesita Director/a
Requisitos: Estudios universitarios avanzados. Experiencia mínima de 1 a 2 años en ventas directas, preferiblemente en el área de servicios. Edad 26 a 32 años. Excelente presentación. Poseer vehículo propio. Buenas relaciones interpersonales.
Ofrecemos: Salario a convenir según experiencia, gasolina, comisiones sobre ventas. Excelente ambiente de trabajo. Oportunidades de crecimiento.
Sueldo compatible con calificaciones
Interesados, enviar currículum a gruporecursoshumanos@hotmail.com

BANCO AZTECA
necesita
10 CONTADORES AUDITORES
Lugar de trabajo ideal: Viña del Mar
- Título universitario
- Mínimo dos años de experiencia
- Flexibilidad horaria
- Deseo de viajar a otras regiones del país
- Capacidad de organización y trabajo

Sueldo atractivo
Interesados, enviar currículum, con fotografía a: Bco. Azteca, 7 Av. 19-28, zona 5

ESTRATEGIA

Gather information strategically to express a decision

When you speak to convey a decision, you need to present your decision and the reasons behind it in an organized and convincing way. Lay out your facts and arguments logically (in your mind or in written notes) before you start to speak.

9-36  Interpersonal

Habla. Escojan un papel. Uno/a es el/la jefe/a de personal de una compañía representada en los anuncios y los otros dos son personas que solicitan el mismo trabajo en esa compañía.

Jefe/a de personal: Entrevista separadamente a dos personas que están interesadas en el mismo puesto. Pregúntales sobre su experiencia, sus estudios, sus preferencias de sueldo, etc., y decide cuál es la persona indicada para el puesto.

Personas que buscan trabajo: Cada uno de ustedes debe escoger un trabajo. Respondan a las preguntas del/de la jefe/a de personal y háganle preguntas para saber más acerca del puesto.

Comprueba
In my conversation …

_____ **I asked questions relevant to the position.**

_____ **I provided answers relevant to the questions asked.**

_____ **I supported my questions and answers with appropriate information.**

En directo

To welcome someone to your office:

Pase/Adelante, por favor./Tenga la amabilidad de pasar. *Please come in.*

Por favor, tome asiento. *Please have a seat.*

Siéntese aquí, por favor. *Sit here, please.*

To put someone at ease:

Por favor, póngase cómodo/a. *Please make yourself comfortable.*

To say good-bye at the end of an interview:

Fue un placer conocerlo/la. *It was a pleasure to meet you.*

 Listen to a conversation with these expressions.

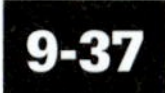

Un paso más. Los jefes de personal y las personas que buscaban trabajo deben informar a la clase sobre lo siguiente.

Informe de las personas que buscaban trabajo:

1. ¿Qué puesto buscabas? ¿Qué requisitos cumples?
2. ¿Qué aspecto de la oferta de trabajo te pareció más atractivo?
3. ¿Crees que vas a recibir la oferta de trabajo? ¿Por qué?

Informe de los jefes de personal:

1. ¿Qué puesto ofrecía tu compañía en el anuncio?
2. ¿Qué cualidades debía tener el/la candidato/a que buscaba trabajo en tu compañía?
3. ¿A qué candidato/a(s) vas a contratar? ¿Por qué?

La manera de expresar la dirección de un negocio o un domicilio en la Ciudad de Guatemala puede confundir a los extranjeros. Por ejemplo, “7 Av. 11-38, zona 9” significa que la casa está en la avenida 7, entre las calles 11 y 12 en la zona 9, y el número de la casa es 38. Las zonas tienen la misma función que los códigos postales (*zip codes*) en Estados Unidos.

Decir la zona es importante, porque los números de las avenidas (que van del norte al sur) y de las calles (que van del este al oeste) se repiten en cada zona.

Comparaciones. ¿Cómo está dividida tu ciudad? ¿Conoces el nombre de algunas zonas? ¿Se incluye el nombre de la zona en la dirección postal?

Note for 9-38
In *Preparación* students exchange ideas to activate background knowledge and help them focus on the topic of the reading and its different subtopics. In *Lee,* students will learn about a specific group of immigrants in the United States from personal, demographic, and economic perspectives. In *Un paso más* they present in a brief paragraph some of the ideas that they have learned through discussion and reading.

Standard 5.1
Students use the language both within and beyond the school setting.
Mexicans and Guatemalans are only two groups of the growing Hispanic population of the U.S. You may wish to encourage students to talk about and perhaps do some research on how their career plans could be expanded and enhanced by having sufficient proficiency in Spanish to use it in their chosen professions.

Note
Other cities with a high concentration of Guatemalans include Phoenix, Houston, Chicago, Miami, Washington, DC, and New York.

Note
Families in Guatemala use 50% of the money they receive from family members in the United States for basic needs such as food and clothing. The other 50% goes for living and health expenses, products for the home, and savings.

LEE

9-38 Interpersonal

Preparación. Lee el título y los subtítulos del texto en la página siguiente. Basándote en esta información y en lo que sabes sobre la inmigración, anota algunas ideas para compartir con tu compañero/a.

1. ¿Son frecuentes los matrimonios interculturales? ¿Conoces alguno? ¿Qué ventajas o desventajas piensas que tienen estas parejas?
2. ¿Cuáles son las nuevas tendencias demográficas en Estados Unidos? ¿Qué grupos de inmigrantes son los más numerosos?
3. ¿Qué efectos puede tener la emigración en la economía de un país?

ESTRATEGIA

Organize textual information into categories

To understand what you are reading, you need to focus on what is being conveyed by the text. By *focus* we mean organizing the information into meaningful categories, which helps you connect the information to what you already know. As you read, focus on the main point of each section. Use the subtitles to help you anticipate the content.

9-39 Interpretive

Lee. Indica a qué categoría pertenecen las siguientes afirmaciones, según el contenido del artículo: información personal sobre una familia (**P**), información general sobre los inmigrantes guatemaltecos en Estados Unidos (**EU**) o información sobre Guatemala (**G**).

1. __EU__ Viven en comunidades donde el grupo predominante son los mexicanos.
2. __P__ Se conocieron en un club de baile.
3. __G__ Reciben dinero de sus familiares que viven en el extranjero.
4. __G__ El dinero que viene del exterior estimula la economía.
5. __EU__ Hay más hombres que mujeres.
6. __P__ Trabaja de obrero y mantiene a su familia en Los Ángeles.

Comprueba
I was able to ...

____ **use the subtitles to anticipate and reflect on the content.**

____ **organize the content into general categories.**

____ **identify the main ideas in the text.**

LOS GUATEMALTECOS EN ESTADOS UNIDOS

MATRIMONIOS ENTRE GUATEMALTECOS Y MEXICANOS

Gustavo Rivera conoció a Marta Rodríguez en un club hispano de Los Ángeles y la invitó a bailar. Marta, que era de la Ciudad de México, se dio cuenta de que Gustavo hablaba español con un acento diferente y que usaba unas palabras diferentes también. Después de un rato, ella le preguntó: "¿De dónde eres, Gustavo?". "Soy de Guatemala", dijo él. Después de esa noche, los dos empezaron a conversar por teléfono y a salir juntos. Pasaron dos años y Gustavo y Marta se casaron; ahora tienen tres hijos.

Esta familia representa una tendencia demográfica en Los Ángeles y en otras ciudades del suroeste: más inmigrantes guatemaltecos y mexicanos, que emigran por trabajo u otras razones, se casan entre sí y tienen hijos, creando familias hispanas mixtas que tienen conexiones con tres países al mismo tiempo. Esa mezcla es ahora tan común que dio lugar al nombre de "guatemexicoestadounidenses" para describir a esas familias.

NUEVAS TENDENCIAS DEMOGRÁFICAS

Hay varias razones que explican esta tendencia demográfica. Primero, el número de personas de ascendencia guatemalteca en Estados Unidos está creciendo. Según la Organización Internacional para las Migraciones (OIM), en el 2010 había más de 1,5 millones de guatemaltecos en Estados Unidos. La mayoría son jóvenes, entre 15 y 44 años, y hay muchos más hombres (72%) que mujeres (28%). Por esta razón, muchos guatemaltecos en Estados Unidos se casan con mujeres no guatemaltecas.

Segundo, cuando los inmigrantes guatemaltecos nuevos buscan vivienda en comunidades hispanas establecidas, conocen a muchos mexicanos, porque son el grupo hispano más grande del país. La constante interacción entre hombres guatemaltecos y mujeres mexicanas da como resultado más matrimonios entre los dos grupos.

IMPACTO ECONÓMICO EN GUATEMALA

Gustavo Rivera es un inmigrante guatemalteco típico. Como el 88% de los guatemaltecos que viven en Estados Unidos, Gustavo se mantiene activo económicamente, trabaja en una fábrica. Como el 33% de los guatemaltecos en Estados Unidos, vive en Los Ángeles. Y como el 93% de los emigrantes guatemaltecos, mantiene contacto con su familia en Guatemala. Llama a sus padres todas las semanas y les envía remesas todos los meses. Según la OIM, más de 600.000 familias en Guatemala reciben remesas de familiares que viven en el extranjero.

  Presentational

Un paso más. En un párrafo, resume las ideas principales del artículo y compártelo con la clase.

Suggestion for 9-40
You can assign this as a pair activity. Have student pairs work together and then present to the class.

Suggestion for 9-41
You may wish to do *Preparación* as a whole-class activity, or at least model for students how to organize their personal information for a specific purpose.

Suggestion for *Estrategia*
Students will be familiar with the notion of writing for a specific audience from their writing classes in English. To help them transfer this knowledge to their writing in Spanish, you may wish to ask them to verbalize what they know.

ESCRIBE

Interpretive

Preparación. Lee el siguiente anuncio de trabajo en Internet y prepara una lista de datos sobre tu experiencia y tus talentos para solicitar el puesto.

Descripción:

Se necesita estudiante para cuidar niños guatemaltecos durante el verano. Imprescindible inglés nativo y saber preparar comidas ligeras.

El trabajo es en Estados Unidos

Detalles generales:

Oferta por: **Empresa Ofertas**
Correo electrónico: empresaoferta@gmail.com

Detalles del anuncio

Número: 13800
Número de visitas: 354
La oferta vence: dentro de 196 días
Fecha: 20/7/2013

ESTRATEGIA

Focus on purpose, content, and audience

To get the job that is right for you, consider the following when responding to an ad in any language:

- Your purpose: What kind of job do you want?
- Your response: What academic degree do you need for the job? What general abilities and job-specific skills should you possess?
- Your audience: What experience does the employer require? What personality characteristics will you need to be considered a serious candidate?

Escribe. Escribe un correo electrónico solicitando el trabajo. En un mensaje breve, organizado y convincente, preséntate y explica por qué tu experiencia, tu conocimiento y tus talentos son perfectos para el puesto.

Comprueba

I was able to …

- ____ appropriately address the potential employer.
- ____ convincingly describe my qualifications for the position.

Un paso más. Comparte tu correo electrónico con tu compañero/a para que te dé su opinión.

En este capítulo…

Comprueba lo que sabes

Go to ***MySpanishLab*** to review what you have learned in this chapter. Practice with the following:

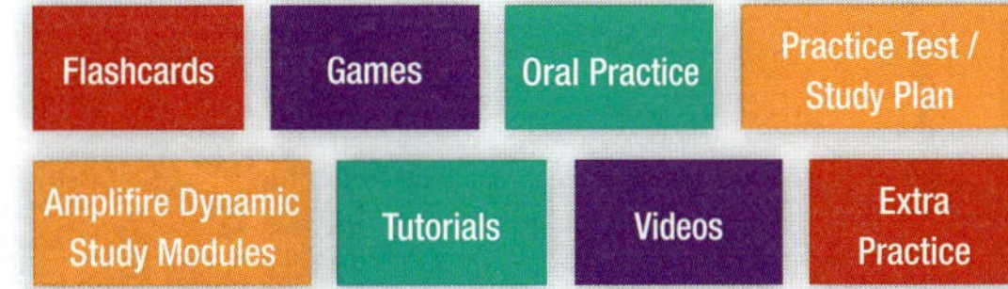

Vocabulario

LAS PROFESIONES, OFICIOS Y OCUPACIONES
Professions, trades, and occupations

el/la abogado/a *lawyer*
el actor/la actriz *actor/actress*
el/la agricultor/a *farmer*
el ama/o de casa *housewife, homemaker*
el/la arquitecto/a *architect*
el/la bibliotecario/a *librarian*
el/la bombero/a *firefighter*
el/la cajero/a *cashier*
el/la carpintero/a *carpenter*
el/la chef *chef*
el/la chofer *driver*
el/la científico/a *scientist*
el/la contador/a *accountant*
el/la contratista *contractor*
el/la ejecutivo/a *executive*
el/la electricista *electrician*
el/la empleado/a *employee*
el/la enfermero/a *nurse*
el/la gerente (de ventas) *(sales) manager*
el hombre/la mujer de negocios *businessman/woman*
el/la ingeniero/a *engineer*
el/la intérprete *interpreter*
el/la jefe/a *boss*
el/la juez *judge*
el/la locutor/a *radio announcer*
el/la médico/a *medical doctor*
el/la obrero/a *worker*
el/la peluquero/a *hairdresser*
el/la periodista *journalist*
el/la plomero/a *plumber*
el/la policía *policeman/woman*
el/la (p)sicólogo/a *psychologist*
el/la técnico/a *technician*
el/la vendedor/a *salesman, saleswoman*

VERBOS
Verbs

apagar *to extinguish, turn off*
cosechar *to harvest*
cultivar *to grow, cultivate*
dejar *to leave*
enviar *to send*
esperar *to wait for*
explotar *to exploit*
llenar *to fill (out)*
mandar *to send*
ofrecer (zc) *to offer*
solicitar *to apply (for)*

LOS LUGARES
Places

el campo *countryside*
la compañía/empresa *company*
el consultorio *office (of doctor, dentist, etc.)*
la finca *ranch, farm*
el terreno *land*

EL TRABAJO
Work

la agricultura *farming*
el anuncio *ad, advertisement*
el/la cliente/a *client*
el currículum *résumé*
la entrevista *interview*
la experiencia *experience*
la exportación *export*
la fuente de ingresos *source of income*
la fuerza laboral *workforce*
el incendio *fire*
el puesto *position*
la solicitud *application*
el sueldo *salary, wage*
la vacante *opening*
las ventas *sales*

RECURSOS NATURALES
Natural resources

el bosque *forest*
el hierro *iron*
la madera *wood*
el petróleo *petroleum*

PALABRAS Y EXPRESIONES ÚTILES
Useful words and expressions

actualmente *at the present time*
agrícola *agricultural*
en realidad/realmente *in fact, really*
lo importante *the important thing*
la industria textil *textile industry*
por cierto *by the way*
propio/a *own*
la señal *signal*
sin embargo *nevertheless*

Introduction to chapter Introduce the chapter theme about food, cooking, and healthy eating. Ask questions to recycle content from the previous chapter. Related questions: *¿Sabes cocinar? ¿Quién en tu familia cocina mejor? ¿Qué tipo de comida te gusta más: la italiana, la china, la india...? ¿Conoces la comida de algunos países hispanos? ¿De cuáles? ¿Qué platos conoces? En general, ¿comes bien o necesitas mejorar tu dieta con más frutas y vegetales? ¿Eres vegetariano/a? ¿Cómo es tu dieta?*

Integrated Performance Assessment: Three Modes of Communication

Presentational: See activities 10-7, 10-8, 10-20, 10-26, 10-27, 10-30, 10-35, 10-40, 10-43, and 10-45.

Interpretive: See activities 10-1, 10-2, 10-3, 10-4, 10-5, 10-6, 10-9, 10-13, 10-14, 10-15, 10-16, 10-18, 10-19, 10-22, 10-23, 10-24, 10-25, 10-26, 10-28, 10-29, 10-31, 10-32, 10-33, 10-34,10-36, 10-38, 10-42, and 10-44.

Interpersonal: See activities 10-1, 10-3, 10-4, 10-5, 10-6, 10-7, 10-8, 10-9, 10-10, 10-11, 10-12, 10-13, 10-14, 10-15, 10-16, 10-17, 10-18, 10-20, 10-21, 10-22, 10-23, 10-24, 10-25, 10-26, 10-27, 10-28, 10-29, 10-30, 10-31, 10-34, 10-37, 10-39, 10-41, 10-46, and all *Situación* activities.

10 ¿Cuál es tu comida preferida?

ENFOQUE CULTURAL
Ecuador

VOCABULARIO EN CONTEXTO
Los productos y las recetas
En el supermercado
La mesa

MOSAICO CULTURAL
Comida callejera

FUNCIONES Y FORMAS
Se + verb constructions
Present perfect and participles used as adjectives
Informal commands
The future tense

EN ACCIÓN
¡Hay que celebrar!

MOSAICOS
ESCUCHA Make notes of relevant details
HABLA Give and defend reasons for a decision
LEE Learn new words by analyzing their connections with known words
ESCRIBE Summarize information

EN ESTE CAPÍTULO...
Comprueba lo que sabes
Vocabulario

LEARNING OUTCOMES

You will be able to:

- talk about ingredients, recipes, and meals
- state impersonal information
- talk about the recent past
- give instructions in informal settings
- talk about the future
- present information, concepts, and ideas about food and public health in Ecuador and other Latin American countries

ENFOQUE cultural ECUADOR

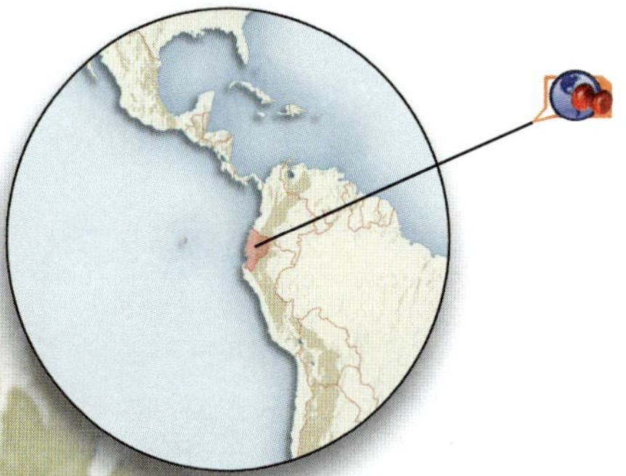

Islas Galápagos

Tortuga de las Galápagos

COLOMBIA

Tulcán

Ibarra

Otavalo

Quito

El distrito histórico de Quito

Textiles de Ecuador

Región amazónica

Manta

Ambato

Riobamba

Guayaquil

Milagro

ECUADOR

La reserva amazónica de Kapawi

Isla Puna

Golfo de Guayaquil

Cuenca

Machala

Loja

CORDILLERA DE LOS ANDES

PERÚ

OCÉANO PACÍFICO

Cartaratas de los Andes

Enfoque cultural

To learn more about Ecuador, go to MySpanishLab to view the *Vistas culturales* videos.

¿QUÉ TE PARECE?

- Charles Darwin visitó las islas Galápagos en 1835. Este viaje influyó en su idea de la evolución mediante la selección natural.
- Ecuador declaró en la Nueva Constitución Ecuatoriana de 2008 que la naturaleza tiene derechos constitucionales. Fue el primer país en reconocer a la naturaleza como sujeto de derecho.
- En Quito, la capital de Ecuador, el punto de ebullición del agua es 90 grados centígrados (194 ºF) debido a la altura de la ciudad.
- Ecuador es el mayor exportador de bananas; produce el 32% de las bananas en el mercado mundial.
- Rafael Correa fue elegido presidente de Ecuador por tercera vez en 2013. Aprendió a hablar quechua durante su año de servicio militar en las montañas.

▲ Este cuadro del siglo XVIII presenta a un indígena yumbo cerca de Quito, Ecuador. Junto a él hay árboles y frutas típicas de su país.

Suggestion for map
Project the image of the map and photos. Call students' attention to the different regions of Ecuador. Have them describe its geographical features: *¿Qué mar u océano está al oeste de Ecuador? ¿Tiene montañas este país? ¿Cómo se llaman?* Ask students to compare: *¿Qué diferencias hay entre la región del Amazonas y la de los Andes? ¿Dónde hace más calor probablemente?* Point out the location of the Galapagos Islands. *¿Qué tipo de animales hay en las islas Galápagos?*

Note
The painting on this page by Vicente Albán is found in the *Museo de América* in Madrid. The Yumbo people, who lived in the northern valleys around Quito, emigrated there from the Amazon after a volcanic eruption around 1500 B.C.

Suggestion for art
Project the image of the painting. Ask students to describe the painting by asking: *¿Qué hay en este cuadro? ¿De qué etnia es esta persona? ¿Cómo va vestido?* You may introduce *lanza* (spear) and *cazar* (to hunt). *¿Qué tiene en la mano derecha y en la mano izquierda? ¿Por qué llevaba estas armas probablemente? ¿Para la guerra? ¿Para cazar?* Make connections: *¿Se puede cazar en Estados Unidos? ¿Qué animales se pueden cazar? (ciervo, pavo, pato, oso, alce, etc.) ¿Qué otros animales comemos? (vacas, cerdos, pollos, ovejas)* Introduce the subject of fruit in the painting. *¿Qué frutas comían estos indígenas probablemente?* Name the fruits in the painting: *piña, papaya, plátano.*

Note for *islas Galápagos*
The tortoises are now considered endangered species and have been protected by the government since 1970. They can grow to 5 feet long and weigh over 100 pounds; they are the largest in the world.

Note for *islas Galápagos*
UNESCO named the archipelago a World Heritage site in 1978. Even though ecotourism is a major portion of the Ecuatorian economy, and the key source of income of the Galapagos National Park, tourism has created problems stemming from contamination, a lack of fresh water, and bringing in plants and animals from the mainland which has changed the balance in the islands.

Note for *Quito*
The capital is in a valley surrounded by the volcanic peaks of the Andes.

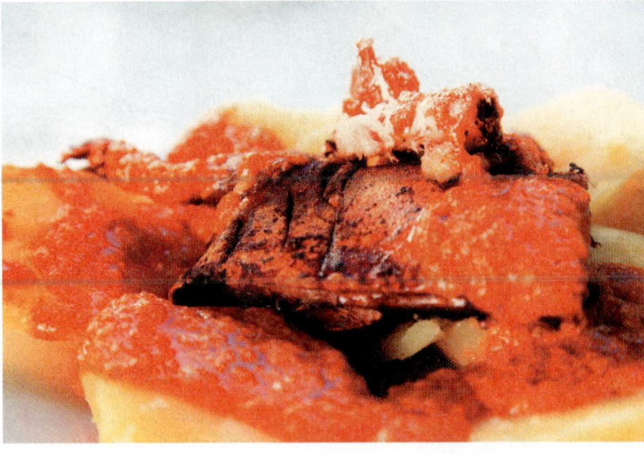

▲ Cuy con papas

Unos típicos platos ecuatorianos son ceviche de camarones, cuy (*guinea pig*), llapingachos (papas con queso), pan de yuca y choclo (maíz) con queso. Se sirve mucha comida con ají criollo (una salsa picante).

Las tortugas de las islas Galápagos son unos animales vertebrados muy antiguos, y pueden vivir hasta 150 años. ▼

▲ Las islas Galápagos tienen plantas y animales que no se encuentran en ningún otro lugar del mundo. El ecoturismo está muy desarrollado en las islas.

Quito fue construida en las ruinas de una ciudad inca. Tiene una rica historia precolombina. Fue designada Patrimonio de la Humanidad por la UNESCO. ▼

¿CUÁNTO SABES?

Asocia la información de las dos columnas.

1. __e__ la capital de Ecuador	**a.** islas Galápagos
2. __a__ territorio ecuatoriano en el Pacífico	**b.** los Andes
3. __f__ llapingachos, cuy y choclo con queso	**c.** Nueva Constitución Ecuatoriana
4. __d__ animal protegido	**d.** tortuga
5. __b__ cadena de montañas	**e.** Quito
6. __c__ protección de la naturaleza	**f.** platos tradicionales

Vocabulario en contexto

Talking about ingredients, recipes, and meals

Los productos y las recetas

MySpanishLab Topic for Pronunciation: Homonyms
Learn more using Amplifire Dynamic Study Modules, Pronunciation, and Vocabulary Tutorials.

En Ecuador se cultiva mucha fruta, sobre todo **piña, limón, melón, papaya, maracuyá** y **plátano.** Mucha de esta fruta se exporta a Estados Unidos y a otros países. Aquí vemos a unas personas trabajando en una compañía de exportación de plátanos cerca de Guayaquil.

En los mercados ecuatorianos, como en los de otros países hispanoamericanos, hay buenos puestos de **pasteles** donde se venden los **dulces** típicos de la región.

El pescado y los **mariscos** son muy importantes en la dieta de algunos países hispanoamericanos como Chile, Perú y Ecuador. En la provincia de Esmeraldas, en Ecuador, uno de los platos típicos es el encocado, pescado que se cocina con **leche de coco.**

Este joven ecuatoriano cuida sus **ovejas** cerca del Parque Nacional Chimborazo. De las ovejas se aprovechan la carne en comida y la lana en suéteres, mantas, etc. Además, los **campesinos** usan la leche para hacer queso y yogur. Junto a la carne de **cordero,** la de **res** y la de **cerdo** son las que más se usan en la comida de Ecuador y se venden en los mercados y en las carnicerías.

En el mercado de Zumbahua se encuentran los productos que se usan en las muchas **recetas** de la comida de Ecuador. La forma de combinar estos productos con el cilantro y otras **hierbas** y **especias** dan fama a la gastronomía ecuatoriana.

PRÁCTICA

10-1  

Escucha y confirma. Match the letter of the photo to the description you hear.

1. d
2. b
3. a
4. e
5. c

Suggestion for *Los productos y las recetas*
Project the online images in class. Ask questions and personalize. Point out that many influences have created great diversity in Hispanic food. When the Spaniards went to the Americas, they discovered a tremendous variety of unknown foods: tomatoes, potatoes, chiles, chocolate, and many others that became staples not only in Spain, but in all of Europe. Certain European culinary traditions, in turn, influenced Latin American cuisine's use of flour, beef, and pork. Climate and geography also explain the great variety of foods throughout the Americas. In general, each region has its special sauces, fruits, vegetables, and methods of preparation. Talk about Hispanic cuisines and the differences among countries and regions; e.g., the difference between Spanish and Mexican *tortillas.*

Remind students that open-air markets are places where food and handicrafts are sold.

Audioscript for 10-1
1. *De la lana de las ovejas se hacen mantas, suéteres y otros artículos.*
2. *Estos pasteles son dulces típicos de Ecuador.*
3. *En Ecuador se cultivan muchos plátanos.*
4. *En el mercado de Zumbahua se encuentran los productos que se usan en las muchas recetas de la comida de Ecuador.*
5. *El pescado y los mariscos son muy importantes en la dieta de los países hispanos.*

Note for 10-3
Explain that *refrito* refers to the fried or sautéed ingredients of the dish to which the other ingredients will be added.

Suggestions for 10-4
Explain that the structure *se + verb* is often used in recipes and will be studied in *Funciones y formas* in this chapter. Encourage student pairs to add another ingredient to the recipe using this structure and present all the steps to the class. You may also want to introduce pizza ingredients: *la masa* (dough), *salchicha* (sausage), *queso* (cheese).

Follow-up for 10-4
To preview the structure *se + verb* ask questions such as: *Típicamente, ¿qué se bebe con la pizza? ¿Se come algo más con la pizza? ¿Se trae la pizza a casa o se come en un restaurante?*

10-2 

Definiciones. Asocia las definiciones a continuación con las palabras que aparecen en los textos y fotos anteriores.

1. una lista de ingredientes y de instrucciones para elaborar una comida receta
2. un animal del que se aprovecha la lana, la leche y la carne oveja
3. una fruta alargada que se pela y que les gusta mucho a los monos plátano
4. un plato ecuatoriano que se cocina con pescado y leche de coco encocado
5. una tienda donde se vende pescado pescadería
6. las personas que cultivan productos del campo campesinos
7. dulces que se venden en las pastelerías y en los mercados pasteles
8. la carne de una oveja pequeña cordero

10-3 

Una receta ecuatoriana. Lean la siguiente receta y clasifiquen sus ingredientes según las categorías. Después, díganse cuál es su comida favorita y por qué les gusta.

1. carnes o pescados: pescado crudo, camarones, almejas
2. vegetales: cebolla, tomate, pimiento
3. condimentos: cilantro, perejil, ajo, aceite, achiote, sal, pimienta, comino
4. frutas: coco

Pescado encocado

Ingredientes:
1 coco
1 libra de camarones
2 libras de pescado crudo

Refrito:
1 cebolla paiteña finamente picada
¼ taza de cebolla blanca finamente picada
1 pimiento picado
4 cucharadas de cilantro picado
4 cucharadas de perejil picado
2 dientes de ajo machacados
4 cucharadas de aceite
1 un tomate grande rojo, pelado y picado
un poquito de achiote
sal, pimienta, comino al gusto

Elaboración:
Haga un refrito con los ingredientes. Agréguele una libra de camarones crudos, pelados y limpios y dos libras de pescado crudo, cortado en trozos. Refríalos durante un rato y luego agregue la mitad de la leche del coco. Tape la olla y deje cocinar durante 20 o 30 minutos. Después, añada la otra mitad de la leche de coco. Sirva inmediatamente, acompañado de arroz blanco y plátano verde asado.

10-4 

Cómo hacer una pizza. Ordenen cronológicamente los pasos para preparar una pizza. ¿Falta algún ingrediente para preparar su pizza favorita? Inclúyanlo y preséntenlo a la clase.

__1__ Se compran los ingredientes para la pizza.

__2__ Se calienta el horno a 350 °F.
__4__ Se echa un poco de aceite (*oil*) antes de poner la masa en la bandeja de horno.
__6__ Se agregan el queso (*cheese*), algún tipo de carne, vegetales y especias.
__5__ Se pone la salsa de tomate.
__3__ Se trabaja bien la masa y se extiende para formar un círculo.
__7__ Se hornea por unos 20 a 25 minutos.

LENGUA

These are some useful words that appear in the recipe: **almejas** (*clams*), **perejil** (*parsley*), **paiteña** (*a type of onion*), **diente de ajo** (*clove of garlic*), **picado** (*chopped*), and **comino** (*cumin*). Other cooking expressions include **picar** (*chop*), **pelar** (*peel*), **machacar** (*crush*), **tapar** (*cover*), **agregar/añadir** (*add*), **taza** (*cup*), and **cucharada** (*spoonful*).

En el supermercado

Las frutas y las verduras

Los productos lácteos y los huevos

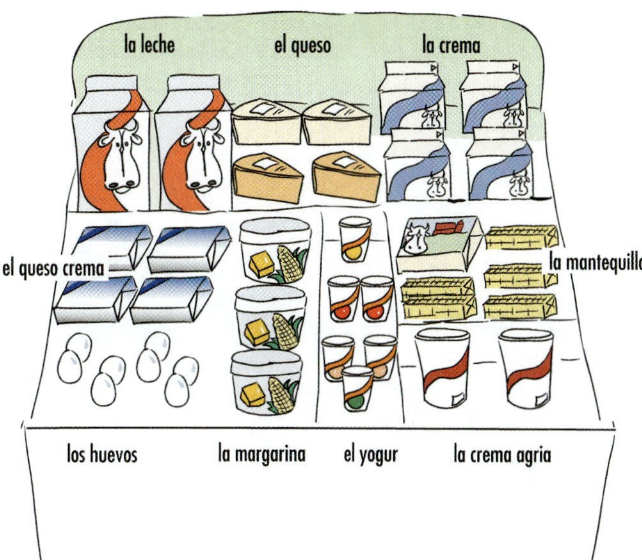

El pescado y la carne

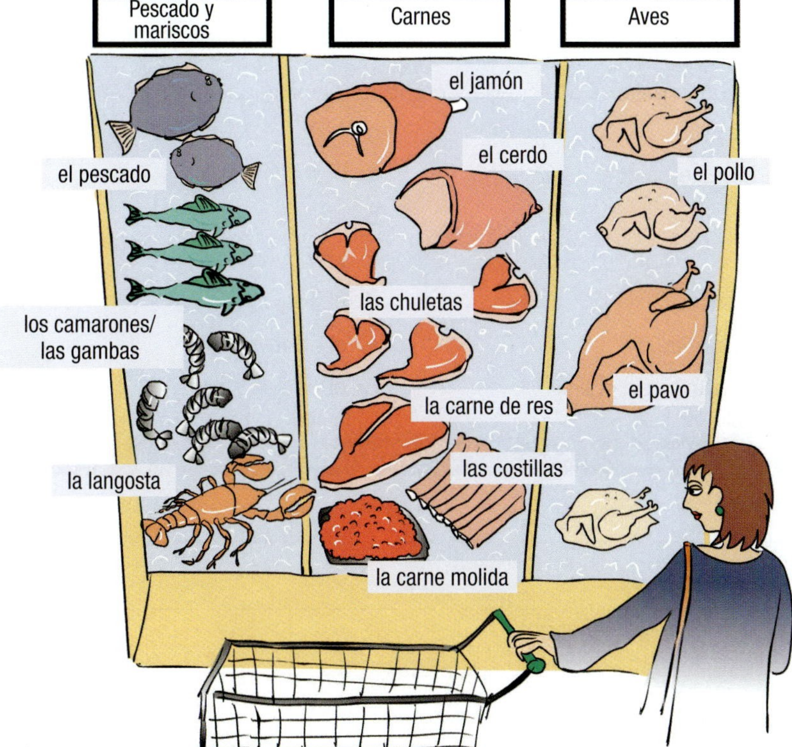

EN OTRAS PALABRAS

The words for some vegetables and spices vary from region to region. **Aguacate** is known as **palta** in some South American countries; **maíz** is known as **elote** in Mexico and in some Central American countries and as **choclo** in parts of South America.

Names of fruits also vary: **plátano** in Spain becomes **cambur** in Venezuela; in other places, **banano** (Colombia) or **banana** (Uruguay) is used. Other examples include **melocotón** (Spain)/**durazno** (Latin America); **fruta de la pasión** (Spain)/**maracuyá** (Colombia)/**parchita** (Venezuela, Mexico).

EN OTRAS PALABRAS

Other names of foods that vary by country are **pavo,** which is **guajolote** in Mexico, and **camarones,** which are **gambas** in Spain. **Puerco** is also commonly used in place of **cerdo.**

Suggestion
Review food vocabulary by talking about your likes and dislikes: *A mí me gustan mucho las zanahorias. Tienen mucha vitamina A. Las como dos o tres veces a la semana. También me gustan las espinacas. Popeye come espinacas y por eso es muy fuerte. Y a ti, ¿te gustan las espinacas? ¿Te gustan las zanahorias? Y a Bugs Bunny, ¿le gustan las espinacas o las zanahorias?*

Suggestion
Bring in menus from a Hispanic restaurant or download them from the Internet. In groups of 3, have students order a meal in Spanish as though they were at a restaurant. Have students play roles of maître d', server, and customer. Encourage students to improvise: the customer complains about the food, the service, etc.

Suggestion for *En el supermercado*
Project images to review other food vocabulary. After you have reviewed a number of items, have students in pairs or groups a) describe items; b) categorize them; or c) put together balanced meals.

Note
The noun *azúcar* has ambiguous gender. It is masculine when alone, but either masculine or feminine when modified: *el/la azúcar moreno/a.*

Los condimentos y las legumbres

la sal
la pimienta
la mostaza
la vainilla
la harina
el/la azúcar
el vinagre
el aceite
el aderezo
la manteca
la salsa de tomate
la mayonesa
los frijoles
las lentejas
los garbanzos

El pan y las bebidas

PRÁCTICA

Warm-up for 10-5
Have students identify certain items: *Se venden con las hamburguesas.* Or *Se usa para cocinar.*

Suggestions for 10-5
Select other foods presented and ask if students like them, how they prepare them, etc. Emphasize the use of the definite article: *Me gustan los frijoles.* Take a class tally of favorite foods in different categories.

10-5  

Para confirmar. Asocien cada explicación con la palabra adecuada y comenten si les gustan o no estos alimentos.

1. __d__ Se toma mucho en el verano, cuando hace calor.
2. __e__ Se pone en la ensalada.
3. __b__ Se usan para hacer vino.
4. __a__ Se come en el desayuno con huevos fritos.
5. __f__ Se prepara para el Día de Acción de Gracias.
6. __c__ Se usa para preparar un sándwich de atún o de pollo.

a. el jamón
b. las uvas
c. la mayonesa
d. el helado
e. el aderezo
f. el pavo

Note for 10-6
Students did a similar activity in *Capítulo 3.* This is an opportunity to recycle *deber + infinitive* and to expand nutrition-related vocabulary.

10-6 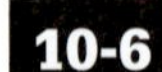 

Dietas diferentes.

PREPARACIÓN. Completen la tabla con las comidas o productos adecuados para estas dietas.

DIETA	SE DEBE COMER	NO SE DEBE COMER
vegetariana		
para diabéticos		
para fortalecer (*strengthen*) los músculos		
para bajar de peso (*lose weight*)		

INTERCAMBIOS. Completen las siguientes oraciones con sus recomendaciones para cada una de estas personas. Digan por qué recomiendan eso.

1. Laura, que es vegetariana,...
2. Mi padre, que es diabético,...
3. Luis, que levanta pesas (*weights*),...
4. Joaquín y Amalia quieren bajar de peso. Por lo tanto,...

Cultura

Muchos hispanohablantes que viven en Estados Unidos mantienen las tradiciones y costumbres alimentarias de su país natal (*native*). Estas tradiciones y costumbres, que varían mucho de un país a otro, se reflejan en las recetas, maneras de cocinar y aun en las horas diferentes de comer. Hay productos, como los frijoles, el arroz, los chiles, los plátanos y el maíz, que constituyen la base de la dieta de muchos países de Hispanoamérica y que se encuentran en casi todos los supermercados de Estados Unidos.

Comparaciones. ¿Qué productos son populares en la comida de tu país o región? ¿Qué platos se preparan con estos productos? ¿Cuáles son los postres especiales? ¿Se comen en una época determinada?

10-7 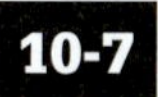 

¿Qué necesitamos?

PREPARACIÓN. Ustedes son estudiantes de intercambio en Ecuador y quieren preparar una cena para su familia ecuatoriana. Describan el menú y hagan una lista de los ingredientes que necesitan.

 **INTERCAMBIOS.** Compartan su menú con otra pareja.

10-8  

Los estudiantes y la comida. **PREPARACIÓN.** Respondan a las siguientes preguntas.

1. ¿Qué comieron hoy?
2. ¿Cuándo y dónde comieron?
3. ¿Cuánto gastaron en comida?

INTERCAMBIOS. Hagan una lista de recomendaciones para una dieta estudiantil más saludable (*healthier*) y compártanla con el resto de la clase.

En directo

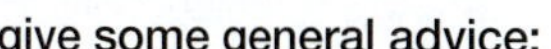

To give some general advice:

Deben + *infinitive* (comer/beber/etc.)...

Para bajar de peso/comer saludable, recomendamos + *noun* (las verduras, el agua, etc.)

Para obtener calcio/proteínas/fibra es bueno + *infinitive* (comer/beber/etc.)

 Listen to a conversation with these expressions.

Note for 10-6, *Intercambios*
Provide a model response so that students know not to use the *se* from the column headers in their responses: *Laura, que es vegetariana, no debe comer...*

Follow-up for 10-6
Present additional vocabulary related to nutrition: *vitaminas, calcio, fibra, proteínas, sin aditivos, calorías, grasa, colesterol.* Discuss preparation methods: *crudo, asado, al horno, hervido, al vapor.* Discuss the pros and cons of vegetarianism.

Suggestion for 10-7
Have students list the types of food that they consider typically American. Ask what food or dishes they would like to share with people from other cultures and why.

Suggestions for 10-8
Have students describe meals during a typical day at home or when they are away at school. Have them prepare a list of what they buy and eat in a typical week.

Note for *En directo*
Before doing activity 10-8, *Intercambios*, have students read the expressions in *En directo*. Then have them listen to the dialogue and encourage them to use the expressions in their own conversation.

Audioscript for *En directo*
DRA. DUARTE: *Bienvenidos al programa* Tu salud. *Estoy aquí para contestar sus preguntas sobre la salud y la comida. Adelante con la primera pregunta.*
HOMBRE 1: *He subido mucho de peso recientemente y quiero perder al menos 5 libras. ¿Qué recomendaciones me puede dar?*
DRA. DUARTE: *Para bajar de peso, debe comer muchas verduras y frutas y también debe beber mucha agua. Claro, también es importante hacer ejercicio.*
MUJER 2: *Mi médica me dijo que debía consumir comidas con calcio. ¿Qué comidas me recomienda?*
DRA. DUARTE: *Para obtener calcio, es bueno comer no solo productos lácteos sino también verduras como la espinaca, frijoles blancos y pescado como el salmón.*

La mesa

Follow-up for 10-10
This is another opportunity to recycle formal commands. Ask what tableware students need to eat or drink various items. *¿Qué (cubiertos) necesitas para comer un bistec? ¿Y para tomar una sopa? ¿Y para comer una ensalada? ¿Necesitas un plato o una copa para beber vino? Y para beber café, ¿qué necesitas?*

Additional practice
Have students list foods they need to buy to prepare meals for a picnic and a Sunday brunch. Have them prepare the menu, the shopping list with approximate prices of each item, and the quantities. Encourage them to look up additional vocabulary.

PRÁCTICA

10-9 

Para confirmar. Indica qué tipo de utensilios se necesitan en las siguientes situaciones. Compara tus respuestas con las de tu compañero/a.

1. para cortar un bistec el cuchillo
2. para tomar sopa la cuchara
3. para beber vino la copa
4. para poner azúcar en el café la cucharita
5. para llevar comida a la mesa la bandeja
6. para cubrir la mesa el mantel
7. para limpiarse la boca (*mouth*) la servilleta
8. para destapar una botella de vino el sacacorchos

10-10 

El camarero nuevo. Ustedes son camareros/as en un restaurante pero uno/a de ustedes es nuevo/a. El/La experto/a debe decirle a la persona nueva dónde debe poner cada cosa de acuerdo con la foto. Después, cambien de papel.

E1: *Pon el cuchillo a la derecha del plato.*

E2: *Muy bien. ¿Y dónde pongo la copa?*

10-11 

Los preparativos. Ustedes deben organizar una fiesta formal para sus mejores amigos que se gradúan de la universidad este año. Primero, preparen un presupuesto (*budget*), una lista de invitados, un menú y una lista de compras. Luego, divídanse el trabajo y dense instrucciones entre ustedes sobre lo siguiente:

1. la decoración del salón
2. la preparación de la mesa
3. la comida y las bebidas
4. los invitados
5. el lugar, la hora, el día
6. ...

10-12 

Una cena. Estuviste muy ocupado/a ayer porque tuviste invitados a cenar. Dile a tu compañero/a todas las cosas que hiciste. Él/Ella te va a preguntar dónde hiciste las compras, a quién invitaste, qué serviste y si lo pasaste bien. Después, cambien de papel.

En directo

To express that you had a good time:

Lo pasé muy bien./Lo pasamos muy bien. *I/We had a great time.*

Fue estupendo. *It was wonderful.*

Estuvo muy divertido. *It was very fun.*

 Listen to a conversation with these expressions.

Cultura

Platos típicos

En Ecuador, al igual que en Perú, el ceviche de pescado o de camarón es muy popular. Otro plato ecuatoriano muy popular es la fritada, una combinación de diversas carnes con plátano (*plantain*) maduro, plátano tostado y maíz. Y entre los postres, además de los pasteles, es muy sabroso el dulce de higos (*candied figs*).

Comunidades. Piensa en los supermercados que hay en tu ciudad. ¿Qué productos típicos de la cultura hispana puedes encontrar en ellos? ¿Cuáles de estos productos se usan en tu casa?

▲ Dulce de higos

10-13 

Una cena perfecta. **PREPARACIÓN.** You will listen to a couple talk about their plans for their dinner party tonight. Before you listen, make a list of four ingredients that you will need for a salad and an entrée. Share your list with a classmate.

 **ESCUCHA.** Now listen to the conversation. As you listen, mark (✓) the appropriate ending to each statement.

1. Rodolfo es...
__✓__ un buen cocinero.
_____ muy perezoso.
_____ vegetariano.

2. Manuela va a...
_____ preparar ceviche.
__✓__ poner la mesa.
_____ llamar a los invitados.

3. Rodolfo va a comprar...
__✓__ pescado y maíz.
_____ limón y camarones.
_____ espinacas y aguacates.

4. Manuela tiene...
_____ todos los ingredientes.
_____ muchos vegetales y frutas.
__✓__ casi todos los ingredientes.

Note for *En directo*
Before doing activity 10-12, have students read the expressions in *En directo*. Then have them listen to the dialogue and encourage them to use the expressions in their own conversation.

Audioscript for *En directo*
JIMENA: *Alex, ¿cómo lo pasaron Ricky y tú en la fiesta anoche?*
ALEX: *Lo pasamos muy bien. Fue estupendo estar con tantos amigos.*
JIMENA: *Y, ¿qué tal el DJ? ¿Tocó música buena?*
ALEX: *¡Sí! Tocó música buenísima. Estuvimos bailando toda la noche. Estuvo muy divertido.*

Audioscript for 10-13
MANUELA: *Rodolfo, esta noche tenemos invitados. Como ellos son estadounidenses, quiero que prepares un ceviche de pescado al estilo del Hotel Colón de Quito. ¿Qué te parece?*
RODOLFO: *Lo que tú digas, Manuela. Tú sabes que a mí me gusta cocinar y, según tú, soy un cocinero excelente. Dime, ¿tenemos todos los ingredientes para el ceviche?*
MANUELA: *Sí, creo que tenemos todo. Solo hay que comprar el pescado porque en casa tenemos todo lo demás: cebollas, tomates, limón, lechuga.*
RODOLFO: *¿Tenemos maíz?*
MANUELA: *¡Ay! No, no tenemos. ¿Puedes comprar maíz, por favor?*
RODOLFO: *Muy bien. Entonces tú pones la mesa y yo hago todo lo demás.*
MANUELA: *¡Estupendo!*
RODOLFO: *Bueno, me voy al supermercado. Si se te ocurre otra cosa me llamas al celular.*
MANUELA: *Gracias, Rodolfo.*

Note
You may wish to remind students that popular foods in the Hispanic world vary from country to country, and even from region to region. People who move to new cities usually miss their traditional food, even among cultures that are traditionally perceived as close.

MOSAICO cultural

Comida callejera

Para Claudia Acosta, encontrar comida en la Ciudad de México no es nada difícil. "La variedad de restaurantes en la ciudad es increíble", comentó Acosta; pero estas opciones no siempre son económicas para una estudiante, especialmente para una que viene de fuera. Por esta razón ha preferido comer en los puestos de la calle durante los cuatro años que lleva viviendo en México y estudiando en la UNAM. "En mis primeros años cuando vine de Ecuador a estudiar aquí, siempre encontraba un puesto de tacos y tortillas cada tres o cuatro calles", dijo Acosta.

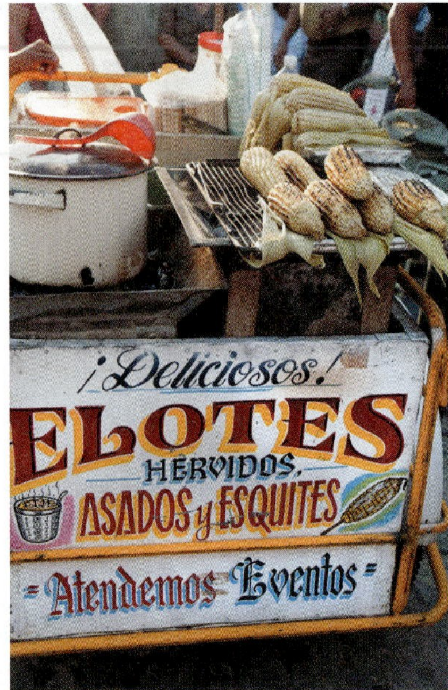

En una ciudad de casi nueve millones de personas, la cantidad de puestos de comida callejera crece constantemente. La mayoría se encuentra en estaciones de metro, áreas de negocios, estadios y parques. Los puestos ofrecen una variedad de carnes, verduras y tortillas para hacer una comida. ¡Y es más barata que en los restaurantes!

Los puestos callejeros han existido en Latinoamérica desde la época de la colonia. Cada país ha mantenido sus costumbres de alimentación y en los puestos se venden productos típicos. En Argentina están los choripanes (pan con chorizo) y las empanadas. En Venezuela se venden arepas rellenas (*filled*) con carnes y vegetales. En todo el mundo hispano se puede conseguir gran variedad de platos típicos. Claudia ha disfrutado de la comida mexicana, pero también ha extrañado (*missed*) la comida de su país: "He tenido días en que cambiaría todo por un buen plato de arroz con menestra y carne asada como el que comía en casa".

Compara

1. ¿Es común encontrar puestos de comida callejera en tu comunidad? ¿Qué tipo de comida venden? Explica detalladamente.
2. En general, ¿cuáles son las comidas que más has consumido en tu vida como estudiante?
3. ¿Se venden comidas extranjeras en tu comunidad?
4. ¿Probaste alguna vez las arepas, los choripanes, los tacos, las empanadas u otras comidas hispanas callejeras? ¿Cómo son en comparación con las comidas callejeras típicas de tu región?

▼ **Empanadas argentinas**

Funciones y formas

1 Stating impersonal information

PROFESOR: En Estados Unidos **se consumen** muchos carbohidratos y mucha grasa. ¿Sabían ustedes que en este país **se comen** 23 libras de pizza por persona al año?

RICARDO: [*piensa*] ¿Cuánta cerveza **se bebe** con 23 pizzas?

PROFESOR: **Se comen** solo 16 libras de manzanas, bla bla bla...

RICARDO: [*piensa*] En esta clase **se duerme** mucho.

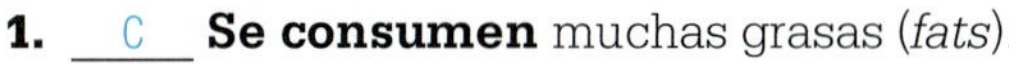

Piénsalo. ¿Cuánto más sabes sobre la dieta estadounidense? Indica si las siguientes afirmaciones son ciertas (**C**) o falsas (**F**), según la información del profesor y lo que sabes.

1. __C__ **Se consumen** muchas grasas (*fats*).
2. __F__ **Se compra** más fruta en el supermercado ahora que en el pasado.
3. __C__ **Se dice** que los niños comen más y hacen menos actividad física.
4. __C__ **Se bebe** mucho café, especialmente en las universidades.
5. __C__ **Se consume** más pizza que manzanas.
6. __C__ **Se recomienda** desayunar todos los días.

Se + verb constructions

- Spanish uses the ***se*** + *verb* construction to emphasize the occurrence of an action rather than the person(s) responsible for that action. The noun (what is bought, sold, offered, etc.) usually follows the verb. The person who buys, sells, offers, and so on, is not mentioned. This is normally expressed in English with the passive voice (is/are + *past participle*).

Se habla español en este restaurante.	*Spanish is spoken in this restaurant.*

- Use a singular verb with singular nouns and a plural verb with plural nouns.

Se necesita un horno para hacer galletas.	*An oven is needed to make cookies.*
Se venden vegetales allí.	*Vegetables are sold there.*

- Use a singular verb when the ***se*** + *verb* construction is followed by an adverb, an infinitive, or a clause. This is expressed in English with indefinite subjects such as *they, you, one,* and *people.*

Se trabaja mucho en ese manzanal.	*They work a lot in that apple orchard.*
Se puede comprar una variedad de manzanas allí.	*You can buy a variety of apples there.*
Se dice que venden sidra excelente también.	*People say they sell excellent cider too.*

¿COMPRENDES?

Completa las oraciones con la forma correcta de **se** + el verbo entre paréntesis.

1. __Se__ __venden__ pasteles en la pastelería. (vender)
2. El ceviche __se__ __prepara__ con pescado. (preparar)
3. __Se__ __puede__ freír o asar la carne de res. (poder)
4. __Se__ __dice__ que la comida de ese restaurante es excelente. (decir)
5. Los llapingachos, tortillas de papas con queso, __se__ __sirven__ en muchos restaurantes ecuatorianos. (servir)

MySpanishLab
Learn more using Amplifire Dynamic Study Modules, Grammar Tutorials, and Extra Practice activities.

Standard 3.1 Students reinforce and further their knowledge of other disciplines through the foreign language. Although the short conversation before *Piénsalo* was written by the *Mosaicos* authors to present a point of Spanish structure (and to insert a bit of humor), it shows that students can learn interesting and useful information about a range of subjects through the medium of Spanish.

Suggestions
Review the *se* + *verb* construction by indicating certain activities that are done in class, as well as those that are not: *¿Se habla francés en esta clase? No, en esta clase siempre se habla español. También se leen y se escriben textos en español.* You may write examples on the board.

Ask other questions comparing singular/plural usage: *¿Se sirve buen pescado en la cafetería de la universidad? ¿Se sirven hamburguesas? ¿Se bebe café colombiano? ¿Se beben refrescos en el desayuno?*

Ask what is done and not done at events such as a business meeting, a party, or a football game.

PRÁCTICA

10-14  

Asociaciones. **PREPARACIÓN.** Asocia las actividades con los lugares donde ocurren. Compara tus respuestas con las de tu compañero/a.

1. __c__ Se cambian cheques en...
2. __a__ Se vende ropa en...
3. __d__ Se toma el sol y se nada en...
4. __b__ Se sirven comidas en...

a. un almacén o tienda.
b. un restaurante.
c. un banco.
d. una playa.

INTERCAMBIOS. Piensa en un edificio o lugar público que te gusta mucho y dile a tu compañero/a qué se hace allí.

Me gusta mucho la zona peatonal (pedestrian area) *de mi ciudad. Allí se camina mucho y en el verano se escucha la música de grupos locales.*

Follow-up for 10-15, *Preparación*
Have students answer these questions: *En casa, ¿qué se hace en la cocina? ¿En el dormitorio? ¿En el comedor?* Ask students to mention typical activities in certain places using the impersonal *se* construction. Have the rest of the class try to guess the place.

Follow-up for 10-15
You may expand this activity as follows: *Marca las cuatro cosas y/o servicios que consideras esenciales en los supermercados hoy en día y compara tus resultados con los de tu compañero/a. Después, en grupos pequeños, escojan las cuatro cosas y/o servicios que obtuvieron más votos y comenten entre todos por qué se necesitan. Comparen sus resultados con los de otros grupos.*

10-15 

El supermercado y las tiendas del barrio. Indica (✓) los productos y/o servicios que se encuentran solo en los supermercados y los que se encuentran en las tiendas de tu barrio. Compara tus respuestas con las de tu compañero/a. Después, dile a tu compañero/a qué productos compras con más frecuencia.

PRODUCTOS/SERVICIOS	SUPERMERCADO SOLAMENTE	SUPERMERCADO Y TIENDA DEL BARRIO
productos lácteos	______	✓
carnes orgánicas	✓	______
frutas de América del Sur	✓	______
detergente para lavadoras	______	✓
alimentos enlatados (*canned*)	______	✓
pescado fresco	✓	______
DVD para alquilar	______	✓

EN OTRAS PALABRAS

The concept of *convenience stores* is expressed differently depending on the country. In Mexico they are **tiendas de conveniencia,** translated directly from English. In Costa Rica the term **tiendas de gasolinera** is used. **La tienda de la esquina** o **del barrio** is frequently used in several Spanish-speaking countries to refer to the small or medium-sized stores located in residential neighborhoods. Convenience stores in Spain that are open 24/7 are called **tiendas de 24 horas.**

10-16 

Recetas creativas.

PREPARACIÓN. Lean estas recetas originales. Luego, intercambien opiniones sobre cuáles les gustaría probar y cuáles no. Digan por qué.

Ponche a la romana: Se muelen (*grind*) unas rodajas de piña. Se mezcla con una botella de champaña y helado de piña; se agrega azúcar; se enfría en el refrigerador antes de servir.

E1: *Me gustaría probar el ponche, pero no bebo alcohol. ¿Se puede preparar sin champaña?*

E2: *Por supuesto, se puede hacer con jugo de piña.*

1. Plátano derretido (*melted*): Se corta un plátano en rebanadas (*slices*) no muy finas. Se echa azúcar. Se calienta en el microondas por uno o dos minutos.
2. Batido de tarta de manzana (*Apple pie smoothie*): Se ponen en la licuadora (*blender*): media taza de jugo de manzana, tres cucharadas de helado de vainilla y media cucharadita de canela (*cinnamon*). Se bate por un minuto.
3. Hamburguesa y salsa con queso (*nacho cheese sauce*): Se calienta la parrilla. Se pone la hamburguesa en la parrilla. Se pone la salsa con queso en el panecillo y se calienta. Se pone la hamburguesa en el panecillo.
4. Ensalada de pollo: Se abre una bolsa de lechuga prelavada. Se cortan en rebanadas dos pechugas de pollo (*chicken breasts*) cocidas, y se corta media libra de queso en cubos pequeños. Se combinan los ingredientes en una fuente (*bowl*). Se agrega un aderezo de vinagre balsámico.

INTERCAMBIOS. Escriban juntos una receta para compartir con la clase. Si es posible, prepárenla para la clase.

10-17 

¿Cómo se prepara este plato? **PREPARACIÓN.** Tu compañero/a y tú quieren darle una sorpresa a otra persona y deciden prepararle su plato favorito. Primero, seleccionen uno de estos platos.

▲ Espaguetis a la boloñesa

▲ Tacos al carbón

Luego, escriban en cada columna una lista de los ingredientes que se necesitan para hacer este plato.

CARNES	VERDURAS/ VEGETALES	ESPECIAS	OTROS

INTERCAMBIOS. Tú sabes cocinar, pero tu amigo/a no. Responde a sus preguntas mientras preparan el plato. Los siguientes verbos pueden ser útiles.

asar	dorar (*brown*)	rallar (*grate*)
cocinar	hervir	(so)freír
cortar	hornear	tostar

MODELO
E1: *Vamos a preparar pollo asado. ¿Cómo se hace?*
E2: *Primero se lava bien el pollo. Luego se ponen la sal y pimienta.*
E1: *¿Y después?*
E2: *Se asa en el horno por dos horas.*

En directo

To propose an idea:

Tengo una idea. *I have an idea.*

¿Qué te parece esto? *What do you think of this?*

Se me ocurrió una idea. *I just thought of an idea.*

To agree with someone's idea:

Me parece perfecto. *That seems perfect.*

Suena muy bien. *Sounds great.*

¡Qué buena idea! *What a great idea!*

 Listen to a conversation with these expressions.

Situación  

PREPARACIÓN. Lean la situación. Luego, compartan ejemplos de vocabulario, gramática y otra información que necesitan para desarrollar la conversación.

Role A. You are an international student who has just arrived in town. A student has offered to help with your orientation. You are not familiar with shopping in the United States, so you ask:

a. where one buys personal items like vitamins and toothpaste (**pasta de dientes**);
b. where on campus one can find a decent meal;
c. where one goes to buy fresh fruit; and
d. where one can get good American pizza.

Ask follow-up questions to be sure you understand the answers.

Role B. You have offered to show a new international student around campus. Answer his/her questions about where one goes to buy different things. Offer several options, and be prepared to answer your new friend's questions.

	ROLE A	ROLE B
Vocabulario	Vocabulary related to food Question words	Vocabulary related to food Question words
Funciones y formas	Asking and answering questions Verifying information Thanking someone	Answering questions Giving instructions on how things are done Making comparisons between options

INTERCAMBIOS. Practica la conversación con tu compañero/a incorporando el vocabulario y las funciones de *Preparación*. Luego, represéntenla ante la clase.

Note for *En directo*
Before doing activity 10-17, first have students read the expressions in *En directo*. Then have them listen to the dialogue and encourage them to use the expressions in their own conversation.

Audioscript for *En directo*
MARTA: *¡Se me ocurrió una idea!*
RUBÉN: *Ah, ¿sí? Dime...*
MARTA: *¿Qué te parece esto? Sabes que el profesor O'Donnell se muda a Cuenca este mes y que es el mejor profesor del mundo.*
RUBÉN: *Es cierto. Nos ha enseñado tantas cosas importantes.*
MARTA: *¿Por qué no le hacemos una fiesta de despedida en el centro estudiantil? Todos podemos contribuir con comida y refrescos.*
RUBÉN: *¡Me parece perfecto! ¡Qué buena idea!*

Suggestion
Talk to students about a trip you have taken: *Yo he visitado Florida muchas veces. He nadado en el mar y he corrido en la playa. He ido a México y a Venezuela, pero no he ido a Ecuador.* Ask: *Y tú, ¿has ido a ciudades en Estados Unidos donde hay muchos hispanos? ¿A qué ciudades has ido? ¿Cuántas veces? ¿Has comido comida ecuatoriana? ¿Has visitado un país hispano? ¿Qué país has visitado? ¿Cuántas veces?*

Suggestion
Review *tener que* + *infinitive.* Give examples contrasting its use with that of *haber* + *past participle: Eduardo no ha terminado el proyecto porque está muy ocupado. Tiene que terminar el proyecto esta noche.*

Suggestions
Review *romper, cubrir,* and *morir* using visuals to illustrate meaning. You may explain that compounds of verbs whose past participles are irregular have the same irregularity: *escribir* → *escrito; describir* → *descrito; volver* → *vuelto; devolver* → *devuelto.* You may wish to introduce related verbs, such as *componer, inscribir, descubrir,* and *resolver.*

Close the text and say: *He cerrado el libro. Ahora el libro está cerrado.* Open the door and say: *He abierto la puerta. La puerta está abierta.*

Suggestion
You may wish to explain to students the difference between *ya* (already) and *todavía* (yet, still).

Ya he leído el libro.
I have already read the book.

Pero todavía no le he dado el libro a Estela.
But I have not yet given the book to Estela.

Note for Present perfect
You may want to point out to students that both Spanish and English have perfect tenses that are used to refer to past actions, events, and conditions. Both languages use an auxiliary verb (*haber* in Spanish, *to have* in English) followed by a past participle. Explain to students that *tener*

2 Talking about the recent past

ALICIA: Hola, César, ¿qué tal?

CÉSAR: Hola, Alicia. ¿**Has visto** a Javier? ¡Estoy muy molesto!

ALICIA: ¿Por qué? ¿Qué te pasa?

CÉSAR: Como sabes, el examen de literatura es pasado mañana y yo no **he leído** el libro todavía. ¿Lo **has leído** tú? ¿Lo **ha leído** Javier? ¿Javier te **ha dado** sus notas? No sé qué voy a hacer sin sus notas. ¡Las necesito para estudiar!

ALICIA: Cálmate, César. Yo **he leído** el libro y **he escrito** unas notas. **He hablado** con Javi. No **ha terminado** el libro todavía, pero va a llamarte esta tarde.

Piénsalo. Lee las afirmaciones e indica a quién(es) se refiere cada una: a Alicia (**A**), a César (**C**) y/o a Javier (**J**).

1. __A__ **Ha hablado** con Javier.
2. __A__ **Ha escrito** unas notas.
3. __J__ **Ha leído** una parte del libro.
4. __C__ No **ha hecho** mucho en su curso de literatura.
5. __A, C__ No **han visto** a Javier.
6. __C__ No **ha abierto** el libro.

Present perfect and participles used as adjectives

- **Present perfect.** Use the present perfect to refer to a past event, action, or condition that has some relation to the present.

He lavado **los platos.** — *I have washed the dishes.*

Cecilia nunca ha vivido **en otro país.** — *Cecilia has never lived in another country.*

- Form the present perfect by using the present tense of **haber** as an auxiliary verb with the past participle of the main verb. In English, past participles are often formed with the endings *-ed* and *-en,* as in *finished* or *eaten.*

PRESENT TENSE OF HABER		+	PAST PARTICIPLE
yo	**he**		
tú	**has**		
Ud., él, ella	**ha**		**hablado**
nosotros/as	**hemos**		**comido**
vosotros/as	**habéis**		**vivido**
Uds., ellos/as	**han**		

Los cocineros **han trabajado** mucho en el banquete. — *The cooks have worked a lot at the banquet.*

Unos miembros de la organización ya **han traído** los manteles. — *Some members of the organization have already brought the tablecloths.*

- All past participles of **-ar** verbs end in **-ado,** whereas past participles of **-er** and **-ir** verbs generally end in **-ido.** If the stem of an **-er** verb ends in a vowel, use a written accent on the **i** of **-ido** (leer → le**ído**).

Lucho, ¿ya **has leído** la receta de la paella?	*Lucho, have you read the recipe for paella yet?*
No, no **he leído** la receta todavía.	*No, I have not read the recipe yet.*

- Some **-er** and **-ir** verbs have irregular past participles. Here are some of the more common ones:

IRREGULAR PAST PARTICIPLES			
hacer	**hecho**	abrir	**abierto**
poner	**puesto**	escribir	**escrito**
romper	**roto**	cubrir	**cubierto**
ver	**visto**	decir	**dicho**
volver	**vuelto**	morir	**muerto**

- Place object and reflexive pronouns before the auxiliary **haber.** Do not place any word between **haber** and the past participle.

¿**Le** has dado las servilletas a César?	*Have you given César the napkins?*
No, todavía no **se las** he dado.	*No, I have not given them to him yet.*

Participles used as adjectives. Spanish uses **estar** + *past participle* to express a state or condition resulting from a previous action.

ACTION	RESULT
Ella preparó la sopa.	La sopa **está preparada.**
Luego cerró las ventanas.	Las ventanas **están cerradas.**

- When a past participle is used as an adjective, it agrees with the noun it modifies.

una puerta **cerrada**	*a closed door*
los restaurantes **abiertos**	*the open restaurants*
unas botellas **lavadas**	*some washed bottles*

LENGUA

To state that something has just happened use the present tense of **acabar** + **de** + *infinitive,* not the present perfect.

Acabamos de volver del supermercado.

We have just returned from the supermarket.

Acabo de probar la sopa y está deliciosa.

I have just tasted the soup, and it is delicious.

¿COMPRENDES?

Escribe la forma correcta del presente perfecto para indicar la acción y la forma del participio pasado para indicar el resultado de esa acción.

Acción	Resultado
1. Yo ___he preparado___ la comida. (preparar)	1. La comida está ___preparada___. (preparar)
2. Nosotros ___hemos comprado___ los ingredientes. (comprar)	2. Los ingredientes están ___comprados___. (comprar)
3. Tú no ___has puesto___ la mesa todavía. (poner)	3. La mesa aún no está ___puesta___. (poner)
4. El niño ___ha roto___ dos ventanas. (romper)	4. Las ventanas están ___rotas___. (romper)
5. Los estudiantes ya ___han hecho___ su tarea. (hacer)	5. Las tareas ya están ___hechas___. (hacer)

MySpanishLab

Learn more using Amplifire Dynamic Study Modules, Grammar Tutorials, and Extra Practice activities.

is never used as an auxiliary verb to form the present perfect.

Suggestion

If needed, you may introduce the present perfect form of *haber. Ha habido* is used with both singular and plural nouns. For example: *Ha habido mucho trabajo últimamente.*

Ha habido varios banquetes. Point out the singular and plural nouns.

Follow-up for 10-18
Have students share information with the class: *Mi compañero/a nunca ha estado en... Nunca ha hecho...* Then take a poll to find out what students have never done.

Preparation for 10-20
One class before doing activity 10-20, prepare students by brainstorming with them the names of famous Hispanics in various fields: film, music, fiction, sports, science, journalism, etc. Assign pairs to gather information about a person of their choice ahead of time.

Suggestion for 10-21
Have students brainstorm 5 or more steps that are involved in preparing a meal. Then have them share their ideas with the whole class. Encourage them to produce both negative and affirmative responses.

Expansion for 10-22
Practice *acabar + de + infinitive* by having students list 5 things that they have just done. Or ask questions: *¿Tienes hambre? (No, acabo de comer.) ¿Tienes sueño? ¿Quieres bailar? ¿Quieres nadar? ¿Tienes sed?*

10-18 

Lo que no he hecho. Tu compañero/a y tú deben decir las cosas de cada lista que no han hecho. Después, comparen sus respuestas con las de otros estudiantes.

1. Yo nunca he estado en...
- **a.** Paraguay.
- **b.** Guatemala.
- **c.** Ecuador.

2. Yo nunca he visto...
- **a.** las islas Galápagos.
- **b.** un volcán activo.
- **c.** un huracán.

3. Yo nunca he comido...
- **a.** aguacate.
- **b.** un postre con leche de coco.
- **c.** langosta.

4. Yo nunca he roto...
- **a.** una taza.
- **b.** un vaso.
- **c.** un plato.

10-19 

Robo (*Robbery*) en un restaurante. El siguiente incidente ocurrió en el restaurante del chef Marco Tovares. Llena los espacios con la forma correcta del participio pasado de los verbos entre paréntesis.

El chef Marco Tovares salió de la cocina para asegurarse de que todo iba bien. Vio que el locutor de televisión Jorge Ramos estaba (1) _sentado_ (sentar) en una mesa con otras personas. Marco vio que la bolsa de una de las mujeres estaba (2) _abierta_ (abrir) y que un hombre en otra mesa la miraba. Como la mujer estaba (3) _distraída_ (distraer), el hombre aprovechó el momento (4) _esperado_ (esperar). Sacó la billetera de la bolsa de ella. Marco lo vio todo. Se acercó a la mesa y le dijo al hombre: "¿Cómo está la comida esta noche?". El hombre parecía muy nervioso, y curiosamente tenía las manos (5) _cerradas_ (cerrar). Marco le dijo: "¿Podría acompañarme, por favor?". El hombre fue con Marco, le dio la billetera (6) _robada_ (robar) y salió. Marco se acercó a la mesa de Jorge Ramos y les explicó lo ocurrido. Todos estaban muy (7) _sorprendidos_ (sorprender). La mujer dijo: "Hace diez años que vivo en Nueva York, y ¡nunca he (8) _sido_ (ser) víctima de un robo hasta esta noche!".

10-20 

Hispanos famosos.

PREPARACIÓN. Piensen en un hispano famoso/una hispana famosa y preparen una lista de cinco cosas que creen que ha hecho para tener éxito (*to be successful*). Después, compartan su lista con la de otra pareja.

E1: *Cameron Díaz es una actriz famosa.*
E2: *Ha protagonizado más de treinta películas...*

INTERCAMBIOS. Digan tres cosas que ustedes han hecho que los/las han ayudado a tener éxito en su vida personal, académica o profesional.

10-21 

Una cena importante.
Ustedes van a preparar una cena para su profesor/a de español. Háganse preguntas para ver qué preparativos ha hecho cada uno/a para la cena.

comprar la carne
E1: *¿Has comprado la carne?*
E2: *No, no la he comprado todavía.*

1. leer las recetas
2. cortar los vegetales
3. hacer el postre
4. decidir qué música tocar
5. poner la mesa
6. decorar el lugar de la cena
7. ...

10-22 

Justo ahora. Digan qué han hecho estas personas. Den la mayor información posible.

Maricarmen y sus amigos ya no tienen hambre.
E1: *Han comido toda la comida.*
E2: *Han dejado la nevera vacía.*

1. Juan y Ramiro salen del estadio.
2. Pedro y Alina salen de una tienda donde se alquilan películas.
3. Mercedes y Paula traen palomitas de maíz (*popcorn*) para todo el grupo.
4. Un hombre sale corriendo de un banco.
5. Jorge y Rubén salen de un supermercado.
6. Frente a todos sus amigos, Rubén le da una sorpresa a su novia.

10-23 

¿Qué ha pasado? Después de unas horas de haber limpiado y ordenado su apartamento, ustedes encuentran todo muy desordenado. Túrnense para describirle al/a la policía lo que han hecho hoy para ordenar el apartamento y lo que ven ahora.

MODELO las ventanas (cerrar, abrir)

E1: *¿Qué ha pasado con las ventanas?*

E2: *Las he cerrado esta mañana... pero ahora están abiertas.*

1. el espejo (usar, romper)
2. la cama (tender, desordenar)
3. el televisor (apagar, encender)
4. las camisas (colgar, tirar al piso)
5. la puerta del apartamento (cerrar, abrir)
6. la comida en el refrigerador (tapar [*cover*], destapar [*to uncover*])

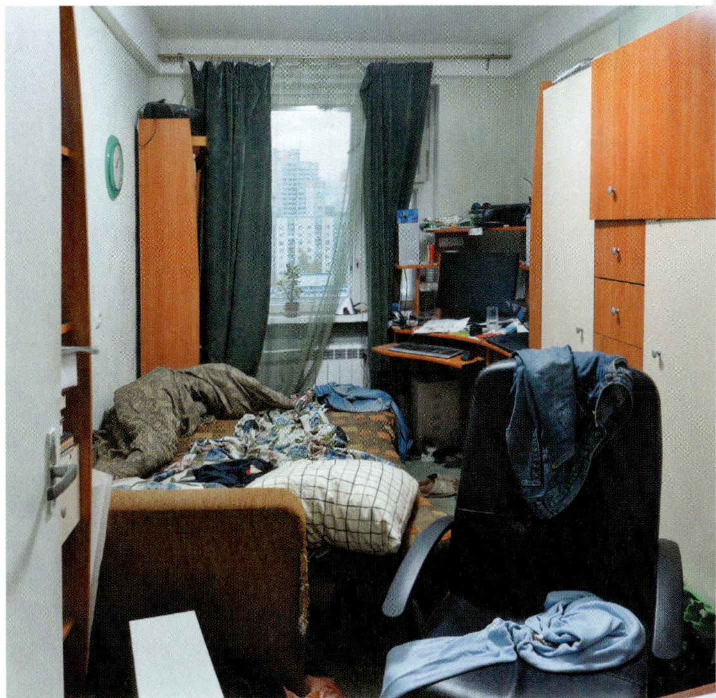

Suggestion for 10-23
Organize students in groups of 3: 1 police officer and 2 victims.

Situación

PREPARACIÓN. Lean esta situación. Luego, compartan ejemplos de vocabulario, gramática y otra información que necesitan para desarrollar la conversación.

Role A. You are a student residence hall assistant at your university. Today you are meeting with a student who lives in the dorm. Explain that other students have complained that:

a. he/she has had parties in the dorm;
b. his/her friends have broken furniture in the public areas; and
c. his/her loud music has bothered everyone on the floor.

Say that you are worried about him/her and ask questions to find out what is prompting this behavior.

Role B. You live in a dorm at your school. The residence hall assistant tells you about complaints that he/she has received regarding your behavior. Respond to his/her comments and questions in detail.

	ROLE A	ROLE B
Vocabulario	University life Music Furniture	University life
Funciones y formas	Talking about the recent past Asking questions Giving advice	Talking about the recent past Stating your case Giving details

INTERCAMBIOS. Practica la conversación con tu compañero/a incorporando el vocabulario y las funciones de *Preparación.*. Luego, represéntenla ante la clase.

Suggestions
Write the *tú* form of some verbs (*cocinas, bebes, escribes*) on the board and erase the final *-s*. Present the following situation to model informal commands. *Mi amiga Luisa quiere preparar una cena espectacular para sus padres. Yo le recomiendo lo siguiente: No prepares platos complicados; cocina un plato sencillo. Primero, consulta un buen libro de recetas. No me consultes a mí porque no soy un buen cocinero/una buena cocinera.*

3 Giving instructions in informal settings

Marcos, la buena alimentación es fundamental para la buena salud. **Desayuna** siempre. Es la comida más importante del día. Para tener energía, **consume** carbohidratos y proteínas en las tres comidas. **Come** carbohidratos complejos, como pasta y pan, pero siempre integrales (*made from whole grains*). **No olvides** las frutas, las verduras y la leche; son muy buenas para la salud. **Evita** comer grasas y azúcares en grandes cantidades.

Piénsalo. Según las sugerencias del enfermero, escoge los alimentos o bebidas que Marcos debe consumir o evitar para alimentarse bien.

1. c, e Come...
2. a, b, f Evita...
3. d Bebe...

a. helado todos los días.
b. pan blanco.
c. manzanas, peras, plátanos, uvas.
d. suficiente leche.
e. pollo y pescado.
f. refrescos.

Informal commands

- To ask a friend to do or not to do something, use an informal command. Use that form with anyone else you address as **tú,** such as someone your own age or someone with whom you have a close relationship.

Pásame la sal.	*Pass me the salt.*
Mira esta foto.	*Look at this photo.*
Lee las instrucciones.	*Read the instructions.*
Préstame tu lápiz.	*Lend me your pencil.*

- To form the affirmative **tú** command, use the present indicative **tú** form without the final -s.

	PRESENT INDICATIVE	AFFIRMATIVE *TÚ* COMMAND
cocinar	cocinas	**cocina**
beber	bebes	**bebe**
consumir	consumes	**consume**

- For the negative **tú** command, use the negative **usted** command form and add the final **-s.**

	NEGATIVE *USTED* COMMAND	NEGATIVE *TÚ* COMMAND
preparar	no prepar**e**	no prepar**es**
comer	no com**a**	no com**as**
subir	no sub**a**	no sub**as**

- Placement of object and reflexive pronouns with **tú** commands is the same as with **usted** commands.

AFFIRMATIVE COMMAND	NEGATIVE COMMAND
Prepárelo (usted).	No **lo** prepare (usted).
Bébela (tú).	No **la** bebas (tú).

- The plural of **tú** commands in Spanish-speaking America is the **ustedes** command.

Cocina (tú).	**Cocinen (ustedes).**
Bebe (tú).	**Beban (ustedes).**
Sube (tú).	**Suban (ustedes).**

- Some **-er** and **-ir** verbs have shortened affirmative **tú** commands, but their negative command is regular.

	AFFIRMATIVE	NEGATIVE
poner	**pon**	**no pongas**
salir	**sal**	**no salgas**
tener	**ten**	**no tengas**
venir	**ven**	**no vengas**
hacer	**haz**	**no hagas**
decir	**di**	**no digas**
ir	**ve**	**no vayas**
ser	**sé**	**no seas**

Sal a las tres si quieres llegar a las cuatro.	*Leave at 3:00 if you want to arrive at 4:00.*
No salgas sin paraguas; va a llover.	*Don't leave without an umbrella; it is going to rain.*
Sé generoso con tus amigos.	*Be generous with your friends.*
No seas impaciente.	*Don't be impatient.*
Dime la verdad.	*Tell me the truth.*
No nos digas mentiras.	*Don't tell us any lies.*

¿COMPRENDES?

Completa la siguiente conversación con la forma correcta del verbo entre paréntesis.

MARIO: ¿Cómo preparo un buen asado?

XIMENA: (1) Compra (Comprar) carne blanda.
No (2) compres (comprar) carne barata.

MARIO: ¿Y luego?

XIMENA: (3) Pon (Poner) sal y pimienta a la carne.
No (4) pongas (poner) demasiada sal.

MySpanishLab
Learn more using Amplifire Dynamic Study Modules, Grammar Tutorials, and Extra Practice activities.

PRÁCTICA

Follow-up for 10-24
Have students write down 5 questions they would ask if they needed advice regarding a healthy diet: *¿Cuánto líquido debo beber todos los días? ¿Debo desayunar o comer algo rápido antes de almorzar?* Then have them exchange roles asking and giving advice using a *tú* command. Ask if classmates agree with the advice given; if not, they should provide their own advice.

10-24 

Consejos. Escoge los consejos más adecuados, según cada situación. Compara tus respuestas con las de tu compañero/a y después añade otra situación. Tu compañero/a te va a dar un consejo.

1. __b, c__ Tu compañero/a comió demasiado en una fiesta de cumpleaños y ahora le duele mucho el estómago.
   - **a.** Come más para recuperarte.
   - **b.** Llama al médico.
   - **c.** Ve a la farmacia y compra medicamentos.
   - **d.** Camina una hora esta tarde.
   - **e.** Practica deportes para olvidarte del dolor de estómago.
   - **f.** No te acuestes.
2. __a, d, e, f__ Tu hermana está enferma. Está congestionada y tiene fiebre.
   - **a.** Toma sopa de pollo.
   - **b.** Come una hamburguesa.
   - **c.** No duermas mucho.
   - **d.** Bebe jugos y agua.
   - **e.** No bebas vino ni cerveza.
   - **f.** No consumas mucha cafeína.
3. __c, d, e__ A tu amiga le fascina la comida basura (*junk food*), por eso, subió diez libras en un mes.
   - **a.** Ve a los restaurantes de comida rápida.
   - **b.** Bebe muchas gaseosas.
   - **c.** Come en casa, no en restaurantes.
   - **d.** No tomes alcohol.
   - **e.** Evita los batidos de McDonald's.
   - **f.** No pidas ensaladas.
4. __a, c__ Tu mamá quiere alimentarse mejor para tener más energía y bajar de peso.
   - **a.** Evita la grasa.
   - **b.** Toma muchos helados.
   - **c.** Come huevos moderadamente.
   - **d.** Compra papas fritas.
   - **e.** Acuéstate y descansa.
   - **f.** Si no tienes energía, consume mucha cafeína.
5. __b, c, d, e__ Tu mejor amigo quiere preparar una cena espectacular para su novia.
   - **a.** Compra pizza.
   - **b.** Haz un plato sofisticado.
   - **c.** No te olvides de comprar un buen vino.
   - **d.** Prepara la mesa el día anterior.
   - **e.** No le pongas chile picante al plato. Ella detesta la comida picante.
   - **f.** Ponle mucha sal a la comida.

Suggestion for 10-25
You may have students do some research on the Internet before doing this activity.

Cultura

Las termas de Papallacta

En la cordillera de los Andes, a una hora de la capital de Quito, se encuentran las termas de Papallacta. Son famosas por sus características curativas. Además, es un gran centro turístico por su ubicación en un área medioambiental muy diversa e interesante, cercana a reservas ecológicas y a la región amazónica.

Comparaciones. ¿Dónde se pueden encontrar baños medicinales en Estados Unidos? ¿Has visitado tú o alguien de tu familia uno de estos lugares? Busca información sobre uno de ellos y descríbeselo a la clase.

Una cura de reposo. Tu amigo/a estuvo muy enfermo/a y su médico le recomendó pasar dos semanas de descanso en las termas de Papallacta en Ecuador. Como tú has visitado este lugar, dile a tu amigo/a qué puede hacer allí. Después, cambien de papel.

disfrutar de la tranquilidad

E1: *Disfruta de la tranquilidad y no escuches música en tu iPod.*

E2: *Y, ¿qué más puedo hacer?*

1. disfrutar del sol
2. respirar aire puro y descansar
3. no hacer la tarea
4. tomar fotos y hacer videos
5. probar un plato típico ecuatoriano
6. salir por las noches y conversar con las personas del lugar
7. tomar baños termales a diario
8. asistir a un concierto de música andina

10-26 

Buenos hábitos alimenticios. **PREPARACIÓN.** Ustedes están preocupados por los hábitos de comida de su amigo/a. Lean lo que esta persona come y bebe en un día típico e identifiquen los problemas que tiene.

> Todos los días se levanta al mediodía. Tan pronto se levanta, toma varias tazas de café. Una hora más tarde, come tres huevos fritos con tocino y tostadas. Toma dos tazas de café cubano con bastante azúcar. Luego, lee el periódico en su dormitorio, mira televisión y come chocolate mientras habla por teléfono con sus amigos. Por la tarde, llama por teléfono al restaurante de la esquina, pide una hamburguesa con papas fritas y toma unas cervezas. Después, duerme una siesta larga. Por la noche, tiene problemas para dormir, por eso, toma un batido.

INTERCAMBIOS. Hagan una lista con cinco recomendaciones o instrucciones que su amigo/a debe seguir. Comparen su lista con las de otros grupos.

10-27 

Cocina paso a paso (*step by step*). **PREPARACIÓN.** Escojan una receta para un plato que se consume en su país y escriban una lista de los ingredientes.

INTERCAMBIOS. Presenten su receta a la clase. Sigan los siguientes pasos: a) describan el plato; b) presenten sus ingredientes; y c) expliquen cómo se prepara.

Warm-up for 10-26
Give examples of healthful and unhealthful foods. Students respond: *(No) es/son sano/a(s)* or *(No) es/son bueno/a(s): la leche, las naranjas, la mantequilla, el chocolate, la pasta en grandes cantidades, la carne de res todos los días, el queso en pequeñas cantidades, una copa de vino por día.*

Expansion for 10-27
You may wish to have pairs of students prepare different dishes, or expand the presentation modes to include live presentations, PowerPoint presentations of recipe preparation done outside of class (for students who are particularly interested in cooking), and/or posters.

Situación

PREPARACIÓN. Lean esta situación. Luego, compartan ejemplos de vocabulario, gramática y otra información que necesitan para desarrollar la conversación.

Role A. To improve your health, you call your friend who is studying to become a nutritionist. Explain what you generally eat for breakfast, lunch, and dinner. Ask questions and answer the nutritionist's questions.

Role B. You are studying to become a nutritionist and a friend calls you for help with eating habits. Ask what he/she eats for breakfast, lunch, and dinner. Advise him/her:

a. to eat fruits, vegetables, fish, and chicken;
b. not to drink soft drinks or alcohol;
c. to consume foods with lots of fiber; and
d. to do physical activity daily.

Answer your friend's questions.

	ROLE A	ROLE B
Vocabulario	Food-related vocabulary	Food-related vocabulary
Funciones y formas	Explaining food habits Asking and answering questions Thanking someone for the advice	Asking and answering questions Giving advice Giving instructions

INTERCAMBIOS. Practica la conversación con tu compañero/a incorporando el vocabulario y las funciones de *Preparación.* Luego, represéntenla ante la clase.

Suggestion
Tell the story shown in a sequence of pictures. For example: *La semana próxima Rafael va a ir en un viaje de negocios a Ecuador. Estará dos días en Quito, donde tendrá varias reuniones de negocios. Su secretaria le hará una reservación en un hotel que le recomendaron unos clientes. Visitará algunas plantaciones de banana en la costa del Pacífico. Al regresar a Estados Unidos, se pondrá en contacto con algunas compañías para importar bananas de Ecuador.*

Note
The *ir a + infinitive* construction is commonly used to express future action; allow students to answer using either construction.

Suggestion
Have students think of a dish they will cook together, whose step-by-step preparation they will describe to the class. Their classmates will guess the name of the dish.
Model the activity: *Prepararemos un plato ecuatoriano. Necesitaremos pescado fresco, mucho limón, aceite, sal y especias. Pedro hará jugo de limón. Mary mezclará las especias con la sal. Jorge limpiará el pescado y Luisa lo cocinará* and so forth. Students will finally guess the name of the dish.

Suggestion
To give students further practice with irregular verbs, have them finish the idea using the verbs *tener, hacer,* or *poder.*
1. *Es la última semana de clase. Los estudiantes... (tener)*
2. *Mario y Ernesto irán de vacaciones juntos. Ellos... (poder)*

4 Talking about the future

CIENTÍFICA: Según los expertos, para el año 2030 la población geriátrica **se duplicará** en comparación con la del presente. La gente **comerá** mejor, **vivirá** más años y **tendrá** buena salud.

JULIA: ¿Y nuestra dieta **será** semejante a la de hoy? ¿Qué **comeremos?**

CIENTÍFICA: Se piensa que **consumiremos** más alimentos naturales, porque más gente **comprenderá** sus beneficios. Al mismo tiempo, muchos alimentos **serán** modificados genéticamente. Los individuos **tratarán** de protegerse de ciertas afecciones y enfermedades, como la diabetes y el cáncer.

Piénsalo. Indica si las siguientes afirmaciones son ciertas (**C**) o falsas (**F**) o no se sabe (**NS**).

1. __F__ **Habrá** menos personas mayores en el futuro.
2. __C__ Las personas **tendrán** una vida más larga.
3. __C__ Más personas **comprenderán** los beneficios de los alimentos naturales.
4. __NS__ La gente **será** más alta.
5. __F__ La gente **podrá** comer grasas y dulces porque la ciencia los protegerá contra las enfermedades.

The future tense

- You have been using the present tense and **ir a** + *infinitive* to express future plans. Spanish also has a future tense. Although you have other ways to express a future action, event, or state, it is important to be able to recognize the future tense in reading and in listening.
- The future tense is formed by adding the endings **-é, -ás, -á, -emos, -éis,** and **-án** to the infinitive. All verbs, **-ar, -er, -ir,** regular or irregular, use these endings.

FUTURE TENSE			
	HABLAR	**COMER**	**VIVIR**
yo	hablar**é**	comer**é**	vivir**é**
tú	hablar**ás**	comer**ás**	vivir**ás**
Ud., él, ella	hablar**á**	comer**á**	vivir**á**
nosotros/as	hablar**emos**	comer**emos**	vivir**emos**
vosotros/as	hablar**éis**	comer**éis**	vivir**éis**
Uds., ellos/as	hablar**án**	comer**án**	vivir**án**

Rafael **visitará** Ecuador el mes próximo.	*Rafael will visit Ecuador next month.*
Él y sus colegas **volverán** después de dos semanas.	*He and his colleagues will return after two weeks.*
Se reunirán con los dueños de unas haciendas de café.	*They will meet with the owners of some coffee plantations.*

- Some verbs have irregular stems in the future tense and can be grouped into three categories according to the irregularity. The first group drops the **-e** from the infinitive ending.

IRREGULAR FUTURE—GROUP 1		
Infinitive	**New Stem**	**Future Forms**
poder	**podr-**	podré, podrás, podrá, podremos, podréis, podrán
querer	**querr-**	querré, querrás, querrá, querremos, querréis, querrán
saber	**sabr-**	sabré, sabrás, sabrá, sabremos, sabréis, sabrán

- The second group replaces the **e** or **i** of the infinitive ending with a **-d.**

IRREGULAR FUTURE—GROUP 2		
poner	**pondr-**	pondré, pondrás, pondrá, pondremos, pondréis, pondrán
salir	**saldr-**	saldré, saldrás, saldrá, saldremos, saldréis, saldrán
tener	**tendr-**	tendré, tendrás, tendrá, tendremos, tendréis, tendrán
venir	**vendr-**	vendré, vendrás, vendrá, vendremos, vendréis, vendrán

- The third group consists of two verbs whose stems in the future tense are quite different from their respective infinitives.

IRREGULAR FUTURE—GROUP 3		
decir	**dir-**	diré, dirás, dirá, diremos, diréis, dirán
hacer	**har-**	haré, harás, hará, haremos, haréis, harán

Los estudiantes **sabrán** más sobre la nutrición después de tomar el curso.	*The students will know more about nutrition after taking the course.*
Tendrán que leer mucho.	*They will have to read a lot.*
También **harán** un proyecto de investigación.	*They will also do a research project.*
¿A qué hora **vendrán** a cenar?	*What time will they be coming for dinner?*
Querrán probar un poco de todo.	*They will want to try a little of everything.*

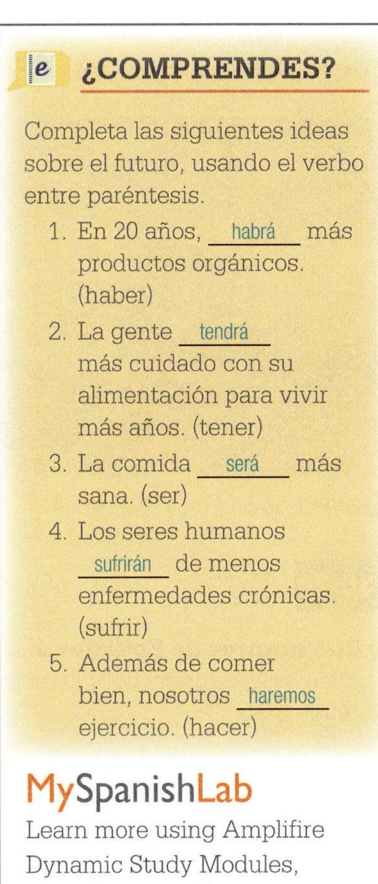

¿COMPRENDES?

Completa las siguientes ideas sobre el futuro, usando el verbo entre paréntesis.

1. En 20 años, __habrá__ más productos orgánicos. (haber)
2. La gente __tendrá__ más cuidado con su alimentación para vivir más años. (tener)
3. La comida __será__ más sana. (ser)
4. Los seres humanos __sufrirán__ de menos enfermedades crónicas. (sufrir)
5. Además de comer bien, nosotros __haremos__ ejercicio. (hacer)

MySpanishLab

Learn more using Amplifire Dynamic Study Modules, Grammar Tutorials, and Extra Practice activities.

PRÁCTICA

Cultura

Quito y Guayaquil

Tanto Quito como Guayaquil son dos ciudades grandes y dinámicas de Ecuador. Quito, la capital, está situada en lo alto de los Andes mientras que Guayaquil está cerca de la costa del Pacífico. Las dos son importantes centros de turismo y de poder económico. El centro histórico de Quito es el mejor preservado de Latinoamérica mientras que en Guayaquil los proyectos de regeneración urbana, como el del Malecón 2000, reflejan su tradición comercial. Aunque muy diferentes entre sí, cada ciudad tiene su verdadero encanto.

Comparaciones. En tu opinión, ¿cuál es la ciudad más importante y dinámica en tu país? ¿Por qué? Explica.

▲ El Malecón 2000, Guayaquil

▲ Basílica del Voto Nacional, Quito

10-28  

¿Qué lugares de Ecuador visitarán estas personas? Completa las oraciones de la izquierda con la acción en la columna de la derecha. Añade un lugar que te interesa y dile a tu compañero/a lo que harás o adónde irás.

1. A Carlos y Eugenia les gusta comer bien. ___b___ al restaurante especializado en la cocina de Guayaquil.
2. A doña Lourdes y a su hija les fascinan la zoología y la botánica. ___d___ un viaje juntas a las islas Galápagos para ver la gran variedad de especies animales.
3. Don Jorge y yo ___c___ el mercado indígena de Cuenca para comprar artesanía ecuatoriana.
4. A ti te gusta disfrutar del aire libre, ver la arquitectura colonial y las montañas. ___a___ por la Plaza San Blas en Quito.
5. A mí... ___Answers will vary___.

a. caminarás
b. irán
c. visitaremos
d. harán

Cultura

Reservas ecológicas

Ecuador tiene muchos parques nacionales y reservas ecológicas cuyo propósito es conservar la riqueza natural de las cuatro regiones del país: las islas Galápagos, la costa, la sierra y la selva amazónica. En las reservas se encuentran muchas especies de flora y fauna. Para los visitantes, hay muchas maneras de explorar las reservas y gozar de la naturaleza.

Comparaciones. ¿Hay reservas naturales en tu país? ¿Dónde están? ¿Qué se protege? ¿Alguna vez has visitado alguno de estos lugares? ¿Qué se puede hacer allí?

10-29

Un viaje a Guayaquil. **PREPARACIÓN.** Ramiro va a Guayaquil a visitar a su familia y a conocer lugares nuevos. Háganse preguntas y contesten según la agenda que preparó Ramiro.

MODELO E1: *¿Qué hará Ramiro el jueves por la mañana?*
E2: *Viajará al Parque Nacional Cajas.*
E1: *¿Cuándo irá al cine con los primos?*
E2: *Irán al cine el martes.*

LUNES	MARTES	MIÉRCOLES	JUEVES	VIERNES
salir para Guayaquil	visitar el Parque de las Iguanas	salir de compras al Mercado Artesanal	viajar al Parque Nacional Cajas	empacar las maletas
cenar con los tíos	visitar a otros familiares	ir a un museo	caminar en la reserva, sacar fotos	almorzar con toda la familia
acostarse temprano	ir al cine con los primos	cenar con unos amigos	dormir en el parque	regresar a Estados Unidos

INTERCAMBIOS. Hagan una lista de cinco actividades que Ramiro probablemente hará al regresar a Estados Unidos. Expliquen por qué.

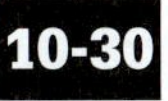

10-30

Planes de fiesta. **PREPARACIÓN.** Planifiquen una fiesta de matrimonio para sus amigos ecuatorianos José y Silvia. Consideren lo siguiente:

- número de invitados
- lugar de la fiesta
- menú que ofrecerán (comida y bebida)
- actividades para los invitados (música, baile, etc.)

INTERCAMBIOS. Compartan sus planes con otra pareja. Hagan una lista de tres semejanzas y tres diferencias entre las dos fiestas.

Note for 10-29
Explain that the Galapagos are a very important natural reserve and that Darwin based his theory of evolution in part on studies he did during his travels in that region. Mention that Otavalo, with its markets of textiles and crafts, is a popular tourist destination.

Note
Beginning in 2000, Ecuador started using the U.S. dollar as its national currency. Use this exercise as an opportunity to mention exchange rates of currencies of several Spanish-speaking countries that they have already studied: *¿Qué otras monedas conoces? ¿Cuál es la moneda oficial de México? ¿Y de Perú?* Students can look up exchange rates on the Internet.

Notes
El Parque de las Iguanas in Guayaquil, also called *El Parque Seminario,* has many types of iguanas. Visitors feed the iguanas mango slices that they buy from park vendors. There is also a pond filled with colorful Japanese tilapia, and an equestrian statue of Simón Bolívar, located in the center of the park. The *Mercado Artesanal* in Guayaquil with its almost 300 stalls is Ecuador's largest handicrafts market. Vendors sell products from all over the country. *El Parque Nacional El Cajas,* located near Cuenca, has extensive hiking trails and a variey of plants and animals. Visitors can stay overnight in rustic shelters, called *refugios.*

Follow-up for 10-31
You may wish to have students discuss what Maricela will do and what she probably won't do, and why.

10-31  

¿Qué recomendaciones seguirá? Maricela sufre de estrés, insomnio y anemia. Después de leer las recomendaciones que le hacen su mejor amiga y su nutricionista, decidan qué hará ella probablemente.

RECOMENDACIONES DE LA NUTRICIONISTA	RECOMENDACIONES DE SU MEJOR AMIGA
1. Coma en pequeñas cantidades por lo menos cuatro veces al día.	**1.** Come cuando quieras. Si subes de peso puedes seguir una dieta.
2. No consuma cafeína para tener energía. Consuma proteínas.	**2.** Para tener energía, come mucho chocolate y, luego, haz ejercicio.
3. Consuma calcio. Beba leche y coma espinacas.	**3.** Toma helado todos los días porque la leche tiene mucho calcio.
4. Para eliminar la tensión y relajarse, haga yoga.	**4.** Escucha música suave y no contestes el teléfono de la oficina.
5. Compre verduras y carnes orgánicas en supermercados especializados en productos naturales.	**5.** Pide ensalada con pollo en los restaurantes de comida rápida y un refresco de dieta.

Situación

PREPARACIÓN. Lean esta situación. Luego, compartan ejemplos de vocabulario, gramática y otra información que necesitan para desarrollar la conversación.

Role A. You are organizing a picnic and some of the guests are vegetarians. Call your nutritionist friend (your classmate) to discuss what food to serve. Say that:

a. you will prepare vegetarian and non-vegetarian food;
b. for the vegetarians, you will make salads and a Spanish tortilla;
c. for the meat eaters, you will serve a chicken salad and hamburgers; and
d. you will serve beer, soft drinks, and juice.

Ask your friend for advice.

Role B. A friend is calling to ask for advice regarding the menu for a picnic that will include both vegetarian and non-vegetarian guests. Give your friend feedback on the proposed menu and offer additional advice.

	ROLE A	ROLE B
Vocabulario	Food-related vocabulary Drinks	Food-related vocabulary Drinks
Funciones y formas	Asking for advice Thanking someone Using proper phone etiquette	Asking and answering questions Giving advice Using proper phone etiquette

INTERCAMBIOS. Practica la conversación con tu compañero/a incorporando el vocabulario y las funciones de *Preparación*. Luego, represéntenla ante la clase.

EN ACCIÓN

¡Hay que celebrar!

10-32 Antes de ver

El restaurante ideal. En este segmento, Esteban invitará a Yolanda a comer en un restaurante para celebrar su cumpleaños. Marca (✓) las cinco sugerencias que tú le harías (*you would make*) a Esteban para elegir el restaurante ideal.

1. _____ Visita el restaurante antes de hacer la reservación.
2. _____ Busca un restaurante en el centro.
3. _____ Acuérdate que Yolanda es vegana.
4. _____ Pregunta si tienen descuento para estudiantes.
5. _____ Mira si el menú es variado.
6. _____ Habla con los camareros.
7. _____ Prueba la especialidad de la casa.
8. _____ Haz investigación en Internet sobre el restaurante.
9. _____ Consulta el libro de quejas (*complaints*).
10. _____ Averigua quién es el chef.

10-33 Mientras ves  

A comer. Esteban, Yolanda, Fernando y Vanesa hablan sobre sus comidas favoritas y sobre las comidas típicas de sus países. Indica si las siguientes oraciones son ciertas (**C**) o falsas (**F**) según la información de este segmento de video. Corrige las oraciones falsas.

En el restaurante:

1. __C__ Yolanda pedirá dos pupusas.
2. __F__ Federico pedirá bistec con ensalada. Federico pedirá bistec encebollado.
3. __C__ Esteban probará la yuca con chicharrones y plátanos.

Comidas típicas de Costa Rica:

4. __C__ Lo más típico de la comida costarricense es el arroz con frijoles.
5. __F__ La *soda* es un tipo de restaurante caro y elegante. La soda es un restaurante pequeño y económico.
6. __F__ El *gallo pinto* es un plato que se come en la cena. El *gallo pinto* se come en el desayuno.
7. __C__ En los restaurantes de barrio se sirve comida fresca.

Las tapas españolas:

8. __F__ Se preparan solamente en casa. Se comen sobre todo en los bares.
9. __C__ El origen de las tapas es muy antiguo.
10. __C__ Se sirven en porciones pequeñas.

10-34 Después de ver 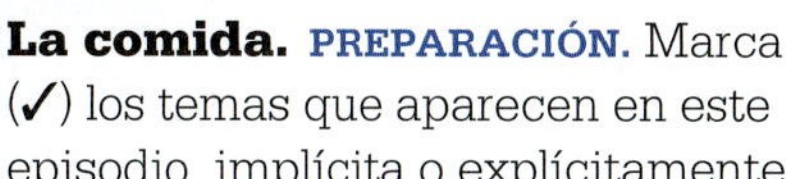

La comida. **PREPARACIÓN.** Marca (✓) los temas que aparecen en este episodio, implícita o explícitamente.

1. __✓__ las comidas tradicionales de algunos países hispanos
2. __✓__ algunas costumbres asociadas con comidas típicas
3. _____ los peligros del consumo excesivo de carne
4. _____ la importancia de hacer ejercicio
5. __✓__ el origen de algunas comidas

INTERCAMBIOS. Comparen sus respuestas de *Preparación* y háganse las siguientes preguntas relacionadas.

1. ¿En qué ocasiones se ve la importancia de la comida como conexión social?
2. ¿Cómo cambiarán nuestras costumbres alimentarias en el futuro? Expliquen o den ejemplos.

Integrated Performance Assessment (IPA)
The activities in each *Mosaicos* section correspond to the three modes of communication as indicated by the tag next to each activity.

Mosaicos

ESCUCHA

10-35 Presentational

Preparación. Antes de escuchar, prepara una lista de productos que compras regularmente y otra de aquellos que solo compras en ocasiones especiales. Compártela con la clase.

ESTRATEGIA

Make notes of relevant details

In previous chapters, you have practiced the strategy of focusing on information that is relevant to your purpose for listening. Note-taking is a useful strategy for remembering important information. Listening more than once also helps you to remember relevant details.

10-36 Interpretive

Escucha. Andrea, Carolina, Roberto, and Darío have each offered to contribute a dish for their friend Óscar's birthday party. Each has bought some kind of vegetable, meat, or seafood to prepare his/her dish. As you listen, mark (✓) the foods that each of them bought. Note that not all the items purchased are listed below.

Audioscript for 10-36
Andrea decidió cocinar dos platos esta vez, paella y una ensalada de papas. Como tenía pescado para la paella en casa, decidió comprar pollo y camarones. Para la ensalada de papas compró zanahorias y papas. También compró aguacates para decorar la ensalada.
Carolina iba a comprar aguacates y tomates para preparar guacamole, pero decidió comprar ajos, cebollas, espinacas, maíz y pollo para hacer una tortilla de verduras y pollo asado.
Roberto pensó que era una buena idea llevar uno de los platos favoritos de Óscar. Por eso compró langosta, sal, pimienta y aguacates.
Darío estaba enfermo y no pudo ir al supermercado. Su hermana hizo las compras para él. Ella compró jamón, papas, aderezo y pimientos verdes. Todos compraron carne molida.

Comprueba
I was able to …

____ distinguish between key and secondary information.

____ listen for and make note of relevant details.

ANDREA	CAROLINA	ROBERTO	DARÍO
____ sal	✓ ajos	____ mermelada	____ huevos
✓ pollo	____ cerdo	____ pepinos	____ ajos
✓ carne molida	✓ espinacas	✓ pimienta	____ fruta
____ azúcar	____ jamón	____ aceite	✓ jamón
✓ zanahorias	____ langosta	____ pavo	✓ aderezo
✓ aguacates	✓ maíz	✓ aguacates	✓ pimientos verdes
✓ camarones	✓ pollo	____ zanahorias	____ pasta

10-37 Interpersonal

Un paso más. Túrnense para hacerse las siguientes preguntas.

1. ¿Cuál es tu plato favorito?
2. ¿Qué productos o ingredientes necesitas para prepararlo?
3. ¿Con quién compartes generalmente tu plato favorito? ¿Por qué?
4. ¿Qué dice esta persona cuando preparas este plato?

LENGUA

Pimienta refers to the spice (*ground pepper*) and **pimiento** refers to the vegetable. Therefore, **pimienta roja** is the red (*cayenne*) pepper that one sprinkles on pizza, and **pimiento rojo** is a red bell pepper. The word for hot, spicy peppers is **chile** or **ají**, as in **chile habanero, chile jalapeño,** and so forth.

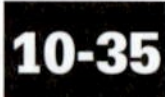

HABLA

10-38 Interpretive

Preparación. Marca cuáles de los siguientes alimentos son más saludables (+) o menos saludables (−).

____ los camarones	____ las espinacas	____ el jamón	____ el pollo
____ la carne de res	____ la fruta	____ las legumbres	____ el queso
____ la cerveza	____ las galletas	____ el pan blanco	____ los refrescos
____ los dulces	____ el helado	____ las papas	____ el vino

Intercambios. Escribe en la tabla los productos o alimentos de *Preparación* que en general producen los siguientes efectos. Explica por qué.

ENGORDAN	NO ENGORDAN	DAN ENERGÍA	AUMENTAN EL COLESTEROL

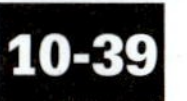

10-39  Interpersonal

Habla. Entrevista a tres compañeros/as para averiguar las preferencias de comida en las siguientes categorías. ¿Qué comida les gusta más y cuál les gusta menos?

MODELO los mariscos

E1: *¿Te gustan los mariscos?*
E2: *Me encantan. ¿Y a ti?*
E1: *A mí no me gustan.*

ALIMENTO	ENCANTAR	GUSTAR MUCHO	GUSTAR	NO GUSTAR
la fruta				
las verduras				
la carne				
los mariscos				
los productos lácteos				
los pasteles				

ESTRATEGIA

Give and defend reasons for a decision

When you make a decision that you wish to communicate effectively to others, it is important to a) state your decision clearly; b) present and explain your reasons logically; and c) urge your listeners to consider your point of view.

En directo

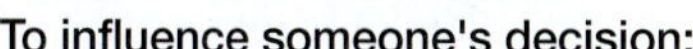

To influence someone's decision:

Es mejor/menos dañino (*harmful*) + *infinitive* ...

¿No te/le(s) parece más saludable + *infinitive* ... ?

¿Qué te/le(s) parece si + *indicative* ... ?

Listen to a conversation with these expressions.

Comprueba

In my conversation ...

____ **I expressed my decision clearly.**

____ **I explained my reasons logically.**

____ **I encouraged my listener to consider my point of view.**

10-40 Presentational

Un paso más. Preparen un informe comparando los resultados obtenidos en la actividad 10-39 sobre las categorías de alimentos que más consumen los estudiantes. Usen las siguientes preguntas como guía. Después, presenten su informe a la clase.

1. ¿Qué tipos de comida se comen más?
2. En general, ¿sus compañeros se alimentan bien o mal? ¿Por qué?
3. ¿Deben ustedes mejorar su dieta? ¿Qué deben hacer?

Suggestion for 10-38, *Preparación*
Model for students ways to state and defend their classifications and their points of view.

Suggestion for 10-38, *Intercambios*
Answers will vary according to students' beliefs about food and health. Model for students ways to state and defend their classifications and their points of view. Encourage them to present and support their points of view, and to persuade their group mates.

Note for 10-39
Inform students that they will need to write a report in activity 10-40 about the results obtained in their interviews. Ask them to walk around the class interviewing at least 5 classmates.

Suggestion for 10-39
Put students in groups of 4 or 6. Ask them to interview each other in pairs and then record their combined results in the group table.

Note for *En directo*
Before doing activity 10-39, first have students read the expressions in *En directo*. Then have them listen to the dialogue and encourage them to use the expressions in their own conversation.

Audioscript for *En directo*
PRIMO: *Prima, estoy un poco preocupado por ti. Veo que ya no estás comiendo bien. Siempre te veo comiendo dulces y frituras. Sabes bien que es dañino comer estas cosas. ¿Qué pasa?*
PRIMA: *Es que siempre estoy corriendo de clase en clase. No tengo tiempo para comer bien.*
PRIMO: *Bueno, acabo de tomar un curso sobre cómo preparar comida saludable en poco tiempo. ¿Qué te parece si te enseño lo que he aprendido?*
PRIMA: *¡¿De veras?! ¡Eres el primo más bueno del universo!*

LEE

Suggestion for 10-41
Encourage students to draw on their general knowledge about food to guess what *fusión culinaria* means. You may draw their attention to the italicized food items in the first paragraph (*California roll, taco pizza*) as examples of *fusión culinaria,* and ask them to figure out what these two items have in common.

10-41  Interpersonal

Preparación. Lean el título y los subtítulos de la lectura en la página siguiente, miren las fotos y lean sus leyendas. Luego, hablen entre ustedes de lo que esperan encontrar en el artículo guiándose por las preguntas siguientes. Expliquen sus respuestas.

1. ¿Qué información esperan encontrar en el artículo?

a. ____ una definición del término *fusión culinaria*

b. ____ recetas para platos de cocina fusión

c. ____ información sobre la influencia china en la cocina de un país

d. ____ información sobre la cocina Tex-Mex

2. Marquen (✓) los elementos que los ayudaron a responder a la pregunta 1.

a. ____ el título y los subtítulos

b. ____ las fotos junto con sus leyendas

3. ¿Qué es la fusión culinaria? Marquen (✓) la definición más lógica.

a. ____ la combinación de la cocina con otras artes, como la decoración de interiores

b. ____ una cocina que combina la influencia de dos tradiciones culinarias

4. Preparen una lista de comidas Tex-Mex que conozcan. ¿Cuáles les gustan más?

ESTRATEGIA

Learn new words by analyzing their connections with known words

As you read in a second language, you encounter words that are unfamiliar to you. In some cases, you can skip over a word and still understand the overall meaning of the sentence or paragraph. In other cases, you should focus on the unfamiliar word and guess its meaning. You can figure out the meanings of unfamiliar words and expand your vocabulary by mentally linking them to words you know that are related in meaning or in grammatical form.

Suggestion for 10-42
You may wish to remind students that dishes that are Americanized versions of other national cuisines are examples of fusion cuisine. You may also ask students to think about when a dish ceases to be considered "fusion" and is seen as native to a particular cuisine. For example, pasta with tomato sauce, considered an Italian dish, actually represents a fusion of influences from China (noodles) and the New World (tomatoes).

10-42  Interpretive

Lee. Según el contenido del artículo, ¿son las siguientes afirmaciones ciertas (**C**) o falsas (**F**)? Si la afirmación es falsa, corrige la información.

1. __F__ El artículo afirma que la cocina fusión se limita a la combinación de influencias asiáticas en la cocina del Oeste. Se refiere a la mezcla de ingredientes y estilos culinarios de distintas culturas en general.

2. __C__ La cocina peruana incorpora influencias culinarias de muchos países.

3. __F__ La inmigración de muchos chinos a Perú empezó al principio del siglo XX. Llegaron en el siglo XIX.

4. __C__ El chifa es un término que se refiere a la cocina chino-peruana.

5. __F__ La cocina Tex-Mex es igual a la cocina mexicana. La cocina Tex Mex y la mexicana tienen diferencias.

6. __F__ Se usa menos carne y menos queso en la cocina Tex-Mex que en la cocina mexicana tradicional. Usa más carne y más queso que la comida mexicana.

7. __C__ Los nachos y los tacos fritos son invenciones de la cocina Tex-Mex.

8. __C__ El chile con carne que se come en San Antonio, Texas, se prepara con especias similares a las que se usan en Marruecos, en el norte de África.

Comprueba
I was able to …

____ **use words I know to guess the meaning of new words.**

____ **understand the main points of the reading.**

LA FUSIÓN CULINARIA: UNA TENDENCIA NUEVA CON UNA HISTORIA LARGA

LA FUSIÓN EN LA COCINA CONTEMPORÁNEA

Todos hemos comido platos que combinan la cocina de dos países o culturas. El llamado *California roll* es un ejemplo; la *taco pizza* es otro. La fusión culinaria, o cocina fusión, ejemplifica la mezcla de ingredientes y estilos culinarios de diferentes culturas en el menú de un restaurante o en un mismo plato. Hoy en día es común encontrar restaurantes en Estados Unidos con nombres como *Roy's Hawaiian Fusion Cuisine* o *Fusion Restaurant and Lounge.* Hay muchas posibles combinaciones, limitadas solamente por la creatividad del chef y los gustos de los clientes.

LA FUSIÓN EN LA HISTORIA CULINARIA

A pesar de la creciente popularidad de estas combinaciones gastronómicas, sería un error pensar que la cocina fusión es un fenómeno nuevo. Dos ejemplos de este antiguo fenómeno en las Américas son la cocina chino-peruana y la cocina mexicano-norteamericana, o Tex-Mex.

EL CHIFA: LA COCINA FUSIÓN DE PERÚ

La cocina peruana es una mezcla de muchas influencias: indígena, española, africana, china y japonesa. El chifa, o cocina chino-peruana, es el resultado de la mezcla de la comida criolla de Lima con la cocina traída por los inmigrantes chinos desde mediados del siglo XIX.

▲ Plato chino-peruano o chifa

Los chinos que fueron a Perú se adaptaron a la sociedad y a sus costumbres, pero siempre mantuvieron sus tradiciones culinarias. Con el progreso económico, importaron de China especias y otros productos esenciales para su comida, pero por lo general tenían que cultivar las verduras que necesitaban o sustituirlas por ingredientes locales.

La cultura chino-peruana revolucionó la gastronomía. Algunos platos considerados típicamente peruanos, como el arroz chaufa (preparado con carne picada, cebollitas, pimentón, huevos y salsa de soja) y el tacu-tacu (una tortilla hecha de un puré de frijoles, arroz, ajo, ají y cebolla) reflejan la influencia de la cocina china.

LA COMIDA TEX-MEX: LA COCINA MEXICANA EN ESTADOS UNIDOS

Un ejemplo de la cocina fusión que se conoce en todas partes de Estados Unidos es la cocina Tex-Mex. Se trata de la fusión del estilo de México y del de Texas. La cocina que conocemos hoy en día como Tex-Mex empezó como una mezcla de la comida del pueblo nativo de Texas y la cocina española.

▲ Nachos, un plato popular de la cocina Tex-Mex

Los indígenas contribuyeron con ingredientes como los frijoles pintos, los nopales (las hojas de un cacto), las cebollas silvestres[1] y el mesquite. La influencia española empezó con la llegada del ganado[2] a la región, traído por los colonizadores al final del siglo XVI. Pero también hay influencias del norte de África. Un grupo de colonizadores de las islas Canarias y de Marruecos inmigraron en el siglo XVIII a lo que es ahora San Antonio, Texas. De ellos vinieron nuevas especias, cilantro y chiles. El *chili con carne* de San Antonio todavía retiene los sabores de la cocina marroquí.

En los últimos treinta años se ha intentado separar *la cocina mexicana* de *la cocina mexicana americanizada,* o Tex-Mex. La Tex-Mex utiliza más carne y usa las tortillas para envolver mayor variedad de rellenos. Los nachos, los tacos fritos, las chalupas, el chile con queso y el chile con carne son invenciones Tex-Mex que no se encuentran en la cocina mexicana tradicional. La costumbre universal en los restaurantes Tex-Mex de servir las *tortilla chips* con salsa picante como aperitivo tampoco existe en la cocina mexicana tradicional.

[1]*wild* [2]*cattle*

10-43  Presentational

Un paso más. PREPARACIÓN. Hagan una lista de platos que se sirven en restaurantes y que son ejemplos de la cocina fusión. Luego, seleccionen uno de estos platos.

INTERCAMBIOS. Preparen una presentación sobre algún plato de cocina fusión que conocen y sus antecedentes culinarios, y preséntenla a la clase.

Suggestion for 10-43
For the presentational part of this activity encourage students to do some research on the Internet and prepare a presentation. As an alternative, they may present about a famous Hispanic chef.

ESCRIBE

Suggestion for 10-44
You may suggest that students start by listing the concepts that they will need to express in their own words in the summary.

10-44 Interpretive

Preparación. Lee una vez más el artículo "La fusión culinaria: una tendencia nueva con una historia larga". Identifica las secciones del artículo y pasa tu marcador (*highlighter*) por las ideas centrales de cada sección.

ESTRATEGIA

Summarize information

A good summary maintains the structure of the original text, synthesizes its principal ideas and information, and accurately captures the central meaning of the original. To write a summary:

- Read the text carefully for the main ideas more than once.
- In your own words, write one or two sentences that summarize the main idea of each section you identify in the text.
- Do not inject your own opinion or add anything not in the original text.

Suggestion for 10-45
To help students who may have difficulty expressing themselves, accept summaries that reproduce ideas verbatim as long as they are able to distinguish the main ideas from the secondary ones.

10-45 Presentational

Escribe. Escribe en tus propias palabras un resumen del artículo, usando las ideas principales que marcaste en *Preparación*.

Suggestion for 10-46
Have students check the following:

1. *¿Representa el resumen una síntesis del texto original? ¿El resumen refleja con precisión las ideas expresadas en el texto? ¿Hay detalles innecesarios?*
2. *¿Sigue el resumen la estructura del texto original?*
3. *¿Hay transiciones claras que muestran las diversas secciones del texto original?*
4. *¿Fluyen las ideas de una manera clara y natural? ¿Hay que aclarar algunos puntos?*
5. *¿El vocabulario y las estructuras son correctas?*
6. *¿La ortografía y la acentuación son correctas?*

10-46  Interpersonal

Un paso más. Envíale tu resumen a un compañero editor/una compañera editora para que te dé su opinión.

Comprueba

I was able to ...

- ____ identify the main ideas in each section of the reading.
- ____ relay the main ideas in my own words.
- ____ focus on factual information rather than my opinion.

En este capítulo...

Comprueba lo que sabes

Go to ***MySpanishLab*** to review what you have learned in this chapter. Practice with the following:

Vocabulario

LAS ESPECIAS Y LOS CONDIMENTOS *Spices and seasonings*

el aceite *oil*
el aderezo *salad dressing*
el azúcar *sugar*
las especias *spices*
las hierbas *herbs*
la mayonesa *mayonnaise*
la mostaza *mustard*
la pimienta *pepper*
la sal *salt*
la salsa de tomate *tomato sauce*
la vainilla *vanilla*
el vinagre *vinegar*

LAS FRUTAS Y LAS VERDURAS *Fruits and vegetables*

el aguacate *avocado*
el ajo *garlic*
la cebolla *onion*
la cereza *cherry*
las espinacas *spinach*
la fresa *strawberry*
el limón *lemon*
el maíz *corn*
la manzana *apple*
el maracuyá *passion fruit*
el melón *melon*
la papaya *papaya*
el pepino *cucumber*
la pera *pear*
el pimiento verde *green pepper*
la piña *pineapple*
el plátano/la banana *banana, plantain*
la toronja/el pomelo *grapefruit*
la uva *grape*
la zanahoria *carrot*

EL PESCADO Y LA CARNE *Fish and meat*

las aves *poultry, fowl*
el camarón/la gamba *shrimp*
la carne *meat*
molida *ground meat*
de res *beef/steak*
el cerdo *pork*
la chuleta *chop*
el cordero *lamb*
la costilla *rib*
la langosta *lobster*
los mariscos *shellfish*
la oveja *sheep*
el pavo *turkey*

VERBOS *Verbs*

agregar/añadir *to add*
batir *to beat*
consumir *to consume*
freír (i) *to fry*
hervir (ie, i) *to boil*
probar (ue) *to try, to taste*
recomendar (ie) *to recommend*
tapar *to cover*

LAS DESCRIPCIONES *Descriptions*

agrio/a *sour*
dulce *sweet*
asado/a *roasted*
frito/a *fried*
lácteo/a *dairy (product)*

OTROS PRODUCTOS *Other products*

los churros *fried dough*
la crema *cream*
el dulce *candy/sweets*
la galleta *cookie*
los garbanzos *garbanzo beans*
la harina *flour*
la leche de coco *coconut milk*
las legumbres *legumes*
las lentejas *lentils*
la manteca/la mantequilla *butter*
la margarina *margarine*
el pan dulce *bun, small cake*
el pastel *pastry*
el queso crema *cream cheese*
el yogur *yogurt*

EN LA MESA *On the table*

la bandeja *tray*
la botella *bottle*
la copa *(stemmed) glass*
la cuchara *spoon*
la cucharita *teaspoon*
el cuchillo *knife*
el mantel *tablecloth*
el plato *plate, dish*
el sacacorchos *corkscrew*
la servilleta *napkin*
la taza *cup*
el tenedor *fork*
el vaso *glass*

PALABRAS Y EXPRESIONES ÚTILES *Useful words and expressions*

el/la campesino/a *peasant*
la receta *recipe*
todavía *still, yet*
ya *already*

Introduction to chapter
Introduce the chapter theme. Ask questions to recycle content from the previous chapter: *¿Qué haces cuando no te sientes bien? ¿Prefieres acostarte o tomas alguna medicina? ¿Te lavas las manos con frecuencia para evitar los gérmenes/microbios? ¿Qué hiciste la última vez que te enfermaste?*

11 ¿Cómo te sientes?

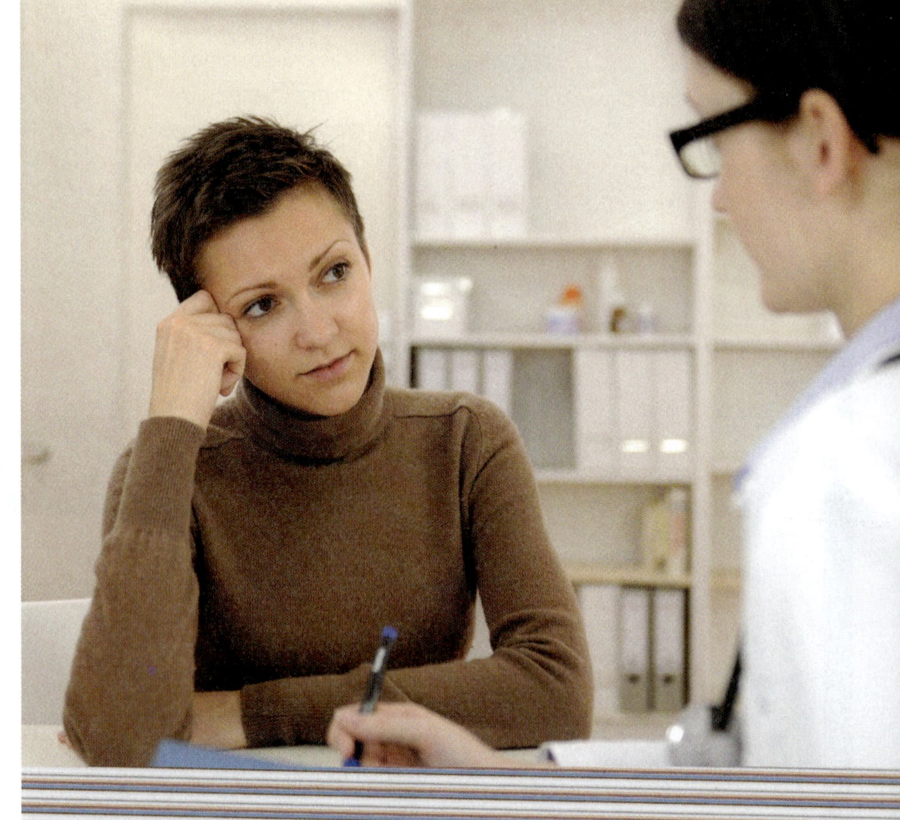

Integrated Performance Assessment: Three Modes of Communication

Presentational: See activities 11-18, 11-22, 11-30, 11-35, 11-38, and 11-40.

Interpretive: See activities 11-1, 11-4, 11-5, 11-6, 11-7, 11-8, 11-9, 11-10, 11-12, 11-14, 11-21, 11-23, 11-31, 11-33, 11-37, and 11-39.

Interpersonal: See activities 11-2, 11-3, 11-4, 11-5, 11-6, 11-7, 11-9, 11-10, 11-11, 11-12, 11-13, 11-14, 11-15, 11-16, 11-17, 11-18, 11-19, 11-20, 11-21, 11-22, 11-23, 11-24, 11-25, 11-32, 11-34, 11-36, 11-41 , and all *Situación* activities.

ENFOQUE CULTURAL
Cuba y República Dominicana

VOCABULARIO EN CONTEXTO
Médicos, farmacias y hospitales
Las partes del cuerpo
La salud

MOSAICO CULTURAL
Los remedios caseros

FUNCIONES Y FORMAS
Introduction to the present subjunctive
The subjunctive with expressions of influence
The subjunctive with expressions of emotion
Uses of *por* and *para*

EN ACCIÓN
No me encuentro bien

MOSAICOS
ESCUCHA Listen for the main idea
HABLA Select appropriate phrases to offer opinions
LEE Focus on relevant information
ESCRIBE Persuade through suggestions and advice

EN ESTE CAPÍTULO...
Comprueba lo que sabes
Vocabulario

LEARNING OUTCOMES

You will be able to:

- discuss health and medical treatments
- express expectations and hopes
- describe emotions, opinions, and wishes
- express goals, purposes, and means
- share information about public health and medical practices in Cuba and the Dominican Republic, and compare cultural similarities

ENFOQUE cultural CUBA Y REPÚBLICA DOMINICANA

El Malecón de la Habana

Un mojito cubano

La Catedral de Santo Domingo

Paracaidismo em el Isla Saona

Enfoque cultural

To learn more about Cuba and the Dominican Republic, go to MySpanishLab to view the *Vistas culturales* videos.

Las divinidades Oxum, Xangó y Yemayá del pintor cubano Almeri

¿QUÉ TE PARECE?

- Vista desde el aire, la isla de Cuba se parece a un cocodrilo. Por eso los cubanos la llaman El Cocodrilo o El Caimán.
- El sistema de servicios de salud está muy desarrollado en Cuba tanto para sus ciudadanos como para los extranjeros. Cuba cuenta con un próspero negocio de turismo médico.
- En Cuba, el béisbol y el dominó son actividades de entretenimiento muy populares.
- El merengue, un estilo de música y de baile, se originó en República Dominicana. Algunos de los artistas más famosos son Juan Luis Guerra, Elvis Crespo y Los Hermanos Rosario.
- En Nueva York viven más dominicanos que en Santiago, la segunda ciudad más poblada de República Dominicana.

Suggestions

Ask what students know about Cuba and the Dominican Republic: *¿Qué tienen en común estos lugares? ¿Qué lengua se habla allí? ¿Cuáles son las capitales? ¿Saben cuál de estas capitales es la ciudad más antigua de Hispanoamérica?* (*Santo Domingo*) Ask: *¿Conocen algunos deportistas, líderes políticos u otras personas famosas…?* Ask about the main industries of these islands (*tabaco, ron, azúcar*). *¿Cómo es el clima?* Talk about *mofongo,* a typical side dish from the Dominican Republic and Puerto Rico that is made from fried plantains or yucca. *¿Conocen alguna costumbre de República Dominicana?*

Suggestion for map

Project the map, point to the photos, and ask: *¿Qué es un mojito? ¿Con qué ingredientes se prepara probablemente?* (*con ron, limón y menta*). Explain that the Malecón is a paved seawall wide enough for strolling and driving. Talk about the other photos: *¿Conocen este deporte que vemos en la foto?* Explain that Punta Cana is one of the most popular Caribbean tourist attractions for Americans. Give some background about the history of these two countries. The island of *Hispaniola* (*La Española*), homeland for Haiti and the Dominican Republic, was the first Spanish colony in the New World. It served as the base of operations for further discoveries. Cuba was the last Spanish colony to fight for its independence, which it did in the Spanish-American War of 1898, with the help of the U.S.

Note for art

The divinities represented in this painting are Orishas of the *Santería* religion practiced in Cuba and elsewhere in the world where there is a large Cuban population. *Santería* is a fusion of the Yoruba religion of the African slaves in Cuba and the Roman Catholicism they learned in colonial Cuba.

Note for *El Malecón*
Although it was originally built to protect Havana from the sea, the Malecón has become a favorite destination for families and couples in the evenings and on weekends.

Note for Columbus
Columbus is said to be buried in the Cathedral of Santo Domingo. However, the Seville Cathedral also has a tomb that is claimed to contain his remains. Columbus's final resting place is a controversial issue, even though he has been dead for more than 500 years.

Note for tourist destinations
La Romana, Punta Cana, and Juan Dolio, east of Santo Domingo, and Puerto Plata in the north, attract thousands of tourists yearly. Samaná, in the northeast, is an important port for cruise ships.

ENFOQUE cultural

◀ El paseo marítimo de La Habana, Cuba, se llama El Malecón.

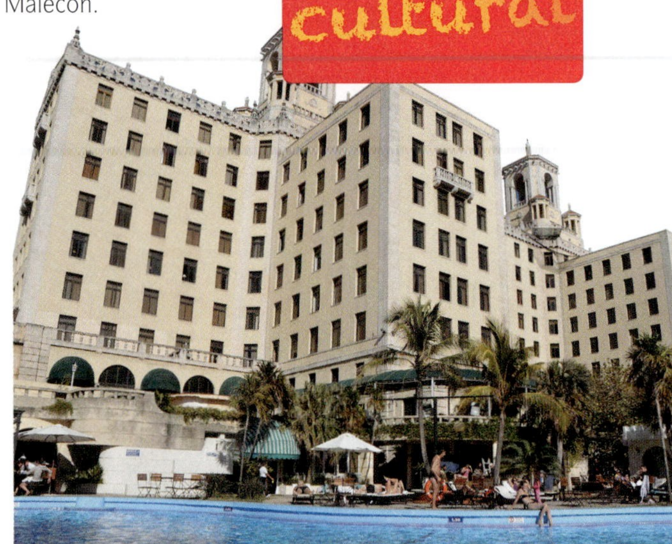

Muchos de los hoteles que se encuentran en Cuba tienen propietarios franceses y españoles. El turismo es una parte importante de la economía cubana. ▶

▲ Cristóbal Colón dio el nombre de La Española (*Hispaniola*) a la isla que hoy comprende las naciones de República Dominicana y Haití. Esta isla se escuentra entre Cuba y Puerto Rico.

▲ Punta Cana es una de las playas más conocidas de República Dominicana y uno de los centros turísticos más populares de la isla. Hay muchos hoteles de enclave (*all-inclusive resorts*) allí.

¿CUÁNTO SABES?

Escribe las palabras que corresponden a las descripciones.

1. El turismo médico es importante en este país. ___Cuba___
2. Esta capital fue la primera ciudad española construida en las Américas. Cristóbal Colón llegó hasta aquí en uno de sus viajes. ___Santo Domingo___
3. Juan Luis Guerra es uno de los artistas de este estilo musical. ___el merengue___
4. Los hoteles que incluyen comidas, bebidas y algunas actividades se llaman así. ___hoteles de enclave___
5. Es una playa turística que se sitúa al extremo oriental de República Dominicana. ___Punta Cana___
6. Es la capital de Cuba. ___La Habana___

Vocabulario en contexto

Talking about health, medical care, and the body

MySpanishLab **PRONUNCIATION TOPIC:** Consonants *ll*, *y*, and *x*
Learn more using Amplifire Dynamic Study Modules, Pronunciation, and Vocabulary Tutorials.

Suggestion for *Vocabulario en contexto*
Project the images and review the vocabulary in context by describing the scenes and asking questions about the photos.

Médicos, farmacias y hospitales

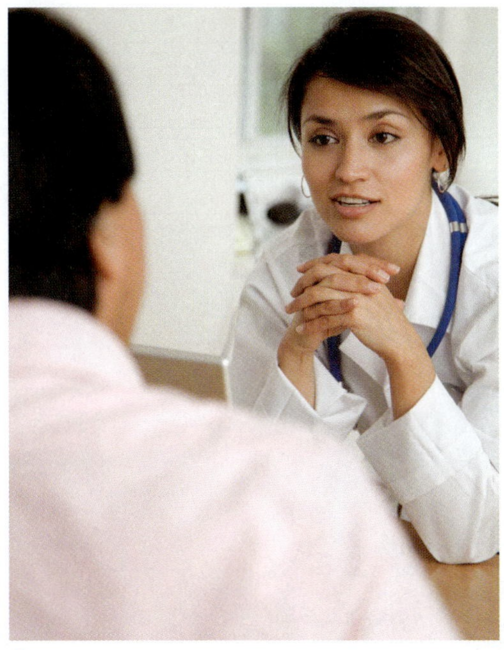

En la mayor parte de los países hispanos existen **hospitales, clínicas** o **sanatorios** y **centros de salud** financiados por el **gobierno** donde los **enfermos** pueden ir sin tener que pagar nada por los servicios o **medicinas** que reciben.

En las **farmacias** se venden todo tipo de **remedios** y **artículos de belleza.** Al igual que en Estados Unidos, en muchos lugares se necesita tener **receta** médica para comprar **antibióticos.** Muchas veces los clientes de la farmacia le preguntan **al farmacéutico/a la farmacéutica** qué remedio deben comprar para **curar** o **tratar** su **enfermedad.**

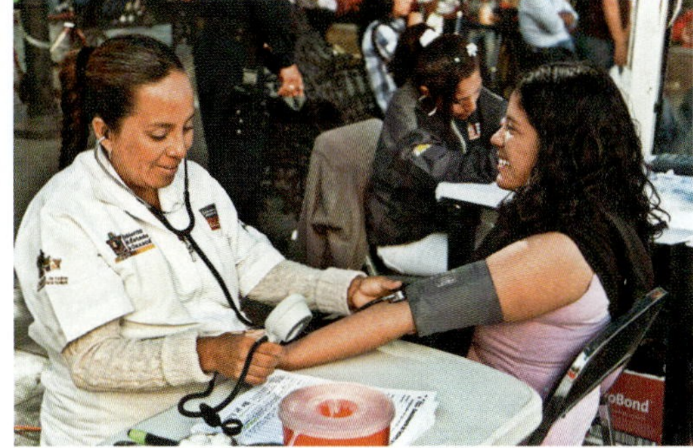

Esta enfermera le toma la **tensión/presión arterial** a una **paciente** en un **sanatorio.**

Algunas personas prefieren curarse con hierbas medicinales. Por ejemplo, para el **dolor de estómago** se recomienda tomar un té de manzanilla (*chamomile*). Otra hierba medicinal muy conocida es la uña de gato (*cat's claw*), que se considera buena para el **tratamiento** de **alergias** y **asma.**

Audioscript for 11-1
1. *el dolor de estómago*
2. *el sanatorio*
3. *el paciente*
4. *la clínica*
5. *la farmacéutica*
6. *el enfermo*

PRÁCTICA

Cultura

Los indígenas del continente americano nos han transmitido muchos conocimientos de medicina natural. Conocían los efectos positivos de las infusiones de hierbas y tenían fórmulas para cerrar las heridas (*wounds*) y curar las úlceras. También trataban fracturas de huesos. Acompañaban muchas de estas prácticas con ceremonias en las que invocaban a sus dioses, pidiéndoles protección y ayuda.

Comparaciones. ¿Qué remedios naturales se usan en tu cultura? ¿Para qué se usan? ¿Recuerdas alguno que se usa en tu familia?

11-1  

Escucha y confirma. Classify the words you hear according to the category to which they belong.

	UN HOSPITAL	UNA ENFERMEDAD	UNA PERSONA
1.		✓	
2.	✓		
3.			✓
4.	✓		
5.			✓
6.			✓

11-2  

Definiciones. **PREPARACIÓN.** Completa las siguientes oraciones con las palabras apropiadas. Compara tus respuestas con las de tu compañero/a.

1. En las ___farmacias___ se venden medicinas y productos de belleza.
2. El té de manzanilla se recomienda para el ___dolor___ de estómago.
3. Los/Las ___enfermeros/enfermeras___ ayudan a los médicos en los hospitales y cuidan de los enfermos.
4. Según la creencia popular, las ___hierbas___ medicinales pueden curar las enfermedades.
5. Los/Las ___farmacéuticos/farmacéuticas___ les venden a sus clientes los remedios que necesitan.
6. El ___gobierno___ financia muchos hospitales y centros de salud en los países hispanos.
7. Los/Las ___pacientes___ son las personas que sufren enfermedades.
8. Algunas personas piensan que la uña de gato es buena para el tratamiento contra el ___asma___.

 **INTERCAMBIOS.** Háganse las siguientes preguntas.

1. ¿Cuándo y para qué vas generalmente a la farmacia?
2. ¿Qué tomas cuando tienes dolor de estómago?
3. ¿Conoces a alguien que tome hierbas medicinales? ¿Para qué enfermedad?

11-3 

Conversación. Háganse las siguientes preguntas para intercambiar información.

1. Cuando necesitas una operación o tienes un accidente, ¿adónde vas? ¿Tienes que pagar o no?
2. ¿Hay muchos hospitales en tu ciudad? ¿Cómo se llama el más importante?
3. Cuando estás enfermo/a y necesitas medicinas, ¿adónde vas a comprarlas? ¿Qué necesitas del médico/de la médica para poder comprarlas?
4. ¿Qué venden en las farmacias de tu país? ¿Por qué venden muchos otros productos, además de medicinas?
5. ¿Usas hierbas medicinales? ¿Para qué las usas? ¿Las usa alguien de tu familia?
6. ¿Te interesa la medicina alternativa? ¿Alguna vez usaste la acupuntura, la homeopatía o alguna otra? ¿Cómo fue tu experiencia?

EN OTRAS PALABRAS

In some Spanish-speaking countries, the word **sanatorio** is used instead of **hospital;** in others, **sanatorio** connotes a hospital that specializes in pulmonary and respiratory diseases. In some countries **clínica** refers to a private hospital. **Hospital** may refer to a government- or church-run facility that may provide free medical care.

11-4 

Una emergencia. PREPARACIÓN. Ustedes están de viaje en República Dominicana y ambos/as están enfermos/as por algo que comieron. Lean este anuncio y decidan cuál es el número más apropiado para llamar.

INTERCAMBIOS. En preparación para su consulta médica, escriban las respuestas a las preguntas que les van a hacer.

1. ¿Cuáles son sus síntomas?
2. ¿Cuándo comenzaron a sentirse mal? ¿Cómo se sienten ahora?
3. ¿Saben ustedes qué causó el problema? Explíquenlo.

Suggestions for 11-4
Explain that pharmacies take turns staying open at times when businesses are normally closed (nights, holidays). The schedule for *farmacias de guardia/de turno* appears in local newspapers. Recycle the vocabulary for giving directions and phone numbers. Have pairs of students perform this activity as a role-play in class.

Suggestion for 11-4, Intercambios
Point out to students that preparing in advance for a conversation or medical interaction is a good strategy that will make the interaction more successful.

Suggestion for *Las partes del cuerpo*
Start by reviewing again the parts of the body that students already know from previous chapters. Then review other body vocabulary by pointing to yourself or projecting the images. Personalize and use gestures to facilitate comprehension: *A mí me gusta esquiar, pero tengo problemas con las rodillas. También tengo problemas con este hombro porque el año pasado me caí. Mi amigo Pedro también esquía. Esquía muy bien, pero el sábado pasado se cayó y se fracturó el brazo. El médico dice que no debe mover el brazo porque tiene un hueso fracturado. Pedro está muy aburrido porque no puede esquiar.* Ask questions to check comprehension.

Name parts of the body and have students point to them. Give commands using parts of the body; recycle *derecho/a* and *izquierdo/a* to make the commands more challenging: *Pongan la mano derecha sobre la cabeza. Pongan la mano izquierda sobre el hombro derecho.* In groups, have students give commands to one another to recycle the informal commands they learned in *Capítulo 10.*

Note
You may present additional words such as *lengua, talón, nalgas, piel, costilla, hígado, riñones.*

Las partes del cuerpo

el pelo/cabello
la cara
la boca
el hombro
los dedos
la espalda
el pecho
la muñeca
la cintura
la cadera
la rodilla
el tobillo
la frente
la oreja
el brazo
el codo
la mano
la pierna
el pie

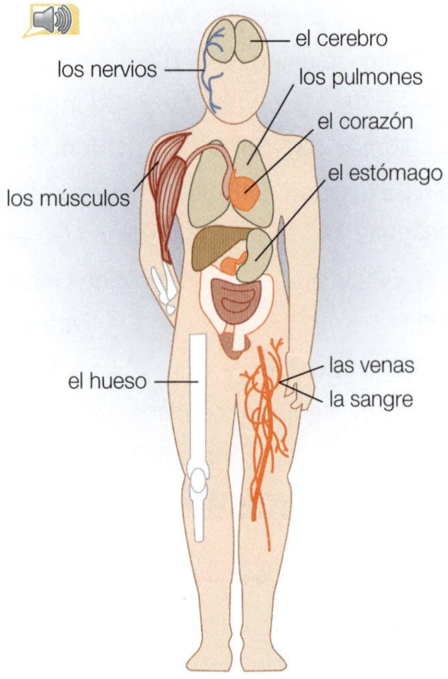

el cerebro
los nervios
los pulmones
el corazón
el estómago
los músculos
el hueso
las venas
la sangre

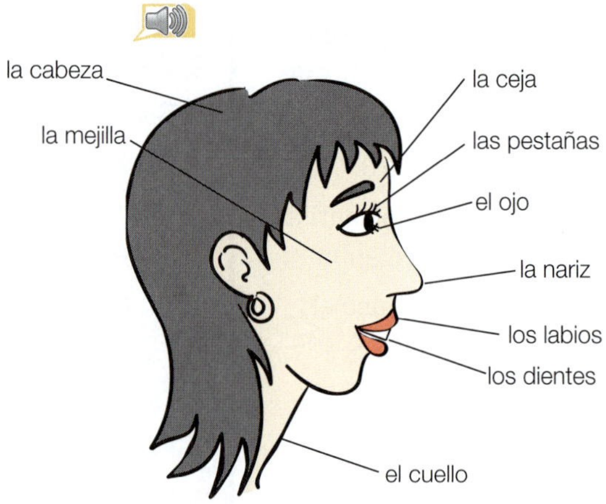

la cabeza
la ceja
la mejilla
las pestañas
el ojo
la nariz
los labios
los dientes
el cuello

PRÁCTICA

11-5 

Para confirmar. Indica en qué parte del cuerpo se ponen estos accesorios y esta ropa.

1. _e_ los calcetines		**a.** la muñeca
2. _f_ los guantes		**b.** la cintura
3. _b_ el cinturón		**c.** las orejas
4. _d_ el collar		**d.** el cuello
5. _c_ los aretes		**e.** los pies
6. _a_ el reloj		**f.** las manos

11-6

¿Para qué sirve(n)? Túrnense para completar las siguientes definiciones. Luego, expresen su opinión sobre la importancia de estas partes del cuerpo.

los brazos	la nariz
el cerebro	los ojos
el corazón	las piernas
los dientes	los pulmones
las manos	la sangre

1. Los brazos unen las manos con el cuerpo.
2. Los ojos permiten que las personas vean.
3. Los pulmones toman el oxígeno del aire y lo pasan a la sangre.
4. La sangre es un líquido rojo que circula por el cuerpo.
5. Las piernas unen el cuerpo con los pies.
6. Los dientes se usan para masticar (*chew*) la comida.
7. Las manos están al final de los brazos.
8. El cerebro le da órdenes al cuerpo.
9. El corazón impulsa la sangre por las venas del cuerpo.
10. La nariz está entre la frente y la boca.

11-7  

Partes del cuerpo. PREPARACIÓN. Indiquen qué parte(s) del cuerpo se relaciona(n) con cada una de las siguientes situaciones.

SITUACIÓN	PARTE DEL CUERPO
1. A Felipe le gusta ponerse aretes.	orejas/nariz
2. María se maquilla todos los días.	la cara
3. Necesito ponerme gafas porque veo mal.	los ojos
4. Un futbolista del Real Madrid le pasa la pelota a un compañero de su equipo.	los pies
5. Se necesitan todos para tocar bien el piano.	los dedos
6. Esta mujer ha perdido 30 libras. La falda le queda ancha.	la cintura/las piernas
7. Daniela lleva siempre el mismo collar.	el cuello
8. El té de hierbas es muy bueno para la digestión.	el estómago

INTERCAMBIOS. Ahora inventen dos adivinanzas para hacer asociaciones con partes del cuerpo.

MODELO E1: *Sirven para besar.*
E2: *Los labios.*

Expansion for 11-5
You may have students work in groups to come up with additional accessories or clothing items for their classmates to associate with parts of the body.

Suggestion for 11-6
You may wish to turn this activity into a contest similar to *Jeopardy!*, in which you state the answer *Unen las manos con el cuerpo* and teams of students compete to come up with the question *¿Qué son los brazos?*

La salud

Jorgito está enfermo

SRA. VILLA: Jorgito, **tienes muy mala cara.** ¿Estás **enfermo?**

JORGITO: **Me siento** muy mal y **tengo dolor de garganta.** Me duele mucho cuando **toso**.

SRA. VILLA: [Le pone el **termómetro**.] Tienes 39 grados de **fiebre.** Enseguida voy a llamar a la doctora Bosque. [En la clínica…]

DOCTORA: Vamos a ver, Jorgito. Cuéntame cómo te sientes.

JORGITO: Ahora **me duele** la cabeza y también me duelen los **oídos.** Además **estornudo** y toso mucho.

DOCTORA: Vamos a **examinarte** los oídos y la garganta. Abre bien la boca y di “Ah”. Tienes una **infección.** No es **grave,** pero es necesario que **te cuides.**

JORGITO: Doctora, no quiero que me ponga una **inyección.**

DOCTORA: ¡No, qué va! Te voy a **recetar** unas **pastillas.** Debes tomarlas **cada cuatro horas.**

JORGITO: Está bien, doctora.

DOCTORA: Además, tienes **gripe.** Debes descansar y beber mucho líquido. Aquí está la receta, señora.

SRA. VILLA: Gracias, doctora.

¿Qué les pasa a estas personas?

Juan **se torció** el tobillo.

Joaquín **se cayó** y **se fracturó** el brazo.

LENGUA

Most words that refer to medical specialists derive from Latin and thus are similar to English: **pediatra** (*pediatrician*), **psiquiatra** (*psychiatrist*), **cirujano/a** (*surgeon*), **radiólogo/a** (*radiologist*), etc. A construction with **de** may also be used: **especialista** or **médico/a del corazón, del estómago,** etc. The primary care doctor is called **médico/a de familia,** or **médico/a de cabecera.**

PRÁCTICA

11-8  

Para confirmar. Indica si las siguientes afirmaciones se refieren a síntomas (**S**) o recomendaciones (**R**). Compara tus respuestas con las de tu compañero/a. Después, añade otro síntoma para Jorgito. Tu compañero/a va a darle una recomendación.

1. _R_ Jorgito tiene que cuidarse.
2. _S_ Tiene dolor de garganta.
3. _R_ Debe tomar dos pastillas cada cuatro horas.
4. _S_ Estornuda y tose mucho.
5. _R_ Tiene que beber mucho líquido.
6. …

11-9  

Remedios y consejos. Elige la mejor recomendación para cada uno de los problemas siguientes. Luego, compara tus respuestas con las de tu compañero/a, y piensen en otras dos sugerencias para cada una de estas personas.

1. _b_ Esteban tiene una infección en los ojos. Le recomiendo…
a. nadar en la piscina. **b.** tomar antibióticos. **c.** leer mucho.

2. _a_ Valeria tiene fiebre y le duele el cuerpo. Le aconsejo…
a. descansar y tomar aspirinas. **b.** comer mucho y caminar. **c.** ir a su trabajo.

3. _c_ Carmen se torció un tobillo. Le sugiero…
a. correr todos los días. **b.** tomar clases de baile. **c.** descansar y no caminar.

4. _b_ Pablo se fracturó un brazo. Le recomiendo…
a. jugar al tenis. **b.** no usar el ordenador por una semana. **c.** hacer ejercicio.

Suggestion for *Vocabulario en contexto*
Project the first drawing to review the vocabulary. Use gestures: *Jorgito no está bien. Está enfermo. Tiene mala cara y se siente muy mal. Tiene dolor de garganta y tose. Su mamá quiere saber si Jorgito tiene fiebre y le pone el termómetro. Jorgito tiene 39 grados (102° Fahrenheit). Ella está más preocupada ahora y llama a la pediatra.*

Ask yes/no questions to check understanding: *¿La mamá está enferma? ¿Jorgito tiene dolor de espalda? ¿Jorgito tiene dolor de garganta?* Point to yourself and say, *Tengo 37°. ¿Tengo fiebre?* Explain that 37° is normal (98.6°F).

Ask questions to personalize: *¿Cuándo vas al médico/a la médica? ¿Qué haces cuando te duele la garganta? ¿Para qué son los antibióticos?*

Act as if you had various aches and pains, complaining, *Me duele(n)…* Remind students that the structure of the verb *doler* is like that of *gustar* and that it has a vowel change in the stem.

Suggestion
When presenting *tiene catarro* and *estornuda,* you may want to introduce the Spanish equivalents of “(God) bless you”: *¡Salud!* or *¡Jesús!*

Follow-up for 11-9
Set up other situations, asking pairs to come up with recommendations. Have each pair share its suggestions with the class.

11-10

¿A quién debo llamar? Explícale a tu compañero/a tus síntomas o necesidades. Él/Ella te va a decir a quién debes llamar según los anuncios. Después, añadan una situación más.

MODELO necesitar un examen médico para el trabajo

E1: *Necesito un examen médico para el trabajo.*

E2: *Debes llamar a la Dra. Corona López.*

1. dolerte la cabeza cuando lees o miras televisión Dr. Amador Cumplido
2. sentirte triste y deprimido/a Dr. Molina Oviedo
3. estar enfermo/a y tener fiebre Dra. Corona López/Dr. Elguezábal
4. no poder dormir Dr. Rodríguez Peláez
5. no poder respirar bien y tener la piel (*skin*) irritada Dr. Shturman
6. dolerte los dientes cuando comes Dra. Jacobo Alcaraz
7. buscar un/a médico/a para tu sobrino de cinco años Dra. Corona López/Dr. Elguezábal/ Dr. Rodríguez Peláez
8. ...

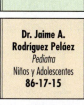

Dr. Fco. Javier Amador Cumplido
Cirugía y enfermedades de los ojos
86-43-57
Consultorio 204

Dra. Silvia Corona López
Medicina Interna
86-51-49

Dr. Héctor Molina Oviedo
Psiquiatra
86-51-49
Consultorio 402

Dr. Jaime A. Rodríguez Peláez
Pediatra
Niños y Adolescentes
86-17-15

Clínica de Asma y Alergias
Dr. Rubén Shturman
Amsterdam 219-A
2° piso
294-3866
584-0153

DR. RAÚL ELGUEZÁBAL R.
Medicina Familiar y Cirugía
86-34-73 EU.
428-4846
Consultorio 309

Dra. Gabriela Jacobo de Alcaraz
Cirujano Dentista
86-48-44
Consultorio 314

11-11

En el consultorio. Tienes un catarro terrible y vas a ver a tu médico/a. Dile cómo te sientes y pregúntale qué debes hacer. Tu médico/a (tu compañero/a) te dará una recomendación y contestará tus preguntas.

MODELO E1: *Me siento.../Tengo...*

E2: *Creo que usted...*

E1: *¿Es bueno...?*

E2: *Es excelente.../No es recomendable...*

LENGUA

Traditionally, law and medicine were professions dominated by men. Therefore, only the masculine form was used in Spanish: **el médico, el abogado.** Now that more women practice these professions, the feminine forms have entered the language. The feminine article is sometimes used before a masculine noun (**la médico, la abogado, la juez**), but it is increasingly common to use the feminine forms of the nouns: **la médica, la abogada, la jueza.**

11-12

Me duele mucho. **PREPARACIÓN.** You will listen to a teenage boy talk to his father about a sports injury. Before you listen, list two symptoms you think he probably has and compare your answers with those of your partner.

ESCUCHA. Pay attention to the general idea of what is said. As you listen, select the letter that indicates the appropriate ending to each statement.

1. __b__ Esteban tiene...
   a. una infección en el dedo.
   b. mucho dolor.
   c. fiebre.
2. __a__ El padre de Esteban cree que...
   a. su hijo se ha fracturado el dedo del pie.
   b. Esteban debe acostarse.
   c. es necesario que Esteban ponga hielo en el pie.
3. __b__ El padre de Esteban quiere...
   a. que Esteban descanse y se cuide.
   b. llevar a Esteban al hospital.
   c. que Esteban tome una aspirina.
4. __a__ El padre de Esteban le dice que...
   a. lo ayuda a caminar para llevarlo al hospital.
   b. decida si prefiere descansar o ir al hospital.
   c. el médico puede verlo esa tarde.
5. __c__ Esteban decide...
   a. no escuchar a su padre.
   b. jugar al fútbol al día siguiente.
   c. ir al hospital con su padre.

Suggestions for 11-10
You may review informal commands: *Llama a la Dra. Corona López.* Encourage students to list other symptoms for themselves or family members. You may also assume the role of a doctor, asking students how they feel. Prescribe accordingly; then have students in pairs play the roles of doctor and patient: *—Todavía me duelen mucho los ojos. No sé qué tengo. —Pues, tiene una infección. Le voy a recetar unos antibióticos.* Review proper salutations and how a doctor and patient address each other. Make sure students use *usted*.

Suggestions for 11-11
Before this activity, brainstorm with students the most common symptoms of a bad cold.

You may also write a list with recommendations that they may get from the doctor: *tomar vitaminas, especialmente vitamina C, beber ocho vasos de agua todos los días, no salir de casa, descansar y dormir más, tomar un analgésico para el dolor de cabeza*, etc.

Warm-up for 11-12
As a pre-listening activity, have students form groups of 4 to discuss if they or someone they know has ever had an injury or accident and what he/she did to take care of him/herself.

Audioscript for 11-12
ESTEBAN: *Papá, tú sabes, esta mañana cuando jugaba al fútbol, me torcí el pie. Mira qué hinchado está. Me duele mucho.*
PADRE: *Esteban, parece que te has fracturado el dedo del pie. Creo que lo mejor será llevarte al médico para que te saquen una radiografía.*
ESTEBAN: *¿Crees que sea necesario? ¿No sería mejor acostarme y descansar? Quizás si tomo una aspirina y me pongo una bolsa de hielo en el pie, me sentiré mejor.*
PADRE: *¿Por qué no quieres ir al hospital? Allí te pueden examinar con cuidado.*

ESTEBAN: *Es que... es que quiero jugar al fútbol mañana y no quiero que el médico me diga que no puedo hacerlo.*
PADRE: *Es necesario que el médico te diga qué tienes y qué puedes hacer. Ven, te llevo al hospital.*
ESTEBAN: *Bueno, si tú lo dices... ¡Ay! Me duele mucho; no puedo caminar.*
PADRE: *Pronto te vas a sentir mejor. Vas a ver. Vamos, déjame ayudarte a caminar, así, poco a poco.*

Note for 11-12
The characters in this dialogue use the subjunctive (*te cuides/ ponga*) in 2 sentences. You may call students' attention to these verbs and tell them that they will study this form later in the chapter.

Note
Remind students that in most Hispanic countries treatment of basic health, including treatment of common conditions and illnesses, is either free or low in cost. Wealthy people may opt for private health care, which is much more expensive. Although this basic coverage extends to everyone, in practice it may be scarce in rural areas far from major cities.

Note
Traditional medicine in Latin America has its roots in practices of indigenous people of each area that involved the use of herbs and other natural products. These traditions were passed down through the generations. Even when the remedies do not have chemically based medicinal properties, they may have a culturally based placebo effect.

MOSAICO cultural Los remedios caseros

Por poco no se realizó el sueño de Miguel Rojas de conocer la fascinante cultura indígena de Paraguay. Tan pronto como llegó a Asunción desde España, empezó a sentir molestias en la garganta y se sentía cansado. Sin embargo, decidió continuar con sus planes de visitar una comunidad guaraní con sus amigos paraguayos.

Ya en el departamento de Guairá, al este del río Paraná, le dolía la cabeza, tenía fiebre, congestión nasal, escalofríos (*chills*), tosía y estornudaba. Quería ir al médico pero sus amigos le decían que era un simple resfriado y bastante típico entre las personas que visitaban Guairá por primera vez. "Tranquilo", le decía su amiga Zunilda. "Te recomiendo que descanses mucho esta noche y

▲ Una mujer guaraní

que te tomes un tereré caliente con una infusión de hierbas".

En Paraguay, como en muchos países latinoamericanos, la medicina occidental y los tratamientos que ofrecen en farmacias y hospitales conviven con la medicina tradicional, cuyo conocimiento ancestral se transmite de generación en generación. El tereré es un tipo de yerba mate que se prepara en Paraguay como una infusión. A

▲ Toma tereré cada cuatro horas para sentirte mejor.

Miguel, por ejemplo, le añadieron en la infusión malva[1] blanca para la congestión de la nariz, saúco[2] para la tos y manzanilla, un relajante natural. Miguel siguió las recomendaciones y al día siguiente se sintió mucho mejor. De esta manera pudo realizar su visita y sacar fotos de su encuentro con la comunidad indígena de Paraguay.

[1]*mallow* [2]*elder*

Compara

1. ¿Te has sentido enfermo/a en algún lugar lejos de casa? ¿Qué tratamientos has seguido en ese caso? Describe tu experiencia con todo detalle.
2. ¿Existe en tu país algún tipo de medicina casera? ¿Es importante en tu cultura? Explica con detalles y ejemplos.
3. ¿Qué le recomiendas a un amigo que tiene gripe?

▼ Los niños posan para una foto.

Funciones y formas

1 Expressing expectations and hopes

ANA: En esta foto estoy con mi madre el día de mi graduación. Ella siempre desea lo mejor para mí: **quiere** que yo **trabaje** mucho, que **tenga** éxito en los estudios, que **piense** en mi futuro.

PEDRO: ¿**Espera** que tú **seas** médica como ella?

ANA: No le importa. **Prefiere** que **tome** buenas decisiones y **siga** mis propios sueños.

Piénsalo. En cada una de estas oraciones, indica cuál es el verbo de deseo (**VD**) y cuál es el verbo de acción (**VA**).

	VD	VA
1. Quiere que yo trabaje mucho.	Quiere	trabaje
2. Quiere que tenga éxito.	Quiere	tenga
3. Quiere que piense en mi futuro.	Quiere	piense
4. ¿Espera que seas médica?	Espera	seas
5. Prefiere que siga mis propios sueños.	Prefiere	siga

Introduction to the present subjunctive

- To form the present subjunctive, use the **yo** form of the present indicative, drop the final **-o** and add the subjunctive ending. Notice that just like the endings of the **usted/ustedes** commands, **-ar** verbs change the **-a** to **-e,** while **-er** and **-ir** verbs change the **-e** and the **-i** to **-a.**

	HABLAR	COMER	VIVIR
yo	habl**e**	com**a**	viv**a**
tú	habl**es**	com**as**	viv**as**
Ud., él, ella	habl**e**	com**a**	viv**a**
nosotros/as	habl**emos**	com**amos**	viv**amos**
vosotros/as	habl**éis**	com**áis**	viv**áis**
Uds., ellos/as	habl**en**	com**an**	viv**an**

- The present subjunctive of the following verbs with irregular indicative **yo** forms is as follows:

conocer: cono**zca,** cono**zcas...** salir: sal**ga,** sal**gas...** decir: di**ga,** di**gas...**
tener: ten**ga,** ten**gas...** hacer: ha**ga,** ha**gas...** traer: tra**iga,** tra**igas...**
oír: o**iga,** o**igas...** venir: ven**ga,** ven**gas...** poner: pon**ga,** pon**gas...**
ver: v**ea,** v**eas...**

- The present subjunctive of **hay** is **haya.** The following verbs also have irregular subjunctive forms:

dar: **dé, des...** saber: **sepa, sepas...** estar: **esté, estés...**
ser: **sea, seas...** ir: **vaya, vayas...**

- Stem-changing **-ar** and **-er** verbs follow the same pattern as the present indicative.

pensar: p**ie**nse, p**ie**nses, p**ie**nse, pensemos, penséis, p**ie**nsen
volver: v**ue**lva, v**ue**lvas, v**ue**lva, volvamos, volváis, v**ue**lvan

Follow-up to *Piénsalo*
To help students understand the relationship between the two verbs in each sentence, show them (or lead them to figure out for themselves) that the verb of volition (*verbo de deseo*) is in the indicative and the resulting verb (*verbo de acción*) is in the subjunctive.

Suggestion
Give examples of the indicative and the subjunctive in context: *Lisa estudia medicina. Sus profesores le recomiendan que estudie cardiología. También sugieren que trabaje en una ciudad grande, porque habla muy bien español.* As you speak, write the indicative verb forms on the board. When you say the subjunctive verb forms, cross out the final *-o* and write the appropriate ending.

Suggestion
Point out the differences between to say (report information) and to tell (direct someone to do something) in these examples. *Decir* is used in both cases in Spanish, but with different meanings and different sentence structures.

Suggestion
Point out to students that since the *yo* form of the present indicative is used to form the present subjunctive, any irregularity in that form also appears in the present subjunctive.

Suggestions
To clarify the change in subject, have students say one thing they want to do and one thing they want a classmate to do: *Quiero cerrar la puerta. Quiero que Clara cierre la ventana.* Ask students to do what you tell them. Point to individual students and say: *Quiero que te levantes. Quiero que abras la puerta.* Then address your instructions to the whole class: *Quiero que ustedes pongan sus libros en el suelo.*
Then tell students *Soy tu amigo/a. Quiero que tú...* Then say to individual students: *Quiero que tú me des tu libro. David, quiero que tú le des tu libro a Susana.*

Suggestion for *Ojalá*
Ask students to list things that they would like to see happen in the future, using *ojalá: Ojalá que yo encuentre un buen trabajo.*

Standard 4.1
Students demonstrate understanding of the nature of language through comparisons of the language studied and their own.

Students are aware that many words in English come from Spanish and from Mexican influence in the American Southwest: *adobe, canyon, hacienda, lasso, vigilante,* and many others. The lexical influence of Arabic on Spanish is similarly pervasive. Common words like *aceite, álgebra, azúcar, café, máscara, ojalá, olé,* and *tarea* come from Arabic. Explain to students that Arabic-speaking Moors from northern Africa ruled the Iberian peninsula from 711 until 1492, and that their culture is still alive in present-day Spain in architectural style, monuments, place names, and language.

LENGUA

Remember that you have seen these same orthographic changes in the formal commands:

Siga las instrucciones.
Follow the directions.

Busque la medicina.
Look for the medicine.

¿COMPRENDES?

Completa las oraciones con la forma correcta del verbo.

1. ¿Estás enferma? ¿Quieres que yo __vaya__ (ir) a tu casa para ayudarte?
2. ¿Quieres que Amanda y yo te __hagamos__ (hacer) una sopa de pollo?
3. Ojalá __te__ __sientas__ (sentirse) mejor pronto.
4. Tus amigos esperan que tú __asistas__ (asistir) al concierto mañana con ellos.
5. Todos dicen: "¡Ojalá Sara __pueda__ (poder) ir con nosotros!"

MySpanishLab
Learn more using Amplifire Dynamic Study Modules, Grammar Tutorials, and Extra Practice activities.

- Stem-changing **-ir** verbs follow the same pattern as the present indicative but have an additional change in the **nosotros/as** and **vosotros/as** forms.

preferir: pref**ie**ra, pref**ie**ras, pref**ie**ra, pref**i**ramos, pref**i**ráis, pref**ie**ran

dormir: d**ue**rma, d**ue**rmas, d**ue**rma, d**u**rmamos, d**u**rmáis, d**ue**rman

- Verbs ending in **-car**, **-gar**, **-ger**, **-zar**, and **-guir** have spelling changes.

sacar: sa**que**, sa**ques**, sa**que**, sa**que**mos, sa**qu**éis, sa**qu**en

jugar: jue**gu**e, jue**gu**es, jue**gu**e, ju**gu**emos, ju**gu**éis, jue**gu**en

recoger: reco**ja,** reco**j**as, reco**j**a, reco**j**amos, reco**j**áis, reco**j**an

almorzar: almuer**c**e, almuer**c**es, almuer**c**e, almor**c**emos, almor**c**éis, almuer**c**en

seguir: si**g**a, si**g**as, si**g**a, si**g**amos, si**g**áis, si**g**an

- Notice in the examples below that there are two clauses, each with a different subject. When the verb of the main clause expresses a wish or hope, use a subjunctive verb form in the dependent clause (the clause that begins with **que**).

MAIN CLAUSE	DEPENDENT CLAUSE
La doctora **quiere**	que Alfredo **respire** profundamente.
The doctor wants	*Alfredo to breathe deeply.*
Espero	que Alfredo no **tenga** asma.
I hope	*Alfredo doesn't have asthma.*

- When there is only one subject, use the infinitive instead of the subjunctive.

Lola **necesita llamar** a la farmacia para pedir una medicina. — *Lola has to call the pharmacy to order some medicine.*

Ella **quiere recogerla** esta tarde. — *She wants to pick it up this afternoon.*

Desea recogerla antes de las tres. — *She wants to pick it up before 3:00.*

- Some common verbs that express expectations, wants, and hopes are **desear, esperar, necesitar, preferir,** and **querer.**

Los residentes del barrio prefieren que la clínica no **cierre** antes de las siete. — *The residents of the neighborhood prefer that the clinic not close before seven o'clock.*

La niña espera que el enfermero no le **ponga** una inyección. — *The girl hopes that the nurse will not give her a shot.*

- The expression **ojalá (que)** (*I/we hope [that]*), which comes from Arabic, originally meaning *May Allah grant that …* , is always followed by the subjunctive.

Ojalá (que) ellos **vengan** temprano. — *I hope (that) they will come early.*

Ojalá (que) **puedas** llevarme a la cita con la médica. — *I hope (that) you can take me to the doctor's appointment.*

PRÁCTICA

11-13 

Comentarios y deseos. Los miembros del Club de Estudiantes de Pre-Medicina están hablando de la fiesta que darán mañana. ¿Cuáles de las afirmaciones siguientes probablemente son comentarios de ellos? Márquenlas (✓) y justifiquen sus selecciones.

1. _____ Queremos que la fiesta empiece puntualmente.
2. _____ Ojalá que no sirvan comida.
3. _____ Preferimos que pongan música caribeña, porque queremos bailar salsa y merengue.
4. _____ Esperamos que también asistan estudiantes de odontología (*dentistry*) y de enfermería.
5. _____ Necesitamos que la fiesta termine temprano.
6. _____ Deseamos que nuestros profesores vayan a la fiesta.
7. _____ Queremos que todos recojan la basura después de la fiesta.
8. _____ Ojalá que nos divirtamos.

Note
The activities in this section present a sequence that moves from input based to open ended. To maximize the communicative experience in the input-based activities, students are encouraged to share or check their answers with a classmate.

Expansion for 11-13
You may also wish to have students explain their reasons for not selecting some of the items.

11-14 

Trabajo voluntario en el hospital. **PREPARACIÓN.** Unos estudiantes trabajan de voluntarios en el hospital. ¿Qué espera la directora del programa de voluntarios que ellos hagan? Túrnense para hablar sobre cada escena.

 MODELO Elena: llevar flores/conversar con los pacientes

E1: *La directora espera que Elena les lleve flores a los pacientes.*

E2: *También espera que Elena converse con los pacientes. Algunos pacientes se sienten muy solos.*

Suggestion for 11-14
Explain to students that object pronouns are placed immediately before the subjunctive verb form.

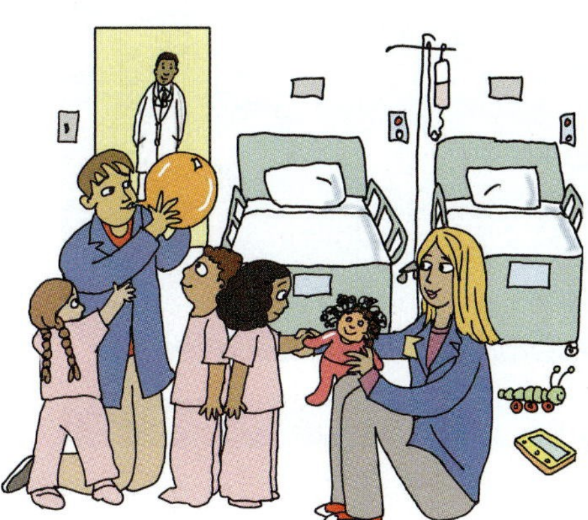

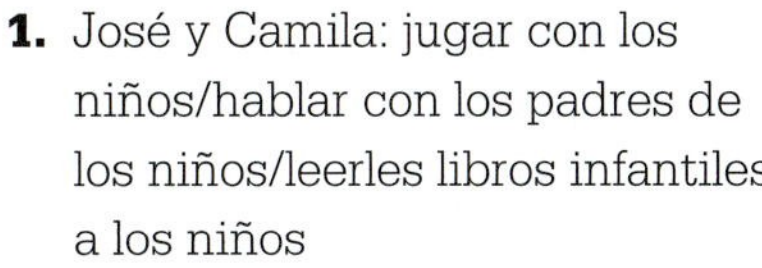

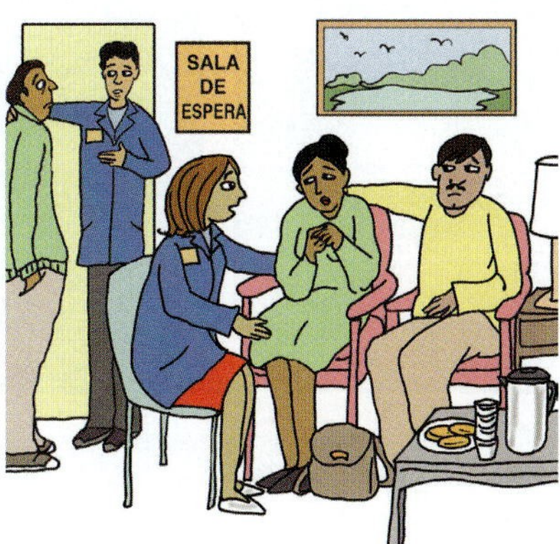

1. José y Camila: jugar con los niños/hablar con los padres de los niños/leerles libros infantiles a los niños
2. Marisa: trabajar en la tienda de regalos/hacerles recomendaciones a los clientes/poner flores frescas en el mostrador de la tienda
3. Sofía y Eduardo: conversar con los familiares de los pacientes/ofrecerles café/darles almohadas si quieren dormir mientras esperan

 **INTERCAMBIOS.** ¿Qué más esperan los pacientes que hagan los voluntarios en el hospital? Escriban una lista de cuatro cosas más.

 MODELO *Los pacientes esperan que los voluntarios les traigan la comida.*

Follow-up for 11-15
After students compare their lists with a partner, those pairs can compare their lists with another pair of students.

Suggestion for 11-15
Give examples using the present tense of *necesitar* followed by a clause with a subjunctive verb: *Necesito que abran la clínica. También necesito que contesten el teléfono.* Then change *necesito* to *es necesario.* You may use a visual (transparency or PowerPoint presentation) with the first two sentences as a first layer, then on the second layer hide *necesito* and write *es necesario.*

11-15 

Clínica de familia. En una semana se abre una nueva clínica y ustedes están ayudando con los preparativos. En la tabla siguiente, escriban una lista de lo que ustedes tienen que hacer y otra de lo que esperan que hagan los empleados.

E1: *Tenemos que pintar la sala de espera.*
E2: *Y también tenemos que limpiar los pisos.*

E1: *Espero que los empleados lleguen a tiempo.*
E2: *Y yo espero que los carpinteros terminen su trabajo.*

LO QUE TENEMOS QUE HACER	LO QUE ESPERAMOS QUE OTRAS PERSONAS HAGAN
____________________	la médica especialista: ____________
____________________	los enfermeros: ____________
____________________	la recepcionista: ____________
____________________	la chofer de la ambulancia: ____________
____________________	el anestesista: ____________
____________________	los empleados de limpieza: ____________

Situación

PREPARACIÓN. Lean la situación. Luego, compartan ejemplos de vocabulario, gramática y otra información que necesitan para desarrollar la conversación.

Role A. You are sick today so you will miss the review session for your Spanish midterm. Call a classmate.

a. Say that you need him/her to take notes for you;
b. tell him/her that you hope it is not too much trouble;
c. say when you want your friend to bring you the notes; and
d. thank your friend.

Role B. When a friend from your Spanish class calls to ask a favor, say that you will be happy to take notes for him/her.

a. Ask how your friend is feeling and what he/she has;
b. ask when your friend wants you to bring over the notes; and
c. say that you hope he/she feels better soon.

	ROLE A	ROLE B
Vocabulario	Expressions related to health and parts of the body	Expressions related to health and parts of the body
Funciones y formas	Asking for a favor Expressing hopes and preferences: Subjunctive with verbs of volition Describing symptoms Thanking someone Making polite requests in Spanish	Replying to requests Asking questions Expressing wishes: Subjunctive with verbs of volition

INTERCAMBIOS. Practica la conversación con tu compañero/a incorporando el vocabulario y las funciones de *Preparación.* Luego, represéntenla ante la clase.

2 Expressing requests

PABLO: ¿Qué me recomienda, doctor?

MÉDICO: Le **recomiendo** que **tome** agua y caldo de pollo. **Quiero** que **duerma** mucho y que no **vaya** a clase.

Más tarde...

ALICIA: ¿Qué dice el médico?

PABLO: **Dice** que **me quede** en cama. También **quiere** que tú me **prepares** un caldo de pollo, que **limpies** mi apartamento, que me **traigas** helado...

Piénsalo. Para cada afirmación, indica quién recomienda la acción y quién va a hacer la acción: **el médico**, **Pablo** o **Alicia.**

	Recomienda la acción	Va a hacer la acción
1. Le **recomiendo** que **tome** agua y caldo de pollo.	el médico	Pablo
2. Quiere que tú me **prepares** un caldo de pollo.	el médico	Alicia
3. Deseo que **duerma** mucho.	el médico	Pablo
4. Dice que **me quede** en cama.	el médico	Pablo
5. Quiere que **limpies** mi apartamento.	el médico	Alicia
6. Quiere que me **traigas** helado.	el médico	Alicia

The subjunctive with expressions of influence

- Verbs that express an intention to influence the actions of others (**aconsejar, pedir, permitir, prohibir, recomendar**) also require the subjunctive in the dependent clause. With these verbs, Spanish speakers often use an indirect object.

El médico **le** recomienda que no **salga** por unos días.	*The doctor recommends that he not go out for a few days.*
La enfermera **me** aconseja que no **coma** por una hora.	*The nurse advises me not to eat for an hour.*

- You may also try to impose your will or express your influence, wishes, and hopes through some impersonal expressions such as **es necesario, es importante, es bueno,** and **es mejor** followed by **que.**

Es necesario que los atletas **duerman** un mínimo de siete horas por noche.	*It is necessary that the athletes sleep a minimum of seven hours a night.*

LENGUA

You have seen that a stressed **i** or **u** requires a written accent when preceded or followed by another vowel (**oír, frío, reúno**). This is because no diphthong results and the vowels are pronounced as two separate syllables. The same rule applies to an **h** between the two vowels (**prohíbo**, **prohíbe**), since the **h** has no sound. When **i** or **u** is not stressed, the vowel combination is pronounced as one syllable, and no accent is required (**prohibir**).

Follow-up to *Piénsalo*
To help students understand the relationship between the two verbs in each sentence, show them (or lead them to figure out for themselves) that the verb of influence (*recomendación*) is in the indicative and the resulting verb (*verbo de acción*) is in the subjunctive.

Suggestions
Using visuals of people engaged in various activities, give examples of *permitir* and *prohibir* followed by the subjunctive and then the infinitive: *El doctor le permite que camine. El doctor le permite caminar. Le prohíbe que juegue al béisbol. Le prohíbe jugar al béisbol.*

Suggestion
Remind your students of the differences between *to say* (report information) and *to tell* (direct someone to do something) in these examples. You may wish to ask them these questions: *¿Qué te dice el médico cuando tienes fiebre? Y, ¿qué le dices a tu profesor cuando no tienes la tarea?*

Es mejor que coman pescado porque tiene menos grasa que la carne de res.	*It is better that they eat fish because it has less fat than beef.*

- If you are not addressing or speaking about someone in particular, use the infinitive.

Es mejor **comer** pescado y pollo.	*It is better to eat fish and chicken.*

- With the verb **decir,** use the subjunctive in the dependent clause when expressing a wish or an order. Use the indicative when reporting information.

Dice que los atletas **consumen** mucha proteína. (*report information*)	*She says (that) the athletes consume a lot of protein.*
Dice que los atletas **consuman** mucha proteína. (*express an order*)	*She tells the athletes to eat a lot of protein.*

¿COMPRENDES?

Completa las oraciones con el infinitivo o la forma correcta del subjuntivo.

1. El médico te aconseja que ___bebas___ (beber) menos café y más agua.
2. Es necesario que nosotros ___nos cuidemos___ (cuidarse) si queremos vivir muchos años.
3. La enfermera le dice que ___haga___ (hacer) más ejercicio.
4. Es importante ___comer___ (comer) bien.
5. El especialista le aconseja al paciente que ___descanse___ (descansar) mucho.
6. Es bueno que ustedes ___pasen___ (pasar) unos días en la playa.

MySpanishLab

Learn more using Amplifire Dynamic Study Modules, Grammar Tutorials, and Extra Practice activities.

PRÁCTICA

11-16

Normas de conducta en el trabajo. **PREPARACIÓN.** Tu amiga Rebeca tiene un trabajo nuevo como recepcionista en un consultorio médico y te pide consejos sobre qué normas de conducta seguir con respecto a los temas de la lista. Escribe cinco recomendaciones para ella y compáralas con las recomendaciones de tu compañero/a.

- llegar unos minutos antes
- llevar chanclas
- almorzar en la oficina
- conversar con los pacientes
- aceptar regalos de los pacientes
- entrar en Facebook

MODELO usar el celular
Te recomiendo que no uses tu celular en el trabajo. Es importante que no hagas llamadas personales.

INTERCAMBIOS. Escriban una carta a Rebeca combinando sus recomendaciones. Léanla a la clase.

MODELO *Juan y yo te aconsejamos que…*

Warm-up for 11-17
Encourage students to use their imagination. Give details: The program is for students in the health professions (*las profesiones de la salud, como medicina, odontología, enfermería, terapia física,* etc.). Ask for ideas about setting up the program, such as publicity to recruit students, location, programming, living arrangements, etc. Write *Es importante/bueno/mejor que…* on the board and ask for students' suggestions.

Suggestion for 11-17
Put students in groups of 3 for this activity. They can change groups, redoing parts of the activity as needed, to play different roles.

11-17

Consejos y sugerencias. Estás organizando un nuevo programa para estudiantes que quieren trabajar en programas de salud en República Dominicana. Explícales a dos compañeros/as los aspectos del programa que aún no están resueltos. Ellos/as te recomendarán qué hacer.

MODELO viajar a República Dominicana
E1: *Hay varias opciones: podemos viajar a República Dominicana en grupo, o cada estudiante puede hacer su propia reservación.*
E2: *Es mejor que viajen en grupo, así se consigue mejor precio.*
E3: *Y también es importante que todos los estudiantes lleguen juntos.*

1. empezar clases de español
2. establecer conexiones con las clínicas en la capital
3. buscar alojamiento (*lodging*)
4. escoger actividades de ocio (*free time*)

Boca Chica

República Dominicana un país que en los últimos años ha desarrollado una próspera industria turística, gracias en parte a su clima ideal y sus extraordinarias playas. Boca Chica es la playa familiar más famosa de República Dominicana por su arena blanca, agua cristalina y proximidad a la capital. Otras playas conocidas son las de Punta Cana, al este del país, donde predominan los centros turísticos privados (*resorts*). Sin embargo, quedan muchas otras zonas de interés cultural y ambiental relativamente poco exploradas.

Conexiones. ¿Por qué crees que algunas personas prefieren ir de turismo a lugares privados sin conocer realmente el país que visitan?

Excursión a República Dominicana. **PREPARACIÓN.** Tu clase está planeando una excursión a la playa Boca Chica en República Dominicana. Escribe una lista de todo lo que hay que preparar en cuanto a alojamiento, transporte y equipaje (*luggage*) para la excursión. Después, compártela con tu compañero/a.

E1: *Es importante reservar los pasajes.*

E2: *Sí, y es necesario que compremos unas mochilas.*

 **INTERCAMBIOS.** En grupos de tres o cuatro decidan qué quieren que haga cada persona de su grupo. Compartan la información con la clase.

MODELO

E1: *Queremos que David reserve los pasajes.*

E2: *Sí, y esperamos que Alicia compre las mochilas.*

E1: *Necesitamos que...*

Follow-up for 11-18
You may create groups of 6 and assign 1 research item to each student. Once they exchange the information they have obtained, encourage them to brainstorm what they will need or have to do to prepare for the trip. Recycle vocabulary for clothes and weather expressions. Example: *¿Qué necesitas llevar para protegerte del sol? ¿Qué ropa es más cómoda para caminar mucho?*

Suggestion for *Situación*
Remind students that this is theater, and that they may have to put themselves in an unfamiliar role when presenting the *Situación*.

Situación

PREPARACIÓN. Lean la situación. Luego, compartan ejemplos de vocabulario, gramática y otra información que necesitan para desarrollar la conversación.

Role A. You are allergic to (**ser alérgico/a a**) cats, and you have just come back from spending the weekend with your friend who has two cats. Now you have a headache, your eyes itch (**me pican los ojos**), your lungs hurt, and it is hard to breathe. Call the clinic.

a. Explain your situation;
b. describe your symptoms; and
c. ask what the nurse recommends that you do.

Ask questions to be sure you understand the recommendations.

Role B. You work as a nurse at the clinic, and someone calls for advice about an allergic reaction. Ask about the person's symptoms and offer advice about what he/she should do.

	ROLE A	ROLE B
Vocabulario	Health symptoms	Health symptoms and remedies
Funciones y formas	Explaining health conditions Asking clarification questions Asking for recommendations Thanking someone Addressing medical professionals appropriately	Giving medical advice Answering questions Wishing someone a prompt recovery

INTERCAMBIOS. Practica la conversación con tu compañero/a incorporando el vocabulario y las funciones de *Preparación*. Luego, represéntenla ante la clase.

Suggestions for *Piénsalo*
Since the subjunctive is a new concept for most students, you may wish to provide guidance by doing the first sentence with the whole class.
As a follow-up, lead students in discovering that the verb that expresses the emotion is in the indicative, and the verb that conveys the action related to the emotion is in the subjunctive.

Suggestions
Introduce the verb *molestar,* give examples, and clarify meaning, i.e., that it does not have any sexual connotations. Give examples using expressions of emotion: *Me alegro de que estén todos aquí. A mí me gusta que todos lleguen temprano y practiquen español con sus compañeros. Me molesta que hablen inglés en clase. Siento que no tengamos películas en español para hoy.* Ask students to finish the following introductory clauses: *Me alegro de que tú… Siento que tú… No me gusta que tú…*

3 Expressing emotions, opinions, and attitudes

ERNESTO: **Me molesta** que **fumen.** Y no me gusta que **hablen** tan alto.

SARA: **Estoy contenta de** que **se vayan** pronto. Ya han terminado de comer.

Ernesto Sara

Piénsalo. Indica si los verbos de cada oración expresan un sentimiento o una acción y escríbelos en el espacio correcto.

	VERBO/FRASE DE SENTIMIENTO	VERBO DE ACCIÓN
1. **Les molesta** que **fumen.**	molesta	fumen
2. No **les gusta** que **hablen** tan alto.	gusta	hablen
3. **Están contentos de** que **se vayan** pronto.	están contentos	se vayan
4. **Es triste** que **permitan** fumar en su restaurante.	es triste	permitan
5. **Es una lástima** que **fumen** en la mesa, tan cerca de otra gente.	es una lástima	fumen

Cultura

Fumar perjudica la salud

Tradicionalmente, los países hispanos han sido más permisivos en el consumo del tabaco en lugares públicos, especialmente por la importancia de cafés, bares y restaurantes en la vida cotidiana. Sin embargo, recientemente la mayor parte de los países han adoptado medidas que prohíben o limitan el uso del tabaco en las zonas públicas. Esto ha producido una gran reducción del consumo del tabaco entre los jóvenes y una mayor concienciación sobre sus efectos nocivos.

Comparación: ¿Cuáles son las normas relacionadas con el uso del tabaco en tu país? ¿Te parecen suficientes? ¿Son excesivas? Explica.

PROHIBIDO
FUMAR EN
TODO EL
RECINTO

The subjunctive with expressions of emotion

- When the verb of the main clause expresses emotion (e.g., fear, happiness, sorrow), use a subjunctive verb form in the dependent clause. Note that the subjects of the two clauses must be different.

Sentimos mucho que el niño **tenga** fiebre.	*We are very sorry (that) the child has a fever.*
Me alegro de que **estés** con él.	*I am glad (that) you are with him.*

- Some common verbs that express emotion are:

alegrarse (de)	*to be glad (about)*	**molestar(le)**	*to bother*
encantar(le)	*to love*	**sentir (ie, i)**	*to feel*
estar contento/a (de)	*to be happy (about)*	**temer**	*to fear*
gustar(le)	*to like*		

- Impersonal expressions and other expressions that show emotion are also followed by **que** + *subjunctive*.

Es triste que el niño **esté** enfermo.	*It is sad that the child is sick.*
¡Qué lástima que no **pueda** ir a la fiesta!	*What a shame that he cannot go to the party!*

¿COMPRENDES?

Completa las oraciones con la forma correcta de los verbos indicados.

1. Juan, me alegro mucho de que tú _vengas_ (venir) a verme las próximas vacaciones.
2. Yo también _estoy_ (estar) contento de que nosotros _podamos_ (poder) pasar tiempo juntos.
3. A mi madre le va a gustar que tú _visites_ (visitar) a los primos durante las vacaciones.
4. Sí, ya sé, es una lástima que nosotros _vivamos_ (vivir) tan lejos.

MySpanishLab

Learn more using Amplifire Dynamic Study Modules, Grammar Tutorials, and Extra Practice activities.

PRÁCTICA

11-19

Estoy enfermo. Asocien cada comentario con la reacción apropiada. Después, túrnense para añadir nuevos comentarios y reacciones.

1. _b_ Estoy muy enfermo/a.
2. _a_ Mis padres llegan hoy para estar conmigo.
3. _c_ Creo que el doctor Pérez me va a operar.
4. _e_ Dicen que es una operación seria.
5. _d_ No voy a poder participar en el campeonato.
6. ...

a. Me alegro de que vengan.
b. Siento mucho que estés tan mal.
c. ¡Qué bueno que sea ese el médico!
d. Es una lástima que no puedas jugar.
e. Ojalá que no tengas complicaciones.

11-20

Una visita. Estás en la clínica para visitar a tu compañero/a, a quien han operado de la rodilla. Tu compañero/a te cuenta sobre su experiencia en la clínica y cómo se siente. Escoge entre las expresiones de *En directo* para responderle e intercambien papeles.

E1: *No me gusta la comida del hospital.*

E2: *Siento que la comida no sea buena. ¿Qué te sirven?*

E1: ...

1. Me duele bastante la rodilla.
2. Tengo fiebre y dolor de cabeza.
3. Estoy mal del estómago porque las medicinas son muy fuertes.
4. Mis amigos me mandan flores y tarjetas.
5. Detesto estar en cama tanto tiempo.
6. Hay tanto ruido que no puedo dormir.
7. Las enfermeras vienen a verme cada media hora.

En directo

To express empathy:

Siento que...

Me alegro de que...

Temo que...

Espero que...

No me gusta que...

¡Qué agradable que...!

Listen to a conversation with these expressions.

Audioscript for *En directo*

DRA. VILLA: *Cati, me alegro de que te sientas mejor, pero temo que tengas que continuar con el tratamiento por dos semanas más.*
CATI: *De acuerdo, doctora. Me duelen mucho las inyecciones, pero espero que me ayuden a curarme pronto.*
DRA. VILLA: *Así será. ¡Qué agradable que tengas una actitud tan positiva!*

11-21 

Reacciones. Túrnense para reaccionar a las actividades que Luisa y Rafael piensan hacer la próxima semana.

Luisa/no desayunar

E1: *Luisa no va a desayunar.* E2: *No me gusta que Luisa no desayune.* E1: *Y yo siento/lamento que…*

PERSONAS	LUNES	MIÉRCOLES	VIERNES	DOMINGO
Luisa	empezar una dieta	ir al gimnasio	hacer ejercicio en su casa	caminar 2 kilómetros
Rafael	trabajar en el hospital todo el día	salir del hospital temprano para ir al cine	quedarse en su casa	reunirse con sus amigos

Follow-up for 11-22
Students list what they like others to do and then share their lists with partners.

11-22 

¿Qué me molesta? **PREPARACIÓN.** Haz una lista de los hábitos que te molestan de otras personas. Compara tu lista con la de tu compañero/a.

Me molesta que mis amigos lleguen tarde.

 **INTERCAMBIOS.** En pequeños grupos, comparen sus listas y escojan seis hábitos que les molestan más a todos y digan por qué. Compartan sus resultados con el resto de la clase.

Situación

PREPARACIÓN. Lean la situación. Luego, compartan ejemplos de vocabulario, gramática y otra información que necesitan para desarrollar la conversación.

Role A. You and your housemate disagree about health and exercise. You exercise regularly, ride your bike, and hike on the weekends, and want only healthful foods in the refrigerator. Your housemate buys a lot of junk food, leaves a mess in the living room and bathroom, and disturbs you with loud music at all hours. You have a serious conversation to tell him/her what is bothering you.

Role B. Your housemate is uptight and conventional and doesn't know how to enjoy life. When he/she tells you what is bothering him/her about your behavior, you should:

a. react to his/her complaints;
b. respond with your complaints about his/her excessive tidiness; and
c. regret that you do not agree on anything.

	ROLE A	ROLE B
Vocabulario	Activities for a healthy lifestyle Household chores Verbs of emotions, likes, and dislikes	Household chores Verbs of emotions, likes, and dislikes
Funciones y formas	Expressing emotion about someone's actions	Expressing emotion about someone's actions

INTERCAMBIOS. Practica la conversación con tu compañero/a incorporando el vocabulario y las funciones de *Preparación*. Luego, represéntenla ante la clase.

4 Expressing goals, purposes, and means

 **Vive más**

- **Para** vivir más no necesitas más dinero. No pagues miles de pesos **por** aparatos de ejercicio. ¡Muévete!
- Sube a tu clase u oficina **por** las escaleras; no tomes el ascensor.
- Cuando vayas **para** el centro, no conduzcas. Es mejor ir a pie.
- Si caminas 30 minutos **por** día vivirás más. Pasea **por** el parque con tus amigos o tu familia y guarda tu dinero **para** cosas necesarias.
- Relájate mientras caminas al aire libre y vive con menos estrés **por** ti y **para** ti.

Piénsalo. Indica si las afirmaciones son ciertas (**C**) o falsas (**F**). Luego, escoge de la lista el significado de **por** o **para** en cada afirmación.

a causa de algo o alguien	en dirección a un lugar
en beneficio de alguien	medio de transporte
duración	objetivo

	CIERTO/ FALSO	SIGNIFICADO DE POR/PARA
1. **Para** tener una vida larga es importante mantenernos activos.	C	objetivo
2. Caminar **por** 30 minutos al día ayuda a vivir más años.	C	duración
3. Es mejor ir en automóvil cuando vamos **para** el supermercado y otras tiendas.	F	en dirección a un lugar
4. Debemos relajarnos y vivir con menos estrés **por** nosotros mismos.	C	en beneficio de alguien

Uses of *por* and *para*

- As you learned in *Capítulo 3,* the prepositions **por** and **para** have several meanings and uses. You have used them easily in some contexts in which they are similar to "for" in English:

  Compré estas vitaminas **para** Anita. *I bought these vitamins for Anita.*

- Other uses of **por** and **para** that are not similar to English can be learned by grouping them into functional categories: expressions of movement, time, purpose, and means.

POR	PARA
MOVEMENT	
• through or by a place Caminaron **por** el hospital. *They walked through the hospital.*	• toward a destination Caminaron **para** el hospital. *They walked toward the hospital.*
TIME	
• duration of an event Estuvo con la médica **por** una hora. *He was with the doctor for an hour.*	• deadline Necesita el antibiótico **para** el martes. *He needs the antibiotic by Tuesday.*
PURPOSE	
• reason or motive Ana fue al consultorio **por** el dolor de garganta. *Ana went to the doctor's office because of a sore throat.*	• for whom something is intended or done Compró el antibiótico **para** Ana. *He bought the antibiotic for Ana.*

- **Por** is also used to express the following:
  - means of transportation

    Mandaron los órganos para el trasplante **por** avión. — *They sent the organs for the transplant by plane.*

  - exchange or substitution

    Irma pagó $120 **por** las pastillas. — *Irma paid $120 for the pills.*

    Cambió esas pastillas rojas **por** las amarillas. — *She exchanged those red pills for the yellow ones.*

  - unit or rate

    Yo camino 5 kilómetros **por** hora. — *I walk 5 kilometers per hour.*

    El seguro de salud cubre el sesenta **por** ciento de las cuentas. — *The health insurance covers 60 percent of the bills.*

  - object of an errand

    Sara fue a la farmacia **por** jarabe para la tos. — *Sara went to the drugstore for the cough syrup.*

    Pasamos **por** ti a las 5:00. — *We'll come by for you at 5:00.*

- **Para** is also used to express the following:
  - judgment or point of view

    Para nosotros, esta es la mejor farmacia. — *For us, this is the best drugstore.*

    Es un caso difícil **para** un médico joven. — *It is a difficult case for a young doctor.*

  - intention or purpose, when followed by an infinitive

    Fueron a la farmacia **para** comprar jarabe para la tos. — *They went to the drugstore to buy cough syrup.*

    Come bien **para** vivir más. — *Eat well to live longer.*

e ¿COMPRENDES?

Completa las oraciones con **por** o **para.**

1. Te llamo __para__ pedirte un favor.
2. Todos los días caminamos __por__ el parque.
3. ¿Puedes pasar __por__ mi casa a las cinco?
4. Es muy fuerte __para__ un niño de siete años.
5. Ella siempre trabaja __por__ mí cuando estoy enferma.

MySpanishLab

Learn more using Amplifire Dynamic Study Modules, Grammar Tutorials, and Extra Practice activities.

PRÁCTICA

11-23  

Un episodio. **PREPARACIÓN.** Selecciona la preposición correcta, según el significado entre paréntesis.

1. Salimos **por/para** el consultorio del médico a las nueve de la mañana. (*toward a destination*)
2. Fuimos **por/para** el túnel para llegar más rápido. (*through*)
3. Ana fue a ver al médico **por/para** su dolor de garganta y tos. (*reason or motive*)
4. El médico recetó un antibiótico **por/para** Ana. (*for whom it is intended*)
5. Yo fui a la farmacia **por/para** el antibiótico. (*object of an errand*)
6. ¿Cuánto pagaste **por/para** el antibiótico? (*exchange or substitution*)

INTERCAMBIOS. Túrnense para hablar del siguiente episodio.

1. ¿Cuándo fue la última vez que fuiste al médico?
2. ¿Por qué fuiste?
3. ¿Qué te recomendó el médico y para qué?
4. ¿Cuánto pagaste por la consulta?
5. ¿Cuánto pagaste por los medicamentos?

11-24

La graduación de un nuevo médico. Completa estos párrafos sobre la graduación de Fernando con **por** o **para,** según el contexto. Luego, de la lista de funciones a continuación, escoge la letra que corresponde a cada uso de **por** o **para.**

El 14 de junio es la graduación de Fernando en la Facultad de Medicina de la Universidad Católica Madre y Maestra de Santiago de los Caballeros en República Dominicana. Sus padres, los señores Rovira, viven en Puerto Plata, pero van a Santiago **(1) por/para** (para, a) asistir a la graduación y quieren llevarle un regalo. El lunes pasado fueron a una tienda y pagaron cien dólares **(2) por/para** (por, d) un regalo muy bonito **(3) por/para** (para, g) Fernando. Graciela, su hermana gemela, vive en Miami y no puede ir **(4) por/para** (por, h) su trabajo. Ella también le compró un regalo y se lo envió **(5) por/para** (por, c) avión porque quiere que llegue **(6) por/para** (para, f) el día de la graduación.

El día 14, los padres de Fernando salieron **(7) por/para** (para, e) la universidad. Estaba lloviendo, y **(8) por/para** (por, h) eso salieron temprano. Normalmente, ellos pueden estar en la universidad en una hora más o menos, pero **(9) por/para** (por, h) la lluvia, el viaje duró casi dos horas. **(10) Por/Para** (Para, b) ellos, que son mayores, el viaje fue un poco largo, pero al final pudieron pasar ese día con su hijo.

To express or indicate...
a. intention or purpose (with infinitive)
b. judgment or point of view
c. means of transportation
d. exchange or substitution
e. toward a destination
f. deadline
g. for whom something is intended or done
h. reason or motive

Suggestions for 11-24
Encourage students to give additional advice, using affirmative and negative commands.

Follow up for 11-24
Ask students to give a brief presentation on one of the places mentioned in the activity.

11-25 

En el laboratorio. Túrnense para averiguar cuándo estarán listos los resultados del análisis (*test*) de unos pacientes. Consulten la tabla para obtener información.

Alfredo Benítez/2:00 de la tarde

E1: *¿Cuándo va a estar listo el análisis del Sr. Benítez?*

E2: *Va a estar listo para las dos de la tarde.*

PACIENTE	RESULTADOS DEL ANÁLISIS
Hilda Corvalán	11:00 de la mañana
Alfonso González	esta tarde
Jorge Pérez Robles	3:15 de la tarde
Aleida Miranda	mañana por la mañana
César Gómez Villegas	martes
Irene Santa Cruz	. . .

Cultura

Nuestra Señora de Altagracia

En un país profundamente católico como República Dominicana, la devoción a Nuestra Señora de Altagracia ocupa un lugar preeminente. Los dominicanos consideran a esta virgen como la protectora de la nación. El 21 de enero celebran con devoción y emoción el día de su festividad. Ese día no se trabaja en República Dominicana y muchas personas peregrinan al templo de Higüey para rezar, dar gracias y pedirle protección.

Comparación. ¿Hay lugares espirituales en tu país donde la gente va para reflexionar o dar las gracias?

Una cura para el estrés. Aconséjale a tu compañero/a que vaya a República Dominicana para curarse del estrés. Sugiérele algunas actividades y escoge de la lista el propósito para cada actividad. Después cambien de papel.

ACTIVIDAD: *caminar por el Jardín Botánico de Santo Domingo*

PROPÓSITO: ver la gran variedad de plantas

Camina por el Jardín Botánico para ver la gran variedad de plantas.

ACTIVIDAD	PROPÓSITO
1. participar en la fiesta nacional de Nuestra Señora de Altagracia en Higüey **2.** ir a la Bahía de Samaná **3.** ir a un club en la Zona Colonia de la capital **4.** explorar la Cueva de las Maravillas cerca de La Romana **5.** salir a cenar en el Mesón de la Cava en Santo Domingo **6.** pasar unos días en las playas de Punta Cana	■ escuchar música y bailar merengue ■ visitar el santuario de las ballenas jorobadas (*humpback whales*) ■ conocer el significado de esta figura espiritual del pueblo dominicano ■ nadar, hacer kayak y tomar el sol ■ explorar las cavernas y ver unas pinturas antiguas hechas por los aborígenes taínos ■ comer comida típica dominicana

Situación

PREPARACIÓN. Lean la situación. Luego, compartan ejemplos de vocabulario, gramática y otra información que necesitan para desarrollar la conversación.

Role A. You hurt your ankle while playing soccer, so you go to the health center at your college or university. Tell the doctor that:

a. you fell during the game;
b. your ankle is swollen (**hinchado**); and
c. you cannot walk.

Ask questions and answer your doctor's questions.

Role B. A patient comes to see you with a sports injury. After you hear how the injury happened, ask:

a. what the coach did for him/her, and;
b. how he/she got to the health center.

After determining that the ankle is not broken, recommend that the patient:

a. rest for three or four days;
b. take medication (**una pastilla**) for the pain; and
c. put ice on his/her ankle to reduce the swelling (**reducir la hinchazón**).

Add that because of the injury, he/she should not play soccer for a month.

	ROLE A	ROLE B
Vocabulario	Health and injuries	Health and injuries
Funciones y formas	Explaining reason for a condition Describing symptoms Asking and answering questions: *Por/para*	Asking and answering questions Giving advice: *Por/para* Subjunctive

INTERCAMBIOS. Practica la conversación con tu compañero/a incorporando el vocabulario y las funciones de *Preparación*. Luego, represéntenla ante la clase.

Suggestion for *Situación*
You may want to assign partners and have pairs create mini-skits using the video-posting feature, *MediaShare*, online.

EN ACCIÓN

No me encuentro bien

11-27 Antes de ver

¿No te sientes bien? Asocia las definiciones de la columna de la izquierda con las palabras de la columna de la derecha.

1. __e__ Vende productos naturales y hierbas medicinales.
2. __b__ Vamos a este lugar cuando estamos muy enfermos o en caso de emergencia.
3. __f__ Lo tomamos cuando tenemos una infección.
4. __d__ Aquí compramos medicamentos con receta médica y también artículos de belleza.
5. __a__ Es un sitio para curas físicas y espirituales.
6. __c__ Es la parte del cuerpo que nos duele cuando comemos mucho.

a. la botánica
b. el hospital
c. el estómago
d. la farmacia
e. el herbolario
f. el antibiótico

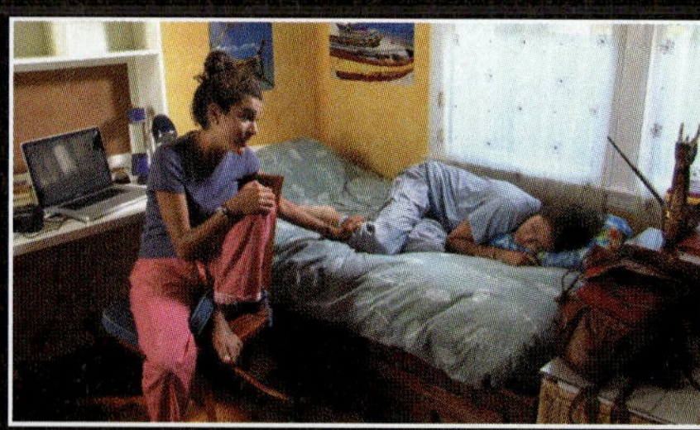

11-28 Mientras ves  

Problemas de la salud. Después de su celebración de cumpleaños, Yolanda no se siente bien. Indica si las siguientes afirmaciones son ciertas (**C**) o falsas (**F**) según la información de este segmento de video. Corrige las afirmaciones falsas.

1. __C__ A Yolanda le duele el estómago porque comió mucho.
2. __F__ Yolanda quiere consultar a su médico. A Yolanda no le gusta ir al médico.
3. __C__ Cuando era niña, Vanesa tomaba antibióticos frecuentemente.
4. __C__ En general, Yolanda goza de buena salud.
5. __C__ La familia de Yolanda prefiere tomar productos naturales y caseros.
6. __F__ El herbolario Morando es uno de los más modernos de Madrid. El herbolario Morando es uno de los herbolarios más antiguos de Madrid.
7. __C__ El herbolario Morando se especializa en plantas medicinales.
8. __F__ En México, las botánicas venden medicinas para enfermedades graves. Las botánicas ofrecen productos para curar enfermedades que no son graves.
9. __C__ Las personas van a las botánicas por problemas de salud y también espirituales.
10. __F__ En Los Ángeles no hay botánicas. Yolanda menciona una botánica en Los Ángeles.

11-29 Después de ver 

Consejos. PREPARACIÓN. Escoge la mejor recomendación para las siguientes situaciones.

1. Yolanda tiene dolor de estómago. Le recomiendo que…
   - (a.) tome un té de manzanilla (*chamomile*).
   - b. coma solamente pasta por unos días.
   - c. beba mucha leche.
2. A Vanesa no le gustan los antibióticos y las inyecciones. Le recomiendo que…
   - a. vaya a la sala de emergencia.
   - (b.) visite un herbolario.
   - c. hable con un farmacéutico.
3. Muchas personas tienen problemas espirituales. Les recomiendo que…
   - (a.) visiten una botánica.
   - b. hagan más ejercicio.
   - c. aumenten la cantidad de agua que toman diariamente.

INTERCAMBIOS. Cuéntense sobre la última enfermedad que tuvieron. ¿Cuál fue? ¿Qué síntomas tuvieron? ¿Qué hicieron para sentirse mejor?

Mosaicos

ESCUCHA

11-30   Presentational

Preparación. Van a escuchar una conversación entre un nutricionista y un grupo de estudiantes universitarios. Antes de escuchar, escriban dos preguntas que los alumnos probablemente le harán al nutricionista y dos sugerencias que les dará el nutricionista. Presenten sus preguntas y sugerencias a la clase, y escriban entre todos una lista.

ESTRATEGIA

Listen for the main idea

You can focus your attention on the main ideas when you listen by following these tips:

1. Rely on knowledge of the topic to make connections.
2. Think about the specific words or concepts you may hear.
3. Pay attention to the introduction and the conclusion, where the main ideas are usually stated.
4. Listen for transitional phrases that signal main ideas, such as **Lo importante es..., Recuerde(n)..., Otro punto importante/central...**

11-31   Interpretive

Escucha. Mark (✓) the statements that best identify the main ideas of what you heard.

1. __✓__ Consultar al médico una vez por año es importante para evitar enfermedades.
2. ____ El consumo de tomates, lechugas, uvas, naranjas, cerveza y carne de res es recomendable para tener energía.
3. __✓__ La buena alimentación y el ejercicio tienen un efecto positivo en la salud.
4. ____ Se recomienda comer bastante y hacer muchísimo ejercicio para mantener una vida saludable.
5. ____ Bajar de peso afecta positivamente la salud y la apariencia de las personas.
6. __✓__ La buena salud requiere disciplina.

Comprueba

I was able to ...

____ use my knowledge of the topic to anticipate what I would probably hear.

____ listen for parts of the conversation where main ideas are about to be presented.

____ identify the main ideas.

11-32  Interpersonal

Un paso más. Háganse las siguientes preguntas. ¿Tienen los mismos hábitos de salud? Comparen sus puntos de vista.

1. ¿Qué hábitos de comida y actividad física tienes? ¿Son tus hábitos buenos o malos?
2. ¿Crees que eres lo que comes?
3. ¿Qué aspecto de tu vida piensas que puedes cambiar para mejorar tu estado físico?

Audioscript for 11-31

NUTRICIONISTA: *Como ustedes saben, es necesario mantener una dieta sana y balanceada para evitar enfermedades y mantener un peso ideal. En primer lugar, es necesario hacerse un examen médico anual, alimentarse bien, mantenerse activo, no fumar ni consumir mucho alcohol.*
FABIÁN: *Pero aquí en la universidad muchos estudiantes toman cerveza para relajarse y divertirse. ¿Qué tiene eso de malo?*
NUTRICIONISTA: *En realidad tomar cerveza o alcohol no es malo. Lo importante es la moderación. La sal, por ejemplo, es buena, pero en altas cantidades puede ser dañina.*
FABIOLA: *¿Y la carne roja?*
NUTRICIONISTA: *Un factor importante es limitar el consumo de grasas animales para evitar el aumento del colesterol en la sangre; el pescado y el pollo tienen menos grasa. Consuman estos últimos con más frecuencia.*
FABIÁN: *En mi casa mis padres comen muchas frutas y verduras, pero a mí no me gustan mucho.*
NUTRICIONISTA: *Es una lástima, porque las frutas y verduras tienen muchos minerales y vitaminas. Además, tienen fibra, y la fibra es buena para la salud.*
FABIOLA: *Yo quiero bajar de peso. ¿Qué debo hacer?*
NUTRICIONISTA: *Mantén una dieta balanceada y haz ejercicios regularmente, por lo menos veinte minutos, tres veces a la semana. Es preferible bajar de peso poco a poco y cambiar los hábitos de comida y ejercicios. Así se puede mantener el peso ideal, mejorar la salud y la apariencia física.*
FABIOLA: *Suena fácil, pero debo tener mucha disciplina.*
FABIÁN: *Sí, sobre todo los fines de semana cuando se socializa con amigos.*
NUTRICIONISTA: *Recuerden, todo con moderación. Buena suerte, y si necesitan más información pueden venir a verme al hospital.*

Suggestion for 11-34
Ask students to prepare a questionnaire. Give them some models to ask related questions: *¿Te mantienes activo/a? ¿Comes verduras regularmente? ¿Bebes alcohol? ¿Con qué frecuencia?*

Note for *En directo*
Before doing activity 11-34, first have students read the expressions in *En directo*. Then have them listen to the dialogue and encourage them to use the expressions in their own conversation.

Audioscript for *En directo*
ENFERMERO: *Te felicito, Juan. Estás en perfectas condiciones. Se nota que te cuidas muy bien.*
JUAN: *Gracias. Como muy bien y hago ejercicio casi todos los días.*
ENFERMERO: *¡Qué bien! Vas a vivir muchos años.*
JUAN: [suddenly becoming very serious] *Entiendo tu punto de vista, pero no estoy de acuerdo contigo. Anoche soñé que estaba muy enfermo. ¡Por eso pienso que me voy a morir muy pronto!* [pause] *¡Ja, ja! ¡Estoy bromeando!*
ENFERMERO: [chuckling] *Me alegro de que seas una persona alegre. El buen humor también es muy bueno para la salud.*

Suggestion for *En directo*
You may provide students with *enhorabuena* as an additional expression to congratulate someone.

Audioscript for *En directo*
MIRIAM: *Mamá, el doctor dijo que es aconsejable que dejes de fumar cuanto antes. ¿Por qué sigues fumando?*
MADRE: *Hija, es bien difícil parar. Cuando fumo, me siento muy relajada.*
MIRIAM: *Lo entiendo, pero si no quieres enfermarte, es importante que busques ayuda ya.*

HABLA

ESTRATEGIA

Select appropriate phrases to offer opinions

When you are talking with someone, it is natural to offer opinions and evaluations of what the other person has said and to express agreement or disagreement. An effective way to do this is to acknowledge the value of what the other person has said and then express your reaction to it.

11-33 Interpretive

Preparación. Marca (✓) los hábitos o condiciones que ayudan a prolongar la vida de las personas.

1. _____ hacer ejercicio físico regularmente
2. _____ trabajar poco
3. _____ poner el cuerpo bajo mucho estrés
4. _____ ser vegetariano/a
5. _____ beber vino con el almuerzo o la cena
6. _____ llevar una vida sedentaria
7. _____ tomar remedios caseros para curar el catarro
8. _____ evitar fracturarse los huesos

11-34  Interpersonal

Habla. Entrevista a tu compañero/a sobre los temas siguientes. Reacciona y opina según lo que escuches. Da recomendaciones cuando sea necesario.

1. sus actividades
2. sus hábitos de comida
3. las bebidas que toma cuando sale con sus amigos

En directo

To congratulate or praise someone:

Felicitaciones por mantenerte en forma.

Te felicito. Te cuidas muy bien.

¡Qué bien! Vas a vivir por muchos años.

To express happiness at someone's success:

Me alegro de que + *subjunctive…*

¡Qué fabuloso que + *subjunctive…!*

To introduce a contrasting opinion:

Lo que dices es interesante, pero mi perspectiva es diferente./Yo lo veo diferente.

Entiendo tu punto de vista, pero no estoy de acuerdo contigo.

 Listen to a conversation with these expressions.

Comprueba

In my conversation, I …

_____ **used the correct expressions to praise and encourage.**

_____ **used the appropriate expressions to acknowledge what the speaker said and then express a different opinion.**

_____ **used expressions effectively to make recommendations.**

11-35 Presentational

Un paso más. Usa la información de la entrevista a tu compañero/a para escribir un informe que incluya lo siguiente:

1. las actividades y hábitos de tu compañero/a.
2. una comparación con los tuyos.
3. tu opinión y recomendaciones para tener una vida más saludable.

En directo

To make a general recommendation:

Es importante/bueno/conveniente/aconsejable + *infinitive…*

To make a recommendation to someone specific:

Es importante que + *name(s)* + *subjunctive…*

 Listen to a conversation with these expressions.

LEE

11-36 Interpersonal

Preparación. De la siguiente lista, indica las enfermedades tropicales que conoces. Después, habla con tu compañero/a sobre las ideas que esperan encontrar en el artículo.

1. _____ la viruela (*smallpox*)
2. _____ la tuberculosis
3. _____ el dengue
4. _____ el virus del Nilo
5. _____ la malaria
6. _____ la enfermedad del sueño

ESTRATEGIA

Focus on relevant information

Identifying the relevant information in a text and disregarding what you think is irrelevant helps you read faster and understand more. Techniques that help you identify what is important include a) reading the titles and subtitles; b) looking at the visuals and reading the captions; c) brainstorming possible content by using your knowledge of the topic; and d) comparing those ideas with what you find as you read.

Suggestion for *Estrategia*
Follow *Estrategia* suggestions *a* through *c* and point out to students what you are doing. Encourage them to follow *d* as they read the text.

11-37 Interpretive

Lee. Según el contenido del artículo en la página siguiente, selecciona las expresiones de la derecha que se relacionan con los siguientes temas.

TEMAS	EXPRESIONES RELACIONADAS
enfermedades tropicales	las infecciones la viruela la tuberculosis el virus del Nilo
desafíos de las enfermedades para los expertos	la infección la adaptabilidad el desarrollo la evolución la resistencia
medidas que los gobiernos toman para enfrentar estas enfermedades	campañas inmunización reproducción vacunas prevención

Comprueba

I was able to . . .

_____ **distinguish between main and secondary ideas.**

_____ **identify key terms related to the main ideas.**

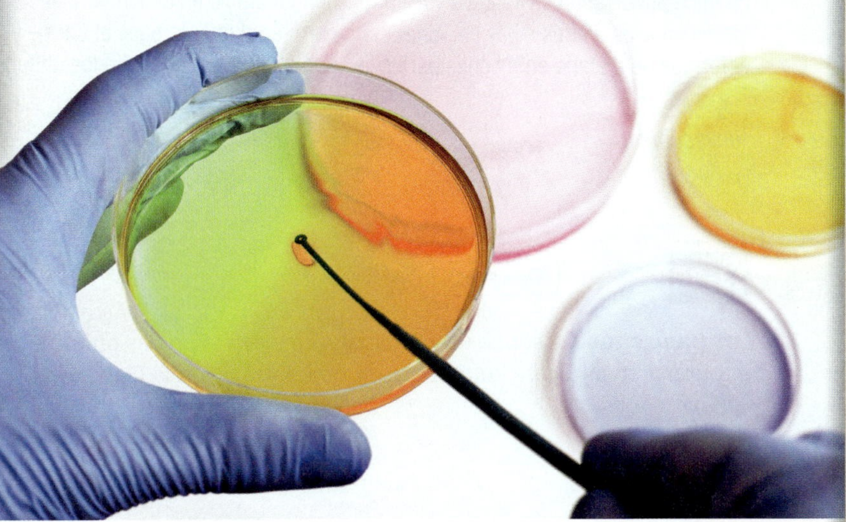

Suggestion for 11-37
Have students find additional *ideas principales* and *ideas secundarias* in the text. Have them explain the difference.

LAS ENFERMEDADES Y LA GLOBALIZACIÓN

Enfermedades tropicales como el dengue, la viruela, la malaria, la tuberculosis y el virus del Nilo que, según muchos expertos, ya no existían, ahora reaparecen y se extienden por todo el mundo. Las causas de su reaparición son evidentes: cambios en el medio ambiente[1] y el constante movimiento de personas entre los continentes. Los turistas, los trabajadores migratorios y los inmigrantes transportan estos virus e infecciones. De la misma manera, los cambios climáticos facilitan la adaptación de los virus a nuevos ambientes y los hacen resistentes.

BACTERIAS, PARÁSITOS Y VIRUS VIAJEROS Y RESISTENTES

Un claro ejemplo de la adaptabilidad de estas enfermedades infecciosas es la tuberculosis. Los científicos pensaban que estaba controlada en los países desarrollados. Sin embargo, los hechos nos muestran que esta enfermedad ha evolucionado y ha retornado.

La Organización Mundial de la Salud (OMS) expresa gran preocupación por la malaria. El mosquito que la provoca puede sobrevivir largos viajes interoceánicos. Por eso, hay personas enfermas de malaria en muchas partes del mundo. La malaria es peligrosa si no se detecta a tiempo. Los médicos sin experiencia en este tipo de enfermedades la pueden confundir con la gripe y tratarla con medicamentos inadecuados.

El virus del Nilo constituye otra enfermedad que afecta a los turistas. Se reportaron 3.500 casos de la enfermedad en Estados Unidos en el 2007, de los que murieron más de cien personas.

LAS ENFERMEDADES MIGRATORIAS

A fines del siglo XX, gracias a una campaña mundial contra la viruela, casi toda la población mundial fue inmunizada contra esta enfermedad. Sin embargo, en Estados Unidos ha sido necesario fabricar vacunas contra la viruela que no se producían desde hacía años.

El dengue es indudablemente la enfermedad más extendida del mundo en los últimos años. Los expertos afirman que es posible que el 40% de la población del mundo contraiga[2] esta mortal fiebre. Geográficamente, el dengue nació en el suroeste de Asia, pero rápidamente pasó al Caribe y Centro y Sudamérica. En los últimos años se han descubierto casos incluso en España.

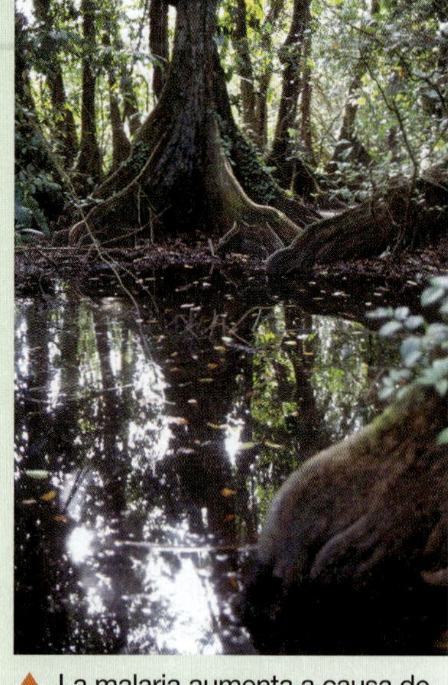

▲ La malaria aumenta a causa de las inundaciones del río Amazonas.

La lista de enfermedades que surgen de nuevo por la movilidad de la población del mundo actual es larga, pero los fondos mundiales para realizar investigaciones sobre las enfermedades que causan el 90% de las muertes en el mundo son mínimos y limitados. Sin duda, la globalización ha resuelto algunos problemas, pero ha creado otros.

[1] *environment*

[2] *contracts*

11-38  Presentational

Un paso más. Escribe un párrafo informativo sobre las enfermedades tropicales y las medidas que los gobiernos toman para enfrentarlas, y compártelo con la clase.

ESCRIBE

11-39 Interpretive

Preparación. Lee este correo electrónico de uno de tus buenos amigos. Después, escribe tres problemas que tiene Tomás y algunas ideas para ayudarlo a resolver cada problema.

Hola:

Perdón por no escribirte antes, pero últimamente no me siento bien. No puedo trabajar un día completo y no tengo apetito. No tengo energía para cocinar, así que a veces como solo sopa enlatada. Otras veces voy a un restaurante de comida rápida. Tomo café constantemente, porque necesito la cafeína para sobrevivir, pero luego no puedo dormir. Mi vida es una pesadilla. Quisiera ver a un médico, pero no tengo dinero. ¿Qué me aconsejas?

Bueno, escríbeme para saber de ti. Te contestaré tan pronto pueda.

Un fuerte abrazo,

Tomás

PROBLEMAS DE TOMÁS	ALGUNAS POSIBLES SOLUCIONES
1.	1.
2.	2.
3.	3.

ESTRATEGIA

Persuade through suggestions and advice

Well-structured suggestions and advice are important for effective persuasion in writing. Remember to ...

- decide whether to address your reader as **tú** or **usted,** based on your relationship (e.g., friend vs. supervisor at work).
- select suggestions that match the nature of your relationship.

En directo

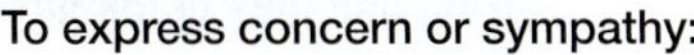

To express concern or sympathy:

Me preocupa (mucho) que...

Siento/Lamento que...

Qué lástima que...

To persuade a friend through suggestions:

Te recomiendo/sugiero/aconsejo que...

Es importante/necesario/urgente/mejor que...

Ojalá (que)...

Listen to a conversation with these expressions.

Suggestion for 11-39
In preparation for the upcoming writing task, you may wish to have students write (type) an anonymous letter—outside of class—to *Querida Dra. Márquez.* The content of the letter should be related to ailments and health issues.

Ask students to bring a printed copy of the letter to class. Collect the letters, and depending on the time you have, you may distribute one to each student or to pairs of students.

Students read the letter and discuss the problem(s) stated or implied in it and write at least two or three specific recommendations.

Point out that recommendations should be given with the intent to modify certain behaviors of the individual who wrote the letter. Also, make students aware of the issue of register.

Alternate
Ask students to e-mail you their letters so you can choose one of them and have the whole class work on only one letter. This will give students the chance to compare analysis of the letter and strength of their persuasiveness.

Audioscript for *En directo*
NIETO: *Abuelo, me preocupa mucho que te hayas torcido el tobillo otra vez. Lamento no poder estar contigo.*
ABUELO: *No te preocupes, mi'jo. Ya me siento mucho mejor.*
NIETO: *Me alegro de que te sientas mejor, pero te aconsejo que te compres un bastón para evitar más accidentes.*
ABUELO: *No quiero un bastón. Es mejor que haga más ejercicio para ponerme fuerte.*
NIETO: *Ojalá que tengas razón, abuelo.*

Suggestion for 11-40
Depending on your group, you may wish to turn this into a paired activity. Weak students may profit from the skills of stronger ones.

Note for *En directo*
Before doing activity 11-40, first have students read the expressions in *En directo*. Then have them listen to the dialogue and encourage them to use the expressions in their own message.

Audioscript for *En directo*
DOCTOR AYUDA: *Queridos radioyentes, les habla el doctor Ayuda, y tenemos nuestra primera llamada. Alicia, ¿en qué puedo servirle?*
ALICIA: *Doctor Ayuda, por un lado, mi médica me dice que estoy muy saludable. Mi presión arterial está muy bien. No tengo dolores. Por otro lado, desde el sábado me siento muy mal. Me duele la cabeza y, además, me pica la piel.*
DOCTOR AYUDA: *Alicia, es posible que necesite volver a su médica. Sin embargo, me pregunto si usted comió algo o está usando algún producto nuevo.*
ALICIA: *Pues sí, Doctor. Ahora que lo pienso, empecé a usar una nueva loción el sábado.*
DOCTOR AYUDA: *¡Ajá! Es posible que usted sea alérgica a esa loción. Le recomiendo que vaya a ver a su dermatólogo.*

Suggestion for 11-41
Ask students to revise their e-mails according to the following:
1. *¿Tiene el correo electrónico una introducción, un cuerpo, un párrafo de cierre y una despedida?*
2. *¿Corregiste la concordancia, la puntuación y la ortografía? ¿Usaste comas, puntos, etc., donde eran necesarios?*
3. *¿Usaste vocabulario apropiado al tema y expresiones de cohesión? ¿Revisaste el tiempo (presente, pasado, futuro) y los modos (indicativo, subjuntivo)?*

11-40 Presentational

Escribe. Responde al correo electrónico de Tomás. Usa la información de la actividad 11-39 y expresa tus sentimientos o preocupación por los problemas. Indícale algunas sugerencias para que los resuelva.

Comprueba
I was able to …

- ____ use a familiar tone to communicate with a friend.
- ____ use appropriate expressions to express concern and sympathy.
- ____ use appropriate suggestions for effective persuasion.
- ____ use transitions effectively to move from one idea to the next.

En directo

To put ideas together coherently:

Por un lado…
On one hand …
Por otro (lado)…
On the other (hand) …
En primer/segundo lugar…
In the first/second place …
Además…
Besides/In addition/Furthermore …

To contrast ideas:

No obstante… *However …*
Sin embargo… *Nevertheless …*

 Listen to a conversation with these expressions.

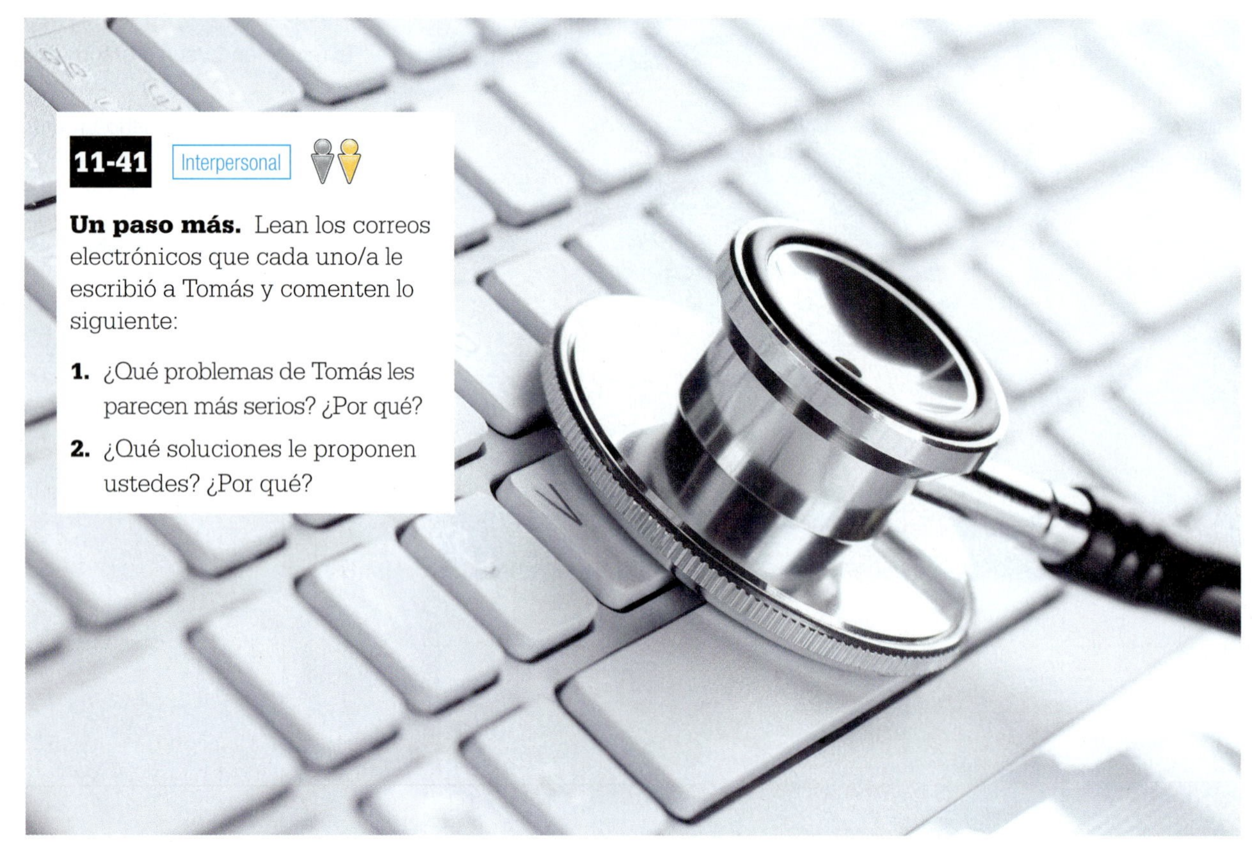

11-41 Interpersonal

Un paso más. Lean los correos electrónicos que cada uno/a le escribió a Tomás y comenten lo siguiente:

1. ¿Qué problemas de Tomás les parecen más serios? ¿Por qué?
2. ¿Qué soluciones le proponen ustedes? ¿Por qué?

En este capítulo…

Comprueba lo que sabes

Go to ***MySpanishLab*** to review what you have learned in this chapter. Practice with the following:

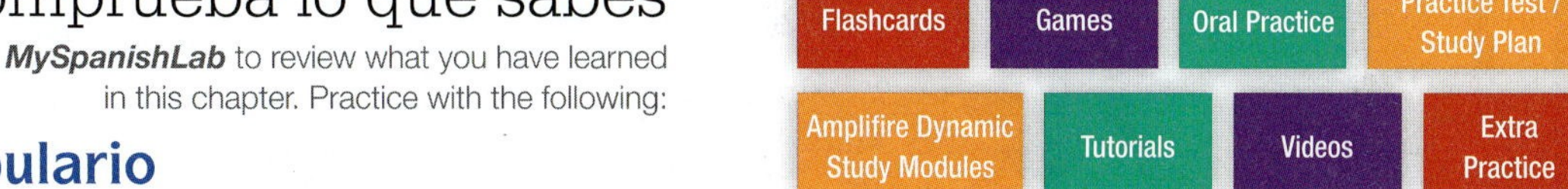

Vocabulario

EL CUERPO HUMANO
The human body

la boca *mouth*
el brazo *arm*
la cabeza *head*
la cadera *hip*
la cara *face*
la ceja *eyebrow*
el cerebro *brain*
la cintura *waist*
el codo *elbow*
el corazón *heart*
el cuello *neck*
el dedo *finger*
el diente *tooth*
la espalda *back*
el estómago *stomach*
la frente *forehead*
la garganta *throat*
el hombro *shoulder*
el hueso *bone*
el labio *lip*
la mano *hand*
la mejilla *cheek*
la muñeca *wrist*
el músculo *muscle*
la nariz *nose*
el nervio *nerve*
el oído *(inner) ear*
la oreja *(outer) ear*
el pecho *chest*
el pelo/cabello *hair*
la pestaña *eyelash*
el pie *foot*
la pierna *leg*
el pulmón *lung*
la rodilla *knee*
la sangre *blood*
el tobillo *ankle*
la vena *vein*

LOS PROVEEDORES DE SALUD
Healthcare providers

la clínica/el centro de salud/el sanatorio *clinic*
el/la farmacéutico/a *pharmacist*
la farmacia *pharmacy*
el gobierno *government*
el hospital *hospital*

LOS TRATAMIENTOS MÉDICOS
Medical treatments

el antibiótico *antibiotic*
la inyección *injection*
la medicina *medicine*
la pastilla *pill*
la receta *prescription*
el remedio *remedy, medicine*
el termómetro *thermometer*

LA SALUD
Health

la alergia *allergy*
el asma *asthma*
el catarro *cold*
el dolor *pain*
la enfermedad *illness*
el/la enfermo/a *ill person*
la fiebre *fever*
la gripe *flu*
la infección *infection*
el/la paciente *patient*
el síntoma *symptom*
la tensión/la presión (arterial) *(blood) pressure*
la tos *cough*

VERBOS
Verbs

alegrarse (de) *to be glad (about)*
caer(se) *to fall*
cuidar(se) (de) *to take care of*
curar *to cure*
doler (ue) *to hurt, ache*
estornudar *to sneeze*
examinar *to examine*
fracturar(se) *to fracture, break*
fumar *to smoke*
molestar(le) *to bother, be bothered by*
recetar *to prescribe*
respirar *to breathe*
sentir (ie, i) *to feel*
temer *to fear*
torcer(se) (ue) *to twist*
toser *to cough*
tratar *to treat*

PALABRAS Y EXPRESIONES ÚTILES
Useful words and expressions

el artículo de belleza *beauty item*
cada… horas *every … hours*
¿Qué te/le(s) pasa? *What's wrong (with you/them)?*
tener dolor de… *to have a(n) … ache*
tener mala cara *to look terrible*

LAS DESCRIPCIONES
Descriptions

enfermo/a *sick*
grave *serious*
serio/a *serious*

Introduction to chapter
Introduce the chapter theme about travel and ask questions to recycle previous content: *¿Cuándo fue la última vez que fuiste de vacaciones? ¿Adónde fuiste? ¿Te divertiste? ¿Por qué? ¿Cómo viajaste? ¿En avión, en tren, en coche? ¿Te quedaste en un hotel? ¿Tenías reservaciones? ¿Cómo hiciste las reservaciones para viajar/del hotel? ¿Nos recomiendas que vayamos allí?*

Integrated Performance Assessment: Three Modes of Communication

Presentational: See activities 12-5, 12-11, 12-27, 12-31, 12-35, 12-39, and 12-37.

Interpretive: See Activities 12-1, 12-2, 12-3, 12-4, 12-5, 12-6, 12-7, 12-9, 12-12, 12-13, 12-14, 12-15, 12-18, 12-22, 12-24, 12-25, 12-26, 12-32, 12-34, 12-36, 12-38, and 12-40.

Interpersonal: See activities 12-2, 12-3, 12-6, 12-7, 12-8, 12-9, 12-10, 12-11, 12-12, 12-13, 12-14, 12-15, 12-16, 12-17, 12-19, 12-20, 12-21, 12-22, 12-24, 12-24, 12-25, 12-26, 12-30, 12-33, 12-36, 12-37, 12-42, and all *Situación* activities.

12 ¿Te gusta viajar?

ENFOQUE CULTURAL
Costa Rica y Panamá

VOCABULARIO EN CONTEXTO
Los medios de transporte
El alojamiento y las reservaciones
Viajando en coche

MOSAICO CULTURAL
El mochilero

FUNCIONES Y FORMAS
Affirmative and negative expressions
Subjunctive in adjective clauses
Possessive pronouns
Subjunctive with expressions of doubt

EN ACCIÓN
Lugares fantásticos

MOSAICOS
ESCUCHA Use background knowledge to support comprehension
HABLA Make your presentations comprehensible and interesting
LEE Focus on logical relationships
ESCRIBE Use facts to offer advice

EN ESTE CAPÍTULO...
Comprueba lo que sabes
Vocabulario

LEARNING OUTCOMES

You will be able to:

- talk about travel arrangements and preferences
- express possession and clarify what belongs to you and to others
- express affirmation and negation
- express doubt and uncertainty
- talk about travel experiences
- share information about the social and economic impact of the Panama Canal

ENFOQUE cultural COSTA RICA Y PANAMÁ

Enfoque cultural

To learn more about Costa Rica and Panama, go to MySpanishLab to view the *Vistas culturales* videos.

Una mola tradicional de los gunas, indígenas de las islas San Blas en Panamá

¿QUÉ TE PARECE?

- Para muchos estadounidenses, Costa Rica y Panamá son países predilectos para retirarse.
- Panamá, también llamada la nueva Suiza, es uno de los centros bancarios del mundo.
- Panamá es el país natal de varios cantantes de reguetón, como Flex (Félix Danilo Gómez), Eddy Lover (Eduardo Mosquera), El General (Edgardo Franco), La Factoría, Makano (Ernán Enrique Jiménez) y Nando Boom.
- Costa Rica es el único país latinoamericano sin ejército.

Suggestion for map
Ask what students know about Costa Rica and Panama. Project the map and ask: *¿Dónde está el Canal de Panamá? ¿Qué océanos conecta? ¿Cuándo se construyó?* (early 1900s) Explain that the distance between New York and San Francisco using the Panama Canal is only 6,000 miles (9,500 kms), compared to 14,000 miles (20,500 kms) going around Cape Horn. Personalize to introduce the chapter topic: *¿Adónde les gusta ir de vacaciones, a la playa, a la montaña?* Explain that tourism is very important in Costa Rica: *En Costa Rica hay playas muy buenas donde se puede hacer surf. ¿Les gusta el surf? También hay lugares donde muchos turistas hacen ecoturismo. ¿Les gusta visitar lugares exóticos?*

Note for art
The *mola* is part of the traditional clothing of the Guna, an indigenous people of Panama and Colombia. In Dulegaya, the Guna language, the word *mola* means "clothing" or "blouse." Typical molas are made in layers of different colors. They are sewn by hand, and some require a great deal of work. Today, the production of *molas* includes dresses, T-shirts, wall hangings, quilts, and blouses.

Suggestion for art
Project the image of the artwork and ask students to describe the shapes and colors of the *mola*. Point to Panama's Islands of San Blas on the map and explain that the Guna now live on a large reservation there. You may explain that San Blas is a tourist destination for cruises (*cruceros*). Producing and selling *molas* is an important source of income for the Guna. Ask: *¿Cuánto cuestan las molas, probablemente? ¿De qué depende el precio? ¿Del trabajo? ¿Del tamaño?* Help students make connections with the art of quilting in the U.S.

Note for *Guna Yala*
In 2011, the government of Panama officially recognized the people's request to change the spelling of Kuna to Guna because there is no equivalent to the letter *k* in the Guna language.

Note for *mola*
The word *mola* is often used for the elaborate embroideries made by the Guna women. The panels usually start as blouses but later are transformed into other objects.

Note for the Panama Canal
The expansion of the canal, scheduled for completion in 2014, will allow larger ships to use the Canal and should help with the traffic.

Note for *Parque Nacional Manuel Antonio*
Manuel Antonio National Park is one of the most visited parks in the world. It forms part of the Central Pacific Conservation Area of Costa Rica. The variety of flora and fauna is incomparable. Visitors can find coral reefs, hiking trails, beautiful beaches, and waterfalls.

Note for *Arenal*
Arenal, an active volcano until 2010, is a favorite tourist attraction. Lake Arenal, at its base, is Costa Rica's largest landlocked lake.

ENFOQUE cultural

La mola es una prenda hecha de varias piezas de tela. Algunas molas son de colores brillantes, otras tienen dibujos geométricos. Los gunas las usan para hacer blusas y fundas de almohada. Algunas molas son verdaderas obras de arte.

El Canal de Panamá tiene 48 millas. El viaje dura unas quince horas y los barcos pasan por tres esclusas (*locks*). El Canal de Panamá une el océano Atlántico y el océano Pacífico.

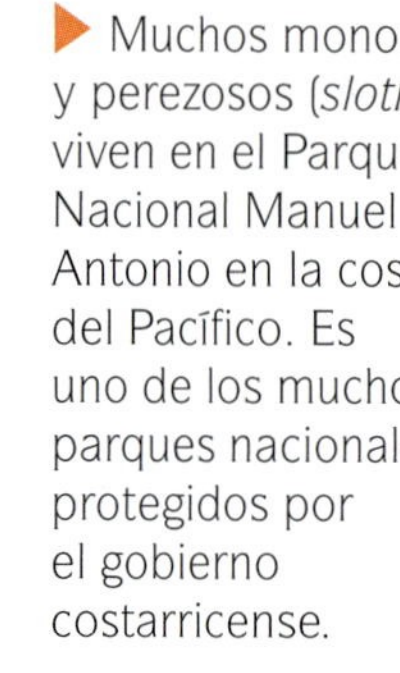

Muchos monos y perezosos (*sloths*) viven en el Parque Nacional Manuel Antonio en la costa del Pacífico. Es uno de los muchos parques nacionales protegidos por el gobierno costarricense.

Costa Rica tiene montañas, volcanes activos, playas bonitas, lagos y mucha diversidad de flora y fauna.

¿CUÁNTO SABES?

Completa las siguientes oraciones con la información correcta.

1. Una de las atracciones turísticas de Costa Rica es __el ecoturismo__.
2. Un animal que vive en los parques nacionales es __el mono/el perezoso__.
3. Los miembros de una tribu indígena que vive en Panamá se llaman __los gunas__.
4. La mola se usa para hacer __las blusas__ y __las fundas de almohadas__.
5. El Canal de Panamá conecta __el océano Atlántico__ y __el océano Pacífico__.
6. Un tipo de música popular en Panamá es __el reguetón__.
7. El único país latinoamericano sin ejército es __Costa Rica__.

Vocabulario en contexto

Talking about travel arrangements and modes of travel

Los medios de transporte

MySpanishLab

Topic for Pronunciation: More practice with linking

Learn more using Amplifire Dynamic Study Modules, Pronunciation, and Vocabulary Tutorials.

Mucha gente usa el transporte público. Los **autobuses** son populares en las ciudades y también para **viajar** largas distancias. Son la solución para las personas que no tienen carro, o a quienes simplemente no les gusta **manejar** en las **carreteras** y **autopistas.** El **metro** es otra forma de transporte eficiente en los centros urbanos, como Madrid, Barcelona, Santiago, Buenos Aires, Caracas y la Ciudad de México.

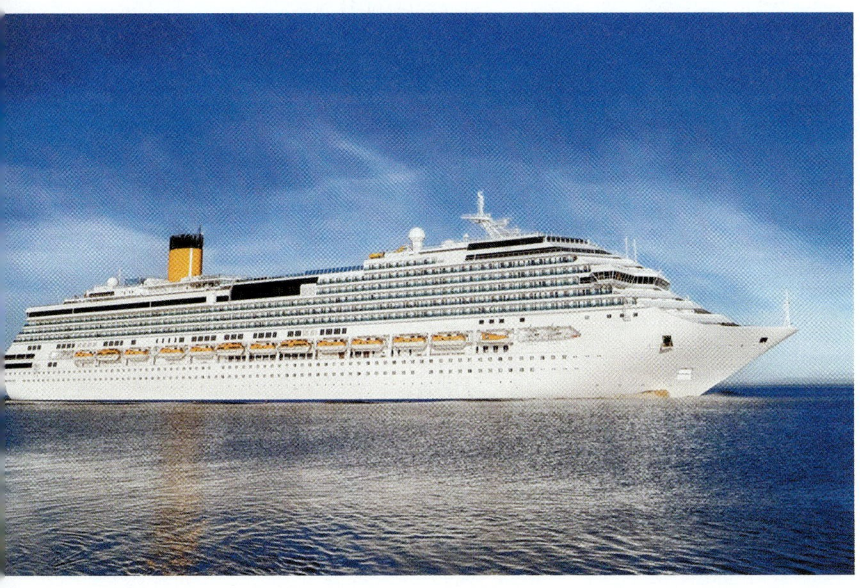

El AVE, el **tren** español de alta **velocidad** entre Madrid y otras grandes ciudades españolas, viaja a unos 300 kilómetros por hora. La RENFE (Red Nacional de Ferrocarriles Españoles) es tan importante en España como las **líneas aéreas** en Estados Unidos. Gracias al turismo se ha recuperado en Costa Rica la antigua tradición de **recorrer** el país en tren. Algunas agencias organizan **excursiones** desde San José a la costa este.

El **crucero** es otra forma de viajar. En **barcos** modernos con una capacidad de 400 hasta más de 2.000 **pasajeros,** se puede hacer de todo. En las **escalas** en los diferentes puertos hay excursiones organizadas y oportunidades para ir de compras. De noche, la diversión continúa en la discoteca, el casino y el teatro. El barco es un medio de transporte y también puede servir para pasar las vacaciones.

Suggestion for *Vocabulario en contexto*
Project the photos and ask questions to practice vocabulary: *¿Vienes a la universidad en autobús? ¿Prefieres venir en autobús o en auto? ¿Te gusta viajar en tren? ¿Qué es el AVE?*

Talk about modes of transportation. *¿Viajaste el año pasado? ¿Adónde fuiste? ¿Cómo viajaste?* Recycle the subjunctive: *¿Qué recomiendan ustedes que hagan los turistas cuando viajan a un país extranjero?*

Standard 3.2
Students acquire information and recognize the distinctive viewpoints that are only available through the foreign language and its cultures.

With the exception of a few large cities, public transportation is utilized much less in the U.S. than in Latin America and Spain. Learning about the various modes of public transportion and how heavily they are used will give students insight into the cultural perspectives and economic factors that affect social mobility in the Spanish-speaking world.

Note for Air Travel
As airlines around the world merge to survive economic strain, so have the two largest airlines in Latin America: LAN and TAM to form LATAM Airlines Group. LATAM is currently the largest airline conglomerate in Latin America.

En el avión

El avión es la manera, aunque más cara, de viajar rápidamente de un lugar a otro, especialmente en zonas como las selvas y en las montañas, donde es difícil construir carreteras por la geografía o el clima. Hoy en día, los viajes en avión son más comunes; se ofrecen **vuelos** domésticos entre muchas ciudades de los países hispanos.

EN OTRAS PALABRAS

Other words for **auxiliar de vuelo** are **azafato/a,** used especially in Spain, and **aeromozo/a,** used mostly in Latin America. To buy a ticket in Latin America you will most likely hear people use the terms **pasaje** or **boleto,** while in Spain the word **billete** is more common.

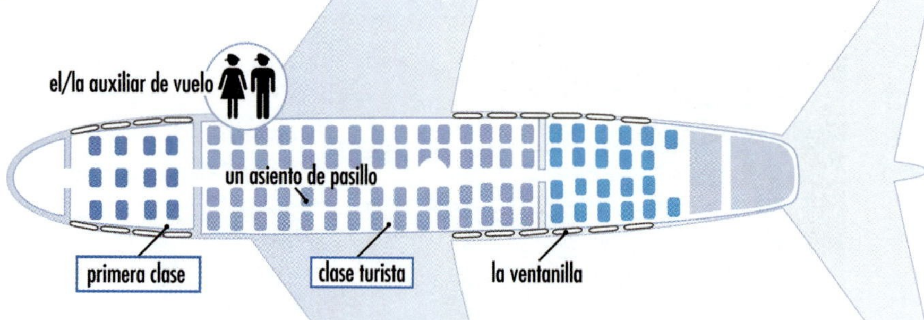

En el aeropuerto

Los pasajeros **hacen cola** frente al **mostrador** de la **aerolínea** para **facturar** el **equipaje,** pedir un **asiento** y conseguir la **tarjeta de embarque** para su **vuelo.** Algunos prefieren hacer esto por Internet.

 **En el mostrador de la línea aérea**

EMPLEADA: Buenos días. Su **pasaporte** y su **boleto,** por favor.

VIAJERO: Aquí están. Y si es posible, prefiero un asiento cerca de una **salida de emergencia.**

EMPLEADA: Muy bien. ¿**Ventanilla** o **pasillo**?

VIAJERO: Pasillo, por favor. Señorita, ¿me puede decir dónde hay un **cajero automático** aquí en el aeropuerto?

EMPLEADA: Sí, hay una oficina del Banco Popular enfrente a la derecha.

VIAJERO: Gracias. ¿Me acreditó los kilómetros a mi programa de viajero frecuente?

EMPLEADA: Sí, y su **pasaje** es **de ida y vuelta,** así que va a tener bastantes kilómetros. Su asiento a San José es el 10F. Aquí tiene su tarjeta de embarque. La puerta de salida es la C20. ¡Que tenga un buen viaje!

PRÁCTICA

12-1 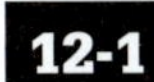  

Escucha y confirma. Listen to the following questions about transportation and select the correct response.

1. **a.** el metro **b.** el autobús
2. **a.** el AVE **b.** la RENFE
3. **a.** el crucero **b.** el avión
4. **a.** facturar el equipaje **b.** hacer escalas
5. **a.** en el mostrador **b.** en el cajero automático
6. **a.** el boleto de ida y vuelta **b.** el pasaporte

EN OTRAS PALABRAS

Depending on the region, different words for **autobús** are used: **camión** (Mexico), **ómnibus** (Peru), **bus, guagua** (Puerto Rico, Cuba), **colectivo** (Argentina), **micro** (Chile), or **chiva** (Colombia).

Audioscript for 12-1

1. *¿Qué medio de transporte se usa para viajar largas distancias?*
2. *¿Cómo se llama el tren de alta velocidad en España?*
3. *¿Qué medio de transporte se usa para pasar unas vacaciones en el mar?*
4. *Si vas a viajar en avión y tienes una maleta grande, ¿qué tienes que hacer?*
5. *Si estás de viaje y necesitas dinero de tu cuenta, ¿dónde lo consigues?*
6. *¿Qué documento se necesita para viajar de Estados Unidos a América Latina?*

12-2  

Asociaciones. Asocia cada palabra con su descripción. Luego, compara tus respuestas con las de tu compañero/a y dile qué medio de transporte prefieres y por qué.

1. _d_ transporte público para viajar por las calles de la ciudad
2. _h_ viaje en un barco grande de pasajeros
3. _a_ persona que atiende a los pasajeros en un vuelo
4. _e_ transporte subterráneo
5. _f_ lugar de inspección al llegar a otro país
6. _b_ identificación necesaria para viajar al extranjero
7. _g_ pasaje para ir y volver
8. _c_ se viaja en un asiento cómodo y se come bien

a. el/la auxiliar de vuelo
b. pasaporte
c. primera clase
d. autobús
e. metro
f. aduana
g. boleto de ida y vuelta
h. crucero

Suggestions for 12-3
As a warm-up, replay the dialogue to practice vocabulary. Ask: *¿Qué prefiere el pasajero, ventanilla o pasillo? ¿Qué necesita? ¿Cuál es su puerta de salida?*

Have students role-play the interaction between an airline agent and a traveler who needs to find out the departure time and gate number for a flight.

Review the phrases *pasaje/boleto de ida y vuelta* and *pasaje/boleto de ida*. Project the image of the airport scene. Ask where the people are, what they are doing, what luggage they have, and so on.

Suggestion for 12-5
You may wish to ask students to choose between **Parque Nacional Isla del Coco** or **Canal de Panamá** in advance. They should research some basic information, such as the location in the country, typical activities tourists may do there, means of transportation to reach this destination, etc.

12-3

Salidas y llegadas. Miren los horarios y la puerta de salida de los siguientes vuelos y háganse preguntas.

MODELO E1: *¿A qué hora sale el vuelo para San José?*

E2: *El avión para San José sale a las tres y media por la puerta 1A.*

SALIDA DEPARTURE	ABORDAR BOARDING	PUERTA GATE	DESTINO DESTINATION
3:30	3:00	1A	SAN JOSÉ
3:50	3:20	4	MANAGUA
4:10	3:40	6	GUATEMALA
4:25	3:55	10	PANAMÁ
4:45	4:15	8	LIMÓN
5:10	4:40	5	MÉXICO D.F.
6:00	5:30	5	KINGSTON

12-4

Problemas en los viajes. Túrnense para completar las conversaciones y resolver los problemas.

MODELO E1: *Estoy en Madrid y tengo que ir a Barcelona inmediatamente.*

E2: *Te recomiendo que tomes el AVE. El tren va muy rápido.*

	ESTUDIANTE 1	ESTUDIANTE 2
1.	No me gusta manejar en las ciudades grandes. ¿Qué hago?	No hay problema. En las ciudades grandes, hay… Te recomiendo que tomes…
2.	No pude imprimir mi tarjeta de embarque en casa porque no tengo Internet. ¿Qué hago?	No es difícil. Al llegar al aeropuerto, tienes que…
3.	Tengo miedo de viajar por avión pero quiero ir de Chicago a Seattle.	Si te gustan los paisajes espectaculares pero no quieres manejar, te sugiero que…
4.	Dejé mi pasaporte en casa y mi vuelo para San José sale en cuatro horas.	¡Ay, qué problema! Te aconsejo que…

Cultura

Parque Nacional de Isla del Coco

El Parque Nacional Isla del Coco se encuentra en el océano Pacífico a unos 550 kilómetros de la costa costarricense. Es un espacio protegido y una reserva natural con numerosas especies animales y vegetales autóctonas. Los visitantes llegan atraídos por la naturaleza salvaje y limpia con el deseo de encontrarse en una isla deshabitada llena de bosques y cascadas donde se puede pescar y caminar. Solo se puede llegar a la isla por barco en un viaje que dura unas 36 horas. Por su interés natural viven allí numerosos biólogos e investigadores del medio ambiente. Debido a la riqueza del ecosistema, el turismo está muy regulado para proteger el equilibrio medioambiental.

Comparaciones. ¿Existe en tu país un parque nacional de características semejantes a las del Parque Nacional Isla del Coco? ¿Qué parque nacional de tu país te gusta más? ¿Por qué?

12-5

Haciendo turismo en Costa Rica o Panamá. Tu compañero/a y tú quieren viajar a Costa Rica o Panamá. Seleccionen su destino y usen la información cultural del capítulo para planear su itinerario. Incluyan en el itinerario la información de la lista. Después, presenten su itinerario a la clase y digan por qué eligieron ese destino.

DESTINOS:	
COSTA RICA	**PANAMÁ**
• Parque Nacional Isla del Coco	• Canal de Panamá

Itinerario:

1. destino y por qué lo seleccionaron
2. fechas de viaje (número de días)
3. tipo de boleto aéreo (primera clase o clase turista) y asiento (ventanilla, etc.) y por qué lo seleccionaron
4. medio de transporte que prefieren utilizar en el lugar
5. sus actividades

El alojamiento y las reservaciones

Buscando alojamiento

EMPLEADO: Buenas tardes. ¿En qué les puedo servir?

SRA. CANO: Buenas tardes. Tenemos dos **habitaciones** reservadas a nuestro nombre, señores Cano.

EMPLEADO: Sí, señora. Tengo una **doble** y una **sencilla.**

SRA. CANO: Muy bien. Una es para nosotros y otra para nuestro hijo. Quisiera dejar los pasaportes en un lugar seguro. ¿Podría usted…?

EMPLEADO: ¿Por qué no los deja en la **caja fuerte** de su habitación?

SRA. CANO: Muy bien.

EMPLEADO: Bueno, aquí tiene dos **tarjetas magnéticas.** Ya no usamos **llaves.** Sus habitaciones están en el segundo piso.

SR. CANO: Y…, ¿nos puede indicar cómo llegar a la Plaza Cinco de Mayo?

EMPLEADO: Sí, cómo no. Mire, **salgan** del edificio y **doblen** a la derecha. **Sigan derecho** por esta calle hasta la próxima **esquina.** Allí, **doblen** a la izquierda y caminen una **cuadra** hasta la plaza que está a la derecha. No pueden **perderse.**

SR. CANO: Muchísimas gracias.

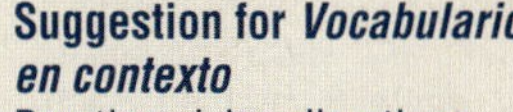

Suggestion for *Vocabulario en contexto*
Practice giving directions by projecting a simple map of the university campus. Mention that *plano* is another word for map, often used to refer to a city map or street map. Tell how to get from one place to the other: *Para ir a la biblioteca, salgo de este edificio y sigo derecho hasta la Facultad de Ciencias. Allí doblo a la izquierda y enseguida veo la biblioteca.* Then give directions to other buildings. If students have maps of the campus, they can follow the directions by drawing a dotted line. For additional practice, use a map of your town or city and have students work in pairs, asking and giving directions.

PRÁCTICA

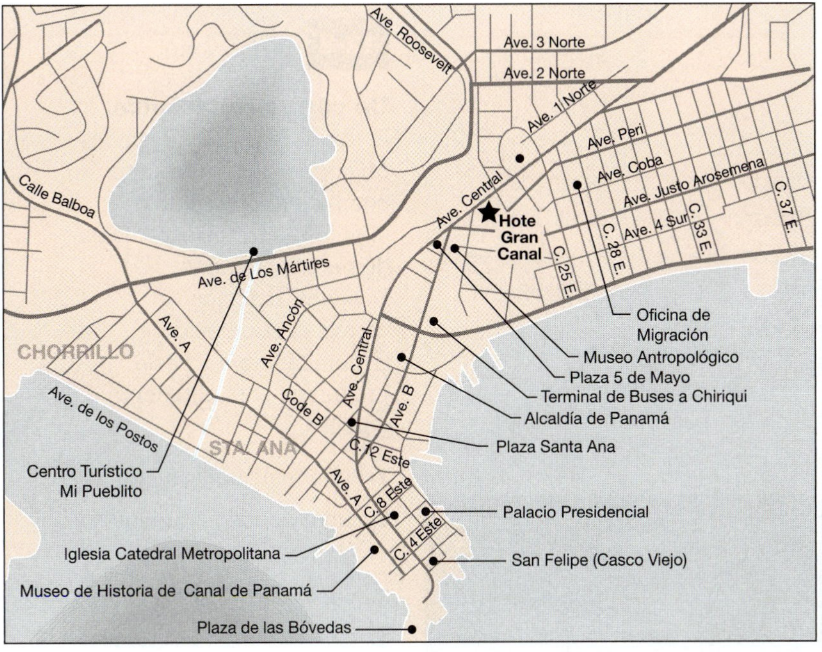

12-6 

Para confirmar. Estás perdido/a en la Ciudad de Panamá. Usando el plano, pregúntale a una persona en la calle (tu compañero/a) cómo ir a ciertos lugares. Tu compañero/a debe explicarte cómo llegar.

ESTÁS EN…	DESEAS IR…
la Plaza 5 de Mayo	al Palacio Presidencial
la Avenida Ancón y la Avenida A	a San Felipe
el Museo de Historia del Canal de Panamá	al Centro Turístico Mi Pueblito

MODELO Estás en el Hotel Gran Canal. Quieres ir a la Oficina de Migración.

E1: *¿Me puede decir cómo llegar a la Oficina de Migración, por favor?*

E2: *Sí, cómo no. La Oficina de Migración está cerca del hotel. Siga derecho por la Avenida Peri. Doble a la derecha en la Calle 27 E. Camine una cuadra y doble a la izquierda en la Avenida Coba. La Oficina de Migración está en la Avenida Coba entre la Calle 27 Este y la Calle 28 Este.*

Suggestion for 12-6
Remind students that since they are talking to a stranger on the street, they should use the *usted* form.

Suggestion for 12-6
You may need to review formal commands to give directions. You may wish to transform the classroom into city streets and do some TPR as follows: Levántense. *Hagan una fila en la calle... Caminen tres pasos. Doblen a la derecha/izquierda. Sigan una cuadra por la calle/avenida...*

Suggestion for 12-7
You may provide additional vocabulary: *ascensor, taxista, inscribirse.* A variation: Each group must find lodging in its price range: *albergue* (hostel), *hotel, hotel de lujo.* Tell students that in lower-price establishments, it is often wise to ask to see the room before deciding to stay there. Remind students of the polite use of *quisiera.* You say rudely, *Quiero una habitación;* students correct you, *Quisiera una habitación.*

Suggestions for 12-8
Students can find the cultural information they need for this activity by using the photos and captions, the *Cultura* boxes, and the *Enfoque cultural* in this chapter.

12-7 

En el hotel. Túrnense para hacer el papel de recepcionista de hotel y cliente en las siguientes situaciones. Usen el vocabulario y las expresiones de la lista. Después, escojan una situación y preséntenla a la clase.

una habitación doble/sencilla	la tarjeta magnética	Quisiera...
la llave	el equipaje	¿Dónde...?
una reservación	la caja fuerte	¿Podría...?

	CLIENTE	RECEPCIONISTA
SITUACIÓN 1	Llega al hotel y necesita una habitación.	Hace muchas preguntas.
SITUACIÓN 2	Necesita una habitación con dos camas para él/ella y su amigo/a pero no tiene reservación.	Solo tiene una habitación sencilla.
SITUACIÓN 3	Quiere reservar una habitación por teléfono, pero no quiere dar su número de tarjeta de crédito.	Para garantizar la reservación debe dar el número de tarjeta de crédito.

Cultura

Bocas del Toro

Isla Colón es la isla principal del archipiélago de Bocas del Toro en el noroeste de Panamá. La ciudad principal lleva el nombre del archipiélago. Esta ciudad es uno de los centros turísticos más importantes de Panamá. Se puede acceder a ella mediante barco o avión, pues cuenta con un aeropuerto internacional. Los turistas viajan a Isla Colón durante todo el año atraídos por las playas y el clima templado. Una atracción turística importante es el surf y la práctica de deportes acuáticos.

Comparaciones. ¿Por qué crees que mucha gente prefiere pasar sus vacaciones cerca del mar? En tu opinión, ¿hay otro lugar mejor para pasar las vacaciones? Explica.

12-8 

Un correo electrónico. Estás en Panamá y le envías un correo electrónico a tu compañero/a. Cuéntale algunos aspectos especiales de tus experiencias. Después, reacciona al correo electrónico de tu compañero/a y hazle preguntas para obtener más detalles.

1. lugar(es) que visitaste
2. lugar donde te quedaste y el tipo de alojamiento
3. personas que conociste
4. experiencias divertidas o especiales que viviste
5. comida nueva que probaste
6. regalos que compraste

Viajando en coche

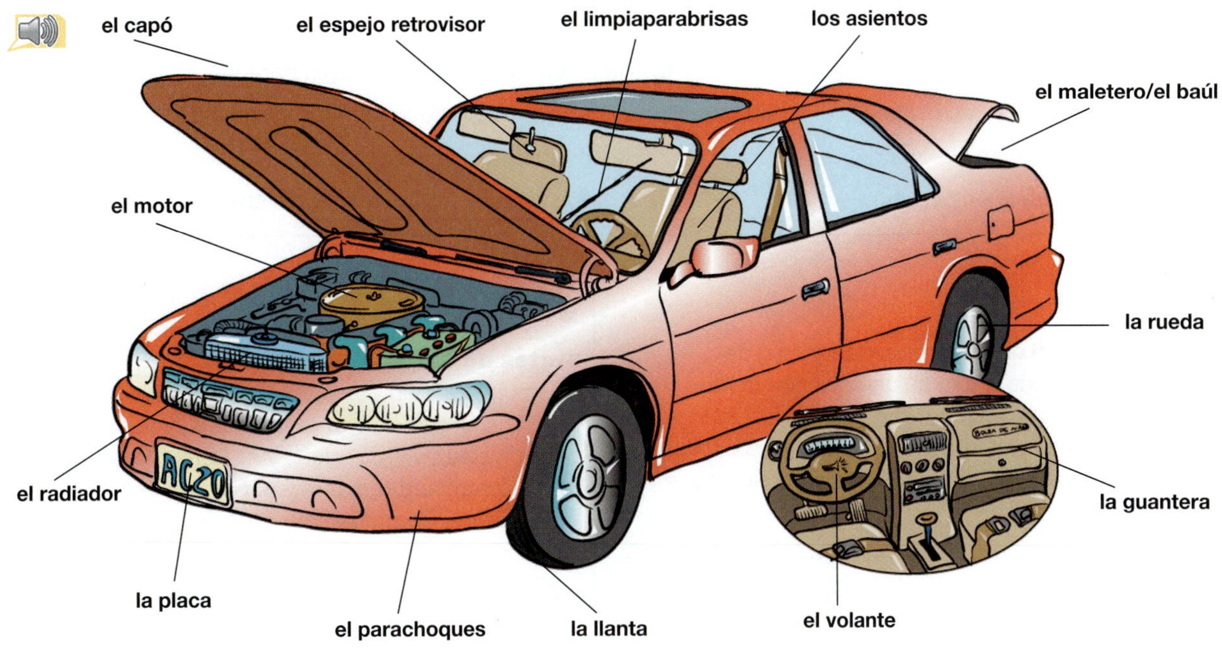

Un episodio desafortunado

Estaba en la **autopista** 95. Mi carro **se descompuso.** Por las **luces** de la consola pensé que era el **radiador** o el **motor.** Saqué el manual de la **guantera.** Traté de bajarme del carro, pero por el **espejo retrovisor** vi que venía una larga fila de vehículos. Mientras esperaba, puse las **luces intermitentes.** Me quedé con las manos al **volante** y quise limpiar el **parabrisas,** pero el **limpiaparabrisas** no funcionaba y el motor se apagó. Me bajé para abrir el **capó** cuando vi un carro patrulla de la policía. Sin decirme una palabra, el policía tomó nota de la **placa** de mi carro, se acercó a mí y me pidió la **licencia de conducir.** Intenté explicarle que tenía problemas eléctricos con el carro, pero me puso una **multa** por estar **mal aparcado.**

Suggestion for Viajando en coche

Expand the car vocabulary by using newspaper or magazine ads. Ask yes/no and either/or questions to review and reinforce vocabulary. Discuss cars with students by talking about *carros/coches pequeños/grandes, consumo de gasolina, contaminación,* etc. Give half the class the picture of a car without the parts identified. The other students say the part of the car, and the first group must label it correctly.

Suggestion for 12-10
Encourage students to use the vocabulary found in this section when talking to their partners about their vehicle preferences.

Suggestion for 12-11
This is a good opportunity to review the use of the subjunctive when giving advice (*Capítulo 11*). You may wish to do a quick review of the forms.

Warm-up for 12-12
As a pre-listening activity, have students in groups of 4 discuss whether they have traveled abroad and where, what documents they had to get before their trip, and what problems they had to deal with.

Audioscript for 12-12
AGENTE: *Buenas tardes, señor. Su pasaje y pasaporte, por favor.*
VIAJERO: *Buenas tardes. Aquí están.*
AGENTE: *Muy bien. ¿Cuántas maletas va a facturar?*
VIAJERO: *Dos. Llevo también un maletín de mano, pero no lo voy a facturar.*
AGENTE: *Muy bien. Ponga las maletas aquí, por favor. Ahora dígame, ¿prefiere ventanilla, pasillo o en el centro?*
VIAJERO: *Pasillo, por favor. Y quisiera uno de los primeros asientos.*
AGENTE: *Lo siento, pero solo quedan asientos después de la fila 27. Le puedo dar el 28C.*
VIAJERO: *Bueno, está bien.*
AGENTE: *La puerta de salida es la número 8. Aquí tiene su pasaporte y tarjeta de embarque. Ahora, pase por seguridad y luego diríjase a la puerta de salida.*
VIAJERO: *Gracias, señor. ¿Tengo tiempo para hacer una llamada?*
AGENTE: *Sí, el avión sale en 45 minutos. No se preocupe. Que tenga un buen viaje.*

PRÁCTICA

12-9 

Para confirmar. Digan la palabra que corresponde a las siguientes descripciones. Después, describan otras partes del coche para ver si otra pareja sabe cómo se llama cada una.

1. Es para poner el equipaje. el maletero
2. Permite ver bien cuando llueve. el limpiaparabrisas
3. Son negras y llevan aire por dentro. las llantas
4. Controla la dirección del coche. el volante
5. Tiene letras y números, y sirve para identificar el coche. la placa
6. Le permite al conductor ver los carros que vienen detrás. el espejo retrovisor
7. Se abre para ver el motor, el radiador, etc. el capó
8. Protege al coche en caso de accidentes. el parachoques

12-10 

Mi auto favorito. Averigüen qué medio de transporte usa cada uno/a de ustedes con más frecuencia. Después, pregúntense cuál es el auto favorito de cada uno/a y por qué. Cada persona debe decir cuatro características del auto para explicar su preferencia.

Los autos y el transporte público

Aunque en los países hispanoamericanos se usa mucho el transporte público, el tráfico y la contaminación son problemas serios en las ciudades grandes. Además, cada vez es más difícil encontrar estacionamiento. Por eso se usan mucho las motos y los carros pequeños.

Comparaciones. ¿Qué medios de transporte hay en tu comunidad? ¿Cuáles son más populares entre los jóvenes? ¿Cuáles son más populares entre los mayores? ¿Qué problemas se asocian con el transporte en tu comunidad y tu región?

12-11 

Para evitar accidentes. Escriban un anuncio con recomendaciones para evitar accidentes de tráfico. El anuncio debe tener la siguiente información:

1. un título o eslogan
2. el nombre de la compañía o grupo que patrocina (*sponsors*) el anuncio
3. tres recomendaciones para evitar accidentes

12-12 

Antes de viajar. PREPARACIÓN. You will listen to a conversation between a man who is checking in at the airport and an airline employee. Before you listen, write two questions you think the employee will ask him and the answers you think the man will provide. Compare your answers with those of your partner.

ESCUCHA. Now listen to the exchange, and choose the appropriate ending to each statement.

1. El empleado le pide al viajero...
   a. su boleto de ida y vuelta.
   b. su tarjeta de embarque.
   c. su pasaporte y su pasaje.
2. El viajero va a facturar...
   a. tres maletas.
   b. un maletín de mano.
   c. dos maletas.
3. El viajero prefiere un asiento...
   a. al lado de la ventanilla.
   b. en el pasillo.
   c. en la parte posterior del avión.
4. El empleado le puede conseguir un asiento...
   a. de pasillo, el 28C.
   b. en el centro, entre la ventanilla y el pasillo.
   c. en la ventanilla en primera clase.
5. El empleado le dice al pasajero que...
   a. tiene tiempo para llamar por teléfono.
   b. puede llamar desde el avión.
   c. no tiene que pasar por seguridad.

MOSAICO cultural

El mochilero

Cuando Edmundo celebró su cumpleaños número 22 —al mismo tiempo que terminó la universidad— decidió hacer un viaje por los lugares más atractivos del mundo hispano. En junio, Edmundo tomó su mochila, que estaba cargada con poca ropa y sus utensilios de *camping*, y se fue de viaje con poco dinero.

▲ **De excursión por el bosque en Panamá**

Edmundo decidió hacer algo común entre los jóvenes hispanos: ser *mochilero*. El plan de *mochilero* significaba viajar sin muchas complicaciones, adaptándose a las circunstancias inmediatas. Edmundo tomaba el transporte que tenía a la mano y dormía en los lugares donde le permitían usar su tienda (*tent*). "Fue un periodo muy bonito, conocí a mucha gente linda y aprendí mucho de la cultura de varios lugares que no conocía", dijo Edmundo.

▲ **Subiendo a la cima de Machu Picchu**

Para empezar, Edmundo tomó un autobús que lo llevó desde su casa en La Paz, Bolivia, hasta Oruro, a mitad del camino entre La Paz y Sucre. Allá acampó por dos días y conoció a un par de mochileros norteamericanos que estaban de visita. Luego de dos días y muchas experiencias, Edmundo salió para Perú. Este viaje le tomó cuatro días, porque lo hizo *echando dedo* (haciendo autostop). Edmundo se ubicaba al lado de las autopistas y esperaba que alguien lo llevara hasta Machu Picchu. Es una forma arriesgada de viajar porque no es muy eficiente y puede ser peligrosa, pero es mucho más económica que comprar boletos de avión. Cuando llegó a Machu Picchu, Edmundo le envió una postal a su mamá: "Mami, pasé por el lago Titicaca, ¡me encantó! Monté en bus, canoa, bicitaxi y ¡en un burro!".

Ir de Bolivia a Perú fue el primer tramo (*stretch*) de un camino mochilero extenso que se conoce como la ruta del gringo. Recibe este nombre por la gran cantidad de norteamericanos que lo visitan. Después de Machu Picchu, otros destinos comunes son Bocas del Toro en Panamá, Antigua y Tikal en Guatemala, Moctezuma en Costa Rica, y por supuesto, Chichén Itzá y Tulum en México. Edmundo viajó por dos meses antes de volver a La Paz.

▲ **La playa Cocles, Costa Rica**

Compara

1. ¿En tu cultura hay una palabra equivalente a mochilero? ¿En qué contextos se usa?
2. ¿Has oído la expresión *echar dedo?* ¿Es algo común en tu país? ¿Has practicado el autostop? Explica con detalles.
3. En tu cultura, ¿existe un viaje simbólico que hacen los jóvenes para ser adultos? Explícalo con ejemplos.
4. ¿Te gustaría tener la experiencia de viajar como mochilero? ¿Qué lugares te gustaría visitar y qué precauciones tomarías?

Remind students how tourism is one of the main economic activities in Central America. Also, tell them that in tropical countries ecotourism is on the rise. Ecotourism follows the premise of environment sustainability and has a lesser impact in nature. Its main target is young people, especially *mochileros*.

For many young Hispanics taking a trip is a coming-of-age activity. There are several great stories about *mochileros* on the web, in personalized blogs that narrate the adventures these young women and men take. Remind students that Che Guevara himself started his socio-political campaign with a road trip across South America.

Explain to students that a *bicitaxi* is a modified bike used in coastal areas to transport passengers. It is an attractive means of transportation to some tourists and also provides jobs for those who live in these areas.

The *gringo trail* is not really a fixed itinerary, but rather a compilation of the landmarks most frequently visited by tourists. You may wish to explain that the word *gringo* refers to tourists who don't speak Spanish, or who don't speak it well. It usually refers to people from the United States or another English-speaking country.

Note
Explain that *nunca* and *jamás* may be used interchangeably, although *jamás* is more emphatic. For dramatic emphasis, you may wish to use them together: *Nunca jamás me van a gustar los viajes largos en auto.*

Funciones y formas

1 Expressing affirmation and negation

JOSEFINA: Alberto, tenemos que hablar de nuestro viaje a Costa Rica. **Siempre** trato de buscar alojamiento económico, pero no me gusta **ningún** hotel de hotelesbaratos.com. **Todos** parecen viejos y malos. Ese sitio web casi **nunca** nos da buenas recomendaciones; no lo voy a usar más.

ALBERTO: A mí **tampoco** me gusta ese sitio. **Nunca** encuentro **nada** que me guste. ¿Por qué no le pedimos una recomendación a tu amiga Maricelle? Es de San José, ¿no?

JOSEFINA: Buena idea. Seguramente tendrá **algunas** recomendaciones.

Piénsalo. Indica quién hace cada una de las afirmaciones a continuación: Josefina (**J**) o Alberto (**A**).

1. __J__ **Siempre** trato de buscar alojamiento económico.
2. __J__ No me gusta **ningún** hotel de hotelesbaratos.com.
3. __J__ Casi **nunca** nos da buenas recomendaciones.
4. __A__ A mí **tampoco** me gusta ese sitio.
5. __A__ **Nunca** encuentro **nada** que me guste.
6. __J__ Seguramente tendrá **algunas** recomendaciones.

Affirmative and negative expressions

- You have already seen and used some affirmative and negative expressions in previous chapters. In this section you will study the most frequently used expressions.

AFFIRMATIVE		NEGATIVE	
algo	*something, anything*	**nada**	*nothing*
todo	*everything*		
alguien	*someone, anyone*	**nadie**	*no one, nobody*
todos/as	*everybody, all*		
algún, alguno/a (-os, -as)	*some, any, several*	**ningún, ninguno/a**	*no, not any, none*
o... o	*either ... or*	**ni... ni**	*neither ... nor*
siempre	*always*	**nunca**	*never, (not) ever*

AFFIRMATIVE		NEGATIVE	
una vez	*once*		
alguna vez	*sometime, ever*	**jamás**	*never, (not) ever*
algunas veces	*sometimes*		
a veces	*at times*		
también	*also, too*	**tampoco**	*neither, not*

- Negative words may precede or follow the verb. If they follow the verb, use the word **no** before the verb.

  Nadie va a ese museo.
  No va **nadie** a ese museo. — *No one/Nobody goes to that museum.*

- **Alguno** and **ninguno** shorten to **algún** and **ningún** before masculine singular nouns.

  ¿Ves **algún** monumento interesante? — *Do you see any interesting monuments?*
  No veo **ningún** monumento interesante. — *I do not see any interesting monuments.*

- Use the personal **a** when **alguno/a/os/as** and **ninguno/a** refer to persons and are the direct object of the verb. Use it also with **alguien** and **nadie** since they always refer to people. Note that negative statements are expressed in the singular.

  ¿Conoces a **alguno** de los guías? — *Do you know any of the guides?*
  No, no conozco **a ninguno.** — *No, I do not know any (of them).*
  ¿Conoces **alguna** de las agencias de turismo? — *Do you know any tourism agencies?*
  No, no conozco **ninguna.** — *No, I do not know any (of them).*

¿COMPRENDES?

Completa las afirmaciones para expresar lo contrario.

1. **Siempre** trato de buscar alojamiento económico. __Nunca__ trato de buscar alojamiento ecónomico. Prefiero los hoteles de lujo.
2. No me gusta __ningún__ hotel de este sitio web porque son baratos y malos. Pero a Marcos le gustan __todos__ porque no tiene mucho dinero.
3. **Nunca** encuentro **nada** que me guste. Maricelle tiene mejor suerte. Ella __siempre__ encuentra __algunos__ hoteles que le gustan.
4. **Algunos** de mis amigos se alojan en albergues cuando viajan. Pero __ningún__ amigo de mis padres se aloja allí. Las personas mayores prefieren los hoteles.

MySpanishLab
Learn more using Amplifire Dynamic Study Modules, Grammar Tutorials, and Extra Practice activities.

PRÁCTICA

Nada de nada. Asocia cada pregunta con su probable respuesta. Luego, comparen sus respuestas y añadan una pregunta más para hacerle a su compañero/a.

1. __e__ ¿Visitaste Panamá alguna vez?
2. __d__ ¿Conoces a alguien en Costa Rica?
3. __b__ ¿Bailas alguno de los bailes típicos de la región?
4. __c__ ¿Sabe alguien quién escribió la novela *Pasiones griegas?*
5. __a__ ¿Conoces alguna canción de Maribel Guardia?
6. ...

a. No, ninguna.
b. No, ninguno.
c. No, nadie.
d. No, a nadie.
e. No, nunca.

Note for 12-13
The author of *Pasiones griegas* is Roberto Ampuero, a Chilean writer based in the U.S. In January 2012 he was appointed the Chilean ambassador to Mexico, and in June 2013 he was named the Chilean Minister of Culture. Maribel Guardia, born in Costa Rica, was elected Miss Costa Rica in the 1978 beauty pageant. In the 1980s she moved to Mexico to develop her acting and singing career. She often appears in TV series and variety shows today, and currently lives in Florida.

Follow-up for 12-14
Have students change partners and share the information they have just gathered with their new partner.

12-14 

¿Con qué frecuencia? Indica con qué frecuencia haces cada una de las actividades de la tabla siguiente y explica por qué las haces. Después pregúntale a tu compañero/a.

 ver una película en español

E1: *Veo una película en español todas las semanas porque me gusta escuchar la lengua. ¿Y tú?*

E2: *Yo nunca veo películas en español porque no me gustan los subtítulos.*

ACTIVIDAD	YO	RAZÓN	COMPAÑERO/A	RAZÓN
viajar a otro países				
salir de vacaciones con amigos				
hacer reservaciones en Internet				
comprar pasajes de avión en Internet				
usar transporte público				
ir a restaurantes mexicanos				
ver películas extranjeras				

Cultura

Ecoturismo

Costa Rica y Panamá, en general, han decidido apostar por un ecoturismo de calidad en vez de un turismo de masas. En este sentido, Costa Rica fue el país pionero. Apoyado en una estabilidad política y económica singular dentro de la zona, Costa Rica fue uno de los primeros países en crear una extensa red de parques naturales y áreas protegidas donde se respetan la biodiversidad y el equilibrio medioambiental. Hoy en día esta red ocupa casi el 25% de la superficie total del país gracias a las decisiones del gobierno costarricense en los años 80.

Comparaciones. ¿Cuáles son las ventajas del ecoturismo? ¿Prefieres hacer ecoturismo o turismo más convencional? Explica.

Warm-up for 12-15
In this activity, since the partner's visit to Costa Rica already took place, students should use the preterit in their questions and responses. Call attention to the verb forms in the *Modelo* and ask some additional questions before students do the activity in pairs.

Suggestion for 12-15
You may wish to have students change roles (asker or responder) midway through the activity or change partners, each time taking a different role.

12-15 

Una excursión de ecoturismo. Estás en Costa Rica y vas a hacer una excursión de ecoturismo. Tu compañero/a ya hizo la excursión y piensa que fue un desastre. Él/Ella va a contestar tus preguntas negativamente. Añade una pregunta más.

 ofrecer excursiones

E1: *¿Ofrecieron excursiones para ver la fauna y la flora?*

E2: *No, no ofrecieron ninguna excursión.*

1. ver tortugas en la playa
2. ver las vistas panorámicas
3. comer un almuerzo típico costarricense
4. dejar entrar a muchas áreas protegidas
5. …

12-16 

¡La negatividad es contagiosa! Después de pasar tus vacaciones con tu amigo/a negativo/a, te sientes influenciado/a y contestas a todo negativamente. Túrnense para preguntarse y añadan alguna actividad más.

 llamar a un amigo

E1: *¿Vas a llamar a un amigo?*

E2: *No, no voy a llamar a nadie. ¿Y tú vas a… ?*

1. visitar Panamá alguna vez en el futuro
2. ver alguna película latinoamericana este fin de semana
3. leer un artículo sobre los siete pueblos indígenas de Panamá
4. invitar a alguien a ver un documental sobre los parques nacionales de Costa Rica
5. …

Comarca Guna Yala

Guna Yala, conocida como San Blas hasta 1998, es una región de Panamá que incluye parte de la costa caribeña de Panamá y numerosas islas pequeñas a las que se accede en barco. Es la tierra de los gunas, un pueblo indígena que ha luchado por sus derechos sobre la tierra. En la tierra de los gunas se mantienen activas tradiciones locales en torno a la agricultura y pesca, aunque últimamente se ha desarrollado una industria turística basada en el ecoturismo.

Comparaciones. ¿Existen en tu país comunidades como las de Guna Yala? ¿Qué tradiciones tienen? ¿Qué actividades se asocian con esta comunidad?

Planeando un viaje. **PREPARACIÓN.** Quieren hacer un viaje a Panamá para conocer su cultura. Comenten qué van a hacer allí.

MODELO pasar unos días en la capital

E1: *Quiero pasar unos días en la capital.*

E2: *Yo también. Es una ciudad interesante.*

1. conocer la Comarca Guna Yala
2. comprar unos textiles de mola, hechos por artesanos indígenas gunas
3. hacer una excursión al Canal de Panamá
4. tomar una clase de cumbia, un baile folclórico
5. asistir a un partido de fútbol

INTERCAMBIOS. Conversen sobre dos o tres actividades que quieren hacer en Panamá. Después, reúnanse con otra pareja, explíquenle sus planes y escuchen los planes de sus compañeros/as. Respondan negativamente a los planes de la otra pareja.

Situación

PREPARACIÓN. Lean esta situación. Luego, compartan ejemplos de vocabulario, gramática y demás información que necesitan para desarrollar la conversación.

Role A. You call a travel agency to purchase tickets for an all-day excursion. When the clerk answers, ask:

a. if sometimes they offer free tickets for students;
b. if they have any tickets for Friday or Saturday; and
c. whether lunch at a restaurant is included in the price.

You may express your annoyance at all the negative answers you receive when you thank the clerk for his/her help.

Role B. You work in a travel agency. A customer calls to ask about tickets for an excursion. Reply that:

a. they never give free tickets to anyone (not students, not young children);
b. there aren't any tickets for the days the customer inquires about; and
c. there will be two breaks for snacks (**merienda**), but not a restaurant meal.

You are in a bad mood and you let it show during the conversation.

	ROLE A	ROLE B
Vocabulario	Question words Travel vocabulary	Travel vocabulary
Funciones y formas	Asking questions Expressing annoyance in a formal setting	Giving information Expressions of negation Expressing annoyance in a formal setting

INTERCAMBIOS. Practica la conversación con tu compañero/a incorporando el vocabulario, las funciones y demás información. Luego, represéntenla ante la clase.

Warm-up for 12-17
Have students tell you what they want to do: *Quiero aprender unas frases en la lengua guna.* You agree: *Yo también.* Then have students tell you what they do not want to do: *No quiero ir a la ópera...* You agree: *Yo tampoco.*

Suggestion for 12-17
You may wish to highlight the cultural information in this activity by referring students to the photos in the chapter opener and the *Enfoque cultural* section of this chapter. You may want to explain that *cumbia* is a popular dance style that began as a courtship dance among African slaves on the Caribbean coast of what is now Colombia, and spread throughout South and Central America, mixing African percussion, indigenous Amerindian flutes, and later, European brass and orchestral instruments. Culturally, *cumbia* is most associated with Colombia. Encourage students to search the Internet for videos of *cumbia* music and dancing.

Suggestion for 12-17, *Intercambios*
Have students brainstorm ways to respond negatively to others' plans: *Nunca voy a los parques nacionales. No me gusta caminar mucho. No he ido jamás a ningún partido de fútbol.*

Suggestions
Use visuals to illustrate existent versus nonexistent antecedents versus antecedents whose existence is unknown. For example, a scene in a bus terminal: *Hay pasajeros que llevan mucho equipaje. Hay personas que están tomando café porque hace frío, pero no hay nadie que esté tomando helado.* Present comparisons: *Sí, hay personas que toman café.* (Existent) *No, no hay nadie que tome helado, porque hace mucho frío.* (Nonexistent) *Los niños buscan una tienda que venda refrescos y dulces.* (Existence unknown)

Suggestion for *Piénsalo*
Guide students to make the connection between situations that exist + the indicative vs. situations that do not exist or that possibly exist + the subjunctive.

Suggestion
The concept of known versus unknown antecedent may be difficult for students to grasp, especially because sentences of both types may have identical English translations. You may wish to provide additional examples in which the personal *a* signals the difference between the two kinds of antecedents: *busco un profesor que enseñe español* vs. *busco al profesor que enseña español.*

Suggestion
Ask questions with *hay,* using the indicative and the subjunctive: *¿Hay una clase que termina/termine a las cuatro?* Point out that when the speaker is not sure or has no knowledge of the existence of the antecedent, he/she uses the subjunctive.

2 Talking about things that may not exist

MUJER: Por favor, ¿dónde está el tren que **sale** a las 9:00?

AGENTE: No hay trenes que **salgan** por la noche, señorita. El último tren salió a las 6:00 de la tarde.

MUJER: ¡Ay, Dios mío! ¿Hay un tren que **salga** temprano por la mañana?

AGENTE: Sí, señorita. El primer tren sale a las 7:00.

MUJER: Bueno, tendré que esperar hasta mañana, entonces. ¿Me puede recomendar un hotel que **esté** cerca? Necesito uno que no **sea** caro.

AGENTE: Sí, cómo no. Le recomiendo el Hotel Colonial. Es un buen hotel que **tiene** precios baratos.

Piénsalo. Para cada oración, indica si la persona habla de algo que existe (**E**), de algo que no existe (**NE**) o de algo que posiblemente exista (**PE**).

1. __E__ ¿Dónde está el tren que **sale** a las 9:00?
2. __NE__ No hay trenes que **salgan** por la noche.
3. __PE__ ¿Hay un tren que **salga** temprano por la mañana?
4. __PE__ ¿Me puede recomendar un hotel que **esté** cerca?
5. __PE__ Necesito un hotel que no **sea** caro.
6. __E__ Es un buen hotel que **tiene** precios baratos (*moderate*).

Subjunctive in adjective clauses

- As you have learned, the subjunctive in Spanish is used primarily in sentences that have two clauses. In this section, you will learn about using the subjunctive in adjective clauses.

LENGUA

Que introduces a dependent clause, and it may refer to persons or things.

El cuarto **que** reservé es muy caro.	*The room I reserved is very expensive.*
Ese es el agente **que** me alquiló el coche.	*That is the agent who rented the car for me.*

Use **quien(es)** after a preposition when referring to people.

Allí está el recepcionista **con quien** hablé esta mañana.	*There is the receptionist with whom I spoke this morning.*

- Both adjectives and adjective clauses provide descriptive information about a noun in the independent clause.

Vamos a ir a un hotel muy **moderno.** (ADJECTIVE)

Vamos a ir a un hotel **que es muy moderno.** (ADJECTIVE CLAUSE)

- Use the indicative in an adjective clause that refers to a person, place, or thing (antecedent) that exists or is known. Use the subjunctive in an adjective clause that refers to a person, place, or thing that does not exist or whose existence is unknown or in question. Study the examples to see the differences.

INDICATIVE	SUBJUNCTIVE
Hay un buen hotel que **queda** cerca de la playa. *There is a good hotel that is near the beach.* (You are familiar with the hotel.)	Busco un buen hotel que **quede** cerca de la playa. *I am looking for a good hotel that is near the beach.* (The existence of such a hotel is uncertain or unknown to you.)
Visité el museo que **tiene** una exposición de molas. *I visited the museum that has a molas exhibit.* (You went there, so there is such a museum.)	Aquí no hay ningún museo que **tenga** una exposición de molas. *There is no museums here that has a molas exhibit.* (There is no such museum.)

¿COMPRENDES?

Completa las oraciones con el indicativo o el subjuntivo de los verbos.

1. Buscamos un guía que (ofrece/ofrezca) excursiones a las pirámides. ofrezca
2. Buscamos a alguien que (trabaja/trabaje) los sábados. trabaje
3. No conozco a nadie que (visita/visite) Costa Rica este año. visite
4. Encontramos un hotel que (está/esté) en el centro. está
5. Hay tres itinerarios que me (gustan/gusten). gustan
6. Necesito un restaurante que (sirve/sirva) comida vegetariana. sirva

MySpanishLab

Learn more using Amplifire Dynamic Study Modules, Grammar Tutorials, and Extra Practice activities..

LENGUA

Use the personal **a** before specific persons or animals that function as direct objects. If the person or animal is unknown or specific, use the subjunctive and do not use the personal **a.** Always use the personal **a** before **alguien** and **nadie.**

Busco **a** la auxiliar que trabaja en ese vuelo.
I am looking for the (specific) flight attendant who is working on that flight.

Busco **una** auxiliar que **trabaje** en ese vuelo.
I am looking for a (any) flight attendant who is (happens to be) working on that flight.

Busco **a** alguien que me **acompañe** al museo.
I am looking for someone who will go with me to the museum.

LENGUA

In questions, use the indicative or the subjunctive according to the degree of certainty you have about the matter. For example, if you want to ask: *Are there any travelers here who are leaving on flight 420?*

If you don't know for sure but think there are, then use the indicative:
¿Hay viajeros aquí que **salen** en el vuelo 420?

If you don't know, but doubt there are, then use the subjunctive:
¿Hay viajeros aquí que **salgan** en el vuelo 420?

PRÁCTICA

12-18

¿Cuál es la respuesta correcta? Selecciona el indicativo o el subjuntivo de los verbos indicados, según el contexto.

1. No hay ningún vuelo que __b__ por la noche. **a.** sale **b.** salga
2. Pero hay un vuelo que __a__ a las 7:00 de la mañana. **a.** queda **b.** quede
3. Me interesa encontrar un hotel (*any hotel*) que __b__ cerca del centro. **a.** habla **b.** hable
4. Hay un hotel que no es muy caro y que __a__ en el centro.
5. Busco al empleado que __a__ inglés.
6. ¿Hay algún empleado (*any employee*) en este departamento que __b__ inglés?

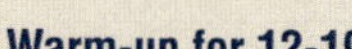

Warm-up for 12-19
You may wish to practice again the use of the indicative and the subjunctive with *hay alguien* and *no hay nadie* before doing the activity:
—*¿Hay alguien/una persona en esta clase que viaje en avión con frecuencia?*
—*Sí, hay alguien que viaja…*
—*¿Quién es?*
—*Es… ¿Hay alguien que haga viajes largos en auto por lo menos una vez al año?*
—*No, no hay nadie que haga…/Sí, hay alguien que hace…*

Suggestion for 12-19
Encourage students to make up additional questions using the subjunctive. You may practice the use of *ningún* and *ninguna* when doing this activity.

Audioscript for *En directo*
CONSERJE: *Hotel Paraíso. ¿En qué puedo servirle?*
CLIENTE: *Señor, ¿tiene un cuarto doble disponible para esta noche?*
CONSERJE: *No tenemos ningún cuarto libre. Estamos con capacidad completa.*
CLIENTE: *Pero, ¿no hay ninguna posibilidad de conseguir un cuarto sencillo?*
CONSERJE: *Lo siento, pero no hay nada disponible, señor.*
CLIENTE: *¡Esto es increíble! Parece que todo el mundo decidió venir a este lugar hoy. No dormiré nada esta noche.*

12-19

Por curiosidad. Túrnense para hacerse preguntas sobre la familia de cada uno/a. Respondan con detalles adicionales.

MODELO tu familia/dormir mucho durante los viajes largos en auto.
E1: *¿Hay alguien en tu familia que duerma mucho durante los viajes largos en auto?*
E2: *Sí, mi hermano siempre duerme mucho en el auto. El año pasado fuimos a la casa de mis abuelos y él durmió durante todo el viaje.*

1. tu familia/viajar mucho
2. tus amigos/trabajar en vez de viajar durante las vacaciones de la primavera
3. tus amigos/conocer los lugares más interesantes de Costa Rica
4. tu familia/saber pilotear un avión
5. tus amigos/ir a esquiar en sus vacaciones
6. tu familia/viajar a Panamá este año

12-20

Emergencia en el aeropuerto. Túrnense para hacer los papeles de dos jefes de personal de una aerolínea que buscan empleados que puedan hacer ciertos trabajos. Sigan el modelo.

programar la computadora (alguien)
E1: *Necesito a alguien que programe la computadora para los itinerarios.*
E2: *No hay nadie en el aeropuerto que pueda programarla.*
E1: *Bueno, es necesario buscar a alguien que lo haga.*

1. hablar inglés, japonés y español para el vuelo a Tamarindo (auxiliar)
2. recibir el vuelo que viene de Puerto Jiménez (agente)
3. darles esta información a los pasajeros del vuelo 562 (empleado/a)
4. llevar a los pasajeros a inmigración (empleado/a)
5. poder trabajar este fin de semana (dos auxiliares)
6. …

En directo

To express annoyance at something in a formal or business setting:

Perdón, pero ¿está seguro/a de que…?
Excuse me, but are you sure that … ?

¡Esto es increíble!
This is incredible.

Perdón, pero ¿no hay ninguna posibilidad de + *infinitive*?
Sorry, but isn't there any chance to …?

Listen to a conversation with these expressions.

12-21 

Un lugar para ir de vacaciones. PREPARACIÓN. Túrnense para hacerse preguntas sobre un lugar adonde ir de vacaciones. Contesten según la información de la tabla.

 hotel/tener piscina

E1: *¿Hay un hotel que tenga piscina?*

E2: *Sí, hay un hotel que tiene piscina./No, no hay ningún hotel que tenga piscina.*

HAY	NO HAY
tiendas/vender ropa para esquiar	autobús/llegar por la mañana
cines/dar películas en español	cafetería/servir comida vegetariana
restaurantes/tener cajero automático	restaurantes/aceptar cheques personales

INTERCAMBIOS. Ahora ustedes deben describir cómo es su lugar ideal de vacaciones, explicando su ubicación, ambiente y atracciones. Después, intercambien ideas con otra pareja.

 E1: *Quiero ir de vacaciones a una isla que tenga playas blancas y un ambiente tranquilo. ¿Y tú?*

E2: *Mi lugar de vacaciones ideal es diferente. Quiero ir a una ciudad que tenga muchos conciertos y obras de teatro.*

Suggestion for 12-21, *Intercambios*
Have students brainstorm in small groups basic requirements they look for in a vacation spot. You may wish to classify the information as follows:
1. *comodidades/atracciones en los hoteles;*
2. *lugares de interés en la ciudad/el pueblo;*
3. *actividades interesantes en el lugar;*
4. *medios de transporte público;*
5. *tipo de tiendas;*
6. *características de los restaurantes/bares, etc.*

Situación

PREPARACIÓN. Lean esta situación. Luego, compartan ejemplos de vocabulario, gramática y otra información que necesitan para desarrollar la conversación.

Role A. Your family owns a small inn near the college that houses international faculty who visit the campus. You need to hire two people for your staff, so you call an employment agency. Explain that you are looking for:

a. a receptionist who speaks French, German, or Spanish (preferably two of those languages) and who has experience as a secretary; and

b. a chef who is familiar with European cuisines and who is able to work nights and weekends.

Role B. You work at an employment agency, and you receive a call from an innkeeper who is looking for a receptionist and a chef. Listen to the innkeeper's requirements and ask about any other qualifications that may be desired. Tell the innkeeper you will start looking right away.

	ROLE A	ROLE B
Vocabulario	Question words Employment qualifications Words and expressions related to cooking Time and schedules	Question words Employment qualifications Words and expressions related to cooking Time and schedules
Funciones y formas	Asking questions Giving information Subjunctive with adjectival clauses to express uncertainty	Asking questions Giving information Subjunctive with adjectival clauses to express uncertainty Expressing reassurance and guarantee of assistance

INTERCAMBIOS. Practica la conversación con tu compañero/a incorporando el vocabulario, las funciones y demás información. Luego, represéntenla ante la clase.

Suggestions
Remind students that pronouns are used to avoid repetition of the noun. Provide examples: *¿Tienes tu mochila? ¿Dónde está la mía? Mi lugar favorito de vacaciones es la playa. Yo siempre hago mis reservaciones para viajar en Internet. Y tú, ¿cómo haces las tuyas? Las maletas que llevo durante mis viajes son viejas. Y las tuyas, ¿son viejas también?*

Practice possessive pronoun forms by holding up items that belong to various students and saying: *¿Es mi mochila? No, es la suya,* etc.

3 Expressing possession

MADRE: Ramiro, mi maleta casi está lista. ¿Y **la tuya?**

RAMIRO: ¡**La mía** no! Después del programa la empaco. ¿Ya empacaste tus libros, mamá?

MADRE: **Los míos** ya están en mi maletín. ¿Y las muñecas (*dolls*) de Susana?

RAMIRO: **Las suyas** están en su mochila, pero **las de** Laurita no sé dónde están.

Piénsalo. Lee las siguientes afirmaciones de la conversación anterior. Indica a qué se refieren las palabras en negrita.

1. *¡**La mía** no!*
   La mía se refiere _____.
   a. al programa de Ramiro
   (b.) a la maleta de Ramiro
2. ***Los míos** ya están en mi maletín.*
   Los míos se refiere a _____.
   (a.) los libros de la madre
   b. las muñecas de Susana
3. ***Las suyas** están en su mochila.*
   Las suyas se refiere a _____.
   a. los maletines de mano
   (b.) las muñecas de Susana
4. ***Las de Laurita** están en su cuarto.*
   Las de Laurita se refiere a _____.
   a. sus libros
   (b.) sus muñecas

Possessive pronouns

- Possessive pronouns express ownership or possession. They are used to avoid repetition of the noun to which they refer.

SINGULAR		PLURAL	
Masculine	**Feminine**	**Masculine**	**Feminine**
el mío	la mía	los míos	las mías
el tuyo	la tuya	los tuyos	las tuyas
el suyo	la suya	los suyos	las suyas
el nuestro	la nuestra	los nuestros	las nuestras
el vuestro	la vuestra	los vuestros	las vuestras

- The definite article precedes the possessive pronoun, and both article and pronoun agree in gender and number with the noun to which they refer.

¿Tienes la mochila de Mario?	*Do you have Mario's backpack?*
Sí, tengo **la suya** y **la mía** también.	*Yes, I have his and mine too.*

- After the verb **ser,** the article is usually omitted.

Esa maleta es **mía.**	*That suitcase is mine.*

- To be clearer and more specific, the following structures may be used to replace any corresponding form of **el suyo/la suya.**

la de usted	*yours* (singular)
la de él	*his*
la de ella	*hers*
la mochila suya → **la suya** or	
la de ustedes	*yours* (plural)
la de ellos	*theirs* (masculine, plural)
la de ellas	*theirs* (feminine, plural)

LENGUA

Stressed possessive adjectives, which have the same forms as possessive pronouns, emphasize to whom a particular object belongs. Because they are adjectives, they always immediately follow the noun to which they refer. They are often used to emphasize a contrast.

El cuarto mío es grandísimo.	*My room is very big.*
La maleta tuya está en la recepción.	*Your suitcase is at the front desk.*
Las llaves nuestras están encima del escritorio.	*Our keys are on the desk.*
Esos primos míos llegan hoy.	*Those cousins of mine arrive today.*

¿COMPRENDES?

Usa una expresión con el pronombre correcto para indicar posesión.

1. mi maleta: __la__ __mía__
2. los pasajes de ustedes: __los__ __suyos__
3. nuestras llaves: __las__ __nuestras__
4. el viaje de ellos: __el__ __suyo__
5. tus planes: __los__ __tuyos__
6. el equipaje de Marta y Sara: __el__ __suyo__

MySpanishLab

Learn more using Amplifire Dynamic Study Modules, Grammar Tutorials, and Extra Practice activities..

PRÁCTICA

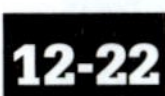  

12-22

¿De quién(es) son estas cosas? **PREPARACIÓN.** En la clase de español decidieron hacer un viaje de estudios a Costa Rica. En este momento van a tomar el bus para ir al aeropuerto. Escoge la respuesta correcta para cada una de las preguntas. Compara tus respuestas con las de tu compañero/a.

1. Miguel, ¿es tuya esta mochila?	**a.** Sí, es mía.	**b.** Sí, es tuya.
2. ¿Son estas maletas de Pedro?	**a.** Sí, son suyas.	**b.** Sí, son mías.
3. ¿El maletín de color café es de Alicia?	**a.** No, es tuya.	**b.** No, no es suyo.
4. Este mapa de San José, ¿es tuyo?	**a.** Sí, es mía.	**b.** Sí, es mío.
5. ¿Son nuestros estos boletos?	**a.** Sí, son suyos.	**b.** Sí, son suyas.

INTERCAMBIOS. Ve por la clase y pregunta a varios compañeros/as de quién son algunos de los objetos que ves o encuentras.

12-23 

¿Quién tiene carro? **PREPARACIÓN.** Entrevístense para saber quién(es) tiene(n) carro. Hablen de sus carros: marca, modelo, año y color. Tomen apuntes sobre la información.

E1: *Mi carro es un Toyota Corolla rojo del 2009. ¿Y el tuyo?*

E2: *El mío es un Ford Focus azul del 2012.*

E3: *Yo no tengo carro, pero mi hermana me presta el suyo de vez en cuando. Es una camioneta negra del 2002.*

INTERCAMBIOS. Combinen la información de todos los grupos y preparen un informe sobre las características más comunes de los carros de los miembros de la clase.

Suggestion for 12-23, *Preparación*
You may create a category of cars owned by friends or family members so that students who do not have their own vehicles may talk about them.

Note for 12-24
GPS in Spanish is *Sistema de Posicionamiento Global.* However, people commonly call it GPS [ge-pe-ese].

Suggestion for *Situación*
For the *Situación,* students may need to prepare ahead of time so they can talk about their ecotourism activities in Costa Rica. Students may want to practice online with a partner. Remind them that they can click on the microphone icon to connect with a partner online and do the activity.

12-24 

Preparándose para un viaje. Van a hacer un viaje en auto y deben tomar varias decisiones antes de salir. Háganse preguntas para decidir lo que van a hacer y den una razón.

 usar mi coche o tu coche

E1: *¿Vamos a usar mi coche o el tuyo?*

E2: *Prefiero usar el tuyo porque es más nuevo.*

1. llevar tus maletas o las de mi hermano
2. usar mis mapas o tus mapas
3. llevar tu cámara o mi cámara
4. llevar tu portátil o mi portátil
5. usar tu GPS o el de mis padres

Situación  

PREPARACIÓN. Lean esta situación. Luego, compartan ejemplos de vocabulario, gramática y otra información que necesitan para desarrollar la conversación.

Role A. On the plane home from an ecotourism trip to Costa Rica, you sit next to a student returning from a similar trip. Ask your seatmate:

a. why he/she went on an ecotourism trip;
b. what national park he/she liked best, and why;
c. one thing he/she learned from the trip; and
d. whether he/she has plans to return to Costa Rica.

Answer your seatmate's questions about your trip.

Role B. On the plane home from an ecotourism trip to Costa Rica, you sit next to a student returning from a similar trip. After answering your seatmate's questions, ask him/her similar questions about his/her trip. Comment on how your experience was similar to that of your seatmate.

	ROLE A	ROLE B
Vocabulario	Greetings Question words Vacation activities Ecoturism activities Future plans	Greetings Question words Vacation activities Ecoturism activities Future plans
Funciones y formas	Talking about a past experience: Possessive pronouns Preterite Discussing plans: Future tense Making small talk	Asking and answering questions about the past and future: Possessive pronouns Preterite Future Comparisons of equality and inequality Making small talk

INTERCAMBIOS. Practica la conversación con tu compañero/a incorporando el vocabulario, las funciones y demás información. Luego, represéntenla ante la clase.

4 Expressing doubt and uncertainty

ANA MARÍA: ¡Qué buenos son! Es seguro que **ganan** el premio.

JULIO: No creo que **sean** tan buenos, y dudo que **salgan** bien en el concurso.

ANA MARÍA: Es posible que **tengan** éxito, ¿no?

JULIO: Creo que no. No tienen ni melodía ni ritmo. Es dudoso que **ganen.**

Piénsalo. Indica (✓) si las siguientes afirmaciones expresan certeza (*certainty*) o duda (*doubt*).

	CERTEZA	DUDA
1. Es seguro que **ganan** el premio.	✓	
2. No creo que **sean** tan buenos.		✓
3. Dudo que **salgan** bien en el concurso.		✓
4. Es posible que **tengan** éxito.		✓
5. Es dudoso que **ganen.**		✓

Subjunctive with expressions of doubt

You learned in *Capítulo 11* to use the subjunctive to express emotions, opinions, expectations, and wishes. In this chapter you will learn to use the subjunctive for a related communicative function: to express doubt and uncertainty.

- When the verb in the main clause expresses doubt or uncertainty, use a subjunctive verb form in the dependent clause (the clause that begins with **que**).

  Dudo que **vendan** libros en español. — *I doubt (that) they sell books in Spanish.*

  Es dudoso que el guía **llegue** tarde a la excursión. — *It's unlikely (that) the guide will arrive late to the tour.*

Suggestion for *Funciones y formas*
You may want to review the *Piénsalo* dialogue. Remind students to make the connection between certainty and the indicative versus doubt/uncertainty and the subjunctive.

Suggestions
Give examples of impersonal expressions followed by the indicative: *Es verdad que mis alumnos hablan español. Es obvio que hablan bien.* Then give related examples of impersonal expressions followed by the subjunctive: *Es probable que estudien los domingos. Es posible que practiquen dos o tres horas todos los días.*

Talk about an upcoming competition with which students are familiar. Students react by using *Dudo que...*

Make statements to elicit opinions from students: *La comida de la cafetería es excelente.* Students answer using *Sí, creo que...* or *Dudo que...* and state their opinion.

¿COMPRENDES?

Completa las oraciones con la forma correcta de los verbos.

1. Es seguro que el avión llega (llegar) tarde.
2. Es posible que llueva (llover) el día de la excursión.
3. Dudo que la compañía nos dé (dar) boletos para otro día.
4. Creo que los autobuses tienen (tener) un horario diferente los domingos.
5. Quizás sea (ser) mejor tomar un taxi.
6. Es verdad que los turistas se divierten (divertirse) mucho en Costa Rica.

MySpanishLab

Learn more using Amplifire Dynamic Study Modules, Grammar Tutorials, and Extra Practice activities.

- Use the subjunctive with impersonal expressions that denote doubt or uncertainty, such as **es dudoso que, es difícil que, es probable que,** and **es posible que.**

Es dudoso que **encontremos** artesanía panameña en ese mercado.	*It is doubtful that we will find Panamanian handicrafts in that market.*
Es posible que **tengan** textiles.	*It is possible that they have textiles.*

- Use the indicative with impersonal expressions that denote certainty: **es cierto/verdad que, es seguro que,** and **es obvio que.** When these expressions are negative, the following verb is in the subjunctive.

Es verdad que el tamborito y la cumbia **son** bailes populares en Panamá.	*It is true that the tamborito and the cumbia are popular dances in Panama.*
No es cierto que los bailes panameños se **conozcan** mucho en Estados Unidos.	*It is not true that Panamanian dances are well known in the United States.*

- When the verbs **creer** and **pensar** are used in the negative, the subjunctive is used in the dependent clause. In questions with these verbs, the subjunctive may be used to express uncertainty or to anticipate a negative response. If the question simply seeks information, use the indicative.

SUBJUNCTIVE	
Hace sol. No creo que **llueva.**	*It is sunny out. I don't think it will rain.*
¿Crees que **haga** calor en San José?	*Do you think it is/will be hot in San José?* (I am not sure.)

INDICATIVE	
¿Crees que **llueve** mucho en la costa?	*Do you think it rains a lot on the coast?* (I think so, and I am seeking confirmation.)

- Since the expressions **tal vez** and **quizá(s)** convey uncertainty, the subjunctive is normally used.

Tal vez el conjunto **toque** un tamborito panameño.	*Perhaps the group will play a tamborito panameño.*
Quizá(s) todos **empiecen** a bailar.	*Perhaps everyone will start to dance.*

PRÁCTICA

12-25 

¿Están de acuerdo? Lee las siguientes opiniones y marca (✓) si estás de acuerdo o no. Luego, compara tus respuestas con las de tu compañero/a. Explíquense las razones de sus respuestas.

	SÍ	NO
1. Yo creo que los bailes folclóricos son fáciles de aprender.	_____	_____
2. Yo dudo que el transporte público sea más popular en Estados Unidos que en América Latina.	_____	_____
3. Creo que los parques nacionales de Costa Rica son muy importantes para la ecología del planeta.	_____	_____
4. Es posible que viajar en tren sea más costoso que viajar en avión.	_____	_____
5. Es obvio que el precio de la gasolina en Estados Unidos afecta el turismo.	_____	_____
6. No creo que los estudiantes hoy viajen a otros países tanto como viajaban los estudiantes hace veinte años.	_____	_____

En directo

To report agreement:

Todos creemos/pensamos que...
We all believe/think that...

Nosotros estamos de acuerdo con que...
We all agree that...

To report different opinions:

No hay consenso entre nosotros/ellos. Unos piensan que..., otros creen que...
We/They do not agree. Some think that..., while others believe that...

 Listen to a conversation with these expressions.

Note for *En directo*
Before doing activity 12-25, have students read the expressions in *En directo.* Then have them listen to the dialogue and encourage them to use the expressions in their own conversation.

Audioscript for *En directo*
ALICIA: *¿Qué planes tiene tu familia este año para ir de vacaciones?*
PALOMA: *Ninguno. Todos tenemos alguna idea pero no hay consenso entre nosotros.*
ALICIA: *Sin embargo, están de acuerdo en que necesitan planear algo, ¿no?*
PALOMA: *Sí, pero no sé cómo lo vamos a hacer. Mis padres piensan que es mejor conocer algún país extranjero. Yo prefiero hacer un crucero y mis hermanos últimamente están obsesionados con la conservación de la naturaleza y el medio ambiente.*
ALICIA: *Espera, quizás yo tenga una solución para todos. ¿Por qué no hacen un crucero a Panamá y Costa Rica?*

12-26 

Opiniones. Intercambia opiniones sobre los siguientes temas con tu compañero/a. Después, comparen sus opiniones con las de otras parejas y compartan sus conclusiones con la clase.

1. los cruceros
2. ir de vacaciones con la familia
3. los bailes folclóricos
4. ver exposiciones de arte

 MODELO el ecoturismo

E1: *Creo que el ecoturismo es aburrido. Prefiero disfrutar de la vida de noche en las ciudades grandes. Y tú, ¿qué opinas?*

E2: *Dudo que las grandes ciudades del mundo sean diferentes de las cuidades grandes de Estados Unidos. Yo prefiero conocer la naturaleza.*

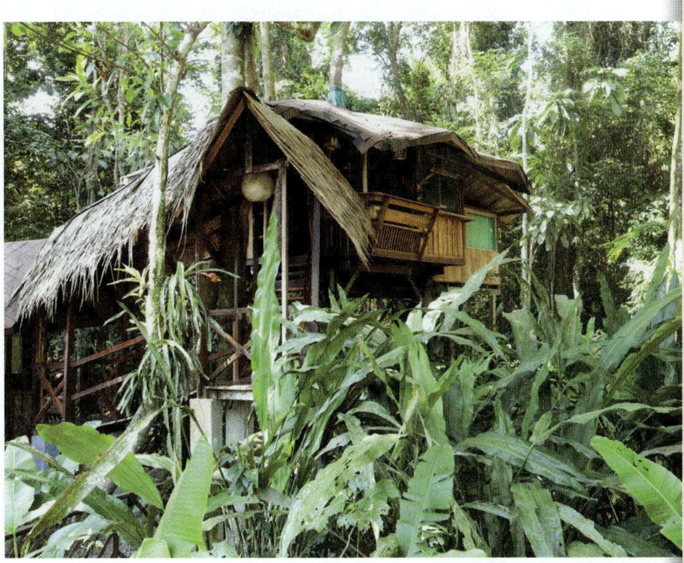

Suggestion for 12-27
You may wish to assign pairs of students ahead of time, and have them select their city and research their lists of 3 things that will probably happen or not happen.

Suggestion
An additional activity to practice this structure is *Dos verdades y una mentira.* Put students in groups of three; each group comes up with three statements about its members, of which two are true and one is untrue. Each group presents its statements to the class, and students contribute expressions of doubt to identify the falsehood; e.g., *Dudo que la familia de Andrea tenga una casa en la playa; No creo que el primo de James sea un jugador profesional de fútbol.*

12-27 

Un viaje. **PREPARACIÓN.** En un concurso, ustedes ganaron un viaje de una semana a cualquier ciudad del mundo hispano. Escojan una ciudad y hagan una lista de tres cosas que posiblemente ocurran durante la semana y tres cosas que dudan que pasen. Expliquen por qué.

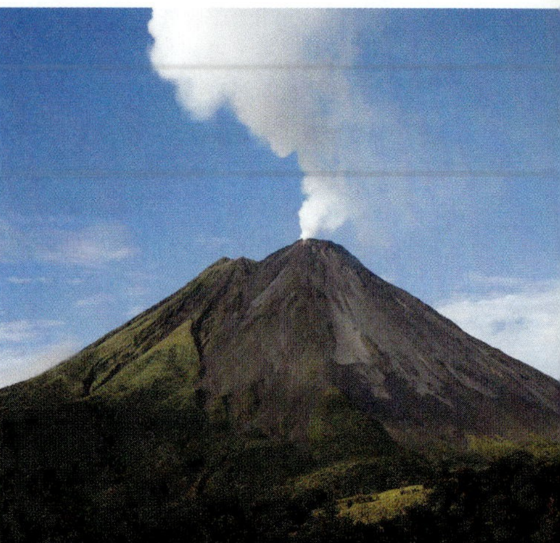

 Puntarenas, Costa Rica

E1: *Esperamos que alguien nos invite a un club porque nos gusta mucho bailar. También es posible que vayamos de excursión al volcán Arenal porque dicen que es muy impresionante.*

E2: *Dudamos que llueva, porque hace buen tiempo casi todo el año. Es poco probable que volvamos otra vez; por eso queremos hacer muchas actividades.*

INTERCAMBIOS. Reúnanse con otra pareja y explíquenle qué ciudad escogieron y por qué. Infórmenle sobre sus expectativas y dudas con respecto a su viaje. Comenten si están de acuerdo con lo que dicen sus compañeros/as.

Situación

PREPARACIÓN. Lean esta situación. Luego, compartan ejemplos de vocabulario, gramática y otra información que necesitan para desarrollar la conversación.

Role A. A friend borrowed your car and brought it back a whole day later than the two of you had agreed, which caused you a lot of inconvenience. Ask your friend for an explanation. Express doubt about at least three reasons your friend gives you. To avoid ongoing conflict with your friend, make sure the situation is resolved.

Role B. You borrowed your friend's car, and you brought it back a whole day later than the two of you had agreed, which caused your friend a lot of inconvenience. Now you have to explain yourself. You don't want to tell the real reason, so you make up a detailed story of what happened. Your friend is skeptical, so you have to try hard to be convincing. To avoid ongoing conflict with your friend, make sure the situation is resolved.

	ROLE A	ROLE B
Vocabulario	Words and expressions related to travel	Words and expressions related to travel
Funciones y formas	Expressing doubts or disbelief Subjunctive with expressions of doubt and disbelief Resolving a problem with a friend	Telling a story Preterit and imperfect Making excuses Apologizing Resolving a problem with a friend

INTERCAMBIOS. Practica la conversación con tu compañero/a incorporando el vocabulario, las funciones y demás información. Luego, represéntenla ante la clase.

EN ACCIÓN

Lugares fantásticos

12-28 Antes de ver

De viaje. Imagínate que vas de vacaciones a un lugar que nunca has visitado. Indica cuáles son las tres actividades más importantes que debes hacer antes de llegar allí.

1. ___ Hacer una reservación de hotel.
2. ___ Comprar un mapa del lugar.
3. ___ Buscar información en Internet sobre los sitios más representativos.
4. ___ Hablar con alguien que viva allí.
5. ___ Hacer las maletas.
6. ___ Despedirte de tus amigos.
7. ___ Comprar ropa para el viaje.

12-29 Mientras ves  

Lugares inolvidables. En este segmento de video se describen tres lugares de interés turístico. Indica si las siguientes oraciones se refieren a las Cataratas del Iguazú (**I**), Costa Rica (**CR**) o San Francisco (**SF**).

1. __SF__ Vanesa siempre ha querido visitar este lugar.
2. __I__ Hay un río que pasa por tres países distintos.
3. __CR__ Es muy popular por su ecoturismo.
4. __I__ Las corrientes (*currents*) son muy poderosas.
5. __SF__ Una de sus atracciones más conocidas es un enorme puente que cruza la bahía.
6. __CR__ Muchas personas van a este lugar para hacer *surf*.
7. __I__ Su nombre viene de una palabra guaraní que significa *agua grande*.

12-30 Después de ver 

Lugares y preferencias. **PREPARACIÓN.** Indica si las siguientes afirmaciones se refieren a Esteban (**E**), a Vanesa (**V**) o a Federico (**F**).

1. __V__ Prefiere los sitios que tengan vida nocturna.
2. __E__ Le encantan los sitios donde se pueda hacer *surf*.
3. __F__ Muestra mucho orgullo al hablar de la industria turística en su país.

Intercambios. Imagínense que Uds. tienen la oportunidad de hacer un video para promocionar un lugar especial. ¿Qué lugar eligen? Describan ese lugar y digan qué actividades pueden hacer las personas allí. Indiquen por qué es especial ese lugar y cuáles son sus principales atractivos. Escriban un eslogan para promocionarlo.

Audioscript for 12-32

SR. HERNÁNDEZ: *Buenos días, señorita, habla el señor Hernández. Viajo a San José dentro de un mes, y estoy buscando un hotel con piscina en el centro de la ciudad. Viajo con mi esposa e hijos.*

AGENTE: *Mire, señor, le voy a dar varias opciones. El Hotel Grano de Oro es un hotel pequeño cerca del centro, y tiene un servicio extraordinario. Tiene algunas habitaciones para cuatro personas, con jacuzzi.*

SR. HERNÁNDEZ: *¡Hummm! ¡Qué bien! ¿Y cuánto cuesta?*

AGENTE: *Este hotel tiene precios muy módicos. Se los doy enseguida.*

SR. HERNÁNDEZ: *Y, ¿qué más tiene?*

AGENTE: *Bueno, tenemos el hotel Buganvilla. Tiene habitaciones bastante grandes, excelente servicio y un restaurante de primera categoría. Además, tiene unos jardines muy bonitos y una piscina muy grande también.*

SR. HERNÁNDEZ: *Bueno...*

AGENTE: *También tenemos otro hotel que es maravilloso, pero está a 45 minutos de San José y es más caro. Tiene una piscina para mayores y otra para niños y unos jardines espectaculares. También se pueden alquilar bicicletas.*

SR. HERNÁNDEZ: *¡Qué bien! Y, ¿cuánto cuesta un cuarto para cuatro personas?*

AGENTE: *120 dólares, con impuestos incluidos.*

SR. HERNÁNDEZ: *Buen precio. Claro que la única desventaja es que no está en el centro, pero voy a hacer la reservación en este hotel. Mi esposa e hijos van a estar más contentos, y yo puedo alquilar un carro o tomar un taxi.*

AGENTE: *Muy buena selección, señor Hernández.*

SR. HERNÁNDEZ: *Sí, espero que sí. Muchas gracias por su ayuda. Hágame la reservación entonces para la última semana de enero.*

AGENTE: *Muy bien, señor Hernández.*

Mosaicos

ESCUCHA

ESTRATEGIA

Use background knowledge to support comprehension

When you listen to a conversation or a lecture in Spanish, your experience may lead you to expect certain content. To support your comprehension, do the following:

Before you listen...

- brainstorm a list of ideas you expect to hear about the topic.
- read about the topic on the Internet if you are not familiar with it.

As you listen ...

- use your prior knowledge to help you understand. For example, when you hear numbers announced at an airport, they probably refer to flight or gate numbers.

12-31  Presentational

Preparación. Vas a escuchar una conversación telefónica entre una agente de viajes y el Sr. Hernández, quien busca un hotel para él y su familia en San José. Antes de escuchar, escribe tres características que el Sr. Hernández probablemente desea que tenga el hotel y tres preguntas que probablemente le hará la agente. Compártelas con la clase.

12-32   Interpretive

Escucha. As you listen to the conversation between Sr. Hernández and the travel agent, check (✓) the statements that best report what was said.

1. _____ El Sr. Hernández dice que quiere un hotel económico que esté cerca del centro de la ciudad.
2. __✓__ La agente tiene varias posibilidades y le describe tres hoteles para que escoja.
3. __✓__ El Sr. Hernández afirma que prefiere que sus hijos y esposa estén cómodos aunque (*even though*) él tenga que tomar un taxi o manejar mucho.
4. _____ La agente le dice al cliente que su elección no es buena porque el hotel es muy caro y está muy lejos del centro de la ciudad.

Comprueba

I was able to ...

- _____ **understand the main points of the conversation.**
- _____ **use experience and logic to confirm what I understood.**

12-33  Interpersonal

Un paso más. Háganse las siguientes preguntas.

1. Cuando buscas un hotel, ¿es más importante que sea económico o que sea de lujo (*luxurious*)?
2. ¿Qué servicios o comodidades prefieres que ofrezca un hotel?
3. ¿Cuál es el hotel más cómodo en el que has estado? Explica.

HABLA

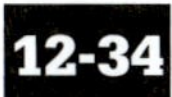

12-34  Interpretive

Preparación. Escojan a una de las personas de la lista. Busquen información sobre esa persona para completar la tabla. También busquen otra información que les interese a ustedes.

Francisco Amighetti	Félix Danilo Gómez
Óscar Arias Sánchez	Manuel Noriega
Rubén Blades	Carlos Ruiz
Franklin Chang Díaz	Juan Santamaría

NOMBRE	DATOS PERSONALES	PROFESIÓN	LOGROS
________	Fecha de nacimiento: ________ Lugar de nacimiento/muerte: ________	________ Contribución a su profesión: ________	

12-35  Presentational

Habla. Hagan una breve presentación sobre la persona que escogieron, usando imágenes y algún tipo de audio para mantener el interés de sus compañeros de clase.

Comprueba

In my presentation…

- ____ I spoke slowly and clearly to make my presentation understandable.
- ____ I used visuals to make my presentation lively and interesting.
- ____ I engaged the audience and successfully answered their questions.

En directo

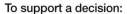

To support a decision:

Hemos elegido a… porque…
We have chosen … because …

Lo que más influyó en nuestra decisión fue/fueron…
What most influenced our decision was/were …

Nuestra decisión está basada en lo siguiente…
Our decision is based on the following …

Listen to a conversation with these expressions.

ESTRATEGIA

Make your presentations comprehensible and interesting

When you give a presentation, your two challenges are to a) keep it simple so your classmates understand it; and b) make it interesting so they will listen.

- Keep it simple. Use words and expressions you know. Don't copy whole sentences from other sources, because your audience may not understand you.
- Practice your presentation. If you have notes, don't read them; instead, use them for reference. If you read, your audience will not understand you.
- Make it interesting. Use PowerPoint, photos, and artifacts to make your presentation more lively and interesting. Do not read from your slides. You may have notes, but only for reference.
- Involve your audience. Make eye contact, ask questions, check that they understand you, and invite them to ask questions.

12-36  Interpersonal

Un paso más. Decidan cuál de las figuras famosas de la actividad 12-34 es la persona más admirable o interesante. Expliquen por qué, usando las expresiones de *En directo*.

Alternative for 12-34
Depending on the time available, you may have students work in pairs or groups to prepare and give their presentations.

Suggestions for 12-34
You may wish to add to the list of individuals. Encourage students to select someone who is not already familiar to them: Costa Rican political figures (Óscar Arias Sánchez, also a Nobel laureate; Juan Santamaría), astronauts (Franklin Chang Díaz), and artists (Francisco Amighetti); Panamanian sports figures (Carlos Ruiz), musicians and actors (Félix Danilo Gómez, known as Flex; Rubén Blades); and political figures (Manuel Noriega). Students may use the cultural information in the chapter and in Internet and print sources to prepare their presentations. Remind them to follow the guidelines in the *Estrategia* box to make their presentations more successful.

Audioscript for *En directo*
PRESENTADOR: *Y ahora, el Presidente de la universidad de Costa Rica va a anunciar el doctorado Honoris Causa de este año.* (*clapping*)
PRESIDENTE: *Los miembros del comité de selección hemos elegido a Franklin Chang Díaz para otorgarle el doctorado Honoris Causa por su contribución a las ciencias nucleares y por su merecido prestigio internacional. Lo que más influyó en nuestra decisión fue que el Dr. Chang Díaz es un ejemplo a seguir para todos nuestros estudiantes. Nuestra decisión está basada en los innumerables éxitos con los que cuenta y en su incansable trabajo como astronauta, físico e ingeniero nuclear...* (*voice fading*)

Note about *Estrategia*
Previous *Estrategias* for reading have highlighted the visual aspects of texts that help readers anticipate the content and the sequence of topics. This *Estrategia* deals with the rhetorical structure of expository texts, which includes advantages and disadvantages, problems and solutions, comparisons, and advice/recommendations.

Suggestion for 12-37
You may wish to have students read the title of the text and, in conjunction with the activity try to guess what the text will be about.

LEE

12-37  Interpersonal

Preparación. Hablen de lo siguiente.

1. ¿Prefieren los viajes en avión o por tierra? ¿Por qué?
2. ¿Les gusta organizar sus propios viajes o prefieren una agencia? ¿Por qué?
3. ¿Qué problema serio ha tenido cada uno/a de ustedes en un viaje?
4. ¿Han tenido problemas semejantes o diferentes?

ESTRATEGIA

Focus on logical relationships

Magazine articles often address current issues, such as identity theft, sedentary lifestyles, or travel tips. When you read an article of this type, you can take advantage of its structure to maximize your comprehension. As you read, look for the issues or problems that the author introduces, and then focus on the logical relationships, such as between problems and their causes, or between problems and their solutions. An individual case often appears at the beginning of the article as an example of the problem, and then returns at the end to illustrate a possible solution.

12-38 Interpretive

Lee. Marca (✓) los problemas que enfrentan los viajeros, según el artículo "Vacaciones o pesadilla". Después, busca en el artículo ejemplos de lo que se indica.

Problemas	Ejemplos
1. ✓ agencias de viajes deshonestas	**1.** tres problemas que tuvieron Isabel y Mario en sus vacaciones
2. ✓ maletas perdidas	**2.** la causa principal de la situación desagradable de Isabel y Mario
3. ✓ vuelos cancelados	**3.** recomendaciones para evitar o minimizar problemas
4. _____ choques de avión	
5. ✓ robo de las tarjetas de crédito	
6. _____ autos alquilados que no funcionan	
7. ✓ problemas para entrar en otro país	
8. _____ enfermedades causadas por la comida	

Ejemplos
1. a. El hotel no tenía vista al mar; b. El hotel no tenía jardines exóticos; c. Las habitaciones eran pequeñísimas e incómodas; d. La comida dejaba mucho que desear.
2. Confiar en una agencia de viajes desconocida que encontraron en Internet.
3. a. Comprar un seguro de cancelación; b. Llevar el pasaporte y otros documentos en una bolsita colgada del cuello que se oculta debajo de la ropa o en un doble bolsillo del pantalón; c. Comprar las bebidas en las tiendas dentro del aeropuerto.

Comprueba
I was able to ...

_____ **identify the problems described by the author.**

_____ **focus on the relationship between different parts of the content to discover key problems, their causes, and their possible solutions.**

VACACIONES O PESADILLA[1]
CÓMO REDUCIR LOS PROBLEMAS EN LOS VIAJES

Isabel y Mario, una pareja estadounidense de origen uruguayo, decidieron celebrar su aniversario de boda en Costa Rica. Para preparar el viaje se pusieron en contacto por Internet con la agencia Viajes Reales. La agencia ofrecía paquetes de excursiones que incluían billete de avión, hotel y coche de alquiler por precios bastante módicos. Las fotos prometían una estancia relajada en un hotel de ambiente exótico al noroeste del país. La variedad de piscinas, la cercanía del mar, la apetecible gastronomía local y los cócteles refrescantes que se veían en lujosas mesitas junto a las hamacas de los afortunados clientes confirmaban que se trataba de un verdadero paraíso.

Isabel y Mario pagaron la cantidad requerida y no dudaron ni un momento de su decisión. Pero al llegar a su destino comprobaron que las fotos no correspondían a la realidad. El hotel no tenía ni vista al mar ni jardines exóticos. Las habitaciones eran pequeñísimas e incómodas y la comida dejaba mucho que desear.

Lamentablemente, esta no es una anécdota aislada entre los viajeros. ¿Quién no ha sufrido alguna vez la pérdida de su equipaje, las incomodidades de un vuelo cancelado, el robo de su pasaporte o sus tarjetas de crédito, los problemas en la aduana por comprar un producto comestible que no se permite pasar?

La experiencia de los viajes nos enseña a ser prudentes y prever los riesgos. La facilidad que proporciona Internet es conveniente, pero cuando se viaja por primera vez es preferible dirigirse a una agencia local para que los especialistas de viajes nos ayuden a elegir las mejores opciones. Frecuentemente es más caro hacerlo así, pero se puede ahorrar tiempo y evitar sorpresas desagradables. Por otra parte, a veces resulta más barato comprar un seguro de cancelación que arriesgarse a perder, por una razón u otra, el costo de un billete de avión.

Algunos incidentes son naturalmente inevitables, pero otros se pueden prevenir. Por ejemplo, es posible minimizar el riesgo de un robo llevando los pasaportes y papeles importantes en una bolsita colgada del cuello que se oculta debajo de la ropa, o en un bolsillo doble del pantalón. En cuanto a los impedimentos en la aduana, hay que tener en cuenta que las medidas de seguridad son cada vez más estrictas. Ya no se puede subir al avión con líquidos de más de tres onzas y solo se permite viajar con las bebidas y comestibles comprados en las tiendas del aeropuerto.

Por suerte, las vacaciones de Mario e Isabel no fueron un desastre total. La pareja pudo disfrutar del maravilloso país en sus excursiones a Puntarenas, Puerto Limón y los parques naturales cercanos a Orosí. También pudieron celebrar su aniversario en un magnífico restaurante. ¡Qué lástima que la experiencia completa no fuera tan agradable! Como dice un conocido refrán[2]: Más vale prevenir… que lamentar.

[1]*nightmare* [2]*proverb*

12-39 Presentational

Un paso más. La agencia Viajes Reales recibe una carta de Isabel y Mario quejándose de los problemas que tuvieron durante su viaje a Costa Rica. Contesta esa carta de parte de la agencia incluyendo lo siguiente.

1. las excusas de la agencia por la mala experiencia de los clientes
2. una explicación por la falsa publicidad
3. la promesa de devolver el dinero o de ofrecer otro viaje

Suggestion for 12-39
As an alternative, you may ask students to write a brief narration of a particularly bad experience that they have had while traveling or on vacation.

ESCRIBE

12-40  Interpretive

Preparación. En un concurso, tu amigo/a ganó diez mil dólares para viajar a San José, Costa Rica. Nunca ha hecho un viaje largo, siente mucha ansiedad (*anxiety*) y te pidió ayuda con la planificación de su viaje. Para ayudarlo, haz lo siguiente:

1. En Internet, lee uno o dos artículos sobre este lugar.
2. Subraya y toma nota de las ideas y los datos concretos más relevantes y útiles.
3. Decide cuáles son tus consejos principales sobre la planificación del viaje, y selecciona la información que lo sustente (*support*).
4. Organiza la información y las ideas en orden de importancia.
5. Selecciona las palabras adecuadas para lograr (*achieve*) el tono adecuado.

ESTRATEGIA

Use facts to offer advice

In your academic work, you are often expected to provide reliable facts, such as statistics and expert opinions. Facts also serve as the basis to support a point of view on an issue. For example, a person may be against texting while driving (personal point of view) because statistics show accidents are caused by drivers who text while behind the wheel (fact). When talking to a friend, facts about different options provide objective support for the advice you give. However, not all sources of information are helpful. Always be sure to …

- consult reliable sources
- acknowledge your sources
- make it clear how your facts are connected to other sources of information, such as knowledge about your friend.

Suggestion for 12-41
Depending on your students' level of proficiency and their interests, you may wish to expand the scope of this writing task. You may give them the option of writing a brief essay on a travel-related issue, such as how to prepare for a long trip, how to plan an adventure trip, or how to book trips using the Internet. This may give students the opportunity to research an area of personal interest and to use the information to write a letter and help others.

12-41 Presentational

Escribe. Escríbele un correo electrónico a tu amigo/a y compártelo con la clase. Incluye la información que preparaste. Además, dale buenos consejos para disminuir su ansiedad.

▲ San José, Costa Rica

Comprueba

I was able to …

____ locate and organize key factual information.

____ give advice based on factual information.

____ use the *En directo* expressions to present and support my perspective.

12-42 Interpersonal

Un paso más. Comparen sus respectivos mensajes. ¿Dieron consejos similares o diferentes? ¿Cuáles son los consejos más importantes? Preparen un informe breve para compartir con la clase.

En este capítulo...

Comprueba lo que sabes

Go to the ***MySpanishLab*** to review what you have learned in this chapter. Practice with the following:

Vocabulario

LOS MEDIOS DE TRANSPORTE
Means of transportation

el autobús/bus *bus*
el avión *plane*
el barco *ship/boat*
el metro *subway*
el tren *train*

EN EL AEROPUERTO
At the airport

la aduana *customs*
la aerolínea/línea aérea *airline*
el asiento *seat*
de pasillo/ventanilla *aisle/window seat*
la clase turista *tourist class*
la llegada *arrival*
el mostrador *counter*
la primera clase *first class*
la puerta (de salida) *gate*
la salida *departure*
la sala de espera *waiting room*
la salida de emergencia *emergency exit*
el vuelo *flight*

LAS PERSONAS
People

el/la agente de viajes *travel agent*
el/la auxiliar de vuelo *flight attendant*
el/la inspector/a de aduana *customs agent*
el/la pasajero/a *passenger*

LOS VIAJES
Trips

la agencia de viajes *travel agency*
la autopista *freeway*
el boleto/el pasaje *ticket*
la carretera *highway*
el crucero *cruise*
el equipaje *luggage*
la escala *stopover*
la excursión *outing, trip*
la maleta *suitcase*
el maletín *briefcase*
el pasaporte *passport*
la tarjeta de embarque *boarding pass*
la velocidad *speed*

EN EL HOTEL
In the hotel

el alojamiento *lodging*
la caja fuerte *safe*
la habitación doble/sencilla *double/single room*
la llave *key*
la recepción *front desk*
la tarjeta magnética *key card*

LOS LUGARES
Places

la cuadra *city block*
la esquina *corner*

LAS PARTES DE UN COCHE
Parts of a car

el capó *hood*
el espejo retrovisor *rearview mirror*
la guantera *glove compartment*
el limpiaparabrisas *windshield wiper*
la llanta *tire*
la luz (las luces) *light(s)*
las luces intermitentes *flashers/hazard lights*
el maletero/el baúl *trunk*
el motor *motor*
el parabrisas *windshield*
la placa *license plate*
el radiador *radiator*
la rueda *wheel*
el volante *steering wheel*

LAS DESCRIPCIONES
Descriptions

bien/mal aparcado *well/badly parked*
lleno/a *full*
vacío/a *empty*

VERBOS
Verbs

descomponerse *to break down*
doblar *to turn*
facturar *to check in (luggage)*
manejar *to drive*
perderse (ie) *to get lost*
recorrer *to cover, travel*
reservar *to make a reservation*
salir *to leave*
viajar *to travel*

PALABRAS Y EXPRESIONES ÚTILES
Useful words and expressions

el cajero automático *ATM*
de ida y vuelta *round trip*
hacer cola *to stand in line*
la licencia de conducir *driver's license*
la multa *fine*
nunca *never*
seguir (i) derecho *to go straight*
una vez *once*

See pages 434 and 435 for a list of stressed possessive adjectives and pronouns.

Introduction to the chapter
Introduce the chapter theme about art and ask questions to recycle vocabulary and structures from previous chapters. Related questions: *¿Qué es arte? ¿Hay alguna diferencia entre el arte que vemos en la calle y el arte que se encuentra en los grandes museos? ¿Quiénes son sus pintores preferidos? ¿Hay algún artista en la clase?*

Note for *grafiti*
Although the word **grafito** now appears in many Spanish-language dictionaries, *Mosaicos* uses the word **grafiti,** which is widely used throughout the Spanish-speaking world.

Integrated Performance Assessment: Three Modes of Communication table

Presentational: See activities 13-5, 13-7, 13-10, 13-11, 13-14, 13-17, 13-19, 13-27, 13-35, and 13-37.

Interpretative: See activities 13-1, 13-2, 13-4, 13-6, 13-8, 13-9, 13-10, 13-11, 13-12, 13-13, 13-16, 13-20, 13-21, 13-22, 13-24, 13-25, 13-26, 13-28, 13-30, 13-34, and 13-36.

Interpersonal: See activities 13-2, 13-3, 13-4, 13-8, 13-12, 13-13, 13-15, 13-16, 13-17, 13-18, 13-19, 13-21, 13-22, 13-23, 13-26, 13-29, 13-31, 13-32, 13-33, 13-38, and all *Situación* activities.

13 ¿Qué es arte para ti?

ENFOQUE CULTURAL
Bolivia y Paraguay

VOCABULARIO EN CONTEXTO
La literatura y el cine
La pintura y el arte
La música y la cultura popular

MOSAICO CULTURAL
El grafiti y la identidad urbana

FUNCIONES Y FORMAS
Review of the preterit and imperfect
The conditional
Reciprocal verbs and pronouns

EN ACCIÓN
¡No te lo pierdas!

MOSAICOS
ESCUCHA Identify the speaker's intentions
HABLA Make your presentations comprehensible and interesting
LEE Focus on multiple meanings when reading poetry
ESCRIBE Write to spark interest

EN ESTE CAPÍTULO...
Comprueba lo que sabes
Vocabulario

LEARNING OUTCOMES

You will be able to:

- talk about art and culture
- express doubt and uncertainty
- hypothesize about the future
- describe states and conditions
- talk about Bolivia and Paraguay in terms of products, practices, and perspectives
- share information about art and culture in Hispanic countries and identify cultural similarities

ENFOQUE cultural BOLIVIA Y PARAGUAY

Enfoque cultural

To learn more about Bolivia and Paraguay, go to MySpanishLab to view the *Vistas culturales* videos.

Detalle de tabla de madera pintada, siglo XVI, Museo Casa de Murillo, La Paz, Bolivia

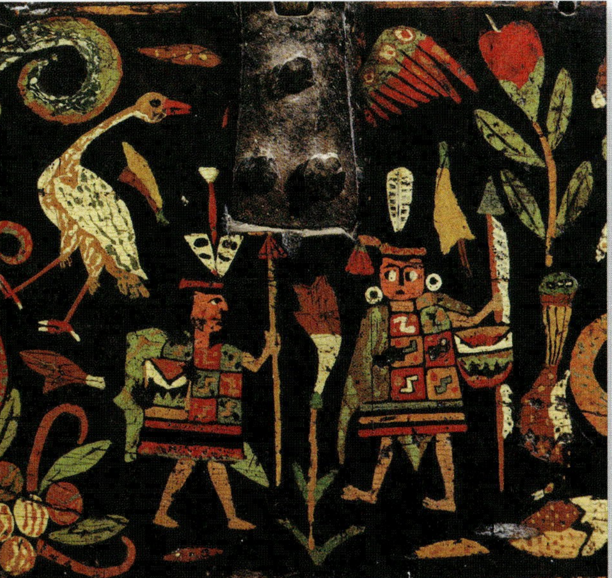

¿QUÉ TE PARECE?

- El Salar de Uyuni en Bolivia es el desierto de sal más grande del mundo y una fuente importante de litio (*lithium*). Tiene hoteles de lujo construidos de sal.
- El Lago Titicaca en Bolivia es el lago comercial y navegable más alto del mundo con una altura de 3.812 metros y es el lago más grande de Sudamérica.
- El presidente boliviano, Evo Morales, salió en el *Daily Show* de Jon Stewart el 25 de septiembre de 2007.
- Paraguay y Bolivia son los únicos países de Sudamérica sin salida directa al mar.
- El español y el guaraní son los dos idiomas oficiales de Paraguay. El guaraní es también el nombre de su moneda.
- El 95% de la población de Paraguay es mestiza, es decir, de ascendencia europea e indígena.

Note for art
This painting on wood dates from just after the arrival of the Spaniards in Bolivia. It combines native and Spanish motifs, representing the encounter of two cultures. In this detail we see representations of indigenous people in colorful clothes, surrounded by birds and lush vegetation.

Suggestions
Discuss the painting and describe the figures and the motifs. You may show photos of indigenous people of Bolivia, who inspired this anonymous artist, and have students describe their appearance and clothing. Mention colors and shapes. Talk about Hispanic art by reviewing some of the painters presented in previous chapters, such as Pablo Picasso, Frida Kahlo, Fernando Botero, and Xul Solar. Ask students to talk about the different styles: *¿Es un cuadro realista?* (Write the word *realista.*) *¿Es un cuadro abstracto?* (Write *abstracto.*) Ask students to express their opinions about some of these paintings: *¿Qué prefieren, el arte realista o el arte abstracto? ¿Les gusta este cuadro? ¿Por qué?* You may wish to find additional examples of both artistic styles on the web.

Suggestions
Point out the photos on the map and make comments to introduce vocabulary as you ask: *¿Cuál es la capital de Bolivia? ¿Y la de Paraguay? ¿Qué países rodean Bolivia? ¿Qué fronteras tiene Paraguay?* Mention that Bolivia is approximately the size of Texas, and Paraguay is slightly smaller than California. Explain that Bolivia was named after Simón Bolívar, whom students studied in *Capítulo 6.* Refer to the photo on the map of the mountains surrounding La Paz and explain that La Paz is one of the world's highest cities, with an altitude of 3,640 meters (11,492 ft.)

above sea level. Visitors to La Paz sometimes suffer from altitude sickness (*soroche*) for a few days until their bodies adjust.
Point out that the Bolivian Constitution of 2009 recognizes 37 official languages; the most commonly spoken are Spanish, Quechua, and Aymara.
Mention that Paraguay has two official languages: Spanish and Guaraní, an Amerindian language spoken by 75% of the population.
Have students search online to see a clip of Evo Morales on *The Daily Show*. Discuss the conversation between Jon Stewart and the Bolivian president in class.

Note for *Sucre*
Sucre is actually the constitutional and judicial capital of Bolivia. La Paz is the seat of government. Thus, technically, even according to the 2009 Constitution, Sucre is the capital.

ENFOQUE cultural

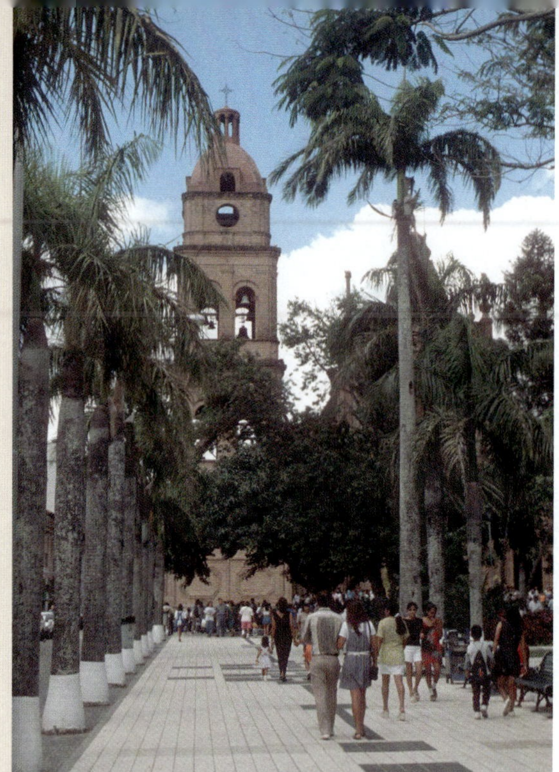

◀ La ciudad de Santa Cruz de la Sierra en Bolivia, ubicada en el corazón del continente, era un puesto fronterizo insignificante de menos de 30.000 habitantes hasta mediados del siglo XX. Hoy en día es la ciudad más grande de Bolivia, con 2,5 millones de habitantes, y produce el 80% de la agricultura del país. Es una ciudad tradicional y sofisticada a la vez, con una multitud de cafés, museos, boutiques y grandes centros de cine.

La Santísima Trinidad de Paraná ▶ forma parte de una serie de misiones fundadas por los jesuitas en el siglo XVII. Siete de estas misiones se establecieron en Paraguay. Hoy en día, solo quedan las ruinas de estos centros urbanos y espirituales creados para los indígenas de la zona.

▲ En 2005, Evo Morales fue el primer indígena elegido presidente en Bolivia. Bajo la constitución de 2009, la República de Bolivia cambió su nombre a Estado Plurinacional de Bolivia, en reconocimiento a los diversos grupos indígenas. El mismo año, Morales fue nombrado *World Hero of Mother Earth* por la Asamblea General de las Naciones Unidas. Morales recibió atención global cuando decretó la *Ley de los Derechos de la Madre Tierra* en 2010. Esta ley, única en el mundo, atribuye a la naturaleza los mismos derechos que a los seres humanos. Refleja la antigua y aún vital creencia de los aimaras y los quechuas en la Pachamama (*Mother Earth*), que el ser humano fue creado de la tierra y así tiene un parentesco fraternal con toda la naturaleza.

◀ La Represa Hidroeléctrica de Itaipú en el río Paraná, entre Paraguay y Brasil, suministra el 90% de la energía de Paraguay y el 25% de la de Brasil. En 1994 fue nombrada una de las Siete Maravillas del Mundo Moderno por la *American Society of Civil Engineers*.

¿CUÁNTO SABES?

Indica si las siguientes afirmaciones son ciertas (**C**) o falsas (**F**), según lo que tú sabes sobre Bolivia y Paraguay.

1. __F__ El río Paraná está en la frontera entre Paraguay y Argentina.
2. __C__ El guaraní es una de las lenguas oficiales de Paraguay.
3. __F__ La capital de Bolivia es Santa Cruz.
4. __F__ Paraguay no produce suficiente energía hidroeléctrica para exportarla a sus países vecinos.
5. __C__ Bolivia tiene grandes depósitos de sal y litio.
6. __F__ La República de Bolivia cambió su nombre a Estado Plurinacional de Bolivia en reconocimiento a la diversidad ecológica del país.

Vocabulario en contexto

Discussing the arts: literature, film, art, music, and popular culture

La literatura y el cine

MySpanishLab **PRONUNCIATION TOPIC:** Pronunciation-based changes in *y* and *o*
Learn more using Amplifire Dynamic Study Modules, Pronunciation, and Vocabulary Tutorials.

▲ Gabriel García Márquez

Gabriel García Márquez (1928), colombiano, es otro escritor que se asocia con el realismo mágico. **A través de** sus **novelas** y **cuentos** ha sabido recrear un mundo mítico de gran riqueza humana. En su novela *Cien años de soledad* (1967) narra en tono épico la historia de una familia y la **fundación** y **desarrollo** de Macondo, un pueblo imaginario. En 1982 este autor recibió el **Premio** Nobel de Literatura. Algunas de sus obras han sido llevadas al cine; por ejemplo, *El amor en los tiempos del cólera* (2007), con el actor español Javier Bardem.

Augusto Roa Bastos ▶

Uno de los **novelistas** más importantes de Hispanoamérica es el paraguayo Augusto Roa Bastos (1917–2005). Su novela *Yo, el supremo* (1974) **trata** sobre el **tema** de las dictaduras. Su **personaje principal** se basa en la figura de José Rodríguez de Francia, dictador de Paraguay en las primeras décadas del siglo XIX. Este **escritor** fue uno de los iniciadores del movimiento literario conocido como realismo mágico, que combina elementos mágicos o irracionales con situaciones de aparente normalidad.

◀ Gabriela Mistral

La **poesía** tiene nombres **destacados** en las letras hispanas. Gabriela Mistral (1889–1957), chilena, fue la primera persona de Hispanoamérica en recibir el Premio Nobel de Literatura, en 1945. Algunos de los temas de su **obra** son **el amor, la amistad** y el mestizaje como característica de la identidad latinoamericana. Otros **poetas** universalmente conocidos son el chileno Pablo Neruda y el peruano César Vallejo.

Iciar Bollaín ▶

El cine hispano ha dado numerosos ejemplos de **calidad** en películas de todos los países. Entre las que han sido **nominadas** o han ganado algún Óscar se encuentran las españolas *Mar adentro* (2004), de Alejandro Amenábar, y *Volver* (2006), de Pedro Almodóvar. La cubana *Fresa y chocolate* (1994), de Tomás Gutiérrez Alea, ganó el Oso de Plata en el festival de Berlín, y la colombiana *La estrategia del caracol* (1993), de Sergio Cabrera, fue premiada en el festival de Valladolid. El cine mexicano ha tenido grandes éxitos en los últimos tiempos con películas de Alfonso Cuarón (*Y tu mamá también*, 2001), de Alejandro González Iñárritu (*Babel*, 2006) y de Guillermo del Toro (*El laberinto del fauno*, 2006). Entre los directores jóvenes más **prometedores** está la española Iciar Bollaín, autora de *Mataharis* (2007) y de *Te doy mis ojos* (2003), que **denuncia** el tema de la violencia doméstica.

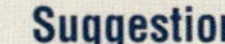

Suggestion
Point out the importance of Spanish and Latin American literature throughout history, from Shakespeare's contemporaries, Pedro Calderón de la Barca and Sor Juana Inés de la Cruz, to modern Cuban writers like José Lezama Lima and Alejo Carpentier. Bring examples of poems by Gustavo Adolfo Bécquer or Alejandra Pizarnik, extracts from novels by Carmen Laforet, or short stories by Juan Rulfo. Read aloud excerpts from a play by Federico García Lorca or Griselda Gambaro. Mention some prominent current literary figures: Carlos Fuentes and Elena Garro from Mexico; Álvaro Mutis from Colombia; Blanca Varela from Peru; and the Chicanas Sandra Cisneros and Ana Castillo and the Dominican Junot Díaz, who are based in the U.S. and write in English.

Note
Realismo mágico is a term that describes a literary genre that became popular among writers of the so-called Latin American boom during the 1960s and 1970s. It refers to works whose story lines appear to be set in real time and places, but in which things happen that are products of the imagination, and even though they would be impossible in the real world, they are presented as natural.

Standard 3.1
Students reinforce and further their knowledge of other disciplines through the foreign language. Although students may be familiar with the Hispanic writers and filmmakers presented in this section, they may not have made the connections that can be gained by learning about them in the context of their Spanish course.

Instructors may lead a discussion in which students say what they know about the artistic figures featured here and the instructor provides relevant historical, geographical, and cultural information.

Suggestion
Talk about some Hispanic films that students may be familiar with. Explain again that some countries, including Mexico, Argentina, and Spain, have an important film industry. If possible, show a Spanish-language movie outside of class and have students talk about its theme, plot, and characters with the help of a viewing guide.

Audioscript for 13-1
1. *Este novelista creó un pueblo mítico en su novela más famosa. Lo llamó Macondo.*
2. *Esta poetisa de Chile recibió el Premio Nobel de Literatura.*
3. *Es una de las directoras más prometedoras del cine actual.*
4. *Este escritor, junto con Augusto Roa Bastos, se asocia con el movimiento literario del realismo mágico.*
5. *En su obra se destacan los temas del amor y la amistad.*
6. *Este escritor basó su obra principal en uno de los dictadores de Paraguay.*

Suggestions for 13-2
Turn this activity into a class discussion by projecting the photos or names of the renowned Hispanic people mentioned in the preceding presentations. Ask if students have heard of them or are familiar with any of their works. Have students locate their countries of origin on a map. You may assign students to research on the web the biography of a particular figure mentioned in the presentation and have them write down two interesting facts to report to the class. Write these facts in the last column of the table. Before doing the *Intercambios,* brainstorm with students some of the Hispanic figures they associate with art, literature, or popular culture. This can serve as a preview for the following sections in *Vocabulario en contexto.*

PRÁCTICA

13-1  

Escucha y confirma. Listen to the descriptions and select the writer or artist it refers to.

	AUGUSTO ROA BASTOS	GABRIEL GARCÍA MÁRQUEZ	GABRIELA MISTRAL	ICIAR BOLLAÍN
1.		✓		
2.			✓	
3.				✓
4.		✓		
5.			✓	
6.	✓			

Cultura

Las nominaciones y los premios son muy codiciados (*sought after*) en el mundo del cine. Las películas que compiten en los festivales de cine suelen adquirir más publicidad y tener más éxito económico. Ganar un Óscar a la mejor película extranjera es una de las aspiraciones de muchos directores de todo el mundo, pero hay otros festivales de cine internacionales que tienen gran tradición y repercusión en el mundo hispano, como los de Valladolid (Seminci) y de San Sebastián en España.

Conexiones. Busca información sobre la Semana Internacional de Cine de Valladolid (Seminci) y el Festival de Cine de San Sebastián. ¿Qué películas fueron premiadas en los últimos festivales? ¿Te parecen interesantes estas películas? ¿Conoces algún director o actor entre los ganadores?

Cineastas (*Filmmakers*) y escritores. PREPARACIÓN. Completen la tabla con la información que leyeron sobre ciertos hispanos prominentes.

NOMBRE	PROFESIÓN	LUGAR DE ORIGEN	DATOS INTERESANTES	OTRO DATO
Sergio Cabrera	director de cine	Colombia	Ganó un premio en el festival de Valladolid.	
Gabriela Mistral	poetisa	Chile	Answers may vary.	
Pedro Almodóvar	*director de cine*	*España*	Es el director de la película *Volver.*	
Iciar Bollaín	directora de cine	*España*	Una película suya denuncia el tema de la violencia doméstica.	
Gabriel García Márquez	escritor	*Colombia*	Ganó el Premio Nobel.	

INTERCAMBIOS. Comparen su tabla con la de otra pareja, y entre todos hagan una lista de otros artistas o escritores hispanos famosos. Pueden incluir a gente del cine, la música, la pintura, el periodismo, la arquitectura, el diseño de ropa, etc. Incluyan el nombre y la siguiente infomación:

1. profesión
2. lugar de origen
3. algunos datos interesantes de su carrera

13-3 

¿De qué trata? **PREPARACIÓN.** Intercambien información sobre un libro que han leído o una película que han visto últimamente. Utilicen las siguientes preguntas como guía.

1. ¿Quién escribió el libro o dirigió la película?
2. ¿Cuál es el tema?
3. ¿Quién es su personaje principal? ¿Cómo es?
4. ¿Te gustó la película/el libro? ¿Por qué?

INTERCAMBIOS. Comparte con la clase la información que has obtenido de tu compañero/a.

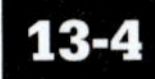

13-4 

Un poema. **PREPARACIÓN.** Lean el siguiente poema de Gabriela Mistral y digan si las siguientes afirmaciones son ciertas (**C**) o falsas (**F**). Si son falsas, den la respuesta correcta.

Dame la mano

Dame la mano y danzaremos;
dame la mano y me amarás.
Como una sola flor seremos,
como una flor, y nada más...

El mismo verso cantaremos,
al mismo paso bailarás.
Como una espiga ondularemos,
como una espiga, y nada más.

Te llamas Rosa y yo Esperanza;
pero tu nombre olvidarás,
porque seremos una danza
en la colina y nada más...

1. __C__ "Dame la mano" es un poema de amor.
2. __F__ El poema habla de tres personas. Habla de dos personas.
3. __F__ El tiempo del poema se relaciona con el pasado. Se relaciona con el futuro.
4. __C__ Es un poema alegre.

INTERCAMBIOS. Marquen (✓) los temas que trata el poema. Luego, escriban el verso o los versos que ejemplifican cada tema.

1. __✓__ el baile
2. __✓__ el amor
3. _____ la familia
4. __✓__ la naturaleza
5. __✓__ la música

Suggestions for 13-4
Model the reading of the poem and have students repeat the verses after you, or choose some students to read the poem aloud. This is an opportunity to practice rhythm and intonation. Have students work with the vocabulary. Use gestures to help them remember the meanings of some of the words and expressions. Model *Dame la mano* and *danzar.* Bring a photo or have a student draw a flower and a hill and introduce the words *espiga* and *colina.* Explain *ondular* and *olvidar* with gestures or examples. Remind them of the meaning of *Y nada más* ("That's all"). Call attention to the repetitions in the poem and to the comparisons (*Como una sola flor, como una espiga*). You may wish to introduce the words *rima* and *verso.* Recycle numbers by having students count the number of lines and the number of syllables in each line. Tell students to add a syllable to lines whose last syllable is stressed.

13-5 

Escritores famosos. Busquen información en Internet sobre uno de estos poetas hispanos y preparen una breve presentación incluyendo la siguiente información.

César Vallejo	Pablo Neruda	Blanca Andreu
Alejandra Pizarnik	Federico García Lorca	Adela Zamudio

1. datos biográficos
2. explicación de uno de sus poemas (tema y características de estilo)

Suggestion for 13-5
You may wish to divide class into small groups (3 or 4) and assign this activity in advance. To avoid repetition, assign a poet to each group.

Suggestions for *La pintura y el arte*
Use the Internet to show paintings by Hispanic painters. Show some by Velázquez and Goya. Use their paintings to review vocabulary associated with colors, numbers, clothes, physical descriptions, etc. Before reading the presentation, ask questions about *Las Meninas: ¿Cuántas personas hay en este cuadro? ¿Qué animal es este? ¿Qué ropa lleva la niña? ¿Quién aparece en el espejo?* Recycle the expressions *a la derecha, a la izquierda, delante,* and *detrás* to describe the painting. Mention Picasso's cubism and Dalí's surrealism and talk about their works. Show some murals by Diego Rivera and point out their social focus. Review the information that students have learned about other painters in the chapter openers.

La pintura y el arte

▲ *Las Meninas* de Diego Velázquez

El Museo del Prado tiene una excelente colección de cuadros de **pintores** españoles, como Diego Velázquez, del siglo XVII, y Francisco de Goya, del siglo XVIII. Uno de los cuadros más importantes de Velázquez es *Las Meninas,* donde **retrata** una **escena** en el palacio real. En esta escena vemos a una hija del rey Felipe IV **rodeada** de sus sirvientas. En el cuadro hay un espejo donde **se reflejan** los reyes. También hay un **autorretrato** del pintor.

La persistencia de la memoria de Salvador Dalí ▶

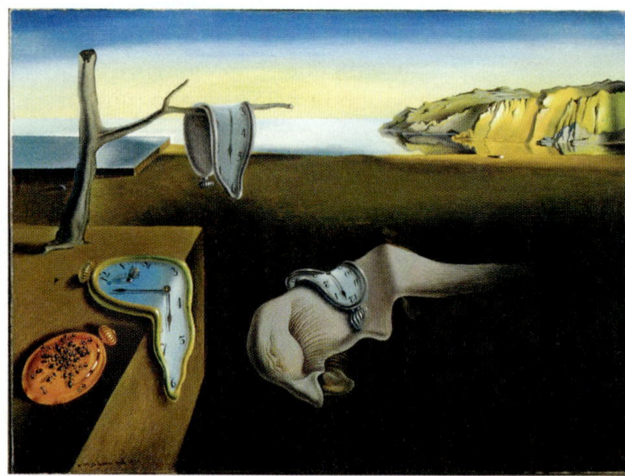

Algunos de los mejores pintores del siglo XX, como Pablo Picasso y Salvador Dalí, también son españoles. En este cuadro vemos el estilo **surrealista** de Dalí, con sus relojes **blandos** y su obsesión por los insectos. Este **paisaje,** con el mar **al fondo,** es un **recuerdo** del pueblo del Mediterráneo donde él vivió, y se repite en muchos de sus cuadros. Picasso desarrolló el estilo **cubista** y fue muy original en el uso de los colores y las **formas.**

◀ *Danza en Tehuantepec* de Diego Rivera

Los mexicanos Frida Kahlo y Diego Rivera muestran en sus **obras** las costumbres y las condiciones sociales de su país. Este cuadro **se titula** *Danza en Tehuantepec* y en él se ve a una pareja bailando una danza tradicional. Rivera es muy famoso por sus grandes **murales.** Algunos de ellos se pueden ver en México, Detroit y San Francisco.

Fernando Botero

El **escultor** y pintor colombiano Fernando Botero es conocido por las voluminosas figuras humanas de sus cuadros y esculturas que **se exponen** en todos los museos del mundo. Botero reconoce la influencia artística de los grandes pintores españoles Velázquez y Goya, así como la de los **muralistas** mexicanos. En su obra, Botero critica con humor una sociedad infantilizada o inmadura en la que **abundan** los **símbolos** de la autoridad y del poder, como clérigos, presidentes y burgueses (*members of the middle class*).

PRÁCTICA

13-6 e

Para confirmar. Relaciona las siguientes afirmaciones con los pintores mencionados anteriormente.

1. __g__ Pinta con humor retratos de figuras poderosas.
2. __d__ Sus cuadros son de estilo surrealista.
3. __f__ Es famoso por sus murales.
4. __b__ Fue un pintor español del siglo XVIII.
5. __a__ Es el pintor de *Las Meninas*.
6. __e__ Es una pintora mexicana que retrata las costumbres de su país.
7. __c__ Su estilo cubista muestra formas muy originales.

a. Diego Velázquez
b. Francisco de Goya
c. Pablo Picasso
d. Salvador Dalí
e. Frida Kahlo
f. Diego Rivera
g. Fernando Botero

Saturno devorando a un hijo de Francisco de Goya

Suggestions for 13-7
You may wish to have students work on their reports in small groups. Encourage them to use visuals in their presentations. You may give them questions to elicit good descriptions of their chosen paintings, for example: *¿Qué ven en el cuadro? ¿Cuántas personas hay? ¿Qué hay delante? ¿De qué color es?*

Suggestions for 13-8
You may wish to review comparisons and model some sentences before having students do the activity: *En el cuadro de Picasso hay más ventanas. En los dos cuadros hay un perro,* etc. You may also guide students by asking questions, such as: *¿Qué cuadro tiene más color? ¿Dónde está el pintor, a la derecha o a la izquierda?*

Cultura

Los aparapitas

Enrique Arnal (1932) es uno de los artistas bolivianos más importantes a nivel internacional. Es muy conocido por una serie de pinturas que se enfoca en la figura del aparapita, cargador indígena contratado para llevar objetos y productos en los concurridos mercados de La Paz. La palabra proviene de la lengua aimara y significa *el que carga*. De procedencia rural, los aparapitas se encuentran en una sociedad moderna, desubicados y aislados socialmente. Arnal capta esta alienación en sus cuadros colocándolos entre portales donde parece que pasan de una dimensión a otra. Para expresar su presunta anonimidad ante el público, Arnal borra las facciones de las caras. Al mismo tiempo que los aparapitas están presentes, pasan sin ser percibidos (*noticed*).

▲ *Doble recinto* de Enrique Arnal

13-7 

Otros artistas. Busquen información en Internet sobre algún pintor, escultor o muralista de Bolivia o de Paraguay. Luego, preparen una presentación visual para la clase que incluya lo siguiente.

1. lugar y fecha de nacimiento
2. título y descripción de una de sus obras más famosas
3. algún acontecimiento (*event*) notable de su vida

13-8 

Comparación. Comparen *Las Meninas* de Picasso con *Las Meninas* de Velázquez. Analicen los siguientes aspectos y expliquen cuál de los dos cuadros les gusta más y por qué.

1. el color
2. la ubicación de los personajes
3. las formas
4. el estilo

▲ *Las Meninas,* Diego Velázquez, 1656

▲ *Las Meninas,* Pablo Picasso, 1957

La música y la cultura popular

◀ El boliviano Piraí Vaca es uno de los **guitarristas** más famosos de la **actualidad**. Aparte de su repertorio clásico, Vaca interpreta las tradiciones de la música popular como el tango argentino y el chopi paraguayo. Entre sus muchas distinciones, Vaca ha sido honrado con el *Fellowship of the Americas* por el John F. Kennedy Center for the Performing Arts y declarado el *Boliviano más Destacado en el Exterior* por las Naciones Unidas para la Juventud. Sus conciertos son **inolvidables** por su impresionante talento musical y su carismática presencia sobre el escenario.

La variedad ▶ de la música hispanoamericana, que va **desde** la música afrocaribeña **hasta** las melodías de los Andes, es impresionante. Entre todas estas formas musicales, el tango siempre **se ha distinguido** por la riqueza de las **voces** de sus más notables **intérpretes,** como Carlos Gardel. El tango **surgió** entre los europeos que emigraron a Argentina a comienzos del siglo XX en busca de una vida mejor.

La danza latinoamericana ▶ tiene una larga tradición, tanto en su manifestación clásica como contemporánea. Alicia Alonso, de Cuba, Julio Bocca, de Argentina, y la **bailarina** mexicana Laura Rocha, quien **dirige** su propia **compañía,** Barro Rojo, se han presentado en muchos países de América Latina, en Estados Unidos y en Europa.

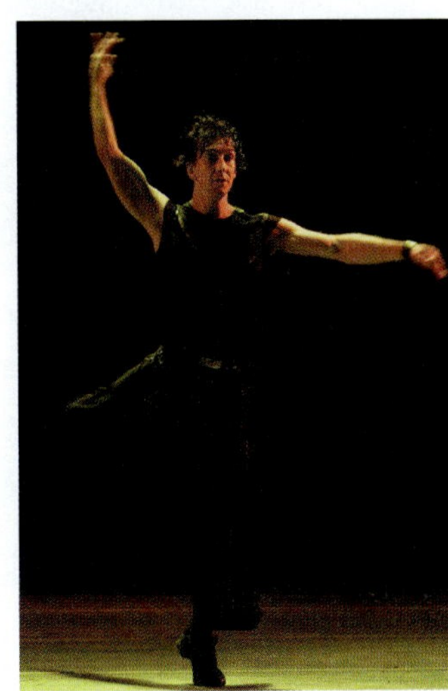

Los actores son a menudo ▶ los protagonistas de las **revistas del corazón.** Los medios de comunicación hablan de sus **éxitos** y de sus **fracasos,** de sus relaciones y de la ropa que llevan. La multifacética actriz Leonor Watling, hija de una británica y un español, ha trabajado en películas tan famosas como *La vida secreta de las palabras,* de Isabel Coixet, y *Hable con ella,* de Pedro Almodóvar. Además, es la cantante principal del grupo Marlango.

Cultura

Los instrumentos musicales

La música de Hispanoamérica incluye una gran variedad de instrumentos, desde los tambores y trompetas de la música del Caribe hasta las quenas y los charangos característicos de los Andes. La quena es una flauta tradicional, generalmente de bambú, y el charango es parecido a una guitarra pero más pequeño. El instrumento típico del tango argentino es el bandoneón, que es como un acordeón con botones a los lados. La música típica de Paraguay incluye en ocasiones el arpa (*harp*).

Comparaciones. ¿Cuáles son los instrumentos más importantes en la música folclórica norteamericana? Selecciona uno y descríbelo.

Suggestion
Have students search YouTube for performances by Piraí Vaca, Carlos Gardel, and Barro Rojo. You may also bring in samples of music to class from different regions of Latin America and Spain. Have students identify the styles (salsa, tango, Andean music, Cuban jazz, flamenco, etc.) and some of the instruments.

PRÁCTICA

13-9  

Para confirmar. Asocia la descripción con la expresión apropiada.

1. __e__ lo contrario del éxito	**a.** un bailarín/una bailarina
2. __f__ un/a artista muy famoso/a	**b.** una compañía
3. __a__ una persona cuya (*whose*) profesión es la danza	**c.** un concierto
4. __b__ un grupo de artistas que hace un espectáculo	**d.** una revista del corazón
5. __c__ un espectáculo de música	**e.** el fracaso
6. __d__ una publicación sobre la vida de los artistas	**f.** una estrella

Cultura

El flamenco

El flamenco es un tipo de música que se originó en Andalucía, en el sur de España, hacia el siglo XV. Inicialmente eran canciones breves, sin acompañamiento instrumental, que los gitanos (*gypsies*) cantaban para lamentarse de sus malas condiciones de vida. A través de los siglos, el flamenco ha continuado su desarrollo y ha añadido instrumentos musicales, principalmente la guitarra. A partir del siglo XVIII adquirió gran popularidad el baile flamenco, que es uno de los más emocionantes y variados del mundo.

Comparaciones. Investiga el origen del *blues* y compáralo con lo que sabes del flamenco. ¿Qué similitudes encuentras?

Suggestions for 13-10
Suggest names of other Hispanic artists for students to research. When students give their presentations, they should keep eye contact with the class rather than read. As an alternate to *13-10,* ask students to role play the interview.

13-10

Personajes célebres. **PREPARACIÓN.** Vas a escribir un breve artículo sobre uno de los artistas mencionados en la página 457. Escribe al menos ocho preguntas relacionadas con los siguientes aspectos de su vida que después investigarás para tu artículo.

1. su lugar de origen
2. su familia
3. algún recuerdo o anécdota de su vida
4. los inicios de su carrera artística
5. sus mayores éxitos y sus fracasos
6. sus planes

 **INTERCAMBIOS.** Busca en Internet información sobre este artista y escribe un breve artículo sobre él/ella incluyendo esta información. Comparte el contenido de este artículo con la clase.

13-11

La cultura en los medios de comunicación. **PREPARACIÓN.** En una revista o un periódico en línea, busca un artículo sobre algún concierto o película que te interese, léelo y resúmelo.

INTERCAMBIOS. Comparte con tu grupo el resumen del artículo que leíste. Incluye la siguiente información.

1. ¿Cómo se llama la revista o el periódico de donde obtuviste el artículo?
2. ¿Quién lo escribió?
3. ¿Cuál es el tema del artículo?
4. ¿Cuáles son las ideas centrales que se presentan?
5. ¿Por qué escogiste este artículo?

13-12

¿Adónde vamos? **PREPARACIÓN.** You will listen to a young couple trying to decide where to go on a Friday evening. With your partner, list three places where you think they might want to go.

ESCUCHA. As you listen, focus on the general idea of what is said. Then select the appropriate ending for each statement.

1. Uno de los eventos culturales a los que Alberto y Josefina consideran ir es...
   - **a.** una exposición de arte precolombino.
   - **(b.)** una lectura de poemas.
   - **c.** un concierto de música popular.
2. Josefina prefiere ir al...
   - **(a.)** concierto de la orquesta sinfónica.
   - **b.** museo de arte latinoamericano.
   - **c.** lugar que sea más barato.
3. Para averiguar si hay entradas, Josefina va a...
   - **a.** usar Internet.
   - **(b.)** llamar por teléfono a todos los lugares.
   - **c.** ir personalmente al centro.
4. Según esta conversación podemos ver que...
   - **a.** Alberto siempre decide a qué lugar van a ir y no escucha a nadie.
   - **b.** Josefina no acepta ninguna sugerencia e impone su voluntad.
   - **(c.)** Alberto y Josefina discuten las posibilidades y deciden juntos.

Suggestion for 13-11
Give students the names of Hispanic magazines such as *People en español, Latina, Vanidades*, etc. They may find the following newspapers on the Internet: *Diario Popular* (from Asunción), *El Diario* (from La Paz).

Note for 13-12
You may want to point out that the *boliviano* is the official currency of Bolivia. One BOB equals approximately fifteen cents.

Audioscript for 13-12
ALBERTO: *Josefina, ¿adónde quieres ir esta noche?*
JOSEFINA: *Mira, yo quisiera ir al Centro de Arte de América Latina. Hoy va a tocar la Orquesta Sinfónica de Puerto Rico. ¿Qué te parece? Empieza a las 8 de la noche y la entrada cuesta 180 bolivianos.*
ALBERTO: *Un poco caro, pero bueno, vale la pena. Hay que ver si hay entradas. Llama por teléfono o mira en Internet. Si no tienen entradas para el concierto, podemos ir a la lectura de poemas de los Nuevos Poetas Bolivianos. Va a ser en el mismo centro, pero en otra sala. Va a incluir a Pedro Shimose, Matilde Casazola y Yolanda Bedregal. ¿Qué piensas?*
JOSEFINA: *¡Me parece excelente!*
ALBERTO: *Empieza a las siete y media. La entrada cuesta 100 bolivianos.*
JOSEFINA: *Bueno, si no conseguimos entradas para ninguna de las dos cosas, ¿qué te parece si vamos al Museo de Arte Latinoamericano? Siempre tienen exposiciones interesantes y la ventaja es que podemos ir ahora mismo sin tener que esperar hasta más tarde. Las entradas son más baratas también.*
ALBERTO: *Bueno, decide tú.*
JOSEFINA: *Voy a llamar a todos los lugares y luego decidimos, pero yo prefiero ir al concierto de la orquesta sinfónica.*
ALBERTO: *Avísame, entonces.*

Suggestion for *Oz Montania*
Have students search online for a video of Oz Montania's graffiti honoring one of the most prominent literary authors in Paraguay: Augusto Roa Bastos. Search terms: *Oz y el mural Roa Bastos.*

Note for *Mosaico cultural*
Emphasize the political mission of graffiti in Latin America. For the most part, graffiti is an expression of political and social protest. It is most common in urban centers and other heavily populated areas. Graffiti often reaches more people than other, more traditional, forms of art, such as literature or theatre.

MOSAICO cultural

El grafiti y la identidad urbana

El grafiti es una manifestación cultural que ha adquirido mucha fuerza en el mundo hispano. Para Oz Montania, un reconocido artista urbano paraguayo, el grafiti es libertad de expresión y es espacio público. Desde los doce años, Oz ha llevado esta forma de arte hasta la gente de una manera absolutamente democrática, como dice él. Históricamente, el grafiti —que es una parte del arte urbano— ha tenido principios políticos: en los periodos de dictadura (*dictatorship*) militar el grafiti fue una de las formas de expresión ideológica más fuerte, especialmente en Argentina, Chile y México. Desde entonces, el grafiti ha ganado importancia entre las otras artes populares, como la música y la danza.

▲ Una calle en la región de Tarapacá, Chile

▲ ¿Arte o vandalismo?

Sin embargo, este arte popular es aún relativamente joven y no es comprendido por algunos sectores de la población. Charqui, un grafitero chileno, ha tenido problemas con la policía porque a veces lo han considerado un criminal y no un artista. "Es probable que las personas no entiendan el humor, la ironía y la inconformidad política de mis grafitis. Quizá por eso piensan que soy un vándalo", comentó Charqui.

Es obvio que esta manifestación artística ha comenzado a definir la identidad de las ciudades. Desde hace años se celebra en Valparaíso el Festival Mundial del Grafiti. En este encuentro se reúnen artistas urbanos de todo el mundo y pintan gran parte de la ciudad de forma colaborativa. Dice Charqui sobre el festival: "El código del grafiti es la solidaridad; la obra de un artista fusionada con el trabajo de otro. Al final, la cultura de la ciudad gana con este proceso artístico".

▲ Valparaíso, Chile

Compara

1. ¿Conoces a algún artista urbano en tu ciudad? ¿Qué tipo de grafiti hace?
2. ¿Piensas que el grafiti es una manifestación artística y que tiene valor cultural? Justifica tu respuesta.
3. ¿Piensas que los grafitis hispanos son diferentes de los estadounidenses? Explica tu opinión con ejemplos.

Funciones y formas

1 Talking about the past

JOSEFINA: Alberto, ¿qué piensas de esta obra?

ALBERTO: Es una expresión magnífica del arte abstracto.

JOSEFINA: ¿Ah, sí? ¿Quién la **pintó?**

ALBERTO: **Fue** un artista que en todas sus obras **pintaba** un ojo abstracto. **Tenía** mucho talento pero **murió** joven. **Empezó** a pintar a los 15 años y **vendió** su primer cuadro a los 17 años. Poca gente lo **conocía.** Sin embargo, **era** uno de los favoritos de los críticos.

JOSEFINA: ¿Qué le **pasó?**

ALBERTO: **Tuvo** un accidente de moto cuando **viajaba** por los Andes. ¡Muy trágico!

Piénsalo. Indica si cada una de las oraciones se refiere a un evento que ocurrió en el pasado (**E**), o si es una descripción (**D**).

1. __D__ En todas sus obras **pintaba** un ojo abstracto.
2. __E__ **Murió** joven.
3. __E__ ¿Quién lo **pintó**?
4. __D__ **Era** uno de los favoritos de los críticos.
5. __E__ **Tuvo** un accidente de moto.
6. __D__ **Tenía** mucho talento.

Review of the preterit and imperfect

- In previous chapters you learned two tenses that Spanish uses to express the past: the preterit (**el pretérito**) and the imperfect (**el imperfecto**). You used the preterit to talk about past events, actions, and conditions that are viewed as completed or ended. You used the imperfect to describe characteristics and conditions in the past; to express habitual or repeated actions, or states in progress at a particular time in the past; and to tell the time and someone's age in the past. In this section you will gain further experience using both tenses to narrate in the past.

REGULAR PRETERIT ENDINGS			
	-ar	**-er**	**-ir**
yo	-é	-í	-í
tú	-aste	-iste	-iste
Ud, él, ella	-ó	-ió	-ió
nosotros/as	-amos	-imos	-imos
vosotros/as	-asteis	-isteis	-isteis
Uds., ellos/as	-aron	-ieron	-ieron

REGULAR IMPERFECT ENDINGS			
	-ar	**-er**	**-ir**
yo	-aba	-ía	-ía
tú	-abas	-ías	-ías
Ud, él, ella	-aba	-ía	-ía
nosotros/as	-ábamos	-íamos	-íamos
vosotros/as	-abais	-íais	-íais
Uds., ellos/as	-aban	-ían	-ían

Refer to *Capítulos 6* through *8* for more information about the past tense.

Suggestion for Review of the preterit and imperfect
The preterit is presented in *Capítulos 6* and *7*, the imperfect in *Capítulo 8*, and the preterit and imperfect together in *Capítulos 8* and *9*. You may wish to go back to some of the activities that have students use preterit and imperfect together, and have students self-assess their understanding of the differences in their meaning and communicative function in the context of storytelling.

Suggestion for 13-13
You may wish to play some Paraguayan music that features a harp. You may compare it with the use of the harp in the music of other Latin American countries, such as Mexico, Peru, Venezuela, Chile, and Argentina. You may also review parts of the body and introduce some new words students may need, such as *uñas, yemas de los dedos,* etc.

¿COMPRENDES?

Escoge entre el pretérito y el imperfecto en cada oración.

1. Durante nuestra visita a La Paz, Marcos y yo (fuimos/íbamos) al Museo Nacional de Arte Contemporáneo. fuimos
2. (Fue/Era) temprano cuando el museo (abrió/abría) sus puertas. Era, abrió
3. (Hubo/Había) un guardia en cada sala del museo. Había
4. Toda la gente (caminó/caminaba) en silencio y (admiró/admiraba) las hermosas obras de arte. caminaba, admiraba
5. Marcos y su familia siempre (fueron/iban) al museo cuando él y sus hermanos (fueron/eran) pequeños. iban, eran

MySpanishLab
Learn more using Amplifire Dynamic Study Modules, Grammar Tutorials, and Extra Practice activities.

PRÁCTICA

13-13  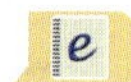

El arpa de Paraguay. Lee la siguiente historia sobre el arpa en la música paraguaya. Completa las oraciones con la forma correcta del pretérito o el imperfecto de los verbos. Luego, compara tus respuestas con las de tu compañero/a.

Los historiadores afirman que los españoles (**1**) __trajeron__ (traer) el arpa a América. Cuando este instrumento (**2**) __llegó__ (llegar) a Paraguay, a los habitantes indígenas de lugar les (**3**) __encantó__ (encantar) la música que (**4**) __tocaba__ (tocar) el español, don Martín Niño. El contacto de la cultura europea y la indígena (**5**) __resultó__ (resultar) en la fusión de dos culturas. De esa unión (**6**) __nació__ (nacer) el arpa paraguaya. Los guaraníes (**7**) __adoptaron__ (adoptar) el arpa y la (**8**) __remodelaron__ (remodelar), usando materiales americanos, como la madera. También (**9**) __crearon__ (crear) su propio repertorio musical. (**10**) __Era__ (Ser) obvio para los jesuitas y los franciscanos españoles que los mestizos (**11**) __tenían__ (tener) gran talento musical. Con cada perfeccionamiento del instrumento musical, los clérigos (**12**) __observaban__ (observar) una mejor sonoridad y claridad en la ejecución del arpa paraguaya. Los mestizos (**13**) __pasaban__ (pasar) sus conocimientos de generación en generación y de esta manera cada una (**14**) __creaba__ (crear) sus propias técnicas. Por ejemplo, (**15**) __usaban__ (usar) las uñas de la mano derecha para crear la melodía. El acompañamiento lo (**16**) __hacían__ (hacer) con la mano izquierda. Con los años el arpa (**17**) __pasó__ (pasar) a ser parte de diversos tipos de música de México, Venezuela, Perú, Chile y Argentina.

Nuestro viaje a Bolivia. Visiten virtualmente las salas del Museo Nacional de Etnografía y Folklore de Bolivia y seleccionen un objeto que les interese. Presenten un informe breve a la clase con la siguiente información.

1. qué tipo de objeto era
2. cuándo y dónde se encontró
3. quiénes lo usaban y para qué lo usaban
4. qué importancia tenía
5. otros detalles interesantes que ustedes descubrieron en su investigación

13-15 

Un espectáculo inolvidable. **PREPARACIÓN.** Piensa en un espectáculo emocionante al que asististe en el pasado. Habla con tu compañero/a sobre el espectáculo e incluye la siguiente información.

1. lo que sabías acerca del espectáculo y los artistas antes de ir
2. lo que esperabas ver allí
3. algo nuevo que descubriste después de ver el espectáculo y los artistas
4. dos actividades que hiciste y dos actividades que no hiciste
5. lo que más recuerdas del espectáculo

 **INTERCAMBIOS.** Determinen cuál de los dos espectáculos fue el más interesante y por qué. Compartan con la clase sus experiencias en el espectáculo.

Situación

PREPARACIÓN. Lean la situación. Luego, compartan ejemplos de vocabulario, gramática y otra información que necesitan para desarrollar la conversación.

Role A. Last week you travelled to La Paz, Bolivia and, on the plane, you happened to be seated next to a movie star. Call your best friend and tell him/her:

a. who the famous person was;
b. what he/she looked like;
c. what he/she was wearing;
d. if you spoke to him/her and what you talked about.

Role B. Your best friend calls you to tell you that he/she met a movie star. Listen to his/her descriptions and information about the encounter. Ask him/her additional information:

a. what he/she did on the plane;
b. what he/she ate;
c. why he/she was sitting in economy class; etc.

	ROLE A	ROLE B
Vocabulario	Physical descriptions Clothes	Airplane and travel expressions Food
Funciones y formas	Using the imperfect to describe Using the preterit for actions Topics of conversation	Using the imperfect to describe Using the preterit for actions

INTERCAMBIOS. Practica la conversación con tu compañero/a incorporando el vocabulario y las funciones de *Preparación*. Luego, represéntenla ante la clase.

Suggestion for 13-14
To make the activity more interesting, divide the class into 4 groups and have each group choose in advance the photo or art piece they will talk about. Have students in each group do some research individually before class on the characteristics of the museum (location, size, etc.) and the type of collections that it holds. In class, have students work together in groups to share the information.

Standard 5.2
Students show evidence of becoming life-long learners by using the language for personal enjoyment and enrichment.
Activities like 13-14 help students combine their interest in history and art with their emerging knowledge of Spanish, which may expand their professional horizons and present new options for leisure travel.

Suggestion for 13-14
Whichever orientation you give the activity, have students make brief presentations to the class. Students in the audience should be expected to react to the content and quality of the information presented by asking questions, offering opinions, and making suggestions.

Note for Hypothesizing
The instruments in the photo are *la zampoña* (also called *el sicu*), a traditional flute of the Andean region, and *el bombo*, a type of drum (*tambor*). Other instruments mentioned in *Piénsalo* are *la quijada* (lit., *jawbone*), a percussion instrument made from the jawbone of a donkey or similar animal, and *la guitarra*. The traditional Bolivian guitar is *el charango*, with five double strings, which was adapted from a guitar brought to the Andean region by the Spaniards.

Suggestions for the conditional
Review the future tense before introducing the conditional and model it in a few sentences: *Este fin de semana pasarán una película española. ¿Irán algunos de ustedes a ver la película? También habrá una presentación de música andina. ¿Asistirás tú al concierto?* Use conditional forms in questions: *De tener tiempo, ¿te gustaría aprender a tocar la guitarra? ¿Qué instrumento te gustaría tocar? Y tú, ¿tomarías clases de alguna lengua indígena?*

You may remind students that the conditional is also used to soften requests and statements: *Me gustaría visitar el museo. ¿Podrías darme la dirección?*

Suggestion for the conditional
Point out that the endings of the conditional are the same as the endings for the imperfect of *-er* and *-ir* verbs.

2 Hypothesizing

GLORIA: Aquí veo solo dos de los instrumentos para el concierto de esta noche. ¿Dónde están los otros?

AMARU: Siempre grabamos digitalmente la música de los otros instrumentos. Yo los **traería** todos, pero **sería** carísimo. **Gastaríamos** demasiado para traer los tambores, las guitarras y las quijadas (*jawbone*), por ejemplo.

GLORIA: ¿Cuánto **costaría** traer los otros instrumentos?

AMARU: Bueno, yo **tendría** que pagar 200 dólares solo para traer mi guitarra. Para traer todos los instrumentos, **pagaríamos** una fortuna.

Piénsalo. Indica (✓) en la columna correspondiente si cada una de las siguientes afirmaciones se refiere a la **realidad** o a una **hipótesis.**

	REALIDAD	HIPÓTESIS
1. Aquí **veo** solo dos de los instrumentos para el concierto.	✓	___
2. Siempre **grabamos** digitalmente la música de los otros instrumentos.	✓	___
3. ¿Cuánto **costaría** traer los otros instrumentos?	___	✓
4. **Sería** carísimo.	___	✓
5. **Tendría** que pagar $200 solo para traer mi guitarra.	___	✓
6. **Pagaríamos** una fortuna.	___	✓

The conditional

- You have used the expression **me gustaría...** to express what you would like. **Gustaría** is a form of the conditional.
- The conditional in Spanish is similar to the English construction *would* + *verb*. It is used to hypothesize about a situation that is not part of the speaker's present reality.

Yo **saldría** temprano para el concierto, pero trabajo hasta tarde. — *I would leave early for the concert, but I work late.*

- When English *would* implies *used to*, the imperfect is used in Spanish.

Cuando era chica, mi papá me **llevaba** a los conciertos al aire libre en el parque. — *When I was little, my father would (used to) take me to open-air concerts in the park.*

- The conditional is easy to recognize. It is formed by adding the endings **-ía, -ías, -ía, -íamos, -íais, -ían** to the infinitive.

CONDITIONAL			
	HABLAR	**COMER**	**VIVIR**
yo	hablar**ía**	comer**ía**	vivir**ía**
tú	hablar**ías**	comer**ías**	vivir**ías**
Ud., él, ella	hablar**ía**	comer**ía**	vivir**ía**
nosotros/as	hablar**íamos**	comer**íamos**	vivir**íamos**
vosotros/as	hablar**íais**	comer**íais**	vivir**íais**
Uds., ellos/as	hablar**ían**	comer**ían**	vivir**ían**

¿COMPRENDES?

Completa las oraciones con la forma del condicional de los verbos.

1. De ser el líder del grupo, yo ___pagaría___ (pagar) dinero para llevar todos los instrumentos a mis conciertos.
2. El público ___preferiría___ (preferir) escuchar la música en vivo que escucharla digitalizada.
3. Nosotros ___ganaríamos___ (ganar) más dinero porque ___asistiría___ (asistir) más público.
4. Los conciertos ___serían___ (ser) un éxito rotundo.

MySpanishLab

Learn more using Amplifire Dynamic Study Modules, Grammar Tutorials, and Extra Practice activities.

- Verbs that have an irregular stem in the future have that same stem in the conditional.

IRREGULAR CONDITIONAL VERBS		
INFINITIVE	**NEW STEM**	**CONDITIONAL FORMS**
haber	**habr-**	habría, habrías, habría...
poder	**podr-**	podría, podrías, podría...
querer	**querr-**	querría, querrías, querría...
saber	**sabr-**	sabría, sabrías, sabría...
poner	**pondr-**	pondría, pondrías, pondría...
salir	**saldr-**	saldría, saldrías, saldría...
tener	**tendr-**	tendría, tendrías, tendría...
venir	**vendr-**	vendría, vendrías, vendría...
decir	**dir-**	diría, dirías, diría...
hacer	**har-**	haría, harías, haría...

Yo **pondría** el cuadro sobre la chimenea. — *I would put the painting over the fireplace.*

¿**Podrías** escribir un poema de amor en español? — *Would you be able to write a love poem in Spanish?*

Suggestions for the conditional
You may wish to remind students that *haber* is the infinitive of *hay, había,* etc. The verbs are ordered according to the categories of the irregularity of their stems.

PRÁCTICA

13-16

¿Qué harías? PREPARACIÓN. Lee las siguientes situaciones y escoge lo que probablemente harías.

1. Es el cumpleaños de tu mejor amigo, quien sigue cursos avanzados de español, y le quieres regalar algo útil.
  a. Le compraría una novela de Roa Bastos traducida al inglés.
  b. Le regalaría *El Quijote* de Cervantes.
  c. Le daría un buen diccionario.

2. El dúo boliviano Tupay va a dar un concierto en tu ciudad este fin de semana.
  a. Invitaría a mi novio/a al concierto.
  b. Llamaría a mis amigos para ir al concierto.
  c. Compraría un charango para tocar con ellos durante el concierto.

3. Van a estrenar (pasar por primera vez) una nueva película de Leonor Watling.
  a. La iría a ver la noche del estreno.
  b. No vería la película porque no me interesa la actriz.
  c. Leería las reseñas (*reviews*) antes de ir a verla.

4. Vas a pasar unos días en Madrid pero tienes poco tiempo para visitar el Museo del Prado. ¿Qué harías?
  a. Pasaría algunos minutos en el museo para conocerlo.
  b. Me informaría sobre lo que se puede ver en el museo.
  c. Solo visitaría las salas donde están las pinturas de mi pintor favorito.

INTERCAMBIOS. Comparen sus respuestas y después digan qué harían ustedes realmente en esas situaciones.

Suggestion for 13-16
Review the cultural material presented in *Vocabulario en contexto* by talking about it and asking some questions. For example, *Augusto Roa Bastos es un novelista latinoamericano importante. ¿Sabes de dónde es? (Paraguay) ¿Cuál es su novela más conocida? (Yo, el supremo) ¿En qué figura histórica está basada? (el dictador José Gaspar Rodríguez de Francia)*

Note for 13-16
All answers are possible. You may wish to have students explain why they chose their answers.

Suggestion for 13-17, *Intercambios*
Maximize the use of the conditional by having students react and comment on their classmates' plans as follows: *Y ustedes, ¿harían lo mismo que proponen sus compañeros/as o harían algo diferente? ¿Por qué harían algo diferente? ¿Sería una buena idea hacer…? ¿O sería aconsejable* + infinitive*?*

Follow-up for 13-17
You may wish to add a writing activity by having the pairs of students combine their proposals into a single essay.

Suggestion for 13-18
You may wish to have pairs compare answers in groups or with the whole class together.

13-17

Desafíos (*Challenges*). PREPARACIÓN. Ganaste una beca de tu universidad. Con los fondos (un millón de dólares), debes despertar el interés de los alumnos universitarios por las artes y las letras. Escribe algunas ideas de qué harías con el dinero y por qué. Considera los siguientes propósitos.

1. promocionar la pintura
2. despertar el interés por las artes populares
3. organizar un foro de expresión artística para los estudiantes con talento artístico

 INTERCAMBIOS. Comenten y comparen sus planes hipotéticos. Luego, seleccionen el mejor plan y explíquenle a la clase por qué lo escogieron.

13-18 

Buscar soluciones. Primero di qué harías en las siguientes situaciones. Después, compara tus respuestas con las de otros estudiantes.

1. Mientras caminas por una calle de tu ciudad, inesperadamente, te encuentras (*run into*) con tu artista favorito/a.
2. Un amigo tuyo es pintor y necesita dinero para montar su primera exposición.
3. Acabas de descubrir que alguien en el campus está vendiendo entradas falsas y muy baratas para un concierto de tu grupo favorito.
4. Alguien confiable (*trustworthy*) te informó que la persona que pintó grafiti en las paredes de la residencia donde vives es uno de tus mejores amigos.

13-19

Músicos aficionados. PREPARACIÓN. Tienen un grupo de amigos que han creado una banda de música muy buena pero no saben promocionarse. Denles ideas de lo que ustedes harían en su lugar.

INTERCAMBIOS. Compartan sus ideas con otra pareja y escojan las mejores para compartir con la clase.

Cultura

Museo Nacional de Bellas Artes

El Museo Nacional de Bellas Artes de Asunción es el más importante del país. En este museo se puede apreciar la historia del país, caracterizada por la importancia de la cultura indígena y por su aislamiento de corrientes artísticas y emigraciones de influencia europea hasta el siglo XX. Hoy en día, cuenta con una importante colección de arte indígena y con obras de los principales artistas paraguayos del siglo XX que siguieron tendencias cosmopolitas. También cuenta con una colección de artistas internacionales.

Comparaciones. ¿Con qué frecuencia visitas los museos de arte? ¿Qué tipo de obras se pueden ver en el museo de bellas artes de tu ciudad o estado?

Situación

Suggestion for *Situación*
You may wish to brainstorm with students what words they know for places to stay while traveling: *hotel, pensión, albergue juvenil.* Explain the differences in quality and services that travelers are likely to encounter.

PREPARACIÓN. Lean la situación. Luego, compartan ejemplos de vocabulario, gramática y otra información que necesitan para desarrollar la conversación.

Role A. You are considering visiting Paraguay next summer so you call a friend who has been there. Include the following in your conversation:

a. ask how much money you would need for food and lodging for a month in Paraguay;
b. tell your friend that you are really interested in seeing and studying the indigenous art of Paraguay;
c. ask your friend to recommend some Paraguayan folk music; and
d. find out how long it would take to learn Guaraní, the indigenous language of Paraguay.

Role B. Your friend is thinking of visiting Paraguay, a country you love and know a lot about. Tell your friend the following:

a. he/she would probably need around U.S. $1,500 for food and lodging for a month if he/she stays at youth hostels (**albergues juveniles**);
b. you would recommend the Museo Nacional de Bellas Artes in Asunción for indigenous art; and
c. the Teatro Nacional for concerts of Paraguayan folk music;
d. he/she would probably be able to learn some basic expressions in Guaraní during the trip, but it's totally different from Spanish.

	ROLE A	ROLE B
Vocabulario	Expressions related to traveling and popular art, such as handicrafts Question words	Expressions related to traveling and popular art, such as handicrafts
Funciones y formas	Asking questions	Answering questions Giving suggestions on hypothetical situations

INTERCAMBIOS. Practica la conversación con tu compañero/a incorporando el vocabulario y las funciones de *Preparación*. Luego, represéntenla ante la clase.

Suggestions for Expressing reciprocity
Introduce reciprocal verbs and pronouns by talking about visuals you bring to class and/or members of your class. For example, look at a student and say: *Yo miro a Pedro. Pedro me mira a mí.* [use hand gesture] *Pedro y yo nos miramos. Él y yo nos respetamos. Nos hablamos en la clase y a veces nos vemos en la cafetería o en un pasillo y nos saludamos.* Practice *llevarse bien/mal.* You may introduce additional vocabulary and expressions such as *darse la mano, extrañarse/echarse de menos.*

3 Expressing reciprocity

En general, los artesanos hispanos forman comunidades donde abundan las relaciones de solidaridad. **Se conocen** entre ellos y, puesto que generalmente viven modestamente, **se ayudan** mutuamente. Así lo indican las afirmaciones de Camilo, uno de los artesanos de este taller. "Mario y yo somos amigos y compartimos casi todo. Cuando uno de los dos no tiene dinero, **nos prestamos** dinero. Pero aún más importante, **nos respetamos** el uno al otro porque **nos necesitamos**".

Piénsalo. Asocia las afirmaciones con su significado.

1. __c__ **Se conocen** entre ellos.
2. __d__ **Se ayudan** mutuamente.
3. __e__ **Nos prestamos** dinero.
4. __a__ **Nos respetamos** el uno al otro.
5. __b__ **Nos necesitamos**.

a. Yo respeto a Mario y él me respeta a mí.
b. Mario me necesita a mí y yo lo necesito a él.
c. Mario conoce a Camilo y Camilo conoce a Mario.
d. Camilo ayuda a Mario y viceversa.
e. Yo le presto dinero a Mario y él hace lo mismo conmigo.

Reciprocal verbs and pronouns

- Use plural reflexive pronouns (**nos**, **os**, **se**) to express reciprocal actions. In English, reciprocal actions are usually expressed with *each other* or *one another.*

Muchos hispanos **se abrazan** cuando **se saludan.**	*Many Hispanics embrace when they greet each other.*
Los artesanos de este taller **se ven** todos los días.	*The artisans in this workshop see each other every day.*
En este centro de arte **nos ayudamos** mucho.	*In this art center, we help each other a lot.*
Nos llamamos cuando hay una nueva exposición de arte para ir juntos.	*We call each other when there is a new art exhibit so that we can go together.*

¿COMPRENDES?

Completa las oraciones para indicar reciprocidad.

1. Mónica y Pablo __se ayudan__ (ayudar) a preparar la exposición de la artesanía que ambos han creado.
2. ¿Por qué tú y yo no __nos vemos__ (ver) después del concierto?
3. Los guardias que cuidan a los artistas famosos __se mandan__ (mandar) mensajes de texto cuando ven algo extraño.

MySpanishLab
Learn more using Amplifire Dynamic Study Modules, Grammar Tutorials, and Extra Practice activities.

PRÁCTICA

13-20 

Indicaciones de reciprocidad. Escoge las ideas que completen las oraciones.

1. __b__ Cuando Mario y Camilo no se ven durante el día, ellos...
2. __d__ El perro y el gato de Mario se pelean todo el tiempo. Ellos...
3. __a__ Alberto y yo somos muy buenos amigos, pero vivimos en ciudades diferentes. No hablamos mucho por teléfono, pero...
4. __e__ Mario y Alicia son novios y se quieren mucho. Cuando se despiden por la noche, ellos...
5. __c__ Mario y Camilo dicen que el secreto de su larga amistad es que ellos...

a. nos mandamos correos electrónicos.
b. se llaman por teléfono.
c. se aprecian y se respetan.
d. se detestan.
e. se abrazan y se besan.

13-21 

¿Qué hacen los buenos colegas? **PREPARACIÓN.** Determinen si los buenos colegas deben hacer lo siguiente, y bajo qué circunstancias.

respetarse

E1: *Yo creo que los buenos colegas se respetan, a pesar de sus diferencias.*

E2: *Estoy de acuerdo. En las reuniones se escuchan con atención y se tratan con respeto siempre.*

1. ____ llamarse todos los días
2. ____ comprenderse
3. ____ ayudarse cuando tienen problemas
4. ____ insultarse y pelearse
5. ____ regalarse cosas
6. ____ darse consejos cuando los necesitan
7. ____ comunicarse constantemente
8. ____ criticarse continuamente
9. ____ pedirse disculpas (*apologize*) después de una fuerte discusión
10. ____ demostrarse empatía

INTERCAMBIOS. Compartan sus ideas con otra pareja. Luego, hagan lo siguiente:

1. Escojan las cuatro actitudes más importantes para mantener una buena relación con la gente. Justifiquen su selección.
2. Escojan las dos actitudes que consideran más problemáticas en las relaciones con otras personas. Den ejemplos de los problemas que podrían causar entre las personas.
3. Compartan sus conclusiones con la clase.

13-22 

Mis relaciones con... Piensa en la gente con quien te relacionas normalmente y explícale a tu compañero/a cómo son las relaciones entre ustedes. Usa los verbos de la lista.

comunicarse	pelearse
detestarse	quererse
odiarse	respetarse

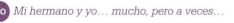

Mi hermano y yo... mucho, pero a veces...

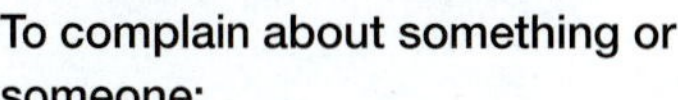

To complain about something or someone:

Tengo una queja. *I have a complaint.*

Quisiera quejarme de... *I would like to complain about ...*

Quisiera hablar con usted sobre un problema que tengo con... *I would like to discuss with you a problem that I have with ...*

 Listen to a conversation with these expressions.

Suggestion for 13-21, *Intercambios*
You may give examples of what students could say when comparing their lists: *Para nosotros, la generosidad es importante en una buena amistad.* You may also wish to do item #1 with the whole class by brainstorming the desirable/undesirable attitudes and values that benefit or hurt work relations, such as: *el respeto, la consideración, la generosidad, la empatía, la sinceridad, la envidia, el chisme, la mentira, la hipocresía.* It may be helpful for students if you write the two lists in columns on the board/transparency.

Audioscript for *En directo*
ROLANDO: *Vamos a terminar un capítulo más de esta novela esta noche.*
MARICARMEN: *Perdón, pero tengo una queja.*
ROLANDO: *¿Cuál es tu queja?*
MARICARMEN: *Hablas demasiado. Quisiera pedirte silencio para concentrarme e inspirarme.*
ROLANDO: *Trato hecho. Guardaré silencio.*

13-23

Consejos. **PREPARACIÓN.** Identifica los problemas de las siguientes personas. Luego, recomienda una solución en cada situación.

1. Rafael y Magdalena son novios, pero no se ven con mucha frecuencia. Él es un pintor que vive en Monterrey, México, y ella trabaja en Los Ángeles. Mantienen una relación a distancia.
2. Catalina y Raquel trabajan en un taller de arte. Cuando Catalina quiere pintar un cuadro, necesita silencio absoluto para inspirarse. Pero cuando ella llega al taller, siempre encuentra a Raquel hablando por teléfono con su novio.
3. Los empleados de Pablo tienen miedo de expresar sus opiniones sobre las piezas de cerámica que él crea porque Pablo siempre toma los comentarios de sus empleados como un ataque personal o parece no escucharlos. Sus colegas evitan hablar con él de este tema.

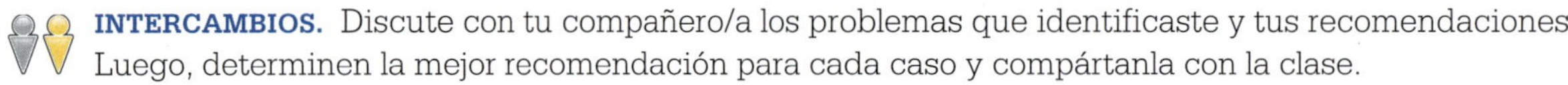

INTERCAMBIOS. Discute con tu compañero/a los problemas que identificaste y tus recomendaciones. Luego, determinen la mejor recomendación para cada caso y compártanla con la clase.

E1: *En el caso de Rafael y Magdalena, el problema es la distancia. Se ven con poca frecuencia.*

E2: *Tienes razón. ¿Qué les recomendarías?*

E1: *Les recomendaría conseguir un trabajo en la misma ciudad.*

E2: *Estoy de acuerdo./No estoy de acuerdo. Deberían terminar su relación.*

Situación

PREPARACIÓN. Lean la situación. Luego, compartan ejemplos de vocabulario, gramática y otra información que necesitan para desarrollar la conversación.

Role A. You are talking with the owner of a popular art studio in your community where you are taking a pottery class (**cerámica**). You are new in town and think this will be a good place to meet people. You trust this person enough to ask the following personal questions:

a. if he/she has many good friends;
b. when he/she met his/her best friend (**conocerse**); and
c. what the key (**la clave**) to a long friendship (**amistad**) is.

Role B. You own an art studio that is very popular in your community. You are talking with a new student who is eager to make friends with people in the class. Share with him/her some of your own experiences. Explain:

a. when you and your best friend met (**conocerse**);
b. how your friendship (**amistad**) started;
c. that you do not see each other every day but you stay in touch (**mantenerse en contacto**); and
d. that you respect each other, although you do not always agree on everything.

	ROLE A	ROLE B
Vocabulario	Vocabulary related to relationships	Vocabulary related to relationships
Funciones y formas	Asking questions Expressing reciprocity	Answering questions Expressing reciprocity

INTERCAMBIOS. Practica la conversación con tu compañero/a incorporando el vocabulario y las funciones de *Preparación*. Luego, represéntenla ante la clase.

EN ACCIÓN

¡No te lo pierdas!

13-24 Antes de ver 

Artistas del mundo hispanoamericano. ¿Con qué artistas asocias las siguientes obras?

1. __d__ *Autorretrato entre México y Estados Unidos*	a. Gabriel García Márquez
2. __a__ *Cien años de soledad*	b. Cervantes
3. __e__ *La estrategia del caracol*	c. Velázquez
4. __b__ *Don Quijote de la Mancha*	d. Frida Kahlo
5. __c__ *Las Meninas*	e. Sergio Cabrera

13-25 Mientras ves  

Manifestaciones artísticas. En este segmento de video, cada uno de los chicos se interesa por distintas manifestaciones artísticas del mundo hispanoamericano. Asocia la persona interesada con cada uno de los siguientes temas.

1. __c__ obras de pintores latinoamericanos	a. Vanesa
2. __a__ música puertorriqueña	b. Yolanda y Federico
3. __d__ teatro infantil	c. Héctor
4. __b__ muralistas latinoamericanos	d. Esteban

13-26 Después de ver 

Preferencias artísticas. **PREPARACIÓN.** Indica si las siguientes afirmaciones son ciertas (**C**) o falsas (**F**) de acuerdo con la información en el video.

1. __F__ El Museo de Arte Latinoamericano tiene una importante colección de obras de artistas hispanos del siglo XIX.
2. __C__ A Héctor le interesan mucho los artistas que hacen un comentario social a través de sus obras.
3. __F__ Fede y Yolanda salen a la calle para entrevistar a un novelista hispano.
4. __F__ En el festival que grabó Vanesa se celebra la cultura y herencia de todos los latinos en Estados Unidos.
5. __C__ Según Choco Orta, la música salsa representa la voz de la gente pobre e invisible.

 **INTERCAMBIOS.** En el video que muestra Héctor se dice que los artistas hispanos enfocan su arte en la realidad política o económica de su país. ¿Están ustedes de acuerdo? Discutan esta idea con sus compañeros e ilustren sus comentarios con la obra de algún artista que conozcan. ¿Ocurre lo mismo en el arte de su propio país? Expliquen con ejemplos.

Mosaicos

ESCUCHA

13-27

Presentational

Preparación. Vas a escuchar a cuatro estudiantes universitarios que hablan sobre actividades culturales. Antes de escuchar, haz una lista de tres actividades culturales que te interesarían a ti. Comparte tu lista con la clase.

ESTRATEGIA

Identify the speaker's intentions

When you listen to a speaker, you can frequently infer his or her intentions from the context. Let's imagine that you get this message: "I have a couple of tickets to a recital. Please give me a call." You immediately know the caller wants to invite you to the recital, even though the word *invitation* was never uttered.

To identify correctly a speaker's intention, follow these tips:

- Hypothesize about what the speaker probably means, making logical connections based on what you hear.
- As you listen, see if you can confirm your hypothesis.
- If you get information that does not fit, form a new hypothesis.

13-28

Interpretive

Escucha. Now read the following statements, and then listen to the students. As you listen, next to each statement write the number of the passage associated with the student who probably uttered it.

__2__ Miguel probablemente quiere escuchar o conversar con los artistas latinoamericanos para decidir sus estudios de posgrado.

__4__ Joaquín es el pintor a quien le gusta más la pintura mexicana.

__1__ Rosa María piensa ir a ver las obras de teatro este año.

__3__ Eugenia es pianista y quiere convencer a otra persona de las ventajas de aprender a tocar el piano.

Comprueba

I was able to ...

____ **identify the activities students are interested in.**

____ **make logical connections between what students say and what they do.**

13-29

Interpersonal

Un paso más. Comparte tu opinión con tu compañero/a.

1. ¿Es importante que los jóvenes aprendan a apreciar las diversas expresiones artísticas (la pintura, la música clásica, el teatro o la escultura)? ¿Por qué?
2. ¿Qué manifestación artística prefieres, la música o la pintura?
3. ¿Cuál es tu pintor o músico favorito? ¿Por qué te gusta?

Audioscript for 13-28

1. *A mí me encantan las comedias y los dramas. Aunque por lo general solo tengo que leer algunas escenas de las obras para mis clases de literatura, yo busco el tiempo para leer toda la obra. Este año vamos a tener otro festival de teatro latinoamericano, donde se presentarán dramas y comedias clásicas y algunas obras de autores bolivianos. El año pasado no pude ir y lo sentí muchísimo, pero este año va a ser diferente.*
2. *Voy a graduarme de la escuela de artes en algunos meses, pero para enseñar necesito estudios de posgrado. Ya he investigado sobre el arte moderno y, en particular, algunos escultores contemporáneos de varios países hispanoamericanos. Afortunadamente habrá una exposición de escultores bolivianos en el salón de exposiciones de la universidad este mes. Esto me ayudará muchísimo para aclarar mis ideas.*
3. *El piano es un instrumento fascinante. Si quieres aprender a tocarlo profesionalmente debes practicar desde pequeño. Si lo haces con dedicación y arte, tendrás muchas satisfacciones. Yo empecé mis clases de piano en la escuela primaria y las seguí durante la escuela secundaria. Ahora voy a casa de mi maestra dos veces al mes para escuchar sus críticas y perfeccionar mis técnicas. Hago esto porque me gusta, y no pienso en el sacrificio ni en las horas que paso haciéndolo. Vale la pena. Nunca lo he lamentado.*
4. *Pinto desde hace varios años. Mi profesor cree que puedo llegar a ser un buen pintor. A mí me gustan las pinturas de Velázquez, Goya y el Greco, pero en realidad, hay algo especial en las obras de los pintores mexicanos con las cuales me identifico más. De hecho, hoy quiero ir a una exposición de arte mexicano. Sé que exhiben*

HABLA

13-30 Interpretive

Preparación. Escoge a una de las personas de la lista y busca la información indicada en la tabla sobre esta persona. También puedes incluir otra información que te interese.

Luis Cañete	Alfonso Gumucio Dagrón
Pablo Casals	Jaime Laredo
Carlos Colombino	Marina Núñez del Prado
Susy Delgado	Maria Luisa Pacheco
Plácido Domingo	Violeta Parra
Carlos Gardel	

NOMBRE	DATOS PERSONALES	PROFESIÓN	LOGROS
	fecha de nacimiento	contribución a su profesión	premios
	lugar de nacimiento/ muerte		reconocimientos

ESTRATEGIA

Make your presentations comprehensible and interesting

When you give a presentation in your Spanish class, your two challenges are a) to make it understandable to your classmates; and b) to make it interesting so they will listen. The following guidelines will help you achieve these goals:

- Keep it simple. If you consulted sources for your presentation, present content in your own words. Look up new words in the dictionary and simplify your speech.
- Practice your presentation, so you can talk, not read, to your audience.
- Use visuals and props to make your presentation more lively and interesting.
- Involve your audience. Make eye contact, ask questions, check that they understand you, and invite them to ask questions.

13-31  Presentational

Habla. Haz una breve presentación sobre la persona que escogiste en la actividad 13-30. Incluye la mayor cantidad de información posible.

Comprueba

I was able to …

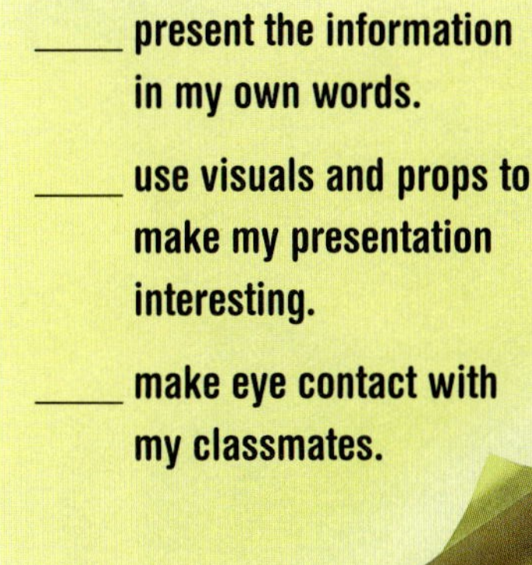

____ present the information in my own words.

____ use visuals and props to make my presentation interesting.

____ make eye contact with my classmates.

En directo

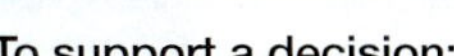

To support a decision:

He elegido a... porque... *I have chosen … because …*

Lo que más influyó en mi decisión fue/fueron... *What most influenced my decision was/were …*

Mi decisión está basada en lo siguiente... *My decision is based on the following …*

 Listen to a conversation with these expressions.

13-32 Interpersonal

Un paso más. Elige a uno de los artistas de la actividad 13-30 como la persona a quién más admiras. Comparte tu elección con tu compañero/a. Dale tres razones para explicar tu elección.

las obras de Kamilo Almanza y José Baray. No me la puedo perder.

Alternatives for 13-30
Depending on the time you have available for class presentations, you may wish to have students do their presentations individually, in pairs, or in small groups.

Suggestions for 13-30
Students will find information on their famous person in the arts on the Internet or print sources. Encourage them to find out about individuals whose names may not be as well known: Carlos Colombino (Paraguayan painter), Alfonso Gumucio Dagrón (Bolivian writer, filmmaker, and photographer), Jaime Laredo (Bolivian-American violinist and conductor), Marina Núñez del Prado (Bolivian sculptor), or add other artists not listed here, such as Augusto Roa Bastos (Paraguayan writer).

Remind students to follow the guidelines in the *Estrategia* box when preparing their presentations.

Suggestions for 13-31
Before their presentations, remind students to engage with their audience and to speak, rather than read from their notes. Students in the audience should take notes, ask questions, and be ready to answer questions from the speaker and from you.

Audioscript for *En directo*
FEMALE SPEAKER: *¿A quién escogiste?*
MALE INTERVIEWEE: *He elegido al músico Pablo Casals. Lo que más influyó en mi decisión fue su interés por hacer de la música un instrumento de la paz en el mundo.*

Suggestions for 13-32
Give students other expressions to use when answering classmates' questions. To acknowledge not having some information: *Lamentablemente, no tengo/tenemos esa información. Lo siento/sentimos, pero no sé/sabemos…* To acknowledge you didn't think of something, but will look into it: *La verdad es que no pensé/pensamos en eso, pero lo averiguaré/averiguaremos.*

LEE

13-33 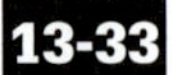  Interpersonal

Preparación. Háganse las siguientes preguntas. ¿Piensan igual o diferente?

1. ¿Tienes algunos objetos favoritos? ¿Por qué son especiales?
2. ¿Les hablas a tus objetos a veces? ¿Qué les dices?
3. ¿Es posible tener una relación personal con tus objetos favoritos, aunque sean inanimados Explica tu opinión.
4. ¿Tienes mascota en casa? ¿Cómo es?
5. ¿Qué relación tienes con tu mascota? ¿Tratas a tu mascota como otro miembro de la familia, aunque sea un animal?

ESTRATEGIA

Focus on multiple meanings when reading poetry

When you read a narrative or journalistic text in Spanish, you have learned to increase your comprehension by going for the main ideas and using your prior knowledge to guess what the text is about. When you read poetry in Spanish, you need different strategies. Start by looking up the meanings of unfamiliar words. Then, with a pencil in your hand, read the poem aloud several times. Circle important, unusual, or repeated words. Draw lines to connect related ideas. Try to unfold the language of the poem by paraphrasing it in straightforward sentences: subject, verb, object. This will help you answer the question: "What is this poem about?"

13-34 Interpretive

Lee. Antes de leer el poema, lee primero la siguiente nota biográfica de la autora. Después, relaciona las cosas y objetos con las acciones.

Gloria Fuertes, poeta española (1917–1998), nació en Madrid. Era de una familia pobre: su madre era costurera (*seamstress*) y sirvienta y su padre limpiaba edificios comerciales. Fuertes comenzó a una edad temprana a escribir cuentos y poemas. De adolescente leía sus poemas en Radio España de Madrid. En 1961, recibió la beca Fulbright para dar clases de poesía española en la Universidad de Bucknell en Pensilvania. Los temas principales de su poesía son el amor, la muerte y los derechos humanos. También le interesa mucho el poder de la poesía de revelar el significado profundo de la vida cotidiana (*everyday*). Dada su afinidad por las letras desde muy niña, no es sorprendente que escribiera también cuentos y poemas infantiles.

LAS COSAS

Las cosas, nuestras cosas,
les gustan que las quieran;
a mi mesa le gusta que yo apoye los codos,
a la silla le gusta que me siente en la silla,
a la puerta le gusta que la abra y la cierre
como al vino le gusta que lo compre y lo beba,
mi lápiz se deshace[1] si lo cojo[2] y escribo,
mi armario se estremece[3] si lo abro y me asomo[4],
las sábanas son sábanas cuando me echo sobre ellas
y la cama se queja cuando yo me levanto.
¿Qué será de las cosas cuando el hombre se acabe?
Como perros las cosas no existen sin el amo.

[1] *dissolves* [2] *I hold it* [3] *trembles* [4] *I look inside*

COSAS	ACCIONES
d 1. las cosas	**a.** estremecerse (*tremble*)
e 2. la mesa	**b.** deshacerse (*dissolve*)
h 3. la silla	**c.** quejarse
f 4. la puerta	**d.** quererlas
g 5. el vino	**e.** apoyar los codos
b 6. el lápiz	**f.** cerrarla
a 7. el armario	**g.** beberlo
c 8. la cama	**h.** sentarse

Comprueba
I was able to ...

____ **understand what the poem is about.**

____ **understand the speaker's relationship to her objects.**

13-35  Presentational

Un paso más. Trabajando en grupos, escriban su interpretación de los dos últimos versos (*lines*) del poema y preséntenla a la clase.

ESCRIBE

13-36 Interpretive

Preparación. Busca información biográfica en Internet sobre una persona hispana que te interese en uno de estos campos: los deportes, las artes, la ciencia o la política. Toma nota sobre los siguientes datos que te ayudarán a expresar información concreta de esta persona.

1. nombre, fecha y lugar de nacimiento: ¿Cuándo y dónde nació?
2. información personal: ¿Es soltero/a, casado/a, divorciado/a? ¿Tiene hijos? ¿Cuántos?
3. estudios y formación profesional: ¿Cuáles son los mayores éxitos personales y/o profesionales de esta persona? ¿Cómo los logró?
4. su comunidad: ¿En qué área se destaca (*stands out*): en la religiosa, étnica, profesional, científica, artística, etc.? Sus éxitos, ¿han beneficiado a la comunidad? ¿Cómo?

ESTRATEGIA

Write to spark interest

To hold the interest of your reader, these tips may prove useful.

1. Be sure you are knowledgeable about the topic before you start to write. Do some research if necessary.
2. Organize the information to keep the text focused on the topic.
3. Vary your vocabulary.
4. When appropriate, add a hint of controversy by including provocative statements or questions.
5. When appropriate, incorporate the element of fun with a personal story or anecdote.
6. Choose a title that will grab the attention of your readers.

Suggestion for 13-37
You may wish to have students become peer editors. Guide students to check the following in their classmate's text:

1. How interesting is the information presented about this famous artist? Did your classmate include any information to spark your interest about this person?
2. Is the information well organized? Does the biography focus on the acomplishments of this person?
3. Is the title appealing?
4. Is the text cohesive? Are there logical transitions and connectors?
5. Is the vocabulary varied and dynamic?
6. Are there any spelling or punctuation problems? Any missing accent marks?

13-37 Presentational

Escribe. Escribe un informe biográfico para una revista electrónica, usando la información obtenida en la actividad 13-36. Tu propósito es despertar la curiosidad de los jóvenes por conocer qué sacrificios han hecho los famosos para tener éxito.

Comprueba

I was able to ...

____ **focus on the topic.**

____ **add an interesting element to spark the reader's attention.**

13-38  Interpersonal

Un paso más. Lee la biografía que escribió tu compañero/a y, luego, hazle preguntas sobre otros aspectos de la vida o carrera de este artista de los cuales (*about which*) te gustaría saber más.

En este capítulo...

Comprueba lo que sabes

Go to ***MySpanishLab*** to review what you have learned in this chapter. Practice with the following:

Vocabulario

LAS PERSONAS *People*

el bailarín/la bailarina *dancer*
la compañía (de danza, de teatro) *(dance, theater) company*
el/la escritor/a *writer*
el/la escultor/a *sculptor*
el/la guitarrista *guitar player*
el/la intérprete *performer, artist*
el/la muralista *muralist*
el/la novelista *novelist*
el/la pintor/a *painter*
el/la poeta *poet*

LAS OBRAS DE ARTE *Works of art*

el autorretrato *self-portrait*
el cuento *story*
la escena *scene*
la forma *shape, form*
el mural *mural*
la novela *novel*
la obra *work*
el paisaje *landscape*
el personaje principal *main character*
la pintura *painting*
el poema *poem*
la poesía *poetry*
el símbolo *symbol*
el tema *theme*
el verso *line*
la voz *voice*

PALABRAS Y EXPRESIONES ÚTILES *Useful words and expressions*

a través de *through*
al fondo *at the back, in the rear*
la amistad *friendship*
el amor *love*
la calidad *quality*
cubista *cubist*
el desarrollo *development*
desde *since*
en la actualidad *at the present time*
el éxito *success*
el fracaso *failure*
la fundación *establishment, founding*
hasta *including*
el premio *award, prize*
el recuerdo *memory*
la revista del corazón *gossip magazine*
surrealista *surrealist*
tener éxito *to be successful*

LAS DESCRIPCIONES *Descriptions*

blando/a *soft*
destacado/a *outstanding*
inolvidable *unforgettable*
prometedor/a *promising*

VERBOS *Verbs*

abrazar (c) *to embrace*
abundar *to abound*
besar *to kiss*
denunciar *to denounce*
dirigir (j) *to direct*
distinguir *to distinguish*
exponer (g) *to exhibit*
grabar *to film, to record*
nominar *to nominate*
pintar *to paint*
reflejar *to reflect*
retratar *to portray*
rodear *to surround*
saludar *to greet*
surgir (j) *to emerge*
titular(se) *to be called*
tratar *to treat, be about*

Introduction to chapter
Introduce the chapter theme about social change and ask questions to recycle previous content: *¿Qué cambios sociales han visto ustedes en los últimos años en Estados Unidos? ¿Y en el resto del mundo? ¿Creen que todos los ciudadanos tienen los mismos derechos y oportunidades en la vida? ¿Qué cambios sociales creen que son los más urgentes? ¿Qué hacen ustedes para lograr cambios en su comunidad?*

Integrated Performance Assessment: Three Modes of Communication

Presentational: See activities 14-3, 14-22, 14-26, 14-31, 14-34, and 14-36.

Interpretive: See Activities 14-1, 14-2, 14-4, 14-7, 14-9, 14-10, 14-11, 14-12, 14-13, 14-15, 14-16, 14-17, 14-18, 14-20, 14-21, 14-22, 14-23, 14-24, 14-25, 14-27, 14-29, 14-33, and 14-35.

Interpersonal: See activities 14-1, 14-2, 14-3, 14-4, 14-5, 14-6, 14-8, 14-10, 14-12, 14-14, 14-15, 14-16, 14-17, 14-18, 14-19, 14-21, 14-22, 14-25, 14-28, 14-30, 14-32, 14-37 and all *Situación* activities.

14 ¿Cómo vivimos los cambios sociales?

ENFOQUE CULTURAL
Chile

VOCABULARIO EN CONTEXTO
Cambios en la sociedad
El papel de la mujer
Temas de hoy: los jóvenes y la emigración

MOSAICO CULTURAL
La migración interna en el mundo hispano

FUNCIONES Y FORMAS
Adverbial conjunctions that require the subjunctive
Adverbial conjunctions that take the subjunctive or indicative
The past perfect
The infinitive as subject or object

EN ACCIÓN
Por un mundo mejor

MOSAICOS
ESCUCHA Identify the speaker's point of view
HABLA Organize ideas to present solutions to problems
LEE Identify the tone of a text
ESCRIBE Use language to express emotions

EN ESTE CAPÍTULO...
Comprueba lo que sabes
Vocabulario

LEARNING OUTCOMES

You will be able to:

- discuss demographics and social conditions
- indicate conditions, goals, and purposes
- express conjecture
- talk about the past from a past perspective
- share information about social change, gender roles, and migration in Hispanic countries and identify cultural similarities

ENFOQUE cultural CHILE

Enfoque cultural

To learn more about Chile, go to MySpanishLab to view the *Vistas culturales* videos.

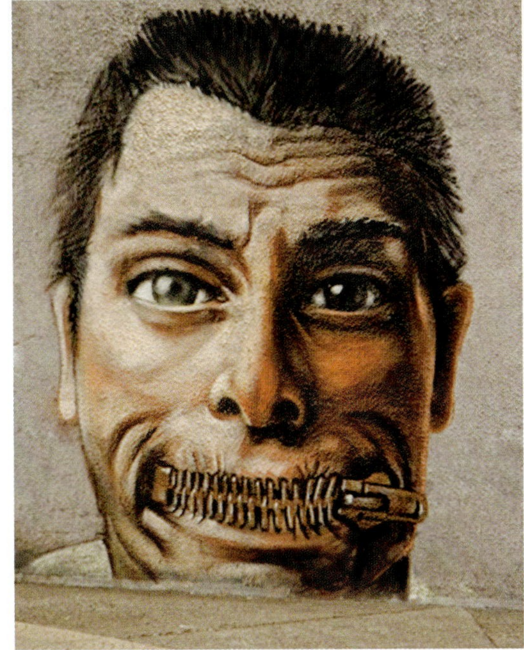

▲ Este mural en las calles de Santiago retrata el sufrimiento y la opresión de los chilenos durante la dictadura militar entre 1973 y 1990.

¿QUÉ TE PARECE?

- Chile es una larga franja de tierra rodeada de montañas: al este, por la Cordillera de los Andes; al oeste, por la cordillera de la costa.
- Sobre su nombre, muchos han especulado que Chile proviene de la palabra quechua *chiri,* que significa frío, helado. Sin embargo, para el cronista Diego Rosales, el nombre probablemente venía de Tili, un cacique picunche, quien gobernó la región de Aconcagua antes de la llegada de los españoles. Hasta hoy no existe consenso del origen del nombre Chile.
- El desierto de Atacama, en el norte de Chile, es el más árido del mundo. Aunque llueve poco, en las últimas décadas, a causa del calentamiento global, el clima está cambiando. En 2013, nevó copiosamente después de 30 años.

Suggestions for map
Ask students what they know about Chile. Point out the photos on the map and make comments to introduce some vocabulary as you ask: *¿Cuál es la capital de Chile? ¿Qué países limitan con Chile? ¿Cuáles son las características geográficas del país? ¿Dónde está el desierto de Atacama? ¿Dónde está el estrecho de Magallanes? ¿Y la isla de Pascua? ¿Por qué es famosa esta isla?* Explain that *isla de Pascua* (Easter Island), also known as Rapa Nui, belongs to Chile. Located in Polynesia, 3,600 km (2,237 mi.) west of Chile, it is a volcanic island known for its large stone statues (Moai). Show the photo of the vineyards and remind students that Chile is a major producer of fruit and wine, much of which is exported to the U.S. The country is also rich in minerals, especially copper (*cobre*), mainly produced in the Atacama desert. Explain that although Spanish is the official language of Chile, some indigenous languages are spoken there, such as Mapuche, which has more than half a million speakers, Aymara, and Quechua. Ask if they know of any famous authors from Chile. Nobel Prize winner Pablo Neruda (1904–1973) is perhaps Chile's most outstanding literary figure.

Suggestion for art
Point out that this image, like many others, was painted on a wall. You may want to show some others, with a different message, on the streets of Valparaíso or Santiago. Ask students to brainstorm words or feelings that the image evokes: *¿Qué sentimientos evoca esta imagen? ¿Alegría o sufrimiento? ¿Qué tipo de sufrimiento: físico, emocional, o ambos?* Ask for reactions to this image: *¿Qué expresa esta imagen, en tu opinión?* Ask students to describe the image. You may recycle some vocabulary: *cara, frente, cejas, nariz, ojos, pelo, calle,* and introduce *cremallera.*

ENFOQUE cultural

Note
In the 1970s, particularly during the oppressive Pinochet years, street art became an instrument of protest and expression when the citizens' voices were silenced by the military Junta ruling Chile. Since the 1990s, with the return of democracy in Chile, the port city of Valparaíso has become the center of organized graffiti for artists throughout Latin America. In 2012, the first Latin American festival of graffiti was organized in Valparaíso.

Note for *¿Qué te parece?*
Picunches were mapuche Indians who lived in central Chile, between the Aconcagua river and Itata river. At the time the Spaniards arrived, they were under Quechua control.

Note for *El desierto de Atacama*
The Atacama Desert covers an area of over 100,000 square kilometers in the northern reaches of Chile and is comprised mostly of salt flats (*salares*), sand, and lava flows. Because of its high altitude, remote location, and clear weather, the Atacama hosts several of the world's most important astronomical observatories, including ALMA (Atacama Large Millimeter Array).

Note for *Santiago*
Santiago is known as an international hub for business and commerce, and serves as the base for one of Latin America's strongest economies. The Chilean economy is also bolstered by the high quality of the country's agricultural products, including many varieties of fruit and wine which it exports across the Americas, Europe, and Asia.

Note for *Punta Arenas*
Punta Arenas, the southernmost city in Chile, was established as a penal colony in 1848. It is located on the Straits of Magellan and is an important port city with approximately 120,000 inhabitants.

◀ El desierto de Atacama, situado en el norte de Chile, es sin duda el más seco del mundo. En él se encuentran riquezas minerales como el cobre, el hierro, el oro y la plata. Los recursos económicos más importantes de Chile son el cobre, el vino, la fruta y el pescado, los cuales exporta a muchos países en todos los continentes.

▲ Santiago, la capital de Chile, cuenta con una población de más de seis millones y medio de habitantes. En esta antigua ciudad capital, ubicada entre el mar y las montañas, conviven armoniosamente lo antiguo y lo moderno. Es una de las ciudades más importantes de Sudamérica por el comercio y por su alta calidad de vida.

El pastel de choclo y las empanadas son considerados dos platos típicamente chilenos. Preparado con choclo, o maíz, carne y huevos, el pastel de choclo usualmente se come durante el verano. Las empanadas suelen ser de carne o de mariscos. Tanto el pastel de choclo como las empanadas se acompañan con vino tinto o blanco. ▶

▲ Ubicada a aproximadamente 670 kilómetros del puerto de Valparaíso, la isla de Pascua forma parte del territorio chileno. Aparte del español, en la isla se habla el rapanui, una lengua indígena. Por su historia y atractivo natural, la isla de Pascua es un lugar visitado por muchos turistas de todo el mundo. En 1996 UNESCO declaró el Parque Nacional Rapa Nui patrimonio de la humanidad.

Punta Arenas, la ciudad más austral del país, está situada al lado del estrecho de Magallanes. Durante el verano, el sol sale (*rises*) antes de las 6:00 de la mañana y se pone (*sets*) después de las 10:00 de la noche. Así, los habitantes de Punta Arenas gozan de más de dieciocho horas de luz natural. ▼

¿CUÁNTO SABES?

Completa las siguientes oraciones con la información correcta.

1. El desierto de ___Atacama___, uno de los desiertos más áridos del mundo, está en el norte de Chile.
2. En ___Santiago___, la capital de Chile, viven más de seis millones de habitantes.
3. Chile exporta ___vino/fruta/productos agrícolas___ a otros países.
4. Punta Arenas es la ciudad más al sur de Chile. Está junto al estrecho de ___Magallanes___.
5. Santiago está entre el ___mar___ y las montañas.

Vocabulario en contexto

Talking about social change, gender roles, and migration

Cambios en la sociedad

MySpanishLab Pronunciation Topic: Intonation
Learn more using Amplifire Dynamic Study Modules, Pronunciation, and Vocabulary Tutorials.

▲ En las últimas décadas ha habido **cambios** muy importantes en el mundo hispano. Varios países, como Chile, Uruguay, Argentina y España, pasaron de tener **regímenes dictatoriales** a ser **democracias** modernas. Michelle Bachelet ganó la presidencia en las **elecciones** democráticas de Chile en 2006 y en 2010 fue nombrada directora ejecutiva de la ONU Mujer. En 2013 anunció su candidatura presidencial por un segundo período. Esta mujer **políglota,** médica de profesión, la primera mujer en llegar a la presidencia de su país, es considerada una de las mujeres más poderosas del mundo.

▲ En Argentina, Cristina Fernández de Kirchner fue **elegida** en 2007 por una **amplia mayoría** y reelegida en 2011. Aunque es la segunda mujer **presidenta** de su país (en los años 70 **gobernó** Isabel Perón), es la primera en ser elegida en un proceso democrático.

Evo Morales, de origen aimara, fue elegido presidente de Bolivia en 2005 y reelegido en 2009. Es el primer presidente indígena de su país desde la conquista española hace 470 años. Desde el comienzo de su carrera política, Morales **se destacó** por su capacidad de organizar a los campesinos en la **lucha** por sus **derechos.** Es un defensor del cultivo de la coca en la región andina. La coca es un producto natural con fines medicinales. Sin embargo, se opone a la comercialización de la coca por las bandas internacionales del **tráfico de drogas.** ▶

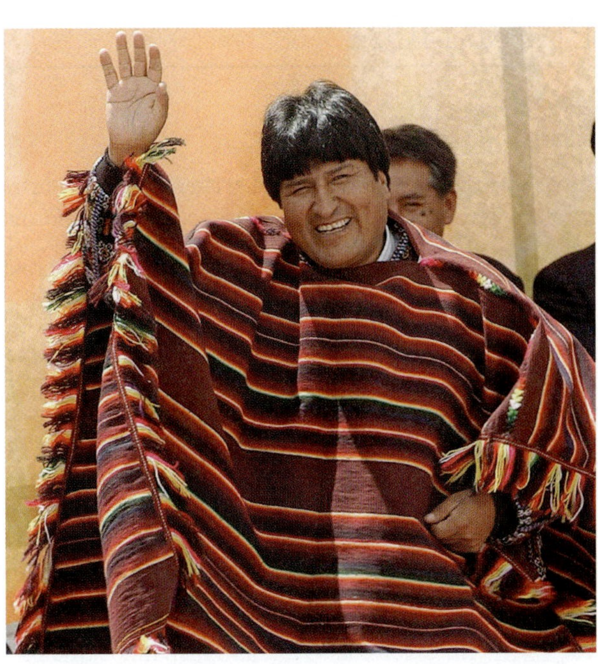

Suggestion for *Cambios en la sociedad*
Prepare students to understand the texts and chart by discussing demographic data and social changes, such as birth, illiteracy, child mortality, and unemployment rates. Introduce the word *promedio* (average). Ask questions such as: *¿Cuál es el promedio de hijos que las familias tienen en tu país? ¿Tienen más o menos hijos que antes? ¿Sabes tú si hay muchas personas analfabetas, es decir, que no saben leer ni escribir, en tu país? En general, ¿crees que hay más analfabetas o más analfabetos en el mundo? Si una persona es analfabeta, ¿puede encontrar trabajo fácilmente en tu país? ¿Hay mucho desempleo donde tú vives?* Also discuss issues related to changes in the last 50 years in family structure, divorce rate, number of children per family, career choices for women and men, and so on, using questions such as: *¿La familia de hoy es diferente a la de tus abuelos? ¿Cómo ha cambiado? ¿Tiene la mujer más oportunidades profesionales fuera de la casa ahora? ¿Crees tú que el promedio de hijos de cada familia ha subido o ha bajado?*

Standard 2.1 Students demonstrate an understanding of the relationship between the practices and perspectives of the culture studied.
Students may be aware that Chile elected a woman as president in 2006. Students may know of current or past presidents of other Latin America countries who are women. These facts can serve as a starting point for discussions that may challenge stereotypes about traditional roles and sexism in Latin American cultures.

Las condiciones de vida aún son difíciles en algunos países de Hispanoamérica donde la **pobreza** y el **analfabetismo** todavía son problemas importantes entre sus **habitantes.** Sin embargo, la economía de algunos países latinoamericanos como Chile, Colombia y México, entre otros, **ha mejorado** considerablemente en las últimas décadas gracias a la **diversificación** de los cultivos, a la intensificación de las **exportaciones** y a mayores índices de educación de sus habitantes. Hoy en día Chile, por ejemplo, exporta cobre, vino, pescado, fruta y otros productos a todo el mundo.

Estos **datos** muestran y comparan algunos de los problemas sociales de Hispanoamérica. Por ejemplo, a pesar de ser un país emergente, el **desempleo** es bastante alto en Colombia. El **porcentaje** de mujeres **analfabetas** es más alto que el de los hombres en casi todos los países. Las mujeres guatemaltecas tienen el **promedio** más alto de hijos. La **esperanza de vida** es en general más alta para las mujeres que para los hombres, y Bolivia tiene la **tasa** más alta de **mortalidad infantil.**

2012-2013	CHILE	BOLIVIA	COLOMBIA	GUATEMALA
Población	17.216.945	10.461.053	45.745.784	14.373.472
Tasa de crecimiento económico (GPD)	5,5%	5,2%	4,0%	3,0%
Esperanza de vida (años)	78,27	68,22	75,02	71,46
Tasa de fertilidad (número de hijos por mujer)	1,9%	2,9%	2,1%	3,8%
Analfabetismo entre los hombres	1,4%	4,2%	6,6%	18,8%
Analfabetismo entre las mujeres	1,5%	13,2%	6,3%	28,9%
Tasa de desempleo	6,4%	7,5%	10,4%	4,1%
Mortalidad infantil (por cada mil nacimientos)	7,19	39,76	15,46	24,32

Fuente: CIA *The World Factbook*

PRÁCTICA

Expansion for 14-1
You may wish to bring to class copies of other infographics and have students work in groups to create statements like those in activity 14-1.

Para confirmar. Determinen si las siguientes afirmaciones son ciertas (**C**) o falsas (**F**) de acuerdo con lo que leyeron. En caso de que sean falsas, corrijan la información.

1. __F__ Cristina Kirchner fue la primera mujer presidenta de su país. Isabel Perón fue la primera mujer presidenta.
2. __F__ Evo Morales fue elegido presidente de Chile. De Bolivia.
3. __C__ Michelle Bachelet habla más de dos lenguas.
4. __C__ El presidente de Bolivia defiende el cultivo tradicional de la coca.
5. __F__ El analfabetismo en algunos países de Latinoamérica ya no es un problema grande. Sigue siendo un grave problema, por ejemplo en Guatemala.
6. __C__ La economía de Chile ha mejorado.
7. __F__ En Bolivia hay menos analfabetismo entre las mujeres que entre los hombres. Hay más mujeres analfabetas.
8. __C__ Bolivia tiene menos habitantes que Guatemala.
9. __F__ Las chilenas tienen más hijos que las guatemaltecas. Las guatemaltecas tienen más hijos.
10. __F__ En Colombia se mueren más niños que en Bolivia. En Bolivia mueren más niños.

Cultura

La natalidad

El índice de natalidad en los países hispanos ha descendido de manera espectacular en los últimos treinta años. Este descenso parece ser la tendencia general, a pesar de las circunstancias particulares de cada país. En Perú y Bolivia, por ejemplo, los gobiernos han apoyado campañas para mostrar las ventajas de los planes familiares y el control de la natalidad. En Venezuela, sin embargo, el promedio de hijos ha bajado en treinta años de 6,7 a 2,7 sin campañas por parte del gobierno. Esto se debe a varios factores, como la crisis económica, la escasez de vivienda y el mayor acceso de las mujeres al trabajo y a la educación. Pero tal vez el caso más extremo de esta tendencia es el de España, que ha pasado de ser el país de Europa con más hijos por pareja en los años sesenta, a ser, junto con Italia, el país europeo con el índice de natalidad más bajo en la actualidad, con un promedio de 1,3 hijos.

Comparaciones. Piensa en el número de hijos en tu familia en las últimas dos o tres generaciones. Después compara tu caso con el de tus compañeros/as. ¿Qué tendencia de natalidad se puede observar? ¿Creen ustedes que hay una crisis de natalidad en Estados Unidos?

14-2 

Los datos demográficos. PREPARACIÓN. Busquen en los textos y en la tabla en la página anterior la información necesaria para contestar las siguientes preguntas. Después comparen sus respuestas con las de otros/as compañeros/as.

1. ¿Cuál de los países en la tabla está más poblado? Colombia
2. ¿Cuál tiene menos habitantes? Bolivia
3. ¿En qué país vive más años la gente? Chile
4. ¿En qué país crece con más rapidez la población? Guatemala
5. ¿De dónde son las mujeres que tienen más hijos? Guatemala
6. ¿Dónde hay más analfabetos probablemente, en el campo o en las ciudades? en el campo
7. ¿En qué país hay menos desempleo? Guatemala
8. ¿En qué país se mueren más niños cuando son bebés? Bolivia
9. ¿En qué país crece más rápido la economía? Chile
10. ¿Qué país probablemente les ofrece más oportunidades educativas a las mujeres? Chile

INTERCAMBIOS. Comparen los datos de los países hispanos en las siguientes áreas con los datos de su propio país.

1. analfabetismo
2. desempleo
3. promedio de hijos
4. mortalidad infantil
5. esperanza de vida

14-3 

Una encuesta sobre las familias.

PREPARACIÓN. Háganse preguntas para obtener los siguientes datos sobre sus respectivas familias.

1. número de personas que forman el núcleo familiar
2. número de hombres y de mujeres
3. edad promedio de los miembros de la familia
4. número de personas que estudian
5. número de personas que trabajan

INTERCAMBIOS. Recopilen (*Compile*) la información obtenida. Con esta información, preparen una tabla que indique el porcentaje de familias que hay en su clase…

1. con menos de tres miembros o más de tres.
2. con mayoría de mujeres o de hombres.
3. con edad promedio de 40 años más o menos.
4. con más o menos de dos personas con títulos (*degrees*) universitarios.
5. donde trabajan más o menos de dos miembros.

Suggestion for 14-2
Ask students to compare the size of these countries. Expect approximate answers. *Intercambios* may require previous research. You may assign it as homework, and have students share their findings in class.

Suggestion for 14-3
To prepare for this activity, you may ask students to write down some of the following data in relation to families they know: 1. *porcentaje de jóvenes entre 10 y 18 años que viven con sus padres;* 2. *edad promedio en la que se casan las personas;* 3. *edad promedio en la que tienen hijos;* 4. *promedio de hijos por pareja.* Then have students compare their results.

Suggestions

Discuss jobs seen traditionally as either "men's work" or "women's work." Ask students if there are jobs commonly held by students that are considered typical of one gender or the other.

Ask students about gender roles in their everyday lives. Do they get different treatment for being male or female? *¿Tienen sus padres las mismas aspiraciones para los hijos que para las hijas? En nuestra sociedad, ¿qué actividades se consideran adecuadas o inadecuadas para un hombre o una mujer? ¿Sufren o han sufrido discriminación alguna vez por ser hombre o mujer? ¿En qué circunstancias? ¿En el trabajo? ¿En los estudios?*

Suggestion for 14-4

You may encourage students to do some research on topics related to the status of women in Hispanic countries in comparison to the U.S. Assign groups to study particular aspects, such as: *diferencias salariales entre el hombre y la mujer; la educación de la mujer; las mujeres en la política.*

Follow-up for 14-4

Ask students to make comparisons between the role of women in the U.S. and in Colombia, according to the information in the excerpts from the articles.

Follow-up for 14-5

Discuss the role of women in U.S. society. You may wish to provide students with the names of female public figures, such as Rosa Parks, Hillary Clinton, and Michele Obama. Personalize by asking: *¿Cuántas mujeres hay en tu familia? ¿Qué trabajo hacen? ¿Fue fácil o difícil conseguir el puesto que tienen? ¿Ha sufrido discriminación de género alguien de tu familia o alguna amiga?*

Follow-up for 14-6

Have each group provide at least one example from their list. Encourage a final summary of predictions for this century.

El papel de la mujer

■ (FEMPRESS) En un reciente estudio **realizado** en 553 empresas colombianas, Luz Gabriela Arango encontró que solo el 23,7% de las directivas están constituidas por mujeres. Con todo, el estudio muestra que en este terreno, así como en otros, ha habido enormes cambios. En los años cincuenta, por ejemplo, todas las **sucursales** bancarias tenían un varón como gerente. En los años noventa, una alta proporción era dirigida por mujeres.

La encuesta "clase empresarial", realizada a ejecutivos, señala que la **confianza** en el desempeño profesional de la mujer es mayor que en el del hombre. De hecho, el 96,8% de los entrevistados le dio la más alta calificación a su **honestidad;** el 80% a la calidad de su trabajo; el 81,6% en materia de confiabilidad; el 79,2% lo dio a su cumplimiento.

En cuanto al manejo de la autoridad, las ejecutivas entrevistadas por *Dinero* consideran que mientras se valora a un hombre por ser **enérgico,** cuando una mujer asume posiciones fuertes puede causar rechazo. En cuanto al poder, se sienten menos ambiciosas y le dan menor prioridad que los hombres.

Las gerencias administrativas y de recursos industriales en manos de mujeres están aumentando. En algunas entrevistas de *Dinero,* se destaca y se apoya la participación de las mujeres en la empresa pues las consideran más responsables, más comprometidas, más honestas, se ausentan menos del trabajo que los hombres, demuestran mayor **eficiencia** en el manejo del tiempo y son más transparentes en el trabajo.

Es interesante ver, dice CIDER (Centro Interdisciplinario de Estudios Regionales), las áreas en las cuales se ha concentrado la presencia femenina. Estas son, en sectores financieros y de servicios en el caso de la empresa privada, y en instituciones de servicio y manejo de relaciones públicas en el sector público, como son los ministerios de salud, educación, trabajo y relaciones exteriores. La mayor concentración de fuerza laboral femenina en un alto **nivel** se ubica en las labores ejecutivas, mientras que solo el 8,2% de los funcionarios hombres está en ese nivel no directivo.

PRÁCTICA

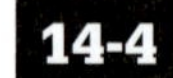 

Para confirmar. Preparen un informe sobre la situación de la mujer en el mundo hispanohablante, utilizando la información que leyeron en las estadísticas (p. 482) y las citas. Comparen su informe con el de otros grupos.

14-5 

Mujeres ejecutivas.

PREPARACIÓN. Cada uno/a de ustedes debe hacer una lista de cinco mujeres que ocupan puestos importantes en países hispanos o en su país. Hablen sobre estas mujeres, basándose en los siguientes puntos.

1. puesto que ocupan y responsabilidades que tienen
2. su personalidad y rasgos (*traits*) de carácter
3. obstáculos que cada una ha tenido que superar en su área de trabajo

INTERCAMBIOS. Ahora, comenten lo siguiente.

1. ¿Qué tipo de personalidad y rasgos de carácter tienen en común estas mujeres?
2. ¿Hacen estas mujeres trabajos tradicionalmente femeninos, o han incursionado en el mundo laboral típicamente masculino?
3. ¿Hay semejanzas entre los obstáculos que estas mujeres han tenido que superar? ¿Cuáles son? ¿Cómo han logrado superarlos?

14-6 

Los tiempos cambian. Conversen sobre los logros de la mujer en este siglo y el pasado. Hagan una lista de los cambios que han afectado a la mujer en las siguientes áreas en los últimos 50 años.

1. la familia
2. el trabajo
3. la casa
4. el gobierno/la política
5. la educación

Temas de hoy: los jóvenes y la emigración

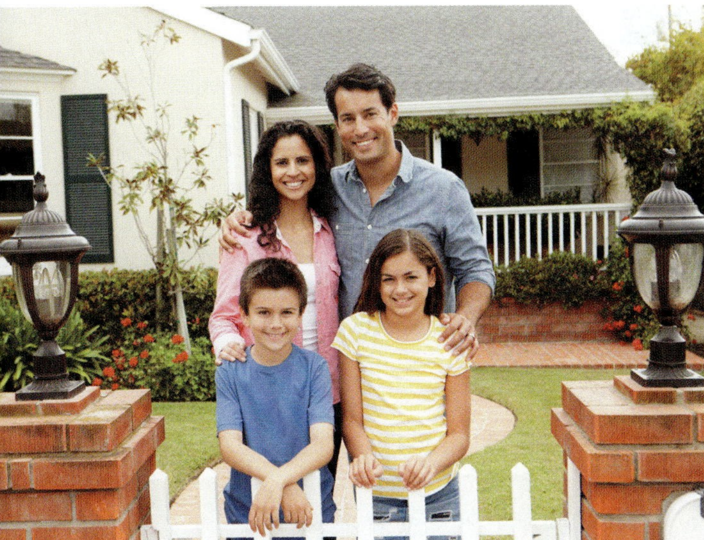

El **desplazamiento** de personas de un país a otro es algo muy común en los últimos tiempos. En general, los jóvenes que emigran de sus países lo hacen por motivos económicos o políticos. Muchos tienen la esperanza de mejorar sus condiciones de vida. Entre los países hispanos, Chile y España son los que más **emigrantes** reciben, aunque debido a la crisis **económica,** la **inmigración** a España ha disminuido en los últimos años.

LENGUA

La emigración refers to the act of *leaving* one's country to settle somewhere else. **La inmigración** refers to *entering* another country for the purpose of setting up permanent residence there.

País de origen de los extranjeros en Chile

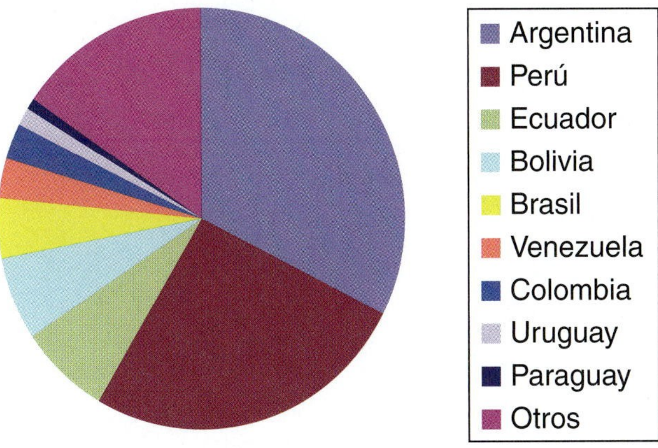

En Chile, los argentinos y los peruanos son los dos grupos de extranjeros más numerosos. En España también las comunidades peruana y argentina son muy numerosas, solo superadas por los **inmigrantes** de origen ecuatoriano. La ventaja de estas **migraciones** interhispanas es que todos hablan la misma lengua y esto hace que las dificultades de **adaptación** sean menores.

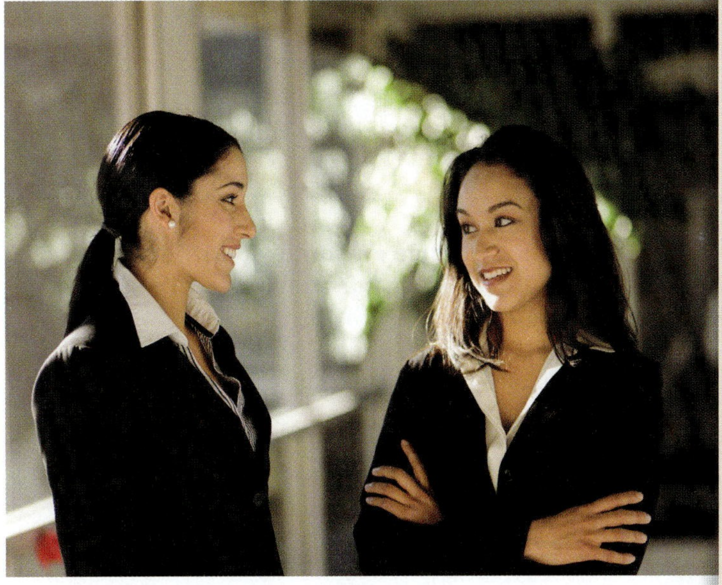

Muchos hispanoamericanos, especialmente mexicanos y caribeños, prefieren **emigrar** a Estados Unidos **en vez de** a Europa en busca de oportunidades económicas y una mayor **proximidad** con sus países. Los jóvenes por lo general se adaptan más fácilmente que sus padres porque aprenden inglés rápidamente. Además, hoy en día las ventajas de ser bilingüe en EE.UU. son evidentes.

Warm-up for *Temas de hoy: los jóvenes y la emigración*
Introduce the theme of immigration by asking students what they know. *¿Cuál es el país o continente de origen de gran parte de la población estadounidense? ¿De dónde eran sus abuelos? ¿Cuántos de ustedes tienen origen europeo, asiático, africano, hispano? ¿Qué comunidades de inmigrantes hay en su estado o en su ciudad? ¿Qué productos de otros países se pueden comprar? ¿Qué restaurantes internacionales conocen?*

Suggestion for *Temas de hoy: los jóvenes y la emigración*
Remind students that the reasons for emigration vary. Many Cubans in the U.S. left their country for ideological reasons. On the other hand, Puerto Ricans are U.S. citizens and a common reason for moving to the mainland is to seek better economic opportunities.

Audioscript for 14-9
REPORTERO: *Buenas tardes, doctora Gómez. Muchas gracias por acceder a esta entrevista.*
DRA. GÓMEZ: *Gracias por invitarme.*
REPORTERO: *Dígame, doctora Gómez, ¿cuál es la situación de la mujer en los países hispanos en la actualidad?*
DRA. GÓMEZ: *Bueno, la situación de la mujer ha cambiado mucho en los últimos años, sobre todo en el aspecto legal.*
REPORTERO: *¿Qué quiere decir?*
DRA. GÓMEZ: *Bueno, las nuevas leyes protegen a la mujer, pero así y todo es más difícil para la mujer conseguir trabajo que para el hombre.*
REPORTERO: *Sí, pero hoy muchas mujeres trabajan.*
DRA. GÓMEZ: *Es verdad. Sin embargo, a las mujeres se les exige más preparación. Además, no se les paga lo mismo que a los hombres.*
REPORTERO: *¿Y ha mejorado la situación de la mujer en el hogar?*
DRA. GÓMEZ: *Muy poco. Algunos hombres colaboran con las labores domésticas y en la crianza de los niños, pero es la mujer la encargada de la casa. La mujer tiene dos trabajos, uno fuera de casa por el que le pagan muy poco, y otro en la casa donde no se le paga absolutamente nada.*
REPORTERO: *¿Usted cree que hay alguna esperanza de que esto cambie?*
DRA. GÓMEZ: *Poco a poco las cosas van cambiando. Hay más mujeres que estudian y no forman una familia tan pronto como antes. Las mujeres ahora quieren ser independientes económicamente. Cada vez habrá más mujeres como jefas de empresas, ministras, médicas, abogadas, economistas.*
REPORTERO: *Bueno, doctora Gómez, muchas gracias por compartir su opinión con nosotros.*
DRA. GÓMEZ: *Gracias a usted.*

PRÁCTICA

14-7 

Para confirmar. Completa las siguientes oraciones con la forma correcta de las palabras de la lista.

bilingüismo	emigración	habitante
condición	emigrante	proximidad

1. En España hay muchos ___habitantes, emigrantes___ de nacionalidad ecuatoriana.
2. Una ventaja para los caribeños que emigran a Estados Unidos es la ___proximidad___ a los países del Caribe.
3. El ___bilingüismo___ es útil para los jóvenes hispanos que buscan trabajo.
4. Frecuentemente las personas se desplazan para mejorar sus ___condiciones___ de vida.
5. La ___emigración___ es un fenómeno de nuestros días que está relacionada con la globalización.
6. Chile es uno de los países de Hispanoamérica que más ___emigrantes___ recibe.

14-8 

Los habitantes de su comunidad. Preparen preguntas para entrevistar a un/a compañero/a sobre sus orígenes y las costumbres de su comunidad o grupo étnico. Usen los puntos a continuación como guía para elaborar su cuestionario.

E1: *¿Cuál es el origen de tu familia?*
E2: *Mis abuelos eran italianos.*
E1: *¿Cuándo emigraron a este país?*
E2: *Emigraron cuando mi padre tenía cinco años.*

1. origen de tu apellido
2. grupo(s) étnico(s) que asocias con tu familia
3. área de concentración en Estados Unidos
4. costumbres e idioma
5. fiestas o celebraciones
6. productos que consumen
7. comida típica

14-9  

La mujer en los países hispanos. You will listen to a conversation between a reporter and a professor of sociology at the Universidad de Santiago de Chile about the status of women in the Hispanic world. Before you listen, write two questions the reporter may ask the professor and the answers that you think she may provide.

As you listen, focus on the main ideas of what is said. Indicate the appropriate ending to each statement.

1. La doctora Gómez dice que la situación de la mujer ha mejorado porque…
   - **a.** más mujeres son jefas de empresas.
   - **(b.)** ahora hay más leyes que las protegen.
   - **c.** hay muchas mujeres que no tienen hijos.
2. Según la doctora Gómez, en comparación con los hombres, las mujeres…
   - **a.** no tienen que trabajar tanto.
   - **(b.)** tienen que estar mejor preparadas.
   - **c.** no estudian tanto.
3. Las mujeres hispanas ganan…
   - **a.** más dinero que los hombres.
   - **b.** tanto dinero como los hombres.
   - **(c.)** menos dinero que los hombres.
4. En los hogares hispanos, el trabajo de la casa y la crianza de los hijos…
   - **a.** son la responsabilidad de los empleados domésticos.
   - **b.** son compartidos por todos los miembros de la familia.
   - **(c.)** están principalmente en manos de las mujeres.

MOSAICO cultural

La migración interna en el mundo hispano

Olga Jaramillo ha vivido en Tegucigalpa, la capital de Honduras, desde hace siete años. Olga nació en una pequeña ciudad llamada Danlí, donde vivía con tres hermanos en una familia campesina (*farming*). “Tan pronto como terminé mis estudios del colegio, supe que quería ir a la universidad”, comenta Olga. Las oportunidades de educación superior son limitadas en las ciudades pequeñas, por eso muchas mujeres como Olga prefieren ir a las ciudades principales. “Cuando mi madre tenía mi edad ya había tenido a mis hermanos. Yo sabía que a menos que saliera de Danlí a estudiar, mi futuro sería similar”, dice Olga. Olga tuvo que dejar a su familia y pasar momentos difíciles adaptándose a la vida de la ciudad. Como muchos otros jóvenes, Olga trabajaba mientras estudiaba, y después de los cinco años de carrera universitaria, consiguió un trabajo estable como dentista.

Esta decisión de Olga demuestra un cambio de mentalidad en los jóvenes hispanos: tener menos hijos y tomarse más tiempo para educarse. Sin embargo, las oportunidades en educación y seguridad social son estables principalmente en las ciudades grandes. El progreso económico vertiginoso de algunas ciudades capitales no es igual al de las ciudades más pequeñas. Por esta razón, muchas personas deciden buscar suerte en la gran ciudad, en un proceso que se conoce como migración interna. Pero llegar a la ciudad no siempre asegura mejores condiciones; en ocasiones, estas personas enfrentan retos de adaptación demasiado grandes y terminan en situaciones de pobreza. Afortunadamente para Olga, este no fue su caso: “Venir a Tegucigalpa fue muy difícil, pero tenía que salir de Danlí o no habría encontrado la estabilidad que buscaba”.

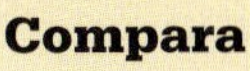

Compara

1. En promedio, ¿cuántos hijos por familia tienen las personas en tu país? ¿Este número ha variado en las últimas décadas? ¿Piensas que esta tendencia varía dependiendo de la región geográfica?
2. ¿Qué importancia social tiene la educación en tu país? Piensa en las regiones que no son predominantemente universitarias. Compara las grandes ciudades con otras zonas más pequeñas.
3. ¿En tu país existe un fenómeno similar a la migración interna? ¿Cuáles son las razones principales de esta migración? Incluye detalles en tu respuesta; piensa en tendencias demográficas que han cambiado en los últimos años.
4. En tu opinión, ¿qué implicaciones sociales tiene la migración interna para las grandes ciudades? ¿Qué ocurre con la economía? ¿Qué ocurre con la seguridad social de los migrantes?

Notes for *Mosaico cultural*
Internal migration is a complex phenomenon in the Hispanic world. People move to new places in search of educational and economic opportunities, but also to escape violence. In countries like Mexico, Guatemala, El Salvador, and Colombia, armed conflict and civil unrest force people to migrate to the capital cities or even other countries.

Although there have been advances in gender equality in the Hispanic world, women have more opportunities in large metropolitan areas. In smaller cities and rural areas, women's access to education may be limited, and they may be held back by traditional ideas about women's roles.

Suggestion for *Mosaico cultural*
You may wish to give examples of the striking social inequalities in Latin America. In the capital cities of some Hispanic countries, the very wealthy and the very poor live in close proximity. In some areas, real estate prices are higher than in Manhattan or Paris, while just a few miles away, an estimated 20% of the population lives on less than two dollars per day. This inequality results from rapid, often uncontrolled economic growth in the major cities, where wealthy investors, a small percentage of the population, are seeing huge profits while the great majority work for very low wages (or cannot find work at all).

Note for Expressing conjecture
Although the purpose of this photo and text is to provide a context for the presentation of a grammatical structure, you may wish to use them as a starting point for discussion of the complex issues of immigration and migrant laborers in U.S. agriculture.

Suggestions for Expressing conjecture
Review uses of the subjunctive in noun clauses (who, what) and adjective (which, what kind) clauses.

Since the structures presented in this section are complex, you may want to stress recognition. Tell students you do not expect them to be able to produce the structure independently at first. Review the functions of adverbs (how, why, when, where) and of adverbial clauses. A mnemonic device to remember the conjunctions that take the subjunctive is *CASPA* (dandruff): *con tal de que, antes de que, sin que, para que, a menos que.*

Note for Expressing conjecture
En caso de que is not presented in the lesson; you may introduce it for recognition only.

Funciones y formas

1 Expressing conjecture

Estos inmigrantes cosechan cebollas en Texas. Según la ley, pueden trabajar en Estados Unidos **con tal de que** tengan estatus legal en el país. Muchos inmigrantes mandan dinero a su familia **para que** sus hijos vivan mejor. Muchos vuelven a su país **a menos que** su familia pueda venir a Estados Unidos también.

Piénsalo. Escoge en la columna de la derecha el significado de las palabras en negrita.

1. __a__ Pueden trabajar en Estados Unidos **con tal de que** tengan estatus legal.
2. __d__ Mandan dinero a su familia **para que** sus hijos vivan mejor.
3. __c__ Volverán a su país **a menos que** su familia pueda venir a Estados Unidos.
4. __c__ Para muchos inmigrantes es difícil conseguir trabajo **sin que** sus amigos los ayuden.
5. __b__ Los hijos de algunos emigrantes pasan muchos años con solo su madre **antes de que** su padre vuelva a casa.

a. si
b. anterioridad de tiempo
c. si... no
d. con la intención

Adverbial conjunctions that require the subjunctive

- Conjunctions are words or phrases that function as connectors in sentences. Some conjunctions introduce dependent clauses known as adverbial clauses, which communicate how, why, when, and where an action takes place.
- Some conjunctions always require the subjunctive when followed by a dependent clause.

a menos que	*unless*	**para que**	*so that*
antes (de) que	*before*	**sin que**	*without*
con tal (de) que	*provided that*		

Las mujeres tendrán una reunión **antes de que** sus representantes **hablen** con los oficiales.	*The women will have a meeting before their representatives speak with the officials.*
Las mujeres votarán por los oficiales **con tal de que** ellos **implementen** los cambios mencionados en la petición.	*The women will vote for the officials provided that they implement the changes mentioned in the petition.*
Las representantes negocian con los oficiales **para que** todos los niños **tengan** acceso a servicios médicos.	*The representatives negotiate with the officials so that all children have access to medical services.*

- Use an infinitive after the prepositions **antes de, para,** and **sin** when there is no change of subject.

Las comunidades ofrecen clases **para que** los inmigrantes **aprendan** inglés.	*Communities offer classes so that immigrants can learn English.*
Los inmigrantes estudian inglés **para aprender** la lengua rápidamente.	*Immigrants study English to learn the language quickly.*

¿COMPRENDES?

Completa las afirmaciones a continuación con las conjunciones más lógicas en cada contexto.

1. Pagamos impuestos ___para que___ haya buenas escuelas.
2. Tenemos que limpiar la oficina ___antes de que___ lleguen los miembros del comité.
3. Votaremos por ellos ___con tal de que___ nos guste su plan para la ciudad.
4. No publicamos el panfleto ___sin que/a menos que___ el presidente lo apruebe.

MySpanishLab

Learn more using Amplifire Dynamic Study Modules, Grammar Tutorials, and Extra Practice activities.

PRÁCTICA

14-10  

En el futuro. **PREPARACIÓN.** Túrnense para leer la primera parte de cada oración y después busquen el final apropiado a la derecha. Fíjense (*Take note*) en el contexto y también en la forma verbal correcta.

1. ___c___ Muchos empleados trabajarán en casa sin...
2. ___f___ Las compañías de limpieza programarán los robots para que...
3. ___h___ Podremos jubilarnos (*retire*) antes de...
4. ___a___ Casi todos los cursos universitarios se ofrecerán en Internet sin que...
5. ___g___ Los jóvenes no tendrán que trabajar a menos que...
6. ___d___ Habrá computadoras de uso gratis en muchos lugares públicos para...
7. ___b___ Los empleados de las compañías multinacionales podrán comunicarse fácilmente con tal de que...
8. ___e___ Después de nacer sus hijos, los padres no volverán a trabajar antes de que los niños...

a. los profesores ni los alumnos tengan que ir a la universidad.
b. tengan aparatos de interpretación simultánea.
c. tener que comunicarse con los clientes o colegas en persona.
d. facilitar la comunicación entre las personas.
e. cumplan 5 años de edad.
f. limpien los edificios sin intervención de los seres humanos.
g. les interese hacer trabajo de voluntariado.
h. los 50 años.

INTERCAMBIOS. Ahora escojan dos de las oraciones de la izquierda y complétenlas de acuerdo con sus propias ideas. Después comparen sus respuestas con las de otra pareja.

14-11 

Una ingeniera se entrevista. La ingeniera industrial María Victoria Martín se entrevista hoy con Sanofi Aventis, una compañía que fabrica medicinas. Para saber qué pasó en la entrevista, completa las oraciones con la forma correcta del verbo apropiado: **decir, hacer, ofrecer, pasar** o **saber.**

María Victoria llega temprano a la cita con la directora, y la secretaria le pide que espere unos minutos antes de (1) ___pasar___ a su oficina. María Victoria trata de tranquilizarse para que nadie (2) ___sepa___ que está muy nerviosa. Piensa que podrá dar una buena impresión con tal de que la directora le (3) ___haga___ preguntas relevantes a su experiencia. Finalmente la directora se presenta y la invita a entrar en su oficina sin que María Victoria (4) ___diga___ una palabra. Al final de la entrevista la directora le ofrece el puesto. María Victoria dice que no puede aceptar la oferta a menos que la compañía le (5) ___ofrezca___ seguro médico. La directora acepta esta condición.

Suggestion for 14-11
This activity requires that students choose between the infinitive and a present subjunctive form. To avoid having students respond without understanding the sentences, you may wish to have them focus on the meaning of the conjunctions.

Alternate for 14-12
You may need to have students brainstorm possible responses for E2, as well as various ways for E1 and E2 to start their sentences. You may decide to do one or two mini-conversations as a group before putting students in pairs to continue on their own.

14-12 

¿Estudio en Chile o no? Estás considerando la posibilidad de estudiar en Chile el próximo semestre. Indica lo que piensas sobre esta posibilidad, usando las expresiones adverbiales de la lista. Tu compañero/a va a responder de forma lógica.

a menos que	antes (de) que	con tal (de) que	para que	sin que

MODELO el programa sea muy caro

E1: *Voy a estudiar en Chile, a menos que el programa sea muy caro.*

E2: *No participes en el programa a menos que te den una beca.*

1. el semestre termine para el 1 de junio
2. mis compañeros y yo aprendamos mucho español
3. viva con una familia amable
4. mi familia me visite durante el semestre
5. haya oportunidades de viajar a otros países
6. mi amigo/a también participe en el programa
7. conozca la cultura mapuche
8. pasemos las vacaciones esquiando en los Andes

Situación

PREPARACIÓN. Lean la situación. Luego, compartan ejemplos de vocabulario, gramática y otra información que necesitan para desarrollar la conversación.

Role A. You are an exchange student who has recently arrived in the United States. Ask your classmate a) what his/her family does to help him/her attend college; b) if in big lecture classes students can use their cell phones and read e-mail without their professors' knowledge; and c) what he/she hopes to accomplish before graduating.

Role B. You have become acquainted with an international student at your university. Answer his/her questions about university life in the United States and ask about university life in his/her country.

	ROLE A	ROLE B
Vocabulario	Academic subjects Technology	Academic subjects Technology
Funciones y formas	Formulating questions	Adverbial conjunctions with subjunctive

INTERCAMBIOS. Practica la conversación con tu compañero/a incorporando el vocabulario y las funciones de *Preparación*. Luego, represéntenla ante la clase.

2 Expressing conjecture or certainty

SRA. LÓPEZ: ¿Qué te interesa hacer **cuando te gradúes**?

VICENTE: **Después de terminar** mis estudios, me gustaría trabajar en otro país para una organización sin fines de lucro (*non-profit*).

SRA. LÓPEZ: Muy bien. **Tan pronto como terminemos** de hablar, te mandaré una lista de organizaciones. No esperes **hasta que te gradúes** para empezar a buscar trabajo. Familiarízate con las posibilidades ahora, **mientras eres** estudiante.

Piénsalo. Indica si la persona que habla se refiere al presente (**P**) o al futuro (**F**).

1. __F__ ¿Qué te interesa hacer **cuando te gradúes?**
2. __F__ **Tan pronto como terminemos** de hablar, te mandaré una lista de organizaciones.
3. __F__ No esperes **hasta que te gradúes** para empezar a buscar trabajo.
4. __P__ Familiarízate con las posibilidades ahora, **mientras eres** estudiante.
5. __F__ Vicente va a buscar trabajo en una organización sin fines de lucro, **aunque gane** poco dinero.
6. __P__ Estas organizaciones siempre apoyan a las comunidades aun (*even*) **después de que** las comunidades **terminan** el proyecto.

Adverbial conjunctions that take the subjunctive or indicative

- Earlier in this chapter you learned about conjunctions that are always followed by the subjunctive. Here you will practice using conjunctions that are followed by a verb in either the subjunctive or indicative, depending on whether the event in the adverbial clause has occurred or not, or whether it is factual or unknown.

aunque	*although, even though, even if*	**en cuanto**	*as soon as*
		hasta que	*until*
cuando	*when*	**mientras**	*while*
después (de) que	*after*	**según**	*according to, as*
donde	*where, wherever*	**tan pronto (como)**	*as soon as*

- These conjunctions require the subjunctive when the event in the adverbial clause has not yet taken place. Note that the main clause expresses future time.

Va a luchar **hasta que** la comunidad **ofrezca** clases gratis para los inmigrantes nuevos.
She is going to fight until the community offers free classes for new immigrants.

Nos reuniremos **después de que comiencen** las clases.
We will meet after classes start.

Me llamará **tan pronto reciba** la aprobación del alcalde.
She will call me as soon as she receives approval from the mayor.

Suggestion for *Piénsalo*
Help students make the proper association between the time frame of the dependent clause (present or future) and the mood of the verb (indicative or subjunctive). Bring sentence 6 to their attention, in which the event in the adverbial clause refers to an activity that always takes place, not to the future. This understanding will be good preparation for the explanation that follows.

Suggestion
A mnemonic device to remember the conjunctions that can take either the subjunctive or the indicative is MATCHED CDS, which stands for:

m ientras
a unque
t an pronto como
c uando
h asta que
e n cuanto
d espués de que
c omo
d onde
s egún

Suggestion
Guide students to notice the sequence of tenses in these examples. A preterit verb in the independent clause usually signals indicative in the dependent clause. A future verb (or **ir a** + *infinitive*) in the independent clause usually signals subjunctive in the dependent clause.

Suggestion
The distinction in meaning between definite/known vs. indefinite/unknown in the dependent clause may be difficult for students to grasp. You may wish to provide additional examples.

- These conjunctions require the indicative when the event in the adverbial clause has already taken place, is taking place, or usually takes place.

  Nos reunimos **después de que comenzaron** las clases.
  We met after classes started.

  Me llamó **tan pronto recibió** la aprobación del alcalde.
  She called me as soon as she received approval from the mayor.

  La organización apoya a los inmigrantes **hasta que se establecen** en la comunidad.
  The organization supports the immigrants until they become established in the community.

- **Donde** and **según** require the indicative when they refer to something definite or known, and the subjunctive when they refer to something indefinite or unknown.

  Vamos a reunirnos **donde** ella **dice.**
  We are going to meet where she says. (She has already announced the place.)

  Vamos a reunirnos **donde** ella **diga.**
  We are going to meet wherever she says. (She has not yet announced the place.)

  Llena el formulario **según dice** el consejero.
  Fill out the form according to what the adviser says. (Instructions have already been given.)

  Vamos a seguir el procedimiento **según diga** el alcalde.
  We will follow the procedure in accordance with whatever the mayor says. (Instructions have not yet been given.)

- **Aunque** also requires the subjunctive when it introduces a condition not regarded as fact.

  Lo compro **aunque es** caro. — *I will buy it, although it is expensive.*

  Lo compro **aunque sea** caro. — *I will buy it, although it may (turn out to) be expensive.*

¿COMPRENDES?

Completa las oraciones con la forma del subjuntivo o indicativo del verbo entre paréntesis.

1. Por lo general, el jefe lee los informes después de que yo se los ___entrego___ (entregar).
2. Comenzaremos la reunión cuando Sandra ___llegue___ (llegar).
3. Haremos lo que el grupo ___decida___ (decidir).
4. No importa la hora; iré a las protestas aunque ___empiecen___ (empezar) a la medianoche.

MySpanishLab
Learn more using Amplifire Dynamic Study Modules, Grammar Tutorials, and Extra Practice activities.

LENGUA

You learned that in Spanish, the subject is normally placed after the verb when asking a question: **¿Les dio instrucciones el alcalde?** (*Did the mayor give them/you instructions?*) You may also place the subject after the verb in statements, especially when you wish to emphasize the subject: **Les habló el alcalde.** (*The mayor talked to them/you.*) To avoid misinterpreting statements with this structure, you should locate the subject first, and not assume that the first noun or pronoun in the sentence is the subject.

PRÁCTICA

Cultura

Regímenes dictatoriales en Latinoamérica

Aunque hoy en día todos los países latinoamericanos tienen sistemas democráticos, a través de la historia ha sido notable la presencia de líderes militares que se han convertido en dictadores de diferentes países. Estas figuras han accedido al poder casi siempre mediante golpes de estado y han consolidado regímenes políticos autoritarios y represivos que han llevado una "guerra sucia" sin respeto por los derechos humanos. Entre otros, se destacan los casos de las juntas militares en Argentina (1976–1983), Chile (1973–1989) y Uruguay (1973–1985) así como las sangrientas dictaduras centroamericanas de Somoza (asesinado en 1979) en Nicaragua, o los escuadrones de la muerte en Guatemala y El Salvador.

Conexiones. ¿Qué tácticas se aplican en una guerra sucia? ¿Qué efecto tienen estas tácticas en la población? ¿Todavía existen regímenes que usen las tácticas de una guerra sucia?

14-13 

¿Cuáles serán los cambios? Escoge la forma verbal correcta para completar las siguientes afirmaciones.

1. A menos que hay/haya elecciones democráticas, un país no puede considerarse democrático. haya
2. Se suprimió el derecho de libre expresión según lo exige/exigió la Junta Militar. exigió
3. Las familias que tenían miembros desaparecidos reclamaron (*demanded*) justicia cuando se recuperó/se recupere la democracia. se recuperó
4. Como resultado, la Corte Suprema ha decidido atender los reclamos de las familias de los desaparecidos para que la sociedad pueda/puede recuperar su confianza en las instituciones jurídicas. pueda
5. Muchas personas dicen que no creerán en la justicia hasta que ven/vean a los culpables encarcelados. vean

Suggestions for 14-13
The activities in this section include the conjunctions presented in the previous section, as well as those presented in this section, to help students internalize the concept of whether the action in the dependent clause has or has not already taken place. You may wish to highlight that concept, especially by pointing out the importance of the temporal information conveyed by the verb in the main clause.

Suggestion for 14-14
You may wish to remind students that when there is no change of subject, they should use *antes de + infinitive* or *después de + infinitive* rather than *antes de que/después de que + conjugated verb.*

14-14 

La educación a distancia. Ustedes toman un curso en Internet sobre la historia de Chile por medio del programa VirtualU de la Universidad de Chile. Todo lo hacen en la computadora y se comunican por mensajes de texto y correo electrónico. Digan lo que van a hacer, completando las oraciones lógicamente con una frase de la siguiente lista.

ser las 12:00	llegar el día del examen final
tener tiempo	escribirme mi compañero/a virtual
ser muy tarde	leer unos mensajes electrónicos de la profesora
tener sus horas de consulta	terminar de leer sobre los regímenes dictatoriales

 Voy a trabajar en la computadora hasta que... empezar las noticias/ser la hora de cenar

E1: *Voy a trabajar en la computadora hasta que empiecen las noticias.*

E2: *Y yo voy a trabajar hasta que sea la hora de cenar.*

1. Voy a hablar con la profesora en cuanto...
2. Comeré después de que...
3. Voy a comprobar los datos tan pronto como...
4. Haré la mayoría del trabajo en nuestro ensayo hasta que...
5. Voy a estudiar el tema de la inmigración chilena esta noche aunque...
6. Le mandaré a la profesora mi informe sobre las lecturas antes de que...

Note for 14-15
Note that this activity has three parts. In *Preparación*, students first work individually and then compare results with a partner. In *Intercambios*, small groups pool their results to create a plan for their community. You may find it helpful to give students instructions for one step at a time, so that the activity can proceed with input from all students in the class.

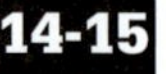 

Después de que termine el año escolar. **PREPARACIÓN.** Quieres descansar y divertirte después de que terminen las clases, pero también quieres hacer algo por tu comunidad. Completa dos de las opciones que más te interesen en cada columna y añade una más para expresar tus propias ideas. Después, comparte tus planes con tu compañero/a.

DIVERSIÓN	AYUDA COMUNITARIA
1. Quiero dormir hasta que...	**1.** Trabajaré de voluntario donde...
2. No voy a abrir los libros aunque...	**2.** Ayudaré en la biblioteca después de que...
3. Haré un crucero por... tan pronto como...	**3.** Les serviré comida a los desamparados (*homeless*) cuando...
4. Iré a la playa todos los días a menos que...	**4.** Organizaré juegos infantiles en el parque para que...
5. ...	**5.** ...

INTERCAMBIOS. Preparen un plan para ayudar a su comunidad. En su plan deben indicar lo siguiente:

1. sector de la comunidad
2. tipo de ayuda
3. frecuencia de su participación
4. medios que van a usar
5. resultados que esperan obtener

14-16

El hombre y la mujer en la sociedad. **PREPARACIÓN.** Indica (✓) si, en tu opinión, las situaciones presentadas en las siguientes afirmaciones existen o no existen hoy en día.

LOS HOMBRES Y LAS MUJERES...	SÍ	NO
1. reciben la misma educación.		
2. son tratados de la misma forma en el trabajo.		
3. ganan el mismo sueldo por el mismo trabajo.		
4. tienen las mismas oportunidades.		
5. hacen las mismas tareas domésticas.		
6. tienen los mismos derechos en un divorcio.		

En directo

To make a polite request or a proposal:

Quiero/Queremos proponer (que)…

Sugiero/Sugerimos (que)…

 Listen to a conversation with these expressions.

 **INTERCAMBIOS.** Ahora compara tus respuestas con las de tu compañero/a. Defiende tus opiniones negativas y di cuándo o bajo qué condiciones crees que los cambios necesarios ocurrirán.

 E1: *Los hombres y las mujeres ocupan más o menos el mismo número de puestos importantes.*

E2: *No estoy de acuerdo. Los hombres ocupan la mayoría de los puestos importantes en las compañías y en el gobierno. Esto va a cambiar cuando las generaciones jóvenes puedan tomar más decisiones.*

Situación

PREPARACIÓN. Lean la situación. Luego, compartan ejemplos de vocabulario, gramática y otra información que necesitan para desarrollar la conversación.

Role A. You make a presentation to the city council (**concejo municipal**) about starting an adult literacy program. Explain how the lives of participants will improve when they know how to read and write well. In response to questions, say that you will a) organize the program; b) hold classes wherever the council says; and c) decide on class schedules according to the needs of the participants.

Role B. You are the president of the city council (**concejo municipal**). After listening to a presentation by a specialist in adult literacy who wants to start a program in the community, ask a) where and when the classes will be held; and b) who will pay for the program.

	ROLE A	ROLE B
Vocabulario	Social problems Dates and time	Social problems Dates and time
Funciones y formas	Expressing conjecture or certainty Adverbial conjunctions that take the subjunctive or indicative	Expressing conjecture or certainty Adverbial conjunctions that take the subjunctive or indicative

INTERCAMBIOS. Practica la conversación con tu compañero/a incorporando el vocabulario y las funciones de *Preparación*. Luego, represéntenla ante la clase.

Suggestion for 14-16
You may wish to have students do some research on the Internet before doing this activity to support their opinions.

Audioscript for *En directo*
CANDIDATO A SENADOR: *Estimados compatriotas. En nuestra sociedad existe discriminación en contra de las mujeres. Quiero proponer una ley que prohíba la discriminación en contra de las mujeres o de cualquier individuo.*
PERSONA DEL PÚBLICO: (shouting) *¡El pueblo le sugiere que primero cree trabajos para todos!*

Suggestion for *Situación*
You may wish to help students prepare for the *Situación* by brainstorming additional arguments for the proposals. This pre-speaking phase will also help students use the appropriate adverbial expressions and the subjunctive as needed.

Note
Point out that the events of Gabriela Mistral's life resonate in the central themes of her poetry, which include betrayal, love, a mother's love, sorrow and recovery, travel, and Latin American identity as seen as a mixture of Indian and European influences.

Suggestion for *Piénsalo*
Draw students' attention to how different verb forms (preterit vs. past perfect) effect a change in meaning (past vs. anterior past). You may also wish to come back to the statements in *Piénsalo* after students have done some of the activities in this section.

Suggestion for the Past Perfect
Present the past perfect in the same manner as the present perfect in *Capítulo 10* (pp. 360–361). You may wish to contrast the use of the two tenses: *Gracias por invitarme, pero ya he comido. Cuando Luis me invitó a cenar, ya había comido.*

3 Talking about the past from a past perspective

VIOLETA: Oye, mamá, mi profesora habló un poco de Gabriela Mistral. ¿Tú sabes algo de ella?

MADRE: ¡Claro que sí! Gabriela Mistral fue una gran poeta chilena que ganó el Premio Nobel de Literatura en 1945. Pero antes de recibir el premio, Gabriela ya **había hecho** muchas cosas importantes.

VIOLETA: ¿Qué **había hecho?** Yo no sé nada de ella.

MADRE: Antes de ser famosa, Gabriela **había tenido** una vida muy difícil. Su padre **había abandonado** a la familia, y eran muy pobres.

VIOLETA: ¡Qué triste la vida de Gabriela, mamá!

MADRE: Sí y no. Ella utilizó su sufrimiento positivamente para lograr mucho. Por ejemplo, a los 15 años, ya **había escrito** sus primeras poesías y **se había graduado** de profesora. Además, antes de ella, ningún escritor latinoamericano **había ganado** el Premio Nobel.

Piénsalo. Indica (✓) las experiencias de Gabriela Mistral y su madre que se refieren a un momento cronológicamente anterior al momento cuando Gabriela se hizo internacionalmente famosa.

1. __✓__ Gabriela ya **había hecho** muchas cosas importantes.
2. __✓__ Su madre y ella **habían tenido** una vida muy difícil.
3. _____ **Ganó** el Premio Nobel en 1945.
4. __✓__ Su padre **había abandonado** a Gabriela y a su madre.
5. __✓__ **Había escrito** poesías antes de cumplir los 15 años.
6. __✓__ Ningún escritor latinoamericano **había ganado** el Premio Nobel.

The past perfect

- Use the past perfect to refer to a past event, action, or condition that occurred prior to another past event, action, or state.

Ningún escritor latinoamericano **había ganado** el Premio Nobel de Literatura antes de Mistral.	*No Latin American writer had won the Nobel Prize for Literature before Mistral.*
Otros escritores **habían sido** nominados para el premio, pero ella lo recibió.	*Other writers had been nominated for the award, but she received it.*

- Form the past perfect with the imperfect tense of **haber** and the past participle of the main verb.

IMPERFECT OF *HABER*		PAST PARTICIPLE
yo	**había**	
tú	**habías**	
Ud., él, ella	**había**	**hablado**
nosotros/as	**habíamos**	**comido**
vosotros/as	**habíais**	**vivido**
Uds., ellos/as	**habían**	

¿COMPRENDES?

Completa las afirmaciones con la forma del pluscuamperfecto del verbo entre paréntesis.

1. Cuando Michelle Bachelet ganó la presidencia de Chile, ya __había trabajado__ (trabajar) por muchos años en el servicio público.
2. El novelista chileno Roberto Ampuero ya __había escrito__ (escribir) varios libros antes de estudiar para su doctorado.
3. Nosotros sacamos muy malas notas en el examen porque no __habíamos leído__ (leer) el material.
4. Cuando invité a mis padres al concierto, me dijeron que ya __habían hecho__ (hacer) otros planes para esa noche.

MySpanishLab
Learn more using Amplifire Dynamic Study Modules, Grammar Tutorials, and Extra Practice activities.

PRÁCTICA

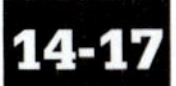 

¡Recuerdos! **PREPARACIÓN.** Para cada afirmación, indica la acción que ocurrió primero.

 Cuando yo cumplí diez años, ya había escuchado discusiones políticas.

1. Cuando cumplimos diecisiete años, mis amigos y yo ya nos habíamos inscrito en un partido político.
2. Cuando terminé la escuela secundaria, mis padres ya me habían comprado un carro.
3. Yo ya había trabajado y había ahorrado (*saved*) algún dinero cuando empecé la universidad.
4. Cuando pasó el primer mes de clases en la universidad, yo ya me había acostumbrado a todo el trabajo que tenía que hacer.
5. Mis padres ya sospechaban que yo me había hecho más independiente cuando los visité después de algunos meses.

 **INTERCAMBIOS.** ¿Cuáles de las acciones de *Preparación* concuerdan (*agree*) con tu experiencia personal? Comparte tus respuestas con tu compañero/a.

Una investigación. **PREPARACIÓN.** Completa la tabla y dile a tu compañero/a si tú o miembros de tu familia ya habían hecho estas cosas antes del año 2013.

 buscar trabajo en Internet antes del año 2013

E1: *Mi hermano y yo ya habíamos buscado trabajo en Internet. En el año 2012, los dos conseguimos trabajo por Internet.*

E2: *Pues, yo nunca había usado Internet para buscar trabajo. En 2012, yo estaba en la escuela secundaria.*

ANTES DEL AÑO 2013	SÍ	NO	¿QUIÉNES?
1. manejar un carro híbrido			
2. hacer trabajo voluntario			
3. votar en las elecciones presidenciales			
4. leer periódicos digitales muchas veces			
5. comunicarse con los amigos por mensajes de texto			
6. comprar un iPod			
7. diseñar una página web			
8. crear una cuenta de Twitter			

 **INTERCAMBIOS.** Hagan una encuesta para averiguar qué tres actividades de *Preparación* marcaron más personas del grupo. Determinen si más hombres o más mujeres hicieron cada una de las tres actividades.

Expansion for 14-17, *Intercambios*
Encourage students to expand on those statements that are part of their personal experience. Provide an example with the *Modelo* as follows: *Cuando yo cumplí diez años, ya había escuchado a mis padres, mis tíos y mis abuelos hablar de política. Mi familia era republicana/demócrata/independiente, pero todos estaban muy comprometidos con los cambios sociales.*

Follow-up for 14-18, *Intercambios*
You may wish to pool responses to create a class tally. To expand, you can have students order all the activities by frequency, or change the date that serves as the reference point. Students may also wish to add items to the list.

Additional practice
You may wish to have students describe the experiences of the *arpilleras* of Chile using the past perfect tense. They may research this topic on the Internet for more information. Explain that: *Durante la dictadura en Chile entre 1973 y 1990, las arpilleras chilenas hicieron tapices en los cuales protestaban por la desaparición o muerte de un familiar. Usen su intuición o conocimiento de la historia para hacer una lista de posibles experiencias que las arpilleras habían tenido durante esa dictadura.*

MODELO *Antes de la democracia, las mujeres probablemente habían mostrado sus tapices en secreto.*

You may wish to give students the following verbs to help them with their descriptions: *escribir, participar, protestar, llorar, pedir ayuda, relatar, luchar, perder, sufrir.*

14-19 

¡Una familia organizada! Los señores Rosales salieron temprano para el trabajo hoy. Cuando volvieron por la noche notaron que sus hijos Carlos, Eduardo y Magdalena habían hecho todo el trabajo doméstico. Túrnense para conjeturar qué había hecho cada uno.

Al salir, les dijeron a sus hijos que iban a llegar un poco tarde y que no tendrían tiempo para cocinar. *Al volver, vieron que Eduardo había cocinado unos espaguetis para toda la familia.*

1. Después del desayuno dejaron los platos sucios en el lavaplatos.
2. Antes de irse a la oficina, la señora Rosales vio que había un montón de libros de la biblioteca en la mesa del comedor.
3. Cuando salía de casa el señor Rosales notó que el garaje estaba sucio.
4. Los dormitorios de sus hijos estaban desordenados; había ropa y libros en el piso.
5. Como tenía prisa, la señora Rosales olvidó mandar por correo unos cheques importantes.
6. No llevaron a la tintorería (*dry cleaner*) una ropa que querían limpiar en seco (*dry clean*).

Situación

PREPARACIÓN. Lean la situación. Luego, compartan ejemplos de vocabulario, gramática y otra información que necesitan para desarrollar la conversación.

Role A. You are interviewing a student for your campus newspaper. Ask a) what he/she had planned to study before coming to the university; b) what other schools he/she had considered before choosing this one; and c) how his/her experience has been different from what he/she had expected.

Role B. You are a student who is being interviewed for the campus newspaper. Provide as much information to the reporter as possible, including your expectations (**lo que había pensado**) before you entered college and the reality you found when you started to study here.

	ROLE A	ROLE B
Vocabulario	Studies Extracurricular activities	Studies Extracurricular activities
Funciones y formas	Asking questions Past perfect	Past tense Past perfect

INTERCAMBIOS. Practica la conversación con tu compañero/a incorporando el vocabulario y las funciones de *Preparación.* Luego, represéntenla ante la clase.

4 Expressing actions

LAURA: Mamá, ¿viste la marcha en la tele? Yo también estaba allí con todos mis compañeros de la clase de sociología.

MAMÁ: **Luchar** por la igualdad entre los sexos es tiempo perdido, hija. No hemos avanzado mucho. Mira, yo continúo trabajando en casa, pero no me importa.

LAURA: Pero **quedarse** de brazos cruzados tampoco es una opción para mí, mamá.

MAMÁ: **Trabajar** duro es lo que debemos hacer. Ninguna protesta nos ayudará.

LAURA: Mamá, ¿cómo puedes pensar así? **Guardar** silencio es **hacerse** cómplice de la injusticia. **Exigir** igualdad y respeto por nuestra dignidad es nuestro derecho.

Suggestion
Show international signs (e.g., a lighted cigarette crossed by a diagonal line) and have students give the Spanish equivalents.

Piénsalo. Indica si crees que las siguientes acciones representan las opiniones de Laura (**L**) o las de su madre (**M**).

1. __M__ **Trabajar** en casa no es un problema para la mujer.
2. __L__ **Protestar** nos ayudará a cambiar la sociedad.
3. __L__ No **resignarse** al trato desigual es fundamental para conseguir el cambio.
4. __L__ **Mantenerse** de brazos cruzados significa aceptar la desigualdad y la injusticia.

The infinitive as subject or object

- The infinitive is the only verb form that may be used as the subject of a sentence. As the subject, it corresponds to the English *-ing* form.

Dialogar es necesario para lograr cambios.	*Talking is necessary for changes to occur.*
Hacer comentarios negativos no es bueno para nuestras negociaciones.	*Making negative pronouncements is not good for our negotiations.*

- Use an infinitive after a preposition.

Llama **antes de ir.**	*Call before going.*
No trates de discutir el tema **sin prepararte.**	*Do not try to argue without preparing yourself.*

- **Al** + *infinitive* is the equivalent of **cuando** + *verb*.

Al recibir su carta de despido, llamó al director.	*Upon receiving his pink slip, he called the director.*
Cuando recibió su carta de despido, llamó al director.	*When he received his pink slip, he called the director.*

- When used in signs and instructions, the infinitive functions as a command.

No **comer** en clase.	*No eating in class.* (Lit. *Don't eat in class.*)
Hablar en voz baja.	*Speak softly.*

¿COMPRENDES?

Completa las oraciones con los siguientes verbos.

abrir	hacer
cerrar	nadar
dormir	participar
fumar	

1. __Fumar__ está prohibido en los edificios de la universidad.
2. __Nadar__ es el mejor ejercicio para el dolor de espalda.
3. La vida es breve: un __abrir__ y __cerrar__ de ojos.
4. Al __participar__ en las protestas, Gonzalo se comprometió aún más con el movimiento.

MySpanishLab
Learn more using Amplifire Dynamic Study Modules, Grammar Tutorials, and Extra Practice activities.

PRÁCTICA

Cultura

Independencia en Latinoamérica

Los países latinoamericanos consiguieron la independencia de España durante el siglo XIX. Las diferentes guerras por la independencia crearon países libres en un tiempo relativamente corto. El primer país en independizarse fue Venezuela, en 1811, y el último Bolivia en 1825. Entre las grandes figuras guerreras independentistas se encuentran Iturbide en México y el "gran libertador de las Américas", Simón Bolívar, que venció a los españoles en la batalla de Ayacucho en 1825. Un caso singular es el de Cuba y Puerto Rico. Tras la guerra entre España y Estados Unidos a finales del siglo XIX, Cuba ganó su independencia en 1898. Puerto Rico, por otra parte, nunca ha sido un país independiente. Primero fue un protectorado de Estados Unidos y posteriormente, un "Estado libre asociado".

Comparaciones. ¿Qué personajes históricos se consideran "grandes libertadores" en la Guerra de Independencia de los Estados Unidos? Prepara una breve presentación.

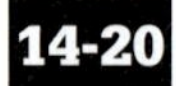 

14-20

Ciudadanos responsables. Asocia lógicamente las opciones de la columna de la izquierda con las ideas de la columna de la derecha y compara tus respuestas con las de tu compañero/a.

1. ___d___ Luchar por la libertad...
2. ___c___ Estudiar idiomas...
3. ___b___ Expresar una opinión...
4. ___a___ Aceptar a los inmigrantes...

a. es indispensable para una convivencia sana dentro de una comunidad.
b. es un derecho.
c. es la mejor manera de aprender sobre otras culturas.
d. es una obligación moral de todos.

14-21 

Opiniones. **PREPARACIÓN.** Indica si las siguientes actividades son necesarias (**N**), opcionales (**O**) o inaceptables (**I**). Después, compara tus respuestas con las de tu compañero/a y explícale las razones de tus respuestas.

ACTIVIDAD	OPINIÓN
1. ofrecer seguro de salud para todos	
2. informarse sobre lo que pasa en el mundo	
3. prohibir la proliferación de armas nucleares	
4. hacer investigación sobre células troncales (*stem cell*)	
5. discriminar a algunas personas por su etnia (*ethnicity*)	

INTERCAMBIOS. Escojan el tema más importante para ustedes de *Preparación.* Expliquen por qué es importante y qué es necesario hacer para lograr la atención de la gente.

14-22 

Interpretar los mensajes. **PREPARACIÓN.** Observen los siguientes letreros y escriban una nota bajo cada uno de ellos.

1. ______________

2. ______________

3. ______________

4. ______________

INTERCAMBIOS. Preparen su propio letrero. Otra pareja tiene que decir dónde sería bueno ponerlo y por qué.

Expansion for 14-22, *Intercambios*
After groups have finished *Intercambios*, have them share their signs with the class.

Situación

PREPARACIÓN. Lean la situación. Luego, compartan ejemplos de vocabulario, gramática y otra información que necesitan para desarrollar la conversación.

Role A. As president of the Student Association, you are designing a campaign to promote cross-cultural understanding in your area. Discuss with a friend: a) what students can do to better understand people from other cultures; and b) how students can reach out to (**comunicarse con**) people from other cultures who live in the community.

Role B. A friend wants to discuss a project to promote cross-cultural understanding in your area. Explain your views about a) what students can do to learn about cultural diversity; and b) how students can reach out to (**comunicarse con**) people from other cultures who live in the community.

	ROLE A	ROLE B
Vocabulario	Social issues Plans and projects	Social issues Plans and projects
Funciones y formas	Expressing opinions Using the infinitive as subject or object *Por/para*	Expressing opinions Using the infinitive as subject or object *Por/para*

INTERCAMBIOS. Practica la conversación con tu compañero/a incorporando el vocabulario y las funciones de *Preparación*. Luego, represéntenla ante la clase.

EN ACCIÓN

Por un mundo mejor

14-23 Antes de ver

Temas de interés social. Asocia las personas o grupos de la columna de la izquierda con los temas de la columna de la derecha.

1. _c_ los techos verdes	**a.** la persecución política
2. _a_ los refugiados	**b.** la discriminación sexual
3. _d_ los indocumentados	**c.** el medio ambiente
4. _e_ los indígenas	**d.** la reforma migratoria
5. _b_ los homosexuales	**e.** las minorías étnicas
6. _f_ los veganos	**f.** la protección de animales

14-24 Mientras ves  

Cambios y más cambios. En este segmento, los chicos hablan sobre sus proyectos. Indica si las siguientes afirmaciones son ciertas (**C**) o falsas (**F**) según la información que aparece en el video. Corrige las afirmaciones falsas.

1. _F_ Yolanda ya ha terminado su proyecto de video. *Yolanda piensa continuar trabajando hasta que termine su proyecto de video.*
2. _C_ El proyecto de Yolanda está relacionado con problemas del medio ambiente.
3. _F_ Esteban cree que la pobreza y el analfabetismo ya no existen. *Hay todavía mucha pobreza y analfabetismo.*
4. _C_ El video de Esteban trata de la inmigración.
5. _F_ La organización Chirla lucha por los derechos de los homosexuales. *Chirla es una coalición para luchar por los derechos humanos de los inmigrantes y refugiados.*
6. _C_ Chirla promociona actividades para que haya una sociedad más justa.
7. _F_ El proyecto de Federico trata de la legalización de la marihuana en Argentina. *El proyecto de Federico trata de los derechos de los gays en Argentina.*
8. _C_ Argentina fue el primer país latinoamericano en legalizar el matrimonio entre personas del mismo sexo.

14-25 Después de ver 

Un mundo mejor. **PREPARACIÓN.** Completa las afirmaciones de la izquierda con las ideas de la derecha.

1. _d_ Para que haya más conciencia sobre los problemas del medio ambiente...	**a.** para que deje de consumir carne y otros productos derivados.
2. _c_ Chirla intentará influir sobre el congresista de Los Ángeles...	**b.** de manera que aumente la conciencia social sobre ellos.
3. _a_ Yolanda hablará con Federico sobre los derechos de los animales...	**c.** para que vote a favor de la reforma migratoria.
4. _b_ Los chicos van a presentar proyectos sobre problemas sociales...	**d.** la organización techos verdes busca cambiar la actitud de las personas en México.

INTERCAMBIOS. El proyecto de video de Esteban está relacionado con los derechos de los inmigrantes y refugiados. Explíquense las diferencias entre un inmigrante y un refugiado. Hablen de los desafíos (*challenges*) de ser inmigrante o refugiado y sugieran maneras de mejorar la situación de estos grupos.

Mosaicos

ESCUCHA

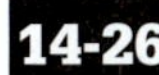 Presentational

Preparación. Dos mujeres mayores conversan sobre los cambios que han ocurrido en la familia hispana. Antes de escuchar su conversación, escribe un cambio que probablemente se mencionará en relación con cada una de estas áreas: los quehaceres de la casa y la crianza de los hijos. Luego, comparte tus ideas con la clase.

ESTRATEGIA

Identify the speaker's point of view

When you listen to someone or see someone talk you may identify the speaker's intention and point of view by paying attention to word choice as well as other cues, such as tone, organization of ideas, and pitch. Identifying the speaker's point of view will help you understand his/her position on the issues.

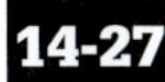   Interpretive

Escucha. Read the statements, then listen to Sonia and Vilma talk about changes in the Hispanic family that have occurred during their lifetime. Pay attention to how each woman organizes her ideas, her choice of words, and the tone she uses to indicate if each statement reflects Sonia's (**S**) point of view or Vilma's (**V**).

1. __S__ Los cambios que han ocurrido en la sociedad han sido positivos.
2. __V__ Ahora nadie se ocupa de los quehaceres de la casa.
3. __S__ No era bueno el papel secundario que tenía la mujer en la casa.
4. __V__ Los abuelos han perdido la importancia que tenían en la familia.
5. __S__ La mujer debe desarrollarse profesional e intelectualmente.

Comprueba

I was able to ...

____ **identify words that helped me understand different points of view.**

____ **identify Sonia and Vilma by the pitch and tone of their voices.**

14-28  Interpersonal

Un paso más. Compartan su punto de vista sobre los siguientes asuntos.

1. ¿Es necesario que uno de los padres se quede en casa mientras los hijos son pequeños? Expliquen su respuesta.
2. Si ambos padres trabajan fuera de casa, ¿cómo se podría resolver la cuestión de la educación de los hijos?

Audioscript for 14-27

VILMA: *¿Qué te parece la sociedad en que vivimos, Sonia? Todo lo que ha ocurrido en los últimos años ha tenido repercusiones en la familia.*

SONIA: *Sí, es verdad, pero los cambios han sido positivos, ¿no crees?*

VILMA: *No sé qué decirte, Sonia. Antes las tareas estaban bien definidas y cada uno sabía lo que tenía que hacer. La responsabilidad del padre era mantener económicamente a la familia, mientras que la madre se ocupaba de las labores domésticas y de la educación de los niños. Ahora, parece que nadie se ocupa de la casa.*

SONIA: *Bueno, pero acuérdate que siempre la última palabra la tenía el padre y él era el rey del hogar. La mujer tenía un papel secundario. Yo prefiero la vida de las mujeres de hoy. Ellas juegan un papel más importante tanto en la familia como en la sociedad.*

VILMA: *Pero ¿cuál es el costo? Antes toda la familia colaboraba en la crianza de los hijos. Los abuelos ayudaban a cuidarlos y todos los miembros de la familia les mostraban cariño. Ahora, los niños están en las guarderías infantiles y los abuelos en las residencias de ancianos.*

SONIA: *Sí, eso sí es triste. Aunque el papel de la mujer en la sociedad sea mejor ahora, no me gusta que los niños pasen tantas horas del día separados de sus padres y abuelos. Debería haber más equilibrio para que la mujer no se sacrifique y no deje de crecer intelectual y profesionalmente.*

VILMA: *Tú eres más moderna que yo, Sonia. Yo prefiero el pasado cuando todo era más sencillo.*

SONIA: *Yo no. Yo prefiero ver a la mujer desarrollarse igual que el hombre.*

HABLA

14-29 Interpretive

Preparación. Investiga sobre un problema (local, nacional o mundial) en una de las siguientes áreas y anota en qué consiste el problema.

Área: *seguridad*

Problema: *terrorismo*

Explicación del problema: *Hoy existen grupos terroristas que atacan y crean caos en el mundo. Nadie se siente seguro.*

ÁREAS

1. economía
2. igualdad
3. educación
4. salud

ESTRATEGIA

Organize ideas to present solutions to problems

When you present your ideas about how to solve a problem, organize them so that you can communicate clearly to your listeners a) what the problem is, to whom it is important, and why; b) how your proposal is to be implemented and how it addresses the problem; and c) the likely consequences of your solution. Your underlying goal is to convince your listeners of the wisdom of your approach.

Suggestion for 14-30
You may wish to point out that the *Modelo* represents opinions at opposite extremes of the spectrum. Whatever the range of the opinions of the group, members should ask each other to explain their opinions in as much detail as possible. It may not be possible to arrive at the consensus suggested in the model.

Audioscript for *En directo*
MADRE: *Después de discutir el tema de la falta de seguridad en las escuelas, nuestro comité ha llegado a la siguiente conclusión. Necesitamos contratar a personal de seguridad e instalar máquinas que detecten armas de fuego.*
ADMINISTRADOR: *A nosotros nos parece que tanto los padres como la administración debemos trabajar juntos para mejorar la protección de todos. Las estadísticas nos muestran que en el 99% de los casos las escuelas seguras son aquellas donde hay colaboración de los padres y la administración en el tema de la seguridad. Los padres pueden mantener sus armas lejos de las manos de sus hijos.*

Suggestion for 14-31
Before students present their reports, you may wish to model how to present and defend a personal or a group position on a controversial issue.

14-30  Interpersonal

Habla. Conversen sobre los problemas que ustedes identificaron en la actividad 14-29. Hagan lo siguiente:

1. Intercambien la información que encontraron sobre los problemas que eligieron. Expliquen cuál es el más serio y por qué.
2. Luego, háganse preguntas relacionadas con ese problema. Utilicen en sus respuestas las expresiones indicadas en *En directo* y tomen nota de las respuestas del grupo.

la falta de seguridad en las escuelas

E1: *¿Creen que haya solución al problema de la falta de seguridad en las escuelas?*

E2: *Sí, la solución es tener/establecer más comunicación con la administración de las escuelas, para que controlen mejor la seguridad de los alumnos.*

E3: *A mí me parece que la solución es instalar máquinas en las entradas de las escuelas que registren a todas las personas que quieran entrar en la escuela.*

En directo

To present a group's conclusion:

Después de hablar sobre el tema, hemos llegado a la siguiente conclusión. Nuestro grupo cree/piensa que...

A nuestro grupo le parece que...

Para nosotros, el problema más serio es...

To support a group's view or position:

No tenemos duda de que es el problema más serio porque...

Si miramos/observamos... nos damos cuenta de que...

Las estadísticas/La opinión de los expertos apoya(n) nuestra conclusión.

Listen to a conversation with these expressions.

Comprueba

I was able to ...

____ inform myself well about the problem, and identify possible solutions.

____ organize my ideas in a logical sequence: identification of a problem and possible solutions to share with my classmate.

14-31 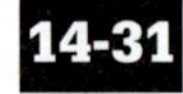 Presentational

Un paso más. Preséntenle a la clase la información y conclusión a la que llegaron en la actividad 14-30. Prepárense para defender su posición.

LEE

14-32 Interpersonal

Preparación. Responde a las siguientes preguntas. Compara tus respuestas con las de tu compañero/a.

1. ¿Qué fábulas conoces o recuerdas de tu niñez?
2. ¿Cuáles son los elementos de las fábulas?
3. ¿Cuál es el propósito de una fábula?
4. ¿Qué diferencias hay entre una mosca y un águila? ¿Qué tienen en común?
5. Imagínate que no eres un ser humano, sino un animal. ¿Preferirías ser una mosca o un águila? ¿Por qué?

ESTRATEGIA

Identify the tone of a text

Identifying the tone of a text is important when reading literature. A writer may use subtle irony or sarcasm to convey social criticism. Sometimes the writer adopts a traditional genre (e.g., fairy tale, fable) to present a message about contemporary life.

Augusto Monterroso (1921–2003) nació en Honduras de un padre guatemalteco y una madre hondureña, pero se crio en Guatemala y siempre se consideró guatemalteco. Por sus actividades políticas, estuvo encarcelado brevemente en 1944 pero escapó y vivió exiliado en Chile y luego en México, donde vivió hasta su muerte. Monterroso, conocido por sus relatos breves que tratan sobre temas complejos del comportamiento humano, es uno de los maestros de la minificción. Su microcuento "El dinosaurio" es considerado uno de los más breves de la literatura universal (*Cuando despertó, el dinosaurio todavía estaba allí.*), aunque el escritor mexicano Luis Felipe Lomelí ha escrito uno más corto de solo cuatro palabras.

14-33  Interpretive

Lee. Desde la perspectiva de la Mosca del cuento, indica cuáles son las ventajas (**V**) y las desventajas (**D**) de ser un águila.

1. __V__ volar por los Alpes
2. __D__ tener alas grandes
3. __D__ tener un cuerpo pesado
4. __D__ tener un pico duro
5. __D__ tener garras fuertes
6. __V__ remontar montañas

Comprueba

I was able to ...

- ____ **understand the story literally.**
- ____ **understand the fly's internal conflict.**
- ____ **apply the message of the story to human behavior.**

Suggestion for 14-32
You may wish to have students discuss how "El dinosaurio" lends itself to various interpretations and raises numerous questions: *¿Quién se despertó? ¿Dónde está "allí"?* You may also wish to show them Lomelí's 4-word story, "El emigrante": *¿Olvida usted algo? —¡Ojalá!*

Standard 1.3 Students present information, concepts, and ideas to an audience of listeners or readers on a variety of topics. The strategies and *En directo* boxes offer students useful information on how to organize and present facts and opinions orally. Such skills can help students not only in their language classes, but in any course where they give oral presentations.

LA MOSCA QUE SOÑABA QUE ERA UN ÁGUILA

Había una vez una Mosca que todas las noches soñaba que era un Águila y que se encontraba volando por los Alpes y por los Andes.

En los primeros momentos esto la volvía loca de felicidad; pero pasado un tiempo le causaba una sensación de angustia, pues hallaba las alas[1] demasiado grandes, el cuerpo demasiado pesado, el pico[2] demasiado duro y las garras[3] demasiado fuertes; bueno, que todo ese gran aparato le impedía posarse a gusto sobre los ricos pasteles o sobre las inmundicias[4] humanas, así como sufrir a conciencia dándose topes contra los vidrios de su cuarto.

En realidad no quería andar en las grandes alturas o en los espacios libres, ni mucho menos.

Pero cuando volvía en sí lamentaba con toda el alma no ser un Águila para remontar montañas, y se sentía tristísima de ser una Mosca, y por eso volaba tanto, y estaba tan inquieta, y daba tantas vueltas, hasta que lentamente, por la noche, volvía a poner las sienes en la almohada.

Monterroso, Augusto. *La oveja negra y demás fábulas.* Alfaguara. México: 2a edición. 1998.

[1]*wings* [2]*beak* [3]*claws* [4]*filth*

14-34  Presentational

Un paso más. En grupos, escriban su interpretación del minicuento y preséntenla a la clase. Enfóquense en cómo se puede aplicar el conflicto de la Mosca al comportamiento humano.

ESCRIBE

14-35 Interpretive

Preparación. Lee el siguiente poema que alude a las emociones de una persona que se siente atrapada en una relación. Luego, indica si estás de acuerdo (**A**) o en desacuerdo (**D**) con las afirmaciones sobre el poema.

Hombre pequeñito
de Alfonsina Storni

Hombre pequeñito, hombre pequeñito,
Suelta a tu canario, que quiere volar…
Yo soy el canario, hombre pequeñito,
Déjame saltar.

Estuve en tu jaula, hombre pequeñito,
Hombre pequeñito que jaula me das,
Digo pequeñito porque no me entiendes,
Ni me entenderás.
Tampoco te entiendo, pero mientras tanto

Ábreme la jaula que quiero escapar;
Hombre pequeñito, te amé media hora.
No me pidas más.

Answers will vary. Encourage students to support their answers.

1. ____________ El poema tiene un tono alegre.
2. ____________ La persona que habla en este poema es un hombre.
3. ____________ La voz del poema expresa un sentimiento de disgusto por la opresión en la que ha vivido.
4. ____________ La persona expresa la esperanza de que su pareja la comprenda en el futuro.
5. ____________ Al usar la palabra *pequeñito* la voz del poema expresa irónicamente su desprecio por su pareja.
6. ____________ La voz del poema quiere continuar viviendo con su compañero/a.

ESTRATEGIA

Use language to express emotions

Poetry is well suited to the expression of emotions. Poets paint with words experiences or feelings of heroism, beauty, love, sadness, loss, or injustice. To compose an effective poem, it is important to think carefully about the feelings we want to convey. Because poetry is a reflection of human experience, it is available to everyone both as readers and writers.

Suggestions for 14-35
You may want to assign this activity as homework and concentrate on the next activity in preparation for writing.

Note for *Alfonsina Storni*
You may wish to provide students with the following background on Alfonsina Storni. She was born in Switzerland in 1892, and then her parents moved to Argentina, where she lived until her death in 1938. Storni was an actress, a cashier, a playwright, a teacher, and a poet. Her book *Languidez* received first prize in the Municipal Poetry Prize competition and second place in the National Literary Prize.

Note for 14-36
This type of simple poem is known as a didactic cinquain. Here is an example:
Hermanito
Pequeño, sonriente
Llorando, gritando, insistiendo
Solo a veces duerme
Amor.

14-36 Presentational

Escribe. PREPARACIÓN. Vas a escribir tu propio poema de cinco líneas. Primero, escoge el tema principal (una persona, un animal, un objeto) y piensa en el tono y las emociones que quieres expresar. Luego, sigue las instrucciones para escribir tu poema.

Tema: ____________

Tono, emociones: ____________________

Comprueba
I was able to …

____ **decide on a topic, tone, and message for my poem.**

____ **follow the instructions to create an original 5-line poem.**

Mi poema de cinco líneas:

Título (el tema en una palabra)	______________________________
Dos adjetivos que describan el tema	______________, ______________
Tres gerundios (*-ando/-iendo*) relacionados con el tema	______________, ______________, ______________
Una frase de cuatro palabras relacionada con el tema	______________________________
Una palabra que exprese lo mismo que el título	______________________________.

  Interpersonal

Un paso más. Lean sus poemas y decidan si evocan las emociones que cada uno de ustedes quería expresar. Luego, háganles preguntas específicas a los miembros de su grupo sobre el uso de las palabras que han escogido.

 *¿Por qué dices en el poema que…?*

En este capítulo…

Comprueba lo que sabes

Go to ***MySpanishLab*** to review what you have learned in this chapter. Practice with the following:

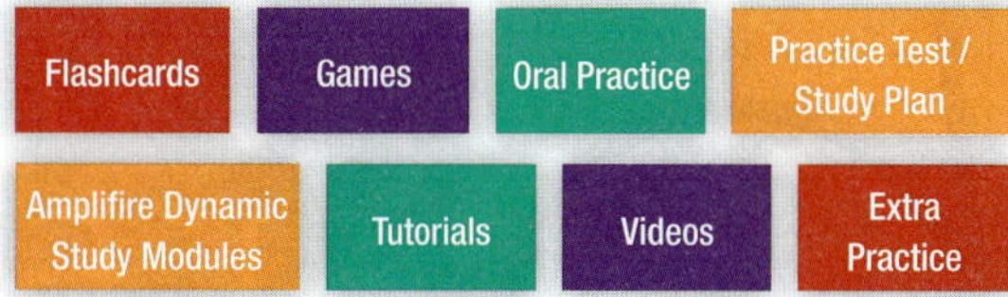

Vocabulario

LA SOCIEDAD
Society

la adaptación *adjustment, adaptation*
el alfabetismo *literacy*
el analfabetismo *illiteracy*
el cambio *change*
la confianza *trust*
la democracia *democracy*
el derecho *right*
el desempleo *unemployment*
el desplazamiento *movement, displacement*
la dictadura *dictatorship*
la diversificación *diversification*
la eficiencia *efficiency*
la elección *election*
la emigración *emigration*
la esperanza de vida *life expectancy*
la exportación *export*
la honestidad *honesty*
la igualdad *equality*
la inmigración *immigration*
la lucha *fight*
la migración *migration*
la mortalidad *mortality*
la pobreza *poverty*
la proximidad *proximity*
el régimen *regime*
el tráfico de drogas *drug trafficking*

LAS ENCUESTAS
Surveys/Polls

los datos *data, information*
la mayoría *majority*
la minoría *minority*
el porcentaje *percentage*
el promedio *average*
la tasa *rate*

LAS DESCRIPCIONES
Descriptions

amplio/a *ample*
analfabeto/a *illiterate*
dictatorial *dictatorial*
económico/a *economic*
enérgico/a *energetic*
infantil *children's*
políglota *polyglot, multilingual*

PALABRAS Y EXPRESIONES ÚTILES
Useful words and expressions

en vez de *instead of*
el nivel *level*
la sucursal *branch (business)*

LAS PERSONAS
People

el/la emigrante *emigrant*
el/la habitante *inhabitant*
el/la inmigrante *immigrant*
la población *population*
el/la presidente/a *president*

VERBOS
Verbs

destacarse *to stand out*
defender (ie) *to defend*
elegir (i, i) *to choose, elect*
emigrar *to emigrate*
gobernar (ie) *to govern*
luchar *fight*
mejorar *to improve*
preceder *to precede*
realizar (c) *to carry out*

See pages 488 and 491 for a list of adverbial conjunctions.

Introduction to chapter
Introduce the chapter theme about the future and ask questions to recycle previous content: *¿Cómo se imaginan Uds. el futuro de nuestro planeta? ¿Creen que habrá grandes cambios ecológicos? En su opinión, ¿cuáles fueron los avances tecnológicos más importantes del siglo XX? ¿Qué avances tecnológicos o científicos veremos en el siglo XXI?*

Integrated Performance Assessment: Three Modes of Communication

Presentational: See activities 15-3, 15-4, 15-7, 15-9, 15-16, 15-27, 15-29, 15-32, 15-35, and 15-37.

Interpretive: See Activities 15-1, 15-2, 15-4, 15-5, 15-6, 15-7, 15-9, 15-11, 15-13, 15-14, 15-17, 15-20, 15-21, 15-22, 15-24, 15-25, 15-26, 15-28, 15-30, and 15-34.

Interpersonal: See activities 15-3, 15-5, 15-6, 15-8, 15-10, 15-11, 15-12, 15-14, 15-15, 15-16, 15-17, 15-18, 15-19, 15-20, 15-23, 15-26, 15-31, 15-33, 15-36, 15-38, and all *Situación* activities.

15 ¿Qué nos trae el futuro?

ENFOQUE CULTURAL
Puerto Rico

VOCABULARIO EN CONTEXTO
La ciencia y la tecnología en el mundo de hoy
La conservación del medio ambiente
Otros retos del futuro

MOSAICO CULTURAL
La investigación tecnológica en Latinoamérica

FUNCIONES Y FORMAS
The imperfect subjunctive
If-clauses
Se for unplanned occurrences

EN ACCIÓN
¡Cuidemos el medio ambiente!

MOSAICOS
ESCUCHA Identify the speaker's intention through the main idea and specific information
HABLA Use drama and humor in telling a personal anecdote
LEE Identify the narrator's perspective
ESCRIBE Use imagination and humor in writing a narrative

EN ESTE CAPÍTULO...
Comprueba lo que sabes
Vocabulario

LEARNING OUTCOMES

You will be able to:

- talk about advances in science and technology
- express wishes and recommendations in the past
- hypothesize and share information about the present and the future
- express unexpected occurrences
- talk about Puerto Rico in terms of its advances in science and technology

ENFOQUE cultural PUERTO RICO

Enfoque cultural
To learn more about Puerto Rico, go to MySpanishLab to view the *Vistas culturales* videos.

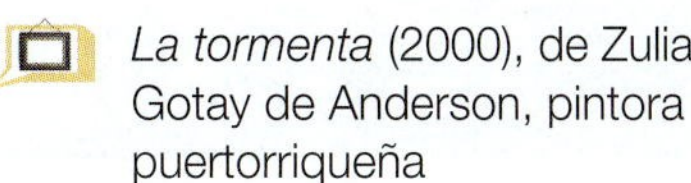

La tormenta (2000), de Zulia Gotay de Anderson, pintora puertorriqueña

¿QUÉ TE PARECE?

- En Puerto Rico se mide la temperatura ambiental en grados Farenheit mientras que la temperatura corporal se mide en grados centígrados.
- En Puerto Rico se usa el sistema monetario de Estados Unidos, pero se han mantenido los nombres de las antiguas monedas españolas. Un dólar se conoce como un peso y la moneda de 25 centavos es una peseta.
- En Puerto Rico hay cientos de especies de bananas. La palabra genérica para esta fruta es guineo porque en la época colonial las importaban del país africano Guinea. En vez de naranja, se usa la palabra china porque esta fruta se trajo de China.
- Puerto Rico participa como país independiente en los Juegos Olímpicos. Ha ganado siete medallas: cinco en boxeo, una en lucha libre y otra en atletismo. Javier Culson es el atleta olímpico más conocido.

Note
Remind students that since 1952, Puerto Rico has been a commonwealth (*Estado Libre Asociado*) of the U.S., which controls all areas of Puerto Rico's government except its internal affairs. The differences between Puerto Rico and the 50 states are its exemption from some aspects of the Internal Revenue Code and its lack of representation in both houses of the U.S. Congress. Puerto Ricans cannot vote in U.S. presidential elections unless they are residents of one of the 50 states. The political status of the island has long been the object of controversy.

Suggestions
Ask students about Puerto Rico: *¿Cómo es el clima? ¿Cuál es la capital? ¿Qué relación tiene con Estados Unidos? ¿En qué ciudades continentales de Estados Unidos viven muchos puertorriqueños? ¿Conocen alguna comida típica de Puerto Rico?* Talk about *mofongo*, a typical dish made from fried plantains or yucca, served with chicken or meat. *¿Conocen alguna costumbre de Puerto Rico? ¿Alguna persona famosa de Puerto Rico?* Ask if students have heard of the *coquí* and point to the photo.

Note
Zulia Gotay de Anderson is a Puerto Rican painter who specializes in female subjects and Hispanic themes. She works mainly in oils and watercolors.

Suggestions
Introduce the words *óleo* (oil painting) and *acuarela* (watercolor) when talking about this artist. Use questions to help students describe the painting: *¿Dónde están estas mujeres? ¿Están felices? ¿Tienen miedo?* Introduce other words that refer to emotions: *Las mujeres están preocupadas. Están aterradas probablemente.* Ask students to explain those emotions: *¿Por qué? ¿Qué pasa en el mar?* Recycle climate

and weather vocabulary: *¿Qué pasa cuando hay una tormenta en el mar?* Help students describe the ongoing actions in the painting.

Ask students about their artistic talents: *¿Les gusta pintar? ¿Prefieren pintar al óleo o con acuarela?* Ask: *¿Alguien en esta clase usa la computadora para dibujar? ¿Qué programas para pintar conocen?*

Note
You may wish to show students images of insects and marine animals that emit the light known as *bioluminiscencia.* Remind them that they are familiar with one such creature, *las luciérnagas* (fireflies).

Note for *Arecibo*
The Arecibo observatory, which provides technical support to scientists worldwide, has a sensitive radio telescope with a surface of 305 meters (1,000 feet) in diameter. Situated in a natural crater in the mountains of Puerto Rico, its dual reflector antenna system sends and receives signals to study planets and asteroids.

Notes for *reguetón*
You may wish to point out that in Spanish, *reggaeton, reggaetón,* and *reguetón* are all commonly accepted spellings. Students may be interested to know that the term comes from the combination of the English word *reggae* with the addition of the Spanish suffix *–ón* which can be used to indicate something big.

Note for *Tego Calderón*
Tego Calderón, a famous Puerto Rican actor and rapper, is credited with having started and named *reguetón.* Students may recognize Tego from his role in *Fast & Furious,* the fourth installment in the action film series *The Fast and the Furious.* The fifth installment was filmed in Puerto Rico.

ENFOQUE cultural

La Parguera, en Lajas, es una bahía llena de casas flotantes y una de las tres bahías de Puerto Rico donde en las noches sin luna se puede observar el fenómeno de la bioluminiscencia. Las bahías sorprenden por la intensidad de la luz emitida por los organismos microscópicos al agitarse. Es como un espectáculo de luces bajo el mar.

El Observatorio de Arecibo, en el norte de la isla, tiene el radiotelescopio más grande del mundo. Allí se filmaron las películas *Contact* y *Goldeneye* del famoso Agente 007. Además ha aparecido en episodios de *X Files* y más recientemente en *Covert Affairs.* Desde 1999 el Instituto SETI ha analizado los datos recolectados por este radiotelescopio en búsqueda de evidencia de la existencia de inteligencia extraterrestre y, por eso, en el mundo del cine muchas veces se asocia con los temas de ciencia ficción.

La expresión musical en Puerto Rico es el resultado de una gran mezcla de culturas. El *reguetón,* una expresión de música urbana, es una fusión del reggae en español que proviene de Panamá, del hip hop y de otros ritmos caribeños. En sus comienzos fue prohibido por sus temas sociales muy controvertidos, pero hoy, gracias a la persistencia de cantantes famosos como Tego Calderón, el reguetón es popular en todas partes del mundo.

Las Fiestas de la Calle San Sebastián, que se celebran cada año en el Viejo San Juan a finales de enero, duran cuatro días. Hay desfiles, música, artesanía y exhibiciones de arte. Con ellas se pone fin a la temporada navideña puertorriqueña. En la Comparsa de los Cabezudos, los cabezudos (muñecos con cabezas enormes) representan a las figuras más destacadas de la historia, la cultura y la política, al igual que a otras figuras populares del momento.

¿CUÁNTO SABES?

Completa estas oraciones con la información correcta.

1. El coquí es una __rana__ que vive exclusivamente en Puerto Rico.
2. El reguetón es una mezcla de ritmos de hip hop, __reggae__ en español y otros ritmos caribeños.
3. Una china en Puerto Rico es una __fruta/naranja__.
4. En Puerto Rico un peso equivale a __cuatro__ pesetas.
5. El Observatorio de Arecibo es famoso por tener el __radiotelescopio__ más grande del mundo y por las investigaciones sobre la vida __extraterrestre__ que se realizan allí.

Vocabulario en contexto

Talking about science, technology, and the environment

La ciencia y la tecnología en el mundo de hoy

MySpanishLab **Pronunciation Topic:** More on regional variations

Learn more using Amplifire Dynamic Study Modules, Pronunciation, and Vocabulary Tutorials.

Antes de salir para la universidad, Ángel, un joven puertorriqueño, **se conecta** con sus amigos por Internet. Entra en Twitter y le manda un *tweet* sobre la nueva película de **ciencia ficción** a Carmen. Luego, baja el último *podcast* para su clase *online* y le envía a su profesor de ciencias naturales un **mensaje** con un **documento adjunto.**

Entonces, Lorena, la hermana de Ángel, le pide que la ayude a bajar una canción de Internet para tenerla en su **tableta.** Por último, entra en el *blog* de su amigo Juanjo para leer las últimas novedades sobre sus **videojuegos** preferidos. Allí encuentra un **enlace** que le interesa.

Actualmente, la ciencia y la tecnología **contribuyen** a un mejor **conocimiento** y comprensión de las diferencias culturales que existen entre los pueblos. Los jóvenes de Europa e Hispanoamérica tienen muchas cosas en común con los de Asia, África o Estados Unidos. El **acceso** a Internet a través de las tabletas, computadoras y **móviles** hacen más fluida la comunicación y facilitan la **diseminación** y el **intercambio** de información.

Hace unos años, se estableció el Instituto de Ciencias y Tecnología (ICT) de la Universidad de Puerto Rico con el fin de **promover** el estudio de las ciencias entre los jóvenes. La Escuela Graduada de Ciencias y Tecnología de la Información (EGCTI), de la misma universidad, tiene una **biblioteca digital** que sirve como una importante **fuente de recursos** para los interesados en el campo de las ciencias de la información.

Suggestion
Have students brainstorm about the impact of technology on their lives. Write their ideas on the board under the heading: *¿Para qué sirve la tecnología?*, then follow the pattern *para + infinitive* (*para cocinar, para escribir a mis amigos,* etc.) You may start the conversation with questions: *¿Usan ustedes la tecnología en la cocina? ¿En la comunicación con sus amigos? ¿Qué invenciones o aplicaciones tecnológicas usan con más frecuencia? En general, ¿para qué se usa la tecnología en tu casa/en la universidad/en la medicina? ¿Hay lugares donde la gente prefiere no usar la tecnología? ¿Qué ventajas tiene usar la tecnología? ¿Y qué desventajas tiene?* Inquire how many hours a day they use their computers or cell phones and for what purposes.

Standard 4.1 Students demonstrate an understanding of the nature of language through comparisons of the language studied and their own. The language of technology and the Internet is increasingly in English worldwide. Students can learn about how languages adapt terms from other languages to make them sound more natural. For example, *iPod* is masculine, *el iPod,* because it is a type of *reproductor.* Perhaps because it is a neologism, its pronunciation is still unstable, varying between *aiPod* and *iPod.* Some words are also directly translated into their semantic equivalents. For example, the word *tweet* is quickly becoming *trino* in many parts of the Spanish-speaking world. You may wish to have students poll native speakers to see how they say such things as "mp3," "tablet," "post" (i.e., *an entry made to a blog*), and "flash/ pen drive."

PRÁCTICA

Suggestion for 15-1
To prepare for this activity have students brainstorm the uses of the Internet: *¿Para qué sirve Internet?* Write down their answers.

Audioscript for 15-1
Cursos de ingeniería y humanidades online. *Regístrate pronto para obtener tu título de maestría. Tenemos las mejores bibliotecas digitales. Nuestros profesores son expertos en recursos digitales para la diseminación de conocimientos. No somos una universidad tradicional: somos la Universidad del Futuro. Usamos las tecnologías más avanzadas para garantizar la mejor calidad de enseñanza y la mayor interacción. Solo necesitas acceso a Internet. ¡Conéctate al futuro!*

15-1  

Escucha y confirma. Escucha el anuncio radiofónico y decide si las afirmaciones son ciertas (**C**) o falsas (**F**). Corrige las falsas, dando la información correcta.

1. __F__ Es el anuncio de una tienda digital.
2. __C__ Según el anuncio se puede obtener un título de maestría *online*.
3. __F__ Se ofrecen clases de humanidades solamente.
4. __C__ Los expertos en recursos digitales son los profesores.
5. __F__ La calidad de la enseñanza es más importante que la interacción.
6. __F__ Los estudiantes no necesitan acceso a Internet.

15-2 

¿Para qué lo usamos? En las siguientes afirmaciones relacionadas con diversos usos de tecnología, indica el uso que *no* corresponde.

1. Internet sirve para...
- **a.** acceder a información sobre muchas disciplinas.
- **b.** ver películas.
- **c.** enviar felicitaciones.
- **(d.)** examinar a un paciente.

2. El correo electrónico se usa para...
- **a.** comunicarse con los amigos.
- **(b.)** hacer fotografías.
- **c.** enviar un documento adjunto.
- **d.** recibir mensajes.

3. La biblioteca digital se utiliza para...
- **(a.)** comunicarse con los profesores de la universidad.
- **b.** encontrar enlaces.
- **c.** bajar artículos.
- **d.** identificar documentación.

4. Los videojuegos sirven para...
- **a.** divertirse con los amigos.
- **(b.)** practicar deportes al aire libre.
- **c.** diseminar ciertos conocimientos.
- **d.** intercambiar información.

Note for 15-3, *Intercambios*
Have students ask each other questions about what technology they used to research and create their presentations. You may then have some groups present to the entire class.

Suggestion for 15-4, *Intercambios*
As an alternative for the *Intercambios*, if some students agree to use their cell phones, you may ask them to leave the class and call those still in the class to comment on the piece of news that they read.

Cultura

Universidad de Río Piedras

La Universidad de Puerto Rico está formada por once campus que se encuentran por toda la isla. El campus de Río Piedras es el más importante de todos y el que cuenta con mayor número de estudiantes, más de 17.000. Está situado en el centro de la zona comercial y cultural de Río Piedras, a las afueras de San Juan. El campus es fácilmente identificable desde diferentes puntos de la ciudad por su llamativa torre.

Comparaciones. ¿Cuál es el campus más importante de la universidad pública de tu estado? ¿Cuántos alumnos tiene? ¿Qué programas, actividades o edificios de esa universidad son los más conocidos?

15-3

Usa la tecnología.
PREPARACIÓN. Usa la tecnología para preparar una presentación sobre Puerto Rico que incluya lo siguiente.

1. ubicación de un lugar en un mapa
2. descripción y tres datos que se refieran a las características físicas del lugar, la gente del lugar y una costumbre del lugar
3. fotos

INTERCAMBIOS. Comparte la información con tu grupo, incluyendo una descripción de los recursos tecnológicos que utilizaste.

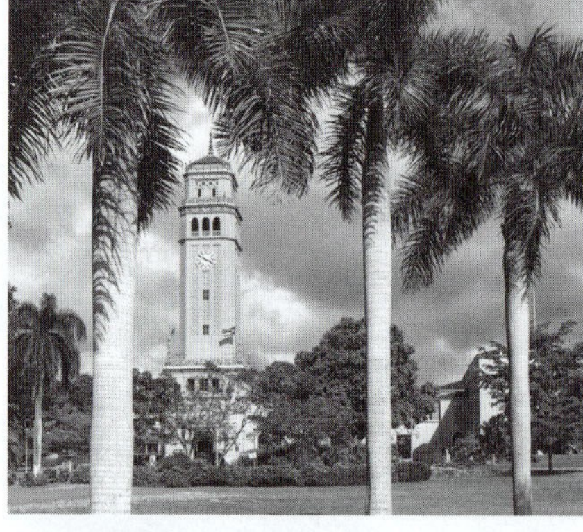

15-4

Una noticia. PREPARACIÓN. Busca una noticia que te interese en un periódico virtual de Puerto Rico. Léela y toma apuntes sobre lo esencial de la noticia.

INTERCAMBIOS. Mándales a tres personas de la clase un mensaje electrónico incluyendo un resumen de la noticia y tu opinión sobre ella.

La conservación del medio ambiente

La contribución de América Latina a la ciencia **se ha enfocado** principalmente en la biología, **debido a** la riqueza de la flora y la fauna, la **conservación** de la **naturaleza,** la agricultura y la medicina. Aunque a veces las **infraestructuras** y los recursos son insuficientes, algunos científicos de esta región han hecho **descubrimientos** importantes. Esta es una foto de El Yunque en Puerto Rico, una de las muchas **reservas naturales** de Hispanoamérica.

¡TODAVÍA ESTAMOS A TIEMPO!
La reserva de la biosfera es nuestra oportunidad

La reserva de la biosfera del Alto Golfo de California y del delta del río Colorado puede ser la salvación de nuestra cultura pesquera. Juntos vamos a desarrollar un plan que nos permita manejar la reproducción y recuperación de los recursos naturales y de esta manera, asegurar nuestro bienestar y el de nuestros hijos.

¡El éxito depende de nuestra participación!

La **cuenca** del río Amazonas cubre un área de más de siete millones de kilómetros cuadrados, región comparable en extensión a dos terceras partes del territorio continental de Estados Unidos. Debido a su densa vegetación selvática, esta zona es conocida como el pulmón del **planeta.** Hoy en día, miles de campesinos llegan a la selva **en busca de tierra** para cultivar. La **deforestación** de nuestros **bosques** se considera una **pérdida** irreparable para el **medio ambiente.**

Suggestion for *La conservación del medio ambiente*
Ask students to mention some ecological problems in the world, such as the damage of the ozone layer, pollution, acid rain, overpopulation, or the destruction of the rain forest. Provide any needed vocabulary. Move the discussion into speculation about the future. For example, in the field of medicine, will there be a cure for cancer, heart disease, AIDS?

Suggestion
Some students may find it helpful for you to explain the metaphor *pulmón del planeta.*

Follow-up for 15-5
Compare the proposals of various pairs of students, emphasizing the variety of ideas presented to solve current ecological problems.

Suggestion for 15-6
Have one student write on the board the advances and changes that students include in their lists. The class can try to reach a consensus on the feasibility of achieving such progress.

PRÁCTICA

15-5 

Para confirmar. **PREPARACIÓN.** Indica cuáles de los siguientes problemas se asocian **a)** con la industria pesquera, **b)** con los bosques tropicales o **c)** con los dos.

1. __b__ la construcción de carreteras
2. __b__ la desertización
3. __b__ la erosión
4. __c__ la exterminación de especies animales
5. __b__ la tala (*felling*) de árboles
6. __a__ la contaminación provocada por aguas residuales (*sewage*) y substancias químicas
7. __b__ la disminución de la capa de ozono
8. __a__ la pesca ilimitada

 **INTERCAMBIOS.** Intercambien ideas y recomendaciones para resolver cada problema.

15-6

Los adelantos (*Advances*) científicos.
PREPARACIÓN. Haz una lista de tres adelantos científicos y tres cambios sociales que esperas que se realicen en las próximas décadas.

ADELANTOS CIENTÍFICOS	CAMBIOS SOCIALES
______	______
______	______
______	______

INTERCAMBIOS. Comparen sus listas y justifiquen la razón de los cambios que indicaron en *Preparación*. ¿Por qué ocurrirán? ¿Son cambios necesarios?

Cultura

El coquí

El coquí es el nombre general para designar de manera popular un conjunto de ranas específico de Puerto Rico. El nombre es una onomatopeya del sonido emitido por las ranas. Debido a los cambios medioambientales su población ha disminuido considerablemente en los últimos años. Muchas organizaciones ecologistas siguen luchando por la protección del hábitat del coquí, que se ha convertido en símbolo nacional de Puerto Rico, y hoy día el coquí llanero está protegido bajo la Ley Federal de Especies en Peligro de Extinción.

Conexiones. Busca información sobre las causas de la destrucción del hábitat del coquí llanero. ¿Qué animales están en peligro de extinción en tu estado o región? ¿Qué hacen los grupos ecologistas y el gobierno para protegerlos?

15-7

Organizaciones ecologistas. Busca información en Internet sobre organizaciones como Greenpeace o el Club Sierra, cuyo propósito es proteger el medio ambiente. Escoge una de esas organizaciones y prepara un breve informe oral con la siguiente información.

1. ¿Qué objetivos tiene la organización?
2. ¿Cómo se financia?
3. ¿Quiénes trabajan o hacen voluntariado en ella?
4. ¿Cuál fue una de sus campañas recientes?
5. ¿Qué objetivos tenía la campaña?
6. ¿Cómo la realizaron?
7. ¿Cuál fue el resultado de la campaña?
8. ¿En qué capacidad crees que podrías ayudar tú?

Otros retos del futuro

LAS CIUDADES

- Se **construirán** ciudades verticales con edificios **climatizados** por medio de **energía solar** o **energía de fusión.**
- El 90% de la población vivirá en las ciudades.
- Todas las basuras urbanas serán **recicladas.**

EL MAR

- El nivel del mar subirá por los **deshielos** debido al **calentamiento** de la atmósfera y causará **inundaciones** y **la desaparición** de algunas costas.
- La contaminación de los mares provocará la **extinción** de los **bancos de peces.**

LA ATMÓSFERA

- El **agujero** de la **capa de ozono** hará aumentar el número de enfermos de cáncer de piel.
- Se cultivarán plantas que mejoren la calidad del aire.

LAS VIVIENDAS

- Todos los hogares estarán conectados a Internet. Las compras se harán siempre **virtualmente.**
- Las puertas y los aparatos electrónicos serán activados por la voz o con sensores que reconocerán a cada individuo.
- Habrá **robots** que se ocuparán de hacer la limpieza.

Suggestion for *Las ciudades*
You may use visual aids to present the city of the future and ask questions.

Brainstorm ideas about the cities of the future regarding: *tipos de vivienda, medios de transporte, energías alternativas.* Also, discuss what technology may be able to accomplish in the future. Bring up topics such as: *la selección genética, el transplante de órganos, la cirugía estética. ¿En qué consistirá la dieta del futuro: alimentos transgénicos, comida orgánica, congelados? ¿Qué tipo de actividades físicas haremos? ¿Será fácil viajar al espacio?*

Ask students if we will have more free time then; if so, how will we spend it? *¿Nos permitirá la tecnología tener más tiempo libre? ¿Por qué? ¿Qué haremos en el tiempo libre?*

EL TRANSPORTE

- Los trenes de alta velocidad conectarán las grandes ciudades y circularán por **rieles** suspendidos a la altura de los edificios.
- Los coches combinarán la energía eléctrica y la energía solar. Serán pequeñas **cápsulas voladoras** que podrán **despegar** y **aterrizar** verticalmente como los helicópteros.
- El tráfico aéreo será controlado por **satélite**.

LA CIENCIA Y LA TECNOLOGÍA

- Habrá **clonaciones** de animales **extinguidos.**
- Los embriones humanos se seleccionarán **genéticamente.**
- Los **chips electrónicos** se implantarán en el cerebro mediante **microcirugía**.
- Se explorarán energías alternativas.
- Se **repoblarán** los bosques con técnicas avanzadas para eliminar la desertización.

Suggestions for 15-8
Have students review comparatives (*Capítulo 8*) before doing *Preparación*. Encourage them to express their concerns about current problems and to speculate about solutions in *Intercambios*.

Follow-up for 15-9
Have students present their primary concern to the whole class. Rank problems by the number of students concerned about the same issue.

PRÁCTICA

15-8

Para confirmar. **PREPARACIÓN.** Tomando como base las fotos y textos anteriores, haz una lista de tus propias predicciones para el futuro en dos de las siguientes áreas: el transporte, la tecnología, las formas de vida, la vivienda o la planificación de las ciudades.

 **INTERCAMBIOS.** Compartan sus predicciones sobre el mundo del futuro.

- Hablen de dos problemas específicos que existen en el mundo contemporáneo.
- Sugieran posibles soluciones para cada uno de los problemas.
- Presenten sus ideas ante la clase.

 MODELO *El tráfico en las ciudades es un problema muy grande. Proponemos construir aparcamientos en las afueras de las ciudades y tener más zonas peatonales.*

15-9 

El reto más serio de hoy. Preparen un informe oral sobre el reto más serio que enfrentan el mundo y el ser humano hoy, según su opinión. Describan detalladamente el problema y ofrezcan algunas soluciones.

15-10

¡El futuro es hoy! Primero, individualmente hagan una lista de cinco cosas (aparatos, sistemas de comunicación, transporte, etc.) que existen hoy y que no existían cuando sus padres tenían su edad. Luego, comparen sus listas y expliquen el impacto y las consecuencias de estas nuevas cosas en sus vidas.

15-11 

Los OVNIS (Objetos Voladores No Identificados). **PREPARACIÓN.** Observen la imagen y contesten las preguntas.

1. ¿Qué va a pasar cuando lleguen las cápsulas voladoras a la Tierra?
2. ¿Qué van a encontrar los extraterrestres?
3. ¿Cómo van a reaccionar los habitantes de la Tierra?

INTERCAMBIOS. Imaginen que visitaron un planeta desconocido. Hablen entre ustedes sobre los siguientes asuntos. Luego, escriban un párrafo sobre sus observaciones para compartir con la clase. Incluyan la siguiente información.

1. nombre y descripción del planeta
2. descripción de sus habitantes
3. descripción de sus ciudades, viviendas y medios de transporte

15-12

Un viaje a Marte. Planeen un viaje a Marte y expliquen con quiénes irán, qué llevarán, cuánto tiempo tardarán en llegar, qué verán allí y cómo se sentirán física y emocionalmente en este nuevo ambiente. Compartan su plan con otros dos astronautas (sus compañeros/as) para formular el mejor plan posible.

Cultura

Agricultura ecológica

Debido a la riqueza medioambiental y a la biodiversidad de la isla, Puerto Rico es un lugar apropiado para la explotación agrícola que respeta la naturaleza y el medio ambiente. En los últimos años, se ha incrementado la práctica de agricultura ecológica que cumple unas normas éticas y de sostenibilidad con el fin de proteger los recursos naturales para las futuras generaciones.

Comparaciones. ¿En qué lugares de tu comunidad puedes comprar productos agrícolas ecológicos? ¿Qué ventajas tienen estos productos?

15-13  

El problema de la alimentación. You will listen to a short talk about the problem of feeding the world's population. Before you listen, list two problems you think the speaker may mention and two solutions you think she may provide.

First, read the following incomplete ideas. Then, as you listen, pay attention to the general idea of what is said and mark (✓) the appropriate ending to each statement.

1. Los gobiernos tienen que solucionar el problema de...
   - **a.** _____ la agricultura tradicional.
   - **b.** __✓__ la falta de alimentos para la población.
   - **c.** _____ las pocas variedades de productos.
2. La tecnología y los científicos...
   - **a.** __✓__ pueden ayudar a solucionar este problema.
   - **b.** _____ trabajan en las islas Filipinas.
   - **c.** _____ desarrollan computadoras de mucha utilidad.
3. Si se aumenta la producción del arroz, los gobiernos pueden...
   - **a.** _____ exportarlo y ganar más dinero.
   - **b.** __✓__ alimentar a más personas.
   - **c.** _____ obtener variedades más nutritivas.
4. Hay que aprovechar los avances de la tecnología, pero también es necesario...
   - **a.** _____ aumentar la productividad en un 70%.
   - **b.** _____ conseguir alimentos básicos.
   - **c.** __✓__ preservar el medio ambiente.

Audioscript for 15-13

Uno de los problemas que tienen que resolver los gobiernos del mundo es el de la alimentación de sus pueblos. Este problema se hace mayor cuando se toma en consideración el crecimiento de la población. La tecnología y los científicos son los que pueden dar una respuesta. En las islas Filipinas se encuentra el Instituto Internacional para la Investigación del Arroz, uno de los alimentos básicos en muchas regiones del planeta, especialmente en Asia. Hoy en día, a través de la ingeniería genética, se han conseguido variedades de arroz que resultan mucho más productivas. Con ellas, la producción de arroz podría aumentar en un 70% y alimentar a un mayor número de personas. Los métodos de cultivo también tendrán que cambiar. La ingeniería genética, unida a nuevos métodos de cultivo, puede ser la respuesta a los problemas que tenemos hoy y que tendremos que resolver en este siglo. Sin embargo, nuevas polémicas surgen con la alta productividad conseguida mediante la manipulación genética. El cultivo de cereales para la producción de biocombustibles ha causado, en opinión de algunos, la alta subida de los precios de los cereales y la escasez de estos en algunos mercados del mundo. Por otro lado, algunos gobiernos se resisten a tomar medidas drásticas contra la contaminación atmosférica para no perjudicar sus industrias. El calentamiento global es otro reto para el que los gobiernos deben buscar soluciones si quieren resolver el problema del hambre en el mundo.

Note for *Mosaico cultural*
Although in recent years the governments of Hispanic countries have increased funding for scientific research and development, most top scientists from these countries still live and work abroad. Institutions and research centers in Europe and North America are usually able to provide greater support for such research. This phenomenon is known as the *fuga de cerebros*. Such is the case of the Colombian neuroscientist Rodolfo Llinás, a founder of the field of brain science.

Note for *Mosaico cultural*
The biopharmaceutical industry has seen a recent surge in growth. Cubans and Puerto Ricans are pioneers in the use of traditional medicinal plants in the making of new, efficient, and accessible drugs.

MOSAICO cultural

La investigación tecnológica en Latinoamérica

En los últimos años, América Latina ha firmado importantes tratados (*treaties*) de comercio con Estados Unidos, Europa, Rusia y China. "Estamos ante un cambio de mentalidad importante", afirma el investigador cubano Pablo Oliveros de la Universidad de Estocolmo. El profesor Oliveros ha dirigido el Departamento de Investigación, Ciencia y Tecnología de esta universidad los últimos cinco años y para esta entrevista le preguntamos sobre el panorama de la investigación tecnológica en el mundo hispano.

"La academia hispana históricamente ha tenido poca participación en avances tecnológicos en el mundo. Aproximadamente el 3% de los ingenieros realizan tareas de investigación y desarrollo en el planeta y solo el 1% de los recursos se invierte con este fin. Por esta razón, muchos científicos preferimos salir de nuestros países hacia Europa o Estados Unidos". A pesar de (*despite*) esto, muchos inventos importantes de hispanos han impactado el mundo: la píldora anticonceptiva (*birth control pill*) del químico mexicano Luis Miramontes, o el test de paternidad, del venezolano Baruj Benacerraf, son dos ejemplos.

▲ Juan Manuel Santos, el presidente de Colombia, y Barack Obama, el presidente de EE.UU., reunidos para discutir el Tratado de Libre Comercio.

▲ Un científico hispano trabaja en su laboratorio.

"Estos científicos tuvieron que hacer grandes esfuerzos para producir avances tan importantes. Los tratados de comercio son buenas oportunidades para la ciencia y la tecnología hispanas. Si hacemos bien las cosas, en el futuro tendremos muchos más investigadores y científicos importantes sin tantos inconvenientes", dice Oliveros. "La verdad es que la inversión extranjera, los grandes avances en educación y estos tratados de comercio comienzan a mostrar a una Latinoamérica menos dependiente; nos veo como una potencia mundial en el futuro." Comenta Oliveros: "El futuro de la ciencia hispana es brillante: gracias a estos proyectos habrá mejores oportunidades, habrá menos desequilibrios sociales y la educación será una base sólida para la comunidad". También es necesario recordar que los cambios demográficos harán que para el 2020 el español sea una de las tres lenguas más importantes, junto con el inglés y el mandarín.

Compara

1. ¿Qué otras invenciones de hispanos conoces? ¿Cuáles son las principales contribuciones tecnológicas de científicos de tu comunidad para el mundo?
2. ¿Qué beneficios sociales trae la investigación científica? ¿Cuáles serán las principales contribuciones de la tecnología hispana? Elabora tu respuesta.
3. ¿Crees que el rol de la comunidad hispana cambiará para el año 2040? ¿Cómo afectará a tu comunidad el incremento de la población hispana? Explica y justifica tu respuesta.
4. ¿Crees que en el futuro será importante hablar español? ¿Cuáles serán las principales lenguas en 2040? Explica tu respuesta.

Funciones y formas

1 Expressing wishes and recommendations in the past

PADRE: ¿Qué quieres que **hagamos** ahora?

NIÑA: Papá, quiero que me **cuentes** un cuento.

PADRE: Muy bien, hija. Cuando mi abuelo era niño, los seres humanos querían que los robots **hicieran** todo su trabajo. Mis abuelos limpiaban la casa, preparaban las comidas, hacían las tareas de los niños…

NIÑA: ¡Qué terrible, papá! Pero luego, ¿qué pasó?

PADRE: Los políticos recomendaron que los científicos **produjeran** robots más complejos. Querían que los robots **tuvieran** computadoras muy potentes (*powerful*). Los científicos temían que los robots **fueran** más inteligentes que ellos, pero los políticos insistieron en que los científicos los **construyeran** con más capacidad intelectual. Entonces…

Suggestions
You may wish to review the *Uds./ellos/ellas* forms of the preterit before introducing the past subjunctive. Do a quick question/answer activity: *¿Salieron ustedes anoche? ¿Adónde fueron? ¿Y qué hicieron allí?* Use related questions to simulate natural conversation and spontaneity. Remind students that they have used the imperfect subjunctive of *querer* for polite requests: *Quisiera comprar un regalo para un amigo.*

Piénsalo. Indica (✓) si las siguientes oraciones se refieren al presente/al futuro o al pasado.

	PRESENTE/FUTURO	PASADO
1. ¿Qué quieres que **hagamos** ahora?	✓	
2. Quiero que me **cuentes** un cuento.	✓	
3. Los seres humanos querían que los robots **hicieran** todo su trabajo.		✓
4. Los políticos recomendaron que los científicos **produjeran** robots más complejos.		✓
5. Querían que los robots **tuvieran** computadoras muy potentes.		✓
6. Los científicos temían que los robots **fueran** más inteligentes que ellos.		✓
7. Los políticos insistieron en que los **construyeran** con más capacidad intelectual.		✓

Suggestion
You may wish to review (or have students review at home) the functions and forms of the present subjunctive, starting with *Capítulo 11.*

The imperfect subjunctive

- In previous chapters, you studied the forms and uses of the present subjunctive. Now you will study the past subjunctive, also called the imperfect subjunctive. All regular and irregular past subjunctive verb forms are based on the **ustedes/ellos/ellas** form of the preterit. Drop the **-on** preterit ending and substitute the past subjunctive endings. Note the written accent on the **nosotros/as** forms.

PAST OR IMPERFECT SUBJUNCTIVE				
	HABLAR (hablar~~on~~)	**COMER** (comier~~on~~)	**VIVIR** (vivier~~on~~)	**ESTAR** (estuvier~~on~~)
yo	habla**ra**	comie**ra**	vivie**ra**	estuvie**ra**
tú	habla**ras**	comie**ras**	vivie**ras**	estuvie**ras**
Ud., él, ella	habla**ra**	comie**ra**	vivie**ra**	estuvie**ra**
nosotros/as	hablá**ramos**	comié**ramos**	vivié**ramos**	estuvié**ramos**
vosotros/as	habla**rais**	comie**rais**	vivie**rais**	estuvie**rais**
Uds., ellos/as	habla**ran**	comie**ran**	vivie**ran**	estuvie**ran**

- The present subjunctive is oriented to the present or future, whereas the past subjunctive generally focuses on the past. In general, the same rules that determine the use of the present subjunctive also apply to the past subjunctive.

  HOY O MAÑANA → PRESENT SUBJUNCTIVE

  Sandra quiere comprar una computadora portátil que **sea** ligera.
  Sandra wants to buy a laptop that does not weigh a lot.

  Hablará con sus amigos para que le **den** unas recomendaciones.
  She will talk to her friends so that they can give her some recommendations.

  AYER → PAST SUBJUNCTIVE

  Sandra quería una computadora portátil que **fuera** ligera.
  Sandra wanted a laptop that did not weigh a lot.

  Habló con sus amigos para que le **dieran** unas recomendaciones.
  She talked to her friends so that they could give her some recommendations.

- Always use the past subjunctive after **como si** (*as if, as though*).

  Gastan dinero en aparatos electrónicos **como si fueran** millonarios.
  They spend money on electronic gadgets as though they were millionaires.

  Hablaba con la científica **como si entendiera** el problema.
  He talked with the scientist as if he understood the problem.

e ¿COMPRENDES?

Completa las oraciones con la forma apropiada del subjuntivo (presente o pasado) de los verbos entre paréntesis.

1. Juan me recomendó que __fuera__ (ir) a ver una película de ciencia ficción.
2. Mi profesora quiere que nosotros __usemos__ (usar) tecnología en nuestras presentaciones.
3. El gobierno les pidió a los científicos que __exploraran__ (explorar) energías alternativas.
4. Los viajeros prefieren que los trenes __sean__ (ser) rápidos y puntuales.
5. Es necesario que los edificios climatizados __conserven__ (conservar) mejor la energía.
6. Era inevitable que la contaminación de los mares __afectara__ (afectar) a los peces.

MySpanishLab
Learn more using Amplifire Dynamic Study Modules, Grammar Tutorials, and Extra Practice activities.

PRÁCTICA

15-14 

Cuando era niño/a. **PREPARACIÓN.** Marca (✓) lo que tus padres querían o no querían que hicieras cuando eras niño/a. Después, compara tus respuestas con las de tu compañero/a.

1. _____ Querían que yo comiera muchos vegetales y frutas.
2. _____ Querían que yo estudiara ciencias.
3. _____ No querían que yo viera programas violentos en la televisión.
4. _____ Querían que yo cuidara el medio ambiente.
5. _____ Querían que yo leyera sobre el programa espacial y los astronautas.
6. _____ No querían que yo estuviera sin hacer nada.

INTERCAMBIOS. Marca con un círculo lo que tú querías que tus padres hicieran cuando eras niño/a. Luego, compara tus respuestas con las de tu compañero/a. Añade otra opción si es necesario.

1. Para divertirme con la tecnología…
   - **a.** yo quería que mis padres me llevaran a ver una nave espacial.
   - **b.** deseaba que mis padres me permitieran jugar a videojuegos muchas horas.
2. Para estar con mis amigos…
   - **a.** yo quería que mis padres me llevaran al parque los fines de semana.
   - **b.** les pedía a mis padres que me permitieran jugar en las casas de ellos.
3. Para pasarlo bien los fines de semana…
   - **a.** yo quería que mis padres me dieran más dinero.
   - **b.** insistía en que mis padres me permitieran hacer fiestas en casa.
4. Para mi cumpleaños…
   - **a.** siempre quería que mis padres me regalaran juguetes electrónicos.
   - **b.** prefería que mis padres me compraran ropa.

15-15

En el laboratorio. Miguel es un estudiante inteligente, pero muy distraído. Hoy hizo unos experimentos con su profesor de química en el laboratorio. ¿Qué le dijo el profesor en estas situaciones? Túrnense para dar respuestas lógicas.

Miguel no se puso los guantes para hacer el experimento.

El profesor le dijo que se pusiera los guantes.

1. Llegó tarde al laboratorio. El profesor le dijo que no llegara tarde.
2. Escuchaba música mientras hacía un experimento. Le dijo que no escuchara música mientras hacía un experimento.
3. Dejó una botella de alcohol cerca de una estufa. Le sugirió que no dejara el alcohol cerca de una estufa.
4. No esterilizó unos instrumentos. Le dijo que esterilizara los instrumentos.
5. Recibió una llamada en su celular. Le pidió que no recibiera/contestara llamadas.
6. La mesa donde Miguel trabajaba estaba muy desordenada. Le aconsejó que ordenara la mesa.
7. No comparó sus resultados con los del ayudante del profesor. Le dijo que comparara sus resultados con los del ayudante.
8. Salió del laboratorio durante un experimento para conversar con su novia. Le dijo que no saliera para hablar con su novia durante un experimento.

EN OTRAS PALABRAS

Cell phones are **teléfonos móviles** or **teléfonos celulares.** The name of these devices is usually shortened to **móvil, celular** o **cel.**

Suggestion for 15-15
You may want to remind students that with the verb *decir*, the subjunctive is used in the dependent clause to express a wish or an order.

Alternate for 15-16
Have students finish the following ideas in a chain:
1. *Mi carro traga* (uses) *gasolina como si…*
2. *Los programadores de computadoras trabajan como si…*
3. *Los pilotos manejan los aviones como si…*
4. *La gente consume gasolina como si…*
5. *Todas las compañías se modernizan con nueva tecnología como si…*

15-16 

Alguien que no nos cae bien. **PREPARACIÓN.** Imagínense que ustedes conocen a una persona arrogante que cree que es mejor que todos. Digan cómo se comporta esta persona en los siguientes aspectos de su vida. Pueden usar los verbos que aparecen más abajo u otros.

MODELO cuando va de un lugar a otro a pie
Camina como si fuera la única persona en la calle.

cambiar	manejar
caminar	usar
discutir	vestirse
gastar	vivir

1. cuando quiere comprar algo
2. cuando se prepara para salir con un grupo de amigos
3. cuando habla con otras personas
4. cuando se sube a (*gets into*) su automóvil

INTERCAMBIOS. Ahora háganse las siguientes preguntas e informen a la clase.

1. ¿Conoces a alguna persona que sea arrogante?
2. ¿Qué hábito o comportamiento de esa persona te molesta? ¿Por qué?
3. ¿Te gustaría que esta persona cambiara? Si es así, ¿cómo te gustaría que cambiara?

Situación

PREPARACIÓN. Lean esta situación. Luego, compartan ejemplos de vocabulario, gramática y otra información que necesitan para desarrollar la conversación.

Role A. You are unhappy with your new digital device (cell phone, tablet, laptop, etc.). You go back to the electronics store and tell the manager:

a. your friend had recommended that you buy this device;
b. you hoped the device would be of better quality; and
c. you want to return it and expect them to give you back your money.

Role B. You are the manager of the computer department at an electronics store. A customer is unhappy with a recent purchase of a digital device and tells you why. Explain:

a. the store does not give refunds (**devolver el dinero**); but
b. you would be glad to exchange the device for a different one; and
c. you hope that the customer will like the new device.

	ROLE A	ROLE B
Vocabulario	Digital technology	Digital technology
Funciones y formas	Expressing wishes Present and past subjunctive	Expressing wishes Present and past subjunctive

INTERCAMBIOS. Practica la conversación con tu compañero/a incorporando el vocabulario y las funciones de *Preparación*. Luego, represéntenla ante la clase.

2 Hypothesizing about the present and the future

MATEO: Oye, Lucía. ¿Has visto la calidad de las nuevas cámaras digitales? ¡Es increíble! **Si** la tecnología **continúa** avanzando así, pronto **producirán** minicámaras para controlar a toda la población, incluso en sus casas.

LUCÍA: **Si** lo **hicieran, pondrían** en peligro las libertades individuales. Pero **si** la ciencia **avanza** tan rápidamente, ¿por qué no **podemos** trabajar por la paz? Yo no quiero que se perfeccione la tecnología para vigilar a la gente y controlarla, sino para protegerla.

MATEO: Tienes razón, Lucía. **Si** los jóvenes no **hacemos** nada para dar un buen uso a la tecnología, **tendremos** problemas en el futuro.

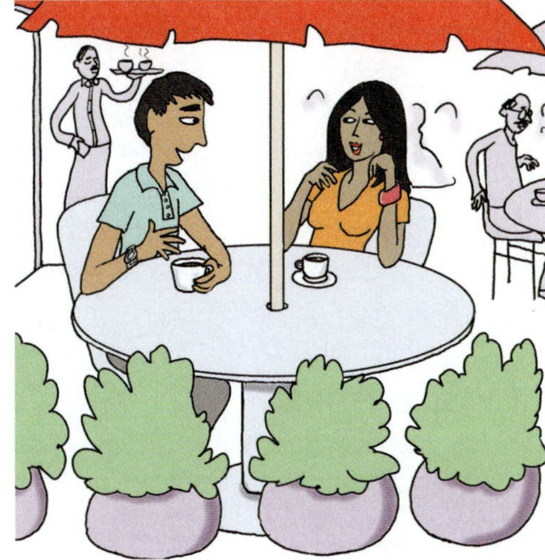

Piénsalo. Indica si las siguientes afirmaciones hechas por Mateo y Lucía indican una condición relacionada con el presente (**P**), con el futuro (**F**) o si indican una condición que es improbable (**I**) que se cumpla (*come to pass*).

1. __F__ **Si** la tecnología **continúa** avanzando así, pronto **producirán** minicámaras para controlar a toda la población, incluso en sus casas.
2. __I__ **Si** lo **hicieran, pondrían** en peligro las libertades individuales.
3. __P__ Pero **si** la ciencia **avanza** tan rápidamente, ¿por qué no **podemos** trabajar por la paz?
4. __F__ **Si** los jóvenes no **hacemos** nada para dar un buen uso a la tecnología, **tendremos** problemas en el futuro.

Suggestion for *Piénsalo*
You may wish to draw students' attention to the sequence of tenses in the P/F vs. I statements. Help students understand the logical relationships between the actions in the two clauses in each type of sentence.

Suggestion for *If*-clauses
Students may grasp the temporal and logical relationships in the statements if they identify whether the action in the dependent clause (the *if*-clause) refers to the present or the future with respect to the time frame established in the dependent clause.

If-clauses

- To express what happens or will happen *if* certain conditions are met, use the present or future indicative in the main clause and the present indicative in the *if*-clause.

  Si **continuamos** cortando árboles, los bosques **van a** desaparecer.
  If we continue cutting down trees, the forests will disappear.

  Si **creamos** tecnología para cuidar los recursos naturales, las generaciones futuras **tendrán** una vida mejor.
  If we create technology to protect the natural resources, future generations will have a better life.

  Puedes obtener información sobre las últimas novedades tecnológicas si la **buscas** en Internet.
  You can get information on the latest technology if you look for it on the Internet.

- To express a condition that is unlikely or contrary to fact, use the imperfect subjunctive in the *if*-clause. Use the conditional in the main clause.

  Si **invirtieran** más dinero en el aeropuerto, el tráfico aéreo **podría** mejorar.
  If they invested more money in the airport, air traffic could improve.

  Si **usáramos** la energía solar en las casas, **ahorraríamos** mucho petróleo.
  If we used solar energy in our homes, we would save a lot of oil.

¿COMPRENDES?

Completa las oraciones con el presente de indicativo o el imperfecto de subjuntivo del verbo entre paréntesis según su grado de probabilidad.

1. Si los habitantes _mantienen_ (mantener) limpias las ciudades, será más agradable pasear por ellas.
2. Si los perros _hablaran_ (hablar), dirían que los humanos estamos locos.
3. Si el gobierno _protegiera_ (proteger) más el medio ambiente, habría menos contaminación.
4. Si los ingenieros _hicieran_ (hacer) un cohete espacial más barato, irían turistas al espacio.
5. Si tú _tuvieras_ (tener) más imaginación, inventarías una máquina para viajar en el tiempo.
6. Si los estudiantes _practican_ (practicar) mucho el español, aprenderán más rápidamente.

MySpanishLab
Learn more using Amplifire Dynamic Study Modules, Grammar Tutorials, and Extra Practice activities.

PRÁCTICA

Cultura

Problemas ecológicos de Puerto Rico

Puerto Rico es una de las islas con mayor densidad de población del mundo. Esto ha causado graves problemas medioambientales que han deteriorado el patrimonio natural. Entre los problemas ecológicos más importantes se puede mencionar la deforestación, la contaminación del aire —a menudo por la congestión del tráfico— la mala calidad del agua y el tratamiento y reciclaje de basura.

Comparaciones. ¿Crees que los problemas ecológicos de Puerto Rico son similares a los que existen en tu comunidad? ¿Cuáles son algunas soluciones posibles a estos problemas?

15-17   

El mundo que todos queremos. Completa cada idea de la izquierda con una de las conclusiones de la derecha. En algunos casos, puede haber más de una respuesta lógica. Luego, compara tus respuestas con las de tu compañero/a.

1. _b_ Si las escuelas tuvieran más dinero…
2. _e_ Si hubiera menos armas de fuego en manos de la gente…
3. _a_ Si cuidáramos más nuestro planeta…
4. _c_ Tendríamos un mundo mejor…
5. _d_ Si hubiera trenes de alta velocidad…
6. _f_ Gastaríamos menos gasolina…

a. no contaminaríamos tanto el medio ambiente.
b. todos los alumnos tendrían acceso a los laboratorios para hacer investigación.
c. si todos nos respetáramos y dialogáramos en vez de pelear.
d. las personas manejarían menos en las carreteras.
e. habría menos homicidios en la sociedad.
f. si usáramos el transporte público.

Suggestion for 15-17
Say what you would do in a hypothetical situation: *Si yo ganara la lotería, compraría una casa en la playa.* Give other examples. Then ask questions to find out what students would do. Explain that the order of the clauses is often reversed: *Iría a Puerto Rico si ganara la lotería.*

Follow-up for 15-17
Have students discuss some of these problems, provide other possible completions, and share them with the class.

15-18

¿Qué pasa si...? Túrnense para decir qué resultados se pueden obtener si se hacen ciertas cosas.

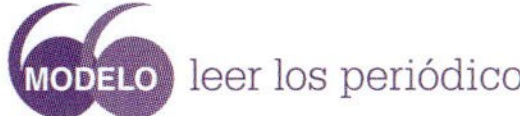

MODELO leer los periódicos

Si todos leen los periódicos regularmente, sabrán qué está pasando en el mundo.

1. usar solamente tecnología para aprender otra lengua
2. inventar aparatos electrónicos desechables (*disposable*)
3. proteger los recursos naturales
4. legalizar las drogas
5. comunicarse solamente por correo electrónico
6. construir más estaciones espaciales

15-19

¿Cómo sería el mundo? Expliquen cómo sería el mundo si se dieran las siguientes circunstancias. Después, compartan sus ideas con otros/as estudiantes.

1. si no hubiera televisión
2. si los seres humanos viviéramos más de 150 años
3. si la clonación fuera legal
4. si no existieran fronteras entre los países
5. si pudiéramos viajar en autos supersónicos a todas partes
6. si toda la educación se hiciera por Internet

15-20

Cambios. PREPARACIÓN. Identifica un problema serio en tu comunidad, en tu país o en el mundo, en cada una de las siguientes áreas en la vida de tu comunidad, de tu país o del mundo. Explica por qué lo consideras un problema serio.

1. la seguridad personal y/o colectiva
2. el consumo excesivo de alcohol entre los jóvenes
3. el transporte público
4. el costo de las necesidades básicas, como la comida y la gasolina

Suggestion for 15-18
You may wish to have a class discussion on a few of the topics in this activity. Encourage students to support their views with logical arguments.

Suggestions for 15-20, *Intercambios*
You may have each group choose a moderator who will lead the group presentation and make sure every group member participates in it. The moderator should also open the discussion with the rest of the class. You may wish to go over the expressions in *En directo*. For further reinforcement, model the *Intercambios* with a strong student.

Follow-up for 15-20
Divide the class in small groups and assign an area to each group. After groups have reached some conclusions, they may share them with the rest of the class.

Audioscript for *En directo*
(We hear the end of clapping in a conference room.)
PRESENTADOR: *Muchas gracias, profesor Urrutia, por esta conferencia tan interesante. Ahora damos la palabra al público.*
(Attendees 1 and 2 speak at the same time.)
MUJER: *Me gustaría saber...*
HOMBRE: *Mi pregunta es la siguiente...*
PRESENTADOR: *Por favor, pidan la palabra.*
MUJER: *Yo quisiera añadir algo a lo que ha dicho el profesor...*
PRESENTADOR: *Por favor, no interrumpan sin pedir la palabra.*
MUJER: *¿Podría agregar algo?*
PRESENTADOR: *Ese señor tiene la palabra...*
HOMBRE: *Profesor, díganos lo que piensa sobre...*
(Fade away.)

INTERCAMBIOS. Ahora digan cuál creen ustedes que es el problema más serio en cada área. Explíquenles a sus compañeros por qué lo consideran serio. Si pudieran, ¿qué harían para eliminar cada problema?

MODELO **ÁREA:** el medio ambiente

PROBLEMA SERIO: *la contaminación del aire y el agua*

RAZÓN: *El mal uso y el descuido* (neglect) *de los recursos naturales como el petróleo han causado el calentamiento del planeta. Todos usamos carros que contaminan el aire. Además, las industrias ponen sus desperdicios* (waste) *en los ríos. Contaminan el agua que todos bebemos.*

PLAN HIPOTÉTICO: *Crearíamos incentivos para usar el transporte público y pondríamos multas* (fines) *muy altas a las compañías que tiran desperdicios en los ríos.*

En directo

To ask that people request the floor before speaking:

Por favor, no interrumpa(n) sin pedir la palabra.
Please don't interrupt without requesting the floor.

Pida(n) la palabra. *Request the floor.*

To request the floor:

Yo quisiera decir/añadir/explicar algo.
I would like to say/add/explain something.

¿Podría añadir/agregar algo?
Could I add something?

To give the floor to someone:

X tiene la palabra. *X has the floor.*

Dinos lo que tú piensas. *Tell us what you think.*

Listen to a conversation with these expressions.

Situación

PREPARACIÓN. Lean esta situación. Luego, compartan ejemplos de vocabulario, gramática y otra información que necesitan para desarrollar la conversación.

Role A. You are a billionaire who believes that education should be radically different. You would give your local college 20 million dollars if they did the following:

a. there would be no required courses; students could choose all their own courses;
b. there would be no exams, only projects and papers; and
c. students would tell the faculty what courses should be taught.

Respond to the reaction of the college president.

Role B. You are a college president. A billionaire (your classmate) would donate 20 million dollars to the college if you agreed to make radical changes. Listen to the potential donor's proposal and respond with your hypotheses of what would happen if:

a. there were no required courses; students could choose all their own courses;
b. there were no exams, only projects and papers; and
c. students told the faculty what courses should be taught.

	ROLE A	ROLE B
Vocabulario	Numbers Academic policies	Numbers Academic policies
Funciones y formas	Talking about hypothetical situations	Talking about hypothetical situations

INTERCAMBIOS. Practica la conversación con tu compañero/a incorporando el vocabulario y las funciones de *Preparación*. Luego, represéntenla ante la clase.

3 Expressing the unexpected

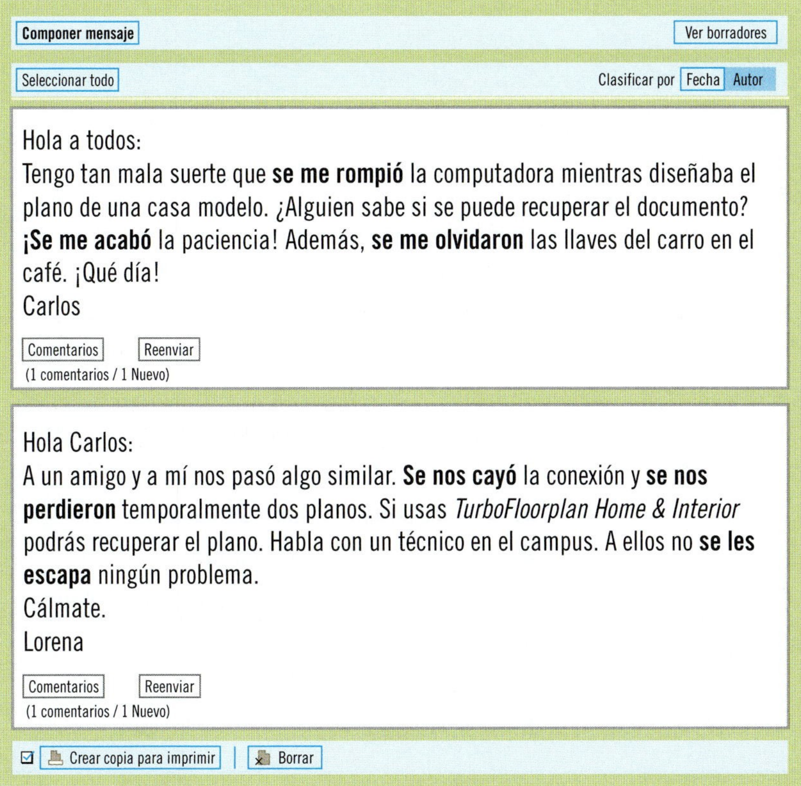

Componer mensaje | Ver borradores

Seleccionar todo | Clasificar por Fecha Autor

Hola a todos:
Tengo tan mala suerte que **se me rompió** la computadora mientras diseñaba el plano de una casa modelo. ¿Alguien sabe si se puede recuperar el documento? **¡Se me acabó** la paciencia! Además, **se me olvidaron** las llaves del carro en el café. ¡Qué día!
Carlos

Comentarios | Reenviar
(1 comentarios / 1 Nuevo)

Hola Carlos:
A un amigo y a mí nos pasó algo similar. **Se nos cayó** la conexión y **se nos perdieron** temporalmente dos planos. Si usas *TurboFloorplan Home & Interior* podrás recuperar el plano. Habla con un técnico en el campus. A ellos no **se les escapa** ningún problema.
Cálmate.
Lorena

Comentarios | Reenviar
(1 comentarios / 1 Nuevo)

Crear copia para imprimir | Borrar

Piénsalo. Indica si en las siguientes afirmaciones se pone énfasis en el evento (**E**) o en la persona responsable del evento (**PR**).

1. __E__ **Se me rompió** la computadora.
2. __PR__ **Rompí** la computadora.
3. __PR__ **Olvidé** las llaves del carro en el café.
4. __E__ **Se me olvidaron** las llaves del carro en el café.
5. __E__ **Se nos perdieron** temporalmente dos planos.
6. __PR__ **Perdimos** temporalmente dos planos.

Suggestions
Pretend to accidentally drop your keys, then deliberately drop them: *Se me cayeron las llaves./Dejé caer las llaves.* Have one individual and a group drop, break, or tear one object, then several objects in order to demonstrate the difference between *Se le(s)* and *cayó/cayeron.* Ask *¿Qué le(s) pasó?*

Se for unplanned occurrences

- Use **se** + *indirect object* + *verb* to express unplanned or accidental events. This construction puts the focus on the unexpected nature of the event rather than on personal responsibility for its occurrence. Some verbs often used with this construction include **olvidar** (*to forget*), **apagar** (*to turn off*), **acabar** (*to run out of something*), **romper** (*to break, to tear*), and **quedar** (*to leave something behind*).

Se les apagaron las luces del carro.	*The headlights of their car went out.*
A él **se le acabó** el dinero.	*He ran out of money.*
Se nos olvidó el código.	*We forgot the code.*
Se te rompió la chaqueta.	*Your jacket got torn.*

- Use an indirect object pronoun (**me**, **te**, **le**, **nos**, **os**, **les**) to indicate whom the unplanned event affects. Place the pronoun between **se** and the verb. If what is lost, forgotten, and so on, is plural, the verb also must be plural.

Se me quedó el DVD en la computadora.	*I left the DVD in the computer.*
Se me quedaron los cables en casa.	*I left the cables at home.*

Follow-up for 15-21
Show visuals and ask *¿Qué le(s) pasó?* Visuals may show someone with a broken leg, a baseball catcher missing the ball, a groom who forgot the ring. Be imaginative!

¿COMPRENDES?

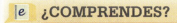

Completa las oraciones con el pronombre de objeto indirecto apropiado.

1. A Miguel se __le__ estropeó la computadora.
2. A mí se __me__ perdió el pasaporte.
3. A Juan y Elisa se __les__ olvidó comprar la comida.
4. A ti se __te__ acabó la tinta (*ink*) de la impresora.
5. A Elena se __le__ apagaron las luces cuando trabajaba.
6. A ustedes se __les__ rompieron los platos.

MySpanishLab
Learn more using Amplifire Dynamic Study Modules, Grammar Tutorials, and Extra Practice activities.

PRÁCTICA

15-21

¿Qué les pasó? Termina lógicamente las ideas de la columna de la izquierda, usando las ideas de la columna de la derecha.

1. __e__ Hablaron con el plomero porque...	**a.** se me quedó el dinero en casa.
2. __a__ Tuve que usar la tarjeta de crédito porque...	**b.** se nos rompió la computadora.
3. __c__ No pude llamarte por el celular porque...	**c.** se me olvidó tu nuevo número de teléfono.
4. __f__ Tuvieron que llamar al electricista porque...	**d.** se me perdió la llave del coche.
5. __b__ Tuvimos que llamar al técnico porque...	**e.** se les inundó el baño.
6. __d__ Llegué tarde a casa de mi novia porque...	**f.** se les apagaron las luces en la casa.

15-22

Problemas. Tú trabajas en un laboratorio de ingeniería genética. Ayer hubo muchos problemas técnicos. Explica qué pasó usando las opciones de la lista u otras.

MODELO El investigador no pudo completar el experimento.
Se le olvidó la fórmula.

perder las llaves	acabarse la gasolina
enfermarse un hijo	romper el microscopio
romper la computadora	escapar el perro en el parque
perder unos datos importantes	quedar documentos confidenciales en un café

1. Los científicos no pudieron hacer el experimento con las bacterias. Se les rompió el microscopio.
2. El director nunca falta al trabajo, pero ayer no fue a trabajar. Se le enfermó el hijo.
3. Los ayudantes llegaron tarde de un viaje a un laboratorio en otra ciudad. Se les acabó la gasolina.
4. La doctora Milán no pudo entrar en el laboratorio durante el fin de semana. Se le perdieron las llaves.
5. El subdirector no recibió un correo electrónico importante. Se le rompió la computadora.
6. El presidente de la compañía estaba histérico cuando llegó a la oficina y se dio cuenta de lo que le había ocurrido. Se le habían quedado documentos confidenciales en un café.

15-23 

Momentos difíciles. Miren los dibujos y túrnense para contestar las preguntas que siguen.

a

b

1. ¿Qué les pasó a las personas en los dos dibujos? Inventen una historia para cada situación: ¿Cuándo y dónde pasó, cómo se sintieron las personas y qué hicieron después?
2. ¿Les ha pasado a ustedes una situación semejante? Cuéntense la historia de su problema y cómo lo resolvió cada uno de ustedes.
3. Si vivieras una experiencia semejante otra vez, ¿harías algo diferente esta vez? ¿Tu respuesta es similar o diferente a la de tu compañero/a?

Suggestions for 15-23
Encourage students to use their imagination to describe and narrate what they see in each drawing. You may wish to have students tell the stories of their similar experiences to the class, or turn them into a writing activity.

Situación

PREPARACIÓN. Lean esta situación. Luego, compartan ejemplos de vocabulario, gramática y otra información que necesitan para desarrollar la conversación.

Role A. You have had a bad day and you call your friend to vent. Say that:

a. you forgot to set your alarm clock so you got up late and missed your first class;
b. you ran out of gas on the highway;
c. you left your homework for your Spanish class at home; and
d. in the cafeteria you accidentally dropped your soup and salad on your friend's backpack.

Role B. Your friend calls to complain about his/her day. Commiserate with him/her and describe what happened to you last night:

a. there was a big storm in your city and the lights went out so you could not watch your favorite TV show;
b. you decided to drive to your parents' house, but when were leaving your apartment, both of your cats accidentally escaped; and
c. when you were walking in the dark (**oscuridad**), you accidentally dropped your wallet and could not find it.

	ROLE A	ROLE B
Vocabulario	Time Problems at school Food	Weather Pets Personal belongings
Funciones y formas	Past tense *Se* for unplanned occurrences	Past tense *Se* for unplanned occurrences

INTERCAMBIOS. Practica la conversación con tu compañero/a incorporando el vocabulario y las funciones de *Preparación*. Luego, represénтenla ante la clase.

EN ACCIÓN

¡Cuidemos el medio ambiente!

15-24 Antes de ver

Un futuro mejor. Marca (✓) las situaciones que contribuirían a mejorar el medio ambiente.

Mejoraríamos el medio ambiente si…

1. __✓__ usáramos más autos eléctricos.
2. __✓__ plantáramos más árboles.
3. _____ elimináramos el transporte público.
4. __✓__ no compráramos agua en botellas de plástico.
5. __✓__ lleváramos bolsas de tela al supermercado.
6. __✓__ aumentáramos el uso de la energía solar.
7. _____ continuáramos la deforestación de nuestros bosques.

15-25 Mientras ves

La tecnología al servicio del medio ambiente. En este segmento de video, Yolanda y Federico comparten sus proyectos con los otros chicos. Indica si las siguientes afirmaciones son ciertas (**C**) o falsas (**F**). Corrige las afirmaciones falsas.

Techos verdes:

1. __F__ Es un programa del gobierno de Estados Unidos para mejorar el problema de la contaminación en México. *Es un programa del gobierno mexicano para mejorar el problema de la contaminación en ese país.*
2. __C__ El principal beneficiario de este programa es la Ciudad de México.
3. __C__ En la Ciudad de México hay muy pocos espacios verdes.
4. __C__ En los techos y paredes de edificios se planta vegetación nativa.

Coches eléctricos y taxis solares:

5. __C__ El gobierno de California está en la vanguardia de la tecnología de autos eléctricos.
6. __F__ El plan ZEV es un programa del gobierno mexicano que promueve la creación de autos con cero emisiones. *Es del estado de California.*
7. __F__ Telsa Motors ofrece autos de energía solar. *Telsa Motors crea autos eléctricos.*
8. __C__ En la Ciudad de México hay algunos taxis ecológicos.

15-26 Después de ver 

¡Bienvenida sea la tecnología! **PREPARACIÓN.** Empareja las oraciones de la columna de la izquierda con las de la columna de la derecha.

1. __b__ Si más ciudades implementaran programas como Techos verdes...
2. __c__ Si no quisiéramos usar nuestros coches de gasolina...
3. __a__ Si otros gobernadores siguieran el ejemplo del gobernador de California...

a. no habría tantas emisiones de monóxido de carbono en la atmósfera.
b. habría más oxígeno en el medio ambiente.
c. podríamos usar autobuses o taxis solares.

INTERCAMBIOS. Comparen sus respuestas de *Preparación* y háganse las siguientes preguntas.

1. ¿Qué otros planes o proyectos conocen ustedes para mejorar los problemas del medio ambiente?
2. ¿Quiénes son los responsables de enfrentar los problemas del medio ambiente? ¿Los individuos? ¿Los gobiernos? ¿Las organizaciones internacionales? Hablen de los beneficios y desafíos de cada una de estas opciones.

La beca. **PREPARACIÓN.** Los estudiantes llevan todo el verano trabajando en sus proyectos cinematográficos. Ahora, te toca a ti decidir quién va a ganar la beca. Vuelve a ver los proyectos finales y decide a quién le darías la beca.

___ Esteban ___ Fede ___ Héctor
___ Vanesa ___ Yolanda

INTERCAMBIOS. Hablen con los otros miembros de su grupo para justificar su selección. ¿Están de acuerdo ustedes en quién va a ganar la beca? Expliquen las razones por las que seleccionaron al ganador/a la ganadora y compartan sus ideas con la clase.

Mosaicos

ESCUCHA

15-27 Presentational

Preparación. Vas a escuchar una breve presentación sobre el futuro de la tecnología en la medicina. Antes de escuchar, escribe dos avances tecnológicos o médicos que, en tu opinión, ayudarán a los pacientes del futuro. Comparte tus ideas con la clase.

ESTRATEGIA

Identify the speaker's intention through the main idea and specific information

To understand what a speaker says, it is necessary to use a number of strategies. To identify the main idea, you should anticipate key concepts that may be associated with the topic and focus on phrases that signal the presentation of the main idea. Keep track of the speaker's message by organizing the information mentally as you listen. Pay attention to the speaker's verbal and nonverbal cues, such as word choice, tone, and gestures.

Warm-up for 15-28
As a prelistening activity, have students work in small groups and discuss what they know about the use of computers and technology in medicine for such purposes as the prevention and treatment of diseases.

Audioscript for 15-28
La tecnología se usa cada día más para tratar a los enfermos y a las personas que han sufrido accidentes. El médico norteamericano Paul Zoll implantó el primer marcapasos, un pequeño generador electrónico que regula los latidos del corazón, en 1952. Desde entonces, el marcapasos ha salvado de la muerte a infinidad de enfermos del corazón y los adelantos en los implantes continúan multiplicándose. Otro adelanto es un implante, mejor dicho una microcomputadora, que se coloca en el oído interno. Con este implante, los sordos pueden oír, pero los sonidos que reciben son diferentes, como si se tratara de una lengua extranjera. Pronto los sordos podrán escuchar los sonidos exactamente como se producen. En la actualidad se están haciendo investigaciones en diferentes áreas; por ejemplo, se están haciendo grandes esfuerzos para crear un implante que funcione como un ojo artificial para que los ciegos puedan ver. También se está trabajando en la posibilidad de diseñar implantes que envíen corrientes eléctricas a los músculos para que los parapléjicos puedan caminar. Sin duda, el futuro de la tecnología y su uso en la medicina es impredecible. Lo que sí es cierto es que probablemente en el futuro dependeremos más de la tecnología en la prevención y el tratamiento de las enfermedades.

Interpretive

Escucha. Read the statements below and then listen to the presentation. As you listen, indicate the statements that reflect the main idea and the supporting details. Then, explain what the speaker's intention is for sharing this information.

	IDEA PRINCIPAL	DETALLES
1. _b, a_ El marcapasos…	**a.** se usa para ayudar a los corredores. **b.** les ha salvado la vida a muchas personas. **c.** es un tipo de tecnología obsoleta.	**a.** regula los latidos del corazón. **b.** se inventó hace diez años. **c.** es una microcomputadora.
2. _a, c_ Con el implante en el oído…	**a.** los sonidos suenan como una lengua extranjera. **b.** los sordos pueden oír muy pocos sonidos. **c.** los sordos no sufren de dolor de oídos.	**a.** el aparato se pone en la parte externa del oído. **b.** el aparato aumenta el volumen. **c.** el aparato se coloca en el oído interno.

3. _b_ What is the speaker's intention in sharing this information?

a. aliviar a los pacientes

b. informar al público

c. entretener a la familia de los pacientes

Comprueba

I was able to …

__ identify the main idea of each section.

__ understand the details in each section.

__ understand the speaker's intention.

Presentational

Un paso más. Trabajen juntos para responder a las siguientes preguntas. Presenten sus repuestas a la clase.

1. Según ustedes, ¿de qué otra forma la tecnología puede ayudar a la medicina?
2. ¿En qué otras áreas, puede ayudar la tecnología? Expliquen.

Note for *Habla, Estrategia*
You may want to remind students to use preterit when recounting a particular moment and imperfect when providing descriptive details surrounding the moment.

Suggestion for 15-30, *Preparación*
Have students identify the dramatic and humorous elements of the sample narratives. They should note the narrators' use of exclamations to express strong emotions, the incorporation of descriptive detail to heighten the dramatic tone, and the humorous comments by the narrator of the second story. You may want to practice with expressions in the *Lengua* box by having students select a logical place for the narrator to insert one of these comments.

HABLA

15-30 Interpretive

Preparación. Lee las anécdotas que les ocurrieron a dos celebridades y luego sigue las instrucciones para analizar las estrategias de las narradoras.

"Hace dos años, una amiga mía vino a San Francisco para visitarme. Como era su cumpleaños, el sábado por la noche fuimos a un restaurante francés muy elegante y caro para celebrarlo. Después de comer muy bien y beber el mejor champán que tenían, me trajeron la cuenta. La cantidad era enorme, pero no había problema, porque mis películas siempre tenían mucho éxito y me pagaban bien. Llevé la mano al bolsillo de mi chaqueta y me di cuenta de que la billetera estaba en casa, no en mi chaqueta. Llamé al camarero y le expliqué la situación. Incluso le dije quién era. Con una mirada irónica y un tono más frío que la Antártida en invierno, el camarero me dijo: Si usted es…, yo soy Brad Pitt. Por favor, no me cuente historias."

"Una tarde de verano decidí ir de incógnito a Manhattan. Iba a pasar unas horas comprando, y luego iba a ver una película. Después de viajar como veinte minutos por la carretera, se me descompuso el Jag. ¡Qué feo! Había mucho tráfico y hacía un calor insoportable. Me bajé del carro, levanté el capó y revisé lo que había allí dentro. Como aparentemente no había ningún problema mecánico, volví al carro. De repente, me acordé de que el marcador de gasolina no funcionaba, y que ¡se me había olvidado llenar el tanque! En ese momento llegaron dos policías y me preguntaron cuál era el problema. Les conté la historia, pero no me creyeron y me pusieron una multa altísima. ¡Claro, estaba en Nueva York, donde todo es carísimo!"

1. En la primera anécdota:
   - **a.** Subraya (*Underline*) los adjetivos que describen el restaurante y la comida.
   - **b.** ¿Qué palabras y frases indican que la narradora se cree rica y famosa? Subráyalas.
   - **c.** Subraya la frase que indica la perspectiva del camarero.
2. En la segunda anécdota:
   - **a.** Subraya las palabras que indican que la narradora se cree famosa.
   - **b.** ¿Qué palabras y frases indican las emociones de la narradora? subráyalas.
   - **c.** Subraya la frase que indica la perspectiva de los policías.

ESTRATEGIA

Use drama and humor in telling a personal anecdote

You learned in *Capítulo 13* to keep your listeners interested in your story by inserting remarks to draw their attention to moments that are particularly funny, frightening, or surprising. You can use these remarks, called *evaluations,* to make your story humorous or to heighten the drama. You can also increase the drama by strategically using descriptive details to slow down the pace and thus create suspense.

LENGUA

Spanish has several expressions with **se** that speakers use daily. Read the following and think of possible situations in which they may be used.

Se me puso la piel de gallina.
I got goosebumps.

Se me fue el alma a los pies.
My heart sank.

Se me fue la lengua.
I gave myself away.

Se me congeló la pantalla.
The screen froze up on me.

Interpersonal

Habla. Prepara una anécdota (real o ficticia) de una experiencia y cuéntasela a tu grupo. Usa las expresiones de *En directo* para que tu anécdota tenga humor y un tono dramático. Cada miembro del grupo debe hacerte preguntas y consultar el segundo recuadro de *En directo* para expresar sus reacciones efectivamente.

Comprueba

I was able to …

___ **organize the events of my story in a logical sequence.**

___ **insert descriptive elements to flesh out the events.**

___ **use exclamations or direct quotes to make my story humorous or dramatic.**

En directo

To make your story dramatic:

¿Y qué crees/creen que pasó después? *And what do you think happened then?*

¡No vas/van a creerlo! *You're not going to believe it!*

Espera/Esperen, que todavía no has/han escuchado la mejor parte. *Wait, you still haven't heard the best part.*

To incorporate humor:

Hacía más frío/calor que… *It was colder/warmer than …*

Me/Nos miró con cara de… *You/He/She looked at me/us with an expression of …*

Me/Nos respondió como si… *You/He/She answered me/us as if …*

 Listen to a conversation with these expressions.

En directo

To express sympathy:

¡Qué lástima!/¡Cuánto lo siento! *I am (so) sorry.*

¡Qué triste/horrible! *How sad/horrible!*

To express happiness:

¡Qué bueno/bien! *Great!*

¡Cuánto me alegro! *I am really happy!*

To express relief after a tense situation:

¡Qué alivio! *What a relief!*

¡Por fin! *Finally!*

¡Gracias a Dios! *Thank goodness!*

 Listen to a conversation with these expressions.

Audioscript for *En directo*
Patricia: *Lorena, tengo que contarte una historia. ¡No vas a creerlo!*
Lorenzo: *Dime, dime.*
Patricia: *Me encontré con el profesor de historia en la discoteca.*
Lorenzo: *¿Qué me dices?*
Patricia: *Me miró con cara de no conocerme.*
Lorenzo: *No me digas. ¿Y le dijiste algo?*
Patricia: *Sí, yo lo saludé como si fuera lo más normal. Pero él no me respondió, como si no me hubiera visto en su vida.*
Lorenzo: *¡Qué raro!, ¿no?*
Patricia: *Pero, espera, espera, que todavía no has escuchado la mejor parte…*
(Fade away)

Audioscript for *En directo*
Julia: *¿Sabes que ayer se nos perdió mi perro en el parque?*
Juan: *¿De veras? ¡Cuánto lo siento!*
Julia: *Sí, no lo encontrábamos por ningún lado.*
Juan: *¡Qué horrible!*
Julia: *Por suerte un señor muy amable lo encontró y lo identificó por la correa.*
Juan: *¡Qué alivio!*
Julia: *Sí, y nos lo trajo a casa.*
Juan: *¡Qué bien! ¡Cuánto me alegro!*

15-32  Presentational

Un paso más. Seleccionen la anécdota más dramática o graciosa de su grupo. Conviertan la anécdota en una pequeña obra de teatro y represéntenla frente a la clase.

Alternate for 15-32
You may want to ask that each group collectively write down their most humorous or most dramatic story, edit it, and e-mail it to you so that you can send the stories of all the groups to the whole class. You may have students vote on the one that is most humorous/dramatic, or you may wish to use the anecdotes for a future class activity.

LEE

15-33  

Interpersonal

Preparación. Comenten entre ustedes cuáles de las máquinas, aparatos o servicios de la lista se encontrarían en una sociedad donde se usa una tecnología avanzada. Expliquen su selección.

1. automóviles voladores
2. electricidad generada por la energía eólica (energía del viento)
3. servicio postal automatizado
4. computadoras nanomecánicas
5. impresoras que escanean, faxean y fotocopian
6. aviones de pasajeros sin pilotos

ESTRATEGIA

Identify the narrator's perspective

A narrative can be told from one of several perspectives. Two important points of view are the perspective of the protagonist (someone who tells his/her own experiences: I, we) and that of a witness (someone who tells what he/she sees or witnesses: he, she, they). Therefore, to identify the perspective of the narrator, the following questions will help you: Who witnesses the event? Who is speaking? Who is responding?

Suggestion for 15-33
The theme of the conversation between the father and daughter robots and accompanying drawing on page 521 is related to the theme of the *microcuento* in this section. You may wish to reintroduce it here and have students hypothesize about how it might relate to the story they are about to read.

Marco Denevi (1922–1998), escritor argentino, fue autor de novelas, obras de teatro y cuentos cortos (entre ellos, cuentos muy cortos o *microcuentos*). También fue abogado y periodista. Tanto en su ficción como en sus escritos periodísticos expresó su preocupación por los problemas políticos y sociales de su tiempo.

Suggestions for 15-34
Point out the use of *hombres* as "human beings." Explain that currently *seres humanos* is more widely used. Situate the story for students in terms of when it was written (1960s) with reference to what the author considered futuristic.

As a warm-up activity, you may wish to divide the class into groups of 4 and have them list five elements they associate with modern life. You may guide them by saying: *El teléfono móvil es un aparato que yo asocio con la vida moderna.* Before reading, explain to students that *quedase* means *quedara*, and *aumentase* means *aumentara.*

15-34 

Interpretive

Lee. Lee el siguiente microcuento escrito por Marco Denevi, un conocido escritor argentino, y luego sigue las instrucciones.

APOCALIPSIS

La extinción de la raza de los hombres se sitúa aproximadamente a fines del siglo XXXI. La cosa sucedió así: las máquinas habían alcanzado tal perfección que los hombres no necesitaban comer, ni dormir, ni leer, ni escribir, ni siquiera pensar. Les bastaba apretar botones y las máquinas lo hacían todo por ellos.

Gradualmente fueron desapareciendo las mesas, los teléfonos, los Leonardo da Vinci, las rosas de té, las tiendas de antigüedades, los discos con las nueve sinfonías de Beethoven, el vino de Burdeos[1], las golondrinas, los cuadros de Salvador Dalí[2], los relojes, los sellos postales, los alfileres[3], el Museo del Prado, la sopa de cebolla, los transatlánticos, las pirámides de Egipto, las Obras Completas de don Benito Pérez Galdós.[4] Sólo había máquinas.

Después los hombres empezaron a notar que ellos mismos iban desapareciendo paulatinamente[5] y que en cambio las máquinas se multiplicaban. Bastó poco tiempo para que el número de los hombres quedase reducido a la mitad y el de las máquinas aumentase al doble y luego al décuplo.[6] Las máquinas terminaron por ocupar todo el espacio disponible. Nadie podía dar un paso, hacer un simple ademán[7] sin tropezarse[8] con una de ellas. Finalmente los hombres se extinguieron.

Como el último se olvidó de desconectar las máquinas, desde entonces seguimos funcionando.

[1]región de Francia famosa por sus vinos [2]famoso pintor y diseñador español conocido por su estilo surrealista y su excentricidad [3]*pins* [4]famoso novelista español (1843–1920) [5]gradualmente [6]*tenfold* [7]*gesture* [8]*stumble*

Marca (✓) la información relacionada con la perspectiva del narrador.

1. ______ El narrador habla de una experiencia que le contaron.
2. ___✓___ El narrador habla de una experiencia que ha vivido.

Marca (✓) la información relacionada con el narrador.

3. ___✓___ Al final del cuento descubrimos quién es el narrador.
4. ___✓___ El narrador habla desde la perspectiva del tiempo futuro.
5. ___✓___ El narrador es una máquina.

Marca (✓) la información relacionada con la trama de esta historia.

6. ______ El ser humano, según el narrador, se dio cuenta de que las máquinas lo estaban controlando, y las destruyó.
7. ___✓___ Al final del cuento, ya no había seres humanos, sino solamente máquinas.

Comprueba

I was able to ...

___ **identify the narrator.**

___ **understand the ending.**

___ **understand the meaning of the title *Apocalipsis.***

Presentational

Un paso más. Respondan a las preguntas y apunten las ideas que salgan en su discusión. Presenten sus respuestas y justificaciones a la clase.

1. ¿Cuál es el significado del título de este cuento? Explíquenlo.
2. ¿Hace un comentario social este cuento? ¿Cuál es el mensaje?
3. ¿Están ustedes de acuerdo con el mensaje? Expliquen sus ideas.

Suggestion for 15-36
Divide the class in small groups to brainstorm possible humorous situations that involve humans and machines, computers in this case.
Remind students that accentuating the negative, exaggerating, and emphasizing the absurd will provoke laughter.

ESCRIBE

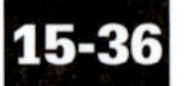  Interpersonal

Preparación. Imagínense que ustedes son las máquinas que quedaron funcionando después de la desaparición de los seres humanos.

1. Intercambien algunas ideas que describan la existencia de las máquinas después de la desaparición del ser humano: ¿Es su existencia semejante o diferente a la del pasado? ¿Es más o menos divertida? ¿Qué hacían ustedes antes que ya no hacen hoy o viceversa?
2. Mencionen tres errores cometidos por el ser humano que, según ustedes, tuvieron relación directa con su desaparición y expliquen por qué.

ESTRATEGIA

Use imagination and humor in writing a narrative

In creative writing you can use your imagination to invent events and characters that would be impossible in real life. You can use fantasy and humor to exaggerate events and characters' behaviors to entertain your readers. To write an imaginative and humorous story, consider the following tips:

- Create situations or behaviors that differ from people's expectations.
- Use contradictions within a character to create humor. The humor will be apparent when you poke fun at the contradictions.
- Base your humor on situations and characterizations that will be familiar to your audience.

15-37 Presentational

Escribe. Ahora, en el papel de una de las máquinas que sobrevivió la desaparición del ser humano, escribe una narración. Usa la información que preparaste en la actividad 15-36.

1. Describe tu existencia antes y después de la desaparición de los seres humanos. Usa humor para captar la atención del lector.
2. Indica con humor algunos aspectos de tu interacción y trabajo cotidianos con los humanos que extrañas con nostalgia.
3. Especula sobre algunos errores que, en tu opinión, provocaron la extinción de la raza humana.

Comprueba

I was able to ...

___ **use fantasy to make my story interesting.**

___ **create a humorous situation by using contradictions or exaggerations.**

Suggestion for 15-38
You may want to give students the following questions to use as a guide for reviewing their classmates' work. *¿Cómo usó ideas y situaciones originales o absurdas para captar la atención del lector? ¿Qué fue lo que más te llamó la atención sobre los personajes? ¿Exageró las descripciones o los comportamientos de los personajes?*

15-38 Interpersonal

Un paso más. Lee la narración de tu compañero/a y escoge una situación o un personaje que te guste de su narración. Haz lo mismo con la de otros compañeros/otras compañeras y revisa tu propia narración incorporando estas nuevas ideas.

En este capítulo…

Comprueba lo que sabes

Go to ***MySpanishLab*** to review what you have learned in this chapter. Practice with the following:

Vocabulario

LA CIENCIA Y LA TECNOLOGÍA
Science and technology

el acceso *access*
el agujero *hole*
la biblioteca digital *digital library*
la cápsula *capsule*
el chip electrónico *integrated circuit*
la ciencia ficción *science fiction*
la clonación *cloning*
el conocimiento *knowledge*
el descubrimiento *discovery*
la diseminación *dispersal, dissemination*
el documento adjunto *attachment, attached document*
la energía solar/de fusión *solar/ fusion energy*
el enlace *link*
la fuente *source*
la infraestructura *infrastructure*
el intercambio *exchange*
el mensaje *message*
la microcirugía *microsurgery*
el móvil *cell phone*
el reto *challenge*
el riel *rail*
el robot *robot*
la tableta *tablet (computer)*
el videojuego *video game*

EL MEDIO AMBIENTE
Environment

el banco de peces *shoal; school of fish*
el bosque *forest*
el calentamiento *warming*
la capa de ozono *ozone layer*
la conservación *preservation*
la cuenca *(river) basin*
la deforestación *deforestation*
la desaparición *disappearance*
el deshielo *thaw, thawing*
la extinción *extinction*
la inundación *flood*
la naturaleza *nature*
la pérdida *loss*
el planeta *planet*
los recursos *resources*
la reserva natural *nature preserve*
el satélite *satellite*
la tierra *land, soil*

LAS DESCRIPCIONES
Descriptions

climatizado/a *air-conditioned*
extinguido/a *extinguished*
ligero/a *light*
reciclado/a *recycled*
volador/a *flying*

VERBOS
Verbs

aterrizar (c) *to land*
avanzar *to progress, to advance*
bajar *to download*
conectarse *to connect*
construir (y) *to build*
contribuir (y) *to contribute*
despegar (u) *to take off (airplane)*
encender (ie) *to turn on*
enfocarse (qu) *to focus*
meter *to insert*
promover (ue) *to promote*
repoblar *to reforest*
unificar (qu) *to unify*

PALABRAS Y EXPRESIONES ÚTILES
Useful words and expressions

debido a *due to*
en busca de *in search of*
genéticamente *genetically*

Appendix **1**

Stress and Written Accents in Spanish

Rules for Written Accents

The following rules are based on pronunciation.

1. If a word ends in *n*, *s*, or a vowel, the penultimate (second-to-last) syllable is usually stressed.

   Examples: ca**mi**nan
   muchos
   silla

2. If a word ends in a consonant other than *n* or *s*, the last syllable is stressed.

   Example: fa**tal**

3. Words that are exceptions to the preceding rules have an accent mark on the stressed vowel.

   Examples: sar**tén**
   lápices
   ma**má**
   fácil

4. **Separation of diphthongs.** When *i* or *u* is combined with another vowel, the two vowels are pronounced as one sound (a diphthong). When each vowel sound is pronounced separately, a written accent mark is placed over the stressed vowel (either the *i* or the *u*).

   Example: gracias día

Because the written accents in the following examples are not determined by pronunciation, the accent mark must be memorized as part of the spelling of the words as they are learned.

5. **Homonyms.** When two words are spelled the same, but have different meanings, a written accent is used to distinguish and differentiate meaning.

Examples:				
	de	*of*	**dé**	*give* (formal command)
	el	*the*	**él**	*he*
	mas	*but*	**más**	*more*
	mi	my	**mí**	me
	se	*him/herself, (to) him/her/them*	**sé**	*I know, be* (formal command)
	si	*if*	**sí**	*yes*
	te	*(to) you*	**té**	*tea*
	tu	*your*	**tú**	*you*

6. **Interrogatives and exclamations.** In questions (direct and indirect) and exclamations, a written accent is placed over the following words: **dónde, cómo, cuándo, cuál(es), quién(es), cuánto(s)/cuánta(s),** and **qué.**

Word Formation in Spanish

Recognizing certain patterns in Spanish word formation can be a big help in deciphering meaning. Use the following information about word formation to help you as you read.

- **Prefixes.** Spanish and English share a number of prefixes that shade the meaning of the word to which they are attached: **inter-** (between, among); **intro/a-** (within); **ex-** (former, toward the outside); **en-/em-** (the state of becoming); **in-/a-** (not, without), among others.

inter-	interdisciplinario, interacción
intro/a-	introvertido, introspección
ex-	exponer (*expose*)
en-/em-	enrojecer (*to turn red*), empobrecer (*to become poor*)
in-/a-	inmoral, incompleto, amoral, asexual

- **Suffixes.** Suffixes and, in general, word endings will help you identify various aspects of words such as part of speech, gender, meaning, degree, etc. Common Spanish suffixes are **-ría, -za, -miento, -dad/tad, -ura, -oso/a, -izo/a, -(c)ito/a,** and **-mente.**

-ría	place where something is made and/or bought: **panadería**, **zapatería** (*shoe store*), **librería**
-za	feminine, abstract noun: **pobreza** (*poverty*), **riqueza** (*wealth, richness*)
-miento	masculine, abstract noun: **empobrecimiento** (*impoverishment*), **entrenamiento** (*training*)
-dad/tad	feminine noun: **ciudad** (*city*), **libertad** (*liberty, freedom*)
-ura	feminine noun: **verdura, locura** (*craziness*)
-oso/a	adjective meaning having the characteristics of the noun to which it's attached: **montañoso, lluvioso** (*rainy*)
-izo/a	adjective meaning having the characteristics of the noun to which it's attached: **rojizo** (*reddish*), **enfermizo** (*sickly*)
-(c)ito/a	diminutive form of noun or adjective: **Juanito, mesita** (*little table*), **Carmencita**
-mente	attached to the feminine form of adjective to form an adverb: **rápidamente, felizmente** (*happily*)

- **Compounds.** Compounds are made up of two words (e.g., *mailman*), each of which has meaning in and of itself: **altavoz** (*loudspeaker*) from **alto/a** and **voz; sacacorchos** (*corkscrew*) from **sacar** and **corcho.** Your knowledge of the root words will help you recognize the compound; and likewise, learning compounds can help you to learn the root words. What do you think **sacar** means?

- **Spanish–English associations.** Learning to associate aspects of word formation in Spanish with aspects of word formation in English can be very helpful. Look at the associations below.

SPANISH	ENGLISH
es/ex + consonant	*s* + consonant
esclerosis, extraño	*sclerosis, strange*
gu-	*w-*
guerra, Guillermo	*war, William*
-tad/dad	*-ty*
libertad, calidad	*liberty, quality*
-sión/-ción	*-sion/-tion*
tensión, emoción	*tension, emotion*

Appendix 2

Verb Charts

Regular Verbs: Simple Tenses

Infinitive Present Participle Past Participle	Indicative					Subjunctive		Imperative
	Present	Imperfect	Preterit	Future	Conditional	Present	Imperfect	Commands
hablar hablando hablado	hablo hablas habla hablamos habláis hablan	hablaba hablabas hablaba hablábamos hablabais hablaban	hablé hablaste habló hablamos hablasteis hablaron	hablaré hablarás hablará hablaremos hablaréis hablarán	hablaría hablarías hablaría hablaríamos hablaríais hablarían	hable hables hable hablemos habléis hablen	hablara hablaras hablara habláramos hablarais hablaran	habla (tú), no hables hable (usted) hablemos hablad (vosotros), no habléis hablen (Uds.)
comer comiendo comido	como comes come comemos coméis comen	comía comías comía comíamos comíais comían	comí comiste comió comimos comisteis comieron	comeré comerás comerá comeremos comeréis comerán	comería comerías comería comeríamos comeríais comerían	coma comas coma comamos comáis coman	comiera comieras comiera comiéramos comierais comieran	come (tú), no comas coma (usted) comamos comed (vosotros), no comáis coman (Uds.)
vivir viviendo vivido	vivo vives vive vivimos vivís viven	vivía vivías vivía vivíamos vivíais vivían	viví viviste vivió vivimos vivisteis vivieron	viviré vivirás vivirá viviremos viviréis vivirán	viviría vivirías viviría viviríamos viviríais vivirían	viva vivas viva vivamos viváis vivan	viviera vivieras viviera viviéramos vivierais vivieran	vive (tú), no vivas viva (usted) vivamos vivid (vosotros), no viváis vivan (Uds.)

Regular Verbs: Perfect Tenses

Indicative										Subjunctive			
Present Perfect		Past Perfect		Preterit Perfect		Future Perfect		Conditional Perfect		Present Perfect		Past Perfect	
he has ha hemos habéis han	hablado comido vivido	había habías había habíamos habíais habían	hablado comido vivido	hube hubiste hubo hubimos hubisteis hubieron	hablado comido vivido	habré habrás habrá habremos habréis habrán	hablado comido vivido	habría habrías habría habríamos habríais habrían	hablado comido vivido	haya hayas haya hayamos hayáis hayan	hablado comido vivido	hubiera hubieras hubiera hubiéramos hubierais hubieran	hablado comido vivido

Irregular Verbs

Infinitive Present Participle Past Participle	Indicative					Subjunctive		Imperative
	Present	Imperfect	Preterit	Future	Conditional	Present	Imperfect	Commands
andar andando andado	ando andas anda andamos andáis andan	andaba andabas andaba andábamos andabais andaban	anduve anduviste anduvo anduvimos anduvisteis anduvieron	andaré andarás andará andaremos andaréis andarán	andaría andarías andaría andaríamos andaríais andarían	ande andes ande andemos andéis anden	anduviera anduvieras anduviera anduviéramos anduvierais anduvieran	anda (tú), no andes ande (usted) andemos andad (vosotros), no andéis anden (Uds.)
caer cayendo caído	caigo caes cae caemos caéis caen	caía caías caía caíamos caíais caían	caí caíste cayó caímos caísteis cayeron	caeré caerás caerá caeremos caeréis caerán	caería caerías caería caeríamos caeríais caerían	caiga caigas caiga caigamos caigáis caigan	cayera cayeras cayera cayéramos cayerais cayeran	cae (tú), no caigas caiga (usted) caigamos caed (vosotros), no caigáis caigan (Uds.)
dar dando dado	doy das da damos dais dan	daba dabas daba dábamos dabais daban	di diste dio dimos disteis dieron	daré darás dará daremos daréis darán	daría darías daría daríamos daríais darían	dé des dé demos deis den	diera dieras diera diéramos dierais dieran	da (tú), no des dé (usted) demos dad (vosotros), no deis den (Uds.)
decir diciendo dicho	digo dices dice decimos decís dicen	decía decías decía decíamos decíais decían	dije dijiste dijo dijimos dijisteis dijeron	diré dirás dirá diremos diréis dirán	diría dirías diría diríamos diríais dirían	diga digas diga digamos digáis digan	dijera dijeras dijera dijéramos dijerais dijeran	di (tú), no digas diga (usted) digamos decid (vosotros), no digáis digan (Uds.)
estar estando estado	estoy estás está estamos estáis están	estaba estabas estaba estábamos estabais estaban	estuve estuviste estuvo estuvimos estuvisteis estuvieron	estaré estarás estará estaremos estaréis estarán	estaría estarías estaría estaríamos estaríais estarían	esté estés esté estemos estéis estén	estuviera estuvieras estuviera estuviéramos estuvierais estuvieran	está (tú), no estés esté (usted) estemos estad (vosotros), no estéis estén (Uds.)
haber habiendo habido	he has ha hemos habéis han	había habías había habíamos habíais habían	hube hubiste hubo hubimos hubisteis hubieron	habré habrás habrá habremos habréis habrán	habría habrías habría habríamos habríais habrían	haya hayas haya hayamos hayáis hayan	hubiera hubieras hubiera hubiéramos hubierais hubieran	
hacer haciendo hecho	hago haces hace hacemos hacéis hacen	hacía hacías hacía hacíamos hacíais hacían	hice hiciste hizo hicimos hicisteis hicieron	haré harás hará haremos haréis harán	haría harías haría haríamos haríais harían	haga hagas haga hagamos hagáis hagan	hiciera hicieras hiciera hiciéramos hicierais hicieran	haz (tú), no hagas haga (usted) hagamos haced (vosotros), no hagáis hagan (Uds.)

Infinitive Present Participle Past Participle	Indicative					Subjunctive		Imperative
	Present	Imperfect	Preterit	Future	Conditional	Present	Imperfect	Commands
ir yendo ido	voy vas va vamos vais van	iba ibas iba íbamos ibais iban	fui fuiste fue fuimos fuisteis fueron	iré irás irá iremos iréis irán	iría irías iría iríamos iríais irían	vaya vayas vaya vayamos vayáis vayan	fuera fueras fuera fuéramos fuerais fueran	ve (tú), no vayas vaya (usted) vamos, no vayamos id (vosotros), no vayáis vayan (Uds.)
oír oyendo oído	oigo oyes oye oímos oís oyen	oía oías oía oíamos oíais oían	oí oíste oyó oímos oísteis oyeron	oiré oirás oirá oiremos oiréis oirán	oiría oirías oiría oiríamos oiríais oirían	oiga oigas oiga oigamos oigáis oigan	oyera oyeras oyera oyéramos oyerais oyeran	oye (tú), no oigas oiga (usted) oigamos oíd (vosotros), no oigáis oigan (Uds.)
poder pudiendo podido	puedo puedes puede podemos podéis pueden	podía podías podía podíamos podíais podían	pude pudiste pudo pudimos pudisteis pudieron	podré podrás podrá podremos podréis podrán	podría podrías podría podríamos podríais podrían	pueda puedas pueda podamos podáis puedan	pudiera pudieras pudiera pudiéramos pudierais pudieran	
poner poniendo puesto	pongo pones pone ponemos ponéis ponen	ponía ponías ponía poníamos poníais ponían	puse pusiste puso pusimos pusisteis pusieron	pondré pondrás pondrá pondremos pondréis pondrán	pondría pondrías pondría pondríamos pondríais pondrían	ponga pongas ponga pongamos pongáis pongan	pusiera pusieras pusiera pusiéramos pusierais pusieran	pon (tú), no pongas ponga (usted) pongamos poned (vosotros), no pongáis pongan (Uds.)
querer queriendo querido	quiero quieres quiere queremos queréis quieren	quería querías quería queríamos queríais querían	quise quisiste quiso quisimos quisisteis quisieron	querré querrás querrá querremos querréis querrán	querría querrías querría querríamos querríais querrían	quiera quieras quiera queramos queráis quieran	quisiera quisieras quisiera quisiéramos quisierais quisieran	quiere (tú), no quieras quiera (usted) queramos quered (vosotros), no queráis quieran (Uds.)
saber sabiendo sabido	sé sabes sabe sabemos sabéis saben	sabía sabías sabía sabíamos sabíais sabían	supe supiste supo supimos supisteis supieron	sabré sabrás sabrá sabremos sabréis sabrán	sabría sabrías sabría sabríamos sabríais sabrían	sepa sepas sepa sepamos sepáis sepan	supiera supieras supiera supiéramos supierais supieran	sabe (tú), no sepas sepa (usted) sepamos sabed (vosotros), no sepáis sepan (Uds.)

Irregular Verbs *(continued)*

Infinitive Present Participle Past Participle	Indicative					Subjunctive		Imperative
	Present	Imperfect	Preterit	Future	Conditional	Present	Imperfect	Commands
salir saliendo salido	salgo sales sale salimos salís salen	salía salías salía salíamos salíais salían	salí saliste salió salimos salisteis salieron	saldré saldrás saldrá saldremos saldréis saldrán	saldría saldrías saldría saldríamos saldríais saldrían	salga salgas salga salgamos salgáis salgan	saliera salieras saliera saliéramos salierais salieran	sal (tú), no salgas salga (usted) salgamos salid (vosotros), no salgáis salgan (Uds.)
ser siendo sido	soy eres es somos sois son	era eras era éramos erais eran	fui fuiste fue fuimos fuisteis fueron	seré serás será seremos seréis serán	sería serías sería seríamos seríais serían	sea seas sea seamos seáis sean	fuera fueras fuera fuéramos fuerais fueran	sé (tú), no seas sea (usted) seamos sed (vosotros), no seáis sean (Uds.)
tener teniendo tenido	tengo tienes tiene tenemos tenéis tienen	tenía tenías tenía teníamos teníais tenían	tuve tuviste tuvo tuvimos tuvisteis tuvieron	tendré tendrás tendrá tendremos tendréis tendrán	tendría tendrías tendría tendríamos tendríais tendrían	tenga tengas tenga tengamos tengáis tengan	tuviera tuvieras tuviera tuviéramos tuvierais tuvieran	ten (tú), no tengas tenga (usted) tengamos tened (vosotros), no tengáis tengan (Uds.)
traer trayendo traído	traigo traes trae traemos traéis traen	traía traías traía traíamos traíais traían	traje trajiste trajo trajimos trajisteis trajeron	traeré traerás traerá traeremos traeréis traerán	traería traerías traería traeríamos traeríais traerían	traiga traigas traiga traigamos traigáis traigan	trajera trajeras trajera trajéramos trajerais trajeran	trae (tú), no traigas traiga (usted) traigamos traed (vosotros), no traigáis traigan (Uds.)
venir viniendo venido	vengo vienes viene venimos venís vienen	venía venías venía veníamos veníais venían	vine viniste vino vinimos vinisteis vinieron	vendré vendrás vendrá vendremos vendréis vendrán	vendría vendrías vendría vendríamos vendríais vendrían	venga vengas venga vengamos vengáis vengan	viniera vinieras viniera viniéramos vinierais vinieran	ven (tú), no vengas venga (usted) vengamos venid (vosotros), no vengáis vengan (Uds.)
ver viendo visto	veo ves ve vemos veis ven	veía veías veía veíamos veíais veían	vi viste vio vimos visteis vieron	veré verás verá veremos veréis verán	vería verías vería veríamos veríais verían	vea veas vea veamos veáis vean	viera vieras viera viéramos vierais vieran	ve (tú), no veas vea (usted) veamos ved (vosotros), no veáis vean (Uds.)

Stem-Changing and Orthographic-Changing Verbs

Infinitive **Present Participle** **Past Participle**	**Indicative**					**Subjunctive**		**Imperative**
	Present	**Imperfect**	**Preterit**	**Future**	**Conditional**	**Present**	**Imperfect**	**Commands**
almorzar (ue) (c) almorzando almorzado	almuerzo almuerzas almuerza almorzamos almorzáis almuerzan	almorzaba almorzabas almorzaba almorzábamos almorzabais almorzaban	almorcé almorzaste almorzó almorzamos almorzasteis almorzaron	almorzaré almorzarás almorzará almorzaremos almorzaréis almorzarán	almorzaría almorzarías almorzaría almorzaríamos almorzaríais almorzarían	almuerce almuerces almuerce almorcemos almorcéis almuercen	almorzara almorzaras almorzara almorzáramos almorzarais almorzaran	almuerza (tú), no almuerces almuerce (usted) almorcemos almorzad (vosotros), no almorcéis almuercen (Uds.)
buscar (qu) buscando buscado	busco buscas busca buscamos buscáis buscan	buscaba buscabas buscaba buscábamos buscabais buscaban	busqué buscaste buscó buscamos buscasteis buscaron	buscaré buscarás buscará buscaremos buscaréis buscarán	buscaría buscarías buscaría buscaríamos buscaríais buscarían	busque busques busque busquemos busquéis busquen	buscara buscaras buscara buscáramos buscarais buscaran	busca (tú), no busques busque (usted) busquemos buscad (vosotros), no busquéis busquen (Uds.)
corregir (i, i) (j) corrigiendo corregido	corrijo corriges corrige corregimos corregís corrigen	corregía corregías corregía corregíamos corregíais corregían	corregí corregiste corrigió corregimos corregisteis corrigieron	corregiré corregirás corregirá corregiremos corregiréis corregirán	corregiría corregirías corregiría corregiríamos corregiríais corregirían	corrija corrijas corrija corrijamos corrijáis corrijan	corrigiera corrigieras corrigiera corrigiéramos corrigierais corrigieran	corrige (tú), no corrijas corrija (usted) corrijamos corregid (vosotros), no corrijáis corrijan (Uds.)
dormir (ue, u) durmiendo dormido	duermo duermes duerme dormimos dormís duermen	dormía dormías dormía dormíamos dormíais dormían	dormí dormiste durmió dormimos dormisteis durmieron	dormiré dormirás dormirá dormiremos dormiréis dormirán	dormiría dormirías dormiría dormiríamos dormiríais dormirían	duerma duermas duerma durmamos durmáis duerman	durmiera durmieras durmiera durmiéramos durmierais durmieran	duerme (tú), no duermas duerma (usted) durmamos dormid (vosotros), no durmáis duerman (Uds.)
incluir (y) incluyendo incluido	incluyo incluyes incluye incluimos incluís incluyen	incluía incluías incluía incluíamos incluíais incluían	incluí incluiste incluyó incluimos incluisteis incluyeron	incluiré incluirás incluirá incluiremos incluiréis incluirán	incluiría incluirías incluiría incluiríamos incluiríais incluirían	incluya incluyas incluya incluyamos incluyáis incluyan	incluyera incluyeras incluyera incluyéramos incluyerais incluyeran	incluye (tú), no incluyas incluya (usted) incluyamos incluid (vosotros), no incluyáis incluyan (Uds.)

Stem-Changing and Orthographic-Changing Verbs *(continued)*

Infinitive Present Participle Past Participle	Indicative					Subjunctive		Imperative
	Present	**Imperfect**	**Preterit**	**Future**	**Conditional**	**Present**	**Imperfect**	**Commands**
llegar (gu) llegando llegado	llego llegas llega llegamos llegáis llegan	llegaba llegabas llegaba llegábamos llegabais llegaban	llegué llegaste llegó llegamos llegasteis llegaron	llegaré llegarás llegará llegaremos llegaréis llegarán	llegaría llegarías llegaría llegaríamos llegaríais llegarían	llegue llegues llegue lleguemos lleguéis lleguen	llegara llegaras llegara llegáramos llegarais llegaran	llega (tú), no llegues llegue (usted) lleguemos llegad (vosotros), no lleguéis lleguen (Uds.)
pedir (i, i) pidiendo pedido	pido pides pide pedimos pedís piden	pedía pedías pedía pedíamos pedíais pedían	pedí pediste pidió pedimos pedisteis pidieron	pediré pedirás pedirá pediremos pediréis pedirán	pediría pedirías pediría pediríamos pediríais pedirían	pida pidas pida pidamos pidáis pidan	pidiera pidieras pidiera pidiéramos pidierais pidieran	pide (tú), no pidas pida (usted) pidamos pedid (vosotros), no pidáis pidan (Uds.)
pensar (ie) pensando pensado	pienso piensas piensa pensamos pensáis piensan	pensaba pensabas pensaba pensábamos pensabais pensaban	pensé pensaste pensó pensamos pensasteis pensaron	pensaré pensarás pensará pensaremos pensaréis pensarán	pensaría pensarías pensaría pensaríamos pensaríais pensarían	piense pienses piense pensemos penséis piensen	pensara pensaras pensara pensáramos pensarais pensaran	piensa (tú), no pienses piense (usted) pensemos pensad (vosotros), no penséis piensen (Uds.)
producir (zc) (j) produciendo producido	produzco produces produce producimos producís producen	producía producías producía producíamos producíais producían	produje produjiste produjo produjimos produjisteis produjeron	produciré producirás producirá produciremos produciréis producirán	produciría producirías produciría produciríamos produciríais producirían	produzca produzcas produzca produzcamos produzcáis produzcan	produjera produjeras produjera produjéramos produjerais produjeran	produce (tú), no produzcas produzca (usted) produzcamos producid (vosotros), no produzcáis produzcan (Uds.)
reír (i, i) riendo reído	río ríes ríe reímos reís ríen	reía reías reía reíamos reíais reían	reí reíste rió/rio reímos reísteis rieron	reiré reirás reirá reiremos reiréis reirán	reiría reirías reiría reiríamos reiríais reirían	ría rías ría riamos riáis/riais rían	riera rieras riera riéramos rierais rieran	ríe (tú), no rías ría (usted) riamos reíd (vosotros), no riáis/riais rían (Uds.)
seguir (i, i) (ga) siguiendo seguido	sigo sigues sigue seguimos seguís siguen	seguía seguías seguía seguíamos seguíais seguían	seguí seguiste siguió seguimos seguisteis siguieron	seguiré seguirás seguirá seguiremos seguiréis seguirán	seguiría seguirías seguiría seguiríamos seguiríais seguirían	siga sigas siga sigamos sigáis sigan	siguiera siguieras siguiera siguiéramos siguierais siguieran	sigue (tú), no sigas siga (usted) sigamos seguid (vosotros), no sigáis sigan (Uds.)

Infinitive Present Participle Past Participle	Indicative					Subjunctive		Imperative
	Present	Imperfect	Preterit	Future	Conditional	Present	Imperfect	Commands
sentir (ie, i) sintiendo sentido	siento sientes siente sentimos sentís sienten	sentía sentías sentía sentíamos sentíais sentían	sentí sentiste sintió sentimos sentisteis sintieron	sentiré sentirás sentirá sentiremos sentiréis sentirán	sentiría sentirías sentiría sentiríamos sentiríais sentirían	sienta sientas sienta sintamos sintáis sientan	sintiera sintieras sintiera sintiéramos sintierais sintieran	siente (tú), no sientas sienta (usted) sintamos sentid (vosotros), no sintáis sientan (Uds.)
volver (ue) volviendo vuelto	vuelvo vuelves vuelve volvemos volvéis vuelven	volvía volvías volvía volvíamos volvíais volvían	volví volviste volvió volvimos volvisteis volvieron	volveré volverás volverá volveremos volveréis volverán	volvería volverías volvería volveríamos volveríais volverían	vuelva vuelvas vuelva volvamos volváis vuelvan	volviera volvieras volviera volviéramos volvierais volvieran	vuelve (tú), no vuelvas vuelva (usted) volvamos volved (vosotros), no volváis vuelvan (Uds.)

Appendix 3

Spanish-English Glossary

This vocabulary includes all words and expressions presented in the text, except for proper nouns spelled the same in English and Spanish, diminutives with a literal meaning, typical expressions of the Hispanic countries presented in the *Enfoque cultural*, and cardinal numbers (found on page 23). Cognates and words easily recognized because of the context are not included either.

The number following each entry in bold corresponds to the **capítulo** in which the the word is introduced for active mastery. Non-bold numbers correspond to introduction of words for receptive use.

A

a *at, to* **P**
a menos que *unless* 14
a pesar de *despite* 15
¿A qué hora es? *At what time is [it]?* P
a sí misma/o(s) *himself/herself/ themselves* 4
a través de *through* **13**
a veces *sometimes* **1;** 3 *at times* 12
abandonar *to abandon* 14
el/la abogado/a *lawyer* **9**
abrazar(se) (c) *to embrace* **13**
el abrazo *hug* 4
el abrigo *coat* **6**
abril *April* **P**
abrir *to open* 10
la abuela *grandmother* **4**
el abuelo *grandfather* **4**
abundar *to abound* **13**
aburrido/a *boring* **1**, 4, 6; *bored* 6
aburrirse *to get bored* 7, **8**
a caballo *horseback* **8**
acabar(se) *to run out of* 9, 15
el acceso *access* **15**
el accesorio *accessory* **6**
el aceite *oil* **10**
la aceituna *olive* **3**
acompañar *to accompany* **8**
aconsejar *to advise* 5
el acontecimiento *event* 13
acostar(se) (ue) *to put to bed; to go to bed* **4**, 7 ; *to lie down* 4
el actor/la actriz *actor/actress* **9**
actual *present, current* **14**
actualmente *at the present time* **9**
la adaptación *adjustment, adaptation* **14**
Adelante. *Come in.* 5
el adelanto *advance* 15
el ademán *gesture* 15
además *in addition* 3, *besides, furthermore* 11
el aderezo *salad dressing* **10**
adiós *good-bye* **P**
adivinanza *guess* 2
adivinar *to guess* 5
¿adónde? *where (to)?* **3**
adornado/a *decorated* **8**
la aduana *customs* **12**
la aerolínea/línea aérea *airline* **12**
el/la aeromozo/a *flight attendant* 12
afeitar(se) *to shave; to shave (oneself)* **4**
las afueras *outskirts* **5**
la agencia de viajes *travel agency* **12**
el/la agente de viajes *travel agent* **12**
agosto *Augost* **P**
agradable *nice* **2**
agregar *to add* **10**, 15
agrícola *agricultural* **9**
el/la agricultor/a *farmer* **9**
la agricultura *farming* **9**
agrio/a *sour* **10**
el agua *water* **3**
el aguacate *avocado* 6, **10**
las aguas residuales *sewage* 15
el agujero *hole* **15**
ahora *now* **1**
ahorrar to save 14, 15
el aire acondicionado *air conditioning* **5**
el ají *pepper (hot, spicy)* 10
el ajo *garlic* **10**
al (*contraction of* **a** + **el**) *to the* **3**
al aire libre *outdoors* 3
al fondo *at the back, in the rear* **13**
al lado (de) *next to* **P**
el ala wing 14
alegrarse (de) *to be glad (about)* **11**
alegre *happy, glad* **2**
la alegría *joy* **8**
alemán/alemana *German* **2**
la alergia *allergy* **11**
el alfabetismo *literacy* **14**
el alfiler *pin* 15
la alfombra *carpet, rug* 5
algo *something* **1,** *anything* 12
alguien *someone, anyone* 12
algún, alguno (-os, -as) *some, any, several* 12
alguna vez *sometime, ever* 12
algunas veces *sometimes* 12
el alivio *relief* 15
el almacén *department store; warehouse* **6**
la almeja *clam* 10
la almohada *pillow* **5**
almorzar (ue) *to have lunch* **4**
el almuerzo *lunch* **3**
¿Aló? *Hello? (on the telephone)* 3
el alojamiento *lodging* **12**
alquilar *to rent* 1, **3**
el alquiler *rent* **5**
alto/a *tall* **2**
el/la alumno/a *student* **1**
el ama/o de casa *housewife, homemaker* **9**
la amabilidad *kindless* 9
amarillo/a *yellow* **2**
el ambiente setting 8
el amigo/la amiga *friend* **P,** 2
la amistad *friendship* 6, **13,** 13
el amor *love* **13**
amplio/a *ample* **14**
el analfabetismo *illiteracy* **14**
analfabeto/a *illiterate* **14**
el análisis *test* 11
anaranjado/a *orange* **2**
ancho/a *wide* **6**
el anillo *ring* **6**
animado/a *lively* **8**
el ánimo *mood* 5
anoche *last night* **6**
la ansiedad *anxiety* 12
ante(a)noche *the night before last* **6**
anteayer *the day before yesterday* **6**
el antepasado *ancestor* **8**

antes *before* **8**
antes de eso *before that* 6
antes (de) que *before* 14
el antibiótico *antibiotic* **11**
antiguo/a *old* **1**
antipático/a *unpleasant* **2**
la antropología *anthropology* **1**
el anuncio *ad, advertisement* 5, 9
añadir *to add* **10,** 4, 15
el año *year* **P**
el año/mes pasado *last year/month* ***6***
el Año Nuevo *New Year's Day* **8**
apagar *to extinguish, turn off* **9,** 15
el apagón *power outage* 9
el apartamento *apartment* **5**
apoyar *to support* 7, 14
aprender *to learn* Pr, **1**
aquel/aquella/aquello *that (over there)* 5
aquellos/aquellas *those (over there)* 5
el árbitro *umpire, referee* **7**
el árbol *tree* **7**
el arete *earring* **6**
argentino/a *Argentinian* **2**
el armario *closet, armoire* **5**
el aro *earring* 6
el arpa *harp* 13
el/la arquitecto/a *architect* **9**
la arquitectura *architecture* **1**
arrepentirse (ie) *to regret* 7
el arroz *rice* **3**
la artesanía *handicrafts* **6**
el/la artesano/a *craftsman/woman, craftsperson* **13**
el artículo de belleza *beauty item* **11**
asado/a *roasted* **10**
el ascensor *elevator* 4
el aserrín *sawdust* 8
el asiento *seat* **12**
el asiento de pasillo/ventanilla *aisle/ window seat* **12**
la asignatura *subject* **1**
asistir *to attend* **1**
el asma *asthma* **11**
asomarse *to look inside* 13
la aspiradora *vacuum cleaner* **5**
atender (ie) *to help* (a customer) 9
atentamente *kindly* 4
aterrizar (c) *to land* **15**
el atletismo *track and field* **7**
atreverse *to dare* 7
aunque *although, even though, even if* 12, 14
el auto *car* **2**
el autobús/bus *bus* **12**
la autopista *freeway* **12**
el autorretrato *self-portrait* **13**
el/la auxiliar de vuelo *flight attendant* **12**
avanzar (c) *to advance* **15**
la avenida *avenue* Pr
averiguar *to find out* 5
las aves *poultry, fowl* **10**
el avión *plane* **12**
ayer *yesterday* **6**
ayudar *to help* 1, **4,** 5
el/la azafato/a flight attendant 12
el azúcar *sugar* **10**
azul *blue* **2**

B

bailar *to dance* **1,** 6
el bailarín/la bailarina *dancer* **13**
la bajada *slope* 7
bajar *to download* 1, **3, 15**
bajar de peso *lose weight* 3, 10
bajo *under* 5
bajo/a *short (in stature)* **2,** 2
la ballena jorobada *humpback whale* 11
el balón/la pelota/bola *ball* **7,** *7*
el baloncesto/el básquetbol *basketball* **7**
el banano *banana, plantain* 10
el banco de peces *shoal; school of fish* **15**
la bandeja *tray 9,* **10**
la bandera *flag* 2
la bañadera *bathtab* 5
bañar(se) *to bathe; to take a bath* **4**
la bañera *bathtub* **5,** 5
el baño *bathroom* **5**
barato/a *inexpensive, cheap* **6**; *moderate* 12
la barbacoa *barbecue pit; barbecue (event)* **5**
el barco *ship/boat* **12**
barrer *to sweep* **5**
el barrio *neighborhood* **5**
bastante *rather* **P**
la basura *garbage, trash* **5**
la bata *robe* **6**
el bate *bat* **7**
el batido *shake* 3; *smothie* 10
batir *to beat* **10**
el bautizo *baptism, christening* **4**
beber *to drink* ***1****; beber(se) 10*
la bebida *drink* **3**
la beca *scholarship* 1
el béisbol *baseball* **7**
besar(se) *to kiss* **13**
el beso *kiss 4*
la biblioteca *library* **1; digital** *digital library* **15**
el/la bibliotecario/a *librarian* **9**
bien *well* **P,** 2
bien/mal aparcado *well/badly parked* **12**
bilingüe *bilingual* **2**
el billete ticket 12
la billetera *wallet* **6**
el bistec *steak* **3**
blanco/a *white* **2**
blando/a *soft* **13**
la blusa *blouse* **6**
la boca *mouth* 10, **11**
el boleto/el pasaje *ticket* **12**
el bolígrafo *ballpoint pen* **P**
boliviano/a *Bolivian* **2**
la bolsa/el bolso *purse* **6**
el/la bombero/a *firefighter* **9**
bonito/a *pretty* **2,** 2
el borrador *eraser* **P**
el bosque *forest* **9, 15**
las botas *boots* **6**
la botella *bottle* **10**
el brazo *arm* 6, **11**
¡Buena suerte! *Good luck!* **1**
buenas noches *good night* **P**
buenas tardes *good afternoon/good evening* **P**
¡Bueno! *Hello? (on the telephone)* 3
bueno/a *good* **1;** *well* (health); *physically attractive* 6
buenos días *good morning* **P**
la bufanda *scarf* **6**
el burgués/la burguesa *middle class person* 13
el buscador *search engine* 15
buscar *to look for* **1,** 11, 15
la butaca *armchair* **5**

C

el cabello *hair* **11**
la cabeza *head* 6, **11**
cada *each* 4
cada día each 3
cada... horas *every ... hours* **11**
la cadera *hip* **11**
caer bien (y) *to like* 6
caer mal (y) *to dislike* 6
caer simpático *to be liked* **15**
caer(se) (y) *to fall* **11**
café (color) *brown* 2
el café *cafe, coffee shop* **1;** *coffee* **3**
la cafetería *cafetería* **1**
la caja fuerte *safe* **12**
el cajero automático *ATM* **12**
el/la cajero/a *cashier* **9**
los calcetines *socks* **6**
la calculadora *calculator* P
la calefacción *heating* **5**

el calentamiento *warm-up* 7; *warming* **15**
la calidad *quality* 6, **13**
caliente *hot* **3**
callado/a *quiet* **2**
la calle *street* Pr, **15**
el calzado *footwear* **6**
calzar (c) *to wear a shoe size* **6**
los calzoncillos *boxer shorts* **6**
la cama *bed* **5**
la Cámara de Representantes *Congress* 3
el/la camarero/a *server, waiter/waitress* **3,** 9
el camarón/la gamba *shrimp* **10**
cambiar *to change, to exchange* 3, **6,** 8
el cambio *change* **14**
el cambur *plantain* 10
caminar *to walk* **1**
el camión *bus* 12
la camisa *shirt* **6; de manga corta** *short sleeve shirt* **15**
la camiseta *T-shirt* **6**
el camisón *nightgown* **6**
la campanada *bell chime* 8
el campeón/la campeona *champion* **7**
el campeonato *championship* **7,** *tournament* 7
el/la campesino/a *peasant* **10**
el campo *field* **7**; *countryside* **9**
el campo de fútbol *soccer field* **7**
canadiense *Canadian* **2**
cancelar *to cancel* 12
la cancha *court, golf course* **7**
la canción *song* **3**
la canela *cinnamon* 10
cansado/a *tired* **2**
cantar *to sing* **3,** *6*
la capa de ozono *ozone layer* **15**
el capó *hood* **12**
la cápsula *capsule* **15**
la cara *face* 4, **11**
el cargador *charger* 5
carmelita *brown* 2
el carnaval *carnaval* **8**
la carne *meat*; **de res** *beef/steak*; **molida** *ground meat* **10**
caro/a *expensive* **6**
el/la carpintero/a *carpenter* **9**
la carrera *race* **7**
la carrera *major* 1
la carreta *cart, wagon* **8**
la carretera *highway* **12**
el carro *car* **2**
la carroza *float (in a parade)* **8**
la casa *house, home* **1**
casado/a *married* **2, 4**
casar(se) *to get married* **4,** *5, 8*
el casco *helmet* 7
casi almost 1
castaño/a *brown* 2
el catarro *cold* 11
la cebolla *onion* **10**
la ceja *eyebrow* **11**
el cel/celular *cell phone* 15
la celebración *celebration* 3, **8**
celebrar *to celebrate* **3**
la célula troncal *stem cell* 14
el cementerio *cemetery* **8**
la cena *dinner, supper* **3**
cenar *to have dinner* **3,** 7
Cenicienta Cinderella 3
el centro *downtown, center* **5**
el centro comercial *shopping center* **6**
el centro turístico privado *resort* 11
cerca (de) *near, close (to)* **3, 5**
el cerdo *pork* **10**
el cereal *cereal* **3**
el cerebro *brain* **11**
la cereza *cherry* **10**
cerrar (ie) *to close* **4**
el certamen *contest* 9
la cerveza *beer* **3**
el césped *lawn* **5**, *grass* 5
el cesto *wastebasket* **P**
el cesto/la cesta *basket, hoop* **7**
el ceviche *dish of marinated raw fish* **3**
chao (chau) *good-bye* **P**
la chaqueta *jacket* **6**
el/la chef *chef* **9**
el chico/la chica *boy/girl* **P**
el chile *pepper (hot, spicy)* 10
chileno/a *Chilean* **2**
la chimenea *fireplace* **5**
chino/a *Chinese* **2**
el chip electrónico *integrated circuit* **15**
la chiva *bus* 12
el choclo *corn* 10
el/la chofer, chófer *driver* **9**
la chuleta *chop* **10**
los churros *fried dough* **10**
el ciclismo *cycling* **7**
el/la ciclista *cyclist* 7
el cielo *sky* 7
cien/ciento *hundred* 3
la ciencia ficción *science fiction* **15**
las ciencias *sciences* **1**
las ciencias políticas *political science* **1**
el/la científico/a *scientist* **9**
cierto *true* **Pr**
el cine *movies* 2, **3**
el/la cineasta *filmmaker* 13
la cintura *waist* **11**
el cinturón *belt* **6**
ciudad *city* **3**
¡claro! *of course!* **3**
la clase turista *tourist class* **12**
la clave *key* 13
el/la cliente/a *client* **9**
climatizado/a *air-conditioned* **15**
la clínica/el centro de salud/el sanatorio *clinic* **11**
la clonación *cloning* **15**
el clóset *closet* 5
la cobija *blanket* 5
el coche *car* **2**
la cocina *kitchen* **5;** *stove* 5
cocinar *to cook* **5**
codiciado/a *sought after* 13
el codo *elbow* **11**
coger (j) *to hold* 13
el colectivo *bus* 12
el collar *necklace* **6**
colombiano/a *Colombian* **2**
el color *color* **2**
el comedor *dining room* **5**
comenzar (ie) *to start 1, to begin 6,* **8**
comer *to eat* **1,** 3, 6
comer(se) *to eat* 10
la cometa *kite 8*
la comida *food; meal; dinner, supper* **3**
la comida basura *junk food* 10
el comienzo *origen* 7; *beginning* **8**
el comino *cumin* 10
¿cómo? *how?/what?* **1**
¿Cómo es? *What is he/she/it like?* **P**
¿Cómo está? *How are you? (formal)* **P**
¿Cómo estás? *How are you? (familiar)* **P,** 2
¡Cómo no! *Of course!* **9**
¿Cómo se dice... en español? *How do you say ... in Spanish?* **P**
¿Cómo se llama usted? *What's your name? (formal)* **P**
como si *as if, as though* 15
¿Cómo te llamas? *What's your name? (familiar)* **P**
¿Cómo te va? *How is it going?* **1**
cómoda *dresser* **5**
cómodo/a *comfortable* 9
el/la compañero/a *partner, classmate* **1,** 2; **de cuarto** *roommate* 2
la compañía (de danza, de teatro) *(dance, theater) company* **13**
la compañía/la empresa *company* **9**
la comparsa *group dressed in similar costumes* **8**
compartir *to share* 4
el comportamiento *behavior* 9
comprar *to buy* **1,** *6*
las compras *shopping* 6
¿Comprenden?/¿Comprendes? *Do you understand?* **P**
comprender *to understand* **1,** *10*
el compromiso *engagement* 8
el/la computador/a *computer* 1

la computadora portátil *laptop* **P**
la comunicación *communication* **3**
comunicarse con *to reach out to* 14
con *with* **1**
con cariño *affectionately* 4
con ellos/ellas *with them* 7
con mucho cariño *with much love* 4
Con mucho gusto *With pleasure / Gladly.* 1
con permiso *pardon me, excuse me* **P**
con qué frecuencia *how often* 1
con quien *with whom* 12
con tal (de) que *provided that* 14
el concejo municipal *city council* 14
la concha *shell* 8
concordar (ue) *to agree* 14
el concurso *contest* 5
el condimento *seasoning* **10**
conectarse *to connect* **15**
conectarse a *to connect to* **4**
confiable *trustworthy* 13
la confianza *trust* **14**
congelar(se) *to freeze* **7**
conmigo *with me* **7,** 7
conocer (zc) *to know* 3, 13
conocer(se) (zc) *to meet; to know (each other)* 13
el conocimiento *knowledge* **15**
el/la consejero/a *adviser* **1**
el consejo *advice* 5
el consenso *consensus* 12
la conservación *preservation* **15**
la consola de videojuegos *games console* 5
construir (y) *to develop* **7,** *to build* **15**
el consultorio *office (of doctor, dentist, etc.)* **9**
consumir *consume* **10**
el/la contador/a, el/la contable *accountant* **9,** 9
contar (ue) *to count* 3, 6; *to tell* 15
contento/a *happy, glad* **2**
contestar *to answer* 4
Contesten, por favor./Contesta, por favor. *Please answer.* P
contigo *with you (familiar)* **7,** 7
continuar *to continue* 15
contraer *to contract* 11
contrario/a *opposing* **7**
el/la contratista *contractor* **9**
contribuir (y) *to contribute* **15**
controlar *to control* 7, **8**
conversador/a *talkative* **2**
conversar *to talk, to converse* **1**
la copa *(stemmed) glass* **10**
el corazón *heart* **11**
la corbata *tie* **6**
el cordero *lamb* **10**
correr *to run* **1**
la correspondencia *mail* 9
la corrida (de toros) *bullfight* 8, 2
la corriente *current* 12
cortar *to cut; to mow (lawn)* 5
la cortesía *courtesy* P
la cortina *curtain* **5**
corto/a *short (in length)* **2,** 2
la cosa *thing* **6**
cosechar *to harvest* **9**
costar (ue) *to cost* **4,** 13
costarricense *Costa Rican* **2**
la costilla *rib* **10**
la costumbre *custom* **8**
la costurera *seamstress* 13
cotidiano/a everyday 13
crear *to create* 15
crecer *to grow* 5
creer (y) *to believe* **5,** 7
la crema *cream* **10**
el crucero *cruise* **12**
el cuaderno *notebook* **P**
cuadra *city block* **12**
el cuadro *picture, painting* **5**
¿Cuál es la fecha? *What is the date today?* **P**
¿cuál(es)? *which?* **1**
cuando *when* 14
¿cuándo? *when?* **1**
¿Cuántas clases tienes? *How many classes do you have?* **1**
¿cuánto/a? *how much?* **1**
¿Cuánto cuesta? *How much is it?* **1**
¿Cuánto tiempo hace que…? *How long has it been since…?* 4
¿cuántos/as? *how many?* **1**
Cuaresma *Lent* 4
cuarto/a *fourth* **5**
el cuarto *room; bedroom* 2, **5**
cubano/a *Cuban* **2**
cubierto *overcast (sky)* **7**
cubista *cubist* **13**
cubrir *to cover* 10
la cuchara *spoon* **10**
la cucharada *spoonful* 10
la cucharita *teaspoon* **10**
el cuchillo *knife* **10**
el cuello *neck* 6, **11**
la cuenca *(river) basin* **15**
la cuenta *bead* 8
el cuento *story* **13**
el cuero *leather* **6**
el cuerpo *body* 6
cuidar(se) (de) *to take care of* **11**
cultivar *to grow, cultivate* **9**
el cumpleaños *birthday* **3**
cumplir *to fulfill* 7
cumplir (requisitos) *meet (requirements)* 9
curar *to cure* **11**
el currículum *résumé* **9**
el cuy *guinea pig* 10

D

dañino/a *harmful* 10
dar *to give, to hand* ***6,*** *6, 10*
dar de comer *to feed* 9
dar órdenes *to order around* 5
dar una vuelta *to take a walk* **8**
darse cuenta *to realize* 14
los datos *data* 14
de *of, from* **2**
de acuerdo con *according to* 4
de color entero *solid* **6**
de cuadros *plaid* **6**
de estatura mediana *average, medium height* **2**
de ida y vuelta *round trip* **12**
de la mañana *A.M. (from midnight to noon)* **P**
de la noche *P.M. (from nightfall to midnight)* **P**
de la tarde *P.M. (from noon to nightfall)* **P**
de lunares *dots* **6**
de moda *stylish* 6
de nada *you're welcome* **P**
de ninguna manera *absolutely not* 2
¿de quién? *whose?* **2**
de rayas *stripes* **6**
debajo (de) *under* **P**
deber *should* **1**
debido a *due to* **15**
débil *weak* **2**
décimo/a *tenth* ***5***
decir (g, i) *to say, to tell* **4,** 6, 7, 10, 11, 15
el décuplo *tenfold* 15
dedicar *to dedicate* **4**
el dedo *finger* **11**
defender (ie) *to defend* 14
la deforestación *deforestation* **15**
dejar *to leave* **9**
del *of the (contraction of de + el)* 1, **2**
delgado/a *thin* **2**
la democracia *democracy* **14**
denunciar *to denounce* **13**
el departamento *apartment* 5
el dependiente/la dependienta *salesperson* **1**
el deporte *sport* 1, 4
el/la deportista *sportsman, sportswoman* 7
la derecha *right* 4
derecho *law* **1**
el derecho *right* **14**

derretido/a *melted* 10
el desafío *challenge* 13, 14
la desaparición *disappearance* **15**
desarmar *to disassemble* 9
desarrollar *to develop* 8
el desarrollo *development* **13**
desayunar *to have breakfast* **4**
el desayuno *breakfast* **3**
descansar *to rest* **3**
descomponerse *to break down* **12**; *to break* 9
describir *to describe* 6
la descripción *description* **1**
el descubrimiento *discovery* **15**
el descuido *neglect* 15
desde *since* **13**
desear *to want to, to wish* **1, 2,** 3, 5
desechable *disposable* 15
el desempleo *unemployment* 5, **14**
el desfile *parade* **8**
deshacer (g) *to dissolve* 13
el deshielo *thaw, thawing* **15**
el desorden *mess* 3
la despedida *leavetaking* **P**
despedir (i) *to fire* 9
despedir(se) (i) *to say goodbye* 7
despegar (u) *to take off (airplane)* **15**
desperdicios *waste* 15
despertar(se) (ie) *to wake (someone up); to wake up* **4**
el desplazamiento *movement, displacement* **14**
después *after, later* **3**
después (de eso) after (that) 3, 6
después (de) que *after* 14
destacado/a *outstanding* **13**
destacarse *to stand out* **14**
destapar *uncover* 10
la desventaja *disadvantage* **5**
detrás (de) *behind* **P**
devolver (ue) *to return an item* 6
el día *day* **P**
el Día de Acción de Gracias *Thanksgiving Day* **8**
el Día de la Independencia de México *Mexican Independence Day* **8**
el Día de la Madre *Mother's Day* ***8***
el Día de las Brujas *Halloween* **8**
el Día de los Enamorados/del Amor y la Amistad *Valentine's Day* **8**
el Día del Padre *Father's Day* **8**
el día feriado *legal holiday* **8**
el día festivo *holiday* **8**
el dibujo *drawing* 5
el diccionario *dictionary* **1**
diciembre *December* **P**
dictadura *dictatorship* **14**
dictatorial *dictatorial* **14**
el diente *tooth* **11**
el diente de ajo *clove of garlic* 10
difícil *difficult* **1**
difundir *to spread, disseminate* 15
difunto/a *dead* **8**
¿Diga?, ¿Dígame? *Hello? (on the telephone)* 3
Dile a tu compañero/a... *Tell your partner ...* **P**
el dinero *money* 4; **en efectivo** *money in cash* **6**
dirigir (j) *to direct* **13**
la discoteca *dance club* **1**
disculparse *to apologize* 7
el discurso *speech* 8
discutir *to argue* **7**
la diseminación *dispersal, dissemination* **15**
el diseño *design* **6**
disfrazarse (c) *to wear a costume* **8**
disfrutar *to enjoy* 5
distinguir *to distinguish* **13**
la distribución *layout* 5
la diversificación *diversification* **14**
la diversión *entertainment* **3**
divertido/a *funny, amusing* **2;** *fun* 4, 10
divertirse (ie, i) *to have fun, to enjoy* 7
divorciado/a *divorced* **4**
doblar *to fold* **5;** *to turn* **12**
el documento adjunto *attachment, attached document* **15**
doler (ue) *to hurt, ache* 2, **11**
el dolor *pain* **11**
domingo *Sunday* **P**
dominicano/a *Dominican* **2**
donde *where, wherever* 14
¿dónde? *where?* **1**
¿Dónde está...? *Where is...?* **P**
dormir (ue) la siesta *to take a nap* **4,** 4
dormir(se) (ue) *to sleep; to fall asleep* **4,** 7, 10. 11
dos veces *twice* 3
la ducha *shower* **5**
duchar(se) *to give a shower to; to take a shower* **4,** 7
la duda *doubt* 14
el dulce *candy/sweets* **10; de higos** *candied figs* 10
duplicar *to duplicate* 10
durante *during* **3**
durar *to last* **7**
el durazno *peach* 10
el DVD *DVD; DVD player* **P**

E

economía *economics* **1**
económico/a *economic* **14**
ecuatoriano/a *Ecuadorian* **2**
el edificio *building* **5**
la eficiencia *efficiency* **14**
el/la ejecutivo/a *executive* **9**
él *he* **P**
el/la *the* **1**
elaborar *to produce* 9
la elección *election* **14**
el/la electricista *electrician* **9**
los electrodomésticos *appliances* **5**
elegir (ie, i) *to choose, elect* 5, 13, **14**
elenco *cast* 4
ella *she* **P**
ellos/ellas *they* **1**
el elote *corn* 10
la emergencia *emergency 9*
la emigración *emigration* **14**, 14
el/la emigrante *emigrant* **14**
emigrar *to emigrate* **14**
empezar (ie) *to begin, to start* **4,** 6, 13
el/la empleado/a *employee* **9**
en *in* **P**
en busca de *in search of* **15**
En cambio... *On the other hand . . .* 4
En contraste... *In contrast . . .* 4
en cuanto *as soon as* 14
en la actualidad *at the present time* **13**
en punto *on the dot, sharp (time)* **P**
¿En qué página? *On what page?* **P**
¿En qué puedo servirle(s)? *How may I help you?* **6**
en realidad/realmente *in fact, really* ***9;*** *actually 9*
en vez de *instead of* **14**
Encantado/a. *Pleased/Nice to meet you.* **P**
encantar *to delight, to love* **6,** 6, 11
encender (ie) *to turn on* 15
encontrar (ue) *to find* **4, 6**
encontrarse *to run into* 13
el encuentro *encounter* Pr
la energía solar *solar energy* **15**
enérgico/a *energetic* **14**
enero *January* **P**
enfadarse *to get angry 7, 7*
la enfermedad *illness* 2, **11**
el/la enfermero/a *nurse* **9**
el/la enfermo/a *ill/sick person* 3, **11**
enfocarse (qu) *to focus* **15**
enfrente (de) *in front of* **P**
el enlace *link* **15**
enojado/a *angry* **2**
la ensalada *salad* **3**
enseguida *immediately* **6**
entender (ie) *to understand* **4**
enterar(se) *to find out* 7
enterrar *to burry* 8
entonces *then* **8**
entrar (en) *to go in, to enter* **6**

entre *between, among* **P,** 7
entregar *to turn in* 9
el/la entrenador/a *coach* **7**
la entrevista *interview* 1, **9**
entrevistar(se) *to interview (each other)* 4
enviar *to send* 3, **9**
en vivo *live* **8**
el equipaje *luggage* 11, **12**
el equipo *team; equipment* **7**
eres *you are (familiar)* **P**
es *you are (formal), he/she is* **P**
la escala *stopover* **12**
la escalera *stair* **5**
el escaparate *store window* **6**
la escena *scene* **13**
escoger *to choose* 4
Escribe. *Write.* **P**
escribir *to write* **1,** 6, 10
escribirse *to write to each other* 4
el/la escritor/a *writer* **13**
el escritorio *desk* **P**
escuchar *to listen (to)* **1**
el/la escultor/a *sculptor* **13**
ese/a *that (adjective)* P
ese/esa/eso *that* 5
esos/esas *those* 5
los espaguetis *spaghetti* **3**
la espalda *back* **11**
el español *Spanish* **1**
español/a *Spanish* **2**
la especialidad *specialty 9*
las especias *spices* **10**
el espejo *mirror* **5; retrovisor** *rearview mirror* **12**
la esperanza de vida *life expectancy* **14**
esperar *to wait for* **9**; *to wish 11*
las espinacas *spinach* **10**
la esposa *wife* **2, 4**
el esposo *husband* **2, 4**
el esquí *skiing, ski* **7**
esquiar *to ski* **7**
la esquina *corner* **12**
está *he/she is, you are (formal)* **P**
está despejado *it's clear* 7
esta noche *tonight* 3
está nublado *it's cloudy 7*
la estación *season* **6**
el estadio *stadium* 7
la estadística *statistics* **1**
el estado libre asociado *commonwealth* 2
estadounidense *U.S. citizen* 2
estar *to be,* **P, 1,** 1, 2, 5, 6, 7, 8, 12
estar aburrido/a *to be bored* 2
estar cansado/a *to be tired* 2
estar contento/a *to be happy* 2, 11
estar de acuerdo *to agree* 11
estar de moda *to be fashionable* **6**
estar en forma *to keep in shape* 7
estar enojado/a *to be angry* 2
estar listo/a *to be ready* 2
estar malo/a *to be ill* 2
estar verde *to be unripe* 2
estás *you are (familiar)* **P**
este/a *this* **1,** 1
este/esta/esto *this* 5
el estilo *style* **5**
estimado/a *dear 4*
el estómago *stomach* 2, **11**
estornudar *to sneeze* **11**
estos/estas *these* 5
estrecho/a *narrow, tight* **6**
la estrella *star* 13
estremecerse *to tremble* 13
el/la estudiante *student* **P**
estudiar *to study* **1**
estudioso/a *studious* **1**
la estufa *stove* 5
¡estupendo! *fabulous!* **3**
la etnia *ethnicity* 14
evitar *avoid* 2, 10
el examen *test* **1**
examinar *to examine* **11**
excelente *excellent* **1**
la excursión *outing, trip* **12**
exigir *to demand* 14
el éxito *success* **13**
la experiencia *experience* **9**
explicar *to explain* 4, 15
explicarse *to explain to each other* 6
explotar *to exploit* **9**
exponer (g) *to exhibit* **13**
la exportación *export* **9, 14**
la expresión *expression* P
la extinción *extinction* **15**
extinguido/a *extinguished* **15**
extrañar *to miss* 10
extrovertido/a *extrovert, outgoing* 4

F

fabuloso/a *fabulous, great* **3**
fácil *easy* **1**
facturar *to check in (luggage)* **12**
la facultad *school, department* **1**
la falda *skirt* **6**
falso/a *false* Pr
la familia *family* **4**
el fantasma *ghost* 8
el/la farmacéutico/a *pharmacist* **11**
la farmacia *pharmacy* **11**
fascinar *to fascinate, to be pleasing to* **6,** 6
favorito/a *favorite* **1**
febrero *February* **P**
felicidades *congratulations* **3**
felicitar *to congratulate* 11
feo/a *ugly* **2**
el festival *festival 8; event or celebration (public)* 8
la festividad, la fiesta *festivity; holiday; celebration* **8;** *(public) festivity* **8**
la ficha *note card* 7
la fiebre *fever* **11**
fielmente *faithfully* 7
la fiesta *party 3; holiday, celebration* 8
fijar(se) *to focus 4; to take note* 14
el fin de semana *weekend* **1**
finalmente *finally 5, 6*
la finca *ranch, farm* **9**
la flor *flower* 2
el/la fontanero/a *plumber* 9
la forma *shape, form* **13**
fortalecer (zc) *to strenghten* 10
la foto(grafía) *photo(graph)* **4**
el fracaso *failure* **13**
fracturar(se) *to fracture, to break* **11**
francés/francesa *French* **2**
la frazada *blanket* 5
la frecuencia *frequency* **1**
frecuentemente *frequently, often* **4,** 5, **8**
el fregadero *kitchen sink* **5**
freír (i) *to fry* **10**
la frente *forehead* **11**
la fresa *strawberry* **10**
frijoles *beans* **3**
frío/a *cold* **3**
frito/a *fried* **3, 10**
la fruta *fruit* **3, 10; de la pasión** *passion fruit* 10
los fuegos artificiales *fireworks* **8**
la fuente bowl 10; *source* 8, **15**
la fuente de ingresos *source of income* **9**
fuerte *strong* **2**
la fuerza laboral *workforce* **9**
fumar *to smoke* **11**
funcionar *to work* 4
la fundación *founding (noun)* **13**
el fútbol (americano) *soccer (football)* 3, **7**

G

las gafas de sol *sunglasses* **6**
la galleta *cookie* **10**
las gambas *shrimp* 10
el ganado cattle 10
ganar *to win* 3, **7,** 12, 14; *to earn (money)* 14
la ganga *bargain* 6

el garaje *garaje* **5**
los garbanzos *garbanzo beans* **10**
la garganta *throat* **11**
la garra *claw* 14
gastar *to spend* **6,** 13
gemelo/a *twin* **4**
generalmente *generally* **8**
genéticamente *genetically* **15**
la gente *people* **8**
la geografía *geography* **1**
el/la gerente (de ventas) *(sales) manager* **9**
el gimnasio *gymnasium* **1**
el gitano *gypsy* 13
gobernante *ruler* 8
gobernar (ie) *to govern* **14**
el gobierno *government* **11**
el gol *goal* **7**
el golf *golf* **7**
gordo/a *fat* **2**
la gorra *cap* **6**
grabar *to record* 13
gracias *thanks* **P**
¡Gracias a Dios! *Thank goodness!* 15
graduarse *to graduate* 14
grande *big* **1**
grave *serious* **11**; *seriously ill* 6
la gripe *flu* **11**
gris *gray* **2**
la guagua *bus* 12
el guajolote *turkey* 10
el guante *glove* **6**
la guantera *glove compartment* **12**
guapo/a *good-looking, handsome* **2**
guardar silencio *to keep silent* 14
guatemalteco/a *Guatemalan* **2**
la guía *guide* 6
la guitarra *guitar* **3**
el/la guitarrista *guitar player* **13**
gustar *to like* **2;** *to be pleasing to, to like* **6,** 11

H

haber consenso *to agree* 12
la habitación *bedroom* **5**
la habitación doble/sencilla *double/single room* **12**
el/la habitante *inhabitant* **14**
hablar *to speak* **1,** 9, 10
Hablen (sobre...) *Talk (about . . .)* **P**
hace *ago* 7
Hace (+ expresión de tiempo) que... *It's been (time expression) since...* 4
Hace buen/mal tiempo. *The weather is good.* **P,** 7
hace fresco *it's cool* **7**
Hace sol. *It's sunny.* **P**
hace un día/mes/año (que) *it has been a day/month/year since* **6**
hace viento *it's windy* **7**
hacer (g) *to do* 1, **3,** 7, 9, 10, 15
hacer cola *to stand in line* **12**
hacer la cama *to make the bed* **3**
hacer malabarismo *to juggle* 9
hacer parapente *to go paragliding* **7**
hacer surf *to surf* **7**
hacerse *to become* 14
hacerse daño *to hurt oneself* 8
la hamburguesa *hamburger* **3**
la harina *flour* **10**
hasta *even* 7; *including* **13**
hasta luego *see you later* **P**
hasta mañana *see you tomorrow* **P**
hasta pronto *see you soon* **P**
hasta que *until* 14
hay *there is, there are* **P**
el hecho *fact* 6
la heladera *refrigerator* 5
el helado *ice cream* **3**
la herida *wound* 11
la hermana *sister* **4,** 1
el hermano *brother* **4**
hervir (ie, i) *to boil* **10**
el hielo *ice* **7**
las hierbas *herbs* **10**
el hierro *iron* **9**
la hija *daughter* **4**
el hijo *son* **4**
el hijo único/la hija única *only child* 4
el/la hincha *fan* **7**
hinchado/a *swollen* 11
la hinchazón *swelling* 11
hispano/a *Hispanic* **2**
la historia *history* **1**
el hockey sobre hierba *field hockey* **7**
hoja *leaf* **5**
hola *hi, hello* P
el hombre *man* **3**
el hombre/la mujer de negocios *businessman/woman* **9**
el hombro *shoulder* **11**
el homenaje homage 8
hondureño/a *Honduran* **2**
la honestidad *honesty* **14**
el hospital *hospital* **11**
hoy *today* **P**
hoy en día *nowadays* **8**
Hoy es (día de la semana). *Today is (day of the week.)* **P**
el hueso *bone* 8, **11**
el huevo *egg* **3**
las humanidades *humanities* **1**

I

la iglesia *church* 8
la igualdad *equality* **14**
Igualmente. *Likewise.* **P**
el impermeable *raincoat* **6**
la impresora *printer* 5
el incendio *fire* **9**
independizarse *to become independent* 5
la industria textil *textile industry* **9**
la infancia *childhood* 7
infantil *children's* **14**
la infección *infection* **11**
influir (y) *to influence* 3, 13
la información de fondo *background information* 8
la informática/la computación *computer science* **1,** 1
el informe *report* 9
la infraestructura *infrastructure* **15**
el/la ingeniero/a *engineer* **9**
la inmigración *immigration* **14,** 14
el/la inmigrante *immigrant* 14
la inmundicia filth 14
el inodoro *toilet* **5**
inolvidable *unforgettable* **13**
el/la inspector/a de aduana *customs agent* **12**
el intercambio *exchange* **15**
interesante *interesting* **1**
interesar *to interest* **6,** *6*
el/la intérprete *interpreter* **9;** *performer, artist* **13**
interrumpir *to interrupt* 15
la inundación *flood* **15**
invertir (ie) *to invest* 15
el invierno *Winter* **6, 7**
la invitación *invitation* 8
invitar *to invite* 8
la inyección *injection* **11**
ir *to go* **3,** 6, 11
ir bien con... *to go well with* 6
ir de bowling *to bowl* 7
ir de compras *to shop* 3, *to go shopping* **6**
ir de tapas *to go out for tapas* 1
ir(se) *to go away, to leave* **7,** 7, 11
irse la luz *to be a blackout* 8
la izquierda *left* 4

J

el jabón *soap* **5**
jamás *never, (not ever)* 12
el jamón *ham* **3**
japonés/japonesa *Japanese* **2**
el jardín *garden* **5**
el/la jefe/a *boss* **9**

joven *young* **2**
el/la joven *young man/woman 3*
la joya jewel 4; *piece of jewelry* **6**
jubilarse *to retire*14
el juego/el partido *game* **7**
jueves *Thursday* **P**
el/la juez *judge* **9**
el/la jugador/a *player* **7**
jugar (ue) *to play (a game, sport)* **4**
jugar (ue) a los bolos/(al) boliche *to bowl* 4, **7,** 7
el jugo *juice* **3**
el juguete *toy* **6**
julio *July* P
junio *June* P
juntos/as *together 4*

L

el labio *lip* **11**
lácteo/a *dairy (product)* **10**
el/la ladrón/a *thief* 8
el lago *lake* **7**
lamentar *to be sorry* 11
la lámpara *lamp* **5**
la langosta *lobster* **10**
lanzar *to throw* 7
el lápiz *pencil* **P**
largo/a *long* **2**
la lástima *shame 11*
el lavabo *bathroom sink* **5**
la lavadora *washer* 5
la lavandería *laundry room* **5**
el lavaplatos *dishwasher* 4, **5**
lavar(se) *to wash (oneself)* ***4***
le gusta(n) *you (formal) like* **2**
la leche *milk* **3**
la leche de coco *coconut milk* **10**
la lechuga *lettuce* **3**
Lee. *Read.* **P**
leer *to read* **1, 7,** 10
las legumbres *legumes* 10
lejos (de) *far (from)* 4, **5**
las lentejas *lentils* **10**
lentes de contacto *contact lenses* **2**
Levanta la mano. *Raise your hand.* **P**
levantar pesas *to lift weights* **7**
levantar(se) *to raise; to get up* **4,** 7
levantarse con el pie izquierdo *to get up on the wrong side of the bed* 7
la libertad *freedom* 14; **de expresión** *freedom of expression* 14
la librería *bookstore* ***1***
el libro *book* **P**
la licencia de conducir *driver's license* **12**
el limón *lemon* **10**
el limpiaparabrisas *windshield wiper* **12**
limpiar *to clean* **5,** 11; **en seco** *to dry clean* 14
limpio/a *clean* **5**
listo/a *smart; ready* **2;** *clever* 6
la literatura *literature* ***1***
el litio *lithium* 13
llamarse *to be called* **4,** 8
la llanta *tire* **12**
la llave *key* **12**
la llegada *arrival* **12**
llegar *to arrive* 1, 6
llenar *to fill (out)* **9**
lleno/a *full* **12**
llevar *to take* 4; *to wear, to take* **6**
llorar *to cry* 8
llover (ue) *to rain* **7**
Llueve./Está lloviendo. *It's raining.* P
la lluvia *rain* **7**
lo importante *the important thing* **9**
lo mismo *the same* 5
lo siento *I'm sorry (to hear that)* **P**
el/la locutor/a *radio announcer* **9**
lograr *to accomplish* 7; *to achieve* 12
los/las *the (plural)* **1**
las luces intermitentes *flashers/ hazard lights* **12**
la lucha *fight* **14**
luchar *to fight* **14**
luego *after, later* **3**
luego *then* 4, 5, 6
el lugar *place* **1**
el lujo *luxury* 12
luna de miel *honeymoon 4*
lunes *Monday* **P**
la luz (las luces) *light(s)* **12**

M

machacar *to crush* 10
la madera *wood* **9**
la madrastra *stepmother* **4**
la madre *mother* **4**
la madrina *godmother* 4
magnífico/a *great* **6**
el maíz *corn* **10**
mal *bad* **P**
la maleta *suitcase* 6, **12**
el maletero/el baúl *trunk* **12**
el maletín *briefcase* **12**
malo/a *bad* **1;** *ill* 6
la malva *mallow* 11
la mamá *mom* **4**
la mami/mamita *mommy* 4
mandar *to send* ***9***
mandar saludos *to say hello* 5
manejar *to drive* **12**
la mano *hand* 6, **11**
la manta *blanket* **5**
la manteca/la mantequilla *butter* **10**
el mantel *tablecloth* **10**
mantener (g, ie) *to maintain* **8**
mantenerse *to stay* 14
mantenerse en contacto *to stay in touch* 13
mantenerse en forma *to keep in shape* 11
la manzana *apple* **10**
manzanilla *chamomile* 11
mañana (adv.) *tomorrow* **P;** 3
la mañana *morning* **P**
el mapa *map* **1**
maquillar(se) *to put makeup on (someone); to put makeup on (oneself)* **4**
el mar *sea* **3**
el maracuyá *passion fruit* **10**
maravilloso/a *marvelous* **8**
la marca *brandname* 6; *brand* 7
el marcador *scoreboard* 5
el marcador/el rotulador *marker* **P;** *highlighter* 10
la margarina *margarine* **10**
el marido *husband* 4
los mariscos *shellfish* 3, **10**
marrón *brown* **2**
marroquí *Moroccan* **2**
martes *Tuesday* **P**
marzo *March* **P**
más (+ adj.) *most (+ adj.) 1*
Más alto, por favor. *Louder, please.* **P**
más de *more than* 8
Más despacio/lento, por favor. *More slowly, please.* **P**
más o menos *about, more or less* **P**
más tarde *later* 3, 4, 5, 6
el/la más... *the most...*8
más... que *more...than* 8
matar *to kill* 8
la materia *subject* **1**
el material *material* 6
el matrimonio *marriage* **4**
mayo *May* **P**
la mayonesa *mayonnaise* **10**
mayor *old* **2**
mayor que *older than* 8
el/la mayor *the oldest* **4**
la mayoría *majority* **14**
me gusta(n) *I like* **2**
Me gustaría... *I would like . . .* 3, **6**
Me llamo... *My name is...* **P**
el médano *sand dune* 7
la media hermana *half-sister* **4**
las medias *stockings, socks* **6, 6**
la medicina *medicine* **1, 11**
el/la médico/a *medical doctor* **9**
el/la médico/a de cabecera/de familia *doctor (primary care)* 11
el medio ambiente *environment* 11
el medio hermano *half-brother* **4**

la mejilla *cheek* **11**
el/la mejor *the best* 8
mejor que *better than* 4, 8
mejorar *to improve* **14**
el melocotón *peach 10*
la melodía *melody* **8**
el melón *melon* **10**
el/la menor *the youngest* **4**
menos... que *less...than* 8
el mensaje *message* **15**
el mercado *market 6*
la merienda *snack* 12
el mes *month* **P**
la mesa *table* **P**
meter *to insert* 15
meter un gol *to score a goal* **7**
el metro *subway* **12**
el metro cuadrado *square meter* 4
mexicano/a *Mexican* **2**
mi amor *(term of endearment)* 3
mi vida *(term of endearment)* 3
mi(s) *mine* 2
mi(s) *my* P
el micro *bus* 12
la microcirugía *microsurgery* **15**
el (horno de) microondas *microwave (oven)* **5**
mientras *while* **3, 8,** 14
miércoles *Wednesday* **P**
la migración *migration* **14**
mil *thousand* 3
millón *million* 3
la minoría *minority* **14**
el minuto *minute* P
mirar *to look (at)* **1**
mismo/a *same* 2
mitad *half* 2
el móvil *mobile* **15**
la mochila *backpack* **P**
mojado/a *wet* 7
módico/a *moderate* 12
moler (ue) *to grind* 10
molestar(le) *to bother, be bothered by* **11**
montar (en bicicleta) *to ride (a bicycle)* **1**
morado/a *purple* **2**
moreno/a *brunette; of African ancestry; of dark skin or hair color* **2**
morir (ue) *to die* 6, 7, 10, 13
la mortalidad *mortality* **14**
la mostaza *mustard* **10**
el mostrador *counter* **12**
mostrar (ue) *to show* ***6***
el motor *motor* **12**
mover(se) *to move* 7
el móvil *cell phone* 15
muchas veces *many times* **1**
mucho *(adv.) much, a lot* **2**
mucho/a *(adj.) many* **2**
Mucho gusto. *Nice to meet you.* **P**
mudar(se) *to move* 5
los muebles *furniture* **5**
muerto/a *dead* **8,** *deceased* 6
la mujer *woman* ***3;*** *wife* 4
la multa *fine* **12,** 15
la muñeca *wrist* **11**
el mural *mural* **13**
el/la muralista *muralist* **13**
el músculo *muscle* **11**
la música *music* **3**
muy *very* **P,** 2

N

nacer *to be born* 8
la nacionalidad *nationality* **2**
nada *nothing* 12
nadar *to swim* **3, 7**
nadie *no one, nobody* 12
la [la naranja] **naranja** *orange* **3;** (color) *orange* 2
la nariz *nose* 6, **11**
la natación *swimming* ***7***
natal *native* 10
la naturaleza *nature* ***7,*** **15**
la Navidad *Christmas* ***8***
necesario/a *necessary* 11
necesitar *to need* **1,** 13
negro/a *black* **2**; *of African ancestry; of dark skin or hair color* 2
el nervio *nerve* **11**
nervioso/a *nervous* **2**
nevar (ie) *to snow* **7**
la nevera *refrigerator* 5
ni... ni *neither . . . nor* 12
nicaragüense *Nicaraguan* **2**
la nieta *granddaughter* **4**
el nieto *grandson* **4**
la nieve *snow* **7**
nigeriano/a *Nigerian* **2**
ningún, ninguno/a *no, not any, none* 12
el niño/la niña *child* **4**
nivel *level* **14**
¿no? *isn't it?* 1
No comprendo. *I don't understand.* **P**
no obstante *however* 11
No sé. *I don't know.* **P**
la Nochebuena *Christmas Eve* **8**
la Nochevieja *New Year's Eve* **8**
nominar *to nominate* **13**
norteamericano/a *North American* **1**
nosotros/as *we* **1**
la noticia *news* 4
las noticias *news* 2
la novela *novel* **13**
el/la novelista *novelist* **13**
noveno/a *ninth* **5**
la novia *fiancée; girlfriend* **4,** 2
noviembre *November* **P**
el novio *fiancé; boyfriend* 2, **4**
nuestro(s), nuestra(s) our **2**
nuevo/a *new* **2**
el número *size (shoes)* **6**
nunca *never* **1** *(not ever)* 12

O

o... o either ... or 12
la obra *work* **13**
el/la obrero/a *worker* **9**
octavo/a *eighth* **5**
octubre *October* **P**
ocupado/a *busy* **4**
ocurrir *to occur* 10
odiar *to hate* ***8***
la odontología *dentistry* 11
la oficina *office* **1**
ofrecer (zc) *to offer* ***9***
el oído *(inner) ear* **11**
Oiga, por favor. *Listen, please.* 1
¡Oigo! *Hello? (on the telephone)* 3
oír *to listen to* 3, **7**
ojalá que... *I/we hope that . . .* 11
el ojo *eye* **2**
la ola *wave* 7
olvidar to forget 10, 15
el ómnibus *bus* 12
ordenado/a *tidy* **5**
el ordenador *computer* 1
ordenar *to tidy up* **5**
la oreja *(outer) ear* 6, **11**
el oro *gold* **6**
la orquesta *orchestra* **8**
oscuro/a *dark 2*
el otoño *fall* **6, 7**
Otra vez. *Again.* P
otro/a *other, another* **3**
la oveja *sheep* **10**
el OVNI *UFO* 15
¡Oye! *Hey!* 1

P

el/la paciente *patient* **11**
el padrastro *stepfather* **4**
el padre *father* **4**
los padres *parents 2,* **4**
el padrino *godfather* 4
pagar *to pay (for)* **6**
el país *country, nation* 1, **3**
el paisaje *landscape* 13
la paiteña *a type of onion* 10
la palabra *word* **P**
las palomitas de maíz *popcorn 10*
los palos *golf clubs* **7**
la palta avocado 10
el pan dulce *bun, small cake* **10**
el pan tostado/la tostada *toast* **3**

panameño/a *Panamanian* **2**
la pantalla *earring* 6; *screen* **P**
los pantalones *pants;* **cortos** *shorts* **6**
las pantimedias *pantyhose* **6**
el pañuelo *handkerchief* **6**
el papá *dad* **4**
la papa *potato* **3**
las papas fritas *French fries* **3**
la papaya *papaya* **10**
el papi/papito daddy 4
para *in order (to); towards* 3; *for, to* 3, **1**
para mí *for me* 7
para que *so that* 14
¿para qué? *why?/what for?* **1**
para ti *for you (familiar)* 7
el parabrisas *windshield* **12**
el paraguas *umbrella* **6**
paraguayo/a *Paraguayan* **2**
la parchita *passion fruit* 10
pardo/a *brown* 2
parecer (zc) *to seem* **6;** to think 14
parecido *similar* 1
la pareja *couple* 4
el parentesco *kinship* 4
el pariente *relative* **4**
el parque de atracciones *amusement park* 3
participar *to participate* **1**
pasado mañana *the day after tomorrow* 3
el/la pasajero/a *passenger* **12**
el pasaporte *passport* **12**
pasar *to spend (time)* **4;** *to happen* 13
pasar (muy) bien/pasarlo bien *to have a good time* 3, **8**
pasar la aspiradora *to vacuum* **5**
la Pascua *Easter* **8**
Pase(n). *Come in.* 5
pasear *to take a walk, to stroll* **4**
el pasillo *corridor, hall* **5**
el paso *step* 5
la pasta de dientes *toothpaste* 10
el pastel *cake* 5; *pastry* **10**
la pastilla *pill* **11;** *medication* 11
la pata *foot, leg (in animals and furniture)* 2
patinar *to skate* **7**
patriótico/a *patriotic* 8
patrocinar *to sponsor* 12
el pavo *turkey* **10**
el pecho *chest* **11**
la pechuga de pollo *chicken breast* 10
pedir (i) *to ask for; to order* **4,** 7; *to request* 15
pedir la palabra *to request the floor* 15
peinar(se) *to comb (someone's hair); to comb (one's hair)* **4**
pelar *to peel* 10
pelear *to argue 4*
la película *movie, film* 2, **3**
el peligro *danger* 8
pelirrojo/a *redhead* **2**
el pelo *hair* **2**
la peluquería *beauty salon, barbershop* 9
el/la peluquero/a *hairdresser* **9**
el penalti *penalty (in sports)* **7**
el pendiente *earring* 6
pensar (en) (ie) *to think (about)* 3, **4,** *6, 11*
pensar (ie) + *infinitive to plan to +* verb **4**
el pepino *cucumber* **10**
pequeño/a *small* **1**
la pera *pear* **10**
percibido/a *noticed* 13
perder (ie) *to lose 7, 15*
perderse *to miss out on* 8; *to get lost* **12**
la pérdida *loss* **15**
perdón *pardon me, excuse me* **P**
¿Perdón? *What?* 1
el/la peregrino/a *pilgrim, traveller* **8**
el perejil *parsley* 10
el perezoso (Zool.) sloth 12
perezoso/a *lazy* **2,** 4
perfecto/a *perfect* 10
el periódico *newspaper* **3,** 1
el/la periodista *journalist* **9**
permitir *to allow* 5, 11
pero *but* **1**
el/la perro/a *dog* 5
la persona *person* **P**
el personaje principal *main character* **13**
las personas *people* **P**
las pertenencias *things you own* 2
peruano/a *Peruvian* **2**
la pesa *weight* 10
la pesadilla nightmare 12
el pescado *fish* **3, 10**
la pestaña *eyelash* **11**
el petróleo *petroleum* **9**
picado/a *chopped* 10
picante *spicy* 8
picar *to chop* 10
el pico *peak* 14
el pie *foot* 2, 6, **11**
la piel *skin* 11
la pierna *leg* 6, **11,** 12
el pijama *pajamas* 6
la píldora anticonceptiva *birth control pill* 15
la pileta *pool* 7
la pimienta *pepper* 10; *ground pepper* 10; **roja** *cayenne* 10
el pimiento *pepper (vegetable);* **rojo** *red bell pepper* 10 ; **verde** *green pepper* **10**
pintar *to paint* 13
el/la pintor/a *painter* **13**
la pintura *painting* **13**
la piña *pineapple* **10**
piscina *swimming pool* **5, 7**
el piso *floor* ***4, 5;*** *apartment* **5**
la pista *slope; court; track* **7**
pitar *to whistle* **7**
el/la piyama *pajamas* **6**
la pizarra *chalkboard* **P**
la placa *license plate* **12**
planchar *to iron* **5**
el planeta *planet* **15**
la planta baja *first floor, ground floor* **5**; *lobby* 4
la plata *silver* **6**
el plátano/la banana *banana, plantain* **10**
el plato *plate* **5,** *dish* **5, 10**
la playa *beach 1*
la plaza *plaza, square 1*
el/la plomero/a *plumber* **9**
la población *population* **14**
pobre *poor* **2**
la pobreza *poverty* **14**
poco después *shortly after* 4
poder (ue) *to be able to, can* **4,** 7, 9, 10, 15
el poema *poem* **13**
la poesía *poetry* **13**
el/la poeta *poet* **13**
polaco/a *Polish* **2**
polémico/a *controversial* 7
el/la policía *policeman/woman* **9**
políglota *polyglot, multilingual* **14**
la pollera *skirt* 6
el pollo *chicken* **3**
poner (g) *to put* 4, 10, 15
poner (la tele) (g) *to turn on (the TV)* ***3***
poner la mesa (g) *to set the table* **3**
poner una película *to show a movie* **3**
ponerse (g) la ropa *to put one's clothes on* **4**
popularizar (c) *to popularize* 13
por *along* 3; *for* 2, 3; *per* 1; *through* 3
por ciento *percent* **3**
por cierto *by the way* **9**
por ejemplo *for example* **3**
por eso *for this reason* **3**
por favor *please* **P**
por fin *at last* **3;** *finally* 15
por lo menos *at least* **3,** *5*
Por otro lado... *On the other hand . . .* 4, 11
por primera vez *for the first time* 3
por qué *why* 3
¿por qué? *why?* **1**
por supuesto *of course* 1, **3**

por último *finally* 4
Por un lado... *On the one hand . . .* 4, 11
el porcentaje *percentage* **14**
porque *because* **1, 3**
portugués/portuguesa *Portuguese* **2**
la posición *position* **P**
practicar *to practice* **1**
preceder *to precede* **14**
el precio *price* **6**
precioso/a *beautiful* **6**
preferir (ie) *to prefer* **4,** 7, 11
el premio *award, prize* **13**
prendas de vestir *articles of clothing* 6
preocupar(se) *to be worried* 11
preparar *to train* **7;** *to prepare* **8,** 11
el preparativo *preparation* **8**
la presentación *introduction* P
Presente. *Here (present).* P
el/la presidente/a *president* **14**
prestar *to lend* **6,** 13
el presupuesto *budget* 10
la primavera *spring* **6, 7**
el primer piso *second floor* 4
la primera clase *first class* **12**
la primera planta *second floor* 4
primer/primero/a *first* 4, **5,** 6
el primo/la prima *cousin* **4**
probar (ue) *to try, to taste* **10**
probarse (ue) *to try on* **6**
la procesión *procession* **8**
producir *produce* 15
el/la profesor/a *professor, teacher* **P,** 2, 4
el promedio *average* 8, **14**
prometedor/a *promising* **13**
promover *to promote* **15**
el pronóstico del tiempo *weather forecast* 7
propio/a *own* **9**
proponer (g) to propose 14
el propósito *purpose* **4**
protestar *to protest* 14
la próxima semana *next week* 3
la proximidad *proximity 14*
próximo/a *next* 5
el próximo mes/año *next month/year* 3
la psicología *psychology* **1**
el/la (p)sicólogo/a *psychologist* **9**
el pueblo *village* 5
el puerco *pork* 10
la puerta *door* **P; de salida** *departure gate* **12**
puertorriqueño/a *Puerto Rican* **2**
el puesto *position* **9**
el pulmón *lung* **11**
la pulsera *bracelet* **6**
el punto de vista *point of view* 11

Q

¿qué? *what?* Pr, **1**
¡Qué aburrido! *How boring!* 1, 3
¡Qué bien! *How nice!* 3
¡Qué casualidad! *What a coincidence!* 1
¿Qué día es hoy? *What day is today?* **P**
¡Qué divertido! *How funny!* 1, 3
¿Qué fecha es hoy? *What date is today?* **P**
¿Qué hay? *Hello? (on the telephone)* 3
¿Qué hora es? *What time is it?* **P**
¡Qué increíble! *That's unbelievable!* 1
¡Qué interesante! *That's so interesting!* 1, 3, 8
¡Qué lástima! *What a pity!* **1**
¡Qué lata! *What a nuisance!* 3
¡Qué maravilla! *How wonderful!* 3
¡Qué suerte! *How lucky!* 3
¿Qué tal? *What's up? What's new? (familiar)* **P,** 2
¿qué te parece? *what do you think?* **3**
¿Qué te/le(s) pasa? *What's wrong (with you/them)?* **11**
¿Qué tiempo hace? *What's the weather like?* **P**
quedar *to be left over; to fit;* **6;** *to leave something behind* 15;
quedar(se) *to stay* 11, 14
quejarse to complain 5, 7
querer (ie) *to want* 3, **4,** 7, 9, 11; to wish 3, 11; to love 8
querido/a *dear* 3
el queso *cheese* **3; crema** *cream cheese* **10**
¿Quién es...? *Who is ... ?* **P**
¿quién(es)? *who?* **1**
la quinceañera *celebration for a girl's 15th birthday* 4
quinto/a *fifth* **5**
Quisiera... *I would like . . .* 3, 6
quitar(se) *to take away; to take off* **4**

R

el radiador *radiator* **12**
el/la radio *radio* **5**
rápido/a *fast* 3
la raqueta *racquet* **7**
el rasgo *trait* 14
la razón *reason* 4
realizar (c) *to carry out* **14**
realmente *actually* 9
la rebaja *sale* **6**
rebajado/a *marked down* **6**
la rebanada *slice* 10
la recepción *front desk* **12**
la receta *recipe* **10;** *prescription* **11**
recetar *to prescribe* **11**
reciclado/a *recycled* **15**
reclamar *to demand* 14
recoger (j) *to pick up* 3, **5**
recomendar (ie) *to recommend* **10,** 11
el reconocimiento *recognition* 7
recopilar *to compile* 14
recordar (ue) *to remember* 2, 4, **8**
recorrer *to travel, to cover (distance)* **7, 12**
el recuerdo *memory* **13**
los recuerdos *souvenirs* 6
los recursos *resources* **15**
la red *net* **7**
las redes sociales *social networks* 3
reducir *to reduce* 11
reflejar *to reflect* 5, **13**
el refrán *proverb* 12
el refresco *soda, soft drink* **3**
el refrigerador *refrigerator* **5**
regalar *to give (a present)* **6**
el regalo *gift* 3, *present* **6**
regar (ie) *to water* 5
regatear *to haggle* **6**
el régimen *regime* **14**
regular *fair* **P**
reír (i) *to laugh* 7
rellenar *fill out* **1**
relleno/a *filled* 10
el reloj *clock* **P**
el remedio *remedy, medicine* **11**
remunerado/a *paid* 9
el renacimiento *rebirth* 8
el rendimiento *performance* 9
reparar *to fix* 5
repetir (i) *to repeat* **4,** *7*
Repite./Repitan. *Repeat.* **P**
repoblar *to reforest* **15**
el repollo *cabbage* 6
la reserva natural *nature preserve* **15**
reservar *to make a reservation* 12
respetar(se) *to respect (each other)* 13
respirar *to breathe* **11**
responder *to respond* **1,** 9
el reto *challenge* **15**
retratar *to portray* **13**
la reunión *meeting, gathering* **3**
la revista *magazine* **3**
la revista del corazón *gossip magazine* **13**
rico/a *rich, wealthy* **2**; *delicious (food)* 6
el riel *rail* **15**
el robot *robot* **15**
rociar *to spray, to sprinkle* 8
rodear *to surround* **13**

la rodilla *knee* 11
rojo/a *red* 2
romper *to break* 10; *to tear* 15
la ropa clothes 6
la ropa interior *underwear* 6
rosado/a, rosa *pink* 2
rubio/a *blond* 2
la rueda *wheel* 12
el ruido *noise* 8
las ruinas *ruins* 5

S

sábado *Saturday* P
la sábana *sheet* 5
saber *to know* 3, 9
el sacacorchos *corkscrew* 10
sacar buenas/malas notas *to get good/bad grades* 1
sacar *to take out* 5, 6
el saco *blazer, jacket* 6
la sal *salt* 10
la sala *living room* 5; **de espera** *waiting room* 12
la salida *departure* 12
la salida de emergencia *emergency exit* 12
salir *to go out* 3; *to leave* 12
el salón de clase *classroom* P
la salsa con queso *nacho cheese sauce* 10
la salsa de tomate *tomato sauce* 10
saludable *healthful* 2, 10
saludar *to greet* 13
el saludo *greeting* P
salvadoreño/a *Salvadoran* 2
el sanatorio *hospital* 11
las sandalias *sandals* 6
el sándwich *sandwich* 3
la sangre *blood* 11
el satélite *satellite* 15
el saúco *elder* 11
Se me congeló la pantalla. *The screen froze up on me.* 15
Se me fue el alma a los pies. *My heart sank.* 15
Se me fue la lengua. *I gave myself away.* 15
Se me puso la piel de gallina. *I got goosebumps.* 15
la secadora *dryer* 5
secar(se) *to dry (oneself)* 4, 5
seco/a *dry* 5
seguir (i) *to follow, to go on* 4, 7, 11
seguir (i) derecho *to go straight* 12
según *according to* 4, 5; *as* 14
segundo/a *second* 5
la seguridad *security* 8
la semana *week* P
la semana pasada *last week* 6
la semilla *seed* 8
sentarse (ie) *to sit down* 4
el sentimiento *feeling* 3
sentir (ie, i) *to feel* 11; *to be sorry* 11
sentir(se) (ie) *to feel* 4, 7
la señal *signal* 9
el señor (Sr.) *Mr.* P
la señora (Sra.) *Ms., Mrs.* P
la señorita (Srta.) *Ms, Miss* P
septiembre *September* P
séptimo/a *seventh* 5
ser *to be* P, 2, 6, 8, 10, 11, 12, 13, 15
ser aburrido/a *to be boring* 2
ser listo/a *to be clever, smart* 2
ser malo/a *to be bad/evil* 2
ser verde *to be green* 2
serio/a *serious* 11
la servilleta *napkin* 10
servir (i) *to serve* 4, 7
sexto/a *sixth* 5
si *if* 3
sí *yes* P
siempre *always* 1, 8, 12
Siga(n). *Come in.* 5
siguiente *following* 12
la silla *chair* P, 5
silvestre *wild* 10
el símbolo *symbol* 13
simpático/a *nice, charming* 2
sin embargo *nevertheless* 1, 9, 6, 11
sin fines de lucro *non-profit* 7
sin nosotros/as *without us* 7
sin que *without* 14
sino que *but rather* 1
el síntoma *symptom* 11
sobre *on, above* P
el sobrenombre *nickname* 5
sobrevivir *to survive* 9
la sobrina *niece* 4
el sobrino *nephew* 4
la sociología *sociology* 1
el sofá *sofa* 5
solicitar *to apply (for)* 9
la solicitud *application* 9
solo *only* 1, 2
soltero/a *single* 2; *unmarried* 5
el sombrero *hat* 6
la sopa *soup* 3
la sorpresa *surprise* 4
el sostén *bra* 6
el sótano *basement* 5
soy *I am* P
su(s) *your (formal), his, her, its, their* 2
suave *soft* 8
subir *upload* 9
subir a *to get into* 15
subir de peso *to gain weight* 3
subrayar *to underline* 15
sucio/a *dirty* 5
la sucursal *branch (business)* 14
la sudadera *sweatshirt; jogging suit* 6
el sueldo *salary, wage* 9
el suéter *sweater* 6
sugerir (ie) *to suggest* 11
el supermercado *supermarket* 6
surgir (j) *to emerge* 10
surrealista *surrealist* 13
sustentar *to support* 12

T

la tableta *tablet* P, 15
la tala *felling* 15
la talla *size (clothes)* 6
los tallarines *spaghetti* 3
el taller *workshop* 9
los tamales *tamales* 3
el tamaño *size* 6
también *also* 1; *also, too* 12
tampoco *neither, not* 12
tan bien como *as well as* 8
tan bueno/a como *as good as* 8
tan pronto (como) *as soon as* 14
tan... como *as . . . as* 8
tanto/a... como *as much . . . as* 8
tapar *to cover* 10
tarde *late* 4
la tarea *homework* 1
La tarea, por favor. *Homework please.* P
la tarjeta de crédito *credit card* 6; **de embarque** *boarding pass*; **magnética** *key card* 12
la tarta de manzana *apple pie* 10
la tasa *rate* 14
la taza *cup* 10
te gusta(n) *you (familiar) like* 2
el té *tea* 3
el teatro *theater* 8
el/la técnico/a *technician* 9
la tela *fabric* 6
el teléfono *telephone* 3; **celular/móvil** *cell pone* 15
el televisor *television set* P
el tema *topic* 4; *theme* 13
temer *to fear* 11
temprano *early* 4
tender (ie) *to hang (clothes)* 5
el tenedor *fork* 10
tener (g, ie) *to have* 4, 7, 10, 11, 12, 13, 14, 15
tener calor *to be hot* 5
tener cuidado *to be careful* 5
tener dolor de... *to have a(n) . . . ache* 11
tener éxito *to be successful* 10, 13
tener frío *to be cold* 5
tener hambre *to be hungry* 5

tener la palabra *to have the floor* 15
tener mala cara *to look terrible* **11**
tener miedo *to be afraid* **5**
tener prisa *to be in a hurry* **5**
tener que *to have to* **4**
tener razón *to be right* **5**
tener sed *to be thirsty* **5**
tener sueño *to be sleepy* **5**
tener suerte *to be lucky* **5**
tener tiempo *to have time* 3
tener... años *to be . . . years old* 5
tengo/tienes *I have/you have* **1**
Tengo... años. *I am ... years old.* **2**
el tenis *tennis* **7**
el/la tenista *tennis player* **7**
la tensión/la presión (arterial) *(blood) pressure* **11**
tercer/tercero/a *third* **5**
terminar *to finish* **4,** 6, 10, 14
el termómetro *thermometer* **11**
la terraza *deck, balcony* **5**
el terreno *land* **9**
la tía *aunt* **4**
el tiburón *shark* 5
el tiempo *weather* **7**
el tiempo libre *free time* ***3***
la tienda *store* **6**; *tent* 12
la tienda de 24 horas *convenience store* 10
la tienda de conveniencia *convenience store* 10
la tienda de gasolinera *convenience store* 10
la tienda de la esquina o del barrio *convenience store* 10
tiene *he/she has; you (formal) have* **2**
¿Tienen preguntas?/¿Tienes preguntas? *Do you have any questions?* **P**
la tierra *land, soil* **15**
tímido/a *shy* 4
la tina *bathtab* 5
la tintorería *dry cleaner* 14
el tío *uncle* **4**
típico/a *typical* 3
titular(se) *to be called* **13**
el título *degree* 14
la toalla *towel* **5**
el tobillo *ankle* **11**
el toca DVD *DVD player* **P**
tocar (un instrumento) *to play (an instrument)* **3**
todas las semanas *every week* **1**
todavía *still, yet* **10**
todo *everything* 12
todos los días *every day* **1**
todos los meses *every month* **1**
todos/as *everybody* **2;** *all* 12
tomar *to drink* 3, 11; *to take, to drink* **1,** 10
tomar apuntes/notas *to take notes* **1**
tomar asiento *to have/take a seat 9*
tomar el sol *to sunbathe* **3**
el tomate *tomato* **3**
tonto/a *silly, foolish* **2**
torcer(se) (ue) *to twist* **11**
el torero *bullfighter* 2
el torneo *tournament* 7
el toro *bull* **8**
la toronja/el pomelo *grapefruit* **10**
la tos *cough* **11**
toser *to cough* **11**
trabajador/a *hardworking* **2**
trabajar *to work* **1,** *10, 14*
trabajo *job 1*
el trabajo *work* **5**
la tradición *tradition* **8**
traducir (zc) *to translate* 7, 7
traer (j) *to bring* **3,** 7, 11, 13
el tráfico de drogas *drug trafficking* **14**
el traje *suit* **6; de baño** *bathing suit* **6**
el tramo *stretch* 12
el tratado *treaty* 15
tratar *to treat, be about* **11, 13;** to try 5, 10
trazado/a *drawn* 3
el tren *train* **12**
trigo *wheat* 2
trigueño/a *of lightbrown skin color* 2
triste *sad* **2,** 11, 15
tropezarse *to stumble* 15
tú *you (familiar)* **P,** Pr
tú *you (familiar)* **P**
tu(s) *your (familiar)* **P**
tu(s) *your (familiar)* 2
turnarse *to take turns* 4
Túrnense. *Take turns* **P**

U

la ubicación *location* 4, 5
último/a *last* **8**
un/una *a, an* **P,** 1
Un cordial saludo. *Yours; Sincerely* 4
un poco *a little* **4**
una semana atrás *a week ago* **6**
una vez *once* 3, **12**
unificar (qu) *to unify* 15
la universidad *university* **1**
unos/as *some* **1**
unos/unas *some (plural)* 1
urgente *urgent* 11
uruguayo/a *Uruguayan* **2**
usar *to use* **2,** 15
usted *you (formal)* **P**
ustedes *you (plural)* **1**
útil *useful* **P**
la uva *grape* **10**

las vacaciones *vacation* **3**
la vacante *opening* **9**
vacío/a *empty* **12**
la vainilla *vanilla* **10**
valer (g) *to be worth* **6**
los vaqueros/los jeans *jeans* **6**
el vaso *glass* 3, **10**
Vayan a la pizarra./Ve a la pizarra. *Go to the board.* P
el/la vecino/a *neighbor* 5
el vegetal/la verdura *vegetable* **3, 10**
la velocidad *speed* **12**
¡Ven/Anda, anímate! *Come on, cheer up!* 3
la vena *vein* **11**
el/la vendedor/a *salesman, saleswoman* **9**
vender *to sell* **6,** 13
venerar *to worship* 8
venezolano/a *Venezuelan* 2
venir (g, ie) *to come* **4,** 7, 8
la ventaja *advantage* **5**
la ventana *window* **P**
las ventas *sales* ***9***
ver *to see* **1,** 10, 13
ver(se) *to look* 6
el verano *summer* **6, 7**
el verbo *verb* **P**
¿verdad? *don't you?, right?* **1**
verde *green* 2; *unripe* 6
el verso *line (poem)* **13**
el vestido *dress* **6**
vestir(se) (i) *to dress; to get dressed* 4, 7
vestuario *lockerroom* 7
el/la veterinario/a *vet* 9
viajar *to travel* **12,** 13
viaje *trip* 3
la vida *life* 2
el videojuego *video game* **15**
viejo/a *old* **2,** 8
el viento *wind* 6
viernes *Friday* **P**
el vinagre *vinegar* **10**
el vino *wine* **3**
la viruela *smallpox* 11
virtualmente *virtually* **15**
visitar *to visit* ***4***
la vista *view* **5**
viudo/a *widower; widow* 4
la vivienda *housing* **5**
vivir *to live* **1,** 8, 5, 10
vivo/a *lively (personality); alive* 6
volador/a *flying* **15**

el volante *steering wheel* **12**
volar (ue) *to fly* 6
el vóleibol/volibol *volleyball* **7**
volver (ue) *to return* **4,** 6, 10,
vosotros/as *you (familiar, plural)* **1**
votar *to vote* 14
la voz *voice* **13**
el vuelo *flight* **12**
vuestro(s), vuestra(s) *your (familiar plural)* 2

Y

y *and* **P**
yuca frita *fried yuca* **3**
Y tú, ¿cómo te llamas? *And what is your name?* **P**
ya *already* **10**
ya que *since* 5
yo *I* **P**
el yogur *yogurt* **10**

Z

la zanahoria *carrot* **10**
las zapatillas *slippers* **6; de deporte** *tennis shoes* **6**
los zapatos *shoes*; **de tacón** *highheeled shoes* **6**
el zarcillo *earring* 6
la zona *area* **5**
la zona peatonal *pedestrian area* 10

Appendix 4

English-Spanish Glossary

A

a little un poco
a lot (adv.) mucho
a week ago una semana atrás
a week ago una semana atrás
a, an un/una
A.M. (from midnight to noon) de la mañana
to abandon abandonar
to abound abundar
about más o menos
above sobre
absolutely not de ninguna manera
access el acceso
accessory el accesorio
to accompany acompañar
to accomplish lograr
according to según, de acuerdo con
accountant el/la contador/a , el/la contable *(Spain)*
to ache doler
actor/actress el actor/la actriz
actually en realidad
actually realmente
ad el anuncio
adaptation la adaptación
to add agregar/añadir
adjustment la adaptación
to advance avanzar
advance el adelanto
advantage la ventaja
advertisement el anuncio
advice el consejo
to advise aconsejar
adviser el/la consejero/a
affectionately con cariño
after después (de) que
after después, luego
again otra vez
ago hace
to agree concordar; estar de acuerdo; haber consenso
agricultural agrícola
air conditioning el aire acondicionado
air-conditioned climatizado/a
airline la aerolínea, la línea aérea
aisle seat el asiento de pasillo
alive vivo/a
all todos/as
allergy la alergia
to allow permitir
almost casi
alone solo/a
along por
already ya
also también
although aunque
always siempre
among entre
ample amplio/a
amusement park el parque de atracciones
amusing divertido/a
ancestor el antepasado
And what is your name? Y tú, ¿cómo te llamas?
and y
angry enojado/a
ankle el tobillo
another otro/a
to answer contestar
anthropology la antropología
antibiotic el antibiótico
anxiety la ansiedad
any algún, alguno (-os, -as)
anyone alguien
anything algo
apartment el apartamento, el departamento, el piso *(Spain)*
to apologize disculparse
apple la manzana
apple pie la tarta de manzana
appliances los electrodomésticos
application la solicitud
to apply (for) solicitar
April abril
architect el/la arquitecto/a
architecture la arquitectura
area la zona
Argentinian argentino/a
to argue discutir, pelear
arm el brazo
armchair la butaca
armoire el armario, el clóset
arrival la llegada
to arrive llegar
articles of clothing prendas de vestir
as . . . as tan… como
as good as tan bueno/a como
as if como si
as much . . . as tanto/a… como
as según
as soon as en cuanto
as soon as tan pronto (como)
as though como si
as well as tan bien como
to ask for pedir
asthma el asma
at a
at last por fin
at least por lo menos
at the back al fondo
at the present time actualmente, en la actualidad
at times a veces
At what time is it? A qué hora es?
ATM el cajero automático
attachment, attached document el documento adjunto
to attend asistir
August agosto
aunt la tía
avenue la avenida
average el promedio
average height de estatura mediana
avocado el aguacate, la palta
avoid evitar
award el premio

B

back la espalda
background information la información de fondo
backpack la mochila
bad malo/a
badly parked mal aparcado
balcony la terraza
ball el balón, la pelota/bola
ballpoint pen el bolígrafo
banana el banano *(Colom.)*, la banana *(Urug.)*, el plátano *(Spain)*, el cambur *(Venez.)*
bank el banco
baptism el bautizo

barbecue pit; barbecue (event) la barbacoa
barbershop la peluquería
bargain la ganga
baseball el béisbol
basement el sótano
basin (river) la cuenca
basket el cesto/la cesta
basketball el baloncesto/básquetbol
bat el bate
to bathe bañar
bathing suit el traje de baño
bathroom el baño
bathroom sink el lavabo
bathtub la bañera, la bañadera, la tina
to be ser; estar
to be . . . years old tener... años
to be a blackout irse la luz
to be able to, can poder
to be about tratar
to be afraid tener miedo
to be angry estar enojado/a
to be bad/evil ser malo/a
to be bored estar aburrido/a
to be boring ser aburrido/a
to be born nacer
to be called lamarse
to be called titularse
to be clever ser listo/a
to be careful tener cuidado
to be cold tener frío
to be fashionable estar de moda
to be glad (about) alegrarse (de)
to be green ser verde
to be happy estar contento/a
to be hot tener calor
to be hungry tener hambre
to be ill estar malo/a
to be in a hurry tener prisa
to be left over quedar
to be liked caer simpático
to be lucky tener suerte
to be not ripe estar verde
to be pleasing fascinar
to be pleasing to gustar
to be ready estar listo/a
to be right tener razón
to be sleepy tener sueño
to be smart ser listo/a
to be sorry sentir, lamentar
to be successful tener éxito
to be thirsty tener sed
to be tired estar cansado/a
to be worried preocuparse
to be worth valer
beach la playa
bead la cuenta
beans los frijoles
to beat batir
beautiful precioso/a
beauty item el artículo de belleza
beauty salon la peluquería
because porque
to become hacerse
to become independent independizarse
bed la cama
bedroom el cuarto
beef la carne de res
beer la cerveza
before antes, antes (de) que
to begin comenzar, empezar
beginning el comienzo
behavior el comportamiento
behind detrás (de)
to believe creer
bell chime la campanada
belt el cinturón
besides además
better than mejor que
between entre
bicycle la bicicleta
big grande
bilingual bilingüe
birth control pill la píldora anticonceptiva
birthday el cumpleaños
black negro/a
blanket la manta, la cobija, la frazada
blazer el saco
blond rubio/a
blood la sangre
blouse la blusa
blue azul
boarding pass la tarjeta de embarque
body el cuerpo
to boil hervir
Bolivian boliviano/a
bone el hueso
book el libro
bookstore la librería
boots las botas
boring aburrido/a
boss el/la jefe/a
to bother, be bothered by molestar
bottle la botella
to bowl jugar a los bolos, jugar (al) boliche, ir de bowling
bowl la fuente
boxer shorts los calzoncillos
boy el chico
boyfriend el novio
bra el sostén
bracelet la pulsera
brain el cerebro
branch (business) la sucursal
brand, brandname la marca
bread el pan
to break fracturarse; romper; descomponerse
to break down descomponerse
breakfast el desayuno
to breathe respirar
briefcase el maletín
to bring traer
brother el hermano
brown marrón, café, carmelita, castaño/a, pardo/a
brunette moreno/a
budget el presupuesto
to build construir
building el edificio
bull el toro
bullfight la corrida de toros
bullfighter el torero
bun, small cake el pan dulce
to bury enterrar
bus el autobús/bus, el camión *(Mex.)*, el colectivo *(Arg.)*, el micro *(Chile)*, el bus/la guagua *(P.R., Cuba)*, la chiva *(Colom.)*, el ómnibus *(Peru)*
businessman el hombre de negocios
businesswoman la mujer de negocios
busy ocupado/a
but pero
but rather sino que
butter la manteca/mantequilla
to buy comprar
by the way por cierto

C

cabbage el repollo
cafe el café
cafeteria la cafetería
cake el pastel
calculator la calculadora
Canadian canadiense
to cancel cancelar
candied figs el dulce de higos
candy/sweets el dulce
cap la gorra
capsule la cápsula
car el auto/carro/coche
careful cuidado
carnival el carnaval
carpenter el/la carpintero/a
carpet la alfombra
carrot la zanahoria
to carry out realizar
cart la carreta
cashier el/la cajero/a
cast elenco
cattle el ganado
cayenne la pimienta roja

to celebrate celebrar
celebration (public) el festival
celebration for a girl's 15th birthday la quinceañera
celebration la celebración/fiesta
celebration la festividad, la fiesta
cell phone el teléfono móvil/celular, el móvil/celular/cel
cemetery el cementerio
center el centro
cereal el cereal
chair la silla
chalkboard la pizarra
challenge el reto, el desafío
chamomile la manzanilla
champion el campeón/la campeona
championship el campeonato
to change cambiar
change el cambio
charger el cargador
charming simpático/a
cheap barato/a
to check in (luggage) facturar
cheek la mejilla
cheese el queso
chef el/la chef
cherry la cereza
chest el pecho
chicken el pollo
chicken breast la pechuga de pollo
to achieve lograr
child el niño/la niña
childhood la infancia
children's infantil
Chilean chileno/a
Chinese chino/a
to choose elegir, escoger
to chop picar
chop la chuleta
chopped picado/a
christening el bautizo
Christmas Eve la Nochebuena
Christmas la Navidad
church la iglesia
Cinderella Cenicienta
cinnamon la canela
city block la cuadra
city council el concejo municipal
city la ciudad
clam la almeja
classmate el/la compañero/a
classroom el salón de clase
claw la garra
to clean limpiar
clean limpio/a
clever listo/a
client el/la cliente/a
clinic la clínica, el centro de salud, el sanatorio
clock el reloj
clock el reloj
cloning la clonación
close (to) cerca (de)
to close cerrar
closet el clóset, el armario
clothes la ropa
clove of garlic el diente de ajo
coach el/la entrenador/a
coat el abrigo
coconut milk la leche de coco
coffee el café
coffee shop el café
cold el catarro
cold el frío; **(adj.)** frío/a
Colombian colombiano/a
color el color
to comb (one's hair) peinar(se)
Come in. Pase(n). Adelante. Siga(n). *(Colomb.)*
Come on, cheer up! ¡Ven/Anda, anímate!
to come venir
comfortable cómodo/a
commonwealth el estado libre asociado
communication la comunicación
company (dance, theater) la compañía (de danza, de teatro)
company la compañía, la empresa
to compile recopilar
to complain quejarse
computer la computadora, el computador, el ordenador *(Spain)*
computer science la computación, la informática *(Spain)*
conclusion la conclusión
to congratulate felicitar
congratulations las felicidades
Congress la Cámara de Representantes
to connect conectarse
to connect to conectarse a
consensus el consenso
to consume consumir
contact lenses los lentes de contacto
contest el certamen, el concurso
to continue continuar
to contract contraer
contractor el/la contratista
to contribute contribuir
to control controlar
controversial polémico/a
convenience store la tienda de conveniencia *(Mex.)*, de gasolinera *(C.R.)*, de la esquina/del barrio, de 24 horas *(Spain)*
to converse conversar
to cook cocinar
cookie la galleta
corkscrew el sacacorchos
corn el maíz, el elote *(Mex./Central America)*, choclo *(South America)*
corner la esquina
corridor el pasillo
to cost costar
Costa Rican costarricense
cough la tos
to cough toser
to count contar
counter el mostrador
country el país
countryside el campo
couple la pareja
court la pista
court (golf) la cancha
courtesy la cortesía
cousin el/la primo/a
to cover cubrir; tapar; **(distance)** recorrer
craftsman/woman, craftsperson el/la artesano/a
cream cheese el queso crema
cream la crema
to create crear
credit card la tarjeta de crédito
cruise el crucero
to crush machacar
to cry llorar
Cuban cubano/a
cubist cubista
cucumber el pepino
to cultivate cultivar
cumin el comino
cup la taza
to cure curar
current actual
current la corriente
curtain la cortina
custom la costumbre
customs la aduana; **agent** el/la inspector/a de aduana
to cut cortar
cycling el ciclismo
cyclist el/la ciclista

D

dad el papá
daddy el papi/papito
dairy (product) lácteo/a
to dance bailar
dance club la discoteca
dancer el bailarín/la bailarina
danger el peligro
to dare atreverse
dark oscuro/a

darse cuenta to realize
data los datos
daughter la hija
day before yesterday anteayer
day el día
dead difunto/a, muerto/a
dear estimado/a; querido/a; mi amor/ vida/corazón *(terms of endearment)*
deceased muerto/a
December diciembre
deck la terraza
decorated adornado/a
to dedicate dedicar
to defend defender
deforestation la deforestación
degree el título
delicious rico/a
description la descripción
to delight encantar
to demand exigir; reclamar
democracy la democracia
to denounce denunciar
dentistry la odontología
department store el almacén
departure la salida
depressed deprimido/a
to describe describir
design el diseño
desk el escritorio
despite a pesar de
to develop desarrollar; contruir
development el desarrollo
dictatorial dictatorial
dictatorship dictadura
dictionary el diccionario
to die morir
difficult difícil
dining room el comedor
dinner la cena
dinner la comida
to direct dirigir
dirty sucio/a
disadvantage la desventaja
disappearance la desaparición
to disassemble desarmar
discovery el descubrimiento
dish el plato
dish of marinated raw fish el ceviche
dishwasher el lavaplatos
to dislike caer mal
dispersal la diseminación
displacement el desplazamiento
disposable desechable
to disseminate difundir
dissemination la diseminación
to dissolve deshacer
to distinguish distinguir
diversification la diversificación
divorced divorciado/a
to do hacer
Do you have any questions? ¿Tienen preguntas?/¿Tienes preguntas?
Do you understand? ¿Comprenden?/¿Comprendes?
doctor (primary care) el/la médico/a de familia/de cabecera; el/la doctor/a
dog el/la perro/a
Dominican dominicano/a
don't you? ¿verdad?
door la puerta
dots de lunares
double room la habitación doble
doubt la duda
to download bajar
downtown el centro
drawing el dibujo
drawn trazado/a
dress el vestido
to dress; to get dressed vestir(se)
dresser la cómoda
to drink beber, tomar
drink la bebida
to drive manejar
driver el/la chofer
driver's license la licencia de conducir
drug trafficking el tráfico de drogas
to dry (oneself) secar(se)
to dry clean limpiar en seco
dry cleaner la tintorería
dry seco/a
dryer la secadora
due to debido a
to duplicate duplicar
during durante
DVD el DVD
DVD player el toca DVD

E

each cada
each day cada día
ear (inner) el oído
ear (outer) la oreja
ear la oreja
early temprano
to earn ganar
earring el arete, el aro, el pendiente, el zarcillo, la pantalla
Easter la Pascua
easy fácil
to eat comer
economic económico/a
economics economía
Ecuadorian ecuatoriano/a
efficiency la eficiencia
egg el huevo
eighth octavo
either ... or o... o
elbow el codo
elder (herb) el saúco
to elect elegir
election la elección
electrician el/la electricista
elevator el ascensor
to embrace abrazar(se)
to emerge surgir
emergency exit la salida de emergencia
emergency la emergencia
emigrant el/la emigrante
to emigrate emigrar
emigration la emigración
employee el/la empleado/a
empty vacío/a
encounter el encuentro
energetic enérgico/a
engagement el compromiso
engineer el/la ingeniero/a
to enjoy disfrutar, divertirse
to enter entrar en
entertainment la diversión
environment el medio ambiente
equality la igualdad
equipment el equipo
eraser el borrador
ethnicity la etnia
even hasta
even if, even though aunque
event el acontecimiento
event el festival
ever alguna vez
every ... hours cada... horas
every day todos los días
every month todos los meses
every week todas las semanas
everybody todos/as
everyday cotidiano/a
everything todo
to examine examinar
excellent excelente
to exchange cambiar
exchange el intercambio
excuse me perdón; con permiso
executive el/la ejecutivo/a
expensive caro/a
experience la experiencia
to explain explicar
to exploit explotar
export la exportación
expression la expresión
extinction la extinción
to extinguish apagar, extinguir
extinguished extinguido/a
extroverted extrovertido/a
eye el ojo
eyebrow la ceja
eyelash la pestaña

F

fabric la tela
fabulous estupendo, fabuloso/a
face la cara
fact el hecho
failure el fracaso
fair regular
faithfully fielmente
to fall asleep dormirse
to fall caer(se)
fall el otoño
false falso/a
family la familia
fan (admirer) el/la hincha
fan el ventilador
far (from) lejos (de)
farm la finca
farmer el/la agricultor/a
farming la agricultura
to fascinate fascinar
fast rápido/a
fat gordo/a
father el padre
Father's Day el Día del Padre
favorite favorito/a
to fear temer
February febrero
to feed dar de comer
to feel sentir(se)
feeling el sentimiento
felling la tala
festival el festival
festivity (public) la festividad, la fiesta
fever la fiebre
fiancé/fiancée el novio/la novia
field el campo
field hockey el hockey sobre hierba
fifth quinto/a
fight la lucha
to fight luchar
to fill (out) llenar, rellenar
filled relleno/a
film la película
filmmaker el/la cineasta
filth la inmundicia
finally finalmente; por fin; por último
to find encontrar
to find out enterarse, averiguar
fine la multa
finger el dedo
to finish terminar
to fire despedir
fire el incendio
firefighter el/la bombero/a
fireplace la chimenea
fireworks los fuegos artificiales
first class la primera clase
first floor la planta baja
first primer/o/a, primer
fish el pescado
to fit quedar
to fix reparar
flag la bandera
flashers las luces intermitentes
flight attendant el/la auxiliar de vuelo, el/la azafato/a *(Spain)*, el/la aeromozo/a *(Latin Am.)*
flight el vuelo
float (in a parade) la carroza
flood la inundación
floor el piso
flour la harina
flower la flor
flu la gripe
to fly volar
flying volador/a
to focus enfocarse, fijarse
to fold doblar
to follow seguir
following siguiente
food la comida
foolish tonto/a
foot (in animals) la pata
foot el pie
football el fútbol (americano)
footwear el calzado
for por, para
for example por ejemplo
for me para mí
for the first time por primera vez
for this reason por eso
for you (familiar) para ti
forehead la frente
forest el bosque
to forget olvidar
fork el tenedor
founding (noun) la fundación
fourth cuarto
fowl las aves
to fracture fracturarse
free time el tiempo libre
freedom la libertad
freedom of expression la libertad de expresión
freeway la autopista
to freeze congelar(se)
French francés/francesa
French fries las papas fritas
frequency la frecuencia
frequently frecuentemente
Friday viernes
fried frito/a
fried dough los churros
fried yuca yuca frita
friend el/la amigo/a
friendship la amistad
from de
front desk la recepción
fruit la fruta
to fry freír
to fulfill cumplir
full lleno/a
fun, funny divertido/a
furniture los muebles
furthermore además

to gain weight subir de peso
game el juego/el partido
games console la consola de videojuegos
garage el garaje
garbage la basura
garbanzo beans los garbanzos
garden el jardín
garlic el ajo
gate (departure) la puerta (de salida)
gathering la reunión
generally generalmente
genetically genéticamente
geography la geografía
German alemán/alemana
gesture el ademán
to get angry enfadarse
to get bored aburrirse
to get good/bad grades sacar buenas/malas notas
to get into subir a
to get lost perderse
to get married casarse
to get up levantarse
to get up on the wrong side of the bed levantarse con el pie izquierdo
ghost el fantasma
gift el regalo
girl la chica
to give (a present) dar, regalar
to give a shower to duchar
to give dar
glad contento/a, alegre
glass (stemmed) la copa
glass el vaso
glove compartment la guantera
glove el guante
Go to the board. Vayan a la pizarra. *(plural)*; Ve a la pizarra. *(sing./fam.)*
to go ir
to go away irse
to go in entrar en
to go on seguir
to go out for tapas ir de tapas
to go out salir
to go paragliding hacer parapente
to go shopping ir de compras
to go straight seguir derecho

to go to bed acostarse
to go well with... ir bien con...
goal el gol
godchild el/la ahijado/a
godfather el padrino
godmother la madrina
gold el oro
golf clubs los palos
golf course la cancha de golf
golf el golf
good bueno/a
Good afternoon. Buenas tardes.
Good evening. Buenas tardes.
Good luck! ¡Buena suerte!
Good morning. Buenos días.
Good night. Buenas noches.
good-bye adiós, chao (chau)
good-looking guapo/a
gossip magazine la revista del corazón
to govern gobernar
government el gobierno
to graduate graduarse
granddaughter la nieta
grandfather el abuelo
grandmother la abuela
grandson el nieto
grape la uva
grapefruit la toronja, el pomelo
grass el césped
gray gris
great magnífico/a
green verde
green pepper el pimiento verde
to greet saludar
greeting el saludo
to grind moler
ground floor la planta baja
ground meat la carne molida
ground pepper la pimienta
group dressed in similar costumes la comparsa
to grow crecer
to grow cultivar
Guatemalan guatemalteco/a
guess la adivinanza
to guess adivinar
guide la guía
guinea pig el cuy
guitar la guitarra
guitar player el/la guitarrista
gymnasium el gimnasio
gypsy el gitano

H

to haggle regatear
hair el cabello, el pelo
hairdresser el/la peluquero/a
half la mitad
half-brother el medio hermano
half-sister la media hermana
hall el pasillo
Halloween el Día de las Brujas
ham el jamón
hamburger la hamburguesa
to hand dar
hand la mano
handicrafts la artesanía
handkerchief el pañuelo
handsome guapo, bien parecido, buen mozo
to hang (clothes) tender
to happen pasar
happy, alegre, contento/a
hard-working trabajador/a
harmful dañino/a
harp el arpa
to harvest cosechar
hat el sombrero
to hate odiar
to have tener
to have a good time pasar (muy) bien
to have a(n) ... ache tener dolor de...
to have a seat tomar asiento
to have breakfast desayunar
to have dinner cenar
to have fun divertirse
to have lunch almorzar
to have the floor tener la palabra
to have time tener tiempo
to have to tener que
hazard lights las luces intermitentes
he él
he/she has; you (formal) have tiene
head la cabeza
healthful saludable
healthy saludable
heart el corazón
heating la calefacción
hello hola
Hello? (on the telephone) ¿Diga?/¿Dígame? *(Spain),* ¡Bueno! *(Mex.),* ¿Aló? *(Arg., Peru, Chile),* ¡Oigo!/¿Qué hay? *(Cuba)*
helmet el casco
to help (a customer) atender
to help ayudar
her su(s)
herbs las hierbas
Here (present). Presente.
herself a sí mismo/a(s)
Hey! ¡Oye!
hi hola
highheeled shoes los zapatos de tacón
highlighter el marcador, el rotulador
highway la carretera
himself a sí mismo/a(s)
hip la cadera
his su(s)
Hispanic hispano/a
history la historia
to hold coger
hole el agujero
holiday (legal) el día feriado
holiday el día festivo, la festividad, la fiesta
homage el homenaje
home la casa
homework la tarea
Homework please. La tarea, por favor.
Honduran hondureño/a
honesty la honestidad
honeymoon la luna de miel
hood el capó
hoop el cesto/la cesta
horseback a caballo
hospital el hospital, el sanatorio, la clínica
hot caliente
house la casa
housewife, homemaker el ama/o de casa
housing la vivienda
How are you? (formal) ¿Cómo está?
How are you? (informal) ¿Cómo estás?
How boring! ¡Qué aburrido!
How do you say. . . in Spanish? ¿Cómo se dice... en español?
How fun!/How funny! ¡Qué divertido!
How interesting! ¡Qué interesante!
How is it going? ¿Cómo te va?
How long has it been since. . .? ¿Cuánto tiempo hace que...?
How lucky! ¡Qué suerte!
how many? ¿cuántos/as?
How many classes do you have? ¿Cuántas clases tienes?
How may I help you? ¿En qué puedo servirle(s)?
How much is it? ¿Cuánto cuesta?
how much? ¿cuánto/a?
How nice! ¡Qué bien!
how often con qué frecuencia
How wonderful! ¡Qué maravilla!
how? ¿cómo?
however no obstante, sin embargo
hug el abrazo
humanities las humanidades
humpback whale la ballena jorobada
hundred cien/ciento
to hurt doler
to hurt oneself hacerse daño
husband el esposo, el marido

I

I yo
I am soy
I am ... years old. Tengo... años.

I don't know. No sé.
I don't understand. No comprendo.
I gave myself away. Se me fue la lengua.
I got goosebumps. Se me puso la piel de gallina.
I have tengo
I hope that . . . Ojalá que...
I like me gusta(n)
I would like ... Quisiera/ Me gustaría...
I'm sorry (to hear that) lo siento
ice cream el helado
ice el hielo
if si
ill person el/la enfermo/a
illiteracy el analfabetismo
illiterate analfabeto/a
illness la enfermedad
immediately enseguida
immigrant el/la inmigrante
immigration la inmigración
to improve mejorar
in addition además
in contrast . . . en contraste...
in en
in fact en realidad, realmente
in front of enfrente (de)
in order (to) para
in search of en busca de
in the rear al fondo
inappropriate inapropiado/a
including hasta
inexpensive barato/a
infection la infección
to influence influir
infrastructure la infraestructura
inhabitant el/la habitante
injection la inyección
to insert meter
to inspect revisar
instead of en vez de
integrated circuit el chip electrónico
to interest interesar
interesting interesante
interpreter el/la intérprete
to interrupt interrumpir
to interview (each other) entrevistar(se)
interview la entrevista
introduction la presentación
to invest invertir
invitation la invitación
to invite invitar
iron el hierro
to iron planchar
isn't it? ¿no?
it has been a day/month/year since hace un día/mes/año (que)
It is (time of the day). Es la/Son las (hora del día).
it's clear está despejado
it's cloudy está nublado
it's cool hace fresco
it's raining llueve, está lloviendo
it's sunny hace sol
it's windy hace viento
It's been (time expression) since... Hace (+ expresión de tiempo) que... **4**
its su(s)

J

jacket el saco, la chaqueta
January enero
Japanese japonés/japonesa
jeans los vaqueros/jeans
jewel la joya
jeweller el/la joyero/a
job el trabajo
jogging suit la sudadera
journalist el/la periodista
joy la alegría
judge el/la juez
to juggle hacer malabarismo
juice el jugo
July julio
June junio
junk food la comida basura

K

to keep in shape estar en forma, mantenerse en forma
to keep silent guardar silencio
key card la tarjeta magnética
key la llave; la clave
to kill matar
kindless la amabilidad
kindly atentamente
kinship el parentesco
to kiss besar(se)
kiss el beso
kitchen la cocina
kitchen sink el fregadero
kite la cometa
knee la rodilla
knife el cuchillo
to know (each other) conocer(se)
to know conocer; saber
knowledge el conocimiento

L

lake el lago
lamb el cordero
lamp la lámpara
to land aterrizar
land el terreno (terrain); la tierra (ground, soil)
landscape el paisaje
laptop la computadora portátil
last último/a
to last durar
last night anoche
last week la semana pasada
last year/month el año/mes pasado
last último/a; por último
late tarde
later después, luego, más tarde
to laugh reír
laundry room la lavandería
law derecho
lawn el césped
lawyer el/la abogado/a
layout la distribución
lazy perezoso/a
leaf la hoja
to learn aprender
leather el cuero
to leave dejar; irse
to leave something behind quedar
leavetaking la despedida
left la izquierda
leg la pierna
legumes las legumbres
lemon el limón
to lend prestar
Lent la Cuaresma
lentils las lentejas
less . . . than menos... que
lettuce la lechuga
level el nivel
librarian el/la bibliotecario/a
library la biblioteca
license plate la placa
to lie down acostarse
life expectancy la esperanza de vida
life la vida
to lift weights levantar pesas
light(s) la luz (las luces)
to like gustar; caer bien
Likewise. Igualmente.
line (in a poem) el verso
link el enlace
lip el labio
to listen (to) escuchar; oír
Listen, please. Oiga, por favor.
literacy el alfabetismo
literature la literatura
lithium el litio
live en vivo
to live vivir
lively animado/a, vivo/a
living room la sala
lobby la planta baja
lobster la langosta

location la ubicación
to lock up encerrar
locker room el vestuario
lodging el alojamiento
long largo/a
to look at mirar
to look for buscar
to look inside asomarse
to look terrible tener mala cara
to look ver(se)
to lose perder
to lose weight bajar de peso
loss la pérdida
Louder, please. Más alto, por favor.
love el amor
to love querer; encantar
luggage el equipaje
lunch el almuerzo
lung el pulmón
luxury el lujo

M

magazine la revista
mail la correspondencia
main character el personaje principal
to maintain mantener
major la carrera
majority la mayoría
to make a reservation reservar
to make the bed hacer la cama
mallow la malva
man el hombre
manager, (sales) manager el/la gerente (de ventas)
many (adj.) mucho/a
many times muchas veces
map el mapa
March marzo
margarine la margarina
marked down rebajado/a
marker el marcador/el rotulador
market el mercado
marriage el matrimonio
married casado/a
marvelous maravilloso/a
marvelously estupendamente
material el material
May mayo
mayonnaise la mayonesa
meal la comida
meat la carne
medical doctor el/la médico/a
medication la pastilla
medicine el remedio; la medicina
medium height de estatura mediana
to meet conocer; **(each other)** conocer(se)
to meet (requirements) cumplir (requisites)
meeting la reunión
melody la melodía
melon el melón
melted derretido/a
memory el recuerdo
mess el desorden
message el mensaje
Mexican Independence Day el Día de la Independencia de México
Mexican mexicano/a
microsurgery le microcirugía
microwave (oven) el (horno de) microondas
middle class person el burgués/la burguesa
migration la migración
milk la leche
million millón
mine mi(s)
minority la minoría
minute el minuto
mirror el espejo
to miss extrañar
to miss out on perderse
mobile el móvil barato/a
mom la mamá
mommy la mami/mamita
Monday lunes
money el dinero
money (in cash) el dinero (en efectivo)
month el mes
mood el ánimo
more . . . than más... que
more or less más o menos
More slowly, please. Más despacio/lento, por favor.
more than más de
morning la mañana
Moroccan marroquí
mortality la mortalidad
most (+ adj.) más (+ adj.)
mother la madre
Mother's Day el Día de la Madre
motor el motor
mouth la boca
to move mover(se); mudarse
movement el desplazamiento
movie la película
movies el cine
to mow (lawn) cortar
Mr. el señor (Sr.)
Ms, Miss la señorita (Srta.)
Ms., Mrs. la señora (Sra.)
much mucho/a
multilingual políglota
mural el mural
muralist el/la muralista
muscle el músculo
music la música
mustard la mostaza
my mi(s)
My heart sank. Se me fue el alma a los pies.
My name is... Me llamo...

N

nacho cheese sauce la salsa con queso
napkin la servilleta
narrow estrecho/a
nation el país
nationality la nacionalidad
native natal
nature la naturaleza
nature preserve la reserva natural
near cerca de
necessary necesario/a
neck el cuello
necklace el collar
to need necesitar
neglect el descuido
neighbor el/la vecino/a
neighborhood el barrio
neither . . . nor ni... ni
neither, not tampoco
nephew el sobrino
nerve el nervio
nervous nervioso/a
net la red
never (not ever) jamás, nunca
nevertheless sin embargo
new nuevo/a
New Year's Day el Año Nuevo
New Year's Eve la Nochevieja
news la noticia
newspaper el periódico
next month/year el próximo mes/año
next próximo/a
next to al lado (de)
next week la próxima semana
Nicaraguan nicaragüense
nice agradable, simpático/a
Nice to meet you. Mucho gusto.
nickname el sobrenombre
niece la sobrina
Nigerian nigeriano/a
nightgown el camisón
nightmare la pesadilla
ninth noveno
no one nadie
no, not any, none ningún, ninguno/a
nobody nadie
noise el ruido
to nominate nominar
non-profit sin fines de lucro
North American norteamericano/a

nose la nariz
note card la ficha
notebook el cuaderno
nothing nada
novel la novela
novelist el/la novelista
November noviembre
now ahora
nowadays hoy en día
nurse el/la enfermero/a

O

to occur ocurrir
October octubre
of de
of African ancestry moreno/a, negro/a
of course por supuesto
Of course! ¡Cómo no!/¡Claro!
of dark skin moreno/a, negro/a
of lightbrown skin color trigueño/a
of the (contraction of de + el**)** del
to offer ofrecer
office (of doctor, dentist, etc.) el consultorio
office la oficina
often frecuentemente
oil el aceite
old antiguo/a
old mayor; viejo/a
older than mayor que
olive la aceituna
on sobre
on the dot (time) en punto
On the one hand . . . Por un lado...
On the other hand . . . En cambio/Por otro lado...
On what page? ¿En qué página?
once una vez
onion la cebolla
only child el hijo único/la hija única
only solo
to open abrir
opening la vacante
opposing contrario/a
orange (adj.) anaranjado/a, naranja; **(noun)** la naranja
orchestra la orquesta
to order around dar órdenes
to order pedir
origen el comienzo
other otro/a
our nuestro(s), nuestra(s)
outdoors al aire libre
outgoing extrovertido/a
outing la excursión
outskirts las afueras
outstanding destacado/a
overcast (sky) cubierto
own propio/a
ozone layer la capa de ozono

P

P.M. (from nightfall to midnight) de la noche
P.M. (from noon to nightfall) de la tarde
paid remunerado/a
pain el dolor
to paint pintar
painter el/la pintor/a
painting el cuadro
painting la pintura
pajamas el/la piyama, el pijama *(Spain)*
Panamanian panameño/a
pants los pantalones
pantsuit el traje pantalón
pantyhose las pantimedias
papaya la papaya
parade el desfile
Paraguayan paraguayo/a
pardon me perdón; con permiso
parents los padres
parsley el perejil
to participate participar
partner el/la compañero/a
party la fiesta
passenger el/la pasajero/a
passion fruit el maracuyá *(Colom.)*, la fruta de la pasión *(Spain)*, la parchita *(Venez., Mex.)*
passport el pasaporte
pastry el pastel
patient el/la paciente
patrotic patriótico/a
to pay (for) pagar
peach el melocotón *(Spain)*, el durazno *(Latin America)*
peak el pico
pear la pera
peasant el/la campesino/a
pedestrian area la zona peatonal
to peel pelar
penalty (in sports) el penalti
pencil el lápiz
people la gente, las personas
pepper la pimienta; **(hot, spicy)** el chile/ají **(vegetable)** el pimiento
per por
percent por ciento
percentage el porcentaje
percibido/a noticed
perfect perfecto/a
performance el rendimiento
performer, artist el/la intérprete
person la persona
Peruvian peruano/a
petroleum el petróleo
pharmacist el/la farmacéutico/a
pharmacy la farmacia
photo(graph) la foto(grafía)
to pick up recoger
picture el cuadro
piece of jewelry la joya
pilgrim el/la peregrino/a
pill la pastilla
pillow la almohada
pin el alfiler
pineapple la piña
pink rosado/a, rosa
place el lugar
plaid de cuadros
to plan to + verb pensar + *infinitive*
plane el avión
planet el planeta
plantain el plátano/la banana
plate el plato
to play (a game, sport) jugar
to play (an instrument) tocar (un instrumento)
player el/la jugador/a
Please answer. Contesten, por favor./Contesta, por favor.
please por favor
Pleased/Nice to meet you. Encantado/a.
plumber el/la plomero/a, el/la fontanero/a *(Spain)*
poem el poema
poet el/la poeta
poetry la poesía
point of view el punto de vista
policeman/woman el/la policía
Polish polaco/a
political science las ciencias políticas
polyglot el/la políglota
pool la piscina, la pileta
poor pobre
popcorn las palomitas de maíz
to popularize popularizar
population la población
pork el cerdo, el puerco
to portray retratar
Portuguese portugués/portuguesa
position el puesto; la posición
potato la papa
poultry las aves
poverty la pobreza
power outage el apagón
to practice practicar
to precede preceder
to prefer preferir
preparation el preparativo
to prepare preparar
to prescribe recetar
prescription la receta

present actual
present el regalo
preservation la conservación
president el/la presidente/a
pressure (blood) la tensión/la presión (arterial)
pretty bonito/a, linda, guapa
price el precio
printer la impresora
prize el premio
procession la procesión
to produce producir
professor el/la profesor/a
promising prometedor/a
to promote promover
to propose proponer
to protest protestar
proverb el refrán
provided that con tal (de) que
proximity la proximidad
psychologist el/la sicólogo/a
psychology la psicología
Puerto Rican puertorriqueño/a
purple morado/a
purpose el propósito
purse la bolsa/el bolso
to put poner
to put makeup on (someone); to put makeup on (oneself) maquillar(se)
to put one's clothes on ponerse la ropa
to put to bed acostar

Q

quality la calidad
quiet callado/a

R

race la carrera
racquet la raqueta
radiator el radiador
radio announcer el/la locutor/a
radio el/la radio
rail el riel
rain forest el bosque tropical
rain la lluvia
to rain llover
raincoat el impermeable
to raise levantar
Raise your hand. Levanta la mano.
ranch la finca
rate la tasa
rather bastante
to reach out to comunicarse con
to read leer
Read. Lee.
ready listo/a
to realize darse cuenta
really en realidad, realmente
rearview mirror el espejo retrovisor
reason la razón
rebirth el renacimiento
recipe la receta
recognition el reconocimiento
to recommend recomendar
to record grabar
recycled reciclado/a
red bell pepper el pimiento rojo
red rojo/a
redhead pelirrojo/a
to reduce reducir
referee el árbitro
to reflect reflejar
to reforest repoblar
refrigerator el refrigerador
refrigerator el refrigerador/la nevera/heladera
regime el régimen
to regret arrepentirse
relative el/la pariente
relief el alivio
remedy el remedio
to remember recordar
to rent alquilar
rent el alquiler
Repeat. Repite./Repitan.
to repeat repetir
report el informe
to request pedir
to request the floor pedir la palabra
resort el centro turístico privado
resources los recursos
to respond responder
to rest descansar
résumé el currículum
to retire jubilarse
to return an item devolver
to return volver
rib la costilla
rice el arroz
rich rico/a
to ride (a bicycle) montar (en bicicleta)
right el derecho; la derecha
to be right tener razón
right? ¿verdad?
ring el anillo
roasted asado/a
robe la bata
robot el robot
room el cuarto
roommate el/la compañero/a de cuarto
round trip de ida y vuelta
rug la alfombra
ruins las ruinas
ruler el/la gobernante
to run correr
to run into encontrarse
to run out of acabarse

S

sad triste
safe la caja fuerte
salad dressing el aderezo
salad la ensalada
salary el sueldo
sale la rebaja
sales las ventas
salesman, saleswoman el/la vendedor/a
salesperson el dependiente/la dependienta
salt la sal
Salvadoran salvadoreño/a
same mismo/a
sand dune el médano
sandals las sandalias
sandwich el sándwich
satellite el satélite
Saturday sábado
to save ahorrar
sawdust el aserrín
to say decir
to say goodbye despedirse
to say hello mandar saludos
scarf la bufanda
scene la escena
scholarship la beca
school of fish el banco de peces
school, department la facultad
science fiction la ciencia ficción
sciences las ciencias
scientist el/la científico/a
to score a goal meter un gol
scoreboard el marcador
screen la pantalla
sculptor el/la escultor/a
sea el mar
seafood los mariscos
seamstress la costurera
search engine el buscador
season la estación
seasoning el condimento
seat el asiento
second floor el primer piso; la primera planta
second segundo
security la seguridad
to see ver
see you later hasta luego
see you soon hasta pronto
see you tomorrow hasta mañana
seed la semilla
to seem parecer
self-portrait el autorretrato

to sell vender
to send enviar, mandar
September septiembre
serious (situation) grave; serio/a
seriously ill grave
to serve servir
server el/la camarero/a
to set the table poner la mesa
setting el ambiente
seventh séptimo/a
several algún, alguno (-os, -as)
sewage las aguas residuales
shake el batido
shame la lástima
shape la forma
to share compartir
shark el tiburón
sharp (time) en punto
to shave; to shave (oneself) afeitar(se)
she ella
sheep la oveja
sheet la sábana
shell la concha
shellfish los mariscos
ship/boat el barco
shirt la camisa
shoal el banco de peces
shoes los zapatos
to shop ir de compras
shopping center el centro comercial
shopping las compras
short (in length) corto/a
short (in stature) bajo/a
short sleeve shirt camisa de manga corta
shortly after poco después
shorts los pantalones cortos
should deber
shoulder el hombro
to show mostrar
to show a movie poner una película
shower la ducha
shrimp el camarón, la gamba *(Spain)*
to shut in encerrar
shy tímido/a
sick enfermo/a
signal la señal
silly tonto/a
silver la plata
similar parecido/a
since desde; ya que
to sing cantar
single room la habitación sencilla
single soltero/a
sister la hermana
to sit down sentarse
sixth sexto/a
size el tamaño **(clothes)** la talla; **(shoes)** el número
to skate patinar
to ski esquiar
skiing, ski el esquí
skin la piel
skirt la falda, pollera *(Arg., Urug.)*
sky el cielo
to sleep dormir
slice la rebanada
slippers las zapatillas
slope la bajada; la pista
sloth el perezoso (Zool.)
small pequeño/a
smallpox la viruela
smart listo/a
to smoke fumar
smothie el batido
snack la merienda
to sneeze estornudar
snow la nieve
to snow nevar
so that para que
soap el jabón
soccer el fútbol
soccer field el campo de fútbol
social networks las redes sociales
sociology la sociología
socks los calcetines, las medias
soda el refresco
sofa el sofá
soft blando/a; suave
soft drink el refresco
soil la tierra
solar energy la energía solar
solid de color entero
some algún, alguno (-os, -as)
some unos/as
someone alguien
something algo
sometime alguna vez
sometimes a veces, algunas veces
son el hijo
song la canción
sought after codiciado/a
soup la sopa
sour agrio/a
source la fuente
source of income la fuente de ingresos
souvenirs los recuerdos
spaghetti los espaguetis, tallarines
Spanish español/a; el español
to speak hablar
specialty la especialidad
speech el discurso
speed la velocidad
to spend gastar; **(time)** pasar
spices las especias
spicy picante
spinach las espinacas
to sponsor patrocinar
spoon la cuchara
spoonful la cucharada
sport el deporte
sportsman, sportswoman el/la deportista
to spray rociar
to spread difundir
spring la primavera
to sprinkle rociar
square la plaza
square meter el metro cuadrado
stadium el estadio
stairs la escalera
to stand in line hacer cola
to stand out destacarse
star la estrella
to start comenzar, empezar
statistics la estadística
to stay quedarse
to stay in touch mantenerse en contacto
steak el bistec, la carne de res
steering wheel el volante
stem cell la célula troncal
step el paso
stepbrother el hermanastro
stepfather el padrastro
stepmother la madrastra
stepsister la hermanastra
still todavía
stockings las medias
stomach el estómago
stopover la escala
store la tienda
store window el escaparate
story el cuento
stove la estufa, la cocina
strawberry la fresa
street la calle
to strenghten fortalecer
stretch el tramo
stripes de rayas
stroke la campanada
to stroll pasear
strong fuerte
student el/la estudiante, alumno/a
studious estudioso/a
to study estudiar
to stumble tropezarse
style el estilo
stylish de moda
subject la materia, la asignatura
subway el metro
success el éxito
sugar el azúcar
to suggest sugerir
suit el traje

suit el traje de chaqueta
suitcase la maleta
summer el verano
to sunbathe tomar el sol
Sunday domingo
sunglasses las gafas de sol
supermarket el supermercado
supper la cena, la comida
to support apoyar; sustentar
to surf hacer surf
surprise la sorpresa
surrealist surrealista
to surround rodear
to survive sobrevivir
sweater el suéter
sweatshirt la sudadera
to sweep barrer
swelling la hinchazón
to swim nadar
swimming la natación
swimming pool la piscina
swollen hinchado/a
symbol el símbolo
symptom el síntoma

T

table la mesa
tablecloth el mantel
tablet la tableta
to take a bath bañarse
to take a nap dormir la siesta
to take a seat tomar asiento
to take a shower ducharse
to take a walk dar una vuelta; pasear
to take advantage aprovechar
to take away quitar
to take care of cuidar(se) (de)
to take llevar
to take note fijar(se)
to take notes tomar apuntes/notas
to take off (airplane) despegar
to take off quitarse
to take out sacar
to take tomar
to take turns turnarse
Take turns Túrnense.
Talk (about ...) Hablen (sobre...)
to talk conversar
talkative conversador/a
tall alto/a
to taste probar
tea el té
teacher el/la profesor/a
team el equipo
to tear romper
teaspoon la cucharita
technician el/la técnico/a
telephone el teléfono
television set el televisor
to tell decir; contar
Tell your partner ... Dile a tu compañero/a...
tenfold el décuplo
tennis el tenis
tennis player el/la tenista
tennis shoes las zapatillas de deporte
tent la tienda
tenth décimo/a
test el análisis; el examen
to exhibit exponer
textile industry industria textil
Thank goodness! ¡Gracias a Dios!
thanks gracias
Thanksgiving Day el Día de Acción de Gracias
that (adjective) ese/a
that (over there) aquel/aquella/aquello
that ese/esa/eso
That's so interesting! ¡Qué interesante!
That's unbelievable! ¡Qué increíble!
thaw, thawing el deshielo
the (singular) el/la; **(plural)** los/las
the best el/la mejor
the day after tomorrow pasado mañana
the day before yesterday anteayer
the important thing lo importante
the most el/la... más
the night before last ante(a)noche
the oldest el/la mayor
the same lo mismo
The screen froze up on me. Se me congeló la pantalla.
The weather is good/bad. Hace buen/mal tiempo.
the youngest el/la menor
theater el teatro
their su(s)
theme el tema
themselves a sí mismo/a(s)
then entonces, luego
there is, there are hay
thermometer el termómetro
these estos/estas
they ellos/ellas
thief el/la ladrón/a
thin delgado/a
thing la cosa
things you own las pertenencias
to think parecer; **(about)** pensar (en)
third tercero/la, tercer
this este/esta/esto
those esos/esas
those (over there) aquellos/aquellas
thousand mil
throat la garganta
through a través de; por
to throw lanzar
Thursday jueves
ticket el boleto, el pasaje, el billete *(Spain)*
tidy ordenado/a
to tidy up ordenar
tie la corbata
tight estrecho/a
tire la llanta
tired cansado/a
to a; para
to the al (*contraction of* **a** + **el**)
toast el pan tostado, la tostada
today hoy
Today is (day of the week.) Hoy es (día de la semana).
together juntos/as
toilet el inodoro
tomato el tomate
tomato sauce la salsa de tomate
tomorrow mañana
tonight esta noche
too también
tooth el diente
toothpaste la pasta de dientes
topic el tema
tourist class la clase turista
tournament el campeonato, el torneo
towards para
towel la toalla
toy el juguete
to turn doblar
track and field el atletismo
track la pista
tradition la tradición
train el tren
to train prepararse
trait el rasgo
to translate traducir
trash la basura
travel agency la agencia de viajes
travel agent el/la agente de viajes
to travel viajar; recorrer
traveller el/la viajero/a
tray la bandeja
to treat tratar
treaty el tratado
tree el árbol
to tremble estremecerse
trip la excursión
trip el viaje
true cierto/a
trunk el maletero, el baúl
trust la confianza
trustworthy confiable

to try on probarse
to try tratar; probar
T-shirt la camiseta
Tuesday martes
turkey el pavo, el guajolote *(Mex.)*
to turn in entregar
to turn off apagar
to turn on encender; (the TV) poner
twice dos veces
twin gemelo/a
to twist torcer(se)
typical típico/a

U

U.S. citizen estadounidense
UFO el OVNI
ugly feo/a
umbrella el paraguas
umpire el árbitro
uncle el tío
to uncover destapar
under bajo; debajo (de)
to underline subrayar
to understand comprender, entender
underwear la ropa interior
unemployment el desempleo
unforgettable inolvidable
to unify unificar
university la universidad
unless a menos que
unmarried soltero/a
unpleasant antipático/a
unripe verde
until hasta(que)
to upload subir
urgent urgente
Uruguayan uruguayo/a
to use usar
useful útil

V

vacation las vacaciones
vacuum cleaner la aspiradora
to vacuum pasar la aspiradora
Valentine's Day el Día de los Enamorados/del Amor y la Amistad
vanilla la vainilla
vegetable el vegetal, la verdura
vein la vena
Venezuelan venezolano/a
verb el verbo
very muy
vet el/la veterinario/a
video game el videojuego
view la vista
village el pueblo
vinegar el vinagre
virtual library la biblioteca virtual
virtually virtualmente
to visit visitar
voice la voz
volleyball el vóleibol/volibol
to vote votar

W

wage el sueldo
wagon la carreta
waist la cintura
to wait for esperar
waiter/waitress el/la camarero/a
waiting room la sala de espera
to wake up despertarse
to wake someone up despertar
to walk caminar
wallet la billetera
to want querer, desear
warehouse el almacén
warming el calentamiento
warm-up el calentamiento
to wash (oneself) lavar(se)
washer la lavadora
waste los desperdicios
wastebasket el cesto
water el agua
to water regar
wave la ola
We hope that . . . Ojalá que...
we nosotros/as
weak débil
wealthy rico/a
to wear a costume disfrazarse
to wear a shoe size calzar
to wear llevar
weather el tiempo
weather forecast el pronóstico del tiempo
wedding la boda
Wednesday miércoles
week la semana
weekend el fin de semana
weight la pesa
well bien
well parked bien aparcado
wet mojado/a
What a coincidence! ¡Qué casualidad!
What a nuisance! ¡Qué lata!
What a pity! ¡Qué lástima!
What day is today? ¿Qué día es hoy?
What do you think? ¿qué te parece?
What for? ¿para qué?
What is he/she/it like? ¿Cómo es?
What is the date today? ¿Qué fecha es hoy?/¿Cuál es la fecha?
What time is it? ¿Qué hora es?
What? ¿Qué?; ¿Cómo?; ¿Perdón?
What's the weather like? ¿Qué tiempo hace?
What's up? What's new? (informal) ¿Qué tal?
What's your name? (familiar) ¿Cómo te llamas?
What's your name? (formal) ¿Cómo se llama usted?
What's wrong (with you/them)? ¿Qué te/le(s) pasa?
wheat el trigo
wheel la rueda
when cuando
When? ¿Cuándo?
Where (to)? ¿Adónde?
Where is ... ? ¿Dónde está...?
where, wherever donde
Where? ¿Dónde?
Which? ¿Cuál(es)?
while mientras
to whistle pitar
white blanco/a
Who is . . .? ¿Quién es...?
Who? Quién(es)?
whose? ¿De ¿quién?
why por qué
Why? ¿Para qué?; ¿Por qué?
wide ancho/a
widower viudo/a
wife la esposa, la mujer *(Spain)*
wild silvestre
to win ganar
wind el viento
window la ventana
window seat el asiento de ventanilla
windshield el parabrisas
windshield wiper el limpiaparabrisas
wine el vino
wing el ala
winter el invierno
to wish desear; esperar; querer
with con
with me conmigo
with much love con mucho cariño
With pleasure./Gladly. Con mucho gusto.
with them con ellos/ellas
with whom con quien
with you (familiar) contigo
without sin(que)
without us sin nosotros/as
woman la mujer
wood la madera
word la palabra

work el trabajo; la obra
to work trabajar; funcionar
worker el/la obrero/a; el/la trabajador/a
workforce la fuerza laboral
workshop el taller
to worship venerar
wound la herida
wrist la muñeca
to write escribir
to write to each other escribirse
Write. Escribe.
writer el/la escritor/a

Y

year el año
yellow amarillo/a
yes sí
yesterday ayer
yet todavía
yogurt el yogur
you (familiar) like te gusta(n)
you (familiar) tú; **(plural)** vosotros/as *(Spain)*
you (formal) like le gusta(n)
you (formal) usted; **(plural)** ustedes
you are (familiar) eres; estás
you are (formal) es; está
you have (familiar) tienes
you're welcome de nada
young joven
young man/woman el/la joven
your (familiar plural) vuestro(s), vuestra(s)
your (familiar) tu(s)
your (formal) su(s)
Yours, sincerely. Un cordial saludo.

Text & Photo Credits

Text Credits

Capítulo 13

p. 453: Gabriela Mistral, "Dame la mano." La Orden Franciscana de Chile autoriza el uso de la obra de Gabriela Mistral. Lo equivalente a los derechos de autoría es entregado a la Orden Franciscana de Chile, para los niños de Montegrande y de Chile, de conformidad a la voluntad testamentaria de Gabriela Mistral; **p. 475:** Gloria Fuertes, "Las Cosas" by Gloria Fuertes from OBRAS INCOMPLETAS, Cátedra, 2006. Used by permission of Fundación Gloria Fuertes

Capítulo 14

p. 506: "La mosca que soñaba que era un aguila" by Augusto Monterroso from EL PARAÍSO IMPERFECTO: ANTOLOGÍA TÍMIDA. Debolsillo, 2013. Used by permission of International Editors Company, S. L.

Photo Credits

Front Matter

p. ix: adimas/fotolia; **p. x:** LUIS ACOSTA/AFP/ Getty Images; **p. xi:** Monkey Business Images/ Shutterstock/Dorling Kindersley, Ltd.; **p. xiii(t):** Marcos Brindicci/Reuters/Corbis; **p. xiii(b):** Eduardo Rivero/Shutterstock; **p. xiv(r):** Christian Kieffer/Shutterstock ; **p. xiv(l):** Skylines/ Shutterstock; **p. xv:** Andresr/Shutterstock; **p. xvi:** Nik Niklz/Shutterstock; **p. xvii:** Jose Luis Stephens/Alamy; **p. xiii:** Fotolia; **p. xxiii(l):** Fotolia; **p. xxiii:** Fotolia; **p. xviii:** Imagery-Majestic/Shutterstock; **p. xxxvi(b):** Elizabeth E. Guzman; **p. xxxvi:** Judith Liskin-Gasparro

Capítulo Preliminar

p. 2: Contrastwerkstatt / Fotolia; **p. 3:** Jeff Greenberg / Alamy; **p. 4(tl):** Mikesch112 / Fotolia; **p. 4(tr):** Atm2003 / Fotolia; **p. 4(c):** Joan Albert Lluch / Fotolia; **p. 4(bl):** BlueOrange Studio / Fotolia; **p. 5:** Zurijeta / Shutterstock; **p. 6(t):** Michael Jung / Fotolia; **p. 7(tl):** Ian O'Leary /Getty Images; **p. 7(tc):** Dorling Kindersley, Ltd; **p. 7(bl):** Shutterstock; **p. 8(tr):** Mike Good / Dorling Kindersley, Ltd; **p. 9(bl):** Bonga1965 / Fotolia; **p. 10-11(tl):** Priganica / Fotolia; **p. 11(br):** Brenda Carson / Fotolia; **p. 13(tc):** Alexmillos / Fotolia; **p. 14(bl):** Vannphoto / Fotolia; **p. 14(b):** Vmelinda/fotolia; **p. 16(b):** Diego Cervo / Fotolia; **p. 18(tl):** Pedrosala / Fotolia; **p. 18(cr):** Alex Havret / DK Images; **p. 18(bc):** StockLite / Shutterstock; **p. 20:** Runzelkorn / Fotolia; **p. 22(b):** Chokniti / Fotolia; **p. 23(tr):** Scanrail / Fotolia; **p. 23(b):** Petr Vaclavek / Fotolia; **p. 24(cl):** Adimas / Fotolia; **p. 24(bl):** Brad Pict / Fotolia; **p. 25(tl):** Faraways / Fotolia; **p. 25(tr):** Paul Bricknell / Dorling Kindersley, Ltd; **p. 25(c):** Barone Rosso / Fotolia; **p. 25(bl):** Andy Crawford / Dorling Kindersley, Ltd; **p. 25(br):** Tim Ridley / Dorling Kindersley, Ltd; **p. 26(b):** Silkstock / Fotolia; **p. 27(cr):** Igor Mojzes / Fotolia;

Capítulo 1

p. 30(cr): Yuraliaits Albert / Shutterstock; **p. 31(c):** Matt Trommer / Shutterstock; **p. 31(cr):** Pilar Echevarria / Shutterstock; **p. 31(tc):** Dorota Jarymowicz and Mariusz Ja / DK Images; **p. 31(c):** Rafael Ramirez Lee / Shutterstock; **p. 31(tl):** Carlos Nieto / Age Fotostock / Robert Harding; **p. 31(bl):** Album / Prisma / Newscom; **p. 32(tl):** Akulamatiau / Fotolia; **p. 32(bl):** Aleksandar Todorovic / Fotolia; **p. 32(cr):** Travelwitness / Fotolia; **p. 32(cl):** Mrks V / Fotolia; **p. 33(cr):** Andresr / Shutterstock; **p. 33(bl):** Pkchai / Shutterstock; **p. 34(br):** Andres Rodriguez; **p. 35(tr):** Jenkedco /Shutterstock; **p. 36:** Roman Sigaev / Fotolia; **p. 38(br):** Hemeroskopion / Fotolia; **p. 39:** Santiago Pais / Fotolia; **p. 40(b):** Tim Draper / Dorling Kindersley,Ltd; **p. 41(tr):** Pearson Education Ltd; **p. 41(br):** Yakor / Fotolia; **p. 41(cl):** Fxegs / Fotolia; **p. 47(cl):** Aaron Amat / Fotolia; **p. 47(br):** Hill Street Studios / Blend Images/Alamy; **p. 48(tr):** JHershPhoto / Shutterstock; **p. 49(tr):** Mimohe / Fotolia; **p. 55(tc):** Spencer Grant / PhotoEdit; **p. 56:** Auremar / Fotolia; **p. 57(tr):** Gabriel Blaj / Fotolia LLC; **p. 62:** Dmitriy Shironosov / Shutterstock;

Capítulo 2

p. 64(cr): Andres Rodriguez / Fotolia; **p. 65(l):** Everett Collection Inc / Alamy; **p. 65(l):** Everett Collection Inc / Alamy; **p. 65(tc):** April Turner / Shutterstock; **p. 65(bc):** Robin Holden Sr / Shutterstock; **p. 65(cr):** Hola Images / Alamy; **p. 65(tr):** EPA / Alamy; **p. 65(c):** Gvictoria / Shutterstock; **p. 65(br):** Images / Alamy; **p. 66(tc):** Alessandra Santarell i/ Jeoff Davis / Dorling Kindersley,Ltd; **p. 66(cr):** Everett Collection Inc / Alamy; **p. 66(bl):** Henryk Sadura / Fotolia; **p. 66(br):** ZUMA Press, Inc. / Alamy; **p. 67(tl):** Andres Rodriguez / Fotolia; **p. 67(tc):** Samuel Borges / Fotolia; **p. 67(tr):** Mel Lindstrom / Mira; **p. 67(l):** Mangostock / Fotolia; **p. 67(br):** Andresr / Shutterstock; **p. 68(br):** Avava / Fotolia; **p. 71(cl):** Wallenrock / Shutterstock; **p. 71(cl):** Dallas Events Inc / Shutterstock; **p. 71(c):** Michaeljung / Fotolia; **p. 71(cr):** Shutterstock; **p. 71(b):** Wong Sze Fei / Fotolia; **p. 72(tl):** EPA / Alamy; **p. 72(tr):** EPA / Alamy; **p. 73(bl):** Greg Roden / Dorling Kindersley,Ltd; **p. 74(tr):** Berc / Fotolia; **p. 75(br):** Max / Fotolia; **p. 75(tl):** Igorigorevich / Fotolia; **p. 75(tr):** Dgmata / Fotolia; **p. 77(br):** Shutterstock; **p. 78(tr):** WavebreakMediaMicro / Fotolia; **p. 78(bl):** Michael Germana / Landov; **p. 78(bc):** Front Row Photos; **p. 78(b):** Taylor Jones / The Palm Beach Post / Zumapress / Alamy; **p. 78(br):** Ramon Espinosa / AP Images; **p. 78(cl):** Max Alexander / DK Images; **p. 80(tr):** AP Images; **p. 81** Tyler Olson / Shutterstock; **p. 86(tr):** Dwphotos / Shutterstock; **p. 87(tr):** Andresr / Shutterstock; **p. 89(tl):** Andres Rodriguez / Fotolia; **p. 89(cl):** ArchMen / Fotolia; **p. 90(tl):** Andres Rodriguez / Fotolia LLC; **p. 91(br):** Andres Rodriguez / Fotolia LLC; **p. 92(tr):** Skylines / Shutterstock; **p. 94(br):** Shutterstock; **p. 95(tc):** Alliance Images / Alamy; **p. 96(br):** Scanrail / Fotolia; **p. 97** Andresr / Shutterstock; **p. 98** Leonidovich / Shutterstock;

Capítulo 3

p. 100(cr): Auremar / Fotolia; **p. 101(tl):** Suzanne Porter / Dorling Kindersley, Ltd; **p. 101(cl):** Mike Von Bergen / Shutterstock; **p. 101(cr):** Shutterstock; **p. 101(bl):** Mireille Vautier / Alamy; **p. 102(tl):** Ocphoto / Shutterstock; **p. 102(cl):** Bob Krist / Corbis; **p. 102(bl):** Richard Smith / Corbis; **p. 102(cr):** Silvia Izquierdo/Reuters/Corbis; **p. 103(tl):** Creatas / Thinkstock; **p. 103(tl):** Tim Draper / Rough Guides / DK Images; **p. 103(tc):** iStockphoto / Thinkstock; **p. 103(tr):** Mangostock / Fotolia; **p. 104** Travel Pictures / Alamy; **p. 105(cr):** Luis Santos /shutterstock; **p. 105(tr):** Giuseppe_R / Shutterstock; **p. 105(br):** Goodluz / Fotolia; **p. 106** Grant Hindsley / AP images; **p. 107(br):** Subbotina Anna / Shutterstock; **p. 107(tl):** Jennifer Boggs / Amy Paliwoda / Alamy; **p. 107(bl):** Cameron Whitman / Shutterstock; **p. 107(tr):** Dinner, Allison / the food passionates /Corbis; **p. 108** Jeff Greenberg / Alamy; **p. 109(bc):** John Van Hasselt / Sygma / Corbis; **p. 110(tr):** karelnoppe / Fotolia; **p. 110(cl):** Segismundo Trivero / Fotolia; **p. 110(br):** Jeff Greenberg / Alamy; **p. 113(br):** James Thew / Fotolia; **p. 115(br):** Kitch Bain / Shutterstock; **p. 116(bl):** Fotolia; **p. 116(bc):** Aaron Oberlander / Getty Images; **p. 116(br):** Oscar Pinto Sanchez; **p. 116(br):** Jeff Greenberg / Alamy; **p. 117(br):** Elenathewise / Fotolia; **p. 122** Germanskydive110 / Fotolia; **p. 124** Zuma Press, Inc / Alamy; **p. 125(t):** Robert Lerich / Fotolia; **p. 125(b):** Neale Cousland / Shutterstock; **p. 134** iPics / Fotolia;

Capítulo 4

p. 136(cr): Andres Rodriguez / Fotolia; **p. 137(tc):** Amra Pasic / Shutterstock; **p. 137(cr):** Pies Specifics / Alamy; **p. 137(cl):** Archivo el Tiempo / El Tiempo de Colombia / Newscom; **p. 137(cr):** Richard Gunion / Thinkstock / Getty Images; **p. 137(bl):** Galyna Andrushko / Shutterstock; **p. 137(br):** Marlborough Gallery; **p. 138(tl):** Luis Acosta / AFP / Getty Images; **p. 138(bl):** Fotolia; **p. 138(tr):** Rodrigo Arangua / AFP / Getty Images / Newscom; **p. 138(br):** Jenny Leonard / Shutterstock; **p. 139(tl):** Paloma Lapuerta; **p. 139(tr):** bst2012 / Fotolia; **p. 139(br):** Blend Images / Shutterstock; **p. 139(bl):** Ton Koene / Horizons WWP / Alamy; **p. 141(b):** JackF / Fotolia; **p. 142(tr):** Montserrat Diez / EPA / Newscom; **p. 142(br):** Fotoluminate LLC / Fotolia; **p. 143(cr):** Lucky Dragon USA / Fotolia; **p. 145(bl):** Dennis jacobsen / Fotolia; **p. 145(br):** Monkey Business Images / Shutterstock; **p. 146(br):** Jose R. Aguirre / Cover / Getty Images; **p. 146(t):** Jupiterimages / Brand X Pictures / Thinkstock; **p. 147(tr):** Scott Griessel / Fotolia; **p. 147(br):** Africa Studio /

Fotolia; **p. 148(tr):** Samuel Borges / Fotolia; **p. 149(bl):** Monkey Business Images / Shutterstock / Dorling Kindersley, Ltd.; **p. 149:** Vision images / Fotolia; **p. 150(t):** Doruk Sikman / Fotolia; **p. 150(b):** Noam / Fotolia; **p. 151(bl):** Monkey Business / Fotolia; **p. 151(tr):** Nick White / Getty Images; **p. 152(tr):** Blend Images / Thinkstock; **p. 154(tl):** Stefanolunardi / Fotolia; **p. 155(br):** Giuseppe R / Fotolia; **p. 155(tr):** Gabriel Blaj / Fotolia; **p. 156(tr):** Blaz Kure / Shutterstock; **p. 157(bl):** Daria Filimonova / Fotolia; **p. 158(bl):** Helen Kattai / Shutterstock; **p. 159(tr):** GalinaSt / Fotolia; **p. 161:** AVAVA / Shutterstock; **p. 163(tc):** Omkara.V / Fotolia; **p. 164(tc):** Orange Line Media / Fotolia; **p. 166(tl):** Shutterstock; **p. 166(br):** Bill Aron / PhotoEdit; **p. 167(br):** Andres Rodriguez / Fotolia; **p. 168(br):** Ra2studio / Shutterstock;

Capítulo 5

p. 170(cr): Rtimages / Fotolia; **p. 171(tc):** Oscar Espinosa / Shutterstock; **p. 171(cl):** Tatiana Popova / Shutterstock; **p. 171(cr):** Getty Images; **p. 171(bc):** Getty Images; **p. 171(br):** Eli Coory/Fotolia; **p. 171(l):** Shutterstock.com; **p. 171(bl):** Cindy Miller Hopkins / Danita Delimont / Alamy; **p. 172(cr):** Christian Heeb / JAI / Corbis; **p. 172(bl):** Tazzymon / Fotolia; **p. 172(tc):** Ariane Citron / Fotolia; **p. 173(cr):** Nik Wheeler / Alamy; **p. 175(br):** Kochneva Tetyana / Shutterstock; **p. 176(br):** Oswaldo Rivas / Reuters / Corbis; **p. 180(br):** Ruth Jenkinson / DK Images; **p. 181(bc):** Andres Rodriguez / Alamy; **p. 181(br):** Robert Harrison / Alamy; **p. 184(tl):** Randy Green / Alamy; **p. 184(c):** Bruce Ayres / Getty Images; **p. 184(cr):** Jan Sochor / Alamy; **p. 188(tl):** Tony Freeman / PhotoEdit; **p. 188(tr):** Fotolia; **p. 188(cr):** Erwinova / Fotolia; **p. 192(tr):** Enigmatico / Fotolia; **p. 199(bl):** Diego Cervo / Shutterstock; **p. 200(tc):** Kablonk Micro / Fotolia; **p. 201(br):** Giovanni Cancemi / Fotolia;

Capítulo 6

p. 204(cr): Conrado/Shutterstock; **p. 205(tl):** E Mike / Fotolia; **p. 205(tc):** Enrique Molina / Age Fotostock; **p. 205(cl):** Gastromedia / Alamy; **p. 205(cr):** Mark Cosslett / National Geographic Image Collection / Getty Images; **p. 205(bl):** Simon Bolivar (1783-1830) (chromolitho), . / Private Collection / Archives Charmet / The Bridgeman Art Library; **p. 205(bc):** Malcolm Schuyl / Alamy; **p. 206** Volff / Fotolia; **p. 206(tl):** Malcolm Schuyl / Alamy; **p. 206(cl):** Volff / Fotolia; **p. 206(tr):** Vladimir Melnik / Fotolia; **p. 206(cr):** Hemeroskopion / Fotolia; **p. 207(tr):** Dan Herrick / Alamy; **p. 207(tl):** Rob Crandall/Stock Connection / Glow Images; **p. 207(tc):** Jeff Greenberg / PhotoEdit, Inc.; **p. 208(cr):** Adam Gregor / Fotolia; **p. 209(cl):** Brand X Pictures / Thinkstock; **p. 212(tr):** lunamarina / Fotolia; **p. 214(c):** Glamour / Shutterstock; **p. 215(bl):** Dorothy Alexander / Alamy; **p. 215(tr):** Scott Dalton / Bloomberg / Getty Images; **p. 220(tr):** Patrick Keen / Getty Images; **p. 220(tl):** JKaczka Digital Imaging / Fotolia; **p. 220(bl):** Yann Arthus-Bertrand / Documentary / Corbis; **p. 220(br):** Juan Silva / The Image Bank / Getty Images; **p. 224(cr):** Carlos / Fotolia; **p. 228(bc):** Gelpi JM / Shutterstock; **p. 228(br):** Jason Maehl / Shutterstock; **p. 228(bl):** East / Shutterstock; **p. 228(bc):** Iko / Shutterstock; **p. 228(cr):** Paco Ayala / Fotolia; **p. 229(bc):** Sauletas / Fotolia; **p. 232(br):** Monkey Business Images /Shutterstock; **p. 232(tr):** Antonio Guillem / Shutterstock; **p. 232(bl):** Kurhan / Shutterstock; **p. 232(cr):** Konradbak / Fotolia; **p. 233(tl):** Goodluz / Shutterstock; **p. 233(tc):** Artem Furman / Shutterstock; **p. 233(tr):** Viacheslav Nikolaenko / Shutterstock; **p. 235(cr):** Julia Pivovarova / Shutterstock; **p. 237(cl):** WoGi / Fotolia;

Capítulo 7

p. 240(cl): Jiang Dao Hua / Shutterstock; **p. 241** Zurbaran Galeria / SuperStock; **p. 241(tc):** Elxeneize / Fotolia; **p. 241(bc):** Christopher Pillitz/Alamy; **p. 241(cr):** Eye Ubiquitous / Robert Harding; **p. 241(tl):** Galina Barskaya / Shutterstock; **p. 242(tl):** Demetrio Carrasco / DK Images; **p. 242(bl):** Nicoletaraftu / Fotolia; **p. 242(br):** Kseniya Ragozina / Fotolia; **p. 242(cl):** Fernando Giani / Fotolia; **p. 242(cr):** Toniflap / Fotolia; **p. 243(tl):** Marcos Brindicci / Reuters / Corbis; **p. 243(bl):** Bikeriderlondon / Shutterstock; **p. 243(cr):** Daily Mail / Rex / Alamy; **p. 244(cr):** Gal Schweizer / Getty Images; **p. 245(br):** Corbis Sports/Corbis; **p. 245(bl):** Tim Farrell / Corbis Sports / Corbis; **p. 245(bc):** Fred Thornhill / Reuters / Corbis; **p. 249(cl):** Photocreo / Fotolia; **p. 250(cl):** Maxi Failla / LatinContent / Getty Images; **p. 250(tr):** Alfredo Herms / LatinContent / Getty Images; **p. 250(br):** Richard Rad / LatinContent / Getty Images; **p. 253(bc):** Fotokostic / Shutterstock; **p. 254(cr):** Cusp / SuperStock; **p. 254(tc):** Carlos / Fotolia; **p. 254(br):** Bikeriderlondon / Shutterstock; **p. 261(tr):** Tobias Titz / Getty Images; **p. 264(bl):** Fotolia; **p. 270(br):** Morten Andersen/Corbis; **p. 272(br):** Nicolas Celaya / Xinhua /Landov; **p. 273(cl):** Fotokostic / Shutterstock; **p. 273(tr):** Fotoember / Fotolia;

Capítulo 8

p. 276(cr): Monkey Business /Fotolia; **p. 277(tc):** Chris Ronneseth / Getty Images; **p. 277(tr):** Steven Allan / Getty Images; **p. 277(bc):** Nathalie Speliers Ufermann / Shutterstock; **p. 277(tl):** Ken Welsh / Age Fotostock; **p. 277(cr):** Kinetic Imagery / Shutterstock; **p. 277(bl):** Frida Kahlo / Museo Nacional de Arte Moderno,2001 Banco de Mexico Diego Rivera & Frida Kahlo Museums Trust/Artists Rights Society (ARS), NY. Av./D.F. Reproduction authorized by the Instituto Nacional de Bellas Artes y Literatura / Christie's Images / Corbis; **p. 278(tl):** Ulga / Fotolia; **p. 278(br):** DK Images; **p. 278(bl):** Danny Lehman / Corbis; **p. 278(tr):** Horticulture / Fotolia; **p. 279(tl):** German_click / Fotolia; **p. 279(tc):** Kim Karpeles / Alamy; **p. 279(tr):** Eduardo Rivero /Shutterstock; **p. 279(bl):** Phil Clarke-Hill / Robert Harding World Imagery / Alamy; **p. 279(bc):** Fabienne Fossez / Alamy; **p. 279(br):** Jan Sochor / Alamy; **p. 280(c):** Orlando Sierra / AFP / Getty Images; **p. 281(r):** Danita Delimont / Alamy; **p. 282(bc):** Nito / Fotolia; **p. 283(tr):** Phase4Photography / Fotolia; **p. 284(cl):** Guillermo Gonzalez / Notimex / Newscom; **p. 285(cl):** Jan Sochor / Demotix / Corbis; **p. 285(tr):** Jan Sochor / Demotix / Corbis; **p. 285(br):** Jmstock / Getty Images; **p. 291(bl):** DmitriMaruta / Shutterstock; **p. 291(bc):** Juriah Mosin / Shutterstock; **p. 291(br):** Anetlanda / Shutterstock; **p. 294(bc):** Dan Bannister / DK Images; **p. 294(br):** Hector Vivas / Jam Media / LatinContent / Getty Images; **p. 295(bc):** John Mitchell / Alamy; **p. 295(br):** Sandra van der Steen / Fotlia; **p. 296(tl):** EPA / Alamy; **p. 296(tr):** Peter Kneffel / EPA / Newscom; **p. 298(tr):** Memofoto / Fotolia; **p. 307(tr):** Mireille Vautier / Alamy; **p. 307(cl):** Holbox / Shutterstock; **p. 308(br):** Michaeljung / Fotolia;

Capítulo 9

p. 310(cr): Goodluz / Shutterstock; **p. 311(tc):** Kschrei / Shutterstock; **p. 311(tr):** Linda Whitwam / DK Images; **p. 311(cr):** Robert Lerich / Fotolia; **p. 311(bl):** Kim Seidl / Shutterstock; **p. 311(bc):** Stefano Paterna / Alamy; **p. 311(bl):** Arte Maya; **p. 312(cr):** Simon Dannhauer / Fotolia; **p. 312(cl):** hotshotsworldwide / Fotolia; **p. 312(bl):** Johan Ordonez / AFP / Getty Images; **p. 312(tl):** Tim Draper / DK Images; **p. 313(br):** EPA / Corbis; **p. 313(bl):** Karl Kummels / SuperStock; **p. 313(bc):** Fernando Morales / AFP / Newscom; **p. 313(tc):** Arte Maya; **p. 313(tr):** Arte Maya; **p. 313(tl):** Arte Maya; **p. 315(tl):** Science Photo Library / Alamy; **p. 315(tc):** Shutterstock; **p. 315(tr):** Kokotewan /Fotolia; **p. 315(bl):** Fotolia; **p. 315(bc):** Tsian / Shutterstock; **p. 315(br):** Wavebreakmedia / Shutterstock; **p. 316(bl):** Gabriela Trojanowska / Shutterstock; **p. 317(cr):** Andres Rodriguez / Fotolia; **p. 318(bl):** Dave Rock / Shutterstock; **p. 318(tl):** Shutterstock; **p. 320(bl):** Monkey Business / Fotolia; **p. 320(br):** Snowwhiteimages / Fotolia; **p. 321(tr):** Blickwinkel / LO / Alamy; **p. 321(cr):** Christian Kieffer / Shutterstock; **p. 321(bl):** Homer Sykes / Photonica World / Getty Images; **p. 324(tl):** Lev Kropotov / Shutterstock; **p. 325(tr):** Yuri Arcurs / Shutterstock; **p. 328(br):** Wavebreakmedia /Shutterstock; **p. 329(tr):** Corepics VOF / Shutterstock; **p. 336(cr):** Scott T. Baxter / Photodisc /Getty Images; **p. 341(bc):** Paul Kennedy / Alamy; **p. 342(br):** Daboost / Fotolia; **p. 342(bl):** Daboost / Fotolia; **p. 342(bc):** Daboost / Fotolia; **p. 343(br):** Mark Harmel / Alamy; **p. 343(tc):** A. Ramey / PhotoEdit;

Capítulo 10

p. 346(cr): Lucky Business / Shutterstock; **p. 347(bc):** Jennifer Elizabeth / Fotolia; **p. 347(tc):** iStockphoto / Getty Images; **p. 347(tr):** Steve100 / Fotolia; **p. 347(tl):** Kletr / Shutterstock; **p. 347(cr):** Andrew Linscott / Alamy; **p. 347(br):** Yumbo Indian from the neighbourhood of Quito, Ecuador, with various fruits and trees (oil on canvas), American School, (18th century) / Museo de America, Madrid, Spain / Index / The Bridgeman Art Library; **p. 348(tl):** Rechitan Sorin / Shutterstock; **p. 348(tr):** PB Pictures / Fotolia; **p. 348(bl):** Alexander / Fotolia; **p. 348(br):** Tommypic / Fotolia; **p. 349(tl):** Owen Franken / Corbis; **p. 349(tr):** Greg Roden / Rough Guides / DK Images; **p. 349(bl):** Arco Images G / Newscom; **p. 349(bc):** Imagebroker / Alamy; **p. 349(tc):** Janice Hazeldine / Alamy; **p. 353(cr):** Redav / Shutterstock; **p. 355(cr):** Santiago Cornejo / Shutterstock; **p. 356(cl):** Sven Schermer / Shutterstock; **p. 356(tc):** Margie Politzer / Lonely Planet Images / Getty Images; **p. 356(br):** Pablo Aneli / AP Images; **p. 359(tl):** Lily / Fotolia; **p. 359(tc):** Paul Brighton / Fotolia; **p. 363(tr):** Sergey Peterman / Fotolia; **p. 366(bc):** John Mitchell / Alamy; **p. 367(cr):** Skylines / Shutterstock; **p. 370(cr):** Greg Roden / Dorling Kindersely,Ltd; **p. 370(cl):** Robert Lerich / Fotolia; **p. 371(tr):** Danita Delimont / Alamy; **p. 377(tr):** Julenochek / Fotolia; **p. 377(tc):** Christian Vinces / Shutterstock; **p. 378(bl):** Pressmaster / Fotolia;

Capítulo 11

p. 380(tr): Mangostock / Fotolia; **p. 381(tl):** Alex James Bramwell / Shutterstock; **p. 381(cl):** Osov / Shutterstock; **p. 381(c):** Elias H. Debbas II / Shutterstock; **p. 381(cr):** Rob Huntley / Shutterstock; **p. 381(bl):** Mireille Vautier / Alamy; **p. 382(tl):** Fotolia; **p. 382(cr):** Brelsbil / Fotolia; **p. 382(cl):** Salazar / Fotolia; **p. 382(tr):** Cstyle / Fotolia; **p. 383(tl):** Andresr / Shutterstock; **p. 383(tr):** Adam Eastland / Alamy; **p. 383(bl):** Dorothy Alexander / Alamy; **p. 383(br):** Nigel Hicks / Dorling Kindersely, Ltd; **p. 384(c):** Simone Voigt / Shutterstock; **p. 390(tc):** Paul Almasy / Corbis; **p. 390(tr):** Greg Roden / DK Images; **p. 390(br):** Jorge Adorno / Reuters / Corbis; **p. 391(tr):** Rob Bayer / Shutterstock; **p. 397(tr):** Donya Nedomam / Shutterstock; **p. 398(cr):** Graham Harrison / Alamy; **p. 401(tl):** Linda Whitwam / Dorling Kindersley,Ltd; **p. 401(cl):** Galina Barskaya / Fotolia; **p. 409(br):** Angellodeco / Fotolia; **p. 410(tr):** BrazilPhotos / Alamy; **p. 411(c):** Pablocalvog / Fotolia; **p. 412(b):** Rangizzz / Fotolia;

Capítulo 12

p. 414(c): vilainecrevette / Fotolia; **p. 415(cr):** Marcus / Fotolia; **p. 415(tr):** Jim Lipschutz / Shutterstock; **p. 415(c):** RJ Lerich / Shutterstock; **p. 415(tl):** Brandon / Shutterstock; **p. 415(cl):** Jon Spaull / Dorling Kindersley, Ltd.; **p. 415(bl):** Kevin Schafer / Alamy; **p. 416(t):** Vilant / Fotolia; **p. 416(cr):** AustralianDream / Fotolia; **p. 416(cl):** Searagen / Fotolia; **p. 416(b):** Fotolia; **p. 417(tl):** Jose Luis Stephens / Alamy; **p. 417(tr):** Prisma Archivo / Alamy; **p. 417(bl):** Aleksey Stemmer / Shutterstock; **p. 419(tr):** Michaeljung / Fotolia; **p. 420(bl):** Ethan Daniels / Shutterstock; **p. 421(tr):** Getty Images; **p. 422(bl):** Alfredo Maiquez / Alamy; **p. 425(cl):** Nik Niklz / Shutterstock; **p. 425(tc):** Ariane Citron / Fotolia; **p. 425(cr):** Greg Roden / Dorling Kindersley, Ltd.; **p. 425(c):** Isaac Koval / The Agency Collection /Getty Images; **p. 425(bc):** Ty Milford / Radius Images / Getty Images; **p. 425(br):** Jordan Siemens / Digital Vision / Getty Images; **p. 425(cr):** Todd Warnock / Stockbyte / Getty Images; **p. 426(tr):** Jarno Gonzalez Zarraonandia / Shutterstock; **p. 428(cr):** Blaine Harrington III / Corbis; **p. 429(cl):** Jarno Gonzalez Zarraonandia / Shutterstock; **p. 439(br):** Stuart Pearce / Age Fotostock; **p. 440(tr):** Tony Northrup / Shutterstock; **p. 442(br):** Maisant Ludovic / Hemis / Alamy; **p. 445(br):** Csaba Peterdi / Fotolia; **p. 446(bl):** Fuste Rag a/ Age Fotostock / Getty Images;

Capítulo 13

p. 448(cr): Bikeriderlondon / Shutterstock; **p. 449(tl):** Shutterstock; **p. 449(cl):** Katarzyna Citko / Shutterstock; **p. 449(cr):** Ildar Turumtaev / Fotolia; **p. 449(br):** Leeman / Thinkstock / Getty Images; **p. 449(tc):** Travelscape Images / Alamy; **p. 449(c):** Vario Images GmbH & Co.KG / Alamy; **p. 449(bl):** Gianni Dagli Orti / The Art Archive at Art Resource, NY; **p. 450(tl):** Julio Etchart / Alamy; **p. 450(cl):** Juan Karita / AP Images; **p. 450(tr):** Aukasz Kurbiel / Fotolia; **p. 450(c):** AdStock RF / Shutterstock; **p. 451(tr):** Ulf Andersen / Hulton Archive / Getty Images; **p. 451(tl):** Piero Pomponi / Liaison / Getty Images; **p. 451(c):** Bettmann / Corbis; **p. 451(br):** Carlos Alvarez / Getty Images Entertainment / Getty Images; **p. 452(bl):** Ppicture-Alliance / Geisler-Fotopres / Clemens Niehaus/AP Images; **p. 453(cr):** Victor Potasyev / Shutterstock; **p. 454(tl):** Francis G. Mayer / Corbis; **p. 454(cr):** The Museum of Modern Art /Licensed by SCALA / Art Resource, NY; **p. 454(bl):** Museum Associates / LACMA/ Licensed by Art Resource, NY; **p. 455(bc):** Ray Roberts / Alamy; **p. 455(t):** Mondadori / Getty Images; **p. 456 (tl):** Enrique Arnal; **p. 456(bl):** Francis G. Mayer / Corbis; **p. 456(bl):** Bridgeman-Giraudon / Art Resource, NY; **p. 456(cl):** Adam Lee / Alamy; **p. 457(tr):** Dale Mitchell / Fotolia; **p. 457(c):** Marcos Brindicci / Reuters / Corbis; **p. 457(cr):** Riccardo Cesari / Splash News / Corbis; **p. 457(br):** Sue Cunningham Photographic / Alamy; **p. 458(cr):** Salah Malkawi / Getty Images; **p. 459(cr):** Robert Harding World Imagery / Alamy; **p. 460(tl):** Brent Winebrenner / Lonely Planet Images / Getty Images; **p. 460(bl):** Benoit Paill / Flickr / Getty Images; **p. 460(tr):** Krzysztof Dydynski / Lonely Planet Images / Getty Images; **p. 462(br):** Fotomicar / Shutterstock; **p. 464(tr):** Thinkstock; **p. 466(b):** RoxyFer / Shutterstock.com; **p. 467(tr):** MJ Photography / Alamy; **p. 474(br):** Paco Torrente / AFP / Newscom;

Capítulo 14

p. 478(cr): Gianni Muratore / Alamy; **p. 479(tl):** Jeremy Horner / Corbis; **p. 479(cl):** Art Wolfe / The Image Bank / Getty Images; **p. 479(tc):** Marc C. Johnson / Shutterstock; **p. 479(c):** Ene / Shutterstock; **p. 479(bc):** Travel Bug / Shutterstock; **p. 479(bl):** Stephanie Jackson / Photographsofaustralia / Alamy; **p. 480(tl):** Nataliya Hora /Shutterstock; **p. 480(c):** Michele Pautasso / Fotolia; **p. 480(tc):** Pablo Rogat /Shutterstock; **p. 480(cl):** Tero Hakala /Shutterstock; **p. 480(tr):** Tifonimages / Shutterstock; **p. 480(bc):** Travel Bug / Shutterstock; **p. 481(tl):** Rodrigo Arangua / AFP / Getty Images; **p. 481(tr):** Jorge Villegas / Age Fotostock / Alamy; **p. 481(br):** Martin Alipaz / epa / Corbis; **p. 483(tr):** Bill Bachmann / Alamy; **p. 485(tl):** Monkey Business / Fotolia; **p. 485(cr):** Db2stock/Blend Images / Corbis; **p. 487(cl):** Philippe Lissac / Godong / Corbis; **p. 487(tr):** Hans Neleman / Corbis; **p. 488(tr):** Jack Kurtz / The Image Works; **p. 493(tr):** Jorge Villegas / Xinhua / Newscom; **p. 496(tr):** Corbis; **p. 499(tr):** Carlos Carrion / Sygma / Corbis; **p. 500(tr):** Prisma Archivo / Alamy; **p. 503(br):** Diego Cervo / Fotolia; **p. 505(cr):** Moises Castillo / AP Images; **p. 506(b):** Africa Studio / Fotolia; **p. 508(b):** PhotoSG / Fotolia;

Capítulo 15

p. 510(cr): Alexander Raths / Fotolia; **p. 511(tl):** David Parker / Science Source; **p. 511(tc):** Lori Froeb / Shutterstock; **p. 511(tr):** Eddtoro / Shutterstock; **p. 511(c):** Joseph / Shutterstock; **p. 511(c):** Richard Ellis / Alamy; **p. 511(bl):** Zulia Gotay de Anderson; **p. 512(tl):** Hemis / Alamy; **p. 512(cl):** Tim Draper / Dorling Kindersley,Ltd; **p. 512(bc):** Thais Llorca / EPA / Newscom; **p. 512(cr):** Torkil Adsersen / EPA / Newscom; **p. 513(tl):** Liv Friis-Larsen / Shutterstock; **p. 513(tr):** Sadeugra / E+ / Getty Images; **p. 513(bl):** Ilolab / Shutterstock; **p. 513(br):** David R. Frazier Photolibrary, Inc. / Alamy; **p. 514(cr):** Interfoto / Alamy; **p. 515(tr):** Jennifer Stone / Shutterstock; **p. 515(bl):** Xico Putini / Fotolia; **p. 516(bl):** Joseph / Shutterstock; **p. 517(tl):** Andrea Crisante / Alamy; **p. 517(tr):** Jack Jackson / Robert Harding; **p. 517(bl):** Ziqiu / Fotolia; **p. 517(br):** Vadym Andrushchenko / Shutterstock; **p. 518(tl):** Antonis Papantoniou / Shutterstock; **p. 518(tr):** Jim West / Alamy; **p. 519 (tr):** iLexx/Getty Images; **p. 519(bl):** Lunatic67 / Shutterstock; **p. 520(cl):** Cesar Carrion / Notimex / Newscom; **p. 520(tr):** Ted Spiegel / Nomad / Corbis; **p. 523(br):** Kirill Kedrinski / Fotolia; **p. 526(cr):** Alberto Paredes / Alamy; **p. 527(b):** WavebreakMediaMicro / Fotolia; **p. 536(c):** Ra2 Studio / Fotolia

Communicative Functions and Learning Strategies Index

actions
  describing, 144, 153, 179
  indicating to whom or for whom they may take place, 222
  organizing sequentially, 145
adjectives, using to enrich your description, 98
advice, giving, 353, 411, 446
affirmation, expressing, 426
agreement, reporting, 439
answering questions
  agreeing to answer, 44
appropriateness (or not), ways of stating, 228
asking for what you need, 16, 60
asking questions, 5, 21, 27, 55
  choosing Indicative or subjunctive for, 431
  interrupting to ask, 44
  to gather information, 60
  word order when, 492
attention, getting someone's, 44
  to an unusual fact, 121
attitudes, expressing, 398
audience
  identifying, 134
  focusing on, 344

brainstorming, 62

characteristics, expressing, 69, 76–77, 83–84, 98
chronological order, indicating, 238, 308
clarification, requesting, 16, 62
closings in correspondence, 134
comparisons
  making, 293
  making contrasts and, 164
  organizing information to make, 164
complaints
  about someone or something, 469
  from a friend or family member, 192
  to a friend or family member, 192
concern, expressing, 411
conclusions, drawing, 305
  presenting group's conclusion, 504
  supporting group's conclusion, 504
conditions, expressing changeable, 83
congratulating, 408
conjecture, expressing, 488
  expressing conjecture or certainty, 491
connecting events, 238

content
  anticipating, 165
  focusing on, 344
  predicting and guessing, 272
  selecting appropriate, 202
context, using to figure out meaning, 237, 339
conversation, maintaining the flow of, 152
convincing someone,121
courtesy expressions, 8

daily activities, talking about, 111, 153
decisions
  defending, 375
  gathering information strategically to express, 340
  giving, 375
  influencing, 375
  supporting, 443, 473
descriptions
  adjective use to enrich, 98
details
  asking for, 268
  providing supporting, 274
  recording relevant, 374
  selecting and sequencing, 308
diminutives, 141
dislikes, expressing, 90, 226
doubt, expressing, 437
dramatic stories, techniques for, 534, 535
duration, expressing, 127, 160

e-mail writing, 134
emotional states, describing, 185
emotions, expressing, 408
  feelings that may change, 83
  in poetry, 507
empathy, showing, 305
endearment, terms of, 134, 140
enlisting the help of a friend or family member, 192
events
  describing, 230
  sequencing, 238, 308
expectations, expressing, 391

facts
  differentiating from opinions, 270
  expressing, 274
  using to offer good advice, 446
familiarity, expressing, 134
feelings, expressing, 147

food, ordering, 109
formal tone, using appropriately, 167
  judging degrees of, 6
future, talking about the, 368
  hypothesizing about, 525

gender, specifying, 50
goals, expressing, 401
good time, expressing, 355
greetings, 7, 9
  formal, 60
guessing, contextual, 237, 339

haggling, expressions for, 236
happiness, expressing, 408, 535
  sharing someone's, 305
hopes, expressing, 391
humor in stories, techniques for including, 534, 535, 538
hypothetical situations, talking about, 430, 464
  identifying the speaker's intentions, 472
  the present and the future, 525

ideas
  contrasting, 412
  discussing, 271, 359
  listening for main, 407
  putting together cohesively, 412
illustrations, using to anticipate content, 165
impersonal information, stating, 357
indirect objects, indicating, 222
inferences, making, 304, 306
informal tone, using appropriately, 167
information
  clarifying, 263
  emphasizing, 263
  focusing on key, 271
  focusing on relevant, 409
  gathering, 340
  introducing information about personality, 95
  introducing information on physical characteristics, 95
  listening for, 94
  organizing, 342
  organizing for a survey, 132
  organizing to make comparisons, 164
  presenting factual, 443

information (*continued*)
summarizing, 378
supporting comprehension with background, 442
taking notes to recall, 235
instructions, giving, 334, 364
intention, expressing, 127
identifying the speaker's intention, 472, 533
interest
engaging, 443
expressing, 268, 305
maintaining, 271, 443
interviews, conducting, 305, 318
introductions, 5
invitations, 105, 283
to enter a room or house, 174

key words, looking for and using, 133
knowledge
stating, 123
using background, 131

likes, expressing, 90, 226
listening for the gist, 59
listening for specific information, 94
location, expressing, 21, 53
of events, 81
logical relationships, focusing on, 444

main ideas, listening for, 407
meaning, using context to figure out, 237
means, expressing, 127, 401
mental images, creating, 197
movement, expressing, 115, 127

narratives, writing effective, 308
identifying narrator's perspective, 536
using imagination and humor in, 538
negation, expressing, 19, 426
notes, taking, 235, 374
number, specifying, 50

objects, describing, 230
obligation, expressing, 157
ongoing actions
expressing, 182
past, 286
opinions
differentiating fact from, 270
expressing, 132, 274, 398, 408
reporting, 439
origin, expressing, 81
ownership, expressing, 87

past, narrating in the, 286, 289
past, talking about the, 216, 219, 248, 251, 256, 259, 266, 286, 289, 330, 461
from a past perspective, 496
talking about how things used to be, 289
wishes and recommendations, 521

people
comparing, 293, 297, 300
describing, 19–20, 67, 70, 75, 95, 230
identifying, 19, 193
pointing out, 193
who might interest you, 73
personal anecdotes, telling, 534
persuasion
through suggestions and advice, 411
physical states, describing, 185
planning,
what you want to say, 198
plans, expressing, 105, 115, 147
poetry
looking for meanings in, 474
using language to express emotions in, 507
point of view of speaker, identifying, 503
in narratives, 536
position, describing, 29. *See also* instructions, giving
possession, expressing, 81, 434
praising, 408
preferences, expressing, 147, 226–227
presentations, making comprehensible and interesting, 473
problem solving, organizing ideas for, 504
proposals, making polite, 495
punctuality (being on time), 27, 105
purpose
expressing, 401
listening for, 163
purpose, focusing on, 344

qualities, expressing inherent, 83
quantity, talking about, 119
questions, answering, 44, 55

reacting
to good news, 121
to what someone says, 48, 114
reading. *See also* texts
organizing information into categories, 342
preparing to read, 165, 199
reciprocity, expressing, 468
recommendations, making, 395, 408
in the past, 521
registers, distinguishing, 5, 6, 336
relief after a tense situation, expressing, 535
repetition
avoiding, 188, 322, 326
requesting, 16, 56
requests, expressing, 395
polite, 495
softened, 207

salutations in correspondence, 134, 167
saying goodbye, 8
saying hello, 7
scanning for information, 61, 96
shopping
expressing displeasure at a high price, 209
expressions for, 207
giving sizes, 211
negotiating a price, 236
showing pleasure at a bargain, 209
speaking
to ask that people request the floor before, 528
to give the floor to someone, 528
to request the floor, 528
states of being, expressing, 53
suggestions, giving, 334, 411
summarizing information, 378
surveys, organizing information for, 132
sympathy, expressing, 399, 535

talking about academic life, 15–16, 42
talking about daily occurrences, 42
telephone
answering the, 24, 60, 105
best time to call, 79
saying numbers, 24
speaking on the, 79, 198
thanking a friend for calling, 247
to find out who is answering, 198
to request to speak to someone specific, 198
texts. *See also* reading
identifying the format of, 61
identifying the tone of, 505
scanning for information, 61, 96
things
comparing, 293, 297, 300
identifying, 193
pointing out, 193
time
asking when an event starts, 27
punctuality (on time), 27, 105
titles, using to anticipate content, 165
tone,
choosing appropriate, 167, 202
identifying tone of a text, 504
topic
asking someone to expand on, 305
asking someone to talk about a, 305

uncertainty, expressing, 437
unexpected, expressing the, 529

weather, talking about, 246
wishes, expressing in the past, 521
words, learning new, 376
workplace, useful expressions for, 340
writing. *See also specific kinds of writing*
brainstorming and, 62
dates, 13
effective narratives, 308
organizing events in sequence, 238
to spark interest, 476
writing correspondence
closings, 168
e-mails, 167
salutations, 168

Index

A

a, 263
  for person or specific animal, 143
  uses, 431
a personal, for direct object nouns, 188–189
abrir, 361
acabar + **de** + *infinitive,* 361
acostar(se), 155
addresses, 24
adjective clauses, subjunctive in, 430–431
adjectives, 68, 69, 70, 76–77. *See also* colors; descriptions
  affirmative expressions, 426–427
  comparative forms, 293–294
  demonstrative adjectives, 193
  negative expressions, 426–427
  past participles as, 361
  possessive adjectives, 87–88
  with **estar,** 83–84, 231
  with **ser,** 83–84, 231
adverbial conjunctions
  that require subjunctive, 488
  that take subjunctive or indicative, 491–492
adverbs
  adverbial conjunctions, 488
  affirmative expressions, 426–427
  comparative forms, 294
  expressing time, 115, 145
    past, 217, 239
  negative expressions, 426–427
affirmative expressions, 426–427
almorzar
  formal imperative, 335
  present indicative, 148
  present subjunctive, 392
alphabet, 18
aprender, 46
arrepentirse, 252
articles
  contractions, 81
  gender of, 50–51, 76–77
  number of, 51, 76–77
-ar verbs, 42–43
atrever(se), 252

B

beber, 364
bilingualism, 78

C

caer bien/mal, 227
calendar, 12
car, meanings for, 89
celebrations, 279, 280, 281, 285
cerrar, 148
cocinar, 364
cognates, 20
  false, 318
colors, 70
comer, 364
  conditional, 464
  future, 368
  imperfect, 287
  imperfect subjunctive, 522
  present subjunctive, 391
  preterit, 216
commands
  formal, 334–335
  informal, 364–365
como si, expressions with, 522
comparisons
  of equality, 297
  of inequality, 293–294
  superlative, 300–301
con, 263
conditional, 464–465
conjunctions, adverbial, 488, 491–492
conmigo, 263
conocer
  past tenses compared, 331
  present indicative, 123
  present subjunctive, 391
construir, 257
consumir, 364
contigo, 263
contractions, 81
costar, 148
courtesy, expressions of, 8
creer, 256
cubrir, 361

D

daily routines, 144
dar
  formal imperative, 335
  present indicative, 223
  present subjunctive, 391
  preterit, 223
dates, 12, 13
days of the week, 12
de, 263
  + **el,** 81
deber + infinitive, 47
decir, 361
  conditional, 465
  future, 369
  informal imperative, 365
  present indicative, 148
  present subjunctive, 391
  preterit, 267
  uses, 223
definite articles
  singular and plural, 50–51
  with parts of the body and clothing, 252
  demonstrative adjectives, 193
demonstrative pronouns, 194
describir, 223
descriptions, 68, 69, 70, 76. *See also* adjectives
  materials, 82
despedirse, 260
direct object pronouns, 188–189
direct objects, 188–189
disculparse, 252
divertirse, 252, 260
dónde + está, 21
dormir
  formal imperative, 334
  present indicative, 148
  present subjunctive, 392
  preterit, 260
dormir(se), 154

E

e, 97
  replacing **y,** 246
empezar
  present indicative, 148
  preterit, 217
encantar, 227
encontrar, 148
enfadarse, 252
entender, 148
-er verbs, 46–47
escribir, 223, 361
estar
  imperfect subjunctive, 522
  + location, 21
  present indicative, 53
  present subjunctive, 391
  preterit, 266
  uses of, 83–84, 231
  with adjective, 83–84
expectations, wants, and hopes, expressing, 392
explicar, 223

F

false cognates, 20, 318
fascinar, 227
formal commands, 334–335
formality, 6
frequency, expressions of, 43, 179
future
  expressions that denote, 115, 183
  verb forms, 368–369

G

goodbye, saying, 8, 9
greetings, 7, 9
gustar, 90–91, 226–227
  verbs similar to, 227

H

haber
- conditional, 465
- imperfect, 287
- past perfect, 496
- present perfect, 360–361

hablar
- conditional, 464
- future, 368
- imperfect, 287
- imperfect subjunctive, 522
- present indicative, 42
- present subjunctive, 391
- preterit, 216, 217

hace
- meaning *ago,* 268
- with expressions of time, 160, 268
- with weather, 14

hacer
- conditional, 465
- future, 369
- informal imperative, 365
- past participle, 361
- present indicative, 111
- present subjunctive, 391
- preterit, 266

hay, 23

Hispanic countries
- Argentina, 4, 14, 75, 79, 106, 110, 121, 146, 174, 181, 215, 241–242, 243, 250, 270, 321, 356, 457, 460, 481, 485, 493, 507, 536–537
- Belice, 307
- Bolivia, 78, 121, 181, 279, 425, 449–450, 455, 457, 481, 482, 483, 485, 500
- Caribbean, 243, 285, 457, 485
- Chile, 41, 89, 121, 174, 243, 451, 460, 479–480, 481, 482, 485, 493, 496
- Colombia, 72, 106, 137–138, 146, 158, 174, 181, 215, 243, 244, 250, 285, 451, 454, 482, 485
- Costa Rica, 358, 415–416, 420, 425, 428, 439, 440, 445, 446
- Cuba, 72, 89, 106, 381–382, 457, 500, 520
- Dominican Republic, 381–382, 397, 404
- Ecuador, 4, 181, 321, 347–348, 355, 356, 366, 370, 371, 485
- El Salvador, 171–172, 198, 307, 493
- Guatemala, 78, 279, 301, 307, 311–312, 318, 321, 341, 343, 425, 482, 493, 505
- Honduras, 171–172, 174, 307, 487, 505
- Mexico, 4, 41, 75, 78, 106, 121, 146, 174, 215, 243, 250, 277–278, 279, 282, 284, 294, 295, 298, 301, 307, 356, 358, 377, 425, 451, 453, 457, 460, 482, 485, 500, 505, 520
- Nicaragua, 171–172, 173, 176, 493
- Panama, 415–416, 422, 425, 428, 429
- Paraguay, 78, 390, 449–450, 451, 460, 462, 467
- Peru, 78, 101–102, 106, 108, 110, 116, 121, 174, 181, 321, 355, 377, 425, 483, 485
- Puerto Rico, 72, 73, 121, 500, 511–512, 514, 516, 519, 526
- Spain, 4, 18, 31–32, 36, 39, 41, 45, 60, 70, 75, 77, 78, 79, 89, 106, 142, 146, 181, 201, 243, 264, 279, 280, 282, 285, 316, 358, 410, 451, 452, 453, 456, 457, 460, 474, 481, 485
- United States, 3, 41, 58, 65–66, 72, 73, 75, 77, 93, 200, 215, 295, 301, 377, 410, 500, 520
- Uruguay, 181, 215, 241–242, 243, 272–273, 481, 485, 493
- Venezuela, 174, 205–206, 220, 356, 483, 485, 500

hispano, 77

I

if- clauses, 525

imperative
- formal, 334–335
- informal, 354–365

imperfect, 286–287, 330–331
- versus preterit, 290–291, 461

imperfect progressive, 330

imperfect subjunctive, 522

impersonal expressions, expressing emotion, 399

indefinite articles, singular and plural, 50–51

indicative. *See also* present indicative
- adverbial conjunctions that take, 492

indirect object pronouns, 222–223

indirect objects, 323

infinitive, 42, 499

interesar, 227

interrogative words, 55–56

introductions, 5

ir
- formal imperative, 335
- imperfect, 287
- informal imperative, 365
- present indicative, 115
- present subjunctive, 391
- preterit, 219

ir + a + infinitive, 115, 330

-ir verbs, 46–47

-ísimo/a, 301

J

jugar
- formal imperative, 335
- present indicative, 148
- present subjunctive, 392
- uses of, 243

L

lavar(se), 154–155

leer, 256

levantar(se)
- present indicative, 154
- preterit, 251

llamar(se), 154

llegar, 216, 217

location, 21

M

maps
- Argentina, 241
- Bolivia, 449
- Chile, 479
- Colombia, 137, 520
- Costa Rica, 415
- Cuba, 381
- Dominican Republic, 381
- Ecuador, 347
- El Salvador, 171
- Guatemala, 311
- Honduras, 171
- Mexico, 277
- Nicaragua, 171
- of nationalities, 70
- of Spanish speaking world, 3
- Panama, 415
  - Ciudad de Panamá, 421
- Paraguay, 449, 485
- Peru, 101
- Puerto Rico, 511
- Spain, 31
- United States, 65
- Uruguay, 241, 247
- Venezuela, 205, 520

months, 12

morir, 260, 361

mostrar, 223

N

nationality, 72, 80
- gender of, 80

negative expressions, 426–427

nouns
- direct objects, 188–189
- gender of, 50–51
  - professions, 389
- number of, 51

numbers
- 0 to 99, 23
- 100 to 2.000.000, 119–120
- ordinal numbers, 173

O

o replaced with **u,** 246

oír, 112
- present subjunctive, 391
- preterit, 257

ojalá (que), 392

opinions, expressing, 148, 398–399

P

para, 127–128, 263, 401–402

parecer (zc), 227

past participle, 360–361

past perfect, 496

pedir, 148
- preterit, 260

pensar
- formal imperative, 334
- present indicative, 148
- present subjunctive, 391
- preterit, 217
- uses of, 150

poder
conditional, 465
future, 369
past tenses compared, 331
present indicative, 148
preterit, 266
poner, 361
conditional, 465
formal imperative, 334
future, 369
informal imperative, 365
present indicative, 112
present subjunctive, 391
preterit, 266
poner(se), 154
por, 127–128, 263, 401–402
possessive adjectives, 87–88
stressed, 435
possessive pronouns, 434–435
preferir
present indicative, 148
present subjunctive, 392
preterit, 260
preparar, 364
prepositions, 263. *See also specific prepositions*
present indicative. *See also* indicative
-ar verbs, 42–43
conocer, 123
-er verbs, 46–47
estar, 53
hablar, 42
hacer, 111
ir, 115
-ir verbs, 46–47
poner, 112
saber, 123
ser, 19, 80–81
stem-changing verbs, 148
subjunctive uses compared, 431
present participle, 182–183, 330
present perfect, 360–361
present progressive, 182–183
present subjunctive, 391–392, 1372–1377. *See also* subjunctive
prestar, 223
preterit, 330–331
of **-er** and **-ir** verbs that end in a vowel, 256–257
of **ir** and **ser,** 219
of irregular verbs, 266–267
of reflexive verbs, 251–252
of regular verbs, 216–217
of stem-changing verbs, 260
versus imperfect, 290–291, 461
pronouns
after prepositions, 263
demonstrative pronouns, 194
direct object, 188–189, 322–323
with indirect object pronouns, 326–327
indirect object, 222–223, 323
with direct object pronouns, 326–327
possessive pronouns, 434–435
reciprocal pronouns, 468
reflexive pronouns, 154–155, 251–252
with direct object pronouns, 327

Q

quedar, 227
quejar(se), 252
querer
conditional, 465
future, 369
past tenses compared, 330–331
present indicative, 148
preterit, 266
quitarse, 154

R

reciprocal pronouns, 468
reciprocal verbs, 468
recoger
formal imperative, 335
present subjunctive, 392
reflexive pronouns, 154–155, 251–252
reflexive verbs, 154–155, 251–252
regalar, 223
reír, 260
repetir
formal imperative, 334
present indicative, 148
preterit, 260
romper, 361

S

saber
conditional, 465
formal imperative, 335
future, 369
past tenses compared, 330
present indicative, 123
present subjunctive, 391
preterit, 266
sacar
formal imperative, 335
present subjunctive, 392
preterit, 217
salir, 112
conditional, 465
future, 369
informal imperative, 365
present subjunctive, 391
salutations, 134
schools, 63
se constructions, 357, 529
daily expressions using, 534
seguir
formal imperative, 335
present indicative, 148
present subjunctive, 392
preterit, 260
sentirse, 252, 260
preterit, 260
ser
formal imperative, 335
imperfect, 287
informal imperative, 365
present indicative, 19, 80–81
present subjunctive, 391
preterit, 219
uses of, 80, 80–81, 83–84, 230–231
with adjectives, 80, 83–84
servir, 148, 260
sin, 263
sobre, 263
spelling-change verbs, preterit, 217
stem-changing verbs
e to **i,** 148
e to **ie,** 148
o to **ue,** 148
present indicative, 148
present participles of, 183
preterit, 217, 260
stereotypes, 75
street names, 24
stressed possessive adjectives, 435
subir, 364
subjunctive. *See also* present subjunctive
in adjective clauses, 430–431
adverbial conjunctions that require the, 488
adverbial conjunctions that take, 491–492
imperfect subjunctive, 522
present indicative uses compared, 431
with expressions of doubt, 437–438
with expressions of emotion, 398–399
with expressions of influence, 395–396
superlative, 300–301

T

technology and family communication, 166
tener
conditional, 465
expressions with, 185
future, 369
informal imperative, 365
present indicative, 148
present subjunctive, 391
preterit, 266
tener que + infinitive, 157
time, 81
being on time (punctuality), 27
hace, 160, 268
telling, 26
in the past, 287
time expressions, 25–26, 43, 145
that accompany the imperfect, 287
that denote chronological order, 308
that denote the future, 115
that denote the past, 217, 239
traducir, 267
traer, 112
present subjunctive, 391
preterit, 267
tu, 13
tú
accent mark with, 13
use of, 5, 6

U

u replacing **o,** 246
usted, use of, 5, 6

V

vender, 223
venir
conditional, 465
future, 369

- informal imperative, 365
- present indicative, 148
- present subjunctive, 391
- preterit, 266

ver, 361
- imperfect, 287
- present indicative, 47
- present subjunctive, 391

verb forms. *See* **-ar** verbs; **-er** verbs; irregular verbs; **-ir** verbs; reciprocal verbs; reflexive verbs; *specific verbs;* spelling-change verbs; stem-changing verbs

vestir(se), 154–155
- preterit, 260

vivir
- conditional, 464
- future, 368
- imperfect, 287
- imperfect subjunctive, 522
- present indicative, 46
- present subjunctive, 391
- preterit, 216, 217

vocabulary
- academic life, 33, 35, 42, 63
- accessories, 207, 239
- appliances, 177, 203
- architecture, 173, 203
- art, 454, 455, 477
- bathroom, 203
- bedroom, 203
- cars, 423
- celebrations, 279–282, 309
- chores, 179
- cinema, 451–452
- classroom, 10, 15–16, 28
- clothing, 207, 210, 213, 239
- colors, 99
- communication, 135
- computers, 37
- courses, 33, 36
- courtesy expressions, 28
- descriptive adjectives, 99
- drinks, 107, 109
- electronics, 178, 203, 523
- entertainment, 135
- environment, 515, 526, 539
- family, 139–143, 145–146, 169
- fish, 379
- food, 45, 107–110, 135, 151, 349–352, 379
- friends, 67
- fruit, 379
- furniture, 77, 203
- the future, 517–518
- garden, 203
- gender roles, 481, 484, 487, 496, 499
- greetings, 28
- health, 383–385, 388, 410, 413
- holidays, 279–280, 279–281, 309
- home life, 173–176, 203
- hotel, 421
- hotels, 447
- immigration/emigration, 485
- introductions and farewells, 28
- kitchen, 203
- leisure activities, 103
- literature, 451, 474–475, 477, 505–506, 536–537
- meat, 379
- music, 309, 457, 477
- nationalities, 99
- nature, 275, 515
- occupations, 313–316, 345
- offices, 345
- painting, 454, 455, 456
- parts of the body, 69, 212, 252, 386, 413
- popular culture, 457, 477
- professions, 313–316, 345, 388, 389
- restaurants, 107–109, 135
- schools, 63
- science, 513, 518, 539
- seasonings, 374, 379
- seasons, 213, 246
- shopping, 207–209, 210–211, 237, 239
- society, 481–482, 509
- spices, 374, 379
- sports, 243–244, 245, 246, 248, 275
- students, 33, 35, 38
- surveys, 509
- table settings, 354, 379
- technology, 513, 518, 539
- traditions, 279–282, 309
- transportation, 417–419, 423, 447
- travel, 417–419, 447
- universities, 33, 35, 38, 41, 63
- vegetables, 379
- weather, 246, 275
- work, 313–316, 345

volver, 361
- present indicative, 148
- present subjunctive, 391
- preterit, 217

W

weather, 14, 246, 275

week, days of, 12

written accents, 13, 56
- **i** or **u** followed by another vowel, 395
- on present participles with direct object pronouns, 189
- **sé** (**saber**), 123
- with direct object pronouns, 189
- with double object pronouns, 327
- with **-ísimo/a,** 301

y, 97
- replaced with **e,** 246

Mar Caribe
OCÉANO ATLÁNTICO
Barranquilla
Cartagena
Maracaibo
Caracas
Barquisimeto
VENEZUELA
Río Orinoco
Salto Ángel
Georgetown
GUYANA
Paramaribo
SURINAM
Cayenne
GUAYANA FRANCESA (Francia)
Medellín
Manizales
Bogotá
COLOMBIA
Cali
CORDILLERA DE LOS ANDES
Quito
ECUADOR
Ecuador
Guayaquil
Cuenca
Islas Galápagos (Ec.)
Río Amazonas
Manaus
Belém
Iquitos
Fortaleza
Río Madeira
Cajamarca
Trujillo
PERÚ
Río Branco
BRASIL
Recife
Machu Picchu
Lima
Ayacucho
Cuzco
BOLIVIA
Salvador
Lago Titicaca
Arequipa
La Paz
Brasília
Cochabamba
Santa Cruz
Arica
Sucre
Potosí
Belo Horizonte
Iquique
Desierto de Atacama
PARAGUAY
Río de Janeiro
São Paulo
Antofagasta
Santos
Salta
Asunción
Trópico de Capricornio
Salto Iguazú
CHILE
San Miguel de Tucumán
ARGENTINA
Río Paraná
Río Uruguay
Coquimbo
Pôrto Alegre
Córdoba
Rivera
Rosario
URUGUAY
Valparaíso
Santiago
Mendoza
Buenos Aires
Montevideo
La Plata
OCÉANO ATLÁNTICO
Río de la Plata
Concepción
Bahía Blanca
Puerto Montt
OCÉANO PACÍFICO
Estrecho de Magallanes
Islas Malvinas (Br.)
Punta Arenas
TIERRA DEL FUEGO
Cabo de Hornos
OCÉANO PACÍFICO
I. Pinta
I. Fernandina
I. Marchena
I. San Salvador
Santa Cruz
I. Isabela
I. Santa Cruz
Puerto Ayora
I. San Cristóbal
Puerto Villamil
Puerto Baquerizo Moreno
ISLAS GALÁPAGOS (ECUADOR)
OCÉANO PACÍFICO
Cabo Norte
Volcán Katiki
Hanga Roa
Cabo Cumming
Mataveri
ISLA de PASCUA (CHILE)

América del Sur